IRISH POLITICAL PRISONERS, 1920–1962

Irish Political Prisoners presents a detailed and gripping overview of political imprisonment from 1920 to 1962. Seán McConville examines the years from the formation of the Northern Ireland state to the release of the last Border Campaign prisoners in 1962.

Drawing extensively and, in many cases, uniquely on archives and special collections in the three jurisdictions, and interviews with survivors from the period, McConville demonstrates how punishment came to embody and shape the nationalist consciousness. *Irish Political Prisoners 1920–1962* commences with the legacy of the Anglo Irish and Irish Civil Wars – militancy, division and bitterness. The book travels from the embedding of Northern Ireland's security agenda in the 1920s, and the IRA's search for a role in the 1930s (including the 1939 bombing campaign against Britain) to the decisive use of internment during the war and the Border Campaign years. This volume will be an essential resource for students of Irish history and is a major contribution to the study of imprisonment.

Seán McConville is Professor of Law and Public Policy at Queen Mary, University of London. He has researched and taught at leading universities on both sides of the Atlantic. His interests and publications range widely, from Islamic criminal law to prison architecture, but have clustered around the philosophy and administration of punishment – historically, comparatively and in current debates. He is the author of the first in this trilogy *Irish Political Prisoners 1848–1922* (Routledge, 2003).

ALREADY PUBLISHED

A History of English Prison Administration
Volume I: 1750–1877

English Local Prisons, 1860–1900
Next Only to Death

Irish Political Prisoners, 1848–1922
Theatres of War

IRISH POLITICAL PRISONERS, 1920–1962

Pilgrimage of Desolation

Seán McConville

Routledge
Taylor & Francis Group

LONDON AND NEW YORK

First published 2014
by Routledge
2 Park Square, Milton Park, Abingdon, Oxon OX14 4RN

and by Routledge
711 Third Avenue, New York, NY 10017

Routledge is an imprint of the Taylor & Francis Group, an informa business

British Library Cataloguing in Publication Data
A catalogue record for this book is available from the British Library

Library of Congress Cataloging in Publication Data
McConville, Seán, 1943-
Irish political prisoners, 1920-1962 : pilgrimage of desolation / Seán McConville.
pages cm
Includes bibliographical references and index.
1. Political prisoners--Ireland--History. 2. Political prisoners--England--History.
3. Political violence--Ireland--History. 4. Government, Resistance to--Ireland--History.
5. Punishment--England--History. 6. Irish question. I. Title.
HV9650.3.M333 2013
365'.450941509041--dc23
2013027592

ISBN: 978-0-415-35096-9 (hbk)
ISBN: 978-0-203-69664-4 (ebk)

Typeset in Baskerville
by Taylor & Francis Books

Printed and bound in Great Britain by
TJ International Ltd, Padstow, Cornwall

FOR FIONA McCONVILLE AND
SARAH WEBLEY

CONTENTS

CONTENTS

READING PATHS

This table shows reading paths by topic, theme and interest thread.

Chapter		1	2	3	4	5	6	7	8	9	10	11	12	13	14	15	16	17	18	19
Jurisdiction	Ireland (Free State, Eire, Republic)	◇		◇		◇	◇						◇	◇				◇	◇	◇
	Northern Ireland		◇						◇		◇	◇			◇	◇	◇			
	Britain	◇		◇						◇						◇				
Type of custody	Internment				◇	◇		◇	◇		◇			◇			◇		◇	◇
	Imprisonment			◇	◇	◇	◇		◇	◇		◇		◇						
	Penal servitude			◇		◇	◇		◇	◇		◇				◇				

ABBREVIATIONS

CID	Criminal Investigation Department
CPGB	Communist Party of Great Britain
CRO	Commonwealth Relations Office
DORA	Defence of the Realm Act
DPP	Director of Public Prosecutions
EOKA	Ethniki Organosis Kyprion Agoniston
GAA	Gaelic Athletic Association
GCE	General Certificate of Education
GHQ	General Headquarters
GOAD	good order and discipline
GOC	General Officer Commanding
GOIA	Government of Ireland Act
GPO	General Post Office
HMG	His/Her Majesty's Government
ICRC	International Committee of the Red Cross
IRA	Irish Republican Army
IRB	Irish Republican Brotherhood
IRPDF	Irish Republican Prisoners' Dependants' Fund
IRPDRC	Irish Republican Prisoners' Dependants' Reconstruction Committee
ISDL	Irish Self-Determination League
NAI	National Archives of Ireland
NDU	North Dublin Union
NIPD	Northern Ireland Parliamentary Debates
NLI	National Library of Ireland
OASA	Offences Against the State Act
OAS(A)A	Offences Against the State (Amendment) Act
OC	Officer Commanding
OTC	Officers Training Corps
PD	preventive detention
POA	Prison Officers' Association
POW	Prisoner of War

PP	Parliamentary Papers
PPC	Political Prisoners' Committee
PRO	Public Record Office (now National Archives)
PRONI	Public Record Office of Northern Ireland
RAF	Royal Air Force
REME	Royal Electrical and Mechanical Engineers
RIC	Royal Irish Constabulary
ROIA	Restoration of Order in Ireland Act
RUC	Royal Ulster Constabulary
SS	steamship
TD	Teachta Dála (member of the Dáil)
UCDA	University College Dublin Archives
UPA	Ulster Protestant Association
USS	United States ship
UVF	Ulster Volunteer Force
WPDL	Women Prisoners' Defence League

AUTHOR'S NOTE

I offer some reflections on the substance of the work in the Introduction and wish here only to address usage and a few other matters.

The Irish state had three names during the years covered by this study. With independence in 1922 it chose to be known as the Irish Free State, a direct translation from the Irish, Saorstát Éireann. When a new constitution was adopted in 1937, the name changed to Éire (translated as Ireland), and then in 1948, with further constitutional change, it became the Republic of Ireland. Writing across these decades I have of course used the name officially established at the time to which the text refers. In addition to this, I have in places, for convenience and ease of style, adopted common usage, referring to the state as 'the South'.

I have also sometimes referred to Northern Ireland as 'the North'. This has been for convenience and to avoid cumbersome forms within particular passages. Upper case has always been used, to show proper respect for the two states and to distinguish political from geographic usage. Sometimes the governments have been referred to as 'Northern' or 'Southern', 'Belfast' or 'Dublin', respectively. The British government appears in places as 'London', 'Westminster' or (if it is the official as distinct from the political part) 'Whitehall'. In all these cases I hope that no sensitivities will be offended or *amour propre* disturbed.

Names can be very contentious in divided societies, and in Northern Ireland there seems to be no halfway house between Londonderry and Derry, referring to both county and city. Use one and gain the approval of the unionist community, the other and nationalists will be pleased. I have chosen fairly random usage as a way out of this dilemma and note that both forms appear fairly widely in the correspondence of officials and politicians in Northern Ireland (though not in public statements). Copy-editors are deeply (and properly) averse to inconsistency, and my wandering usage may have been tidied up rather more than randomness would indicate, but the reader will at least know my intentions.

A similar issue arises with the names of individuals, some of which changed in form over the years. The usual transition was to a Gaelicised form of an English name. There is no easy way to decide which form to use in this narrative. I have tried to keep to the name that was in use at the time the reference is made. Two problems remain. Both forms may have been in use at the same time – one in court proceedings and newspaper reports for example, and the one at that time preferred by the individual. The second difficulty is that the rules for Gaelicisation seem to have been rather loose, and there was no guiding authority for the exercise. First names which are given in their English form generally have a recognised equivalent in Irish, but surnames can be more difficult. In some cases the solution was easy: an Irish family name which had been Anglicised was simply re-Gaelicised. With non-Irish family names, the procedure seems to have been to opt for some kind of phonetic similarity. This, as might be imagined, was somewhat arbitrary, at times fanciful, and spelling and intended phonetic rendering seem in some cases to have changed over the years. My aim, amid these possible uncertainties, has been to make it clear to whom I am referring, whatever form of their name they have chosen or were using at the time, and in the text to use the form then current, provided it does not lead to confusion. I would be foolish to claim complete accuracy in my navigation out of these perplexities, and I hope the reader will grant some latitude.

By far the greater part of this book is based on primary sources: archives, contemporary material and interviews. This has brought into the story a number of figures who have not previously appeared in the public record. I have given first names and whatever relevant additional details might be available, but in some instances, without a wholly disproportionate amount of labour and with success not certain, this has not been possible. Similarly, official, police and army correspondence is often – and for the researcher infuriatingly – addressed in general form from one office to another or from one incumbent to a counterpart, without the names of individuals being given. Correspondence to and from prisoners, because it is personal and domestic, frequently refers to a person by first name only, and beyond that is a blank wall. Where the record is fleshed out, I have in all but a very few instances provided the reader with what I have discovered. Always where personal details and other information are essential to an understanding of what is happening in the narrative they have been pursued as far as the available record allows.

The same approach of proportionate use of resources has been applied to biographical notes. Those who occupy public office or who are well-known activists are relatively easy to research, and there are good books and other sources of reference. Despite the difficulties, we have in many instances been able to piece together information about minor figures and private individuals. But of some officials and others we have had to remain largely uninformed. Looking at the biographical notes in general, the groups with which these pages are populated have been dealt with fairly and proportionately: Catholic, Protestant, English, Irish, Northern Irish, members of the IRA, prisoners, politicians, officials and police.

Documents are instruments of business and in public administration are usually intended to be registered and filed. Many are, nevertheless, the work of the hour and the day, frequently composed under pressure and despatched in haste. In consequence, some lack even basic information which would assist the researcher (author, origin and date). We have pursued these details and have usually been successful in obtaining them or in providing a context but occasionally have not been able to go further than the incomplete record.

In the citation of newspapers and certain journals the letter following the page number indicates the column. Some newspaper files, such as Irish editions of English newspapers, have not survived. In these cases the cited item has been accessed through a cutting or fragment and therefore page and column information cannot be provided.

Where I have used secondary sources, full acknowledgement has been given, and, indeed, all sources, primary and secondary, are named. Permissions have been obtained, where necessary. I wish to pay tribute to three authors in particular who in their books put on record important information that otherwise would have been lost or exceptionally hard to retrieve: the late Uinseann MacEoin, Tim Pat Coogan and J. Bowyer Bell. All three deserve the gratitude of those who study these events.

Finally there is the question of notes. I prefer footnotes, and it was my intention and that of Routledge to provide these here, in a format uniform to the first volume. However, the text is at the physical limit of what can be bound into one book, and this problem is appreciably eased by using endnotes rather than footnotes. The alternative, of publishing in two parts, did not appeal and would have rendered the work prohibitively expensive. I trust that the endnotes will be tolerated and hope to return to the footnote format for the third and final volume in this series.

ACKNOWLEDGEMENTS

There are certain communications which, because they are so conventional, are pallid and drained of feeling even before one embarks on them: congratulations and condolences are probably two that most of us will write with something of a struggle to pass beyond the usual formula. Thanks and acknowledgements present the same difficulty. The anticipation of their being written is pleasant to contemplate because a project has been brought into harbour and from the satisfaction and ease of completion the author wants to share relief and express gratitude. But the problem of composition remains. The acknowledgements that follow are necessarily expressed in conventional form and may seem both unoriginal and repetitive. It is with genuinely heartfelt thanks, however, that I acknowledge that this work could not have been completed without the support, kindness and hard work of a number of individuals and the funding of several organisations: I am truly indebted.

This has been a long and complicated project, endlessly engrossing and instructive, and unrelentingly demanding. Of wide scope and considerable depth, it has taken more than a decade to complete. It has involved library, archive and interview research in the three jurisdictions of the study, with additional visits to Australia and to the United States. Such work is expensive and could not have been attempted without the necessary funding. I happily acknowledge the financial contributions and moral support of the following bodies and agencies: the Atlantic Philanthropies; the Department of Justice, Equality and Law Reform (Dublin); the Harry Frank Guggenheim Foundation; the Home Office (London); the Leverhulme Trust; the Northern Ireland Office (London and Belfast); Queen Mary, University of London; and the Royal Irish Academy. I have also had valuable support from the Prison Service for England and Wales (now the National Offender Management Service, NOMS), the Irish Prison Service and the Northern Ireland Prison Service. Private donations met the expenses of a key component of the work.

Introductions have to be made, support expressed and the way smoothed to undertake even the initial stages of work of this sensitivity. I am especially grateful to Sir Martin Narey, Sir Joseph Pilling and to Seán Aylward, who from the outset supported the broad aims of the research. This early endorsement was crucial. A number of others gave energetic and important support and encouragement at critical stages: Dáithí O'Ceallaigh (sometime Irish Ambassador in London), Sir Jonathan Phillips (Northern Ireland Office), Phil Wheatley (Director General of NOMS), Professor Eunan O'Halpin (Trinity College Dublin) and the late Garret FitzGerald. I am grateful also to Duncan Bain, Jim Mitchell, Tim Dalton, Michael McDowell and Robin Masefield.

Without the encouragement and indulgence of colleagues, no long-distance academic researcher can hope to reach the finishing line. This is especially so in the busy and demanding environment of a leading law school, with all the heavy and pressing demands of teaching, research and administration: toleration, trust and forbearance are demanded in sometimes unreasonable quantities and at inconvenient junctures. The late Professor John Yelland, Head of Department during the first phases of the research and writing, was both understanding and supportive, a good and trusty colleague whose sly, penetrating but always generous and good-natured humour I am far from alone in missing. Professor Peter Alldridge, a succeeding Head, created an important opportunity at a key juncture, for which I shall long be grateful. My current Head, Professor Valsamis Mitsilegas, has continued along this most helpful path. I am lucky to have worked in the midst of an exceptionally friendly, able and supportive group of research-minded academics, and I thank them all for their interest, encouragement and constant stimulation.

Able and dedicated support staff are indispensible to the academic enterprise, and I wish to acknowledge my indebtedness to Nerys Evans, our current (and indeed first) Department Manager: she has an unwaveringly positive approach to all the administrative underpinnings of academic work and is always helpful in overcoming obstacles and finding solutions. For close on twenty years Jacqueline Dufaur has dealt with the financial side of my successive research projects. Her constant support and high level of skill have advanced the work in many practical ways. She held me to my fiduciary responsibilities in a tirelessly loyal manner, thereby saving me a deal of grief. Anett Loosz has taken over from Jacqueline in the Department in a most reassuring, skilful and invariably helpful and friendly way.

Queen Mary, a large multi-faculty college of the University of London, sets high standards for its scholars, whether academics or students, and I have been fortunate over the years to have benefited from the achievements of a succession of particularly talented management teams. The importance of a sympathetic and forward-looking ambiance is hard to overstate. Special thanks are due to former Principal Sir Adrian Smith, to Vice Principal Professor Philip Ogden (a friend since my first arrival at Queen Mary) who both took a particular interest in the work and went out of their way to be helpful; and to the current Principal, Professor Simon Gaskell, who has done all possible to facilitate the concluding stages of research and writing.

Among those who have helped me undertake the project and provide a reliable base of high-quality research for the writing I must first name Dr Anna Bryson, who joined the project at the outset as a highly recommended and promising young scholar. As Research Officer she was exceptionally diligent and frequently ingenious in seeking out and accessing many of the diverse sources upon which this book is based. She has a true feeling for the work and the material upon which it draws. Anyone who has ever engaged at this level will know how many hours, days and weeks of hard and often tedious toil it entails, whether they be in the library, at an archive or in the preparation and conduct of an interview: sometimes the end seems impossibly far away. A slip of the eye, an impatiently taken shortcut or a lack of zeal in verification can flaw the research. Anna has not only adhered to the highest standards but has passed them on to others. I am grateful for her loyalty, enterprise, application and flexibility, and gladly acknowledge myself to be the beneficiary of her numerous skills.

At the end of this volume, I list the principal archives and libraries I have used. Many thanks are due here: without good librarians and archivists we researchers simply could not work. I wish particularly to thank the following for their assistance and interest and always positive response to our queries and requests: Seamus Helferty of University College Dublin, Archives Department; Catriona Crowe and Tom Quinlan of the National Archives of Ireland; David Huddlesfield and Patricia Kernaghan of the Public Record Office of Northern Ireland (PRONI), and Aileen McClintock, its current Director and Deputy Keeper of the Records. I am also indebted to Yvonne Murphy, Linenhall Library, Belfast; Janette Martin, late of the Labour History Archive and Study Centre, Manchester (now at Huddersfield University); and to the Working Class Movement Library, Manchester. In Dublin, Commandant Victor Laing took a helpful interest in the project and greatly assisted our access to the Military Archives.

Several people gave me access to privately held material of considerable interest: Eamonn Boyce (memoir); Mairead Casey (Casey letters); Noel Kavanagh (material on the Curragh Internment Camp); Art McMillan (letters and memoir); and Seamus Murphy (Collins memoir). To all of these I am very grateful: these were important papers, informative and distinctive.

I have drawn on a number of interviews. A portion of these I conducted myself, but I could not have committed the time to cover more than a fraction. I may have overused the word 'sensitive' in describing this research, but none other is apt for the interviews: personal skills of a high order, integrity, engagement, lightness of touch, and a lively and attentive intelligence are essential. Anna Bryson made a particularly important contribution to this work, developing all the necessary skills, mastering a broad range of topics and conducting the greater portion of the interviews. Janette Martin (who also worked with me on the preceding volume) ably assisted with a specific group of interviews, as did Maggie Donnelly: both were resourceful and sensitive. Transcribing interviews is a skilled and difficult task, and Margaret Kallen tackled it with verve and brio. Violet Mogg performed the same work at an earlier stage.

It is no easy matter in this field to get people to contribute to a research and writing project: prospective interviewees are apt to be cautious and, indeed, suspicious – and have reason to be both. Endorsement and support from figures of standing are essential. I am grateful to the following for their trust, their sympathetic interest, for making introductions and giving advice: Eamonn Boyce, Brendan Culleton, Sean Heading, Noel Kavanagh, Commandant Victor Laing, Michael McCorry, the late Uinseann MacEoin, Jim Neeson, Sean O'Mahony and Peter Rigney. There are others, who, for a variety of reasons, may not be named but to whom I am also indebted.

Some material in this volume looks forward to the next and final part of this trilogy (1966–2000). In addressing that I had generous help from a number of people and organisations, including Gabriel Cleary, Coiste na nIarchimí, John Gawned (Australia), Tom McCaughren, Laurence McKeown, William McQuiston (Ulster Political Research Group), Seán Curry and Seán O'Hare (An Eochair), Gerard Murphy (Tar Isteach), Tom Roberts (Ex-Prisoners Interpretive Centre) and Finlay Spratt (Prison Officers' Association). The late David Ervine and Ruairí Ó Brádaigh were particularly important in giving their time and making introductions.

A number of part-time researchers gave essential assistance, particularly on archives, newspaper files and special collections. This was an immense task, as the reader will see. Somewhere in the region of 100,000 pages of archive material were photographed, and many hundreds more were noted; a great number of newspaper files were searched. I owe sincere thanks to the following: Alda Balthrop, Eamon Darcy, Darragh Gannon, Brian Hanley, Helen Kelly, Eoin Kinsella, Matt Lyus, Anne Marie McInerney, Kevin O'Sullivan, Justin Dolan Stover, Máiréad Ní Choileáin, Aoife Ní Lochlainn and Ciaran Wallace. All worked with skill and a good heart. Kate O'Malley (now at the National Archives of Ireland) gave much valued support in the early days, when I was finding my feet with the multiplicity of sources.

Finally, we come to the production of the book. Because of my manner of composition, and my reliance above all on primary sources, portions of this text have been drafted and redrafted many times, and some chapters have in a most natural, but occasionally irritating, way delivered themselves of others. Several valued colleagues have turned manuscript into typescript and have struggled not only with my handwriting but with loops and arrows and a disorderly zoo of marginal instructions. I thank them all for their patience and skill. Susan Hemp, lately of Queen Mary, typed most of the script, in first and sometimes multiple drafts. Margaret Kallen prepared a good portion of the later drafts, and Margot Doran and Janet Alkema saw me across the line.

I have published with Routledge for almost forty years and have always had the support, flexibility and understanding that authors most value. Despite the pressures and changes that have swept the world of publishing, Routledge has maintained the highest standards in its lists, on which I feel honoured to appear. Victoria Peters was commissioning editor for this and the previous volume; her successor, Eve Setch, saw the book through to completion with skill and unwavering support. I am grateful to my agent, Susan Smith of MBA, whose patience and belief in the undertaking have been both remarkable and frequently tested.

We have reached almost to the end of this roll-call of gratitude, but not to the tail end of importance. As copy-editor, Liz Hudson was part of the production team for the first volume of the trilogy, and I was delighted that she was able to take on this book as well. Her technical ability, sense of style, appreciation of the nuances and niceties of the various topics and controversies – and her candour and curiosity – have made an important contribution to the finished volume.

I should like to thank Maurice Hayes for reading the final script and making helpful comments. In laying down my pen I want to recall and acknowledge the sustained encouragement of the late Professor Norval Morris, of the University of Chicago Law School. A scholar of exceptional liberality of outlook and generosity of spirit, Norval has imposed on those of us who had the good fortune to have him as a mentor and friend an obligation to follow on and pass on something of his magnaminity.

Having inveighed against the conventional phrase, I must in conclusion now turn to it. I have sought and received advice, and I have had much assistance, as the reader will see, but I affirm that all errors and omissions, all judgements and interpretations, are mine alone, as is every word, well or ill chosen.

Seán McConville
Department of Law, Queen Mary,
University of London

INTRODUCTION

This is the second volume in what will be a trilogy, dealing with Irish political prisoners from 1848 until 2000, or shortly thereafter. The first volume commenced the tale with the Young Irelanders of 1848 and ended with the establishment of the Free State, in 1922. We here take a small backward step to the autumn of 1920, the formation of Northern Ireland and the establishment, within the UK, of its devolved government and administration. The book concludes in 1962, with the release of the last men imprisoned for their part in what came to be called the Border Campaign. This was a series of attacks by the IRA and splinter organisations which were mainly launched along the border between the Republic of Ireland and Northern Ireland. The final volume, now in hand, will take the story forward to the Good Friday Agreement of 1998 and its immediate aftermath. Together spanning a narrative extending over a century and a half, each volume is complete in itself.

In the notorious trial of Stephen Ward in 1963, one of the witnesses, when confronted with what another had said, and which contradicted her account, made the response, 'He would [say that], wouldn't he?' Not original, but forcefully to the point, it has since been used (and in more salubrious settings) to denote patently self-serving explanations. Perhaps I should not invite the reader to recollect the exchange because I am going to venture onto that very ground. Every author of a work of this size will respond to reproaches about prolixity, and even sharper remarks about self-indulgence, by pointing to the complexity of the story, the multiplicity of events, characters and circumstances, and the need to address all, fully and fairly. This is certainly my plea, and before it is peremptorily dismissed, let us hasten to the facts.

This is a story of four tumultuous decades, told across three states, each with its own politics, laws, courts and system of penal administration. Nor is the figure at the centre of events easily described. The 'political' part of the term is in itself contentious, but even 'prisoner' is not straightforward. The latter term is generic (basically anyone who is a captive) and embraces several different types of custody. In ranking of notional onerousness, these range from a person on remand (awaiting trial), to executive-ordered detainees and internees, to those who have been convicted and sentenced. This last subdivides into the ordinary prisoner (whose months or years have been ordered with or without hard labour), Borstal trainee and those serving sentences of penal servitude. Prisoners in this last category were more commonly known as convicts. Each category of prisoner was confined under somewhat different conditions and was subject to its own penal regime of deprivations and privileges. Loss of freedom is by far and away the most salient commonality, but beyond this each group had different experiences and tales to tell.

In the categories of imprisonment, a further division must be made. Men and women adapt differently to confinement, as both historical and sociological studies show. No person can leave at the gate of the prison the experience, attitudes, skills and motivations of their free lives. It would be unrealistic, therefore, to imagine that a community of women would live in the same way as that of men. Apart from the early years of this narrative, women make few appearances, but in the period around the Irish Civil War they left a distinctive mark, a deal of which, thankfully, they recorded.

I have used the term 'political prisoner' in the title of the book, and, since it is the focus and substance of my study, it must be explained and justified. I know that the expression will puzzle or even offend some, yet be taken for granted by others. With one exception – that of internees – my usage does not imply that these were persons imprisoned simply because of their political beliefs. And even with internees, whether they were north or south of the border, arrest and custody were not supposed to relate to political views only. In a probable minority of cases (though the proportion varied with circumstances and events), views and views alone were the dominant consideration in the decision to arrest and detain. In the balance of instances, attachments, associations and activities, which were observed or suspected but could not be proved in court, were decisive factors. Informants and other sources of information had to be protected; the case was there, but not strong enough; and the normal processes of law could not be followed – or so the authorities argued. At other times, campaigns of intimidation of juries, complainants and witnesses blocked the path to fair trials and paralysed the normal processes of justice. A solution had to be found were the law to be upheld and the fabric of the state protected, and internment was introduced. In a democracy, this is, or certainly should be, a solution of last resort. Its ineradicable problems are obvious: the detainee cannot confront witnesses; evidence is not tested; and a person's freedom may be taken on the basis of hearsay, fleeting observation and interpretation of motives. All systems of justice make flawed and wrong decisions from time to time, but internment by executive decision, as we shall see, is particularly prone to do so.

Many, including those who ordered it, would concede the grave drawbacks of internment, even while justifying it as a last resort, a temporary and unavoidably necessary evil. But what of applying the term 'political prisoner' to those who were charged, brought to trial, convicted and sentenced? They have had the full benefit of law, and their guilt has been established in open court according to the rules of evidence and criminal procedure and the requirements of law. They are simply criminals, many would argue: drop the 'political' part of the term. But, as we will find here, the motivation of these offenders cannot be ignored, nor can it usefully or plausibly be maintained that there is no difference between those who break the law for reasons of personal gain or passion, or moral turpitude, and those who do so in pursuit of a political programme. One may consider the political objectives foolish and misconceived and the methods utterly wicked, but there is a significant difference in intent and state of mind and even in normal jurisprudence these factors are important. This is not to preclude a finding of greater culpability against the political rather than the individual offender: that is a matter of judgement.

As far as I have been able to establish, with very few exceptions, and those usually of a trivial nature, the character and antecedents of the politically motivated offender differ from those of the ordinary criminal. The former usually have no criminal record (in the sense discussed here), whereas the latter have usually ascended a ladder of offences, as they work their way into prison. Some may, it is true, commit a grave offence as their first and only crime. (Murder in a domestic setting is the classic example of the first-time lifer.) As will be seen, the IRA and other physical-force republican organisations emphasised the differences between the two categories of offender. In theory, the organisation did not countenance any casual or individual law-breaking, insisting that authority be given for each and every action. Most of those who, at various times, dealt with these prisoners tacitly accepted that these were not run-of-the-mill criminal prisoners – whatever politicians, senior officials and police told the public.

None of this should be taken to palliate the offences which are chronicled here. All states are entrusted with wide reserve powers over property, the daily essentials (food, water and power) and the life of the citizen. Since all authority tends to be abused, the constitutions and law of democratic states provide a variety of checks, balances and safeguards. One may criticise their effectiveness, the consistency with which they are applied, and, from time to time, our reservations and suspicions are confirmed when shocking injustices occur and instances of grave neglect and concealment are uncovered. But, though not infallible, these systems are based on the rule of law and are equipped with robust procedures. They are deliberative, accessible and accountable and are intended to exclude arbitrariness and acts of great and petty tyranny.

Not so the paramilitary organisation, no matter how lofty its aims and majestic its declarations. It would claim accountability and point to its processes. No member of the organisation, it would say, may act in its name without authority, and sanctions, up to the death penalty, will be imposed on those who break these rules. But when the source of its authority is sought, the answer will be a tautology: history or the good of the nation – as divined by the organisation that takes life-and-death powers unto itself.

In the tale which we here unfold it will be seen that grievous harm was done to people and to property: lives were taken violently, often with apparent indifference, usually without remorse, sometimes with satisfaction and triumph.

Intimidation, physical and moral, cast a wide and deep shadow, and young men (and a few young women) were caught up in a movement that could thwart their chances of domestic happiness and modest material achievement.

To all of this the activist would – and did – reply that there was but one law in the land and that was the one by which they lived. Most would point to the moral claims and entitlements of that law and the burden of acceptance and obligation it entailed. They would insist that there was a paramount but usurped authority to which all who claimed to be Irish owed an inalienable duty. They would point to an apostolic handing on of authority, going back to the 1916 Easter Rising and perhaps to the Fenian Brotherhood of 1858. In the name of that living entity they were authorised – obliged – to act, and for it they would bear any cost, be it long years of imprisonment, or even death. And, it must be conceded, never forgetting the price that they forced on others, that over the decades to this cause they came and took the consequences. Many suffered long years of imprisonment, and some were executed. Yet in ranks of varying size they rallied, age by age and generation by generation, before and during the period covered by this study.

The state of mind of political prisoners is closely related to the stance and condition of their organisation beyond the walls. The strategic objectives and the tactics of the IRA in its various phases must therefore be a large part of the narrative. Beginning with a civil war fought and lost, we see, over a decade and a half, an insurrectionary organisation blundering dangerously and occasionally preposterously about in search of a role. This is followed by a formal declaration of war on Britain, bombs in British cities, loss of life and damage to property. Years of captivity followed in the three jurisdictions: the newly named Éire, Northern Ireland and Britain. The organisation was ground down and all but destroyed, eating itself in recrimination and internecine spite. Yet, in another decade and a half, we see the launch of the Border Campaign. At each point, the lives of the prisoners and the success or failure of the organisation are intertwined.

In this exploration, full consideration must be given to the laws and security measures of the three states. These are numerous and varied but easy enough simply to list. Behind each initiative there is a process of formation. Laws and administrative measures are debated within the legislature and bureaucracy, options are considered, objections raised and decisions taken with varying degrees of perceptiveness, rationality and fairness. Events and emotions, as well as leadership and skills, always have an influence, and the process is far from neat.

The tale of prisoners – political or ordinary – is far too often told without reference to their custodians and thus is incomplete and apt to be distorted. Between captor and captive there can be a connection as remote as a face glimpsed through the wires of a detention camp or the intimacy of exchanges of domestic news and concerns and conversations ultimately extending to hours and days but conducted in bits and scraps over several years. In these circumstances, prisoner and staff recognise that each may to some extent shape the life of the other, that mutual respect is possible, and that they must find a way of living together. Both live prison lives, with all the pressures that are only partly grasped and never fully understood by those at liberty. This is a powerful bond, though both sides would probably deny it.

Lest we trip over the edge into sentimentality and notions of false domesticity, let us recognise that despite that which they share there are two very distinct tribes in prison. The political and indeed the ordinary prisoner is far from unfettered in relating to staff. No place of confinement is without its underground life involving contraband and illegal activities such as unauthorised contacts with the outside world. Carelessness or mischance may threaten this important commerce, but far more feared is the threat of the informer. Prisoners are ever alert for signs that a comrade is giving information – for favours, in malice or through naivety. Conversations between a prisoner and a member of staff, unless there is a context, or a witness, can raise suspicions and entail sometimes serious outcomes. The IRA developed mutual surveillance and accountability into a system, in ways and with consequences which I describe. It should be noted that staff are also constrained and colleagues will watch for signs of inappropriate closeness or undue familiarity with the other side.

Prisons are as omnipresent as the other features of our urban way of life, and we generally take them for granted. There may be a small frisson when first we notice a prison, or one is pointed out, but thereafter it becomes a scarcely visible part of the landscape. In most accounts of imprisonment, and certainly of politically motivated prisoners, the physical elements of the prison – its walls, cells, landings, gates, doors and yards – similarly fade away, or become a type of wrap-around adjective or backdrop in a narrative whose focus is on personality and events. Yet the provision and management of custodial premises – prisons, camps and occasionally ships – can entail many problems of politics, finance and administration. That tale also must be told, together with the effect of the physical environment on the lives of prisoners and staff alike.

For the past century and a half, and more, political imprisonment has periodically been at the centre of public events in Ireland. It has put its mark on Anglo-Irish and Intra-Irish relations, as well as the two religious and political communities of the island. The use of detention, internment and imprisonment, and the imposition of the death penalty, have frequently driven political and private discussion and debate. The new Irish state was launched in 1922 with the release of many hundreds of internees and prisoners in British and Northern Ireland custody (including some who were under sentence of death) and the near-simultaneous arrest of thousands more and their internment, imprisonment or execution under the authority of the Free State. Northern Ireland replenished its stock of internees and sentenced prisoners at the same time. Within the following few years in London and in Belfast the strict requirements of the law were pragmatically, and not without misgivings, bent to the requirements of political necessity. This contest between two forms of the public interest – law and politics – will be seen repeatedly throughout this narrative.

This is the material, taking us from the fugitive revolutionist in the rented back room to the deliberations of the higher levels of the judiciary, from reports of water and sanitation engineers to the prisoner choosing to forgo food or refuse the uniform as protest of last resort. Our story takes us from the heat and hatred of civil war to humorous or bad-tempered exchanges between prisoners and their guards, some of these not lacking in a certain kind of inventive satire. There is much that is merely the tedium and monotony that define imprisonment but also instances of extreme emotion and endeavour – humanity and true compassion and charity, as well as degradation, petty hatred and scurrility.

The people of this narrative range widely, from those, be they officials, politicians or prisoners, who merely followed their organisation's current line and did so within the approved glossary of terms, to those whose imagination and spirit took them in a different direction, sometimes with the charm of self-mockery. In research and writing I have tried to keep the human element foremost where possible and always prominent. I confess, before the reader finds me out, that I have sometimes twitched the tiller to sweep an attractive tale – or character – into the script. To regain the colour and reanimate the drama the picaresque must be tolerated and at times encouraged.

Working with such a mass of material, from legal decisions and statutory instruments to the recorded recollections of individuals, requires a deal of flexibility and an aptitude in blending. While I hope that in general I have succeeded in this difficult task, I am sure that some shortfalls will be uncovered and am well aware of my own inadequacies. It is a difficult leap from the vividness of an event relived in interview – the more gripping because it sometimes deals with pain or loss or triumph – to the tangible and intriguing nuances of the carefully considered, systematically debated and closely worded memorandum that perhaps prompted a change in public policy, that saved or took a life. Readers will themselves judge the mixture, the connection and the interweaving. I will only insist that the ingredients are necessary and that their force has been inescapable.

There remains the matter of approach. There is a self-evident obligation to give the facts as fully as they can be gathered and to present them even-handedly. In following this course here no relevant facts that I have uncovered and only a very few names have been withheld. Yet it would be foolish to claim impartiality. The revolutionary would disdain neutrality and the great majority would despise anything other than commitment to the cause and veneration of its guiding principles. The politician and the official might insist that the picture may be drawn in a few simple strokes – here the law, there the transgression and punishment and from that the duty of submission and obedience.

One can navigate between these demands but always in short courses: each instance has its facts, claims and counterclaims; every personality is more than two-dimensional. The law had its undoubted authority, for example, but sometimes it was conceived with too much regard to the narrow entitlements of the state rather than the spirit of democracy; its application was uneven and occasionally flawed by a partisan spirit. The prisoner or internee sometimes had just cause for protest but often simply sought a fight – the armed struggle continued in a different form, or mere release from impotence and boredom. Judgements have to be made in the telling, and these are usually no more and certainly should be no less than an assessment that conscientiously strives to be full and fair. Others may choose to see the picture differently and to draw their own conclusions.

This is basic and obvious, but narration and analysis pose a deeper challenge: how do we approach the actors in events that have long since played out and whose conclusion is known? What attitude and manner of demeanour should we adopt? Or, to consider the issue from a slightly different angle, how do we relate to times that are not our own and whose spirit is to some extent alien, perhaps unattractive, and whose pulse has a different beat from our own? And, in effecting that approach, how do we cope with the inequality of the relationship between the observed and the observer and the inevitable lack of humility in the latter?

Any introduction to historical method will point to the so-called Whig fallacy: the tendency in some histories to define as worthy only those events and person- ages which in the manner of a narrow family genealogy have contributed to the present arrangement of society. Facts and values which are at odds with this line of merit are excluded, minimised or derided because they may contain hints that other courses were possible and that perhaps the outcome was far from inevi- table or even desirable. No matter how conscious one is of the Whig fallacy (and for a generation or so some historians became so sensitive to it that narrative became intolerable to them), it is impossible to study the past without some kind of vantage point. One needs to make that explicit. I have no reluctance in declaring my preference for law and ballot box over any kind of extra-legal movement and for gradual and considered change rather than root-and-branch programmes, chimerical promises and millenarian hopes. This will be obvious from the substance and style of this volume, but perhaps it needs affirmation.

This, however, leaves another problem. How does one deal with people and with courses of events with which one disagrees or even disparages? What then of even-handedness? The last, it seems, requires that one should lay out the facts, as uncovered, and that when judgements are made – as they must be – to apply criteria with consistency across the board. To condemn cruelty and callousness in one set of actors, for example, but to minimise or overlook it in others, would be literally injudicious. To impute bad faith to one group but without direct evidence to accept good intent elsewhere would be indefensible.

Yet agreement on this point – and surely it is elementary – does not resolve all questions about approach. In a work that has posed challenges and spurred debate for some eighty years, the philosopher Michael Oakeshott made a number of criticisms of historians and historiography. One is particularly pertinent here. He notes that the historian often undertakes the task of constructing an unbiased account of events and confuses this with the achievement of a world of facts uninfluenced by experience. But this may in turn mislead, since the historian may suppose that the notionally unbiased account, by being 'independent of the ideas and prejudices of this own place and time must be what is altogether independent of experience'. That, Oakeshott observes, is absurd. The writing of history encapsulates and is impossible without experience.[1]

The logic is that the historian must try to live in two worlds at once – which is very difficult – and always strive to be aware of this straddling of realities. Here we are constructing a narrative, but there we are also encountering a sequence of events, truly encountering, trying to make sense of them in their own terms. The duality is critical, since narrative is impossible without judgement. One must approach this difficult posture with some humility. The qualities that must be summoned up go beyond notions of empathy and sympathy – words so often invoked that they have lost a deal of meaning. Some effort must be made to reduce one's own stature and to curb the arrogance that the living display towards the dead. We sit as gods, watching our subjects in their endeavours, knowing from the outset that their hopes are futile, their actions essentially blind, at other times cheering them on to the race already won. This is true self-indulgence. We know the end of the tale (or think we do) and sate ourselves in delusions of omniscience.

The poet Wisława Szymborska ponders such questions, and in the poem 'The Letters of the Dead' expresses well the susceptibility to illusion to which historians are prone: 'We read the letters of the dead like helpless gods, / but gods, nonetheless, since we know the dates that follow.'[2] The words 'like helpless gods' are completely apt, and the poem's thrust, that we too are the dead in waiting, must, if properly embraced, sober us, abate arrogance and push us to the comforts of acknowledged fallibility. To see history as a chessboard and to observe the pieces move about is an illusion more about ourselves than the past, full of its own sadness.

I am sure that in places I have slithered into these and other pits and traps of perception and construction. What has kept proportion has been the undeniable roundness of character of my subjects, their appeal in adversity as well as success and my continuing desire to understand them. It is easy with some to enter into their concerns and to have some kind of conversation with them. Others – and it may not be the obvious ones – are without appeal or easy point of contact and are the greater challenge, the fences at which we fall.

One final point before I step aside into the shadow of the material and its exposition that properly obscure authors. Throughout the events that this book chronicles, I have been struck by the importance and recurrence of the concept of will. In this narrative it means far more than determination or persistence. It has moralistic and dynamic components, in Irish nationalism particularly expressed as endurance. Its centrality in republican ideology is undoubted. It may be seen across the decades from the Fenians' notion that will and sacrifice could triumph over circumstance and win corporality for the proclaimed and virtual republic. It was the focus of that supremely well-conceived, and in some ways sublimely enacted, political pageant, the Easter Rising of 1916. Belief in the triumph of will fed the hunger-striker and clothed the naked uniform-refuser.

It is easy to see how revolutionary movements grasp and disseminate the notion of the concept: often it is their only resource.

But use the phrase – say it out loud – and its appropriation by the mighty and the despotic comes immediately to mind. Should the lesser currents of life be gathered into the service of a political or religious will; and, if so, can limits be set and respected? As I write these words, historic communities in the Middle East are being torn apart for the advancement of religious will, for purity and exclusivity of doctrine. We have reason ever to fear the pursuit of the perfect and simultaneously to cherish and bewail the flaws and weaknesses of the everyday, the imperfections that so accurately and infuriatingly express the great and abiding strength of our humanity, common and, indeed, enduring.

And so I have tried to bring this narrative together, grateful for the opportunity, seized and instructed by the ideas and events, but above all by lives imagined, attempted and lost. Is this not who and what we are?

Notes

1 Michael Oakeshott, *Experience and Its Modes* (Cambridge: Cambridge University Press, 1995), p. 94. He further points out that discovery without judgement is impossible.
2 Wisława Szymborska, *Views with a Grain of Sand: Selected Poems*, trans. Stanisław Barańczak (London: Faber & Faber, 1995).

1

LOYALTIES

Britain and Ireland

Bleak landscape, troubled times

A hard, bitter and imperfect peace began on 11 November 1918 as the echo faded of the Great War's last shot. Lesser wars continued in the Baltic, Russia, Asia Minor, the Middle East and Ireland. Boundary changes and a clutch of new states altered maps and political balances and stirred new passions. The foundations of the world financial system had been undermined. European economies were prostrate; the Treasury of the United States of America could scarcely contain its vast reserves of bullion.[1] Revolution had shattered tsarist Russia and was the spectre that stalked central Europe. The most perspicacious strained to see ahead. The major conflict had lasted for fifty-one months; it was to be as long again before an uneasy and profoundly insecure armistice took hold across the Continent and its offshore islands.[2] Some of the post-war conflicts were social: working-class risings inspired by Marxist, anarchist or socialist doctrine; crumbling and discredited ruling classes and castes were swept aside, with others yet to triumph and consolidate. Authority was elusive in substance and frequently experimental in form. Blood was spilled for language and ethnicity, for irredentist or expansionist opportunities, and in a quest for safety in the unfamiliar and dangerous landscape emerging from the debris of the German, Austro-Hungarian, Russian and Ottoman empires. Struggles based on language and ethnicity were shot through and stiffened by religious confrontations: Christian against Muslim, Protestant against Catholic, Catholic against Orthodox, and a growing temper of anti-Semitism. Dragon's teeth were sown aplenty, fed and watered well and promised an early and bountiful harvest.

That place, blood, belief and language will fuel murderous conflicts is now a notion of domestic familiarity, headlines more tedious than shocking. Is it insecurity that leads communities to abandon neighbourliness, the routines and rewards of a peaceful and settled life – humanity itself – and take the awful plunge into violence? Must that violence, once loosed, fuel a chain reaction that endures and taints the generations? Is a longing for 'freedom' so devouring that it places this or that form of government, culture, people or language so far above another that deeds of depraved cruelty and violence are rationalised, excused and even glorified? By some appalling alchemy does simple distrust mutate into hatred of the different that drives a war of religion or language? Is the perennial longing and fighting lust of young men a force in itself or merely potential, an instrument in the orchestra of malignity?

There was much to be taken, freely or at little cost, in the weeks, months and years following the 11 November armistice of 1918. Exclusion multiplies opportunity for the victorious: homes become vacant, employment and promotion available. When in the 1940s European Jews were finally driven out for slaughter, their stolen property was minutely recorded, carefully stored and recycled to reward the regime's supporters. Those occupying the vacated houses and apartments, filling the jobs and taking the promotions, those behind the directors' desks of the workshops and factories seized from the outcasts, those who took their time from another's watch: each had opportunity, comfort and good fortune to still conscience and to keep prejudice and hatred warm. All of this had been enacted on a smaller scale twenty years before.

But these mass movements transcend mere avarice. In whatever combination of malign and benign, men and women cannot be induced to step outside the customary and domestic round, to smother conscience and the instincts of pity and decency, to risk all, indeed, simply for material gain. National and religious movements channel the energies of many idealists and make devotees and disciples of those who seek a new dimension in their lives, who wish to be of service, to partake of transcendent forms of passion and joy, to be significant. This psycho-spiritual longing is the extra charge that makes so many conflicts truly ferocious. The grabbing of land, property and jobs has some boundaries of risk, some calculation of cost and benefit; the sordid and the selfish have human dimensions: there are only so many hours in the day for consumption, and most appetites can be sated. The transcendent cause and spiritual plunge are dangerously without calculation and seem to have no boundaries. There is a repulsive inhumanity in these quests for the perfect – and yet they are inseparable from our condition. Joy in death and delight in anticipation would seem perverse and over-imagined were it not for the astonishing fact that we now hear of them on a daily basis.

Ireland and Britain provide examples of many of these phenomena in the aftermath of the First World War. Victorious, the British Empire had been destroyed.[3] Carnage so vast inevitably subjects institutions of authority to question and challenge. This cultural, social and industrial turbulence of the inter-war decades is well documented.[4] The Anglo-Irish struggle finds its context here. Between a great swathe of nationalist, Catholic Ireland and Britain a fierce and brutal war raged between 1919 and 1921, in its causes and conduct part spiritual, part political and part material. Waged by peoples long intermingled and interconnected, it had the qualities of disillusionment and bitter shards of emotion of a shattered family. A ceasefire in July 1921 found fruition in a hard-negotiated Treaty the following December. Neither party was fully satisfied: the document was a thing of thin politeness, strained beliefs and only half substantial; the negotiators had cared far too little about reconciliation. The Irish secured independence, but it was hedged about, denied burnish and glory, was not gen-erously given, and did not extend to the whole of the island.[5] A part of the Empire's mother-country had been torn away, and Britain faced a new neighbour, alive with deeds and rumours of republicanism. Imaginative generosity was needed from both sides, but the wars had dried up the springs. And there was a fatal triangle. Ulster unionism, which had watched, deplored and feared the long negotiations and ambiguous agreement of the other two, now faced many deadly uncertainties.

In those three states – Britain, the Irish Free State and Northern Ireland – the events of the First World War, the complex Anglo-Irish relationship and the several years of armed struggle in Ireland, had thrown loyalties up in the air. They had fallen hither and yon, new patterns replacing the old. Their working out would shape Irish history for the rest of the century, eventually returning Irish issues to the heart of British politics.

Britain: the reluctant midwife

Surviving a trauma, individuals and institutions often seek the comfort of familiar and now deeply cherished pathways. Never dominant, this current cut a path through inter-war political, social and cultural life; grievous loss vented in nostalgic longings. And yet with the losses and changes came possibilities which had to be evaluated, lived with, seized and exploited. Nor was this a period of change for which other great peace-tides provided a guide. The Paris Peace Conference was no Congress of Vienna. No obvious balances and bulwarks had been established. Punishing, draining and humiliating Germany would have seemed both vulgar and dangerous to a modern Castlereagh. Such cautionary voices were raised unheeded. The now-shattered frontiers of the old Europe were per-haps the least important changes. The fierce certainties of nationalism and ideology almost immediately began to whirl about and gather the storm that would renew Europe's unfinished war.

Following a convulsion of such proportions, the term 'victory' must be empty, misleading and, ultimately, mocking. Britain's endurance, its survival, had cost almost a million men, three-quarters of whom were from the UK. The war memorials are widely distributed. In great city centres, tiny villages and institutions as varied as churches, cathedrals, gentlemen's clubs, schools, universities, factories, offices and railway stations, they are so commonplace that we fail to see them. The death of youth on such a scale, the living reminders provided by the several million maimed and afflicted survivors, and the anguish of the bereaved ensured that, directly or indirectly, the war ate at the heart of all but the most isolated and insu-lated. The joy of peace, its profound relief, found expression in those public out-pourings that still flicker and jerk in old movie newsreels. But after the Bacchanal came anger and cynicism, powerful solvents of the politics of pomp, presumption and grand gesture, it is true, but also of national confidence and ease.

Britain was deeply in the red. The National Debt had risen to fourteen times its pre-war level, and its servicing ate up nearly half the taxation take. Fiscal concern and the international financial order dominated policy discussions. Owing the USA £850 million, Britain was unable to collect the large sums due from other wartime allies. There was a pervasive sense of skating on very thin ice: frugality and retrenchment seemed inescapable. Within two years of the armistice, restrictions in government expenditure combined with severe market downturns, unemployment and a rise in left-wing ideology in the labour movement to corrode workplace relations. The miners faced a lockout from April 1921 and were beaten back to work three months later with nothing gained. Humiliation bred hatred, and class warfare released more toxins.

British political possibilities seemed changed with the election of December 1918. A nominal Liberal, David Lloyd George, still bestrode the political land-scape. His stature as wartime prime minister, his absolute conviction in his own indispensability and his need to continue in a coalition ministry fed disarray among his party colleagues and helped destroy the old Liberal Party. This rout was almost as comprehensive as that of Redmond's Irish Parliamentary Party.[6] The Liberal–Irish alliance, which had dominated Anglo-Irish affairs for half a century and more, simply evaporated. Sinn Féin's refusal to sit at Westminster meant that the unionist and imperialist outlook achieved an overwhelming parliamentary dominance.

Lloyd George's desire to continue as national leader required him to placate the Conservative and Unionist Party, now riding the political tide. Coalition Liberals were very junior partners in what was an alliance, but no longer a partnership. In the improbable event that Lloyd George wished to reconstruct Liberalism and make an alliance with Labour, the Conservative majority would have remained at an unshakeable 120 seats. Had Sinn Féin sacrificed its dearest principles – its *raison d'être* – and come to Westminster to join an anti-Conservative alliance, it would have counted for little: Conservatives would have retained an overall majority of around fifty. But this was the stuff of a disordered political imagination. Convinced that almost alone he had the ability and authority to make the peace and establish a new order among the nations, Lloyd George continued to lead the government, to display tactical virtuosity, and to hope for who knows what kind of political deliverance.[7]

British foreign policy was dominated by the need to reach an agreement with the defeated but unstable and still dangerous Germany, to restrain France, to deal with American plans for peace and reconstruction, to combat Bolshevism and to find productive relations with the new nations of central Europe. No one in the leadership thought it possible or even worthwhile to attempt to synchro-nise foreign and monetary policy. Maintenance of the Empire was an axiom. It was unthinkable in the immediate aftermath of a war in which it had so desperately and narrowly prevailed, that Britain should join the defeated empires which were stripped of possessions. The ruin and pathos of the van-quished hardened feelings against any change in the make-up of the UK; an obligation to honour the sacrifices of the dead and maimed meant loyalty to the Empire.

By war's end, the Irish insurgency which had begun in 1916 was again boiling up. The awful years of terror and counter-terror, of murders, ambushes, executions, retaliations, atrocities of all kinds, arson, intimidation, a gendarmerie and soldiery amok and a population conscripted for subversion, all drained the cup of human feeling between the two nations and their leaderships. Beset with difficulties on all sides, struggling to find a place in a world in which the tremors of shifting foundations were frequently felt, Lloyd George and his colleagues worked out an agreement with the rebellious Irish.

This peace had been snatched from seemingly irresolvable disagreements by means of Lloyd George's deftness and lack of scruple. In an act of political philandering, Carson and Craig, Collins and Griffith had been courted and made quite different and irreconcilable promises. In Ireland, personalities (living and dead), utopianism, elements of nihilism and revolutionary metaphysics then fuelled a civil war. From Westminster, the view was sombre and deeply unsettling: the Irish were at it again. But although British intervention was talked about, there was a sufficient sense of the trap that had been laid, of the consequences of reuniting and further enraging Irish republicanism, for caution and restraint to prevail. Instead, Lloyd George found common cause with those Irish leaders who saw the Treaty as a stepping stone. Enormous political capital was invested by unionist imperialists such as Churchill and Birkenhead. Public and parliamentary opinion was reassured and restrained. On a tide of destruction and hate-filled recrimination, the Irish Free State came into being. In the north of the island a new state stood by its ramparts and also claimed British support. British policy in the Irish Civil War easily found its course: support order, oppose extremism.

Fixing the boundary posts

More difficult the post-settlement claims of the Northern and Southern Irish states. Two elements in the Treaty had swung waverers on the nationalist side (and the agreement had been approved by the thin Dáil majority of sixty-four to fifty-seven): a Boundary Commission and a Council of Ireland. The implied promise of both was a united Ireland: this was Lloyd George's nod and wink. There were large areas in Northern Ireland in which Roman Catholics were in the majority, and any plebiscite would record their wish to join the Free State. The Council of Ireland, intended to be a forum for the Free State and Northern Ireland governments, was solid gossamer, supposedly expressing the 'Irish dimension' and appearing to derogate from the separate status of Northern Ireland.

This was a reality only for those who strained in self-deception. Since the Council of Ireland lacked executive power and sanctions for non-participation, the Belfast government simply declined to attend, and the Council was stillborn, formally discontinued in 1925. The Boundary Commission was the nationalists' great and unfounded hope. There was (and is) a greater sense of county identity in Ireland than in Britain, and this was something of a problem. Electoral boundaries followed county, district and urban lines, but population divisions of politics and religion were otherwise ordered. In contriving a land area for their new state, Ulster unionists sought the optimum balance between county areas and population. The full nine counties of the Province of Ulster would have brought within an uncomfortable range of parity the voting power of nationalists and unionists. A land area maximising unionist homogeneity might have proved to be geographically and economically – and perhaps psychologically – unsustainable. The fine-tuning of a district-by-district plebiscite was ruled out by the interspersed distribution of the two populations. Psephological state-building of this kind would have produced an ungovernable patchwork of mini-cantons and the risk of civil turmoil and forced resettlements. By choosing the six-county area, Sir James Craig and Edward Carson obtained the electoral dominance they sought. Roman Catholics – overwhelmingly nationalist – were sufficiently dispersed within it and, once proportional representation had been discarded, were excluded from political influence because they constituted only one-third of Northern Ireland's population. In critical local areas where the arithmetic of the first-past-the-post electoral system failed to give a unionist majority, gerrymandering secured the desired result.[8] London closed its eyes to the injustice, and no politician was far-seeing enough to worry about the long-term stability of such a state.

Westminster could have given teeth to the Boundary Commission. But the man who had hinted at a further distribution of territory and perhaps more was gone. On 19 October 1922, the Conservative Party, meeting at the Carlton Club, voted down the coalition. Andrew Bonar Law, one of Ulster unionism's greatest champions, became party leader and in the subsequent general election won a majority of seventy-seven over the other parties combined.[9] In office for only seven months, Bonar Law died within a year, but his administration was perhaps the least likely of all to read the Treaty favourably towards the Irish Free State. Stanley Baldwin, his successor, was by nature a conciliator, but Ireland was not on his agenda. He went to the electorate on the issue of trade protection, lost, and was succeeded by Ramsay MacDonald, who headed Labour's first and minority government.

MacDonald's was a weak administration with a maximum programme of showing that his party could be trusted to govern. Labour, together with independent and indeed many Coalition Liberals, had been appalled by certain policing and security policies and practices during the Anglo-Irish War, but this did not translate into a desire to revisit or amend the Treaty. The public mood was utterly unpropitious, political energy was low, and even had MacDonald such an intention he could not have carried it through Parliament. In any event, he was brought down in late September 1924 by a combined Liberal and Conservative vote of censure. In the ensuing election (the fourth in two years), the Conservatives secured 419 seats, Labour 151 and the Liberal remnant (once again under Lloyd George's leadership) only forty. The realignment of British politics had been largely completed: Labour the largest party of the left, and the Liberals in third position.

During these turbulent years, one finds but few mentions of Ireland in the columns of *Hansard*. The contrast with the pre-war years is marked. In Redmond's day, every session – or so it seemed – had its rash of Irish questions. These often descended to the parish pump – a railway crossing or sub-post office here, a minor public preferment there. In the years of the settlement of Irish matters, 1920–2, there were debates and disputes at a grander level, but these were concentrated bursts of attention. For the rest, Westminster politicians were happy to be free from Irish concerns and wished Belfast and Dublin to get on with their business: many of their constituents wished them to go to the Devil.[10] Even Northern Ireland, part of the UK, was, in its internal affairs, deemed by the Speaker to be outside the remit of the Commons.[11]

This was the background to the final settlement of territory. On 15 March 1924, T. M. Healy, Governor General of the Irish Free State wrote to J. H. Thomas, Colonial Secretary in MacDonald's first Labour cabinet, asking that the Boundary Commission be set up, as provided under Article XII of the Treaty.[12] Thomas received the letter with a deal of perturbation and sent a lengthy and closely argued reply (from its tone and style personally drafted), counselling delay. He completely accepted the Free State government's right to make its request but asked ministers 'before taking a step they cannot retrace to consider whether, in their calm and dispassionate judgement, an irrevocable fixture of the boundary will help to bring nearer the voluntary union of all Ireland'. He begged them to pause and to take counsel with their friends 'before insisting on rights fraught with danger to the interests dearest to their heart'.

There was no way to know how the Boundary Commission would decide on the allocation of territory, but should it award to the Free State those border areas in which Catholics were a majority, the results would be injurious rather than beneficial. The separation of Catholics and Protestants would be even greater, 'and the forces tending to perpetuate partition strengthened thereby'. Any award of territory, moreover, would be confined to areas near the Border, and the bulk of Catholics 'will remain in the Northern area more isolated than ever'.

It might be hoped that a Northern Ireland state with diminished territory would, for financial reasons, be obliged to seek admission into the Free State. Thomas addressed this. The creation of Northern Ireland had been accepted by its Protestants only under protest; its formation had also been strenuously denounced by the Catholic minority and by every party in the South. He reminded the Irish government that there was another option: 'Were Northern Ireland to sue for reincorporation in the UK on the footing which these counties occupied before 1920, I know not what reasons a British government or parliament could give for refusing their request.'

The Free State should concentrate on the substantive obstacles to reunification: 'unrest, insecurity, and a sense of injustice and oppression in minorities'. It was his deep conviction 'that the union of all Ireland will be near when every man in it feels himself secure in the enjoyment of civil rights'. Thomas summarised his advice: 'Deliberate inaction, boldly adopted and consciously self-imposed with the concurrence and approval of the legislature, would, I believe, accelerate the union of Ireland by years.'[13]

Cosgrave and his colleagues did not accept Thomas's advice. It is likely that the determination to press ahead despite such friendly cautions arose from a need to outflank republican political activists and to draw the sting of critics who questioned the nationalist credentials of the Free State. Thomas had dwelt on the dangers of an award of territory to the Free State while emphasising that he had no means of predicting the decision of the Commission. As it turned out, the vague language of that part of the Treaty proved fatal to Free State hopes. The wording allowed scope for the Conservative friends of Northern Ireland to block what had been represented to Collins and Griffith as the 'poison pill', a possibly decisive loss to the new state of territory in the border areas where there existed a Roman Catholic majority and nationalist preferences.[14] It is clear that at least some of the British signatories to the Treaty at the time had anticipated and accepted a possible loss of territory to Northern Ireland, including two of its six counties. Chamberlain told the Commons that had the clause not been inserted in the Treaty the Irish would not have signed it; Churchill reiterated this and recognised that the deliberations of the Boundary Commission could result in revisions adverse to the Northern Ireland government.[15]

Such had been the explicitness of the Commons warnings that Sir James Craig had at an early point indicated that his administration would shun the Boundary Commission were it to be set up. No other course would have made sense for unionists. They had not wanted Home Rule and had it forced upon them; in subsequent negotiations to which they were not party, the territory which they had chosen as the basis of a viable state was exposed to the risk that it would be significantly reduced, crippling their ability to survive. The Sinn Féin delegation may or may not have been misled, but that was their problem: 'not an inch'.[16]

Faced with the Northern government's tactical refusal to nominate a representative to the Boundary Commission, a special Bill was introduced in August 1924, authorising the British government to make the nomination. Parliament assembled in special session on 30 September 1924 to carry the legislation.[17] The Commission's membership and terms of reference then became the issue. The British nominated Ulster unionist Joseph R. Fisher to the place that Craig had refused to fill, allowing the unionists to refuse their cake and eat it. The Free State nomination was Eoin MacNeill, then its minister for education. As chairman, the two governments agreed on Mr Justice Richard Feetham, a South African judge.[18] Nationalists made much in retrospect about the imperial past of Richard Feetham. It was open to the Free State government to have considered the matter more carefully and to have pushed the case for a more neutral figure. It would not have been prudent for the British government to nominate someone whose views were distinctly removed from their own. Afrikaaners had indeed shown themselves sympathetic to the national aspirations of the Irish, but this did not hold for South Africa's English-speaking community, which was reflexively imperialist and therefore pro-unionist. Given that the third man and chairman of the Commission had a casting vote, it is hard to understand why the Free State government failed to see the crucial significance of this appointment and to dig its toes in.

Lloyd George's reputation was mottled during his lifetime and has undergone no startling transformation since. He practised politics with fewer restraints of principle than one would expect to find in one who held such high office. The Irish politicians who dealt with him knew his reputation and at the very least should have discounted his private undertakings. And quite apart from Lloyd George's deviousness (a type of moral rot not in itself ignoble were it enrolled in the pursuit of peace), it is written in the first pages of the negotiator's chapbook that no agreement should be assented to that depends on or offers a variety of interpretations. A family solicitor of the most modest competence would not let a client buy a house in this way never mind agree the deeds for a new state. Like many deals struck in politics (and business), the Anglo-Irish Treaty had an element of the confidence trick about it: certainly there was bluffing and wishfulness on both sides. The difficulties multiplied later when, with the principal Irish leaders (Collins and Griffith) dead and Lloyd George out of office, the small print mattered.

Following Judge Feetham's appointment (5 June 1924) but before the Commission began its deliberations, a flurry of letters hit the press. They dealt with the Treaty itself, as well as with the changed political situation. Article XII provided that if Northern Ireland exercised its entitlement to opt out of the Irish Free State (which it did in January 1923) then the Boundary Commission should determine the boundary between the two states 'in accordance with the wishes of the inhabitants, so far as may be compatible with economic and geographic conditions'.[19] The second clause is such a powerful qualification that it all but robs the first clause of value (or indeed meaning). The argument was also used that a significant amount of time had passed since the establishment of Northern Ireland and even since the exercise of the option, and therefore the new state had a *prima facie* claim for its territorial integrity to be respected: squatters' rights.

Lord Birkenhead had, on the day after he signed the Treaty, deplored the suppression of the nationalist-dominated Tyrone County Council by the Northern Ireland government: 'we propose that a Boundary Commission shall examine into the boundary lines with a view of rendering impossible such an unhappy incident'.[20] Four months later, however, in a confidential letter to Arthur Balfour, a man who had liberally mixed coercion with conciliation during his tenure as Irish Chief Secretary, Birkenhead was on a different tack.[21] Article XII treated Northern Ireland as an existing state and not (as another reading would have it) as a new state coming into existence upon ratification of the Treaty.[22] The only permissible interpretation of such a reading was to confine the Commission to minor changes, such as the correction of obvious local anomalies and inconveniences. Lloyd George also took a very different line from that which he had pressed on Collins, although still allowing himself steerage room. He endorsed Birkenhead's view as 'the only responsible interpretation of that important clause'. He referred to the ability, integrity and impartiality of Feetham and concluded, 'I cannot imagine he will come to wild and unreasonable decisions which would tear up the territory of Ulster and leave it as a province with nothing but an unconsidered remnant of its land and population.'[23] Winston Churchill, another signatory, took a similar line. The Treaty had indeed contemplated a united Ireland, friendly to Britain, but the Article was intended to lead to nothing more than 'minor readjustments of boundary'.[24]

Other letters followed. A campaign had been mounted, with whatever degree of organisation and forethought, to pre-empt the scope and deliberations of the Boundary Commission. Ulster unionists took strength from these influential supporters, but, to dispel all doubt, Craig, in a rousing speech of 7 October 1924 to mark the opening of the Northern Ireland Parliament, underlined his government's position. Should the Boundary Commission produce unfavourable findings, he would, 'if no other honourable way out is open', resign his premiership and lead the people to defend any unfairly transferred territory.[25] This recalled the semi-treasonable threats of Carson and Law – repeated because they had served so well. The impact now was even greater since, far more than the Ulster Volunteers of 1914, Craig and his colleagues could possibly call on the services of a paramilitary Royal Ulster Constabulary (RUC) of around 2,500 strong – or at least the greater part of it. In addition, there was a territorial Special Constabulary, exclusively Protestant, of more than 35,000 men.[26] But all of this was unnecessary speculation: the notion of the British Army enforcing the secession of South Armagh, Tyrone and Fermanagh, and other border areas to the Free State, was far beyond the realm of realistic politics. And on the other side of the Border, as we shall see, the pragmatic leaders of the Irish Free State recognised that, whatever injustice they felt about it, the Boundary Commission would not produce a united Ireland. Replying to a militant critic of Free State policy, Kevin O'Higgins, Minister for Home Affairs, pointed to the chaos and destruction of the Civil War years and noted with characteristic acerbity that some people still wondered why 'the Orangemen are not hopping like so many fleas across the Border in their anxiety to come within our fold and jurisdiction'. If boundary changes came from the Commission, 'I shall consider that the British are an almost superhumanly wise people politically.' If there were no changes, the British would be foolish, 'but not nearly so foolish as ourselves'.[27]

The British and Free State governments made the best accommodation they could. The Commission, apart from a few trifling local changes, proposed no major adjustment other than the transfer from the Free State of a sizeable area of Co. Donegal. Eoin MacNeill had bound himself, with astonishing naivety, to signing the final report. In effect, this meant that he was in the hands of Mr Justice Feetham and Joseph R. Fisher. When at last he realised that the other two took a line very different to himself, his position became untenable, and, on

20 November 1924, he resigned.[28] This precipitated a crisis in the Free State government, reinforced by a leak in the Tory *Morning Post* of the proposed terms of the Commission's report.[29] There was a distinct possibility that Cosgrave's Cumann na nGaedheal government could fall, with very grave consequences for the peace and barely established stability of the Free State and thereby for Northern Ireland. The last gave the Irish some leverage.

In its advice to government, the Judicial Committee of the Privy Council had indicated that, once published, the Boundary Commission's report would have the force of law. It was imperative, therefore, that publication should not proceed.[30] On 27 November 1924, two days after MacNeill's resignation, a Free State delegation crossed to England. After discussion (including sessions between Kevin O'Higgins and Sir James Craig), it was decided that the difficulties could be overcome only by British and Free State legislation. This would deal with Article XII and (as a political inducement and help for Cosgrave in selling the boundary settlement to his electorate) Article V. The latter dealt with the financial obligations of the Free State in respect of its proportion of the war debts. It was agreed that the Irish share would be cancelled and that the Free State would increase the level of compensation to be paid to those who had suffered property losses between July 1921 and May 1923. The Council of Ireland was effectively wound up by being transferred to the Northern Ireland government (whose share of the war debt was also cancelled). With the exception (in 1938) of the handing back of the Treaty Ports, this was the final territorial settlement between the British and Irish governments.[31]

This agreement was one of the first acts of Stanley Baldwin's incoming government. It sat very well with his general policy of 'business as usual' uneventfulness and conciliation in domestic and foreign policy, which had so attracted the electorate. Although no one was completely satisfied, there seemed no basis for further trouble with Ireland. Republican insurgents had by then been conclusively defeated by the Free State. Craig had indeed taken on a substantial and resentful Roman Catholic and nationalist minority. However unhappy, that minority's armed element was no danger – especially in the light of the Free State's conciliatory policy and denial of a Southern hinterland and military refuge.

Intent on consolidating its own authority, recovering from the Civil War and finding a place in the community of nations, the Free State government entered into a period of cordial relations with Britain and with what was now called the Commonwealth rather than the Empire. Behind the scenes there were even reasonably cordial relations between individual members of the Free State and Northern Ireland governments, although neither openly attempted to improve neighbourliness or to give it more formal mechanisms.[32]

The Commonwealth was undergoing great change. At the 1923 Imperial Conference, the Free State had made little contribution, being both a newcomer and preoccupied with its civil war. Three years later, there was security at home and allies to be made abroad.[33] Smarting from what it considered to have been an improper interference in its internal affairs, arising from vestiges of a now outdated view of dominion status, Canada was determined that the independent nature of members of the Commonwealth should be fully and openly acknowledged.[34] Having recently emerged from a world war in which their sovereignty and resources had to some extent been subordinated to British needs and policies, there was a general sense among the dominions that the constitutional relationship between Commonwealth nations needed a new framework: legality rather than sentiment, convention and precedent. Two countries alone of these had been involved in armed struggle with Britain: South Africa and the Irish Free State.[35] Both looked backward and forward in finding a loosening of imperial ties desirable. On the British side there was a recognition that a new framework would have benefits for all. Arthur Balfour (who had succeeded Curzon as Lord President) found a formula of words that fitted the times. Great Britain and the dominions were 'autonomous Communities within the British Empire, equal in status, in no way subordinate to one another in any aspect of their domestic or external affairs, though united by a common allegiance to the Crown, and freely associated as members of the British Commonwealth of Nations'.[36] Such acknowledgement of the realities of the relationships between this group of nations became the basis for the 1931 Statute of Westminster.[37] In an ironic twist, this in turn provided a legal basis and cleared the political ground for an Irish repudiation of the Treaty. Cosgrave's pledge that this would not happen became a nullity the following year when de Valera's Fianna Fáil came into office and immediately began working towards 'external association' and all the trappings of independence to go alongside what was undoubtedly already the substance.

But this lay ahead. Throughout the decade following the foundation of the Irish Free State, relations between the British and Irish governments became ever more 'normalised' and stable. Successive British governments accommodated to the passage from Empire to Commonwealth and within that broad change its relationship with Ireland. This had been a source of strife and complications for centuries, and of death and destruction just a few years before. The Irish, North and South, were now handling their own affairs, and the heart of Empire had not ruptured. Rather, the new relationship between London, Belfast and Dublin was in tune with the temper of the times. At the end of that first decade, peace seemed unchallenged – as was the British determination not again to become involved in internal Irish affairs.

Despite this political understanding, social, cultural, economic and institutional ties were more complicated and certainly more difficult to disentangle – even where such severance was sought. Language, kinship, shared legal and educational institutions, the impact of Irish literature and drama, Irish workers in British cities, offices, factories and fields; English journals, newspapers, cinema, broadcasting, books and, of course, commerce and manufacturers throughout Ireland: all these maintained many powerful links and everyday shared experiences. A common currency and apparatus of public life also contributed to the sense that neither nation was truly foreign to the other: the lack of passports for travel between the two states confirmed this, as did reciprocal voting arrangements. A divorce indeed, but with lingering and tolerable elements of cohabitation. Yet, as in many such arrangements, there was distance and a residual bitterness, a sense reviving on both sides from time to time of betrayal, bad faith, unaddressed injury and irreparably sundered fidelity.

Ireland: who is the custodian?

In times of peace, such episodes of violence and disorder as may occur have a monstrous quality, distressing yet oddly reassuring to those not directly affected and who, with gratitude, continue in the routine of their lives. These aberrations simply confirm the virtues of the quiet, unremarkable and predictable, and when they are past assert the solidity of the structures of the normal. By 1922, Ireland had endured a decade of political upheaval unmatched since the times of Elizabeth I, Oliver Cromwell or William of Orange. Although unevenly inflicted, the destruction of life and property extended to many parts of the country, and insecurity was experienced by all. Sectarian hatreds led to murder, pogrom and retaliation in the six counties of Northern Ireland. With its overwhelming Roman Catholic majority, and quite a different history of interdenominational relations, sectarianism manifested itself differently and was more diffuse in the twenty-six counties of the Free State – though there were also localised episodes of murder, arson, robbery and intimidation.[38]

In further contrast to Northern Ireland, the First World War was a divisive topic in public discourse. Conscription had not been extended to Ireland, though its threat inflamed opinion, united all shades of nationalism and drove further home the wedge between Ulster unionism and nationalist Ireland. But even without conscription, Irish participation was considerable. Great Britain enlisted 24 per cent of its adult male population in the armed forces, Ireland only 6 per cent. But this amounted to around 206,000 men: some 27,000 Irishmen lost their lives.[39] These deaths and other casualties had their effect across the land: losses and sufferings intensified by the return to civilian life in Ireland. Some of the demobilised found their way into the Irish Republican Army (IRA), others into the Black and Tans and the Auxiliary Division. Many of those ex-servicemen who simply returned to their hearths felt the nation sweep on by them, their sacrifice and that of their comrades marginalised, even nullified, by an insecure sense of nationhood that abhorred, excluded or, at the very least, was embarrassed by the British connection.[40]

All that had happened since the Home Rule campaigns of 1912 combined to sweep masses of people into militant organisations, to agitate and intensify feelings, to blunt sensibilities and to erode constraints. The Ulster Covenant of 1912, the formation of the Ulster Volunteers and then the Irish Volunteers, gun-running into Larne and Howth were, in retrospect, gentle and misleading preludes. Rhetoric and posturing passed into reality and deed: hundreds of thousands of young men placed themselves under military discipline and turned their emotions and ambitions from the worlds of work and domesticity to the transforming romance of bravery, sacrifice, death and national renown.

To move from such fancies to action is a terrible awakening. For the loyal sons of Ulster there was the Somme, the first battle of which produced a carnage over an eighteen-day period then as remarkable and awful as any in the long history of wars.[41] Judged by the volume of its deaths and maimings, the Easter Rising and the two years or so of the Anglo-Irish War were hardly remarkable – a total of casualties seen in a few hours of a skirmishing attack on the Western Front.[42] But those terrible battlefields of the First World War were removed from the lives of most non-combatants. What developed in Ireland was an urban guerrilla war, increasingly permeating civilian life, apt at any time to touch with tragedy and loss the most sheltered of existences. Terror and counter-terror were endured in a manner that in the old life would have seemed inconceivable; humans are wonderfully and tragically adaptable.

The motives of those who become involved in insurrection, rebellion and civil war are many, often passing their own understanding. At its most rational, there was a conviction that the national grievances of Ireland were so great that they called for immediate resolution and that, after a long but ultimately frustrated parliamentary campaign, no means were open but force: a national uprising was morally justified, and civic duty demanded participation or support. A considerable number of people, many of whom were intelligent, educated and with a position, prospects and property to lose, took this view. In later life, in their political and private actions, they showed themselves to be reasonable and ethical. We cannot, it is true, conclude from later actions and beliefs that on embarking on insurrection or revolution they were so reasonable, but we can say that they were not cast in some perverse mould of violence and unreason. Even at the time of their departure from the law they seemed capable of envisaging political goals well within the bounds of reason. It was from these ranks that many leaders of post-revolutionary, post-war political life were drawn.

But the ranks of revolutionaries included many types and sub-types. A Hardyesque twist of fate pitched some into violent action. It was seemingly a chance meeting with a student colleague that drew Ernie O'Malley into insurrection, terror and civil war and made him a much-wounded and legendary fighting man.[43] Had there been no encounter that Easter Monday, would O'Malley, who not long before had thought of following a brother into the British armed services, have found himself on the side of established law and order, pursuing an unremarkable career in medicine? Perhaps. Or another type again: in his seventeenth year, Tom Barry had joined the British Army 'for no other reason than that I wanted to see what it was like, to get a gun, to see new countries and to feel a grown man'.[44] Campaigning in Mesopotamia, news of the Easter Rising reached Barry several weeks after the event, but this was enough to take him into the first ranks of IRA fighters on his return home three years later. Was he a born soldier whose desires for war, danger and glory were only partly met by service in the British Army and who found a more perfect satisfaction in leadership in the Anglo-Irish War?[45]

Even more directly and more literally, some were accidental soldiers. There were those in Volunteer ranks who, on Easter Monday 1916, thought they were going out on yet another of the mock skirmishes that had become so familiar in Dublin in preceding months and were shocked to find themselves in action.[46] Some, no doubt, returned to civilian life when and how they could; others were turned into genuine revolutionaries by the camaraderie of battle and the months of internment that followed. Yet another group enjoyed the local status – and power – that came from membership of the IRA. And there were those opportunists, always ready to surface in times of upheaval and disorder, who grasped the chance to kill, to loot, to bully, consumed by the grievance of their exclusion from the established order. Another group again may have sought escape from the tedium of plough, cowshed and orchard: Tom Barry writ small. In a predominantly agricultural country where many had a poor and uncertain living, participation in Sinn Féin or in the IRA – especially after the Truce of 1921 – may have been a means of reserving a place in the queue for a government or local-government preferment in the great redistribution that was to come.

The strength and quality of the commitment to armed struggle therefore varied immensely. At one extreme there were those who went firmly before the firing squad or took the hangman's hand, fortified or enraptured with the righteousness of their cause, humbled by the usefulness and appropriateness of their sacrifice and fortified by the conviction of a shriven and certain passage to Paradise. A code of loyalty and bravery saw others through – to death or to the grey years of peace.[47] And options close to those who have dwelt in a brotherhood of death: the need to keep faith with their dead was for some far greater than politics or revolutionary doctrine or organisational discipline.

It could, of course, be a long and complicated journey into revolution. Padraig Pearse travelled from Home Rule through Gaelic culture, language, literature and games to the oath of the Irish Republican Brotherhood (IRB) and then to a carefully crafted sacrifice.[48] James Connolly had come from international socialism, syndicalism and Marxism to a most unlikely terminus in militant nationalism.[49] Others found in the death of the 1916 leaders, and in those who followed them, an anchor for a passionate spirituality that commingled national and personal salvation. For these, the Republic was to be the enthronement of perfection, the joyous realisation of man's hopes, a wholly new beginning, the arrival of the beloved. Mary MacSwiney (whose brother Terence had recharged the republican movement by his Brixton hunger strike and death) wrote in 1922 to Richard Mulcahy, the head of the Free State Army.[50] Was the Treaty worth all the unhappiness (of the pending civil war), she demanded? 'Do you not realise that we hold the Republic as a living faith – a spiritual reality stronger than any material benefits you can offer – cannot give it up. It is not *we* who have changed it is you.'[51]

The unsettling and distorting effects of war upon the personalities of participants need little further comment. Those are often severe and persistent when war is joined in a regular army, with all the mental and physical controls, restrictions and support of military structures and discipline. When war, however terrible it may be, is experienced on a battlefield and far from soldiers' homes, there is, on demobilisation, a reasonable possibility of finding a new phase in one's life. Memories – happy, miserable, fearful and exultant – will remain. That they form one of the pillars of adult life is attested to by the associations, reunions and parades of comrades. For some, indeed, military service and war will remain the most intense experience of a lifetime: adventure, danger, comradeship, achievement, loss and survival have a piquancy of youth and romance which may in secret be mourned.

The man or woman involved in revolution and guerrilla war experiences all of the emotions, tests and demands of the regular soldier, and more. Always under threat of discovery or capture, injury or death, some can pass the dangerous months and years with little or no involvement in military action, confined perhaps to watching, carrying, hiding, sabotage, espionage or an occasional and inconclusive ambush. Others can experience intense action, the joy of survival, the power of life and death, the responsibility of command, a type of fame – and this at a young and unformed age. And there are, as twentieth-century history revealed all too clearly, many for whom war ruptures the crust that keeps them in a netherworld of their own instincts, fancies and desires. Those who rejoice in domination, aggression and violence find a golden chance to cross from imaginings and longings to action: to destroy, to humiliate and degrade, to inflict pain and fear, to kill – all such may satisfy a dark lust. Those who are full of envy and resentment get their opportunity to even scores, to demean, to devalue and scorn. Loathsome when fully exposed, the fortunes of war may of course make these worrying but far from unknown figures effective and much commended soldiers.

There is an opposite view. Those who from some distance of space and time contemplate war frequently fixate on the notion of sacrifice and contrast that nobility to the self-absorption and venality of peace. War is seen as a cleansing fire and a purge of all that is base: it is the birthing pangs of a new world, as the revolutionary cliché inevitably has it. Padraig Pearse found such joy in this destructive prospect that in the midst of the Great War's unprecedented horrors he described the times as 'the most glorious in the history of Europe'. By most accounts a kind and sensitive man, an intense but perverted vision allowed him to proclaim, 'It is good for the world that such things should be done. The old heart of the earth needed to be warmed with the red wine of the battlefields.'[52]

But to be charitable, we now know, far more than he, the evil that clings to such phrases. A country is not a briar patch to be reduced by a fire to fertile ashes and purified earth. Human beings, no matter their defects and vices, are not the same as weeds, and any political thought, any rhetoric, metaphor or violence of expression that suggests so is profoundly and inexcusably wicked and destructive. War destroys the talented and the benign as easily as the corrupt and malign; it blights lives and destroys the patrimony of generations as easily as it consumes the institutions of pride and unjustified privilege; it deals misery out equally to the innocent, the ordinary and the guilty. As war proceeds, ebbs and flows, intensifies and dwindles, much of this may be obscured by the tumult and the haze, by blood-lust and righteous exultation.

Civil War

The foundation of the Irish Free State is a well-known story, often rehearsed; we need not here recapitulate it in any great detail.[53] The Sinn Féin negotiators, able but inexperienced and acting as plenipotentiaries, signed the Treaty under great (and expertly stage-managed) pressure. Even the hour, 2 a.m. on 6 December 1921, betokened the desperation of the occasion – real and contrived. Lloyd George, whose experience *was* immense, would doubtless have insisted that manipulation was necessary and was a deed of grace: he was utterly convinced that drift meant disaster, giving opponents of the Treaty on both sides of the Irish Sea a chance to regroup. These were difficult decisions to swallow. The British, whose negotiators included several of the Empire's most stalwart unionists, and convinced imperialists, agreed to the dismemberment of the UK, to them the world's ultimate bastion of civilisation and decency. They had met as delegates, shaken hands with and come to agreement with those who had wrecked British institutions in Ireland, men who had only recently been described as members of a 'murder gang'. The massive political effort that the British politicians had made, and continued to make, unsurprisingly went unremarked and unapplauded in Ireland.[54] These were not the times for a broader or generous view.

The Irish had given up the Republic. This was the overriding sacrifice and immediate cause of the Civil War which would follow. The Republic had been a part of the solemn oath of the IRB since its foundation in 1858 and was by that undertaking declared to be virtually established, the entity to which allegiance was sworn. Its material triumph had been the goal of Fenianism through the decades that followed, an abiding compact, sealed by death and sacrifice. It had been the central focus of the 1916 Rising and of the first Dáil Éireann. The Republic had enjoyed a significant political and administrative existence throughout the Anglo-Irish War, its authority accepted, or enforced by arms. The acts of insurgents were not its only basis. In 1918 and again in 1920, the Irish electorate had shown its support, overwhelmingly and emphatically, for Sinn Féin and the Republic it upheld. At the moment of the signing of the Treaty, all the delegates plenipotentiary took their authority not from Sinn Féin alone but from the Irish Republic, yet the solemn agreement to which they put their signatures required the dissolution of the Republic.

Both sides were keenly aware of the difficulties they would face in selling the settlement to their followers, and that it would inevitably produce pockets of inflamed and indeed enraged opposition. The British negotiators knew that the non-republican name of the new state, the oath of allegiance and fealty, and membership of the British Empire, were essentially stage props to distract attention from actual independence.[55] It was inconceivable that the British electorate or even the Commons would at some future time countenance a reconquest of Ireland on the issue of an oath, a name or even 'membership' of the increasingly fluid British Empire. Yet the stage props, so necessary for British politics, the symbolism and the sacred words, violently divided Irish opinion. Concentrating on the ceding of the Republic, the Irish delegates seem not to have recognised that through the agreement Ulster unionism had obtained a permanent veto over Irish unity.

For exercising their plenipotentiary powers and signing without reference back to the cabinet, the Irish delegates were criticised in the strongest terms by anti-Treaty colleagues. After intense discussion, the vote to accept the Treaty split the cabinet by four votes to three, with Éamon de Valera in the minority. The issue then went to the legislature. Several subsequent weeks of intense lobbying and debate ended, as noted, with a narrow Dáil majority (sixty-four to fifty-seven) in favour of ratification.[56] The British Parliament had met in special session three weeks before, and the Commons, after thorough and sometimes acrimonious debate, voted overwhelmingly (401 to fifty-eight) for ratification.[57] The stage props were a necessary face-saver, but, beyond a doubt, the guarantee to Ulster was the factor that enabled Conservatives to override deeply held convictions. The agreement was not to his liking, but Conservative leader Bonar Law admitted that he saw no alternative: the Irish should be given a chance to carry it through.[58] The Lords, ever the final bastion in reactionary thinking about Ireland, ratified by a smaller but still decisive majority of 166 to forty-seven. The Lords' debate included Carson's vitriolic personal attack on Birkenhead, who, he said, had abandoned Ulster once it ceased to serve his ambition. Curzon he accused of humbugging all during the anti-Home Rule campaign; others, including Lloyd George, got an equally savage drubbing.[59]

The voting done, there came the complicated business of carrying the Treaty into effect. There was, first of all, the question of the transitional authority. There existed a House of Commons for Southern Ireland, which, under the GOIA, had been elected in May 1921.[60] Sinn Féin had refused to participate in this body, and its candidates who had triumphed at the polls constituted them-selves as the Second Dáil Éireann, meeting in Dublin's Mansion House on 16 August 1921, in the name of the Irish Republic. The Irish Commons never-theless existed (and indeed had had an inaugural meeting on 28 June 1921) and had therefore had to be dissolved. On 14 January 1922, it met formally for the second and final time. Only those Sinn Féin members in favour of the Treaty attended, and they, together with the four Unionist members for Trinity College Dublin, approved the Treaty and elected the ministers of the Provisional government. A continuity of authority (which was at the same time a genesis) had been achieved. This interim government was to act as an executive until (as provided by the Treaty) the Irish Free State came into existence on 6 December 1922.

There were now two governments in existence in the twenty-six counties of Southern Ireland, and, in the continuing presence of its armed forces, its functioning civil service and the Lord Lieutenant, a substantial vestige of the old regime. Northern Ireland had had its legislature and government for several months. So, by any reckoning, this small island had four governments: authority, multiply expressed, hung on gossamer. The Dáil ministries and the Provisional government largely overlapped and were occupied by the same persons. Arthur Griffith, elected President of Dáil Éireann after de Valera's resignation, did not join the Provisional government, although he shared responsibility for implementing the Treaty. Michael Collins became chairman of the new government and Richard Mulcahy its minister for defence, combining that position with minister for defence in the Dáil government.

This last duality has a Gilbertian ring about it yet was of great importance, since the Treaty had split the IRA. Many of its members had, however, taken an oath of loyalty to the Dáil, which, while it at first appeared to reinforce the anti-Treaty position, had, in reality, the opposite effect. It was imperative for the new government to buy time to build up a pro-Treaty regular army in place of the IRA, which had a tradition of autonomy that many members were straining to regain. Evading rather than confronting the issues of IRA ultimate authority and loyalty could only gain that breathing space. The narrow pro-Treaty majority that had been won in the Dáil was the basis for this manoeuvre. Mulcahy's Janus-like position and his gnomic statements were also immeasurably valuable in heading off immediate IRA action against the Treaty: in this he showed political skill of a high order. On 13 January 1922, he declared that the IRA could not be transferred to the authority of the Provisional government. The Dáil was the government of the Republic and the IRA its army. This reassured many Volunteers but obscured the fact that a majority of the Dáil had voted for the Treaty, and a prime figure in the Treaty negotiations, Arthur Griffith, was now its president. In practical terms, it mattered little therefore that the IRA was subject to the authority of the Dáil rather than that of the Provisional government. What did count was the military inaction of the anti-Treaty faction and the willingness of the remainder either to leave off soldiering or to serve the Free State.

Under cover of this impasse the new army was rapidly being organised. It had conventional ranks and command structure and was loyal to the Provisional government, which was its paymaster and source of appointments and promotions. Soldiers and officers were drawn from pro-Treaty IRA units and individuals, together with persons unconnected with the IRA. The sense of impending violence, the vast difference between the life, style and resources of a disciplined professional army and that of a guerrilla army and the uncertain authority of the Provisional government all made the creation of the new force a difficult and complicated task. But, despite many problems, within its first six months the National Army had expanded from a small nucleus to about 10,000 men.[61]

This new body was the rock on which the Free State had to be built. A state that depended on the British Army would not have gained the trust of the Irish people, or at least of a substantial section of them, and that would have invited republican resurgence. British military evacuation began almost immediately, demonstrating adherence to the Treaty and, at the same time, reducing the danger of clashes with republican forces. Arrangements for the demobilisation of the residue of 233 officers and 5,764 men of the Royal Irish Constabulary (RIC) were well advanced within six weeks of the formation of the Provisional government.[62] Despite his government's difficulties, weakness and lack of resources, Michael Collins well understood that evacuation strengthened its position. In mid-February there had been some suggestion in the English press that British evacuation had been slowed in order to assist the Provisional government. Collins took the rumour to Churchill:

> The best way in which the British Government could help us at the present time is not by suspending the carrying out of the Treaty but by so adhering to its spirit and letter that Ireland will be convinced that Britain is really delivering the goods this time. Many people in Ireland believe that even at this late hour England will again trick us and this belief is used as much as possible to our disadvantage by those who oppose us.[63]

At the heart of Britain's coalition government was a group particularly well suited to steer its end of the Anglo-Irish relations through the tumultuous and unprecedented events that followed. Lloyd George had the necessary combination of ruthlessness, detachment, experience, guile and commitment to persuade, push and pull his cabinet colleagues. Winston Churchill, impetuous English patriot, had a deal of generosity and personal loyalty in his make-up and, together with Birkenhead, Chamberlain and Law, defended the Treaty and the Provisional government from unionist criticisms that ranged from the worried to the outraged. This quintet was certainly tested as events in Ireland headed, it would have seemed to any reasonable observer, towards disorder and breakdown.

The IRA had taken an oath to the Dáil at a comparatively late point in the Anglo-Irish War.[64] During the spring of 1922, it, and uncompromising Sinn Féiners, looked for a way forward. There remained sufficient heat in the old ties of comradeship and affection to prevent an immediate attack on the pro-Treaty units, now reforming into the National Army, efforts instead being concentrated on trying to revive a common front against the British. This proved to be the strategic blunder of its military arm that doomed the republican cause – though whether it would have prevailed in an immediate struggle in which they would also have had to face a reactivated British Army is at best questionable.

The republicans' political cul-de-sac was an insistence that there was a mandate beyond the popular will. It had become obvious that when it came to be put before the electorate the Treaty would secure their support. Various formulae were sought to square this political circle. De Valera, an intelligent and deeply logical man, put the case with apparent fatuousness: 'The people had never a right to do wrong.'[65] This was a curious doctrine for a republican of any hue, as de Valera must in his heart have recognised. He was in the frustrating position – not unfamiliar to conventional politicians – of knowing what was best for the country but seeing the people take the wrong course.[66] They often do, but it is precisely that right which is the essence (and occasional flaw) of democracy. In the more ideological and purest ranks of republicanism there was an ambivalent, uncertain and shifting attitude to democracy. Part of the reasoning behind the 1916 Rising was that the Irish people had become politically debased and needed a violent shock and the spectacle of sacrifice to call them to their national duty. This divination of the best interests of the people always was part of the special talent of revolutionaries, from Robespierre to Clarke and from Pearse to Lenin. In the autumn of 1922, republicans were infuriated by an observation in the Catholic bishops' pastoral letter on the Civil War: 'A Republic without popular recognition behind it is a contradiction in terms.'[67] If the objective of the armed struggle had not been to secure the right of the people to govern themselves (and therefore to make bad as well as good choices), then what had it been?

The Provisional government focused on an electoral mandate, which it linked to the rapid build-up of an army subject to political authority. Voters would be given the conditions of security within which to ratify or repudiate the Treaty and the Constitution (still being negotiated with the British) which was to flow from it. Through intimidation and attacks on polling stations, electoral officials, candidates, meetings, canvassers and supporters, irreconcilable republicans could have prevented the election or rendered it so uneven as to be meaningless. This would have created an impasse in the political revival of the country and, possibly, a break with the British. The last would almost certainly have led to a blockade and partial reconquest.[68]

To minimise these possibilities, Collins entered into a pact with de Valera to put forward a joint panel of Sinn Féin candidates, proportions to be in accordance with the voting strengths of the two groups in the existing Dáil. The coalition government that would follow this curious 'election' would include non-oath-taking 'external' ministers, heading departments but not voting in cabinet. The British were having none of it. Churchill pronounced the pact to be a violation of the Treaty, a rigged election to deprive the electorate of its voice on the Treaty and to clear the way for the Republic. Level talking, especially from Griffith, convinced the British negotiators that the pact was a sensible tactic and that Collins had stolen an important advantage from de Valera.[69] By this point, a great deal hung on the personal commitment, integrity and mutual trust of the Irish and British negotiators: vital national interests were involved, but it was personal ties and credibility that swung the deal.

The general election was fixed for 16 June 1922. From the outset, it became apparent that Sinn Féin would not have it all to itself.[70] The pact had nevertheless been a tranquillising influence, and, given the general state of disorder, the election campaign was tolerably peaceful. Some candidates (especially from the Farmers' Party) were threatened by local republicans and withdrew; it is also impossible to compute how many would have liked to offer themselves but were deterred by intimidation and the general perception of danger in public life. The pact had involved some rigging, but not nearly as much as London had feared: only thirty-four Sinn Féin candidates stood unopposed. By agreement, seventeen came from each faction of the party, but one must wonder whether and by what means other parties were dissuaded from coming forward in these constituencies.[71] Far from perfect – but for all the intimidation, direct and indirect, and the unpropitious atmosphere, there was established an acceptable basis for a contested and authoritative election: with a certain amount of throat-clearing, the democratic voice was to be heard.

There were two significant and last-minute developments. On 14 June 1922, speaking on his home ground in Cork, Michael Collins addressed a large crowd, withdrawing the exhortation to vote for the Sinn Féin panel and urging the electors instead to support the candidates they most preferred.[72] This precisely timed repudiation of the pact, dirty but effective politics, wrong-footed the de Valera group.[73] Given what would emerge as the mood of the country, it is difficult to assess whether it swung votes; it is also hard to know how many of the rural electorate got to hear of it. Coming from Collins, however, it was a clear promise that the entitlement to a free vote would be respected. It is likewise difficult to gauge the effect of the Free State constitution, which was published only on the morning of election day. The timing was not a Provisional government ploy but rather the effect of the intense and protracted negotiations to obtain an agreement that the document conformed to the Treaty. It was only on 15 June 1922 that the Law Officers were able to make that declaration. The Irish had contrived to push the language of the document as far away as possible from any suggestion of continued British domination. On their side, the British had sought to purge it of republicanism.[74]

But these two last-minute developments were no *deus ex machina*. Most commentators agree that they had a marginal impact. There was a turnout of only 60 per cent, the electoral register was undoubtedly out of date and inaccurate, there were several worrying incidents on election day, and the traditional injunction to 'vote early and vote often' was doubtless piously observed. But, in the end, the voice of the people was heard.[75] Some 620,000 votes were cast, 60 per cent going to the Sinn Féin panel candidates. This bald figure masked an overwhelming defeat for the anti-Treaty side, which won only 131,000 first-preference votes, some 21 per cent of the total cast. Pro-Treaty Sinn Féin votes were almost twice that number (239,000), not far short of 40 per cent. Independents and Farmers between them won 115,000 (18 per cent) and Labour 133,000 (21 per cent – greater than anti-Treaty Sinn Féin).[76] Under the system of proportional representation, and because seventeen of its candidates had been elected unopposed, the anti-Treaty party secured more seats in the Dáil than these figures warranted. The government had fifty-eight seats, anti-Treaty

Sinn Féin thirty-six, Labour seventeen, Independents ten (including four from Trinity College) and the Farmers' Party seven. In all, ninety-two of the 128 Dáil seats were held by pro-Treaty members: the most determined casuistry could not conceal the fact that de Valera's prediction, given some months before, had come true.[77]

During the constitutional negotiations, and the election campaign, strenuous efforts had been made to reunite the IRA: this was seen as an essential step were civil war to be avoided. Discussions were complicated because there were several strands of opinion in the IRA, personalities and localism played important parts, and alliances frequently shifted. It was the unshakeable belief of the irreconcilable faction that the Treaty betrayed the Republic the IRA had sworn to defend and that that obligation transcended all others. Sections of this group favoured some form of military dictatorship – a logical consequence of the doctrine that right could transcend democracy. Before the election, on 13 April, anti-Treaty IRA units occupied the Four Courts and other Dublin buildings. Barracks were seized elsewhere, and within weeks there were clashes with the National Army. Despite these provocations, and much to the fury and deepening concern of the British Cabinet, the Provisional government pursued a softly-softly policy, where possible avoiding confrontation and keeping the door open for reconciliation. This last reflected, at least in part, the personal anguish of many on both sides at the prospect of violence between comrades. Collins, pivotal in the military struggle against the British, had run his underground organisation with a great emphasis on personal loyalty and now found himself particularly torn. The stand-off could not continue, however, and the Provisional government had to act or surrender.

During the weeks of meetings and negotiation, neither side had been idle in preparation. Republicans had robbed banks and post offices for the funds that government had denied them; motor vehicles, fuel, food and other supplies were commandeered, and numerous buildings were occupied. The National Army continued rapidly to expand and had begun to take in experienced soldiers from the British and US armies; it had also been supplied with a considerable amount of British *matériel*.

For some weeks, London had been pressing for action against those engaged in robberies, seizures and other acts of defiance. Cabinet had reached the point where it was prepared to use its own troops: an order to that effect was actually issued to General Sir Nevil Macready, Commander-in-Chief of British Forces in Ireland. For its part, the anti-Treaty IRA could not go on simply occupying buildings, robbing banks and confiscating supplies: these were means rather than ends. But still, it was reluctant to attack the Provisional government. A plan was made to attack the remaining British garrison with the intention of bringing on a reunifying general melee.[78] But events were to take quite a different course. On 22 June 1922, Sir Henry Wilson was murdered on the doorstep of his home in central London.[79] Years of speculation have not determined who ordered the killing. A substantial body of opinion holds Collins responsible – either in the form of an earlier instruction not cancelled or as a response to the police and military advice and political support that Wilson was giving to the Northern Ireland government.[80] This involvement in Northern affairs particularly inflamed opinion in the South because of the actions then being taken against Roman Catholics in Belfast and elsewhere.[81] The British government had no reliable intelligence but not illogically assumed the assassination had been ordered by the anti-Treaty IRA headquartered at the Four Courts; the two IRA men arrested near the scene of Wilson's murder said nothing to indicate otherwise.[82] The killing had outraged British opinion, reinforced the unionist and diehard element in the Conservative Party and increased parliamentary pressure on the British Cabinet to resolve the situation in Dublin.[83]

Four days after Wilson's murder, one of the republicans' senior officers, Commandant General Leo Henderson, was arrested, in Ernie O'Malley's words, 'enforcing the boycott on a Dublin firm', that is, taking fifteen cars and a quantity of fuel at gunpoint.[84] The anti-Treaty GHQ (General Headquarters) decided to take hostage an officer of equal rank in the National Army and to hold him in the Four Courts against Henderson's release. The shortlist of candidates included Michael Collins, Chairman of the Provisional government; Richard Mulcahy, Minister for Defence; and Lieutenant General 'Ginger' O'Connell, Deputy Chief of Staff in the National Army.[85] Circumstances made O'Connell an easy seizure. The National Army command was informed that he would be swapped for Henderson. At the same time, an attack on the remaining British garrison was imminent.[86] All of this heaped potentially lethal contempt on the Provisional government. Churchill's public demand for immediate action complicated the situation. At its meeting on 27 June, notwithstanding the risk that it would be accused of dancing to a British tune, the Irish cabinet authorised an attack on the Four Courts and requested the necessary field-guns from the British garrison. That night, preparations were made, including the assembly of a small battery of eighteen-pound guns (apparently the heaviest that could be used without trained British gunners). At 3.40 a.m. on the morning of 28 June 1922, an ultimatum was delivered to the Four Courts, demanding surrender within twenty minutes. As expected, this was not forthcoming, and at 4 a.m. the National Army launched its attack.[87] Although skirmishes of sorts had been going on for some months, and lives had indeed been lost, the tide of civil war now began its flood: all was swept before it.

This war has been much considered and written about, and, while it is not necessary to duplicate that material, a number of observations bear restating.[88] Popular support for the republican side was not great, strong in pockets but unevenly distributed, and it dwindled rapidly. War-weariness was widespread, and there was a general readiness to accept the Treaty: this had been conclusively demonstrated in the general election. The need to commandeer and forage caused deep resentment and eroded republican discipline, and in towns such as Cork and Limerick it gave the anti-Treaty side the character of an occupying army. Their destruction of transport links also caused widespread hardship. The Civil War was hugely destructive to an economy already shattered by several years of insurrection and disorder. The vulnerability of a poor agricultural country would, even under the best of circumstances, have been more than evident as the post-war downturn took hold in the major manufacturing countries. Civil war made the situation immeasurably worse and set the scene for a half-century of economic underdevelopment; it also destroyed utterly and comprehensively whatever faint reunification prospects might have existed. Unionist fears of republicanism and nationalism seemed amply justified: insurrection, subversion and guerrilla war stretching back to 1916 and beyond, and now a further outbreak of blood-letting and destruction. Finally, a crop of internecine hatred was sown that affected Irish life for generations.

Beginning with the odds stacked against them, the republican side adopted tactics that guaranteed defeat. Taking and holding buildings in Dublin made no military sense: it was little more that a reprise of the 1916 Rising, yet all were aware of how speedily that had been crushed by a relatively modest application of conventional military power. Indeed, tactics were hopelessly muddled, constantly attempting to combine the oil and water of political and military objectives. The republican leadership tried to be symbolic, evocative and inspirational and at the same time to be militarily effective. This last, we need hardly remind ourselves, means eliminating the enemy by the application of superior force. The Four Courts served as the republicans' GHQ, yet it had no store of food, inadequate munitions, no plan for outpost defence, deployed no scouts or roving patrols, was close to concentrations of Provisional government and British soldiers, was easily surrounded and was occupied without an escape or breakout plan: this was voluntary entrapment. The true importance of the Four Courts to the IRA leadership was, indeed, that it replicated the General Post Office (GPO) of 1916, was scene-setting in a pageant, intended to set loose a surge of patriotic feeling. In line with this, a proclamation was drawn up and posted around Dublin. The historical stage was everything: script, characters, lighting and mood music were all in place. Hours before surrender, Ernie O'Malley (who had taken over as garrison commander – ranks, function and military courtesies seeming to increase in importance as options narrowed and hopes faded) told a sympathetic visiting priest, 'We're not men just now, we're a symbol.'[89]

Likewise, in the countryside, there was an attempt to hold territory, even the brief establishment of a 'Munster Republic'.[90] A weaker force can succeed only if it has considerable mobility, determination, ferocity and the tacit or active support of a sufficient section of the people. Attempts to hold territory are futile when faced by a numerically superior enemy that has greater access to transport, supplies and artillery. Ferocity was absent from the beginning, and one can well understand the dilemma. A massacre of National Army troops in barracks, on parade, or on patrol could doubtless have been arranged, but it would have forfeited what was already dwindling political support. There were indeed fierce clashes at later stages in the Civil War – and atrocities by both sides – but the game had by then been lost. It is also worth noting the military consequences of operating in the midst of a population at best neutral: information, shelter and other forms of support essential to the guerrilla are withheld.

By European standards, the toll in deaths and casualties of the Irish Civil War was small. It was said that some 800 National Army troops were lost between January 1922 and April 1924. Records, understandably, were poorly kept, and, even on the government side, such figures are not wholly reliable. Republican deaths, even more difficult to compute, probably amounted to just under 300 (including seventy-seven who were executed). Three or four times that number could be expected to have been wounded. Civilian deaths were numerous, but no accurate calculation can be given.[91] Loss of private property and damage to public property and the infrastructure was reckoned to be some £50 million, a huge sum in money values for the times and a very significant portion of Irish national wealth.[92] Casualties and destruction considerably exceeded those of the years 1916–21, particularly when the relative brevity of the conflict (eleven months) is considered.

Soldiers inevitably became brutalised and behaved accordingly. In Co. Kerry there occurred terror and counter-terror as bad or worse than anything that happened during the Anglo-Irish War. In the early hours of 5 March 1923, four Free State soldiers, following up false intelligence about a dugout, were killed and another wounded by a booby-trap.[93] It was decided that thenceforward prisoners would be used to clear mines, but circumstances suggest that this was simply cover for murder. Two days later, nine captive republicans were taken to a mined barricade at Ballyseedy Bridge, near Tralee, Co. Kerry, where they were tied together and the mine detonated. Eight men were killed. The same tactics were followed in succeeding days, killing four men at Countess Bridge near Killarney and five at Cahersiveen. Addressing the Dáil and citing the Army's Court of Inquiry into the bridge incident, Richard Mulcahy, Minister for Defence, in effect approved of these tactics.[94]

Desperation begat increasing ruthlessness. On 27 November 1922, Liam Lynch, anti-Treaty Chief of Staff, responded to new emergency powers promulgated by the Army Council and sanctioned by the Dáil. This had granted extensive powers to Military Tribunals, including imposition of the death penalty.[95] There followed the execution of four republican rank-and-file combatants and then of Erskine Childers, the republicans' chief publicist and a nationally known figure in the Anglo-Irish War. Lynch's 'Orders of Frightfulness', issued three days after Childers's execution, set out fourteen categories of persons to be shot on sight by Republican forces. Sean Hales, a member of the Dáil, and Pádraic Ó Máille, Deputy Speaker of the Dáil, were shot on 7 December; Hales died and Ó Máille was wounded.[96] The threat to kill legislators and others was a deadly thrust at the vital organs of the new state. As reprisal, the Free State government (which had come into existence only the previous day) selected and shot four republican leaders who had been in custody since the fall of the Four Courts. The circumstances of the executions – the absence of any form of judicial process, rousing the men in the early hours and telling them that they were shortly to be shot – reflected in equal measure the government's desperation and its ruthless determination. A savage sundering of ties of comradeship was evident in the fact that one of the executed, Rory O'Connor, had the year before been best man at the wedding of Kevin O'Higgins – Minister for Home Affairs and one of those who authorised the reprisal killings.[97] The reprisal, as a clear demonstration of will, seems to have been effective, though it would remain a stain on the character of the Free State government. The government had several thousand republicans of varying ranks in custody, who now could be presumed to be hostages. Political assassination ceased, and republican attacks were thereafter largely – not wholly – confined to the destruction of property.[98]

The war shifted from the semi-conventional to the guerrilla, persisting despite several attempts at peace-making. As the republicans' military capabilities waned, the political element became more important. De Valera had put himself at the head of a Republic which existed only in name but which had departments, issued communiqués and, of course, possessed stationery. In theory, this body should have controlled the Republican Army, but in reality it was entirely subordinate to it. As the republican leaders were harried and killed, one by one, and military defeat became an inescapable outcome, authority flowed back to de Valera. He remained a national figure of great importance, always associated in the public mind with the 1916 Rising. After a final and wholly fanciful peace attempt at the end of April 1923 (which would in effect have necessitated a repudiation of the Treaty by the now victorious Free State government), de Valera declared what was a ceasefire in name but which was a surrender in fact.[99] The Civil War ended on 24 May 1923.

De Valera and many other republican figures, political and military, did what they could to avoid joining more than 11,000 of their comrades in Free State custody. W. T. Cosgrave, President of the Free State's Executive Council (cabinet), had promised de Valera and his colleagues full participation in a free political process, provided they accepted the principle that the majority vote should prevail and provided that arms were surrendered. These conditions were not met (arms were cached, not surrendered, and there remained the commitment to a Republic rejected at the polls). The republican leadership was, in consequence, condemned to an underground existence. With the Civil War behind him, Cosgrave decided to seek a fresh mandate, in a general election to be held on 27 August 1923. In the election run-up, de Valera was arrested on ground of his own careful choosing, attempting to address a meeting in the historically significant constituency of Ennis, Co. Clare. In the election itself, however, he was returned with a more than two-to-one majority over his opponent, Eoin MacNeill. His Sinn Féin party also did well, increasing its number of seats by eight. Other irreconcilable republicans were also returned, Mary MacSwiney and Constance Markievicz among them. Cumann na nGaedheal, the newly and belatedly formed party of the government, took sixty-two seats, de Valera's Sinn Féin forty-four, and other parties (almost entirely pro-Treaty) forty-six.[100] The government again had an overwhelming working majority, but the electorate had shown some sympathy with the underdog, had reaffirmed its regard for individual candidates, had expressed dissatisfaction with the executions and large-scale imprisonment and had shown that there remained support for a more republican type of politics. In a paradoxical way, this strengthened the new state: democracy cannot function without criticism, opposition and restraint of the executive.

It was not wholly unexpected, but certainly an irony, when two and a half years later, in March 1926, Sinn Féin narrowly reaffirmed its policy of not entering the Dáil (a 'usurping legislature') and de Valera immediately detached himself ('I am from this moment a free-man').[101] Within weeks, he announced the formation of a new political party, Fianna Fáil, with a strongly nationalist political, social, economic and cultural programme, drawing heavily on republican traditions. This expanded rapidly throughout the Free State, establishing the vital infrastructure of local branches, feeding what was clearly a widespread appetite for this type of political association, voice and outlet. There was appeal in blood and thunder revolutionary rhetoric which went no further down that road than words – nationalist fervour, nostalgia, vicarious struggle – then safely home to hearth, cocoa and bed. De Valera well understood this psychology and was adept in pandering to it, making speeches that blurred the boundaries between his new party and the old, enlisting the powerful ranks of the martyred to reassure the living. He drew considerable support from IRA members throughout the country, and their practical electoral work (canvassing and getting the vote out) contributed to his early and continuing success in elections. In the general election of June 1927, Fianna Fáil was able to breathe down the neck of Cumann na nGaedheal with forty-four seats to its forty-seven. Again, Labour, Independents, Farmers and others helped to make up a pro-Treaty majority. In a decisive development of immense importance to Irish politics (and history), republican voters had followed de Valera: Sinn Féin was crushed and won only five seats.

Events thereafter moved swiftly, in an unpredicted and tragic way. On 10 July 1927, Kevin O'Higgins, the able and steely Minister for Home Affairs (and a man who excited hatred and admiration but not indifference), was assassinated in a Dublin suburb on his way to mass. In response to what was feared might be a new onslaught on government and state, two Bills were rushed through. The Public Safety Act, 1927, gave extensive powers to deal with treasonable or seditious activities. Military courts were authorised to hear certain cases and to impose any penalty available to the Central Criminal Court, including death.[102] The running sore of abstention by Fianna Fáil – a continuing questioning of the legitimacy of the state – was also dealt with. The Electoral Amendment Act required candidates to undertake to take their seat and to subscribe to the oath if elected. The undertaking was by means of an affidavit, and a candidate who failed to comply with the requirement would automatically be disqualified.[103] To copper-fasten this legislation and to prevent further piecemeal tinkering, the constitutional provision that allowed for a voter initiative and referendum (to which de Valera had recently turned) was repealed.[104]

Fianna Fáil now had to choose between constitutional and unconstitutional action. If it wished to continue in politics, the party would have to accept the oath and the legitimacy of the Free State Dáil. A practical man wholly unattracted to fringe politics, de Valera had probably long since made up his mind. The new legislation was something of a gift. Here was a reason to abandon Fianna Fáil's abstention policy yet to respect the sentiments of his supporters. It was now, in the jargon of modern politics and marketing, a presentational issue. After some discussion and manoeuvre, Fianna Fáil deputies agreed to change their stance, and on 11 August 1927, de Valera and his colleagues entered the Dáil and signed the oath.[105] Almost immediately, Fianna Fáil flexed its muscles and, in alliance with Labour, attempted to oust the government on a confidence motion. On the Speaker's casting vote, this was lost. Two government by-election victories shortly thereafter encouraged Cosgrave to consolidate his position by means of a general election. Held on 15 September 1927, the poll allowed Cosgrave's Cumann na nGaedheal again to take government, supported by the Farmers' Party and Independents.[106] Fianna Fáil and Labour formed the now loyal opposition.

The final act in this process of legitimisation occurred following the general election of 16 February 1932. Fianna Fáil, with a narrow majority provided by the Labour Party, was able to form its first administration. Despite rumours of a *coup d'état*, the police and army remained loyal to the state and accepted the democratic verdict, as did the civil service. The handover proceeded smoothly. The outgoing government conceded gracefully, and the country could at last have confidence that democracy was truly rooted in a state born of war, revolution, disorder and fratricide.

The machinery of state

The state apparatus that responded to the Fianna Fáil victory in 1932 was only ten years old yet was possessed of the essential characteristics of the administration of a mature democracy.[107] The police (now known as An Garda Síochána) had, to varying degrees, the imperfections of police forces the world over, and its political division had undoubtedly abused its powers and acted unlawfully on behalf of the status quo.[108] But, that aside, and whatever petty influences politicians, the clergy and others could bring to bear at a local level, the force in general seems to have been largely uncorrupt as an institution and was an instrument of stability. The Army, as has been noted, had expanded hugely and rapidly during the Civil War and had almost as quickly been reduced in size thereafter. That, and its very mixed nature (Old IRA, ex-British Army, new recruits) led to a mutiny in March 1924 by officers of the Old IRA. That had been overcome by a combination of firm action by senior officers, resolution by ministers and some deft recourse to smoke and mirrors. Thereafter, although there was a certain amount of continuing unrest over conditions, dismissals and demobilisation, the Army was firmly under civilian control and, in organisation and ethos, became a professional instrument of the state.[109]

The civil service which greeted de Valera on his accession to office was, in all the circumstances, an impressive instrument. Local government had for decades been an integral part of Irish party politics. Patronage exercised by the Irish Party and the Unionist Party in their respective bailiwicks had been levers to ensure electoral loyalty in an employment-hungry country. A young man helped into secure employment remained in the position of client and was a conduit through whom other local-government favours could be passed. The result was a mess of seemingly ineradicable cronyism, favouritism and straightforward corruption. The Local Government Board in Dublin exercised some control, but all except the most outrageous transactions were left undisturbed.[110]

To deal with those issues, which independence had apparently affected no more than to reorder the channels for preferment, it was necessary to develop a mechanism which could be efficient and fair, removing patronage from local and national politicians, clerics and other persons of influence. Important enough in peaceful times, this was a critical check on those who, irrespective of their suitability, felt that their service in the War of Independence or in the Civil War gave them a claim for employment in public service. Some seventy years earlier, almost exactly, patronage and nepotism had been tackled in Britain by the 1854 Northcote–Trevelyan Report. This had led, *inter alia*, to the establishment of the Civil Service Commission, a body free from political interference, which oversaw the process of appointment through open competitive examinations and certification of physical health.[111] The result was, within a generation, the transformation of the British civil service.[112] As much as the imperial behemoth, perhaps more, and certainly more urgently, the infant Free State required an independent and able civil service. It is a tribute to the perspicacity of inexperienced young ministers then running the country that in August 1923, with the Civil War only recently ended and its ruinous effects still straining all available resources, a reform of local government was pushed through.[113] Three years later, the patronage powers of the Minister for Local Government were discontinued. A three-man Local Appointments Commission was given exclusive authority to fill professional and senior appointments. Decisions on the lower grades continued to be made locally. Centrally, appointment and management were reorganised and put on a new footing.[114] In 1924, a Civil Service Commission was established to oversee central government appointments, which were by general competition. Tenure, remuneration and pensions were regulated by statute. The same principles were followed in army and police recruitment.[115]

It is important to grasp the strong moral position of those who are appointed on demonstrable merit and whose tenure is guaranteed during good service, and which stands in contrast to those whose position comes from patronage and splits loyalty between public service and private obligation. Civil servant and politician serve substantially (but not wholly) different functions. The legitimacy of the ballot-box is fundamental to democracy, but it is vital for public confidence that it should not be used to overwhelm or to politicise officials, to circumvent rules or to produce unfair decisions. Officials appointed through political patronage and serving at will certainly find it almost impossible to resist their patrons. The legitimacy conferred by the open competitive examination therefore helps to establish a balance favourable to democracy. But the corrosive effects of patronage and favouritism were not the only threats to fairness and account-ability in the new state. To deal with the dangers of subversion and disloyalty, another measure was needed, and those appointed to or promoted within the civil service or local government were obliged to make a formal declaration of allegiance to the state.[116] This was no light matter in a country where an oath had been a cause of civil war.

There were two elements that contributed to political influence in the distribution of posts in the public service, after 1922, whether central or local, or one of the semi-state enterprises that were established during this period. The first was the enduring expectation of political influence in appointments, which had been inherited from the decades of the Irish Party, and which was a feature of the system so usual that no one objected.[117] To this was added the demand, inevi-table after a revolutionary or radical political change of government, that those who had put themselves at risk, or who suffered for the new order, should be rewarded. This, in itself, was shored up by the argument (which, of course, has substance) that a new and inexperienced administration needs loyal backing, and that, most unequivocally, comes from those who stood by its cause while it still struggled for power. Having been 'out' in one or another stage in the Irish nationalist struggle did not therefore convey privileges so unexpected or outrageous that they were unacceptable to the population.[118]

Various filters were established to regularise political access to public-service posts. Those were essential to show that there was a degree of system and fairness in selection. Competitive examinations were retained, but to these were added conditions.[119] The most obvious of these, favouring those who had been schooled in the nationalist traditions (and thus very few Protestants) was the addition of the Irish language to the selection process. Former army officers were exempted altogether from the examinations for both the higher and executive grades. At the lower end of the civil service, a range of basic (but, of course, secure and pensioned) posts were reserved for former soldiers of the Free State Army. (The same entitlement was granted in Britain and Northern Ireland to those who had served in the British armed forces.)

A civil service cannot be reconstituted overnight, and there were many specialised posts in finance, agriculture and fisheries, transportation, commerce, education, public health and the like, that needed continuity of service. This meant that the overwhelming bulk of the civil service was constituted of those who had served under British rule; no other arrangement would have been possible, even had there not been a civil war that necessitated as much stability as possibility in the new administration, were it to survive.

Some who had served under the British had been disloyal and had been dis-missed. Others had given their service to the republican cause, covertly, had survived in office and now served under the new dispensation. Those who had been dismissed could (and many did) apply for readmission to the civil service. Their claims were considered, and, if substantiated, they were re-employed. But those numbers were not great: only eighty-eight regained their positions in this way. Compare this, and the 131 officials who had served in Sinn Féin's parallel administration, to the 21,000 hold-overs from the old regime.[120]

While ordinary members of the previous civil service suffered no disability, those who had opposed the Free State in the Civil War, and who had been interned or imprisoned, were dealt with severely.[121] Those amounted to some hundreds of men (and a few women). The grades affected were mainly in the Post Office (which had been a significant reservoir of republicanism throughout) and also schoolteachers. Civil servants who had remained in post throughout the Civil War but whose sympathies with the anti-Treaty side had, in some fashion or another, become overt, were dismissed. The vacancies variously created were available to supporters of the government side, who had no problem in making the mandatory declaration of loyalty.[122]

Democracy, it is frequently assumed, is defined by free elections and an independent legislature. These are certainly required but equally indispensable is the rule of law and an independent judiciary. Equality before the law and access to it by individuals, together with processes for the enforcement of private contracts, derive from these principles and are themselves essential for a free and orderly life. The chaos and disorder of the Anglo-Irish War notwithstanding, there existed in the Free State a climate of opinion favourable to the reception and establishment of a legal structure. This was a conservative society that respected private property and legal rights. A number of Irish lawyers had participated in the protracted negotiations that had led to the Treaty and the Constitution: these and others were present at the birth of the Free State. Before the Anglo-Irish War, Ireland had a sophisticated system of courts, a well-developed legal culture and a sturdy legal profession. Irish lawyers practised in Britain, both as solicitors and barristers, a number rising to the top of their profession and to public prominence. The years of war had certainly bitten deeply into all this. Sinn Féin's establishment of a parallel civil administration, including courts, severely affected the existing system of justice. Rural disputes (land and livestock) were the principal issues brought before the Sinn Féin courts, while the British courts were boycotted, either because of political preference or the application of menace.[123] As fairly simple and inexpensive forms of arbitration, the Sinn Féin panels may have been reasonably successful. More complicated matters in contract, tort and commercial and financial law were utterly beyond them. But even where the British courts were used, civil order had so widely broken down that many court orders were unenforceable.

Court reform was an urgent priority were normal life quickly to be resumed and that confidence fostered which is essential to manufacturing and other forms of commerce, as well as investment. It is definitive of a functioning state that it administers justice: this is a vital service to the citizenry, and where it is absent little or no loyalty can be expected. This was demonstrated during the Civil War when republicans used their courts to challenge the authority of the new state. Accordingly, on 24 July 1922, the Provisional government withdrew authority from the Dáil (Sinn Féin) courts. (A Judicial Commission was later established to deal with the Dáil courts' unfinished business.[124]) Elements of the British system were also discontinued at this time, magistrates' courts and the grand jury. New courts of summary jurisdiction (equivalent to the magistrates' courts) were established on 31 August 1922. These were to be called district courts and conducted by district justices.[125]

A further step was taken the following year when, in September 1923, the Courts of Justice Bill was introduced. This replaced existing county courts with circuit courts. Because of the determination of the Dáil and Senate rigorously to preserve judicial independence from the Executive, this legislation was a full eight months in the making, passing only in May 1924.[126] The higher courts were also adaptations of the British model but shorn of titles and procedures and imbued with a republican plainness, more appropriate to the new form of government in Ireland. Judicial appointments (critical to public confidence) were governed by legal service and seniority as well as by the requirements of state service.[127] Security of tenure completed the safeguards against political or other improper interference. All new courts were open for business by 1925, another indication of the establishment and stabilisation of the new state. A sense of change met some popular expectations, while a degree of continuity met others. It became possible – increasingly easily – to give civic loyalty to this new entity. Public servants – central and local government officials of varying levels of seniority, public employees from medical specialists to the various grades of the semi-skilled and labourers, as well as judges, police and soldiers – these, and others, and their kin, became defenders of the state. The disorders of the war against British rule, and the Civil War, had taken their toll. Now party politics rolled on, the state persisted and in itself promised an ordered and peaceful life for the citizen, dignity and international recognition for the country. To be against the state became a form of national subversion; to be against the government was a different matter altogether: a right, a periodic necessity – even a national inclination. But this commendable civic scepticism and criticism, the heart and lungs of democracy, were only possible because of the persistence of the state. That was worth defending.

Looking backwards, looking forward

Permanent revolution

It had been a difficult birth, but the infant had survived and was daily stronger. Civil war sows a bitter crop, vigorous, ineradicable, perennial in living memory, too often evergreen and malignant for children and grandchildren. It is, perhaps, easier for surviving combatants, in old age, to reach an accommodation and even a reconciliation. This can be a period when veterans, grateful to have survived, put their lives in perspective and reflect on the common identity of hardships shared and on the cruelties and injustices perpetrated by both sides.[128] Those who merely hear the tales, sing the songs, read the memoirs and live the events vicariously may find it hard to leave the frisson of old wrongs behind.

Revolutions invariably cry justice and denounce tyranny, be it national or social, but they have an uncomfortable habit of taking up and supercharging the oppressive methods of the *ancien régime*. This is not an invariable rule but was demonstrated with appalling frequency in the twentieth century.[129] One factor in this phenomenon may be the comparative strength of the triumphant revolution. Some of the dire and inhumane actions of the Bolsheviks were perpetuated and rooted in the period of their greatest weakness, following the October Revolution. Pitilessness was lauded as a cardinal virtue, a personal strength, as they sought to hold then consolidate their power against tsarism (in civil war) and against foreign intervention. Ideology and ruthlessness in their leadership also played a great part; the weight of the various elements is hard to discern. The Portuguese revolution of April 1974, by contrast, peacefully dismantled the apparatus of repression of the Salazar decades, and in fairly short order set the country on the road to full democracy and regeneration. The leadership of the revolution then stepped aside.[130]

The Irish Free State emerged from its turbulent foundation as a reluctantly authoritarian democracy. The rule of law had, on occasion, been egregiously violated in the name of national destiny, then of state security and military necessity. As peace took hold once more, the government showed its willingness to submit to the law and to uphold the process of democracy. But it continued to possess, and was willing to use, extensive repressive powers, more sweeping and severe than those the British had deployed in their catch-all Restoration of Order in Ireland Act (ROIA).[131] A significant section of the population had shown an undiminished appetite for bright green republican politics when, in June 1927, it returned forty-four Fianna Fáil deputies to the Dáil (increased to fifty-seven in the snap election three months later). Outside the electoral politics with which de Valera and his followers had now, albeit grudgingly, decided to engage, there remained the far from inconsiderable remnants and scattered *matériel* of a secret army. The assassination of Kevin O'Higgins, the Minister for Home Affairs, on 10 July 1927, confirmed for its opponents the continued desire of irreconcilable republicanism to destroy the state and, at least on occasion, its ability to reach out with lethal effect. The sweeping Public Safety Act that followed the O'Higgins assassination was inevitable: democratic scruple was held at arm's length in democracy's name.

In its way, that legislation was a minor victory for the IRA (the leadership of which, as far as can now be ascertained, had not given its permission for the O'Higgins murder).[132] It is conventional wisdom among revolutionaries, of many types (but particularly on the left), that the state they seek to overthrow is stronger when it hides its repressive powers; that those powers are always in place; and that the task of revolutionaries is to pull aside the mask of power, thereby demonstrating the state's corrupt and hypocritical nature to the people. This is the logic that justifies a campaign of provocation, seeks to draw in innocent and unattached civilians and finds hope in deaths and overreaction by the security forces. Such actions are not the substance of revolution, but preparation for revolution. In the inter-war decades, there were many inflammatory actions by the IRA and republican activists outside its ranks. In most instances, however, the supposedly oppressive nature of the state was demonstrated only to those already in the republican fold. To others, the state apparatus was thereby given sufficient justification. At a purely pragmatic and prudential level, it would have seemed foolish to dismantle it.

The policies and actions of the IRA are a principal focus of this book, but at this point, as we leave the formative years of the Irish State, a few preliminary observations may be helpful. The organisation had been defeated militarily, but this was a conquered and colonised country, and this was reflected in attitudes towards authority. There existed an instinctive, culturally fortified suspicion, at times amounting to an aversion, to government, broadly defined, and to the courts, police and prisons in particular. Informers and turncoats were reviled. There was always a ready, full and fairly easily tapped reservoir of sympathy for the underdog. Noble defeat and fidelity unto death had, after all, been woven into Irish nationalist history, literature and song for centuries, reaching a powerful apotheosis in the Easter Rising. Then there was, in addition, the messy and indecisive nature of the split in republicanism and the lingering regard that many on both sides had for individuals on the other and for the scattered shreds, themes and echoes of their cause. (This did not preclude detestation for their respective organisations.) Sympathy for the rebel, always a reflex, was almost impossible to extinguish: it could be roused by the fox fleeing across the landscape, hounds in pursuit. This difficulty was an intrinsic problem of legitimacy faced by all regimes that have come to power by revolutionary means. Questions of purity and of sufficient adherence to the founding doctrine are always there, as are easily brought charges and challenges. So was that most difficult of questions: if it was right to overthrow the oppressor, then why not the apostate?

Whether set to music or not, scenes from republican mythology rolled on. For the government, there was an abiding difficulty in this because its leaders claimed a place in the creation myth and were enraged when cast as traitors, snakes in what had been the perfect garden. It was a largely futile policy to attempt to set things right by commandeering the lexicon, but words and labels so brimmed with emotion that the attempt nevertheless had to be made. The term 'republican', with a capital or without, was particularly contested. As in the Dáil debate of December 1921–January 1922, on the terms of the Treaty, there were mutual denunciations of 'bad faith and worse'.[133] So it was also for the term 'IRA'. On the government side, augmented and reorganised, large sections had morphed into the National Army. Anti-Treaty forces claimed the name (and with it, of course, the glory of the rebel story); the government insisted that there was no continuity and no entitlement: in all government pronouncements, the non-compliant IRA was described as 'anti-Treaty forces' or 'Irregulars'. In the course of time, the term 'subversive', with its more negative and odious overtones, was preferred. So important was the naming of things in the political struggle that the government issued precise directives to civil servants on terminology. Under censorship rules, the press was similarly instructed.[134]

Soft revolution

Stalin is reputed to have sneered, 'The Pope! How many divisions has he got?'[135] The implication of the question was that while Stalin could deploy his tanks and divisions, the power of conquest and coercion, the Pope had authority that, while intangible, could nevertheless move masses of the faithful. In modern political discussions, a distinction is frequently made between 'hard' and 'soft' power. This is the point that Stalin's implied ignorance was meant to illustrate. The defeated anti-Treaty forces, military and political, were, in the mid-1920s, able to exercise a surprising amount of soft power, certainly a spiritual division or two. De Valera's performance in the elections of 1927 showed that; a widespread unease with condemnation of the IRA did not amount to support, but it was a constant reminder to the government that public sentiment was complicated. There was an overwhelming desire for peace, but that was seen in complex terms – conciliation as well as containment. Republicans were seen as wayward relatives, generally not ill-disposed intruders and, by their votes, a substantial section of the electorate wished to remind politicians that they should not forget their family history.

The contribution of political romanticism and the Irish literary revival of the 1890s and early 1900s to the political events that followed has long been debated.[136] It would be perverse to argue that the rich effusion of prose, poetry and plays had no political effect: art often runs ahead of politics, perhaps more frequently than it trails behind. It was not idle or egoistic for Yeats to wonder whether his play had sent men out to die.[137] Revolution must have a romantic core, just as it is always an act of faith and frequently – and perhaps necessarily – a repudiation of the rational. It must exalt in and of itself, become an object so consuming that death is a consummation. This is the stuff of musical, poetical and visual romanticism that meshed so well with philosophical and political romanticism throughout Europe from the 1840s onward.[138]

In Catholic and rural Ireland, these notions had particular resonance and ready vernacular forms. Notions of sacrifice were part of the spiritual life of the people, as were the persisting pre-Christian beliefs in a parallel spirit world of beings that inhabited the countryside and exercised powers in the lives of ordinary people. Nor was the romantic appeal confined to those who lived on and off the land. In a persuasive account of the imagery of the Easter Rising, Declan Kiberd draws attention to the ways in which the event took the form of a play and drew inspiration as much from drama as from politics.[139] He also points out that the leaders of the 1916 Rising adhered to the concept of 'the triumph of failure'. In a glorious cause, even if one should lose one's life – particularly if one lost it – one would save it. This is also, of course, a recurring theme in the New Testament.

This was not the only motive in Irish republicanism, as the state emerged from civil war. It is far easier (and much more plausible) to embed the 1916 leaders in the romantic tradition than the leaders of the War of Independence. Urban guerrilla warfare of bombing, arson, man-tracking, assassination and terror, one reasons, must surely drive out all notions of romantic nationalism. In many men who hunted down targets and killed at arm's length, other motivations must surely have been paramount. It seems surprising that even a notorious, irreconcilable republican such as Ernie O'Malley believed fervently in the old Fenian notion of the virtual Republic realised and now defended. But sublime objectives justified the most sordid of tactics.[140]

Those two dispositions came out of the Civil War: an attachment to the idea of the Republic that abhorred pragmatism and, because of the dead, rejected (and indeed could not deal with) the compromises of politics. If those were possible now, believers demanded, then why not in 1920, before the death and destruction? The Republic lived on, in the juridical sense, in the surviving members of the Second Dáil and in the Army Council of the IRA. This virtual, righteous and legitimate government had been usurped, betrayed and defeated in the field, but its claims and rights were not invalidated. For such a cause, to redress a monstrous wrong, all possible methods of clandestine warfare were not simply permissible but mandatory.[141]

Undying loyalty and unbreakable attachment are ubiquitous themes in all forms of romantic art, as is the sense of life lived with and enhanced by loss. Add to this the celebration of deeds of valour, audacity, ingenuity and resistance, praise for the fallen and the excoriation of traitors, and one has the rich material for insurrectionary art. The Free State government had at its disposal all the instruments of state and was faced by a scattered and riven opposition. The persistence of that clandestine and fugitive force can be explained in many ways, from the disputed Treaty to the blood debts of civil war, but it is impossible to account for its durability and periodic reanimation in political and organisational terms alone. Republican traditions, attachments and emotions drew strength from the very music, images and legends they inspired. This form of transmission, as with all folkish art, is never fixed, leaves abundant space for invention, embroidery and adaptation. A gathering of familiar symbols, tropes, tunes, terms and sentiments, together with a scabrous vocabulary of denunciation, energised and enlarged the core material. By this means, the republican tradition was kept fresh and given topical bite, enabling it to reach out to new audiences, enlisting new sympathisers and inducting supporters.

The Devil, it has been suggested, has all the best tunes. This observation might be extended to protestors and rebels (as indeed Lucifer supposedly was). There is a reason for this. Authority lectures and admonishes, justifies, congratulates and inflates itself with self-righteousness and therefore lapses into tedium, pomposity and, inevitably, self-pity. There has always been tension when either a sacred or a secular power is artistic patron. As the Venetians found, together with princes and potentates throughout Europe, glory is best reflected by the beneficence of identifying talent and commissioning the artist or composer, unleashing creativity. The closely stipulated hymn to the patron all too often becomes a dirge; the flattering portrait may contain sly little glances or shades that satirise. For the art of subversion and protest, no such dilemmas arise. Protest, whether it be blues or ballad, poster, cartoon or satirical theatre, needs no greater patron than the audience; it carries its own coherence. The influence of popular culture has always been embedded in Irish nationalism, and within that music has been pre-eminent.

The ballad sits at the heart of republican music. With simple, catching and familiar tunes providing energy and tapping emotions, ballads are apt for simple, inexpensive and appealing community entertainment and participation. They are adaptable and readily topical. Lamentation, celebration, defiance and satire are equally easily accommodated: heroic deeds, tragic deaths, remarkable characters and affecting homilies are conveyed enjoyably, memorably and with-out a sense of preaching, wrapped around in beat and melody. Radio access increased dramatically in Ireland in the 1920s but was still a rarity in rural districts and in the poorer quarters of urban areas. Entertainment, in public houses, halls and private residences was live and local. Music for dancing and the singing of ballads was at the heart of these activities. Emotions stirred and sometimes soared, and a sense of community through participation became tangible. Amidst the range of life's themes – love, loss, home and exile, for example – nationalism and republican messages found easy rest. In the singing, the listening and the joining in, identity was affirmed and celebrated.

The ballad is a form of substance and endurance and has a history easily traced to mediaeval times. It has always been a thing available to, made and enjoyed by the people, as distinct from religious or art music. Ballads have been published as broadsheets and in collections, but they usually have no easily identified point of origin, or authoritative text, and are orally transmitted. This makes them elusive and enticing, the ideal vehicle for rebels and protestors, spanning the range from the insurgent under arms to the straight-faced satire of village and farmstead.[142] Because their structure can easily be mastered, they are particularly suitable for commenting on or memorialising changing events. An uncomplicated rhyming scheme means that no great poetical ability is required for composition, though many ballads have been clever, ingenious and moving.[143] The metre is a quatrain of three and four stress lines, with matching end-rhymes on the second and fourth. Of equal convenience, the melody has four pulse-beats, and (to match the rhymes) the tunes place emphasis on the ends of second and fourth lines.[144] To ease things yet further, there is a familiar repertoire of perhaps two dozen tunes into which all manner of words may be fitted.

The rebel cause is never lost in this type of popular music. Territory, men, arms and organisation may have gone down, but the good old cause lives on in

music where it is protected from questioning and realities. It cannot be suppressed by law (though that has been attempted) and, being intangible and
ethereal, cannot be interrogated by reason. All music has the capability of being
inserted in the personality, becoming part of the subconscious, creating and
meeting needs simultaneously. Even though it is simple in form – perhaps *because*
it is simple – the ballad has this quality to a marked degree. Learnt, sung,
modified and enjoyed, a ballad of protest or rebellion can become a force and
influence even greater than a law or institution. Such were the divisions that
republicans brought to the fields of battle: firepower of a different kind.

Notes

1 See Liaquat Ahamed's brilliant exposition of these events, their national and international ramifications: Liaquat Ahamed, *Lords of Finance: 1929, The Great Depression, and
the Bankers who Broke the World* (London: Windmill Books, 2010), especially Chapters 7–9.

2 Some territorial disputes such as those between Poland and Czechoslovakia, Roma-
nia and Hungary remained heated and unsettled up to the Second World War and
into our own times. See P. M. H. Bell, *The Origins of the Second World War in Europe*
(London: Longman, 1997), pp. 29–32.

3 The British economy had been driven into steep decline, both relatively and absolutely. The authority on which the Empire based itself, part ideology, part utility and
part power, no longer rang true. The USA had crossed its eclipse whilst the European
powers entered theirs.

4 See, for example, Sean Glynn and John Oxborrow, *Interwar Britain: A Social and
Economic History* (London: George Allen & Unwin, 1976). Harold Macmillan offers
the interesting perspective of an active 'one nation' Conservative politician in his
Winds of Change, 1914–39 (London: Macmillan, 1966). A. J. P. Taylor's *English History,
1914–1945* (Oxford: Oxford University Press, 1965), almost half a century on,
remains an instructive, provocative and incisive account of these decades. For an
account of the social and cultural developments, see Chapters 5–11.

5 It cannot, however, be denied that Churchill's speech commending the Treaty to the
Commons was a generous and warm-hearted one. His peroration paid tribute to
Irish indefatigability. How had it happened that Ireland had in successive genera-
tions exacted such a toll on British politics? 'Whence does the mysterious power of
Ireland come?… Ireland is not a daughter state. She is a parent nation. The Irish are
an ancient race. "We too are," said their plenipotentiaries, "a far-flung nation"…
How much have we suffered in all these generations from this continued hostility'
(5 *Hansard*, vol. 149, col. 182, 15 December 1921).

6 Of the non-coupon (i.e. non-Lloyd George) Liberals, only twenty-six were elected in
1918. Lloyd George's majority was massive: 339 Coalition Unionists and 134 Coalition Liberals. Labour had increased its representation from thirty-nine to fifty-nine,
but this, even combined with the independent Liberals, was insignificant in the face
of Lloyd George's 338 majority.

7 Michael Kinnear is instructive on the anatomy of the coalition and the ambitions
and tensions in contained. See *The Fall of Lloyd George: The Political Crisis of 1922*
(London: Macmillan, 1973), especially Chapters 1 and 5.

8 The City of Londonderry is the much quoted example of gerrymandering, but there
were many others. See John Darby, *Conflict in Northern Ireland: The Development of a
Polarised Community* (Dublin: Gill & Macmillan, 1976), p. 51. Parliamentary constituencies seem to have been less susceptible to gerrymandering and boundary

changes unfavourable to Catholics. See John Whyte, 'How Much Discrimination Was There under the Unionist Regime, 1921–68', in Tom Gallagher and James O'Connell (eds.), *Contemporary Irish Studies* (Manchester: Manchester University Press, 1983). In parliamentary debates on the Treaty, Lloyd George had insisted that '[t]here is no doubt… that the majority of the people of two counties prefer being with their Southern neighbour to being in the Northern Parliament' (Fermanagh and Tyrone had nationalist majorities; 5 *Hansard*, vol. 149, col. 40, 14 December 1921).

9 Andrew Bonar Law (1858–1923) was born in Canada and was leader of the Conservative and Unionist Party from 1911 until 1921. He held various ministerial posts in Asquith's and then Lloyd George's coalitions, including Chancellor of the Exchequer, and was a member of the War Cabinet, 1916–18. He became Prime Minister in October 1922, already in poor health. Seven months later he was diagnosed with throat cancer. He immediately resigned and was replaced by Stanley Baldwin. Law's 1912 speeches in support of Ulster unionism came close to a breach of the Treason Felony Act (11 & 12 Vict., c.12), which ironically had been introduced in 1848 to deal with the Young Ireland agitation and insurrection.

10 Parliamentary time had been given to these minutiae for decades. During one afternoon of questions in the pre-war Commons the following topics were raised: Irish foot-and-mouth disease and the cattle trade; gun-running in Ireland and the possible involvement of lieutenants and deputy lieutenants of counties, as well as magistrates; post-office wages in Belfast; taxation in Ireland; Home Rule protests in Belfast; police action at a trade-union congress in Dublin; steamrolling roads in Waterford; land purchase in Ireland; a national school on Achill Island, Co. Mayo; an old-age-pension case in Co. Limerick; clerical staff at Irish Land Registry offices; the use of Drogheda port for the export of fat cattle; three labourers' cottages at Enfield, Co. Meath (5 *Hansard*, vol. 62, cols. 1561–1619, *passim*, 18 May 1914).

11 This could be said to start with the case of Cahir Healy, Sinn Féin Westminster MP for Fermanagh and Tyrone. Healy had been elected whilst interned and had campaigned on an abstentionist platform. These elements did not, however, sway the Speaker when Healy's internment was raised as a possible breach of privilege. Rather, the challenge of breach of privilege failed because the detention had been ordered by the 'competent authority of Northern Ireland under the powers of the criminal law for the punishment of crime or the maintenance of order' (5 *Hansard*, vol. 159, col. 294, 27 November 1922). This was a seemingly perverse decision, since the Government of Ireland Act (GOIA), which had established Northern Ireland, had affirmed the supremacy of Westminster (Government of Ireland Act, 1920: 10 & 11 Geo. V, c.67). Besides the general weariness with things Irish, there was a pragmatic administrative judgement in the self-denying ordinance: Westminster could not be put in the position of routinely second-guessing the Northern Ireland parliament and administration. Should this have become an established convention, there could have been a paralysis of authority. Half a century later, Westminster did intervene, when a crisis demanded. But how, in setting up the division of responsibilities and authority between the two legislatures, could one provide a legislative format to distinguish between fundamental and merely domestic Northern Ireland issues? The failure even to attempt to establish a fallback power of review and intervention was a fatal flaw. It gave one party power without ultimate responsibility and the other responsibility without sufficient and convention-backed intervention powers. On Cahir Healy, see below, pp. 352–60.

12 *Articles of Agreement for a Treaty between Great Britain and Ireland* (London: HMSO [Cmd. 1560], 1921). Timothy Michael Healy (1855–1931), Irish Party MP for Wexford (1880–3), then Co. Monaghan, South Londonderry, North Longford, North Louth successively and finally (1910–18) East Cork. A conservative and clericalist Roman

Catholic, he took a bitterly anti-Parnell stance when the Irish Party split. He lost his place in electoral politics in Sinn Féin's 1918 landslide. First Governor General of Irish Free State. James Henry Thomas (1874–1949), Labour MP for Derby. Started work on the Great Western Railway, where he became an engine driver and eventually General Secretary of the National Union of Railwaymen. Colonial Secretary in Ramsay MacDonald's first administration and held various ministerial positions thereafter in MacDonald's second Labour cabinet and then in the National Cabinet.

13 PRO HO/144/3915/5, Sir John Anderson Papers, J. H. Thomas (Colonial Secretary) to T. M. Healy (Governor General, Free State), 25 March 1924.

14 There are numerous references to the representations that Lloyd George made on the issue of the proposed Boundary Commission. The key interview seems to have been a meeting between Lloyd George and Michael Collins on the morning of Monday, 5 December 1921, during which he noted the probability that the Boundary Commission would add parts of Fermanagh and Tyrone to the Free State. See Geoffrey Shakespeare, *Let Candles Be Brought In* (London: MacDonald, 1949), p. 86; Thomas Jones, *Whitehall Diary*, ed. K. Middlemas, 3 vols. (Oxford: Oxford University Press, 1969–71), vol. III, pp. 131 and 155–8.

15 See 5 *Hansard*, vol. 149, col. 357, 16 December 1921; vol. 150, cols. 1271–2, 16 February 1922.

16 The slogan is forever associated with Sir Edward (later Lord) Carson and Sir William Craig.

17 See 5 *Hansard*, vol. 177; cols. 27–282, 30 September 1924 and 1 October 1924; cols. 363–471, 2 October 1924. The Bill was carried by a large majority, becoming the Irish Free State (Confirmation of Agreement) Act: 15 & 16 Geo. V, c.77.

18 Joseph R. Fisher (1855–1939) was born in Co. Down. After a career in English newspapers in 1891, he became Managing Editor of the *Northern Whig*. Eoin Mac-Neill (1867–1945) was born in Co. Antrim. The first Professor of Early and Medieval Irish History at University College Dublin, he inspired the foundation of the Irish Volunteers of which he became Commander-in-Chief. Deceived by Pearse and MacDonagh, he countermanded orders for the Easter mobilisation. After release from prison for his part in the events that led up to the Easter Rising he returned to activity in Sinn Féin, holding ministerial offices in the Dáil. He supported the Treaty and held ministerial portfolios in the Provisional and Free State governments. Richard Feetham (1874–1965) was born in South Africa and educated in England. At the time of the Commission he was a judge in the Supreme Court, Transvaal Province.

19 See Ronan Fanning, Michael Kennedy, Dermot Keogh, Eunan O'Halpin (eds.), *Documents on Irish Foreign Policy*, vol. I: *1919–1922* (Dublin: Royal Irish Academy, 1998), p. 358.

20 *The Times*, 7 December 1921, 7f.

21 Arthur James Balfour (1848–1930). Irish Chief Secretary, 1887–91; Prime Minister, 1902–5; leader of the Unionist Party until 1911. Nephew of Lord Salisbury and in 1921 a figure of continuing importance within the Party and British political life.

22 In the Article, Northern Ireland 'is regarded as a creature already constituted having its own Parliament and its own defined boundaries'. *The Times*, 8 September 1924, 13b. Balfour had received Birkenhead's confidential letter in March 1922 and was only now making it public.

23 *The Times*, 11 September 1924, 14b.

24 *The Times*, 26 September 1924, 14b.

25 *Northern Ireland Parliamentary Debates* (hereinafter *NIPD*), vol. 4, col. 1207.

26 This was an unpaid body whose rudimentary training and light armament was more than compensated for by strong motivation, excellent local knowledge and ties and a

large enlistment. See Sir Arthur Hezlet, *The 'B' Specials: A History of the Ulster Special Constabulary* (London: Tom Stacey, 1972); Michael Farrell, *Arming the Protestants: The Formation of the Ulster Special Constabulary and the Royal Ulster Constabulary, 1920–27* (London: Pluto, 1983).

27 Terence de Vere White, *Kevin O'Higgins* (Dublin: Anvil Books, 1986), p. 206.

28 Eamon Phoenix, *Northern Nationalism: Nationalistic Politics, Partition and the Catholic Minority in Northern Ireland, 1890–1940* (Belfast: Ulster Historical Foundation, 1994), p. 330.

29 *Morning Post*, 29 November 1924, 9e.

30 The Report has never been published, although the Commissioners did attempt to serve it on representatives of the Free State and Northern Ireland governments who were in London on 28 November 1924. Since neither delegation wished to see the Commission, something of a three-door farce ensued when all moved to Chequers for the weekend and Mr Justice Feetham turned up. See St John Greer Ervine, *Craigavon: Ulsterman* (London: Allen & Unwin, 1949), pp. 503–4.

31 For a detailed account of the settlement, see Phoenix, *Northern Nationalism, op. cit.*, Chapter 8.

32 Of course, each had to operate within the constraints of their respective electorates and party structures. For a view of the good personal relations between Cosgrave and Craig, see Ervine's account of the 1924 agreement and the exchange between Cosgrave and Craig (*Craigavon, op. cit.*, p. 507).

33 See D. W. Harkness, *The Restless Dominion: The Irish Free State and the British Commonwealth of Nations, 1921–31* (London: Macmillan, 1969), pp. 52–5.

34 See Robert MacGregor Dawson (ed.), *Constitutional Issues in Canada* (London: Oxford University Press, 1933), pp. 72–94; Harkness, *Restless Dominion, op. cit.*, pp. 84–5.

35 South Africa came to the 1926 Imperial Conference demanding a statement of full dominion equality (Harkness, *Restless Dominion, op. cit.*, pp. 84–6).

36 *Imperial Conference, 1926: Summary of Proceedings:* PP, 1926, XI [Cmd. 2768], 545, 14.

37 Act to Give Effect to Certain Resolutions Passed by Imperial Conferences Held in the Years 1926 and 1930, 1931: 22 & 23 Geo. V, c.24.

38 See, for example, Peter Hart's *The IRA and Its Enemies: Violence and Community in Cork, 1916–1923* (Oxford: Clarendon Press, 1998).

39 David Fitzpatrick, 'The Logic of Collective Sacrifice: Ireland and the British Army, 1914–18', *Historical Journal*, 38 (4) (1995): 1017–30; see also David Fitzpatrick, 'Militarism in Ireland, 1900–1922', in Thomas Bartlett and Keith Jeffery (eds.), *A Military History of Ireland* (Cambridge: Cambridge University Press, 1996), pp. 379–406.

40 This indifference and hostility were not uniform, and there remained in Ireland a substantial group of ex-servicemen who made their service public at commemorative events. In an interesting essay on Dublin's Armistice Day commemorations, Jane Leonard points out that in 1923 and 1924 thousands assembled after memorial services in the Roman Catholic Pro-Cathedral and the Church of Ireland's St Patrick's Cathedral: 500,000 British Legion poppies were sold in the Dublin area in 1924. Some 20,000 veterans marked the customary silence, with an attendant crowd more than twice that number. Scuffles and disruption caused the ceremony to be moved to the Phoenix Park in 1926. A procession of ex-servicemen from central Dublin to Lutyen's elegant Irish National War Memorial Park at Islandbridge was an annual fixture until 1970, when they were discontinued on police advice. Jane Leonard, 'The Twinge of Memory: Armistice Day and Remembrance Sunday in Dublin since 1919', in Richard English and Graham Walker (eds.), *Unionism in Modern Ireland: New Perspectives on Politics and Culture* (Basingstoke: Macmillan, 1996), pp. 99–114, at pp. 102–3. See the *Irish Times*, 12 November 1925, 6c, 7a and 8c. The last

procession from the city centre took place on 8 November 1970, with no reports of disturbances (*Irish Times*, 9 November 1970, 8a and b).

41 On 1 and 2 July 1916, the attacking British forces, including the 36th (Ulster) Division (comprising the Royal Irish Fusiliers, the Royal Irish Rifles and the Royal Inniskilling Fusiliers, all of which contained substantial elements of the Ulster Volunteer Force [UVF]) had almost 60,000 casualties, of which just over 19,000 were deaths. Four members of the 36th (Ulster) Division were awarded the Victoria Cross for action on 1 and 2 July. This and five further VCs awarded on the Somme in later battles were (and remain) sources of great pride to many Northern Ireland Protestants. See Peter Hart, *The Somme* (London: Weidenfeld & Nicolson, 2005). The Second World War produced more dreadful tolls, civilian and military. In the final battle for Berlin, for example, although estimates vary, perhaps 300,000 Russian and German soldiers and German civilians were killed. The concluding battles lasted from 22 April 1945 until the German surrender on 2 May 1945. See Anthony Beevor, *Berlin: The Downfall* (London: Viking, 2002).

42 The Easter Rising resulted in 450 fatalities, including 132 soldiers, seventy-nine insurrectionists (fifteen of whom were executed) and around 250 civilians (Fitzpatrick, 'Militarism in Ireland', *op. cit.*, p. 392). Estimates of deaths during the Anglo-Irish War vary but are in the range of 3,000 upward. See, for example, Michael Hopkinson, *The Irish War of Independence* (Dublin: Gill & Macmillan, 2002), pp. 201–2.

43 Ernie O'Malley, *On Another Man's Wound* (Dublin: Anvil Books, 1962), pp. 23, 28–9.

44 Tom Barry, *Guerilla Days in Ireland* (Dublin: Anvil Books, 1999), p. 2. Implicit in seeing 'what war was like' was the opportunity to kill and to risk one's life.

45 Barry's formation ('column') operated with a great deal of independence; such was the state of communications, the vestigial staff apparatus of the IRA's central command and the profound loyal sentiments of Barry and his followers, that no other course was possible. The sense of being an independent power and command was to persist into the Irish Civil War and well beyond, with significant consequences.

46 Seán McConville, *Irish Political Prisoners, 1848–1922: Theatres of War* (London and New York: Routledge, 2003), pp. 419–20.

47 See Ernie O'Malley's account of what was thought to be a last meeting with Robert Barton and Patrick Fleming in Mountjoy Prison, in Free State custody; '"You've cheated us," said Paddy. "We go first."… A knock on the door. *Beannacht Dé leat*, Éarnan. "I'll see you on the other side."' Ernie O'Malley, *The Singing Flame* (Dublin: Anvil Books, 1992), p. 219. This belief in the afterlife is so strong it can be expressed in terms almost geographical, like a medieval representation of the cosmos.

48 Patrick (Padraig) Henry Pearse (1879–1916) remains one of the principal figures in Irish republicanism. Born of an English father and Irish mother, he was, from an early age, gifted with a vivid imagination and sympathetic instincts and wrote poetry in Irish and English. Educated at the Royal University, he was called to the Irish Bar but did not practise. He immersed himself in the Gaelic Revival and established St Enda's School at Rathfarnham, Co. Dublin. A founder member of the Irish Volunteers and a member of the IRB, he was at the centre of republican conspiracy. Commander of the insurrectionary forces in the Easter Rising, tried by court martial, sentenced and executed.

49 James Connolly (1868–1916). Another republican figure of immense stature, born in Edinburgh of Irish parents. Served in the British Army and thereafter followed the path of the socialist agitator and labour organiser in Dublin, the USA, then again in Ireland. Attempted a synthesis of Marxism and nationalism but in the end opted for the latter. Commander of the Dublin forces in the Easter Rising, in which he was badly wounded. Tried and condemned by court martial and, because he was unable to stand, faced the firing squad in a chair.

50 Richard Mulcahy (1886–1971) was second-in-command in a relatively successful detachment of the Irish Volunteers in the 1916 Rising. Escaped serious punishment (probably through faulty intelligence) and was interned at Frongoch, North Wales. On release, became Deputy then Chief of Staff of the IRA (as the Volunteers had come to be known). Supported the Treaty and became a successful minister in the Provisional and then Free State governments; a founder member of Fine Gael.

51 UCDA, Richard Mulcahy Papers, P/7a/175. Mary MacSwiney played a leading part in the campaign to support her brother Terence in his epic and fateful hunger strike for release from prison. For an account of this, see Seán McConville, *Irish Political Prisoners, 1848–1922* (London: Routledge, 2003), pp. 740–50, *passim*. See also biographical note below, pp. 266–7, n. 21.

52 Padraig Pearse, *Political Writings and Speeches* (Dublin: The Talbot Press, 1952), p. 216.

53 A useful and detailed account is given by Joseph M. Curran, *The Birth of the Irish Free State* (Tuscaloosa, Ala.: University of Alabama Press, 1980). See also Tom Garvin, *1922: The Birth of Irish Democracy* (Dublin: Gill & Macmillan, 1996).

54 Immediately after the signing Michael Collins wrote to a close friend: 'I believe Birkenhead may have said an end to his political life. With him, it has been my honour to work.' Rex Taylor, *Michael Collins* (London: Hutchinson, 1958), p. 189.

55 Perhaps Churchill should be excepted from accusations of showmanship. Over the following decades, he condemned what he saw as de Valera's betrayal of the Treaty: he excoriated the man with the same heat that he condemned his doctrine. In an article in the *Daily Mail* in March 1932, following de Valera's election victory the previous month, Churchill proclaimed the immutability of the Treaty. Were the Oath of Allegiance abolished in the Free State, the Treaty would have been broken: 'the Free State will cease to exist as a political entity and would become a foreign country outside the Empire'. Churchill commended Michael Collins and Arthur Griffith, who had risked their lives for the Treaty. Indeed, the British Parliament had approved the Treaty because it believed an Irishman's word was his bond: 'Michael Collins gave his life to prove that this was true.' Yet de Valera's poll victory represented 'Irish hatred of England' (*Daily Mail*, 29 March 1932, 'Plain Words on the Irish Treaty', 8c–f). See also *Daily Mail*, 15 February 1933, 'What Isolation Means to a Free State', 10c–e.

56 *Dáil Debates*, vol. T, col. 345, 7 January 1922.

57 5 *Hansard*, vol. 149, col. 360, 16 December 1921.

58 5 *Hansard*, vol. 149, col. 209.

59 5 *Hansard* (Lords), vol. 48, cols. 36–53, *passim*. This reference to Birkenhead (Lord Chancellor and sitting on the Woolsack, only a few feet away) was unmistakable. He hoped to lose friendships of thirty years which were not based on confidence and trust: 'And of all the men in my experience that I think are the most loathsome it is those who will sell their friends for the purpose of conciliating their enemies, and, perhaps, still worse, the men who climb up a ladder into power of which even I may have been part of a humble ring, and then, when they have got into power, kick the ladder away without any concern for the pain, or injury, or mischief, or damage that they do to those who have helped them to gain power' (cols. 44–5). At times Carson's anger seemed to consume him.

60 GOIA, s.1(1).

61 Eunan O'Halpin, *Defending Ireland: The Irish State and Its Enemies since 1922* (Oxford: Oxford University Press, 1999), p. 16. Just under a year later manpower peaked at about 55,000.

62 All but a few men of the most hated units (the Auxiliary Division of the RIC and the Black and Tans) seem to have been removed by February 1922. 5 *Hansard*, vol. 150, col. 2078, 23 February 1922.

63 NAI TAOIS/S/4562, Michael Collins to Winston Churchill, 16 February 1922.

64 In May 1920, and with some reluctance by officers and units. See Ernie O'Malley, *On Another Man's Wound* (Dublin: Anvil Books, 1962), pp. 138–9; see also David Fitzpatrick, *Politics and Irish Life: Provincial Experience of War and Revolution* (Cork: Cork University Press, 1998), p. 166.

65 Speech at Killarney, 19 March 1922: *Irish Independent*, 20 March 1922, 5f; Donal O'Sullivan, *The Irish Free State and Its Senate* (London: Faber & Faber, 1940), p. 59. The point could have been expressed with less haughtiness and might thereby have become more persuasive. What should a democrat do if the electorate vote in effect to end democracy? The German elections of March 1933 gave the Nazi Party a majority in the German parliament; Hitler had campaigned on an anti-democratic platform and had made it clear that he would dismantle the apparatus of democracy. Three weeks after the election, his parliamentary majority allowed him to take dictatorial powers. How can the 'will of the people' be held sacrosanct in these circumstances? Would preventive action have been justified? Similarly, in December 1991, the Islamic Salvation Front, an anti-democratic party, won the first round of Algeria's elections. A few weeks later there was a military coup, the second round of the elections cancelled and the ruling party continued in power. Where should a democrat have stood? De Valera might argue that his conundrum has not been resolved.

66 He was a politician with remarkable confidence in his own powers of perception and judgement, declaring in the course of the Dáil debate on the Treaty, as he offered his resignation as President, 'The first fifteen years of my life that formed my character were lived amongst the Irish people in Limerick; therefore, I know what I am talking about; and whenever I wanted to know what the Irish people wanted I had only to examine my own heart and it told me straight off what the Irish people wanted' (*Dáil Debates*, vol. T, col. 274, 6 January 1922).

67 *Irish Independent*, 11 October 1922, 5b.

68 British forces had by mid-May 1922 been reduced to a garrison of 5,000, concentrated in Dublin (PRO CP/3993, Report of General Sir Nevil Macready, 20 May 1922, Cab, 24/136). Plans had been drawn up for partial reoccupation and a blockade that would starve out rebel areas.

69 Curran, *The Birth of the Irish Free State, op. cit.*, p. 195; 5 *Hansard*, vol. 154, cols. 2126–8, 31 May 1922. Churchill emphasised the British government's continued adherence to the Treaty, as demonstrated by its various actions. He counselled patience and continued good faith and determination to make the Treaty work. But if, in spite of all of this, there was a failure in the process, Britain would have placed itself on the strongest ground 'to encounter whatever events may be coming towards us' (col. 2141).

70 As many as forty-seven non-Sinn Féin candidates were nominated, all of whom, with varying degrees of commitment, supported the Treaty (*Irish Independent*, 7 June 1922, 5d).

71 Certainly there were several occasions on which armed men prevented or attempted to prevent candidates from speaking (*Irish Independent*, 7 June 1922, 4b and 5f).

72 *Irish Independent*, 15 June 1922, 7f.

73 Although Tom Garvin (*1922, op. cit.*, p. 128) points out that there had been attacks on the homes of forty-seven Dáil candidates long before Collins repudiated the pact.

74 For a clear and concise account of these discussions, see Curran, *The Birth of the Irish Free State, op. cit.*, Chapter 14.

75 See the *Irish Times*, 13 June 1922, 8c; 22 June 1922, 17c; *Irish Independent*, 17 June 1922, 5a. In many areas the elections proceeded quietly and peacefully. Much seemed to depend on local IRA commanders.

76 Figures rounded up. See Richard Sinott, *Irish Voters Decide: Voting Behaviour in Elections and Referendums since 1918* (Manchester: Manchester University Press, 1995), Appendix 2.

77 De Valera had admitted in private that an election victory for the pro-Treaty parties was inevitable: people would vote for peace (Garvin, *1922, op. cit.*, p. 124).

78 O'Malley, *The Singing Flame, op. cit.*, p. 86.

79 *The Times*, 23 June 1922, 10e, 14 (photographs), 23b (editorial), 18a–c (obituary). Sir Henry Wilson (1864–1922) was born at Edgeworthstown, Co. Longford and was commissioned into the Royal Irish Regiment in 1884. An outstandingly successful military career culminated with his appointment as Chief of the Imperial General Staff and promotion to Field Marshall. On his retirement, elected MP for North Down; advised the Northern Ireland government on security matters. Wilson was killed by an improbable duo. Reginald Dunne (who had served in the British Army in the First World War) was an OC (Officer Commanding) of the IRA's London Brigade and a student at the Roman Catholic St Mary's College (which trained teachers). Joseph O'Sullivan was a long-standing IRA activist, born in London, where he had lived all his life. During service in the British Army he had lost a leg. This made him a curious choice for a daytime assassination in the heart of London. The two men (captured whilst trying to flee the scene) were sentenced to death at the Old Bailey on 18 July 1922, and executed at Wandsworth prison on 16 August 1922.

80 Peter Hart argues that there is insufficient evidence to conclude that Collins ever authorised the killing. Peter Hart, *The IRA at War, 1916–1923* (Oxford: Oxford University Press, 2003), p. 162.

81 See below, p. 69.

82 *The Times*, 19 July 1922, 10e.

83 *The Times*, 23 June 1922, 10d, 17b; the newspaper denounced the murder in the strongest language as a deed which had not been approached since the murders of Cavendish and Burke in the Phoenix Park (17b). Sir James Craig, Prime Minister of Northern Ireland, had no doubt as to the motive for assassination and proclaimed that Wilson had laid down his life for Ulster. The Northern Ireland Parliament was adjourned as a mark of respect. *NIPD*, vol. 2, cols. 823–6, 22 June 1922.

84 *Irish Times*, 27 June 1922, 5d.

85 O'Malley, *The Singing Flame, op. cit.*, p. 88.

86 This was well publicised. O'Malley even persuaded some newly trained civic guards to hand over their small arms on that basis. Tom Barry and Rory O'Connor had done even better, winning over the guard at the Curragh Camp (where the guards were trained) and taking the arsenal. O'Malley, *The Singing Flame, op. cit.*, pp. 81–2.

87 O'Malley, *The Singing Flame, op. cit.*, pp. 95–7; Michael Hopkinson, *Green against Green: The Irish Civil War* (Dublin: Gill & Macmillan, 1988), Chapter 15.

88 See Hopkinson, *Green against Green, op. cit.* Tim Pat Coogan and George Morrison have provided a remarkable and at times deeply moving collection of war photographs and surrounding events. Tim Pat Coogan and George Morrison, *The Irish Civil War* (London: Orion, 1999).

89 O'Malley, *The Singing Flame, op. cit.*, p. 117. Of Rory O'Connor, Chairman of the Military Council of the anti-Treaty IRA, O'Malley observed, 'The fight [at the Four Courts] to him had been a symbol of resistance. He had built a dream in his mind and the dream was there; failure did not count and he evidently did not sense defeat' (p. 124).

90 Hopkinson, *Green against Green, op. cit.*, p. 129.

91 See Ronan Fanning, *Independent Ireland* (Dublin: Helicon, 1983), p. 39. See also n. 42 above.

92 See Hopkinson, *Green against Green, op. cit.*, pp. 272–3.

93 Niall C. Harrington, *Kerry Landing: August 1922* (Dublin: Anvil Books, 1992), pp. 148–9.

94 *Dáil Debates*, vol. 3, cols. 134–5, 17 April 1923.

95 Statutory Instrument, 2 October 1922, Military Courts: General Regulations as to Trial of Civilians. See also *Dáil Debates*, vol. 1, cols. 1734–8, 18 October 1922. David Fitzpatrick observes that the military courts established under the Act had powers

'exceeding the most egregious instruments created by the British or Northern Governments'. David Fitzpatrick, *The Two Irelands, 1912–1939* (Oxford: Oxford University Press, 1998), p. 133.

96 It was a poignant mark of the nature of civil war that Hales was, at the time, a republican officer in Cork.

97 The other three were Liam Mellows, Joe McKelvey and Richard Barrett. Rory O'Connor (1883–1922) graduated from UCD in Arts and Engineering. Fought in the 1916 Rising and became IRA Director of Engineering. Directed IRA's English campaign. Liam Mellows (1892–1922). Born Ashton-under-Lyme, near Manchester, and raised in Co. Wexford. Led Galway contingent of Volunteers in a number of minor actions in 1916. Fled to the USA, where he worked with the veteran Fenian John Devoy. Involved in arms purchases for IRA. Joe McKelvey (?–1922). Born in Stewartstown, Co. Tyrone. Defended Catholic minority during riots of 1920. OC 3rd Northern Division IRA, 1921. Richard Barrett (1889–1922). Acting Brigade Commander, West Cork Brigade. Arrested by British, March 1921, imprisoned at Cork. Released under amnesty.

98 Kevin O'Higgins was singled out for particular attention. His father, Dr Thomas F. O'Higgins, was shot dead by republicans in front of his family on 11 February 1923, and O'Higgins was himself assassinated on 10 July 1927.

99 Demonstrating his considerable political talent and rhetorical ability, de Valera's order took the form of an address to the 'Legion of the Rearguard'. He acknowledged that 'those who have sought to destroy the Republic' had secured military victory and promised that other means would be sought 'to safeguard the nation's right'. His defeated followers were, at the same time, instructed to cache their weapons, thereby indicating that the armed struggle remained a prospect in more propitious times. Arthur Mitchell and Pádraig Ó Snodaigh (eds.), *Irish Political Documents, 1916–1949* (Dublin: Irish Academic Press, 1985), pp. 161–3. De Valera doubtless had cause to regret this open-ended subversion when he came to office in the 1930s (see Chapter 6, below).

100 The Chamber had been expanded.

101 The Sinn Féin Ard Fheis met from Tuesday, 9 March to Friday, 12 March 1926. De Valera resigned following the failure of a motion that members should enter the Dáil were the oath abolished.

102 Public Safety Act, 1927, s.25 (1 and 2). Should murder or treason be proved ('found' might be more accurate), the court was obliged to impose the death penalty. No appeal was allowed from decisions of the tribunals, nor could civilian courts interfere with their proceedings.

103 Electoral (Amendment No. 2) Act, 1927, s.2 and Schedule.

104 This was clause 48 of the Free State Constitution which provided that a referendum provision could be put to the vote on the petition of not fewer than 75,000 voters. If the electorate then approved, a referendum clause would be inserted in the Constitution. Referendums could then be initiated by not fewer than 50,000 voters.

105 Even while signing, de Valera proclaimed that he was not doing so, theatrically removing a bible from the table and covering the wording of the Oath with some papers. The event went almost unreported in the Irish newspapers.

106 Cosgrave secured sixty-one seats, Independents twelve and the Farmers six. Fianna Fáil had fifty-seven seats, Labour thirteen, the National League two, and there was one Communist. The working majority was only five, however, since Cosgrave himself had been returned for two constituencies but held only one Dáil vote.

107 The development of this has been examined in Martin Maguire's impressive work, *The Civil Service and the Revolution in Ireland, 1912–38* (Manchester: Manchester University Press, 2008). For the developments after the Civil War, see Chapter 5.

108 See Fitzpatrick, *The Two Irelands*, *op. cit.*, pp. 168–70.

109 O'Halpin, *Defending Ireland*, *op. cit.*, Chapter 2.

110 On local government, see Mark Callanan and Justin F. Keogan (eds.), *Local Government in Ireland: Inside and Out* (Dublin: Institute of Public Administration, 2003), especially Richard Haslam's essay 'The Origins of Irish Local Government', pp. 14–40. See also Mary E. Daly, 'Local Appointments', in Mary E. Daly (ed.), *County and Town: One Hundred Years of Local Government in Ireland* (Dublin: Institute of Public Administration, 2001), pp. 45–55.

111 *Report on the Organisation of the Permanent Civil Service*, PP, 1854 [1713], XXXVII, 1. The Civil Service Commission was established in May 1855.

112 I discuss this in Seán McConville, *English Local Prisons, 1860–1900: Next Only to Death* (London and New York: Routledge, 1995), Chapter 12.

113 Local Government (Temporary Provisions) Act, 1923.

114 The Civil Service Regulation Act, 1924, established a unified civil service under the authority of the Minister for Finance. The previous system, under which various sections had devolved budgets and recruited staff, was abolished. There was a tussle over the authority of the legislature's oversight of the civil service. This culminated in agreement that accountability would follow the indirect path of untrammelled executive oversight and responsibility. The executive was, of course, accountable in this, as in all other matters, to the Dáil. See a portion of the discussion at *Dáil Debates*, vol. 6, cols. 1451–66, 27 February 1924.

115 Tom Garvin concludes that, by and large, the functions of politicians and civil servants were successfully separated by these measures and correctly sees this as a major achievement. Tom Garvin, 'Democratic Politics in Independent Ireland', in John Coakley and Michael Gallagher (eds.), *Politics in the Republic of Ireland* (London and New York: Routledge, 1999), pp. 350–64. See also Martin Maguire's clear and detailed narrative: *The Civil Service and the Revolution in Ireland, 1921–38 op.cit., Chapters 3 and 4. For a pre- and post-independence sweep (including the courts), see Lawrence W. McBride*, The Greening of Dublin Castle: The Transformation of Bureaucratic and Judicial Personnel in Ireland 1892–1922 *(Washington, DC: Catholic University of America Press, 1991)*.

116 This had been a requirement since the inception of the new state. From August 1922, a declaration of fealty was required from all members of the still-unamalgamated (i.e. Dublin Castle and Dáil Éireann) civil service. The form reflected the turbulence of the time and the Civil War still raging. 'I have not taken part with, or aided and abetted in any way whatsoever the forces in revolt against the Irish Provisional Government and I promise to be faithful to that government and to give no aid or support of any kind to those who are engaged in conflict against the authority of that government'. NAI FIN/E326/1; circular E326/5, 22 August 1922.

117 Whether from the contribution of the emigrant Irish or other groups, political influence became a seemingly ineradicable part of municipal administration in the large cities of the USA. The great social observer Milton L. Rakove encapsulated this in the title of his account of the reign of Richard J. Daley in Chicago: *We Don't Want Nobody Nobody Sent: An Oral History of the Daley Years* (Bloomington, Ind.: University of Indiana Press, 1979).

118 The pre-qualification did, of course, multiply the number of claimants. O'Malley and others noted the substantial expansion in the ranks of the IRA following the Truce of July 1921. As late as the 1950s, Dublin wits commented on the improbable number of beneficiaries from the public purse, whose claim was based on having been 'out'.

119 Competitive examinations for the civil service in British-ruled Ireland began in 1855 and were uniformly required by 1871 – much the same chronology as in Britain. See

Michelle Millar and David McKevitt, 'The Irish Civil Service System', in A. J. G. M. Bekke and Frits M. Van Der Meer (eds.), *Civil Service Systems in Western Europe* (Cheltenham: Edward Elgar, 2011), pp. 36–60, at p. 39.

120 McBride, *The Greening of Dublin Castle*, *op. cit.*, pp. 307–8; Ronan Fanning, *The Irish Department of Finance, 1922–58* (Dublin: Institute of Public Administration, 1978).

121 Under the terms of the Treaty, those unwilling to continue service had been allowed to retire on a pro-rata pension or to seek service in Northern Ireland. Those options ensured that those who remained were willing or, at least, compliant employees.

122 The loyalty test superseded the requirement imposed by the Provisional government in August 1922.

123 Fitzpatrick, *The Two Irelands*, *op. cit.*, pp. 82–3. The Dáil had issued its decree establishing local arbitration courts in June 1919, but the measure was unevenly implemented.

124 The Dáil Éireann Courts (Winding-up) Act, 1923, provided for the judicial commissioners to deal with outstanding Dáil business.

125 On 30 October 1922, the Dáil decree establishing its courts was rescinded for lower courts in the provinces. District judges were assigned to their various courts in early November 1922. Mary Kotsonouris, *Retreat from Revolution: The Dáil Courts, 1920–24* (Dublin: Irish Academic Press, 1994), pp. 14–15.

126 Courts of Justice Act, 1924. The Act was complex and weighty, extending to 104 sections.

127 The new judges seem to have been fairly evenly balanced between newcomers and those who had served under the British. This exemplifies the way in which the need for continuity was balanced with legitimising innovations throughout the system.

128 See, for example, Niall C. Harrington's memoir of fighting in Kerry in August 1922. Harrington had been a soldier of the Free State and, in the course of researching events of the time, had contacted men who had served with the Irregulars (as government called the anti-Treaty IRA). As he walked an old battleground with those men, still holding bitter memories, all rancour was set aside. Niall C. Harrington, *Kerry Landing: August 1922* (Dublin: Anvil Books, 1992), p. 153 and *passim*.

129 To take but two examples from left-wing revolutions (nationalist and right-wing counterparts could be chosen as well). Tsar Nicholas II was an autocrat, but the constitution of Russia during his reign bore no comparison in oppressiveness to that of his successors. Stalin, when captured by the authorities in 1902 and in 1913, was ordered into a Spartan but endurable exile for his revolutionary banditry. When in power, he dealt with his opponents (real, but mainly supposed) with utter ruthlessness and cruelty and presided over the deaths of millions. Fidel Castro was sent to prison for his 1953 rising against Batista but was released under an amnesty. Throughout his rule of nearly half a century, merely political and conscientious opponents were ruthlessly suppressed. No overt action was needed: mere dissent lay close to treason. Many were executed or done to death in prisons and camps. One of his erstwhile comrades, Armando Valladares, was locked up in solitary confinement, the door of his cell welded up (studied sadism) to underline the hopelessness of his fate: he was to envisage solitude, contempt and suffering unto death. Valladares survived a long and terrible captivity and was released in response to outside pleading and pressure. See, respectively, Simon Sebag Montefiore, *Young Stalin* (London: Weidenfeld & Nicolson, 2007); Armando Valladares, *Against All Hope: The Prison Memoirs of Armando Valladares* (Sevenoaks: Coronet, 1987). It is instructive to speculate on the dialectical transformation and magnification of oppression by certain successful revolutionaries. Their rage is unappeasable, it seems: even the oppressiveness of the displaced regime is held in contempt and surpassed.

130 Reaching further back, General George Washington's surrender to Congress of his command of the Continental Army on 23 December 1783 was a significant step in

the development of democracy and constitutional legality in the USA. The submission of an army commander (especially a successful one) to civilian rule is a delicate stage in transition from revolution to state-building.

131 Restoration of Order in Ireland, 1920: 10 & 11 Geo. V, c.31.

132 Tim Pat Coogan, writing with authority and on the basis of inside information, describes the assassination as impetuous and unauthorised. Tim Pat Coogan, *The IRA* (London: Fontana, 1980), pp. 79–80. It is something of an irrelevance whether it had been ordered or not. The organisation sought, in every way, to topple the Free State, its defeat in the Civil War merely blocking a frontal assault. It execrated the new state, denounced its ministers as traitors and hirelings and, in every way, justified their murder, restraint coming only from expedient calculation. Taking one of the oldest statutes on the offence – Treason Act, 1351: 25 Edw. III, St 5, c.2 – the IRA stood guilty (as it would have been proud to admit) of compassing the monarch's death (read, ministers of the new state) and of levying war when it could.

133 *Dáil Debates*, vol. T, especially sessions on 3–10 January 1922. The debate is also notable for the weight of emotion attached to symbols and the utter rejection by some leading republicans of pragmatic argument as a form of desecration and moral taint.

134 See below, p. 235, n. 238; p. 273, n. 90.

135 The remark may be apocryphal, but it has survived because it is a striking way of reflecting on power and authority. It was supposedly made by Stalin to Pierre Laval, in 1935. Quoted in Winston S. Churchill, *The Second World War*, 6 vols. (London: Cassell & Co., 1948), vol. I, p. 105.

136 The literature on this development is considerable. Declan Kiberd has brought a great deal of the material together in his masterly work of narrative and interpretation, *Inventing Ireland: The Literature of the Modern Nation* (London: Jonathan Cape, 1995).

137 'Did that play of mine send out certain men the English shot?' in 'The Man and the Echo', *The Poems of W. B. Yeats*, ed. Richard J. Finneran (New York: Macmillan, 1983), p. 345.

138 This topic has also produced numerous essays, books and surveys. For the European picture, see, for example, Charles Pouthas, 'The Revolutions of 1848', in J. P. T. Bury (ed.), *New Cambridge Modern History: The Zenith of European Power, 1830–70* (Cambridge: Cambridge University Press, 1960), pp. 389–415. For instructive and humane insights into identity and nationalism, see Rebecca West's classic *Black Lamb and Grey Falcon: A Journey through Yugoslavia*, 2 vols. (London: Macmillan, 1942). Michael Ignatieff is always perceptive and thought-provoking, and his exploration of aspects of nationalism's modern forms is essential reading for those seeking connections between the various strands of the phenomenon. See Michael Ignatieff, *Blood and Belonging: Journeys into the New Nationalism* (London: BBC Books, 1993). There is a warehouse of material on romanticism and nationalism in Ireland, and from it two contrasting books are instructive: R. F. Foster's *W. B. Yeats: A Life*, vol. I: *The Apprentice Mage* (Oxford: Oxford University Press, 1997) is outstanding in drawing together so many threads and laying bare dynamics. Colm Tóibín's *Bad Blood: A Walk along the Irish Border* (London: Vintage, 1994) gives shocking glimpses of the two nationalisms of the island of Ireland: it is a haunting account, similar in some ways to Rebecca West's unpicking of the Balkan tangle.

139 Kiberd's is a comprehensive review of revival drama, full of compelling examples, including *Cathleen Ní Houlihan*, a 1902 play by Yeats. Cathleen was a withered remnant who would be restored to queenly glory and radiant youth only if young men were willing to kill and die in her cause. Kiberd, *Inventing Ireland, op. cit.*, p. 200; n. 137 above.

140 See O'Malley's chronicle of his activities in the Anglo-Irish War, *On Another Man's Wound, op. cit.*; and O'Malley, *The Singing Flame, op. cit.*, especially Chapter 7.

141 In theory, and certainty, republican theory provided no guide to restraint. A large loss of civilian life, the infliction of bestial tortures and other actions seemingly lay beyond the range of permissible activities, but as much because of who the revolutionaries were as of any political doctrine. A deal of this was prefigured and justified in the raucous and unforgiving divisions that emerged in the Dáil Debates on the Treaty. See n. 56 above.

142 Grove notes that ballads usually deal with popular themes, including events which are tragic and adventurous: 'They may be based on some historical event, but the incidents related seldom correspond closely with verifiable facts, being distorted by bias, rumour and hearsay… Nevertheless, they are truthful in the sense of reflecting once current states of mind, which may at last harden into belief.' Stanley Sadie (ed.), *The New Grove Dictionary of Music and Musicians*, 29 vols. (London: Macmillan, 1980), vol. II, p. 71.

143 Some were loved and became memorable because of their unabashed awfulness, notably the compositions of the great doggerel poet, William Topaz McGonagall (1825–1902) (born in Dundee, Scotland, to an Irish father). His ability (if such is the word) to chronicle contemporary events in outrageously bad verse won him a great following.

144 Sadie, *New Grove Dictionary*, *op. cit.*, p. 73. For a useful survey of the broader musical context in Ireland, see vol. IX, especially pp. 316–18.

2

NORTHERN IRELAND
Ourselves alone

To have and to hold

By the mid-1920s, North–South divisions were stronger than ever. No body of people could contemplate casting their fate in with those engaged in civil war; nor would the memory of those events soon fade. Disorder, destruction and loss of life in the South confirmed the views of many Northern Protestants (and probably some Catholics) that loss of the British connection would simply unleash the dark side of Irish nationalism: its violence, propensity for secret societies, grudges, feuds and hatred of all that was not Catholic and Gaelic. At government level, this image was moderated, it is true, by the determination of the Free State to suppress armed insurrection and to uphold democracy under law. Successive elections showed that the great majority of Free State voters sought stability and rejected violence. But the nature of the state's nativity and those first turbulent years animated long-held fears and reinforced distrust.

At the popular level, the increasing power of the Roman Catholic Church within the Free State was a major concern. Northern Ireland was itself deeply religious and conservative in social thought and policy, frowned on divorce, indecency (as it was seen) in literature and the arts, and in matters such as sabbatarianism was more than willing to allow religious considerations to shape public policy. But rejection of 'Rome Rule' lay at the heart of Protestant traditions and fed its stereotypes, and many developments in the Free State confirmed the validity of these concerns. Constant calls for Irish unity and the abolition of the Northern state were completely counterproductive. The 1921–2 raids across the border (discussed below) demonstrated that at least some republicans were intent on conquest and coercion; the activation of the Boundary Commission suggested that even the Southern government hoped to destroy Ulster with salami-slice tactics.

There was an aspect of Northern Ireland's religious and social make-up which nationalist and republican leaders certainly knew, but which they failed fully to ponder. Unlike their co-religionists in Southern Ireland, Ulster's Protestants were a majority and were to be found substantially distributed across all classes and occupations and in all parts of the province. A portion had their feet firmly planted in the soil with which they had an affinity quite different from the Anglo-Irish Protestants of the South. Another portion formed the bulk and the backbone of the extensive manufacturing section of the Northern economy. Northern Catholics might contemplate the historic injustice of the conquests, confiscations and plantations and long for restoration and reparations, but Protestants had an equally strong sense of entitlement and their own history of grievances and experience of atrocities.

These mutual perceptions were powerful drivers of sometimes fearful hostility. At the political level, the rhetoric of Ulster unionism could be fervid and exaggerated and, at times, outrageously sectarian, triumphalist and calculatingly hurtful. Republican rhetoric was more divided. Irish unity was a matter of pious observance in the speeches of Southern politicians but was not a part of practical politics. Northern nationalists pined for unity with the South but in practical matters found themselves largely ignored by their erstwhile countrymen. Their politics were defensive, and their narrative often seemed no more than a series of unavailing protests. And all the time, the two societies – very different even when administratively united under British rule – developed separately and distinctively. Some British politicians had envisaged a national and general growing together of the two states. Fifty years after Partition, Ireland would be more divided than ever.

Northern Ireland had been created by a Westminster Act variously unwanted by Ulster unionists and by nationalists and republicans alike.[1] Division was rejected by dogma originating in the formative days of modern Irish nationalism. The doctrinal fervour of Southern nationalists was matched by the intense practical objection of most Northern nationalists and Catholics that they would be left as a large but helpless minority in an unsympathetic and even hostile unionist and Protestant state.[2] The history of bitter sectarian divisions and periodic outbreaks of communal violence gave an edge of fear to the objections of the Ulster Catholics.

The passage of time has obscured the initial antipathy of Ulster unionists towards the proposed new state. This shifted to ambivalence, to approval and then to visceral loyalty. At the core of Ulster unionism was a belief that they were a distinct British people living in the island of Ireland. Their forefathers had conquered their territory and defended it with determination and sacrifice: this was a patrimony worthy of defence. It was axiomatic that the freedom, safety, welfare and economic advancement of their community required a continuation of the tie between Britain and Ireland and, failing that, between Northern Ireland and Britain. The mixture of religion, politics, economics and social exclusiveness made a powerful bond indeed. Unionists were sometimes derided for their archaic celebration of Williamite victories more than two centuries previously, but those battles, the array of forces and the settlement of the Glorious Revolution informed and framed the Ulster Protestant's view of the world. History had passed and had embedded a sense of siege and a fear that a triumphant and almost exclusively Catholic nationalism meant the yoke of servitude.

That a large portion of the island had decided upon an alteration of the relationship with Britain deeply alarmed them. That their own state had been brought into existence as a form of compromise was also unsettling especially since, in the selling of the Anglo-Irish Treaty to its supporters by the pro-Treaty section of Sinn Féin, there had been much play upon the temporary nature of Partition. For Ulster unionists there was the realisation that if something as basic as citizenship could be altered and boundaries shifted, deals on national destiny sealed in the small hours in a London room, nothing was guaranteed. This view of events saw the Treaty as a reward for violence. To the Ulster unionist, aghast at acceptance of Home Rule in 1920, there remained much more safety in a relationship with Westminster, the Empire and, above all, the Crown – uncomplicated by devolution.[3] That organic tie could be understood, expressed and defended: it was above politics and politicians. Only thus could unionists escape the sense that they had been pushed from brotherhood to cousinship within the British family – from the status of Sussex or Yorkshire to that of a less integral, remote and possibly disposable territory. To those devotees of Glorious Revolution, an earthquake had unmade the landscape. Disloyalty, treason and violence had been rewarded; loyalty and respect for the law devalued and repudiated.[4]

But there was another side to this analysis. Besides the doctrine of the Protestant Succession, the central components of the 1701 Act of Settlement were the conditional nature of monarchy, its subordination to law and therefore the possibility of its lawful termination.[5] The core of the Act was the concept of government by consent. This replaced the Stuart doctrine of the divine right of kings and reconciled monarchy with mechanisms of accountability. The condition of consent passed into British political life and thence over time (and not without hindrance) into the apparatus and procedures of state: legislation, law enforcement and the administration of justice. This doctrine should have been transferred in its totality to the new state of Northern Ireland. The end of British rule in the rest of Ireland certainly confirmed the need to obtain the consent, if not the support, of the governed and showed what happened when this was forfeited. It is ironic and tragic that the principal fruit of the Glorious Revolution should have been so misunderstood or marginalised by the *soi-disant* Williamite devotees who founded Northern Ireland: there can be no legitimate government without consent, and a people who are ruled without consent are unfree and have the right, and, some will inevitably proclaim, the duty, to rebel. The notion of one group dominating another by providential right was a doctrine more expressive of the later Stuarts than of William and Mary.

Such doctrinal consistency and political clarity required qualities of statesmanship far beyond those current in Northern Ireland at the time of its foundation. It is certainly tragic that this long view was not taken – and may not have been politically possible. The genesis of Northern Ireland was insecurity rather than a desire for freedom. This meant that the machinery of state would be defensive and inevitably repressive of the minority. A state must declare itself to be *for* something, to have some purpose: it needs myth, legend and style.

Northern Ireland came into being for protective reasons, and that would define its ethos for the following half century. Watchfulness, distrust of the other and loyalty to one's own would shape style and determine method. In its wider, truer, sense, Northern Ireland could never be truly unionist.

That sense of insecurity (and a deal of distrust of British politicians) had, in the end, convinced Ulster unionists of the need for their own state. A Northern parliament set up and an administration created, it would be no little matter to reverse the process. The lopping off of territory (through the Boundary Commission, for example) would be more easily inflicted on an entity that did not have the standing and resources of a state.[6] Perhaps, therefore, a devolved unionist state – odd creature though it sounded – might be the better option after all? Its parliament would have a voice that could not easily be stilled or, as at Westminster, submerged in a greater volume and wider representation of British domestic and imperial interests. Its apparatus of state and relationship to the Crown would invest it with a dignity and lend a quality of immovability. And then there were the direct-force aspects of Ulster unionism: the accumulation of arms, the training of volunteers and the rhetoric that went to the edge (and perhaps over) of sedition and treason. Would it not be better to keep that armed and organised element of loyalism in the kraal and within the law? Surely it was possible to place it under the direction of a regular authority responsible to a parliament in which unionists would have an unshakeable and perpetual majority? Rather than a stepping stone to a united Ireland, was not the new state a stout wall of stone, a means of preserving the Union, from Sinn Féiners, the fickle fortunes of Westminster parties and the deviousness of Whitehall alike?

There was also much unhappiness and foreboding among Southern unionists. Partition was not in their interest: far better to be part of a large and resourceful Protestant minority in a unified Irish state with a Home Rule constitution, with most of the familiar British institutions left intact and with ultimate power reserved to Westminster. The Easter Rising and the War of Independence nullified this option, so the least worst outcome was a unified Irish dominion, under Free State rule.[7] With the six counties of Northern Ireland removed from the new entity, Southern Protestants were reduced to a mere 10 per cent of the population.[8] Despite the repeated assurances of the Free State leaders, Protestants felt that their interests would be subjugated and that political defeat would be followed by cultural, religious and demographic erosion and eventual effacement. The interests of the two groups of unionists were thus very different, as were their cultures and antecedents. As the doctrines of the Catholic Church increasingly infused and dominated key aspects of public policy in the South, the plight of their co-religionists confirmed the followers of Carson and Craig in their creed.

Once the principle of Home Rule for Northern Ireland had been accepted, Ulster unionists had further decisions to make. As noted, calculations on the viable area of the new entity led one group to press for inclusion of all nine counties of the ancient province of Ulster. In this they were encouraged by several British politicians, even though a four-county state had been canvassed as a compromise only eight years before.[9] But the intervening years had shown what passions and hatreds lay within these disputes. There were, moreover, strong geographical, economic and psychological arguments for the larger unit. On presentational and substantive grounds, a larger unit in which Protestants comprised 57 per cent of the population was preferable to a smaller one with a two-thirds Protestant majority.[10] It could reasonably be anticipated that a relatively balanced population would oblige both sides to compromise and accommodate; and alliances such as Labour might even be made across sectarian lines: this process in itself could make for stability. Another view – possibly held by the same people – was that nine-county demographics made Irish unity more likely and perhaps not too long postponed.

The British Cabinet's Irish Committee, which was entrusted with the task of drawing up the Government of Ireland Bill, wavered. On 17 February 1920, it opted for nine counties.[11] As a result of representations from James Craig and other leading Ulster unionists, this position was abandoned a week later.[12] Craig and his colleagues had taken a close look at likely constituency outcomes. With nine counties, the Ulster Unionist Party could look for a majority of only three or four in a fifty-two seat assembly. Even this might be reduced by Labour or another party attracting working-class votes across sectarian lines. A lost vote in the new parliament could overnight pass the Northern state into a united Ireland, since the unwritten British constitution did not provide for entrenched legislation. Six counties and no more it would have to be. Fewer than six counties would encourage another danger: Westminster at some point taking the view that the new state was an unviable anomaly. Commerce, manufacturing and investor confidence and market psychology demanded a hinterland.

Children of disobedience

The pathway of these decisions has been outlined from the perspective of unionism, but nationalists and republicans saw things very differently. One of the curiosities of Irish political discourse over half a century was the insistence by all parties that they adhered to the doctrines of democracy. The Southern Irish insisted that the vast majority of the Irish as a whole wanted Irish unity, and this was confirmed by the sweeping Sinn Féin victories in the last all-Ireland election in December 1918: Ulster should bow to the democratic will. Unionists insisted that theirs was not a minority vote but a majority within an entity and a people quite different and distinct from that of Southern Ireland. Into our own times many unionists have insisted that power-sharing within Northern Ireland is undemocratic and that the will of the majority, simply expressed, should prevail. Their opposite numbers within republicanism have equally fervently proclaimed Northern Ireland to be a gerrymandered state, and therefore without legitimacy. Thousands of lives and many billions of pounds have been consumed by this dispute.

Within an island where a vigorous localism had survived all the pressures of transformed communications, where townland, village, parish, town, district and county – bush, tree, hedge and field, indeed – have shaped and held identity, it could be misleading to refer to differences between Ulster and the other Irish provinces. All geographic units, to some considerable extent, preserved and valued local and regional distinctions; all nurtured a degree of parish-pump xenophobia. But in its history, and particularly in its majority and type of Protestants, Ulster was different from other parts of Ireland, and the differences within did not block a deep sense of common identity.

Though few said it at the time (and very few probably saw it), a continuation of Westminster rule would have served Ulster Catholics and therefore Ulster Protestants far better. Diluted by the broader concerns of a large and prosperous country and empire, carried along by its pace and held to far stricter and fairer standards of public life, sectarian and communal divisions would have been less oppressive and remedies more easily sought. But union with Britain had already been staked out as the ground of Ulster unionism and nationalism did not have the flexibility of tactics, still less the strategic vision, to question what form that union should take and what strategic political advantages it might hold. Nationalist (particularly republican) doctrine fixated on the notion of one exclusive nationality that fitted all who lived on the island of Ireland. There was indeed a point where Ulster unionism could have been encouraged to follow its instincts and to demand the union be left undiluted by devolution. Pressure from Irish nationalism, North and South, could have assisted this outcome: it is hard to see what element in the British Cabinet would have resisted it.

Shocked by the thwarting of their hopes, and fearing what lay ahead, Northern Catholics generally failed to embrace the new realities and withheld their allegiance from the new state; some tried to imagine it away. As though it were an option that cantons were part of the new order, certain local authorities run by nationalists declared loyalty to Dublin rather than to Belfast. Teachers in some Catholic schools initially refused to accept Northern Ireland salaries, and some were, for a short time, paid instead from Dublin.[13] Nationalist politicians (and these were, for the most part, the remnants of the Irish Parliamentary Party) decided not to participate in the new legislature; republicans continued to seek its destruction. The Roman Catholic hierarchy refused to establish formal relations with the organs of state.[14] Labour, whose doctrines emphasised the overriding common identity and unity of interests of all working people, could not evade the Partition issue and consequently split. Some attempts were made to make the new state more palatable to Catholics, but these lacked the drive and vulnerability of sincerity, or the allure of imaginative generosity; suspicion and gracelessness multiplied on all sides. The most significant concession was to recruit Roman Catholics for the new police force, the RUC. Had this been proportionately achieved, one-third of the constabulary would have been Catholic, and a critical state institution might perhaps have become more acceptable to the minority population.[15]

Abstentionism led all too easily to exclusion.[16] Nationalism, which, unlike republicanism, was entirely peaceful and constitutional, and Catholicism were treated as forms of disloyalty and therefore as dangers to the new state. In the sense that most Catholics did not wish Northern Ireland to exist, it was true that they were not loyal to it. But this was an opinion to which they were surely entitled. To act on it (other than within the law) was quite a different matter. Nor did attitude to the state necessarily determine one's attitude to one's employing organisation. Conversely, Protestant and Orange affiliations commended themselves to many public and private employers. There were various strands to this. Protestant and Catholic workers were frequently at each other's throats at this time: openings were few and fiercely guarded. To many employers, a mixed workforce may simply have been a potential for friction, best avoided. It was not easy to leave the troubles and tensions of the wider community at the factory gate. But, in some instances, refusal of employment to Catholics was simple bigotry and a sharing of the spoils with one's own. Times were hard, becoming harder, and it seemed simple enough to answer the question of who should have jobs in a flat or contracting economy. But, particularly in sensitive fields of public employment – police, prisons, the post office and middle and higher reaches of the civil service – there may have been an additional and perhaps more pragmatic reason for caution. Had not the IRA under Michael Collins skilfully subverted British rule by recruiting or placing agents at all levels in the public services? This became obvious in the setting up of the Free State and the concurrent emergence and rewarding of some of those agents. And, within a few years, all of this was confirmed and celebrated by the memoirs and historians of the Anglo-Irish War.[17] In 1925, an oath of allegiance was instituted for all public appointments (a requirement also in the Free State). This was no light matter or mere form of words in a society in which religious obligations and scruples were a central part of everyday life and where an oath was binding. But even this solemn declaration was seen as an insufficient guard against treachery. Catholics were found places in the public services but were concentrated overwhelmingly in the lower grades. Denominational affiliation was a bar (not consistently or predictably enforced) to recruitment and promotion. As this became known, and possibly exaggerated, Catholics stopped applying and so heightened their self-perception as an excluded and disadvantaged minority.[18] A self-sacrificing process had been set in motion.

The relationship between politicians and the electorate is never static, with constant see-sawing. On many issues, and for most of the time, voters are content to follow their chosen party: they have bought a package and stick with it. But politicians who move too far away from their followers risk their authority (and create opportunities within their own parties for those who would dispute them). This has been repeatedly confirmed in Northern Ireland as moderate unionist leaders have been rejected by their party or have struggled to keep control. It is all too easy to overlook or minimise the political restrictions within which James Craig worked in the first uncertain months and years of his new state. Having acknowledged this, and accepting the fact that Craig abhorred violence and did what he could to ensure peaceful stability, there was an unhappy narrowness in his political vision. He occasionally allowed himself to yield to the temper of the moment and made public statements that rubbed salt into Catholic wounds, thus creating or adding to deeply felt feelings of resentment. He gave little weight to the need to bind up his riven community, to conciliate and incorporate. He preferred to tackle nationalism head-on rather than to attempt to bypass it, to speak directly to nationalist voters and shift the direction of debate. Nor was this confined to the first turbulent and rather desperate years of the new state. More than a decade after Northern Ireland had been stabilised and secured, Craig told its House of Commons that he had held high office in the Orange Institution for many years, 'and I prize that far more than I do being Prime Minister. I have always said that I am an Orangeman first and a politician and Member of this Parliament afterwards.'[19] Whatever his private feelings, this was not a proper statement for a prime minister of a religiously divided state to make; and, quite apart from propriety, it was bound to be dangerous and counterproductive.

Yet James Craig was a moderate in his government. No member of his cabinet had been educated at university level; most were narrow and provincial, and some were decidedly sectarian in outlook. Only Craig and the Marquess of Londonderry had had ministerial experience at Westminster. Edward Archdale, Minister for Agriculture, in 1925 expressed satisfaction at the fact that there were only four Catholics employed by his department.[20] Other ministers pandered to Orange Order complaints about the employment of disloyal people in the public service: 'disloyal' being a thinly veiled code for Catholic. John Andrews, Minister for Labour, in 1933 ordered an investigation into an Orange Order claim that the majority of porters at the Stormont Parliament building were Roman Catholics. Of the thirty-four porters, he found only one, a temporary appointment, was a Catholic.[21] A year later, a Stormont gardener was dismissed because of allegations of republican sympathies, even though he had a good British Army record and had been in the service of the Prince of Wales.[22] Around the same time, the Minister for Home Affairs, Sir Dawson Bates, refused to have Catholics employed in his department, even in the most junior positions.[23] In 1934, he discovered that one of the Stormont telephonists was a Catholic and thereupon refused to use his telephone until the unfortunate telephonist was transferred.[24] When Minister for Agriculture, Sir Basil Brooke, told a Twelfth of July crowd at Newtownbutler, Co. Fermanagh, that a great number of Protestants and Orangemen employed Roman Catholics, but he himself had not a Roman Catholic about his own place.[25] Wherever possible, loyalists should employ 'good Protestant lads and lassies'.[26] What is noteworthy is that these and kindred remarks were made more than a decade after the establishment of Northern Ireland. No Catholic would need a particularly thin skin to feel bitterness and rancour at such utterances: these indeed were the waters of Babylon.[27]

The sectarian remarks of the Northern ministers and politicians – and they can only be read as sectarian in intent as well as in meaning – must be given context, though hardly excuse. From their point of view, the Roman Catholic minority had several characteristics that led unionist politicians to make such remarks and to feel comfortable in doing so. First, Catholicism was largely synonymous with support for the Nationalist Party or republicanism. Only a very small number of Catholics voted Unionist, and almost certainly none was (or was permitted to be) active in that party.[28] Ulster Liberalism had predeceased its parent in Britain, and Labour was weak and divided. The issue went beyond what in another setting would have been party affiliation. Constitutional nationalism and republicanism alike questioned the very existence of the Northern Ireland state. This was emphasised when Craig, in an angry Stormont debate, referred to the disloyal person as anyone out to break up that Constitution established by Great Britain.[29] The disloyal should be denied employment for several reasons. Roman Catholics, Craig claimed, liked to employ their co-religionists 'and leave our people to employ those they cannot employ themselves'. But those – and only those, he implied – who supported the Constitution should benefit from it. He added the saving grace that this should hold whether or not they agreed with government policy. But since policy was defined by the Union, and no other government was likely to hold office in Northern Ireland, this was tongue-in-cheek sophistry. An additional reason for not employing the disloyal was that every one of them was 'a potential voter for destruction of this country'. Finally, 'there is grave danger in employing men who at the first opportunity will betray those who employ them'.[30]

There may have been some truth in Craig's observations. This was a sectarian society, and on both sides co-religionists were doubtless preferred employees. But surely he was too sweeping, too pessimistic and too shallow. Certainly, this parliamentary debate, and a number of others, were sad, mean-spirited affairs, studded with jeering, baiting and mutual contempt. It is hard to see how any who took part in them maintained their self-respect, still less respect for their opponents. Most Northern Catholics would indeed have preferred to be part of an all-Ireland Free State. Sincere Catholics wished the conversion of 'heretics';[31] sincere nationalists wished the reunification of Ireland. These views, provocative no doubt, were matters of opinion and even conscience. Those coming from a Protestant tradition by definition took their stand in a repudiation of Catholicism as unreformed, erroneous and imperfect Christianity loaded with the sacramental accretions and pretensions, a vessel of medieval corruption. One of the central tenets of Protestantism, especially in its political manifestations, was opposition to the intolerance and overweening claims of the Catholic Church. But non-Protestant and non-unionist views, as long as they found no expression in illegal activities, should have been tolerated and certainly should not have affected Catholics' rights as citizens of Northern Ireland. Even in the 1920s they would have had little if any effect on their civic (as distinct from social) standing elsewhere in the UK.[32] Yet Sir James Craig's precepts excluded Catholics from the most basic of rights: to disagree with impunity. They also withdrew the state from an important duty of care: to promote the welfare of all its citizens and to help them provide themselves with a livelihood, or, at least, not to impede their ambitions and efforts. The Northern Ireland state defined itself by loyalty to the Crown, but the Crown was based on that freedom of conscience and politics established by the Williamite victories, the Glorious Revolution and the Act of Settlement. That Roman Catholicism had been the historic enemy derived from Rome's attempted hegemony and intolerance (as well as the track of European history and politics). There was profound historical irony in the anti-Catholicism, real or rhetorical, of Craig, Brooke and others. The supreme value and virtue of British political culture – its tolerance – was being limited, even denied, by the leader of a state that had come into being ostensibly to protect those basic liberties. The superiority of a state based on the British Constitution could be demonstrated only by including, not excluding, its dissident minority.

But it takes at least two to conciliate, and Craig and his ministers could argue that they had no partners. Roman Catholic and nationalist leaders had little appreciation of British constitutional history and no inclination to put unionism to its own test – possibly little notion that such a test existed. Indeed, most conformed to the ultramontane Catholicism then approaching its zenith in Ireland and had no intellectual apparatus or steerage room to take the fight to the Protestant state by invoking its antecedents. There was, of course, the threat and only slowly receding tensions arising from the IRA campaign against the Northern state (which we examine below). But even ballot-box politicians withheld recognition, and it was not until 1925 that Nationalist MPs took their seats in the Northern Ireland Parliament. As in the Free State, Sinn Féin condemned this step and continued to insist upon abstention. By that time, the mould may have been set, and, despite good personal relations between Joseph Devlin (the Nationalist leader) and Sir James Craig, and some gestures of reconciliation, Ulster unionism continued on its way, indifferent to the wishes and interests of the minority, unaware that it daily forged a weapon for its enemies.[33]

Authority lost, power confirmed

It had been anticipated that the constituency-based simple majority rule of the British electoral system would not prove adequate as an instrument of democracy in such a rigidly divided community. First-past-the-post voting would condemn the minority to perpetual exclusion from office. Accordingly, proportional representation had been provided by the GOIA as an equitable and protective device.[34] One of the first acts of Craig's government had been the withdrawal of proportional representation for local elections, a far-reaching matter, considering the patronage powers of local authorities.[35] Instructively, this reneging on a key safeguard evoked not a single comment, much less protest at Westminster. Proportional representation was retained for parliamentary elections, and by 1927 there were ten Nationalist MPs and two (abstaining) republicans. This was not, nor could ever be, a threat to the Unionist majority, yet in 1929 proportional representation was also abolished for parliamentary elections. Joseph Devlin continued to sit in the Northern Ireland Parliament, but in May 1932 he and his party walked out, returning only in October 1934. Thereafter, the Nationalists (who had never accepted the status, privileges and responsibilities of an official opposition) distanced themselves from the institution, attending only spasmodically and, in effect, leaving the Unionists without an effective opposition until 1963.[36] For those thirty years, the Nationalist Party limited itself to anti-Partitionism and protesting against anti-Catholic discrimination: a 'well-worn rut of sulkiness and whinging' as Marianne Elliott observes.[37]

In all of this, it is important to remember the scale of the Northern Ireland Parliament, its limited powers and the pace at which it operated. With a House of Commons of fifty-two members and a Senate half that size, the Commons was less than a tenth the size of the Westminster House of Commons, and the Senate was little more than 3 per cent of the 800-or-so-strong House of Lords. At the same time, it was disproportionately large, considering the respective sizes of Great Britain and Northern Ireland.[38]

Like the legislatures of several of the smaller and more sparsely populated American states, Northern Ireland's was essentially a part-time legislature, meeting for only a few months in each session. Since its powers were subordinate to those of Westminster, it followed the rule that it would not discuss matters which were 'excepted' (foreign relations) or 'reserved' (services financed exclusively by the Westminster budget). On its part, as we have seen, Westminster denied itself questions and debate on matters that fell within the powers exercised by the Northern Ireland Parliament. Today, this arrangement would be called 'subsidiarity' and would be lauded by the European Union as an essential democratic device. Given conditions in Northern Ireland, however, this framework of exclusions and self-denying limitations had an undemocratic and ultimately destructive effect.

So narrowly limited, with one party enjoying an unchallengeable majority in perpetuity and with ministers who held office for long periods – two prime ministers (James Craig and Basil Brooke) held office for twenty years each, four-fifths of the life of the Northern Ireland government – debates were narrow and repetitive. Everyone had heard what everyone else had to say, in every possible way. When sparks did fly, it was almost invariably on Catholic–Protestant, North–South issues, often given a twist by minutely recited local claims, grievances and counter-assertions. Discussions then followed a predictable course, often degenerating into mutual and necessarily unproductive recrimination; spite was vented self-indulgently. The overall impression created was that of an inward-looking county council in a backward area, overlaid with Swiftean caricature and touches of Samuel Butler's Erewhonian fantasy.

Given the political stalemate, the attitude of the Roman Catholic hierarchy was of considerable importance. The tale is simple and short: it shunned the Northern Ireland government from the beginning. Since Nationalist members initially boycotted the Northern Ireland Parliament, no Catholic chaplain was appointed (an unwise omission on Craig's part). This decision is the more curious since there had been no problem in asking the Catholic Church to nominate chaplains to prisons, where (initially) they were paid a modest fee for services and attendance.[39] In 1925, Nationalists decided to enter the Northern Ireland House of Commons. The Speaker, Sir Hugh O'Neill, asked Cardinal O'Donnell, the Roman Catholic Primate and Archbishop of Armagh, to appoint a chaplain. The request was referred to the Bishop of Down and Connor in whose diocese Stormont was located: no more was heard of the matter. Two years later, the Nationalists had ten MPs. Successive primates and bishops maintained the policy of non-involvement and non-cooperation.[40] As a result of this stubbornness and ill-will on both sides, laid down in strata of resentment, the first official meeting between a Northern Ireland prime minister and a primate of the Roman Catholic Church in Ireland did not take place until 25 February 1971, more than fifty years after the foundation of the state.[41] A Roman Catholic chaplain had been appointed to Stormont not long before the meeting. Better late than not at all, but this is a significant record of irresponsibility, of bigotry and of mutual and mischievous disregard, wherever the balance of fault lay.

As noted, the other source of authority for Northern Catholics was Dublin. The sense of abandonment caused by the Treaty probably never faded. As the Free State struggled to survive, it displayed an uncertain and complex attitude towards Northern Ireland. A treaty had been signed that accepted Partition. In its first critical couple of years, the Southern government was being sustained in office substantially through British good offices and material support, but, for the initial months at least, was playing a double game. The Northern Ireland government wanted peace and stability in the South and was defending its own territory only.[42] Yet, sectarian riots in various Northern towns, and especially in Belfast, showed the position of Ulster Catholics to be precarious, with rogue elements in the security forces of the new state being involved in acts of serious violence and even murder. Thousands of Catholics were driven from their workplaces and homes; churches and other properties were destroyed.[43] Collins, who had shown a particular interest in the fate of the Northern minority, and who may eventually have found a pragmatic politics to support his concerns, was killed in a civil-war ambush on 22 August 1922. With his death, the Free State lost a highly talented leader. One of the consequences was that the country turned inwards, accepting Northern Ireland as an established state and leaving Northern Catholics to make the best of the conditions in which they found themselves.

Despite the supposed hopes of successive Southern governments and political leaders, the two parts of Ireland, historically and culturally distinctive in any event, moved further apart. The 1932 advent to office of Éamon de Valera deepened the divergence. Always strong in the rhetoric of anti-Partitionism (though far less so on Irish unity), de Valera had in 1922 split from his comrades over the Treaty – not on the issue of Partition, but on continued membership of the British Empire of that portion of Ireland which had secured its independence. His assertive republicanism, erasure of the final symbolic links with Britain, assertion of *de jure* sovereignty over the territory of Northern Ireland and gratuitous confirmation within his 1937 Constitution of the special status of the Roman Catholic Church, hardened divisions in the island and reinforced Partition. It is incomprehensible that he or his advisers could have imagined otherwise. Yet, among Ulster Catholics, the desire still persisted to belong to the Southern state: they felt deeply that they had no other home. The Irish tricolour became a symbol of that longing, as was the orientation to Dublin for cultural and sporting links. But from the South came little more than words and the cold comfort of brandished emblems, and these often at election time when nationalist sentiments were obligatory ornaments for manifestos and addresses to constituents. Northern Catholics' sense of Southern betrayal was considerable. This survived the generations, with Eddie McAteer, leader of the Nationalists, declaring in the 1960s, 'we are the bastard children of the Republic. Sometimes, they must needs acknowledge us, but generally speaking they try to keep their distance.'[44]

The sinews of state

A major but seldom-considered factor in the state of insecurity that developed in Northern Ireland was the status of the Truce. Momentum for this came from the conciliatory speech delivered by George V on the opening of the Northern Ireland Parliament on 22 June 1921, a reaching out that was the essential first step in ending the Anglo-Irish War. The Truce was signed by Major-General Sir Nevil Macready, GOC (General Officer Commanding) of British Forces in Ireland. It was authorised by the British government and by de Valera in his capacity as President of the Irish Republic. The terms were negotiated by Robert Barton and Eamonn Duggan, representatives of the IRA who had been specially released from British custody for the purpose; the document was signed on 9 July 1921 and came into effect two days later. No Northern Ireland official or politician was party to the Truce, nor were they consulted. It would appear that the first Sir James Craig knew of it was from the newspapers.[45]

By this time, Northern Ireland had existed *de jure* as an entity for seven months and nineteen days, and *de facto* for rather longer. The situation in its six counties was quite different from that prevailing in the rest of Ireland. The IRA had not conducted an offensive campaign along the lines it had been able to follow in the south and west of Ireland and in Dublin. In addition to the Army and the RIC, it was confronted by its loyalist and unionist equivalent, the UVF. This body had been formed by Sir Edward Carson in 1912 to resist by force of arms, if necessary, the imposition of Home Rule in Ulster; it had claimed a membership of 100,000 men and appears to have had many well-equipped and trained units. Through mass enrolment in the British Army (notably the 36th [Ulster] Division) during the First World War, it had ceased to exist as a functioning organisation, although many of its members and an amount of its armament continued to be available.[46]

Faced with what by 1920 had become a major and acute threat to British rule in Ireland and the possible imposition not only of Home Rule but of an all-Ireland and wholly independent republic, steps were taken to re-establish the organisation, the leading part in this being taken by Sir Basil Brooke, a highly decorated soldier and later Prime Minister of Northern Ireland. This organisation began to function before the Northern Ireland state came into existence, and the members of the reactivated body did what they could to counter the IRA in rural areas and to supplement the RIC, which, severely decimated by the IRA and demoralised by its impending disbandment, had been reduced to a poor level of effectiveness. The reconstituted UVF, at least in theory, had the same status as the IRA: it was an unofficial and probably illegal body under the ROIA. UVF members had no more right than the IRA to bear arms and, unless they knew that its members were well disposed towards them, had to hide weapons when they encountered an RIC or army patrol.[47]

For several months in 1920, therefore, there existed a loyalist paramilitary organisation, Protestant in membership and with a partisan and probably sectarian ethos. This body carried out patrols, mounted roadblocks and occasionally engaged in actions against the IRA. It was poorly armed and undermanned, with a leadership of uneven quality and experience, but it had the advantage of considerable local knowledge, a constant flow of intelligence (especially in rural areas) and a relationship to the regular forces of law enforcement that allowed a degree of freedom of action. It had the considerable drawback, however, of being seen by the Catholic population as a sectarian Protestant body. Patrols, roadblocks and searches provided numerous opportunities for encounters fraught with sectarian and personal hostility, which thus heightened tensions. As far as can be ascertained, no UVF member was arrested during these months for the illegal possession of arms or for other forbidden acts. With this force in the field, uncertainty about the application of the Truce to Northern Ireland, the impending demise of the RIC, restricted operations by the Army, IRA regrouping and upsurges in sectarian tensions, there would be many occasions for violence and disorder and uncertain instruments to counter them.

The Anglo-Irish Treaty formally excluded Northern Ireland from the Free State – but it had already excluded itself. Under the 1920 Government of Ireland Act, an administration had been set up and was rapidly being consolidated. This speed was in large part driven by the threats to the new state, both internal and external. As the Anglo-Irish War reached its crisis, relations between the Protestant and Catholic communities in the Northern cities worsened considerably. The Protestant working class feared that they were being railroaded into an Irish republic (Home Rule plus and Rome Rule unrestrained). There was, sadly, a long history of intercommunal confrontation and violence, but the tensions of the war and then the Truce fuelled a particularly savage series of riots in July 1920.[48] Who initiated this disorder and the exact sequence of events is now hard to discern. To anyone familiar with Northern Ireland, July and August – the 'marching season' – are sensitive, strained and at times dangerous. Catholics would have had it that following the Truce they were attacked and that units of the IRA defended them. The fledgling Northern administration insisted that there was an attack on the police by the Belfast IRA on 14 July 1921 (just five days after the Truce was signed) and that this provoked rioting and sniping.[49] The end result was clear enough: some 8,000 Catholics were driven out of their jobs in the Belfast shipyards and factories, and hundreds of others fled their homes. There was a great destruction of property, and at least forty-eight people were killed, with several hundred wounded and injured.[50]

These events were of the greatest import for Ulster unionism. With no effective forces at its direct disposal, the Northern Ireland government was unable to protect property and lives, and its standing with its Protestant supporters was severely strained; Catholics were further alienated. The British government continued to have responsibility for law and order, yet did not appear to be acting with sufficient vigour. London, constrained by the terms of the Truce, genuinely wanted peace and did not wish to provoke Sinn Féin and the IRA by a clampdown. There was a serious failure in communication and an appearance of drift. Leadership of the loyalist population began slipping away from the Ulster Unionists and into the hands of communal groups.[51] The Northern state might have then imploded and, at best, come under British military rule for a period, with all the concomitant political uncertainties. The IRA, a substantial section of which did not expect to reach a final settlement with Britain, continued to rearm, train and regroup, in violation of the Truce.[52] The IRA's Northern divisions, unlike those in the South, functioned primarily as Catholic defence forces. Its rearmament was understandable and yet intolerably threatening to Protestants: it further increased the very conflict that it was arming against. The embattled, beleaguered and fearful state of mind of loyalists is not usually given sufficient weight by those who take a look backwards from the surviving state and the grandly entrenched Stormont of the later decades. None of this justified the appalling attacks on the minority, which were themselves corrosive of authority, but it does help explain why it was so difficult to establish order.

Grossly aggravating these internal problems, Northern Ireland faced cross-border raids. This external threat may have been worsened by the Treaty. After this was ratified by the Dáil, on 7 January 1922, IRA and Sinn Féin prisoners and internees were released. Many hastened to join or rejoin active units of the IRA. According to Northern Ireland government sources, this was a factor in renewed sniping and intercommunal violence in Belfast and also in the strengthening of the groups engaged in cross-border raids. The Treaty also led to a split in the IRA and eventually to civil war. In the months preceding an out-and-out clash between the pro- and anti-Treaty forces, the British government transferred a considerable quantity of *matériel* to the Free State's rapidly expanded National Army. Vital British interests rode on the survival of the Free State, and, certainly at infantry level, aid was not stinted. At the same time, Collins, an accomplished clandestine operator, exchanged some of the incoming British arms for those already in the IRA's possession.[53] His intention was twofold: to bring a degree of *rapprochement* to the IRA factions in the South and to resupply IRA units in Northern Ireland with weapons that could not be traced, if captured.[54]

The last raises the question of Collins's objective in supporting IRA activities in Northern Ireland. Was this an offensive strategy, intended to bring down the new state, or was it a primarily defensive move to protect Northern Catholics from murderous attacks? It would be a natural assumption that, having fought the British Army to a standstill, a divided Northern state would pose no insuperable obstacle to what Collins saw as total victory. A close analysis by Collins's sympathetic and well-informed biographer, Tim Pat Coogan, shows that he principally sought the destruction of Northern Ireland and that on this issue he acted deceptively and certainly in bad faith in his contacts with the British and Northern governments, and even with his own cabinet. Indeed, the majority of his Provisional government colleagues wanted to concentrate resources on defeating the anti-Treaty IRA and postponing to another time the issue of Partition.[55]

On the surface, Collins appeared to desire reasonable working relations with the Northern Ireland government and, above all, to protect Northern Catholics. At a meeting with Sir William Craig on 21 January 1922, agreement was reached on five points.[56] This envisaged a further meeting to consider, *inter alia*, an alternative to the Council of Ireland as a means of conducting North–South relations. Other points were more specific, though not necessarily achievable. Craig agreed to seek the reinstatement of the several thousand Catholics who had been intimidated and driven from their jobs; Collins agreed to call off the boycott of Northern goods. The issue of republican prisoners held in Northern Ireland would be considered at a future meeting of the two men. It was also agreed that, instead of convening the Boundary Commission to fix the frontier between the two states, Collins and Craig would work this out themselves.

There was a mixture of guile, duplicity and pragmatism on both sides. The clauses on the Boundary Commission, a constitutional meeting and republican prisoners were vague and non-committal. The more specific undertakings were in the interest of both states: Collins wanted Catholics reinstated in their workplaces, and Northern manufacturers and traders wanted the Free State boycott lifted. Even here, of course, both Craig and Collins could resile, whilst insisting that they had done their best. But they could not control their followers.

The first Collins–Craig pact made little difference in the level of disturbances. If anything, attacks, home-burnings, murders and kidnappings appeared to increase over the weeks that followed. Craig and Collins were brought together again on 30 March 1922, and the following day the results of their meeting were published in the form of a second agreement – a fairly frank acknowledgement that earlier hopes had been thwarted, which opened with the promise that 'Peace is today declared.' The main issues of contention were again addressed, and both governments pledged to cooperate in restoring peace in affected areas. Steps were to be taken to help form a more religiously balanced police force in

Northern Ireland. A joint committee of Protestants and Catholics would be established to look into complaints of violence and intimidation, and people driven from their homes would be encouraged to return. Relief works would be funded by a £500,000 Westminster grant, with two-thirds of the created jobs going to Protestants and one-third to Catholics (reflecting their proportions in the general population). The IRA would cease its activities, and, subject to agreement between the parties, political prisoners would be released, provided their offences had been committed before the agreement was published.[57]

Behind the politeness and faux earnestness, North–South tensions had worsened. Collins and his close associates continued to support IRA activities in the North, including an attempt by members of the pro-Treaty forces to rescue from Londonderry Prison the three IRA men who had been condemned to death for an earlier escape attempt on 2 December 1921, in the course of which a constable and special constable on duty in the prison had been killed.[58] An armed party of IRA men from the 5th Northern Division, masquerading as footballers, were arrested in Dromore, Co. Tyrone, on 14 January 1922, on their way to rescue the condemned men.[59] This led to a further round of countermeasures. The Dromore prisoners claimed that they were, by the terms of the Truce, allowed to carry arms. Collins pressed Craig for their release. Craig advised Collins that the men should apply for bail and that he would instruct the Northern Ireland Attorney General not to oppose it. Bizarrely, although he had been in talks with Craig, presumably on the basis that he was Prime Minister of Northern Ireland, Collins and his associates would not agree to this application for bail, since it entailed a recognition of the Northern Ireland courts. Eoin O'Duffy, Chief of Staff of the National Army, agreed and instead proposed to Collins that 100 men prominent in the Orange Order should be kidnapped in Fermanagh and Tyrone and held as hostages in the Free State. These could then be traded for the republican prisoners in the North. In a memorandum to Collins outlining the scheme, O'Duffy said that the raids would proceed the following evening unless he had a countermand from Collins.[60]

The operation, for reasons that are now unclear, was delayed for a further week when forty-two people were kidnapped in night-time raids and taken into the Free State. These included 'numerous leading citizens' and twenty members of the Special Constabulary.[61] In a flurry of telegrams thereafter, Lloyd George warned Collins that 'if anything approximating to this has happened', the Treaty itself was imperilled.[62] Relying on the camouflage provided by the disorder of the brewing civil war, Collins pleaded ignorance. He claimed that because of the three men under sentence of death in Derry he had made 'special efforts' to prevent acts of violence. He would do everything he could for the safety of the captured men and to ensure they were returned to their homes.[63] Collins got away with this denial of complicity solely because anti-Treaty forces were more plausible culprits and because in the Free State he was actively engaged in outflanking and defeating them.

It may have suited Lloyd George and his colleagues to affect to believe Collins and his Provisional government colleagues: muddle was preferable to confrontation, as long as the general trend was towards peace and stability. But weekly reports from General Macready minced no words. Attacks in Northern Ireland by the IRA's 2nd Northern Division in counties Tyrone and Derry were so extensive and well coordinated that there could be no doubt but 'that they form part of a deliberate plan'. It was therefore difficult to believe 'that the whole affair was not known to the IRA leaders in Dublin, if not actually planned by them'. Macready noted that Commandant General McKeon (he apostrophised the rank), 'a leading assistant of Collins and Mulcahy', had made a speech in Mullingar on St Patrick's Day referring to a corps being raised for operations against the North and for which he requested recruits, being willing to lend the body himself.[64]

Macready did not think that a full-scale attack was being mounted against Northern Ireland. The objects of the IRA's operations, he judged, fell short of that and were threefold: to show that large portions of Northern territory were disaffected; to show that the Northern Ireland government could not maintain law and order; and, by operations in Northern Ireland, to relieve IRA forces on the border and in Belfast.[65]

The kidnappings intensified sectarian tensions and violence in Northern Ireland: Protestants felt that in the fog of war the threat had come to their own doorstep, accompanied by lies and dissimulation. Many had always believed that nationalists (read Catholics) were crafty, underhand, secretive and intent on revenge and destruction: here was proof. These tensions led to a stepping up of the forces on either side. As a precaution and warning, Winston Churchill, now Secretary of State for the Irish Office, halted the evacuation of British troops from the Free State and reinforced units in Fermanagh. A-Specials (full-time constables) were sent into the area, and, for the first time since the Truce, B-Specials (part-timers) were mobilised. Almost inevitably, this gathering of forces engendered its own malign momentum. Because Ireland had a unified train network, a party of eighteen Specials, en route to Enniskillen (in Northern Ireland) on Saturday, 11 February 1922, passed through a Free State salient and were attacked by a much larger group of uniformed IRA soldiers as they changed trains in Clones, Co. Monaghan. Five were killed, nine wounded, and five captured.[66] However it was regarded by nationalists, the Special Constabulary was a lawfully constituted crown force. The Clones ambush could not but appear to Protestants as an atrocity and a provocation. Anger boiled over, and the resultant sectarian rioting in Belfast produced thirty-one deaths, many more injured and wounded and considerable destruction of property.[67]

Craig had sought authority for hot-pursuit cross-border raids by his Specials. This had been vetoed by Churchill, who saw it as placing the future of the Provisional government in great danger.[68] He understandably and correctly feared a national and perhaps uncontainable conflagration. Sections of the IRA would have welcomed such raiding by columns of Specials as a means of forcing the hand of the Provisional government and reuniting republicanism. The British continued to focus on shoring up and stabilising the Provisional government, continuing its own evacuation and concentration of forces while countering the resurgence of militant republicanism in the South. Indeed, only two weeks after the kidnappings, Churchill supported Collins's request for an additional 1,000 rifles and some armoured cars.[69] With the other Treaty negotiators on the British side, Churchill believed in the ultimate integrity of the individuals with whom he was negotiating and in the personal commitment and obligation of all the signatories to see the Treaty implemented, in spirit as well as in the letter. He was convinced of Collins's good faith, or at least his caution. The British 'softly-softly' policy was a source of great frustration and anger for loyalists and unionists – and for their IRA counterparts. Without a fresh deployment of British troops, which London saw as a possible violation of the Truce, Belfast had to look to a major expansion in the Special Constabulary to protect its territory and outlying districts. Even there, the going was not straightforward since Churchill feared that a large and heavily armed Special Constabulary could tempt Craig into rescue missions and pre-emptive raids. Reinforcement and augmentation were, accordingly, limited to a level appropriate for 'defensive purposes'.[70] In a storm of rumour, alarm and panic, it was an almost impossibly difficult and skilful balancing act by a master politician. Craig, in the meantime, continued to increase his strength in men and *matériel* and to improve their organisation; he also took further legal powers to deal with republican activities.

In a move that was to be fateful in a way he could not have imagined, the newly elected Ulster Unionist Westminster MP for North Down, Field Marshall Sir Henry Wilson, was appointed to advise on security. Wilson was Ulster-born, recently retired as Chief of the Imperial General Staff, unquestionably one of the leading soldiers of his generation and a resolute unionist.[71] Major-General Arthur Solly-Flood was appointed commander of all Northern Ireland police forces on 20 April 1922, and a number of other senior army officers were also seconded for this service.[72] This was a formidable array of command talent and experience.

Policing

In much the same manner as the Provisional government was straining to build its regular army to ensure the survival of the state, Craig and his colleagues maximised the number of their men under arms. As a subsidiary part of the UK, there could be no question of Northern Ireland having its own army. A police force could, however, be developed along the lines of a paramilitary gendarmerie rather than the 'civilians in uniform' model of policing in Great Britain. The soon-to-be-extinct RIC, moreover, was seen as an apt model of a para-military force, under strong central control, well armed and mobile, suitable for Irish conditions. Unlike the British constabulary, this force should be prepared to police without the consent of the population if necessary.

In September 1920, the British Cabinet agreed that there should be established a special constabulary for use in the six counties of what was to become Northern Ireland.[73] Detailed planning had been undertaken by that part of the Irish civil service which had been earmarked for relocation to Belfast in anticipation of Partition.[74] Details of the scheme were published on 22 October, and advertisements inviting applications were placed in Northern newspapers on 1 November.[75] Although the announcement referred to a special constabulary for the whole of Ireland, it stated that this would be established 'area by area as circumstances may require'. In those last months of 1920, it was far from clear what direction the Anglo-Irish War might take: uncertainty was the only certainty. Three classes of constable were envisaged. Class A would be full-timers enlisted to serve in the RIC, but only in the divisional area from which they were recruited. These would be paid £3 17s. 6d. per week and would be armed and equipped as the RIC. The second class, the B-Specials, were enrolled for occasional duty, weekly drill and duties in their local area. These received a nominal six-monthly payment of £5 'to cover wear and tear of clothes and boot-leather'.[76] For drills in excess of one per week they would also be paid 2s. 6d. They would usually be provided with the same arms and equipment as the RIC. B-Specials would have their own officers, who would come under the direction of the local police authority. The third class, C-Specials, were a reserve, to be used only in case of what would have been a national emergency. They received no payment and were drilled only occasionally.[77] The scheme was put into operation two counties at a time. Proclamations were issued in the individual counties, signed by the deputy lieutenant, using powers long in abeyance 'to raise a militia'.[78] Within months, many units of A-Specials had been formed and deployed. A shortage of arms and the inevitable delays in completing the training of part-timers delayed the deployment of the B-Specials until the late spring of 1921.

This was a considerable force, combining efficiency with location and reach with economy. The A-Specials were to have an establishment of 2,000. The B-Specials were a much larger group – 4,000 in Belfast alone – and a proportionate deployment throughout the province. The reserve C-Specials were to be 6,000 strong.[79] The first two classes could act as a cadre, allowing the enrolment of a much greater number at short notice, whilst the organisational structure and lines of communication and supply provided the necessary infrastructure for an extensive and, if necessary, rapid expansion.[80] In mid-December, the Specials were put under the charge of Charles Wickham, an experienced and versatile soldier who had served with distinction in the Boer War and the First World War and then in Siberia, where he had been promoted to Lieutenant Colonel. He had joined the RIC in November 1920 as Divisional Commissioner.[81]

The new paramilitary RUC had two roots. The first was the UVF. This acted as a stop-gap auxiliary from the late spring until mid-autumn 1921. During this period, the UVF retained its unofficial status, and its members were unpaid and, indeed, acting in defiance of the law.[82] This popular militia largely faded away in the autumn of 1920, as the official police forces took shape. Some safeguard was provided against an influx of sectarian or other undesirable elements into the newly formed RUC by establishing a selection committee composed of magistrates. The UVF tried to circumvent this barrier. Its commanding officer, Lieutenant Colonel Wilfred Spender, envisaged a mass enrolment of his men, with the applications vetted and submitted via his organisation.[83] This was not permitted, but many UVF activists were nevertheless drawn into full- or part-time service with the new police body. The second root of the new police force was the RIC. As noted, by the middle of 1920 this had begun to buckle under the weight of the IRA attacks, threats and intimidation. Being an all-Ireland force, it comprised a high proportion of Roman Catholics. As ideas began to form about a new police force for Northern Ireland there arose several objections to a simple transfer of a section of the RIC to the new government: this was the approach outlined in the 1920 GOIA.[84] Unionists were uneasy or unhappy about the high proportion of Catholics that would have been involved in such a transfer. The efficiency of such a force, its willingness to confront the IRA and, ultimately, its loyalty to the Northern state all seemed to be in doubt. For their part, many Southern Catholics would not have sought or accepted transfer to a new force, operating in such fraught circumstances and requiring allegiance to a Protestant-dominated government and administration. The atmosphere of danger and intimidation in which they had latterly worked, an understandable reluctance to start again in a new organisation and the comparative generosity of pension and severance arrangements for those who wished altogether to discontinue their service were additional weights in the scales, all together blocking the apparently pragmatic RIC-to-RUC transformation.

With the GOIA likely to become law in the autumn of 1920, however, practical arrangements for policing had to be made. The widespread sectarian violence of the summer of 1920 was the background to the British government's acknowledgement that it did not have sufficient forces at its disposal to enforce order in Northern Ireland. The transition from the national mobilisation and vast army of the First World War to peacetime soldiering had been made, and any reversal would have been politically unacceptable.

The transitional demands upon British forces in the rest of Ireland, the need to keep a margin of military capability in reserve as well as the innumerable commitments of Empire made it almost inevitable that Ulster's loyalists should have to take a major hand in defending themselves: this was both their tradition and present desire.

The RIC continued in existence throughout 1921, though as a much-diminished and demoralised force, dwindling and fading away. Sectarian violence (in which some of the B-Specials played a part), a vigorous IRA campaign in the South and a great deal of political uncertainty led sections of the Northern Ireland government to wish to go beyond the Special Constabulary scheme and to have what amounted to Northern Ireland's own army. Field Marshall Sir Henry Wilson, military adviser to the new government, wanted to have both the RIC and the Specials disbanded and placed under military command. This body would be joined by 20,000 UVF men who had been reactivated by Lieutenant Colonel Fred Crawford, a major figure in direct-force Ulster unionism, who had organised the 1912 gun-running. To arm this force, the Northern Ireland government had asked London to supply 26,200 rifles and 5,240,000 rounds of ammunition.[85] The British government refused, anxious as it was to come to terms with Sinn Féin and to prevent any possibility of a North–South confrontation. It may also have been mindful that it was Wilson's alarming view that all of Ireland should be reconquered by Britain.[86]

Withdrawing from most of the area of the Free State and concentrating its men in special demobilisation centres, the RIC began a final, phased run-down in February 1922. There was a formal winding-up parade at the RIC's Phoenix Park headquarters on 4 April, though the processing of men out of the force continued for another four months. Throughout this time, demobilised RIC men were locally harassed, attacked, threatened and frequently forced to leave the country. This rout, the indignities, humiliation and violence offered to faithful servants of the Crown, and the dilatory response and general pusillanimity of the British government added to unionist fears: loyalty was being put away as an embarrassment, it seemed.

Westminster, constitution and law had blocked the way to an Ulster army but allowed the reorganisation of the police to proceed. Following a Committee of Inquiry under the chairmanship of Lloyd Campbell, MP, Belfast decided that it would have a regular constabulary, to be a province-wide body, initially 3,000 strong. Of this, one-third would be Catholics, one-third Protestants from the RIC and one-third from the Special Constabulary. That portion of the RIC then serving in Northern Ireland would be disbanded, not later than 31 May 1922.[87] In late April, it was announced that the King's permission had been obtained to call the new body the Royal Ulster Constabulary. The necessary legislation passed the Northern Ireland Parliament the following month, and the RUC came into existence on 1 June 1922.[88] Against a brief campaign of protest, Charles Wickham became its first head, with the old RIC title of Inspector-General.[89] He would remain in post until 1945.

The Campbell Committee, in setting out the shape of the new force, had identified a number of contentious issues. Some of these would remain unresolved, attracting criticism throughout the RUC's existence. Serving such a fractured and religiously sensitive community, representativeness and therefore denominational composition were of critical importance. Campbell and his colleagues recommended a quota of one-third Roman Catholics. This was to be made up through suitable transfers from the RIC, with any shortfall filled by new recruits. Such an apportionment would never be achieved, the percentage of Catholics in the RUC being 21 per cent at its highest, averaging 17 per cent over the years and dropping steadily throughout the years to 7 per cent in 1995.[90]

A second, far-reaching recommendation addressed the organisational structure and oversight of the RUC. Although the counties of Northern Ireland had much the same machinery of governance as those in Britain, it was decided not to follow the British tradition of a locally controlled constabulary. This was partly a consequence of taking the RIC, a national service on gendarme lines, as a foundation for the new body, and partly a means of excluding local religious and political influences. Had several local constabularies been established, Belfast and some of the larger towns, as well as the counties, would have qualified for their own forces. It is likely that at least some of these would have been controlled by police committees in which Roman Catholics predominated. One can see that this might have led to difficulties in the conditions of disorder prevailing at the time, but, in the longer term, local control might have had the benign consequence for the new state of encouraging Roman Catholic participation and a nationalist sense of inclusion (or at least less exclusion). The decision to shut out local interests meant that the dominant unionist influence would override all others: an immediately attractive course to those struggling with the difficulties of the time but an obvious and ultimately fatal canker.

It would have been extraordinarily difficult, though not impossible, to prevent the RUC being seen by the nationalist minority as a blunt instrument of unionist hegemony. As we have already noted, Sir Dawson Bates was convinced that Roman Catholics were intrinsically disloyal.[91] It was a matter of concern to him that any were in public employment in positions of sensitivity: what could be more important to the survival of the state that the wholehearted allegiance of its police? Despite the Campbell Committee's formula, therefore, determined efforts were made to restrict the Catholic proportion in the RUC.[92] Almost from the outset, the Ministry of Home Affairs and unionist politicians favoured making up the RUC numbers by taking men from the Specials (exclusively Protestant) rather than by transfers from the RIC.[93] By June 1924, the number of former Special Constabulary members was roughly in balance with the number of former RIC men: 1,391 to 1,353.[94] But the Specials, numerically dominant or not, had unquestionably established their distinctive presence within the new organisation. A bias towards Protestant recruitment is, of course, only part of the reason for the under-representation of Catholics.[95] At this distance, it is impossible to quantify, but Catholic reluctance to join the new force, for both individual and community reasons, was also an important factor. Given levels of unemployment and the number of former members of the armed services in the Catholic community, there cannot have been a shortage of suitable men. In May 1925, Sir James Craig told the Northern Ireland Parliament that only 500 Roman Catholics had come forward to fill the 1,000 places which had been kept open for them.[96]

There were attempts to draw Northern Catholics into the workings of the Police Committee, but for reasons not now entirely clear these floundered throughout the spring and early summer of 1922. In April, Craig wrote to Collins asking for his nominations and suggestions for membership of the Committee, to represent the Catholic and nationalist interest. Collins replied that he hoped to be able to offer 'the names of our representatives' within a day or two.[97] From the correspondence, it seems that while Craig and his colleagues were not prepared to accept nominations directly from Sinn Féin, they were willing to accept a Collins nomination – presumably of a non-party and uncontroversial Catholic.[98]

It had been mooted in the Craig–Collins discussions that Catholics would form the police force for Catholic areas, at least on an interim basis. There was some concern about this in unionist circles and unhappiness that Craig was willing to countenance the immediate filling of the Catholic quota for the A-Specials. Spender told Craig that the Ministry would do what it could to achieve that, but that he assumed the instruction applied only to Belfast. It had been hoped that the Catholic quota could be met by transfers from the RIC (thereby, no doubt, assuaging concerns about background, loyalty and the like, as well as getting the services of trained constables). Spender noted that older members of the RIC were not volunteering in satisfactory numbers but that there were 'a large number of Roman Catholic volunteers with little Police experience'.[99]

For a time, Bates seems to have been confident enough about securing sufficient Catholic participation to stabilise the new police force. Certainly, in late April he thought that he could establish a Catholic police committee without Collins's cooperation.[100] A week or so later, however, it appeared that Bates had re-evaluated and that he had misgivings about going ahead as planned. Officials pressing for a decision on the commencement of training for the Catholic B-Specials found Bates unwilling to agree to the initial steps to summon the Catholic volunteers and to train them. Spender proposed that the Catholic B-Specials should follow the ordinary Special Constabulary course and that the County Commandant and City Commissioner should call the first meeting. Volunteers would then be told the objects of the force and patrol areas, and other arrangements could be made.[101] For some reason, this proposal did not go forward.

The final remnant of these tantalising exchanges and possibilities came on 7 June 1922, when Spender informed Craig that the (presumably first) meeting of the Roman Catholic Police Committee was to take place that afternoon and that 'Father Laverty has asked for a safe conduct [for] Dr McNab for whom an order has gone out for arrest and imprisonment.'[102] Again, it is not recorded what happened to this request, but the Roman Catholic Police Committee failed to develop and certainly made no impact. This seems to have been an initiative that ran into the sand and was not recovered.[103]

In these early years, two approaches to Northern Ireland policing were possible. One was to navigate a course through sectarian tensions and sensibilities to a service which, although predominantly Protestant, would be demonstrably balanced and could lay claims to an impartial enforcement of the law. This may have been beyond the practical political abilities of Craig and his colleagues; it may have been beyond anyone's. The other, easier and more immediately practical, course was to ride the wave of alarmed and militant loyalism and to benefit from its fierce commitment, even allowing such recruits to see themselves as members of a Protestant militia. It is easy in retrospect, and with modern standards of public service, to condemn the Northern Ireland government's choices. They were certainly wrong, short-sighted and ultimately destructive, but they were perhaps unavoidable in the circumstances then prevailing, with the political talent available and in an atmosphere heavy with suspicion on both sides and devoid of creative generosity.

The RIC had exercised a firm policy forbidding its members from participating in politics or from membership of secret societies such as the Hibernians or the Orange Order.[104] The intention was to prevent any compromise or apparent compromise of police loyalties. If, in the larger geographical area, less religiously tense and more mixed population of an all-Ireland jurisdiction, this restriction was thought essential, how much more necessary might it be in Northern Ireland, where the denominational ratios were so finely balanced and where feelings were so easily inflamed. But, again, the government's choice was propitiatory and immediate rather than looking to the long term. In June 1922, in the midst of yet more sectarian upheavals, Bates was asked whether members of the RUC could privately and in civilian clothes attend meetings of the Orange Order. On 18 July 1922, a standing order was issued by Major-General Arthur Solly-Flood, military adviser to the Northern Ireland government and in charge of establishing the new police force. Members of the RUC were allowed to be members of the Orange Order and to attend its meetings, but not in uniform or to the detriment of their duties.[105] The purpose of the Orange Order was to resist what was seen as Catholic social, political and religious hegemony and to do so by preserving the links with the Crown and upholding the Protestant Succession. It took an uncompromising line which insisted that civil and political liberties were incompatible with membership of the Roman Catholic Church.[106] By departing from the policy of the RIC, established and reiterated in statute, and by allowing membership of this and similar organisations, a significant statement was being made about the RUC's political and religious ethos and about its civic priorities.

Political limits

A stronger line came to be taken about the involvement of RUC members or Specials in any kind of party-political activities. The danger here was that of more extreme loyalists outflanking the government and using police services as a personal credential and police connections as an organisational framework. These possibilities were forcefully brought home to the Northern Ireland government in 1923 and 1924 through the activities of District Inspector John William Nixon, an able and energetic member of the RIC, who had transferred to the RUC.[107] Nixon became the Worshipful Master of the Sir Robert Peel Memorial Loyal Orange Lodge, which, taking advantage of the special dispensation to join societies, had been established for an exclusively RUC membership. He had strong connections with leading unionists, and the first annual general meeting of the Sir Robert Peel Memorial Loyal Orange Lodge was addressed by Sir Dawson Bates.[108]

In January 1924, Nixon addressed the Lodge, making a number of political points of some sensitivity.[109] These remarks were reported to the government, which was concerned about this overt and challenging connection between policing and politics. It cast an unwelcome light on the connection between the RUC and Orangeism and seemed to indicate that Nixon had political ambitions that could perhaps threaten the unionist leadership. The speech was particularly provocative to government because, following similar remarks at the Lodge on 3 January, there had been an oblique rebuke. This took the form of a general statement of policy, issued on 17 January 1924, by Charles Wickham, Inspector-General of the RUC. Unlike the RIC, the circular pointed out, members of the RUC were allowed to be members of certain secret societies and to vote at parliamentary elections. In order to retain public confidence in the impartiality of the RUC, its members 'should not... take part by speaking or entering into discussions where political or sectarian opinions are expressed'. During election campaigns and at certain other times the Inspector-General could give permission 'to attend, strictly individual and in their private capacity' meetings in their district. Attendance was solely for the purpose of hearing candidates' views and in no circumstances should uniform be worn when attending.[110]

Timing and form showed that Nixon was the sole and unmistakeable target of the circular, and he immediately accepted the challenge. Less than a fortnight later, he spoke again on a number of political topics at a lodge meeting.[111] By his contrivance, newspaper reporters were present, together with MPs and a member of the government. This was an open and calculated act of defiance. Disciplinary proceedings were initiated, went uncertainly forward and culminated in an interview with Wickham at which Nixon was obliged to answer 'yes' or 'no' to a list of questions. On 28 February 1924, not much longer than a month after the offending speech, he was dismissed from the RUC, on full pension. (He had by then served twenty-five years as a police officer but was well short of pensionable age.) Nixon's previous good connections with senior unionists were of little avail. Craig and his colleagues rejected all pleas from their own benches. For several months, Nixon's case was raised in Parliament, as opportunity permitted. The government would not countenance reinstatement – and indeed would have lost its Inspector-General and a deal more besides had it been tempted to do so. The pugnacious ex-policeman entered politics, obtaining office as an Independent Unionist, first as a Belfast councillor and after some years as a member of the Northern Ireland Parliament. He would be a vociferous presence in Ulster politics for many years to come. During the period of Nationalist boycott of the legislature he had the distinction of being the sole opposition.

The visceral connection between policing and Northern Ireland politics, the dangers for both parties and the range of sensitivities involved were demonstrated in quite a different way in a parallel case a year later. Sir Basil Brooke, a Fermanagh unionist and landowner who would succeed Sir James Craig as Prime Minister of Northern Ireland, and one of the pioneers of the Protestant protective militia that evolved into the Ulster Specials, raised his banner of militant unionism. He was convinced that the B-Specials had been vital to Ulster's survival, and he himself exemplified the connection between policing and unionist politics.[112] He had been highly decorated for service in the Great War and was County Commandant of the Fermanagh Specials. On 28 March 1925, the *Northern Whig* reported a speech that he had delivered from the chair at a Unionist meeting at Brookeborough. An election was imminent, and Brooke had taken a tilt at faint-hearted and faltering Unionists and at the Nationalists. He also referred to allegations that the electoral register had been 'stuffed with Specials' and observed that Fermanagh had 'given as many men to the Special Constabulary as any other two counties in Ulster, and those others were only taking their places'.[113]

Officials of the Ministry of Home Affairs expressed concern at the speech. In the light of what had transpired the year before in Nixon's case, action was unavoidable. Brooke was written to, and on 16 April 1925 he replied, expressing regrets but explaining that he had not known that the Inspector-General's order 'applied to leading Officers of the Special Constabulary'. He pointed out that when the Special Constabulary was formed, people with county interests were asked to help raise the force 'more as a patriotic duty than for any other duty'. He himself paid considerable taxes and rates on his property and, in consequence, had a deep interest in local and general politics. If, however, it was the government's wish that he should not take part in political meetings, he was prepared to abide by those orders.[114] Brooke remained in office as County Commandant until May 1929, when he discontinued his service in the Specials.[115] Nixon might have reflected that wealth had its privileges, or, alternatively, that a little more tact when he had been called to account might have left him in his place in the RUC. More likely, politics had always been his intent, all the more easily followed on a full police pension.

These strictures on open political involvement apart, the RUC ethos had been established and accepted. Hopes of a representative police service had been rejected or at least scaled down. The mechanism was similar to that of the other branches of the Northern Ireland public service. Unease, suspicion, bigotry, discrimination, rewarding one's own and rejection of Catholics on the one hand; reciprocal bigotry, nationalist antipathy to crown service, rejection of Partition, revanchism and an unwillingness to become involved on the other. Once established, these perceptions fuelled a self-sustaining chain reaction. They were underpinned by republican intimidation of Catholics who entered the service of the state – extending in some cases to violence and murder. Such extreme reactions apart, Catholic and nationalist disapproval was in itself uncomfortable for those in public service who lived within their confessional communities. The life of a Catholic in police or prison service cannot have been easy, with rejection by most of their co-religionists, and with wariness and perhaps even suspicion from some Protestant colleagues.[116]

Police atrocities

With fateful rapidity the sectarian perception of policing in Northern Ireland was dipped in the fixative of police-related atrocities. On Thursday, 23 March

1922, two Specials on patrol in the centre of Belfast were killed by the IRA. There was a swift reprisal. In the small hours of the following night, five gunmen forced their way into the home of Owen McMahon, a Catholic publican. All seven men in the family, together with a male lodger, were collected together in one room and shot. Five died, and two more were wounded (one later dying in hospital). The youngest son (aged eleven) was unhurt. The rumour circulated that the assassins, who had worn raincoats to conceal their inner clothing, were policemen in uniform.[117] Over the years that followed, the name of District Inspector John Nixon was associated with this dreadful event.[118] No substantial connection has ever been made, however, and Nixon may have been linked to the atrocity because he already had a degree of notoriety. No one was or ever would be arrested for the McMahon murders. This was a test of the impartiality and determination of those responsible for leading the police (and the government), and they failed.[119]

Within days, there was a further Belfast outrage, and, once more, Craig's government failed to react. Brown Street barracks covered the Shankill Road area, a bastion of militant loyalism. On Saturday, 1 April 1922, George Turner, an RIC man from the barracks, was shot dead whilst on foot patrol on the Old Lodge Road.[120] In reprisal, it was alleged that a group of Brown Street Specials went on a violent rampage. Three Catholic men were killed, all in their homes; one was battered to death with a sledgehammer. This man's seven-year-old son was shot in the head and died the following day. No arrests were made, though it is inconceivable that the identities of the perpetrators were unknown. Several requests from the Provisional government for information went unanswered. It seemed as though a degree of sectarian counter-terror would be countenanced by the Northern Ireland government. Some in the Roman Catholic community may have feared that they were being held hostage against the deeds of the IRA. Such, perhaps, was the fear that the attacks were intended to kindle.

Three months later, this fear was appallingly confirmed by an incident, known as the 'Cushendall Massacre'. Hot on news of Wilson's assassination in London on 23 June 1922, a combined party of ten Specials and a number of soldiers travelled in four or five lorries from Ballymena, Co. Antrim (a Protestant town) to Cushendall, Co. Antrim (a Catholic town). By the time they left Cushendall, three Catholic men (John Gore, aged twenty-two; John Hill, twenty-six; and James McAllister, eighteen) had been killed and two others wounded.[121] On this occasion, the killings and shootings had been witnessed by credible persons of standing who gave detailed accounts of the event. Instead of an immediate promise of an independent investigation, however, the Northern Ireland government put out a wholly fictitious account of an IRA ambush in the course of which the Specials returned fire and killed four of the ambushers in the course of a 'desperate fight'.[122] There was also a clumsy attempt to distract attention from Cushendall with an atrocity story from the South. The *Northern Whig* ran a story of a sectarian raid on an unnamed Protestant home in Co. Tipperary on 22 June, in the course of which several men raped the woman of the house.[123]

From Westminster, this delayed publication and juxtapositioning of the two reports in the *Whig* looked like a crude manoeuvre. Lionel Curtis, Secretary to the Provisional Government of Ireland Committee, wrote, at Churchill's behest, to Sir James Masterton-Smith, Permanent Under-Secretary at the Colonial Office. Sinn Féin could be countered not by counter-propaganda but by investigations. Churchill had received a letter from the nationalist leader Joseph Devlin, enclosing an eye-witness account of the affair from Mrs Nancy Letts, widow of a distinguished professor of chemistry at Queen's University, Belfast.[124] The upshot was that a month later Devlin and Craig met in Churchill's room at the Colonial Office. It was agreed that Devlin would ask a parliamentary question and that, as crown forces had been involved, the British government would take charge of the inquiry: this would give authority and credibility that a Northern Ireland investigation could not hope to have.[125] Churchill told the Commons that Sir James Craig, 'while not desiring himself to initiate the inquiry, has intimated his willingness to give all possible facilities'.[126]

Initially it was proposed that the inquiry should be conducted by General Sir Archibald Rice Cameron, GOC Northern Ireland, but, on reflection, Churchill instead asked for a civilian. Frederick Temple Barrington-Ward, KC, Recorder of Hythe, agreed to take charge.[127] This was strongly resisted by General Macready. It was without precedent, he protested, for a civilian to conduct an inquiry into a military matter, and, without legislation, Barrington-Ward would have no authority to do so. Macready also objected to the proposed power to compel witnesses to attend, to administer the oath and to cross-examination by those bringing the complaints – in short, to an independent inquiry with teeth.[128] Mark Sturgis, now at the Colonial Office (having been Sir John Anderson's assistant at Dublin Castle during the preparation for the British handover), assured General Macready that such an inquiry was not envisaged. Barrington-Ward had not been given powers to compel the attendance of witnesses or to administer the oath. Churchill was insistent that all witnesses should be voluntary and that the questions be put by Barrington-Ward alone. Macready would have been further reassured by Barrington-Ward's decision to conduct the inquiry in private.[129] These decisions, while ensuring military cooperation, almost certainly diminished Catholic confidence in the investigation.

The verbatim record of the inquiry (which was closed for more than half a century) was indicative of the bitter state of feeling then existing in Northern Ireland, the insecurity and the general background of violence. There was some suggestion – certainly plausible – that the B-Specials' raid had been retaliation for the shooting of Sir Henry Wilson three days before the massacre. One of the Cushendall victims pleaded that he was an ex-serviceman. He was told that it did not matter: the man who shot Wilson was also an ex-serviceman.[130] Another factor was recent IRA activities in the Glens of Antrim (a Catholic area). The presumed assumption was that the local population had been acquiescent or complicit.[131] This conjecture was tendered in support of the claim that the joint patrol had been fired on as it entered Cushendall. This was certainly contested by local people, but visitors supposedly confirmed that the police had been fired on.

The counterclaims were a mere smokescreen, blown away when Barrington-Ward concluded that no one except the B-Specials and the military had fired and that there was no indication of provocation by the people of Cushendall. He also found that two men were wounded by the Specials and that James McAllister, John Gore and John Hill had been murdered by one of the ten Specials. He was not able to identify the killer. The military was exonerated. The sequence of events he recounted started with the despatch of an army patrol to Cushendall to investigate a reported IRA concentration in the Glens of Antrim. The patrol had called at various police stations on its way to Cushendall, and, at Ballymena, a party of ten B-Specials had asked to join them. This had been agreed, although the request from a locally based unit to leave their district should have tripped a warning. En route, the party encountered what it took to be an IRA grouping, but Barrington-Ward concluded that this was an innocent gathering.

Barrington-Ward's investigation substantiated Devlin's Commons' allegations. A cover-up immediately followed. On 16 September 1922, Craig wrote to Curtis at the Colonial Office asking that publication of the report be stayed until he had a chance to consult both Barrington-Ward and Churchill. By Churchill's direction, the report was printed and circulated to the Cabinet, marked 'Very Secret'. Some modification had been made at Craig's request, but the essence of the report was unaltered and was damning. It was agreed that publication would be held back lest prejudice bar the way to a fair trial. Sir John Anderson, the Permanent Under-Secretary at the Home Office, however, took the view that all ten Specials could be prosecuted for murder.[132]

But responsibility for law and order in Northern Ireland had been handed over to Belfast. Churchill had initially supposed that a court martial would be the best way to proceed, but the B-Specials were deemed not to be under army jurisdiction (though they could have been so brought, if wished, by proceeding under the ROIA). Since imperial jurisdiction had been declined, the case had to proceed as an exclusively local matter: London would have no say. The Northern Ireland Deputy Inspector-General of the RIC and the Chief Crown Solicitor disputed Barrington-Ward's findings and, bizarrely, concluded that there was no *prima facie* evidence on which to go to trial. Richard Best, the Northern Ireland Attorney General agreed, as did Bates.[133] These senior officials did not seem unduly perturbed that the report was not to be published, that there were to be no prosecutions, and yet three British subjects were dead and two wounded, and the gravest allegations against crown forces remained untested.

The afflicted persons (survivors of the murdered men and the two who had been wounded and maimed) submitted their claims for compensation against Antrim County Council. A year later, these were dismissed in proceedings at Ballymena Court. Assistant County Court Judge Bates, KC, contradicted Barrington-Ward's findings to conclude that the police had been fired on. But even if they had not, he did not think that the crimes allegedly committed by the

Specials met the test of 'unlawful assembly' which was necessary for the applicants' claim to succeed. Crimes had indeed been committed, but without a finding that there had been an unlawful assembly the County was not liable.[134] This effectively ended matters as far as procedural remedy went. On 10 April 1923, the new Cabinet's Irish Affairs Committee (Churchill was not a member of Bonar Law's short-lived administration) agreed that Barrington-Ward's report should not be published, since British troops had been exonerated.[135] In the autumn of 1923, the appeal against the County Court's refusal of compensation was heard before Northern Ireland's Lord Chief Justice, Sir Denis Henry, and was dismissed.[136]

At the time of the Cushendall murders, the Irish Civil War was in its initial stages. Before and during those hostilities, waves of lawlessness, some politically motivated, others simply criminal, had battered all parts of the island. Assault, wounding, robbery, rape, arson and murder in all their ghastly forms had proliferated and were aggravated and made terrible by a general sense of state impotence. Civilians were kidnapped, homes invaded and property stolen and destroyed, and, in the climate of frightfulness, comment, if any, was muted. Protestants suffered massacres as terrible as that at Cushendall. On 17 June 1922, less than a week before the Cushendall events, six Protestant civilians were murdered in or near the townland of Altnaveigh, close to Newry, Co. Down. The perpetrators were members of the IRA's 4th Northern Division, and this, as far as can be seen, was an official action. The victims were of both sexes, from nineteen to pensionable age. All that the killings and destruction (a dozen or more homes were burnt or bombed) had in common was that the victims were Presbyterians.

The Cushendall massacre could be lost in the pattern of atrocity and counter-atrocity of the times. But it was this very fact that give it distinction. The forces of law and order must be precisely that, or they lose their essence and purpose. Acting atrociously under colour and cover of law, they are more reprehensible than those who deny and wish to bring down the law by means of atrocity and outrage. Cushendall was a test, and, assuming he would not be compelled to act by the moral imperative alone, the wise politician and his party would have seen it as an opportunity to demonstrate tenacious fidelity to the law and to the high purposes of state. Perhaps in the fog of war, in the insecurity of a new administration, in the anger of followers, and in the destructive atmosphere of sectarianism, no other option was open to Craig but to close the door and move away. But it was another fateful decision.

Fear of the Free State

The cross-border attacks of 1922 (sniping, arson, bombings, skirmishing and kidnappings) naturally reinforced unionists in their perception that the Free State harboured malevolent intent and remained unreconciled to the existence of Northern Ireland. Details are now murky, but it seems that it was not only the

IRA that engaged in these actions. Claims were made that the National Army also engaged in cross-border attacks. Given the newness of the Army, the rushed training of recruits, the lack of indoctrination, deepening divisions within republicanism and nationalism and the turbulence of the times, it seems entirely possible that there were instances of army sniping.[137] This was a fresh memory, both in fact and in perception, in the spring of 1924, when the Free State's activation of its Boundary Commission option raked over the coals of Northern insecurity. An additional and potentially destabilising factor was Craig's illness. Probably caused by stress and exhaustion, this was sufficiently serious for him to take a month's leave, cut off from work. London and Dublin, as well as Craig's colleagues, realised his vital importance in keeping the whole of the complex relationship on an even keel.[138]

The Free State's decision to release de Valera from prison on 16 July 1924 further stirred Northern anxieties. At this point, he was the leader of a group of forty-four Sinn Féin members of the Dáil, all of whom regarded the Free State as an illegitimate entity and the Northern Ireland government as an out-and-out enemy. Now at liberty, de Valera would be able to use his considerable political talents, network of adherents and substantial public support to rally republican sentiment. An electoral shift could see the pro-Treaty parties reduced to a minority and de Valera granted a popular mandate to take the country along a republican and revolutionary road, with all the martial and material resources of the state at his disposal. This was the nightmare view from Belfast, and it would precipitate a secret clash with the British government.

On 11 August 1924, the Northern Ireland government expressed its concerns about 'the recent significant political developments in the Free State'. It requested the Imperial government to provide a 'clear statement' of preparations to be taken in the event that a republic were established in the Free State, taking a hostile attitude to Northern Ireland. In particular, Belfast worried about the small numbers and limited detachments of British troops stationed in the province. It recognised that any reinforcement might be misinterpreted by the Free State, but, should the situation develop unfavourably, it might become necessary to mobilise the Special Constabulary. The threat might be such that even this would be an insufficient deterrent: 'The Northern Government are aware that the Free State is equipped with artillery and that it has recently increased its Air Force, and they think it right to point out that there is no warlike material in Northern Ireland competent to meet and cope with these instruments of war.' Any incursions similar to those of 1922 would make it difficult for the Northern authorities to maintain law and order.[139]

The War Office was asked for comment. A week later it replied, setting out two scenarios: (1) a republic is set up in the Free State; and (2) the Free State government continues to exist, but hostile incursions on an extensive scale are made 'by troops purported to be from the Irish Republican Army'. Responsibility for dealing with external aggression rested with the Imperial government. Instructions had been issued in December 1922 to deal with possible Southern aggression, and General Cameron had drawn up a defence plan. Certain military facts had to be taken into account. Cameron had at his disposal five battalions and one armoured-car company. One battalion would probably be tied down in Londonderry. The remaining force was too small to watch more than a small fraction of the 200-mile frontier. Although desirable for military reasons, it would be politically unwise to reinforce the Northern Ireland garrison before incursions actually occurred. Troops had to be kept concentrated in order to retain their mobility and to deal with any threatened point. The consequence of these requirements was that there could be no thought of troops relieving the RUC and Specials of their frontier duties until considerable reinforcements had arrived: even then the police would still have to be deployed on the frontier.[140]

In the light of these operational considerations, there should be consultation between the GOC Northern Ireland and the Inspector-General of the RUC. These discussions would deal with the conditions under which the police would come under military control, arrangements to attach staff and army-liaison officers to the police and the division of operational duties between the army and the police. Appropriate military reinforcements were being identified (but not sent). These would, in the first instance, include units of artillery and engineers, and, should the South use its air force, an anti-aircraft unit as well as a unit of aircraft. Following this, an infantry brigade would be sent, together with further units of artillery and engineers. All of this was to deal with the large-scale incursions by regular military units of the Free State. The Army assumed that minor raids by republicans, sniping and kidnappings would, in the first instance, be dealt with by the RUC and Specials on their side of the border and by the Free State Army on the other. Military units might be moved in support of the police, but such situations, as long as the police could deal with them, would not be defined as 'external aggression'.[141]

Within a few weeks of this memorandum, Ramsay MacDonald's government lost a vote of confidence. Stanley Baldwin's second administration did not take office until November 1924, and thus it was almost five months before Belfast received a reply to its letter. The Home Office tackled the obvious point first: the Northern Ireland government was speculating rather than proceeding on the basis of any reliable intelligence: 'Sir William Joynson-Hicks has no reason to think there is any probability of the situation contemplated in this letter arising the near future.' It was desirable, however, that the two governments should understand their respective functions and duties. Defence was a matter reserved to the British government under s.4 of the GOIA, 1920. Cooperation between the Army, police and Special Constabulary would be necessary for defence, and the relevant planning should be undertaken. Minor raids across the border were matters for the Northern Ireland government. To avoid any confusion as to what was a minor raid and something greater, there should be army–police consultations.[142]

These discussions were speedily arranged and were attended by the various police and army officers directly concerned, as well as Sir James Craig, Sir

Dawson Bates and General Sir Archibald Rice Cameron, who submitted a memorandum on army–police cooperation. It was agreed that the Specials should be assigned to border-watching duties and the troops deployed as mobile reserves. There was some backtracking by the Northern Ireland side, which agreed that, unless a hostile republican government were set up in the South, border incursions were likely to be on a scale within police capabilities. In certain mountainous areas, however, the best way to deal with incursions might be to deploy joint police–army flying columns. There was nothing objectionable so far, but the memorandum went on to propose a policy of cross-border hot pursuit. Craig had broached this with Churchill three years previously, and it had immediately and emphatically been rejected: 'it would be advantageous if such columns could follow any raiding party, *if necessary beyond the frontier*'. This clause was slipped in, and the letter ended on an emollient note.[143]

There was not the slightest chance that such an alarming proposal would pass unnoticed in Whitehall. Anderson immediately marked the offending words and wrote to the War Office, asking for their account of the army–police conference; particular reference was made to the hot-pursuit proposal. It was important to make clear to the Northern Ireland government, Anderson wrote, that 'His Majesty's Government are not prepared to give any countenance to the possibility of police or Specials crossing the border.' Should circumstances ever arise when armed forces might have to cross the border, the whole situation would have to be reviewed by the government and instructions would be issued to the GOC. But unless and until then, 'it is most important to prevent any violation of the border'. The Home Secretary requested the observations of the Army Council on the army–police conference.[144]

The Army Council agreed with the Home Office; had they not, the issue would have gone to Cabinet. On 18 March 1925, Anderson wrote to S. G. Tallents (Imperial Secretary in Belfast) for the information of the Northern Ireland government. Hot pursuit was emphatically forbidden: 'Any attempt by the Police Forces of Northern Ireland to take action outside the jurisdiction of the Northern Government would, of course, be illegal and would be open to the greatest possible objection.' If there was any reason to think that this was not clearly understood, the government of Northern Ireland was asked to ensure that all police and Special Constabulary officers were instructed that their forces should not cross the frontier.[145]

This was, altogether, a curious episode. To raise the threat of invasion from the South in 1925 when there was no evidence whatsoever such a possibility was likely, when security within Northern Ireland was at a high level and constantly improving and when Anglo-Irish relations and mutual trust were in a similar good state, was odd indeed. De Valera had an undoubted following, but there was no concrete sign that he would advance to office in the near future, or that if he did he would launch an invasion. Nor, given the importance of the issue for Northern Ireland, were de Valera's military ambitions (as distinct from his political utterances) probed. Imperial government had an unequivocal responsibility to defend Northern Ireland, and, in the whole of British party politics, there was no sign that this guarantee would not be honoured. Equally, no mature politician (and Craig was that) could imagine that, holding such a grave responsibility, any government would be prepared to grant to another a power such as cross-border hot pursuit, to be decided locally and on the hoof. Whether the Northern Ireland Cabinet had frightened themselves with the spectre of de Valera or whether Craig was playing another game is hard to say. Were his references to the artillery and air-force capabilities of the Free State an oblique bid for some version of the still-desired Northern Ireland Army? Perhaps all that Craig wanted was a reiteration of the British government's guarantee of the territorial integrity of his state. That was what he got, together with an absolute ban on any kind of police or military adventurism. Within his state Craig possessed a great degree of autonomy and discretion – but these stopped at the border.

Special powers

Civil war in the South, cross-border raids, IRA activity in Belfast and elsewhere, a disaffected Roman Catholic minority and volcanic eruptions of sectarian violence were the background to the taking of emergency powers. The deeper background was a struggle of more than four decades to avoid submergence in a Catholic-dominated state. Beyond that there were religious, social and cultural divides maintained by both sides with undying zeal. An ineradicable sense of siege, of precariousness and of unseen forces of subversion was the patrimony of Northern Ireland. Every state has a right to defend itself, a duty to secure the lives and prosperity of its citizens and, certainly in any entity that claims to be a democracy, a continuing obligation to allow them to go peacefully about their business. In times of exceptional danger, a temporary extension of power and authority into spheres from which the state is normally excluded may reluctantly be agreed. The judgement that democracies make is how far these powers should go and for how long they should be kept. Facing its own challenges, Britain had provided itself with the far-reaching Defence of the Realm Act (DORA) and its offspring, the Restoration of Order in Ireland Act (ROIA).[146] The Free State also had no hesitation in bringing in a number of Emergency Powers Acts.[147]

No matter how great the emergency, the prudent legislator will proceed without enthusiasm and with caution. The taking of exceptional powers must be justified by special and pressing circumstances, and these must be real and verifiable, not imaginings and rhetorical possibilities. The matching of means to ends must be set out comprehensively and meticulously, not only as a whole but also in relation to each component and provision: there should be no gratuitous loading of onerous restrictions on the citizen, or back-door concessions to bureaucratic convenience, or ambition, or the lèse-majesté anxieties of politicians and functionaries. One must be aware of the peril of unintended consequences. This is a balancing act of short- against long-term risks. Such special legislation must have no greater lifespan than is necessary. If the likely end of the period of emergency cannot be predicted or discerned, there should be a sunset clause to guarantee that the measure will, within a fixed period, be brought before the legislature, once more to be fully reviewed and justified.[148] In the operation of the measures, powers of oversight and restraint must be provided, both by the legislature itself and by the higher courts. Recognising the essential yet easily displaced and damaged balances between legislature, executive and judiciary, and between the state and the individual, constitutional doctrine should always be thoroughly investigated so that it may be respected. Reluctance, unease and a constant self-questioning – all that is the opposite to haste and enthusiasm – should govern the use of such measures. Emergency powers are justifiable only if they are vital to protect democracy and the rule of law; they are, like some cancer treatments, toxic and damaging and, if prolonged, are invariably destructive. On all these grounds of approach, motive and structure, the Civil Authorities (Special Powers) Act (Northern Ireland), 1922, trespassed on or violated basic principles of constitutional law and wise governance.[149]

In the discretion it conveyed to the executive, the Special Powers Act went to the very limits of democratic legislation and justiciability. By exempting the working of the Act from several key restraints by the judiciary, habeas corpus, juries, justices of the peace and coroners, an almost perfect instrument of dictatorship was implanted within a democratic framework. Even its sunset clause was eventually removed. It is true and of critical importance that the Northern Ireland legislature was subordinate to that of the UK. *In extremis*, this would have been a backstop, but Westminster had entered into a self-denying (and self-indulgent) ordinance that allowed Belfast a wide latitude in matters of law and order. Notions of civil rights as a distinct concern and body of jurisprudence had yet to develop: this was not the common-law method or style. It is also important to acknowledge that Sir James Craig and his colleagues were not the material from which dictatorship can be fashioned: they subscribed to the basic values of the British Empire: respect for law, restraint in government and Christian ethics in public affairs. The awful circumstances of Northern Ireland's birth combined with a narrow political and essentially sectarian outlook would nevertheless blind them to the deeply un-British nature of the Special Powers Act, as would their sweeping definition of 'disloyalty'.[150] Their ultimate safeguard was that of the modified oligarchy of the older democracies: put good and sound men at the top and they will always do the decent thing and never abuse their powers.

A line-by-line analysis of the Act and subsequent amending and extending measures is not possible here, but we may briefly examine its principal features. The keystone was the delegation to the executive of virtually unlimited law-and-order powers. It granted equally extensive powers of secondary legislation by giving the Minister for Home Affairs authority to make, revoke and vary regulations (seemingly of any kind) under the Act.[151] On his part, the Minister could delegate many of his powers, conditionally or unconditionally, to any police officer. Unlike delegated legislation in Britain, where regulations or subsidiary laws are laid before Parliament for a period and are at least in theory submitted to a positive or negative challenge, regulations under the Special Powers Act could be revoked only by a parliamentary petition to the lieutenant-governor (the senior functionary of the ornamental part of the Constitution), who would, of course, act on his government's advice. The same party held office in Northern Ireland for more than half a century, from the foundation of the state until the 1972 suspension of its parliament. The opposition in those years was inadequate and frequently unengaged and could never hope to overturn the ruling party's legislative majority. The accountability or otherwise of the government to the legislature in the matter of special powers, or any other instrument, might therefore be thought to be of no great import. But the need periodically and publicly to justify amended regulations and actions under such powers would, even in a state dominated by one party, would have been some restraint. From the debates on the Bill, moreover, we know that there was within unionism (itself a coalition on non-Union issues) some unease about certain powers: liberal unionism was not entirely dead, and the entry of the Nationalist Party into the Northern legislature in 1925 would (if only marginally) have augmented its vigilance.[152] The unwritten British constitution is frequently criticised for failing to make a sufficiently clear distinction between the executive and the legislature.[153] This has at certain points appeared to be a weakness: if so, measures such as the Special Powers Act have the undoubted capacity to turn a flaw into a crack and that into a fissure in the political fabric.

Besides its un-British character, the Act was far from 'Special'. Catastrophic and extraordinary times demand fitting remedies. As noted, once the emergency has passed, the normal, expected and comfortable ought to be restored: that, after all, is the object and justification for emergency legislation: to preserve and restore and then, as part of that desired return to normality, for the distasteful remedy to expire or be repealed and to vanish from the scene. When first introduced, the Special Powers Act had an expected life of one year; thereafter, it had to be renewed by the Northern Ireland Parliament. These annual renewals continued until 1928. Then, with peace, law and order so well established that white gloves (signifying no criminal business) were presented to judges in a number of districts, the Special Powers Act was, remarkably, extended for five years.[154] With that unjustified extension about to end, an amending Act was brought in that made the 1922 Act permanent.[155] In his 1927 memorandum to the Northern Ireland Cabinet, Bates pointed out that the Act had been little used. During 1927 there had only been one conviction, and that for an offence committed in 1926. He said, however, that this tranquil state of affairs was probably due 'to the moral effect of the Act and Regulations being in force'.[156] In this he may have been partly correct, as we shall see, but it was not the 'moral effect' of the Act that gave it such potency.

Far more to the point, the annual renewals gave an opportunity for questioning the need for such a measure and for challenging its provisions in Parliament or elsewhere. Some of the powers, Bates admitted, were 'very drastic as part of the enactment'. As we have seen, the Northern Parliament had handed to the executive far-reaching powers and, in respect to the Act and its workings, reduced itself to a cipher. Bates was not satisfied with this, however. Annual renewal afforded an opportunity for 'hostile, ill-informed criticism of its provisions; such criticism being especially bitter when it has been found necessary to utilise any of the powers of the Act'.[157] There would be considerable opposition to making the measure permanent: 'it would be represented as an attempt to override the Habeas Corpus Act and a serious infringement of the rights and liberties of the people'. But this objection notwithstanding, permanence was better: Anthony Babbington, the Attorney General, agreed with him. They had been influenced in reaching this conclusion by the fact that 'certain disloyal elements' were continuing their activities 'though in a somewhat suppressed form'.[158] It is a telling comment on the quality of cabinet government in Northern Ireland that no one resisted Bates's logic: there was little or no subversive activity that necessitated action under the Act, yet somehow or other grounds for making it permanent were conjured up. Some doubts may have been raised since it was decided to take a more gradual approach. For whatever reason, Bates went for a five-year extension rather than attempting at this time to force the more drastic course. Perhaps this was a testing of the water; with little opposition from Britain and the Free State, or from Ulster's Catholics, permanence could be the next step. This happened in 1933 when a further Special Powers Act was brought in.[159] The renewal clause of the 1922 Act (s.12) was simply amended, making the Act permanent.[160]

The catch-all nature of the measure is to be found not only in its wide-ranging provisions and in the power to issue regulations on virtually any aspect of daily life but in an 'in-case-I've-forgotten-something' clause that any legislature concerned with the rule of law, or capable of more than basic political calculations, or desirous of justifying its existence, should have thrown out:

> If any person does any act of such a nature as to be calculated to be prejudicial to the preservation of the peace or maintenance of order in Northern Ireland not specifically provided for in the regulations, he shall be deemed to be guilty of an offence against the regulations.[161]

This allowed the prosecution and conviction of a person for an action, which, at the time it was done, was not prohibited by law but which could be construed by the authorities as being prejudicial to peace and order. Such a provision introduces deep uncertainty, is irremediably speculative, violates basic doctrines of common law and British constitutional thinking and calls to mind Soviet jurisprudence in the 1930s, which turned law into an ever-flexible political tool, making the very concept of law a deceptive sham.[162] Having regard to the extraordinary scope of the specific provisions and regulations, it is inconceivable that this section was necessary.

There already existed a wide range of ordinary statutory powers to deal with conspiracies, violence and damage to property. Statutes such as the Treason

Felony Act, 1848, and the Explosive Substances Act, 1883, had been introduced to deal with extreme Irish nationalism, and had proved effective.[163] The Special Powers Act piggybacked these and other measures, making them even more severe in Northern Ireland by attaching the power to flog male offenders. Section 5 allowed flogging upon conviction for any offence under the Explosive Substances Act, 1883, the Firearms Act, 1920, and any firearms or explosives offence under the regulations arising from the Special Powers Act.[164] In addition, flogging could be imposed for demanding money with menaces or for arson.[165] Severe penalties (up to life imprisonment) were already allowed by the Explosive Substances Act, but s.6 of the Special Powers Act provided that offences under ss.2 and 3 of the Explosive Substances Act *shall* be a crime punishable by death.[166]

In addition to these supplementations of existing laws, a number of new offences were created. Such was the elasticity of the 1922 Act and the vastness of the discretionary powers it conferred that it is impossible to enumerate these. Confining ourselves directly to those set out in the Act and Regulations, we can mention the following: curfew violation, causing disaffection, withholding information, failing to answer questions, failing to inform of a violation (past or prospective) of the Special Powers Act and possessing (even privately) or displaying republican flags, emblems or symbols.[167] Other offences included harbouring and the disposal of property taken or about to be taken into government possession.[168]

The power to impose capital punishment for explosives and firearms offences was undoubtedly drastic and severe and, to modern eyes, disproportionate. It matched the powers that would be taken under martial law, and, doubtless, the Northern Ireland government considered that they were in such a situation of dire and pressing necessity in 1922 (as did the Provisional government in Dublin). What may be more difficult to justify is the use of flogging for politically motivated offences. This penalty was to be in addition to any term of imprisonment arising from the breach of law in question. Corporal punishment had by this time substantially declined in use. By the early 1920s, very few floggings were ordered by the courts in England and Wales. These sentences were usually imposed where a particular element of brutality or moral infamy was present in the crime or where public sentiment was particularly outraged. Assaults of a ferocious nature, or on the vulnerable, or pimping, would be typical offences thought to merit flogging. This special and exceptional (and archaic) punishment was intended to express the community's outrage, to humiliate the offender, to inflict a level of pain and extreme indignity that would crush resistance and bring home to him of the nature of his offence. Some judges would also have additionally argued that the sentence was a deterrent, both for the person punished and more generally in the example set. Certainly a flogging was a devastatingly painful and traumatic experience. Six strokes could severely lacerate the back; twelve could scar for life.[169] While the punishment was being carried out, the prisoner would almost certainly shriek, cry out and sometimes lose bladder and bowel control; he would certainly be stripped of dignity. For more than sixty years, the courts in Britain have not had the power to order flogging, and the very notion is alien to modern jurisprudence (though it still has populist advocates). But, thinking ourselves back into the conventions of the time, was a political opponent, even one who resorted to violence, on the same level as a pimp or assailant of the elderly? The framers of the 1922 Act thought so, and members of the Northern Ireland Parliament wholeheartedly agreed.[170]

The police obtained wide powers under the Special Powers Act, some provisions enlarging their discretion as constables, others arising from their deputed designation in the term 'Civil Authority'. Those constabulary powers included arrest without warrant, stop and search of persons or vehicles anywhere, search of premises without warrant and seizure of property. Arrest without warrant was allowed for any person suspected of acting, having acted or being about to act in a manner prejudicial to the peace.[171] In addition (an important matter in an island so recently divided and where rural access to markets had immediate impact), the police could, without warning, block, close or render impassable roads, paths, ferries and bridges.[172] These powers were granted to the two sections of the Northern Ireland police: the RUC and the Special Constabulary. Police powers, moreover, were exercisable, irrespective of whether the officer was in uniform or, indeed, on duty.

As noted, the habeas-corpus procedure had long been withheld from Ireland. Eventually conceded in the late eighteenth century, it was an irritant to successive administrations which had to deal with a troublesome population and periodic eruptions. From the middle of the nineteenth century, and earlier, the safeguard had periodically been suspended in Ireland to deal with campaigns such as the Young Irelanders, the Fenians and the Land League. The power of the subject to seek a writ of habeas corpus has its origins in the prolonged struggle to limit the power of the executive (originally the Crown, of course) to intervene in legal matters: it is a critical part of the British Constitution.[173] The purpose of an application is to bring a detained person before the courts, where the case against him may be scrutinised and, should the Crown have insufficient evidence, for liberty to be ordered or other direction issued. The writ has survived as an easily accessible remedy for executive oppressiveness, as well as for mistakes and tardiness; it was, and remains, a safeguard against unlawful arrest and detention. The Special Powers Act vitiated habeas corpus in several respects. Regulation 23, as we have seen, allowed for arrest without warrant on suspicion alone of having acted, acting or being about to act against peace and order. Following arrest, a person could be detained for an indefinite period without charge or trial. The decision as to charging, continued detention without charge, or release, rested entirely with the Civil Authority, that is, the Minister for Home Affairs and those to whom he had delegated his powers.

The power to intern was given by Regulation 23b: no probable cause or reasonable suspicion test was necessary. The Minister could intern any person for any length of time, and his decision was not justiciable or subject to superior and effective review by any court, panel or tribunal. Visitors and letters to internees required the consent of the authorities, as did internees' access to advice and assistance. Given the long history of abuses behind prison walls and the popular suspicion of cloaked and sequestered power (these sentiments being especially strong in the nationalist community), it is remarkable that the Ministry of Home Affairs equipped itself with such powers of isolation. But suspects were not the only ones to feel the weight of the Special Powers Act. In some jurisdictions (notably those of the USA), material witnesses in criminal cases may be and are regularly detained should there be concern that they might flee or be subject to intimidation or interference.[174] The Special Powers Act allowed detention and removed safeguards. Regulation 22b permitted the arrest of a witness, not on grounds that he or she might flee but only that they were thought to be able to give information on suspected offences. Such witnesses were then subject to private examination. No other person might be present during their questioning by a resident magistrate (unless with the magistrate's consent).[175] There was no entitlement to legal assistance, and, should the witness refuse to answer a question, he or she committed an offence. No protection was provided against self-incrimination – and it is to be remembered that this was an arrest as a potential witness, not as a suspect. Regulation 22b(3) provided that the witness 'shall not be excused from answering any question on the ground that the answer thereto may criminate or tend to criminate himself'. The Court of Star Chamber may have blanched at such powers and procedures.[176]

Finally, habeas corpus was also set aside by Regulation 23a, which empowered the Civil Authority to make an Exclusion Order. This could be applied to any person, whether domiciled in Northern Ireland or not, and could prohibit him or her from entering any part of Northern Ireland. The order could also specify place of residence, reporting to the police, restrictions of movement and other conditions. Banishment of a resident from the territory of Northern Ireland would have contravened the GOIA, 1920 (which, because it was a Westminster statute, overrode local legislation), but, by directing people to live in certain areas and by excluding them from others, a similar outcome could be obtained since life could be made all but impossible by the sundering of social ties and by restricting the possibilities of earning a living. A person so confined might have had no alternative but to leave Northern Ireland.[177] Family and work life could be cast into utter disarray, and property and assets of all but a personal and portable kind could be placed beyond use and benefit.

Persons accused of violating the provisions of the Special Powers Act were brought before special courts. These were not conducted by justices of the peace, but two or more resident magistrates.[178] The proceedings were summary only, which meant that accused persons had no right to jury trial, notwithstanding the fact that the special courts could impose maximum sentences of two years' imprisonment or a fine of £100, or both. (The special punishments of flogging and the death penalty for explosives or firearms offences could only be imposed by a higher court.) Appeals against sentence by a special court were to a recorder or county court judge. It may be pertinent to point out that Northern Ireland's resident magistrates were almost all Protestants. Precise information is not available for 1922, but in 1936, the National Council for Civil Liberties reported that only one of the eleven resident magistrates then serving was a Roman Catholic.[179] This gross disparity could not but add to a sense of probable prejudice, unfairness and injustice in the operation of the special courts.

The office of the coroner is one of the oldest in the UK, dating back to 1194 in England. It originated in times when local magnates could abuse their powers and was intended to extend the protection of the Crown even into remote places. In modern times it has continued to find a place because of universal agreement that it is vital that suspicious or unexplained deaths should be reported and deliberated upon by an independent office. The coroner and his jury have carried out this important work for more than eight centuries. Particular concerns and suspicions must arise when the duties of the coroner are taken over or curtailed by the executive.[180] The Special Powers Act allowed the Minister for Home Affairs to prohibit the holding of inquests in any part of Northern Ireland 'either absolutely or except in such circumstances or on such conditions as may be specified in the order'. The Minister could substitute for the coroner and his jury any other officer or court that he chose.[181]

The intention is quite clear: to remove the possibility that blame might be attributed for a death in which the Northern Ireland government and its police had been involved. The drafters of the Act would no doubt have had in mind the numerous findings of coroners' juries in Southern Ireland, which had been unfavourable to government and to crown forces during the various phases of the Anglo-Irish War. In a country where locality and religious affiliation could be so interchangeable as denominators, it was more than likely that a jury empanelled in a predominantly Roman Catholic district would return a verdict inconvenient to and of some embarrassment to the government – perhaps, it should be said, even perversely so. Whether such rare occurrences posed such a challenge to government (which had full powers of further investigation at its disposal) as to justify the possible removal of such an age-old safeguard against cover-ups by authority of unlawful or criminal deaths is extremely doubtful. Suppression of a coroner's inquest would surely be taken as a sign that the authorities had something to hide. Rumour and suspicion would deliver a much greater blow to the credibility of government – and one of greater durability in effect – than the verdict of a demonstrably partisan jury.

This discussion merely opens rather than exhausts the possibilities of the Special Powers Act. The numerous combinations and cross-multiplications of powers, extraordinary discretionary powers and the lack of restriction and accountability meant, in essence, that short of unquestionably criminal actions such as assault, robbery, rape or murder, the Civil Authority could do virtually anything to anybody and his or her property and yet claim the protective cloak of a virtually unchallengeable and endlessly adaptable authority. As will be seen, the Special Powers Act was rarely, if ever, used against extremist loyalists. This was, in large part, due to the fact that they had every reason to support rather than subvert the status quo. But even when, in times of sectarian tension, loyalist groups stepped over the line and acted against the peace and welfare of the community, the Special Powers Act was not invoked either as a preventive or punitive measure. Its stated purpose was to contain and suppress violent Irish nationalism and anything that tended to support, encourage or represent such a movement. Its actual effect was to reduce overt protest to the minimum, to damage democracy by making non-parliamentary opposition (otherwise legal) a crime and, in sum, to expose to the arbitrary exercise of authority much of the Roman Catholic working-class population. Such instruments can, of course, be effective for many years, but, as numerous instances in many different political and cultural settings have shown, they cannot but intensify resentments and drive underground and frequently into extremism many different and varied currents of opposition.

Postal censorship

Catholic suspicion, lack of trust and alienation would have been further reinforced had it become know that an extensive programme of postal censorship had been instituted at this time. Edward Archdale, Northern Ireland's Minister for Agriculture and Commerce, raised the issue with Churchill towards the end of May 1922.[182] He wanted a general censorship of all the province's mail. The justification was the continuing IRA campaign, subversion and gun-running. A general censorship would have been a huge undertaking, similar in scale to that maintained during the Great War. The War Office was dismissive: without closing the Free State land frontier, instituting a naval blockade and proclaiming martial law, the scheme was inoperable.

A subcommittee of Churchill's Provisional Government of Ireland Committee submitted a secret paper to Cabinet on 14 June 1922. The understanding throughout was that the censorship was directed at republicans in Northern Ireland and the Free State: there was no mention of extremist loyalists. The subcommittee confirmed the War Office's opinion that a general censorship would be impossible. The option of local censorship centres was also impractical because 'the local Post Office staffs cannot be relied upon'. Instead, a roaming censorship team was proposed, to be supplemented by surprise local inspections. The primary object was not intelligence but rather the creation of a continuing uncertainty about detection sufficient to induce republicans to resort to couriers and other methods; these could more easily be watched. New legislation could be avoided if s.56 of the 1908 Post Office Act were used.[183]

Belfast had no authority over the Post Office since by the 1920 GOIA this had been reserved to Westminster.[184] The Home Office, which was responsible for postal warrants, had the responsibility to keep any interception within the law. Sir John Anderson had considerable doubts about the legality of a general warrant. (This would have exceeded the authority conferred by s.82 of the 1908 Act.) And, indeed, the device finally settled upon sailed very close to the wind. On 26 June 1922, a warrant was drawn up instructing the Postmaster General at Belfast to inspect any letters, telegrams or postal packages which the Northern Ireland Minister for Home Affairs 'may have reason to believe to emanate from or be destined for disloyal persons'. Churchill approved of this wording on 5 July 1922, as subsequently did Frederick Kellaway, the Postmaster General (a Liberal minister in the coalition government). The latter remained very cautious. The action could provoke 'deep resentment' and lead the Provisional government to do the same; he also wondered whether the benefits would outweigh the objections. Despite these misgivings, however, the warrant was issued, but for two months only.[185]

A power once given is reluctantly surrendered; governments, institutions and individuals find multiple and pressing reasons to justify retention. As the warrant's two-month validity expired, Belfast pressed for renewal. We do not know how widely the Ministry of Home Affairs interpreted the phrase 'disloyal persons' in exercising the warrant, but we know what Bates thought about Roman Catholics, and it hardly seems reckless to conclude that the mail of virtually any Catholic could be intercepted – and that on grounds that would not have to meet the minimal test of 'reasonable suspicion'. Details are now unknown, but it seems likely that constitutional nationalists were caught in the same net of surveillance as violent republicans. In the first ten weeks (up to 8 September 1922), 7,318 items of mail had been opened and 276 extracts had been taken: a 'hit' rate of less than 4 per cent. About 175 items were being opened every working day. This had little interfered with the post, it was reported: the average time spent in opening, copying, resealing and despatching was just under twenty-three minutes. No practical problems stood in the way of continuing the exercise, nor was there a likelihood of discovery. At this point, the project acquired another supporter: military intelligence considered preliminary results to have been 'most valuable' and recommended continuation. Thirty-one towns had been visited by mobile censorship teams: all were in Catholic areas. London agreed to extend the warrant for a further two months.[186]

Early in 1923, Sir Geoffrey Whiskard, Colonial Office Permanent Under-Secretary, and Sir John Anderson, his Home Office counterpart, apparently agreed that general security in Northern Ireland had much improved. The justification for roaming censorship was not so strong, and there should therefore be only a one-month renewal of the warrant.[187] A tussle subsequently ensued, with the Northern Ireland government unilaterally extending the censorship until 31 March 1923. This was unquestionably *ultra vires*, and, since neither the Post Office nor the Home Office had been consulted, it was in fact an illegal action – wilfully so, given London's prior warnings and explanations. The Post Office, as we have seen, was an imperial responsibility, explicitly excluded from the remit and powers of Belfast. The only reaction from Whitehall, however, was a mild request that Northern Ireland should regularise the position.[188]

The longer the censorship lasted and could be said to be efficiently administered, the stronger the demand for retention. The RUC's Inspector-General reported that much useful information had been collected, 'particularly in locating persons who had left their homes in suspicious circumstances'. Parcels of prohibited literature had been seized and (though this was given less emphasis) information gathered on the IRA.[189] Warrants were extended over the next several years. Baldwin's Conservative government was inclined to go along with requests from Craig's administration, provided there were no political repercussions, or financial commitments. There remained concern about the legality of the operation, backed as it was by what in essence was a general warrant, but the cloak of secrecy gave adequate protection from a legal challenge. On 8 July 1924, Cahir Healy, a Nationalist MP newly released from internment, put down a parliamentary question. This was easily evaded.[190] Two years later, there were repeated concerns about the general nature of the warrant. By this time, RUC intelligence was able to give a schedule of names and addresses. This focused the operation, enabling it to be run on specific warrants rather than on the dubious general-trawling warrant. Concerns were sufficiently allayed for a further renewal to be granted.[191]

Ramsay MacDonald's second, more confident and assertive, Labour administration came into office in June 1929. With J. R. Clynes at the Home Office what had become by now a fairly standard process of warrant renewal was queried. The number of names on the warrant for interceptions had grown from 548 to 585. An increase rather than a decrease ran counter to expectations arising from what was agreed to be an improvement in security. The Home Office pointed this out, adding that 'The new Government may desire to raise this question as a matter of general policy.'[192] It apparently never did, and postal censorship continued as before.

By the early 1920s, the shape of the Northern Ireland state had been formed, much of its detail completed and its style displayed. It was a defensive structure with a number of oppressive features and, despite sailing under unionist colours, was not and never could be a unionist state. Legal, administrative, electoral and civic standards would never during the years of devolved government reach in fairness or equity – or ambition – those of Britain. It is instructive that the issue that brought Stormont down in 1972 was control of security. For the unionist politicians who had run the province for over half a century, it was better to bring down the house than to agree to cede security powers to Westminster. Control of law and order, from legislation to the administration of the courts, police and prisons, was a central focus of Ulster unionism from 1920 until 1972. That preoccupation was always going to curb generosity, stifle imagination and baulk acts of political bravery. A state built solely or mainly on defensiveness will always live off its own substance and, therefore, must fail. Expansiveness, inclusiveness, flexibility and openness to change are political virtues, but not that alone: they build strength and ensure survival.

Sir James Craig and his colleagues would have dismissed some or all of this as irrelevant to the conditions that set their agenda and dictated their priorities and limitations in those terrible months of late 1920. It was the tragedy of their years that there was much truth in this putative dismissal. The people they represented, and over whom they exercised authority, were gripped by the deep feelings and cultural patterns of sectarianism, as they had been for many generations. This was a binary society of inclusion and exclusion, corrosive and static at the same time and oblivious to the possibilities of dynamic engagement, each with the other. Unionist and nationalist politicians alike tended this dark garden and harvested its fruits.

If internal processes accounted for the greater part of the nature of the new state, we cannot ignore external conditions. Irish nationalism had overwhelmingly pivoted from methods of moral force to physical force and had broken up the UK. This was a remarkable and, to unionists, profoundly worrying achievement. It reinforced perceptions of Irish nationalists and the British political class alike: neither was to be trusted. 'Ourselves alone' was the inevitable and ultimately fatal choice.

Notes

1 GOIA, 1920. Independent Liberals, some Conservatives and Labour members also opposed it in the House of Commons, both generally and in detail. See, for example, 5 *Hansard*, vol. 129, cols. 1904–2016, 2099–214, 2 June 1920. Sir Edward Carson was passionate, despairing and scathing at several points during this debate. Nationalists condemned the measure, some, even in mainstream and constitutional parties, regarding it as the 'ultimate crime against Ireland' (*Weekly Irish News*, 20 November 1920, 4c).

2 Not all Northern Catholics were separatists (see below, p. 60). For the most part, however, Catholics favoured a united Ireland independent of Britain.

3 Carson, who still favoured an unaltered continuation of the Union, condemned the 1920 Act as asking the people of Ulster 'to take a Parliament which they have never demanded, and which they do not want' (5 *Hansard*, vol. 123, col. 1198, 22 December 1919).

4 As is well known, Liberalism was split by William Ewart Gladstone's first Home Rule Bill (1886). Ulster Liberalism was particularly affected by this issue, with all but a tiny minority assuming a Liberal Unionist identity. There was, however, another strand within the Liberal tradition that saw a solution in some form of separate Ulster state. This was almost totally overshadowed by the anti-Home Rule campaign that grew so militant from 1910 onwards. See 'An Ulster Presbyterian', *Ulster on Its Own; or An Easy Way with Ireland, Being a Proposal of Self-Government for the Five Counties Round Lough Neagh* (Belfast: Carswell, 1912). The reactions (and actions) at this time of the loyalist population of one area of Northern Ireland, South Derry, are related in a direct and unadorned way by Wallace Clark in his *Guns in Ulster* (Upperlands: Wallace Clark, 2002).

5 Act of Settlement, 1701: 12 & 13 Will. III, c.2.

6 Even Carson warned, 'You cannot knock Parliaments up and down as you do a ball, and, once you have planted them there, you cannot get rid of them' (5 *Hansard*, vol. 123, col. 1202, 22 December 1919).

7 See the discussion of the views of the Southern unionists who followed Lord Midleton (*Irish Independent*, 7 March 1921, 4d).

8 The 1911 Census showed that some 90 per cent of the population of the future Free State declared their religious affiliation as Roman Catholic; Patrick Murray, *Oracles of God: The Roman Catholic Church and Irish Politics, 1922–37* (Dublin: University College Dublin Press, 2000), p. 11.

9 T. C. Agar-Robertes had hinted at this notion during the passage of the third Home Rule Bill. His compromise was rejected by H. H. Asquith's government (5 *Hansard*, vol. 37, col. 2162, 2 May 1912).

10 In the six-county area there were 430,161 Roman Catholics and 820,370 Protestants (Anglicans, Presbyterians, Methodists, Baptists, etc.), 34 per cent and 66 per cent respectively.

11 See Patrick Buckland's succinct account of these events in his *James Craig: Lord Craigavon* (Dublin: Gill & Macmillan, 1980), pp. 42–7.

12 Sir James Craig (1871–1940). First Viscount Craigavon, first Prime Minister of Northern Ireland. Son of a wealthy whiskey distiller. Served in the Boer War and then in the Great War (though ill-health prevented active service in the latter). Entered politics as a Unionist and was elected for East Down in 1906. After the war he was elected for Mid-Down, serving until 1921. Began a ministerial career at Westminster but abandoned this to become leader of the Ulster Unionist Party (after Sir Edward Carson's resignation) and first Prime Minister of Northern Ireland. A Presbyterian, Craig's unionism was based on religious as well as political convictions.

13 These payments were made from the Free State's Secret Service Estimate. UCDA, Hugh Kennedy Papers, P/4/386/15–18, letter to Minister, 21 February 1923.

14 The bishops opposed Partition, and some had supported the Sinn Féin boycott of Belfast goods. At a conference on 7 February 1926, however, the Roman Catholic Vicar General of Dromore, Dean M. McPolin, urged Nationalist MPs to take their seats in the Northern Ireland Parliament. This appears to have been the view of many senior clergy, though not of the Roman Catholic Primate of All Ireland, Archbishop (later Cardinal) Joseph MacRory. See Eamon Phoenix, *Northern Nationalism: Nationalist Politics, Partition and the Catholic Minority in Northern Ireland, 1890–1940* (Belfast: Ulster Historical Foundation, 1994), pp. 339–46.

15 Marianne Elliott, *The Catholics of Ulster* (London: Allen Lane, 2000), pp. 379–80. The predecessor force, the RIC, had, of course, been substantially Catholic, so there was in this transition period at least the opportunity to recruit Catholics. Reflecting on the small proportion of Catholics in the public service, Graham Walker observes that initial attempts to induce them to take up a quota of places in the RUC 'were in effect abandoned'. See Graham Walker, *A History of the Ulster Unionist Party: Protest, Pragmatism and Pessimism* (Manchester: Manchester University Press, 2004), p. 61. In the Craig–Collins agreements that had followed the establishment of the Provisional government, there had been attempts to provide for constructive relations between North and South. One such was an Advisory Committee to encourage Roman Catholic participation in the RUC. The Committee met on only three occasions and appears to have had no effect whatever on policing. See Chris Ryder, *The RUC, 1922–2000: A Force under Fire* (London: Arrow Books, 2000), pp. 55–6. IRA and simple sectarian intimidation by co-religionists of any Catholic inclined to join the RUC also played a major part in diminishing the proportion of Catholics in the ranks. This is often ignored in accounts of the times. But, whatever the balance of causes, failure to persuade the Catholic community to support the RUC and to induce Catholics to join the force in proportionate numbers would have grave consequences and would eventually contribute to the fall of the Stormont government.

16 Maurice Hayes, who has played a distinguished part in promoting cross-community and cross-border relations, served in both the local and national civil service in Northern Ireland. As he advanced in seniority in the latter, he sometimes found himself the only Roman Catholic in his grade. As a reasonably dispassionate observer, he refers to the 'double myth', which goes back to the establishment of Northern Ireland. The unionist version is that Catholics rejected the state and refused to participate; the Catholic take is that they were rejected and oppressed by the new state.

Hayes wryly observes that, '[t]he trouble is that both myths are, in part, true'. Maurice Hayes, *Minority Verdict: Experiences of a Catholic Public Servant* (Belfast: Blackstaff Press, 1995), p. 7.

17 See, for example, Piaras Béaslaí, *Michael Collins and the Making of a New Ireland* (London: Harrap, 1926); Michael Collins, *The Path to Freedom* (Dublin: The Talbot Press, 1922); C. H. Bretherton, *The Real Ireland* (London: Black, 1925). Although published seventeen years after the formation of the Northern Ireland state, Dorothy Macardle's *The Irish Republic* (London: Gollancz, 1937) also detailed the extent and success of subversion during the Anglo-Irish War. That those and other revelations and celebrations of duplicity were a source of dismay and concern to unionists is confirmed by the novelist and playwright St John Greer Ervine, an enthusiastic critic of Irish separatism and republicanism and equally uncritical (but informative) supporter of the Northern Ireland government. See St John Greer Ervine, *Craigavon: Ulsterman* (London: Allen & Unwin, 1949), pp. 462–5.

18 This exclusion was, to some extent, a continuation of long-established *local* practice. A Commons Select Committee of 1891 was informed that only two of the ninety-one paid officials of Belfast Corporation were Roman Catholics. Under pressure from Dublin Castle, this had changed over the succeeding three decades, and the March 1922 minutes of Belfast Corporation recorded that thirty-three paid officials of the Corporation were Catholics. See Phoenix, *Northern Nationalism, op. cit.*, pp. 455–6. In pre-Partition Ireland, civil-service rules provided for appointment according to merit. In the new Northern Ireland state, some of that equity and protection was removed. No more than a trickle of Roman Catholics entered the administrative grades of the Northern Ireland civil service. In the nine years up to 1934 it was found that of the 833 members of the administrative grades, only thirty-seven were Catholics. All top fifty-five posts were held by Protestants. Catholic representation at all levels of the public services had fallen since Partition. See Patrick Buckland, *The Factory of Grievances: Devolved Government in Northern Ireland, 1921–39* (Dublin: Gill & Macmillan, 1979), p. 20; PRONI CAB/9/A/90/2, FIN Diary, 15 February–16 May 1943, ff. 120–1, 151, 166. Conversely, Roman Catholics who joined the RUC seem to have progressed more than proportionately to senior ranks. They comprised just over 21 per cent of the RUC on its foundation. This fell away to an average of 17 per cent and then, in the years after 1969, to about 10 per cent. The proportion of senior officers, however, remained remarkably stable. Chris Ryder points out that at the beginning of 1925 nine of the thirty-eight district and two of the eight county inspectors were Roman Catholics (*The RUC, op. cit.*, p. 60). During the 1970s, when the proportion of the rank-and-file Catholics in the RUC was much smaller, Catholic representation in senior ranks remained much the same as in 1925, at about 25 per cent.

19 *NIPD*, vol. 16, col. 1091, 24 April 1934. In the same debate, he told a Nationalist opponent that the politicians in the South had boasted of theirs being a Catholic state: 'All I boast of is that we are a Protestant Parliament and a Protestant State' (col. 1095). This rash and heated remark would be endlessly repeated by his nationalist critics, North and South, who would also point out that every prime minister of Northern Ireland was a member of the Orange Order, as were all but three members of its cabinet. Craig had added to his observation, 'It would be rather interesting for historians of the future to compare a Catholic State launched in the South with a Protestant State launched in the North and to see which gets on the better and prospers the more... I am doing my best always to top the bill and to be ahead of the South' (col. 1095). This somewhat blunted the sectarian edge of the remarks but was generally omitted from quotations.

20 Three of these, he said, 'were civil servants, turned over to him whom he had to take'. He added that he had recommended people not to employ Roman Catholics

'who were 99 per cent disloyal' (*Northern Whig*, 2 April 1925, 9d). Edward Archdale (1853–1953) had a farming background. He entered the Navy from the Naval School, Portsmouth. Served in China, the Mediterranean, the Cape and West Africa stations. Retired and returned to farming in 1950. MP (Westminster) for various Fermanagh constituencies, 1898–1921 and then MP (Northern Ireland) for Fermanagh and Tyrone. Northern Ireland Minister for Agriculture and Commerce, 1921–5, and then (the post being split) of Agriculture until 1933.

21 Henry Harrison, *Ulster and the British Empire 1939: Help or Hindrance?* (London: Robert Hale, 1939), pp. 86–7. John Miller Andrews (1871–1956). Mill owner and landowner. MP (Northern Ireland) for various constituencies of Co. Down, 1921–53. Northern Ireland Minister for Labour, 1921–37. Minister for Finance, 1937–40. Prime Minister, 1940–3. Grand Master, Orange Institution, 1948–54.

22 The man had charge of the Prince of Wales's horse during the Great War (Buckland, *The Factory of Grievances, op. cit.*, p. 23).

23 See the *Irish Times* article by G. C. Duggan (former Comptroller and Auditor-General of Northern Ireland), 4 May 1967, 6g–h. Sir Richard Dawson Bates (1876–1949) was a solicitor, as were his father and grandfather. A vice-president of the Ulster Unionist Council, he was one of the founders of the UVF Hospitals and of the UVF Patriotic Fund. He had been prominent in the organisation of the great anti-Home Rule demonstrations. Minister for Home Affairs, 1921–43.

24 PRONI CAB/9/A/901, Sir Dawson Bates to C. H. Blackmore (Assistant Secretary to the Northern Ireland Cabinet), 14 August 1934; Blackmore to Bates, 17 August 1934. More generally, see *The Times*, 30 November 1934, 13b.

25 Sir Basil Stanlake Brooke (5th baronet, later 1st viscount) would serve in the Northern Ireland cabinet for thirty years, during twenty of which he would be Prime Minister. His strong and unwavering unionism, as well as his war service and his initiative during the formation period of Northern Ireland made him a pillar of the Ulster Unionist Party and a presence seldom forgotten by supporters and opponents alike. For a biographical note see below, p. 819, n. 61.

26 *Fermanagh Times*, 13 July 1933, 8g.

27 The Orange Institution played a leading, if not dominant, part in the political life of Northern Ireland. As noted, all prime ministers were members, as were 95 per cent of all elected Unionist MPs. See John F. Harbinson, *The Ulster Unionist Party, 1882–1973: Its Development and Organisation* (Belfast, Blackstaff Press, 1974), p. 95.

28 Almost half a century after the establishment of Northern Ireland, Sir James Cameron found that in many, if not most, areas of Northern Ireland, 'effective membership of the Unionist Party is not open to Roman Catholics'. He also pointed out that the Orange Order 'does in fact exercise influence within the Unionist Party'. See Sir James Cameron, *Disturbances in Northern Ireland: Report of the Commission Appointed by the Governor of Northern Ireland* (Cameron Report) (Belfast: HMSO [Cmd. 532], 1969), paras. 52–3. It is worth noting that Cameron records that the practical exclusion of Catholics from the Unionist Party 'was admitted with little or no reservation'.

29 *NIPD*, vol. 16, col. 1118, 24 April 1934.

30 *NIPD*, vol. 16, col. 1120, 24 April 1934. The words 'our people' are instructive as to how he saw himself and his government, and the community for which they were responsible. There emerges from time to time in statements of both unionist politicians and their supporters a sense that ordinary Roman Catholics were sources used by the enemies of the state for information- and intelligence-gathering. The belief that one's neighbours were not what they seemed but spies and targeters apparently grew stronger during the modern period of conflict.

31 The Roman Catholic Church has, since time immemorial, claimed to be the one true church and has made strident claims for universal jurisdiction. Nor is this

a theological formality. Cardinal Cormac Murphy-O'Connor, sometime Roman Catholic Primate of England, recalled in his autobiography that during his days in training at the English College in Rome in the 1950s, the seminarians would, before lunch each day, say prayers for the conversion of England. Cormac Murphy-O'Connor, *At the Heart of the World* (London: Darton, Longman & Todd, 2004), p. 23. But the doctrine goes back to the earliest days of the Church: 'Salus extra ecclestiam non est' (No salvation exists outside the Church) wrote St Augustine (*Oxford Dictionary of Quotations* (Oxford: Oxford University Press, 1979), 21: 19). Whilst it is fair to note, however, that some Protestant churches have made similar statements on scriptural authority, the impact of the doctrine on Northern Protestants, with their particular history of resistance to papal claims, was profound. At a community level, the age-old Catholic prohibition on even attending a Protestant service – be it worship, marriage, baptism or a funeral – was corrosive. For an indication of the rigour with which this doctrine was enforced, see John Bennett Black's account of the 1583 mission of the Jesuits, Edmund Campion and Robert Parsons, to England: John Bennett Black, *The Reign of Elizabeth, 1558–1603* (Oxford: Clarendon Press, 1959), p. 181; see also Peter Ackroyd, *Tudors* (London: Macmillan, 2012), Chapters 22 and 31 for descriptions of the domestic and international aspects of the wars of religion. For descriptions of the comprehensive (and exclusive) claims of the Roman Catholic Church, and its methods of ensuring compliance and adherence, see Tom Inglish, *Moral Monopoly: The Rise and Fall of the Catholic Church in Modern Ireland* (Dublin: UCD Press, 1998), pp. 36–9. See also Louise Fuller, *Irish Catholicism since 1950: The Undoing of a Culture* (Dublin: Gill & Macmillan, 2002).

32 There has, until modern, more secular, times, been a current against Roman Catholicism in Britain, in the same way as there was an exclusionary anti-Semitism. I recently spoke to a former civil servant of senior rank, whose career in the English civil service began in the late 1960s. He confirmed an awareness that there would be some kind of issue with his Catholicism. Within a rising tide of secularism, one would expect this type of friction, however minor, to fade away.

33 On Devlin's death, Sir James Craig paid a warm personal tribute, deploring 'the loss of a great Ulsterman' (*NIPD*, vol. 16, col. 279, 7 March 1934).

34 Speaking for the government at the committee stage of the Bill, Sir Laming Worthington-Evans confirmed that proportional representation, which, in the single transferable vote version, applied to the South as well as the North, had been included in the Bill 'as one of the safeguards by which it was intended to protect minorities' (5 *Hansard*, vol. 130, col. 1206, 15 June 1920). See also GOIA s.14(3); Representation of the People Act, 1918: 7 & 8 Geo. V, c.64, s.20(3).

35 Local Government (Northern Ireland) Act, 1923. Patrick Buckland's archival investigations have shown that the sole concern in these changes in the electoral process was to advance the interest of the Unionist Party (*The Factory of Grievances, op. cit.,* pp. 233–6, *passim*). Writing more than forty years after the withdrawal of proportional representation, Lord Cameron and his colleagues concluded that the arguments deployed when proportional representation was removed from local government 'mainly rationalised a determination to achieve and maintain Unionist electoral control' (Cameron Report, para. 136).

36 For Devlin's speech on leaving the Parliament, see *NIPD*, vol. 14, col. 1339, 11 May 1932. It is quite clear that Devlin was not withdrawing himself and his party from Parliament but, rather, from what he called 'this sham discussion'. The budget was being debated, and Post Office revenue had been raised by Cahir Healy, the Nationalist MP for South Fermanagh. The Speaker ruled the topic out of order (the Post Office being a matter reserved for the British government). This provoked Devlin to withdraw but was doubtless the occasion rather than the cause. It is remarkable, whatever one might think of abstentionism, that for three-fifths of its

existence before direct rule was instituted in 1972 Northern Ireland lacked a parliamentary opposition, so indispensable to this form of government.

37 Elliott, *The Catholics of Ulster, op. cit.*, p. 397.

38 It was smaller than the Dáil, which had 132 seats in 1921, and the Free State Senate (sixty members), but the ratio of representatives to electors was broadly comparable.

39 PRONI HA/9/2/115, Roman Catholic chaplains, 1903–50.

40 St John Ervine is precise about this, stating that the invitation was sent to Cardinal O'Donnell on 29 April 1925 (*Craigavon, op. cit.*, p. 419). The then Catholic Bishop of Down and Connor was the irreconcilable Dr Joseph MacRory, who two years later became Archbishop of Armagh and Primate of All Ireland. It seems inevitable that he would ignore the invitation. Marianne Elliott, however, insists that the first invitation was extended in 1968 and that it then took the bishops three years to respond positively (*The Catholics of Ulster, op. cit.*, p. 471). The record of abstention included arrangements for the morale-raising Festival of Britain in 1951. Whereas in Britain there was Roman Catholic participation in the Festival's Advisory Committee of Christian Churches, in Northern Ireland there was abstention. See Gillian McIntosh, *The Force of Culture: Unionist Identities in Twentieth Century Ireland* (Cork: Cork University Press, 1999), p. 111. See also PRONI CAB/9/F/123/18, Graasden to Cooper, 6 July 1944.

41 *Irish Times*, 26 February 1971, 1a; *Irish Independent*, 26 February 1971, 1e.

42 Though Craig breached more than once with London the possibility of cross-border 'hot pursuit' by Northern forces: these proposals were always unequivocally rejected (see below, pp. 69 and 85–6).

43 The woeful statistics of those disturbances are unreliable and contested. With these limitations in mind, the weekly reports of the GOC British Forces in Ireland are apt to be at the more reliable end of the scale. These can be found in the British Cabinet Papers. See, for example, the report for the week ending 25 March 1923, which notes that twelve were killed (five Protestants, twelve Roman Catholics and two police officers) in Belfast alone (PRO CAB/24/136/9). A number of publications deal with these disturbances. See John Hassan (pseud. G. B. Kenna), *Facts and Figures: Belfast Pogrom, 1920–1922* (Belfast: Donaldson Archives, 1997), pp. 15–16; Jim McDermott, *Northern Divisions: The Old IRA and the Belfast Pogroms, 1920–22* (Belfast: Beyond the Pale, 2001), pp. 52 and 249; Paul Bew, Peter Gibbon and Henry Patterson, *Northern Ireland, 1921–2001: Political Forces and Social Classes* (London: Serif, 2002), *passim*; Thomas Hennessey, *A History of Northern Ireland, 1920–1996* (Basingstoke: Macmillan Press, 1997), pp. 26–7; Andrew Boyd, *Holy War in Belfast* (Tralee: Anvil Books, 1969).

44 C. McCluskey, *Up Off Their Knees: A Commentary on the Civil Rights Movement in Northern Ireland* (Galway: Conn McCluskey and Associates, 1989), p. 16.

45 See Seán McConville, *Irish Political Prisoners, 1848–1922* (London and New York: Routledge, 2003), p. 653 for an account of the Truce and its political and military context. See also the *Irish Times*, 9 July 1921, 5d–e; 11 July 1921, 11d–e; *Freeman's Journal*, 9 July 1921, 5a–e.

46 Some 35,000 rifles and ammunition survived and were stored under RUC control until the outbreak of the Second World War. They were then purchased from the Northern Ireland government by the UK's Ministry of Supply, to be used by the Home Guard (Ryder, *The RUC, op. cit.*, p. 60). See also H. Montgomery Hyde, *Carson: The Life of Sir Edward Carson* (London: Constable, 1974); Timothy Bowman, *Carson's Army: The Ulster Volunteer Force, 1910–22* (Manchester: Manchester University Press, 2007). For a broader context, see David Fitzpatrick, *The Two Irelands, 1912–1939* (Oxford: Oxford University Press, 1998).

47 Clark, *Guns in Ulster, op. cit.*, p. 25.

48 See Catherine Hirst, *Religion, Politics and Violence in Nineteenth Century Belfast: The Pound and Sandy Row* (Dublin: Four Courts Press, 2002), pp. 14–18. See also Phoenix, *Northern Nationalism, op. cit.*, Chapters 1 and 2; Bryan A. Follis, *A State under Siege: The Establishment of Northern Ireland, 1920–25* (Oxford: Clarendon, 1995), p. 16; John F. Harbinson, *The Ulster Unionist Party, 1882–1973: Its Development and Organisation* (Belfast: Blackstaff Press, 1974), p. 89.

49 PRONI CAB/4/9/2, Cabinet Conclusions, 15 July 1921.

50 Provisional committees of loyalists had been formed, together with armed units (PRONI HA/20/A/1/2, Report to Northern Ireland Cabinet by Sir Dawson Bates, 10 September 1921). See also *Irish Times*, 26 July 1920, 5d; 17 October 1921, 6a; 1 September 1921, 5c; *Irish Independent*, 30 July 1921, 6g.

51 See Walker, *History of the Ulster Unionist Party, op. cit.*, pp. 12–13, and 54–86. See also PRONI D/3480/59/34, Edward Carson to Robert Lynn, 28 August 1920.

52 Mulcahy Papers, P/7/A/II/23, Report of 3rd Northern Division, IRA to GHQ, August 1921, ff. 44–6.

53 Macardle, *The Irish Republic, op. cit.*, pp. 761–2.

54 Tim Pat Coogan, *Michael Collins* (London: Arrow Books, 1991), pp. 350–1.

55 Coogan, *Michael Collins, op. cit.*, p. 340; see Chapter 11 generally for Coogan's analysis.

56 See *NIPD*, vol. 2, cols. 221–6, 28 March 1922 for Craig's account of the agreement and its aftermath. Agreement was reached in Churchill's House of Commons Room on 21 January 1922. *The Times*, 23 January 1922, 11d; NAI PG/G/1/1, 23 January 1922. Intriguingly, at this meeting Craig had proposed that the somewhat abstract and ill-defined Council of Ireland should be replaced by working meetings of the Northern and Southern cabinets. Nothing came of this suggestion, which would at least have had the great virtue of bringing the two sides' senior political leaders into a working relationship.

57 *NIPD*, vol. 2, cols. 308–15, 4 April 1922; *The Times*, 31 March 1922, 13b.

58 See p. 388.

59 *Irish Times*, 16 January 1922, 5f.

60 Coogan, *Michael Collins, op. cit.*, p. 344.

61 PRO CAB/21/254, Sir James Craig to Lloyd George, 8 February 1922. The High Sheriff of Fermanagh was among those seized.

62 PRO CAB/21/254, Lloyd George to Michael Collins, 8 February 1922.

63 PRO CAB/21/254, Michael Collins to Lloyd George, 8 February 1922. The kidnapped men were not freed until April.

64 PRO CAB/24/136/9, Report for Week Ending 25 March 1922.

65 *Ibid.* Macready also referred to cross-border sniping.

66 PRONI FIN/18/1/681, 'The Clones Inquiry'; *Daily Herald*, 13 February 1922, 1d–e.

67 The *Herald*'s correspondent in Belfast had been told by a 'high official' of the Northern Ireland government that the Clones ambush was 'an act of war' (13 February 1922, 1d). Over that weekend, every available Special was mobilised and sent to the border. See also Craig's statements to Parliament, *NIPD*, vol. 2, cols. 11 and 21, 14 March 1922.

68 PRONI HO/5/15, Churchill to Sir James Craig, 13 February 1922. There were three telegrams from Craig to Churchill on this topic on this day.

69 PRO CAB, Provisional Government of Ireland Committee, 20 February 1922; see also NAI PG/G/1/1, 27 February 1922, the receipt of funds from the British government.

70 PRONI HO/5/15, Churchill to Craig, 13 February 1922; HO 5/CIM/604/1/3.

71 When, on 22 June 1922, Wilson was assassinated on the doorstep of his London house, Craig gave the news to the Northern Ireland Commons with the observation

that 'Sir Henry Wilson laid down his life for Ulster. Of that we have no doubt whatever' (*NIPD*, vol. 2, col. 823, 22 June 1922).

72 PRONI HO/5/15, Sir James Craig to Major-General Solly-Flood, 30 March 1922. See Paul McMahon, *British Spies and Irish Rebels: British Intelligence and Ireland, 1916–1945* (Woodbridge: Boydell Press, 2008), pp. 151–3; Chris Ryder, *The Fateful Split* (London: Methuen, 2004), p. 45; Richard Doherty, *The Thin Green Line: The History of the Royal Ulster Constabulary* (Barnsley: Pen & Sword, 2004), p. 19.

73 See Sir Arthur Hezlet, *The 'B' Specials: A History of the Ulster Special Constabulary* (London: Tom Stacey, 1972), a sympathetic account; and Michael Farrell, *Arming the Protestants: The Formation of the Ulster Special Constabulary and the Royal Ulster Constabulary, 1920–7* (London: Pluto, 1983), a more critical view.

74 On the background to the formation of the new civil service, see Martin Maguire, *The Civil Service and the Revolution in Ireland, 1912–38: 'Shaking the Blood-Stained Hand of Mr Collins'* (Manchester: Manchester University Press, 2008), Chapter 3.

75 See *Irish News*, 23 October 1920, 5e.

76 *Irish News*, 23 October 1920, 5e; Clark, *Guns in Ulster, op. cit.*, p. 28. A Special would additionally be paid a bounty of £25 for each year of service, in lieu of pension.

77 *Irish News*, 23 October 1920, 5c; see also Sir William Craig's explanation of the functions of the three classes of Specials: *NIPD*, vol. 2, cols. 1092–3, 19 October 1922.

78 See, for example, the recruitment of the Derry and Antrim units: *Irish Times*, 30 November 1920, 6d. The powers of the Lieutenancy derive from the Crown, but the office is local.

79 Sir James Craig described the C-Specials as 'merely the old men… of the force… The Cs have a more – shall I call it – military formation, although under the same jurisdiction as the rest of the Constabulary.' He added that the C-Specials had been conceived 'because there is always a feeling in my mind that perhaps our military would be taken away, and that having no military we have no military formation to take their place' (*NIPD*, vol. 2, col. 1092, 19 October 1922).

80 The cost of the new force was subsumed into the police vote for Ireland. For the first quarter of the financial year, 1921–2, the cost of the RIC and the Special Constabulary was in excess of £2 million (5 *Hansard*, vol. 143, cols. 2170–1, 29 June 1921).

81 Follis, *A State under Siege, op. cit.*, p. 15. Charles Wickham (1879–1971) had been educated at Harrow, entering the Army in 1899. Boer and Great War service were followed by soldiering in Siberia, as an officer in the British Expeditionary Force in its anti-Bolshevik intervention. Following retirement from the RUC in 1945, he had assignments in Greece and in Palestine. This was a man well acquainted with the political dimensions of policing.

82 See above, p. 65.

83 Wilfred Spender (1876–1960) went from Winchester, via a commission in the militia, into the Royal Artillery. He served in several countries throughout the Empire and was also posted to the General Staff. He formed an early and abiding concern about the strategic implications of the loss of Ireland and opposed Home Rule. A year before the First World War, Spender moved to Belfast, working full-time for the UVF, supported by his army pension and private income. He served with distinction in the First World War, returning to Ulster in 1920, being appointed in 1925 as Secretary of the Ministry of Finance in the Northern Ireland administration. He argued that the state should encourage and reinforce ties with loyalist Catholics; he also believed that full union under Westminster was preferable to devolved government.

84 Section 60(1). This proscribed tenure, terms and conditions and salaries of serving members of the RIC and the Dublin Metropolitan Police.

85 Ryder, *The RUC*, *op. cit.*, pp. 45–7.

86 See *Irish Independent*, 9 March 1921, 4d.

87 *NIPD*, vol. 2, cols. 347–380, 5 April 1922. Henry Lloyd Campbell (1868–1950) was MP for North Belfast between 1921 and 1929. He was the Chairman of H. Campbell & Co., flax spinners. He had been a member of the UVF and was a Freemason and a member of the Orange Order.

88 Constabulary (Ireland) Act, 1922: 12 & 13 Geo. V, c.56. A sum of £735,864 was voted for the new force on 31 May 1922, to meet costs until 31 March 1923 (*NIPD*, vol. 2, col. 767). See also Doherty, *The Thin Green Line*, *op. cit.*, p. 16.

89 *Irish News*, 31 March 1922, 4b.

90 Ryder, *The RUC*, *op. cit.*, pp. 60, 70–1. See also Doherty, *The Thin Green Line*, *op. cit.*, p. 21; Graham Ellison and Jim Smyth, *The Crowned Harp: Policing Northern Ireland* (London: Pluto Press, 2000), p. 25.

91 This was a belief almost as old as Protestantism. Much of the domestic policy of Elizabeth I was conducted against the international ramifications of the Papal Bull of 1570 by which Pius V excommunicated her. The effect of this edict was to sanctify, i.e. to legitimise, any attack on the Queen in person, or on her authority. Roman Catholics, already objects of suspicion, thus acquired a character of disloyalty, or uncertain loyalty. Suspicion and prejudice against Catholics persisted into modern times within public (and sometimes private) life in Britain. And not only in Britain. In the then WASP-dominated USA only half a century ago, the fact of his Catholicism was thought to be an insupportable barrier to John F. Kennedy's possible presidency, before his narrow election victory. Would he be loyal to the Pope or to the USA, commentators worried. See Albert J. Memendez, *The Religious Factor in the 1960 Presidential Election: An Analysis of the Kennedy Victory over Anti-Catholic Prejudice* (Jefferson, NC: McFarland & Co., 2011). See also M. C. Questier and E. H. Shagan, *Elizabeth and the Catholics* (Manchester: Manchester University Press, 2005).

92 Some functionaries were frank about their preferences. In May 1924, Colonel W. B. Spender (Secretary to the Northern Ireland Cabinet) listed the two principal qualifications for a member of the RUC: '1. Ulster birth, 2. Experience and a good record in the Special Constabulary' (PRONI PM/8/4, W. B. Spender to Colonel H. Knox, 2 May 1924).

93 Four members of the Police Committee (William Coote and William Grant, Northern Ireland MPs; Senator Joseph Cunningham; and Sir Joseph Davison, head of the Orange Order in Belfast) all submitted addenda to the Report of the Interim Committee urging more recruits from the A-Specials and a reduction in the RIC quota (Ryder, *The Fateful Split*, *op. cit.*, p. 190). *Irish Times*, 1 February 1922, 5f.

94 PRONI HA/4/119, Monthly Return of Admissions to the RUC, 1923–7. See also *NIPD*, vol. 4, col. 948, 15 May 1924.

95 With the RUC just 100 short of its establishment target, R. D. Megaw, Parliamentary Secretary at the Ministry of Home Affairs, reported that 23 per cent of its members were Roman Catholics (Ryder, *The Fateful Split*, *op. cit.*, p. 71).

96 *NIPD*, vol. 6, col. 823, 26 May 1925.

97 PRONI FIN/30/F/C/13, Michael Collins to Sir James Craig, 11 April 1922. This file contains several letters between Collins, Craig and Churchill, the last being Secretary of State, Irish Office at that time.

98 PRONI FIN/30/F/C/13, W. S. Spender to Sir James Craig, 10 April 1922.

99 *Ibid.*

100 PRONI FIN/30/F/C/13, W. S. Spender to Sir James Craig, 25 April 1922.

101 PRONI FIN/30/F/C/13, W. S. Spender to Sir James Craig, 2 May 1922.

102 PRONI FIN/30/F/C/13, W. S. Spender to Sir James Craig, 7 June 1922.

103 *Ibid.* There was no mention of a Catholic police committee in Craig's last letter in these exchanges, on 16 June 1922.

104 Constabulary (Ireland) Act, 1836: 6 & 7 Will. IV, c.13, s.18 by stipulated oath of office prohibited any participation in politics and (with the exception of the Society of Freemasons) membership of any secret society. The Constabulary and Police (Ireland) Act, 1916: 6 & 7 Geo. V, c.59, schedule 3, removed (but not retroactively) the exemption for Freemasons. This was an issue of considerable importance, not apt for executive decision. For some discussion of this point, see Brian Griffin, 'A Force Divided: Policing Ireland 1900–1960', *History Today*, October 1999, 25–31.

105 Since the Orange Institution was represented on the Ulster Unionist Council, the governing body of the Unionist Party, the Minister's decision was perhaps inevitable, if short-sighted.

106 See S. E. Long, *The Orange Institution* (Belfast: House of Orange, 1978), p. 11; Anon., *The Future Is Orange and Bright* (Glasgow: Grand Lodge of Scotland, c.2003), p. 3.

107 John William Nixon (1880–1949) had risen to the rank of District Inspector in the RIC before moving to the RUC. Following the political speech that incurred the anger of Sir James Craig, Nixon was dismissed. He secured a seat on Belfast Corporation as an Independent Unionist and in 1929 was elected as the Northern Ireland MP for the staunchly Protestant constituency of Belfast Woodvale, holding the seat for the following twenty years, until his death. An effective Parliamentary speaker, with a strong popular following, he was dogged throughout his life by rumours and accusations of involvement in a group of men who targeted and killed Catholics.

108 *Irish News*, 16 April 1923, 8a.

109 *Irish Times*, 16 February 1924, 17d; *Irish News*, 3 March 1924, 8d.

110 PRONI HA/32/1/455; *NIPD*, vol. 4, col. 67, 12 March 1924.

111 *NIPD*, vol. 4, cols. 66–96, 12 March 1924. *Belfast Newsletter*, 30 January 1924, 11c.

112 See author's foreword to Clark, *Guns in Ulster, op. cit.*

113 PRONI HA/32/1/455; *Northern Whig*, 28 March 1925, 7c.

114 *Ibid.*

115 Brian Barton, *Brookeborough: The Making of a Prime Minister* (Belfast: Institute of Irish Studies, 1988), p. 54. On resigning as county commandant, he said that it had been an honour to lead the loyal men of his native county.

116 See, for example, the blanket condemnation of Catholics in police service on grounds of imputed disloyalty and deputations demanding their removal (Doherty, *The Thin Green Line, op. cit.*, p. 23).

117 *Derry Journal*, 27 March 1922, 3e; *Irish Times*, 1 April 1922, 2b; *Irish News*, 25 March 1922, 5a–b.

118 Nixon was successful in two libel suits against publishers who had alleged his involvement in reprisal murders, including the McMahon family: £1,000 against the *Derry Journal* and £1,250 against book publishers Methuen.

119 See Joe Baker, *The McMahon Family Murders and the Belfast Troubles 1920–22* (Belfast: Glenravel, c.1996), p. 8.

120 *Belfast Telegraph*, 3 April 1922, 7b.

121 *Irish News*, 26 June 1922, 5a–b. The two wounded men were Daniel O'Loan and John McCallum, both of whom were maimed. The *Irish News* reported that as far as could be ascertained the military took no part in the shooting, remaining onlookers.

122 The *Northern Whig* carried the statement of the Ministry of Home Affairs, 26 June 1922, 5f.

123 *Northern Whig*, 26 June 1922, 5d. See also 5 *Hansard*, House of Lords, vol. 51, cols. 196–8, for Lord Carson's description of the incident. There are significant discrepancies between the *Whig*'s version and that of Carson, but that it was a revolting atrocity there can be no doubt.

124 PRO HO/144/3089/3.

125 PRO HO/144/3089/5.

126 5 *Hansard*, vol. 157, cols. 663–4, 27 July 1922.

127 Frederick Temple Barrington-Ward (1880–1938) was called to the Bar in 1905; KC in 1919. He was a Fellow of All Souls and in 1930 was appointed a Metropolitan Stipendiary Magistrate, sitting at Thames Magistrates' Court.

128 PRO HO/144/3089/8.

129 PRO HO/144/3089/15.

130 PRO HO/144/3089/17. There had been a report on Wilson's death in the Northern Ireland newspapers on the morning of the attack, and this detail had been included.

131 There had been an attack on the Cushendall police barracks, and the bank had been burned, together with a number of houses, including Shane's Castle (seat of the O'Neill family) (*Freeman's Journal*, 2 May 1922, 5d).

132 PRO HO/144/3089/19. This was on the basis of the doctrine of joint enterprise.

133 PRO HO/144/3089/23.

134 PRO HO/144/3089/26; *Irish News*, 4 July 1923, 5a–b, 6a–d; *Northern Whig*, 4 July 1923, 5g and 6f.

135 PRO HO/144/3089/26.

136 *Irish News*, 30 October 1923, 5c and 6d; 31 October 1923, 5c and 6d–g; 1 November 1923, 5e–f.

137 See the case of farmer Robert Scott, whose widow claimed that he had been killed by Free State soldiers firing across the Co. Monaghan border on 26 March 1922. Scott's widow lodged a compensation claim. Because Scott was not a member of the crown forces, the Northern Ireland government would not pay and asked the British government to seek Free State compensation. In a covering letter, Spender wrote: 'At this period sniping from across the Border into Northern Ireland was prevalent and in consequence some of the inhabitants… had to vacate their farms.' The Free State authorities disputed Mrs Scott's story and refused to pay (PRO HO/144/22345). See also *Irish Times*, 24 March 1922, 5a.

138 PRO HO/144/3915, Anderson Papers, Duke of Abercorn (Governor) to Arthur Henderson, Home Secretary, 10 March 1924; J. H. Thomas, Colonial Secretary, to W. T. Cosgrave, President Executive Council, Free State, 25 March 1924.

139 PRO HO/144/21367, C. H. Blackmore, Assistant Secretary to the Northern Ireland Cabinet, to S. G. Tallents, Imperial Secretary, 11 August 1924. The Imperial Secretary was London's representative and, to a significant extent, monitor, in Northern Ireland. Stephen Tallents (1884–1958) was, on Churchill's suggestion, appointed to this post in June 1922. His confidential reports to London were factual and, in general, calming. He remained in Belfast, liaising and reporting, until recalled early in 1926 when, in more peaceful and stable conditions, the post was abolished. A similar position was found necessary and useful during the modern troubles in Northern Ireland.

140 PRO HO/144/21367/2, Anderson Papers, War Office to Home Office ('Secret'), 25 August 1924.

141 *Ibid.*

142 PRO HO/144/21367/4, Anderson Papers, Sir John Anderson to S. G. Tallents ('Secret'), 1 January 1925.

143 PRO HO/144/21367/5, Anderson Papers, Colonel W. B. Spender, Northern Ireland Cabinet Secretary, to S. G. Tallents, Imperial Secretary ('Secret'), 29 January 1925, my italics. The conference had taken place on 23 January 1925.

144 PRO HO/144/21367/6, Anderson Papers, Sir John Anderson to Army Council ('Secret'), 9 February 1925.

145 PRO HO/144/21367/7, Anderson Papers, Sir John Anderson to S. G. Tallents ('Secret'), 10 March 1925. Eunan O'Halpin points out that, even after 1922 and

Irish independence, London assumed that it retained responsibility for the external defence of the island of Ireland, its seas and airspace. This basic strategic necessity, a cornerstone of British policy for centuries, casts Craig's desire to strike the IRA in its hinterland in an even more improbable light. See Eunan O'Halpin, *Spying on Ireland* (Oxford: Oxford University Press, 2008), p. 5.

146 Defence of the Realm Act, 1914: 4 & 5 Geo. V, c.29 (and successive Acts).

147 And, indeed, in many respects, the Free State legislation entailed a greater abridgement of civil and legal rights and far more drastic punishments of offenders. On 28 September 1922, the Dáil authorised the establishment of military courts. These had extensive powers of punishment, which, together with their elastic jurisdiction, their summary procedures and restricted recognition of the rights of the accused, made them far more formidable instruments of state power and repression than any permitted in the British and Northern Ireland jurisdictions. Proceedings under the measures of 28 September 1922 and subsequent extensions led to severe punishments, including seventy-seven executions. The lack of proportionate legal safeguards led Thomas Johnson (Labour) to try to amend the provisions, to include a lawyer to preside over each tribunal: this proposal was resoundingly rejected (*Dáil Debates*, vol. 1, cols. 899–900, 28 September 1922). Nor was such legislation repealed after the IRA was defeated in the field. In August 1923, a number of public-safety and emergency-powers Acts were brought in. Finger-pointing from the Free State was unjustified against this background of ruthless (some would argue justifiable) protection of state interests. For a useful and succinct summary of these measures and their use, see David Fitzpatrick, *The Two Irelands, 1912–1939* (Oxford: Oxford University Press, 1998), Chapter 4.

148 Fionnuala Ní Aoláin discusses these precepts thoughtfully in her *Law in Times of Crisis: Emergency Powers in Theory and Practice* (Cambridge: Cambridge University Press, 2006); see especially pp. 172–3 in relation to the points made here.

149 Civil Authorities (Special Powers) Act (Northern Ireland), 1922: 12 & 13 Geo. V, c.5 (hereafter Special Powers Act, 1922). For an informative review and discussion of emergency legislation, see Ben Brandon, 'Terrorism, Human Rights and the Rule of Law: 120 Years of the UK's Legal Response to Terrorism', *Criminal Law Review*, December 2004, 981–97. It may also be noted that there was a long history of sweeping legislation under the British Administration in Ireland. Looking back at the century before the Special Powers Act, we can see several points of similarity and indeed continuity between the Suppression of Insurrections (Ireland) Act, 1822 (3 & 4 Geo. IV, c.1) and the Habeas Corpus Suspension (Ireland) Act, 1822: 3 & 4 Geo. IV, c.2, and the Special Powers Acts.

150 After his involvement in the early 1920s, Churchill showed little interest in Ireland, North or South. His own attitude to special powers cannot be in doubt. At the height of the Second World War, Herbert Morrison, Home Secretary in the Coalition government, decided to release from detention under Regulation 18B of DORA, the Fascist leader Sir Oswald Mosley and his wife Diana. These and others like them would undoubtedly have formed the class of collaborators had the Nazi invasion plans succeeded. Morrison's decision provoked a considerable amount of dissatisfied comment and popular anger. Churchill, nevertheless, sent a telegram to Morrison, approving the release: 'The power of the executive to cast a man into prison without formulating any charge known to the law, and particularly to deny him the judgement of his peers, is in the highest degree odious and is the foundation of all totalitarian government, whether Nazi or Communist.' See also Cornelius P. Cotter, 'Emergency Detention in Wartime: The British Experience', *Stanford Law Review*, 6 (2) (1954): 238–86. There was reference to Mosley's release in the *Irish Press*, 18 November 1943, 1e. Certain Irish nationalists recalled Mosley's sympathy towards the Irish cause.

151 Special Powers Act, 1922, ss.I(1 and 2).

152 Opposing the 1922 Bill, George B. Hanna, who later became a member of the Northern government, observed that it gave the Minister for Home Affairs 'power to do whatever he likes or let someone else do what he likes for him' (*NIPD*, vol. 2, col. 102, 21 March 1922). He also insisted that the Bill was so comprehensive that, were it passed, the House would have nothing more to do with it. The Minister for Home Affairs could, moreover, pass his vast authority to a police officer, '[a] man of whom he may never have heard, and he has then full authority of this House after it has abandoned its fundamental function of restoring order' (*NIPD*, vol. 2, col. 101, 21 March 1922).

153 This is a basic constitutional division in the unwritten British constitution, fastened and secured by convention, practice, legislation and case law. See, for example, A. W. Bradley and K. D. Ewing, *Constitutional and Administrative Law*, 15th edn (London: Longman, 2011), Chapter 4; see also Hilaire Barnett, *Constitutional and Administrative Law*, 8th edn (London and New York: Routledge, 2011).

154 The kernel of the argument was put by the Attorney General, Anthony Babington. Order had indeed been restored, yet those opposed to the renewal of the Act wished to discard a measure that had been instrumental in combating disorder. Were trouble to break out again the advantage of retaining the Act was that it would be unnecessary 'to go through the long and laborious process' of re-enactment, thus avoiding the possible loss of life and damage to property that such a delay might entail (*NIPD*, vol. 8, col. 1963, 12 October 1927: debate on the Expiring Laws Bill).

155 Civil Authorities (Special Powers) Act (Northern Ireland), 1933: 23 & 24 Geo. V, c.12 (hereafter Special Powers Act, 1933), s.12.

156 PRONI CAB/4/208/27, Memorandum for the Cabinet, ff. 2–3.

157 PRONI CAB/4/208/27, Memorandum for the Cabinet, f. 3.

158 *Ibid.*

159 This was, ironically, steered through its second reading by George B. Hanna, who had expressed strong concerns in 1922. Hanna denied that the Act was to be made permanent. The amendment, he disingenuously pointed out, simply secured the Act on the statute books 'until Parliament otherwise determines' (*NIPD*, vol. 15, cols. 847–8, 14 March 1933).

160 Special Powers Act, 1933.

161 Special Powers Act, 1922, s.2(4).

162 See Peter H. Solomon, 'Soviet Criminal Justice under Stalin', *American Historical Review*, 103 (5) (1998): 1657, *et seq.* For one of many examples of the effectiveness of Stalinism's stage-setting by means of legal forms and its effective deceptive character, see also the memoir of a former US Ambassador to the Soviet Union at the height of the show trials: Joseph E. Davies, *Mission to Moscow* (London: Victor Gollancz, 1942). (Davies was gulled and became an apologist.)

163 Explosive Substances Act, 1883: 46 & 47 Vict., c.3.

164 Firearms Act, 1920: 10 & 11 Geo. V, c.43. This was a comprehensive measure, dealing with the purchase, possession and use of firearms; the granting of firearms certificates; sale and manufacture and forfeitures. Section 7 of the Act linked possession with intent to injure to s.5(3) of the Explosive Substances Act, 1883, and thus equipped the court with a possible maximum sentence of life at penal servitude.

165 Demanding money with menaces was dealt with by s.30 of the Larceny Act, 1916: 6 & 7 Geo. V, c.50. Arson was defined either by common law or statute or any offence punishable on indictment under the Malicious Damage Act, 1861: 24 & 25 Vict., c.97.

166 My italics. Section 2 of the 1883 Act provided for a sentence of up to life at penal servitude for causing an explosion with intent to endanger life or property. Section 3

provided for up to twenty years' penal servitude for attempting or conspiring to cause an explosion with intent.

167 In sequence, these offences arose from Regulations 1, 15, 18, 22A; s.2(b) of the Act and Regulation 24A.

168 Section 2(2) of the Act; Regulation 8.

169 See Henry Stephens Salt, *The Flogging Craze* (London: Allen & Unwin, 1916), p. 76. See also Seán McConville, *English Local Prisons, 1860–1900: Next Only to Death* (London and New York: Routledge, 1995), pp. 247–8, for observations on the regulation of flogging in the late nineteenth century.

170 *NIPD*, vol. 2, col. 86, *et seq.* During the second reading of the Bill, R. D. Megaw, the Home Affairs Parliamentary Secretary, referred to the flogging clauses: 'The use of bombs and explosives is one of the most nefarious means that one can think of in the commission of crimes… intended to do injury to life or property, in the most cowardly, sneakish fashion, and the person who is so degraded as to use a bomb certainly merits no leniency at the hands of justice' (*NIPD*, vol. 2, col. 90). The imposition of flogging for explosives and other offences met with general approval, R. J. Lynn calling for the possession of a bomb, on person or premises, to be made a capital offence (*NIPD*, vol. 2, col. 92). S. McGuffin also considered flogging to be an inadequate penalty for carrying a bomb (*NIPD*, vol. 2, col. 94). Such sentiments were to be repeated elsewhere in the debates on the Bill. This was a hanging as well as a flogging parliament.

171 In order, s.7 of the Act, Regulations 3 and 21, 3 and 18, 3 and 18c and 23.

172 Regulation 7A.

173 The history of habeas corpus is long and complex. Many defects in arrangements were remedied by the Habeas Corpus Act, 1679 (31 Cha. II, c.2), 1816 (56 Geo. III, c.100) and 1862 (25 & 26 Vict., c.20). For a discussion of background and for detail, see T. P. Taswell-Langmead, *English Constitutional History*, ed. T. F. T. Plucknett, 11th edn (London: Sweet & Maxwell, 1960), pp. 432–6. There was considerable resistance throughout the following century to campaigns to extend habeas corpus in Ireland, successive lords lieutenants and law officers claiming that conditions there were too uncertain.

174 It is rare that in Britain a material witness (or possibly complainant) is detained, but it has happened even in modern times. It is not uncommon for witness summonses to be issued (for example in cases of alleged domestic violence). This process could, in rare instances, lead to imprisonment.

175 The resident magistrate was a stipendiary as distinct from a lay magistrate (justice of the peace). The latter office is of great antiquity, traceable at least as far back as the 1360s. Urbanisation made it necessary to introduce full-time paid magistrates – a controversial innovation since it was thought that they would be overly subject to government control. By the 1790s, Dublin had stipendiary police magistrates, and they were appointed in the provinces in 1814. The office and title of resident magistrate (RM) was created in 1822. By 1912, there were sixty-four RMs in Ireland. The office was retained in Northern Ireland after Partition. Their role in the administration of justice was consolidated in 1935 when legal qualifications were required of new appointees. At the same time, justices of the peace were deprived of their judicial powers. See Summary Jurisdiction & Criminal Justice (Northern Ireland) Act, 1935: 25 & 26 Geo. V, c.13, s.3(1). Northern Ireland's RMs were renamed district judges in June 2008, in line with a similar change in Britain.

176 That court, often unfairly represented as no more than an instrument of executive power, conducted all its proceedings in public and had jurisdiction over all matters touching on public order and security as well as violations of royal commands, proclamations, grants and the like. The span of responsibility was in some ways similar

to that addressed by the Special Powers Act: only three centuries and equity separated them. See Black, *The Reign of Elizabeth, op. cit.*, pp. 210–11; see also M. Stuckey, 'The Evolution of the "Star Chamber"', *Australian Law Journal*, 68 (9) (1994): 670 *et seq.*

177 Internal exile was a measure frequently used in tsarist Russia and (in a more severe form) by the Soviet Union. Banning and exclusion orders would be extensively used by the Apartheid government in South Africa. See the case of Cahir Healy, below, pp. 352–60.

178 A hearing before lay justices of the peace would at least have opened the possibility of a more obvious ventilation of a case. Rightly or wrongly, RMs might be seen as being too close to the police. Those holding equivalent office in England from the late eighteenth until the early twentieth centuries were informally and popularly known as 'police magistrates' who sat in 'police courts'.

179 *Report of a Commission of Inquiry Appointed to Examine the Purpose and Effect of the Civil Authorities (Special Powers) Act (Northern Ireland) 1922 & 1933* (hereafter NCCL Commission Report) (London: National Council for Civil Liberties, 1936), p. 25. The Commission also noted that more than half the resident magistrates were former military or police officers and that three of the eleven had no legal qualifications.

180 As has happened recently in terrorist-linked cases in the UK.

181 Sections 10(1 and 2).

182 PRO HO/144/10534/1. Perhaps because of his background Archdale was seen to embody an especially assertive form of unionism. In constituents' minds his long service in the Royal Navy was as indicative of his awareness of unionist sensitivities as was his farming in the always uneasy and territorially sensitive county of Fermanagh. For a biographical note see above, pp. 99–100, n. 20.

183 Post Office Act, 1908: 8 Edw. VII, c.48. This section of the Act provided little direct guidance in itself, merely referring to the opening of postal packages by authority of a secretary of state's warrant. Had the matter ever gone to a court for review, however, the wording 'in obedience to an *express warrant* in writing under the hand of a Secretary of State' (my italics) could have caused difficulty. The implication is that a warrant should be issued for each case in which interception was intended. If the words 'express warrant' have significance, it must be in the sense of a warrant being particular, and that would entail specification of the name and address of the recipient of post and the duration of any warrant. Section 82 of the Act referred to regulations and warrants and required any new regulation to be laid before both Houses of Parliament. The making of any general policy of interception in Northern Ireland could not, therefore, have been concealed. There is a further and perhaps more intractable problem in that the arrangement entered into in June 1922 involved delegation of the power to the Minister for Home Affairs. Legislation conferred no power of this kind, and it is certainly a long way from the restrictive wording of s.56. It is hard to resist the conclusion that Northern Ireland's postal censorship was illegal or extra-legal from the outset. How far the Northern Ireland operation had stretched s.56 of the 1908 Act may be gleaned from an earlier statement on interception, made in May 1909, in which Herbert Gladstone referred to the use of the power 'to trace the perpetrators of serious crimes' and to intercept 'grossly indecent literature' coming from abroad (*Hansard*, vol. 5, cols. 538–9, 19 May 1909).

184 GOIA s.9(2).

185 PRO HO/144/10534/7–8. Given the tendency for Sir Dawson Bates to believe that Catholics in general, and nationalists in particular, were intrinsically disloyal, this was loose and politically risky wording for Churchill to agree. He must by this time have had a fair grasp of the opinions of Bates and some of his colleagues.

186 PRO HO/144/10534/9.

187 PRO HO/144/10534/11.
188 PRO HO/144/10534/13. How 'regularisation' was to be effected was not explained.
189 PRO HO/144/10534/16.
190 5 *Hansard*, vol. 175, col. 1984, 8 July 1924. Interestingly, the reply to Healy's question included the information that the Governor of Northern Ireland had some authority in the matter. For a biographical note on Cahir Healy see below, pp. 364–5, n. 49.
191 PRO HO/144/10534/27. Besides its questionable legality, the general programme of censorship was bound to be enormously costly and, *pace* the army and police, largely ineffective. The interception of the post of individuals in whom the police were definitely interested was quite another matter – though, of course, much depended on the quality of the initial informers and the willingness of the subjects freely to use the post.
192 PRO HO/144/10534/50.

3

CLOSING THE BOOKS
Britain and Ireland, 1920–6

Gate fever

A truce between the IRA and British forces in Ireland was signed on 9 July 1921 and came into effect two days later. This was not a final settlement between the parties but cleared the way for Sinn Féin, the IRA's political counterpart, to enter into discussions with the British government. The document set out the steps for military disengagement and committed both parties not to attack each other and also to refrain from aggressive preparations.[1] In theory, it was a command of 'freeze' to all involved; the reality was otherwise. The IRA undertook staff work, intelligence gathering, planning, training, re-equipping and regrouping; local units and individuals raided and confronted British forces.[2] On its part, the British Army planned and prepared for action in the event of a return to hostilities – an event that, when the Truce was signed, seemed more likely than not. In theory, these manoeuvrings violated the agreement, but in everyday life they were inevitable: 'freeze' is possible only at children's parties.

Republican prisoners in Britain, numbering more than 500, were electrified by the news. Was release now imminent? Did British recognition of Sinn Féin as a negotiating partner mean that conditions of confinement would change? The captives fell into four categories. The first and largest consisted of some 220 persons convicted in Ireland, sentenced to penal servitude and removed to prisons in England for reasons of security and because of a lack of suitable accommodation in Ireland. These were held at three English convict prisons with the main concentration (about 190) at Dartmoor. A second group had been sentenced to imprisonment (as distinct from penal servitude) for offences committed in Ireland. These 277 men were dispersed over thirty-three prisons.[3] (The Home Office would have preferred to spread the convicts in similarly small groups but did not have the accommodation to do so.) Another category was made up of fifty-five persons convicted in Britain and sentenced in the usual way.[4] Their offences clearly arose from the Anglo-Irish struggle, but members of this group were denied the political status which was generally (but not invariably) granted to transferees from Ireland. The fourth and smallest group consisted of persons remanded in custody in Britain for politically motivated offences but against whom proceedings had not yet been completed.

Understandably, the prospect of imminent release, a material change in their conditions or the dropping of proceedings greatly unsettled all these prisoners. Five days after the Truce came into effect, and in a well-timed action, some eighty Irish convicts mutinied at Dartmoor. Less than half the usual complement of warders was on duty (it was a Saturday afternoon). On command, the men, who, most unwisely, had been allowed to exercise together, refused to return to their cells. They began instead to sing and shout and to throw their clothes on the ground. Staff at the relatively remote and self-contained community of Princetown (where Dartmoor Prison is located) lived near the prison and were swiftly called back by the alarm bell. The protesters were forced back to their cells, staves being used by the warders. Six convicts and four warders were injured. A military guard was temporarily posted at the prison, and plans were drawn up (but not implemented) to redistribute what had become a truculent and potentially unmanageable group of fit, organised and well-motivated prisoners.[5]

Michael Collins unintentionally stirred things up when he took time off from the Anglo-Irish negotiations to pay a comfort visit to Pentonville Prison on 14 October 1921. After Collins's pep talk, Pentonville's thirty-six political prisoners demanded changes. Their first act of defiance was to talk during exercise, which was strictly prohibited. Cautions were issued at first, then punishments. This led to the familiar spiral of misconduct, punishment, confrontation, increased punishment, further and more serious misconduct, and so forth. Some prisoners began to destroy their cells; others refused food. Since peace talks were under way, the men wanted immediate release. Failing this, they demanded suspension of the silence rule, separation from ordinary criminal prisoners, better food, permission to smoke and to be exempted from work. Major Wallace Blake, the governor, got little support from the Home Office but managed to avoid further confrontations.[6] These were the blessed days of falling prison populations and empty cells and wings. Blake made use of his spare accommodation to separate the Irish politicals from the criminal prisoners. He may have been intrigued by these men and spent some time talking politics and reasoning. Familiarity bred a deal of respect, and he reported to the Home Office that, '[t]hey are really very decent fellows, merely suffering from the characteristics of their race – obstinacy, pugnacity and an imaginary sense of injustice'.[7] With some grumbling, the Home Office agreed to let things be but insisted that Pentonville would not be a precedent for the other thirty-two local prisons in which Irish political offenders were confined.

Of the fifty-five men convicted of pre-Truce offences in Britain and sentenced to penal servitude, the largest single group comprised sixteen men involved in the Erskine Street Club conspiracy.[8] With sentences ranging from three to fifteen years' penal servitude, these had been sent to Dartmoor but were not held on D Wing with the other Irish prisoners, who had been convicted and sentenced in Ireland. Shortly after the mutiny, the Erskine Street men demanded to be located with those they saw as their comrades. Their leader, Patrick O'Donoghue (Michael Collins's man in Manchester and a participant in de Valera's Lincoln Prison escape) petitioned to be moved to D Wing. He pointed out that his offence was purely political and that he was an IRA officer. As was customary, he also protested at the humiliation of being forced to associate with the criminal classes. His petition was refused, and the Erskine Street group threatened a general disturbance by all the Irish prisoners at Dartmoor.[9] This did not come off.

That autumn of 1921 was a far from easy time in English prisons, either for staff or for prisoners. The convict regime, inflexible and severe, was a daily dose of gall for men who scented freedom; local prisons, with the emphasis on separation and hard labour, were little easier to bear. Back in Ireland, men from IRA units walked openly, triumphantly and in arms, protected by the Truce: the contrast in conditions could not have been greater. The tedium and discomfort of prison life and the sense of time and opportunities passing were suffocating. But relief eventually did come. When the Anglo-Irish Treaty was signed on 6 December 1921 there was an immediate release of some 2,000 persons detained in Ireland under Regulation 14b of the ROIA.[10] Those who had actually been convicted (with the exception of five women immediately released) had to wait for another month until, by a slender majority, the Treaty was ratified by the Dáil. Five days after that (a weekend, and no little uncertainty and turmoil had intervened), Dublin Castle, now in the service of the Provisional government, telegraphed a request to the Home Office that all those Irish prisoners convicted of politically motivated offences in the twenty-six counties of the Irish Free State should be released. By 23 January 1922, all had been freed except for one man who was too unwell to travel and another whose political status was in question.

Those who had committed offences in England, largely during the IRA bombing and arson campaign, had to wait for a further three weeks for their cases to be reviewed and the necessary official procedures to be completed. And how those days must have dragged by: drudgery interspersed with runs and riffs of rumour and alarm. These cases had been considered by a subcommittee of Winston Churchill's Provisional Government of Ireland Cabinet Committee. On 30 January, the Cabinet authorised freedom for all those convicted or held in custody for pre-Truce offences. On 11 February, Downing Street requested the Home Office to go ahead with the releases. The extent to which political and executive interference in judicial processes may be pushed can be seen in the fact that, even in these circumstances of historic change, the Director of Public Prosecutions (DPP) had wished to free only six and to reduce the sentences of seven. DPP advice was overruled and, indeed, was inappropriate to the political circumstances. On 11 February, fifty-five persons convicted of offences committed between 24 January and 18 July 1921 were released by royal warrant, their sentences having been remitted.[11] There remained fifteen, who had been convicted between 5 November 1921 and 15 February 1922 for offences committed after the Truce had been signed. Sentences were mainly short terms of imprisonment, but on J. P. Connolly, said to be the IRA's chief arms agent, operating in south Wales, a sentence of fourteen years' penal servitude was imposed.[12] The Provisional government naturally felt itself under a moral obligation to these men (and one woman) who had been part of the republican enterprise. As we have seen, the IRA continued to train, regroup and acquire arms during the Truce period. Those now in the Dublin government had, to varying degrees, been complicit in some violation of the Truce terms. Kevin O'Higgins, who at this point was the principal Provisional government minister liaising with the British government, pressed the prisoners' case for amnesty. Within Churchill's sub-committee there had been some debate and disagreement. On the face of it, the offences had been dishonourable, since they violated an agreement; public opinion also had to be considered. Eventually, the desire to draw a line and move on – and London's interest in buttressing the Provisional government – prevailed, and the fifteen were freed on 1 April 1922.[13]

With those releases, the books had been largely, but not totally, closed, at least as far as the British government was directly concerned. The few remaining cases would have been a political step too far. All governments view with particular repugnance (and some fear) soldiers who violate their oath of allegiance. Especially in those years, with the memory of the immense losses, bravery and sacrifice of the Great War so raw, painful and omnipresent, no other response was imaginable. Even fifty years before, in comparatively peaceful times, British soldiers who had violated their oath by enlisting in the Fenian Brotherhood had been denied amnesty for several years after their civilian comrades.[14] Similar issues now arose with the Connaught Rangers, sixty-one of whom were serving sentences of between two years' imprisonment and twenty years' penal servitude for their part in the mutiny at Jalandhar in the Punjab on 28 June 1920.[15] There was also the case of Joseph Dowling, who, as a prisoner of war (POW) of the Germans, had joined Roger Casement's notorious and ill-fated Irish Brigade. In British eyes this was bad enough: Dowling had almost certainly brought himself within the reach of the Treason Act under which Casement had been tried and hanged. The aggravating factor, bringing the case even closer to Casement's, was that Dowling had, on 12 April 1918, landed on an island off the coast of Galway on a secret mission organised by the Germans (the purpose and details of which are still apparently unknown).

Within the British government, and within Parliament, there was great reluctance to put these men on the same footing as civilians who in various ways had conspired, organised or taken up arms in Ireland or Britain. The excesses of the Auxiliaries and, even more notoriously, the Black and Tans, had become widely known and had, to a large extent, rebalanced the moral and political scales that affected public opinion: it was easy to accept that there had been wrongs on both sides. Many, even outside republican circles, nevertheless looked with some compassion on the Connaught Rangers, whose mutiny had been sparked by reports of Black and Tan atrocities and excesses in Ireland. Irish former officers of the British Army lobbied on behalf of the Rangers. This plea was taken up by the Free State government, and the thirty-nine remaining in custody at five

English prisons were released in January 1923.[16] Dowling's case lingered, since the British government was anxious not to create a precedent for several similar cases (not Irish).[17] Relations between the Free State and British governments had rapidly grown in confidence and warmth, and, as one of the fruits of this strengthening relationship, Dowling and men involved in a few other difficult cases were eventually released. The introduction of an Indemnity Act by the Free State, and the need to cover President Cosgrave's position against his domestic critics, provided the necessary impetus for clemency to be granted.[18]

Difficult decisions

Francis Breen

There still remained prisoners who, for various reasons, failed to meet even the much liberalised criteria for clemency. These cases lingered as an item on the Anglo-Irish agenda throughout the 1920s. One such case was that of Francis Breen, who became something of a cause célèbre in English liberal circles and eventually a focus for veteran republicans. His case can represent others and is therefore worth recounting in some detail. Breen's first political conviction, in July 1921, had been for the possession of explosives and firearms and for conspiracy to commit treason. He was a major figure in arms procurement and had been caught in flagrante delicto with an associate, John McGallogly, whilst visiting an arms dump. His father, John Patrick Breen, and brother, Gerald (sometimes Gerard), were arrested later.[19] Whilst on remand, Francis Breen had submitted the first of what would be several petitions, asking for political or POW status: his offence was purely political. He also argued that by signing the Truce the British government had recognised the IRA, in which he was a volunteer. The Home Office simply minuted his petition: 'A mere protest – not strictly speaking a petition. Lay by.'[20] Francis was brought to trial and sentenced to five years' penal servitude.[21]

Within ten days of arriving at Dartmoor, Breen petitioned again. As a member of the IRA, he wanted (as had the Erskine Street men) to be transferred to D Wing, to be with those convicted in Ireland. The Dartmoor governor understandably thought that this mutinous group did not need another desperado.[22] This was of little consequence, however, since Breen was to spend rather less than six months at Dartmoor. His sentence was remitted by royal warrant as part of the general release on the ratification of the Treaty. But this was the beginning rather than the end of his prison career.

Smouldering for months, civil war broke into luxuriant flame in the Irish Free State on 28 June 1922. The republican movement, already in bitter dispute, now divided into two major and a number of minor factions.[23] This splintering was reflected in the ranks of overseas sympathisers and activists. In Ireland itself, anti-Treaty IRA operatives were immediately deprived of funds and supplies and took to seizures, requisitions and robberies to maintain their organisation, personnel and operations.[24] Robberies were also authorised in England and Scotland. In a ham-fisted and badly bungled operation, Francis Breen and three others held up a bank at Prestwich, near Manchester, and stole £244. Three of the four were armed. Two of the raiders (Bartley Iago, sometimes Igo, and John Foley) were arrested soon thereafter at Bolton. Francis Breen and Patrick Joseph Gavin (sometimes Galvin) escaped to the Free State. The Lancashire police confirmed that the proceeds of the robbery were to go to the opponents of the Provisional government.[25]

In one of the first instances of Anglo-Irish police cooperation under the new dispensation, the Home Office wrote to its Dublin counterpart, the Ministry of Home Affairs, on 24 August 1922, giving details of the crime, the likely Dublin address of Breen and Gavin and requesting their arrest on Lancashire warrants.[26] Almost by return, Dublin promised that Irish police would energetically pursue the men. Arrest was not so easy to effect, however, since Breen was an active republican, under cover for several months and knew well how to duck and dodge. Eventually, his luck ran out, and, on 6 May 1923, he was handed over to Lancashire police.[27]

Back in Manchester prison, Breen asked again for a petition form. He now wanted to be handed over to the Free State Army. It was a bizarre plea. He claimed that he had committed far more serious offences in the Free State than in England, including attacks on soldiers and complicity in the shooting of Detective Inspector Matthew Daly of the Dublin Crime Investigation Department (CID).[28] Breen disingenuously denied that he had it in mind that he would be released in Ireland on the cessation of hostilities. On the contrary, he pointed out, were he returned to the Free State, he would very likely be tortured and executed for his crimes.[29] Despite the notion that greater retribution lurked on the other side of the Irish Sea, the Home Office preferred the bird in hand. In a volte-face, at Manchester Assizes on 23 July 1923, Breen pleaded guilty to armed robbery, larceny, four counts of using firearms and the possession of firearms. He pleaded guilty, he said, to avoid being returned to Ireland where he was wanted and would be shot.[30]

Breen was sentenced to penal servitude for life. Next only to the death penalty, this was the most severe penalty available to English courts, and it was hardly surprising that in the weeks and months following sentence Breen entered a period of rage, disgust and despair. Some of his ire turned against former comrades, and whilst at Manchester Prison he made extensive disclosures about his IRA activities. At the time of his 1921 arrest, he stated, he was a member of the Manchester brigade of the IRA, shipping arms to Ireland under the orders of IRA headquarters, then composed of Richard Mulcahy ('now described as Commandant in Chief, National Army'), Piaras Béaslaí ('now described as Commander General') and several other men.[31] He went on to name those from whom he had received arms, all now officers in the Free State Army.[32] Other accomplices who had returned to Ireland (and who presumably had taken the Free State side in the Civil War) were also named. He detailed his gun-running operation and named the principal figures: 'When all these men are arrested I will give evidence against them at their trial.'[33] The apparent intention of these revelations was to drive a wedge between the Irish and British governments. Breen also wished to vent his spite by giving up former comrades to the police. But this was naivety. London had not the slightest intention of raking over the ashes of the recent conflict and was even less inclined to disrupt its vital relationship with the new Irish government. Breen's offer of testimony was marked 'Lay By'.[34] In conflict, as in many other spheres, the rule is 'woe to the losers'.

The Dartmoor of the 1920s was as strict, harsh and challenging as its nineteenth-century overseers, Sir Joshua Jebb and Sir Edmund Du Cane, had intended. The object was to grind down the spirit and to mortify the body in toil, drudgery, stultifying routine and unremitting deprivation and discomfort. Only the tiniest of ameliorations were offered as inducements for compliance. It was an impressive and minutely considered apparatus of suffering in which the full repressive powers of the state were brought to bear. Some found that the best way to cope with this ingenious little world of torment was to disengage from the outside, to subside into a type of hibernation and to live as a creature drifting on the tide of routine. Abandoning hope and living only in the present, pain was lessened, endurance strengthened. This was not Breen's way. He seethed with defiance. His accomplices had received sentences of ten years. Even more unjustly and provocatively, others were now in secure and attractive state employment in Ireland. His 1921 gun-running conviction, Breen thought, had prejudiced his judge. He had been amnestied for that offence and the slate had thereby been wiped clean: his record should not therefore be taken as an aggravation, meriting extra punishment. Officials saw things differently. Apart from the fact that he had not been amnestied for his 1921 gun-running but had had his sentence remitted (a not wholly technical point), the longer sentence was merited because he was the ringleader of the robbery. The government saw the survival of the Free State as a British national interest and looked fiercely on those who sought to wound or kill the fledgling.

Breen's anger envenomed his every twist and turn; constraint and humiliation made him the instrument of his own punishment. The Dartmoor chaplain described him as 'sullen & at enmity with mankind in general'. He called himself a freethinker but the chaplain thought him a Bolshevist. There was even less restraint in the governor's four-year report to the Prison Commission:

> Slippery as an eel – Sinn Feiner. Will stick at nothing – would rob a blind kitten of milk if it would benefit himself. At one time a great friend of Conlon – Sinn Feiner who was here & who recently escaped from Belfast. They quarrelled & I gained information from Breen which helped me watch Conlon. He has read a lot – but not the right stuff. Considers that he has been severely & unjustly sentenced. Requires watching all day & night.[35]

This last proved all too accurate. On 5 February 1928 Breen and another prisoner attempted to escape. Captured and brought to account, he insisted that he had been driven to escape by a long and unjust sentence. The Home Office was unimpressed.[36]

Had he followed the 'submarine' strategy and shown himself to be reasonably compliant at Dartmoor, then in the spirit of Anglo-Irish reconciliation, a degree of latitude might have been possible. But anger drove Breen into persistent rebellions and unruly behaviour. A year after his failed escape, and still on the escape list, he submitted a petition for his forfeited smoking and association privileges to be restored. His tone was so defiant and contemptuous that the Visiting Committee thought he should be given further punishment: 'The "privilege" is nothing to me & I don't want it, & would refuse it if offered, but I emphatically object to the petty official tyranny which, in its psychological effects at least, is infinitely worse than the brutality of "the good old days".'[37] The ceaseless pangs and regrets of captivity and daily servitude now wholly possessed and drove him, and Breen seemed set to serve another decade or more. The Home Office was content to leave him to the inevitable debilitation of the years and the heavy attrition of convict discipline.

Here was an unlikely subject for a clemency campaign. A petty criminal before becoming an IRA man, he had in custody, and with mean and spiteful intent, revealed all he knew about former associates and had offered to turn King's Evidence (though it is hard to say how widely this treachery to his cause was known). By his own admission, he had been party to the killing of a Dublin CID man. His prison behaviour crossed far over the border from the defiance of fortitude into an undignified and constant truculence.

But times were changing, both in Britain and in Ireland. Ramsay MacDonald's second Labour administration took office on 5 June 1929. Although the largest party, Labour had no overall majority. This obliged it to adopt a relatively neutral programme, needing Liberal support on most issues: MacDonald nevertheless looked set for a full term.[38] There were immediate approaches from prisoner-support groups. First off the stocks was the Nelson Branch of the Irish Self-Determination League (ISDL), which wrote to the Home Office just four days after Labour took office. Enclosed was a list issued by the Women Prisoners' Defence League (WPDL), which had its office in Parnell Square in Dublin.[39] This Dublin organisation was to be at the centre of the amnesty campaign which then got under way. A briefing for J. R. Clynes, the new Home Secretary, shows officials' irritation and a deal of contempt.[40] The WPDL was 'an organisation of old ladies of advanced Republican views'. These campaigned for the release of 'alleged political prisoners' as well as ameliorations in their treatment: 'Mrs Maud Gonne MacBride is the leader and the whole group consists only of about 20 females who hold regular weekly meetings in Dublin rather analogous to our Sunday meetings in Hyde Park. It is regarded as of no importance by the Irish Free State Police Authorities.'[41] This last was to prove a considerable misjudgement, and in due course the 'old ladies' would show that they still knew how to ring bells and pull levers.

Their first move was to warm the teapot by sending a note of congratulation to MacDonald and each member of his cabinet. Labour's accession was 'a hopeful and inspiring sign' making for peace and unity and relief of unemployment. Fairly briskly this led on to the proposition that, as a token of goodwill, the new government should at once release four Irish political prisoners: Breen (Dartmoor), Iago, Foley and Gavin (Maidstone). With some disregard for the facts, the WPDL contended that these cases were relics of the Anglo-Irish War (the bank robbery had been a year after the Truce) and that the men's continued imprisonment simply kept bitter memories alive. Their robbery had not been for personal gain; they had acted under orders. Nor were they forgotten in Ireland. Their names were read out at weekly public meetings, and even non-republicans resented their continued detention. Clemency would be greatly appreciated by the Irish at home, in England and in America. The letter was signed by Maud Gonne and Bridie O'Mullane, Honorary Secretaries of the League.[42]

The WPDL instigated a campaign of letter-writing, being careful to extend this beyond the usual republican front organisations and more obvious fellow-travellers. They had little difficulty in getting support from the Irish section of the Women's International League, which shared a deal of common membership and connections. The League's International General Secretary was Chicago-based Jane Addams (highly respected and shortly to win the Nobel Prize for Peace), and a Home Office note described the British section of the organisation as 'thoroughly constitutional'. The League had cleverly addressed its plea to Margaret Bondfield, MP and later the first British woman to achieve ministerial rank.[43]

And there were, of course, letters from openly republican organisations, such as the Roger Casement Sinn Féin Club. (A combination of names more likely to produce a Home Office spasm is hard to imagine.) To make the correspondence thoroughly comprehensive, the Adjutant-General of the IRA also wrote to the Home Secretary on 6 January 1930, using the army's very own letterhead, 'General Headquarters, Dublin'. The purpose of the letter is hard to gauge, unless it were explicitly to confirm Breen, Gavin, Iago and Foley as members of the IRA, a fact that none disputed. The letter did note that the bank robbery was 'duly authorised by the Competent Authority here'. Much of the rest was a caricature of IRA speak: rhetoric, name-calling, jargon and formulaic phrases and sentences – a revolutionary's letter-by-numbers. There was, however, some attempt to reason. For stealing a sum of only £300, the sentences, even supposing the men to be ordinary criminals, were far too heavy. English judges took a very poor view of robbery with violence, and the firing of shots was a substantial aggravation. But the writer still had a point: the sentences were heavy, and Breen's was excessive – were his record to be disregarded in sentencing. Having made the basis of a rational case, the pen again slipped into purple ink: 'In honesty you must concede that racial hatred, and perhaps even panic dictated these savage sentences at the time.' Recalling the Labour Party's statements about liberty and justice whilst in opposition, the Adjutant-General hoped it would now act accordingly and concluded, '[h]aving set out the facts of the particular case mentioned, I hereby demand that these prisoners should be set at liberty without delay, and thus repair in some measure a long-standing injustice, and a breach of the recognised rules of warfare in regard to prisoners of war'.[44] Full marks for chutzpah, nil for diplomacy.[45] To the other letters on this subject, Clynes, following the advice of his officials, sent the same stonewalling reply: he was not justified in recommending remission of sentence for Breen and others now in English prisons; communications concerning any Belfast prisoners had to be sent to the Northern Ireland Minister for Home Affairs.[46]

Maud Gonne and the other old ladies had been immersed in radical politics for so long that official rebuffs were the very stuff of encouragement. Indeed, some of them had helped develop and refine the basics of attritionary (as distinct from persuasive) campaigning. The Labour Party included a significant radical element, even in Parliament, and liked to don the raiment of idealism. The government was, moreover, dependent on a close-to-total commitment of votes by its MPs. The point of vulnerability could not have been clearer. The WPDL first persuaded members of the Parliamentary Labour Party to write to the Home Secretary.[47] Questions were raised in the House, and an issue was created around visits to the men.[48] Ever secure in its citadel, the Home Office was unyielding: such requests from MPs did not come within the rules governing visits.[49] Clynes insisted that the offences of Breen, Foley, Iago and Gavin were not of a character that came within the terms of the amnesty.[50] John Scurr, MP (who had himself been briefly imprisoned), wrote to the Free State government: he had been told that, were it to agree, Breen and the others would be released.[51] The Free State government replied that it had no information on the matter.[52] Fenner Brockway, MP, another old lag, asked about Breen's health and was told that it was good (he had by now been transferred to Parkhurst Prison), except for some slight eye problems.[53]

Intelligent and definitely a cut above the average though they were, these remained fairly standard lobbying tactics, and after nine months or so, they seemed to have run into the sand. The WPDL raised the stakes. On St Patrick's Day 1930, Charlotte Despard and Hanna Sheehy-Skeffington opened a campaign of public meetings.[54] The first of these, under the auspices of the Manchester Irish Political Prisoners' Committee, was held in the constituency of John Clynes, the Home Secretary. The audience was largely republican in sympathies, and Sheehy-Skeffington threatened to send speakers all over England until the men were released.[55] Whether this would have had any effect is hard to say. Certainly had the meetings been concentrated on the less safe Labour seats where there was a significant Irish population (and there were a number of these), it could have been uncomfortable for the MPs concerned.

As we have seen, there had been a deal of sympathy for the WPDL campaign. Concerns had been raised, and not only among the rank and file. Sir Charles Trevelyan had been President of the Board of Education in MacDonald's first administration and returned to that post in 1929.[56] When he received his copy of the IRA's letter of 6 January, he immediately wrote to Clynes. He was surprised that such prisoners were still being held. Under the misapprehension that Francis Breen was the brother of Dan Breen (he was not), he went on:

> He may have committed deeds to shock us during that war; so did the Black and Tans who were fighting for us. The brutalities of the past ought to be buried in forgetfulness. Whatever the particular offence it is probable that the main motive of the men's action was originally a love of freedom.[57]

The Home Office, ironside and dreadnought, rebuffed all without fear or favour. Sir Charles got the standard response: there was no reason to interfere with the men's sentences.

But for some of the men the time remaining to be served was running out, and a little magnanimity would be possible without doing great violence to the principles of sentencing, the separation of powers and the administration of penal servitude. The Free State authorities had been impervious to appeals that they should intercede on behalf of the men. This was hardly surprising, given that all were staunchly anti-Treaty, that their robbery had been intended to fund the anti-Treaty side and that Francis Breen had been an active and apparently effective 'irregular'. Eventually, however, two pillars of the Free State establishment – arms and consciences doubtless yanked by the old ladies – did write privately to Clynes. Senator Maurice Moore, a distinguished officer in the Connaught Rangers for more than thirty years, was joined in an appeal for clemency by George Gavan Duffy, a signer of the Treaty.[58] Wisely, they did not seek to excuse the four men but asked for mercy 'as a matter of grace'. Their enquiries about the bank raid revealed that the men had believed that they were acting under orders from organisations in Ireland (the IRA, in other words). In fact, the organisation had not issued the orders, but others, whom Breen and his companions believed to be authorised, had done so: 'they were the tools of others; they were mistaken and, though we have no sympathy with such actions in any case, we do think that after such long sufferings this mistake may be laid to their credit'.[59]

In the case of Foley and Iago, Clynes felt able to grant clemency. In the normal course, their release, with remission for good behaviour, was only weeks away. Foley's date was 30 May 1930, but he was released on 2 May; Iago's release date was 9 June, but he was also freed on 2 May. Breen and Gavin remained in prison. Gavin was serving ten years, but, unlike Foley and Iago, he had not been arrested until two and a half years after the offence. Breen, a lifer, was in a different category altogether. Clynes made a Commons statement on the men's release and wrote to Moore saying that he could add nothing to that statement.[60]

The WPDL, in the meantime, had not ceased from its campaign directed at the Parliamentary Labour Party. A petition was drawn up and circulated. By 15 October 1930, 155 of Labour's 288 MPs – well over half – had signed, and the petition was still circulating.[61] In December, Maud Gonne wrote to Clynes again. It was a long and rambling letter, and the Home Office officials immediately minuted against release: Breen was serving life and Gavin had served only half his ten-year sentence. These cases were very different from the marginal indulgence that had allowed the release of Foley and Iago. But Clynes, mindful of the strength of feeling within the Parliamentary Labour Party, overrode his officials: 'I have given much thought to these two cases and have decided, in view of all the circumstances, to recommend the release of Breen and Gavin before Christmas.'[62] That decision was made on Friday, 19 December 1930 and received by Clynes's officials on the Monday. The following day, both men were freed. Breen went to Dublin, Gavin to Salford.[63]

The story, long and involved as it was, had a coda. Clynes had exempted both men from the obligation to report periodically to the police (the usual requirement for convicts released on licence), but they found it difficult to shake off the past and to pick up the threads of their lives. Both had spent a turbulent decade or more either involved in IRA activities or in prison. Both had acquired notoriety. Neither appeared to have an established and lawful means of earning a living. Nevertheless, Gavin seems to have eventually found his way to some sort of ordinary and unremarkable life and vanished from the official record. Breen took a different path and returned from Dublin to Salford, where, on 12 September 1932, he was arrested for loitering with intent outside a jeweller's shop. Salford CID reported that he had associated with a much-convicted thief and another accomplice in a shop-breaking plan and produced an intercepted letter that set out the scheme sufficiently to convict the men. Breen's accomplice was put on probation for twelve months. Breen, despite his previous conviction for dishonesty, received the comparatively lenient sentence of three months' hard labour.

Given that Breen was a lifer, and until he died at large only on licence, a much greater punishment now loomed: his licence could be revoked, and he could be returned to serve his sentence of life at penal servitude. He recognised his danger well and immediately petitioned for mercy. He outlined his attempts to earn a living and his financial difficulties: 'I am thirty seven years of age & am a totally different man to the man I was ten years ago… I have no connection with the IRA now, & I wish for none.' The Home Office took the benign view that this was not a relapse to his original pattern of offending and decided not to revoke Breen's licence. It did, however, withdraw the exemption he had been given from reporting to the police.[64] Having served his three months' hard labour, Breen returned to Dublin and opened a boot-repair shop. A Special Branch report to the Home Office indicated that he was continuing to live in the demi-monde of ex-convicts and political desperadoes: 'The house is under observation and the police are of the opinion that it is a meeting place for criminals where plans for their activities are discussed.' Breen had 'pronounced Communistic tendencies' and was associated with the Communist Party of Ireland up to 1933 when he was expelled because that organisation thought him to be an undesirable. The Gardaí regarded him as 'a dangerous type of individual who would not hesitate to engage in armed outrages'.[65]

There was a final intriguing twist. In May 1936, Breen (he was still on licence) applied to the Home Secretary for permission to come to England in connection with the Oxford Movement. Either he had made an astonishing journey – from freethinking, Bolshevism and extreme Irish republicanism to the Anglo-Catholic wing of Anglicanism – or he was poking fun at the Home Office. In either event, the permission to travel was denied. Britain had exhausted its appetite for Francis Breen.

Other cases

We have looked at Breen's case in some detail since it can stand for others and is a good snapshot of the dilemmas facing politicians and officials and of the lobbying tactics of the times. It also shows the conflict between the normal processes of law and the override of executive power. Certainly not unique to Breen, though it took many forms, were the enduring personal consequences of imprisonment, beyond the shortest terms. There were other, less serious and comparatively minor sentences, served out in obscurity. In the wake of the murder of Sir Henry Wilson, numerous raids were made on the houses of known republicans.[66] Some of these, in turn, led to trials and convictions. One such was nineteen-year-old Post Office Savings Bank clerk, Herbert Leo Wrigley, who was sentenced to twelve months' hard labour for possessing a revolver with intent to endanger life. Wrigley, an Englishman who had lived in Ireland for sixteen years and who appears to have had a romantic and probably fantasist attachment to revolutionary causes, was lucky not to have faced graver charges. A number of incriminating documents were found in his room, including a list of possible arson targets.[67] The Home Office noted that Wrigley was in touch with various revolutionary movements and was an associate of persons 'believed to be connected with outrages in this country'. He was regarded as 'a dangerous fanatic' who might commit acts of violence against the Free State. With such a background, and given that he was serving a relatively short sentence, it was decided not to intervene in his case: 'The question of [early] release sh[oul]d not be entertained', minuted Sir John Anderson.[68]

Elizabeth Eadie was the only woman to be arrested, charged and convicted as a result of the Wilson raids. Aged thirty-seven and widowed, she was said to be a clerk at the Ministry of Pensions. More to the point, it was believed that she was a sister of James Connolly, who had been co-leader of the Easter Rising.[69] For this he had been condemned to death and shot on 12 May 1916. Famous in the Free State, he was given an equal weight of notoriety in Britain. Eadie had been born in Dublin but had lived in London since childhood, supporting the anti-Treaty side in the Civil War. In the aftermath of Wilson's assassination, Eadie was one of several known IRA contacts to be raided. At her Bayswater flat, police uncovered a box containing eleven bombs. On 21 July 1922, she was convicted at the Old Bailey, the DPP leading for the Crown.[70] She was indeed lucky that the judge, possibly deciding that she was analogous to a suffragette, had decided to sentence her under the Malicious Damage Act, 1861.[71] Had she been sentenced under a statute, which, arguably, was equally applicable, the 1883 Explosive Substances Act, she would have faced a long term of penal servitude.[72] The Home Office regretted her good fortune: 'She is regarded as one of the most prominent extreme Republicans in this country, and there is reliable information that she assisted in the collection of arms for opponents of the Provisional government and was in touch with their leaders here and in Ireland.' In the ordinary course she would be released from Holloway (London's female prison) on 17 March 1924: Anderson minuted that she was not to be released before that time.[73] The Free State government had reasons to be not particularly sympathetic to Mrs Eadie and, in her case, as in that of Wrigley, undertook in advance to accept the decision of the Home Office.

The IRA, as an underground organisation, had imperfect and intermittent communications with many of its units. This was a fact of some consequence in deciding for the purposes of amnesty which offences had been committed under the authority of the organisation's chain of command and which were merely freelance criminal activities. This question was central to the cases of William Coleman, Thomas Duddy and Patrick Dempsey. The three, all West Lothian miners, had committed robbery with violence (taking a purse and £1 5s.) on 9 July 1921. On 26 August 1921, they held up a car, struck the driver and stole £2,000 – wages destined for a mine.[74] Coleman was further charged with firing revolver shots with intent to murder. The likelihood that these were freelance crimes rather than IRA actions was perhaps indicated by the timings. The first offence, which seems a particularly mean one, was committed within a week of the ending of the national lockout of the miners. This dispute had lasted three months and had cast mining communities into desperate hardship. The offences had also been committed during the period of the Truce, during which the IRA and British forces had promised to refrain from aggressive actions.

At the men's trial, no political motivation was claimed, nor did they make any of the traditional gestures of republicanism such as refusing to recognise the court. During the general clearing up of cases of disputed character that followed the signing and ratification of the Treaty, the Free State government, through its Minister for Defence General Richard Mulcahy, stated that the men had acted on erroneous orders from within the IRA. The Free State government hinted that elements in the IRA command structure at that time (probably a reference to Liam Mellows) had issued the robbery orders in an attempt to derail the peace treaty.

The British side was not at first disposed to order the men's release on the say-so of Mulcahy alone, but when this was backed up by an official assurance from the Free State government, a more favourable view was taken. The Scottish Office was asked to enquire into the men's antecedents, 'particularly as to whether there is any previous criminal history & whether they have been associated with any Communist or other non-Irish subversive movement'. No information of this kind was recorded.[75] On 27 March 1923, Lionel Curtis reported a conversation he had with Desmond FitzGerald, Free State Minister for External Affairs. FitzGerald agreed that, following the embarrassment recently incurred by both governments over deportation, they 'would be made to look extremely foolish if these men were released and were afterwards found to be plotting against the Free State'.[76] His proposed solution was to find sureties satisfactory to the Scottish Office, who would guarantee that in the event of their being freed the men would abstain from political action, 'criminal or otherwise'.[77] This course, which would have been of doubtful legality, was not taken. The Irish government offered to repay the stolen £2,000. That, and the assurances of Cosgrave and FitzGerald, cleared the way for the men's freedom.[78]

Northern Ireland prisoners in Britain

A number of prisoners tried, convicted and sentenced in Northern Ireland were transferred to England. There was no convict prison in Northern Ireland, so when, on 22 November 1921, the new state assumed responsibility for law and order, it acquired the duty but not the means to carry out sentences of penal servitude. Prior to Partition, convicts (those sentenced to penal servitude), from any part of Ireland, would have been transferred from the committing local prison to Maryborough (now Portlaoise).[79] Dublin's Mountjoy was mainly a local prison, but it did have limited convict accommodation. Partition deprived Northern Ireland of access to Portlaoise, and whilst Belfast Prison (Crumlin Road) was slowly being altered to hold them, Northern Ireland's convicts had to be sent to England or to Scotland.[80] With the establishment of the Free State and the disentangling of the component parts of the UK jurisdiction, Northern Ireland convicts already at Maryborough were transferred to English prisons.[81] Unlike persons sentenced to ordinary imprisonment, convicts could be moved easily from one British jurisdiction to another, simply by ministerial directive.[82]

By early 1924, there were seventy-two Northern Ireland convicts in English convict prisons and seven Borstal boys. It is hard from the brief descriptions provided of the men's offences to be completely certain as to their motivation – political or ordinary criminal. Taking the stated offence and counting murder and manslaughter offences as having been mainly political (though a few cases were probably not), between fifteen and twenty convicts were non-political. This would leave around fifty who were serving time for politically motivated crimes. Armed robbery and assault, possession of guns and explosives, manslaughter and murder were the principal offences. Fourteen men were held at Dartmoor, thirty-eight at Maidstone and twenty at Parkhurst. Some of the Borstal boys (whose offences are not given) may have been politicals: they were assigned to the Borstal wing of Wandsworth Prison and to Feltham and Borstal (Kent).[83]

There was no legal problem in the transfer of convicts, but individual cases raised particular and untested legal issues. One of these concerned William

Conlon, Irish-born but a naturalised citizen of the USA. With three others, Conlon had been tried for murder (committed during an ambush) at the Ulster Winter Assizes on 20 December 1920.[84] The men had held up the cashier of a manufacturing firm at Gilford, Co. Down, who was returning from a Banbridge bank having drawn cash for wages. About £1,300 was taken from the cashier, and his driver was shot and killed. The Northern Ireland government, newly established and still without law-and-order powers, did not regard Conlon's as a political crime but as 'sheer deliberate and cold-blooded murder'. H. M. Pollock contrasted the case with others, including murder, but observed that 'the murders in these cases were not connected with sordid robbery, as in the case of Conlon'.[85] The jury at the first trial failed to agree a verdict, and, following the Christmas break, the case was to have been resubmitted to the Winter Assizes. The Attorney General, possibly because of a fear of jury intimidation, indicated that the case should be held over for the next Down Assizes.[86] Conlon was instead tried by general court martial on 19 and 20 April 1921, under the ROIA.[87] He and two companions were sentenced to death, but, on the Irish Chief Secretary's intervention, this was commuted to life at penal servitude. The men were removed from Belfast Prison to England: Conlon went to Dartmoor, Francis O'Boyle and Hugh Rogers to Maidstone.[88]

Conlon petitioned to be treated as a political prisoner. There was an odd twist in his representation. Since arriving at Dartmoor he had, because of the manner of his trial, been classified as a misdemeanant. This had the effect of barring him from outside working parties – which was a hardship. The reason for this exclusion was that Dartmoor's armed patrols had legal authority to shoot at escaping felons but not at misdemeanants. The curious consequence was that misdemeanants who, in general terms, were convicted of less serious offences were not allowed outside the prison walls. Conlon threatened to have his uncle (who he said had been a Nationalist MP for twenty years) to raise a question in the House. As a naturalised US citizen, he wished to contact the US Consul and added – for good measure – that as an Irish prisoner he wished to be transferred back to Ireland.[89]

The Directors of Convict Prisons opted for a pragmatic response and decided to treat him as a felon and therefore to allow him to join an outside working party. This decision was made in the face of a Law Officers' Opinion that a court-martial conviction was not a felony conviction but an offence against military law. The application to Conlon's case came in the rider: 'nevertheless if such a convict whose offence *w[ou]ld under civil law have been a felony* attempted to escape, it w[ou]ld be lawful to shoot at him'. Specifically, the Law Officers concluded that having been convicted under the ROIA of an offence that was a felony, Conlon could be treated as a felon.[90]

This was further confirmed on 18 September 1923, when Conlon asked permission to sign a blank cheque in favour of his wife. The Northern Ireland government raised no objection and passed the matter back to the Home Office. Harry Simpson, Assistant Secretary at the Home Office and head of the Criminal

Department, pointed out that there was some doubt as to Conlon's status.[91] Were he a felon, Conlon could not write a cheque, but it was not clear that he was (despite his serving a sentence of penal servitude).[92]

Following the 1916 Rising, the British administration in Ireland took the view that persons convicted by court martial of treason or felony were felons. The following year, the Attorney General reversed this, and prisons were instructed not to treat these offenders as felons. The Law Officers were further consulted and advised that non-felonious status be confined to those convicted under the Army Act.[93] Since Conlon had been convicted under the ROIA, however, murder was, for all purposes, a felony. Conscious perhaps that this was making heavy going of a mere domestic arrangement, Simpson concluded that it was not clear whether Conlon's payment to his wife of a cheque for £10 would be invalidated by the Forfeiture Act. Accordingly, he was to be allowed to make the transaction.[94]

When a wing of Belfast Prison was converted and made ready for convicts, Conlon and his accomplices were among those repatriated to Northern Ireland. But on 9 May 1927, the three men (Conlon, Rogers and O'Boyle) escaped. They were joined by Edward Thornton, who was serving twelve years for a violent and vile attack on a girl in a railway carriage between Hollywood, Co. Down and Belfast.[95] The four men had overcome a prison officer, whom they bound and gagged. They took his keys and a revolver and gained entry to the prison yard. From there they managed to scale the perimeter wall, using a rope of knotted sheets. The escape had been well planned, and accomplices were waiting in what was described as a high-powered red car.[96] Conlon was recaptured, but the other two made their way to the Free State, where Northern Ireland warrants could not be executed.[97]

Some other cases also merited attention at the higher level. Geoffrey Whiskard (formerly Assistant Under-Secretary at Dublin Castle, now handling Irish affairs in the Colonial Office) was a temporising influence, his eye always on the broader development of Anglo-Irish relations.[98] At the end of 1922, he drew attention to the cases of David McKinstry (seven years' penal servitude), James Laverty and John Kearney (five years' penal servitude each). On 21 October 1921, they had been convicted and sentenced by field general court martial at Belfast for 'having firearms and ammunition not under effective military control'.[99] The background was the bloody sectarian warfare then raging in Belfast, including attacks on Roman Catholic workmen repairing tramlines. The men were arrested by an RIC patrol near a group of such workmen. Police sent to protect the workers found the three men already there, 'lurking in a ditch by the side of the Antrim Road, with loaded automatics in their trouser-legs'. McKinstry had, in addition, six flat-nosed bullets, possession of which was viewed particularly seriously by the military (and which was almost certainly why he received an additional two years' penal servitude). Explaining themselves to the police, the men said that they had been sent from St Mary's Hall to protect the work party. At their trial they refused to recognise the court; no character evidence was produced.[100]

The IRA, with much justification, contended that the Truce allowed its members to carry arms. The Northern Ireland government took a different view and, in general, seems to have excluded its own territory from the agreement. Whiskard contended that the men could not be regarded as criminals or even rebels, 'but merely as wrong-headed men acting under wrong-headed instructions'. He could not believe that their release would have any ill-effects in Northern Ireland but was sure that it would improve relations between the two governments, North and South. He also referred to the Collins–Craig pact of 30 March 1922, Article 10 of which had provided that the two governments 'shall, in cases agreed upon between the two signatories, arrange for the release of political prisoners in prison for offences before the date hereof'.[101] Because certain other articles had not been implemented, Article 10 had not come into operation, but, Whiskard observed, 'it can hardly... be doubted that had the agreement been carried into effect these 3 men w[oul]d have been released'.[102]

This view was also taken by Sir John Anderson, an important and weighty voice in Irish affairs.[103] With characteristic insight and decisiveness, he pointed to the background: 'These men were convicted before responsibility for law & order had been transferred to the Gov[ernmen]t of N. Ireland. H.M. Govt have therefore a clear status in the matter & the question of release might properly be taken up with N[orthern] Govt.'[104] Legally and politically this was the correct course, and Messrs Kinstry, Kearney and Laverty were, in due course, freed.[105]

But not all cases were treated so leniently, even where there were broader political considerations. On behalf of the Free State, President W. T. Cosgrave pressed for the release of two men particularly well connected to the new political establishment. John McCurtain and John (sometimes Shaun) Flood had been convicted at the Co. Fermanagh Spring Assizes, 1922.[106] Arrested in Enniskillen with nine others in two motor cars while taking part in a kidnapping operation on the homes of James Cooper, MP, George Elliot and others, they had been sentenced under the Firearms Act, 1920, and the Explosive Substances Act, 1883. Refusing to recognise the court, they had each been sentenced to a total of ten years' penal servitude.[107] What Cosgrave could not disclose to the British government was that both men, and the raiding party, had been armed by and were acting with the connivance, and indeed encouragement, of the then Provisional government and in accordance with the understanding that Michael Collins had forged with the IRA.[108] British military intelligence had a very good idea of what was going on, and General Macready had reported to Cabinet on the movement of arms.[109] In any event, the Home Office would have been alerted to this possibility by the men's connection but did not wish to take official notice of the background.

John McCurtain was the brother of Tomás MacCurtáin, Lord Mayor of Cork and IRA Commandant, who had been killed in his home by members of the RIC in April 1920.[110] John Flood was the brother of Frank, who had been hanged on 14 March 1921 at Mountjoy Prison for his participation in a Dublin ambush.[111] The Home Office noted that Flood 'is said to have great influence in Republican circles, partly owing to his brother's death, but to be a strong adherent of the Free State'. Cosgrave's request for clemency stressed that both men had excellent characters and that his government's interests would benefit from their release. Winston Churchill (as Secretary of State for War) had had much correspondence with the government of Northern Ireland on these and other cases, but no conclusion had been reached. In the light of this, and the circumstances of the offence, Sir John Anderson could see no ground on which to press their cases.[112]

Public opinion in Southern Ireland was always apt to be stirred by reports about republican prisoners. This was a potential political danger, which made it sensible for the Free State government to maintain a watching brief for persons convicted and sentenced in Northern Ireland and transferred to England. Irish patriots in English prisons, the 'Felons of Our Land' drew on a long tradition of symbolic as well as substantive sacrifices and touched on sensitivities within both constitutional and revolutionary nationalism. In the medium term, Dublin sought not only releases but also, pending these, improvements in prisoners' conditions. In May 1924, President Cosgrave asked Lionel Curtis of the Colonial Office (who had been a go-between in 1921–2 and who was well known to a number of the Free State leaders) whether it could be arranged for these long-term prisoners to have 'internment treatment', with any additional expense this might entail being met by his government.[113]

Curtis, who would be an architect of the emerging Commonwealth, and who was sympathetic towards the Free State government, may have thought that this request – politically advantageous at little cost – could easily be met.[114] With Cosgrave, who had himself been imprisoned and interned in England, Curtis doubtless hoped that more lenient conditions for the prisoners would ease some of the pressures relating to internees and prisoners which the Free State government was then experiencing.[115] Neither man fully understood the legal constraints. With simple imprisonment a change in status might have been effected, allowing the prisoners the privileges of first-class misdemeanant status.[116] In effect, this regime meant civil detention: one's own clothes, one's own food (if it could be purchased), a comfortable cell and a generous allowance of letters, parcels and visitors, even an ordinary prisoner paid to clean and tidy the detainee's cell. It was still captivity, but shorn of many of the petty hardships, restrictions and humiliations. This was the regime which the 1918–19 internment of Sinn Féin leaders and activists resembled, which Cosgrave would have remembered from his internment at Reading Prison in great contrast to his earlier time as a convict at Dartmoor and Lewes. But the prisoners for whom he wanted this status were not internees, nor ordinary prisoners even, but were serving sentences of penal servitude. These men were governed by the requirements of the Penal Servitude Act, and the Home Secretary had no executive powers in the matter.[117]

These legal considerations were irrelevant if the Northern Ireland government decided not to cooperate. Cosgrave had probably been attracted to the possibility of internment status because Art O'Brien and Sean McGrath had been treated as first-class misdemeanants in the course of their legal battle against deportation.[118] The Home Secretary referred to this but also made it clear that the British government could not intervene to change the status of the Northern Ireland prisoners.[119] This was confirmed in a letter from Curtis to Cosgrave on 13 June 1924. Home Rule in Northern Ireland was a key part of the Irish settlement. As we have seen, responsibility for law and order had been passed to Belfast on 22 November 1921, and, quite apart from the legal barriers, the British government had very strong reasons not to undermine Sir James Craig's authority. It therefore spelt out the constitutional and administrative position. The English and Scottish prison authorities were no more than agents of the Northern Ireland government, which was making use of their respective prisons because of its own lack of accommodation: all questions as to the treatment of these prisoners therefore had to be directed to Belfast.[120]

Notwithstanding the legal and constitutional niceties, it was in the end – and inevitably so – a matter of political will. Freedom for its political prisoners, a safe homecoming, was an important issue for the Free State in the continuing battle for guardianship of the republican heritage. The prisoners themselves were not the issue. As enemies of his own government as well as of the British one, Cosgrave more than likely deplored and condemned them. The British government was supportive of Cosgrave but itself saw no urgent or necessary reason to press Belfast for a change in the prisoners' treatment. That a political decision could overcome many barriers in law, regulation and interpretation was acknowledged by Harry Simpson as he reviewed the exchanges. Having studied the files, he pointed out that for the Fenian convicts there had been little in the way of special arrangements, 'but considerable relaxations were allowed in the case of the Sinn Féin convicts after the Rebellion of 1916 and as Mr Cosgrave & other members of the F[ree] S[tate] Gov[ernmen]t were among the convicts they will know of personal experience that special concessions were made!'[121]

Arising from the painful births of their respective states, Belfast and Dublin had no established channels of direct communication at a political level. Meetings between the respective leaders were episodic and crisis-related. This greatly impeded the prospect of a general deal on issues such as the political prisoners and meant that some negotiations had to be conducted at arm's length, via London. From November 1924, the British government was again Conservative, which, an outside observer might have imagined, tilted any granting of favours towards Belfast. But there was a substantial Irish community in Britain and therefore possible sources of additional pressure on issues of Irish interest. On 28 April 1925, George Buchanan, Labour MP for the Gorbals, raised the possibility of a relaxation in visiting regulations for Northern Ireland prisoners being held in Scotland's convict prison at Peterhead.[122] There followed consultation between the Home and Scottish Offices. A tabulation showed that the prisoners had few visits – two of them only when they had temporarily been transferred to Edinburgh for medical treatment. Only one of the thirty-four had been visited at

Peterhead: 'no doubt owing to the distance and expense of the journey'.[123] This was true of other non-political Irish prisoners at Peterhead. Although sentenced in another jurisdiction, the Irish prisoners were, for practical reasons of management, held under Scottish (not Northern Ireland) rules, and these provided for visits from relatives and friends but not from other persons or societies. In any event, it was not desirable 'to make any discrimination in this matter between certain prisoners and others who are similarly situated'. The governor had discretion to allow extra letters for any legitimate purpose, and this had been done. As to Buchanan's suggestion that prisoners might have visits from a society for the purpose of ventilating complaints, this function was already carried out by the prison's Visiting Committee.[124]

The Free State government had not given up. A few months later, L. S. Amery, the Colonial Secretary, visited Dublin, and the matter of the Peterhead men was put to him 'very earnestly' both by Cosgrave as President of the Executive Council and Timothy Healy as Governor-General.[125] This was a particularly sensitive time for both the Free State and the Northern Ireland governments, and the issue of the prisoners became a deal more important and urgent. It was widely expected that the Boundary Commission would report in the autumn of 1925.[126] Whether there was to be a major redistribution of territory, or none at all, could prove politically explosive. Were Craig to release the Peterhead convicts, his position as leader would almost certainly be damaged if, at the same time, Northern Ireland were to lose territory. The same reasoning applied to Cosgrave, but, for him, the disappointment of strong public expectations of gaining territory was the cause of concern. Peterhead releases might to some extent divert and placate his nationalist constituency.

The political context was well understood by the Home Office. Harry Simpson reminded the Home Secretary that the Peterhead men had repeatedly been mentioned in Parliament but that on each occasion their case was referred to the Northern Ireland government. Were the British government to approach Sir James Craig unofficially and tentatively, there was a risk that the intervention would leak out, causing political and constitutional embarrassment. Cosgrave wanted the men released and 'the sore healed' before the Boundary Commission report. But this was not a wholly convincing argument for freeing men who had been arrested raiding over the border: 'Such an action by the N.I. Government might be read as an encouragement to N. Ireland people to resort to violence if the boundary is now shifted towards the North.'[127]

The Permanent Under-Secretary, Sir John Anderson, was clearly irritated by the matter: 'This is one of the normal sequelae of a visit by a British Minister to Dublin. We have had many such requests before.' Some of them had been passed on to the Northern Ireland government; others had not. In the case of Thomas Hueston, 'Strong pressure was brought to bear; but always with negative results.'[128] That the issue was one of politics rather than security was made clear from further minutes. The men could now be released quite safely:

The release of a much larger number of prisoners convicted in G[rea]t Britain, at a time when conditions in Ireland were much less settled was followed by no untoward consequences; & it is inconceivable that this handful of men would wish, or be able, to make trouble if let loose now.

But this was not an argument for the British government to act 'at this juncture'. Craig had his own constituents to consider and might find himself in a difficult position over the Boundary Commission: 'We must hope that he will then be able & willing to use his influence on the side of moderation.' With that in prospect, it would be a grave mistake 'to start setting the extreme section of his supporters by the ears at the present time, as any action on his part which could be construed as weakness would be bound to do'. The Colonial Office should be told that the Home Office was willing to send a memo to the Northern Ireland government setting out the request and arguments but would exert no pressure. Sir William Joynson-Hicks, the Home Secretary, agreed with all of this but thought that action should not even go as far as a neutral memo to the Northern Ireland government: 'I will see the C[olonial] Secretary personally.'[129]

A month later, Robert Duke wrote from the Scottish Office. There were now twenty-eight Northern Ireland prisoners at Peterhead.[130] Sir Richard Dawson Bates, the Northern Ireland Minister for Home Affairs, hoped to take all back by the end of the year ('though somewhat slowly'). In the meantime, the Minister was most anxious not to be pressed to remove the remaining men.[131]

The three governments soon discovered the danger that lay in the Boundary Commission. Justice Richard Feetham, its Chairman, and the Ulster Unionist nominee J. R. Fisher had interpreted its brief in a manner favourable to Northern Ireland.[132] To forestall publication, which would have given legal force to the Commission's findings, an agreement was reached on 3 December 1925 to leave the boundary between the two parts of Ireland as determined by the Treaty and by the GOIA, 1920.[133] An attempt was then made to settle all outstanding issues between the three states – financial, political and territorial.[134] The outcome was an agreement, signed on 3 December 1925. As a side pocket to this resolution of major issues, Sir James Craig gave an undertaking to Stanley Baldwin, the British Prime Minister, that the cases of the Northern Ireland political prisoners 'convicted in Northern Ireland in respect of offences during the period of disturbance' would be reviewed by the British government, 'whose decisions in each case shall be accepted by the Government of Northern Ireland'.[135]

To give maximum reassurance to Ulster Unionists, and to protect Craig from protests from the more militant of his supporters, it was decided that the review of cases would be undertaken by Lord Birkenhead, former Lord Chancellor. Birkenhead was one of the principal negotiators of the Treaty and, less than a decade before that, as F. E. Smith, had been one of Ulster Unionism's most militant (and dashing) supporters in its conflict with Liberalism and Home Rule. On their part, Cosgrave and his colleagues would have drawn some reassurance from Birkenhead's positive role in the Treaty negotiations and thereafter and the high regard in which he was held by Michael Collins.[136]

Although oversight and the all-important imprimatur came from Birkenhead, the detailed work fell to the Ministry of Home Affairs and the Home Office. On 11 December 1925, the Northern Ireland Minister for Home Affairs, Dawson Bates, wrote to the Home Office about the Craig–Baldwin agreement.[137] It was not clear to him when the 'period of disturbance' began and ended. Law-and-order powers and responsibilities were transferred to the Northern Ireland government on 22 November 1921, 'and comparative peace was restored by the 30th September, 1923'. He undertook to supply all the details of each case: crime, circumstances, sentence, date of likely release and any previous convictions. Bates, who was on the more irreconcilable side of Ulster Unionism, and who was probably opposed to or uneasy about the Craig–Baldwin agreement, either misunderstood what it was intended to do or deliberately attempted to put obstacles in its way. When considering remission of sentence, it was Northern Ireland practice, he informed Joynson-Hicks, to consult the relevant judge and to see the police report. Constitutional procedure required the Ministry of Home Affairs to submit the files to the governor, 'and no doubt your Department will in each case state their reasons for recommending remission'.[138]

This last irritated the Home Office, which, as a major department of state, did not intend to submit its judgments to a comparatively minor functionary such as the Governor of Northern Ireland – or to Dawson Bates. There may also have been some unease as to the substantive, as distinct from the procedural, nature of such submissions. The Governor, the Duke of Abercorn, was a former Conservative MP and had been a nominee of the Ulster Unionist Party.[139] It would be awkward, at the very least, were he (or one of the judges) to go beyond the constitutional form and state an opinion. In any event, Sir James Craig had bound his government to accept the decision of the British government in each case. The arrangement proposed by Dawson Bates was of a very different nature and could delay or unnecessarily complicate outcomes.

The Home Office reply, from Sir John Anderson, neatly and without confrontation set Dawson Bates's proposal to one side. What was intended was not the exercise of the Royal Prerogative (which was the procedure outlined by Dawson Bates) 'and the responsibilities for advising the Government of Northern Ireland will rest not with the Home Secretary but with the Government as a whole'. It was not an invariable rule to consult the judge when remission of sentence was being considered 'as a mere act of clemency'. Such consultation in this instance 'might be rather embarrassing'.[140]

Dawson Bates supplied the Home Office with a list of forty Northern Ireland political prisoners, including details of seven who had served their sentences and who had been released and four named persons who were not in custody. The twenty-nine serving prisoners had release dates (assuming full remission) that ran from one month thence (December 1925) to 1942. The men fell into several groups. Ten men, including John Flood and John McCurtain, had been involved in the border kidnapping raids of 7 and 8 February 1922.[141] Four other men, shortly to be released, had been arrested for the kidnapping of fourteen Roman Catholics who were in dispute with the IRA. The captives were held at the Hibernian Hall, Cranagh, Co. Tyrone, and were released following a police raid during which shots were exchanged. A house near the hall was found to contain an arms dump, including landmines, arms and ammunition. Thomas Hueston had been sentenced to penal servitude for his part in the Wattlebridge ambush of 7 February 1922.[142] Bernard McCreesh and Joseph McGuire had been identified as being among the Belcoo raiders of 28 March 1922. The raiding party had escaped to the Free State (with their RIC prisoners) but McCreesh and McGuire were later arrested when they returned to Northern Ireland. Four more men had been sentenced for their part in a raid on Pomeroy RIC barracks (Co. Tyrone) in which arms and various munitions were seized. Incidents of raiding, shooting and possession of arms and ammunition made up the balance of the offences, apart from a trio comprising the most controversial of all the prisoners.

These last had been involved in an IRA escape at Londonderry Prison on 2 December 1922; one had been a temporary warder in the prison at the time.[143] A well-planned operation, involving a copy master-key, a rope ladder, a traitor within and the use of chloroform, went tragically wrong when Constable Michael Gorman of Malin, Co. Donegal, and Special Constable William Lyttle, of Magherafelt, Co. Derry, both on duty at the time of the escape, were killed by the chloroform. Patrick Leonard (the treacherous warder), Patrick Johnston (a prisoner who had taken an active part in the escape) and Thomas McShea (another prisoner) were duly found guilty of murder at Belfast Winter Assizes on 12 January 1922.[144] The most serious view was taken of Leonard's case, and the Northern Ireland Cabinet decided that in his case the death sentence should be carried out. The Cabinet recognised the lesser roles of Patrick Johnston and Thomas McShea and recommended that their death sentences be commuted to fifteen years' penal servitude. The Cabinet was overruled by the Lord Lieutenant in Patrick's case, and life at penal servitude (usually twenty years before release) was substituted for the death penalty.[145] The decision was not finalised until the day before the planned execution and did not reach the prison, or the men, until that evening.[146]

Overall, therefore, this was a very mixed bag, but the result of the review was foregone. All bar the Derry prisoners were recommended for release, the calculation probably being that these three were the most controversial cases and that their amnesty would have kindled most ill-feeling amongst the loyalist supporters of the government.[147] Before the recommendations were put to the British Cabinet for a final decision, Dawson Bates sought to exclude prisoners O'Boyle and Rogers, who, with William Conlon, had been convicted of a murder in the course of robbery at Banbridge on 3 September 1920.[148] There was no political element in their crime, but the men, who had been sentenced to death, had been reprieved on the advice of the Irish Chief Secretary. The names had not been put on the schedule by Anderson, and it is curious therefore that he raised them at all. It seems likely that he used this case to head off what he may have feared was a general release. The Imperial government, he wrote, should have regard to the effect that their decision might have 'on our ability to maintain the existing peaceful conditions'. He mentioned a Protestant who, for two or three years, had been on the 'wanted' list for shooting a Sinn Féiner. The man had eventually been arrested in Canada and brought to trial: 'I need not elaborate how our position with regard to this man and others whose crimes are yet unpunished would be affected if the recommendations made by the Imperial government go too far in the cases of convicts at present serving their sentences.'[149]

This plea was not favourably received. There was a deal of impatience in London, where the expectation was an uncomplicated and speedy implementation of the political decision that had already been made. Anderson knocked the ball back into Dawson Bates's court by asking whether there were any Protestants that should be brought within the terms of the amnesty. The reply, given the fierce and murderous intercommunal strife of the preceding years, must have been instructive. 'We have no Protestants at present in custody who are serving sentences in respect of crimes such as were committed by persons (all members of the Irish Republican Army) whose names were contained in the lists which you forwarded.'[150]

While Dawson Bates was stalling, Cosgrave's government was asking for action by Christmas. This had become the traditional time of year for clemency, in republican eyes. A list of the men whose releases were being sought appeared in the *Irish Independent* on 10 December 1925 – publication no doubt inspired by a government leak.[151] If this caused Craig some embarrassment, it was not obvious in his statement to the Northern Ireland Parliament.[152] Cosgrave and Craig had met on 24 November 1925, when both men were in London to seek final agreement of outstanding issues under the spur of the imminent report of the Boundary Commission.[153]

Despite Cosgrave's wishes, there was to be no Christmas homecoming (from which, no doubt, he would have reaped useful kudos). At a meeting of the British Cabinet on 19 January 1926, Birkenhead's decisions on the prisoners were confirmed. Leonard, Johnston and McShea were denied further clemency, but it was agreed that their already commuted sentences might be reviewed after a further five years. The decision was telegraphed to Belfast and acknowledged by Dawson Bates for immediate action. Cosgrave was informed at the same time but asked to keep the information to himself until all formalities were completed.[154]

There was another and unexpected obstacle to be overcome. Dawson Bates, who had been unhappy with the releases, had, on receiving confirmation of the Cabinet decision, immediately announced his intention to exclude from Northern Ireland those who were to be released, 'except in localities where their presence is not likely to constitute a danger to the public peace'. The police force was depleted, and the men's presence might prove to be 'a source of grave danger'.[155] This decision appalled Baldwin, to whom it was immediately communicated. It smacked of bad faith, meanness and backtracking and could nullify the political advantages of the agreement in the Free State.

On Anderson's initiative, Baldwin now intervened, and, going over the head of Dawson Bates, he telegraphed Craig, urging him not to issue the exclusion orders. He was anxious that Britain and Ireland as a whole should benefit from the releases and the good feelings they had produced. Exclusions would be seen as being inconsistent with the Supplementary Agreement (of 3 December 1925) and with the exercise of royal clemency. It was also to be noted that the majority of the men would in any event have been due for release during 1926. This message was circulated to Cabinet, Baldwin explaining that he had of necessity acted immediately and had made the decision himself because colleagues involved with Irish affairs had not been available for consultation.[156]

Baldwin's telegram arrived late in the evening, and Craig's reply came back within the hour: one can imagine a fairly firm conversation between Craig and his minister. A climbdown letter followed smartly, with Dawson Bates explaining why he had wanted the exclusion orders. In his letter to Baldwin, Craig tried for a positive gloss. There had been no intention of cutting across the December agreement: 'I hope you realise that our suggestion was intended to be in their own best interest, as with one meagre Police Force we are quite unable to afford personal protection to so large a number of marked men.'[157] That may indeed have been the case, but it is equally certain that this was not Dawson Bates's thinking: nothing in the previous correspondence had mentioned the safety of the released prisoners.

All of this was a tidying up of consequences that had their origin in revolutionary times and in a deal of chaos. It was inevitable that the Londonderry Prison murderers would eventually be released. Those enjoying peace and restored stability in the Free State were always likely to have feelings of unease and sympathy for men who, as they saw it, had been caught up in turbulent times and events. Young men had acted if not under the direct then certainly under the indirect orders and authority of those now holding office in the new Irish state. A sense of fairness required that steps be taken to restore these captives to freedom. Such sentiments were communicated to Irish politicians, and the Dublin government continued to lobby for further leniency. Throughout the first part of 1926 there were several such approaches, which encountered caution and reluctance in London. An increasing sense of stability and security, north and south of the border, eventually allowed mercy to be granted, and, on Saturday, 17 July 1926, Leonard, McShea and Johnston were released.[158] The three travelled to Dublin, where they were welcomed by the father of James Monaghan, who had been released in January. A few days later, there was a public meeting.[159]

The great deportation fiasco

Grasping the nettle

We have seen how, following the signing of the Treaty, the republican move-ment in Britain split in much the same way as it did in Ireland. The principal public organisations were, in England, the ISDL and, in Scotland, Sinn Féin. Intelligence reported that these organisations' rank and file supported the Pro-visional government but that many office-holders were persons of extreme views and were bitterly opposed to it.[160] At this distance it is impossible to gauge the respective strengths of the pro- and anti-Treaty factions, but it seems reasonable to assume that they were distributed as in Ireland, with a solid majority favouring the Treaty. As Ireland moved to civil war, sharp differences of opinion shattered the republican organisations in Britain. The same intelligence report was prob-ably correct in its claim that the IRA in England and Wales 'practically ceased to exist', with many activists and supporters taking the view that Irish indepen-dence had been established by the Treaty.[161] The strength of the ISDL consequently ebbed away.

Determined efforts were made by the anti-Treaty side to regain ground, and from March 1922 onwards there were reports of a reorganisation and re-estab-lishment of republican forces in Britain, with particular anti-Treaty IRA strength in Glasgow and Liverpool – each having large Irish populations and convenient contact and transportation points for Ireland. Art O'Brien, who had been one of the principal representatives of Irish republicanism in both its public and underground organisations, now fiercely against the Treaty, led his faction to victory in the struggle to capture offices and to control the ISDL. In consequence, the League campaigned strongly against the Provisional government.

O'Brien had moved effortlessly from a representation of the republican movement as a whole to propaganda against the new Irish government. In the early months of 1922, the issue of the unreleased prisoners provided a con-venient way station to this outright opposition. Militants and sympathisers could continue along the path of anti-British agitation and indignation while at the same time the Provisional government could be criticised and condemned by association. On Sunday, 12 February 1922, O'Brien addressed a large demon-stration in Trafalgar Square, ostensibly calling for the release of the imprisoned Connaught Rangers but also laying claim to be the leader of uncompromising republicanism.[162] By the end of the year, attacks on the Provisional government were explicit and vehement. On the first anniversary of the signing of the Treaty, O'Brien organised a protest meeting at the Public Hall, St Pancras Baths, London. His publicity asserted that in Ireland 'thousands are imprisoned without charge or trial, prisoners are cruelly tortured and secret court-martials are a regular feature'. He reproduced a handbill distributed outside some Dublin churches before and after masses on Sunday, 26 November 1922: 'Fidei Defensores: Cromwell Could Not Destroy Our Faith and Neither Can the

Bishops.' The ISDL observed that the leaflet was 'a timely protest against the political and anti-national partisanship of Catholic Church dignitaries in Ireland'.[163]

Covert activities were organised, although with much-diminished resources, and apparently fairly thoroughly penetrated by both British and Free State intelligence. Experienced IRA men were sent to Britain. There was secret drilling and purchases of arms from the USA and from Germany. The arms, together with chemicals and money, were then forwarded to Ireland, though much harassed and interrupted by a high level of police raiding and captures, both of *matériel* and personnel.[164] Towards the end of 1922, as the tide turned ever more strongly against the Irregulars, there were renewed pleas to supporters overseas to send money and weapons. A Home Office report pointed out that there was a sense of desperate urgency, underlined by phrases such as 'now or never' and 'a bullet now is worth ten later on'. Patrick (Pa) Murray, sent over to act as OC Britain, emphasised this message of most urgent necessity to the various IRA commands.[165]

Intercepts disclosed that the IRA's ambition was a re-run of the campaign of arson and bombings that had inflicted so much damage and had caused such alarm in Britain in 1920–1. On 9 January 1923, Liam Lynch, IRA Chief of Staff, wrote to his OC in Britain. Murray, he understood, would prefer to be fighting in Ireland, but he could render more service in Britain, where, 'owing to the advanced development of [the] situation here', Lynch was considering a second front of 'active hostilities'. This would involve 'general destruction'. Following this, the IRA's Director of Chemicals ordered the setting up of workshops in London and elsewhere for the manufacture of explosives and incendiary devices: 'I did not mean stuff should be made there for export to Ireland but... for use in England if and when such an exigency should arise.' The Quartermaster General made the message even clearer: 'I am having some aluminium alloy grenades made and packed with shrapnel, which I hope will be effective.These should be tested this week. If successful I may be able to send you some.'[166]

From the commencement of the Irish Civil War (and indeed before overt conflict), the British insisted that the Irish government should fully, and through such force as was necessary, assert its authority. To this end, a deal of assistance would be given. From the documents it is clear that there was, in addition to military and logistical assistance, some intelligence support. It is hard to say how formal this assistance was, and it is certain that neither the British nor the new Irish intelligence agencies could fully trust each other. For some time, London must have feared that persons who so recently had been actively engaged against the Crown might again be enemies: even in times of untroubled peace and tranquillity the firmest of allies withhold some sources and intelligence, and Dublin and London were only in the preliminary stages of trust-building. A cold-eyed assessment would have concluded that the Provisional government was fighting for its life and its files might at some stage pass into enemy hands. Some of its officials, moreover, might have divided loyalties, and worse. Irish intelligence agents had in some cases gone from belligerents to allies in a breathtaking matter of months, and it was inevitable that they would be equally wary. And, while the Civil War was still undecided, there must have been some loyal servants of the Provisional government who worried about republican victories sufficient to provoke British military action in Ireland and therefore a possible realignment of republican forces.

There were powerful reasons for both sides to cover their cards, but, as the weeks and months passed and the victory of the Provisional government became more certain, relations grew easier. Atrocities on both sides of the republican divide hardened allegiances and dissolved doubts. Lists of active anti-Treaty republicans in Britain were jointly prepared by the British and Irish authorities. What should be done to neutralise them? There were two options. Where evidence warranted (and could be used), criminal proceedings could be instituted. Alternatively, suspects could be interned under the ROIA and its attendant regulations.

There were obvious difficulties in taking suspects to courts. Much of the evidence against them, coming from informers, agents and interceptions, could not be revealed without damaging sources and methods. There also had to be considered the quality of the evidence, strong enough for an intelligence dossier but in many cases far short of what would constitute criminal proof. A few convictions, perhaps not involving the more serious activists, was a small return for disclosing so much about British intelligence. The Free State government also cautioned that even a limited number of prosecutions would provide an opportunity for further anti-Treaty propaganda.

Internment had therefore clear appeal. But how did the ROIA stand, now that the Irish Free State had been established? The Law Officers advised that the Act and its regulations continued in force. They recognised that this view might be challenged in the courts but thought that it would prevail. With this assurance the British and Irish authorities prepared their lists. These were supposed to be reviewed, case by case, in a process lasting some four weeks. On 7 March 1923, internment orders were signed by the Home Secretary and (for persons residing in Scotland) the Scottish Secretary. These directed removal from Britain and internment in the Free State. On the night of Sunday/Monday, 10/11 March 1923 – generally in the small hours – 110 people considered to be key anti-Treaty republicans were arrested.[167] Within hours they were en route to Dublin, where the Free State government took them into custody and lodged them – 102 men and eight women – in Mountjoy Prison.[168] The British insisted that the step had been taken none too soon. On 7 March 1923, the Deputy Chief of Staff of the IRA had written to the OC Britain informing him that the Chief of Staff (at this time Liam Lynch) wished operations in Britain to be started at once: 'He says that days now count.'[169] And, indeed, the IRA, pulverised by the increasingly powerful Free State Army, was within days of comprehensive defeat. Aid from Britain, the USA or elsewhere would at this stage have made no difference.[170]

Regulation 14b of the ROIA was directly derived from the powers of internment and removal conferred by the regulation of the same number promulgated under the authority of the 1914 DORA.[171] There was here a certain curiosity, if not historical irony. In the tense year before the 1916 Easter Rising, an unprepared but increasingly perplexed and perturbed Irish administration had used DORA to prosecute some 500 persons whom it saw as firebrands, poised to exploit the opportunities for subversion and rebellion created by the Great War. Deportation, exclusion orders and residence requirements were backed up by short terms of imprisonment. At that point, the deportation was from Ireland to Britain, where the Volunteer and Sinn Féin activists, it was hoped, might be removed from associates and supporters and from the possibility of action. Among the deportees, to complete the irony, was Ernest Blythe, now Minister for Local Government and Public Health in the Free State government.[172]

From the outset, there was a problem in the reasoning behind the 10-11 March arrests and the subsequent removals and detention. Internment was supposed to aid the restoration of order in Ireland, yet the justifications for arrest related largely to Britain. However much the British government wished to strengthen the Irish Free State, the legal, administrative and organic relationship that had existed when both countries were part of the UK had been transformed with Irish independence. The legal consequences of stretching the power of the Home and Scottish Secretaries would soon be revealed. In the meantime, the two governments were gratified when, following the arrests, intercepted correspondence from the OC Britain to Liam Lynch lamented, 'you knew the possibilities of operations before, judge for yourself the possibilities now'.[173] This assessment was confirmed a few days later in another letter to Lynch, this time from the IRA's GHQ in Dublin. Having reviewed the situation, the writer concluded, 'I am afraid the chances of operations in Britain are now negligible, if not altogether impossible.'[174]

Pain and discomfort

In the closing weeks of the Civil War, conditions were extremely difficult in Ireland, both for a swathe of the civilian population and for the surviving anti-Treaty forces. Liam Lynch had been killed by government troops on 10 April 1923 as IRA leaders dispersed following a meeting of their executive. There followed weeks of inconclusive discussion and disagreement between the surviving leaders and unavailing attempts to get terms from the government. But the Free State had survived, and even its most steadfast opponents could see that it was now militarily unassailable. On 24 May 1923, the IRA conceded defeat and issued a ceasefire and dump-arms order. The Irish government had, by this time, over 10,000 prisoners on its hands – an enormous responsibility, considering its resources. Killings, reprisals, sabotage, destruction, hatred and general disorder had ravaged the community, which had endured seven years of such pestilence. Pro- and anti-Treaty activists had each experienced bitter loss and much suffering: nationalism was riven, the shared republican dream a ruin, and hatred was woven into the fabric of political life and a good deal of ordinary life as well.

Times were hard for the free civilian, and there was much difficulty in everyday life. In these bleak circumstances, prisoners coming into Ireland would necessarily experience material hardship and a great deal of hostility. Years of neglect and the limitations of public finance in a country at war meant that conditions were worse than in English prisons, basic though they were. Those in charge would perhaps be unsympathetic to internees who had given aid and comfort to the anti-Treaty side. Prison staff, given the turnover that accompanied independence, included a proportion who were both inexper- ienced and politicised. Soldiers, most of whom were newly recruited and poorly trained, had guard duties at Mountjoy, some on the perimeter and others inside the prison. The government may have won, but nobody could be certain that the victory was secure. The fear of riot, organised breakout or an outside attack kept everyone on edge. It was indeed an overcrowded, poorly nourished, nervy, anxious and unhappy home to which the unwilling guests were brought.

The prisoners' hardships began with their arrests in Britain. The object of the round-up was to get them out of the country without delay; due process was minimal. Requests to consult solicitors or to see senior police officers were refused. A habeas corpus application was to be avoided by every means: one success could lead to an avalanche of others. There was a certain amount of rough handling of those who were not fully cooperative. In some instances, homes were searched without a warrant, and there were the usual indignities – perhaps necessary to the operation but irksome and provocative to those arrested: manhandling, searching and the anxious uncertainties of confinement in police cells.[175] Some were told only that they were to be taken to the local police station and so took no changes of clothing or toiletries and made no prepara- tions.[176] Men from Manchester were manacled together on their journey to Liverpool; others were handcuffed between detectives. At Liverpool, the internees were embarked for Dun Laoghaire (formerly Kingstown) on board a naval cruiser, under a guard with fixed bayonets. From Dun Laoghaire they were transferred to a destroyer for transit to Dublin's North Wall, a matter of a few miles. While some found this taxing and intimidating, at least one of the eight women deportees referred to her time in naval custody as 'the only redeeming feature' of her arrest and noted 'the extreme kindness and con- sideration of the officers and all ranks on board the cruiser'.[177] 'All the Nice Girls Love a Sailor', a popular song of the day declared, and this encounter showed reciprocity.

But it was not gallant sailors who ran Mountjoy Prison but an ill-prepared, poorly resourced, perplexed and possibly indifferent administration. These were unconvicted persons, at the very least entitled to the privileges of remand pris- oners. On reception they were told that they could send and receive one letter a week, but this was subsequently denied them, as were newspapers, writing materials and parcels from friends; no visits were allowed.[178] The prisoners' money had been taken from them. This was (and is) customary on reception, but, unlike ordinary remand prisoners, they were denied the use of it to buy food and toiletries. The prohibition of cigarettes and pipe tobacco was, of course, keenly felt. There was a shortage of beds, and the prisoners had to sleep on dirty mattresses on the floor with poor bedding and without pillows; soap and towels were not supplied.[179]

The small group of women deportees had the tougher time. At Mountjoy, they were squeezed into whatever accommodation was available on the female side. Only the fairly makeshift top-floor hospital was available. This consisted of three ordinary cells knocked into one. 'Absolutely filthy' was how Kathleen Brooks, a thirty-six-year-old London-born schoolteacher, described the condition of this large cell. She added that, 'The sanitary arrangements were filthy beyond description.' There had been minimal preparations: 'There was not even a table or a camp bed or anything of the sort which an ordinary convict is provided with.' Mugs, plates, knives and forks were not issued during the first two days (quite how the internees managed to eat is not clear). There was a delay of more than two weeks before beds were provided. In the interim, the women slept on the floor on mattresses; the army blankets with which they were provided were too musty to use.[180] Rosina Killen said that the cell was 'fearfully overcrowded' and their beds 'most inconvenient'.[181] Having travelled from London to see her, Kathleen Brooks's brother was turned away; the prison also refused to accept a letter for her. He complained that his sister had had no change of clothing since her arrest and was told that the prison doctor could authorise a change, but only into the prison uniform.[182]

The women also had to endure what was described with only a limited amount of hyperbole as a 'state of terror', but this, gender-blind, was inflicted on all. During the time that Kathleen Brooks was at Mountjoy, there was 'ceaseless and indiscriminate' firing by the guards. She claimed that 'Drunken soldiers threatened to fire if a light showed, even though it were a light permitted by the regulations.' There was also firing from the corridor into the cells 'if anyone so much as showed themselves at a window'.[183] This certainly happened and was described in some detail by Ernie O'Malley, who was in the prison at the time. It was also raised in the House of Commons.[184]

Mountjoy's governor was Phil Cosgrave, brother of the Free State leader; the day-to-day work was done by Paudeen O'Keefe, the Deputy Governor. Both men were said to overindulge in drink.[185] O'Keefe, at one point, whether through drink or ill-temper, or both, appears to have got carried away in a way that was both frightening and cruel. Two women had complained of what appears to have been (the language is delicate and oblique) a bout of diarrhoea – hardly surprising if the lack of hygiene was as severe as the internees reported. Medical treatment was requested for the two, and, in circumstances that were not quite clear, the entire complement of women were visited in their cell at midnight by O'Keefe, accompanied by eight or nine soldiers. The women subsequently insisted that O'Keefe was intoxicated and that he harangued them for fifteen minutes or so, apparently angry that he had been disturbed. Torches were shone in the women's faces as they lay on their mattresses or on the floor, and revolvers were flourished. They should, he said, have asked for medical attention when he was in the prison earlier in the day. Despite the women's pleas, O'Keefe said that he would keep them all locked up for as long as he wished. The cell door was not unlocked until 11.30 the following morning. During that time, there was no access to a lavatory, and the two unwell women were in extreme distress. Eventually, Maria Killen, one of the internees, persuaded a wardress to let one of them out to the lavatory. She did so, 'although she said Mr O'Keefe would make her pay dearly for it'.[186]

Altogether, these women were treated with far less regard than ordinary criminal prisoners and certainly worse than the male detainees. It is only fair to note, however, that, no fading violets, they managed to sustain an *esprit de corps*, Kathleen Brooks looking back on classes and activities that kept them 'jolly and smiling'.[187] Their Mountjoy experiences were likely to distract and obscure their republican activities when related by a press instinctively sympathetic to young women. On the night of 30 April 1923, the women were removed to the North Dublin Union (NDU) – a former workhouse.[188] Here were conditions improved.[189] But they were to spend just over two weeks at the Union, and Mountjoy was the core of their prison experience – and of their court testimony.[190]

The Advisory Committee

As with earlier versions of internment and deportation, an Advisory Committee was established to consider appeals. This gave some gloss of elementary fairness to a process almost completely devoid of the elements of natural justice. The committee comprised Lord Trevethian (Chairman), Sir Henry Mather-Jackson and Sir Matthew Wallace.[191] Both governments recognised that the British, in the words of Mark Sturgis, the ubiquitous fixer, 'had gone to the extreme limits of our legal powers'. Appearances and presentation demanded that the Advisory Committee should appear to be an independent and freely available safeguard and corrective. Sturgis thought that for persons domiciled in Ireland there would probably be no political difficulty arising from their deportation and internment in Dublin. Persons born in Britain, or who had lived in Britain for a long time, were another matter and had to be given every facility to make representations.[192]

The obvious administrative difficulties of operating a London-based committee for prisoners held in Dublin do not appear to have been thought through, increasing the impression that the committee was no more than a fig leaf. Logistics were still being sorted out several days after the deportations, even though the liberty of the subject and concerns about wrongful detention (or misidentification) should have been matters of urgent concern. Writing from the Home Office to a Dublin-based Colonial Office colleague, Sturgis proposed that those who wished to appear before the Committee should be brought over to London in batches of ten.[193] In fact, only eight deportees applied for review. This lack of candidates was open to two interpretations. The government could point to the small number as a demonstration that it had got the round-up more or less right. Prisoners, however, insisted that an appeal was in some way an admission of guilt, and, therefore, possible applicants were deterred. From Mountjoy, Art O'Brien and his comrades argued that the Advisory Committee was a mockery of justice since it presumed guilt and forced detainees to prove their innocence to some hidden charge.[194] Though they did not say so, the republican gorge was apt to rise at the notion of humbly petitioning an instrument of the Crown.

From the outset, Labour and Liberal MPs had been frequent, vigorous and persistent critics of the arrests and deportations.[195] As noted, the Advisory Committee was an important part of the government's defence against such criticisms. Within days of the arrests, questions were being raised in the Commons. How could the prisoners present themselves to the Advisory Committee and were they able to get legal advice to enable them do so?[196] But the government's core defence was whether it had got it right and had indeed rounded up pikes rather than minnows. The list of detainees seems to have been well put together, probably because it was a joint effort of the Irish and British intelligence. This was shown by the evidence presented to the Committee on appeal cases and also by the surviving dossiers of those who chose not to appeal. A few examples will suffice.

Miss Mary Finan, a twenty-five-year-old teacher, Liverpool-born, admitted to being the captain of the Liverpool branch of the Cumann na mBan at the time of her arrest.[197] This branch had been infiltrated by a Free State intelligence officer and was known to be actively involved in arms transportation and storage.[198] The branch's other work was to support the IRA by carrying messages, raising funds and providing accommodation. One member, Miss Murphy, acted as a forwarding agent for letters addressed to Miss M. Brooks (in fact Kathleen Brooks). These were known to British authorities (through intelligence and interception) as communications from de Valera, Liam Lynch and others to the IRA OC Britain and to Sean Moylan in the USA.

All of this was set out in a report to the Advisory Committee from Colonel J. F. Carter, head of Special Branch. He also explained the aims and methods of Cumann na mBan, emphasising its support role for those involved in active operations and its importance in the Irregulars' communications network. He cautioned against releasing Mary Finan. This would allow her to resume her activities 'and thus encourage the others to continue'. Her representations were that she did not fully understand the organisation in which she held office. Colonel Carter urged the Committee to reject this disingenuous explanation.[199]

The Committee agreed with Carter, and Mary Finan was retained in custody (to be freed in the general release of 16 May 1923). Carter communicated the news of Mary's continued detention to Diarmuid O'Hegarty, head of Free State Army intelligence, at Portobello Barracks, Dublin, who expressed relief at the decision whilst regretting that Kitty Furlong had been released. ('She is a very able woman.') O'Hegarty wrote that he was 'rather ashamed of the little assistance we have been able to give' in Advisory Committee cases. Despite the large number of internees being held in the Free State, there was very little documentary evidence 'and in the case of the English prisoners we have hardly any'.[200] That certainly would have been a problem had more prisoners chosen to put their cases to the Advisory Committee, but they did not do so, unaware of the embarrassment they could have caused.

Kathleen Brooks was prominent among the women deportees, largely because of her illness at Mountjoy, and also her evidence when she claimed compensation. As noted, she had been under police surveillance for some time in connection with her role as IRA postmistress. Following one of the elementary precepts of intelligence (product rather than enforcement), it was decided by the police that the arrangement would be left in place subject only to the most discreet and distant observation of the family. A simple double-envelope method was used, with the inner envelope addressed to P. Healy, a *nom de guerre* of Pa Murray, the OC Britain. It is evident from the dossier that surveillance and interception continued for some time and therefore a mass of IRA correspondence must have been obtained. Brooks's brother Bernard was followed to meetings with republicans in London. Their sister, Nora, prudently disappeared after the police raid that netted Kathleen.

When Kathleen actually appeared before a tribunal to press her compensation claim for £2,000, she was ill prepared and palpably evasive and untruthful. Were the government able to show her involvement in IRA activities, her compensation would be reduced on the basis that she had contributed to her own detention. Naturally, she wished to avoid that, as well as to maintain the propaganda advantage of representing herself as a much-wronged innocent. Although Kathleen's middle name was Mary, when confronted by Special Branch Detective Sergeant Victor Anger and his warrant, she said that there was no Miss M. Brooks in the house. (The outer envelope of the stream of letters had been addressed to Miss M. Brooks.) When cross-examined by Sir Douglas Hogg, the Attorney General, at her compensation hearing, she denied ever having received such letters. She could not explain why and how they kept arriving at the house (where she lived with her five brothers, a sister and a servant) without anyone else receiving them. She explained the photograph of de Valera at the house as being simply a family possession, given to her brother in America. When asked why she had refused to release herself by signing the Free State government's form of undertaking, she replied, 'They had no right to take me, and I was not going to sign a form which looked an admission of guilt.' She also claimed, implausibly, not to know that Art O'Brien was a great friend of one of her brothers.[201]

The biter bit

In the years following the Easter Rising, Art O'Brien had been one of the most active republican organisers in Britain, publicly linked to Sinn Féin and to organisations such as the Irish National Relief Organisation (for prisoners and dependants) and the ISDL. Behind the scenes, using his public militancy and notoriety as a double bluff – hiding in the open – he was involved in the clandestine activities of the IRA, helping with finance, procurement, publicity and legal aid.[202] At the time of his deportation he described himself (in court proceedings) as 'the representative in London of the Irish Republican Government'.[203] Not a lawyer himself, he had worked closely with solicitors representing prisoners and internees and had a good knowledge of the relevant parts of the law and of the legal system and its possibilities for baulking and harassing government and obtaining redress. He also had access to funds and was in contact with sympathetic and reliable solicitors. He decided to challenge the legality of the deportations. The weakness in the government's position was obvious: after the establishment of the Irish Free State, had the ROIA (1920) lapsed?

To test this, an application for a writ of habeas corpus was made to the King's Bench on 10 April 1923, four weeks after the round-up and deportations. At the heart of the application was the Irish Free State Constitution Act, 1922, the Free State Constitution itself and the implied repeal of the statute under which deportation and internment had been ordered.[204] The ROIA had been passed at a time when the Imperial government was responsible for law and order in Ireland and when the Anglo-Irish War was in full spate. It no longer had that governing responsibility, and, therefore, it was contended that the statute was void. Giving judgment against the applicant, Lord Hewart, Lord Chief Justice, sidestepped the argument that when the purpose of a law ceased so also did the law. Whether the ROIA was no longer valid in Ireland, as the Irish courts had suggested in the Childers Case, was beside the point: that judgment (of which only a newspaper report was offered) did not address the issue of whether the statute continued to be in force in England.[205] There was the Home Secretary's statement to Parliament on 19 March 1923, and indeed that 'the [Irish] Government whose coming into existence was said to have impliedly repealed this regulation [14b] was the very Government which asked that it might be set in operation'.[206] Then there was the wording of the Act itself, which 'expressly contemplated that the need for the Regulation might continue beyond "the end of the present war"'. Lord Hewart also dismissed the argument that Ireland was no longer a British isle (relevant because of the wording of the Regulation).[207] Geographically, Ireland remained part of the British Isles; constitutionally, the Free State had become a British dominion. The applicant had argued that the Home Secretary could not deport someone to a place where he had no legal control. But he could not have it both ways: his application contended that the Home Secretary was the proper person to whom the rule of the court should be directed. Judgment was accordingly given for the applicant.

Application was immediately made to the Court of Appeal, which, on 13 April 1923, agreed to hear the case. Arguments were made on 23 and 24 April, and the Court gave judgment on 9 May. All three justices (Lords Bankes, Scrutton and Atkin) emphasised the great importance of issues bearing on the liberty of the subject. Lord Justice Scrutton set out the classic arguments of liberalism, as though John Stuart Mill were speaking through him. In particular, he emphasised that care for this liberty was not to be less vigilant because the person in question 'may not be particularly meritorious'. It was a test of belief in principles if one applied them to cases with which one had no sympathy at all. Moreover, the subject could be deprived of liberty only by due process of law: 'A man undoubtedly guilty of murder must yet be released if due forms of law have not been followed in his conviction.'[208]

In deciding that the Home Secretary's order was not legal, the Court began by considering the question of the independence of the Irish Free State and therefore of the relations between it and England.[209] These had been determined by the Irish Free State (Agreement) Act, 1922, the Irish Free State Constitution Act, 1922, and the Treaty between Great Britain and Ireland set out in Schedule 2 of the latter and which was thereby given the force of law.[210] In the view of Lord Justice Bankes, 'these provisions point irresistibly to the conclusion that since the establishment of the Irish Free State an order cannot lawfully be made by the Home Secretary for the internment of a person in the Irish Free State'.[211]

The judges considered the case from several points, but always coming back to the illegality of the Home Secretary's action. The government's case was hardly strengthened by the Orders in Council which had been made to remove doubts as to the validity of its action under the ROIA.[212] These Orders failed to address the central weakness in the government's case – could not do so – which was the fact of Irish independence. In any event, no new regulations had been issued under the Order. The making of the Orders reeked of panic and seemed ham-fisted and inept. Had they directly affected the case being heard it was more than probable that a serious confrontation would have developed between the judiciary and the executive. Lord Justice Scrutton certainly made this clear when he referred to the second Order having been made 'during the actual argument of the case on appeal'.[213] It was perhaps beyond the function of His Majesty's judges to criticise the advice which His Majesty's ministers give in issuing Orders in Council, 'but it may be permissible to say respectfully that it adds a new terror to litigation with Government officials if they can make Orders in Council while a case is being argued, to assist their argument'.[214]

One other point remained, and Lord Justice Scrutton dealt with it briskly. The Attorney General, in a move that hardly reflected well on the integrity and obligations of government, had argued that since the applicant was in the Free State he was no longer under the executive authority of the Home Secretary, and, therefore, the writ of habeas corpus was not returnable against him. Had this argument been accepted, O'Brien would have been left in a legal and political limbo: the Home Secretary had ordered his deportation and detention for an indefinite period but, according to this reading of the law, could not order his release. This contention was somewhat undermined by statements made by the Home Secretary in the House of Commons which suggested that he was under the impression he had not lost control over the persons who by his order had been interned in the Irish Free State. It was true that, as stated in the Home Secretary's affidavit, the Governor of Mountjoy Prison was an official of the Free State government and not under the control of the British government, but the question remained of what arrangement the Home Secretary had made with the Free State government.[215] Lord Justice Atkin took the same line, noting that the applicant had been in the custody and control of the Home Secretary, 'by an order which we have held to be illegal'.[216] Actual physical custody was not essential, as shown by the Lords' judgment in the case of *Bernardo* v. *Ford*.[217] 'There is', he continued, 'grave doubt whether he is not still in the custody or control of the Home Secretary'. *Bernardo* v. *Ford* provided ample ground for the Court to order the writ to go to the Home Secretary. If, in fact, he no longer had control over the applicant, he had fully to show how that had come about.[218]

This was a comprehensive rout for the government side and a significant political embarrassment. The effect was total and immediate. Following an emergency cabinet, the decision was telegraphed to Dublin, with the request that all the deportees be released.[219] Relations between the two governments were cordial, but the Home Office must have breathed a sigh of relief when the men were released from Mountjoy and the women from the NDU.[220] The Free State government was still at war with the anti-Treaty republicans, and, while victory was certain, the ceasefire and dump-arms order would not come for another fortnight (24 May 1923). The Dublin government must have seen the liberation and departure of some of its most bitter and able opponents with deep regret and must have been at least passingly tempted to retain them.

The civil servants who had advised the Home Secretary so poorly and who had encouraged him through persistent Commons' criticism, were now left to put the best possible face on things. A memorandum by Harry Simpson two weeks after the Appeal Court ruling rehearsed the reasons for making the deportation orders: the seriousness of the IRA threat in England; the imminence of a campaign of bombing and arson; the role of the auxiliaries in Britain in raising funds and procuring explosives, ammunition and arms; and the difficulty in bringing the activists to court, because of the nature of the evidence and the threat to intelligence sources and techniques. The Appeal Court decision had resulted in the release of the majority of the deportees, but in eleven cases (including O'Brien's) proceedings had been brought in the criminal courts on the basis of the evidence to hand.[221] A careful watch would have to be kept, but 'His Majesty's Government have no doubt, and this view is shared by the Free State government, that the deportations have inflicted a smashing blow upon the Irregulars from which they will not recover.'[222]

This last was true – at least in the medium term. A total of 111 people (one had been added to the original 110) had been arrested and deported. This was an uncomfortable and punitive experience. Upon release, most were able to pick up the threads of their lives again – not an impossible thing to do, after a relatively short confinement. But some had lost employment and opportunities, and all now knew that they had been and would continue to be under close surveillance.[223] The fear of postal interceptions, of being watched and, of course, of informers and even agents provocateurs would have been extremely demoralising, if not paralysing. It is most unlikely that trust, self-confidence and the brio necessary for clandestine activity could be re-established. New recruits would have been extremely hard to find. But, well beyond this, there was the awful reality of the total military triumph of the Free State and the crushing of resistance. Were the deportations really necessary, and did they contribute in any significant way to this outcome?

In the autumn, the bill had to be paid. Concerned at the possible scale of damages, the personal liabilities of ministers and the uncertainties of legislation, and to protect the Home Secretary immediately, an Indemnity Bill was rushed in.[224] This provided for cases to be processed by a tribunal rather than by the courts. A Compensation Tribunal was set up. With more than a hundred lawsuits pending, with their attendant legal as well as unpredictable substantive costs, this verged on retroactive legislation, but it passed.[225] The claimants were saved the expense, procedural delays, uncertainties and complexity of civil action. Fault was admitted at the outset, and the Tribunal heard evidence as to damages. This included the manner of arrest, conditions of confinement and effects on employment or business and health. It was the usual tussle: strong claims of distress and loss on the plaintiff side and an attempt to mitigate on the part of the Crown by examining the claimants on their activities, which, it suggested, had put them in the path of the illegal order.[226] The first awards were announced at the end of November 1923, with most in the £300 to £400 range but with some reaching between £600 and £900. By 30 November 1923, a total of £24,283 had been awarded in forty-four claims, with another twenty-two pending.[227] But it was not all bad news for the Treasury. Almost half the deportees lodged no claim: through either disdain or a desire to avoid further anxiety, they had decided not to submit themselves again to the British legal process.

Notes

1 The terms of the Truce are set out in *Arrangements Governing the Cessation of Active Operations in Ireland* (London: HMSO, 1921), Cmd. 1534; see also Public Record Office (hereafter PRO), HO/45/20094.

2 Ernie O'Malley, *The Singing Flame* (Dublin: Anvil Books, 1992), pp. 15–41.

3 PRO HO/144/1734/221. Penal servitude was imposed for sentences of three years and over. Persons subject to this sentence were called 'convicts' and were sent to one of the five convict prisons where the regime of penal servitude was administered. Sentences of imprisonment could be imposed for up to two years and were served in

one of the forty local prisons in operation in England in 1921 or twelve local prisons in Ireland. See *Forty-Second Report of the General Prisons Board, Ireland, 1919–1920*, PP, 1921, XVI [Cmd. 1375], 469, iii; *Report of the Commissioners of Prisons and the Directors of Convict Prisons*, PP, 1922 (Sess, 2), II [Cmd. 1761] 1017, 53, Appendix 3. For a description of the development of penal servitude, see Seán McConville, *History of English Prison Administration, Vol. I: 1750–1877* (London: Routledge & Kegan Paul, 1981), pp. 385–92; for an account of nineteenth-century 'ordinary' imprisonment, see Seán McConville, *English Local Prisons, 1860–1900: Next Only to Death* (London and New York: Routledge, 1995). This was a period during which prisons were taken out of use on both sides of the Irish Sea. Eight English prisons were closed during 1922 and a further two by 1928 (5 *Hansard*, vol. 215, col. 571, 22 March 1928).

4 These were either involved in the IRA's wave of arson, explosions and criminal damage or had been convicted of procuring weapons. This British campaign was ordered by Rory O'Connor of the IRA's GHQ, as a retaliation, it was asserted, for the Black and Tan action in Ireland. Sentences ranged from fifteen months' hard labour to fifteen years' penal servitude (PRO HO/144/4645/102e). As part of the mutual Anglo-Irish indemnities, the Provisional government of the Free State agreed to pay £1 million for damage to property and persons in Britain during the Anglo-Irish War. The sum was to be settled over a three-year period in twelve quarterly instalments of £83,333 6s. 8d. (PRO HO/144/4645/103).

5 For some background to the Dartmoor mutiny, see PRO HO/144/1734/225; see also Seán McConville, *Irish Political Prisoners, 1848–1922: Theatres of War* (London and New York: Routledge, 2003), pp. 760–2.

6 McConville, *Irish Political Prisoners, op. cit.*, pp. 763–4; see also Major Wallace Blake, *Quod* (London: Hodder & Stoughton, c.1923).

7 PRO HO/144/1734/217. Blake was himself Irish.

8 A schedule of these prisoners, their offences and sentences, and a commentary on the offences, is to be found at PRO HO/144/4645/102e. See *The Times*, 4 April 1921, 10f; *Manchester Guardian*, 4 April 1921, 8a, photograph 5c–d. The Irish Club, located in Erskine Street, in the Hulme district of Manchester, was raided during the night of 2 April. Police were looking for those involved in a number of arson attacks which had been mounted that morning on three hotels, and on offices, a cotton warehouse and a café. During the raid on the Erskine Street premises, shots were fired from the club, and police returned fire. One man, John Morgan, was shot dead and another, Shaun Wickham, was wounded. Three policemen received slight wounds. Morgan was found to be in possession of a list of further targets in Manchester, with drawings and other incriminating papers. Several revolvers and fire-setting materials were discovered on the premises. Many of an estimated forty men in the club escaped through a lavatory window.

9 PRO HO/144/1734/208.

10 The Irish releases were immediately welcomed by Lansbury's *Daily Herald* (12 December 1921, 1a and b, 4b), which urged immediate release of all those imprisoned in connection with the Irish war. The *Herald* also wanted amnesty for all those in prison for offences in connection with the Labour, socialist and Communist movements.

11 PRO HO/144/4645/106; PRO P.Com./7/260/412340/116. Pardons were not granted in these cases and – at least in theory – they could have been obliged to serve out their original sentences in the event of a further conviction.

12 PRO HO/144/4645/103.

13 PRO HO/144/4645/116; PRO P.Com./7/260/412340/116.

14 See McConville, *Irish Political Prisoners, op. cit.*, pp. 165–8, 252–5, 209–12.

15 For the background to the mutiny, see Anthony Babbington's *The Devil to Pay: The Mutiny of the Connaught Rangers, India, July 1920* (London: Cooper, 1991); Sam Pollock,

Mutiny for the Cause (London: Sphere, 1971). For the initial cabinet paper on the matter, which went no further than to agree to a partial remission of sentences, see PRO CAB/24/132/89, Cabinet Paper 3690, 4 February 1922. The Cabinet agreed, on 21 February 1922, to review the sentences on the Connaught Rangers in accordance with the proposal of the Secretary of State for War (PRO CAB/23/29/12). In 1936, in belated recognition of the contribution that the mutineers had made to the cause of Irish independence, the de Valera government made provision for their pensioning with the Connaught Rangers (Pensions) Act.

16 PRO HO/144/3724/1–5. A number had already completed their sentence. See the letter from W. T. Cosgrave to British Prime Minister Bonar Law, on 16 December 1922, in which he pointed out that the continued detention of the Connaught Rangers mutineers was causing him difficulty as he sought to bring in the Amnesty Bill. This and the British response are at PRO CAB/23/32/8, 16 and 18 December 1922 respectively.

17 PRO HO/144/3724/3; PRO CAB/23/32/9; PRO CAB/23/46/11.

18 PRO HO/144/3724/4. See the Indemnity (British Military) Act, 1923.

19 Police had been watching a Manchester shed for two days and found the following: 618 detonators, 1,719 rounds of ammunition, 2,583 high-explosive charges and 100 feet of fuse, together with twenty-five rifles, four pistols and eight bayonets. A further 300 cartridges were found later when Breen's father and brother were arrested, including fifty dum-dum bullets. The latter were viewed with particular repugnance by the authorities (*Daily Chronicle*, 27 May 1921, 6b; 5 July 1921, 6b; PRO HO/144/20092). On approaching the shed, Breen saw that the padlock had been broken and exclaimed to McGallogly, 'We are done; we are sold.' At this point, the two were rushed by police (see also PRO HO/144/4645/102E).

20 PRO HO/144/20092.

21 It was disclosed at sentencing that both Breen and McGallogly had previous non-political convictions (stealing guttering from a handcart) for which they had pleaded guilty and had served a nine-month prison term in 1919–20 (*Manchester Evening News*, 15 July 1921, 5c).

22 PRO HO/144/20092/2.

23 See above, pp. 23–7.

24 See above, p. 23. There was probably also a certain amount of freelance booty-taking. Almost from the outset, the Provisional government, anxious to strip its armed opponents of their claim to republican legitimacy, directed that they should be known as 'Irregulars'. Government forces were to be called the 'National Army'. Both sides fiercely contested the title 'republican'.

25 PRO HO/144/20092/2a. There is some speculation in the files, however, that the robbery may not have been for political purposes.

26 The Provisional government had used some of the forces at its disposal to penetrate and covertly police anti-Treaty groups and the IRA in Britain. Insufficient liaison with the local police led to the arrest in Carlisle of Arthur Nolan of the CID and John O'Hara, a Free State intelligence agent. They were found to be in possession of ammunition, but their credentials were quickly established, and the ammunition (which they had intercepted en route to anti-Treaty forces) was handed over to the Free State (PRO HO/144/21356/14).

27 *Irish Independent*, 8 May 1923, 6a; *Irish Times*, 8 May 1923, 5c.

28 This highly political unit was one of the principal instruments of the Provisional and Free State governments in the Civil War. It was deeply hated by the republicans against whom it waged a ruthless campaign. For an account of its activities, see Eunan O'Halpin, *Defending Ireland: The Irish State and Its Enemies since 1922* (Oxford: Oxford University Press, 1999), pp. 11–15.

29 PRO HO/144/21356/14/4; *Manchester Guardian*, 4 July 1923, 11e. He was, he said, more afraid of torture than execution.

30 *The Times*, 4 July 1923, 11g; *Manchester Guardian*, 24 July 1923, 9c; *Freeman's Journal*, 24 July 1923, 7d.

31 'The man Mulcahy was the organiser of the outrages of 2 April 1921, and was also the organiser of the plot to blow up Stuart Street Power Station, Bradford, Manchester [*sic*]. The documents relating to this plot are, I believe, in the hands of the authorities' (PRO HO/144/20092/8); for a report on the wave of arson to which Breen referred (and a fatal exchange of shots at the Erskine Street Club), see *The Times*, 4 April 1921, 10f.

32 These were James Coyle, Sean Golding, Scanlon, Connolly (South Wales) and Purcell.

33 PRO HO/144/20092/8. He named Mathias Lawless, Richard Hurley and Joseph Dillon as accomplices and Michael Fitzgerald and others as gun-runners. Two men named Wofer had smuggled arms to Dublin on the SS *Elban*. He later named Henry Trummel as a gun-runner and a Communist.

34 PRO HO/144/20092/8. He continued to make statements to the police and, in August 1924, claimed that Bartley Iago and John Foley were innocent of the robbery charges on which he had been convicted. He provided a detailed account of the operation and stated that there were at the time only half a dozen 'Irregulars' in Manchester and only a couple of these were capable of bank robbery. Men had come over from Ireland to help. The Lancashire police dismissed Breen's statement, which was contradicted by Patrick Joseph Gavin, the fourth man on the raid.

35 PRO HO/144/20092/8/26. On William Conlon, see pp. 127–9 below.

36 PRO HO/144/20092/8/28. Harry Simpson, Assistant Secretary, minuted that since Breen had served only four and a half years of his life sentence it was too early to set a date when he might be released.

37 PRO HO/144/20092/8/37, 22 February 1929.

38 Labour had 288 seats, the Conservatives 260 and the Liberals fifty-nine. The first Labour administration (1924) had survived only ten months.

39 PRO HO/144/20092/37a. The League was of course known to the Special Branch and the Home Office as being firmly in the hands of anti-Free State forces.

40 John Robert Clynes (1869–1949). MP Platting division of Manchester, 1906–31 and 1935–45. Trade-union background. Chairman Parliamentary Labour Party, 1921–2. Lord Privy Seal and Leader of Commons, 1924. Home Secretary, 1929–31.

41 PRO HO/144/20092, 28 June 1929.

42 PRO HO/144/20092/38. The League also mentioned William Conlon, who was in Belfast Prison. They did not regard him as a political prisoner but asked for a retrial in his case. Another Belfast man (George Nash) was a political prisoner, and they added his name to those of Breen and his comrades (see pp. 117–20 above). Bridie O'Mullane was a colleague of Hanna Sheehy-Skeffington, who also worked in the WPDL. O'Mullane had been imprisoned in Kilmainham in 1923. See Trinity College Dublin Archives, Kilmainham Diary of Cecilia Saunders Gallagher; see also NLI MS. 33,606 for prison collaboration between O'Mullane and Sheehy-Skeffington. O'Mullane was a recruiting officer for Cumann na mBan during the Anglo-Irish War.

43 PRO HO/144/20092/40, 26 June 1926. Margaret Grace Bondfield (1873–1952). Trade-union background. Labour MP for Northampton, 1923–4; Wallsend, 1926–31. Minister for Labour, 1929–31.

44 PRO HO/144/20092/56.

45 Should the Home Office have desired to acknowledge receipt of this curious letter, instructions were given how to do so. A copy had been sent to various Cabinet

members. The Home Office passed a copy to the Dominions Office for forwarding to His Majesty's Government of the Free State.

46 PRO HO/144/20092/38.

47 John Beckett, MP, for example, wrote on 12 August 1929 and E. Thurtle, MP, on 16 October (PRO HO/144/20092/53 and PRO HO/144/20092/55).

48 See John Beckett's questions (5 *Hansard*, vol. 226, cols. 537–8, 7 March 1928; 325, cols. 579–84, 13 February 1930).

49 PRO HO/144/20092/58.

50 *5 Hansard*, vol. 225, cols. 582–3, 13 February 1930.

51 John Scurr (1876–1932). Born in Brisbane. Active in labour movement in East End of London and imprisoned in 1921 with twenty-nine other Poplar councillors for rates equalisation activities. Labour MP for Stepney. He spoke from Labour's heartland.

52 PRO HO/144/20092/60.

53 PRO HO/144/20092/74, 30 March 1930. Archibald Fenner Brockway (1888–1988). Journalist, peace campaigner and anti-colonialist. A major figure on the left of the labour movement. Imprisoned four times during the Great War for his anti-conscription activities, including a sentence of two years' hard labour. Lifelong commitment to anti-colonial causes. Labour MP, East Leyton, 1929–31. Opposed Ramsay MacDonald and joined the Independent Labour Party of which he was a leader until 1946 when he rejoined the Labour Party. Labour MP for Eton and Slough, 1950–64, when he lost a controversial election in which race and immigration were issues. Life Peer, 1964.

54 Charlotte Despard (1844–1939, née French) was the sister of Lord French, the penultimate Lord Lieutenant of Ireland. She became known to the authorities as a leading member of the troublesome 'old ladies'. See below, p. 269, n. 42, for a biographical note. Hanna Sheehy-Skeffington (1877–1946) was also a suffragette and had been imprisoned in 1912 for breaking windows in protest at the exclusion of the female franchise from the Home Rule Bill. Her husband Francis, a pacifist, was murdered by a British officer during the 1916 Rising, but Hanna refused to accept compensation. She became a member of Sinn Féin and a judge in the Dáil courts. She took the anti-Treaty side in the Civil War. An energetic, lifelong and uncompromising radical.

55 *Manchester Guardian*, 18 March 1930, 15e.

56 Sir Charles Philips Trevelyan (1870–1958), 3rd baronet. Educated Harrow and Trinity, Cambridge. Secretary to Lord Crowe when he was Lord Lieutenant of Ireland. Labour MP, Central Newcastle, 1922–31.

57 PRO HO/144/20092/57. Dan Breen (1894–1969) was the instigator of the Soloheadbeg ambush which is generally taken to mark the beginning of the Anglo-Irish War. His subsequent activities were such that the British government offered £1,000 for his capture. Breen was an emblematic figure for many republican activists, to whom he embodied decisiveness and derring-do. See below, p. 234, n. 234, for a biographical note.

58 Maurice Moore (1854–1939) settled in Ireland after his military career. He had sought clemency for Roger Casement and, more recently, for the Connaught Rangers mutineers. He was a supporter of Home Rule and then – surprisingly – a founder member of de Valera's Fianna Fáil. George Gavan Duffy (1882–1951) was the son of the Young Irelander, Sir George Gavan Duffy. He was one of the plenipotentiary delegates during the Treaty negotiations. He became Minister for Foreign Affairs in the Second Dáil government but resigned as a protest against the suppression of the Supreme Court. He had a distinguished legal career in Ireland, in 1946 becoming President of the High Court.

59 PRO HO/144/20093, 30 April 1930.

60 5 *Hansard*, vol. 228, cols. 1074–5, 7 May 1930; PRO HO/144/20093/85.

61 PRO HO/144/20093/105.

62 PRO HO/144/20093/107, 19 December 1930.

63 PRO HO/144/20093/110.

64 PRO HO/144/20093/115–17.

65 PRO HO/144/20093/117.

66 See above, p. 23–4.

67 He had made notes at work on the savings account of an RIC man who had been transferred to police service in England. He had also collected information on petrol pumps, timber, an acetylene gas manufacturer's premises and underground power stations (*Manchester Guardian*, 27 July 1922, 13b). The jury at his first trial failed to agree, largely, it seems, because he had no ammunition for his revolver (*The Times*, 25 July 1922, 5e; 26 July 1922, 5g; *Manchester Guardian*, 27 July 1922, 13b). At his second trial, he was convicted. Mr Justice Benson, taking a lenient view of the offence (why is not clear) passed a sentence of twelve months' hard labour (*Irish Times*, 9 September 1922, 10b; *Freeman's Journal*, 9 September 1922, 5e).

68 PRO HO/144/20093/85. Wrigley was due to be released from Wandsworth early in September 1923.

69 It is not at all clear that Eadie was a sister of James Connolly. The usual biographical sources state that he was the youngest of a family of three boys (see *The Dictionary of Irish Biography*, for example). It is possible that she was a natural half-sister of Connolly; more probable is a mistake at the Home Office. Eadie's husband had served with the Post Office Rifles in France. For the trial, see *The Times*, 30 June 1922, 7d; 22 July 1922, 7c.

70 *Irish Times*, 22 July 1922, 5c; *Freeman's Journal*, 25 July 1922.

71 This Act had been used repeatedly in connection with the suffragettes' campaign of violent destruction (see, for example, the aftermath of the arson attack at Kew Gardens on 20 February 1913: *Morning Post*, 21 February 1913, 7g, 8a; 8 March 1913, 8g).

72 The maximum term for making or possession under suspicious circumstances was fourteen years' penal servitude (s.4 [1]).

73 PRO HO/144/3724/3.

74 *Scotsman*, 29 August 1921, 4b.

75 PRO HO/144/3742/3. The Free State asked for the men's freedom as an act of grace, whilst reprobating their acts. Cosgrave also pointed out that his government would be faced with a continual agitation whilst the men remained in custody. Sir John Anderson, who eventually agreed to the men's release, and who had been a key figure in Anglo-Irish negotiations in 1921–2, sourly noted, 'we were assured over & over again by the Irish leaders that the seizure of money from private persons had never been authorised by the "political organisation"'.

76 See below, pp. 148–51.

77 PRO HO/144/3724/7, Lionel Curtis to Sir Mark Sturgis, 27 March 1923. Lionel George Curtis (1872–1955). New College, Oxford, then called to the Bar. Served in the Boer War and in Transvaal local government. Returned to Oxford. Fellow of All Souls. Secretary to Treaty talks, 1921. Adviser on Irish affairs at Colonial Office, 1921–4. Published extensively on Commonwealth and peace issues. Companion of Honour, 1949.

78 A paper was presented to Cabinet in March 1924, which considered whether Irish (and other) political prisoners could or should be subject to a special and more lenient regime. This option was rejected on both substantive and practical grounds (PRO CAB/24/166/14, 27 March 1924).

79 At first spelt as Portlaoighise, then simplified to Portlaoise. Some republicans until recent times insisted on Maryborough, to emphasise the continuity between British and what they saw as illegitimate Irish administration. See, for example, Uinseann MacEoin, *The IRA in the Twilight Years, 1923–1948* (Dublin: Argenta, 1997), *passim*.

80 Belfast Prison, like almost all Victorian city and county gaols built in the UK after 1842, had followed the Pentonville, separate-cell model. Since prisoners were expected to spend all or most of their sentences in their cells, little or no provision was made for workshops and association facilities. Penal servitude, by contrast, once the initial separate ('probationary') stage was passed, enforced extensive hard toil on the convicts. For this, and other purposes, association was required – allowing prisoners to congregate for work, exercise or (very limited) recreation. This in turn meant that convict prisons had a different design from the separate-system local prisons. Belfast Prison, with its limited footprint and restricted opportunities for labour, would always remain unsatisfactory for the implementation of the convict regime.

81 See the schedule for the first quarter of 1924 at PRO HO/144/6065/8. This shows that of seventy-seven Northern Ireland convicts in English prisons, all came from Belfast bar four from Maryborough and two from Londonderry. Most, but not all, were political.

82 Penal Servitude Act, 1857: 20 & 21 Vict., c.3, s.6.

83 PRO HO/144/6065/8. Borstal training took its name from the establishment in Kent, where it had been originally devised.

84 The WPDL did not categorise Conlon's murder as political, and for this view they almost certainly had IRA authority. They took an interest in his case ostensibly because they thought he had received unfair treatment, having been arrested by the army as he left court after the jury at his first trial disagreed. Conlon was secretary of a Sinn Féin club, and it was probably for this reason that the WPDL sought a retrial (PRO HO/144/20692/38, schedule of April 1929). The other defendants were William McConville, Francis O'Boyle (or Boyle) of Beragh, Co. Tyrone, and Hugh Rogers of Sixmilecross, Co. Tyrone (see *Down Recorder*, 25 December 1920, 3c; *Banbridge Chronicle and Downshire Standard*, 25 December 1920, 3a–d, 4a–e, 5a–e). In his summing up for the jury, the judge, Mr Justice Pim, had commented that 'the case was entirely one of circumstantial evidence'.

85 PRONI CAB/4/239, H. M. Pollock (Acting Prime Minister, Northern Ireland) to George Lansbury, MP (First Commissioner of Works), 24 October 1929.

86 *Banbridge Chronicle and Downshire Standard*, 8 January 1921, 3d. Bail was refused, as was a further application to King's Bench in Dublin by William McConville (*Banbridge Chronicle and Downshire Standard*, 19 February 1921, 1d).

87 Section 1(2). It is not clear why it was chosen to proceed by court martial, but the newspaper report suggests that Conlon had been a soldier in the Norfolk Regiment and still had some connection. Conlon's solicitor objected to his client being tried under Article 67 of the ROI Regulations on two grounds: (1) Conlon was an American citizen and (2) the ROI applied to cases where law and order had broken down, and this was not true of Co. Down. Both arguments were rejected. William McConville was, however, granted a separate trial (*Banbridge Chronicle and Downshire Standard*, 23 April 1921, 1f; see also 30 April 1921, 3f, 4e, 5a–d). McConville (who may have been assisting the Crown) was found not guilty of misprision of felony (i.e. failing to report a felony) and no evidence was offered on the murder charge against him. At this distance it is impossible to be definite, but the newspaper reports suggest that Conlon may have been the principal target for the prosecution. This might explain why his case was taken up so vigorously by those who sought clemency.

88 PRO HO/144/6065/8.

89 PRO HO/144/6026.

90 PRO HO/144/6026/3.

91 Harry Butler Simpson (1861–1940), Winchester and Magdalen College, Oxford (Double First), was legally qualified and a key figure in many of the decisions involving prisoners – political and non-political alike. His career is dealt with *in extenso* by Jill Pellew in her authoritative account, *The Home Office, 1848–1914: From Clerks to Bureaucrats* (London: Heinemann, 1982). See also Martin J. Wiener, *Reconstructing the Criminal: Culture, Law and Policy in England, 1830–1914* (Cambridge: Cambridge University Press, 1990).

92 Under the Forfeiture of Property Act, 1870: 33 & 34 Vict., c.23, s.9, the property of convicts passed to trustees during their confinement. Section 8 of the Act disqualified the convict from making any contract.

93 The Army Act was an annual Act that provided, *inter alia*, for the jurisdiction and powers of courts martial. For 1916, see 6 & 7 Geo. V, c.5.

94 PRO HO/144/6026.

95 Thornton, aged thirty-six, had cut the girl's neck with a razor. See *Irish Independent*, 12 May 1927, 10b; *Weekly Irish Times*, 14 May 1927, 6d; *Irish Times*, 16 May 1927, 7c.

96 See *Irish Times*, 10 May 1927, 7g. The Ministry of Home Affairs offered a reward of £500 for information leading to the men's recapture.

97 *Irish Independent*, 16 May 1927, 6f; PRONI CAB/4/239, H. M. Pollock (Acting Prime Minister, Northern Ireland) to George Lansbury, MP (First Commissioner of Works), 24 October 1929. There was a protest from Bundoran Urban Council (Co. Donegal) because it was thought that orders had been issued for the arrest of the escapees in the Free State (*Irish Times*, 26 May 1927, 7f).

98 Geoffrey Granville Whiskard (1886–1957). Educated at St Paul's and Wadham College, Oxford. Home Office, 1911. Assistant Secretary, Dublin Castle, 1920–2. Colonial Office (Irish Section), 1922–5. Distinguished civil-service career. KCB, 1943.

99 For the arrest, see the *Irish News*, 12 October 1921, 5c; the general situation, General Macready commented, was 'one of grave anxiety and the danger of the epidemic of reprisal and blood feud spreading to the Border is already apparent' (PRO CAB/24/136/9).

100 PRO HO/144/3724. St Mary's Hall was the location of the IRA headquarters in Belfast and a major arsenal until it was raided by the RUC on 18 March 1922.

101 PRO HO/144/3724; *The Times*, 31 March 1922, 12a and b; see also 13b and 17g.

102 PRO HO/144/3724.

103 Sir John Anderson (1882–1958) had a brilliant civil-service and political career, becoming an independent MP in 1938, then Home Secretary (1939–40) and Chancellor of the Exchequer (1943–5). Created Viscount Waverley, 1952.

104 PRO HO/144/3724.

105 See PRO HO/267/228.

106 Committal hearings took place before a special court in Enniskillen on 20 February 1922. The prisoners were produced under heavy guard and were handcuffed throughout. Altogether, fifteen men had been captured by the Special Constabulary and the RIC; they were found to have bombs (probably grenades), arms and ammunition in their possession. The men had been taken in flagrante delicto, and the explanations that were offered by a few were pitifully incredible. (For committal, see *Irish Times*, 20 February 1922, 6e–f.) Evidence showed that this had been a carefully planned operation mounted mainly by members of the Leitrim IRA units guided by local men. At Fermanagh Assizes, all were found guilty, and heavy sentences were imposed of between five and ten years' penal servitude (*Irish Times*, 13 March 1922). Astonishingly, one of the men (John Griffin) was carrying incriminating documents including details of shootings, accounts, lists of arms and ammunition and

the names of leading IRA figures. To carry such items at any time was reckless, but to do so when going on an operation was carelessness almost beyond belief. This free and easy attitude to documents was a minor but persistent theme in IRA operations.

107 As noted, the sentences of the other eight men (only two of whom were from Northern Ireland) ranged from five years (for the drivers of the cars) to ten years for John Griffen, who, it was said, was in possession of 'some of the worst documents' (PRO HO/144/6065/39; *Irish Times*, 15 March 1922, 6e).

108 Collins's double-dealing on this is well documented. See, for example, John M. Regan's account in *The Irish Counter-Revolution 1921–1936: Treatyite Politics and Settlement in Independent Ireland* (Dublin: Gill & Macmillan, 1999), pp. 61–5. See above, pp. 68–70.

109 PRO CAB/24/136/9, Report by the GOC-in-Chief on the situation in Ireland for the week ending 25 March 1922.

110 See McConville, *Irish Political Prisoners, op. cit.*, pp. 686–7.

111 For an account of Frank Flood's trial and execution, see Tim Carey's *Hanged for Ireland: A Documentary History* (Dublin: Blackwater Press, 2001), pp. 98–100, 124–6; see also *Irish Independent*, 22 January 1921, 5f; *Sunday Independent*, 13 March 1921, 1a.

112 PRO HO/144/3724/5, Sir John Anderson to Sir James Masterton-Smith, 9 January 1923. See also Geoffrey Whiskard to Arthur Locke on the cases of John McCurtain, John Flood and Felix O'Byrne, 3 January 1923. For confirmation of Cosgrave's attempts to persuade Sir James Craig to release, see NAI S5750/13, Northern Prisoners.

113 PRO HO/144/6065/8.

114 See pp. 115–16, above.

115 There were numerous questions in the Dáil about the release of internees and a growing sense that wars (Anglo-Irish and Civil) were over and it was time for a return to some kind of normal life. See, as but one example, *Dáil Debates*, vol. 7, cols. 863, *et seq.*, 16 May 1924. There were many sessions of that nature. On 21 May 1924, there was a major debate on the release of political prisoners, initiated by the Farmers' Party (*Dáil Debates*, vol. 7, cols. 1111–48). These questions and debates referred to Free State prisoners and internees, but the concerns expressed by those who wanted accelerated releases were part of a general political and popular mood and growing consensus.

116 See McConville, *English Local Prisons, op. cit.*, pp. 373–7 and 454 n.74, for an account of this division of imprisonment and the powers of the authorities to commit to the various classes.

117 PRO HO/144/6065/8, Alexander Maxwell (Chairman of the Prison Commission) to Lionel Curtis, 6 May 1924: 'They are "convicts" for whom no question of treatment as "first class misdemeanants" can arise.'

118 See pp. 148–50 below; see also PRO CAB/23/48/5, 7 May 1924, item 4.

119 5 *Hansard*, vol. 182, col. 437, 25 March 1925; see also vol. 185, cols. 2773–4, 2 July 1925.

120 PRO HO/144/6065/8.

121 PRO HO/144/6065/8. For a description of the Fenians' imprisonment, see McConville, *Irish Political Prisoners, op. cit.*, Chapters 4–6.

122 5 *Hansard*, vol. 183, cols. 129–30, 28 April 1925. See also cols. 138–9. George Buchanan (1890–1955). Trade unionist. Started political career as town councillor. Member of Independent Labour Party. Labour MP for the Gorbals, 1922–48. Minister for Pensions, 1947–8.

123 Peterhead Prison, located some 30 miles north of Aberdeen, on Scotland's east coast, was difficult and expensive for Irish prisoners' families to reach.

124 PRO HO/144/6065/26. In fact, the tabulation showed, some of the thirty-four Northern Ireland prisoners at Peterhead had, up to 4 May 1925, not used up their normal allowance of letters. One of the men was illiterate.

125 Leopold Stennett Amery (1873–1955). Born India, educated Harrow and Balliol. Fellow of All Souls, Oxford. Correspondent of *The Times* in South Africa during the Boer War. Assistant Secretary, War Cabinet, 1917. Unionist MP, Sparkbrook division of Birmingham, 1911–45. Colonial Secretary, 1924–9. Secretary of State for India and Burma, 1940–5.

126 See above, pp. 5–11; 134.

127 PRO HO/144/6065/32: 'For this reason I feel that it would be the more awkward for the British Gov[ernment] to suggest an amnesty.' S. G. Tallents, Imperial Secretary, had offered, on his return to Belfast, to take the matter up with Prime Minister Craig 'in whatever degree of formality was wished'.

128 Thomas Hueston had been convicted of attempted murder and of arms offences in connection with the Wattlebridge, Co. Fermanagh, ambush (7 February 1922) and at the Belfast Assizes was sentenced to ten years' penal servitude (PRO HO/144/6065/39; *Fermanagh Herald*, 13 January 1923, 3d). The offences had taken place about one mile from the border, on the Northern Ireland side. The captured policemen had been held for a fortnight and were released at Cavan Railway station with travel warrants home and a glass of rum (*Irish Times*, 21 November 1922, 7f).

129 PRO HO/144/6065/32, 21 August 1925. Sir William Joynson-Hicks (1865–1932) had previously been Postmaster General, Financial Secretary to the Treasury and Minister for Health. He had been Home Secretary since the previous November.

130 One appears to have been released on the expiration of his sentence. Five more had been transferred to Belfast on 28 August 1925: The five had 'given a good deal of trouble at Peterhead and were exercising a bad influence over the others, to such an extent that serious trouble was apprehended at their instigation from the other North Irish prisoners' (PRO HO/144/6065/32a, 24 September 1925).

131 PRO HO/144/6065/32a, 24 September 1925; see also Frank Aubrey Newsam (Home Office) to Geoffrey Whiskard, 25 September 1925 (PRO HO/144/6065/32). Robert Duke (1893–1969) was a principal in the Scottish Office. He had served throughout the Great War, rising from Second Lieutenant to Brigade Major, completing his Oxford BA in 1919. Newsam (1893–1964) was in the early stages of what would be an outstanding career of public service.

132 See above, pp. 10–11.

133 Section 1(2).

134 See above, pp. 5–11.

135 PRO HO/144/6065/37, Sir Richard Dawson Bates to Sir William Joynson-Hicks, 11 December 1925; PRO CAB/23/51/13, 16 December 1925.

136 Tim Pat Coogan, *Michael Collins* (London: Arrow Books, 1991), pp. 236–7.

137 Richard Dawson Bates. MP for the Protestant heartland of East Belfast from 1921 to 1943, during which period he was also Minister for Home Affairs. For a biographical note, see p. 100, n. 23 above.

138 PRO HO/144/6065/37.

139 James Albert Edward Hamilton, 3rd duke (1869–1953). Long-established Scots, then Ulster family. Former Conservative MP (City of Londonderry) in the UK Parliament. Northern Ireland Senator, 1921.

140 PRO HO/144/6065/37, Sir John Anderson to Sir Richard Dawson Bates, 15 December 1925.

141 The schedule setting out names, offences, sentences, etc., is to be found at PRO HO/144/6065/39. Another man, Francis Reilly, had also been captured on 8 February 1922. He was not part of the two Enniskillen groups, though taken within a few miles of the town. The floor of his car was covered with blood, and firearms, ammunition and bombs were also found (see above, p. 130).

142 Hueston pleaded guilty to possession of explosives and attempted murder. He had previous firearms and wounding convictions for which he had also received long sentences of penal servitude. He had been released in the general amnesty of January 1922 (PRO HO/144/6065/39).

143 Patrick Leonard, the temporary warder, may have secured his position through family connections. His father was a principal warder in the Free State, at the Clonmel Borstal Institution.

144 Altogether, fourteen political prisoners, in addition to Leonard, went on trial, facing various charges (*Freeman's Journal*, 5 December 1921, 5g; 7 December 1921, 6g; see also *Irish Independent*, 8 December 1921, 7h–g). Six men (Patrick Leonard, Patrick Tully, Hugh J. Timmins, Henry O'Loan, Thomas McShea and Patrick Johnston) faced murder charges at the Winter Assizes. Tully, Timmins and O'Loan were, on the direction of the Lord Chief Justice, acquitted and discharged at the conclusion of the evidence. Leonard, McShea and Johnston were convicted and (the penalty was mandatory) sentenced to death (*Irish Times*, 21 January 1922, 3d). Execution was fixed for Thursday, 9 February 1922, in Londonderry Prison.

145 *Irish Times*, 8 February 1922, 6c.

146 *Irish Times*, 8 February 1922, 6c; *Fermanagh Herald*, 11 February 1922, 5g.

147 The schedule is simply marked (possibly by Birkenhead) 'All except nos. 29, 30 & 31.'

148 See above, p. 128.

149 PRO HO/144/6065/39, Dawson Bates to Sir John Anderson, 23 December 1925.

150 PRO HO/144/6065/40a, Dawson Bates to Sir John Anderson, 18 January 1926. Against the background of the violent sectarian warfare of the preceding years, this is a curious admission.

151 *Irish Independent*, 8 December 1925, 6d; 10 December 1925, 7c.

152 *NIPD*, vol. 6, col. 1858, 9 December 1925. Reference to 'an act of grace' was buried within the longer, celebratory and generally conciliatory statement on the settlement around the Boundary Agreement. At this point, Craig – if he is to be taken at his word – hoped for friendly and cooperative relations with the Free State.

153 *The Times*, 27 November 1925, 14d. The men, each on their own, met British ministers and then together met Baldwin, the Prime Minister, for some two hours. There is no report of Craig and Cosgrave holding bilateral discussions. The British approach was to encourage the two leaders and their governments to resolve issues between themselves (see also *Irish Independent*, 27 November 1925, 7a; *Manchester Guardian*, 26 November 1925, 11e).

154 The press notice was issued on 23 January 1926 and appeared in *The Times* two days later. Only thirty-three prisoners were released, the thirty-fourth having died. The Scottish Office wrote to the Home Office pointing out that there were still six Northern Ireland convicts at Peterhead. Since their release had not been ordered, it was assumed that they were non-political (PRO HO/144/6065/42).

155 PRO HO/144/6065/41, W. A. Magill, Assistant Secretary, Ministry of Home Affairs, to Sir John Anderson, 20 January 1926.

156 PRO HO/144/6065/41.

157 PRO HO/144/6065/41.

158 This was a considerable departure from an agreement by the British Cabinet earlier in the year to recommend to the Northern Ireland government that the cases of the Derry prisoners be reviewed 'in five years' time', that is, in 1931 (PRO CAB/23/52/1, 19 January 1926).

159 *Irish Times*, 19 July 1926, 5c. A few days later, there was, however, a public meeting to celebrate Leonard's return to Galway. Thousands assembled, there was a procession, and tar barrels were burned. On their release in Belfast, the three men had

been served with deportation orders (see also *Irish Independent*, 20 July 1926, 8c; *Leitrim Observer*, 24 July 1926, 1f).

160 PRO HO/144/3746/131, 'The Irish Deportation'.

161 PRO HO/144/3746/131.

162 *Daily Herald*, 13 February 1922, 1e. It had been announced that certain other prisoners were to be released. This was not enough: all must be freed.

163 PRO HO/144/21356/18. The Home Office thought it best not to bring criminal proceedings arising out of speeches made at the meeting, unless some breach of law or of the peace in England was apprehended (see also *Daily Herald*, 13 February 1922, 1e and 4c).

164 An intercepted letter from Liam Lynch, IRA Chief of Staff, referred to the scale of the interdictions: 'Q[uarter] M[aster] G[eneral] have passed on accounts of OC London for July to December 8th. Out of a total of £833 odd scarcely any supplies reached Ireland. This was of course due to captures' (PRO HO/144/3746/131).

165 PRO HO/144/3746/131.

166 PRO HO/144/3746/131. Such grenades were for maiming and killing and were largely ineffective in attacks against property. The envisaged campaign was therefore to go beyond that of 1920–1, in the direction of terrorism and the deliberate targeting of civilians. It is not clear if this departure had been discussed within the IRA leadership. The tactic was intended to serve the more general strategy of reinvolving British forces in Ireland, thus opening the way for a realignment of republican forces. It was also no doubt thought appropriate that the British puppet-masters (as they were seen by the anti-Treaty side) should be punished.

167 Forty came from Scotland, the rest from England and Wales (see *Irish Times*, 6 October 1923, 5b).

168 *Irish News*, 12 March 1923, 5a; 13 March 1923, 4c. The operation was immediately raised in the Commons. See 5 *Hansard*, vol. 161, cols. 1043–7, 12 March 1923. There was vigorous questioning of the legality and propriety of the police action by Ramsay MacDonald and others.

169 PRO HO/144/3746/131.

170 Liam Lynch was cornered in the Knockmealdown mountains and shot by government forces on 10 April 1923. He was succeeded by Frank Aiken, who had, with de Valera, urged the cessation of hostilities.

171 For an analysis of the legal background, see *O'Brien* v. *Secretary of State*, *Times Law Reports*, 10 May 1923, 7a–g.

172 See McConville, *Irish Political Prisoners*, *op. cit.*, p. 421.

173 PRO HO/144/3746/131, letter of 30 March 1923.

174 PRO HO/144/3746/131, letter of 5 April 1923.

175 *The Times*, 16 October 1923, 17d. Many details of the treatment of the deportees may be found in the reports of the Compensation Tribunal, established later in 1923 (see below, p. 151). The proceedings have to be read with some caution because those who appeared before the Tribunal had an obvious interest in exaggerating the degree of their hardship, both for pecuniary and for political reasons. That said, the fundamental tort – unlawful detention – could not be denied. The only issue to be considered was the degree of its aggravation and the quantifiable losses to income and the like. The Crown sought to mitigate damages by demonstrating that the claimants were not as innocent as they claimed (and some certainly were not) and that in some way they had contributed to their own arrest. See, for example, the submission of the Attorney General to the Tribunal on 16 October 1923, in the case of Kathleen Brooks (*The Times*, 17 October 1923, 9d).

176 Kathleen Brooks told a later compensation tribunal that when police came to her house they said they had a warrant for Miss M. Brooks. On being told that there was

no one of that name (a disingenuous if not downright deceitful response, since this was the name to which IRA correspondence – for redirection – was addressed) the police inspector in charge demanded that one of the sisters go with him. Kathleen (who was in fact the postmistress) went but did not take clothes for the journey that lay ahead of her, imagining that she was simply to be taken to a local police station, and not having been informed otherwise (*The Times*, 16 October 1923, 17d).

177 And this despite extreme sea-sickness. These details were taken from a letter of protest from internees on the C Wing of Mountjoy Prison, dated 19 March 1923 and addressed to the Home Secretary, William Bridgeman. This was probably drafted by Art O'Brien and ran to more than five typed foolscap pages. A sizeable portion of the document is hectoring polemic of the shriller and more pointless kind, but many of the details of arrest and confinement have the ring of truth and are supported by other accounts. A transcription of the letter is at PRO HO/144/3746/55. The security precautions in Dublin were to reduce as far as possible the distance of road travel and indicate the concerns of the Irish Army, even in an area that appeared to be firmly under its control.

178 Assurances as to letters and visits were given to the House of Commons on 14 March 1923 by Bridgeman. He was careful, however, to promise that the Free State authorities 'will' give these privileges. The exchanges showed that Bridgeman, in truth, had little idea of what was happening in Dublin (5 *Hansard*, vol. 161, cols. 1548–53). A Labour Party delegation, which travelled to Dublin to report on the deportations, met Cosgrave and Hugh Kennedy, Attorney General. The delegation was told that the denial of letters and parcels to prisoners was a response to the IRA declaration of a period of 'mourning' during which the population was ordered not to attend cinemas, theatres, etc. The restrictions imposed on prisoners (including the deportees) was temporary. PRO HO/144/3746/90, Parliamentary Labour Party, 'Report on the Irish Deportations', by J. W. Muir, MP, and Arthur Greenwood, MP, Press Release, p. 6.

179 PRO HO/144/3746/55.

180 *Westminster Gazette*, 16 October 1923, 6a. The female wing at that time was already holding a number of female republicans, so it is hard to account for the lack of supplies for the deportees other than poor administration. It seems likely that, for reasons of security, or simply poor planning, the Mountjoy administration was not informed of the English arrests until the internees had embarked at Liverpool.

181 *Irish Times*, 17 October 1923, 9b.

182 PRO HO/144/2852. The unsanitary conditions of confinement for the women deportees was raised in the Commons on 22 March 1923 by pacifist (and Baptist minister) Revd Herbert Dunnico, Labour MP for Consett (5 *Hansard*, vol. 161, cols. 2781–3).

183 *Westminster Gazette*, 17 October 1923, 6d.

184 O'Malley, *The Singing Flame*, *op. cit.*, pp. 206 and 226. It was perhaps not quite the reign of terror described by Kathleen Brooks and others, and the firing does not appear to have been wholly indiscriminate. Lights were forbidden in the cells after 10 p.m., when the gas was shut off. The prisoners improvised candles, and when light from these was seen by the soldiers, they fired at the offending window. It was also forbidden to show oneself at a cell window, possibly to prevent communication between cells. Apparently to unnerve the guards, some of the prisoners, in O'Malley's words, 'provoked them by a jack-in-the-box appearance at a cell window' (p. 206). The prisoners ducked when the sentry swung his rifle up and reappeared when the shot had smashed the glass or chipped the embrasure. But, if not indiscriminate, the shooting was certainly draconian and frightening, and the possibility of injury or death from a ricochet was ever present. O'Malley, an experienced fighting man, found the situation severe and draining.

185 O'Malley, *The Singing Flame, op. cit.*, pp. 206–7; *The Times*, 16 October 1923, 17d; *Manchester Guardian*, 16 October 1923, 5a. George Lansbury, the veteran pacifist and venerable Labour leader, told the Commons about the firing of live rounds inside Mountjoy Prison. When he mentioned that prisoners had been shot, there was a deal of merriment in the Chamber, presumably from the Unionist benches (5 *Hansard*, vol. 161, cols. 2105–6, 19 March 1923).

186 *The Times*, 16 October 1923, 17d; *Manchester Guardian*, 16 October 1923, 5a; 17 October 1923, 15e. Relations between the women and the wardresses were good. Rosina Killen told the Compensation Tribunal that the wardresses 'were always kind and sympathetic, and did all they could to ameliorate the conditions that prevailed' (*Irish Times*, 17 October 1923, 9b).

187 Kathleen Brooks to Nora Brooks, from Holloway Prison, 24 April 1923 (PRO HO/144/2852/8). O'Malley reports the women prisoners singing 'We'll hang Dick Mulcahy [Free State Chief of Staff and Minister for Defence] on a crab apple tree'. 'Tales of their escapades', he continues 'were reported by the medical orderlies or by note' (*The Singing Flame, op. cit.*, pp. 214–15). This account is somewhat at odds with that of a vanquished, oppressed and fearful sorority. They managed to maintain morale until the end. When, on 17 May, they returned to England, they were met at Holyhead by a correspondent from the *Manchester Guardian*. The captain of the steamer, *Lady Curlow*, reported that the deportees had given no trouble of any kind during the crossing from Dublin: 'They were a happy, jovial lot… and passed the time singing Irish songs and ditties.' As the *Lady Curlow* came alongside, the women deportees shouted 'Are we downhearted?' and responded with loud shouts of 'No!' and more singing and laughter (*Manchester Guardian*, 18 May 1923, 10d; see also *Irish News*, 18 May 1923, 5a–b).

188 The decision had been made to concentrate all female prisoners at the Union, so the deportees joined women who were moved from Kilmainham the same night (see below, pp. 252–54).

189 One woman took a different view, claiming that 'The Union was in a filthy condition, and as a result two women had scarlet fever, and others suffered severely from septic throats' (*Manchester Guardian*, 18 May 1923, 10d). On conditions at the Union more generally, see below, pp. 247–48.

190 The transfer to the Union was accompanied by some violence, responsibility for which was disputed. One of the female deportees from London (possibly Rosina Killen) told the *Manchester Guardian* that their treatment was 'incredible' and that the women searchers had been 'insolent to a degree, and that despite the fact that we did not offer any resistance'. One woman (Miss McDermott), who appears to have raised objections (and perhaps more), was, it was claimed, 'brutally ill-treated'. Men were called in to assist the wardresses, and it was claimed that while Miss McDermott was held down 'women searchers were beating her face with the soles of her boots' (*Manchester Guardian*, 18 May 1923, 10d).

191 Lord Trevethian had been Lord Chief Justice of England, 1921–2. High Court Judge, 1904–21. President of the War Compensation Court, 1920. Sir Henry Mather-Jackson was a barrister and Chairman of Monmouthshire Quarter Sessions. Sir Matthew Wallace was a former president of the Scottish Chamber of Agriculture and also a member of the War Compensation Court; he was a Justice of the Peace.

192 PRO HO/144/2852/8.

193 PRO HO/144/2852/8/12, Mark Sturgis to Norman Loughnane, 26 March 1923. (Loughnane was at this time the Colonial Office representative in the Free State.)

194 PRO HO/144/2852/8/55.

195 There had been numerous questions, both general and particular, and it was evident that considerable dissatisfaction persisted. See, for example, the adjournment motion

debate on 19 March 1923 (5 *Hansard*, vol. 161, cols. 2205–62); 147 members voted against the government.

196 See the questions by Shapurji Saklatvala (Britain's first Communist MP), Sir John Simon (Liberal), Sydney Webb, James Maxton (the Glasgow socialist), Ramsay MacDonald (Labour) and others (5 *Hansard*, vol. 161, cols. 1548–53, 14 March 1923). Conservatives and Unionists seem to have been less concerned about the matter.

197 Six of the eight women were or had been teachers: Kitty Furlong, Kathleen Brooks, Mrs Margaret Leonnard (former teacher), Grace Lally, Mary Finan and Maria Killen.

198 PRO HO/144/2866.

199 'Mary Finan's rank and education make her the more dangerous. It is difficult to believe that "this extremely clever young woman" did not fully appreciate the meaning of the Constitution of her organisation and that her actions were intended to further civil war in Ireland' (PRO HO/144/2866/B, 9 April 1923).

200 PRO HO/144/2904/2a, Diarmuid O'Hegarty to Carter, 1 May 1923. The nascent Free State intelligence service was at this point struggling with the last, messy and seemingly interminable stages of the Civil War and had neither energy nor resources to spare. See Eunan O'Halpin, *Defending Ireland: The Irish State and Its Enemies since 1922* (Oxford: Oxford University Press, 1999), Chapters 1 and 2, for a detailed account of the background.

201 *The Times*, 16 October 1923, 17d. Despite Kathleen Brooks's unconvincing performance before the Tribunal, she was granted £562 in compensation, well above the average, reflecting the Tribunal decision to concentrate on what was an illegal arrest rather than on Kathleen's contributory actions.

202 See McConville, *Irish Political Prisoners*, *op. cit.*, pp. 476, 483–4, 549, 750–2.

203 *The Times*, 10 May 1923, 7c.

204 See Irish Free State Constitution Act, 1922: 13 Geo. V, c.1, Schedule 1.

205 The Erskine Childers case involved a habeas-corpus application for Childers, who had been tried by military court on the capital charge of possessing a revolver. The application in this case, and in eight others, was refused. The Master of the Rolls held that, owing to the state of war then prevailing, he had no jurisdiction in these cases (*Irish Times*, 24 November 1922, 5c). Nine months later, in the case of Mrs Connolly O'Brien and Mr Eamon Donnelly (seeking writs of habeas corpus), the Lord Chief Justice and Lord Justice Ronan stated that it had not been proved to their satisfaction that a state of war or armed rebellion existed in Dublin (*Irish Times*, 2 August 1923, 3a).

206 5 *Hansard*, vol. 161, cols. 2091–8 and 2105–6, 19 March 1923. See cols. 2097–107 generally for what was a heated series of exchanges, with the Attorney General (Sir Douglas Hogg) and the Home Secretary (William Bridgeman) under considerable pressure and failing to convince the opposition. The matter was reopened the same day, cases of constituents who had been deported having been put to the Home Secretary for Written Answer: see cols. 2146–8. *The Times*, 11 April 1923, 5c. The following account of the initial application is taken from this source.

207 The regulation provided that the Secretary of State could order a person 'to reside or be interned in any place in the British Isles'.

208 See *The Times*, 14 April 1923, 5d; 24 April 1923, 5a and b; 25 April 1923, 5a, and 10 May 1923, 7a–g; *Irish Times*, 15 May 1923, 7a–b.

209 The Home Secretary in this matter exorcised authority in relation to his English duties. In Scotland and Northern Ireland, these were undertaken by other ministers.

210 Irish Free State (Agreement) Act, 1922: 12 & 13 Geo. V, c.4.

211 *The Times*, 10 May 1923, 7b.

212 On 27 March, an Order was made to exclude the Irish Free State from enactments made before its establishment that contained references to 'the United Kingdom',

the 'United Kingdom of Great Britain and Ireland', 'Great Britain and Ireland', 'Great Britain or Ireland', 'the British Islands' or 'Ireland'. Exceptions were specified in the Order, and it was stipulated that in any Act passed after the establishment of the Free State, the term 'British Islands' would include the Irish Free State. The second order, made on 21 April ('remarkable not only because of the date at which it is issued, but also because of what it purports to do'), in effect provided that all the regulations made on 13 August 1920 (under the ROIA) were to apply to the Free State.

213 See *The Times*, 14 April 1923, 5d; 24 April 1923, 5a and b; 25 April 1923, 5a, and 10 May 1923, 7a–g; *Irish Times*, 15 May 1923, 7a–b.
214 *The Times*, 10 May 1923, 7e.
215 *Ibid.*
216 See *The Times*, 14 April 1923, 5d; 24 April 1923, 5a and b; 25 April 1923, 5a, and 10 May 1923, 7a–g; *Irish Times*, 15 May 1923, 7a–b.
217 HL 1892 AC 326.
218 *The Times*, 10 May 1923, 7f.
219 See PRO CAB/23/45/26–8, 14–16 May 1923, items 3, 1 and 1 respectively.
220 *Manchester Guardian*, 18 May 1923, 10d; *Irish Times*, 18 May 1923, 7a–b; PRO CAB/23/46/1, 24 May 1923, item 5.
221 The decision to arrest and bring conspiracy charges against O'Brien and perhaps half a dozen others was taken in Cabinet on 14 May 1923 (PRO CAB/23/45/26, item 1). Proceedings were to start as soon on O'Brien's and the others' 'landing in Great Britain'.
222 PRO HO/144/3746/131, 22 May 1923.
223 As indeed had been ordained by Cabinet (PRO HO/144/3746/131).
224 Restoration of Order in Ireland (Indemnity) Act, 1923: 13 & 14 Geo. V, c.12; PRO CAB/23/45/26.
225 See also 5 *Hansard*, vol. 166, cols. 1566–7, 12 July 1923. The Bill was rubber-stamped through the Commons, but there was a thoughtful and concerned Lords' debate: *Hansard* (Lords), vol. 54, cols. 356–82, 4 June 1923. The Tribunal was preferred to a parliamentary committee, both on grounds of confidentiality of proceedings and to avoid problems arising from party issues (PRO CAB/23/45/28, 16 May 1923, item 1; PRO CAB/23/46/1, 24 May 1923; PRO CAB/23/46/3, 13 June 1923).
226 The cases were widely and sensationally reported. See *The Times*, 16 October 1923, 17d; 17 October 1923, 9d; *Westminster Gazette*, 16 October 1923, 6a; 17 October 1923, 6d; *Star*, 16 October 1923, 1d, 9c; *Daily Express*, 16 October 1923, 3b; *Evening News*, 17 October, 5b; *Manchester Guardian*, 17 October 1923, 15e.
227 *The Times*, 30 November 1923, 9b. This contains a full list of the awards to date. See also the *Daily Mail*, 30 November 1923, 12d.

4

AN INSTRUMENT OF WAR

Free State prisoners, 1922–4

The Irish prison estate

The late-nineteenth-century organisational history of the Irish prisons closely parallels that of their English counterparts. Legislation in 1877 provided for the nationalisation of Irish local prisons.[1] From 1 April 1878, thirty-eight local prisons and ninety-five bridewells passed from the control of grand juries and boards of superintendence to the General Prisons Board.[2] A central argument for nationalisation was that substantial savings could be made through rationalisation, and, as in England, the Board immediately undertook a programme of closures and consolidations, with a view to eliminating the smaller and more costly establishments.[3] Twelve prisons were immediately discontinued. The bridewells were subjected to an even more drastic culling, and fifty-two were closed in August 1878.[4] Prison numbers were comparatively low at this point, and the average daily population had been fairly static since 1860 at around 2,500. Committals had been less stable, fluctuating between 30,000 and 45,000 per year.[5] Bridewell intakes had dropped drastically, from 22,421 in 1860 (and much higher before then) to 4,830 in 1878.[6] Committals to the convict prisons were much smaller: 1,631 at the beginning of 1860 and 1,114 in 1878.[7] The contraction continued, and twenty-one years later there were two convict prisons (Maryborough and dedicated parts of Mountjoy), nineteen local prisons, six minor prisons, one district bridewell and thirteen bridewells.[8] Efficiency, economy and a greater access to railways had produced the further closures.[9]

The Anglo-Irish War and its mass sweeps and continuing arrests strained available prison accommodation, but when the problem looked as though it might become acute or, perhaps, unmanageable, considerable capacity was made available by opening detention camps. On the signing of the Treaty, some thousands of men and some women were being held as internees in camps and prisons.[10] One of the very first fruits of the agreement was the release and joyous homecoming of these detainees in large numbers. Throughout this period, the ordinary criminal-justice system continued to operate, albeit severely disrupted, and prisons were used for a mixture of political, ordinary criminal and civil prisoners: those awaiting trial, serving sentences or persons who had proved refractory or who were a security risk in the camps. A small number of condemned men were also held, awaiting execution.

At first the Anglo-Irish War barely registered on the prison numbers. Although exempt from conscription, a substantial number of Irishmen, North and South, had enlisted.[11] This, and the shortage of labour due to the demands of a wartime economy, helped to keep a considerable number of young men from the usual courses of criminality. In 1913, there were 25,251 committals to Irish prisons; by 1916 this had fallen to 15,519, and the average daily population all but halved, dropping from 2,130 to 1,267. The Troubles (as they were called) further skewed the figures and complicated their interpretation. By the end of 1919, the RIC was under severe attack from the IRA, as were the courts and all elements of the legal process. Disorder, political and civil, became acute, while the instruments of the law were increasingly disabled in dealing with ordinary crime; even the recording of incidents became difficult.[12] That year, the number of committals dropped to 7,276 and the average daily population to only 759. The two years that followed showed a marked growth in these numbers. In 1920, there were 9,678 committals and an average daily population of 1,014; in 1921, 10,720 and 1,656 respectively. The General Prisons Board noted the increase in political prisoners. In the first year of Free State administration there was a dramatic fall, both in the number of committals and in the average daily population to 3,550 and 570, respectively. Their annual report does not say so, but it seems clear that these were almost entirely ordinary civil prisoners; the returns apparently excluded political prisoners.[13]

In the best of times, prisons are never at the forefront of public funding. Even by the standards and expectations of customarily ungenerous budgets, by 1922 the Irish prison estate had endured eight hard years and was becoming ever more dilapidated. The priorities of the Great War drained the prisons of funds and staff.[14] The War of Independence and its aftermath provided a further test. Exact figures are hard to come by, but as compared to 1916, the prison establishment was much changed.[15] The prison rules for various classes of prisoners – remands, convicts and hard labour – and the regulations and standing orders for staff, were unchanged from the old regime. But, even with this basic template intact, transitional problems were inevitable. The administration and running of a prison requires a range of aptitudes, skills and experience, and these were now substantially unavailable. A career in the prison service had very rarely found a place in the ambitions of nationalists, much less republicans.

In 1922, there were fourteen prisons in the Free State.[16] Two were mere lock-ups; others were large and complex establishments, able to perform several functions. The Provisional government concluded that the customary administration of prisons could not meet the challenges of civil war and the influx of its turbulent captives. The principal prisons were, accordingly, placed under military direction. Soldiers guarded the perimeter and, as military police, worked inside, alongside regular staff, and they were available as a reserve in case of disturbances or other emergencies.[17] The Prisons Board continued to be responsible for general administration and maintenance.

British-style management had long been based on the controlled intermingling of staff and prisoners. One of the consequences of these crisis arrangements, however, was that staff distanced themselves from their charges: hostility, intimidation and an unwillingness to obey any orders other than those issued by prisoners' own officers put great pressure on those who patrolled the landings and halls, carrying out the manifold tasks of their custodial duties. The inevitable consequence was their withdrawal from the body and life of the prison, to the detriment of intelligence collection and control. Staff only went among prisoners for locking, unlocking, to supervise inmate movements and to conduct cell changes and searches. Prisoners had considerable control over their routines and in the way they filled the days. They existed in the same physical space as staff but did their utmost to construct a social space that excluded them. These were times of revolutionary change, and, at least for a time, it was impossible to predict who would become the political masters of the country. Elementary prudence dictated that all public servants, but especially those in the institutions of state control, should adopt carefully neutral attitudes.

As we have seen, the Free State inherited from British administration a binary system of imprisonment: convict and ordinary. Convicts served sentences of three years and over; their regime was known as penal servitude.[18] This was divided into stages of modestly stepped disciplinary ameliorations, promotion through which was secured by a combination of time served and compliant or good behaviour. Remission of part of the sentence imposed by the court was marked by a daily allocation of marks. Ordinary prisoners (as distinct from convicts) served sentences of up to two years. (Extremely rarely, two such sentences could simultaneously be imposed, to be served consecutively, raising the total to three or four years.) Courts directed the sentence to be served with or without hard labour. The latter consisted of three divisions of varying degrees of lenity and latitude. Division I (sometimes also called Class I or first-class misdemeanant) conferred significant privileges as to food, visitors, letters, own clothing and furniture and amounted to little more than civil detention; such prisoners were kept strictly apart from other classes. Classes II and III, in Ireland initially restricted to prisoners between the ages of sixteen and twenty-one, were more penal but were still granted ameliorations that spared the prisoner the intentional punitive degradation of the hard-labour regime.[19] By a rule of 1911, the General Prisons Board was empowered to extend such indulgences to suitable adult offenders not sentenced to hard labour whose offences did not involve 'dishonesty, cruelty, indecency or serious violence'. Such ameliorations could not be greater than those granted to first-class misdemeanants. Key privileges for political offenders were the wearing of one's own clothes and separation from ordinary prisoners – a highly important point in a society with an overdeveloped sense of social contamination. The regime for first-class misdemeanants was to allow the court to reflect the lack of moral turpitude of the offence. By making assignment to the first class a sentence of the court rather than a matter for executive decision, it was intended to give an objective quality to the punishment and to exclude political intervention and favouritism. In practice, sentencers used these options in a muddled and inconsistent way. Certainly the full range of custodial options was rarely deployed: imprisonment with hard labour was the reflexive sentence for many judges and magistrates.

In addition to sentenced criminal prisoners, local prisons (as the non-convict prisons were called) held those remanded for trial or sentence as well as those committed because they could not or would not pay a fine, find a surety or deposit a security. There were also non-criminal prisoners, committed for contempt of court or for debt. These last were known as civil prisoners and were, by law, supposed to be kept strictly separated from criminal offenders. Usually (though sometimes the accommodation did not permit it) they enjoyed their own comparatively liberal regime, with a good deal of time out of their cells, association in day rooms, their own clothes and other privileges. Theoretically at least they were being held for coercive rather than punitive reasons.

There was one other category of prisoner, which had grown out of a modification of the convict system, to fit it better for comparatively serious young offenders aged sixteen to twenty-one. These prisoners, kept separately from adults, were managed in a special way, with an emphasis on work, training, encouragement and resettlement. Their sentences were indeterminate, up to three years, and early release on licence was granted to those who were deemed suitable and meritorious. Help was given to find employment on release, and the Borstal Association (a body of volunteers) took a paternalistic interest in their progress, both during sentence and afterwards. The courts in Britain made quite extensive use of Borstal sentences, but there was only one Borstal institution in Ireland.[20] As far as can now be ascertained, no political offenders were sent to the Irish Borstal.[21]

To accommodate this array of prisoners, the General Prisons Board had in 1922 both single- and multi-purpose institutions. Convicts were held at Maryborough (later called Portlaoise) and part of Mountjoy (Dublin). The various classes of ordinary prisoners were assigned to certain wings at Mountjoy as well as to Cork (Western Road), Cork (Sunday's Well), Dundalk, Galway, Limerick, Sligo and Waterford. In addition, the Board had bridewells at Birr and Ballina. There was a Borstal institution, which, after some peregrinations necessitated by the Civil War, settled for a while in Kilkenny. Two of the Board's disused prisons, Kilmainham and Kilkenny, had been refurbished and taken into commission for republican internees.[22] On the eve of the outbreak of the Civil War, the country's prisons held only 652 prisoners. This number would expand by a factor just short of twenty, imposing enormous financial, staffing and logistical strains.[23] At the outset, the system was running at under a quarter of its capacity, in large part reflecting the breakdown in the ordinary processes of the criminal-justice system. On 27 January 1922, the General Prisons Board advised the Provisional government that it had accommodation for 647 women and 2,038 men.[24]

Maryborough convict prison had been used by the British military authorities during the Anglo-Irish War and was handed back to the Prisons Board as the

British began their evacuation in January 1922. Civilian convicts were shortly thereafter transferred to Maryborough, only to be removed again in April 1922 when the Free State Army requisitioned the prison as a place of internment. Maryborough thereupon entered upon a period of turmoil. The result of this hard use was sorrowfully recorded by the Prisons Board: 'It is to be regretted that this prison – the most modern and up to date in the Free State – suffered serious damage at the hands of the Internees, amounting to several thousands of pounds.'[25]

With the exceptions of Mountjoy and Maryborough, the Irish prisons were small. Sligo had only twenty-one cells and Waterford ten. Average daily populations in 1922 ranged from 15.35 at Waterford to 265.15 at Mountjoy. For females, the equivalent figures were 1.13 and 49.7.[26] Prisons had to be maintained and staffed irrespective of level of occupancy; female prisoners had to be in the sole custody of wardresses at all times. With such a low and dispersed general population, the cost of servicing the courts and transferring prisoners between establishments was high. In 1922, the annual cost per prisoner was calculated by the Prisons Board at £63 18s. 7d. In the smaller prisons, and for women and juveniles, the cost could have been two or three times greater.[27]

The ordinary criminal prisoner was tractable and, with few exceptions, easily managed. Usually they were individuals, often struck with shame and remorse, anxious only to complete their sentence with as little trouble as possible. They were frequently socially isolated and generally were not disposed to combine with others against the authorities; some, indeed, were apt to seek advantage by informing. The political prisoner had quite contrary characteristics and instincts: imprisonment was a badge of honour, a confirmation of fidelity, entry onto another battlefield on which collective action was a duty, an opportunity and a privilege. One of the consequences of this state of penal exultation was a continuous attack upon the fabric and furnishings of the prison and periodic outbreaks of considerable destruction. This in turn led to even higher annual costs for maintenance and repair. It is notable, however, that no prison staff were killed by prisoners during the Civil War.

The NDU, a former workhouse, had abundant accommodation.[28] Laid out in wards, rather than cells, it was not thought suitable for men. At the end of March 1923, the Ministry of Defence asked the Department of Public Works to prepare the building for occupation.[29] At a meeting on 22 April 1923, attended by General Richard Mulcahy, Free State Minister for Defence and Chief of Staff, other officers, the Vice Chairman of the North Dublin Unions, and T. MacMahon of the General Prisons Board, it was agreed that the NDU's east wing should become a place for female internment. A military governor would be appointed, and the army would assume responsibility for victualling, guarding and the like. The General Prisons Board was asked to provide female staff – initially a female superintendent and thirty female officers. Provision was to be made for an additional thirty wardresses, as the internee population increased. The Prisons Board would, in the first instance, take responsibility for paying the female staff, recovering the funds in a manner to be decided by the government: all arrangements were to be pursued with urgency. Kilmainham Prison was to be retained for a limited number of women, the remainder to be transferred to the NDU on 26 April 1923. The Prisons Board was asked to muster as large a staff as it could, ready to receive them; the remainder of the wardresses would be deployed as soon as possible.[30] The occupation went ahead as planned, but the NDU's use as an internment camp lasted only eight months, until December.[31]

As the war swung decisively in favour of the government in 1923, the Army returned the prisons to civil control, starting in March 1923 with the men's prison in Cork. Mountjoy male prison was handed back in January 1924 and Kilmainham the following month; Dundalk was finally relinquished in March 1924. The Clonmel Borstal institution was the last to be handed over (in July 1924).

Something of the tensions that had arisen between the civilian prison staff and the military may be gleaned from a letter sent, at the end of 1923, by The MacDermott, Vice Chairman of the General Prisons Board, to the Ministry of Justice. It was couched in the querulous tones of an official whose previously quiet, predictable and sheltered corner of public administration had been rudely and violently disrupted. There remained no establishment in which normal conditions existed: 'Signs of demolition are everywhere in evidence before the eyes of the prisoners. The cell walls and woodwork still announce to them the views of the Irregulars.' Civil staff had been demoralised by having to work alongside the military, and their consequent lack of authority was having an influence on the conduct and attitude of the prisoners. There were various difficulties in reconstruction. Portlaoise had been so badly damaged that the hundred or so convicts engaged in the work there were having to be accommodated three, four or even five to a cell, and that lit only by candles. Virtually all prison workshops had ceased to operate, and it was necessary to purchase the items of clothing, bedding and furniture that had previously been made by inmate labour. Some of this was reflected in comparative expenses. He cited only one, but it was telling: under civil administration during the first half of 1922, Mountjoy had cost £909 to light; under joint civil and military control for the same months the following year, the bill was £3,265. Only 200 military prisoners were occupying Mountjoy male prison with its 500 cells. The immediate evacuation of the military was an essential first step if the penalties of the law were to be seriously enforced 'and if we are once for all to write finis to wanton destruction of public property and violence and mutiny from prisoners'.[32]

MacDermott's ire had boiled over, but his difficulties were far from fanciful. There were two consequences arising from the military use of civil prisons. The first and by far the most serious was the damage done during the occupation. This was caused mainly by the prisoners, but soldiers also took a hand, as demonstrated by the extensive use of warning shots to enforce orders at Mountjoy. The Army, knowing its occupation was likely to be of short duration, was not particularly likely to treat premises or equipment with any particular care. This was especially so since the Prisons Board remained responsible for administration and maintenance, even with the Army in occupation. As the Army left, the civil authorities fully assessed damages, and the bills rolled in. In 1924, some £19,000 was expended on structural repairs and a further £2,685 on ordinary repairs and re-equipment. The cost of reopening Kilmainham and Kilkenny prisons for military use had been £10,000. Particularly extensive damage had been caused at Mountjoy. Cork female prison (which had been used for males) had been reduced to such a state that it was uneconomical to repair it. Maryborough 'was gutted by fire, all internal wood and iron work including equipment having been damaged or destroyed'. There was much internal but no structural damage at Kilmainham. All the smaller prisons suffered, but to a lesser extent.[33] It was not until the beginning of 1925 that restoration work was completed. But even making use where possible of prisoners' labour, an additional expenditure of £5,780 was necessary.[34]

A second consequence of the military occupation of such a large swathe of the civil accommodation was that ordinary prisoners had to be concentrated, as far as possible. This overcrowding affected discipline and living conditions and also meant that prisoners' labour, formerly used to some extent to offset prison expenses, was almost totally unavailable for productive purposes. Here was another source of the increase in prison expenditure.

The camps

During the summer months of 1922, it became ever more clear that the capture and imprisonment of active republicans was a prime strategic task for the Provisional government. The position of those who surrendered in the course of hostilities, or who were taken whilst in arms, reflected the conflict: to the Free State Army they were military prisoners, but to republicans they were POWs; nomenclature denoted status and entitlements.[35] Combatants had to be supplied with food, shelter, communications and intelligence, and, as the war entered its guerrilla phase, those who gave any form of material or intelligence support, or who were suspected of doing so, were rounded up. On 26 September 1922, the Dáil passed the Army Emergency Powers Resolutions. This provided for the removal to a place of detention of 'any person taken prisoner, arrested, or detained by the National Army'. In effect, any person ('within or without the area of jurisdiction of the Government') could be held on whatever grounds the Army thought sufficient: no other criteria or limits were provided.[36] The inevitable consequence was a rapid and considerable rise in the numbers detained. In its prosecution of the war, this was seen as an overriding necessity by the Provisional government. It meant, however, that there was a desperate scrabble to find secure and suitable accommodation.

The Provisional government attempted to resolve two related internal pressures. First there was the need of the Department of Justice and the General Prisons Board to return the principal civil prisons to their primary purpose – holding remand, civil and sentenced prisoners. Simultaneously, the Army had realised that guarding a number of prisons was a major drain on manpower: experienced and reliable officers were needed to manage the prisons, and custodial duties were no less exacting for the rank and file. The need to prosecute the war was the greater priority, and these men would be more useful on active service. The answer was to concentrate all the internees in one or two large camps at Newbridge, Co. Kildare, and Gormanston, Co. Meath. The latter provided the most immediate solution since it could readily be adapted to hold 4,500. This meant, however, that the motor-repair depot it housed would have to be moved to the Curragh, Co. Kildare, or to Dublin, and the Army blocked this. There was also a water-supply problem at Gormanston, which would mean a daily limit of 10 gallons per head, a ration that could have been difficult to enforce.[37]

The problem was batted to and fro, but the influx of prisoners forced a decision. Were money and time available, a wholly new camp might be established at one of the aerodromes (Tallaght and Baldonnel in Co. Dublin or Collinstown, Co. Westmeath) or at an empty workhouse (Navan, Kells or Trim, Co. Meath, or Drogheda, Co. Louth). The aerodrome sites could hold up to 2,000 and the workhouses up to 1,000: whichever were used, there would be a considerable delay before occupation. An alternative was to move soldiers out of a section of the Curragh complex, which could then be made ready to receive prisoners within a few weeks.[38]

The Office of Public Works was pressured for other solutions. One suggestion was to adapt five blocks of stable buildings and to erect twenty-seven huts at Newbridge Camp. This would provide for 1,200 men. Somewhat out of the blue came a fairly obvious proposal to use double bunks 'as in steamers' instead of beds. Were this thought to be acceptable for internees, ventilation of the huts could be improved and existing camps could almost double their capacities. Using double bunks, moreover, would enable Hare Park Camp at the Curragh to hold 1,700 men; 1,000 if only beds were installed. Another advantage of the Curragh was that the existing supply system for soldiers could be used also for the internees, thus reducing set-up and use costs.[39] The last was the most practical solution, and, by the end of October, General Richard Mulcahy, Chief of Staff and Minister for Defence, reported to the Provisional government that, using the Curragh in addition to the existing camps, 12,000 internees could be accommodated. There was no need to expand Gormanston or other centres, and he hoped to release most of the civil prisons from army use by 1 December 1922.[40] He set out the accommodation in tabular form (see Tables 4.1 and 4.2).

In the original tables, the addition of the capacity figures for males had been wrongly totalled at 10,267 and actual male population at 10,307. These were simple errors in addition, but had the effect of showing that the population was greater than capacity, whereas, by a small margin, the opposite was the case.

In the first desperate rush to find accommodation, two small ships were chartered and brought into use as temporary holding places, the SS *Arvonia* and *The Lady Wicklow*. The first came into use as a means of easing the gross overcrowding at Limerick Prison. On 30 August 1922, 550 men from the prison

Table 4.1

Prison or camp	Prisoners
Portlaoighse	728
Athlone	659
Newbridge	1,865
Harepark	1,077
Gormanston	972
Cork	490
Mountjoy	679
Kilkenny	366
Dundalk	289
Tralee	310
Limerick	241
Waterford	85
Templemore	31
Kilmainham	53
Athy	42
Wellington	22
Thurles	10
Navan	8
Sligo	100
Tipperary	7
Mullingar	6
Naas	6
Westport	6
Beggars Bush	7
Trim	3
Portobello	2
Carrick-on-Shannon	4
Galway	270
Total	8,338

Source: NAI, TSCH, S1/369/1.

were transferred to the ship at Limerick docks. The vessel immediately sailed for Dublin, arriving there at 6 p.m. the following day. The IRA OC on board reported that most of the men were on hunger strike. He also claimed that there were fifty Fianna boys, aged from twelve years, and that these were in a prostrate condition, having been denied medical treatment.[41] This accommodation was, however, of a temporary kind, and the prisoners were transferred on shore once space had been created for their reception.

Staffing

Warders and other discipline staff

When the Provisional government took over in January 1922, there were 408 civilian staff members in the prisons.[42] By the early autumn of 1924, a few

175

Table 4.2

Prison or camp		Capacity	Number detained
		Males	
Curragh			
	Tintown No. 1	462	462
	Tintown No. 2	1,500	1,468
Hare Park		1,150	1,135
Newbridge		2,000	1,952
Mountjoy		900	783
Galway		354	354
Tralee		150	118
Cork		540	411
Gormanston		1,000	961
Limerick		300	471
Dundalk		346	346
Templemore		75[a]	64
Athlone		400	519
Sligo		130	138
Maryborough		570	554
Kilkenny		380	382
Waterford		100	89
Total		10,357	10,207
		Females	
North Dublin Union		N/A	285
Kilmainham		N/A	99
Total			384

Source: Military Archives A/6983, Irregulars, General File
[a]This figure is queried in the original table.
Note: No capacity figures are given for the female prisoners. Women had been held at other places of detention, not listed here. On 22 November 1922, a question was raised in the Dáil about a young woman, Miss Coyle, who for eight weeks had been in custody at Rock Barracks, Ballyshannon, 'during which time she has not been allowed to see any one of her own sex'. On 11 November, Miss Coyle went on hunger strike and five days later was removed to the Military Hospital, Buncrana, 'where', General Malcahy reported, 'she in charge of a female attendant' (*Dáil Debates*, vol. 1, col. 2293, 28 November 1922).

months after the last of the republican leaders had been released, staffing totals (excluding the military police) showed the impact of the Civil War. There were nine prisons in operation on 1 October 1924.[43] These were staffed by a total of 348 males and fifty-three females. The rapid expansion that had been necessary during the Civil War was indicated by the division between permanent and temporary staff. Of the male officers, 172 (just under half) were temporary, and of the females thirty-nine were temporary, almost exactly three-quarters.[44] Five years later, the contrast with staffing levels in more peaceful times was apparent. There were still nine prisons, but only 287 male and forty-nine female staff.

About one-third of the male staff and three-quarters of the female staff were temporary employees.[45]

Unlike the RIC, prison staff had not been subject to IRA attacks during the Anglo-Irish War. However, because of the frequent hunger strikes and disturbances, as well as executions and the public demonstrations attached to all of these, prisons had notoriously become an expression of British rule. Ordinary staff, whose whole prior experience had been of criminal and civil prisoners, and whose lives had been an unremarkable round, became increasingly uneasy. Theirs was an occupation that was always likely to produce ambivalence in the general population. As Sinn Féin's following grew and was confirmed in the 1918 election, staff became conscious of the likelihood of great changes in their own position. Max Green, Chairman of the General Prisons Board, reported that 'the greatest uneasiness exists throughout the service'. This was confirmed by the social ostracism experienced by those connected with prisons 'because we are and have been loyally carrying out the policy of the Executive for the time being'.[46]

As part of the Treaty arrangements, the RIC had been progressively withdrawn and was eventually disbanded. Staff worried that the Provisional government would similarly wish to have a major turnover in the prisons. On 25 October 1922, the matter was raised in the Dáil, by Ailfrid Ó Broin, on behalf of the Prison Officers' Association. What was the government's policy towards those who wished to continue their services, and what terms would be given to those who wished to retire or leave the service because of the change in government? Was it the intention of government to dispense with prison officers' services once 'the present critical period' (the Civil War) had passed?[47]

Kevin O'Higgins, the Minister for Home Affairs, replied. It was not intended to dispense with existing prison officers, 'merely because they were servants of the British Government'. Any staff who retired as a consequence of the change in government, or who was discharged, would, under Article 10 of the Treaty, be entitled to compensation on terms not less favourable than those provided by the GOIA, 1920.[48] Similar considerations applied to senior staff members of the General Prisons Board, governors, medical officers and others.

The chaplaincy

Given that all but a handful of republican prisoners were Roman Catholics, their chaplains were of great importance. At liberty, it would seem, a determined man or woman could probably find a friendly or complaisant priest who would be careful not to broach the subject of, or who would overlook, IRA membership, thus clearing the way for the important sacraments of confession and communion.[49] In prison, no such searching out of a sympathetic pastor was possible. Chaplains were appointed by both Church and State and received clear and emphatic instructions regarding persons who were in rebellion against lawful authority. After the Treaty came into operation, that authority was the Provisional government and then the Free State. The bishops' pastoral letter of

10 October 1922 left no scope for doubt – certainly not in the minds of the chaplaincy. The general elections of 1922 and 1923, with their clear pro-Treaty majorities, reinforced the thinking of the hierarchy, leading it to condemn the anti-Treaty side. 'A Republic without popular recognition behind it is a contradiction in terms.'[50]

The memoirs, journals and letters of republican prisoners frequently refer to difficult conversations or confrontations with chaplains. A deal of anger arose out of these encounters and, when recorded and reflected upon, entered into republican tradition. Ernie O'Malley wrote with some contempt of the Mount-joy chaplain, Father MacMahon, referring particularly to his attempts to get men who were sick and in some pain to sign a form of renunciation before he could give them the sacraments. The priest also came to O'Malley after the surrender call by Liam Deasy, evidently expecting a similar declaration from him.[51] Other republican prisoners had similar experiences. These were so frequent that only a few may be mentioned. In his prison diary, Frank Gallagher recounts a number of encounters with the Gormanston internment camp chaplain. His refusal to admit Gallagher to absolution was defended by a combination of political and religious reasoning.[52] In May 1923, the Gormanston chaplain attempted to apply further pressure. The internees were barred from the sacraments because they would not repent of their deeds and promise amendment. It was the duty of Catholics to come to the sacraments, and, should they not do so, they would be liable to excommunication. Father MacMahon insisted, in a subsequent discussion with the IRA camp staff, that he was within his rights in this declaration but agreed, when pressed, to explain to the men that he meant *liable* to be excommunicated, rather than immediately subject to the penalty.[53]

Military prisoners

There can, of course, be accidental shootings and even temporary or mistaken arrests, but when a mechanism is established to process and hold prisoners, a conflict of some duration is anticipated, or is already under way. The enmities of civil war had been coalescing well before the Dáil ratified the Treaty on Wednesday, 7 January 1922. Less than three weeks later, the Provisional government was asked by the (pro-Treaty) Adjutant General of the IRA to set aside one wing of Mountjoy Prison for army use.[54] Hardly perceptible at first, momentum increased rapidly throughout the spring months; angry words became irrevocable deeds. Seizures of property, occupations of buildings, the formation of garrisons and separate commands all came to a head with the storming of the Four Courts in the early hours of Wednesday, 28 June 1922. By the Friday afternoon, the interior of the building had been destroyed by artillery, fire and explosives, and the trapped republicans, including many key leaders and their GHQ, surrendered; more than 100 were taken into Free State custody.[55] This was the first large batch of military and political prisoners, a number that, within a year, would balloon to some 12,000 men and women. The ranks of the incarcerated were then sieved, sorted and selectively released until only handfuls remained. The last of the republican leadership was released on the 16 and 17 July 1924.[56]

For the following decade, prisoners were never to be far removed from the centre of public attention and from the cares and counsels of the government. There were the inevitable ironies of revolutionaries in power.[57] The greatest of these is the rebellious captive turned cunning captor, but there were others. Whilst it was operating its own prisons and camps and filling them with its armed opponents, their supporters and suspects, the Free State government continued to seek the release of republicans held in Northern Ireland and in Britain.[58] Methods of furthering revolutionary struggle through the plight of the prisoners – real and supposed – were now turned against the Free State. The difficulty faced by the republican camp was that the prison experience of those now in power had been gained behind the same bars and on the same prison landings as themselves.[59] A cold eye indeed would be cast on hunger strikes while the desires and tactics of the insubordinate captives would be countered by those with the knowledge and skills of insiders. The hardness of steel and heart engendered by civil war ran through it all.

Only the Free State could hold prisoners. In the opening stages of the Civil War, the republicans held territory, principally in Munster. This included a number of towns, including Cork. On 12 August 1922, Cork was captured by Free State forces, and, a week later, Liam Lynch, the IRA Chief of Staff, directed that any large IRA formations were to be broken up.[60] His judgement was that any attempt at conventional warfare would, from this point on, prove to be disastrous, given the numbers, equipment and logistics of his opponents. Thereafter, the IRA conducted ambuscade, hit-and-run operations, with as much mobility as possible. The inability to hold prisoners was a significant handicap. Captives could indeed be interrogated, but, thereafter, almost invariably they had to be released.[61] Murder as policy was out of the question: at this juncture, fratricide had its limitations. Efforts were made to neutralise those who were released by asking for their word of honour not to return to the field of combat, but this was never likely to be a successful manoeuvre: soldiers in the field cannot promise to disobey their orders.[62]

Because of their numbers, those who had surrendered at the Four Courts were speedily transferred to Mountjoy, after first being held in Jameson's Distillery on Bow Street, Dublin. Mountjoy was the only available prison with capacity and what looked like sufficient security. In this first major engagement, the Free State Army and the CID (effectively the political police) were apparently unprepared to conduct interrogations and to collect and manage intelligence. The Provisional government, indeed, probably had no idea of the nature and extent of the conflict that was to follow. As the war developed, prisoners were more liable to be subject to interrogation and to ill-treatment. Many men were given a beating with fists and boots, but other forms of pressure and intimidation were also used. Since this happened at the preliminary stage, the ill-treatment was usually in barracks, rather than in prisons.[63] The republican publicity machinery referred to these cases, but, even allowing for calculated exaggeration, there can be no doubt that many brutal acts took place: the reports are too many and from too many sources for it to be otherwise.[64] Prisoners, moreover, could expect to spend some weeks in the detention rooms of barracks, awaiting the completion of interrogation and then for a transfer to prison. The Political Prisoners' Committee (PPC) reported overcrowding and unsanitary conditions at Wellington Barracks: 'The prisoners' ration consists of the leavings of the Guard-room, for which they are said to "forage".'[65]

As the Civil War proceeded, there was an increased ruthlessness, on both sides, in dealing with prisoners. In December 1922, the IRA's Adjutant General raised the issue with Liam Lynch, evidently proposing that a prison be captured and used to hold spies. His letter has not survived, but the Chief of Staff's withering reply was, 'far bigger military schemes than procuring a prison have had to be cancelled. When the enemy is continuing executions we do not need wasting time with prisoners we're about to take... it is ridiculous to talk of prison for spies.'[66]

One of the government's first decisions concerned the status of captives. Were they ordinary criminals, political offenders or POWs? The day after the Four Courts fell, the Provisional government concluded that those taken there and elsewhere should be treated as military captives.[67] The choice of term was significant. Rather than 'political prisoners' or 'prisoners of war', the most restricted status, short of criminal, was being conferred. Irregulars (the government's preferred term) were not seen as ordinary criminals, but neither were they to be treated as prisoners from an enemy army, with rights conferred by the usages and conventions of warfare. Still less were they to be accorded the easements, liberties and martyr's garb of political status. They were 'military captives' in the factual sense that they were being held by the Army, which would permit a wide latitude in their treatment.[68]

There was also an important element of control in this definition. 'Order No. 1', issued at Mountjoy on 3 July 1922, informed the prisoners that the institution had been designated a military prison. They were to be treated as 'military captives, still within the area of operations'. The implication of this last phrase was that military necessity would determine their treatment, particularly should security be threatened, whether by internal revolt or by internal threat. This was spelt out: 'The position of prisoners, therefore, is that any resistance to their guard, or attempt to assist their own forces, revolt, mutiny, conspiracy, insubordination, or attempt to escape, will render them liable to be shot down.' Nor was the status of 'military captive' more than a temporary one, since it was given to review 'as soon as military operations in Dublin cease'.[69] This stern warning was based on the opinion of the Law Officer, who had advised that, for the purpose of regaining control, it would be lawful to shoot prisoners attempting to escape or resisting the guard.[70]

It was extremely unlikely that these threats would be followed through. While the public might well understand the necessity of shooting prisoners in a mass escape, or in an armed revolt, it would have been a great deal less sanguine about shooting as a response to insubordination or conspiracy. And how many prisoners could be shot in the event of an uprising without a political backlash, perhaps even a rift within the still-shifting ranks of the pro-Treaty forces? The response from Joe McKelvey (signing himself 'Chief of Staff, IRA') was certainly uncowed. He rejected the designation of military captive and demanded full POW status.[71]

During this exchange, the prison was in the midst of a major riot, of which the government had been informed the previous day. The bulk of the Four Courts' prisoners and those from other Dublin actions were now held in Mountjoy.[72] By 4 July 1922, those totalled 308 men, with another twelve being held temporarily at a police station.[73] Eamonn Duggan, then Minister for Home Affairs reported that the Irregulars had escaped from their cells, which they had wrecked.[74] Encouraged by the sounds of continued fighting in the city, they had used iron bars torn from the windows as weapons and as tools to attack the masonry of the embrasures; walls and floors had also been destroyed, as the men 'tunnelled' between cells. Large crowds of sympathisers assembled outside the prison and were able to have shouted communications with the inmates.[75] Since this was one of the country's principal prisons and an important part of the apparatus of government and of war, and since the rioters seemed intent on wrecking it, a strong response was inevitable. Riot and destruction were rational, calculated and disciplined military actions against the Provisional government: no other conclusion was possible. All civil prisoners were removed and the establishment designated an exclusive military prison; male criminal prisoners were transferred to the Mountjoy female prison. Diarmuid O'Hegarty was then in command as Military Governor, with the rank of Commandant.

O'Hegarty drew on the government's statement of intent.[76] Prisoners would not obey orders to get down from the windows, which was a security problem since they were shouting to each other and to outside supporters. He warned that this rendered them liable to be shot.[77] He particularly objected to an exchange of signals between men at the windows and persons outside the prison. Fighting in Dublin had been much reduced, but there was fear of an attack on the prison, coordinated with an uprising of the prisoners. It was also highly undesirable that the prison should become a focus for anti-government demonstrations. Not only were these threatening in themselves but they evoked the events of the Anglo-Irish War, when there had been similar demonstrations, and thus cast the government in the same role as the departed British. The fighting mood of the prisoners, and the presence among them of leading IRA officers, added to the tension of the situation.[78] Most jumped down from their cell windows as firing began (which was at first intentionally wide). Thereafter, sentries fired into the cells of those who appeared at windows. Prisoners were transferred from the heavily damaged D Wing to the disused C Wing, where they were locked in cells.[79] The transfer to C Wing brought only short-term peace. Almost immediately, the men, who had agreed among themselves not to destroy their new cells, took steps to loosen staff control. Using a simple and effective method for breaking cell-door hinges (a book jammed between the hinge and the door-frame and the door then slammed), the prisoners made it impossible for anyone to be locked in. The Governor responded to this tactic by placing sentries on platforms from which they could fire along the wing. Any prisoner who appeared outside his cell after 11 p.m. would be fired upon.[80] The Governor asked the government for twenty 'picked men' to act as warders, for the guard to be strengthened and for the deployment of an armoured car.[81]

That O'Hegarty's concerns about signalling had been well founded was soon confirmed. Nor was it only a matter of men shouting from the windows to egg on demonstrators, and vice versa. On Wednesday, 12 July 1922, a prisoner named O'Brien was granted parole. (He had probably been ordered by the IRA command in prison to apply for release in order to liaise with the organisation outside.) On being searched, preparatory to release, a message concerning signalling and 'speeding up' was discovered. This was taken to mean that a tunnel was being dug into the prison. By some means, this was pinpointed, and troops were sent to two houses in the adjacent Glengarriff Parade. The first house (No. 11) yielded nothing, but, as the troops approached No. 28, a party of men came out and surrendered. Eleven men and one woman had been in the house, led by Seán MacEntee, on whom tape measures and a compass were found.[82] Evidently the dig had just begun. There was a hole some six feet deep in the kitchen, and the distance to the prison was some 30 yards.[83] Although squashed at the outset, this was a serious matter. Freeing the Four Courts leaders, with or without a mass breakout, would have greatly embarrassed, compromised and undermined the Provisional government and heightened tensions with London, whilst heartening and strengthening the insurgents. The ability to imprison had been shown to have two sides: reassuring to the public and damaging to the Irregulars if the government ensured safe and controlled custody, but all the time holding the authority and reputation of the government hostage to fortune.

The attempted Mountjoy breakout opened a season of incidents at various prisons. Defiance and the costly destruction of property by prisoners further hardened government attitudes, and it resolved, wherever possible, to use the ordinary criminal law where there was sufficient evidence. Desmond FitzGerald, in charge of publicity for the Dáil, was instructed to visit the prison and to obtain details of the riot from O'Hegarty so that the public could be informed of what had happened.[84] At the same time, it was recognised that there could be political (as well as financial) advantage in drawing a distinction between leaders and followers, allowing the conditional release of the latter.[85] Applicants had to pledge that they would not take up arms against the state; peaceful opposition was not in question. This undertaking would prove contentious over the years to come. There was no perceptible sense of inconsistency when, a few weeks later, the Provisional government advised IRA members and supporters interned on board the prison ship *Argenta* in Larne Lough not to give their bail to the Northern Ireland authorities.[86]

By 15 July 1922, the Provisional government was assured that order had been established at Mountjoy.[87] Something of the post-riot conditions may be inferred from the Governor's request that furniture should be provided for each cell, 'on a guarantee from each prisoner that these articles would not be misused or damaged'. It was also agreed that a set of underclothes be issued to each man from the prison stock. Security nevertheless continued to cause great concern. In the first days of military administration, there had been suspicions that an attack was being planned on the prison – thus the sensitivity over hand signals from and to those at the cell windows. It was now decided to discontinue visits 'on any pretext'.[88] This move was only partially successful as a communications barrier, since some members of staff were willing to act as couriers. There were, of course, letters that passed through regular channels which were censored. On 18 July 1922, Colm Ó Murchadha, the new military governor, asked that J. J. Sheehan, a civil servant, be assigned to him for this work.[89] There is no indication that the censoring of mail was conducted within the structure of military intelligence.

Throughout the rest of the summer of 1922, as government forces mopped up pockets of resistance in Dublin and elsewhere, prisoners flooded in to Mountjoy. The riot had taken all of D Wing out of operation, and more accommodation was urgently required. The problem was discussed on 7 July 1922, and four days later it was announced that Kilmainham Prison had been placed under a military governor, Commandant Sean O'Muithuile, with Captain Eamon Dorkan as his deputy.[90] There had apparently been some lack of cooperation on the part of the Secretary of the Prisons Board in preparing the prison for its new occupants, and this spat was reported to the Provisional government.[91]

By mid-July 1922, the military authorities had taken over a number of prisons. Male civil prisoners from Maryborough and Dundalk were transferred to the female prison at Mountjoy. The unfortunate women whose accommodation they took were relegated to the basement, and a review was undertaken by the Recorder of Dublin and by magistrates to ascertain which of them could be given early release to ease the situation. Sligo prison was being used as a barracks, and the occupying soldiers were moved elsewhere. The prison's only two women prisoners were released forthwith, and the ordinary male prisoners moved into their wing, freeing the male section of seventy-three cells for military prisoners. It was understood that, if necessary, each cell could be used for three men. A similar course was followed at Galway: females freed, civilian prisoners removed to the vacated wing and ninety-five cells released for military use. Cork female prison was remarkably ample for ordinary criminal-justice needs: 153 cells but only thirteen occupants. Its male counterpart had 225 cells for fifty-eight prisoners. It was decided to discharge the women and to use their prison for male civil prisoners from Limerick, Waterford, Galway and Cork. This put the 225 cells at Cork male prison and those at Galway, Limerick and Waterford at the disposal of the Army. With triple occupancy, these prisons could hold about 1,200 in total. Enquiries were made about workhouses, and a prison camp for 5,300 was proposed for Lambay Island, Co. Dublin.[92]

In the months following the capture of the Four Courts, republican volunteers and supporters were rounded up and captured in battle throughout the country.[93] Once inside, many energetically embarked on campaigns of disobedience, attrition and destruction of the buildings and fittings. This was entirely to be expected: prison disturbances had been a major element in the campaign against the British from 1916 onwards. With a barely trained staff, inadequate in number and uncertain in morale, threats of lethal force inevitably and all too quickly became a first rather than last recourse for those seeking to maintain order and control. This initiated a dangerous process of disproportionality. As any parent knows, if they are to retain credibility, threats must, from time to time, be carried out. The divisions of sentiment between the republican and Free State rank and file were so uncertain at this point that thirty soldiers of the Mountjoy guard resigned in protest at the use of firepower as an instrument of control. The reaction of the authorities was instructively mild; the soldiers were sent back to their barracks.[94] At other prisons there were also great difficulties. On 27 July 1922, the IRA blew a gap in the wall of Dundalk prison and 105 men escaped.[95] A couple of weeks later, the Post Office discovered a bomb in a parcel intended for a Dundalk prisoner, the intention obviously being an encore. All privileges were withdrawn from the prisoners and a military governor and deputy governor were appointed.[96] Portlaoise was severely damaged by republican prisoners on 29 August 1922; there had also been a hunger strike at the prison.[97]

Republicans saw Free State imprisonment as further proof of the shameless apostasy of their erstwhile comrades. That was to be expected, and the rhetoric, protests and denunciations that flowed from it could be set aside by what was an undoubted popular majority on the Treaty side. Such support could not, however, be taken for granted, especially where there was a suspicion that prisoners might be ill-treated. Questions were repeatedly raised in the Dáil, especially by Labour TDs (Teachtaí Dála), but also by other independent-minded and respected deputies. On 9 October, Dublin Municipal Council established a committee to investigate the treatment of prisoners and to take sworn evidence. When the Council asked the Provisional government to give safe conducts to witnesses, it was told that such an inquiry was illegal, and, should it continue, prosecution would be considered.[98]

Among republicans, much bitterness was caused by ill-treatment by intelligence officers during interrogation. Ernie O'Malley (admittedly a highly partisan commentator) referred to a room at Portobello Barracks which was known as the 'knocking shop', in which prisoners were abused. He claimed that the doomed Erskine Childers received a bad kicking and was in pain as a result. (Childers was executed on 24 November 1922, having been in custody for a fortnight.[99])

Séamus Robinson, an IRA commander, was also beaten after arrest, and, according to O'Malley, money, valuables and papers were taken from him.[100] Initially, at least, this type of abuse also occurred at Mountjoy. Men who were sent to the punishment cells were beaten by an intelligence officer, 'but this did not last for long'.[101]

In late 1922, there developed on the Free State side the practice of taking hostages. Con Casey and three other Irregulars were captured after an attack on Free State soldiers in Cork. They were sentenced to death and held in Tralee Prison. Notices were widely posted that, in the event of any hostile action, the four men would be shot.[102] Since Erskine Childers and a number of others were executed in Dublin at this time, it was obvious to one and all that the threat was not an empty one. After six weeks, the sentences on the four were commuted to ten years' penal servitude, and the men were transferred to Mountjoy. The strain of the six weeks was considerable, however, 'not knowing but than any morning we might be shot'.[103]

On or about 20 January 1923, Liam Deasy, a senior IRA commander, had been captured.[104] A military court sentenced him to death, and, during the night before his scheduled execution, he accepted Free State terms of an immediate and unconditional surrender. This was issued as an appeal to all IRA units and clemency was granted to him. On this basis, the government sought to encourage a more general surrender. For obvious reasons, Deasy's appeal seems to have been largely ignored by his comrades. On 8 February 1923, an amnesty was offered to all in arms against the government who surrendered with their weapons.[105] The offer also had only a limited effect, though many may, then and later, have surrendered unofficially by simply dropping out. The offer of clemency having been made, the government could go forward, justified in adopting a more stern policy towards those who remained in the field.

The struggle for Mountjoy Prison

The first military governor of Mountjoy prison was Commandant Diarmuid O'Hegarty, who, with Colm Ó Murchadha as his deputy, was appointed on 2 July 1922.[106] Both men were replaced within weeks. O'Hegarty was followed briefly by his deputy and then by Commandant Sean O'Muithuile. On 30 August, he in turn was succeeded by Phil Cosgrave, brother of W. T. Cosgrave, President of the Provisional Government.[107] Phil Cosgrave had been active in Sinn Féin during the Anglo-Irish War but had no military experience. Whilst holding the governorship, he continued to be politically active and took a lesser part in day-to-day administration of the prison than Patrick (Paudeen) O'Keefe, his deputy governor.[108] Having served for eleven months, Cosgrave, ill since his appointment, was replaced by Commandant Dermot MacManus; O'Keefe was replaced by Commandant Sean Fitzpatrick.[109] MacManus immediately strength-ened physical security. More barbed wire was installed, and additional raised sentry posts were constructed.[110] He then attempted to bypass the prisoners' structure of command and, in effect, to regain control of the daily life of the prison.[111]

On 24 May 1923, Frank Aiken, IRA Chief of Staff (succeeding Liam Lynch, who had been killed), ordered his men to cease fire and to dump their arms.[112] This was not a surrender and meant that the Free State authorities would continue round-ups and arrests, since dumped arms could be retrieved and attacks on state forces recommenced at any opportune time. The camps and prisons continued to fill until, on 1 June 1923, there were 11,989 in custody. Legislation had been brought in to authorise internment, and criminal cases were being prepared against a number of IRA leaders. By the autumn, although numbers had dropped significantly, the prisons and camps had become extremely tense.[113] A general election on 21 September confirmed popular support for the Treaty and the government.[114] One consequence of this was to increase the frustration of republican prisoners. With no military or immediate political hope left to them, riot and disorder became ever more likely. Prisoners could not understand why they were still in prison several months after the IRA had ceased operations. For their part, the governors of prisons and camp commandants could not allow their prisoners to continue to stake such strong claims to run their establishments. A decisive clash was inevitable.

The extent to which the Mountjoy republicans had established their alternative command structure and controlled the prison routine and movement within the building itself may be seen in O'Malley's account of a prisoner 'going on the run' in C Wing. This was Paddy Coughlan, C-Wing OC. Following a dispute with MacManus, attempts were made to take Coughlan to the punishment cells. He evaded the military police, who acted as warders, and, in an act of defiance and provocation, continued to conduct his language class and to carry out his OC duties. So poor was the control of prisoners' movements that Coughlan slept each night in another wing, to which the C Wing prisoners had managed to effect an entrance. He was eventually taken, and confined in a basement punishment cell. Men in the cell above then broke through the floor and pulled him out with roped blankets; his life as a prison fugitive resumed.[115] This extraordinary sequence shows the prisoners' defiance, their physical control of the interior for much of the day and the general level of administrative disorganisation. From various reminiscences, it seems that some prison staff turned a blind eye to prisoners' smuggling and related activities; a few actively aided them. A civil war was in progress whose outcome was not certain, loyalties were freshly sundered and not yet set: it was probably easier to go along with the rebellious prisoners than to confront them.

The outcome of this uncertainty became manifest on 10 October 1922.[116] Mountjoy, like most Victorian prisons, is built on a radial plan around a central hub ('circle'). From this core a full view may be had down all the wings. Each wing was secured by its own gate and barrier, stretching floor to ceiling. Prisoners somehow smuggled mines and guns into the prison, and a plan was made to capture the circle (the central control point of surveillance), to seize arms and to stage a general breakout. Prisoners opened fire in the circle and killed two military police guards (Thomas Gaffney and James Kearnes). Fire was returned by soldiers: one prisoner (Peadar Broslin) was killed, and another (John Harbourne) wounded.[117] Unsurprisingly, an ugly mood developed among staff and CID men who had joined them. There was talk of shooting any prisoner found to be involved. Paudeen O'Keefe controlled the situation, much to the prisoners' relief. His abusive and obscene language towards them seemed to still the staff rage by venting it. Some of the leaders were removed to punishment cells, and the staff used the cover of a search to destroy the men's food and property. There were no further killings, though it must have been a very fine balance.[118] A military inquiry was set up to look into the event.[119]

All of this suggested a dangerous loss of authority. MacManus's countersteps had full government support. Once control had been re-established, the screw could be tightened further. At its last meeting in 1922, the Executive Council decided to discontinue many privileges. Ernie O'Malley had ruefully observed, 'we were up against jailors who had themselves been prisoners, and who knew the ropes'.[120] The government therefore knew what it was doing when it recommended that the military command reduce the number of incoming letters to one a week; parcels were totally prohibited.[121] Tobacco, which the prisoners fiercely craved, was to be an instrument of control and punishment. Individual supplies were prohibited; it was ordered in bulk to be distributed in small amounts by the prison authorities. The Executive Council stated that it had taken these steps because of 'the continuance of outrages in Dublin'.[122] Prisoners were to bear some consequences for the activities of their comrades.

As we have seen, the Mountjoy prisoners had waged their campaign of attrition throughout the summer months of 1922. They were mainly young men, many of whom had been plucked from the unsettled life of the irregular soldier; they hated their guards as lackeys and apostates and were increasingly frustrated by captivity. A Mountjoy version of 'chicken' provided an outlet for some. Prisoners would play 'jack in the box' at a cell window or simply show a light after 10 p.m. Sentries would warn and then shoot. Firing both warning and targeted shots thus became commonplace from the days of the first Mountjoy riot. In many cells, windows had been shot out.[123]

To the extent that its harassed and increasingly depleted state permitted, the IRA sought to prop up its captive comrades. Their prisoners' morale, well-being and ability to continue to use their captivity for training were of some importance within the overall campaign. Defections or recantations could be as damaging as defeat in a military skirmish. The regulations for ordinary remand prisoners came closest to the political-status custody the IRA sought. The untried in criminal proceedings, who were, of course, legally innocent, could wear their own clothes, freely obtain newspapers and books, write and receive letters virtually without restriction, have parcels, shave themselves and smoke. Additionally, they could have visitors every day (not more than two people) for up to fifteen minutes. They had walking exercise for up to two hours daily or could do work of their choice (within reason) for five hours. Should they be able to afford it they could have their meals sent in.[124] This last, the IRA Adjutant General observed, was unnecessary since the prison diet for the untried was good enough for anyone.[125]

But untried status, liberal though it was, still had a number of custodial restrictions. The IRA therefore sought four further privileges: (1) complete separation from non-political prisoners, especially at exercise; (2) association with each other for four or five hours a day and whilst at classes and debates; (3) smoking in cells as well as at exercise; and (4) lights out extended until 10 or 11 p.m. These four modifications, the IRA Adjutant General observed, 'would make political treatment'.[126]

This was the package for which IRA Volunteers should agitate: 'they may as well go out for the whole hog as for one or two privileges'. The critical moment came on entry into the prison. All except first- and second-division prisoners could be ordered to change into prison uniform.[127] Refusal would usually mean immediate removal to the punishment cells. The uniform would be left in the cell: this was seen as the critical psychological moment. Refusal to wear the uniform, with all its criminal stigma, was of propaganda value to the IRA, but 'something silly' such as a hunger strike would probably end in fiasco. Various forms of coercion were used, such as taking the naked prisoner out and putting him in a cold bath 'and other stunts like that'. But should the ordinary prisoner persist and get his own clothes, 'he will have very little difficulty in getting at least all 2nd Division privileges'. Prisoners should be instructed to accept their privileges in instalments but without giving guarantees as to future behaviour.[128]

There was other advice on tactics. Prisoners (whose republican reflex was to shun what they saw as illegitimate authority) should not demur at taking their application to the Prisons Board. The goal was to be accepted as political, not military, prisoners: 'political' would include non-army men 'and possible non-official republicans who are there on definite political changes against the National Army'. Prisoners in the different classes should make every effort to keep in touch with each other. Finally, as to demonstrations, the best time for 'stunts' (evidently a favoured word) would be after 6 p.m. – '10:00 p.m. for smashing, shouting, singing, etc. to undermine the whole jail system'.[129]

The last suggestion had been and would be freely followed. Such disruption could not continue without a full-scale riot and destruction of the prison, leading perhaps to a mass breakout. An additional danger for the government was a panic reaction on the part of the guard in the face of rioting and disorder: a massacre was possible. Throughout 1923, steps were taken to regularise the system of control and administration. This was felt by the prisoners, who sought to keep their own military structure and the relative freedom they had secured within prison walls.

The Military Governor reported to his superiors that the Mountjoy men had built up an effective military organisation in the prison. All contacts with staff, and with the outside world, were monitored and subject to close and complete IRA control. An inmate 'military policeman', wearing an armlet, was stationed at the barrier between each wing and the circle. No contact was permitted with staff. Of particular concern was the ability of the inmate command to control prisoners' correspondence. Every item, besides passing through the hands of the prison censor, also had to be submitted to the IRA censor. The authorities attempted to counter this by having staff go into the wings to hand their post directly to the prisoners. Letters out had to be handed directly to the prison officer handling mail. This tactic was easily countered by the prisoners' command, which simply issued an order to continue as before. The Civil War had ended several months previously. A general election on 21 September had increased government representation in the Dáil and confirmed its mandate. The authorities, by this point, were anxious to begin the process of emptying the prisons and camps and wished to be able to receive the forms that those who wished to be considered for release should sign. At a later point, when prisoners were given the opportunity to conform with the regime, several immediately submitted petitions for release.[130]

MacManus's steps to regain control of Mountjoy were having an effect, and, in response to an escape, he decided to control movements further. As we have seen, cell-door locks had been smashed, but a sufficient number were repaired by 12 September to confine men to their cells on A Wing. The following day, the same procedure was followed on C Wing. There was to be no general opening-up in the morning. Cells were unlocked one by one and breakfast was doled out by military police; visits to the lavatories were conducted under armed guard. This was an attempt to return the prison to the cellular discipline which was the lot of ordinary criminal prisoners. On 13 September 1923, about 200 men in B Wing formed up and began to drill, under command. When attempts were made to stop this, there was violent resistance and destruction. The men again broke their door hinges, making it much more difficult to impose order.[131] In addition, prisoners equipped themselves with makeshift weapons, and at one point some military police were disarmed. Notionally, at least, no wing could communicate directly with another, save through the circle. Gates are let into the security barriers, which are locked and unlocked to control movement. In response to the mass demonstration in B Wing and the refusal to disperse, the Military Governor brought in reinforcements, including a mounted machine gun. An armoured car was brought into the yard to back up the detachment of fully armed soldiers in the prison. The officer in charge of the detachment ordered all prisoners back to their cells. The order was ignored, since it had not come from the prisoners' OC. A volley was fired over the prisoners' heads, upon which the OC ordered the men to their cells.[132]

The cell blocks having been subdued, the men were then ordered out of their cells, to assemble in the yard. This order was refused, and the prisoners were instructed by their OC to resist passively. Men were manhandled out of the cells, and high-pressure hoses were brought into use. Resistance was futile, given the imbalance of forces, and, amid the destruction of much of the men's property, all the able-bodied were eventually forced into the yard. Once outside, the men were told that they would be given food if they re-entered the cellhouse one by one. They refused food, except that served by their own orderlies. A stand-off began, with the men in the yard directly covered by machine-guns and rifles. This continued until the evening, when, at 6.30 p.m., en masse, the men were readmitted to the cell block.[133]

It is a *sine qua non* that movement is controlled within a prison. Without that, none of the basics can be accomplished: prisoners cannot be counted; crowds can assemble; disorder and riot are difficult to prevent; vulnerable prisoners may be bullied and attacked; staff are at risk of being mobbed or taken hostage. Nor can this disorder be contained. A crowd of prisoners, especially if it is cleverly led and willing to accept orders, can create an opportunity to storm walls and gates. These precepts were set out in a report from Mountjoy's military governor to his superiors:

> There are certain vital essentials of control without which the safe custody of prisoners in a gaol cannot possibly be guaranteed. Every individual prisoner or group of prisoners must be prepared to enter his cell on the orders of the Military Governor; also to enter the exercise ground from the wing or the wing from the exercise ground. In addition to these two points open military training and drill cannot be permitted – otherwise imprisonment becomes a farce.[134]

The IRA well understood these propositions and were prepared to test them whenever opportunity permitted.

On the night of 15/16 September, twelve Mountjoy men – presumably thought to be leaders and driving spirits in the prisoners' insubordination – were transferred from Mountjoy to Arbour Hill, where they were subject to close custody. A week later, they wrote to the Military Governor, protesting about the conditions of their confinement. The troubles at Mountjoy, they insisted, had been caused by MacManus's overturning the arrangements whereby the prison had been run as an internment camp, with the internees' own organisation fully recognised, as in other camps throughout the country, and as it had been in Ballykinlar and Frongoch (under the British). The prisoners had kept their part of the bargain – resisted the new arrangements, in other words – and, as a result, had been brutally and scandalously ill-treated. The twelve were now locked in their cells at Arbour Hill, 'deprived of exercise, association, correspondence, newspapers, parcels and other rights to which we are entitled'. They protested at this as well as the ill-treatment at Mountjoy.[135]

On the men's return to their Mountjoy cellhouse, apparently in good fettle, the struggle for control continued. Since they would accept letters and parcels only from their own orderlies and refused to take them individually from the guards, these items were withheld. Food parcels had been used to substitute for or supplement prison rations, but now only prison food was available, and this of poor quality. The evening order to return to cells was refused until the OC issued it. The OC was forbidden to issue his orders, and announcements and warning shots were fired when he continued to do so. Other staff orders were ignored and frequently had to be enforced at gunpoint. Exercise was further limited, and relations between guards and prisoners, already dire, continued to deteriorate. The men found their situation intolerable as, no doubt, did the staff. Prisoners remained unwilling to submit, and, without submission, their deprivations would continue and intensify. Various courses of action were discussed, including the destruction of the prison, a general assault on the guards and a breakout; a tunnel was being driven through the basement of the prison.[136]

Prisons and camps outside Dublin

As Dublin's principal prison and the place where several hundred IRA men would be concentrated, it was to be expected that clashes and disturbances would be most intense and most decisive at Mountjoy. A dozen and more other prisons and camps were in operation, and dissent and resistance took a number of forms in these. A section of the Campa Imtheorannacta (Curragh Camp), known to inmates and staff alike as Tintown because of the many huts which had formerly housed part of the British garrison, comprised two main camps: Tintown 1 and Tintown 2. Within these camps there were further subdivisions or compounds. This was conventional and basic army accommodation, of the kind used to house soldiers and, when required, prisoners. There was also an isolation prison for those who were to be separated from the main body of prisoners or who were under punishment.[137] Huts were either of the corrugated-iron Nissen type, or were of wood, with felted roofs and mounted on short brick piles. Each contained about thirty-six beds. By the winter of 1923-4, they were in dilapidated condition, a combination of neglect by the outgoing British, poor maintenance, the damage and wear that inevitably occurred when the tenants were several hundred resentful and poorly supervised men, and the destruction that came from clashes with the camp guards. Windows lacked panes, and floorboards had, where possible, been torn up for firewood. Prisoners were locked in and were inspected and counted during the night. The camp was enclosed by rows of barbed wire, which prisoners could not approach, even during the day. At night there were searchlights and roaming patrols; raised sentry boxes provided surveillance and firepower when needed.[138] Physical security and the threat of deadly force were formidably combined.

Since the purpose was detention rather than punishment or reformation, there was little need for prisoners and staff to interact. That was reflected in camp layout and a daily routine that amounted to a POW regime. The emphasis was on perimeter security, prevention of tunnelling and interdicting other means of escape. Inspections, a close and careful watch on all that was happening and the collection of whatever intelligence was available were all essential measures. Within the secure perimeter, prisoners were allowed to organise their own routine, subject to the timetables of inspection, head-count and lock-up. In contrast to Mountjoy, there appear to have been few clashes over these arrangements. Prisoners improvised their own breakfasts; other meals were drawn from the cookhouse by orderlies. Cleaning and related duties were carried out by fatigue parties appointed by the prisoners.[139]

The prisoners' determination to exercise self-governance as far as possible offered significant administrative and manpower assistance to their captors. But cooperation could also be withdrawn, and this would happen some months after the camp opened. A policy of non-engagement and passive assistance was announced by the prisoners' leaders. This arose out of escapes from Tintown 1 on 24 April 1923, by means of a tunnel. The authorities immediately initiated searches for other tunnels, and a number were discovered in Tintown 2 and in the Hare Park Camp. These were destroyed, much to the chagrin of the diggers and other aspiring escapers. The Military Governor then, perhaps naively, approached the prisoners' command, asking for the names of the men who had got away. In this, as Mulcahy told the Dáil, the Governor had scant success, and, indeed, he met orchestrated opposition. The identification of escapees would have allowed their details to be circulated to the police and army and would have assisted in their rearrest. Further searches uncovered a document setting out the prisoners' policy of opposition. This basically was a series of steps to stop counting and identification from taking place, thus frustrating the identification of the fugitives. There was to be 'an absolute refusal to produce a man for the Free State'. In addition, there would be obstruction during hut inspection, the count to be rendered as difficult as possible and a refusal by hut commanders to order men in the huts to stand by their beds.[140] This confrontation was eventually resolved, or shelved, it would seem, and a degree of cooperation was restored. This accommodation did not spring from any reduction in mutual animosity or from warmer feelings between the two parties but strictly because each side benefited in some way.

Commodious though the Curragh accommodation was, it could not provide all that was required. Besides places for its rapidly growing number of prisoners, the Provisional government also had to provide for its even more rapidly expanding army. One of the encampments of the complex, Hare Park Camp, which had been used by the British for internees, had been taken over by the national army.[141] It was subsequently found possible to move the 800 soldiers to another section of the Curragh.[142] The sites of two former camps were nearby: Rath and French Furze camps. Although the buildings had been removed from these sites, some of the old hut stands remained, with most of the water and drainage systems and the fences intact.[143] By the following spring (March 1923), much work had been carried out, and Hare Park was in operation, as were the other three camps around the Curragh.[144] They would be known by prisoners, guards and officials alike as Tintown 1 and 2 and then the subdivisions within 1 and 2 as Tintown 3 and 4.[145] The camps could by then hold about 5,000 prisoners, as well as their guard and support services. By this point, the IRA was obviously defeated, and its ceasefire was only weeks away. Demand for prison and camp places had peaked and would now begin to decline.

In August 1922, in Portlaoise, the prisoners issued an ultimatum regarding their political status. This was ignored, and on 29 August they attempted to fire the prison.[146] According to republican accounts, it was agreed that, to avoid injury and possible loss of life, the fires would be set from the top landing down (each wing had four tiers of 'landings' in prison terminology). Everything on the east side of the prison was burned: bedding, furniture and the prisoners' own property. As the fire took hold, an army formation was drawn up in the exercise yard to prevent a mass escape. The prisoners were ordered to stay in smouldering cell blocks, and, when they rushed out, shots were fired over their heads.[147] Once control had been asserted, they were then removed to the Curragh Camp.[148]

In the first weeks of the Civil War, the Provisional government estimated that it would need 500 places in camps, in addition to those already available in prisons to be taken over from the civil authorities. Michael Collins instructed the Department of Public Works to commence construction and adaptation at two former British camps, Gormanston and Newbridge, accommodating between 2,000 and 3,000 together. In these calculations, allowances had to be made for barracks, mess-halls and the like for what would be quite a large guard.[149] By October, 2,500 places had been provided at these two camps, but the original estimates had been taken over by events: a further 7,500 places were now required. An additional consideration was the need, as far as possible, to concentrate the accommodation. Security and economy could not be optimised with a number of small sites.[150]

Newbridge Camp was a former British cavalry establishment, with stone buildings rather than huts. The 1,000 prisoners were held in all parts of the barracks. In October 1922, the Commissioners of Public Works proposed to adapt five stable blocks and to add twenty-seven huts, thereby providing for an additional 1,200 men at a cost of some £13,000. Memoirs suggest that little was provided by way of activities. Prisoners dug tunnels, but apparently none were successful. They did, however, discover a large sewage drain, running from the barracks to the nearby river Liffey, with an opening into a carpenter's shed on the river bank. On Saturday, 14 October 1922, a sizeable number escaped through the drain. The following day, another group were discovered, using the same drain. The guard opened fire, and several were wounded – some reportedly quite seriously. The majority but not all of the men were recaptured.[151]

Gormanston Camp was a well-equipped RIC base (latterly used by the Black and Tans), with accommodation for 4,500. A survey in July 1922 suggested that 2,500 internees could be accommodated in dormitories in four large hangars; huts could hold another 2,000. On consideration, the hangars were deemed unsuitable. The Army insisted that it needed the RIC's large motor-transport depot at the camp. These amendments to the original scheme cut the accommodation to 1,500. This was ready by 23 August but could not immediately be put into use because of a shortage of manpower for guard duties.[152] Pressures elsewhere then necessitated a very rapid takeover, and, by 12 October 1922, the camp was fully occupied.[153] Haste in occupation, poor preparation and the lack of custodial experience by those involved all contributed to an immediate escape of thirty men.[154] Despite the assurances of the Office of Public Works, prisoners had discovered that part of the perimeter fence had not been fully secured. On 7 September, Tom Barry, a noted republican leader escaped through the incomplete perimeter entanglements.[155] Most prisoners were from the South of the country, but their command structure was dominated by the IRA's Dublin Brigade.[156]

Athlone had long been a major British garrison, strategically situated on the Shannon river and near the geographical centre of the country. The extensive barracks complex accommodated soldiers as well as two separate places of detention. The first, Pump Square, was an ordinary barracks, adapted for prisoners. In this were held internees and ordinary sentenced prisoners. Garrison Detention, formerly a British military prison, had regular cells and was used for those facing serious charges or who those had been convicted before Military Tribunals. A number of executions were carried out at this prison in the spring of 1923.[157] There was a short hunger strike, from 30 August to 2 September 1922.[158]

A Free State base was established at Drumboe Castle at Stranorlar, Co. Donegal.[159] During the Civil War it was also used as a place of detention and acquired a sinister reputation among republicans. On 14 March 1923, four republicans, Charlie Daly, Daniel Enright, Seán Larkin and Timothy O'Sullivan, were executed there. They had been part of an eight- or ten-man IRA column, captured on 2 November 1922 at Meenabul, Dunlewey, Co. Donegal, and had been held at the Castle in the intervening period. (Later the men would become known to republicans as the 'Drumboe Martyrs'.)[160] The government's justification for the executions after such a long captivity was that it was retaliation for the shooting of Captain Bernard Cunnon at Creeslough, Co. Donegal. The four executed men were officers in the IRA, and this may have been the reason they were chosen for execution. Of their guilt there was no doubt, since they had been in possession of arms, ammunition and bombs when captured. The death sentence had been imposed by a military court, but its implementation was delayed. Had it not been for the killing of Captain Cunnon, the sentence may not have been carried out. The lapse of some months made its eventual implementation seem vindictive, but it should be noted that the other four men in the group were not executed. The Drumboe executions were not the last of the Civil War; another twelve would follow (the final two on 2 May 1923) to make up the seventy-seven memorialised by republicans.[161]

But these executions were not the only reason for Drumboe Castle's reputation. Three weeks after Seán Larkin was arrested he had managed, through his brother, Father James Larkin, to get a complaint to the government. This reached the Ministry of Defence via the Ministry of Education. The letter was given weight be being countersigned by the parish priest of Donaghmore, Co.

Tyrone. Father Larkin complained that his brother and other prisoners in Drumboe Castle were being ill-treated. The men had refused to work, 'which work would seem to be of the most menial character', and, in consequence, they had been put on a punishment diet of bread and water for the previous ten days. The conditions were squalid, nine men in one cell, ten in another, 'and the place is infested with rats'.[162]

Father Larkin appealed to Eoin MacNeill, Minister for Education, 'as member for Derry City and County in Dáil Éireann, to bring this case before the military authorities. I feel certain they would not tolerate such tyranny on the part of their subordinates. My brother's record is at least as good as any of the authorities at Drumboe.'[163] The arrival of the letter coincided with the ending of the Provisional government and the inauguration of the Free State government. On 9 December, Mulcahy wrote to the *Ard Chongantóir* stating that President W. T. Cosgrave had asked for an assurance that 'energetic steps' were being taken to prevent the ill-treatment of prisoners by 'certain undisciplined officers, against whom there are general grounds of complaint'.[164]

This implied rebuke drew a vigorous response from the officer responsible for the Drumboe area, S. Mac Loclainn. He pointed out that Larkin had been taken in arms and that captured with him was a man named Lane, 'who led the ambush at Drumkeen where two of our men were killed, and their dead bodies robbed'. The prisoners had been asked to work when they were brought to Drumboe Castle. Having refused, they were indeed put on bread and water. It was also true that there were nine prisoners in one cell, 'and it is infested with rats, so are the Officers' Quarters in the Castle'. Mac Loclainn was indignantly unapologetic. 'The treatment he got was as good as he had any right to expect... John Larkin's record is *not* as good as that of some of the Authorities at Drumboe.'[165] An army unit in the field, likely to be under fire and taking casualties, does not take kindly to criticism, even from the head of government.

The military post at Carrick-on-Suir, Co. Tipperary, was also brought into use as a temporary prison. In September 1922, a prisoner gave an account of the accommodation, which was a former workhouse. In one of the vagrancy wards (intentionally the bleakest of all workhouse provision), fourteen prisoners from the IRA's 3rd Tipperary Brigade were confined. 'The floors and ceiling of the ward were in a filthy condition... no plates or mugs were supplied; the only article of this kind which they were allowed was one knife, stolen from the kitchen by a criminal prisoner and handed to them.' The prisoner complained that eight criminals were held in an adjacent room and that they were better treated. He claimed that the IRA prisoners got the criminals' leftovers at mealtimes. The IRA men were held for sixteen days before transfer to the barracks at Kilkenny.[166]

Complaints about conditions

By the autumn of 1922, the Provisional government was in constant receipt of correspondence about overcrowding and poor conditions. In some areas, prisoners were having to be released because of a lack of accommodation. The Minister for Defence was reminded by his colleagues that he had, on 30 October 1922, reported that 12,000 places were being created at the Curragh. What progress had been made and was there any assistance that might speed matters up?[167] The evasive reply was nine days in the writing. Prison overcrowding had been inevitable but 'the matter will be disposed of satisfactorily at a very early date'. Likewise, the Curragh work was 'being pressed forward with all possible despatch'.[168]

There were political as well as operational reasons for urgency. Complaints were being made by people in no manner associated with the IRA. These held credibility and were hard to resist. The threat of an epidemic originating in one of the prisons because of poor conditions, and then sweeping beyond its walls, caused an even greater shift in public sentiment. Limerick Prison was a particular concern. Eamonn Roche, the Sinn Féin TD for East Limerick, described conditions as 'something appalling'. There was poor food and neither bed nor blanket for the majority of the men. A boy had collapsed and was unconscious in the prison hospital, but his mother had been refused a visit. The PPC (not an impartial source, it must be said) confirmed the shortage of blankets and claimed that cells built for one person now held eight. Sanitary arrangements were primitive: filthy bedclothes, no underclothing of any kind, no baths and no medical arrangements. (This last, we know from Roche, was not true: medical provisions may have been inadequate, but they did exist.) There were problems with meals, and some prisoners were not served breakfast until 2 p.m.[169]

Although republicans may have exaggerated some of the conditions at Limerick, there seems no doubt that things were very bad indeed. Bishop Denis Hallinan of Limerick telegraphed Cosgrave on 11 November 1922: 'There is very serious overcrowding in prison here. Could it be remedied immediately.'[170] The reply was also telegraphed: 'Arrangements had already been made to relieve overcrowding this week. Every effort will be made to do so in course of two or three days.'[171] In a follow-up letter, Bishop Hallinan detailed the dangerous state of the prison, which was holding three times its built capacity.[172] Limerick Corporation had appealed to the bishop, and he in turn had gone to General Michael Brennan, the military commander for the area. Brennan told Hallinan that he had twice been to Dublin about the matter. The bishop had been informed by 'a reliable source' (possibly Brennan) that there was plenty of accommodation in Cork; could not the men be transferred at once?[173]

That the bishops had, if anything, understated the difficulties was confirmed by a short official report. In the south-west of Ireland, from Clifden in Connemara to Tralee in Co. Kerry to Thurles in Co. Tipperary, there were two safe prisons: Galway and Limerick. Because the majority of Galway, Clare and Connemara prisoners were sent to Limerick, together with the county's own prisoners, those from Kerry and a large part of the counties of Tipperary and Cork, the prison had become vastly overcrowded. There was accommodation for 120, but 600 were being held, with an extra 100 shortly to arrive: 'The cooking and sanitary arrangements unable to cope with the situation and the numbers of prisoners.' Overcrowding on this scale resulted in inefficiency and an increased risk of disease and escape.

Some complaints were fairly obviously prepared as propaganda.[174] The PPC issued a statement quoting a letter sent to a prisoner's wife from Maryborough, asking her to 'send all the cigarettes you can, as there are a lot of poor lads here who are not receiving any parcels, so we can help them all we can... the grub here is desperate... it would break your heart to see fine men dropping down at your feet from want and exposure... only for the parcels we would be down and out long ago'.[175] No other accounts of life at Portlaoise mention men dropping for 'want and exposure'. There may have been an ignoble and venial intent to the letter: to persuade the man's wife to send as large a parcel as her resources would allow – and perhaps even more. Men in prison (political and ordinary criminal alike) can become extraordinarily self-centred and demanding of their womenfolk.[176]

The dimensions of Victorian cells were carefully calculated, with a number of penal objectives in mind: security, separation and seclusion. The designers had also been deeply conscious of the need to preserve health. Heating and airflow were factored into the dimensions and design.[177] Each cell had been built for single occupancy, but pressure for space now led to two, three and sometimes more prisoners being crammed in. As the weather began to warm in the second year of the Civil War, the Military Governor of Mountjoy, Phil Cosgrave, forwarded to his brother (now President of the Executive Council of the Free State) a letter from five internees. Four of them had medical degrees, the fourth was the D-Wing OC. The authors insisted that the cells were large enough for one occupant only, and, consequently, they had advised the men to 'take down' (i.e. demolish) the windows in order to provide enough fresh air for two men. In cells in which there were three, however, even the removal of the windows would not provide sufficient ventilation. The problem had been drawn to the attention of the Prison Medical Officer, Dr Brandt, and also the Sanitary Officer of the Dublin Command (of the Army): 'Both these gentlemen agree that the ventilation was insufficient.'[178] It is not clear from the record what, if any, action followed this letter.

As internment continued after the cessation of hostilities, complaints about conditions matched the increasing frustration of those who, having fought and lost, longed to go home and to resume their lives. On 28 March 1924, towards the tail-end of internment, a question about the conditions at Hare Park was put in the Dáil.[179] The suggestion was that things were so bad that the prisoners were becoming dangerously ill, that a disproportionate number were in the camp infirmary and that, in general, the camp was a source of concern. This was denied by the government, which gave the population on 26 March at 663, of whom twenty-three were in hospital, none seriously ill.[180]

Mulcahy was asked by Patrick Baxter, TD, if he would appoint a committee to inspect the camp, and, a few days later, on 2 April 1924, an internal government memorandum reported that arrangements were almost complete for such an independent body. This was evidently on the pattern of existing Visiting Committees (part of the governance of prisons retained from the British administration). The committee was to be charged with the inspection of the camp and with visiting prisoners.[181] The fact that such a body was deemed necessary showed that there was a level of public concern – respectable, weighty and beyond republican ranks – to which the government felt obliged to respond.

The government's sensitivity to this, and its desire to fend off criticism from any source that might be seen to be independent and to carry particular moral authority had been demonstrated in its response to a Quaker request to visit military prisons and places of internment. The clerk to the Dublin Yearly Meetings Committee of the Society of Friends wrote to Mulcahy on 17 November 1923, making the request. The letter was simply minuted 'No'.[182] There could be no question about the integrity of the Society of Friends, its pacifist philosophy, its non-partisan stance and the sincerity of its desire to relieve suffering where possible. That, indeed, was the problem. That reputation could make any statement of the Society, or any implication that might be drawn from its actions, an embarrassment to the government. Better therefore to ride whatever criticism that might arise from failing to give them access to prisoners and internees than to face substantive comment from such a body.[183]

This was the twilight of internment, and the inmates were understandably in a depressed and truculent state. The men refused to wash out their huts, and the Hare Park Military Governor, Michael Love, then stopped letters and parcels. In this tense atmosphere, one of the internees wrote to Mulcahy insisting that conditions were so bad that one man had attempted to cut his own throat. Love responded that the man in question had since been released, and that he had attempted suicide because of the treatment he had received from other prisoners when he asked to sign himself out of the camp.[184]

In deciding the order of release from internment, the sick had an obvious claim for clemency and priority. Here, however, humane and security concerns could be in conflict. Patrick Baxter pressed the prisoners' case, asking how many were being held in military hospitals and why they had not been released.[185] He was told that forty-one were in hospital, of whom eleven had been sentenced to terms of imprisonment (and who were therefore not eligible for release), and a further six were being prosecuted. Ten men who fitted into neither category were being held because they were considered to be dangerous. The cases of the remaining fourteen prisoner-patients were under consideration.[186] With the last embers of the Civil War fading, however, it was undoubtedly becoming more difficult to justify the retention of sick men in custody.[187]

Some releases and a great expansion in accommodation, combined with improved organisation in the prisons and camps and the effectiveness of government control through the country, vastly improved conditions by the end of 1923. The propaganda value of prison and camp stories to the IRA was considerable. A note to the IRA Chief of Staff from the organisation's Director of

Medical Service, dated 11 December 1923, dealt with the situation following the general hunger strike. He lamented that the reports he had received did not have much publicity value on the grounds of ill-treatment, 'except in the case of Mountjoy'. Enclosed was a communication from the OC at Newbridge camp. Conditions had improved when the men called off their strike. They had been allowed their own orderlies, light, coal, clothes and three letters a week; 'in fact, anything we thought of asking at the time, we got'. There were musical entertainments organised by the prisoners in the huts from 7 to 10 o'clock each evening, 'and this helps to cheer the fellows up a bit'. The report had probably been written to show the benefits that the prisoners had won through their struggle and firm dealing with the authorities, but it contained no sustenance for republican propagandists, whom it must have irritated. Overall, the OC concluded, 'the treatment by the Staters is as good as can be expected. In fact I have no complaint about their treatment of us.'[188]

Who's one of us?

Not everyone being held for acts of rebellion, subversion, violent disorder or the like was a member of the IRA. This was a matter of some importance since republican prisoners wished to establish the exclusive authority of their command structure, and freelancers and non-affiliates could be a problem in the close quarters of a prison. Thought had therefore been given to the question of who qualified for the designation. After the IRA ceasefire of 24 May 1923, this point became even more pressing. A high proportion of whatever republican resources remained available was now concentrated in the prisoners. The war had been lost in the field, but the activists hoped to regroup, reorganise and fight again another day: the organisation had to be preserved. Camps and prisons held some of the most experienced and committed IRA men, whose continued adherence was critical. In its attitude towards and efforts on behalf of the prisoners, the IRA knew that it was being tested. Had its defeat and dissolution progressed so far that ties of loyalty and obligation had been cut? Alternatively, could the organisation begin to re-establish morale and take the first steps in reconstructing a fighting spirit by standing by the prisoners and their dependants?

Having been relatively broad and generous earlier in the year, a highly restrictive definition of IRA membership was proposed by its adjutant general on 22 July 1923: 'A Volunteer or civilian who was convicted for an act carried out with the authority, sanction or approval of either the military or civil Republican Authorities.'[189] In the circumstances of the Civil War, however, this formulation avoided a number of difficult questions, some of which were also addressed by a Maryborough prisoner in May 1923. The writer, who cannot be identified from the remaining records, was penetrating and articulate, if at times ponderous. His approach was more flexible and inclusive: 'A prisoner who is considered to be a traitor by his political opponents.'[190] His justification of the proposition was instructive. Since in war there is much taking of life and seizure or destruction of property, the issue of criminality arose: those who carried out the acts insisted that they were not criminal; their opponents insisted they were. How, over the course of the previous ten years, were these deeds, criminal in themselves, to be regarded as acts of patriotism? (Since many of the Free State leaders had, in their time, been accused by Lloyd George of being members of a 'murder gang' and had repeatedly been denounced in the Commons as criminals, this was a pertinent line of questioning.) To get out of the difficulty, the writer proposed that '*conscience* is the supreme arbiter and *motive* and *circumstance* the ruling factors'. Applying these criteria, acts of war were not criminal.[191]

Civil war made it difficult to apply the criteria. Some men were fugitives, unable to return home; others could go home but not find employment; many were starving, as were their families. Men had to depend on chance and on the generosity of their neighbours; the IRA war chest 'was a minus quantity', and officers and men were in the same position. Supposing a man took food or clothing from a person or company that could easily bear the loss, would he be a criminal? And should he have to take a car to escape, would he be a criminal? In these cases, the answer must be no. The same reasoning applied to someone who carried out an act whilst following a superior order. Such men were all political prisoners, 'and those who treat them as criminals are themselves criminals'.

This letter was forwarded to the IRA HQ under the pseudonym of John Hogan, IRA OC at Maryborough. Hogan had informed some republican prisoners some time previously that their status was not recognised by the IRA. In reply, one of the prisoners had given him the foregoing analysis 'What is a Political Prisoner?' Hogan thought it unnecessary to give his own views or those of the others who were 'recognised' by the IRA: 'Suffice it to say that this cause has our sincerest sympathy and we hope and pray that HQ will take an enlightened view (of at least a good many of these cases) as circumstances will permit.' This referred not only to incorporation into the IRA structure in the prison but also to material support for families and upon release.

But the IRA had ceased to be a fighting organisation. The spirit of petty bureaucracy, which always struggles for the soul of revolutionary organisations, had triumphed. HQ responded not to the substance of the argument but with a burst of indignation at what it took to be a breach of chain of command, committed when the paper had been forwarded: 'I do not like the idea at all that it is the prisoner who wrote this that is officially communicating with us and if any other person could be got to communicate with official prisoners, he should be dropped at once.' The Maryborough OC was instructed that the document's author was on no account to be recognised as an official (i.e. IRA) prisoner. Further enquiries were to be made about the status of all prisoners. The OC was directed to provide a list to the HQ Director of Intelligence, and each case was to be considered 'minutely' at HQ. When IRA officers visited the home areas of prisoners, moreover, they were to make further enquiries and to report back to

HQ. The Adjutant General's concern was to husband funds available in those lean and unpromising times to those prisoners whose membership and adherence to the IRA was unquestioned.[192]

The issue continued to perplex the IRA's GHQ even after the last republican leaders had been released in mid-July 1924.[193] A number of men remained in custody, having fallen outside the terms of the government's criteria for release.[194] Sinn Féin's Director of Publicity, Mary MacSwiney, asked Frank Aiken for directions on the standing of those who had been sentenced or who were awaiting trial for unauthorised acts. Two examples were given. One concerned man called O'Kane, from Carlow, whose action was described by MacSwiney as 'rank dishonesty'. The other involved Dempsey, McCarthy and O'Donovan of Skibbereen, Co. Cork, who had acted against the IRA's ceasefire order 'but probably had great provocation'. These three could not be put in the same category as O'Kane, 'yet how can GHQ stand over their action'? And what was to be done about bail? In addition, many of the exploits of Keogh were unauthorised, 'but one can't repudiate Keogh.'[195] MacSwiney's view was that the IRA would probably have to take disciplinary action for breaches of the ceasefire, 'but there are certain men who cannot be let down by us outside GHQ even if they did do unauthorised things'. In the campaign for immediate release of republican prisoners, which prisoners should Sinn Féin mention and which were to be left 'severely alone', she asked.[196]

There is some indication that there were in government those who were aware of the demoralising effects of internment, especially after the IRA ceasefire, and who wished to explore its use further to fracture the organisation. At the end of August 1923, three months into the peace, Colonel M. Costello wrote to the Director of Intelligence for the Minister for Defence. Information had been received from a reliable source that showed that 'too much attention cannot be paid to the task of segregating prisoners and creating internal disputes in their various compounds'. The information was that there was a great deal of ill-feeling between the wives and relatives of those who had been killed, those who were still free and those who were inside: 'they are constantly finding fault with each other'. The inference was that this fault-finding was most connected to the limited funds that were available for relief. The informant noted that if any prisoner received exceptional treatment, 'the outside party at once falls out with that prisoner's relatives'. This tendency could be exploited by 'having different treatment for different Irregulars'.[197]

This type of manipulation is akin to that of 'psychops' in a modern army: psychological and propaganda activities intended to split and disrupt army forces.[198] It required experience, resources, secrecy, flair and a deft hand to be successful, and, if any of these are absent or if, by simple bad luck, the ploy should fail, it can be wholly counterproductive. There are no indications that the Free State Army (or the government) had the ability to undertake such operations during or after the Civil War. Simply meeting the security and logistical demands of holding several thousand prisoners strained resources. But the observations throw light on the in-fighting and corrosive jealousies that attended defeat.

And since you are one of us...

Those prisoners who were officially recognised accepted in turn their continuing obligations to the IRA, which remained unyielding in its claim that it was the sole body in the land entitled to such loyalty. On 27 September 1922, Lynch issued a general order strictly forbidding IRA men from giving any undertaking or signing any document as to their future actions: 'They will only accept release unconditionally.' Any breach of the order would entail a court martial. Those who had already signed or given undertakings were ordered to rejoin their units and, in default, were to be court-martialled for desertion.[199] A further order followed three months later. Confrontation and rejection of the spurious authority of their captors was to commence from the earliest point of captivity. IRA men should refuse to recognise the jurisdiction of the court, affirm allegiance to the Republic and demand POW treatment. Pragmatism was allowed to peep around the corner, and an exception to the non-recognition injunction was made for those facing a capital charge. These could engage a solicitor to contest the charges, but, in framing the defence, lawyers were to be directed to safeguard the republican position – pragmatism evidently could go too far. In pressing for POW status, members were not to resort to hunger strike without GHQ authorisation.[200]

Even with the war palpably lost and hopes dwindling by the day, the issue of signing out continued to be one of principle rather than pragmatism for the IRA. In the face of all the other demands on their shrinking resources and personnel, time and effort were devoted to courts martial to try and punish those who had 'signed out' in violation of General Order No. 8. Oscar Traynor, who had been a leading commander during the Anglo-Irish and Civil wars, was thus dealt with under this General Order on 30 January 1924.[201] Those discharged from prison were required to report to the IRA, and the organisation took a close interest in prison conduct. As far as conditions of time and place allowed, incidences of signing out were to be recorded and seem to have merited attention not only at the individual level but also as an index of the morale and cohesiveness of the organisation.[202] Such was the strength of the taboo that the government took the view that the signing of an undertaking neutralised or at least compromised IRA prisoners. There is some indication that threats, including the threat of capital punishment, were used to coerce signatures.[203]

Hunger strikes

As we have seen, frustration, ennui and a desire for action built up in the months following the ceasefire. These were vented in a hunger strike that commenced at Mountjoy on 13 October 1923 and quickly spread to other prisons and camps. The prisoners issued a manifesto pointing out that although hostilities had ended on 28 April, almost six months before, they remained in custody. They also protested at their treatment for failing to obey what they considered to be degrading orders: 'the hosings of prisoners here, their forcible expulsion, then saturated, into the exercise rings, there to suffer exposure in bitter weather for thirty seven hours, and to be hosed again and again on subsequent days, and bedding cells, clothing etc., also hosed; the beating and kicking'.[204] Their strike was for unconditional release rather than non-criminal status because they believed that, even were such status granted, they had no guarantee that it would last: release alone would save them from slow death. Their action would begin on the night of 13/14 October 1923. Evoking the defiance of the republican martyr Terence MacSwiney, they promised that they would persist until they had achieved 'freedom or the grave'.[205]

Republican leaders had good reason to be wary of hunger-striking, a double-edged weapon. Persisted in, the Free State might be brought to concede demands. The death of a prisoner – and such an awful, lingering and pitiful death – could evoke compassion and inflame public opinion. On the one side was the suffering captive; on the other implacable and seemingly cruel authority. The inevitable distraught family and ashen-faced cleric were powerful, heart-tugging images. The administrative and political demands on the government and officials coping with a hunger strike could in themselves be an effective part of war by attrition. All this was on the positive side, as were the possibilities for additional recruitment and fund-raising arising from associated protest and sympathy campaigns. But there was also grave political risk. Organisation and all the necessary support and publicity activities could be as draining for the various front organisations and for the IRA as they were for the state in countering them, and, strained though it was, the state had immeasurably greater resources. A further problem – perhaps the key one – was the consequence of an unsuccessful hunger strike. The morale of those coming off the strike would undoubtedly plummet, as would that of their wider circles of supporters and sympathisers. And should deaths occur and the state still fail to yield, the loss would be greater still: an IRA failure brought about by a display of resoluteness and ruthlessness could all too easily transmute into a tale of pig-headed indifference to the individual and could strengthen both government and state.

The IRA ceasefire and order to dump arms was emphatically not a surrender; it was an attempt to have it both ways: to stop fighting without acknowledging defeat. The IRA made a point of underlining this, as did de Valera in his stirring proclamation to 'the Legion of the Rearguard', when he acknowledged that 'military victory must be allowed to rest for the moment with those who have destroyed the Republic'. The overt intention was to renew the battle when circumstances permitted, and to communicate this to friend and foe alike. Even had there been an unconditional surrender, there would have been no immediate opening of the prison gates. As it was, the infant Free State had to show minimal prudence and to proceed cautiously. Releases would be driven in part by a desire to shed the economic burden of such relatively large-scale imprisonment, but their pace had to be regulated by security above all. Understandably, prisoners did not share this view.

On 25 July 1923, the Mountjoy prisoners had sought GHQ guidance on hunger strikes. The IRA Executive had already unanimously agreed that, in the light of all the imponderabilities, particularly the state of public feeling and government control of the press, it could not recommend this action. It did not, however, issue a definite prohibition and gave the IRA Army Council authority to make tactical decisions. In the meantime, the government had called a general election. To the Army Council, this was a tactical opportunity, allowing hunger-strike publicity to be ventilated at the hustings. But even so, the decision to refuse food must rest solely with the prisoners. In a cautionary note, HQ emphasised that a prospective hunger-striker should realise that he had to stick it to the end 'and that considering the brutal and inhuman record of the enemy a number of the men will probably die in the fight'. Prison councils were directed to be 'particularly careful to discourage any man who is not perfectly satisfied he can carry it through to the end'. Men not physically fit were emphatically forbidden to go on hunger strike.[206]

As had happened on several previous occasions, the prisoners stumbled into hunger-striking for want of an alternative. Nor was there any serious attempt to learn from past experience. In consequence, two fundamental mistakes made failure inevitable. All such actions are as strong as the weakest link. Instead of selecting a small group of the most reliable and determined men and women, hard-core, hard-headed and fully prepared to die, all prisoners who wished to participate were allowed to do so. Inevitably, given the fervency of the prison culture and the need to exclude all doubt and dissent, the vast majority raised hands and voices, swore to do or die and drew comfort from anticipated glory.[207] But before the glory came starvation – an extended mental and physical ordeal of the most testing kind – and a willingness to embrace death. Few there were that could take such a journey, and that alone in a prison cell. A falling-off was utterly inevitable. The fracturing of the strike would become cumulative, progressive and demoralising, placing an unendurable strain on a diminishing group of stalwarts and soaking the drop-outs in a flood of guilt. The other mistake, which any consideration of precedents would conclusively have demonstrated, was the maximalist nature of the demand. This was foolishly devoid of calculation. Were the government to release all the prisoners unconditionally, its authority would be fractured, even shattered: having prevailed in a bitter and consuming war, it manifestly was not going to allow this to happen. Its determination was reinforced by a strong popular mandate and by the country's unmistakable desire for peace and order. The government's policy of phased releases, proceeding at a rate of about 3,000 a month in the autumn of 1923, allowed it to draw a distinction between the relatively harmless rank and file and the more dangerous, the irreconcilables and the leadership.[208] It also presented a face of reasonableness to the public. An unexpected consequence of this policy, however, was to confirm the notion that some internees and prisoners would be held for protracted periods, or indefinitely.[209]

Having many former prisoners in its ranks and the counsel of many more, the government was, of course, aware of the hunger-strikers' weaknesses. It sought to develop these by separating leaders from followers. The Mountjoy OC, Mick Price, together with Seán MacBride, Ernie O'Malley and others, were transferred to Kilmainham – a thrust somewhat blunted when, en route, Price, Seán MacBride and Dáithí O'Donoghue managed to escape.[210] At Kilmainham, a group of mainly senior IRA officers was assembled, including figures such as Frank Gallagher, Gerald Boland, Austin Stack and Peadar O'Donnell.[211]

At first the advantage seemed to lie with the strikers. This was, after all, a form of protest that had deep roots in recent political history and in popular consciousness. It was surely unthinkable that an Irish government in this newly formed state would allow political prisoners – erring brethren – to starve themselves to death. The circumstances demanded leniency: the rebels had been so comprehensively routed and had given in – surely mercy was appropriate. As the strikers became weaker, the Church, which had withheld its sacraments from unrepentant republicans, demanding political apostasy for spiritual comfort, softened its line.[212] There was also an easing of secular tensions. Prison staff, according to O'Malley, became more willing to carry letters into and out of the prison.[213] The authorities, now keen to get the men to eat, allowed previously forbidden parcels to be sent in and did not object to the prisoners' adjutant delivering them.[214] The government also declared that the process of release that had been under way would not be suspended but that persons on hunger strike, who might otherwise have been released, would remain in custody.[215]

But shifts in tactics by the authorities were no more than that: there was no slackening in the determination to prevail. In this, as in other matters, the republicans had seriously misread the political runes. After a comparatively short time it began to seem that the Irish people would not be outraged by an Irish government seeing through a republican hunger strike: it had been granted a clear mandate in free elections and had fought a civil war to defend the right of the democratic majority. A strike for better prison conditions, buttressed by accounts of squalor and hardship, of which there were many, might have put the government in a more awkward position than the demand for unconditional release. An opening of the gates and a plethora of triumphal homecomings would be widely understood as a surrender, washing away the foundations of the government's still shaky authority: all knew this from the latter days of British rule.

And, indeed, almost from the outset, from the days after the gung-ho declarations, the rank and file began to drop away. By 29 October 1923, the government was claiming that 3,200 had, in the previous five days, begun to accept food.[216] This showed the utter impossibility of success in an unrestricted and inclusive strike. The collapse was dramatically confirmed on 19 November when Con Moloney, OC of Mountjoy's D Wing, accepted food.[217] This was a disastrous blow, especially since Moloney immediately informed all the Mountjoy men of his decision. Frank Aiken tried to put the best face on it, but this was a whirl of words – a bluster so contrived that it could only have depressed the strikers. It was only natural, Aiken wrote, that the strikers should find this defection disheartening, but it was entirely possible for the outcome to be very different: 'the strikers will be convinced once and for all that no matter who may go off strike there are upwards of 250 men who are determined to win out'. The Free State leaders knew the big post-war test had arrived. If the other strikers followed Con Moloney, the struggle was lost to them, but if the strikers held on, the government would lose: 'Every Volunteer was proud of the men in D Wing who held on when their O/C and Adjutant have given in. They will have greater reason to be proud of all the men in Mountjoy who stick it out now.'[218]

The previous day, and before he had received news of Moloney's decision, Aiken had revealed how much was riding on the strike. Writing to the Mountjoy OC, he exhorted

> [K]eep a stiff upper lip, A Mhic. Things are going fine. Under no circumstances, even should a comrade die, are you to call off the hunger-strike – of course you have no power to *order* a man off. I believe your fight will do more for the cause than a thousand years war.[219]

The desperate IRA had placed its remaining chips on the table, hoping that, at this utmost ebb, there would be a turn. Moloney's defection squashed that last thin hope.

Aiken's attempt to shore up the strike was futile, and, indeed, damaging. A core had been firm from the beginning, but the pace of desertion had been inexorable, and it now gained momentum. The various camps abandoned the strike fairly quickly.[220] On 20 November 1923, Denis Barry died at Newbridge Camp. Andy O'Sullivan was transferred to hospital because of his grave condition; he died on 22 November after a forty-day fast.[221] Barry's body was refused entry to a Cork church, Bishop Daniel Cohalan denouncing republicanism as a wicked and insidious attack on the Church.[222] Other prisoners were declining rapidly, yet, despite the representations of some public bodies, the government would not yield. The longer the hold-outs persisted, the harder it became for either side to give way, or so it seemed. The deaths of Barry and O'Sullivan provided moral reinforcement for the strike: those who at this point left the ranks made their sacrifice futile. A conciliatory appeal by Cardinal Logue, however, may have shifted positions. At the end of the fifth week, on 23 November 1923, the Kilmainham OC consulted his officers and decided to end the strike.[223] Two men (Tom Derrig and David Robinson) requested permission to leave the prison to inform those in Mountjoy, the Curragh camps and the NDU.[224]

This was a demoralising defeat for the IRA, removing it as a moral as well as a military threat to the Free State. The strike benchmarked the government's future responses. Under the Cosgrave and, an ironical twist, successive de Valera administrations, it became clear that general campaigns of hunger-striking would not succeed and that the government, whether green or deeper green, would accept any passing opprobrium that might come from resultant deaths.

The IRA's miscalculation is all the harder to understand because over the preceding months there had been indications that the government understood well the dynamics of the hunger strike and had formed the necessary intent. In protest at being made to associate with ordinary prisoners, Máire Comerford and Sheila (Sighle) Humphreys had refused food at Mountjoy in January 1923.[225] The Executive Council decided to sidestep them by seeking sufficient accommodation 'to segregate the two women and any other women who might be tried and convicted by the Military Tribunal'.[226] (Women who had been arrested but not tried and sentenced were to be held at Kilmainham, but the government did not wish to mix the two categories.[227]) There was a similar move to head off a hunger strike ten weeks later, when Dr Con Murphy refused food at Mountjoy.[228] The Prison Medical Officer reported that Murphy was beginning to show signs of cardiac failure, and the Executive Council decided immediately to prepare and serve criminal charges. This did not persuade Murphy to take food, and his strike continued, to back his demand for unconditional freedom. The response from the government was firm: 'Arising out of this case and those of other prisoners in similar circumstances, it was decided that no prisoner can be permitted to secure his release by hunger-strike.'[229]

This decision was announced to Dr Murphy, who, on 18 April 1923, a month into his protest, signed a declaration that he had not taken any part in warfare against the Free State and that he had no intention of doing so. He was then immediately released.[230] The requirement that an undertaking be signed appeared so reasonable and unproblematic to a person of good faith that it could not but stifle potential sympathy. Refusal would indicate the prisoner's malign intent towards the state; a signature was a solemn promise, which, if broken, would discredit the man or woman who had given it.

This approach was immediately taken with Miss Kathleen (Kitty) Mary Costello and two other women.[231] Letters of intercession had been received from the Roman Catholic Archbishop of Dublin, Dr Edward Byrne; the Chairman of the Seanad, Lord Glenavy; and Kathleen Costello's mother – the latter asserting her daughter's innocence. The women were offered, but refused, the same declaration that Dr Con Murphy had signed. For the next ten days or so, a stand-off continued, with the government demanding signatures and the weakening women refusing. Further pleas on behalf of the women were received from Trinity College TDs and others.[232]

A small group of women continued to be held in the NDU through the autumn of 1923. By the middle of November, only fourteen remained in custody. Releases in early December reduced this to four. Two women were freed over the fortnight that followed with their two remaining comrades being released on 22 December.[233]

The government rejoiced in a significant victory when Dan Breen, who had been on hunger strike, signed himself out. His declaration was unambiguous: 'It is not my purpose to oppose by force of arms the Government elected by the people.'[234] This and other prominent submissions confirmed to all but the most foolish and obdurate that, with the IRA defeated in the field, continued efforts by prisoners to challenge and wish away the authority of the Free State were futile. Seán T. O'Kelly, a leading republican on the political side (and future president of Ireland) evidently had no difficulty in signing himself out of Gormanston Camp to visit his seriously ill mother.[235] The undertaking he signed became the standard requirement for other prisoners who were given temporary parole on compassionate grounds. That these forms were signed and that undertakings were given was a further indication that the Free State had received *de-facto* recognition from republicans.

Training

During the aftermath of the 1916 Rising and the imprisonment and internment arising from the Anglo-Irish War, the IRA realised that captivity, whilst to be avoided by every means possible, held its own attractions and opportunities. It could provide a base for a continuation of the war of attrition against official-dom and against the apparatus of the state; it could also be a stage on which sympathetically to dramatise the cause. Classes and military instruction were undertaken to whatever extent the regime, organisation and layout of the prison or camp allowed. A strict cellular regime will limit the possibilities, which is why one of the first demands was always for free association and maximum out-of-cell time. The typical camp regime of free association within a secure perimeter and self-regulated hut living maximised the training opportunities – cultural, educational and military – as well as possibilities to maintain and promote physical fitness. In such a setting, the prisoners' structure of command and discipline could flourish and ties of loyalty and mutual dependence be tightened.

Imprisonment had its own built-in tests of commitment, and these were also useful. It measured leadership qualities, and its hardships and deprivations ensured that the summer soldier would fade away once freed. Conversely, if adversity can truly be shared in a common cause, it provides a powerful and lasting bond. To this end, a tough regime and continuous clashes between prisoners and staff could be particularly useful, were these handled with deftness by a leadership able to command loyalty. If, however, the balance of skill and determination lay with the authorities, such struggles and concomitant adversity could go quite the other way: desertion, disloyalty, recrimination and denuncia-tions could exercise a disastrous influence, wounding and disabling for the indi-vidual, divisive, corrosive and self-consuming for the organisation. The prison and camp experiences of 1923–4 weakened, demoralised and diminished the IRA. The failed hunger strike was a significant defeat, but it was not the only one. Yet the lesson was not taken. Ernie O'Malley, one of several seasoned IRA leaders who opposed but nevertheless joined the hunger strike, was content to allow the daily experience of imprisonment to provide raw nutriment which he saw as strengthening the IRA. His Mountjoy memoir dwelt on discipline and solidarity among the prisoners as well as the reinforcement of personal ties.[236] From these he doubtless drew personal and political consolation as well as justification for the course he had followed. In his view, the prison chapter was an important contribution to the republican struggle, to be remembered and analysed. Writing to Lynch on 14 January 1923, he reported, 'I am getting people to write the history of Mountjoy.' The months of confrontation and hardship in captivity were in some ways equivalent to combat experience. Such was the recourse to warning shots from guards that the men had been hardened by being under fire. O'Malley thought it extraordinary so few had been hit by what he called 'the miscellaneous firing'.[237]

Publicity battle

The prisons and camps were battlefields for popular support. A sophisticated publicity machine had been developed by Sinn Féin during the Anglo-Irish War. It was far more nimble than the British apparatus, which, by comparison, seemed sclerotic. Some talented publicists had delivered a string of important successes that had helped to shape opinion in Ireland, Britain, the USA and elsewhere. David fought Goliath on a regular basis, and David nearly always won. Throughout the Civil War, republicans rated highly the value of stories of prison hardship and ill-treatment; these authenticated claims of the anti-Treaty side to be the true and faithful heirs of patriotic sufferers for the cause of Irish nationalism. The more they could represent internment and imprisonment as the undeviating *via dolorosa* of patriots and the Free State as a witting or unwitting instrument of British imperialism, the more they hoped to mobilise their supporters and to increase the number of their sympathisers. The government was equally aware of the need to set the tone and to control the content of reports of imprisonment. Press censorship had been initiated on 29 June 1922, and steps were taken to project the government's version of events.[238] Newspapers outside Ireland were in a stronger position to give an independent account, but these could also be courted by both sides, and, were the government sufficiently provoked, enough individual issues of an offending publication could be banned to inflict a financial penalty through lost sales and advertising revenue.[239] Editors and journalists would also have been aware that the IRA had in the past struck at newspapers that displeased it, and might do so again.[240] A deal of self-censorship to avoid provoking either side was prudent and inevitable.

Threats could be avoided to some extent by picking one's way carefully between the two sides. On 13 November 1922, the *Freeman's Journal* published a letter of complaint from Stiofáin Ó Madagáin and Ruairí Ó Conchubhair, respectively OC and Medical Officer of the republican prisoners in Limerick Prison.[241] They claimed that the Limerick cells were damp and cold, that prisoners lacked bedclothes as well as knives and forks and that they had to eat their meals off their cell floors.[242] They also complained of gross overcrowding, an insufficient number of lavatories and broken cell windows and claimed that there was an influenza epidemic under way.[243] In a newspaper interview a fortnight later, Kevin O'Higgins, the Minister for Home Affairs, gave the government version of events. All fixtures, heating pipes, bedding and cell tables had been destroyed by the prisoners, as had cell windows 'whenever they would get away with it'. He agreed that there was insufficient space for exercise and sidestepped the claim that on the night of 30/1 October shots had been fired into the cells, wounding one man.[244] But whatever gloss O'Higgins put on it, these were dire conditions in which to keep prisoners of whatever status, much less persons who had not been charged with any offence – so much so that a Northern Ireland official appended a note to a clipping of the report, proposing that it should be displayed in the library of the internment ship *Argenta*, then moored in Larne Lough, where apparently much better (but certainly Spartan) conditions failed to avert complaints.[245]

Besides the press, each party sought to win for their cause the considerable influence of the Roman Catholic hierarchy. There were private injunctions to show mercy and humanity, but the bishops firmly backed Cosgrave's government.[246] Sentiment in overseas communities was also of considerable importance, determining republicans' abilities to raise cash and to exert international influence. In the tense autumn of 1923, both sides were active in Australia, which had the largest overseas Irish community outside the USA. Irish-born Archbishop Daniel Mannix of Melbourne had taken a strongly nationalist position during the War of Independence and continued to be sympathetic to the republican cause.[247] In October and November 1923, he was contacted by the Irish Republican Prisoners' Dependants' Fund (IRPDF). P. J. Ruttledge wrote as acting president of the organisation, explaining why the prisoners had undertaken a hunger strike and asking Mannix to intensify his efforts on behalf of the IRPDF 'to bring succour to those helpless ones on whose behalf this noble Organisation is so heroically asserting itself'.[248] The letter, which includes a number of religious allusions, had been intercepted by the Free State government, as was another, a month later. On 27 November 1923, Kathleen Barry, General Secretary of the IRPDF, wrote to Mannix more directly and practically, setting out the difficulties within which the organisation was operating. The autumn hunger strike, she claimed, had resulted in thousands being released and this in turn meant a further drain on funds until those freed secured employment.[249] Her letter crossed with a telegram to Cosgrave from Mannix, forwarding a resolution from Irish societies in Victoria asking for the release of the prisoners. This, Mannix, cabled, 'I wholeheartedly endorse'.[250]

With Archbishop Mannix's patronage, the Irish Distress Appeal Australia was raising money for republican relief. Understandably, the Irish government considered that this strengthened the anti-Treaty cause. In particular, it claimed that a portion of the funds was being used to support the military campaign. With the two IRPDF letters to hand, Cosgrave cabled James Duhig, Archbishop of Brisbane (Mannix he doubtless believed to be a lost cause).[251] The IRPDF, Cosgrave contended, had been taken over by the anti-Treaty side on the outbreak of the Civil War in July 1922. Although 12,000 had been interned (by 3 January 1923), now fewer than 2,000 were being held. As for the October–November 1923 hunger strike, Cosgrave insisted that rather than speeding releases it had impeded them. Many who had 'blindly followed de Valera in his orgy of destruction' now saw that their cause was mistaken and criminal and had determined to turn their energies to more profitable and patriotic objectives.[252] The Archbishop's response took some months to arrive but was gratifying: 'every one of our priests who has been home, has come back a convert to the Free State, and Australia is slowly but surely permeated with a favourable impression regarding all of you who have stood out against the extremists'.[253]

The hunger strike was also the basis for an attempt to enlist the sympathies of the Irish medical profession. This appeal, the authors claimed, was not issued in a 'petty party spirit' but rather in an attempt to prevent the disaster of some 8,000 prisoners hunger-striking to death. They had been driven to the action by the conditions of prisons throughout the country. Three men were being held in cells designed for one – 'over-crowded, unsanitary and badly ventilated'. Many were being denied exercise, and in some places this had persisted for up to six weeks. Human waste was not being removed daily from the cells and blocks and had been allowed to accumulate for as long as ten days. Soap was in short supply, and underclothing was not being changed. There was random firing into cells, wounding many prisoners and causing some fatalities. Prisoners had been hosed and left in their dripping clothes; men had been manacled in their cells for days, in some cases without stools to sit on or with chamber pots. There had been cruel beatings, and tubercular prisoners, who should have been released, were still in custody. These conditions were 'a disgrace to a Christian country and a crime against humanity'. The circular called for an investigation to be carried out by a committee of the Medical Association.[254]

There was no response to this circular by the Medical Association or by any other professional body. Conditions in the prisons and camps were hard, in some instances extremely unsanitary and unhealthy, and, in truth, they were a disgrace to the country. The inescapably political nature of hunger strikes and the divided state of the nation (with a substantial majority of the middle-class vote going to the Free State) ensured that few doctors would want to intervene in a dispute that had unseen dimensions and in which any opinion or action on their part would become ammunition for one side or the other.[255]

Releases and after

Although technically it was not a surrender, the IRA's ceasefire and order to dump arms was an acceptance of defeat, and this made it possible to contemplate a staged and gradually accelerated release of prisoners. For a poor country, whose infrastructure and economy had been shattered by several years of war, the burden of some 12,000 prisoners and an army in excess of 50,000 could not too soon be put down. A sizeable portion of the Army was deployed in staffing the various prisons and camps. With all the demands on the depleted coffers of the new state, and the continued credit-worthiness of its bonds on international markets a matter of vital importance, a rapid move away from a war footing was a priority, even if some arrests had to continue.[256] On 16 June 1923, the Executive Council agreed to set up a mechanism for releasing 'the more or less harmless type whose detention was no longer really necessary in view of the rapid trend of conditions towards normal'.[257] A committee of officers of the various military commands was set up to review lists of prisoners. State solicitors and county committees would be consulted, and the committee would formulate a recommendation to the Minister for Defence on each case.[258]

Releases proceeded rapidly, reflecting the government's strong and growing confidence and its rapidly diminishing apprehensions that there could be any kind of military resurgence by anti-Treaty forces. On 1 June 1923, there were 11,989 prisoners; six months later, this number had more than halved to 5,495.[259] Of the leaders, those on the political side were understandably the first to be released (apart from the most senior); equivalent military figures still posed too much of a risk. On 10 December 1923 it was decided to release four members of the Dáil as well as Robert Barton (Erskine Childers's cousin), a former Dáil member and minister.[260] Three days later, a further five Sinn Féin TDs were released on the same terms.[261] Steps were also taken to free persons who had been tried and sentenced (as distinct from internees), with the sick among them receiving first consideration. The case of Joseph McEvilly was considered by the Executive Council on 4 February 1924. He was serving the very heavy sentence of fifteen years' penal servitude but had been diagnosed as tubercular – then a most serious condition. In other such cases it was agreed that where the prisoner's medical condition was sufficiently grave the Minister for Defence could make a release recommendation to the Minister for Home Affairs.[262]

By the early summer of 1924, the country had moved sufficiently from conflict and disorder to halt further criminal proceedings against many who had already been convicted on other charges. It was decided that such prosecutions should in general not go forward, but information on the charges should be passed from the military to the Garda Síochána, thus allowing local police files to be updated and a watch kept on the released men.[263] There was an increasing flow of questions in the Dáil, both in relation to individuals and on the general policy and tempo of releases.[264] Case-by-case reviews were time-consuming and expensive: officials are, by nature, risk-averse and always apt to be cautious about appending their signatures. With numbers much diminished, on 5 July 1924, it was decided that the remaining political prisoners (the term 'non-criminal' was preferred) should be released in daily batches of about twenty.[265] Drawing on their own experience of the recent past, when they were fighting the British, ministers were insistent that

there should be no general release in order to avoid demonstrations and celebrations (though the festive spirit had long since deserted republican ranks). A
Dáil statement on the review of sentenced prisoners was made by the Minister for
Defence.[266] In a similar spirit, it was decided quietly to exhume the bodies of the
men who had been executed and buried on army property. As part of the winding
down of military operations, several barracks and bases would be evacuated, and
it would invite demonstrations were the remains of the executed to be left on the
vacated premises, to be reclaimed by relatives and friends. Exhumed bodies
were to be reinterred in the nearest military post designated for permanent
occupation.[267] The implication was that the remains would stay in long-term or
permanent army custody. This could be read as pure vindictiveness or continuing insecurity – neither flattering to the government. Almost immediately, there
were second thoughts. Given the importance, especially in rural areas, of family
and community obsequies, and the history of prison interments of those executed
under the British administration, there was a risk of stirring up particularly hostile
feeling and that to little advantage, were the families to be deprived of the final
consolation of a funeral. Wisely, it was decided to give way, and, on 6 October
1923, the Executive Council agreed to hand over remains to any family that
applied.[268] This also applied to the remains of those who had been executed by
the British during the War of Independence.[269]

As the releases progressed, two important issues arose.[270] The first would dog
the Free State for another decade: what should be done about those who had taken
up arms or who were actively involved in the struggle against the Free State, who,
before arrest, had been in public employment and now sought reinstatement, or,
indeed about those who were applying for such a post? This led to a number of
further considerations. The Free State had a badly damaged and stagnant
economy.[271] Positions in the public sector were much sought after since they
offered reasonably remunerated and secure employment and the prospect of a decent
pension. Should such posts be restricted to those who had supported the government
or, at the very least, who had played no overt part in armed struggle and republican
politics? To reward loyalty, should there be a distribution of the spoils, along Tam-
many lines? Alternatively, in the interests of national reconciliation and efficiency in
the public sector, should employment be offered to all on an open and competitive
basis? Policy would evolve over a period but in this immediate post-war period,
with little else at its disposal by way of reward, the government's decision was to link
employment to loyalty.[272] It was ordered that those interned or imprisoned for
republican activities and who consequently had been absent from employment
without leave from official duties at any time after 1 July 1922 should be dismissed. In no case was payment to be made for the period of absence. Dismissed
persons were to be given an opportunity to appeal.[273]

The IRA had been remarkably successful in subverting key offices and services
of the British administration in the years following its post-Rising reconstruction
and during the Anglo-Irish War. The subversive effectiveness of the leakage of
confidential and secret information was personally known to several members of

the Free State Executive Council. To address this, a declaration of loyalty was instituted in the summer of 1922 for all those in transferring from Dáil to government service or applying for public employment.[274] Unconscionable to many if not most with republican sympathies, the declaration was a deterrent to many applications and served as an additional restraint on those who had signed undertakings to secure release from prison or internment; it was also a device to bar or remove those of questionable loyalty.[275] In some respects, the wording was not as prohibitive as it might have been. Read carefully, it provided republicans with a loophole. It required fidelity to the government rather than to the state: governments could, of course, change, so the declaration simply sought a willingness to accept the democratic verdict.[276] But the declaration effectively excluded those who had been on the republican side in the Civil War, whether as fighters or as anything more than merely passive supporters. It was a solemn declaration, not a religious oath: should republican rank-and-filers (leaders were self-evidently excluded) cross their fingers or make a mental reservation and sign? IRA GHQ was asked for comments.

The IRA Chief of Staff (Twomey) set out the dilemma:

> Of course refusing to give it will only play into the hands of the F.S. 'government' as they will be only too delighted to dispose of such persons and fill positions with their own nominees. Moreover the dismissal of resignation of the vast majority of the civil servants who are republicans would not in the least inconvenience the Free State, as I am sure they made certain that the higher officials are not republicans.[277]

Given the highly local nature of Irish society, the importance of extended family and personal connections and the many ambivalences of life in the new state, it was inevitable that the declaration would not be uniformly enforced. Just as it had been possible for IRA men to find a sympathetic priest who would not too zealously enforce the bishops' pastoral letter, it was not too difficult for a sympathetic official to tell a new employee that the declaration was required and then take no further steps to enforce it. All that would be required then was a degree of discretion from the newcomer.[278]

But even where the oath was taken fully and conscientiously rather than of necessity and with reservations, security considerations limited the prospects of former activists, especially in central offices of the civil service. Four and a half years after the ending of the Civil War, Miss Ethan O'Byrne, formerly a clerk in the Dáil Department of Labour, had applied for reinstatement. This went before and was considered by the Executive Council (showing how seriously such cases were viewed). Re-employment was approved when a suitable vacancy arose, but not for any post where she might have access to confidential documents.[279]

Another issue was full of irony. At the height of their use, the various camps and prisons throughout the country, as well as the barracks, had brought supply and service business into their localities. The procurement of supplies of all kinds and the domestic and personal spending of soldiers, prison staff and civilian support staff had all injected cash into areas that sorely missed it when the National Army moved on and scaled down operations to peacetime levels. The Executive Council received appeals from the Newbridge and Curragh areas both about the hardship arising from closures and about contracts which had been given to non-local suppliers.[280] There was little that the government could do or say in response: the artificial, inflationary and haphazard effects of the war economy had to give way to the different but also testing demands of the market, a hard peace and an ungenerous community of nations.

The IRA had also to involve itself in the release process. The leadership had a moral obligation to members who were facing difficult and uncertain prospects as they picked up the threads of their lives in bleak and depressing circumstances. It continued to regard itself as the defender of the usurped Republic and needed to salvage networks and renew the ties with as many of its activists as possible. Pragmatically, the organisation of support for ex-prisoners and campaigns for those still to be released were means of preserving its wider circles of supporters and sympathisers.

The daunting task of rallying prisoners in the wake of the ceasefire order was given considerable priority. The IRA's Director of Intelligence reported to the Army Executive some six weeks later that most of his department's resources had been concentrated on communications with prisons and camps. From these he asserted that 95 per cent of the captives continued in their 'uncompromising Republicanism'.[281] This, as we shall see, was wishful thinking. The momentum had gone, and when that happens, an insurrectionary movement rapidly goes into a tailspin, since it does not have the institutional structures and routines, or the physical resources and locations necessary to stabilise and sustain it. Coherence, adhesion and a fanatical spirit come from a forward goal, actively and relentlessly pursued, and if this is removed dissolution follows. Indeed, merely a prolonged lull in action can damage the fragile mechanism of revolution and insurrection. Apart from a handful of zealots, mere organisational maintenance fails to provide that heady sustenance.

A letter to the Mountjoy prisoners from the IRA HQ some six weeks after the ceasefire is instructive. There was an acknowledgement (implicit, of course) of defeat and of the passing of the baton to another generation which will act in other times. The organisation was being maintained 'so that any body of Irishmen can use at any future date any means best suited to obtain their ideals'. All Volunteers had been ordered to do what they could to avoid capture. In contradiction to what everyone knew to be the reality, there was the pro-forma and therefore empty assertion that among Volunteers there prevailed a spirit of hopefulness and confidence. Educational work in the prisons was very satisfactory, 'and it is very encouraging to see that our men are utilizing the opportunity they now have of preparing themselves for the future'. This last, had the prisoners heard it, may have evoked a cynical or simply weary response from those enduring the drab, stagnant, life-wasting and dispiriting life of camp and prison: here was indeed an 'opportunity' they would most happily forgo. Much more pressing for Mountjoy prisoners was information about families. On this vital issue there was disconcerting and telling vagueness: 'Every effort is being made by the Army, CnaB and Sinn Féin Cumainn to look after prisoners' dependants.'[282] Here was the central and abiding worry of most prisoners – self-centred though they can be and often are.[283] The various prisoner-support groups were intended to address it by raising funds and distributing at least minimum cash doles. For reasons of principle as well as expediency, this obligation had always been part of the calculations of the IRA's operational costs. As the IRA's strength ebbed in 1923 and public feeling became more unfavourable, support groups stretched ever-diminishing resources at a time when demands were increasing substantially.

Ostensibly under the control of civilians, the relief committees were supposedly drawn from as wide a range of political views and social classes as possible in order to ease the consciences of the non-political and to optimise appeals to neutral yet potentially sympathetic members of the public. This seemingly disengaged and purely humanitarian face was never more than window-dressing and, in a society as compact as 1920s Ireland, deceived few people. The relief committees, even where they were not directly established by the IRA, existed only with its agreement: they were franchises. This close relationship was essential to the IRA and to its members. There was a need to control policy and to steer the public pronouncements of the committees: careless wording, for example, might cause confusion or even lead some members or supporters to think that a key line had changed; the effect on those still in custody also had to be considered. It was also important that anybody offering material support and guidance with employment and housing should be seen to be part of the republican family. Prisoners and ex-prisoners and their families should feel that the broader reaches, the ancillaries of the IRA, were looking after them. Finally, but nevertheless of core importance, there were issues of security. Support organisations, in the course of providing relief, acquired a great deal of information about prisoners and their families, and also about the persons, networks and assets of the republican movement. Only trusted individuals could be allowed to have that information. The organisation could also make good use of information that travelled the other way: what was the state of a family; for example, was a wife or other relative steadfast in the cause, wavering or even putting pressure on a prisoner to disengage?[284]

This is the background to IRA participation in the several prisoners' support groups. In 1923–4, the organisation had representatives on the IRPDF, the Irish Republican Prisoners' Dependants' Reconstruction Committee (IRPDRC) and the PPC. The IRA Adjutant General was an ex-officio member of the Executive Committee of the IRPDF but attended meetings only for important issues. In May 1925, he reported that they had ceased to operate as a working committee.[285] He had attended the IRPDRC's initial meetings (this committee was reorganised in December 1922) but had thereafter asked the Director of Communications to attend as his representative.[286] The PPC seems to have been viewed as the most important of these bodies and had two IRA representatives, one from the

Adjutant General's department and one from the Director of Intelligence.[287] From their knowledge of IRA records and reports, these two representatives gave the committee updates on individual prisoners. There were two other relief committees active at the time: the White Cross and the Students' Aid Committee. The IRA had no representative in the former.[288] The Adjutant General had attended the latter, but it eventually ceased to exist.[289]

Since most of the prisoners were young men, their loss of earning power often affected a wider group of dependants. In the absence of any but the most rudimentary social provisions, extreme hardship would affect all. Where there were children or the elderly, other charities might provide relief, but these were small and uncertain doles.[290] An analysis of the IRA men in Mountjoy's A Wing (probably compiled in the latter part of 1922) gives a fuller picture of family needs. Some had a wife or mother dependent on them; others had a wife and several children. What would today be regarded as a large family was then not uncommon. One man (Seán Kennedy, a Dubliner) was the sole support of his parents and two brothers; another (James Donnelly, also of Dublin) maintained his sister and her child. Aunts and cousins, fathers, mothers, sisters, sisters-in-law as well as the man's own wife and children appear in the list.[291]

Quite apart from the perennial shortage of funds, relief committees operated in very difficult circumstances. There was a certain amount of police harassment, and, because of their intelligence value, many papers were seized.[292] The Free State authorities argued that the long-established PPC had been taken over by the anti-Treaty faction and that it went well beyond the provision of succour and relief in its work. That apart, the organisation had to conduct its operations (often complex) in a fair and accountable manner. One of the vulnerabilities of the republican movement from the days of the Fenians had been recurring demoralising and damaging scandals about stolen, missing or misapplied funds and favouritism in their disbursement. Combined with the need to distribute the relief in a fair and accountable manner, this meant that there was an element of delay and bureaucracy in the committees' operation. Acknowledging the difficulties in securing employment that would inevitably be faced by those with a prison record, the Reconstruction Committee gave seed funding so that ex-prisoners might set themselves up in a small way in trades and handicrafts. The thinking was that those activities, rather than small shops, were more likely to give employment to members and former members of the IRA. The loans (on which no interest was charged) were for the purchase of stock, advances on rent, tools and materials and the like and seldom exceeded £50. The IRA vetted all applications.[293] And, indeed, for those without trades, professions, resources or capital, it was a daunting task to find a foothold in the post-war, post-prison score-settling and recommendation-dependent world. The relief and support available through republican organisations barely addressed those difficulties. Such favours as could be done by those adherents or sympathisers who had employment to offer were particularly helpful and enabled some to get started again. Others with a certain burden of notoriety and who were disinclined to enter politics (such as Ernie O'Malley) cast a cold eye on their prospects and left the country.

The use of imprisonment by the Free State provided a number of solutions in the campaign to maintain and consolidate power. The experience of imprisonment, for captor and captive alike, also laid down a number of patterns that would be followed by both during later confrontations. Republicans would never again be able to challenge the elected government of the Free State and its successors by force of arms as they had during the Civil War, but they continued to see it as a wholly illegitimate body. Not even Fianna Fáil's accession to power in 1932 would change that.

Imprisonment had long been incorporated into the repertoire of rebellion. Daniel O'Connell, the Young Irelanders and the Fenians had found ways to turn captivity against the captor, as had the rebels of 1916 and the IRA of the War of Independence. The great, significant and, to the republicans, shocking difference was that an Irish government was even more willing than the British had been to use executive detention (internment), to equip the courts with powers to impose heavy sentences and to bring in Military Tribunals as deterrent and retributive backstops administering summary and drastic justice. A Rubicon had been crossed: the new Irish state had demonstrated that it would use all its powers, civil and military, to protect itself. When challenged at a later point, and with a wholly different political leadership, it would again resort to these measures. Successive elections would show that, provided cause could be demonstrated, and the state's coercive powers were used proportionately, Irish electors would back strong government. Consciences were eased by a certain amount of ineffectual and sentimental (and even seasonal) regard for the underdog. But everyday necessities overrode the vicarious pleasures of rebel music and rhymes. Family life and ambition, as much as business and commerce, require stability and predictability if they are to flourish.

For their part, republicans had confirmed that political prisoners could be a kedge-anchor for supporters and sympathisers. But they had also learnt that when public opinion became indifferent or hostile to their cause the plight of prisoners also ceased to attract sympathy – and even executions or hunger-strike deaths failed to have an impact beyond those already attached, in some form, to the IRA. More positively for them, the powers of attrition inherent in imprisonment had been demonstrated. Even if the population beyond the walls proved largely hostile or indifferent, state resources could be sapped and diverted by protests, petitions, applications, non-cooperation and obstruction and combative publicity. The prisons were, without question, important instruments of state at the height of the Civil War, but they were also labour-intensive and hugely expensive. Anything that could add to that drain on resources was a form of support for those in direct combat with the Army beyond the walls, a flank attack by the battalions of the immobilised.

Republicans also had cause to reflect on the experience of imprisonment as an element in promoting or diminishing loyalty and attachment to the organisation. Shared hardship boosted camaraderie, but much depended on the broader political and military context. To be a captive when there was hope for the cause would strengthen one's vision of ultimate triumph; to be on the losing side in the closing phases of a struggle was debilitating and frequently divisive. The war might be lost, but small tactical victories could continue to be won by the losers. These held back the state's days of magnanimity. To those in internment or under sentence, each of these essentially hopeless victories was time added to their confinement, extending intolerable, corrosive and gnawing uncertainty.

Keeping an army in the field, even an insurgent and clandestine one, is an expensive business; money undoubtedly provides the sinews of war. The counterpart to the state's struggle to finance large-scale imprisonment was the IRA's even more desperate struggle to honour its compact with its activists. Men could not be expected to fight and to remain disciplined in prison (refraining from signing out, for example) if dependants were suffering and in want. And what lesson would activists take when, at some future point, the call to battle was renewed? The survival of the organisation rested to a large extent on its ability to keep faith with those removed from the field of action. And beyond the organisation, the supply of foodstuffs, tobacco and comforts to internees and prisoners was a direct drain on family resources, for many a decisive strain added to an already over-large pile of worries. No family, moreover, whatever its material resources, emerges unscathed from the imprisonment of one of its members. Resentments flow both ways: from the wife or dependent parent left to shift for themselves – not simply materially but psychologically also; and from the former prisoner who cannot convey his experience to his family and for whom, on occasion, the comradeship, emotional support and intimacy of prison friendship will never be matched. And for most ex-prisoners and their families in Ireland in the 1920s, the uncertain basis of liberty was a continuing concern. Unless one had unequivocally renounced subversive republicanism, publicly turning one's back on one's comrades, there remained the possibility of rearrest and the probability of police surveillance and harassment, of varying degrees.

The state was strengthened in the Civil War. Republicans believed that no cause was ever established and validated were there not a blood sacrifice. Two types of republican had confronted each other over the Treaty, and both could certainly claim to have made such a sacrifice. The forces of the state, wavering and uncertain at first, had gathered momentum and strength, and had become overwhelming. In that triumph, imprisonment had played its part, and successor governments could now be certain that they had the capacity to round up, hold and incapacitate those among their opponents who were willing to use, support or be complicit with insurrectionary violence.

Notes

1 General Prisons (Ireland) Act, 1877: 40 & 41 Vict., c.49.
2 Thirty-three were county prisons; five were borough or city prisons; and three (Galway, Kilkenny and Waterford) were joint county and city (*First Report of the General Prisons Board, Ireland*, PP, 1878–9 [C.2447], XXXIV, 353, p. 5).

3 Generally speaking, those prisons with the lowest average daily population were the most expensive to run on a per-capita basis since certain staffing costs (including twenty-four-hour staffing) were spread over a small number of prisoners.

4 Most of the bridewells were lock-ups for short-term or remand prisoners, up to eight days were the committal made by two justices, and three days if by one justice. Persons convicted of drunkenness could be confined for up to forty-eight hours. Another small group of four bridewells could be used for longer remands and sentences. Parsonstown in King's County could hold prisoners for trial or for up to four months if sentenced. Three others could take persons sentenced up to seven days or on remand. (*First Report of the General Prisons Board, op. cit.*, p. 7). See also NAI GPB/ XB-2, Deeds of Prisons and Borstals in Ireland.

5 *First Report of the General Prisons Board, op. cit.*, p. 15. These figures excluded debtors.

6 *First Report of the General Prisons Board, op. cit.*, p. 16.

7 *First Report of the General Prisons Board, op. cit.*, p. 18.

8 *Report of the General Prisons Board, Ireland*, PP, 1899 [C.9439], XLIII, 585, p. 5.

9 For evidence on the decline of offences of violence in Ireland between 1860 and 1914, see Mark Finnare, 'A Decline in Violence in Ireland? Crime, Policing and Social Relations, 1860–1914', *Crime, History and Societies*, 1 (1) (1997): 51–70.

10 Because of the pressures and administrative breakdowns arising from the Anglo-Irish War, reliable figures are elusive. See *Forty-Fifth Report of the General Prisons Board, Ireland* (Dublin: Stationery Office, 1924), p. iv. See also Peter Hart, *The IRA at War, 1916–1923* (Oxford: Oxford University Press, 2003); Michael Hopkinson, *The Irish War of Independence* (Dublin: Gill & Macmillan, 2002).

11 Exact figures are difficult to source and compare. Taking a broad view, however, Philip Orr offers an approximation of around 200,000 Irishmen in the Armed Forces during the First World War, with the majority serving in infantry regiments. See John Horne (ed.), *Our War: Ireland and the Great War* (Dublin: Royal Irish Academy and RTÉ, 2008). As in Britain, there were enlistments from the Prison Service.

12 See Hart, *The IRA at War, op. cit., passim.*

13 *Forty-Fifth Report of the General Prisons Board, op. cit.*, p. iv. Camps and military prisons were excluded. The difficulty in interpreting the figures is that sometimes institutions that had both military and civil wings are mentioned, without it being made clear if all or only some inmates were included in the returns. See, for example, the *Forty-Fifth Report of the General Prisons Board, op. cit.*, p. 1. Eleven prisons are listed as being under the control of the Board. In addition the refurbished prisons of Kilmainham and Kilkenny are mentioned, even though they were under military administration as, apparently, were the bridewells at Birr and Ballina.

14 NAI PG/34(A), S1813/22, 11 October 1922.

15 However, staff costs had tripled, rising from some £50,000 to just under £150,000. Even allowing for post-war inflation, this growth in outlay indicates a vastly expanded and therefore much altered establishment of staff, with many temporary and new members. See *Thirty-Seventh Report of the General Prisons Board, Ireland* (Dublin: HMSO, 1917), p. 15; *Forty-Third Report of the General Prisons Board, Ireland* (Dublin: Stationery Office, 1922), p. 10.

16 See *Forty-Fifth Report of the General Prisons Board, op. cit.*, p. 1.

17 For some details on the administrative and practical work of the Army's takeover of civil prisons, see NAI FIN/1/1841 and FIN/1/110.

18 See Seán McConville, *A History of English Prison Administration, Vol. I: 1750–1877* (London: Routledge & Kegan Paul, 1981) for an account of the development of penal servitude.

19 The background to the various classes of imprisonment is set out in Seán McConville, *English Local Prisons, 1860–1900: Next Only to Death* (London and New York: Routledge, 1995), Chapter 8.

20 Borstal sentences were imposed under the Prevention of Crime Act, 1908: 8 Edw. VII, c.59. For an account of Borstal in England, see Roger Hood, *Borstal Reassessed* (London: Heinemann, 1965); see also Victor Bailey, *Delinquency and Citizenship: Reclaiming the Young Offender, 1914–1948* (Oxford: Clarendon, 1987), Nial Osborough, *Borstal in Ireland: Custodial Provision for the Young Adult Offender, 1906–1974* (Dublin: Institute for Public Administration, 1975); and Conor Reidy, *Ireland's 'Moral Hospital': The Irish Borstal System, 1906–1956* (Dublin: Irish Academic Press, 2009).

21 At a later point, several IRA activists – most notably the irrepressible rebel (and later playwright) Brendan Behan – were given Borstal sentences in England. See below, pp. 447–59. Reporting for 1923, the General Prisons Board distinguished between civil and military prisoners in all the relevant institutions, except the Borstal Institution (*Forty-Fifth Report of the General Prisons Board, op. cit.*, p. 13).

22 *Forty-Fifth Report of the General Prisons Board, op. cit.*, p. iii. The bridewells had greatly declined in use. When Irish local prisons were centralised under the control of the General Prisons Board in April 1878 (to match a similar nationalisation in England) there were ninety-five bridewells. These were closed for reasons of economy and efficiency, and by 1923 only two remained; the General Prisons Board recommended their closure.

23 On 6 May 1922, numbers were as follows: Cork Male, 48m 8f; Cork Female, 7; Dundalk, 35m 3f; Galway, 20m 3f; Kilkenny, nil; Limerick, 21m, 15f; Mountjoy, 244m 60f; Sligo, 33m 2f; Waterford, 27m 6f; Clonmel Borstal Institution, 144m (NAI JUS/H78/17, Returns – Prisoners and Prison Officials 1922).

24 NAI JUS/H78/17, 27 January 1922.

25 *Forty-Fifth Report of the General Prisons Board*, p. v.

26 *Forty-Fifth Report of the General Prisons Board*, Appendix, p. 6, Table IV.

27 In England, with its larger prisons and more concentrated population, costs were lower: £55 10s. 11d. in local prisons in 1922–3: *Report of the Commissioners of Prisons and the Directors of Convict Prisons*, PP, 1923 [Cmd.2000], XII, Pt. 2, 379, Appendix 10(B), p. 95. In weighing these comparative costs it must also be remembered that the British economy was of a different order of strength and diversity, with a commensurate tax take.

28 For a brief account of the history of the NDU, see Jacinta Prunty, *Dublin Slums, 1800–1925: A Study in Urban Geography* (Dublin: Irish Academic Press, 1998), pp. 218–21. Prunty refers to 'its immense size and physical layout, whereby blocks of building were arranged around separate yards' (p. 221).

29 NAI FIN/I/1/1839, Public Works to Secretary, Ministry of Finance, 4 June 1923. An expenditure of £2,000 was necessary to prepare the east wing, including refurbishment, security and equipment.

30 NAI JUS/H170/113, Vice Chairman, NDU, to Department of Home Affairs, 23 April 1923. The three categories to be retained at Kilmainham were (1) women awaiting a decision on internment; (2) women convicted by military courts and awaiting final location; (3) refractory women transferred from the NDU, awaiting trial or other decision.

31 NAI JUS/H170/113, note from Ministry of Defence, 22 December 1923.

32 NAI JUS/H78/33, The MacDermott to Ministry of Home Affairs, 19 December 1923.

33 *Annual Report of the General Prisons Board, 1923–1924* (Dublin: Stationery Office, 1925), p. iv. From this report on, the Board dropped sequential years from the title page, presumably to emphasise the break with British administration. In all other respects,

however, they followed the established template. The members of the Board, appointed by the British, remained in office. The Vice Chairman, Tuhe MacDermot, was the most senior official until his retirement in 1928, by the end of which year the Board consisted entirely of Free State appointees.

34 *Annual Report of the General Prisons Board, 1924–1925* (Dublin: Stationery Office, 1926), p. iv.

35 See the statement by Kevin O'Higgins, Minister for Home Affairs in the new Free State government on 13 September 1922 (*Dáil Debates*, vol. 1, cols. 207–8). At this point military prisoners were being denied visits, even from professional advisers.

36 *Dáil Debates*, vol. 1, cols. 791–2, 26 September 1922; cols. 925–32, 28 September 1922.

37 NAI TAOIS/S1369/1, Department of Public Works to Provisional government, 12 October 1922.

38 *Ibid.*

39 NAI TAOIS/S1369/1, Department of Public Works to Provisional government, 14 October 1922.

40 NAI PG/49(A), 1 November 1922.

41 MA, BMH, CD/6/40/1, folder September 1922. Madge Daly, on hearing of the removal, went to the docks with parcels of shirts for the men, having been told they were needed. She claimed to have been ill-treated by the guards as she attempted to deliver the goods. See also NLI, Austin Stack Papers, MS. 17,082, Prison Ship in Dublin Bay.

42 NAI FIN/1/1720, General Prisons Board Estimates.

43 The nine were Clonmel Borstal Institution, Cork, Dundalk, Galway, Limerick, Mountjoy, Portlaoise, Sligo and Waterford.

44 NAI JUS/H263/1, Distribution of Staff in the Prisons, 1 October 1922.

45 NAI JUS/H263/1, Distribution of Staff in the Prisons, 1 October 1929. Temporary staff had four immediate advantages to the administrator: they could be hired and fired to match the needs of the institution; their rate of remuneration was lower; they were not eligible for promotion; and they had no pension rights. There was a fifth advantage: when permanent positions became available there was a pool of known and well-tested staff from whom a selection could be made.

46 NAI RF 1934 1116/1221. Max Green (1864–1922) was the son-in-law of the Irish National Party leader, John Redmond. An engineer by profession (Trinity College Dublin and the Royal College of Science), he entered the Irish Prisons Department in that capacity, eventually becoming Chairman of the Prisons Board. He was shot and killed in St Stephen's Green, Dublin, on 3 March 1922, 'by a robber flying from Justice' (see *Freeman's Journal*, 4 March 1922, 6e).

47 *Dáil Debates*, vol. 1, cols. 1903–4, 25 October 1922.

48 *Dáil Debates*, vol. 1, col. 1904.

49 The position of those who were in danger of death or facing execution seems to have been, at the same time, more flexible and inconsistent. Some of those about to be executed were denied the sacraments because, even on the point of death they would not repent their deeds and republican affiliations. Others, including O'Malley, were given the sacraments when thought to be dying but turned away when they recovered. Ernie O'Malley, *The Singing Flame* (Dublin: Anvil Books, 1992), p. 196.

50 *Irish Independent*, 12 October 1922, 5a and 8b. The hierarchy also insisted that 'No republican can evade this teaching by asserting that the legitimate authority in Ireland is not the present Dáil or Provisional Government.'

51 O'Malley, *The Singing Flame, op. cit.*, pp. 215–16.

52 Trinity College Dublin Archives, Frank Gallagher Papers, MS. 10051, diaries and notebooks. See 6 January 1923, 1 April 1923, 6 May 1923. Frank Gallagher (1893–1962) was an able publicist for the republican cause, working with Erskine Childers for the first Dáil. A close associate of Éamon de Valera, he became the first editor of the

Irish Press (1931). Subsequent career included radio, government information and the National Library. He participated in a number of hunger strikes. Author of several memoirs.

53 Gallagher Papers, 6 May 1923. For more of the background and a discussion of contacts between some of the bishops and Seán T. O'Kelly, the representative of the anti-Treaty 'Irish Republican Government', see Patrick Murray, *Oracles of God* (Dublin: University College Dublin Press, 2000), pp. 56–7 and 50–135, *passim*.

54 NAI, Executive Council, 25 January 1922, G1/1, item 9, p. 29.

55 Various versions are given for the number taken prisoner. Seán MacBride recalled 'about a hundred and eighty'. He also noted that in the process of marshalling the prisoners into temporary holding accommodation at Jameson's Distillery five men escaped, including the diehard republican leader Ernie O'Malley. Uinseann MacEoin, *Survivors: The Story of Ireland's Struggle as Told through Some of Her Outstanding Living People Recalling Events from the Days of Davitt, through James Connolly, Brugha, Collins, Liam Mellows, and Rory O'Connor, to the Present Time* (Dublin: Argenta, 1980), pp. 117 and 323; see also O'Malley's account of the escape in *The Singing Flame, op. cit.*, pp. 123–6.

56 For the figures of political prisoners in Free State custody during the latter half of 1923, see NAI TAOIS/S1369/21, note of 31 December 1923. On 1 June 1923 there were 11,989. By 1 December 1923, this had fallen to 5,495. It is not clear if these figures included any non-military and non-political prisoners. (These figures are given by the General Board, though in the circumstances of the times a deal of uncertainty was inevitable.)

57 In captivity, however, some republicans insisted that the Free State understood their qualities no better than the British. Ernie O'Malley insisted 'they understand our psychology as little as the English did'. UCDA, Maurice (Moss) Twomey Papers, P/69/7/2, Ernie O'Malley to Liam Lynch, 14 January 1923. But O'Malley was a rare and spirited type, and it is probable that the Free State authorities understood very well indeed the psychology of imprisonment.

58 See above, pp. 126–32, *passim*.

59 And the same held for the military conflict itself, where networks of supporters, safe houses and hideaways were known to both sides. Mary Humphries had the task of finding safe houses for the IRA during the Anglo-Irish War. In this she was hard-pressed by Richard Mulcahy, later Free State Minister for Defence. During the Civil War, when they were on opposite sides, Mary often regretted having disclosed so many useful addresses (MacEoin, *Survivors, op. cit.*, p. 342). May Dálaigh makes much the same comment about Free State soldiers raiding houses in which before the Civil War they had received refuge (MacEoin, *Survivors, op. cit.*, p. 366).

60 See Twomey Papers, P/69/2/11 and P/69/1/27, Operations Order No. 9, 19 August 1922. This directed the formation of active service units. None was to exceed thirty-five men, and (underlining mobility), '[a] number of cycles should always be at the disposal of each Active Service Unit'. Liam Lynch (1890–1923) commanded the IRA's 2nd Cork Brigade in the War of Independence. Opposed the Treaty but for the first few months of 1922 sought to avoid a split; disagreed with the seizure of the Four Courts but joined the IRA garrison just before attack; escaped Dublin and took command of the Southern Division of the IRA and then assumed position of Chief of Staff. Shot by Free State soldiers on 10 April 1923 and died some hours later.

61 See Dorothy Macardle, *The Irish Republic* (London: Victor Gollancz, 1937), pp. 789–90.

62 For such an incident, see O'Malley, *The Singing Flame, op. cit.*, pp. 135 and 139.

63 Four accounts of ill-treatment (among the many that survive) may be found in what appears to be an IRA document, prepared for publicity purposes: NLI, Austin Stack MS. 17,082. See also (again, only an example) the statement by Thomas Lynch who

was arrested by Free State soldiers in O'Connell Street on 18 July 1922. He refused to give his name and address and was so badly beaten up that when his brother was brought to his cell he could not recognise him (MA, BMH, CD/6/40/1).

64 Allegations of soldiers' ill-treatment of captives were denounced as propaganda in the Dáil (*Dáil Debates*, vol. 1, cols. 262–3, 14 September 1922).

65 UCDA, Sighle Humphreys Papers, P/106/1307/3, untitled leaflet, c. September/ October 1922. This document also claimed ill-treatment at Beggars Bush Barracks and on board the prison ships *Avonia* and *The Lady Wicklow*.

66 Twomey Papers, P/69/13/104, Liam Lynch to Adjutant General, 7 December 1922.

67 NAI PG/45 S1249–22, 1 July 1922.

68 They were in a legal limbo not dissimilar to that which the US government, under George W. Bush, contrived to establish at Guantánamo Bay and which, at the time of writing, still has not been, and shows no prospect of being, resolved. They were not, however, held extra-territorially; their numbers and conditions of confinement did not allow an information blackout; and there were the restraints of Irish religious and community values. The knowledge that all would have to live together when conflict ceased may have tempered enmity with caution.

69 Signed Diarmuid O'Hegarty, Military Governor, 3 July 1922 (NAI TAOIS/S1369/1).

70 The Law Officer was Hugh Boyle Kennedy (1879–1936). He became the first Attorney General of the Free State (1922–4) and then the first Chief Justice (1924–36). NAI PG/46 S1349/22, 2 July 1922.

71 NAI PG/46 S1349/22, Joe McKelvey to Diarmuid O'Hegarty, 3 July 1922. McKelvey listed the conditions that attached to the prisoners' rightful status: 'No. 1. Our being kept in a camp, under our own officers. No. 2. The allowing of parcels containing articles not to be used for purposes of escape. No. 3. Adequate medical supplies and attendance. No. 4. Suitable accommodation. No. 5. Issuing of adequate food supplies by our own men. No. 6. Supplies of cooking utensils. No. 7. No interference with internal organisation or work of prisoners. In addition we require three visits per week per person' (punctuation added).

72 The men captured from the Four Courts were aghast and bitterly frustrated by the turn of events, and the more experienced and thoughtful realised that they had suffered a strategic defeat. According to Peadar O'Donnell, there was an 'angry mood in the thronged cells of Mountjoy Jail'. The men wanted to know how the IRA had let itself be overrun by much weaker military forces. Some of the dire frustration and bitterness was bound to be taken out on the fabric of the prison. Peadar O'Donnell, *There Will Be Another Day* (Dublin: Dolmen Press, 1963), p. 9.

73 NAI TAOIS/G1/2/49, Provisional Government Minutes (abstracts), 4 July 1922.

74 Eamonn Duggan (1874–1936) had fought at the GPO in 1916 and was subsequently interned. He was imprisoned again during the Anglo-Irish War and was one of the Irish team in the Treaty negotiations. He subsequently held posts as a Minister without Portfolio, Minister for Defence and a member of the Senate.

75 Peadar O'Donnell, *The Gates Flew Open* (London: Jonathan Cape, 1932), pp. 13–16.

76 NAI TAOIS/S1369/1, Official notice, 2 July 1922. Later in July Michael Collins noted that the necessity of appointing a military governor and a deputy governor to the various prisons and places of detention was disadvantageous to the Army. For this reason, he preferred to concentrate internees in one or two large camps (NAI TAOIS/S1369/1, Michael Collins, Commander-in-Chief, to Provisional government, 23 July 1922).

77 On the evening of 6 July 1922, at 8.30 p.m., the Military Governor reported that a man had stood on a wall adjoining the prison and had attempted to communicate with the

prisoners using hand signals. A sentry ordered him to stop and, when he refused, opened fire and wounded him (NAI TAOIS/S1369/1, Governor to Arthur Griffith, 6 July 1922).

78 And there was encouragement from supporters outside the prison. Some of these may merely have been venting their frustrations at the fall of the Four Courts. Others may have been more purposeful.

79 O'Donnell, *The Gates Flew Open*, *op. cit.*, p. 23; see also NAI TAOIS/S1369/1, Report of Governors.

80 O'Donnell, *The Gates Flew Open*, *op. cit.*, p. 24.

81 NAI PG/60, S1349/22, 14 July 1922.

82 See p. 192 for accounts of tunnels in camps.

83 NAI TAOIS/S1369/1, Report to Provisional government, 13 or 14 July 1922; *Irish Independent*, 14 July 1922, 8g. For a prisoner's account of the event, see Tony Woods, interviewed by Uinseann MacEoin in *Survivors*, *op. cit.*, pp. 324–5. See also *Freeman's Journal*, 14 July 1922, 3b.

84 Desmond FitzGerald (1889–1947). Fought in the GPO in 1916 and, as one of the recognised leaders, was sentenced to a long term of penal servitude. Director of Propaganda during the Anglo-Irish War; became Minister for Foreign Affairs in the Provisional and Free State governments and then Minister for Defence (1927–32); member of the Senate (1938–47). Published widely, including poetry, drama and philosophy. Father of Garret FitzGerald (Taoiseach, 1981–2 and 1982–7). NAI PG/53, S1349/22, 7 July 1922; see also PG/61, agreeing to publish the names of the Mountjoy prisoners 'subject to the consent of the army authorities'. This was probably a response to anxious enquiries from relatives.

85 NAI PG/55, S1555/22, 10 July 1922. Application for release had to be made in writing. The forms on which this should be set out were available by mid-July but were issued only on request, either by those who applied for release or by those acting on their behalf (PG/64, 18 July 1922). The making and preservation of a record of submission was, as we shall see, an important part of the process of neutralising 'signers'.

86 NAI PG/77, S1444/22, 31 July 1922. Bail involved an undertaking to a Northern Ireland court, and thus explicit recognition of its authority. The Provisional government preferred that its supporters remain in custody than accept the jurisdiction of Northern courts.

87 *Irish Times*, 17 July 1922, 6e.

88 NAI PG/61, S1349/22, 15 July 1922. The prohibition was still in force in September and was defended in the Dáil by Home Affairs Minister Kevin O'Higgins. Prisoners who signed the required undertaking to not take up arms against the government again were released 'with minimum delay'. It followed, O'Higgins contended, that those who remained in prison were there because they would not give the undertaking, and it was therefore proper that they should receive no visitors: 'there is no particular hardship in expecting such persons to communicate in writing with their solicitors' (*Dáil Debates*, vol. 1, col. 208, 13 September 1922).

89 NAI TAOIS/S1369/1.

90 NAI TAOIS/S1369/1, Official Notice, 11 July 1922.

91 NAI PG/55, 10 July 1922.

92 NAI TAOIS/S1369/1, Letter to Michael Collins, 17 July 1922. Lambay Island, approximately one by three miles in area, is off the coast of Co. Dublin. Like many island prison schemes, the initial attractions were soon dimmed by practicalities. Lambay ran into the predictable difficulties of construction and supply costs, water supplies and drainage. Difficulty of access, while a security advantage, would prolong construction times and greatly increase costs. The proposal was finally abandoned on 23 July 1922. An even more unlikely proposal was the use of Saint Helena. This was mooted on 19 September 1922. British consent would have been forthcoming, but the practical obstacles were immense; it is also likely that this revival of a form of

transportation would have evoked bitter memories across the political spectrum in Ireland. See, for example, the concern expressed in the Dáil by the much-respected George Gavan Duffy on 20 October 1922 (*Dáil Debates*, vol. 1, col. 1829). The proposal was finally abandoned by the Executive Council on 18 January 1923 (NAI TAOIS/S1369/1; see also cabinet and then executive-council minutes 19 September 1922, 16 November 1922, 23 November 1922, 18 January 1923). This determined but rather desperate search for prison accommodation underlines what a powerful part prisons played in the war.

93 The principal camps and prisons used for internment during the Civil War were as follows: Athlone, Athy, Beggars Bush Barracks, Carlow, Carrick-on-Shannon, Cork (municipal, military and county), Curragh (Tintown 1, 2, 3 and 4), Dundalk, Galway, Gormanston Camp (Co. Meath), Kilmainham, Kilkenny, Limerick, Maryborough, Mountjoy, Mullingar, Naas, Navan, Newbridge, NDU, Portobello Barracks, Sligo, Templemore, Thurles, Tipperary, Tralee, Trim, Wellington Barracks (now Griffith Barracks), Waterford, Westport. Other gaols and bridewells (lock-ups) were used as required. See above, Tables 4.1 and 4.2.

94 NAI PG/60, S1349/22, 14 July 1922.

95 NAI PG/73, S1361/22, 27 July 1922. See *Irish Independent*, 29 July 1922, 5c.

96 NAI PG/80, S1555/22 and S1361/22, 3 August 1922.

97 NAI PG/104, S1361/22. On 24 July 1922, Michael Collins, Commander-in-Chief, had appointed Commandant John Twomey as Military Governor. See *Irish Times*, 30 August 1922, 5d.

98 NAI PG/60A, S1814/22, 14 November 1922.

99 Childers was arrested on 10 November 1922 and sentenced to death by a military court a week later. At the time of his execution an appeal was pending. Erskine Childers (1870–1922) was one of the most remarkable figures of a generation of revolutionaries. Born in England of Anglo-Irish parents, he was orphaned in childhood and went to live in Co. Wicklow. An English public-school education followed (Haileybury and Trinity, Cambridge) and with a law degree he entered the staff of the Commons. Initially an imperialist and opposed to Home Rule he took up the Irish nationalist cause, running guns in 1914. Despite this, on the outbreak of hostilities he volunteered for military service, serving in naval flying and intelligence. In the post-war period he became involved with Sinn Féin and was secretary to the Irish delegation in the Treaty discussions. He subsequently took the anti-Treaty side and played a major part in publicity and propaganda. He was a figure about whom feelings were never less than strong and was detested by Churchill and by many of the 'Irish-Irish' in the nationalist and republican causes he served. For accounts of Childers's arrest and a report of his execution, see, respectively, *Connacht Tribune*, 18 November 1922, 3c; *Freeman's Journal*, 25 November 1922, 5a. See *Dáil Debates*, vol. 1, cols. 2357–76, 28 November 1922 for the initial bitter debate on Childers's execution.

100 Séamus Robinson (1890–1961) took part in the 1916 Rising. He was a leading military figure during the Anglo-Irish War, from the Soloheadbeg ambush onward. A close associate of Ernie O'Malley, he took the anti-Treaty side in the Civil War. Robinson later became a member of Fianna Fáil. In his early career he was to the left, politically. See Emmet O'Connor, 'Communists, Russia and the IRA, 1920–23', *Historical Journal*, 46 (1) (2003): 115–31.

101 Twomey Papers, P/69/7/2, Ernie O'Malley to Chief of Staff, 14 January 1923.

102 *Irish Times*, 23 December 1922, 2b.

103 Con Casey in MacEoin, *Survivors, op. cit.*, pp. 376 and 378.

104 *Irish Independent*, 31 January 1923, 7e; *Freeman's Journal*, 30 January 1923, 5b.

105 *Irish Times*, 7 February 1923, 5a; NAI TAOIS/S1369/1.

106 See above, pp. 31–32. *Irish Independent*, 6 July 1922, 10d.

107 NAI PG/104, S1813/22, 30 August 1922.

108 O'Keefe was appointed Deputy Governor of Mountjoy Military Prison on 13 August 1922 (NAI TAOIS/S1369/1, Official Notice, 14 August 1922). Formerly Secretary of Sinn Féin, he was described by one of his inmates as '[a] tubby little man in a Free State captain's uniform... more a figure of fun for most of us than one we could take seriously. Flashes of crude humour, alternated with curses and epithets, from him.' It was O'Keefe's duty to wake up and prepare for execution the four IRA leaders who were shot in the early hours of 8 December 1922 as an act of retaliation and deterrence (Peadar O'Donnell interview in MacEoin, *Survivors, op. cit.*, p. 27; see also pp. 118–19). A different light on the man was given by Tony Woods, another Mountjoy prisoner. After an escape attempt on 10 October 1922, during which a soldier was killed, an angry party of the soldier's comrades surrounded the failed escapers. Injury or death would have resulted had not O'Keefe ordered the soldiers to fall in; he then marched them around the exercise yard (pp. 324–5). An amusing and not unaffectionate portrait is provided by Peadar O'Donnell in his memoir *The Gates Flew Open, op. cit.*, Chapter 7, prefaced by the observation that 'no tale of Mountjoy is complete without some tidings of that Deputy-Governor, *Paudeen* O'Keefe'. He seems to have done his best to maintain decent living conditions for the prisoners and took his custodial duties seriously. He was known for his jocular boast 'Nothin' escapes here but ghas' (O'Malley, *The Singing Flame, op. cit.*, p. 242). O'Keefe had himself been a prisoner in Mountjoy in September 1919 but was released after a hunger strike.

109 *Irish Independent*, 23 October 1923, 7c. Phil Cosgrave died on 22 October, the *Independent* noting that he had carried out his duties in a kindly way and that no complaint had ever been made against him.

110 O'Malley, *The Singing Flame, op. cit.* MacManus had served in the British Army and then in the IRA. He took the pro-Treaty side and had been in the attack on the Four Courts.

111 See IRA leaflet, 'Mountjoy Atrocity', MA, BMH, CD/6/40/4. The leaflet claimed that MacManus's refusal to recognise the prisoners' OC was an act of humiliation, intended to break the men's organisation. The civilian governor of the prison, Charles Munro, took no part in the custody of the political prisoners. The female prison was taken over for the male criminal prisoners, with Munro in charge. An experienced governor, he had served in the Indian police and, on joining the Irish prisons in 1902, had been appointed to Londonderry as Governor. See Tim Carey, *Mountjoy: The Story of a Prison* (Cork: Collins Press, 2005), pp. 187–8 and 198. See also Sandie Byrne, *The Unbearable Saki: The Work of H. H. Munro* (Oxford: Oxford University Press, 2007), p. 24. There is an unfortunate reference to Munro from an earlier period in Sean Milroy's memoir, *Memories of Mountjoy* (Dublin and London: Maunsel & Co., 1917), p. 4.

112 Frank Aiken (1898–1983) had a remarkable career which in many ways reflected the transition of a section of direct force republicanism to constitutionalism. He was a close and trusted colleague of Eamon de Valera. For a biographical note see below, pp. 320–1, n. 129.

113 For numbers, June to December 1923, see NAI TAOIS/S1369/21.

114 In an enlarged Dáil, the government increased its representation and obtained sixty-three seats. Sinn Féin gained eight seats for a total of forty-four. The government had secured 411,000 first-preference votes, Sinn Féin 280,000. The other parties and Independents, pro-Treaty, obtained between them forty-four seats. This was an unquestionable endorsement of the Free State (see *Irish Times*, 5 September 1923, 4f).

115 O'Malley, *The Singing Flame, op. cit.*, p. 240. To confuse the administration, the prisoners refused to give their names and also moved around the cells. They had the

daily head count, and so staff knew how many they had in custody but not the identities of the less prominent prisoners. At a later point, fingerprinting was introduced to deal with this tactic (see MacEoin, *Survivors*, *op. cit.*, p. 376).

116 See also below, n. 125.

117 *Dáil Debates*, vol. 1, col. 1445, 10 October 1922. *Freeman's Journal*, 11 October 1922, 5a.

118 O'Donnell, *The Gates Flew Open*, *op. cit.*, Chapters 11 and 12.

119 NAI PG/34(A), S1813/22, 11 October 1922; *Dáil Debates*, vol. 1, cols. 1444–6, 10 October 1922; *Freeman's Journal*, 11 October 1922, 5a.

120 O'Malley, *The Singing Flame*, *op. cit.*, p. 230.

121 Even with a full and experienced staff operating in times of tranquillity, searching parcels for contraband and censoring letters were time-consuming tasks.

122 NAI TAOIS/G2/1, Executive Council Minutes, 29 December 1922. Deputy Governor O'Keefe had from time to time taken his own measures as a collective punishment on the prisoners. These included cutting off gas, and thus lighting, from the wings and withholding cigarettes (O'Donnell, *The Gates Flew Open*, *op. cit.*, pp. 70 and 81).

123 O'Malley, *The Singing Flame*, *op. cit.*, p. 226. 'Some nights I had to listen to shot after shot.' But, writing to Lynch early in 1923, O'Malley reported that '[s]hooting here has died considerably', adding, 'I expect it is… close season'. Twomey Papers, P/69/7/2, Ernie O'Malley to Liam Lynch, 11 January 1923. At Kilmainham there seems to have been a less tense atmosphere; however, shots were fired there too. The design of the prison allowed A-Block prisoners from certain of the washrooms to converse with relatives on the road outside. Soldiers of the guard would threaten and occasionally shoot at the windows from which the shouted conversation was being conducted (Emmet Humphreys, in MacEoin, *Survivors*, *op. cit.*, p. 436).

124 Not being convicted, remand prisoners had traditionally, and through several sets of rules, been exempted from all rules which had a penal or degrading overtone. The notion (though often it was no more than that) was that only the restrictions arising from security and safe detention were justified for the unconvicted (see NAI GPB RL12, Statutory Rules and Orders 1920, No. 1361: Rules 198, 201, 203–8 and 210).

125 Twomey Papers, P/69/12/67, IRA Adjutant General to Liam Lynch, Chief of Staff, 5 February 1923.

126 *Ibid.*

127 See SAI GPB/RL12, Statutory Rules and Orders, 1915, No. 347, Rules 1, 7, 10 and 15 (First Division) and Rules 21, 23, 26, 29 and 30 (Second Division).

128 Twomey Papers, P/69/12/67, IRA Adjutant General to Liam Lynch, Chief of Staff, 5 February 1923.

129 *Ibid.*

130 These details are taken from the report of the Military Governor to his superiors. See *Dáil Debates*, vol. 5, cols. 436–7, 31 October 1923.

131 *Dáil Debates*, vol. 5, col. 436, 31 October 1923.

132 O'Malley, *The Singing Flame*, *op. cit.*, pp. 242–4. For O'Donnell's account of these events, see *The Gates Flew Open*, *op. cit.*, Chapter 33. There can be little doubt that the detachment would have opened fire with lethal intent had the order been ignored.

133 See the IRA leaflet, 'Mountjoy Atrocity', which gave the republican version of events. In this publication the members of the military command (the Governor and others) were named: 'The distinguished FS Officers who attacked unarmed prisoners should have the credit of their deeds of prowess' (MA, BMH, CD/6/40/4). See also O'Donnell, *The Gates Flew Open*, *op. cit.*, pp. 245–7. The report to IRA HQ claimed that most of the military police refused to baton the men and that the Governor himself mercilessly beat prisoners who stood with folded arms (pp. 245–7). Ernie O'Malley's account does not fully agree with this (see *The Singing Flame*, *op. cit.*, pp. 244–7). For a full statement by the Military Governor, relayed to the Dáil by

Richard Mulcahy, see *Dáil Debates*, vol. 5, cols. 436–41, 31 October 1923. The prisoners' version is given in a petition submitted by the B-Wing prisoners to Commandant MacManus on 19 September 1923 (NAI TAOIS/S1369/3).

134 *Dáil Debates*, vol. 5, col. 437, 31 October 1923.

135 MA, BMH, Robert C. Barton Collection, CD/264/53/12, Protest on Behalf of Twelve Prisoners to the Governor of Arbour Hill Detention Barracks, 23 September 1923.

136 The tunnel was not discovered until 14 October, by which time it had been driven seventy yards and was estimated to be within ten days of completion (*Dáil Debates*, vol. 5, col. 440, 31 October 1923). Seán MacBride had been actively involved in the tunnel. Ingeniously, it began on the top floor of the prison. Access to the basement was down one of the great ventilation chimneys, and the spoil was stored in the prison's roof space. MacBride thought that some of the subsequent rough handling of the prisoners was because of the Governor's fury when the tunnelling works were discovered (see his interview in MacEoin, *Survivors, op. cit.*, p. 120). This was one of several escape attempts, including at least two tunnels, an attempt to bluff an exit in Free State uniform, a shoot-out and a tunnel driven from the outside (p. 324).

137 The brutal traditions of the days when the prison had been a disciplinary barracks for recalcitrant soldiers continued under the Free State, Peadar O'Donnell claimed. These abuses included semi-hangings and mock crucifixions (*The Gates Flew Open, op. cit.*, p. 121).

138 See O'Donnell, *The Gates Flew Open, op. cit.*, Chapters 17–21, for an account of life at Tintown No. 1 camp at the Curragh. O'Donnell was particularly active in organising the digging of tunnels.

139 O'Malley, *The Singing Flame, op. cit.*, pp. 272–3.

140 This captured document was sent to the Dáil by Mulcahy, see *Dáil Debates*, vol. 5, col. 435, 31 October 1923.

141 Faced with the full occupancy of Ballykinlar (Co. Down), the British authorities had opened Rath Camp in 1921, with 1,200 to 1,500 extra places. The camp was also used by the Black and Tans prior to their move to Gormanston (see Commandant Desmond A. Swan, 'The Curragh of Kildare', *The Barracks and Posts of Ireland*, May 1972, p. 63).

142 The Commissioners for Public Works estimated that each new camp place cost about £50. For each prisoner who could be placed in an existing building, between £30 and £50 could therefore be saved, depending on the amount of adaptation required (NAI TAOIS/S1369/1, Public Works to Provisional government, 12 October 1922).

143 NAI FIN/1/1204, Commissioners of Public Works to Secretary, Ministry of Finance, 11 November 1922.

144 NAI FIN/1/1204, letters of 20 March and 3 April 1923.

145 Hare Park eventually reclaimed its nomenclature in official documents. Because of the rapid expansion and the lack of experience of officials there was some confusion in the manner of referring to the various camps. Sometimes numbers were used as designations, other times letters were used. Most unhelpfully it cannot be determined whether correspondents knew or agreed upon the various references – either in letters or numbers.

146 NAI TAOIS/S1369/1, Governor Civil Prison to Dublin Castle, telegram, 29 August 1922.

147 NAI TAOIS/S1369/1, Governor Maryborough to Prisons Board, telegram, 29 August 1922. See also Tomás Ó Maoileoin's account of the incident in MacEoin, *Survivors, op. cit.*, pp. 99–100.

148 The Governor, Jack Twomey, also moved to the Curragh. Tomás Ó Maoileoin (an experienced escaper) wrote to his wife shortly after arrival. The Governor, through

whose hands the letter passed, added a postscript: 'Tom is alright, Peig, but be assured he will not get away this time.' Such was the intimacy of civil war. But Tom did escape and, in his memoirs, Ó Maoileoin claims that he was home before the Governor's letter arrived (MacEoin, *Survivors, op. cit.*, p. 100).

149 NAI FIN/1/1200, Commissioner of Public Works to Secretary of the Provisional government, 12 October 1922.

150 *Ibid.*

151 *Irish Independent*, 17 October 1922, 6c.

152 NAI TAOIS/S1369/1, Office of Public Works to Ministry of Defence, 7 September 1922. See also NAI TAOIS/G1/2, 24 July 1922.

153 NAI TAOIS/S1369/1, Office of Public Works to Secretary of Provisional government, 12 October 1922.

154 MacEoin, *Survivors, op. cit.*, p. 436.

155 *Freeman's Journal*, 9 September 1922, 5c.

156 MacEoin, *Survivors, op. cit.*, p. 273. Among the prisoners was Seán T. O'Kelly, who would later become President of Éire and, later, the Republic of Ireland.

157 MacEoin, *Survivors, op. cit.*, p. 293.

158 MA, BMH, Contemporaneous Documents Collection, CD/6/40/1. A note on conditions in Athlone Military Barracks is presented in this file.

159 The castle had been the home of the Hayes family between the late eighteenth century and 1912. During the Civil War it was the National Army Headquarters in Co. Donegal.

160 Daly had previously been OC of the Old IRA's 2nd Northern Division (covering the counties of Fermanagh and Derry). Larkin was OC of the anti-Treaty IRA's 3rd Northern Brigade and, when arrested, was in arms and thus liable to the death penalty. For more detail on the anti-Treaty IRA's divisional structures, see Michael Hopkinson, *Green against Green* (Dublin: Gill & Macmillan, 1988).

161 Macardle, *The Irish Republic, op. cit.*, p. 1023; *Irish Times*, 24 March 1923, 2g. The last gives a detailed account of the men's arrest and the arms which were in their possession. These executions brought the number to sixty-seven: there would be seventy-seven acknowledged executions, though the number is probably greater.

162 MA A/7078, Prisoners: Alleged Cruelties, etc. (Donegal), Father James Larkin to Eoin MacNeill, 23 November 1923.

163 MA A/7078, Prisoners: Alleged Cruelties, etc. (Donegal), Father James Larkin to Eoin MacNeill, 23 November 1923.

164 MA A/7078. The title *Ard Chongantóir* is not easily rendered into English, but it may be the equivalent of the provost marshal or head of the military police.

165 MA A/7078. S. Mac Loclainn (rank not given) to Adjutant General, 8 January 1923.

166 MA, BMH, Contemporaneous Documents Collection, CD/6/40/1, folder September 1922.

167 NAI TAOIS/S1369/1, Government to Minister for Defence, 20 November 1922; PG/40(A), Provisional Government Minutes, 30 October 1922.

168 NAI, Department of Defence to Government, 29 November 1922.

169 Humphreys Papers, P/106/1307/1, 'Limerick Gaol' (no publication details, but almost certainly the PPC). The leaflet contrasted the conditions for which Fionán Ó Loinsigh (now Commandant General in the National Army's South Western Command) had gone on hunger strike when a prisoner of the British with the conditions he ordered for Limerick Prison. No visits were allowed 'under any circumstances' except with the permission of GHQ, Dublin. As for complaints about conditions, 'You will say you will do what you can about cooking, bedding and medical arrangements.' Prisoners were to be warned that any interference with the locks would be regarded as attempted escape and the sentries had been instructed to deal with it by firing to kill. It was emphasised that hunger-striking would not alter

conditions. More generally, '[t]he government cannot see its way, at the moment at any rate, to add further to the burden of the Irish taxpayers for providing clothes for persons who have destroyed wholesale the property of the Irish people'.

170 Humphreys Papers, Bishop Hallinan to President W. T. Cosgrave, 11 November 1922.

171 Humphreys Papers, Cosgrave to Hallinan, 12 November 1922.

172 Humphreys Papers, Hallinan to Cosgrave.

173 Humphreys Papers, Hallinan to Cosgrave, 11 November 1922. In the same letter, the bishop referred to the phrasing of the draft constitution, then under way.

174 The newspaper *Poblacht na hÉireann* ran various tales about the ill-treatment of prisoners. Tony Woods, who had been in the Four Courts surrender, recalled one about Patrick O'Keefe, the Deputy Governor of Mountjoy. Entering his cell in an inebriated state, he addressed Woods: 'Your mother, the oul battleaxe is enquiring how you are… Drunken Paudeen O'Keeffe [*sic*] is battering the prisoners again.' Woods commented, 'Paudeen never battered anyone; he was repeating what *An Phoblacht* was writing about him' (MacEoin, *Survivors*, *op. cit.*, p. 324). See also *Poblacht na hÉireann*, 16 August 1922, 1b; 21 August 1922, 1b. The latter contained a piece under the heading 'The Adventures of Paidín O'Keefe, Ex T.D.'.

175 Humphreys Papers, P/106/1307/2, Political Prisoners Committee, 'Things Bad Begun', c. September 1922. From the literary style and framing of the leaflet, Maud Gonne may have been the author. In this and in other publications, the Committee (and other republican bodies) refer to 'Maryborough', sometimes 'Maryboro', rather than 'Portlaoighse', the Gaelicised place-name adopted by the Free State. The intention seems to have been to emphasise the continuity of the identity of the prison under the British and now the Free State regime.

176 See p. 238, n. 283, below.

177 See McConville, *English Local Prisons*, *op. cit.*, Chapter 7, for an account of these matters.

178 NAI TAOIS/S1369/1, Phil Cosgrave to President W. T. Cosgrave, Executive Council (with enclosure), 16 May 1923.

179 *Dáil Debates*, vol. 6, cols. 2735–6, 2 April 1924. Patrick Francis Baxter (1891–1959) was a farmer and would later go on to a career in the Seanad. Others raised questions about Hare Park around this time. See, for example, *Dáil Debates*, vol. 6, cols. 2603–4, 28 March 1924 for questions from Seán Ó Laidhin, John Lyons, Thomas Johnson and Patrick Baxter.

180 *Dáil Debates*, vol. 6, cols. 2603–4, 28 March 1924.

181 MA A/11701, Prisoners, Hare Park, Curragh.

182 MA A/7361, Prisoners Irregular, Red Cross Investigation.

183 Nevertheless, Quaker relief went ahead on a modest scale. Internees at the Park thanked the Friends' Relief Committee for parcels and games, as did those at Kilmainham, who had received six chess sets, to enable them to play a tournament. (MA A/7361).

184 MA A/7361, Military Governor Michael Love to Adjutant General, GHQ, 12 May 1924.

185 *Dáil Debates*, vol. 6, cols. 792–3, 12 February 1924.

186 MA A/11377; *Dáil Debates*, vol. 6, col. 2736, 2 April 1924.

187 The last of the interned women had been released from the NDU on 22 December 1923 (NAI TAOIS/S1369/4, Secretary to the Executive Council, 24 December 1923).

188 MA, BMH, CD/6/41, IRA Director of Medical Services to Chief of Staff, 11 December 1923, enclosing report from OC Newbridge, 5 December 1923.

189 Twomey Papers, P/69/12/14, Adjutant General to Director of Intelligence, 22 July 1923.

190 This and following quotations are taken from the Twomey Papers, P/69/12/16, letter from S. O'S., Maryborough Prison, to IRA HQ, 20 June 1923. (The letter was dated 1926, but a note in the file states that 1926 was substituted for 1923 as a form of concealment or deception.)

191 The writer was almost certainly not a trained lawyer, but this was a sound attempt to consider *mens rea*, the mental element that, together with the act, constitutes or fails to constitute a criminal offence.

192 Twomey Papers, P/69/12/14, Adjutant General to Director of Intelligence, 22 July 1923.

193 NAI TAOIS/S1369/4. Nine sentenced men at Hare Park were transferred to the custody of the Civil Governor at Mountjoy.

194 Serving sentences, on remand or awaiting trial. See NAI TAOIS/S1369/4, Secretary, Department of Defence, to each member of the Executive Council, 21 June 1924. This lists the twenty-nine persons whom the Director of Intelligence recommended should be retained in custody. They included well-known anti-Treaty figures such as Liam Deasy, Gerald Boland, Ernie O'Malley, Seán Russell and, of course, Éamon de Valera. The Executive Council was informed by the Department of Defence that on the evening of 6 July 1924 there remained in custody 197 IRA prisoners: three at Arbour Hill, 192 at Hare Park and two on parole. See also Twomey Papers, P/69/15/11, Statement by the Publicity Department of the IRA, 28 August 1924.

195 This was probably IRA Commandant Jack Keogh, who in 1924 was sentenced to ten years' penal servitude. In May 1926, George Gilmore, Secretary to Seán Lemass, Minister for Defence in the shadow republican government, rescued Keogh from Dundrum Asylum, Dublin, where he was being held. See *Irish Times*, 26 July 1924, 9e; *Irish Independent*, 14 May 1926, 7f. Keogh was described by a prison official as 'one of the most turbulent prisoners the authorities ever had to deal with. He had, it was, alleged, broken all prison regulations and observed no prison discipline' (*Irish Independent*, 14 May 1926, 7f).

196 Twomey Papers, P/69/15/15, Mary MacSwiney, Director of Publicity, to Frank Aiken, Chief of Staff, 23 July 1924. Imprisoned several times herself, and always particularly sensitive on all matters concerning prisoners, MacSwiney had chided Aiken ten weeks previously on the IRA's policy: 'what are you doing to get the prisoners released more than twelve months after the cessation of the fighting?' Twomey Papers, P/69/17/10, 7 May 1924. Dempsey, McCarthy and O'Donovan were convicted of having assaulted two civil guards in Skibbereen and were each sentenced to ten years' penal servitude. Remarkably, the judge directed that the sentences were not to be put into effect if the men entered into recognisances. From MacSwiney's note it is evident that the men refused the court's clemency rather than acknowledge its authority by entering into recognisances (see *Irish Times*, 26 July 1924, 9e). A week or so later, Aiken directed MacSwiney to remove the name of John O'Brien from a list of IRA prisoners which she had circulated to the press. The name had not been supplied by GHQ, or by an IRA officer, and 'we cannot accept responsibility for his acts'. MacSwiney was accordingly to write again to the press, saying that a mistake had been made and that 'John O'Brien is not a soldier of the IRA and that the IRA General Headquarters accepts no responsibility for his acts.' Twomey Papers, P/69/15/14, Frank Aiken to Mary MacSwiney, 31 July 1924. Status as a member of the IRA was taken very seriously indeed by the organisation.

197 MA A/7361, Colonel M. Costello to Director of Intelligence, 29 August 1923.

198 See, for example, *Report of the Bloody Sunday Inquiry* (London: HMSO, 2010), vol. X, Chapter 178.

199 Twomey Papers, P/69/2/35, General Order No. 8 from Chief of Staff.

200 Twomey Papers, P/69/1/17, Order No. 13 from Chief of Staff. This order was followed by a note from the IRA Adjutant General, giving a list of sympathetic solicitors.

201 Twomey Papers, P/69/20/405, 10 February 1924. The IRA court martial reduced him to the ranks for his breach of discipline. Traynor was already on the journey away from the IRA that would lead him to become a founding member of Fianna Fáil and thence to high ministerial office. For a biographical note see below, p. 1042, n. 4.

202 Twomey Papers, P/69/4/107 and P/69/3/10.

203 Twomey Papers, Seamus O'Donovan (Director of Chemicals) to Chief of Staff, 27 March 1923.

204 This was a reference to the aftermath of the confrontation and disorder of 13 September 1923. See above, p. 189.

205 MA, BMH, Simon Donnelly Collection, CD/62/13/11; see also the Sinn Féin pamphlet 'Freedom or the Grave: The Final Hunger Strike' (CD/62/13/12). The Madame Czira (Sidney Gifford) Collection (CD/186/7/1) contains important extracts from the correspondence passing between camps and prisons and the IRA GHQ, together with an account of the strike negotiations and the developments in the principal camps and prisons.

206 Twomey Papers, P/69/3/23, Department of Chief of Staff to OCs and Prisoners, Mountjoy, 31 July 1923.

207 Peadar O'Donnell looked back on the hunger strike as a climacteric in republican resistance, which it nearly broke: 'No one was ordered on to it, but then no one felt they could stay off it' (MacEoin, *Survivors, op. cit.*, p. 51). See also his account in *The Gates Flew Open, op. cit.*, Chapters 34–8.

208 See, for example, *Irish Independent*, 17 October 1923, 5d.

209 See the letter from Dr McCurtan to the *Irish Independent*, making this point (23 October 1923, 5e).

210 *Irish Independent*, 23 October 1923, 7f. At the time of escape, the men were being taken to hospital, presumably for further examination, in a Red Cross ambulance. Their condition was nowhere near as debilitated as the authorities imagined, but such experienced men could easily feign feebleness.

211 Gerald Boland (1885–1973) fought in 1916 and in the Civil War. Founder member of Fianna Fáil. Extensive ministerial career including Minister for Justice (1939–48 and 1951–4). As Minister, took stern measures against the IRA. Austin Stack (1880–1929). Kerry Commandant during 1916 Rising. TD and Minister in First Dáil. Prominent anti-Treatyite. Captured in April 1923. Peadar O'Donnell (1893–1986). Member of Four Courts garrison and taken into custody on surrender. Escaped in 1924 and became a member of IRA Executive and Army Council (1924–34). Lifelong socialist agitator and commentator on social conditions. Published several works of literature and two memoirs. These were men of character and depth.

212 But relations between the prisoners and church authorities and chaplains remained bitter. See O'Donnell, *The Gates Flew Open, op. cit.*, Chapter 8.

213 O'Malley, *The Singing Flame, op. cit.*, p. 260.

214 The temptation must have been acute. Neil Gillespie, a member of the IRA's 2nd Northern Division, was detained at Newbridge Camp. He recalled the hunger strike as 'sheer, mad ravenous hunger. Even when asleep… you would dream of food, creamed potatoes, chicken, bacon and cabbage, the sort of thing some of us had not seen for years' (MacEoin, *Survivors, op. cit.*, p. 164).

215 *Irish Independent*, 26 October 1923, 7d.

216 *Irish Independent*, 29 October 1923, 8c. By 12 November 1923, only 330 were said still to be refusing food (*Irish Independent*, 29 October 1923, 6c).

217 For a short obituary of Con Moloney, see the *Irish Press*, 12 March 1951, 4e.

218 Twomey Papers, P/69/16/3, Chief of Staff to Mountjoy Volunteers, 20 November 1923.

219 NLI, Austin Stack Papers, MS. 17,091, Frank Aiken to Mick Price, OC Mountjoy, 19 November 1923.

220 For details on the numbers on hunger strike and the falling off of the action, see the comprehensive file at NAI TAOIS/S1369/10, General Hunger Strike. O'Malley was told of the breakdown of the strike in one of the camps (he does not identify it): 'men, mad with hunger, armed with knives, had rushed the quartermaster's stores in the dark, slashing and hacking at raw meat and flitches of bacon... They did not wait to cook, but gorged it on the way back to their huts' (*The Singing Flame, op. cit.*, p. 269). He had seen the participation of the other prisons and camps as a weakness rather than a strengthening through solidarity. To O'Malley, the strike was not a gesture but an acceptance of death were release not granted (*The Singing Flame, op. cit.*, p. 253).

221 Macardle, *The Irish Republic, op. cit.*, p. 901; *Irish Times*, 21 November 1923, 5c. The newspaper reported that Barry had been on hunger strike for thirty-four days. That there was a fatal outcome after such a short strike may indicate that he had an underlying health problem. More usually death might be expected somewhere between fifty-five and seventy-five days in a healthy person. On Barry, see the biography by his relative and namesake: Denis Barry, *The Unknown Commandant: The Life and Times of Denis Barry, 1883–1923* (Cork: Collins Press, 2010).

222 For Bishop Cohalan, see the *Dictionary of Irish Biography*.

223 O'Donnell, *The Gates Flew Open, op. cit.*, p. 224. The final decision was taken by Tom Derrig, Frank Gallagher, Michael Kilroy and Peadar O'Donnell.

224 O'Malley, *The Singing Flame, op. cit.*, p. 262. At the time of his arrest in March 1923, Derrig had been Adjutant General of the IRA. He later became a Fianna Fáil education minister. David Robinson was a friend of Robert Barton, who had been the swing vote (reluctantly) in the signing of the Treaty, but who went on to take the anti-Treaty side.

225 For Máire Comerford, see the short obituary in the *Irish Press*, 6 September 1949, 5a; for Sighle Humphreys, see the *Dictionary of Irish Biography*.

226 NAI G2/1/C/1/36, Executive Committee Minutes, 27 January 1923.

227 NAI G2/1/35/S/1724 and S1361, Executive Committee Minutes, 23 January 1923.

228 Con Murphy was a lifelong republican and a scholar of both French and Irish. See *Irish Independent*, 29 December 1947, 5h.

229 NAI TAOIS/G2/1, Executive Committee Meetings, 9 April 1923 and 14 April 1923.

230 NAI TAOIS/G2/1, Executive Committee Meeting, 19 April 1923.

231 The other strikers were Miss Annie O'Neill and Miss Nellie O'Ryan. All were described as 'female Irregulars'. See NAI TAOIS/S1369/3, Women on Hunger Strike at Kilmainham.

232 NAI TAOIS/G2/2, Executive Council Minutes, 19 April 1923, 24 April 1923 and 27 April 1923.

233 See MA CW/P/06/01, NDU Releases, 1923.

234 NAI TAOIS/G2/2, Minutes of 24 September 1923. Dan Breen (1894–1969) had been a major figure during the War of Independence and a gunman at the Soloheadbeg ambush in January 1919. In 1921 he went to the USA but returned to take part in the anti-Treaty struggle. He advocated a compromise within the IRA, to avoid civil war. He was elected as a Sinn Féin member of the Dáil in August 1923 and in April 1927 was the first republican to take the Oath of Allegiance. He briefly mentioned his Mountjoy hunger strike – six days of refusing water and twelve refusing food – in his memoir, *My Fight for Irish Freedom* (Dublin: Anvil Books, 1989), p. 187; he did not mention his declaration.

235 NAI TAOIS/G2/2, Executive Council Minutes, 24 September 1923. The declaration read: 'I hereby give my parole to return to Gormanston Camp by 12 noon on Saturday, 29th September 1923, and I undertake not to interfere in matters military or political during that time while on parole.' Seán T. O'Kelly (1883–1966) had been a staff captain during the 1916 Rising and was subsequently interned. Thereafter he took political rather than military roles. He supported the anti-Treaty side and was imprisoned on the outbreak of the Civil War. A founder member of de Valera's Fianna Fáil, he occupied a number of ministerial posts when that party came to power. He became President of Éire in 1945, and, when Éire became the Republic of Ireland, he continued as President until 1959, when he was succeeded by Éamon de Valera.

236 O'Malley, *The Singing Flame, op. cit.*, Chapters 12–16.

237 Twomey Papers, P/69/7/2.

238 See NAI PG/G1/1, 28 June 1922. Bill Kissane notes that following a similar line of concern, the government prohibited the importation, distribution or sale of newspapers which had not been approved by the censor. Some newspapers were still thought to be unhelpful to the Provisional government, and the editors of the *Freeman's Journal* and the *Irish Times* were summoned and spoken to. This resulted in what the government deemed to be 'a considerable improvement'. Bill Kissane, *The Politics of the Irish Civil War* (Oxford: Oxford University Press, 2005), p. 81. A great deal of helpful detail is given by Peter Martin in his *Censorship in the Two Irelands, 1922–39* (Dublin: Irish Academic Press, 2006); see especially pp. 15–24. See also Dorothy Macardle, *The Irish Republic, op. cit.*, p. 765. She particularly notes that the censorship applied to foreign as well as Irish publications.

239 The English newspapers therefore continued to be a cause of concern. See NAI PG/G1/2, 2 July 1922 and 7 July 1922.

240 The *Freeman's Journal* was attacked on 29 March 1922. Its presses were completely destroyed, together with its irreplaceable collection of photographic plates, reputedly the finest in the country and of immense historic value. The newspaper had displeased a section of the IRA by its report on the Army Convention of 26 March 1922.

241 The letter had been sent to the Mayor of Limerick, Stephen O'Mara, and to the city's branch of Cumann na mBan. The latter had forwarded it to the *Freeman's Journal* (13 November 1922, 6h); see also PRONI HA/32/1/46, Report on Internments, 1922–4.

242 An important republican reference to the imprisonment of the Fenian, Jeremiah O'Donovan Rossa, who, under punishment for misbehaviour, was illegally hand-cuffed in his cell in Portland convict prison in July and August 1869. In consequence, with his hands behind him, he had to eat his meals from a dish placed on the floor of his cell. This was a powerful tale of republican heroism. See Seán McConville, *Irish Political Prisoners, 1848–1922: Theatres of War* (London and New York: Routledge, 2003), pp. 179–80. By making this reference, however elliptically, roles were being assigned within the morality play then being enacted in the prisons and camps.

243 *Freeman's Journal*, 13 November 1922, 6h.

244 *Freeman's Journal*, 27 November 1922, 6d–e. The last, he said, was a matter for the military. Given what was happening at Mountjoy, there can be little doubt that shots had indeed been fired and that there was a high probability that the prisoners had provoked them. By 28 November 1922, O'Higgins was able to tell the Dáil that 400 prisoners had been transferred from Limerick Prison in order to deal with the bad conditions that had arisen because of overcrowding (*Dáil Debates*, vol. 1, col. 2323, 28 November 1922.

245 PRONI HA/32/1/46, Reports on Internments, 1922–4. See the *Daily Herald*, 2 November 1922, for the *Argenta* complaints.

246 See Murray, *Oracles of God, op. cit.*, p. 84. Republican prisoners were almost uniformly bitter at the bishops' stance (see p. 21 above). The hierarchy had switched horses in the period 1916–21 (away from British administration) but, going back as far as the Fenians of 1865 – and beyond – the bishops were suspicious of both the doctrines and mode of organisation of republicanism and invariably recoiled from what they saw as extremism. But the majority of prisoners continued to hold to their Catholic beliefs. See, for example, Sinéad McCoole, *No Ordinary Women: Irish Female Activists in the Revolutionary Years, 1900–1923* (Dublin: The O'Brien Press, 2003), p. 115, in describing the beliefs of Margaret Buckley.

247 Daniel Mannix (1864–1963). Born in Co. Cork. A distinguished career in Catholic scholarship and teaching culminating in the Presidency of Maynooth College (1903–12). Co-Adjutor Bishop of Melbourne (1912–17); Archbishop (1917–63). In his early career he was sceptical about the Gaelic revival and steered away from political involvement. Like many others, however, he was stirred by the Easter Rising and its aftermath. Regarded by the British government as a dangerous influence in the volatile circumstances then prevailing, he was intercepted by destroyer whilst en route to Ireland in August 1920 and was landed in England. He became a supporter and friend of de Valera.

248 NAI TAOIS/S1369/21, Civil War Prisoners, 1922–4. P. J. Ruttledge to Archbishop Daniel Mannix, 30 October 1923. This document is a typed copy. Patrick J. Ruttledge (1892–1952), a solicitor by profession, was imprisoned during the Anglo-Irish War. He took the anti-Treaty side and served on the IRA's Army Council and Executive in 1922 and acted as President of the anti-Treaty Republic whilst de Valera was imprisoned. Entered the Dáil in 1927; various ministerial appointments in Fianna Fáil cabinets (1932–41), including Minister for Justice (1933–9).

249 NAI TAOIS/S1369/21, Civil War Prisoners, 1922–4. Kathleen Barry to Archbishop Daniel Mannix, 27 November 1923. At that point the outgoings of the IRPDF amounted to £700 per week, but for the previous eight months less than £600 per week had come in. It was now easier to collect money, but, because of the financial strain experienced by republicans for the previous seven years, to a large extent the IRPDF would have to depend on funds raised abroad.

250 NAI TAOIS/S1369/10, 31 October 1923.

251 James Duhig (1871–1965) was born in Co. Limerick but emigrated to England with his family and then emigrated to Brisbane in 1885. He engaged in lay work for the Catholic Church and was selected for further study in Rome. A successful career as priest and bishop followed. He saw himself as both Irish and British, denouncing both the 1916 Rising and the manner of its suppression. Supported the Treaty. In 1959 he accepted a knighthood. He lived to become the world's longest-serving Catholic bishop.

252 NAI TAOIS/S1369/21, Civil War Prisoners, 1922–4, W. T. Cosgrave to Archbishop James Duhig, 3 January 1924.

253 NAI TAOIS/S1369/21, Civil War Prisoners, 1922–4, Archbishop James Duhig to W. T. Cosgrave, 22 July 1924. Sinn Féin had better-than-expected results in the August 1923 election (forty-four seats against sixty-three for Cosgrave's Cumann na nGaedheal). This, wrote Duhig, 'gave us rather a shock. To me [it] was proof of the unreliability of the people as a whole in matters of national concern.'

254 PRONI HA/32/1/12, IRA Circular, 23 October 1923, signed Conchubhar Ua Lusaigh (Conor Lacey), Director of Medical Service. The circular claimed that approximately 15,000 were being held without trial.

255 In Northern Ireland, the circular was passed by the RUC to the Ministry of Home Affairs, where the claim that conditions in its prisons were even worse was dismissed as 'absurd' (PRONI HA/32/1/12).

256 In the last months of the Civil War, IRA seizures and destruction of property and goods continued. Given the fractured nature of the organisation, it was difficult in

many instances to distinguish between IRA operations and robberies and thefts for private gain. These possibly freelance operators were pursued, as were prominent republican figures (such as de Valera) who could assist in rallying and reorganising the movement. See, for example, the cases set out in a number of Department of Finance files at FIN/1396, 1402, 2573, 1638 and 1188. See also *Irish Times*, 27 June 1923, 7a.

257 There appeared to be no awareness of the irony in the use of the term 'more or less harmless type' and certainly no latter-day recognition that the net might have been flung too widely.

258 NAI G2/2/C/1/123/S1555, Executive Committee Minutes, 16 June 1923. In order to expedite the release of Irregular prisoners 'of the more or less harmless type' and whose detention was no longer necessary as normal conditions were re-established, 'it was suggested' (note the diffidence) that committees be established in the various commands. These would consider lists of prisoners of the harmless type. After consultation with the local state solicitor and the county committee of order, a report and recommendation would be submitted to the Minister for Defence. Where the prisoners were from Dublin, the CID would be consulted. All details would be arranged by the ministers of defence and justice.

259 NAI TAOIS/S1369/21, Ministry of Defence Communication, 31 December 1923.

260 The others were Seán T. O'Kelly, Dr James Ryan, Dr Patrick McCarville and Charles Murphy. No undertakings were required for these releases, which were at the discretion of the Minister for Defence (NAI TAOIS G2/3). See also *Irish Independent*, 14 December 1923, 7e; 19 December 1923, 8d; *Eire*, 22 December 1923, 4b.

261 Sean Buckley, TD, Patrick Cahill, Charles Murphy, Brian O'Higgins and Patrick Smith (NAI TAOIS G2/3).

262 NAI TAOIS G2/3, Executive Minutes.

263 NAI TAOIS G2/3, Executive Minutes, 12 June 1924.

264 See, for example, the Adjournment Debate on 27 June 1924 (*Dáil Debates*, vol. 8, cols. 75–84).

265 NAI TAOIS G2/3. On 1 July 1924 it was disclosed that there remained in custody 123 internees and eighty-six persons sentenced for political offences (*Dáil Debates*, vol. 8, col. 89).

266 *Dáil Debates*, vol. 8, cols. 88–9, 1 July 1924.

267 NAI TAOIS G2/3, Executive Committee Minutes, 5 July 1924.

268 NAI TAOIS G2/4.

269 As in the case of Patrick Casey of Ballybricken, Co. Limerick, who had been executed on 2 May 1921 and whose remains had been interred at Cork Prison (*Dáil Debates*, vol. 9, col. 14, 22 October 1924).

270 Even as late as November 1924, some more recently arrested persons remained in internment under the Public Safety (Powers of Arrest and Detention) Temporary Act, 1924. Philip O'Dwyer of Kilkenny and Edward O'Dwyer of Callan, Co. Kilkenny, for example, had been detained in May 1924 on suspicion of involvement in the wounding of two members of the Garda Síochána. Both were still detained in custody on 4 November. They had not been charged, and neither had made application to have his case reviewed (*Dáil Debates*, vol. 9, cols. 650–1, 4 November 1924).

271 Though, starting from this low base, economic growth would outstrip that of Northern Ireland in the period 1926–38. See Kieran A. Kennedy, Thomas Giblin and Deirdre McHugh, *The Economic Development of Ireland in the Twentieth Century* (London and New York: Routledge, 1988), p. 118.

272 This had two components: reward for past support and the procurement of security within the public service. As in Northern Ireland, the last remained an unavoidable consideration.

273 NAI TAOIS G2/3, Executive Committee Minutes, 13 November 1923. A further complication at this point was the application of reinstatement in civil- and public-service positions of those who had, for nationalist or republican sympathies or actions, been dismissed by the British in the period 1916–21. These had organised themselves in the Association of Victimised Civil Servants and had effective means of promoting their cause. Some individuals were dismissed by the British, reinstated by the Provisional government and dismissed again for taking the anti-Treaty side. See Martin Maguire, *The Civil Service and the Revolution in Ireland, 1912–38* (Manchester: Manchester University Press, 2008), pp. 170–1.

274 See Maguire, *The Civil Service and the Revolution, op. cit.*, p. 137; NAI PG/G1/2, 26 July 1922 and 8 August 1922.

275 See above, pp. 32; 214.

276 The declaration was as follows: 'I declare that I have not taken any part with or aided or abetted in any way whatsoever the forces in revolt against the Irish Free State government and I promise to be faithful to that government and to give no aid or support of any kind to those who are or may in future be engaged in conflict against the authority of that Government.' The declaration had to be signed, witnessed and dated. The witness had to declare his rank, which suggested not only an official position but a degree of endorsement of the person making the declaration. In many circumstances, a declaration of loyalty to the state rather than to the government, would have provided the necessary leeway to the politically active and conscionably scrupulous: this was a contrary situation since it was the state to which republicans took exception. If, of course, one believed that no element of a usurping state could be legitimate (a not unreasonable deduction), the declaration could not be acceptable.

277 Twomey Papers, P/69/8/224, Chief of Staff's Department to GHQ members, 9 January 1925.

278 Dan Gleeson, a well-known IRA activist from Co. Tipperary, was appointed as a local-government assistance officer in the post-Civil War period under exactly these circumstances (see MacEoin, *Survivors, op. cit.*, p. 274).

279 NAI TAOIS G2/7, Executive Council Minutes, 5 November 1928. For Miss Ethan O'Byrne's personal file and the information that led to her dismissal, see NAI TAOIS/S8077A, Personal File, which includes a note from the Executive Council Minutes of 28 August 1925. On de Valera's accession to power in 1932, Miss O'Byrne was reinstated in the public service. This suggests that under the previous administration it was not found expedient to re-employ her even without access to confidential documents (NAI TAOIS G2/9, Executive Council Minutes, 12 August 1932).

280 NAI, G2/4/C/2/132, Executive Council Minutes, 27 January 1925.

281 Twomey Papers, P/69/11/136, Department of Intelligence to Chief of Staff (for Executive Council), 6 July 1923.

282 Twomey Papers, P69/3/23, Chief of Staff's Department to OCs and Prisoners, Mountjoy, 31 July 1923.

283 Confinement and lack of change and stimulation have an inevitable tendency to cause prisoners to dwell on their own circumstances. This can manifest itself in demands upon already hard-pressed families and relatives to provide comforts. In the midst of the Mountjoy hunger strike in the autumn of 1923, Ernie O'Malley noted that the stoppage of parcels must have benefited families: 'Some women sent much more than they could afford; often wondered if some of our men realised that' (*The Singing Flame, op. cit.*, p. 249). But this selfish tendency notwithstanding, most men would have been aware of their family obligations and worried about their inability to meet them.

284 The importance of this work may be gauged from the fact that it was assigned to Michael Collins after his release from Frongoch Camp in 1916 and was almost certainly a factor in the re-establishment of the clandestine organisation and Collins's emergence as a leader.

285 Twomey Papers, P/69/8/32, 11 May 1925.

286 On the reorganisation of the IRPDF under anti-Treaty auspices, see UCDA, Kathleen Barry Moloney Papers, P/94/55. The Constitution of the organisation is at P/94/50.

287 Twomey Papers, P/69/8/32, 11 May 1925.

288 The White Cross was established in 1921 to provide relief for Catholics who suffered in the sectarian conflicts in Belfast and elsewhere in Northern Ireland. See Twomey Papers, P/69/43/41, Note by Director of Irish White Cross, 15 August 1924.

289 Twomey Papers, P/69/43/41. The Students' Aid Committee gave financial assistance to those whose studies had been interrupted by the Civil War. Some thirty students were helped to finish their courses.

290 Social provision in the 1920s Free State was extremely limited, with a high reliance on voluntary, church-sponsored bodies. There was some unemployment insurance, and relief was also provided through public-works schemes. Relief for the indigent was also provided along Poor Law lines, and the Free State struggled with both policy and administration in this area. See, for example, NAI PG/G1/2, 12 May 1922. For public works (reconstruction and new schemes), see *Dáil Debates*, vol. 12, cols. 166–7, 3 June 1925; and vol. 14, col. 1351, 10 March 1926. For a statement on Poor Relief, see *Dáil Debates*, vol. 32, cols. 442–4, 30 October 1929. The difficulty for former IRA men (and women) was that whatever patronage was available, public or private, was more likely than not to be steered away from them.

291 Humphreys Papers, P/106/1285/5, Prisoners in A Wing, Mountjoy. (The compilation – thorough, neat and exact – was almost certainly the work of the women of the PPC.)

292 See, for example, the letter from Áine Ní Rathghaille, IRPDF, to editors of the various Irish newspapers, protesting that government forces had, on recent raids, confiscated large sums of money. MA, BMH, Contemporaneous Documents Collection, CD/6/40/1, February 1924. See also *Irish Times*, 22 January 1924, 3b.

293 Twomey Papers, P/69/8/116, note to IRA GHQ, 6 March 1925.

5

WOMEN IN PRISON

An intensity of experience

History is not the mere passage of time, an accretion of years, months and days. Its essence lies in human perception and creation, in the imposition of patterns and meaning. We focus on events that we consider to have consequences or to be outcomes, and, as we develop an understanding and create a coherence, we draw in ever more factors and make new links. There can be no final history, since our understanding is constantly changing, always limited. These elementary cautions are essential when one attempts to denote any factor in a narrative as being especially significant. For all kinds of reasons it may not be as important, or even as sound a judgement, as one imagines, but it may nevertheless provide a point of purchase to pull us onward.

In political, social and economic history, such points of purchase are not uncommon: a group, person or idea may demonstrably animate political life; the establishment or breakdown of a convention may have wide social consequences; and a development in technology, sometimes apparently marginal, may affect many areas of life. Spurts, crises and surprises match inertia, lulls and continuities. Into this mosaic we drop revolution, war and the challenges of order. Exceptional times call for, or permit, exceptional people to come forward, both of moral nobility and of depravity. Abilities and proclivities that may have been obscured, ignored or absorbed in other circumstances become prominent and efficacious. These qualities may have long-lasting effects, or may be no more than sounds and flashes, distantly glimpsed, soon forgotten.

These preliminaries are possibly unnecessary, but they are a prelude to the claim that there can be exceptional generations, just as we have exceptional individuals. By 'generation' we do not mean the whole of an age cohort but usually a group within it: artists, writers, musicians, scholars – or political activists. Such was the group of republicans who, in Ireland, launched the Rising of 1916 and who followed the pathways of war, violence, struggle, split and recrimination in the years and decades thereafter. Among these was a quite remarkable group of women. They come into our story because many made their way into prisons or, as agitators, took their places by their walls and gates.

These women lived through and were deeply affected by events of historical decisiveness and by movements that left a deep imprint on Irish and Anglo-Irish history. A watershed is easily discernible in the Irish cultural revival which began to get under way in the 1880s. This was, in part, driven by women and certainly was particularly accessible to them. With its creative energy directed to literature, drama, poetry, music, games and the nurture of the young in all things Irish, it was likely to attract female participation. 'Revival' suggests the restoration of something already in existence, but this movement was in substantial part a matter of reconstruction, invention, innovation and interpretation. Those involved in it were making a personal journey in identity as well as taking their part in a political and cultural reshaping of the notion of Irishness.

The immediate watershed was part of a more extensive system, a continental divide. The venerable movement for women's rights had acquired new perspectives, coherence and urgency through the broadening of the male franchise. This, inevitably, put a sharp and inescapable question into the public arena: how could it be just that the least worthy and most irresponsible adult male was entitled to vote, whilst an educated woman, a person of property – or indeed a woman with the grave responsibilities of motherhood – was denied it? A range of organisations began to campaign on the issue, baulked, it seemed to them, only by the desire of those in power to protect male prerogatives. Quite apart from its fervour and substance, moreover, the various suffrage and feminist organisations gave training in procedure, structure and public campaigning, as well as injecting individuals with potent doses of self-confidence.

Yet other social currents swirled about those entering womanhood in these decades. Socialist, social-democratic and labour movements addressed the conditions and expectations of working people. The cooperative societies that spread through Britain and Ireland in the latter part of the nineteenth century dealt with the welfare of the household and also offered women the chance to participate in organisation-building and management. The temperance movement, whether religious or political, sprang from a belief in and buttressed domesticity. Other developments both reflected and influenced social and cultural change. Dress reform promised to free women from impossibly constraining and impracticable garments; cycling offered ordinary young women the chance to travel considerable distances from their homes, informally and in the company of others of their age and cast of mind, and of both sexes. Organised hiking and youth hostels were other tools to advance this desire for personal liberation. Among sections of the middle classes, early forms of contraception allowed women to control their fertility.[1] Confined largely to women in the upper reaches of society, and in cities, the very notion offered a chance to reshape the female identity. Marie Stopes's brave and shocking *Married Love* was, in 1910, a few years off publication, but was already in the making in the choices and interests of some women.[2]

Some breaches had been made in the outer walls of male privilege, and pioneering women advanced through them in small but always growing numbers.

Girls' education (at least for the middle classes) had already advanced several stages in the long process of reform, shifting from an exclusive concentration on preparation for the duties of wife and mother to notions of choice and to the acquisition of cultural competence, self-confidence and self-sufficiency – the female identity as more than a series of limitations and renunciations. The most determined and able women had penetrated some of the realms of professional exclusiveness, and, albeit grudgingly and with a degree of unease, universities and some professional bodies were coming to terms with a female presence. Even for those who could not aspire to a degree or professional qualification, the living proof that women had the capacity for such achievement was a source of pride and encouragement. In Ireland, from the late 1850s, the English high-school movement (including, for example, the pioneering work of Dorothea Beale at Cheltenham Ladies' College and Frances Buss at North London Collegiate School) had an impact, introducing a rigorous academic curriculum for girls.[3] The effect of the possession of such an education is as hard for us now to understand as are the consequences of its absence: knowledge indeed confers freedom.

There was a flowering of female leadership in republican politics and activities before and after the Anglo-Irish War, during the Civil War and, on a declining trend, thereafter. This was a shift within physical-force nationalism. Women had taken scarcely any part in Fenianism. This was, it seems, not simply a matter of unacknowledged contributions but of the nature of the organisation, with its aspirations to raise an army and its emphasis on soldierly honour and bravery.[4] This exclusion held less firmly in the years of Parnell and the Land Wars, and women participated in both lawful organisations and in clandestine activities.[5] This was a trend which would grow but, *pace The Times*, Parnellism was not Fenianism, and the agrarian outrages, local confrontations and intimidation arising from the Land Wars could not be described as insurrection. A detailed analysis might disclose more direct links, but the social and political currents to which I have alluded, together with the destruction, loss, horror and transformative effect of the First World War, seems to have wrought a generation of women activists like none other in Ireland's modern history. This was a conflux, driving the energies of nationalism's women activists in directions and with a force not previously seen.

One must not overdraw the picture. Involvement in republican bodies – the Volunteers, the IRA and the post-Treaty IRA – was still remote, even as the object of contemplation, from the lives of most women; many, no doubt, would have regarded the prospect with horror. For the select group that did become involved, through Cumann na mBan or another avenue, the contribution was likely to be that of an auxiliary: cook, courier, housekeeper, nurse or typist. It is true that in the closing years of British rule and then during and after the Civil War, women were prominent in prisoners' aid, family support, and in organising and participating in protests outside prisons. These were extremely useful activities, but none opened the gate to leadership roles.

A sisterhood

Those women who were the mothers, sisters, wives or fiancées of men executed in 1916, or who had died in the Anglo-Irish or Civil wars, had a particular status. With the tide of republicanism at full flood they became objects of popular interest and indeed veneration. Their men were seen as martyrs and heroes, and the women were encouraged by militant republicanism to voice the sentiments and to take the positions that (by selective conjecture) the departed would have taken. This meant that the dead voices they channelled were inevitably fixed at their most militant, the instant of revolutionary sacrifice, of immovable and eternal defiance. Had they lived, the glorious dead might have changed their views, developing or repudiating previously held opinions, as had many of their companions who had lived and who had to contend with the demands of life and change, or who had simply concluded that they had been wrong. Almost uniformly, this group of survivors joined a Sophoclean chorus – cautioning, admonishing, calling to duty, repudiating and castigating. Accorded some of the veneration of the Sibyl, during the years of war and death they reached too far. Overuse of the status and the rancorous, repetitive, sometimes absurdly expressed and other times abusive exhortations and bitter words inevitably led to a fading away of influence. Beyond that lay pity and then ridicule.[6]

But in the years that their voices reached beyond the ranks of political activists to sections of the ordinary public, the women showed passion, flair, imagination and daring in protest and publicity – abilities and qualities that they shared with and which may partly have derived from the militant female suffragists of the immediate pre-war years.[7] Simply by protesting in public these republican women were able to attract attention, since they were breaking with the convention that femininity required unobtrusiveness and meekness, its influence – were there to be any – to be exercised through men.[8] Having discarded these social fetters, blending and bonding with others who had done the same was a heady, frisky experience. Far from ending, moreover, the world became far more interesting: this was women's liberation. Hunger strikes inside and outside prisons, vigils and prayer gatherings at the gates, placard processions, slogan-painting, strong letters to public figures and heckling the meetings of opponents, were all well-tested methods of protest and disruption and fitted well with these new perspectives and capabilities. To these the militant republican women added well-crafted leaflets and pamphlets and, as the 'Ghosts' campaign showed, were not averse to intimidation of courts and juries.[9]

Inevitably, many came from comparatively well-off and secure sections of society. A working-class woman had limited opportunities to participate in protest and agitation, and not many had the experience or confidence to do organisational work – though there were some prominent exceptions (especially in the trade-union and labour movements). Sighle Humphreys was the daughter of a doctor; Mary MacSwiney, although the child of a far-from-affluent family became a teacher, and her sister-in-law Muriel (Terence's widow) was the daughter of a wealthy distillery-owner. Maud Gonne (English but claiming Irish family connections) became a considerable heiress and was a noted beauty. Charlotte Despard, also English and also from a wealthy background, first visited Ireland on her honeymoon, when she was twenty-six. Her brother was Lord Lieutenant during the War of Independence and was greatly embarrassed by her activities.[10] Constance Markievicz, the only woman commander in 1916 (she held rank in Connolly's Citizen Army) and possibly the only woman to fire a shot during the Rising, was born into the wealthy and substantial ranks of the Anglo-Irish landowning gentry and married into the Polish nobility. That these and other women had crossed social and political divides so decisively showed spirit, contrariness and, in some (Despard, Gonne and Markievicz, for example), bohemian style.

As I have noted elsewhere, politically motivated prisoners are generally of a very different cast from ordinary criminal prisoners.[11] The latter, sporadic bravado notwithstanding, are isolated, marginal figures, governed by an inescapable sense of failure and subscribing to a 'convict code' elastic enough to allow preying on their weaker fellows. Politicals, particularly in the Ireland of rebellion and war, were buoyed up by their convictions and a certainty of solidarity and support within and beyond the prison. For the women we are discussing, these assurances were adamantine. Suffering and persecution, as they saw it, burnished and endorsed their convictions and confirmed the moral failure and dissolution of their opponents. The leaders were a special group, long accustomed to the world of political ideas and debate, drawn to utopian visions, resolute, articulate, demonstrably self-sacrificing, unbowed, unafraid and convincing. They were aware of the indulgences and protections extended to their sex, as well as the limitations and disadvantages imposed upon it. In addition, they were frequently colourful, imaginative and dramatic; they could infuse politics with credible emotion and could politicise the minutiae of everyday life and certainly understood the dynamics and routines of institutions. Unabashed, they looked beyond the official persona to the personality of the office-holder and were wont to emphasise moral responsibility and choice rather than allowing these to be attributed to and displaced by organisational processes and structures of authority. All encounters with officialdom, and certainly those of a hostile nature, were conducted with confidence, in moral security, characterised by personal challenge and carelessly veiled disdain. Women in prison, sociological studies suggest, tend to associate in a family-like manner.[12] These leaders provided a focus for respect, embodied feminine strengths, transmitted confidence to their followers and helped all to draw together to meet the hardships of confinement.

Captives or captors?

During the Civil War and its aftermath, anti-Treaty women were interned and imprisoned. The former group attracted the attention of the Free State authorities by their associations, agitational activities and auxiliary work for the anti-Treaty forces. The last included customary Cumann na mBan tasks such as producing, caching and distributing literature and carrying communications, weapons and ammunition, as well as intelligence and other military activities; some were also arrested while operating under cover of the Red Cross. By September 1922, a sizeable group was being held. An estimated 400 or more would pass through the prisons in the course of the Civil War.[13] They could be ingenious, unruly, relentless and particularly difficult to handle; some were seasoned campaigners with a considerable ability to organise themselves and a repertoire of disruptive tactics to match. They knew to a very fine point how far they could push their indiscipline. This included a calculation of the limited range of sanctions and punishments available to their captors. Although they attacked persons in a few instances only, they were willing and more than able to smash prison cells and fittings. Because of this, and the shortage of female warders, they were given a predominantly male guard. It proved easier to hold them in a prison set aside for that purpose than in a wing of a male prison. On 7 September 1922, the Provisional government decided to equip Kilmainham to hold women who had been arrested for directly assisting the IRA. They were to be subject to the same regulations as the men.[14] Kilmainham had recently been used and left in a poor condition by the military, however, and much refurbishment was required. It was not until late October that the building was pronounced fit for reoccupation.[15]

Dublin was the principal holding place for women prisoners. By the end of March 1923, some 300 were being held, with transfers from provincial towns adding twenty-five to thirty each week.[16] Earlier that month new regulations had been brought in, withdrawing letters and visits from the women in Kilmainham.[17] This was intended to stop them from furthering their cause by sending and passing out letters about prison conditions. The women immediately went on hunger strike, and, after several days, the privileges were restored.[18] The authorities had again picked the wrong fight with these doughty females, but skirmishing of this kind would continue throughout 1923. However difficult they were to manage, it was hard to justify an embargo on their communications with friends and families: persons convicted of serious criminal offences were not denied correspondence. Women, moreover, were thought to have particular and important family responsibilities. Moreover, cutting off letters and visits was counterproductive as a sanction for ill-discipline, since it allowed rumours to multiply and to become fantastical.

As with prisons throughout the country, Kilmainham conditions were over-crowded and sordid. The building itself was of an old design, having been built in 1796 and with few of the features of later buildings constructed to the Pentonville pattern; it was also poorly maintained. Sighle Bowen (probably OC of the women prisoners) complained about the B-Wing conditions, which she described as 'appalling', with some fifty women sleeping on the floor; the wing itself had been condemned as unfit for human habitation (by whom it was assessed she did not say). She reported, however, that the food 'on the whole is good enough'. But neither overcrowding nor dilapidation improved escape possibilities: 'I'm nearly grey exploring avenues of escape. But it seems hopeless.'[19]

Women presented a number of political and logistical problems, and, in general, their imprisonment reinforced the anti-Treaty side in a manner quite disproportionate to their numbers.[20] They included many who had played prominent parts in the 1916 uprising or in the Anglo-Irish War, or whose husbands, sons or brothers had been prominent figures. Kathleen Clarke was the widow of the veteran and venerated Fenian, Thomas Clarke, whose name had been the first of those on the 1916 Proclamation; her father and uncle were also Fenians (the latter a prominent activist), and her brother, Edward Daly, was one of those executed in 1916. Mary and Ann MacSwiney were the sisters of Terence MacSwiney, whose death in Brixton Prison on the seventy-fourth day of his hunger strike was a pivotal event for all republicans: Muriel MacSwiney was the widow: attractive, personable and an excellent ambassador for the anti-Treaty cause. Countess Markievicz was the only woman leader in the 1916 Rising and would then, but for her sex, have been shot; she was the most famous woman republican and was affectionately regarded by many of Dublin's poor. Hanna Sheehy-Skeffington was the widow of the murdered Francis (who had been a pacifist), but she was also a notable suffrage, social and anti-war activist in her own right before turning to Sinn Féin. Maud Gonne was also a widow. Her estranged husband John MacBride had fought on the Boer side and had been executed for his (minor) part in the Rising. Gonne was herself a well-known anti-British campaigner from the earliest days of Sinn Féin and its predecessors.[21]

The list could be extended to other names perhaps not so familiar nowadays but instantly recognisable through much of nationalist Ireland in the 1920s.[22] There was an undoubted political cost to having such women against the Treaty – rather as though the widows and sisters of the signers of the US Declaration of Independence had survived to take sides in the American Civil War. As a general rule, in Ireland women were accorded the deference that went with their special role in family life, in the theology, social doctrine and organisation of the Roman Catholic Church, and as the embodiment of the compassionate spirit. In nationalist literature and imagery, Ireland was often portrayed as a grieving woman. The spectacle of any politically active women, but especially republican icons (women who directly and indirectly had paid a considerable price for Irish independence) behind the walls, gates and bars of an Irish prison, disturbed and deeply perturbed many nationalists who did not share the women's passionate politics. For their part, the women were well aware of the sensitivity of their incarceration for the Free State and were deft in their tactics of harassing officials, embarrassing politicians and representing themselves to the public. To their immediate captors they were civil, if occasionally troublesome; of the Free State leadership they were deeply contemptuous and wont to vent these feelings in full and angry statements, slogans and songs.

Gonne was arrested on 5 January 1923 and released twenty-seven hours later.[23] An experienced prisoner, having spent several troubled and troublesome months in Holloway Prison in 1918, she was prone to tubercular ill-health and unlikely to be fit for this latest detention.[24] She immediately wrote to

Max Wright, a journalist, expressing her mock gratitude to 'the ignorant young ape of a Free State officer' who, by arresting her, had unwittingly given her a chance to act as a visiting justice or sanitary officer at Mountjoy Prison: 'You know the Free State Gov[ernmen]t have suppressed sanitary officers and visiting justices in the prisons – so the unfortunate prisoners have no possible means for getting complaints heard or redressed.'[25] Sickly herself, she complained particularly about the quality of medical treatment. The doctor did not make his daily round as with ordinary criminal prisoners but came to the political prisoners only when requested, and then only after a long delay.[26] Although she had not experienced it personally, Gonne confirmed that the soldiers of the guard were firing into the cells. She had seen bullet holes in the windows and marks on the walls opposite. The practice (she wrote) seemed to amuse the soldiers. She had seen an 'officer' (her quotation marks) empty his revolver at the windows of one of the wings, which held ordinary criminals.[27] The overcrowding was 'shocking'. Forty-three women were being held two or three to a cell; she had heard that conditions for the men were even worse. Staffing was as chaotic: 'Disorder, drunkenness seem the rule of the officers, so-called guards.' She concluded with a plea to Wright to make the facts public.[28]

A different account was rendered by Sighle Humphreys, with the intention of showing republican women as indefatigable and defiant. Writing from the NDU, which, because it had been a workhouse, she designated as Tig na mBocht (the poorhouse), she described the transfer of the women from Mountjoy to the NDU on the night of 26/7 April 1923.[29] At this point, Kilmainham was for sentenced women; the NDU held internees. There had been ten women internees on Humphreys's wing, all of whom expected imminent release (forty women had been freed over the preceding days). Instead, they were told that they were immediately to be taken to the NDU: 'We had a lovely drive thro' the city and got a great reception here. We are quite settled now for the winter.' It was cold, since they had no coal, but not as cold as Mountjoy's B Wing, 'and we have great Rounders'.[30] About eighty women had been released, with some 145 remaining at the NDU. Besides playing rounders, time was passed in reading: books seem to have been sent in with little trouble. Humphreys indicated the range of the women's literary tastes, from Lewis Carroll's *Alice in Wonderland* to Karl Spindler's account of Roger Casement and gun-running.[31] The letter ended with a mischievous postscript intended to irk the prison censor (though it seems equally possible that the authorities were bypassed and this was a clandestine communication): 'The last day you were up [visiting the prison] I was dying to tell you of a tunnel we were making and which I was just working at when I was called to see you. I missed your valuable help very much. It was discovered alas.' All a great girls' adventure, it would seem. The letter concluded in just that tone: 'don't be too reckless with your motor bike'.[32]

Some women (Humphreys being an especially prominent example) remained involved in prison matters throughout their lives. For others, it was simply an episode, albeit one that made a profound impression: days of danger, strangeness, crisis, deep emotions and intense comradeship. Writing to Humphreys a decade and a half after her imprisonment, Mary Lambert recalled it as 'the happiest days I ever had – though I must confess, I often got nervous [with] all the tricks we played and never got caught.'[33] Nell Humphreys, matriarch of the redoubtable Humphreys family, was herself incarcerated. Her prison letters, or letters to her from other women who had been inside (either as internees or sentenced prisoners) convey the sense that there had been lots of fun, socialising, devising pastimes, planning, chatting, writing, sleeping and eating (whilst not on hunger strike). She herself recalled playing charades and commented that she 'never had such an enjoyable time since I was at school'.[34]

Black sheep

Some families – Protestant, unionist and prosperous – could not believe that their daughters had been arrested for any good reason: surely a mistake had been made? Such was the case with Dorothy Macardle, a teacher of English at Alexandra College, Dublin.[35] She was arrested almost by accident whilst on what she insisted was a mission of mercy, but it is likely that the authorities were looking for her.[36] Her father made various anxious enquiries, and, on 19 December 1922, he wrote to W. T. Cosgrave, head of the government. He explained that he should like to visit his daughter and wished to take her to London for six months 'until all this trouble is dead and gone'.[37] Sir Thomas Macardle gave the archetypal perplexed and poorly informed father's account of how his daughter had come to be involved in such matters: her successful efforts to secure reprieves for Edward Potter and William Conway (convicted of taking part in the Bloody Sunday massacre of British intelligence officers) during the Anglo-Irish War.[38] How he imagined that this subsequently came to count against her in the Free State cannot be said.

But Dorothy had form and was known to be deeply involved in republican activities – far more than her father knew. In the desperate straits of civil war, a great deal of latitude had necessarily been given to the Army by the politicians. Despite intercessionary pleading, Richard Mulcahy, Minister for Defence and Commander-in-Chief, refused to bend the rules. He informed Cosgrave that detainees were not allowed to have visits but that Macardle would be considered for release.[39] A review was conducted, and a fortnight later Mulcahy reported that Macardle had refused to sign the required undertaking and that, in view of her previous record, he did not intend to release her.[40] Lady Macardle was the next to try. Her daughter and other girls had been led astray 'by the woman you released last week after 24 hours in a jail' (i.e. Gonne). It was useless to ask Dorothy to sign anything, since she was too loyal to her friends to do so. Should Dorothy be released, however, she would do her best to keep her out of Ireland.[41]

Macardle's loyalty (or obduracy) confirmed her place in the ranks of those the Free State regarded as diehards: Mulcahy had been correct in his assessment. Against that perception, her parents' efforts were futile. Sir Thomas continued to lobby for her. In April 1923, J. J. O'Neill of the *Manchester Guardian* offered her a position as a journalist – probably through her father's influence. Thanking O'Neill, Sir Thomas insisted that his daughter had never been a militant but had by chance become friendly with Gonne and Charlotte Despard in the cause of prisoners.[42] On his part, O'Neill immediately wrote an intercessionary letter to Cosgrave:

> my own view is that she has been so influenced by some of the mad women who have been prominent in the Irish affairs that she has been persuaded to act as if she is in agreement with them… there is no comparison between her and Mrs. Comerford or the MacSwiney people. She is altogether a different type – an educated type.[43]

But Macardle's friends and contacts were against her, as was her age. She was thirty-three and could not plausibly be portrayed as an innocent led astray. Despite lobbying, she was held until 5 May 1923.[44]

Another middle-class activist was also arrested in a general swoop; again an absent mother and child were involved. This was Rosamund (Rose) Jacob, a humanist of Quaker origins and a feminist – not a member of Sinn Féin.[45] She was a friend of Hanna Sheehy-Skeffington (doubtless from the days when Hanna was also a pacifist). Hanna embarked on a US tour to promote the anti-Treaty cause. Whilst she was away, she arranged for Rose to look after her son and house. Sinn Féin publicity activities were being organised on the premises, and Rose was picked up in an army raid.[46] Other than her friendship with Sheehy-Skeffington, Rose had no involvement with Sinn Féin or the IRA, though she was known to have anti-Treaty sympathies. Whilst in Mountjoy, she shared a cell with Dorothy Macardle. Rose's imprisonment was fleeting, and she was released on 25 January 1923.[47]

Mary MacSwiney's hunger strike

Of the half dozen or so especially fiery and stubborn women at the heart of the female republican *prominente*, none was more of a fighter nor mistress of the tactics of attrition than Mary MacSwiney.[48] Intelligent, energetic, single-minded and direct to the point of bitterness in her manner of expression, during the 1916 internment of her brother Terence in England, Mary stalked and berated Home Office officials on his behalf, establishing, even with the most senior functionaries, a fearsome reputation as a termagant. Terence's arrest and ultimately fateful hunger strike in 1920 drove her to proportionately greater confrontations with officialism: she had the distinction of being ejected from Brixton Prison – one of a very select company so treated in the history of that establishment.[49] Hers was a particularly eminent place in the republican leadership because of these defiant and well-publicised actions. Her standing was reinforced by her utterly uncompromising opposition to the Treaty.[50] Arrested on 3 November 1922, she refused food forthwith and demanded to be released. She relished the opportunity to take on the Provisional government and was equally dismissive of the Roman Catholic hierarchy which, on 10 October 1922, had issued a pastoral letter insisting that those actively supporting the republican cause could not be admitted to the sacraments of confession and communion.[51]

The odds looked all in the government's favour, but such was the abiding feeling in Ireland and across the Irish diaspora about Terence MacSwiney's hunger strike – widely represented as one of the most heroic episodes of modern Irish nationalism – that her arrest and hunger strike unleashed a great storm. Even a moment's dispassionate reflection would have led to the conclusion that the fledgling Provisional government could under no circumstances afford to have a second MacSwiney die on hunger strike, this time in Irish custody.

MacSwiney first tackled the Church. Like the government, it was in an impossible position. She most emphatically would not conform to the bishops' 10 October pastoral letter, but were she to persist in her refusal of food and then, approaching death, request the sacraments, could the Irish Catholic hierarchy refuse her this final (and, for the faithful, most fateful) of all comforts? She may have known this when she wrote to Archbishop Edward Joseph Byrne two days into her hunger strike.[52] Whatever right he had as a citizen to take political sides, she insisted, he was not entitled to do so on behalf of the Church. The morality of republican acts of war depended on the justice of their fight, and of these she had no doubts: 'If our cause is wrong today, then every fight carried on for freedom in Ireland was wrong; the men of 1916 were the murderers some of the Bishops called them then; my brother was a suicide; Kevin Barry and his comrades were lawfully executed.'[53] Facing death, she was utterly confident and indeed exultant: 'it will not take me so long to die as it took my brother. I am offering my sufferings and death as he offered his for the immediate triumph of the Republic and also for the conversion of those renegade Irishmen whose surrender brought all these evils on our country.'[54] This last was an expression of sentiments widely held by republicans and by many of their supporters and sympathisers.[55]

The Archbishop's response was restrained and cautious but uncompromising and to the point: he knew he had to tread carefully. It was, he pointed out, his duty to guard and interpret the law of God. He repeated the pronouncements of the bishops' pastoral. Those who participated in such crimes (against the state) 'are guilty of the gravest sins and may not be absolved nor admitted to Holy Communion if they purpose to persevere in such evil courses'. He loved his country and his people as much as many who made more open professions of patriotism.[56] Both for spiritual and political reasons, the Archbishop was deeply concerned to prevent another MacSwiney tragedy, and so, a week later, he wrote privately to Cosgrave strongly urging that she should not be allowed to die. He had little sympathy with her, 'and politically none', but she was untried and unconvicted, and to let her die 'would in the public mind give a taint of inhumanity'. He was afraid of making a heroine out of MacSwiney, considering especially her brother's death.[57]

As noted, Terence MacSwiney's long-drawn-out and appalling death had evoked deep feelings of sorrow and anger from Irish communities around the world and was one of the founding episodes in republicanism, close to the Rising as sacrificial validation. Support networks in those communities were still very active, and letters and telegrams began to land on President Cosgrave's desk. Militantly republican and blustering in tone, some presumably had little influence on government thinking or inclinations. The American Association for the Recognition of the Irish Republic cabled its protest: 'millions of Americans will hold you personally responsible for murder of Mary MacSwiney if she dies'.[58] The Terence MacSwiney Council similarly warned Cosgrave that thousands of Americans would hold him responsible for torturing MacSwiney. Letters and cables arrived from Kentucky, Rhode Island, New York, New Jersey, Ohio, California, Massachusetts, Connecticut and many other places. On the other side of the world, republican organisations in Australia voiced concerns in varied tones of militancy, bluster and civility. Closer to home, there were pleas and protests from Cork (MacSwiney's family's home town), a subcommittee of Dublin Corporation and a number of prominent Irish citizens, not all of whom were sympathetic with MacSwiney's politics.[59] Irish organisations in Britain also wrote and wired. Three other Mountjoy women and a male prisoner briefly joined her hunger strike but by 10 November 1922 were again taking food.[60] The same day, Ann MacSwiney, in a tonal reprise of letters directed at British officials and politicians two years earlier, violently threatened the Governor of Mountjoy, Phil Cosgrave: 'I'll hold you and Richard Mulcahy responsible for the murder of my sister. Murderers and traitors will be punished as they deserve.'[61]

Officials also brought discreet pressure to bear. The Army's Director General of Medical Services, Major-General M. Hayes, on the fifth day of the hunger strike, fretted about MacSwiney's symptoms, which, given her age, he thought were most likely due to the menopause. The Senior Medical Officer at Mountjoy concurred that her 'disturbed mental equilibrium from the climacteric may conceivably culminate in unhinging her mind'.[62] Hayes reported again within days. MacSwiney was showing no inclination to take food, entering into what he termed 'the dangerous zone', which, he explained, 'is the period of hunger strike when a collapse is to be feared'.[63]

The protests and pleas widened. Sir John Harley Scott, High Sheriff of Cork, sent a telegram on 20 October: 'At the request of many citizens I venture to urge release to an outside hospital.' Trade-union branches added their voices, and a hundred and more women marched to Archbishop Byrne's Drumcondra residence, asking him to intervene.[64] The prison-gate vigil, particularly effective during the last years of British rule, was now revived. On 17 November 1922 there was a procession from Dublin's Mansion House to Mountjoy, where the demonstrators recited the rosary. A number, including Annie MacSwiney, then stayed outside the prison, having declared that they would fast until they were allowed to see her.[65] Annie remained at the Mountjoy gates for three days and nights, with no sign that the authorities would relent.[66] But the sister hunger-striking at the gate and the other starving herself within was a tableau with a considerable moral impact and political effect. Finally Cosgrave blinked and, on the evening of 27 November 1922, decided that Mary should be freed. A military ambulance took her to a nursing home in Eccles Street, and Annie was borne dramatically away on a stretcher carried by members of Cumann na mBan. The Provisional government had faced the inevitable.[67] And because it was Mary MacSwiney, because of her family's special history and the fact that she had been released not following conviction and sentence, but merely detention, the government probably lost little authority in its backing down. Her self-inflicted death would almost certainly have thrown off balance a state already unsteady.

The Kilmainham transfer

Such confrontations were not easily avoided. MacSwiney was energised by a seemingly inexhaustible reserve of anger and was, besides, temperamentally combative: day by day, indeed hour by hour, the new government enraged her. On 12 April 1923, she was again arrested and taken to Kilmainham. With Kathleen O'Callaghan (another member of the Second Dáil), Count George Noble Plunkett and some others, she had been en route to the Tipperary funeral of Liam Lynch, the IRA Chief of Staff who had been killed by Free State troops two days before. The government could not accept such an incendiary presence at what in any event was an enormously emotional event. MacSwiney and O'Callaghan were taken to Kilmainham Prison.[68] A hunger strike was already under way, and the two immediately joined it. Through no action on her part, MacSwiney became the focus of what appears to have been a brutal confrontation between the detainees, military police and the CID. A prisoners' council had been formed at Kilmainham and had become a channel of communication with the authorities. On Monday, 30 April 1923, the Council was informed that eighty-one women were forthwith to be moved to the NDU. Since MacSwiney and O'Callaghan were eighteen days into their hunger strike, the others refused to be transferred without them, reasoning, no doubt, that they should not be deprived of moral support. O'Callaghan was, however, released late that evening, leaving MacSwiney alone on hunger strike.[69] O'Callaghan's release failed to shift her comrades from their refusal to be moved. Just before midnight, a substantial body of CID men and women searchers entered the prison with military police and began to remove the internees. The women subsequently alleged that this was done with excessive force and violence. Annie Hogan insisted that, in turn, each woman was kicked, beaten and dragged along and that several were pulled by their hair. Having taken seventy-nine, the operation was concluded. Hogan, reporting the physical ill-treatment of the women, insisted 'on my word of honour… all I have said is true without exaggeration'.[70] It is also true, however, that the women were resisting removal, and it is significant that Hogan fails to mention how they did so.

The official account partly confirms the women's claims, but it also contends that the removal was violently resisted. Indeed, the prisoners had vowed that they would not be moved, and it is unimaginable that they would have been purely passive in their resistance. The Military Governor of the NDU gave his version of the confrontation. He had been ordered to transfer his new charges to the NDU from Kilmainham, and they had refused to go unless Mary MacSwiney and Kathleen O'Callaghan were released. He was therefore compelled to use force, but this was as 'gentle as was compatible with efficiency'. 'But', he continued, 'if you consider that the prisoners had to be dragged or carried down two flights of stairs you will realise that gentleness was not possible.' Soldiers and police had acted with 'commendable forbearance', and one policeman had suffered a very severe cut on his face. None of the prisoners was injured, he claimed. The operation began at 11.50 p.m. and was completed at 5 a.m. the following morning.[71]

Annie Hogan's account was supported by others. Miss O'Harte, who had been arrested at the Mansion House while collecting for the Prisoners' Dependants' Fund, who gave the number of CID officers, men and women, as fifty, and who claimed that they had come into Kilmainham, charged up the stairs and assaulted the prisoners. Dorothy Macardle and Iseult Stuart concurred, neither mentioning defiance or resistance by the women. Stuart claimed that, when the women had arrived at the NDU, no beds were provided and sixty had to sleep outside in the yard; she also insisted that the women had been 'brutally man-handled'.[72] The Hon. Albinia Brodrick (sister of Lord Midleton, leader of Southern unionists prior to the Treaty) had also testified to conditions but does not appear to have witnessed the transfer incident. She was a Red Cross nurse, arrested whilst working in Kerry (a republican area). She had been released from the NDU after fifteen days on hunger strike and described conditions as poor and the doctor as a bully.[73]

Opinions about their new place of confinement varied, but the wards, communal rooms and greater ease of movement at the NDU, bleak though it was, cannot but have commended it to some as an alternative to Kilmainham's close confinement. Margaret Burke thought that the NDU would be 'much healthier than Kilmainham', with a much bigger exercise ground and green spaces and trees. Interestingly, her transfer complaint was rather short of the traumatic: 'We were kept a long time waiting in the cold.' The transferees had not been allowed to take luggage with them, but it had just arrived (a delay of only a day). The food was not very good but she expected it to improve once the women had settled in.[74]

That there was another side to accounts of unprovoked brutality and victim-isation is also suggested by the state of Kilmainham after the NDU transfer. Writing to the Ministry of Home Affairs a few days later, The MacDermott, Vice Chairman of the General Prisons Board, referred to the destruction of B Block, the female section, by the women. Repair work had been completed just prior to the transfer incident, and the Board did not intend to again make good.

It would appear that B Block had been rendered largely uninhabitable, since MacDermott indicated that the main prison would be sufficient for the number of committals anticipated by the Department of Justice: 'Should B Block be required later, we can submit the question of repair.'[75] The block, which can be viewed by visitors to the preserved and restored building, was a particularly claustrophobic piece of prison design, barely habitable even when in pristine condition.

The Kilmainham and Mountjoy transfers and the associated violence and use of force show the pitch of militancy and solidarity reached by the women detainees at this point. The frustrations of confinement were intensified by the sense of defeat, betrayal, loss and anger as the anti-Treaty forces were pounded into the May ceasefire. The women seem to have expressed these extremely strong feelings in their resistance to and attacks upon the Free State's two most hated bodies: the National Army and the CID. If they had hopes that their sex would allow them a free run in the confrontations, these were confounded. On their part, the soldiers and the CID had reason for anger – particularly the loss of comrades – and the confrontations allowed some settling of accounts. At no future point would women prisoners, whether in the Free State or in Northern Ireland, be held in such numbers, be willing to confront the authorities so directly and violently, or be able to attract such strong public sentiment to their cause.

The autumn hunger strikes

Hunger-striking was undertaken and continued throughout the autumn of 1923 and, sporadically, in 1924, usually for the maximum demand: unconditional release. In all but a few instances, these were untried women, and their insistence that they be charged or released was politically difficult to field; they had at least the basis of a case. Quite erroneously, and with a deal of condescending sentimentality, they were seen as less of a threat than their male comrades and were therefore more easily accepted as objects of public sympathy. On 10 April 1923, Gonne wrote on behalf of the WPDL to 'each member of the Colonial "Free" State Parliament'. She reported that three women were hunger-striking against unlawful imprisonment. Nell Ryan of Wexford had been in gaols in Ireland and England and had declared that she refused to allow her brother-in-law, Richard Mulcahy (Minister for Defence and Commander-in-Chief), to inflict any more imprisonment on her.[76] Miss O'Neill, also of Wexford, was on the twentieth day of her fast and Kitty Costello on the fifteenth.[77]

The women took part in the general hunger strike of republican prisoners in the autumn of 1923, though the experienced among them had doubts as to the wisdom of the action.[78] Their relatives and friends outside had similarly mixed feelings. In some ways, it must have been far worse to contemplate the lot of those inside whom one loved and for whom one cared, than to be on hunger strike, dealing with one's own weakness.[79] At the NDU, Anna Humphreys was one of the strikers. Her letters to her mother Nell made up a gentle but vivid narrative. On 28 October 1923, four days in, she reported that some fifty NDU women were refusing food. She and her sister Sighle 'had not suffered anything', and the authorities had treated them fairly, allowing them letters, newspapers and plenty of coal in the dormitories.[80] Three days later, she reassured her mother that she was quite well and asked for a bottle of eau de cologne for herself and Sighle: 'We talk about food but we are no longer really hungry.'[81] The women were allowed to have consultations with their own doctors, and Anna, in a letter to her brother, described a visit from Dr Kennedy (presumably the family doctor) as being 'as good as a nice dinner'. But, despite the brave show, the strike took its inevitable toll, mental and physical. Some began to eat again, but Anna, reporting this to her brother, emphasised that they were 'not our crowd'. As with many hunger-strikers, she evidently enjoyed conjuring up meals and feasts and at this time expressed her wish for 'a bit of goose and apple sauce'.[82] Some days later, it was evident that her physical resources were dwindling. She asked her mother not to believe public reports of their condition. Sighle was well, under the circumstances: 'I am fairly, but you could not expect me to be as good as S. in her youth.' She confessed that she could not longer write to anyone as she was 'unable'.[83]

The strike ended on 23 November, the decision having been made by senior male IRA officers at Kilmainham. The authorities allowed Thomas Derrig and David Robinson, the IRA officers, to visit all the hunger-strikers, and Anna described how they came to the NDU, having completed a forty-one-day hunger strike themselves but not yet having eaten. She and her comrades were all delighted to see them, and were recovering well, though she compared herself to a scarecrow. As Anna was writing her letter, Markievicz was visiting the NDU women and was 'the greatest company to us all'.[84] By the end of the month, most of the NDU women were released.[85] At this point, the privations of imprisonment and the suffering of the hunger strike seemed of little account. The IRA had been defeated in the field and the republican cause seemed to have lost popular support and even interest. Sighle Humphries recalled, 'we were flattened. We felt the Irish public had forgotten us. The tinted trappings of our fight were hanging like rags about us.'[86]

The hunger strike had been an action to support the men rather than an independent initiative.[87] But earlier in the year there had been a wholly female action. Some forty women at Kilmainham had gone on hunger strike on 23 June 1923, not for their own release but for the transfer to hospital of Cissie Doherty of Dungloe, Co. Donegal. A letter from Eilís Ní Mhurchadha claimed that 'when this young lady was being arrested she was kicked in the side and ill-treated by Brig. Gen. James McCole of the F.S. Army. The assault lacerated her side, tore her muscles, broke a rib and injured the kidney and other organs.' Though various doctors had said that she needed an operation, nothing had been done.[88] The matter was resolved (how is not clear), and the women came off hunger strike.

Prisoner-support committees

Although there was considerable overlap in support and membership, prisoner-support groups were of two kinds: those that agitated for releases and those who raised funds for the relief of dependants. Women played a leading part in each. There were some who, though prominent and vocal in their support for the anti-Treaty cause, seemed to be untouchable. Constance Markievicz directly and Maud Gonne indirectly had been involved in the 1916 Rising, and their imprisonment would have incurred for the government a particularly heavy penalty of opprobrium. But there were limits to their immunity, and both may also have taken care (or had others to take care on their behalf) not to connect themselves directly to the IRA, through operational or other direct support activities. Charlotte Despard was certainly in this category and, with the other two, gave no cause to the authorities, beyond voice and pen, to suspect her of involvement in republican activities. There was bound to be a heightened emotional impact when a woman spoke from her own prison experience about the plight of those still detained. Here Hanna Sheehy-Skeffington was a figure of great authority. Her experience of imprisonment went back to the 1912 suffrage campaign to modify the electoral provisions of the ill-fated Home Rule Bill; she had also undertaken hunger strikes under both British and Free State governments. An obvious leader and speaker on prison matters, she was called upon on many occasions.[89]

During the Civil War and in its immediate aftermath, the press was controlled, by directives from the government, by editorial sympathy (pro-Treaty for the most part) and by protective self-censorship.[90] Public demonstrations were a poor substitute, being able to reach only spectators, but they were one of the few ways in which anti-Treaty republicans could publicly express their views (albeit at the risk, were attendance or participation habitual, of attracting police attention). The campaign to release the prisoners provided a focus and was an issue which, by its nature, would reach out to persons beyond the ranks of activists and supporters. With so many men in prison and apt to be arrested, women took a leading part in organising these demonstrations. In addition to demands for releases, they also protested at what they described as summary executions in the course of Free State military activities.[91]

As the months passed after the IRA ceasefire and dump-arms order of 24 May 1923, those still in captivity, most of whom had only minor and peripheral roles in the Civil War, felt increasingly depressed by the apparently indefinite nature of their confinement and the consequent hardships for their dependants. But a state that had come close to being smothered at birth was not inclined to err on the side of magnanimity. The women's protests, almost ritualistic in their form and frequency, were one way of keeping releases on the government's agenda. There were a number of other pressures, of course, and an overarching need to return the country to the normal paths and preoccupations of peace, but the irritant of frequent demonstrations, speeches and placards imparted some quality of urgency. This would scarcely have been possible had the women's protests not been led by figures so close to the militant coalescence of nationalism, success in the Anglo-Irish War and therefore the foundation of the state itself.

In the autumn of 1923, there was a sense that releases could be effected if only public opinion could be ratcheted up. From the releases of Christmas 1916 onward, the British had been induced to open the prison and camp gates in the season of peace and reconciliation. Part of the thinking was to derive maximum benefit from seasonal sentimentality. Could the Free State be induced to follow suit? At one of the weekly meetings in Sackville Street, Hanna Sheehy-Skeffington demanded better conditions for the prisoners, proclaiming that a convicted murderer was treated better than the detainees who had not even had a charge proffered against them. At the current pace of releases, it would take a further year and a half to free all. They were not going to wait for that time, she added, in a vaguely threatening manner.[92]

Besides the weekly meetings in Dublin, women were prominent in prisoner-support demonstrations in the provinces. At a meeting in Limerick in the summer of 1923, for example, Kathleen O'Callaghan, a Sinn Féin member of the outgoing Dáil, demanded that those who had ill-treated women republican prisoners 'should be hounded out of public life'.[93] She and others made sure that the release of the prisoners would be an issue in the general election of September 1923.[94] A protest meeting had been held in Sligo several weeks before. Again, the leading speakers enjoyed a degree of immunity. Mrs Mulcahy, Acting Secretary of the Technical Institute, presided, and the principal speakers were Mary MacSwiney and an Irish-American priest, Father Fagan, of Ohio. MacSwiney's was an election speech and Fagan's a tilt at the Irish hierarchy. A resolution was adopted, demanding the release of the prisoners.[95]

A week later, Caitlín Brugha, widow of the republican hero killed in a shoot-out with Free State forces in the first days of the Civil War, was a leading speaker at a similar type of meeting held on the Mall in Waterford. Her late husband had been a member of the Dáil for the constituency of East Waterford, and, drawing on his memory, she told her audience that it would be a lasting disgrace if imprisonment continued. The Free State ministers called on their electoral mandate to support their authority, but it was not the will of the people that prisoners should rot in jail. She appealed to the public to contribute as generously as possible to the dependants' fund.[96]

The protest meetings continued in Dublin beyond the general releases of detainees, when those who remained in custody had been convicted of various offences. A fortnight after the release of Éamon de Valera (16 July 1924), Charlotte Despard and Maud Gonne led a demonstration consisting of a meeting in what was now O'Connell (previously Sackville) Street along the usual lines and then a banner procession to Mountjoy Prison.[97]

Quite apart from protest meetings calling for the release of the prisoners and generally condemning the government (and such gatherings, entirely, it would seem, of the faithful, were held weekly in O'Connell Street), the plight of the prisoners' dependants was a matter of genuine humanitarian concern. Whether the relief organisations could be trusted to disburse the funds strictly in accordance with their public pledges was doubted by the government, and when Sinn Féin premises at Harcourt Street were raided by the Army and the CID on 5 January 1923, funds which the Irish Republican Prisoners' Dependants' Fund later claimed to be theirs were seized. The authorities took the view that finance was the lifeblood of military activity and that Sinn Féin was actively engaged in raising it. The Dependants' Fund, through its Honorary Secretary, Anna O'Rahilly, insisted that it was a 'purely charitable organisation' and that the contributions it received and disbursed were intended solely for the relief of women and children.[98]

In a tradition going back to the Anglo-Irish War, activists leafleted and made collections at Sunday masses. Attendance rates were extremely high, and these were likely to be the largest assemblies in parishes (apart, perhaps, from major sporting events, which were less frequent) and were also least likely to be interfered with by the authorities. And in relation to prisoner support, moreover, those who had been at their religious devotions were perhaps more inclined to compassionate reflections. These Sunday activities therefore constituted a major resource and propaganda opportunity for the anti-Treaty side, with little chance of arrest in or near church premises in the midst of congregations coming and going.

Secular authority might by convention stop at the churchyard gates, but ecclesiastical authority was not inclined to step aside. In November 1922, the Bishop of Cork, Dr Daniel Cohalan, denounced republican collections at churches. He pointed out that these contravened a decree by the National Synod of Maynooth, whether made on church premises or at gates opening on to church property.[99] On 10 October 1922, as we have noted, a joint pastoral from the Irish bishops had been issued, to be read in all churches after the principal masses on 22 October. It condemned physical-force republicans, but, '[n]otwithstanding this condemnation, a number of women stand near the church doors on Sundays distributing political leaflets and collecting money for the support, directly or indirectly, of the movement which has been declared unlawful by the Bishops'.[100]

Dr Cohalan had been angered by an incident at a church not long before. A priest had attempted to stop a woman collecting near his church. At a time when the laity was reverential and submissive in its dealings with the clergy, the woman's reply, 'It is not from you I have got my orders', was regarded by Cohalan as a scandalous affront: 'This', he observed, 'is a part of the disregard for all public law and public order, civil and ecclesiastical, which has appeared amongst us.' He went on to assure his flock that, were the prisoners' dependants in need, no one would turn them away. Indeed, the St Vincent de Paul Society (a Roman Catholic charity) 'will not refuse to make provision for anyone in need, be he Free State or Republican'. Cohalan concluded by appealing to the faithful to help in ending what he termed 'this abuse' by refusing to make a contribution to 'these women collectors'.[101]

But if the integrity of the Dependants' Fund was open to question by the government, there was far less doubt about the scale of the relief problem, which, since it concerned families, seemed a particularly appropriate arena for female activism. By early June 1923, republicans estimated that there were 15,000 of their supporters in custody, some awaiting trial or under sentence but for the most part internees in the various prisons and camps.[102] The Dependants' Fund calculated that some 5,000 families were, as a consequence, in need or actually destitute. To provide relief for this number, the organisation required £2,500 per week, which was a very substantial sum indeed. The Dependants' Fund was not the only body providing relief, it is true, but the plight of the families gave them a strong moral position. Well beyond the ranks of the anti-Treaty forces and their sympathisers, the families' need was seen as a pressing national difficulty. The Lord Mayor of Dublin acknowledged in June 1923 the size and gravity of the problem. It would, he warned, be a 'terrible reflection on the country' were aid not forthcoming. He put into words what many, of all political persuasions, may have felt: 'No doom of law condemns to privation and penalty the relatives of imprisoned men, or the families of the sentenced dead.'[103]

In terms of the military and political struggle, the plight of dependants (not all of whom were women and children; some being elderly and infirm) cut both ways. The need to have breadwinners meeting their obligations was a strong argument for their speedy release, and continued detention could make the government seem callous or vindictive, or both. And not only republican activists or sympathisers would take such a view: many uncommitted people were moved to concern or protest; the churches were also apt to be uneasy, given their pastoral roles and the universal emphasis upon family in their doctrines.

But the pressure was not all one-way. By signing a pledge not to oppose the government by violent means, all internees, and many others who had been convicted, could have obtained their release. Such was the stigma incurred by those who 'signed out' that only a very small number ever took this step, but the psychological and emotional pressures on those who knew that dependants were suffering was no doubt considerable. This, in turn, was a strain on the anti-Treaty movement at large. Considerable resources from what was a militarily defeated, demoralised and much diminished organisation had to be devoted to the maintenance of prisoners' dependants. The experience of prolonged and uncertain confinement and its impact on family life and work and career prospects, the knowledge of defeat and the hard life of a bitter liberation must have turned many from active republicanism or, indeed, from politics of any kind.

Secure in the victories of the Free State forces, middle Ireland wanted peace and accepted that, in the accommodation that had to follow hostilities and mass imprisonment, concessions had to be made across the political spectrum. Compassion and magnanimity in victory emanated from and helped to consolidate and moderate that opinion on which the hopes of the new state were based. To take but one telling example: Alice Stopford Green had been a close friend of Roger Casement (and had struggled desperately to the last to secure his reprieve); she had also been prominent in the fund-raising that made possible the landing of arms in 1914.[104] Not a republican, she had disapproved of the 1916 Rising but nevertheless was a firm supporter of the Treaty and became a member of the Free State's first senate. She was a member of the Free State political establishment, and her views were quite far removed from those who approached her for intercession. Unimpeachable in her loyalty to the Free State and with a record as an early and long-time supporter of Irish nationalism, she could ensure the serious consideration of any approach she made to the government.[105]

Contacts with the Red Cross

In the spring of 1923, operating under the cover of the government of the Irish Republic, women activists attempted to involve the International Committee of the Red Cross (ICRC) in Irish prison and camp conditions. Had this succeeded (and the hope was for an adverse report), the Free State government, taking its first steps in the international arena, would have come under pressure from an important arbiter of standards of humanity. (The government of the Irish Republic would also have secured some recognition.) The details of the episode merit some attention, since the outcome was to enhance rather than to diminish the reputation of the Free State in this sensitive, indicative and emotionally charged area of public administration.

A submission was made to the ICRC through the Irish Republic's representative in Paris and by the Irish Women's Republican Federation. On 7 April 1923, the ICRC wrote to say that the memorandum was of interest to them, that they were studying it closely, and that they were considering what course of action they might take.[106] Despite an ICRC promise to keep in touch, and further letters of enquiry from Gonne, nothing more was heard from the ICRC for some weeks. On 11 May 1923, Gonne was sent a press release that was being issued that day, outlining the findings of an ICRC delegate who had visited Ireland at the end of April. She and her colleagues had not previously known of this.

In parallel with this exchange, there had been another, apparently quite separate contact with the ICRC in Geneva, by Charlotte Despard. Despard had outlined her concerns about Irish prison conditions and requested that the Red Cross do what it could to ensure that the Irish government treated its detainees as POWs. Miss O'Brennan was then despatched to Geneva with letters of introduction to the ICRC and to the International Women's League for Peace and Freedom. The contacts seemed promising, with Red Cross undertakings to investigate. Finally, Despard was informed that delegates would be sent to Ireland and that they would make contact immediately they arrived, so that she might provide relevant information. In the event, all that she heard was that the delegation had come and gone; she had no opportunity to make submissions to them. Despard tried to remedy the situation by sending information to Geneva and by emphasising that the complaints she had received were from the barracks and prisons where thousands were detained rather than the 'show' internment camps. There was no response to this letter.

In the aftermath of what had been a debacle for those campaigning on prison conditions, it emerged that there had been a further, equally frustrating set of contacts. Dr Kathleen Lynn had also gone to Geneva and, on 8 December 1922, had made submissions to the ICRC, on behalf of the Irish Women's Republican Federation.[107] She was promised an inquiry and was also told that the ICRC representatives would get in touch when they arrived in Ireland. This did not happen, and, quite by chance, on 19 April 1923, Lynn heard that two Red Cross representatives were in Dublin. She then called on them at their hotel, accompanied by Áine Ceannt and Madeleine ffrench-Mullen.[108] But there was further disappointment, since one of the delegates, M. Schlemmer, was in London. M. Haccius, who received the three women, 'appeared rather taken aback at being discovered by us', Dr Lynn noted.

Haccius was presented with updated reports about conditions in Kilmainham and Maryborough prisons. Dr Lynn emphasised that there were some 300 women in Kilmainham and that the prison was in Dublin (and, by implication, easily accessible). Haccius urged the women to keep the Red Cross presence in Dublin secret for a few days, in order to avoid prisoners' relatives calling at the delegates' hotel and also to avoid any difficulties in getting access to prisons. These reasons sounded plausible enough, and Haccius gave some reassurance by saying that he would accept written statements about prison conditions and forward them to Geneva. Thus concluded the only meeting between the ICRC delegates and prison campaigners in Ireland.

The investigation by Schlemmer and Haccius was, in the view of the prison campaigners and republicans, extremely limited. Gonne and her colleagues particularly objected to the dismissive attitude towards the 300 women and girls in Kilmainham, 'the most notorious prison in Ireland', where the prisoners were held 'in conditions scandalous to any modern state'. According to Gonne, the delegates thought it unnecessary to visit Kilmainham, since they had 'no reason to believe that the treatment there is different to that adopted at Mountjoy'. It is hard to find justification for such an approach, but it may additionally have been urged on the delegates that Kilmainham was shortly to cease holding women and that they would do better to visit the NDU, then being prepared to receive the Kilmainham women.

Whatever transpired between the delegates and the government, Kilmainham was not visited, but the still-vacant NDU was inspected. Exactly how the delegates thought they could inspect and evaluate empty premises to any degree of reliability is unclear, but the impression such a procedure created inevitably looked biased towards authority and dismissive of prison campaigners and republicans. The statement that the NDU buildings would 'fulfil all desirable hygienic conditions' was, at the very least, speculative. Writing when the NDU had been occupied, the ICRC observations gave room for a vehement denunciation by Gonne. She listed three baths for the 300 women, unclean conditions, an unequipped hospital and 'intolerable overcrowding' as features of the NDU, which the delegate could not have foreseen 'when he made his complaisant report'.

But the delegates had come and gone. They had been summoned from Geneva by various activists in the hope that they would inspect and condemn (and indeed there was much to condemn) and thereby provide support for the accelerated release of prisoners, and that they would more generally pronounce, at least in this sphere of public administration, against the Free State government. But the delegates had limited resources and took considerable care not to become a rallying point in the post-war bitterness then enveloping the country. The ICRC was a body with a deal of experience of the politics of conflict and post-conflict and also knew its own limitations. To inspect the range of places of detention in Ireland; to interview even a small sample of the 12,000 or so persons in custody (and, by the logic of balance, a proportionate number of administrators, staff, officials and ancillaries) would have required both manpower and time. Whatever came from such an extensive investigation would have attracted controversy and hostility. (And, indeed, they might have remarked, look at what a limited mission produced.)

For the prison activists and their republican colleagues, it would have been better had the ICRC not visited. Despite what, in places, were deplorable conditions, the government had the general excuse of lack of resources due to the Civil War and the specific counter-complaint that the prisoners had, wilfully and maliciously, caused tens of thousands of pounds' worth of damage across the system.[109] Following the visit of Schlemmer and Haccius, Richard Mulcahy, Minister for Defence (under whose authority the political prisoners were accommodated) was able to point to his government's willingness to receive the ICRC delegates and to facilitate their inspection. He also acknowledged the humane mission of the ICRC, together with its experience and the impartiality of its investigations. With these preliminaries, Mulcahy's quotations from the ICRC report were all the more impressive.

Haccius had visited the principal camps in which a total of 7,369 were held. His observations were a blow to the prison activists and to republican propaganda. The treatment of the prisoners, he was able to say, 'is devoid of all hostile spirit and the general principles adopted by the 10th International Conference of the Red Cross are observed'. He noted that, although the government refused to grant POW status to those it held, it 'in reality treats them as such'. Nowhere did Haccius find a sick or wounded prisoner without treatment: 'The serious accusations made on this subject appear to him unfounded.' Whilst he considered complaints about overcrowding at Mountjoy to have some justification, he found no basis for complaints about correspondence with prisoners' families, sanitary conditions and food in the camps.[110]

There was a deal of weight in the complaints by Gonne and her co-signatories of the letter to the *Irish Independent* about the failure to visit Kilmainham. The delegates offered the feeble excuse – absurd, indeed – that there was no reason to believe that the treatment there was different from Mountjoy (which had been visited). An indication of the more substantive and actual reason was given in Haccius's reference to the hunger strike. This was not for an improvement in conditions but had been undertaken by women from the day of their arrest in order to obtain their trial or immediate release. Haccius had not thought it his duty to insist on contacting these women, he noted, because he feared that his intervention misinterpreted 'would only encourage them to persist in their attitude, and give rise to a new case of strike [*sic*]'.[111]

Dispersal

For most of the women we have met, imprisonment was only one episode in careers of political and public commitment and activity. Unlike the 1848ers or 1968ers, it would be hard to capture all the women's interests in a single generational cohort. This, in part, is because their activities and achievements were so varied, their paths to prison merging but from many different points of origin. Feminism and female suffrage is perhaps the most common factor, though not all agreed on the method, or perhaps on the destination. Cultural revival and nationalism is another commonality, though early pacifism cuts across that for Hanna Sheehy-Skeffington. Social justice and public health were other important motivators. It is hard, when coming to know them, even a little, to avoid their sense of sisterhood.

Female suffrage was both pragmatic and millenarian. Certainly for the Women's Social and Political Union of the Pankhursts and their followers, the achievement of female suffrage was seen as the radical and comprehensive answer to a host of social ills. The woman's view and vote, translated into legislation and wise policies, would, it was argued, produce solutions to problems as varied as drunkenness, working-class emancipation and many crimes. For some of the women of Kilmainham and Mountjoy, the Republic proclaimed in 1916 was possessed of such a potential for universal beneficence: they saw it as much in terms of social justice, or at least as a broader highway thence, as of national self-realisation. In the Republic, both ideals fused. These women were more truly radical than most of their male comrades. Reading the letters, diaries and memoirs, there is little doubt that much of what they wanted was not on the mainstream republican agenda and could never find a place there.

They would have said that the Republic was not achieved and therefore that its promise was not tested. If one passed beyond mere politics to issues of profound social concern, to unfulfilled promises of social transformation and to the deep sadness of social inertia or retrogression, the lost prize is all the more passionately mourned. That sense of loss, of indignation and of allocating personal responsibility for opportunities betrayed lies behind the fierceness with which some regarded the Free State and its leaders, and later the apostate de Valera.

Being radical in this sense meant that many could not find rest in Cosgrave's independent state. A few did, and yet more accepted de Valera's vision and incremental advance to a version of the lost Republic. The times, national and international, economic restraints, engrained and reflexive social conservatism, an ultramontane church and timid polity, all emphasised the radicalism of those who stayed the course on which they had embarked at various points in or around the turn of the century. Isolation and political impotence thrust some into a spiral of sectarianism and bitter recrimination. The mundane and personally preoccupying concerns of the population left but limited purchase for transformative ideas. The poetic vision and apotheosis of Pearse, Connolly and the others could not be renewed and inevitably became contested emblems on a fairly conventional political tilting-ground.

Despite their concern with social reform, the women of Mountjoy and Kilmainham (and the camps) subsequently had little to say about penal reform. It may be that their experience of imprisonment was such a small episode in full and varied lives that it faded into a narrative that was largely political. They may also have recognised that their conditions of confinement were so specific and special that beyond the restrictions of custody they knew little of the ordinary processes of criminal imprisonment. For the most part they were well endowed with compassion, and many continued to be involved in or to support practical work to improve the lot of the poor and disadvantaged. Not unreasonably, they may have taken the view that solutions to the problems of crime and punishment were to be found well beyond the walls and gates of the penal estate.[112]

Notes

1 Analysing the 1911 Census, Joseph Banks pointed out that the decline in fertility had begun fifty years before, if not earlier, and that although part of a general movement, it was most rapid in the Registrar-General's Class I and, within that group, the upper professionals. J. A. Banks, *Victorian Values: Secularism and the Size of Families* (London: Routledge & Kegan Paul, 1981), p. 97.

2 Marie Stopes, *Married Love: A New Contribution to the Solution of Sex Difficulties* (London: A. C. Fifield, 1918). The book went through multiple editions in its first year, provoked wide and heated debate (and condemnation) and remained in print for decades.

3 For a survey of this important social and political landscape in Ireland, see the collection of informative and thoughtful essays edited by Judith Harford and Claire Rush (eds.), *Have Women Made a Difference? Women in Irish Universities, 1850–2010* (Berne: Peter Lang, 2010), especially Chapter 2.

4 For some discussion of the nature and organisation of feminism and republicanism, see Seán McConville, *Irish Political Prisoners, 1848–1922: Theatres of War* (London and New York: Routledge, 2003), Chapters 3 and 4.

5 Patricia Groves, *Petticoat Rebellion: The Anna Parnell Story* (Dublin: Mercier Press, 2009), pp. 174–80. Anna was Charles's sister and became the founding President of the Ladies' Land League. Parnell opposed the notion of the League because he thought it invited ridicule for the movement as a whole by involving women, yet they showed their effectiveness in hindering British government policy whilst the male leaders of the Land League were imprisoned under the Coercion Acts. See Robert Kee's excellent biographical study, *The Laurel and the Ivy: The Story of Charles Stuart Parnell and Irish Nationalism* (London: Penguin, 1994), p. 329 and *passim*. On the suppression of the Ladies' Land League by the parent body and the 'retirement' of the women, see F. S. L. Lyons's classic biography, *Charles Stuart Parnell* (London: Fontana, 1978), p. 228. See also the succinct account of Anna and Fanny Parnell in Marian Broderick's *Wild Irish Women* (Dublin: The O'Brien Press, 2002), pp. 187–91.

6 See, for example, Yeats's poem 'In Memory of Eva Gore-Booth and Con Markievicz', in which he refers to Constance Markievicz, whom he recalls fondly, as a beautiful and graceful girl, and then being condemned to death and pardoned (for her part in the 1916 Rising): 'Pardoned, drags out lonely years / Conspiring among the ignorant'. W. B. Yeats, *The Poems*, ed. Richard J. Finneran (New York: Macmillan, 1983), p. 233.

7 The connection was close. The Irish Women's Franchise League and its journal, *The Irish Citizen*, provided a platform for the anti-conscription campaign which, in turn, was directly linked to both constitutional and physical-force nationalism. Constance Markievicz, Padraig Pearse, James Connolly, Thomas MacDonagh and other leaders of the Rising contributed to *The Irish Citizen*. The Irish Socialist Party used the same premises, the Antient Concert Rooms in Dublin. See *An Phoblacht*, 11 February 1933, 3b.

8 Even Nell Humphreys, whose children were formidable campaigners for irreconcilable republicanism (and who herself was imprisoned) confessed that she had considered the Volunteer activities of her daughter Sighle (aged sixteen or seventeen) in the period before the Rising to be 'unwomanly'. She later revised this view. Writing to her sister-in-law, a nun in Australia, she asked if she had heard of the part that women had played in the Rising: 'I used to feel ashamed of Sighle, as being unwomanly, when Anna told me that at times it was difficult to keep her from taking a shot herself, that the way she glorified when the enemy fell was actually inhuman, and that her nerve during the whole thing was wonderful. But it is only the spirit of the age, every girl in every centre, the G.P.O., Jacobs, the College of Surgeons, was just as cool and brave. They gave the men invaluable help, and kept things normal. The only place where they were not present, Boland's Mills (as de Valera the commandant would have none of them) they became so highly strung that a young volunteer lost his head and shot one of their best men.' Humphreys Papers, P/106/384/13. Some punctuation added.

9 On the 'Ghosts' campaign, see Margaret Ward's *Unmanageable Revolutionaries: Women and Irish Nationalism* (London: Pluto Press, 1983), pp. 205–9. For examples of the 'Ghosts' letters, see Humphreys Papers, P/106/1457 and 1458. The latter was a letter to members of a jury panel from which would be drawn the jury for the trial of Sean McGuinness, an escapee: 'We know there is no necessity to ask you to acquit him of this charge as any others who have been arrested were already acquitted.' The sting in the letter was its delivery to the jurors' home addresses.

10 These were in general support of republicanism. Following the Treaty, which Despard opposed, she became a founding member of the WPDL.

11 See, for example, McConville, *Irish Political Prisoners, op. cit.*, pp. 3–5.

12 See the pioneering work by David A. Ward and Gene G. Kassebaum, *Women's Prison: Sex and Social Structure* (London: Weidenfeld & Nicolson, 1966). The social structure of male prisons, by contrast, is generally competitive, frequently exploitative, concerned with status, power and control of scarce resources.

13 Ward, *Unmanageable Revolutionaries, op. cit.*, p. 190. By the spring of 1923, as we have seen, there were between 10,000 and 12,000 internees in camps and prisons (*Dáil Debates*, vol. 3, col. 354, 20 April 1923).

14 NAI PG/110, S1724/22.

15 NAI TAOIS/S1369/1, General Prisons Board to Ministry of Home Affairs, 26 October 1922. There was a last-minute hitch when the Army started to use the former female block for its own delinquent soldiers. The Board asked for the removal of these military prisoners and their guards. The key to the female block had to be handed over the Board, the letter continued, and instructions issued by the Army that the female portion of the prison was to remain in charge of the Board's officers. On 27 January 1923, it was decided to give the whole prison over for female prisoners (NAI TAOIS/S1369/1, Minister for Home Affairs to Minister for Defence).

16 Dorothy Macardle, *The Irish Republic* (London: Victor Gollancz, 1937), p. 871. A number of the women were arrested in connection with publicity and logistical activities. The CID raid on the IRA's publicity HQ in North Great George's Street on the evening of 20 March 1923 resulted in fourteen arrests, of whom six were women, and, of these, three were described as 'leading members of Cumann na mBan'. Besides thousands of copies of the republican *Daily Bulletin* and other literature, guns were discovered under floorboards and materials for the manufacture of explosives in a garden shed. As they were removed from the premises, the women prisoners, it was reported, 'laughed, cheered, and shouted "Up the Republic"' (*Irish Times*, 22 March 1923, 8e). The government had evidently lost patience with republican publicity women. Four months earlier, there had been an army raid on the republican publicity offices at 23 Suffolk Street. The press reported that the raiders had found 'only a number of girls and one or two middle-aged women on the premises'. These were regarded with such disdain that they were released and told to go home. The raiders then concentrated on destroying the books and other propaganda material in the offices (*Irish Times*, 10 November 1922, 5d). In the intervening period, someone in the government had worked out that the essence of propaganda was not the materials, easily destroyed and equally easily replaced but rather those who worked in this department of the republican organisation. 'Girls and middle-aged women' could do a lot of damage, it was now seen: best to lock them up.

17 *Irish Times*, 29 March 1923, 5d. According to Maud Gonne, the stoppage of parcels, letters and newspapers, which began in mid-March, extended to all Free State prisons and internment camps.

18 Macardle, *The Irish Republic, op. cit.*, p. 872; *Irish Times*, 3 April 1923, 5f.

19 MA, BMH, CD 6/40/1, Sighle Bowen to IRA Director of Publicity, 24 March 1923. Bowen reported that the matrons (wardresses) were no use (i.e. could not be used as couriers, etc.) and that the women did not come into contact with the Army (who guarded the perimeter of the prison).

20 At the Cumann na mBan Special Convention in Dublin on 5 February 1922, the vote was reported to be 419 to sixty-three against the Treaty (*Irish Times*, 11 February 1922, 5e). This vote has acquired the patina and durability of an historic monument. In her thoroughly researched account of the meeting, Ann Matthews points out that the vote was a rejection of a pro-Treaty amendment not the substantive resolution. This, when later put, was carried by a show of hands, producing a majority of 312 delegates (out of a notional 600) in favour of the anti-Treaty resolution. Ann Matthews, *Renegades: Irish Republican Women, 1900–1922* (Cork: Mercier Press, 2010), pp. 318–20. The organisation was much more divided than republican historiography allows, particularly between the Dublin leadership and the provincial branches. The start of the Civil War increased pressures, and the organisation began to shed a substantial portion of its membership.

21 Kathleen Clarke (1878–1972) married Tom Clarke in 1901. She returned to Dublin in 1907 and engaged in the production of republican publications and in organisational work. After the Rising, she had the ordeal of visiting her husband and brother before their respective executions on 3 and 4 May. Thereafter at the heart of Sinn Féin and Cumann na mBan activities, imprisoned by the British and taking the anti-Treaty side in the Civil War. Long-time activist on behalf of prisoners' dependants. A Fianna Fáil founder member, she was critical of de Valera's leadership. First female Lord Mayor of Dublin (1939–41) and strong supporter of women's rights. Mary MacSwiney (1872–1942) was born in the working-class district of Bermondsey (London) of an English mother and Irish father. The family moved to Cork in 1879 and over the succeeding years Mary struggled with her health and to complete her education, eventually becoming a teacher and (at the age of forty) obtaining her BA from

University College, Cork. She supported a number of reform and radical causes, from female suffrage to physical-force nationalism and republicanism. Achieved national and international fame during and after her brother Terence's hunger strike (August–October 1920). Took anti-Treaty side and twice secured her release from Free State prisons by hunger-striking (November 1922 and April 1923). Broke utterly and bitterly with de Valera in 1927 and remained an irreconcilable republican until her death. She was elected to the (pre-independence) Dáil and thereafter was a participant in increasingly sectarian and marginalised political groupings. See Charlotte H. Fallon's comprehensive (and partisan) biography, *Soul of Fire* (Cork: Mercier, 1986). Muriel MacSwiney (1892–1982) came from a substantial middle-class background and was educated at home and then in a convent in England. Involved as a supporter and helper in what turned out to be the inconsequential events of 1916 in Cork. Married Terence MacSwiney in June 1917, despite her family's strong disapproval. Equivocal about her husband's hunger strike. Active in republican publicity in the USA in 1920 and again (in the anti-Treaty cause) in 1922. Declared herself to be an atheist and embraced left-wing causes, spending much of the 1920s and 1930s on the Continent, settling in England with the fall of France in 1940. In 1950 was granted a pension by the Republic of Ireland.

22 Including, for example, Áine Ceannt, the widow of Éamonn Ceannt, one of the executed leaders of the Rising; Mary (Molly) Childers (née Osgood) widow of Erskine, executed by the Free State on 24 November 1922; and Nora Connolly O'Brien, the second eldest daughter of James Connolly, a first-aider in the Rising and, for a time, paymaster of the anti-Treaty IRA. There were also the three O'Brien sisters – Anne, aged sixteen, Lily, eighteen, and Eileen, sixteen – who had been stationed at Marrowbone Lane with the Volunteers during Easter Week. Cecilia Gallagher (née Saunders) married Frank Gallagher, the Sinn Féin publicist and journalist, who, during the Anglo-Irish War, was on hunger strike at Mountjoy Prison for forty days, a well-known anti-Treaty activist. Elizabeth (Lily) O'Brennan was the sister of Áine Ceannt. She had been a secretary to the Treaty delegation and then to the Provisional government's Arthur Griffith. Changing sides, she became secretary to Erskine Childers and was arrested at the Sinn Féin offices in Suffolk Street.

23 *Irish Times*, 8 January 1923, 7e. Gonne attributed her speedy release to the fact that she was well known abroad, particularly in America, and also because Charlotte Despard (see below, n. 42) had immediately informed the press that she had been arrested. Shortly after her release she addressed a hastily arranged public meeting in Dublin's Sackville Street.

24 See McConville, *Irish Political Prisoners, op. cit.*, pp. 631–5.

25 National Library of Ireland (NLI), MS. 15, 001, undated but almost certainly shortly after her release. For an account of visiting justices who were appointed to visit the prisons and report on conditions, to hear complaints and to adjudicate on the more serious breaches of discipline, see Seán McConville, *English Local Prisons, 1860–1900: Next Only to Death* (London and New York: Routledge, 1995), Chapter 10. The Free State did not discontinue Visiting Committees but in the administrative chaos of the times they became inactive. They were fully re-established in 1925, appointed by central government rather than by grand juries as had been the arrangement before independence. See Shane Kilcommins, Ian O'Donnell, Eoin O'Sullivan and Barry Vaughan (eds.), *Crime, Punishment and the Search for Order in Ireland* (Dublin: IPA, 2004), pp. 41–2. See also Prisons (Visiting Committees) Act, 1925, ss.2(1–4) and 5(5). The rules for Visiting Committees were set out in a Statutory Instrument (unnumbered) of 3 June 1925. Rules 3 and 4 obliged members of the Committee to visit the prison 'at frequent intervals'; Rule 14 directed them to report to the Minister any abuses or required repairs. The point of Gonne's complaint was that in 1923 this valuable and

corrective instrument of external inspection had ceased to operate. See *Dáil Debates*, vol. 10, cols 262–4, 18 February 1925.

26 In the case of Kathleen Barry, Gonne claimed, there had been a serious misdiagnosis. Barry had been ill in bed for three weeks, suffering from typhoid but having been diagnosed with 'hysteria'. Eventually the doctor realised her true state, and she was transferred to the Mater Hospital. Gonne was misinformed about prison doctors. Whilst they would have visited the infirmary daily to see patients, they had no obligation and indeed no need to visit the general population of the prison. It was, however, the legal duty of the governor or his deputy to visit all parts of the prison.

27 Gonne claimed that one of the criminal prisoners had a few weeks previously been shot in the eye whilst in his cell: 'he lost his eye and is now in a Dublin hospital' (NLI, MS. 15, 001). Máire Comerford, who was in Mountjoy in January 1923, was shot in the leg by a sentry: she had been waving at other women prisoners. See Uinseann MacEoin, *Survivors* (Dublin: Argenta, 1980), p. 49.

28 NLI, MS. 15,001.

29 NAI S1369/3/7, Office of Military Governor, NDU, to Adjutant General, 6 June 1923. See also (for the Mountjoy transfer) NAI S2151, Violent Resistance of Transfer to NDU on 26–7 April 1923.

30 NLI, Hearn Papers, MS. 15, 994, Sighle Humphreys to Máire Comerford, 5 October 1923. A critical difference in the new accommodation was that it was not cellular, as were Kilmainham and Mountjoy, but consisted of day rooms and wards or dormitories. This meant that the women were not cramped together in overcrowded cells and that they had greater freedom of movement. By the end of October, a problem with heating seems to have been resolved, with Sighle's sister Anna reporting that plenty of coal had been allowed in the dormitories (see p. 255 below).

31 Karl Spindler had been captain of the German gun-running ship *Aud*. He had published a memoir the previous year: *Gun Running for Casement in the Easter Rebellion, 1916* (London: Collins, 1921).

32 Humphreys's unconcern at being a prisoner (real or feigned) was taken by the authorities as defiance, and, when she and Máire Comerford had pressed for improved conditions at Mountjoy, both were put in punishment cells. They responded to this with a hunger strike and were restored to their comrades within a few days. The concessions were granted. MacEoin, *Survivors, op. cit.*, p. 347.

33 Humphreys Papers, P/106/1194, Mary Lambert to Sighle Humphreys, 24 August 1937.

34 Humphreys Papers, P/106/393, Nell Humphreys to Emmet Humphreys (her son), 4 January 1923.

35 Dorothy Macardle (1889–1958). Supported the 1916 Rising and was a prominent republican publicist during the Anglo-Irish War. Took the anti-Treaty side and was a devout follower of de Valera, becoming a member of the first executive of Fianna Fáil. Her account of the emergence of modern Irish nationalism, although that of a de Valera loyalist, was written to high scholarly standard. Her father was a wealthy Dundalk brewer. Alexandra College was (and is) a highly regarded Church of Ireland girls' school.

36 Muriel MacSwiney, on a speaking tour of the USA, had placed her child in the charge of Madame O'Rahilly. Sister of the 1916 tragic and romantic hero, The O'Rahilly, she had been arrested, as had Mary MacSwiney, the child's formal guardian. Macardle was asked to find out who had the child but on visiting the Suffolk Street headquarters of Sinn Féin was arrested in a raid. The network of friendship between these republican women is further illustrative of what was in effect an extended family. See *Freeman's Journal*, 13 November 1922, 6f. Tours by republican activists and sympathisers were a key part of the reaching out to Irish

America and the garnering of political support and, vitally, finance. They had begun during the years leading up to and after the 1916 Rising, had increased in volume and importance during the Anglo-Irish War and were part of the contested ground of the Civil War. Women became key figures in these campaigns. For further detail and analysis, see Joanne Mooney Einhacker's interesting and extremely useful study, *Irish Republican Women in America: Lecture Tours, 1916–1925* (Dublin: Irish Academic Press, 2003).

37 NAI TAOIS/S1369/18, Imprisonment of Miss Dorothy Macardle.

38 Macardle had taken their case to Fleet Street and had interviewed or otherwise asked a number of prominent English figures to intervene. These included Margot Asquith, Bonar Law, Lord Haldane, Sir John Simon and Sir Hamar Greenwood. Sir Thomas observed, 'as far as I know this got her into looking after the prisoners, and that was the main thing that occupied her attention outside her own business' (NAI TAOIS, Sir Thomas Macardle to R. J. Baker, Secretary to President Cosgrave, 19 December 1922). The fond father evidently did not know the strength of his daughter's convictions nor the extent of her subversive activities. For Conway and Potter, see the *Irish Independent*, 1 March 1921, 5c; and *Freeman's Journal*, 7 March 1921, 3c.

39 No communication – letters or visits – was then permitted to any detainees.

40 NAI TAOIS/S1369/18, Mulcahy to W. T. Cosgrave, 13 January 1923.

41 NAI TAOIS/S1369/18, Lady Macardle to W. T. Cosgrave, 17 January 1923. The frustrated mother surely had a point about the comparative degrees of culpability and punishment.

42 Charlotte Despard (née French) (1844–1939). Born into an Anglo-Irish family in Co. Roscommon. Her brother, Lord French, was a distinguished soldier, commanding the British Expeditionary Force in France (1914) and in May 1918 becoming an uncompromising Lord Lieutenant of Ireland, a position he retained throughout the most bitter period of Anglo-Irish conflict. Charlotte was a militant suffragette and socialist. She opposed the Treaty and in later years supported attempts to build a Communist party in Northern Ireland, across the sectarian divide. Her brother disowned her and even on his deathbed in 1925 refused to receive her. Hers is a familiar form and face in the newspaper photographs of the various prison-gate vigils on behalf of political prisoners, both British and Free State.

43 NAI TAOIS/S1369/18, J. J. O'Neill to W. T. Cosgrave, 18 April 1922.

44 NLI, MS. 32, 582 (44), Rose Jacob Diary. The release was followed by a deal of socialising and agitation: 'When we were just writing for Owen to come for tea, Dorothy Macardle entered, gorgeously dressed. She was going over to W.B.Y. [William Butler Yeats] in a great hurry – was released on Saturday and was publishing news of Kilmainham… I went with her to Merrion Square and heard something about the C.I.D. affair at Kilmainham when they were transferred to the N[orth] D[ublin] Union. She was released unconditionally and ascribes it to her father' (entry of Monday, 7 May 1923).

45 Rosamund (Rose) Jacob (1888–1960). Born in Waterford of a well-established Quaker family, but her parents, radically for the times, held humanist and agnostic views. She had a lively and enquiring mind and became active in a number of causes – feminist, republican and vegetarian; she had socialist and later pacifist sympathies. She sided with the anti-Treaty side but wished to see a reconciliation and, in July 1922, with other female activists and prominent personalities, urged a ceasefire on both parties.

46 *Irish Independent*, 22 January 1923, 6g. See also Rosemary Cullen-Owens, *Louie Bennett* (Cork: Cork University Press, 2001), p. 53.

47 NLI, MS. 32, 582(43). Jacob recorded the details of her release: 'Paudeen [the Mountjoy governor] walked in with letters and we continued the applause, louder and louder. He called to me. "Which is your cell?" "Clear that cell." Dorothy

[Macardle] and Nora O'Shea were in it. He then told me I was released and locked me in, first with Dorothy and then with a wardress, to pack. The wardress was to search my luggage. They all came up in a crowd in the hall to shake hands and cheer.'

48 See p. 44, n. 51 above.

49 See McConville, *Irish Political Prisoners, op. cit.*, pp. 483 and 735–53 for an account of Mary MacSwiney's activities at this time.

50 Hers was recognised as perhaps the most irreconcilable and anti-British Dáil speech on the Treaty (*Dáil Debates*, vol. 3, cols. 108–27, 21 December 1922). Among the many fiery passages in her long speech she warned that, should people of the country set up the Free State, 'I will be a rebel, a deliberate rebel, for the first time in my life.' She evidently discounted her struggle against what she considered to be the illegitimate authority of British rule. She also took the line to which she would adhere thereafter: 'I speak for the living Republic, the Republic cannot die… The Irish Republic was proclaimed and established by the Easter Week, 1916. The Irish Republican Government was established in January 1919, and it has functioned since under such conditions that no country ever worked under before' (col. 126). This was the definitive republican position in the years and decades that followed.

51 See p. 21 above.

52 Edward Joseph Byrne (1872–1940). Educated Dublin and Rome (Royal University of Ireland and Irish College, respectively). Early clerical posts in diocese of Dublin before returning to Rome as Vice-Rector of the Irish College. Appointed Auxiliary Bishop of Dublin in 1920, becoming Archbishop in August 1921, thus holding senior positions through the bitterest periods of the Anglo-Irish War. Favoured the Treaty but sought to promote peace between the sides. Attempted to stop the summary executions of 8 December 1922 and also sought to end the republican hunger strikes. His support for the new state was tempered by a caution about the moral limitations of state power.

53 NAI TAOIS/S1369/9, Mary MacSwiney to Archbishop Edward Byrne, 5 November 1922. See also UCDA, Mary MacSwiney Papers, p. 48. Her argument, as it often did, switched to hyperbole: 'you are supporting perjurers, job-hunters, materialists and driving away those who stand for truth, honour and the sanctity of oaths'.

54 MacSwiney Papers, p. 48. Only two years ago, as her brother's body was brought home, snatched by the British and buried surrounded by armoured cars, who would have thought that 'Dick Mulcahy, one of his closest friends, would condemn his sister to the same suffering for the same cause'.

55 The bishops' pastoral of 10 October 1922 had provoked a furious response from republicans, who, with Mary MacSwiney, saw it as the enlistment of religion in the cause of the Free State. Prisoners' letters and memoirs abound with expressions of this indignation, which was a theme running back to a similar stance of the bishops during the years of the Fenian campaigns of the 1860s and 1870s. During the Civil War, there was a special bitterness at the refusal of chaplains to offer the consolations of their religion to the condemned. The pastoral letter also stimulated several pamphlets. See, for example, Proinsias Ó Gallchobhair, *The Bishops' Pastoral: A Prisoner's Letter to His Grace the Archbishop of Dublin* (Glasgow: Kirkwood & Co., n.d.) (a copy is to be found in the Dorothy Macardle Collection at the MA, BMH, CD 9/6/4). In the same vein, see Anon. ('A Priest'), 'Reply to the Pastoral Issued by the Irish Hierarchy, October 1922' (in the Fintan Murphy Collection at MA, BMH, CD 227/34/76).

56 NAI TAOIS/S1369/9. See also MacSwiney Papers, p. 48. Archbishop Edward Byrne to Mary MacSwiney, 8 November 1922. Two points are of interest in this response. The theological basis for the bishops' pastoral is not made clear: their authority alone seems to be conclusive. Byrne also seemed to hint at a 'don't ask,

don't tell' solution. Referring to the prison chaplain's duty, he observed that, 'If anyone in Mountjoy *openly manifests* to the chaplain *an intention of contravening* this authorised teaching' then he had no option but to follow the directions set out in the pastoral (my emphasis). This careful wording suggests that the Archbishop would have welcomed discretion as a means to circumvent the prohibitions that he was defending. His clergy might have felt that this shifted an unfair burden of interpretation to them.

57 NAI TAOIS/S1369/9, Archbishop Edward Joseph Byrne to W. T. Cosgrave, 16 November 1922.

58 NAI TAOIS/S1369/9, Michael A. Kelly (New York City) to W. T. Cosgrave, 8 November 1922.

59 NAI TAOIS/S1369/9.

60 *Freeman's Journal*, 11 November 1922, 5d. The three women were Sighle Humphreys, Miss H. Murphy and Madame O'Rahilly. The male prisoner was unnamed.

61 NAI TAOIS/S1369/9. It says something of the degeneration of temper and the seeming acceptance of such abuse in public discourse that Annie was not arrested for what was a death threat. Officials may have concluded, however, that she was seeking not merely to vent her rage but to join Mary in Mountjoy.

62 NAI TAOIS/S1369/9, Report from M. H. O'Connor, Senior Medical Officer, Mountjoy, 8 November 1922.

63 NAI TAOIS/S1369/9, Report of Major-General M. Hayes, 11 October 1922.

64 *Irish Times*, 20 November 1922, 5e; 21 November, 5e. The Archbishop had ordered the gates of his property closed against the women, but a number nevertheless entered. Some sat on the entrance steps to the residence whilst others explored the grounds. Eventually Dr Byrne relented and a deputation was allowed to make their case. This consisted of Maud Gonne, Charlotte Despard and Constance Markievicz. No statement was issued as to the exchanges.

65 *Irish Independent*, 18 November 1922, 5f. The Dublin Corporation Committee on the Treatment of Prisoners had been meeting at the Mansion House. It was decided, because of the absence of Mr Lynn, who had been representing the prisoners, to adjourn proceedings. The women in attendance expressed their dissatisfaction, and Gonne invited the committee members to accompany her to Mountjoy to hear from Annie MacSwiney, who was keeping vigil at the prison gate. The invitation was declined, but the women left in procession.

66 *Irish Times*, 21 November 1922, 5e.

67 NAI TAOIS/S1369/3/7; *Irish Times*, 28 November 1922, 5e.

68 Kathleen O'Callaghan (1888–1961) was a member of the Second Dáil for Limerick City–Limerick East (1921–2). She retained her position in the 1922 election but refused to take her seat in the Third Dáil and was defeated in the 1923 election. She also had a close connection to a republican martyr, for which she was known throughout the country and beyond. Her husband Michael had been Mayor of Limerick, as well as a leading figure in the IRA. On 7 March 1921, she saw him murdered by Black and Tans, who had come to their home. On the same day, George Clancy, the serving Mayor of Limerick, was also shot and his wife wounded as she tried to shield him. The murders became a national and international cause célèbre.

69 *Irish Independent*, 1 May 1923, 4f. O'Callaghan was released because of medical certification that she was in a dangerous state of health. Mary MacSwiney was also said to be in a serious state but at that point evidently insufficiently so to persuade the authorities that they should release her.

70 NLI, MS. 5815, Irish Prison Conditions, Civil War, Letter of Annie Hogan, 1 May 1923. The forcible removal to the NDU became part of republican folklore. See the

ballad 'The Transfer of Women Prisoners from Kilmainham Jail to NDU' in Humphreys Papers, P/106/1061, 1 May 1923.

71 NAI TAOIS/S1369/3/8, Military Governor, NDU, to Adjutant General, 6 June 1923. The Governor named Mrs Gordon and Bridie O'Mullane as having assaulted the police and female searchers.

72 NLI, MS. 5815, Irish Prison Conditions, Civil War, Iseult Stuart, Statement of 16 May 1923. Stuart had been in custody for one month (10 April to 11 May). Iseult Stuart (1894–1954) was Maud Gonne's natural daughter from her relationship with Lucien Millevoye. In childhood she was concealed from Gonne's circle of friends and was raised in France. Gonne entered into a spectacularly disastrous marriage with John MacBride (shot for his part in the Rising) during which Iseult allegedly became his sexual victim. She was closely acquainted with W. B. Yeats, at first through her mother and then as the object of Yeats's romantic attachment. Iseult married Francis Stuart in 1919. Twenty years later, he took up a position at Berlin University. Through his recommendation, the German agent, Hermann Görtz, made contact and stayed at Iseult's Wicklow home. She was subsequently arrested and put on trial by the Irish authorities but was acquitted. A remarkable and in many ways tragic life.

73 NLI, MS. 5815, undated statement. There were allegations of a similar violent removal of women from Mountjoy on 26 April 1923. A statement by Nora Spillane on behalf of Sorcha MacDermott referred to this operation. Máire Comerford was so badly beaten about the head that she needed three stitches. Mary McDermott had her wrist broken. The clothing of other women was cut off as they were thrown down the steps in the cell block (Statement of 28 April 1923). Whatever the precise truth of these events, there clearly was rough handling and high feelings of antagonism on both sides. The Military Governor of Mountjoy, E. Cahill, confirmed that there was violent resistance to the women searchers and that there were injuries (NAI S2115). Máire Comerford got something of her own back, when she and several others managed to slip through the inexpertly laid barbed wire at the NDU. To the embarrassment of the authorities, she was at large for a month and, when rearrested, went on hunger strike at Kilmainham. She was released after twenty-seven days. See MacEoin, *Survivors*, *op. cit.*, pp. 49–50.

74 UCDA, Margaret Burke Papers, P/30/7, Margaret Burke (writing from the NDU) to her sister Nora, 1 May 1923. She concluded by thanking Nora 'for the two parcels of cake'. Things cannot have been too bad.

75 NAI JUS/90/16/566, The MacDermott, Vice Chairman of the General Prisons Board, to Secretary of Ministry of Home Affairs, 3 May 1923. It is relevant that the transfer of female prisoners from Mountjoy to the NDU on the night of 26/7 April was also accompanied by disturbance. See above, pp. 252–4; MA, BMH, CD 6/40/1, folder May 1923.

76 Nell Ryan (?–1959) had carried despatches for the anti-Treaty forces, was arrested in Wexford and transferred to Kilmainham. In later years she was active and prominent in Fianna Fáil, occupying a number of public positions in Wexford. She, her sister Phyllis, and her brother Jim took the anti-Treaty side. Another sister (Min) was married to Richard Mulcahy. See Sinéad McCoole, *No Ordinary Women: Irish Female Activists in the Revolutionary Years, 1900–23* (Dublin: The O'Brien Press, 2003), pp. 206–8.

77 NLI MS. 5815, Maud Gonne to members of the Dáil, 10 April 1923.

78 On 24 October 1923, the women's OC wrote from the NDU to the Director of Intelligence of Cumann na mBan, listing the women who would begin their strike that day. The issue had divided the prisoners, she noted. Some believed that the hunger strike was a new phase in the struggle and that 'we would be shirking our duty to the Republic if we did not fall in line with the men'. Others, however, saw it

as a publicity campaign or as being illogical since NDU conditions were 'fairly decent'. Some also argued against their strike on the grounds that it diverted public attention away from the treatment of the Mountjoy prisoners and others held elsewhere. Personally, and for many reasons, she did not agree with the action. Instead of helping the Mountjoy men, 'who struck for very definite reasons', a strike by the women would only divert public attention from 'the vile treatment the Mountjoy prisoners received'. She also considered that 'very few of the girls here are fit subjects for a protracted hunger strike and if they were released after 40 or so days would need a great deal of care and attention which very few of them could afford' (Humphreys Papers, P/106/1172, OC to Director of Intelligence, Cumann na mBan, 24 October 1923).

79 Mary O'Rahilly, writing to Elgin (Eileen), her mother, on 30 October 1923, confessed that she did not know whether she was 'sorry or glad'. She said that she felt terrible and, with everyone, was 'absolutely miserable thinking of you all', adding 'you two kids are much too young to be on'. Anxious to help, she asked if any hunger-striker who did not have relatives in Dublin wanted anything sent in: 'lemons, soda water, etc.' UCDA, Elgin O'Rahilly Papers, P/200/92/1, Mary O'Rahilly to Elgin, 30 October 1923.

80 Humphreys Papers, P/106/197, Anna Humphreys to Nell Humphreys, 28 October 1923.

81 Humphreys Papers, P/106/198, Sighle Humphreys to mother, 1 November 1923.

82 Humphreys Papers, P/106/199, Anna Humphreys to Dick Humphreys, dated November 1923. The imaginative creation of meals seems to fall more in the category of self-torment than consolation, but it was not uncommon.

83 Humphreys Papers, P/106/200, Anna Humphreys to Nell Humphreys, dated November 1923.

84 Humphreys Papers, P/106/201, Anna Humphreys to Nell Humphreys, 25 November 1923. She continued, 'I was going to write a nice long letter but she came in and started talking and now I am too hungry and am only to have milk and biscuits before going to sleep when we could eat a loaf of bread.'

85 NAI TAOIS/S1369/4, Return(s) of Military Prisoners in Custody. The last two were freed on the evening of 22 December 1923.

86 MacEoin, *Survivors, op. cit.*, p. 347.

87 These women, republicans all, were not members of the IRA and therefore not subject to its discipline. Since the point of their action had been to support the men, it would have been pointless for the women to have continued alone. There is no indication in the surviving documents and memoirs that they were involved in discussions about the cessation of the strike. The visit by Derrig and Robinson was to communicate a decision already made rather than to consult.

88 NAI TAOIS/S1369/3/8, Eilis Ní Mhurchadha to unnamed (presumably W. T. Cosgrave), 28 June 1923; NLI, Sheehy-Skeffington Papers, MS. 33, 606.

89 Thus, in late December 1924, with most of the republican prisoners released, Sheehy-Skeffington was enlisted by the PPC (whose members included Maud Gonne) to speak at a protest meeting in O'Connell Street, Dublin. Sheehy-Skeffington Papers, MS. 33, 606, letter of 11 December 1924.

90 See Peter Martin's valuable study, *Censorship in the Two Irelands* (Dublin: Irish Academic Press, 2006). Newspaper censorship began in the Free State in July 1922. The newspapers were expected to censor themselves, and there were curbs on the sale of English newspapers and journals. Piaras Béaslaí, as *pro tem* Publicity Director of the National Army, was a central figure, his restrictions ranging widely, from reports of the sales of coffins to IRA publicity and criticism of the authorities. See Martin, *Censorship in the Two Irelands, op. cit.*, pp. 15–18, 21 and 24, for example.

91 There are photographs of such demonstrations in the impressive photographic account of the times by Tim Pat Coogan and George Morrison, *The Irish Civil War* (London: Orion, 1999). See Plates 302, 303, 326 and 330.

92 *Irish Times*, 8 October 1923, 3b. Gonne also spoke at the meeting, protesting at the restrictions on exercise for the men in Mountjoy but making no reference to the prisoners' behaviour, which the authorities cited as the reason for the tightening of custody.

93 *Irish Independent*, 23 July 1923, 7b. Mary MacSwiney also spoke at length at the meeting, noting, *inter alia*, that 'the war was temporarily over'. Mary Clancy, the widow of George Clancy, the murdered Mayor of Limerick, was a member of the platform party at the demonstration but apparently did not speak.

94 *Irish Times*, 3 September 1923, 6f.

95 Fr. Fagan denounced what he described as the muzzling of bishops who were sympathetic to the republican cause, together with priests. The Irish press was similarly muzzled, and, he proclaimed, '[t]he only thing to do was to throw the damned muzzle to hell' (*Irish Times*, 10 July 1923, 6a).

96 *Irish Times*, 18 July 1923, 6c. Professor McCaffrey, chairman of South Dublin Rural council, joined Caitlín Brugha on the platform. Both were relatively immune from arrest.

97 *Irish Times*, 28 July 1924, 6a. The established format was to make speeches and then, with placards denouncing various aspects of the prisoners' confinement, to march to the gates of Mountjoy. It also seems to have been usual during these months for Gonne to play a leading role. Richard Fox, a close friend, recalled of these meetings that '[i]n some strange fashion her presence filled that great audience with a sense of irresistible power'. The demonstration had a definite feminine quality: 'She carried a huge bouquet of flowers and looked radiant.' Richard Michael Fox, *Rebel Irishwomen* (Cork: Talbot Press, 1935), p. 13.

98 *Irish Times*, 9 January 1923, 6g.

99 Cohalan referred to the conclusions of National Synod no. 114. Daniel Cohalan (1858–1952). Born in the nationalist Kilmichael district of Co. Cork, served as Bishop of Cork from 1916 to 1952. During the War of Independence, he had criticised both the British forces and the IRA. He was particularly strong in his condemnation of the treatment of Terence MacSwiney. With a strong stance against violence, Cohalan was a powerful critic from within the nationalist camp.

100 *Irish Independent*, 21 October 1922, 6f; see also *Irish Times*, 17 November 1922, 4f.

101 *Irish Independent*, 21 October 1922, 6f. Men also collected at church gates and on occasion confronted the clergy. On 26 November 1922, a group of young men were rebuked at the gates of a Lurgan (Co. Armagh) church. A policeman was in attendance, and, as the incident developed, four of the young men drew revolvers 'and became very defiant towards priest and policeman' (*Freeman's Journal*, 27 November 1922, 5c).

102 The Red Cross, on the basis of government figures, estimated that there were rather fewer than 12,000 in custody in April 1923 (NAI S1369/3/6), quoting ICRC visits in April–May 1923.

103 *Irish Independent*, 2 June 1923, 4a; *Anglo-Celt*, 23 June 1923, 5b.

104 See McConville, *Irish Political Prisoners, op. cit.*, pp. 578–9.

105 See NLI, MS. 5815, Irish Prison Conditions, Civil War 1922–4, Conn Mac Marcada (Sinn Féin HQ) to Alice Stopford Green, 24 October 1923. This was a plea for her intercession in the October–November hunger strike, but it was expressed in intemperate language which can scarcely have appealed to her.

106 This and following details of the incident are taken from a lengthy letter from Gonne and others published in the *Irish Independent* on 11 July 1923, 8e. The other signatories

were Charlotte Despard, Mary MacSwiney, Marlon K. Malley, Albinia Brodrick, Kate Boland and Sarah Mellows.

107 Kathleen Lynn (1874–1955), the daughter of a Church of Ireland priest. Had an extended international education, graduating from medical school in 1899. Espoused female suffrage as well as nationalism and joined the Irish Citizen Army. Following the Rising was imprisoned in Kilmainham. Taking the anti-Treaty side was elected (as an abstentionist) to the Dáil in 1923. A natural advocate of prisoners' causes.

108 Áine (aka Frances, Fanny) Ceannt (née O'Brennan) (1880–1954). Came to nationalism and republicanism through the Irish language revival. Met and was courted by Éamonn Ceannt, who played a prominent part in the Rising. Following his execution, involved herself in Cumann na mBan, Sinn Féin and public life generally. Continued to be involved in prisoner-relief works through a later generation of IRA activities and was a founding member of the Irish White Cross (see p. 217 above). Madeleine ffrench-Mullen (1880–1944). Joined the Irish Citizen Army on her return from several years in Belgium and Germany. Participated in the Rising as a nurse. Arrested with Markievicz, was briefly interned in Kilmainham. Together with Kathleen Lynn, in 1919 she established an infants' hospital. She was a member of Sinn Féin and urged it to adopt a social charter.

109 To take but one example, see the complaint by James Everett, Labour member for Wicklow about the appalling conditions of Wicklow Prison. The complaint was not gainsaid by the government. Mulcahy acknowledged the 'unsatisfactory conditions' at the prison but blamed the destruction wrought by prisoners elsewhere in the system for the lack of resources. See *Dáil Debates*, vol. 4, cols. 96–102, *passim*, 3 July 1923.

110 *Dáil Debates*, vol. 4, cols. 103–5, 3 July 1923. Details were also given of visits to Tintown (Curragh) and Grangegorman camps, as well as Mountjoy.

111 *Dáil Debates*, vol. 4, cols. 103–5, 3 July 1923. He noted that, during his sojourn in Ireland, three of the striking women were released.

112 Many of the suffragists and pacifists imprisoned in England in the years preceding, during and following the First World War were, by experience, similarly convinced of the need for reform and a more humane approach to penal policy. Their interest either dwindled upon release or was subsumed into agitation on wider social issues. Those who attempted to follow the path of prison reform had remarkably little success, considering their talent and the first-hand insights that they could bring to public and politicians. For more on this, see Seán McConville, 'Hearing, Not Listening: Penal Policy and the Political Prisoners of 1906–21', in Lucia Zedner and Andrew Ashworth (eds.), *The Criminological Foundations of Penal Policy: Essays in Honour of Roger Hood* (Oxford: Oxford University Press, 2003), pp. 238–68.

6

THE INTER-WAR YEARS
IN THE SOUTH

What is to be done?

The IRA's military defeat, culminating in the ceasefire and dump-arms order of 24 May 1923, began half a century of sporadically interrupted decline and isolation from the mass of the Irish people. Although often treated as two distinct periods in the organisation's history, the years of Cosgrave rule up to March 1932 and de Valera's pre-war governments are merely episodes in this longer process. With Cosgrave in office, the IRA's purpose seemed clear enough: regroup for a second round of civil war and assert the power of the Republic, already in existence but betrayed by those who had signed and upheld the Treaty. When de Valera came to office there was at first the hope that, despite his apostasy and break with Sinn Féin, the Republic would be redeclared and the apparatus of the state subsumed. De Valera and his followers took the opposite view, that with Fianna Fáil now in power the IRA had no purpose and should dissolve itself. When the IRA failed to see this a clash became inevitable. There could only be one master in the republican household.

Devotion to the cherished but desolated Republic was not enough for revolutionaries. There had to be action, and that needed purpose. During the fifteen years from the ceasefire until the IRA began preparations for its bombing campaign in Britain it struggled to answer the question, 'what is the IRA for?' Over almost half a century, up to the beginning of the Northern Ireland troubles in the late 1960s, the failure convincingly to address those outside its ranks was far more debilitating than the 1923 military defeat. How can an army regroup, retrain and rearm unless it has a strategic purpose? Under Cosgrave, the objective might have been stated simply: to overthrow traitors and take power by force of arms. But this clarity faded in the process of the IRA's reconstruction: means replaced ends and were all the more rewarding for that: short-term action, swagger, flourish and tail-twisting here and now, tangible and measurable, against an increasingly abstract and elusive Republic.

The republican movement in conflict with the British appeared monolithic, but this was misleading. Sinn Féin and the IRA were separate organisations, with very different origins. Largely the difference lay in their character: one a military body under discipline and the other a relatively open political organisation. They agreed on the general objective – a united Irish Republic – but there were sufficient doctrinal distinctions for differences in the pace of travel and in emphasis and tactics. In the inter-war period, tensions were bound to emerge. Cumann na mBan remained unwaveringly devoted to the 1916 Republic and was constantly on the alert for any backsliding. Its purpose was auxiliary to the IRA, but its influence was considerable. Na Fianna Éireann, founded by Constance Markievicz and Bulmer Hobson in 1909, functioned as a republican boy-scout movement and IRA cadet force. In addition to these, dwindling away by the attrition of years, was the anti-Treaty section of the Second Dáil. The Nicene Creed of republicans held that this body, elected on the last all-Ireland franchise, had never dissolved itself and had merely been usurped. This remnant and the government it chose (of which Éamon de Valera was until 1926 the President) had long since lost all practical executive power, but the preservation of the entity – however theoretically – was basic to republican claims of legitimacy. (This doctrine, and the various steps in a continuous succession, has persisted into modern times, the basis of claimed organic links to the Easter Rising and its Proclamation.) But towering over all of these and giving them purpose and pace was the IRA itself, which, at the end of the Civil War, had an active membership in the region of several thousand (including those in prisons and camps) with a much larger body of supporters of varying degrees of involvement.[1] It was a key point in its later history (and one insisted on in modern times) that although defeated in the field the IRA had not surrendered its weapons, merely ordered that they be stored. Equally, it had not left the field but had ordered the cessation of all offensive actions.[2]

With peace regained after seven years of fairly continuous strife and much destruction, Cosgrave and his colleagues bent every effort to the consolidation of the Free State: police, army, courts, civil service, local government and all the other instruments of governance. The IRA engaged in a parallel exercise, reconnecting with its units, recruiting, training and rearming. These subversive preparations inevitably provoked special legislation, and, in June 1925, the government brought in the Treasonable Offences Act to replace the recently lapsed Public Safety Act.[3] The Act was comprehensively directed at the legislature, government, administration and armed force which the IRA represented to be the alternative state in waiting.[4] The Firearms (Temporary Provisions) Act, 1924, placed severe restrictions on the possession of guns.[5] The police force was reorganised in April 1925 by amalgamating the Civic Guard (which had replaced the RIC) and the Dublin Metropolitan Police. The new body was to be known as the Gárda Siothchána (later spelt Garda Siochána).[6]

Sinn Féin had won forty-four seats in the 1923 general election. Since the Treaty was anathema, there could be no question of entering the Dáil (which Sinn Féin referred to as 'Leinster House', as distinct from their genuine and perforce underground Second Dáil). In the months after the last internees returned home, a succession of by-elections began to restore Sinn Féin's electoral fortunes. The Cosgrave government's humiliating ham-fisted handling and rout on the Boundary Commission, together with the everyday pains and grumbles of a country returning to the routine ambitions and frustrations of peace, presented political opportunities to its opponents. To all with experience of practical politics, however, it was clear that whatever satisfaction electors may have achieved by bloodying the nose of the ruling party and supporting abstentionist Sinn Féin candidates, republicanism needed to offer much more were it to hope for a parliamentary majority.[7]

The republican movement, like all political bodies, was a coalition and contained elements which, in the new circumstances, could not live together. On 13 and 14 November 1925, the first step was taken in divorce proceedings. Meeting in general convention, IRA delegates carried a motion noting that the government of the Republic had 'developed into a mere political party', and the organisation therefore cast off its (largely theoretical) subordinancy to the Second Dáil. Thenceforward the IRA would act under an independent executive, empowered to declare war when a suitable opportunity arose.[8]

The second step was de Valera's. He was set far apart from his contemporaries by his strategic vision, political skills and personal control, all artfully bound together by an outstanding ability to touch his constituency. By 1925 he could see no likelihood of a forcible overthrow of the Free State: it was stronger and more entrenched than ever and, without a republican opposition in the legislature, was shaping the country ever more into a dominion. Institutions were being built and habits consolidated that in time might prove impossible to shift. But how to provide an opposition and to take with him the body of his supporters? He had, after all, been the leader of leaders who had led the country into civil war over what could not now be represented as a quibble. The alternative was to sit out the years waiting for a culmination that looked ever more improbable. De Valera wanted power, and that was impossible while he was corralled among fervent but irrelevant purists. Any entry into a usurping Dáil would be seen as a betrayal of the republican ideal and of all who had suffered and died for it. The substantive issue could never be settled for some except by the extirpation of the Free State. But surely there were others who would be satisfied with the removal of unacceptable symbols? At the apex of these was the oath of fealty and allegiance to the Crown. Were that removed, de Valera calculated, he could lead his followers – or at least a sufficient proportion of them – into the Free State Dáil: Sinn Féin's programme at that point would be the realisation of the Republic in incremental and constitutional but nevertheless transformative steps.

The artful politician, like a good tradesman, and unlike the amateur, knows that he must spend more time on preparation than execution. He will, for instance, sometimes espouse one position while aiming for another.[9] There was, therefore, a deal of sounding and of testing once de Valera had made his decision. By the time the Sinn Féin Ard Fheís met on 9 March 1926, he was sure of his course, whatever decision the delegates reached. As it happened, de Valera's resolution was carried by a narrow margin, but with a killer amendment. The way was thus blocked to Sinn Féin's entry into the Dáil. This was a rebuff for which he was ready, with his supporters gathered behind him. Two days later, he resigned as President of the Republic and left Sinn Féin. A month later, his new party, Fianna Fáil, was formed and on 16 May 1926 was inaugurated at its first public meeting in Dublin's La Scala Theatre.[10] An Ard Fheís was announced for 14 November, and in the intervening months branches were organised throughout the country, staff appointed and fund-raising put in hand.

A general election had to be held in 1927, and de Valera and his followers, remarkably, had created sufficient momentum to have reasonable hopes of displacing the Cosgrave government. Once elected, de Valera intended to implement his step-by-step programme. The precise sequence was probably not clear to him at this stage but with the oath removed his party would certainly enter the Dáil. In the June 1927 election, Fianna Fáil won forty-four seats to Cumann na nGaedheal's forty-seven. With a number of other parties returning deputies, albeit in smaller numbers, de Valera was on the threshold of political power. The obstacle remained the oath. But to do the deals to put together the necessary votes to form a government, de Valera had to be in the Dáil. On 23 June, he led his followers into Leinster House but could not get past the Clerk to the Dáil, who insisted on the little preliminary of the oath.[11] The politicians trooped out again, vowing never to take an oath to a foreign king. De Valera indicated that he might use Article 47 of the Free State Constitution to demand a referendum on the oath.[12]

Before this and other options could be explored, however, a shocking incident convulsed the nation and shifted the political balance. Around midday on Sunday, 10 July 1927, Kevin O'Higgins, Minister for Justice and External Affairs, seen as the Cosgrave government's strongman by its opponents, was mortally wounded in a brutal shooting. Opinion was further incensed when it became known that he was attacked while walking to mass at Booterstown church, not far from his home. The shooting was immediately and universally assumed to be the work of the IRA, which had reason to hate him.[13] Despite the organisation's denial of involvement, a number of prominent members were rounded up. Intensive police efforts failed to link any of those arrested to the murder.[14]

No government that wished to survive could fail to respond to such a challenge, and a government so recently put to the test by civil war least of all. Three emergency measures were enacted. A Public Safety Act allowed the government to declare illegal any association that aimed to use force to overthrow the state; membership of such an organisation could be severely punished. The Act, which passed into law on 10 August 1927, also provided extensive rights to search and authorised the setting up of a Special Court with powers to impose the death penalty, or long terms of penal servitude, for the possession of arms. As previously noted, it was conceded that these powers were an exceptional invasion of civil rights, and the measure was repealed sixteen months later when the crisis was deemed to have passed.[15]

Four years after the end of the Civil War, the paramount need was for a fully functioning political system. This could not be secured without the participation of the principal opposition party. Without that, no matter what was said or meant, the legitimacy of the state was in question: de Valera's abstentionism was a constant if passive challenge to the political settlement and indirect encouragement to others to take up arms. Two measures addressed this. The Electoral (Amendment No. 2) Act dealt with the most venerable and potent of Sinn Féin's weapons: seeking a popular mandate for abstention and then constituting an alternative forum or legislature that would drain authority from the established body. To block this tactic, it was provided that every candidate should, when nominated, swear that, if elected, he or she would take the parliamentary oath. Failure to do so within a set time following election would vacate the seat. The Constitution (Amendment No. 10) Act, 1928, blocked off de Valera's referendum option by restricting the right to requisition a referendum to members of the Dáil who had taken the oath. The Act also removed the procedure by which a referendum could alternatively be sought by popular petition.[16]

De Valera had been boxed in. He had travelled too far down the constitutional path and had soiled the hem of his raiment too much to be readmitted to the temple of republican purity. Nor did this wish dwell within even the most remote realm of his ambitions. Despite a civil war having been fought largely on the issue, he now declared the oath to be 'an empty political formula'.[17] On 11 August 1927, he again led his followers into the Dáil, this time signing the book recording acceptance of the oath.[18] This was more than an embarrassment, whatever gloss he put upon it – but in politics even the most painful embarrassment can be endured if the prize is sufficiently desired.[19] To the government and to much of the country, de Valera's turnabout was a blessed relief; to a section of republicans the blackest treachery.

There had been a discounting of de Valera's stock, however, and the strength of indignation and outrage was probably less than he had feared. Mary MacSwiney, Márie Comerford, Sighle Humphreys, Maud Gonne and other republican women who had been close to him were the most vociferous; Constance Markievicz would doubtless have joined them had she not recently died.[20] The IRA's reaction was rather muted. This was due both to the rapid unfolding of events and possibly to the hope that, despite all, Fianna Fáil's step might simply be a ploy to take the Free State from within. Once in the Dáil, de Valera had immediately gone on the attack, joining with Labour in a no-confidence vote. This was a thrilling close-run thing, buoying his followers with the hope of victories to come.[21] Cosgrave survived, but only on the Speaker's casting vote and with a bit of skulduggery.[22] To remove doubts, another election was called, returning Cosgrave with sixty-seven seats and de Valera with fifty-seven.[23] On 10 October 1927, Cosgrave's parliamentary position was secured in a seventy-six to seventy Dáil vote of confidence. The next chance to transfer of power would be in 1932.

While Fianna Fáil deputies honed skills in parliamentary procedure and politics and, in the usual way, promoted the interests of constituents, they also did business with their Dáil colleagues, including Cosgrave's Cumann na nGaedheal. Give and take is the nature of such relationships, and some of the ferocity and bile drained from party politics when faces and names became part of the workaday world. De Valera sought allies among the smaller parties (Labour in particular), but these also had their interests and agendas, and who was to know the necessities of majority-making in 1932? Doors had to be kept open and calculation as well as decency dictated mutual respect. Participation meant a degree of incorporation, but it also changed the process that was joined. Cosgrave and his ministers now saw the lifting of the siege: whatever the eventual electoral outcome, they had prevailed in the larger matter.

The uncertain trumpet

Outside parliamentary politics, the path ahead was not so clear, and the IRA still faced its existential question. Bitterly condemned by some, de Valera's stature as a founding father was such that it was impossible to extinguish the affectionate regard in which he was held by many in the IRA and Sinn Féin, who in some areas assisted Fianna Fáil in getting out the vote. Many agreed with Peadar O'Donnell's editorial in *An Phoblacht* the year before: 'One Movement: Two Groups'.[24] It was also undeniable that many excellent men and women had followed de Valera into Fianna Fáil, persons whose republican credentials could not easily be gainsaid. But none of this pointed the way for the IRA. Mere existence without a strategy would embroil it in conflicts and not be of the most advantageous kind: it would drift and turn in the eddies of events and must ultimately wither into a sect, benign or malign almost entirely by chance.

Unable to attack government forces, IRA units satisfied their need for action in attacks on individuals and other soft targets. These were such a recurrent, persistent and at times outrageous feature of Irish life in the inter-war years that only a massive chronology could cover them.[25] Something of the flavour and impact can be given here. Targets included (at the public-order end of seriousness) shops and other premises displaying British emblems (as often happened on Armistice Day) and films deemed to be pro-British. More deadly were threats and attacks on persons known or suspected of being police agents, as well as witnesses, complainants, police and jurors who were wont to attend too closely to the evidence. The last was a particularly potent threat to law and order, well tested and successful in the war against the British. Jurors were written to and their names were circulated in an obvious invitation to do them harm. A group of men invaded the home of a jury foreman on 23 January 1929 and seriously wounded him.[26] The government responded with a Juries Protection Act.[27] There was, in all this, a deeply worrying sense of increasing violence and gathering disorder. Of all targets, the unarmed police were among the softest and most vulnerable. There was widespread shock when on 11 June 1929 four members of the force were lured to a supposed arms dump and one was killed in a murderous booby-trap explosion. An anonymous letter had been sent to Detective Officer Timothy O'Sullivan of

Knock Station, in Co. Clare. The writer claimed to have found a box of ammunition and papers. He was so frightened of getting into trouble that he had discarded it in a ditch. When O'Sullivan and his colleagues retrieved and tried to open the box, it exploded, killing O'Sullivan immediately and wounding two others.[28]

It was a persistent thread in republican thinking that if the Free State, or elements within its machinery, could be brought into collision or conflict with Britain, revolutionary unity could be regained and the work of the 1916 Rising completed. This had probably lain behind the attack on unarmed British personnel (including dependent women and children) disembarking from Cobh Pier from Spike Island on 21 March 1924. Four men in Free State Army uniforms opened fire with machine guns, killing a British soldier, Private Herbert Aspinall and wounding twenty-eight, two women amongst them.[29] Swift action, including compensation payments and an unqualified apology to the British government, ensured that this grave incident did not block the way to what had become noticeably improved relations between the two states.

There were two alarming incidents in connection with prisoners the following year. In an attempt to rescue Jim Killeen, the IRA leader, and two others, some twenty armed men raided Hill of Down railway station on 6 November 1925, destroying all means of communication. The train on which Killeen was being transported had left minutes earlier so the rescue failed, but the scale of the operation was of great concern.[30] Far more serious was the successful escape of nineteen political offenders from Mountjoy Prison on Friday, 27 November 1925. The audacious, carefully planned and imaginative operation included the entry of six armed men into the prison, successfully passing themselves off as gardaí.[31] Among those who got away were Jim Killeen (whose rescue had failed three weeks before), Seán Russell, Michael Carolan and David Fitzgerald. A month later, on 28 December 1925, Garda Thomas Dowling, unarmed and coming off duty, was ambushed and killed at Fanore, Co. Clare.[32] On the evening of Sunday, 14 November 1926, there were twelve coordinated raids on garda barracks and one on a military post. Telephone and telegraph wires were cut and roads blocked by felling trees. At Cork, Sergeant James Fitzsimmons was killed; and at Hollyford, Co. Tipperary, Garda Henry Ward was wounded at St Luke's Barracks. (Private Thomas Maloney was shot in the stomach when he refused to surrender his revolver.)[33] These attacks continued, on 20 November at Crumlin, Co. Dublin, and at Knockmore, Co. Waterford. Records and equipment seem to have been the principal objectives, though the strategic intention was to undermine the police and to render them inoperative, as had happened with the RIC in the last stages of the War of Independence. The death of two of their colleagues, however, far from cowing the Gardaí, seems to have strengthened their determination to suppress the IRA. Some evidently became enraged, and there were attacks on men in police custody who had been gathered up in connection with the raids. As sometimes happens in such circumstances, zeal had turned into unlawful brutality, and a departmental committee of inquiry was established under the chairmanship of Charles Kenny.[34]

Throughout the post-Civil War years and in the 1930s, attacks on organisations with British connections, cultural, political, economic or other, were a prominent part of the IRA's repertoire. The incidents are too numerous to catalogue here, but a few examples will show their nature and temper. There is a 'nothing better to do' quality about the attacks and, occasionally, an undercurrent of spite directed at Irish Protestants, who, as well as a substantial number of Catholics, still found value in these forms of British connection. Armistice Day (11 November), commemorated with poppies, was a trigger for such attacks. Two cinemas were raided on 9 November 1925 and the films they were showing were seized; the action was justified on the basis that *Ypres* and *Prince of Wales* were British propaganda. The same day, the British Legion office in Kildare Street, Dublin, was raided and documents were removed. The British Legion was (and is) an ex-servicemen's welfare and representation body. On Armistice Day itself, shots were fired into La Scala restaurant in Dublin, where ex-servicemen were at supper.[35]

It would be tedious to continue to trace such activities through the whole of the inter-war years, but a brief description of some events before the 1932 transfer of power to de Valera's Fianna Fáil may be helpful in providing the background to the organisation's presumptions about itself and the incoming administration. The upsurge in raids and violence in 1926 were intended to demonstrate that the IRA was back in the game and that it had intelligence, reach and determination. In the opening weeks of that year it certainly seemed that the IRA was arming and reorganising for a more general challenge to the Free State. There was, in addition to the attacks on the police and (occasionally) the Army, continued threats and attempts to subvert the jury system by direct and indirect intimidation.[36] Thus, on 2 June 1926, armed men raided the office of the Sheriff in Dublin and removed lists of names and addresses of persons liable for jury service.[37] Along similar lines, with a view to garnering popular support, there were raids on money-lenders, some of whose records were removed and destroyed. The mere fact of having been raided by armed men was threat enough in itself. Similar raids had been mounted on landlords' agents and rent-rolls seized.[38]

Some of this was little more than local cock-of-the-walk intimidation. Uinseann MacEoin wondered how much of it arose from the temporary removal of Moss Twomey, newly appointed IRA Chief of Staff.[39] Were the numerous raids on garda barracks that followed an attempt at coordinated protest or were they a consequence of a vacuum of authority within the IRA?[40] Roads were blocked by felled trees, cars were commandeered, telephone wires cut and a number of people were threatened by armed men. The raids and other activities took place across five counties on the weekend of 13–14 November 1926.[41] An apprehensive government had rushed a Public Safety Bill into law in mid-November 1926.[42] This became law, and, on 19 November 1926, a State of Emergency was proclaimed and small-scale internment followed. Ministers seem to have been convinced that the raids on barracks were not going to continue and that they did not constitute a continuing threat to state security. Those arrested for unlawful acts were processed through the courts, and, on 14 December 1926, all detained under the Public Safety Act were released.[43]

The IRA's 1926 upsurge in activities was, in truth, little more than revolutionist's make-work. Groups of young men had been brought together, introduced to weapons and schooled in a few key concepts, such as the IRA's apostolic authority, the outlines of its doctrines, the chain of command. They were also drilled and took part in elementary infantry exercises and weapons training. Republican ideology was added to the mixture, and the whole was simmered over the frustrations of unemployment, underemployment, truncated education, poor prospects and, probably, the boredom and lack of wider interests of many working-class young men in both rural and urban Ireland. A civil war, with its rich harvest of grudges, was scarcely past, Ireland's economy was fragile and inflexible, and, despite independence, elements of the colonial mentality remained burdensome. All of this contained difficulties for the ordinary civil population, but for an idealistic organisation of would-be warriors, constraint and immobility were intolerable: activity had to become an end in itself. Tactical purpose was given scant consideration, and there was no strategy other than to stay in existence, bang the drum and wave the flag.

Whether because of the strong political and public reaction to the murder of Kevin O'Higgins, or for other reasons, there was a lull in IRA activities in the latter part of 1927. That there had been little change in the organisation's outlook or determination was confirmed early the following January when three IRA men fired shots at Principal Warder Robert Grace of Mountjoy Prison.[44] Five days later, Intelligence Officer Seán Harling was attacked in his home, shots being fired by two men. In a return of fire, one of the two attackers, Timothy Coughlan, was mortally wounded.[45] Such attacks on individuals who had, for one reason or another, offended the IRA, continued over the next few years, but generalised attacks, such as those that had been mounted on the garda stations in November 1926, were either not possible or were deemed by the IRA command to be too provocative. But well-publicised attacks on individuals, the organisation hoped, would cast wide a useful shadow of intimidation.

The harassment of gardaí and prison staff, short of wounding and killing, continued into the new decade. On 27 July 1930, a warder from Mountjoy Prison was handcuffed and chained to the railings of a nearby church, placarded with a slogan about the treatment of political prisoners in Mountjoy.[46] Garda Farrell was similarly treated three months later, his inscription reading 'Informer Farrell Arrests Republicans'.[47] An attack with potentially greater consequences was mounted on 28 November 1930, when Sergeant O'Regan, Army Special Unit, was shot and wounded while on protection duties at the residence of the Ceann Comhairle (Speaker of the Dáil).[48]

There is in these years a tedium of repetition in the IRA's activities. Unable to mount a full-scale insurrection or guerrilla war, and without a significant political agenda or organisation, the IRA followed its round of individual attacks and killings, intimidation and destruction. The years before de Valera's accession to power, and immediately thereafter, are of particular interest. On 30 January 1931, Patrick Carroll was murdered in Crumlin, Co. Dublin. Carroll was shot twice in the head and was also blown up by a grenade or similar device. A member of the IRA, Carroll was suspected of being an informer.[49] Seven weeks later, Superintendent John Curtain was shot five times at his home in Tipperary and died within hours; he had been a leading figure in anti-IRA activities.[50] One of Curtain's informants, John Ryan, had given evidence in a prosecution for illegal drilling and was murdered at Boyle, Co. Tipperary. A placard hung around his neck announced 'Spies and Informers Beware. IRA'.[51] Within two months, William McInerney, a building contractor, of Kilrush was shot and seriously wounded while standing at his front door, examining a 'Spies Beware' notice that had been pinned there.[52] Two days after that, a Thompson sub-machine gun – increasingly the IRA's weapon of choice – was used in an attack on the home of James Lynch, State Solicitor for Co. Clare.[53]

Short of violent and terrible incidents, the IRA flexed its muscles in other ways throughout the late 1920s and early 1930s. There was jury tampering, of course, but also intimidating and roughing up prison staff, putting up threatening posters, open drilling and pressure on the police.[54] Shopkeepers and others were threatened and attacked for selling certain goods (a Cumann na mBan drive against British confectionary, for example), for displaying British emblems or for showing British films with patriotic themes. The campaign against usury seems to have been motivated mainly by a desire to prevent the exploitation of the poor. In Limerick, however, it developed an anti-Semitic cast, particularly as a result of the sermons of Father John Creagh, and led to a two-year boycott of Limerick's Jewish shopkeepers and traders.[55] Behind all of this was an erosion of the ties of civil society by means of IRA menaces: only a very foolish man would act in any way that might attract their attention; holders of certain public offices, of course, had no option.

De Valera might have been safely gathered into Leinster House, but a left-inclined section of the IRA was making a deal of progress with its new political party Saor Éire, which was strongly syndicalist and advocated extra-parliamentary action on a number of its campaign issues. This threat alarmed the Roman Catholic bishops, who on 18 October 1932, assembled at Maynooth, issued a pastoral condemning Saor Éire and the IRA as 'sinful and irreligious... no Catholic can lawfully be a member of them'.

It would be misguided to imagine that the IRA activities, individual and usually sporadic, were simply instances of civil disorder that could be safely consigned to the police. In their aggregate, they had a destabilising effect, and there was a deepening sense of crisis, beyond political developments and IRA actions. The country, with its narrow, vulnerable and agriculture-based offshore economy, only partly recovered from its debilitating war years when it caught the wash of the world depression in trade. A state still less than a decade old had meagre stocks of confidence on which to draw. The government could not be seen to dither, and, when the Dáil reconvened in the autumn of 1931, a new public-safety measure was announced. Sweeping police, court and executive powers were provided, and the Act, *inter alia*, established the Constitution (Special Powers) Tribunal and inserted into the Free State Constitution Article 2A, which conferred powers to proscribe organisations. Within days of the measure coming into force, a wide range of republican and left-wing organisations were banned and a number of police raids were mounted.[56]

Several men and women were brought before what became known as the Military Tribunal, which began its work in late November.[57] By early December, the brothers George and Charlie Gilmore had been sentenced (five years' and three years' penal servitude, respectively) for membership of the IRA, control of a substantial quantity of arms and ammunition and conspiracy.[58] Others joined them, including Sighle Humphreys (for her activities with 'Ghosts', under which name a series of jury-tampering leaflets and messages had been issued), T. J. Ryan (a prominent Clare leader) and Seán O'Farrell of Leitrim.[59] The IRA did not have the means, nor probably the will, to respond to the government's crackdown with force. A general election was imminent. The consensus of a wide spectrum of public opinion was that Cosgrave had to be removed from office and that the only body that could do that was de Valera's Fianna Fáil. The IRA Army Council withdrew its General Order, which forbade its members from working in Free State or Northern Ireland elections, and IRA men were thus free to help Fianna Fáil in the general election called for 16 February 1932. Cosgrave's party, in power in one form or another for a decade, had run out of steam. Its ministers were exhausted; it had no policies beyond more of the same; and the electorate were unenthusiastic or actively wanted change; Cosgrave also ran a very poor campaign. Voting for Fianna Fáil, getting out the vote and engaging in the usual amount of multiple voting all helped, but the IRA could hardly claim to have put de Valera in its debt. The results were conclusive: Fianna Fáil secured seventy-two seats, Cumann na nGaedheal fifty-seven.[60] In a chamber of 153 and with Labour support, de Valera could govern.

A short and turbulent honeymoon

Fianna Fáil's victory was a mixed blessing for the IRA. It could reasonably expect pressure from the police and military courts to ease, and, indeed, as soon as their appointments were ratified by the Dáil, the new Ministers for Justice and for Defence (James Geoghegan and Frank Aiken, respectively) went to Arbour Hill military prison and spoke to the prisoners in their cells, twenty of whom were released the next day.[61] Just over a week later, Article 2A of the Constitution was suspended, and the Military Tribunal was dissolved.[62] On 12 March 1932, the IRA organ, *An Phoblacht*, banned by the Cosgrave government, was again available. These were symbols and tangible tokens that a new spirit would prevail in politics and public affairs. This, and the importance of the prisoners, was reflected in a large demonstration in College Green in the heart of Dublin, celebrating the releases.[63] More was to come, of course, as de Valera advanced constitutionally towards his vision of the Republic, but the immediate willingness of the new government to use its executive powers to relieve fellow republicans was powerful, encouraging and misleading news for the IRA. At the same time, elements of what had been the victorious side in the Civil War, whose party had now been democratically ejected from office, began to regroup in a fashion that carried the undercurrent of menace.[64]

But when the picture was tilted even slightly, the prospect was not so clear. Successive elections had shown the country to be fairly evenly divided on issues which were most central to republicans. There was now in office a successful political party that claimed to carry the republican baton, making its electoral appeal under a leader with the status of a founding father. What room did that leave for the stern republicanism of the IRA and Sinn Féin? More difficult still, de Valera's accession to power again raised the basic question of the purpose of the IRA. Did it have the will to launch an armed assault on this new government? How would it justify such a move? How many of its members and supporters, never mind the population at large, would support renewed war?

The portents of conflict were always there, were the curtain of comforting optimism pulled aside. The IRA's response to the release of seventeen prisoners from Arbour Hill military prison within days of de Valera forming his first Free State government was hardly reassuring. Far from wanting to merge itself with the newly inaugurated process of peaceful institutional politics, or even to accept some form of reconciliation or pragmatic cooperation, Seán MacBride, speaking to the celebratory rally at College Green, insisted that the IRA had no intention of disbanding or of deviating from its purpose.[65] At various private meetings, de Valera tried to draw IRA leaders to his programme. His argument was that once the process of institutional transformation upon which he had embarked had been completed, the Republic would be at hand. Partition would remain an issue, of course, but short of this, with the emergence of a policy which all republicans could accept, there was no further need for the IRA. The realisation that the two parties of former comrades, both drawing deeply on all the springs of republicanism, were destined to become even more implacable enemies than Cosgrave and the IRA had been, came not immediately, but came still fairly rapidly. The ultimate fierceness of the conflict issued from the affinity of the two groups. The ground fought over was too narrow. There was no room for the respect and even curious friendliness that political opponents from different traditions sometimes grant each other. Bitterness and deep anger would infuse this fraternal conflict, accompanied by accusations of inexcusable treachery and irredeemable bad faith. This was more than a contest for power: it was a grasping for the mantle and claim to the spirit of Irish republicanism.

Partly out of conviction, and also out of a desire to neutralise any challenge on his republican flank, de Valera moved quickly on core issues. The Statute of Westminster – great irony – had confirmed the sovereignty of all dominions and their right to be free from the authority of the British Parliament less than four months before.[66] There was no longer a barrier to the changes that a decade ago might possibly have renewed the Anglo-Irish War. Collins had been right in his reading of the Treaty as the first step to a more complete state of independence. Following British constitutional theory, the Irish parliamentary body was supreme. Subject as it was to easy amendment by the Dáil, the Free State Constitution was not entrenched legislation. In theory, a simple statute, introduced on 20 April 1932, should have removed the Oath, but Seanad opposition held it back for a year.[67] The office of Governor General was demolished by an ingenious and indeed satirical device. The Cosgrave-nominated incumbent was ignored and in October 1932 replaced by a Fianna Fáil placeman, who then chose to drop the trappings of office, lived in his suburban home rather than the Vice Regal Lodge in the Phoenix Park and did little more than sign the documents delivered to him by the government: it was effective theatre as well as a democratic parable.

Those were safe, ingenious and elegant solutions to problems that had gripped and inflamed republican opinion: maximum effect with minimum cost. Such was the importance of symbols to republicans that de Valera, speaking after some twenty months in office, was baffled that his changes had not brought about cooperation between all republican organisations.[68] His decision to withhold land annuity payments involved a deal more pain and, in the trough of the 1930s, initiated a damaging economic war of tariffs and sanctions with Britain that had the long-term effect of making even more inefficient an economy which was static or decaying.[69] But this was another emotional issue, symbolic as well as financial, looking back to conquest and dispossession and touching on sovereignty. Payments by farmers did not cease (or were not supposed to), but the funds that would have been remitted to Britain were retained by the Irish government. Default on an international financial agreement seemed both wrong and self-damaging to Cosgrave supporters and to business and commercial interests, but that was not the way it played among the less monied in cities and towns and, above all, in Fianna Fáil's rural hinterland.

With such initial successes and manoeuvres to his credit, de Valera followed Cosgrave's tactic and sought a more conclusive mandate from the voters. In the election of 24 January 1933, Fianna Fáil achieved an overall majority, albeit the smallest possible, with seventy-seven seats.[70] Labour again offered support, providing the necessary leeway to govern with little hindrance. Once more the IRA had put its organisational weight behind de Valera in the election, but he had made it clear that there was no place in his plans for a parallel state, particularly any form of militia: 'No section of the community will be allowed to arm. All arms shall be completely at the disposal of the elected representatives of the people.'[71] Some militant republicans took this as mere election fluff, intended by de Valera to reassure the faint-hearted and to widen his vote: this was a serious misperception.

In his second term, de Valera rode the horse with confidence and gathered the reins more closely. He dismissed Eoin O'Duffy as head of the Garda Síochána.[72] O'Duffy then embarked on a foolish political venture that aped

European fascism and ultimately led to the political wilderness. His Blueshirts, growing out of the Army Comrades' Association (the organisation for former pro-Treaty combatants), alarmed the country and (importantly for our story) gave the IRA at least a short-term answer to its questions about the purpose of life. De Valera, now well aware of the consequences of direct political action, prudently chose to rely on the courts, army and police to deal with Blueshirt posturing. He had changed the top personnel of the Detective Division, and now, under different management, a number of former but post-Civil War IRA men were recruited. They were inevitably known as the 'Broy Harriers' (a play on the name of the new commissioner, Colonel Eamon Broy, and a well-known Co. Wicklow sporting club, the Bray Harriers). Well armed, amply funded, these men knew their business, were determined and had no difficulty in switching loyalty to this new republican government. They were an effective instrument against the Blueshirts (whose paramilitary organisation was known as the National Guard). A march on Dublin (mimicking Mussolini's October 1922 march on Rome) collapsed ignominiously in the face of determined government preparation. IRA delight at these events was seemingly undiminished by any reflection that having drawn steel de Valera might use it in many other ways.

The government had its obligations, and whatever tolerance it had for republican rhetoric and sabre-rattling, the gathering menace of street warfare could not be tolerated: there were vivid examples of the consequences to be had from events in Italy and Germany. On 11 August 1933, the Executive Council had issued an Order bringing into operation Parts II to V of Article 2A of the Constitution and re-established Special Courts, popularly known as the Military Tribunal. Further, to show that it meant business, the government (via the Minister for Defence) also promulgated regulations allowing it to intern or imprison persons at Arbour Hill Detention Barracks, the Military Detention Barracks at the Curragh (the Glasshouse) and other places. Rules were set out for the conduct of detention or imprisonment under Article 2A.[73] Pressure was ratcheted up in the months that followed. Equally importantly, a precedent had been created and an instrument had been placed in the hands of those who in opposition had denounced it.

To provide a legitimate outlet for the patriotic and military-minded young men, and to act as an alternative to subversive organisations, de Valera established the Volunteer Reserve. With its play on the Old IRA (whose members had been known as Volunteers) and its offer of a uniform and military training (some in residential camps), the new body seems to have succeeded in its purpose. The IRA sought to counter it by intimidating recruits, and there were numerous incidents in which recruits' uniforms were seized and threats were made by armed men.[74] This was inflammatory action since the new body was a division of the national armed forces, and actions against it could not but be a challenge to the regular army.

De Valera and the IRA had enjoyed a relatively brief honeymoon, based (as such interludes sometimes are) on mutual wilful illusion. The real world inevitably intruded, and both sides realised that a clash of authority was inevitable. As part of the IRA's attempts to find an effective role for itself, there had been a boycott of the British-owned Bass beer – economic nationalism and the tariff war between Britain and the Free State providing context and justification. The issue was but a means of flexing republican muscles and attracting recruits. In the prosecution of this campaign, persuasion and menace were mixed: the IRA generally had only to threaten for a publican to comply, though in September 1933 leaders of the raiding parties began to carry revolvers.[75] Beer battles took a more dangerous turn when O'Duffy's Blueshirts took it on themselves to provide protection for publicans. This led to clashes that threatened public order and to arrests and imprisonment. The disorder of street politics sometimes passed beyond fists and clubs to the use of firearms. There was a continuous round of marches and counter-marches, demonstrations and disorder.[76] There was also victimisation and retaliation: Italy and Germany on a studio stage. On 25 October 1933, an IRA member, John O'Connor of Inishannon, Co. Cork, was made to perform forced labour whilst being threatened by firearms. Four days later, two Blueshirts, Hugh O'Reilly (also of Inishannon) and John O'Leary of Bandon, Co. Cork, were taken away and badly beaten. O'Leary was, in addition, shot in both legs; O'Reilly died two months later of his injuries.[77] On 6 October 1933 there was a marshalling of forces in a determined attempt to prevent O'Duffy from speaking in Tralee, Co. Kerry; tear gas was used to control the resulting ruckus, and soldiers, bayonets fixed, were deployed.[78] IRA men began to be brought before the Military Tribunal. This was de Valera's lenient and conciliatory phase, and sentences were doled out in months rather than in years, but clear warning had been given.[79] Fianna Fáil was certainly opposed to O'Duffy's movement, but violent action against him was an indirect move against the government and could swiftly have contributed to an unravelling of authority and order in the revolutionary spiral for which the IRA longed.

The mild prison sentences passed by the Military Tribunal were not heeded. Without a strategy, action – any action – was compelling for the IRA, and there was always hope of a more general conflagration. In the early months of 1934 there were further worrying incidents. Most seriously, Cornelius Daly, a Blueshirt supporter, publican and farmer, died after injuries sustained in a street attack by IRA men in Dunmanway, Co. Cork.[80] A bomb was placed in the Dundalk house of Joseph McGrory, who had given identity evidence against two republicans charged with robbing a United Ireland Party collector. The blast caused extensive damage to adjacent buildings; the man's mother was mortally injured, and two children suffered lesser injuries.[81] Blueshirt and IRA clashes continued throughout the spring and summer months with garda and military courts seemingly marginalised. At the heart of its teachings, fascism and its derivatives emphasised triumph of the will, leadership and the organic nature of politics. Its logical outcome was a coup or another type of challenge to established institutions. The supporters of the Blueshirt campaign undoubtedly included a violent element, intent on brawling. But these were also men of property and position, intrinsically conservative, to whom any kind of radicalism was repugnant and a threat to their fundamental desire for order and to their material interests. By early autumn, O'Duffy was forced out of the organisation he had inspired and headed. The paramilitary methods and trappings he had introduced were rapidly discarded by the now dominant conservative faction.[82] The party thenceforward confined itself to parliamentary action. Again, this was a mixed blessing for the IRA. They had taken on the street politics of a right-wing faction and had prevailed, as they saw it, over reaction and anti-republicanism. But with O'Duffy and his followers a spent force, there remained only one extra-legal organisation of significance in Ireland, and one government determined to have its way; there were no alibis, no stalking horses and no intermediaries.

IRA activity and pugnacity was certainly at full flood, and it may not have been possible to stem or divert them. A strong denunciation by the Roman Catholic hierarchy was a twig in the stream.[83] In terms of intimidation and influence and its aspirations to be an alternative court of appeal, the organisation had undoubtedly made a mark. To some whose means or caste put them beyond the normal legal processes, it had a Robin Hood appeal. This led to the organisation in Co. Longford becoming involved in a dispute between the Sanderson estate and its tenants.[84] On 9 February 1935, a group of men broke into the house of the land agent, Gerald More O'Ferrall, near Edgeworthstown, Co. Longford. In the ensuing scuffle, More O'Ferrall's son Roderic was shot; he died twelve days later. A reward of £1,000 produced information on the attack and a number of men were arrested. The trial cast the IRA and the government into a new trial of strength. This had been an authorised IRA operation, and the organisation's capacity to menace and record of violence made it difficult to get convictions. The first jury failed to agree a verdict, and a second trial led to an acquittal.[85] In May 1935, General Richard Mulcahy, now a Fine Gael TD, set out a catalogue of IRA incidents over the preceding months, alleging police inaction and demoralisation and party-political interventions in favour of persons connected to Fianna Fáil. There had been open drilling, he claimed, robberies, instances of the possession of arms being overlooked and, in all, a lack of effective action by the authorities or evidence of a sense of urgency.[86]

An even more direct confrontation came in early March 1936 with a Dublin bus and train strike. This was an especially emotive event for republicans, since a similar strike in September 1913 had been met with a lockout by employers. The violent confrontations between police and workers that had followed were regarded as important elements in the sequence of events and perceptions of injustice that culminated in the 1916 Rising. Three weeks into the 1936 strike, the government began to use army lorries as a means of easing Dubliners' transportation difficulties. The IRA opened fire on the lorries, attempting to shoot out their tyres. Attacks were made on the police, and in two separate incidents three gardaí were wounded. Following the second shooting, forty-four republicans were arrested in Dublin.[87] Intelligence was good, and so many of the leading figures had been lifted. Some were released fairly swiftly, but others went before the Military Tribunal on a variety of charges. By historical standards, the sentences remained light – months rather than years – but by mid-April more than 100 republicans were in prison.[88]

Accustomed to daily tales of intimidation and violence as it was, much of the nation was shocked and morally outraged when, in the late evening of 24 March 1936, an IRA assassination team shot the seventy-two-year-old Vice Admiral Henry Somerville in his home in Castletownshend, Co. Cork. Somerville had been known to supply references to local young men seeking to join the British armed forces. Times were very hard, unemployment and emigration high, and few would have conceived that the Vice Admiral's reference-writing remotely merited the death penalty. That Somerville was a Protestant, and that West Cork had the unique distinction of having 'cleansed' itself of certain Protestant families in 1922, were undoubtedly factors in this brutal and bloody action.[89] Most importantly, however, was the desire of local units for action and the paucity of targets. Nor was this simply the action of local hotheads: IRA headquarters had been consulted and had approved.[90] The following month there was GHQ approval for another murder. This time it was a young man denounced as a traitor by a local unit in Co. Waterford and shot dead in Dungarvan.[91]

There had been repeated accusations from the opposition in the Dáil that the government, feeling its way to a policy on the IRA, had undermined respect for law, had left the police confused with regard to political crime and had failed to bring miscreants to justice.[92] This was to change. Gerald Boland, a man who would prove to be the hammer of the IRA, was shifted from Posts and Telegraphs to Justice on 24 March 1936, to cover for P. J. Ruttledge, who was seriously ill. There followed greater firmness on the part of government.[93] The IRA Chief of Staff Moss Twomey was brought before the Military Tribunal and sentenced to three years' penal servitude and three months' imprisonment, concurrently.[94] Jim Killeen, escaper and well-known IRA leader, was also dealt with by the Tribunal. The prohibition on the IRA, which had been lifted on 18 March 1932 on de Valera's first accession to office, was reinstated.[95] The annual republican pilgrimage to Bodenstown, Co. Kildare, burial place of Wolfe Tone, was banned. This annual event provided an opportunity to the IRA to show off its strength and to issue a call to members, supporters and the nation. Unlike the Cosgrave government, which had also banned the Bodenstown processions in 1931 and had failed to carry through (damaged its standing thereby), de Valera and his colleagues enforced their order with pre-emptive arrests, train and coach cancellations, massed gardaí, 400 soldiers and, above all, an unmistakable will.[96] The days were past when the IRA could set up a more or less open headquarters in Dublin while functioning as a secret army.

As the government's patience with the IRA ran dry, and as the organisation refused to alter course or to temporise, the Public Safety Act exacted a toll. Special Branch, reorganised and reoriented, knew what was expected. On 18 June 1936, acting under the instrument they had reviled in previous years (Article 2A), the Executive Council declared the IRA to be an unlawful organisation.[97] Leading

IRA men were, within weeks, either in custody or on the run. Twomey, whose identity as Chief of Staff was known throughout the land, was serving three years for membership of an unlawful organisation. Con Lehane, a lawyer and member of the Army Council, had also been arrested but was released on giving a written undertaking that he had severed his IRA connections. Donal O'Donoghue, editor of *An Phoblacht*, was a fugitive for some time but was arrested in Kerry on 8 July 1936. Whilst awaiting trial, he went on hunger strike and was released after about four weeks – but by then was exhausted and spent.[98] Other prominent IRA leaders, including Seán Russell and Seán MacBride, went into precautionary hiding.

In the Dáil, Boland, Acting Minister for Justice, referred to the murders of Somerville and Egan.[99] Stern action had to be taken against any organisation that claimed life-or-death powers over fellow citizens or ex-members: 'I now give definite notice to all concerned that the so-called Irish Republican Army or any organisation which promotes or advocates the use of arms for the attainment of its object will not be tolerated.' The government, Boland claimed, had smashed the Blueshirts, 'and we are going to smash the others'. Persons who knew where arms were being held should 'do their civic duty and tell the police where they were, and if any form of reward was necessary, to obtain the information, government would pay it'.[100]

The legislature had authorised coercive and deterrent measures giving this more determined government a freer hand to secure order and control. At the same time, it deflected accusations of backsliding on its own republican agenda. The Senate, the scrutinising and advisory part of the legislature, established in part to give a voice to Irish Protestant and unionist sentiment that could not be represented from the ballot box, was abolished on 28 May 1936.[101] British politicians had washed their hands of Ireland: the high imperialist sentiment, so vigorous from the 1890s until the mid-1920s was ebbing rapidly. Churchill, who had kept a jealous eye on Ireland, dwelt in political twilight. Grave dangers were gathering in a resurgent Germany and an ever more confident Soviet Union, both sources of international tension and disorder. Ireland had moved well down the British agenda, no longer an object of passion, more likely to be a subject of policy discussions in connection with relatively minor fiscal and trade matters. De Valera, always an astute tactician, seized the Abdication Crisis of the autumn of 1936, in the course of which all Commonwealth leaders were consulted, to remove the Crown from the symbolic side of Irish politics. (It no longer had any practical significance.)[102] This was a logical extension of a number of earlier measures such as compensation for those republicans who had lost property during the Civil War and pensions for republican wounded and disabled; an army pension for former IRA volunteers had been introduced in 1932.[103] Against this practical and compassionate assistance to those who had shown loyalty to republican ideals, to many former supporters the rhetoric and violent actions of the IRA seemed to be mistaken, misplaced and irrelevant.

To tie his symbolic and structural measures together, de Valera consulted widely and (formally) on a new constitution. This, when unveiled to the Dáil on

10 March 1937, fell short of declaring a republic. On 1 July he again put himself before the electorate; the constitutional referendum was held on the same day. A week later the results were declared. De Valera was returned, but without a majority in the Dáil; his constitution, though carried, failed to get a plurality of the votes.[104] For a man who claimed that he had only to look into his own heart to know the desires of the Irish people, these were sobering results. But a win is a win, and on 29 December 1937 the Free State, with its Treaty constitution, was replaced by the all-but-Republic Éire: de Valera's tide had covered nearly all that foreshore claimed by the IRA.

On an international scene dominated by conflicts and the threat of war, Britain's Prime Minister sought peace on his country's western flank. In April 1938, in a move deplored by Winston Churchill, and which even today is difficult to categorise either as appeasement or statesmanship, Neville Chamberlain concluded what would be a final and complex agreement with the Irish state, now called Éire, sixteen years after independence. The tariff war between the two countries was brought to a close. More importantly, and a triumph for de Valera's statesmanship, Britain relinquished the Treaty Ports, care and maintenance parties finally withdrawing on 11 July 1938. The first part of the agreement would guarantee Britain access to Irish agricultural produce in the event of war; the second made Irish neutrality in such a war a practical possibility. Territory is at the nerve endings of all nationalism, and de Valera reaped great acclaim for recovering the Treaty Ports, and for doing so peacefully. On 17 June 1938, he went to the country yet again, seeking its endorsement of the agreements he had procured and – very much to the point – in search of an overall Dáil majority. This time he was suitably rewarded. Whatever vexation the electorate may have felt at being called yet again to the poll was not sufficient for them to punish the government. Once more with seventy-seven seats, the changed position of the other parties meant that Fianna Fáil had a comfortable majority of sixteen over all the other parties combined. De Valera had achieved the vision of his old adversary Michael Collins and had used the Treaty as a stepping stone to complete independence. He had outmanoeuvred the party that traced its legitimacy back to Collins's government, while at the same time marginalising his republican flank: a masterclass in both tactical and strategic politics.

Despite the cool and sometimes brutal powers of observation which made him such an effective party politician, de Valera retained a romantic streak in his make-up. It was this perhaps that had dominated and produced uncharacteristically wishful thinking regarding the IRA. Notwithstanding all that had passed, he and his Fianna Fáil colleagues apparently entertained bouts of hope that republican unity would be restored. This they envisaged as the outcome of the series of measures that had incrementally dissolved institutional ties with Britain and had set on firm foundations a Gaelic, Catholic and republican Irish state. Since these objectives were shared with the IRA, de Valera's advances towards them, and the demonstration of his intent to go further, would, he thought, somehow convince if not the leadership then the mass of the IRA that the organisation was no longer needed and should therefore dissolve. For many of those IRA members, supporters and sympathisers, he did in fact make this case. On its part, the IRA leadership and active core imagined that de Valera would give some form of institutional reality to the Second Dáil and the Republic of which for several years he had been President and which nationally was still in existence. Both parties colluded in evading the basic issue: was it the ballot box or the ideals of republicanism that provided the basis for legitimacy?

But now that the remaining British ties had been almost totally severed, de Valera's message was clear. Republicans had, in the past, been blocked in attempts to pursue their political objectives, had been robbed of gains bought with blood and sacrifice. The oath and all the paraphernalia of dominion status had made it impossible for them conscientiously to participate in the political process and hobbled independence. To that extent (though de Valera was careful never to say so in precise terms), extra-parliamentary opposition and perhaps the IRA itself had been justified: both had fostered a body of republican opinion and had created a momentum. To give time for the new modus vivendi to be established, there had initially been a halt to the Cosgrave government's vigorous pursuit of the IRA. Training camps and public marching by large bodies of armed men had been tolerated. Militant and inflammatory statements had been ignored by the authorities; all political prisoners had been released. Its side of a tacit bargain fulfilled, in the government's view, there remained no legitimate basis for extra-legal or extra-parliamentary republican or other paramilitary activity.[105] The IRA did not see things that way and declined to pass through the garden gate. Another portal now loomed.

Prison conditions

The period is studded with ironies. Civil war had turned former fugitives into policemen and soldiers, prisoners into gaolers, and comrades into prisoners. There was to be a re-run when, after a relatively brief interlude, republicans were again imprisoned by republicans, and the now routine protests at prison conditions resumed, inside and outside the walls. Tracing the prison events and their connections is rather like watching a long run of a theatrical production: the actors change (though some return for a new season) but the roles, plot, costume, scenery and props are the same – just a little more tarnished, threadbare and certainly familiar. Here, repeatedly, we have the prison as a theatre, the prison as a pageant of justice contested.

By 1925, all but a handful of IRA Civil War prisoners had been released. Those that remained had been convicted of offences which in some way precluded pardon. John McPeak absconded with his Free State armoured car in 1923 and delivered it to the IRA. His sentence of six years' penal servitude reflected the seriousness of what was seen as an act of treachery. The Free State took much the same view as the British: mercy would be withheld from a soldier who broke the bond of loyalty.[106] Men convicted of raids on police barracks were also treated severely, even though these actions had been carried out during the Civil War. John Hogan (pro-Treaty) had been convicted in 1922 of killing James Cullinan (anti-Treaty), whom he said had tried to disarm him, on 31 October 1922. He was sentenced to death, later commuted to penal servitude for life.[107]

The Civil War had not long ended before there began to accumulate a number of prisoners sentenced for post-war offences, though the terms imposed were not particularly lengthy. As we have seen, the Gilmore brothers were given hefty sentences for their part in the spectacular escape of nineteen prisoners from Mountjoy on 27 November 1925.[108] A two-year sentence had been imposed on J. McCarthy, who had been convicted of the possession of arms – an offence which, during the Civil War, had been punished by death. Six-month sentences were imposed for fairly low-level disruption – a raid on a landlord's rent-rolls, and the like. A number of persons had also been remanded in custody, charged with politically motivated offences.[109]

In the months and years following, the number of prisoners increased, as did the range and gravity of offences, reflecting the IRA's restored ambitions, increased pace of reorganisation and rearmament, as well as the expanding campaign on the issue of land annuities. Only two political prisoners were under penal servitude: John Hogan, at Portlaoise (formerly called Maryborough), serving a life sentence for murder under strict conditions, and Con Healy (known as the 'One Eyed Gunner'), who had been sentenced to five years for shooting at a detective.[110] Ordinary imprisonment had been imposed, in the main, for arms possession, although the land-annuity campaign continued to produce convictions, as did possession of IRA documents, action against what the Republican Prisoners' Committee describes as informers and interfering with the actions of bailiffs.[111]

In 1930, there was a reduction in the number of political prisoners. Hogan and Healy remained at Portlaoise (the former would be released in March 1932, when Fianna Fáil came to power and immediately freed the political prisoners). Three men were each serving two years' hard labour in Mountjoy for arms offences. In Cork Prison, Denis Coughlan was similarly serving twelve months, with an additional six months in default of a £50 fine. At Waterford, Daniel McEvoy was in custody awaiting trial on a charge of possessing ammunition.[112] Eighteen months later the picture had hardly changed. The two penal-servitude men remained at Portlaoise. Mountjoy had one man (Seán McGuinness) serving two years, and Arbour Hill held nine sentenced men: the Gilmore brothers, George and Charles, serving five and three years respectively and the others between three and six months.[113] Arbour Hill had now begun to acquire a sinister reputation to which the PPC drew attention in their leaflet, 'In Jail for Ireland Christmas 1931.'[114]

Cumann na mBan was, by mid-1931, using the prisoners as a call to arms. They were living proof of the existence of tyranny and showed that the Free State and Northern Ireland governments were joint enemies of the Irish people. A leaflet published in June listed those in prison, skated over their offences, cast their conditions as unfavourable as possible and tried to kindle a sense of outraged decency. The annual cost of the Free State and Northern departments of justice (quotation marks were freely used) was put at £1,824,950 and £1,078,210, respectively. But it was not merely a matter of funds. The prisoners could not be held without police and prison officers: 'The members of the ROYAL ULSTER CONSTABULARY AND THE FREE STATE POLICE are the people really responsible for this ill-treatment of prisoners. THESE MUST BE SHUNNED AND BOYCOTTED BY EVERY SELF RESPECTING IRISHMAN, unless they decide they will not act as agents of the British Government in Ireland.'[115]

This was ritual rhetoric, chanting before the altar. The intention was to attract recruits to the IRA and its supporting organisations, to rouse sentiment and to raise funds. Such had been the objective a few months previously when the Republican Prisoners' Committee, using the arrest of Father John Fahy, urged protests against 'illegal imprisonment'.[116] A more menacing exhortation followed. Words alone were not enough: 'Your enemy holds your country and your prisoners by force of Arms. Only by force of Arms will you obtain release of both. You… Young Men who have no arms – Sell your shirt and buy one.'[117] The incendiary language made the WPDL (the parent organisation of the Republican Prisoners' Committee) an obvious target for banning when, in October 1931, Article 2A of the Constitution was brought into effect.[118]

The treatment of those in police rather than prison custody became a more effective cause célèbre than the political prisoners and formed one of the last chapters in the life of the Cosgrave administration. De Valera, after several years fund-raising and manoeuvring, had, in September 1931, launched the *Irish Press*, a daily newspaper intended to publicise the ideas and promote the cause of Fianna Fáil.[119] It immediately showed its effectiveness as a political instrument, and, within a few months, its first editor, Frank Gallagher, had come into head-on collision with the government.[120] The difficulty for Cosgrave was that Gallagher was not calling for revolution, but for the law to be upheld. The decision to bring him before the Military Tribunal raised issues about the freedom of the press that disturbed people far beyond the ranks of Fianna Fáil and militant republicanism. The case was a godsend to the fledgling newspaper: the decision to prosecute Gallagher for seditious libel can only have brought joy to the *Irish Press* circulation manager.

On 22 December 1931, Gallagher ran an article, 'A Grave Public Concern', that detailed police brutality towards suspects and stated that it was widely believed that the beating up of suspects had become part of the administration of the law. There was, he also claimed, a considerable section of the Irish population 'placed outside the pale of legal protection and even of justice'. Political prisoners in military custody were denied all communication with their relatives and with each other. Persons arrested on suspicion in some cases had been 'savagely assaulted' and in bitter weather confined in unheated cells. Anxious relatives who came enquiring had been insulted at the prison gates. 'Christmas parcels have been refused to tried and untried prisoners, and finally, a priest has been refused admission to those who desired his spiritual aid.'[121]

This was a far weightier blow than any landed by the Republican Prisoners' Committee, Cumann na mBan, the IRA or any part of the direct-force republican alliance. Gallagher based his article on two signed statements which had been passed to him by Frank Fahy, TD, who assured him that they were 'authentic and reliable'.[122] One was from John Burke of Loughrea, Co. Galway, detained on 5 December 1931. Arrested returning from a fair on a day of drenching rain, Burke claimed to have been kept for forty-eight hours in the wet clothes in which he had been taken. He also alleged that during that time he had been assaulted in bouts of kicking, choking, beating and punching. A detective had battered him against the wall, 'until my jaws, throat, tongue, neck and head was one sore'. He was then taken from the garda barracks to Loughrea Lake and threatened with drowning; back at the barracks the threat was shooting. Detectives wanted information about IRA meetings at his home. Throughout, Burke refused to answer questions, which in itself would have convinced the police that he was a guilty party. On this, Gallagher reassured his readers, 'We are informed that John Burke is not a member of any organisation other than Fianna Fáil. He is the son of a widow.' A second statement from Peter Plower described similar CID brutality.[123]

Gallagher's trial provided even more publicity (in what was the immediate run-up to a general election). His piece had been cleverly written but posed some difficulty for a defence based on justification. Were the brutalities detailed in the statements 'isolated and wholly unusual incidents in which the Detective Division of the Garda got out of hand they would still be of grave concern and a matter in which the Government should instantly take action'. But, Gallagher continued, there was reason to believe that such abuses were widespread, and 'there is reason to fear that in this particular district and in others a system of "beating-up" those suspected of refusing information has become "part of the administration of the law"'.[124] The statements of Burke and Plower could, to some considerable extent, be circumstantially substantiated by others – not direct observers, but people who had seen their condition before and after arrest. It would be much more difficult in the time available to Gallagher's defence, and the resources to hand, to provide support for the more general claim.

Neighbours and relatives duly testified that when released both Burke and Plower had black eyes. The process of examination and cross-examination also provided excellent copy. Detective Sergeant Breen denied 'having the vilest tongue of any human being this side of hell'.[125] The case came much closer to the government itself when Colonel David Neligan, head of the CID (a section of which acted as the political police), gave evidence. He insisted that Frank Fahy, TD, and Father John Fahy (himself from Loughrea) had concocted Burke's statement. His informers had told him that Fahy had been interviewing Irregulars (the term used for members of the IRA), trying to get statements from them that they had been beaten.[126] The outcome of the Tribunal did not matter – and, to a large extent, was wholly predictable: soldiers are not jurists. Numerous opportunities were provided to tilt at the government's complacency in the face of abuses by its own agents, who were portrayed as violent and foul-mouthed bullies. *Irish Press* readers were galvanised. When Gallagher and the *Press* were each fined £100, contributions poured into the newspaper's office, frequently accompanied by supportive letters. There was tabloid-type schmaltz, of course, and a little boy sent a sixpenny piece to help Gallagher 'pay that fine'.[127] The Tribunal refused to award prosecution costs to the state (a strong hint that the officers had found an element of justification in the defence case). Certainly, the liberal *Manchester Guardian* considered the prosecution to have been heavy-handed: 'There was nothing in the articles which the average newspaper reader would construe as exceeding the limits usually allowed to the opposition press.'[128]

De Valera was probably set to win the 1932 election, the electoral cycle having moved in his favour. Even so, electoral fortunes are sometimes determined by last-minute and unforeseen developments. Reactions to the *Irish Press* trial thus provided helpful leeway. De Valera would not capture office on the basis of any deep concern for civil or political liberties, and these were not elements either of his politics or personal style. When the conflict between his administration and the emboldened IRA required it, he was not a whit less willing than his predecessor to vigorously defend elected government. Two key appointments, as far as prisoners were concerned, were Defence and Justice. To the former he appointed Frank Aiken, a former Chief of Staff of the anti-Treaty IRA.[129] James Geoghegan became his Minister for Justice, a somewhat surprising appointment since Geoghegan had been a member of Cosgrave's Cumann na nGaedheal.[130] It has been suggested that de Valera foresaw difficulties in Justice in the years ahead and that Geoghegan's former attachment to the Treaty party offered a degree of insulation from the political opprobrium that was to come.[131]

No government, of whatever complexion, can be other than deeply concerned about an armed body operating on its territory, and by the summer of 1933, as we have seen, the Fianna Fáil government was convinced that the process of reconciliation and absorption had failed and that the IRA's activities threatened the country's stability. Over the months that followed the government would move from a relatively placatory and liberal attitude towards its political prisoners to a determination to use the prisons as an instrument of suppression of politically motivated offences. This would lead it to develop and defend what may have been the most punitive and repressive episode in the imprisonment of political offenders, in Ireland or Britain.

The build-up was slow, and there were fits and starts, but by the spring of 1934 there was an appreciable body of republicans in Arbour Hill and the Curragh, together with a smaller but still significant group of Blueshirts. The routine of control and resistance was by now well established and predictable, with the various advances and retreats, twists and turns, feints and swings, as familiar and reflexive to both sides as often-practised ballroom steps. At this point, the de Valera administration did not claim, as Cosgrave and the British had, from time to time, that politically motivated or not, the prisoners were merely criminals.

Initially the prison regulations were liberal, especially in comparison to those that applied to ordinary criminal prisoners. Indeed, the dietary was superior to that of serving soldiers, comprising of their full allowance, with the addition of a supper of half a pint of milk, a quarter pound of bread and one ounce of butter. If such rations failed to satisfy, political prisoners could purchase additional items of food. They wore their own clothes and could receive further items of apparel, without restriction; the needy had clothing supplied. There was access to a library, and prisoners could also buy books. Smoking was allowed at all times, and tobacco and cigarettes could be freely purchased. There was free association during daytime hours – from after breakfast until 9 p.m. in summer (8 p.m. in winter). Classes were allowed, up to a maximum of four hours a day, with the proviso that the teachers had to be qualified. (This was probably intended to prevent or at lease impede prisoners running all the classes themselves.) There were facilities for various games – handball, table tennis, draughts, chess, cards and the like. Prisoners could wash their own clothes, and basins and drying racks were provided.[132]

These conditions approximated more to civil detention, such as might be enjoyed by a debtor, contempt-of-court prisoner or internee, than to criminal imprisonment. Any captivity must, in degrees, be constraining, intrusive, demeaning and frustrating, but this was a regime that allowed prison life to be as little irksome as was practically possible and that therefore acknowledged the non-criminal and emphasised the non-penal nature of the detention. Two regulations failed to match the liberality of the others: both involved security and staffing. Although prisoners could receive all letters written to them, only one a week could be sent out. Censorship, deemed essential for paramilitary prisoners, who might be planning an escape or a move against the government, or whose letters might be seen as a source of intelligence, was a considerable drain on staff resources. Similar considerations applied to visits, which had to be closely supervised, although the entitlement to one per month was somewhat restrictive even allowing for staffing requirements. Special visits for family or other compassionate reasons could be allowed at the governor's discretion.[133]

There was here little of the grounds for protest that arise when a government insists that all its sentenced prisoners are, by definition, criminal and will be treated as such, irrespective of motivation. Ministers knew that the denial of political status provides effective *matériel* with which to wage a campaign of attrition against the authorities. Instead, the conflict between gaolers and captives focused on the privileges that could be expected by persons convicted of political offences. Earlier exchanges between the government and Seán Ryan, IRA OC at Arbour Hill Prison, are instructive.[134] On 5 March 1934, Ryan, threatening 'certain steps', listed the convicted political prisoners' demands. None was extravagant or, on the face of it, unreasonable. The men wished for reveille to be put back from 6.30 to 7.30 a.m., for all newspapers and letters to be delivered to them and wanted to be able to send out two letters a week. They also wanted exercise after the evening meal, between 6 and 9 p.m., and the same routine over weekends as weekdays.[135]

Ryan had put a four-day deadline on his demands, backed by 'certain steps', were a favourable reply not forthcoming (this referred to hunger-striking). Though the response came within the time limit, only a compromise was offered. Reveille was put back to 7 a.m. 'except on Sundays and Holy Days when it will be at 6:30 a.m.'. Prisoners would be allowed all their letters, but no newspapers. The outward allowance of letters would not be altered – one letter per week. The entitlement to visits (one a month) would not be varied. Hours of exercise were slightly expanded – one hour after the evening meal 'as conditions permit'. Weekend out-of-cell time was brought into line with weekday levels, except for classes.[136]

Both parties knew that there was a short-, medium- and long-term game, in which these were the opening moves. This was a select group of committed and experienced activists who would give only one answer to the question, 'Do you want to be a soldier or will you allow them to make you a prisoner?' Concessions were in no sense a deal or bargain to be agreed, after which they could settle down to serve their time. Instead, they merely cleared the way and stimulated further demands. The primary objective was not an easing of the conditions of confinement or improved amenities and comforts. These were active soldiers on a harassing campaign to be conducted by administrative skirmishes and attrition.

In accordance with this programme, on 3 April a further set of demands was lodged: a letter a day out; two visits a week (instead of one per month), a daily newspaper (own purchase) and unlimited parcels and books. Most important was the demand for virtually unrestricted contact between prisoners: cells were to be opened from 8 a.m. to 10 p.m., and there was to be free association during those hours. Were these demands not granted by noon on 4 April, four named prisoners would go on hunger strike.[137] The staffing and financial implications of these changes, let alone increased control, security and political risks, meant that there was no chance of their being conceded.

The Arbour Hill and Curragh prisoners continued to campaign in the months that followed. That they should receive more privileges than ordinary criminals could be justified by the government, anxious to insist that it was not acting through weakness, and able to cite customary practices going back to the origin of the state. They were a class apart from all other prisoners because they had been sentenced by the Military Tribunal and were being held in special prisons. For the men, however, the objectives remained: a campaign behind the lines, maximalist demands, and the engineering of situations to show them in a favourable light and the government in a poor one. Far from sophisticated by today's standards of spin, the men and their support organisations sought whatever favourable publicity could be harvested.[138] Prisoners regarded their incarceration as a further iniquity of an illegitimate government; the government saw imprisonment as a well-merited punishment for challenges to lawfully constituted authority and detention as an outer wall in the defences of the state. There was also indignation that the IRA's gratuitous and ungrateful activities should continue even as de Valera moved the state towards the Republic. Both parties appealed to the wider circles of republican voters and supporters. As with Cosgrave before him, de Valera had to avoid being cast as heavy-handed in his dealings with honest and unselfish, if perhaps misguided and excessively zealous patriots. At the same time, he could not afford to relax prison conditions to the point where the government appeared or indeed actually did relinquish critical controls. Such a spiral could have dangerous outcomes. The game of demand, response, concession, counter-demand and veto had to be played with attentiveness and flexibility and a constant awareness of the gallery as well as the stalls.

Hard time

The de Valera government had drawn on the support of many voters who were now distinctly uneasy about the imprisonment of IRA men, thinking that such repression (as they saw it) had gone out with Cosgrave.[139] They were understandably shocked when they heard that the disciplinary regime at the Curragh and at Arbour Hill was in some ways tougher than that imposed by the despised Treaty government. There were, in consequence, many letters to Aiken and de Valera from their supporters. E. Drummond, from Tralee (a strongly republican area), wrote that he was so disturbed by reports from the Curragh, where his two sons were held, that he had gone there himself to see them and to allay family anxieties. The Curragh Governor had refused to see him and had sent a soldier to turn him away:

> As one of the unfortunate republican parents who has been absolutely deceived by your government and one who did his utmost for the election of your party. I take it upon myself to remind you of one of your own statements when speaking in Tralee, *viz.* 'Fool me once, shame on you, Fool me twice, shame on me.'[140]

There had been many public-order arrests in the autumn of 1934 as a result of the IRA's anti-Blueshirt campaign and also Blueshirt militancy. Throughout the early months of 1935, protests were lodged by Fianna Fáil members and supporters, concerning because the dissent was coming, in many cases, from core de Valera supporters. The impact on ministers was shown by the fact that Aiken replied personally to several letters. His tone was far from apologetic, especially when the letter-writing appeared to be following a republican campaign. He was well aware that whatever he wrote would be circulated and discussed in the locality and beyond and was careful to avoid giving a message that could be turned against the government. One group in particular infuriated Aiken as the recipients of undeserved solicitude. They had been charged with assaulting two off-duty soldiers at Lismore, near Tralee, Co. Kerry on the night of 27 October 1934. The defendants had behaved in what was seen as a disrespectful and contemptuous manner during proceedings before the Military Tribunal. The Tribunal Chairman or the Prosecutor had evidently complained to Aiken. He sent the men to the Glasshouse at the Curragh to serve six months for contempt of court. To ensure that the message was driven home, all privileges, including visits, were withheld. Aiken was determined to punish what he saw as loutish behaviour, and to make an example. At face value, however, without details of the background, these prisoners could be represented as victims of a vindictive government.

Several correspondents wrote from the heartland republican counties of Kerry and Tipperary; there were also protest resolutions from public bodies. Because of extensive IRA disturbances and attacks in the Tralee area and a number of arrests and prosecutions, there were several protests and expressions of concern. Daniel Curran, a member of the Tralee Urban District Council, had a son in the Curragh, as a consequence of one of these incidents.[141] Curran had complained that his son had been imprisoned simply for refusing to give an account of his movements. Not so, Aiken fulminated: he had been part of a mob that had, in a brutal manner, 'overpowered, stripped and beat a couple of unarmed Volunteers'.[142] In addition, he had comported himself before the Tribunal as if he were proud 'of the cowardly and blackguardly act with which he [was] charged'. If innocent, why not say so at the first opportunity? Alternatively, had he, 'in a wild and unthinking moment', taken part in the attack, why not express regret and make it clear he would not do the like again? Had this been his course of action, Aiken observed, 'I feel sure that little or no punishment would have been inflicted on him.' Aiken had been to the Curragh the week before and had found Curran's son in perfectly good health. He had been on hunger strike for a few days, but had been taking food since Christmas Day. Aiken regretted that the rumours of ill-treatment had caused anxiety and pain. Surely Curran should have guessed that the stories were untrue and 'only part of the unscrupulous propaganda of those who are out to damage the government'. Everything possible was being done to keep the prisoners healthy, and he advised Curran to find out who had started the rumours and point out to them that this type of propaganda 'as well as being mean, is unfair to the relatives of the prisoners'.[143]

Curran was a Fianna Fáil member of his Urban District Council and therefore a person of local and party importance. It was therefore understandable that the Minister for Defence should write at such length and go personally to the Curragh, the more emphatically to refute rumour. Ireland was a small country, in which county, town and townland – and interlocking family loyalties – ran deep and meant a great deal. In the 1930s, moreover, local government had a more substantial part in governance than it has today – more discretion and a more direct access to its funding. Majorities in the Dáil were small, and every seat mattered. On the same day that Aiken wrote to Curran, the Tralee Urban District Council passed a resolution protesting at the 'torture and ill-treatment' of IRA prisoners at Arbour Hill, Belfast Prison and the Glasshouse. At the Glasshouse, 'the son of our respected member, Mr Curran, is with six other Tralee boys suffering'.[144] A similar resolution was also passed by the local Thomas Ashe Fianna Fáil Cumann, asking that their members be allowed to visit the Curragh. Aiken must have been furious at this representation of the facts but replied in vigorous but courteous terms. The prisoners, whom he had seen himself, were all in perfectly good health. Visits were not being allowed at the Curragh, and he could not therefore give cumann members access. Some people would like to see the prisoners ill-treated so that they might have a real grievance against the government: 'As they have no legitimate grievance they are busily engaged in making false charges and even if every member of Fianna Fáil in Tralee were to see the prisoners it would not stop these charges being circulated.'[145]

A well-attended public meeting in Tralee on 11 January 1935 protested at the alleged ill-treatment.[146] Other Fianna Fáil branches in Kerry and Tipperary wrote to Aiken. Denis Daly, Kerry Fianna Fáil TD, warned about the state of public feeling. The Curragh men were not being as well treated as those at Arbour Hill and were being held in solitary confinement. Certain Gaelic Athletic Association (GAA) clubs in the county had decided to cease all activities until the Kerry prisoners were removed from the Glasshouse. This would have well-publicised consequences on the forthcoming Gaelic football match between Munster and Ulster, for which ten Kerry players had been selected to play. The Munster Council of the GAA would make an official announcement on the abstention of the Kerry players and there would be publicity. Daly recommended immediate action 'to alleviate the tension and bitterness arising from this alleged "Glasshouse affair"'.[147]

Aiken was no more placatory towards his Dáil colleague than he had been to the Tralee protestors. Daly, he wrote, was wrong to suppose that Arbour Hill and Curragh conditions were the same. There were a number of differences between the two regimes, 'which I published in the newspapers two or three times'. The Curragh prisoners were not allowed association, visits or smoking: 'They are getting four hours a day exercise, however, and all the books they want.' He had been prepared to move the Kerry prisoners back to Arbour Hill had he received any assurance from them that they would not behave at their trial 'as if they were proud of being charged with beating up Volunteers'. He referred Daly to his earlier reply to Curran: 'This letter contained my view on the whole matter. The people have given us a job to do and we must prevent any section interfering with our progress.'[148]

Another tack was taken by Duagh Fianna Fáil Cumann, Kilmorna, Co. Kerry. This time the letter went to Eamonn Kissane, the local TD, requesting his intercession; he forwarded it to Aiken. Leniency was requested for a number of local boys in Arbour Hill. They were farm workers, and their detention would cause a severe hardship to a badly hit section of the community, who, up until then, had helped Fianna Fáil, 'and I daresay will again'. The men had 'got a fright they won't soon forget and it seems their company don't given them any credit'.[149]

As we have noted, at this time and for a while thereafter, a section of the political prisoners consisted of members of organisations affiliated to Eoin O'Duffy's Blueshirts.[150] Republicans were concerned that no undue privileges should be granted to their opponents. Seosamh O'Ceannaigh contacted Aiken on 6 April 1935, saying that he had reliable information that Arbour Hill Blueshirt prisoners had been allowed to hold a meeting without supervision. The military policeman on duty was asked by one of the prisoners to leave the room. He refused but was subsequently instructed to do so by a senior officer. If Aiken wished to have further information, O'Ceannaigh would provide it.[151]

Despite this concern that neither group should have favourable treatment, prisoners, even avowed enemies, find surprising degrees of common cause against their captor. An intercepted letter from a Blueshirt prisoner, Kevin Holland, to Eoin O'Duffy complained that the Arbour Hill leader of the League of Youth, the Blueshirt organisation for young people, a man called Quinlan, had struck up too close a relationship of cooperation with Seán Ryan, his IRA counterpart. Ryan was a particular *bête noir* of the Blueshirts because of his role in attacking one of their meetings in Tralee, when several members were injured. It seemed particularly outrageous to Holland, therefore, that Quinlan had spent several hours in consultation with Seán Ryan. The result of the meeting had been agreement on joint action for further privileges: 'We have now received orders which is as follows, receive no visits write no letters do nothing regarding the general cleanliness of the prison do no washing clean no lavatorys draw no coal and to say all do nothing'.[152] Holland deplored cooperation with an organisation that had opposed freedom of speech and had attacked and murdered so many Blueshirts. He asked Duffy to remove Quinlan as the Blueshirt prisoners' leader in Arbour Hill. He set out the demands for which the non-cooperation campaign was being waged: 'One is a raido [*sic*] to be installed in here (2) the daily papers ever [*sic*] day (3) a swimming pool (4) a handball alley in the compound, are those demands made by any sane man.'[153]

From June through to October 1935, the opposing groups had made a number of demands wildly beyond any possibility of being granted. Among those had indeed been a wireless and a swimming pool. By the standards of the day, both requests were outlandish. The wireless had become a common feature of many Irish homes above the poorest, but the idea that one should be installed in a prison would have provoked a deal of derisive incredulity. At a time when few if any schools or indeed localities had a swimming pool, the notion of prisoners splashing about was not to be entertained, except as a form of satire.

The IRA did not pursue the swimming-pool dream and soon dropped their demand for a wireless. In support of their other demands, in the first week in June the Blueshirts refused to take exercise, but prisoners looking out on the summer weather they were missing may have reflected on the folly of a protest that inconvenienced no one but themselves: it petered out after a few days. The IRA prisoners stuck to their demands that their food be served by an orderly of their own choice, the issue being the right to appoint the orderly. De Valera – himself one of the great prisoner campaigners and tacticians, a pioneer of the extension of political campaigning into prisons – well knew what was at stake and was determined to stand firm.

Within a few months, the struggle between the IRA and the prison administration had become manifest, as had the government's determination to defend its authority. (The Blueshirts were largely irrelevant.) The IRA wanted to resurrect the regimes that had been granted in Mountjoy during the first weeks of the Civil War, with parcels, letters and food being distributed by the men's own orderlies, acting under the instruction of their OC. By mid-1935, Aiken had tightened control at Arbour Hill and the Glasshouse. On or about 16 May 1935, he issued an order that in future no books, cigarettes or, with the exception of clothing, parcels would be accepted from relatives on their monthly visits.[154] The contest of wills continued through the summer and into the autumn of 1935. It was later claimed that the non-cooperating prisoners had been induced to call off their campaign on 14 October, on a promise that they would be allowed to receive parcels and to appoint orderlies. The Governor, it was said, reneged on the agreement and refused to allow the prisoners' orderlies to take meals to the cells. Only twenty of the prisoners were released for exercise. Their comrades then barricaded the cells in protest. The men claimed that they had subsequently, on the instructions of their OC, dismantled the barricades. The exact sequence is unclear, but a substantial body of military police arrived to restore order. They removed the barricades and stripped the cells of furniture (which had been used for the barricades) and personal property.

There was a conflict between the IRA GHQ and the Arbour Hill OC over the conduct of the protests. In September 1935, the authorities intercepted a letter sent out of the prison. Con Lehane indicated that the men's protest had not been orchestrated by him and that he had had difficulty in controlling it.[155] He had undertaken a solo hunger strike in protest at conditions. The men had then given him an ultimatum that unless he ordered them to stay barricaded in their cells – and this, he said, was tantamount to an order to refuse food – they would go on hunger strike indefinitely in sympathy with him. He did not want this, presumably aware of the impossibility of carrying through a general hunger strike. As a compromise, he ordered them to remain barricaded for four days, when both they and he would end their actions. This was done, but it had no effect in altering conditions.[156]

At this point IRA HQ suggested that the Arbour Hill protests be discontinued and that the men should again agree to take exercise. Lehane bridled at this, pointing out that, as the man on the spot, he was the more competent judge. The men would take it very badly if, having stuck it out for sixteen weeks, the protest were called off. While HQ had only suggested that the protest be called off, it was Lehane's view that it must now be continued to the end: 'Particularly on the "recognition" end, any concession on the parcels issue would satisfy their pride.' He felt that the men who had started and continued the thing, before he came into prison, were entitled to have their views considered. For himself, being confined to a cell was no great discomfort since it gave him 'a certain seclusion and privacy that I would not otherwise have'.[157]

The government placed the blame for the fracas and its aftermath on the prisoners who, it insisted, were frustrated by the stalling of their non-cooperation campaign. They had twice barricaded themselves in cells, and some had assaulted staff. While prisoners received only a few minor bruises, two of the military police were injured to the extent that one had to take a fortnight's sick leave and the other three days'. Some prisoners, it was claimed, were found to have sharpened their table knives 'into the form of daggers', and, as a precaution, the knives of all participants in the protest were confiscated. Likewise, the men who had barricaded their cells were deprived of furniture (except bedding) for a month. Those who had acted most violently during the altercation forfeited remission of sentence, and two were punished by a bread and water diet for three days.[158]

How are we to choose between these two completely different accounts of events? Quite impossible at such a distance, and without independent eye-witnesses; probably impossible even at the time. The prisoners were far from being the passive and peaceable victims portrayed in the PPC and Cumann na mBan statements. It is equally probable (if general prison history in all countries at all times is anything to go by) that their guards were not models of rule-bound rectitude. Two groups of fired-up and physically fit young men facing up to each other in a confined space will almost certainly result in an exchange of more than hard words. It is reasonable to assume, however, that had the IRA and the Blueshirts not directly challenged authority there would have been no violent encounters. The accounts of political imprisonment in Ireland up to this point shows that, for the most part, prisoners and staff fairly easily and instinctively lived in a condition of mutual toleration and even a degree of workaday friendliness.

The prisoners claimed that when the most serious confrontation took place the military police were under the influence of drink, and, in that condition, they attacked and variously injured several men.[159] Writing to Mrs Leddy, wife (or possibly mother) of Charles Leddy, one of the men who was allegedly beaten, the Secretary General of the Department of Defence denied that Leddy and his fellow prisoner Broderick had been beaten. The allegations were 'absolutely without foundation and are merely part of the propaganda which the government has to contend with from foreign and, unfortunately, also Irish sources'. Some of the Arbour Hill men, he conceded, including her husband, had refused food for a few days.[160]

With the full backing of de Valera and other ministers, Aiken refused to soften the regime. At the end of 1935, the Executive Council decided that conditions were sufficiently stable to justify the release of thirty-five men from Arbour Hill.[161] The remaining prisoners then conformed to the restricted regime which Aiken had introduced. On 1 May 1936, twenty-six remaining Arbour Hill prisoners were transferred to the Glasshouse at the Curragh.[162] Twenty-seven men awaiting trial before the Military Tribunal were then moved from Mountjoy to Arbour Hill. These immediately began a campaign for free association within the prison, in support of which they refused exercise, one man hunger-striking for two days. Aiken responded to this by withdrawing tobacco and issuing an even tighter set of regulations. These initiated a contest of wills and confinement of exceptional strictness.

The protests were hampered by the severely restricted communications between the men, who were confined in their cells for twenty-four hours a day.[163] The impact of this can be seen in the sporadic and rather desperate attempts by various IRA officers to make use of the chapel to issue orders and exhortations. More often than not, hunger-striking was on an individual rather than collective basis; sometimes meals were accepted or rejected alternately. At the beginning of May 1936, however, a group of twenty-six men refused exercise to back their demand for free association.[164] By mid-May several men had gone on individual hunger strikes, the twenty-six continued to refuse exercise (though four others took it). After a hunger strike of ten days, Seán MacSweeney was temporarily transferred to St Bricin's hospital. Christopher Aherne, described as a 'Mental Case', was removed to the same hospital on 14 May 1936 and was released altogether by order of the Military Tribunal eleven days later. Whether his condition was pre-existing or arose out of his imprisonment was not clear.[165]

The Military Tribunal had begun to hand out sentences of between three and twelve months. Moss Twomey was committed to Arbour Hill on 23 May 1936 and almost immediately assumed a leadership role – scarcely surprising since before arrest he had been Chief of Staff. His presence did little to loosen the tight control under which the men were being held. Concerned about the effects of prolonged solitary confinement on what, with a few exceptions, was a group of young and largely inexperienced men, Twomey advised them to accept the exercise under the conditions offered and to seek to subvert the regime by any other available means. Only a few men joined him, however, when he went out, and he then reverted to the men's position. He had given his advice on his second Sunday at Arbour Hill by suddenly coming to the front of the gallery of the church, calling the congregation to attention and giving his message.[166] Twomey was not long among the remands, since on 19 June he was sentenced to three years' imprisonment by the Military Tribunal.[167]

The regulations allowed convicted prisoners at Arbour Hill four hours of exercise a day, when practicable. No communication was permitted, and the exercise had to be taken on the march, with a gap of four paces between the men.[168] Remand prisoners took their exercise under the same conditions and were also forbidden to communicate with each other. Smoking was not permitted during exercise, but a prisoner who had taken exercise could, with the Governor's permission, be allowed to smoke in his cell for the rest of the day.[169] At the core of this regime, in other words, was cellular confinement and the control of tobacco. Curragh prisoners had a markedly more liberal regime. They were not confined to their cells and could exercise and associate between 9 a.m. and 8 or 9 p.m.; they could, with the Governor's permission, smoke in their cells or at exercise.[170]

The Arbour Hill conditions, which lasted for some three months in their most severe form, were intended to be repressive and deterrent. At the individual level, men were to be brought to a realisation that misbehaviour in custody would entail Spartan living conditions and the ordeal of near isolation. As examples, the

Arbour Hill men would demonstrate that IRA activities were no longer to be punished by relatively short intervals in prison or camp under civil detainee conditions. This model of active punishment was not a new one and had been the basis for the Victorian convict regime as well as the short sharp shock of local prisons.[171] Whether Frank Aiken knew about this historical background is uncertain, but doubtful: a desire to move from the passive punishment of mere custody, with its deprivations cushioned by companionship and privileges, to one that would impart a quota of additional uncomfortable and irksome restrictions and demands lay behind the move. Officials had found their way, by trial and error, to a regime of severity, of cold comfort and psychological pressure.

Christy Quearney was arrested in May 1936 and sentenced to twelve months for membership of an illegal organisation and for drilling. He arrived at Arbour Hill from Mountjoy shortly afterwards. Exercise, he recalled, was offered for two hours a day (officials claimed it was for four) on condition that the men walked three paces apart and there was absolutely no communication. The prison had sufficient accommodation to provide an empty cell on each side of an occupied one. This prevented communication by tapping on the wall, a particularly severe hardship for those who had chosen to forgo exercise under what they saw as demeaning conditions.[172]

By September 1936, the prisoners, numbering around forty, attempted to stage hunger strikes.[173] Any kind of collective activity was extremely difficult under conditions of complete cellular confinement and almost total isolation. For example, Twomey had no idea that strikes were being staged. The men communicated in the only way they could: at church. According to Aiken, 'discreditable scenes were created after mass in Arbour Hill church on more than one occasion by way of protest'.[174] Three prisoners were give short spells of dietary punishment, and one was deprived of tobacco. Demonstrations then ceased.[175] In the summer of 1936, Finbar McCarthy of Innishannon, Co. Cork, was released from Arbour Hill and made a statement about his experience.[176] This became the centrepiece of an appeal by the relatives of Arbour Hill prisoners.[177] McCarthy painted a picture of an austere and punitive regime. In his wing, he claimed, there were just four other prisoners, all of whom were denied contact with each other and were held in complete solitary confinement in absolute silence. The military police were forbidden to speak to the prisoners; prisoners could not speak to each other and were not allowed to sing, hum or whistle.[178] Breach of silence could result in removal to 'the dungeons' (basement punishment cells).[179] Prisoners were allowed out of cells to exercise only if they had agreed to march around the exercise yard, five paces apart and not to speak; refusal of these conditions meant twenty-four-hour lock-up.[180] Visits, cigarettes and newspapers were not allowed, and the privilege of buying fruit had been withdrawn. At mass the men could see each other but could have no contact, since each was guarded by a military policeman. Communicants were accompanied to the altar rails by two policemen. The relatives' statement described this regime as 'unnatural and unchristian' and, appealing especially to the

Roman Catholic hierarchy, held that such treatment was 'against all religion'. They asked for immediate action to secure the release of their relatives 'and until & in time as they are released at least human treatment'.[181]

The Arbour Hill Governor, Commandant T. Duffy, asked to comment on McCarthy's letter, gave a somewhat different account. McCarthy was incorrect in stating that there were five prisoners on his wing: there were twelve. This seemed a rather academic point, since it was agreed that prisoners had no contact with each other; however, except for those who refused exercise, they were not in solitary confinement (the reasoning being that the non-communicating marching exercise provided the contact that turned solitary into separate confinement). He agreed that absolute silence was maintained: staff were allowed to speak to prisoners only on necessary prison matters; singing, humming and whistling were indeed prohibited. A prisoner who, when ordered, refused to stop singing had been put in a basement cell, but only for two hours. 'A number' of prisoners who took exercise were allowed to smoke in their cells. Similarly, on the recommendation of the prison medical officer, 'a number' had fruit purchased for them by staff (the implication being that conformity and submission opened the way for ameliorations). Each prisoner was guarded by a military policeman whilst in chapel because some had attempted to use the occasion to make political speeches and to issue orders. It was untrue that prisoners were accompanied to the altar rails by two policemen. The priest gave communion immediately before mass, and any member of staff who wished to receive it went up with the prisoners 'so as not to delay the Priest'.[182]

When the two versions of events are compared, it is clear that they were substantially in agreement, except for the issue of a police escort to the altar rails. An unsigned document, almost certainly issued by the IRA or by one of its support groups, set out the regime more or less as described here. It differed on some points and added a few more details. Exercise was for two hours, and, to ensure complete control, prisoners were brought into the yard in batches of four and five. After exercise they were each escorted back to their cells by two armed and silent guards. Exercise and the handing of food into the cell were the only easements in solitude. The document claimed that this life of isolation and silence had extremely adverse effects. Released prisoners claimed that on several occasions they had heard screams from other cells and that those betokened either men losing their minds, or receiving a beating from the guards, or both.[183]

The period of cellular isolation and silent exercise at Arbour Hill came suddenly to an end on Monday, 14 September 1936. The previous day, a long and time-crawling prison Sunday, Seán Glynn had committed suicide by hanging himself in his cell.[184] In a panic, correctly anticipating a strong public reaction, all the prisoners were immediately released for exercise. The previous conditions of non-communication and marching a set number of paces apart were abandoned. The regime at Arbour Hill was not dismantled, as the prisoners had demanded. Talking was allowed during exercise, but apart from that and their chapel attendance, the men remained in their cells: separate but not solitary confinement. There was none of the free association and appointment of their own orderlies that had been the basis for the earlier prison protests. The inquest on Seán Glynn was an embarrassment for the government. Moss Twomey was called to give evidence. He considered himself a tough man, he said, but the Arbour Hill conditions were the worst he had experienced.[185]

By the middle of the 1930s, two questions had been given unambiguous answers: the IRA would not accept the Fianna Fáil settlement, its legal and pending constitutional changes: it stood by the All-Ireland Republic proclaimed in 1916 and that alone, with all the overturning it involved, would do. In personal terms, Éamon de Valera, Harry Boland and Frank Aiken were assigned to a robustly tended demonology. Their circle of the inferno contained renegades, apostates, turncoats, recreants and backsliders of which there were, in the IRA view of history, many. On their part, de Valera and his execrated ministers rested on their own military and political records and their successive mandates from the electorate. The IRA had neither legitimacy nor a practical programme; it was an organisation that wished to blow a doctrine of grievances into a conflagration of civil and Anglo-Irish wars. Individuals who broke with the organisation would be allowed to find another path in life; those who remained obdurate would encounter an array of state responses. The organisation's leaders would be thwarted, pursued and, if necessary, contained for prolonged periods and broken in spirit.

The IRA had not in those years answered the question of purpose and, to a significant extent, survival displaced its wider ambitions. Defiance of the usurper and loyalty to ideals, structures, rules and comrades was enough to keep the organisation alive. It had entwined itself with rebel spirit in Irish political and popular culture. Its deeds, characters and ballads gave it a vitality that would be hard to suppress; it would claim sympathy and a surprising amount of low-level complicity on this basis. But, as with all revolutionary organisations, it had to acknowledge a fundamental axiom: to be is to do. It had tried a range of essentially unconnected things, from social campaigning to intimidation to killing, but it had failed conclusively or convincingly to demonstrate a purpose.

On the side of the government, and facing such a resilient organisation, a question had been answered at the level of method, if not objective. Practical politics excluded a revival of Victorian methods of silence, separation and hard labour to crush IRA offenders. Ireland was too deeply rooted in family and community for its inhabitants to be indifferent to the plight of errant young men in prison, especially if authority were seen as oppressive, single-minded and disproportionate. The Consolidated Regulations of 1936 acknowledged this: politically motivated offenders had to be contained, but containment was sufficient precaution and punishment in itself. Aiken and de Valera had gone beyond the limits they had clearly sensed and, in consequence, had turned perpetrators into victims.

Notes

1 J. Bowyer Bell's *The Secret Army: The IRA, 1916–1979* (Cambridge, Mass.: MIT Press, 1983), Chapter 4, provides useful background but, understandably, few precise

figures. Uinseann MacEoin's indispensable *The IRA in the Twilight Years: 1923–1948* (Dublin: Argenta, 1997), provides a mass of detail and first-hand accounts.

2 Frank Aiken, Chief of Staff, issued the proclamation on 27 April 1923; all offensive operations were to cease at noon on 30 April.

3 This measure, the Public Safety (Emergency Powers) Act, had been introduced in June 1923 to provide authority for the continued detention of around 12,000 internees. The Act had a sunset clause and was periodically renewed.

4 The Act defined treason fairly widely: levying war against the state, aiding those who levied war, conspiring to or inciting the levying of war. Attempts to levy war were also defined as treasonable. All these crimes were subject to the death penalty (see s.5[1] and Schedule). Penalties were also provided for attempts to create an alternative administration and for certain other offences (s.3). See also ss.4–7.

5 This also has a sunset clause and was renewed in 1925.

6 See *Irish Police News* (which at this point covered both the Garda Síochána and the RUC), 18 April 1925, 17a. Some 1,200 members of the Dublin Metropolitan Police entered the Gárda Siothchána.

7 Since one of the movement's roots went back to Griffith's notion of using a majority to back fundamental change, the target was more than simply tactical. An organisation that claims to embody the true interest, if not the voice, of the people must always be particularly frustrated when the electorate fails to do its duty. Like the faithful spouse awaiting a homecoming, it can keep a vigil but only for a few parliamentary cycles. Thereafter, a Penelope posture is apt to become at first pitiful, then ridiculous.

8 Bell, *The Secret Army, op. cit.*; see also MacEoin, *The IRA in the Twilight Years, op. cit.*, pp. 121–2.

9 Numerous examples of delay, circuitousness and divination of timing are provided in Doris Kearns Goodwin's highly accomplished biography of Abraham Lincoln, *Team of Rivals: The Political Genius of Abraham Lincoln* (London: Penguin, 2009). Not as great a figure as Lincoln and treading a stage diminutive by comparison, de Valera was possessed of a number of similar qualities, entwining necessary horse-trading, medium-term pragmatism and strands of idealism.

10 *Irish Independent*, 17 May 1926, 6d–e.

11 Cumann na nGaedheal (the government party) had won forty-seven seats. Instructively, in the first test after the split, Sinn Féin had taken only five seats (all of which were abstentionist). Other results were Labour, twenty-two; Independents, sixteen; Farmers' Party, eleven; and the National League (founded in 1926 by Captain William Redmond, son of John), eight.

12 *Evening Herald*, 23 June 1927, 1c–g; *Irish Independent*, 24 June 1927, 9f–g and 10a–c.

13 O'Higgins's father, Dr Thomas F. O'Higgins, was shot dead in his home by anti-Treaty IRA men on 11 February 1923, as a reprisal for government executions. His wife and two teenage sons were in the house at the time. *Evening Herald*, 11 July 1927, 1a–c, f–g, and 3e; *Irish Independent*, 11 July 1927, 7a–e, 8a–e; *Irish News*, 11 July 1927, 5a–e. On O'Higgins, see Terence de Vere White's now slightly dated (and hagiographical) *Kevin O'Higgins* (Dublin: Anvil Books, 1986). There can be no doubt, party politics aside, that the country lost a very considerable political and administrative talent – and a growing breadth of vision.

14 *Evening Herald*, 12 July 1927, 1a–b; *Irish Independent*, 13 July 1927, 7d. Ten men were arrested on 18 July 1927 in connection with the shooting and remanded in custody (*Evening Herald*, 18 July 1927, 1a–b; *Irish Independent*, 19 July 1927, 10b). All were released without charge a week later when gardaí offered no evidence in court (*Evening Herald*, 25 July 1927, 1a–b; *Irish Independent*, 26 July 1927, 9b). Tim Pat Coogan, well informed about republican activities, and drawing on sources alive in the 1960s, stated that the shooting was carried out by two young IRA men acting independently

of their organisation. Neither was brought to justice. Tim Pat Coogan, *The IRA* (London: Fontana, 1980), pp. 79–80. Later evidence, published by Uinseann MacEoin in Harry White, *Harry: The Story of Harry White as Related to Uinseann MacEoin* (Dublin: Argenta, 1985), confirmed that the murder had been an official IRA action and named the three men as Timothy Coughlan, Archie Doyle and Bill Gannon. See also the account in MacEoin, *The IRA in the Twilight Years*, *op. cit.*, pp. 136–7.

15 The Public Safety Act, 1927, was a comprehensive measure, amending the Constitution, and, in twenty-eight sections and a two-part schedule, dealing with unlawful associations, the publication of documents and journals of such bodies, expulsion and search orders, police powers, court processes, parental responsibility and forfeitures. It also authorised the establishment of special courts (laying down membership requirements that would be followed in successive Acts thereafter). The Firearms Act, 1925, was strengthened by additional penalties for possessing or carrying firearms: these started with three years' imprisonment and extended to the death penalty.

16 Electoral (Amendment No. 2) Act, 1927, ss.2 and 3.

17 This was part of a Fianna Fáil statement; see *Irish News*, 11 August 1927, 5a.

18 *Irish Independent*, 12 August 1927, 7a–b. See also *Irish News*, 11 August 1927, 5a–c; *Evening Herald*, 11 August 1927, 1a–b.

19 It is an indication of how closely de Valera had guarded and disguised his intentions that the Fianna Fáil's newspaper *The Nation* of 13 August 1927, which had gone to press before the decision to enter the Dáil had been revealed, denounced precisely the course that he had taken: 'If all the Fianna Fáil deputies published tomorrow a signed declaration that in their opinion the oath in the Free State Constitution is an unsworn undertaking, the oath would still remain the oath and to swear to it falsely would still continue to be perjury.'

20 Mary MacSwiney, writing some years later to her former comrade Seán T. O'Kelly, was still gripped by fury, much of it personalised. Did he and de Valera and Ruttledge really think they were going to smash the IRA? 'Are you such fools as to think you can succeed where your predecessors have failed?' She was not pleading with him for loyal Irishmen 'who are being gaoled or hunted by Aiken's bullies today, as they were by Mulcahy's bullies a few years ago, by the Black and Tan bullies earlier still… I am pleading with you against your own dishonour and disloyalty to all you ever professed.' MacSwiney Papers, P/48A/139 (1936).

21 *Dáil Debates*, vol. 20, cols. 1670–748, 16 August 1927. Seán T. O'Kelly (speaking in Irish) was the only Fianna Fáil contributor to the debate; the attack was led by Thomas Johnson, Labour leader. See also *Evening Herald*, 16 August 1927, 1c–e; *Irish News*, 17 August 1927, 7a–b; *Irish Independent*, 17 August 1927, 7a–b.

22 Alderman John Jinks, one of the members of Redmond's National League, was, it is said, waylaid by Major Bryan Cooper, an Independent, intent on supporting the Government. A hearty lunch with copious wine kept Alderman Jinks from voting, while Cooper returned to the Dáil to vote for the government. See MacEoin, *The IRA in the Twilight Years*, *op. cit.*, pp. 138–9; F. S. L. Lyons, *Ireland since the Famine* (London: Fontana, 1973), p. 500. Unlike British parliamentary practice, which can see a government with a narrow majority repeatedly tested and ambushed, the emerging Free State convention was to leave in office a party which had survived a no-confidence vote. This vote, however, had been so clearly secured by dubious means that another was inevitable. That being the case, the government had either to reconcile itself to another test of confidence in short order or to another election.

23 The other results were Farmers' Party, six; Labour, thirteen; National League, two; Independents, twelve; Independent Labour, one. Sinn Féin won no seats.

24 *An Phoblacht*, 16 April 1926, 3a.

25 Such a chronology was assembled by the de Valera government in 1941 and remains an invaluable guide to IRA activities between 1931 and 1940: UCDA, P/104/3712, 'Departmental Notes on Events from 1 January 1931 to 31 December 1940'. Uinseann MacEoin (*The IRA in the Twilight Years, op. cit.*, pp. 69–410) has assembled an equivalent and equally informative chronology with an oppositionist, IRA, bent.

26 'Departmental Notes', *op. cit.*, p. 216.

27 Juries (Protection) Act, 1929. This provided for secret jury selection, protection of juries and imprisonment for refusal to recognise the court.

28 *Irish Independent*, 13 June 1929, 9a–b.

29 According to press reports, the British soldiers, and their women and children, were fired on from a Rolls-Royce car by four men in Free State officers' uniforms; two Lewis guns were used (*Irish News*, 22 March 1924, 5a–c; *Irish Independent*, 22 March 1924, 7a–c; *Northern Whig*, 25 March 1924, 7d). The victims were stationed at one of the 'Treaty Port' bases. The Free State immediately apologised, offered to pay compensation and posted a £10,000 reward for the apprehension of five named suspects. See MacEoin, *The IRA in the Twilight Years, op. cit.*, p. 101, for a brief description of the incident.

30 *Irish Independent*, 7 November 1925, 6a; *Irish News*, 7 November 1925, 7c; *Northern Whig*, 7 November 1925, 8c. Killeen (aka Grace) and two other members of the IRA were being escorted to Mullingar Circuit Court. Foiled in the rescue, the armed party then raided the railway-station office and the local post office (at Longwood, Co. Meath, some three miles away), presumably in search of funds.

31 *Nenagh Guardian*, 28 November 1925, 5g; *Irish Independent*, 28 November 1925, 7a–b; *Irish News*, 28 November 1925, 5a; 30 November 1925, 5d (confirmed list of escapers); *Northern Whig*, 28 November 1925, 8b; 30 November 1925, 8c; MacEoin, *The IRA in the Twilight Years, op. cit.*, pp. 122–3. In what would be an astonishingly persistent theme in IRA operations, the rescue nearly failed because of transport difficulties: only one taxi turned up to take the men away from the prison.

32 *Irish News*, 30 December 1925, 5c; *Northern Whig*, 30 December 1925, 5g. It was said that Dowling had been singled out 'for being too nosey' (MacEoin, *The IRA in the Twilight Years, op. cit.*, p. 124).

33 *Irish News*, 15 November 1926, 5a–b; *Northern Whig*, 15 November 1926, 7c. According to reports, Garda Ward's injuries were not too serious and despite his having been shot twice in the face, he was able to walk from the ambulance to the train. See also *Irish Times*, 16 November 1926, 7b and 9b; *Manchester Guardian*, 16 November 1926, 11e.

34 *Irish News*, 17 December 1926, 5e. In line with perennial practice, blame was fixed on these comparatively low-ranking detectives, who were reprimanded and demoted to uniform.

35 The *Irish News* (10 November 1925, 5a–b) reported that the raiders were after Poppy Day documents, including lists of collectors (presumably for retaliation) but left empty-handed. See also *Northern Whig* (10 November 1925, 7g) for incidents in connection with Armistice Day. Other reports appeared in the *Irish News* (12 November 1925, 5f–g) and the *Northern Whig* (12 November 1925, 7d). Many of the incidents occurred in the vicinity of Trinity College Dublin.

36 There were concerted attacks on garda barracks on the night of 12/13 November 1926: twelve in Cork, Kerry and Meath; twenty-four in Co. Waterford (MacEoin, *The IRA in the Twilight Years, op. cit.*, p. 129).

37 MacEoin, *The IRA in the Twilight Years, op. cit.*, p. 126.

38 MacEoin, *The IRA in the Twilight Years, op. cit.*, p. 128.

39 MacEoin, *The IRA in the Twilight Years, op. cit.*, p. 129. Elsewhere MacEoin notes that 'the restless companies of the IRA had to be given tasks, and one such from time to

time in different areas, could be a local trade boycott; burning a pro British film, or the destruction of newspapers' (pp. 133–4).

40 *Irish Times*, 16 November 1926, 7b and 8b. The raid on St Luke's Barracks was one of several – all seeking arms and documents.

41 *Manchester Guardian*, 16 November 1926, 11e.

42 Public Safety (Emergency Powers) Act, 1926.

43 *Irish News*, 15 December 1926, 5e; *Northern Whig*, 15 December 1926, 7e.

44 Although wounded in the leg, Grace chased the attackers, stopping only when he collapsed because of a lack of blood. *Irish News*, 24 January 1928, 5e.

45 *Irish News*, 30 January 1928, 5f.

46 *Irish Independent*, 28 July 1930, 8d.

47 MacEoin, *The IRA in the Twilight Years, op. cit.*, p. 187.

48 *Irish Independent*, 24 November 1930, 9a–b; *Irish News*, 24 November 1930, 5c.

49 As noted, a calendar of IRA activities, including acts of violence, threats, training, the stockpiling of arms and explosives, and government and police responses, was compiled in 1941 on the orders of Harry Boland, Minister for Justice. This provides a systematic and (as far as can be seen) comprehensive account of these years. See 'Departmental Notes', *op. cit.* See also *Irish News*, 31 January 1931, 5d. Detective Superintendent Ennis told the subsequent inquest that Carroll had indeed been a police informer (*Irish News*, 24 February 1931, 5e). See also *Irish News*, 2 February 1931, 5d; *Irish News*, 3 February 1931, 5d.

50 *Irish Independent*, 23 March 1931, 9a–c.

51 Ryan had received a note from the IRA on 29 April, warning him to leave the country, on pain of death (MacEoin, *The IRA in the Twilight Years, op. cit.*, p. 198).

52 *Irish Press*, 14 September 1931, 1e. The notice also displayed the skull and crossbones device.

53 This attack was apparently not an attempted murder but an effort to destroy documents relating to Land Annuities. *Irish Press*, 16 September 1931, 1c–d; *Irish News*, 16 September 1931, 5f.

54 See, for example, the open letter from Ghosts to James Fitzgerald Kennedy, criticising his 'brutal ill-treatment' of political prisoners (Humphreys Papers, P/106/1457, June 1930). Even more pointed, see the circular issued to the jury in the case of Seán McGuinness, charged with prison escape in 1926. There was no threat whatever in the letter, which simply made a political case. But the fact that 'Ghosts' knew the juror's address was threat in itself (Humphreys Papers, P/106/1458, 20 April 1931). Jury tampering (and jury packing) had been features of political trials for generations and under British rule had at times been blatant and shameless. It was therefore a wholly familiar part of the repertoire. Máire Comerford, Sighle Humphreys and Helena Moloney had been charged with the offence of endeavouring to induce jurors to disregard their oaths (*Evening Herald*, 9 December 1926, 1b–c). Humphreys had also been arrested in April 1928 for disrupting the court during the trial of Florence McCarthy.

55 Constitution (Amendment No. 17) Act, 1931, Part II. On Creagh, see the curiously incomplete obituaries in the *Irish Times* (27 January 1947, 6b) and the *Sunday Independent* (26 January 1947, 1b).

56 Ten organisations were banned, including the IRA and its support bodies, extending to the WPDL. Several left socialist and Communist bodies also found a place on the list: Friends of Soviet Russia, the Irish Labour Defence League, the Workers' Defence Corps, the Irish Working Farmers' Committee and the Workers' Research Bureau (*Iris Oifigiúil*, 23 October 1931). None of these could reasonably be said to be a threat to the state, and their inclusion, alongside the IRA, reflected a growing concern about what were seen as the gathering forces of Communism. (See, for example, *Dáil Debates*, vol. 51, cols. 1089–92, 1210–24, 20 March 1934.)

57 The official name of the Tribunal was the Constitution (Special Powers) Tribunal. Five army officers were appointed on 20 October 1931 (*Iris Oifigiúil*, 23 October 1931).

58 The Gilmores were sentenced on 9 December 1931 on a variety of charges: assisting in the formation of an illegal military organisation, possession of arms, conspiracy and contempt of court (*Irish News*, 10 December 1931, 5f). See also the *Irish Times*, 12 December 1931, 11a–b. Gardaí had uncovered a large arms dump in the vicinity of the Gilmores's isolated dwelling in the Dublin mountains. It included an assortment of rifles, ammunition, explosives and a Lewis machine gun. Equally damning was a large store of IRA documents.

59 The Tribunal showed that where there was willingness to renounce the IRA, leniency would be shown. The first step was for the defendant to recognise the court. Daniel McKiernan, of Drumdiffer, Co. Leitrim, was charged with the possession of firearms and with IRA membership, as was Patrick Mitchell. Character references were submitted, home circumstances (an elderly father and small farm in McKiernan's case) outlined and a detailed statement of repentance and renunciation was read to the court. There were also promises to assist the police and to do all possible to persuade comrades to break their connection with the IRA. The court directed that the men be released once they had entered into recognisances (*Irish Times*, 12 December 1931, 13a). A number of other cases from Co. Mayo, Co. Clare and Co. Kerry were reported at the same time.

60 The other results were Labour, seven; Farmers' Party, four; Independents, thirteen.

61 Tim Pat Coogan, *De Valera: Long Fellow, Long Shadow* (London: Hutchinson, 1993), p. 463; Donal O'Sullivan, *The Irish Free State and Its Senate* (London: Faber & Faber, 1940), p. 295. Ominously, the Dublin Brigade of the IRA paraded under military command, accompanied by uniformed members of Cumann na mBan.

62 UCDA, Frank Aiken Papers, P/104/2804/2, Constitution (Special Powers) Tribunal, memorandum, July 1936.

63 The IRA deployed in uniform and under military command, as did the Cumann na mBan.

64 The Army Comrades' Association, part of which would mutate into the Blueshirt movement, met in convention on St Patrick's Day, appointed a national executive and demanded the reinstatement of preferential employment opportunities for ex-members of the Irish Army (*Irish Times*, 18 March 1932, 9f).

65 *Irish Times*, 14 March 1932, 7f–g; see also *An Phoblacht*, 12 March 1932, 1a–d, for articles by Moss Twomey, IRA Chief of Staff, and Peadar O'Donnell.

66 The Statute passed into law on 11 December 1931 as the Act to Give Effect to Certain Resolutions Passed by Imperial Conferences Held in the Years 1926 and 1930. Through its participation in imperial conferences and its relations with other dominions, the Free State had played a leading part in preparing the way for the measure.

67 Constitution (Removal of Oath) Act, 1933. The Seanad inserted an amendment requiring negotiation of the Oath's removal with the British government. After a further general election (1933), the Bill went again to the Seanad and again was held up, pending negotiations. After a sixty-day delay and some subsidiary legislation, the Bill was finally passed in May 1933, without negotiations with London.

68 Speech at Fianna Fáil Ard Fheis, 9 November 1933. 'All Republican organisations' was a scarcely veiled reference to the IRA and its auxiliaries.

69 Land annuity payments originated in the land reforms of previous decades whereby the government bought out landlords and tenants purchased the land they farmed by small annual payments. The Anglo-Irish Financial Agreements of 1925 and 1926 provided that these repayments were forwarded to the British Exchequer, which had funded the original buy-out. Republicans of all degrees of militancy found it

iniquitous and intolerable that Irish taxpayers should underwrite what was in effect the purchase of lands seized in the British conquest.

70 The other results were Cumann na nGaedheal, forty-eight; Labour, eight; Independent Labour, one; Independents, eight; and Central Party, eleven.

71 *Irish Press*, 11 January 1933, 1f–g.

72 O'Duffy was dismissed on 22 February 1933, a month after Fianna Fáil's victory. He was offered but declined another civil-service post. A special Act was brought in (the Garda Síochána Pensions Act, 1933) so that O'Duffy could be paid his pension at the maximum rate. De Valera had signalled his intention to be rid of him when, on 17 December 1932, he removed Colonel David Neligan from his post in charge of the Detective Division, replacing him with the trusted Colonel Eamon Broy. The Detective Division dealt, *inter alia*, with political crime, and its head could not but be political. Broy moved up again, taking over from O'Duffy as Commissioner of the Garda Síochána.

73 *Iris Oifigiúil*, 11 August 1933; *Irish Times*, 14 August 1933, 6c. Under the measure (which had been repealed in 1928 but which was now revived), the Executive Council could declare an organisation which had certain objectives and characteristics to be an unlawful organisation. The unlawful elements included an intention forcibly to overthrow the state, the promotion or encouragement of the unlawful possession of firearms, the encouragement of non-payment of rates and taxes, and the like (Public Safety Act, 1927, s.4[1–4]). Membership of an unlawful organisation could be punished by between three and five years' penal servitude or up to two years' imprisonment, with or without hard labour (s.5).

74 Such incidents are too numerous to list, but the Military Tribunal took a serious view of them. On 14 October 1934, armed men raided a house in Tralee and seized a Volunteer uniform. A member of the IRA raiding party was brought before the Tribunal and sentenced to two years' imprisonment. The victim of the attack was subsequently beaten by armed and masked men ('Departmental Notes', *op. cit.*, p. 27). In February 1935, Moss Twomey urged his men to smash the Volunteer Force, and a number of attacks followed ('Departmental Notes', *op. cit.*, p. 34).

75 'Departmental Notes', p. 16. The campaign had been started by the Boycott British League and was then taken over by the IRA in August 1933.

76 See, for example, the reports of Blueshirt marches and counter-demonstrations in the cities of Cork, Limerick and Waterford on 20 August 1933.

77 O'Reilly died on 29 December 1933 (*Irish Press*, 30 December 1933, 7b; see also *Irish Independent*, 30 December 1933, 9f–g and 11a–d). The *Irish Press* reported that a week before the attack the two men had been named in a piece in *An Phoblacht* under the caption 'Imperialist Hooligans' (see *An Phoblacht*, 21 October 1933, 8d). 'Departmental Notes', *op. cit.*, pp. 17–18.

78 *Irish Press*, 7 October 1933, 1a–b; *Irish Independent*, 7 October 1933, 9a–e.

79 In retaliation for their part in protecting O'Duffy from the counter-demonstration at Tralee, the Garda barracks was attacked with rifles and revolvers. Twelve men were brought before the Military Tribunal for their part in the Tralee disorders, and each received sentences of three months' imprisonment ('Departmental Notes', *op. cit.*, p. 17).

80 Daly had been attacked around 3 a.m. on Christmas morning, after attending midnight mass. He died at his home on 4 January 1934, without regaining consciousness (see *Irish News*, 5 January 1934, 5c; *Irish Press*, 5 January 1934, 7g). Joe Collins, active in the IRA in Dunmanway, Co. Cork, claimed in his memoirs that the organisation had no hand in Daly's murder and that he and five IRA companions had found him lying in Main Street, unconscious. It appeared to them that Daly had been in drink and had fallen over and cracked his skull. There are complaints about police attempts to make a murder case against the men but no fear of a perjured witness:

'We knew that was not likely because anyone who did so would know he was probably signing his Death Warrant'. Joe Collins, 'Memoirs', unpaginated.

81 *Irish News*, 12 February 1934, 5a–b; *Irish Press*, 12 February 1934, 1a–b and 2b. Four Dundalk men were brought before the Military Tribunal, charged with the murder of Mrs McGrory. After a trial lasting five days, all were acquitted.

82 A section of the debate on the Wearing of Uniform (Restriction) Bill, 1934, is instructive on these events and the perspectives of the parties (*Dáil Debates*, vol. 51, cols. 537–98, 13 March 1934).

83 See the Pastoral Letter of the Bishop of Waterford and Lismore, read in Waterford Cathedral on Sunday, 6 January 1935. By joining or remaining members of the IRA, Catholics were putting themselves in opposition to the Church's teaching, imperilling their immortal souls and 'cutting themselves off from all that is glorious in the historic past of their native land' (*The Standard*, 11 January 1935, 1a–c and 2a–b).

84 The estate was owned by Miss Maria E. Sanderson. She had been certified as being of unsound mind and so the estate was under court administration. At first the management was conducted by a member of the family, but in the summer of 1935 Gerald More O'Ferrall was appointed to the position of estate manager.

85 *Irish Press*, 13 July 1935, 1a–c; 11 December 1935, 5c; *Irish Independent*, 13 July 1935, 9g, 10c–f.

86 *Dáil Debates*, vol. 56, cols. 305–22, 2 May 1935; see also cols. 368–99, *passim*, 3 May 1935.

87 'Departmental Notes', *op. cit.*, p. 38.

88 For lists of prisoners' names and offences, 1934–6, see UCDA P/104/2802 (1–19).

89 *Irish Press*, 26 March 1926, 1e; *Irish Independent*, 25 March 1936, 9a–b. It is possible that Somerville's involvement in the British Secret Intelligence Service during and after the First World War was known to the IRA and that this was a factor in his assassination. For an account of the murder, see Joseph O'Neill's *Blood-Dark Track* (London: Granta, 2001).

90 Bell, *The Secret Army*, *op. cit.*, p. 126. Tim Pat Coogan (*De Valera*, *op. cit.*, p. 480), on direct interview evidence, states that Tom Barry, the famous fighter of the Anglo-Irish War and an IRA leader, gave the order. No one was arrested in connection with the murder, but in late April there was a major round-up of Cork activists. The Military Tribunal imposed sentences of between three and twelve months' imprisonment.

91 The victim was John Egan, aged twenty-four. He was shot in the street and died in the nearby house of a priest (*Irish Independent*, 28 April 1936, 9a–c; *Irish Press*, 28 April 1936, 1a–b and 7c). Michael Conway was sentenced to death for the murder, but the sentence was commuted to life at penal servitude. Three others were brought before the Military Tribunal in connection with the offence.

92 See, for example, the intervention of Professor O'Sullivan (Fine Gael) in a supply debate on 7 May 1935 (*Dáil Debates*, vol. 56, cols. 415, *et seq.*)

93 Boland denounced Somerville's murder as 'a cowardly crime' and expressed the government's determination to do all that was possible to bring the culprits to justice (*Dáil Debates*, vol. 61, col. 364, 26 March 1936).

94 Twomey was arrested on 21 May 1936 and brought to trial on 19 June charged with membership of an unlawful organisation and refusing to give an account of his movements. A large number of IRA documents had been taken from Twomey on arrest. He was found guilty of membership of an illegal organisation, the reason for his lengthy sentence, it being unquestionable that he was the IRA Chief of Staff. Little information is given on this in his military detention file (MA, Civilian Prisoners, 1937); *Irish Press*, 20 June 1936, 7d–e; *Irish Independent*, 20 June 1936, 8c–e.

95 *Iris Oifigiúil*, 20 June 1936.

96 *Irish Press*, 22 June 1936, 1a–b and 2c–d. See also Frank Gallagher's article at 10b–c; *Irish Independent*, 22 June 1936, 9a–c and 10d.

97 Statutory Instrument (SI) No. 172/1936, Constitution (Declaration of Unlawful Association) Order, 1936.

98 *Irish Independent*, 8 August 1936, 12f–g; *Irish Press*, 8 August 1936, 1e.

99 See p. 318, n. 89 and 91.

100 *Dáil Debates*, vol. 62, col. 2410, 16 June 1936; col. 2617, 17 June 1936.

101 Constitution (Amendment No. 24) Act, 1936.

102 Constitution (Amendment No. 17) Act, 1931. An analysis by Sir Harry Batterbee of the Dominions Office of de Valera's speeches and intentions, is of interest. Batterbee noted that de Valera had to take some action in regard to the Crown because of the abdication. He also noted the reasonable and pragmatic tone that de Valera had adopted on this and on Northern Ireland and Commonwealth relations: 'The extraordinary thing about him as a politician is that he is so cool headed and cal-culating.' It would not be in the British interest to challenge de Valera on his con-stitutional changes. Other Commonwealth countries might take his side, and Commonwealth unity was desirable. Another consideration was that in the event of 'international trouble', a friendly Free State was essential. PRO DO/35/399/6, Batterbee memorandum, 24 December 1936.

103 Army Pensions Act, 1932. See s.5 for the definition of beneficiaries. De Valera and his colleagues saw this provision, brought in so early in the Fianna Fáil administra-tion, as the settlement of a debt of honour.

104 Fianna Fáil obtained sixty-nine seats; Fine Gael, forty-eight; Labour, thirteen; and Independents, eight. The Dáil had been reduced in size, from 153 to 138 members, though the number of constituencies had been increased from thirty to thirty-four. See Electoral (Revision of Constituencies) Act, 1935. The constitutional referendum was only slightly more satisfactory: for, 686,042; against, 528,296. The majority was 157,746, but 560,662 of the electorate had failed to vote.

105 This view was summarised by Frank Aiken, Minister for Defence, in March 1935, writing to the father of an IRA prisoner: individuals or groups could not be allowed to disrupt the country and hinder its defence and economy: 'We have secured that all who have a national or sectional policy can advocate and vote for it inside and outside the Dáil in a peaceful manner without being hindered by an Oath or other obstacle any more than they are on Local Bodies. There could be no excuse for anyone using violence for political or social ends and such actions would be stopped, whether they had a malicious or reckless character' (Aiken Papers, P/104/2804/1, quoting letter of 7 March 1935).

106 See p. 106 above.

107 The jury at Hogan's trial made a strong recommendation for mercy, and commu-tation followed a week later. See also Humphreys Papers, P/106/1341, Political Prisoners' Committee, Official Statement no. 8 (October 1927). At this date there were five republican prisoners serving sentences of penal servitude for periods between three years and life.

108 See above, p. 282.

109 For a complete list of political prisoners in Ireland (North and South) and in England, see the Political Prisoners' Committee, Official Statement no. 8, *op. cit.*

110 On 27 August 1927, Healy had shot Detective O'Donnell near Mallow, Co. Cork. The two had met on the road, and Detective O'Donnell had recognised the dis-tinctive Healy as a wanted man. MacEoin, *The IRA in the Twilight Years, op. cit.*, p. 20; 'Departmental Notes', *op. cit.*, p. 214.

111 A notable arrest was made on 16 April 1929 when Father John Fahy took part in the recovery of two cattle seized by a bailiff as a result of payments withheld in the annuities campaign. This caused the Republican Prisoners' Committee to issue a leaflet headed 'God Bless Father Fahy'. Humphreys Papers, P/106/1346.

112 NLI, MS. 10, 559, Political Prisoners' Committee, Statement no. 14 (July 1930).

113 The Gilmores had, on 7 December 1931, been convicted by the Military Tribunal of being members of an illegal organisation and of being in possession of arms. See above, p. 286.

114 Humphreys Papers, P/106/1352. This may have been a Cumann na mBan publication.

115 Humphreys Papers, P/106/1349, 'Boycott the Jailors of Irish Patriots!' (Cumann na mBan leaflet, June 1931).

116 For Father John Fahy, see below, p. 320, n. 126.

117 'Boycott the Jailors of Irish Patriots!'

118 SI No. 72/1931, Constitution (Operation of Article 2A) Order, 1931. The declaration was made by the Executive Council on 17 October 1931. The list of unlawful associations was made three days later. The list was as follows: 'Saor Éire; The association styling and calling itself the Irish Republican Army, sometimes known as the IRA or Óglaigh na hÉireann; Fianna Éireann; Cumann na mBan; Friends of Soviet Russia; The Irish Labour Defence League; The Workers' Defence Corps; The Women Prisoners' Defence League; The Workers' Revolutionary Party (Ireland); The Irish Tribute League; The Irish Working Farmers' Committee; The Workers' Research Bureau.'

119 For an account of de Valera's founding of the newspaper, see Tim Pat Coogan (himself an editor of the *Irish Press* or at a later time and an unrelenting critic of his former boss), *De Valera, op. cit.*, pp. 414–21.

120 Frank Gallagher (1893–1962) had taken part in several hunger strikes whilst imprisoned by the British during the Anglo-Irish War. See his memoir, *Days of Fear* (London: John Murray, 1928). He opposed the Treaty. His later career was at Radio Éireann, the Government Information Bureau and then the National Library of Ireland.

121 *Irish Press*, 22 December 1931, 6b; 24 December 1931, 6b.

122 Frank Fahy (Fianna Fáil) represented the Galway constituency. He was a barrister and teacher and could not be regarded as a lightweight.

123 *Irish Press*, 22 December 1931, 6b–c.

124 *Irish Press*, 22 December 1931, 6b–c.

125 *Irish Independent*, 28 January 1932, 7b–c; 29 January 1932, 6b–g; 30 January 1932, 11c–d. The other officer named was District Officer McCann.

126 David Neligan (1899–1983), known as the 'Spy in the Castle', had been one of Michael Collins's most important agents. He later became Director of Intelligence in the Irish Army. He was known to republicans as 'the Butcher of Kerry' because of his Free State Army service during the Civil War. Father John Fahy (1893–1969) was from time to time an associate in land campaigns of the left-wing republican Peadar O'Donnell. In March 1929 he had been sentenced to six months' imprisonment for helping to free two cows which had been seized in default of land annuity payments. He had a reputation as a firebrand and would eventually be placed under an order of silence by his bishop. This and other episodes in land agitation are described in Peadar O'Donnell's *There Will be Another Day* (Dublin: Dolmen Press, 1963). See also Uinseann MacEoin's brief account in *The IRA in the Twilight Years, op. cit.*, pp. 865–6.

127 *Irish Press*, 12 January 1932, 6a.

128 *Manchester Guardian*, 22 January 1932, 4f. The trial concluded on 9 February 1932, with judgment delivered on 17 February.

129 Frank Aiken (1898–1983) was born in Co. Armagh. He joined the Irish Volunteers in 1913 and became Commandant of the IRA's 4th Northern Division during the Anglo-Irish War. Taking the anti-Treaty side, he succeeded Liam Lynch as Chief of Staff when Lynch was shot by Free State troops in April 1923. Upon de Valera

splitting from Sinn Féin, Aiken followed him, becoming a founder member of Fianna Fáil. He was de Valera's Minister for Defence until 1939 and then occupied other ministerial offices, retiring in 1969.

130 James Geoghegan (1886–1951) entered the Dáil in a 1930 by-election, representing Longford-Westmeath in the Fianna Fáil interest. From his post at Justice he moved (in December 1936) to the Supreme Court.

131 Bell, *The Secret Army*, *op. cit.*, p. 464. This type of calculation would certainly not have been out of character for de Valera, who knew the value of keeping his own counsel and who at times effectively thought several moves ahead.

132 These provisions are taken from what seems to be a draft (dated 18 September 1936) for a public statement (Aiken Papers, P/104/2804/2). The Regulations were set out in SI No. 206/1936, Article 2A of the Constitution, Consolidated Regulations, 15 July 1936 (hereafter, Consolidated Regulations). The liberality of the regime was confirmed in a letter to Hanna Sheehy-Skeffington by a man who had spent a month in Arbour Hill; she had asked him to speak at a protest meeting. In reply, he hoped that Madam MacBride would not think him a Fianna Fáil propagandist when he said that Arbour Hill prisoners were well treated 'compared with those unfortunate individuals in Mountjoy and Maryboro!' The worst feature was the loss of liberty, and even the amenities of the Shelbourne Hotel would not make up for that. NLI, Sheehy-Skeffington Collection, MS. 33, 607, Joseph Dennigan to Hanna Sheehy-Skeffington, 24 January 1934.

133 Consolidated Regulations, 24 and 27(1).

134 Seán Ryan was a prominent Tralee republican who would spend much of the next two decades in and out of prison.

135 Aiken Papers, P/104/2801, Seán Ryan to Arbour Hill Governor, 3 March 1934.

136 Aiken Papers, P/104/2801, Frank Aiken to Adjutant General, 7 March 1934.

137 Aiken Papers, P/104/2801, OC to Governor, 3 April 1934. The designated hunger-strikers were Michael Herlihy, John Curtain, James Finnegan and Matt McCrystal.

138 They were severely disadvantaged by lack of sympathy in the Dáil: both major parties were hostile. The press may have been less monolithic, but favourable comment or sympathy would have been hard to find.

139 The number of Blueshirt-associated persons convicted before the Military Tribunal between 1 September 1933 and 5 February 1935 was almost three times that of IRA related convictions: 375 to 138 (*Dáil Debates*, vol. 54, cols. 1759–60, 13 February 1935). The Blueshirt organisations (the Young Ireland Association and its successor, the League of Youth) were only temporary strayers from the path of lawfulness; the IRA was more seriously committed in both senses: the gravity of their offences and their persistence. As another indication of the level of police activity, the Minister for Justice reported that during 1934, 964 persons had been detained under Article 2A and released without charge. Of these, 732 (more than three-quarters) came from five counties: Co. Cork (369), Co. Galway (56), Co. Limerick (82), Co. Tipperary (88), and Co. Waterford (137) (*Dáil Debates*, vol. 54, col. 2080, 20 February 1935; my calculations). The Blueshirt organisation, the League of Youth, was particularly active in Co. Cork, Co. Waterford and Co. Tipperary. The IRA was active throughout the country in attacks upon the League of Youth (particularly at dance halls) and other Blueshirt-related targets.

140 He urged de Valera to turn back before he had gone too far down 'that wretched coercion road… which brought the Cosgrave Regime to disgrace and destruction'. His family had suffered much, having lost a brother and son in the War of Independence and the Civil War and by having had their home made a continuous target 'for CID thugs, past and present'. Drummond declared his firm belief that

'Republican Ireland will not lie down under Tyranny now no more than they did in 1931–32.' Aiken Papers, P/104/2801/117, E. Drummond to Éamon de Valera, 4 January 1935.

141 Patrick Curran and six others were brought before the Military Tribunal on 18 December 1934, when they were sentenced to six months' imprisonment for contempt. The principal charges against them were not proceeded with. On 21 May 1935, they were brought again before the Tribunal, and six of them received sentences of a further three months (one man was effectively discharged). Attacks on Volunteers had been coordinated by the Tralee IRA, virtually all of whom took part in the incidents on 27 and 28 November 1934. This had been no chance or hot-blooded confrontation but part of an IRA attempt to counter the Volunteer Reserve. 'Departmental Notes', *op. cit.*, pp. 29–30.

142 'Volunteer' was the venerated IRA term for 'soldier', in this case referring to a private in the Volunteer Reserve.

143 Aiken Papers, P/104/2801/113, Aiken to Curran, 10 January 1935. This and a number of similar exchanges would be used by Aiken later in the year when putting together a statement for the Dáil on the prisoners and their course of behaviour (see P/104/2804/2 *et seq.*).

144 Aiken Papers, P/104/2801/113. See the *Kerryman*, 12 January 1935, 4a–d, 8f–g and 10e–g for reports of IRA units parading through Tralee, followed by a public meeting of protest.

145 Aiken Papers, P/104/2801/113, Frank Aiken to Secretary of Thomas Ashe Fianna Fáil Cumann, Tralee, 14 January 1935. Thomas Ashe (after whom the cumann was named) was a republican hero. He had fought in the 1916 Rising and had died as a consequence of forcible feeding in September 1917.

146 The IRA ran a strong campaign on the issue. See, for example, *An Phoblacht*, 12 January 1935, pp. 1 and 6. In addition to the parades and protest meeting in Tralee, there was, at this time, a reception and fund-raising dance for released republican prisoners in Milford, Co. Donegal (*Irish News*, 14 January 1935, 5d).

147 Aiken Papers, P/104/2801/83, Denis Daly to Frank Aiken, 5 February 1935.

148 Aiken Papers, P/104/2801/82, Frank Aiken to Denis Daly, 11 February 1935.

149 Aiken Papers, P/104/2801/78, Duagh Fianna Fáil Cumann to Eamonn Kissane, TD, 8 February 1935.

150 On the Blueshirts, see Mike Cronin, *The Blueshirts and Irish Politics* (Dublin: Four Courts Press, 1997). See also Eunan O'Halpin, *Defending Ireland: The Irish State and its Enemies since 1922* (Oxford: Oxford University Press, 1999), pp. 112–21. These men were mainly imprisoned for acts of violence and serious public-order offences in 1933–5. It was to be the only period before the modern troubles in Northern Ireland when republicans and their paramilitary opponents would be in prison together.

151 Aiken Papers, P/104/2801/70, Seosamh O'Ceannaigh to Frank Aiken, 6 April 1935.

152 Aiken Papers, P/104/2801/67, Kevin Holland to Director General, League of Youth, 3 June 1935. Spelling and punctuation as in original.

153 Aiken Papers, P/104/2801/67, Holland to Director General, League of Youth. He was writing, he claimed, under the penalty of being expelled from the organisation 'and cast out to exercise in the condemned [*sic*] ring with the other cast off'.

154 Letter to *Irish Press* from Cumann na mBan, Republican Political Prisoners' Committee (10 July 1935, 6g).

155 Con Lehane (1911–83), a graduate of University College Dublin, later became a solicitor and partner of Seán MacBride. Having joined the IRA at the age of seventeen, he was imprisoned twice in the 1930s and was interned in September 1939. He undertook a hunger and thirst strike and was thereafter released. In the 1948 election he became a Clann na Poblachta TD, losing his seat three years later

in the Church–State 'Mother and Child' confrontation. He remained active in legal practice, often representing republicans in dire circumstances.

156 Aiken Papers, P/104/2804/9, Con Lehane, Arbour Hill OC, to IRA GHQ, 17 September 1935 (intercepted and copied letter).

157 Aiken Papers, P/104/2805/3–4.

158 Aiken Papers, P/104/2804/8, draft statement. The statement itself was made in the Dáil on 13 December 1935, by which time Aiken was able to lend weight to his case by quoting from prisoners' letters. *Dáil Debates*, vol. 59, cols. 2669–73, 13 December 1935.

159 These details are taken from a letter from William Norton (TD and leader of the Labour Party) to Frank Aiken, 6 December 1935. Norton enclosed a statement by John Morton, recently released from Arbour Hill. He claimed that Charles Leddy of Belfast and Michael O'Leary of Dublin were among several men who had been brutally beaten. Other victims included Jack Fitzsimmons and Thomas Quin (aged sixty). Quin was made to walk in his bare feet on broken glass on the floor. Batons as well as fists were used (Aiken Papers, P/104/2801/28). This version of events was carried in a special edition of *Republican Congress* (11 November 1935, p. 1). For the Government's version of events, see the extensive statement in the Frank Aiken Papers, P/104/2804/2–15.

160 Aiken Papers, P/104/2801/45, 14 October 1935. The 'foreign sources' may have been a reference to Clan na Gael or other Irish-American groups. Leddy's brother, Peter, a priest with the Maynooth Mission to China, made a personal appeal to Aiken ('As a man of the North yourself') to have his two-year sentence commuted. The sentence had been imposed by the Tribunal for taking part in an IRA summer training camp. Charles Leddy had been a student at Queen's University, Belfast. While there he had taken an active part in Gaelic cultural and sporting activities. He had been imprisoned in Belfast for a lengthy period and, in consequence, had had to give up his course, just as he was about to be admitted to an English university (Aiken Papers, P/104/2801/49, Revd Peter J. Leddy to Frank Aiken, 23 September 1935).

161 An indication of the government's thinking was given in the Dáil by de Valera on 28 November 1935. The government was not ready to revoke the Order that had brought into effect the provisions of Article 2A. There had been 'a decided improvement in the situation' in recent months but organised acts of violence, with which the ordinary courts could not cope, were continuing. *Dáil Debates*, vol. 59, col. 1535, 28 November 1935.

162 *Irish Press*, 2 May 1936, 1e; Aiken Papers, P/104/2805/2. A list of the remand prisoners is to be found in this document. The Curragh Governor reported that more than half the newly arriving prisoners had drink taken. One prisoner (Patrick Curtain) had been struck on the head with a revolver, presumably by one of the escort, and needed medical attention.

163 Regulation 18(1) provided 'when practicable' four hours of exercise a day (Consolidated Regulations, *op. cit.*). The wording was sufficiently loose to allow continuous cellular confinement. In practical terms it would have been all but impossible to bring the matter before the courts, both because of judicial attitudes and because of the practical difficulty of obtaining access to, and instructing, a solicitor.

164 The protest began on 2 May 1935. On that day, Seán McSweeney refused all meals and told staff that he was on hunger strike for unconditional release. Aiken Papers, P/104/2805/2.

165 Aiken Papers, P/104/2805/3–4.

166 A melee followed, with the guards drawing their batons (MacEoin, *The IRA in the Twilight Years*, *op. cit.*, p. 845).

167 Aiken Papers, P/104/2805/5.

168 Consolidated Regulations, *op. cit.*, 18(1). Four hours' marching exercise a day, in silence, would in itself have been extremely demanding. The regulations did not mention rest periods, and, indeed, it is hard to see how they could have been permitted if at the same time the silence rule was enforced. The intention may have been to tire the men, but, except for the very fit, tiredness may have crossed into exhaustion.

169 Consolidated Regulations, *op. cit.*, 28(1)(A). The intention here was to ensure that prisoners took their exercise and did not choose to remain in their cells as a form of protest.

170 Aiken Papers, P/104/2804/6.

171 For this background, see Seán McConville, *English Local Prisons, 1860–1900: Next Only to Death* (London and New York: Routledge, 1995) and *A History of English Prison Administration, Vol. I: 1750–1877* (London: Routledge & Kegan Paul, 1981).

172 MacEoin, *The IRA in the Twilight Years, op. cit.*, p. 772.

173 MacEoin, *The IRA in the Twilight Years, op. cit.*, p. 348, but note that Moss Twomey, who was in Arbour Hill at the time, recalled, when interviewed in 1959 by MacEoin, that there were sixty men in Arbour Hill in the autumn of 1936 (*The IRA in the Twilight Years, op. cit.*, p. 845).

174 This series of protests started when Twomey attempted to speak to prisoners after mass on 31 May 1936. He addressed them as officers and men of the IRA and said that they were going to fight for their rights as political prisoners. He ordered them to the exercise yard to assert their rights, but himself sat down when ordered. That evening, some prisoners who attempted to talk during exercise were ordered back to their cells (Aiken Papers, P/104/2805/4). Similar incidents, calling for protests against the use of solitary confinement, occurred on 11, 14 and 21 June 1936. On 5 July there was another attempt to address the prisoners, and W. O'Donoghue and Tomás MacCurtáin were forcibly removed from the chapel.

175 Aiken Papers, P/104/2805/4.

176 Finbar McCarthy had been remanded to Arbour Hill on 30 April 1936. Appearing before the Tribunal on 26 May he was sentenced to nine months' imprisonment. He stood the Arbour Hill discipline for three weeks before giving an undertaking to keep the peace and be of good behaviour and was released on 20 June 1936 (Aiken Papers, P/104/2801/11). See also *Irish Press*, 25 June 1936, 12d; MacEoin, *The IRA in the Twilight Years, op. cit.*, p. 350.

177 The appeal was addressed to the Nuncio Apostolic, the Cardinal, Archbishops and Bishops, 'the members of the present Free State government and Public Bodies of Ireland' (Aiken Papers, P/104/2805/12, no date, but late June or early July 1936).

178 Consolidated Regulations, *op. cit.*, 31(10) provided that a prisoner who 'sings or whistles in a noisy manner, or makes any unnecessary noise or gives any unnecessary trouble' committed an offence.

179 This incident appears to have occurred on 3 May 1936, when Patrick O'Leary started singing in his cell and refused an order to stop: he was removed to the basement cell. Aiken Papers, P/104/2805/3, Report of Arbour Hill Governor to Provost Marshal, Department of Defence, 15 July 1936.

180 Prisoners mentioned different distances of separation at exercise – probably estimates. The prescribed distance was four paces between each marching prisoner, though how the guards enforced this with any precision is hard to say.

181 Aiken Papers, P/104/1201/12. See also NLI, MS. 17,082, draft of letter to Dublin Corporation, no date, but apparently September 1936.

182 Aiken Papers, P/104/1201/11, Captain T. Duffy (Governor of Arbour Hill) to Provost Marshal, Department of Defence, 6 July 1936. He confirmed that on one

occasion a member of staff who was not a communicant went to the altar rails with the prisoners in error. This part of the explanation was an undoubted fudge.

183 NLI, MS. 17, 082. From internal indications it would seem that the document was drawn up in the autumn of 1936, with the intention of persuading Dublin Corporation to set up an inquiry into Arbour Hill.

184 *Irish Independent*, 14 September 1936, 9a; *Irish Press*, 14 September 1936, 1d. Glynn's offence dated back to the Bodenstown commemoration on 21 June 1936, when he was one of a group involved in taking a car without permission. On 11 July he was convicted of being a member of an unlawful association and sentenced to nine months' imprisonment, six months to be suspended if he kept the peace. Glynn was given an IRA funeral in Limerick on 15 September, with a tribute from a firing party. Mary MacSwiney led the prayers at the graveside. The inquest jury found that Glynn had committed suicide, adding that he was not fit for solitary confinement but that he had not otherwise been ill-treated by civil or military police.

185 MacEoin, *The IRA in the Twilight Years*, *op. cit.*, p. 772. See also *Irish Independent*, 15 September 1936, 11c–f; 19 September 1936, 8a–g; 23 September 1936, 9f–g and 20a–d; *Irish Press*, 15 September 1936, 1a and 7e–g; 19 September 1936, 9d–e, 6a–c; 23 September, 6a–g and 14c. Moss Twomey, attending the inquest under military guard, told the Coroner that 'Arbour Hill today would not be good for Jack Dempsey' (*Irish Independent*, 23 September 1936, 10c). Dempsey was World Heavy-weight Boxing Champion in the 1920s and remained a well-known public figure – the epitome of hardiness.

7

NORTHERN IRELAND

Internment in the 1920s

IRA activities

As in the South, the IRA in the North concentrated in the inter-war years on reorganisation, retraining and rearming after its comprehensive defeat in the Civil War.[1] There were no great campaigns in either part of the island, but a number of sporadic actions against targets as diverse as foreign beer, cattle ranchers, informers and supposedly harsh or overzealous police or prison officers. A number of IRA men (and a few women) were in prison at the start of this period, some for their part in cross-border raids and others for activities in Northern Ireland.[2] Others joined the ranks of prisoners as convictions were obtained for various offences. The Northern IRA had none but the most distant hopes of overthrowing the state, and certainly none at all on its own. It nevertheless seems to have avoided much of the sense of purposelessness and splits that ravaged the organisation in the South. It was embedded in the Catholic working-class community, and, although many were in disagreement with it in various ways and turned more towards the Nationalist Party, Labour or one of the few Independents, its role as a Catholic defence organisation gave it a capacity for robust endurance. It was the ultimate backstop on occasions of sectarian disorder. Since most of the Catholic minority were apparently alienated from the Northern state, those disposed towards republicanism had no rival for their affections, unlike their counterparts in the Free State.

It is clear from the extensive police and ministry files that through observation, local knowledge, infiltration and informers, IRA and Sinn Féin activities were closely watched and individuals' movements and contacts were kept under constant review. That intuitive knowledge worked both ways, of course, but the IRA was rarely in a position to use its intelligence. Internment in 1922 cast a wide net, but in with the many minnows were a number of larger and more important fish. Internment served both as an incapacitating measure and as a deterrent. These objectives would at various points be sought both in individual arrests and by small-scale revivals of internment, involving limited groups.

Internment

In response to the cross-border attacks and civil disorders of the spring of 1922, the Northern Ireland government, using its powers under the Special Powers Act, which had become law on 7 April 1922, introduced large-scale internment.[3] Raids and arrests commenced on the night of 22/3 May. That night, 202 people were picked up, and within a few weeks almost 300 persons – almost all Roman Catholic males – were detained, most to be served with internment orders.[4] A further 150 orders were imposed during July and August.[5] From then until May 1923, around twenty persons were interned each month; after that there were few new cases.[6] Within two and a half years, a total of 732 persons were interned. They were drawn from across Northern Ireland, as follows: Belfast, 217; Antrim, twenty-six; Armagh, seventy-two; Down, ninety-eight; Fermanagh, sixty-four; Derry, seventy-five; Tyrone, 180. Those committed at a later point fell into three categories. The first two were obvious: persons who had fallen under suspicion since the first round-ups and suspects returning to Northern Ireland from the Free State and elsewhere. The third group showed with what determination the net was being stretched: those released from imprisonment or penal servitude having completed sentences for crimes of violence 'and who could not safely be allowed at large'.[7]

Very few women were interned. At this point (and for several decades to come) they could not join the IRA, though they were members of active support organisations. From the records it is not easy to determine whether the small number arrested was because of their sparse numbers as activists, because it was thought impolitic to round them up or because of a shortage of female accommodation. Probably all three factors were involved. On 6 June 1922, in the midst of continuing civil unrest in Belfast, the Ministry of Home Affairs wrote to Lieutenant Colonel M. M. Haldane, the Military Advisor. Two women had been arrested the previous night, one with arms concealed on her person and the other for helping a man to conceal a bomb. What was to be done with them? 'In the opinion of a great many people well qualified to judge, the Cumann-na-mBan is the most dangerous organisation with which we have to deal.' Women had been almost exempt from emergency measures, and it was essential that they were dealt with firmly. There was no reason why they should not be interned, '[a]lthough there will probably be very strong sentimental opposition to any such action'.[8]

Colonel Henry Toppin put this proposal to Samuel Watt, Secretary at the Ministry of Home Affairs. Where there was evidence (as with the two women who had been arrested), there should be prosecution. Internment had been widespread in 1920–1, but, although a total of some 4,000 had been held, women were largely excluded: 'It was considered that the supply of fanatical women was practically inexhaustible and that scope enough for the government activities was provided by men.' Women who were of such pronounced criminal tendencies should be interned if evidence against them could not be gathered.[9] Watt evidently suggested that the Military Advisor submit a list of likely women (the correspondence has not survived); Toppin demurred. He would, of course, carry out the Secretary's directions, but, instead of compiling a list, would it not be better to let things follow their natural course and to 'wait until women obtrude themselves'. Only one woman had so far been interned: Mary Josephine Kerr, who was being held in Armagh Prison.[10]

Given Northern Ireland's very limited prison accommodation, the search for custodial places was even more urgent than in the Free State: this almost certainly influenced the timing and pace of arrests.[11] A well-tried expedient was to hold the prisoners on board a ship. From the time of the eighteenth-century hulks, these had been used in emergency, offering speedy availability and security but few facilities for protracted confinement.[12] The SS *Argenta*, previously a cargo boat, was purchased for £3,000, modified by the shipbuilders Harland & Wolff, and finally taken over by the Ministry of Justice on 20 June 1922.[13] By midnight, 273 men were brought on board, under police and prison staff escort. At a later point, the total on board rose as high as 345. The ship was moored at first in Belfast Lough but on 22 August 1922 it was moved to Larne Lough, close to Islandmagee, Co. Antrim.[14] It remained in use until 30 January 1924 when its 101 men were transferred to Larne Workhouse.[15]

The building had been taken over from the Larne Board of Guardians during the summer of 1922.[16] Since the 1834 Poor Law had sought to make poor relief as unattractive as possible – sustenance of very last resort – its workhouses were both custodial and deterrent. Few alterations were therefore needed to receive internees. Barbed-wire fences and entanglements were laid down to heighten security and for defence against an IRA attack. Within the camp (as it came to be called), baths, showers and lavatories were constructed in the yards.[17] On 25 September 1922, operations commenced with the receipt of sixty-eight *Argenta* men, a number eventually rising to 264. Larne Camp functioned until Christmas Eve, 1924, when its last inmates departed.

Staffing problems

The scale of internment, the urgency of implementation, the pinched and makeshift nature of accommodation and the largely untrained warder staff all created management problems.[18] These came to a head in late 1922. On 2 December, a general search was announced. Since this involved an examination of all personal possessions, there was much scope for aggravation of the friction that already marked relations between warders and internees, drawn broadly as they were from opposite sides of the political and religious divides. Internees (and possibly some complicit staff) additionally feared that some petty contraband would be uncovered. The response to the announcement, therefore, was a hunger strike and a smashing of the ship's fittings. Special constables were ordered into the living quarters, and quietness was restored. On the following day, the men again refused food, threw that which had been issued and the contents of slop-buckets through the wires, and generally threatened staff. A. D. Drysdale, the Governor, came on board and summoned James Mayne, the principal inmate leader.[19] The two men, according to a later whistle-blowing complaint by a warder, discussed the dispute over lunch. Thereafter, there is a sharp difference in recollection between the warders and Drysdale. The warders claimed that Mayne had been allowed to go to the kitchen and direct that before lock-up the men should have a meal with extra tea, margarine and bread. They also insisted that the internees were told that the search had been irregular and unauthorised and that in future they would be excused the labour of unloading food supplies from the tender, SS *Lull*. Furious at having to perform duties previously carried out by their prisoners, staff refused to handle the supplies.[20] This last was the only point agreed between the Governor and the warders.[21] The exact sequence of events is unclear, but the warders were unhappy that the internees had come off better in the dispute and that staff were now having to perform internee tasks.

Sir Dawson Bates, Minister for Home Affairs, was concerned. With both staff and inmates resentful and refractory things could easily get out of hand. Colonel F. S. Pountney, of the office of the RUC's Inspector-General, was sent to investigate. Following his visit on 5 December 1922, he concluded that the *Argenta* warders' insubordination had had 'the effect of destroying the last vestige of control over the internees'. Living quarters were filthy because internees refused to keep them clean; latrines were deliberately being blocked; and the ship's fittings were being destroyed. The internees were refusing to handle their own food supplies and had even made an attempt, partly successful, to cut a way out of the ship. All of this was being done with impunity because the ship's authorities were unable to reassert themselves. A bad situation would get worse 'unless immediate and thorough measures be taken to restore discipline'.[22]

It was a balance, but the principal difficulty was probably the warder staff, hastily recruited, inefficient and discontented, and for the most part utterly unsuited to take control back from the inmates. The majority knew nothing of the work and took no trouble to learn, 'chiefly because no adequate inducement is given to them in the way of pay'. Drysdale's duties had been extended to Larne Camp, and this had made it impossible for him to be in direct and constant command of the *Argenta*. It was, in any event, very much more difficult to handle internees than ordinary prisoners. Firmness and tact had to be artfully blended, and it was impossible to subject them to penal discipline. Any attempt to do so was as paraffin on a red-hot stove of discontent. The two places of confinement, moreover, were particularly susceptible to being tampered with from the inside and were vulnerable to outside attack, and it was impossible to segregate 'dangerous characters' or to carry out disciplinary punishment by way of close confinement.

Staff ought to be trained warders, recruited in Scotland and England, and Pountney contended that Ulstermen, 'particularly Belfast men', were unsuitable. Those they had to guard were 'in ordinary conditions' their neighbours, and they were always faced with possible retaliation. There was in addition 'the old racial and religious antagonism': 'This constantly bursts into flame and causes outbreaks of mutual recrimination which destroy discipline and puts moral ascendancy on the part of the warders out of the question.' All his observations about the *Argenta*, Pountney concluded, applied 'though in a less urgent manner' to Larne Camp. The Ministry was unwilling to go as far as Pountney recommended, to install English and Scots staff. This would have been time-consuming, complicated to arrange and would doubtless have been a deal more expensive; there would also have been adverse comment from the government's working-class supporters, to whom even the *Argenta*'s short-term employment was a boon in hard times. It was hardly certain, moreover, that English or Scottish staff, prison-trained, could have coped with the more fluid and less structured management of internees and all the nuances of religion, localism and politics in Ulster. There were no dramatic changes. Four additional warders joined the *Argenta* staff, and it was agreed to remove certain internee leaders to Londonderry Prison.[23]

Confident and able clergy would have been a stabilising and emollient influence, but there were problems in finding suitable chaplains. Father Daniel Murphy was appointed to the *Argenta* in July 1922, and no query was subsequently raised about his service. Father Daniel McGuckian of Cloughmills, Co. Antrim, was appointed to serve Larne Camp, but a subsequent RUC security check revealed that he was but recently ordained and that his two brothers were IRA suspects. One had been on the run since May, and the other was actually an internee. On occasional visits to his home the RUC District Inspector had always found McGuckian in the company of suspects. Something of an outrage generally occurred during his visits home, and there was speculation that he was to blame. He was not at all suitable for appointment as chaplain, and the RUC considered that 'he would do all in his power to defeat the ends of justice'.[24] One of the Larne priests, Father Burns, was nominated instead. He declined to take the oath of allegiance, and a police report was requested.[25] This was favourable, Burns being described by the District Inspector as a quiet and inoffensive man who took no part in politics: 'He is suspected locally to be a unionist and is on good terms with all the Protestant clergymen in Larne.'[26] On the strength of these findings, he was appointed at a salary of two guineas a week. On Burns's resigning the post in August 1923, his replacement, Father Black, also baulked at the oath. He seems to have carried on nevertheless, although there was a subsequent disagreement about the payment of his expenses. The oath was also an issue at Belfast and Londonderry prisons. In January 1925, it was noted that both chaplains had refused to take it. Their employment was terminated, but were reinstated when they subsequently relented.[27]

Regime

Besides the *Argenta* and the Larne Camp, internees were also held at Belfast and Londonderry prisons, numbers peaking at 575 in May 1923. The regime for internees was based on but was more liberal than that for remand prisoners: own clothes, no prison labour, a liberal allowance of letters, a degree of free association, tobacco and smoking allowed and an enhanced dietary; internees could also make and send out handicraft items.[28]

The *Argenta* routine was very much more that of camp than prison. The intention there, and in the workhouse, according to A. D. Drysdale, the Governor of both, was to provide safe custody with a modified discipline, 'which would leave as little bitter feeling as possible behind at the expiry of internment'.[29]

In Drysdale's view (though he was making a comparison with the ordinary criminal system in which he had served), the dietary was 'of the most generous description', and to increase variety internees were allowed 'considerable latitude' to prepare food. Three meals a day were provided, and there were few hunger strikes on the ship, Drysdale noted somewhat wryly. When started, they never extended beyond one meal and were followed by a request for the one that had been missed.[30] Importantly for a generation that indulged so heavily in tobacco, smoking was freely allowed when men were on the upper deck. Custody pens were unlocked at 7 a.m., and men then had free access to the upper deck until 8 p.m. Discipline was lax, the only constraints being security and whatever weight of opinion the internees could bring to bear on each other. Cahir Healy recalled what had been for some an intolerable pattern of young men rising late and socialising into the small hours.[31] The men did their own cleaning and cooking, by rota, in working parties, but this presumably matched in quality the pattern of socialising. Apart from those housekeeping duties, during the thirteen hours of access to the upper deck and open air they had activities available such as deck quoits and dancing; less active pastimes included chess, draughts and cards. Initially library books were issued, but since they all unaccountably disappeared there was no exchange or second issue.[32] The men were permitted to have newspapers sent in by friends. Parcels were not allowed at this point, although this policy was later relaxed.[33]

No matter how well regulated, the close confinement of a large number of men – up to 345 – for several months on board a hastily adapted ship had undoubted health risks. While the men's general condition was said to be good, and there were claims that it improved during the time of their confinement, there were outbreaks of skin disorders. Some, it was claimed, had been verminous and suffering with scabies on reception. In these close quarters, such conditions were easily transmitted. Scabies cases were removed to Belfast Prison for treatment and then to an isolation ward in the Larne Workhouse.[34] Eighteen years later, when involved in negotiations again to procure a ship on which to hold internees, the Secretary at the Ministry of Home Affairs commented that the *Argenta* experience had caused officials to resist the idea of another ship for, 'as you know, the conditions on the "Argenta" were not at all good. In fact, they were so bad that it would be difficult to stand over them now'.[35]

Police access

Internment provided the police with opportunities to gain intelligence and possibly to recruit sources.[36] A month or so after the first and major wave of internments they sought access to the men. The proposed interrogations, it was emphasised, were not to be cross-examinations intended to get confessions. This was to be an intelligence-gathering exercise: 'a series of quiet talks… with a view to getting further information on which we can act'. Lieutenant Colonel M. M. Haldane, intelligence officer at the CID Divisional Commissioner's Office, Belfast, assured the Ministry that '[w]e used to do a lot of this in Dublin, but I believe some order is necessary to authorise the Governor of the Prison to admit the interrogator'.[37] The Ministry was cautious about this exercise, since police interrogation of a person in preventive custody could be represented as a form of ill-treatment, or at the very least undue and inappropriate pressure. The internees had not been charged, and to go on an information trawl now simply because they were available could be regarded as an improper use of internment. There were various ways in which this might be unfavourably represented, the Ministry may have worried, not least by the Provisional government in Dublin, and by some in London. Toppin somewhat enigmatically warned Haldane of the original principle that 'only hares and not rabbits' should be arrested.[38]

Some interrogation permits were granted, but Toppin dragged his feet over others. When Haldane wrote again, Toppin consulted Samuel Watt, Secretary at the Ministry of Home Affairs. By requiring that the CID return a copy of each access order to him as it was used, Toppin sought to control the interrogations. The CID had failed to comply, and, together with his more general reservations, Toppin asked whether the interrogation of persons already in custody should continue. This access to prisoners was a measure justifiable 'in times of acute disorder' but liable to be bitterly attacked during a period of comparative calm: 'It will be remembered how bitterly the Govt. General Maxwell and Major Price were attacked over the interrogation by the last named of Prof. McNeill in Mountjoy Prison in 1916.'[39] A great deal depended on the discretion of the CID and of the Special Constabulary acting on their orders. However energetic and resourceful Special Constabulary officers might be in carrying out searches and similar operations, Toppin was not sure that they had sufficient police training 'to ensure their acting with discretion in more delicate matters and I am sure we cannot rely on the discretion of the CID'.

Toppin's central concern was that the Ministry of Home Affairs, through the Prison Service, had responsibility for the safe custody of the internees and prisoners and could not enter into an arrangement where this responsibility was not matched by full control. He recommended that Haldane be asked to provide examples of useful results arising from interrogations of prisoners, giving sufficient detail to allow the Ministry to decide whether access should be continued. It is not clear from the files if this was done, but on 28 September 1922, Haldane was told that future access to internees would be limited to cases which the Minister had personally sanctioned, having been informed why the visit was considered necessary.[40] The political risks, including the provision of propaganda opportunities to nationalists and republicans, were considered too great to allow any but the more defensible of interrogations to continue.

There survives in the files some indication that the pressures of internment resulted in information being volunteered in hope of release. One report concerned men from the IRA's 3rd Northern Division returning to Belfast from Dublin. Whether they had a particular objective in mind the internee could not say, but he did know that they had had special training in Dublin: 'I overheard this in a conversation this morning.' He had also heard that Edward Malone, an internee who had been granted release on condition that he leave Northern Ireland within twenty-four hours, had returned. The letter concluded with a plea for his own release, 'which if granted I will do all in my power to assist the authorities'.[41] In a covering letter, Drysdale reported that the information which had been given had been conveyed to the brothers Henry and Hugh Marks by their mother who had visited them on the day that the letter was written.[42]

Strife on shore

The daily round at Larne Camp was similar to that of the *Argenta* but was implemented in roomier and more adaptable conditions. Dining halls remained open until 9 p.m. and were available for recreational activities including short dramatic sketches. Apart from acts of collective disobedience (discussed below), there were the usual problems. No matter how unlike an ordinary prison (and conditions were never as agreeable as Drysdale represented), men – most in their twenties and early thirties – were being deprived of their liberty and were understandably resentful and frustrated. The regime was custodial rather than penal, but sentenced prisoners had at least had a release date; even remands had their trials in view. In the politically uncertain months of 1922–3, internees could see no end to their custody, and that in itself fired sometimes unmanageable frustration. There was also the very severe moral and psychological test of confinement: the lack of almost any personal privacy and the many petty, constant and irking frictions of communal life and unremitting company. Some fellow captives were known and liked, no doubt, but some may have been disliked, and yet others were strangers. Even so, there seems to have been relatively little misbehaviour; Drysdale mentions few punishments either on the *Argenta* or in the camp. At the former, only sixteen men were given dietary punishments, although Drysdale noted that there were some whose offences were so serious or persistent that they were moved to the camp (where there were cells which could be used for close-confinement punishment) or to Belfast or Derry prisons.[43] At the camp there seems to have been more individual misbehaviour, and Drysdale observed that a number of men were found to be unsuitable for association with their fellows because of objectionable language and personal habits as well as destructiveness. He also mentioned vandalism, the perpetrators of which were hard to detect, since the damage was usually committed at night.[44]

A letter smuggled out and published in Northern Ireland's major Catholic newspaper took issue with the benign picture painted by the authorities, especially the Prime Minister, Sir James Craig. Craig had claimed that the internees were well clothed and that those who worked were paid. Not so, insisted the author of the letter. The food was sometimes unfit for human consumption and had to be refused. This protest ensured a temporary improvement, but after a few days the food deteriorated and the whole process was repeated. There were other problems, the letter claimed. The men's clothes were in such a state of raggedness that were they to appear in public they would probably be arrested, and it was only at that point they were replaced.[45] Of the 253 men in the camp, only four were paid (at a rate of nine shillings a week): two were shoemakers, 'the other two make the mattresses for their fellow victims'. All the other work of cooking and cleaning was done by the internees, without pay, 'for their own comfort'.[46]

Reporting to the Ministry, the Londonderry Governor also painted a picture of continued dissatisfaction and insubordination, which he blamed on the laxity permitted by Dublin Castle before Partition. (This was a theme that would find repeated expression in a number of contexts.) Being a cellular prison, the Derry men were individually locked up, and, in theory at least, this improved control. The Governor continued to implement the stricter discipline introduced by his predecessor, but the internees 'appeared to delight in causing as much trouble and petty annoyance to prison officials as their ever ready minds could devise'. He attributed this to 'clever scheming by the leaders or commanders'. These were secretly chosen from among the better class of internees, and their identities were sometimes concealed from the authorities. He also claimed that a favourite pastime was to shout 'party expressions' (political and possibly religious slogans) to other categories of prisoners from cell windows or over the walls in the exercise yards. His main lament, indeed, was of the adverse effect the internees had on the discipline of the ordinary prisoners.[47] This was another theme to which governors entrusted with the custody of internees would return through the decades that followed.

Instances of individual misbehaviour are rare among the official papers dealing with internment in the Free State at this time. In large part this was because the internees were members of the anti-Treaty IRA, their command structure was intact, and they enforced and almost universally adhered to their own code of discipline. The position in the North was more fragmented. In 1922, there were at least three groups among the internees. The majority (as with the Northern republicans generally) were almost certainly pro-Treaty and had been interned because in some overt fashion they refused to recognise the legitimacy of Northern Ireland. Some, but not all, of these may have taken a hand in or been complicit in IRA attacks then being mounted in border areas, with the clandestine support of Michael Collins and some members of the Provisional government. These men looked to Dublin for direction and assistance.[48] The second, minority, group was anti-Treaty and may also have been involved in attacks on Northern Ireland, or have been supporters or auxiliaries. As the Civil War developed in the South, they necessarily developed a keener sense of their republican identity, setting up their own command structures in internment. The third group was of nationalists whose political beliefs led them to reject or to deny the legitimacy of the Northern Ireland state but who had not been involved in IRA activities, though some may have been supporters of pre-Treaty Sinn Féin. Some, such as Cahir Healy, appear to have been interned simply because of their prominence.[49] This mix meant that some of the enmity of the prisoners was directed at each other; it also meant, unlike in the Southern prisons and camps, that a number of individuals could squeeze between the cracks of any structure of inmate authority, acting and fending for themselves.[50]

The Free State government, as we shall see, took a close interest in the Northern internees and had lines of communication to several of them. An interned teacher from Belfast, Francis Crummey, writing from Larne Workhouse to Frank O'Duffy, Secretary and Aide to the Free State Minister for Education, reported that there were three 'governments' on the *Argenta*: 'The Irregulars have an Army Council. Those loyal to the Treaty have an Army Council and then there is Mayne's council which is supposed to be the government of the ship.'[51] The powerfully placed Kevin O'Shiel, assistant legal adviser to President Cosgrave (and himself a Tyrone man), had particular responsibility for advising on developments in Northern Ireland.[52] He reported to Cosgrave in July 1923 that of the 500 Northern internees the majority were supporters of the Free State government, 'the greater number of the remainder being colourless neutrals more inclined towards us than against us'. The number of Irregulars, according to O'Shiel's information, was quite small.[53]

Hunger strikes

Despite the fragmentation of allegiances among the prisoners – indeed, what must have been a degree of antagonism – there were hunger strikes. These required degrees of coordination and agreement that, predictably in the circumstances, simply were not there. Without a unified command and sense of common purpose the men could neither prepare for nor endure the ordeal. Unlike earlier groups of hunger-strikers in Ireland and Britain they had no definite outside constituency, and this was utterly fatal to the action. Northern working-class Catholics, to whom they might have looked for sympathy, had been through several years of civil disturbance and now sought safety in their own areas. Any public demonstrations that republicans were able to mount in the Free State were small, but they did take place – especially when women were the principal participants. It was inconceivable that anything of this kind could have been mounted in the North without provoking public disorder, a violent sectarian response or action from the state.

The first strike on the *Argenta* took place only four days after the initial receptions. The ostensible cause was a demand for an increase in the margarine ration. Until this had been conceded, the men announced, they would undertake neither cooking nor cleaning. Unless working parties were turned out within the hour, Drysdale warned, all internees would immediately be placed on a bread-and-water diet. The leaders who had initiated the strike were replaced, and within the ultimatum hour cleaning and cooking resumed. There were some later threats of hunger-striking, but all collapsed.[54] This inability to sustain common action was hardly surprising. The authorities held all the cards, and most of the men may have asked themselves whether it made sense to volunteer for additional and futile hardship.

On 13 October 1922, IRA prisoners and internees in the Free State began their hunger strikes.[55] Since the majority of the Northern internees were not anti-Treaty, there was no direct inducement to follow suit; political and social conditions in Northern Ireland, moreover, were very different.[56] Twelve days after the commencement of the hunger strike at Mountjoy and elsewhere in the South, nevertheless, 131 men on the *Argenta* (less than half) refused food. Their demand, foolishly, was unconditional release. All were immediately transferred to Belfast Prison, with the intention of breaking the action by confining them separately in their cells.[57] A sympathy strike by sixty-five men got under way at Larne Workhouse on 29 October 1922; 108 of their fellows refused to join them. The authorities' reaction was the same: all sixty-five were removed to Belfast and Derry prisons. By 31 October 1922, a total of 209 were on hunger strike, 113 in Belfast, sixty-nine in Larne and twenty-seven in Derry prison.[58]

The government was alarmed but not sufficiently so to contemplate giving way. Major A. W. Long, Governor of Belfast Prison, gave a mixture of good and bad news in his reports. A large number had been forced into the strike and were afraid to take food. The chief grievance was against the Advisory Committee, about which there was great bitterness. Men had gone before it, agreed to meet its conditions, and yet had not been freed.[59] Some had no ill-feeling against the Northern Ireland government, but there were also diehards who refused to recognise it, even at arm's length, by appearing before the Advisory Committee: 'Several have stated to me that they have been interned so long that life is not worth living and that they will either die or be unconditionally released.' It was a resolute hunger strike, and at least some were determined to go on to the bitter end and might die. Long was nevertheless in no doubt as to the course that the government should take. Were it to yield he did not see how it would be possible to hold any interned prisoner in future; he also thought that there could be the same trouble with ordinary (presumably he meant convicted political) prisoners serving long sentences.[60]

The following day, Sir Dawson Bates nailed his colours to the mast in a speech to the Pottinger Unionist Association, delivered at Albertbridge Road Orange Hall in Belfast. His attitude was exactly the same as his Free State counterpart, he told the audience. Men could not be allowed to challenge the law and the fabric of the state 'by the woman's weapon of the hunger strike'. The government was responsible for law and order and would not yield.[61]

Sir James Craig was in London but had requested regular reports on developments. Sir Dawson Bates now took a direct part in the affair. A meeting of medical officers, governors and ministry officials convened under his chairmanship on 2 November. It was agreed that every inducement to take nourishment would be given. In a reassuring letter to Craig, Bates emphasised that he had followed his suggestions, sought to establish a common policy across the various establishments, 'and one as humanitarian as could be under the circumstances'. He realised that should any of the strikers 'go under' there would be a campaign of misrepresentation against the Northern Ireland government. The political situation in Britain had to be considered (presumably this was a reference to the likely general election). Craig had suggested that an official experienced in handling hunger strikes be brought over from Britain, but neither the head of the English or Scottish prison services would want to be involved unless they had the direct approval of their superiors, 'and in the case of England this, of course, would be [Sir] John Anderson' (a prime Northern *bête noir*). Bates was also worried lest a visiting expert recommend use of the Cat and Mouse Act or that any other similar measure should be introduced.[62] In plain words, he did not wish a fudge to be forced on the government: he wanted to face down the hunger strike. He regretted the situation, especially the fact that at the time of writing there were two men whom he feared would 'go under' (he repeated the phrase). From a broader point of view, 'if not alone from the humanitarian point of view' there was no option but to stick by the policy they had agreed. To give way would make gaol administration 'absolutely impossible', with serious consequences for the peace of the community.[63]

In fact, the strike was less firm than Bates and his governors feared, and their background intelligence was surprisingly sparse and poor. The biggest error was to overestimate internees' unity and coherence. It is likely that Bates and his advisers were also blinded by their own political assumptions, which had tended to cast all who held nationalist, or even anti-unionist, views as Sinn Féiners, gunmen *manqué*. Yet, as we have seen, there was a major rupture between pro- and anti-Treaty factions, there was an undecided or neutral group, and there were many who had no affiliation. Even with a unified group of prisoners, an effective chain of command, full knowledge of what a strike until death entailed, a well-organised outside body of supporters (including public-relations expertise) and broad circles of sympathisers, a hunger strike was an enormously difficult thing to bring off. A mass strike with (it seems reasonable to suppose) a number of lukewarm conscripts, could not prevail should the government stand firm for even a short time. Far more than the Free State, which was forcing its own hunger-strikers to give in at this very time, Craig's government could afford not to budge. The fear of serious public disorder in response to a death was perhaps its main concern; not too far behind that came the likely reaction of its own supporters should government falter.

A mass hunger strike is a hollow thing, and this quality had already begun to show when Bates wrote to Craig. By 3 November 1922, seventy-seven men had begun to accept food; two days later this had risen to ninety. There had been particular concern about the health of the two mentioned by Bates, but both began to take nourishment.[64] Once the spiral of submission gets under way it is utterly impossible to stop it, and a week later all was over. One man held out, but he too capitulated after seventeen days. This was the last attempt by the internees to mount a general hunger strike. Craig reported the outcome to the Duke of Abercorn, Governor of Northern Ireland. He was delighted, the Duke replied, and the collapse reflected great credit on Bates and his associates. He was all the more pleased since the outcome was a great rebuff against 'that mischievous and stuffy Prelate, Dr McCrory [*sic*], the R.C. Bishop of Down'.[65]

Opposition grows

Internment of 752 people, and the continuance of the measure for some thirty months, could not but have a significant effect on the nationalist population. With the Northern government so well equipped with instruments to restrain and suppress protest, especially the catch-all Special Powers Act, little could be done to bring pressure on it. In the midst of its own civil war, with prisons and camps overflowing with several times the number of internees being held north of the border, the Free State was in no position to intervene or even to intercede. Kevin O'Shiel suggested to President Cosgrave in July 1923 that Northern internment was being prolonged as a bargaining chip in the forthcoming boundary negotiations and as a reason to maintain the Special Constabulary on active service, thus continuing the payment of British government grants. It was, he wrote, 'impossible for us to move hand or foot on their [the internees] behalf whilst we were contending with the Irregular conspiracy'.[66] At a later point, it is true, both Stanley Baldwin, the outgoing British Prime Minister, and Ramsay MacDonald, the incoming one, urged Craig to look again at aspects of internment.[67] There were no other sources of external influence or pressure. Unlike the Free State, Northern Ireland's hunger-strikers had not benefited from American support, and the protests of Irish-American groups tended, if anything, to confirm the Northern government in the correctness of its policies. Most obviously and crucially, all or most of the supporters of Ulster unionism (two-thirds of the community) supported or were indifferent to the policy of internment.

There was, however, much unfavourable comment from the nationalist press, some merely sensationalist, some rather more accurate. Even here, of course, there could be no gainsaying the uncomfortable fact that most of the nationalist press, North and South, supported the Free State government and therefore its policy of interning its republican opponents. In August 1922, the *Irish Independent* ran an exposé of conditions under the banner 'Craig's Death-Trap for Political Prisoners; Hunger and Disease in Floating Gaol; Shocking Conditions; "Northern" Government Unmoved by Recent Exposure'. The piece referred to the scabies outbreak and what was claimed to be inferior food. It also deplored the use of bunk-beds, 'one on top of the other, after the fashion of a third-class berth on an inferior cross Channel boat'. It drew attention to the hours that men were locked below deck in 'a veritable black hole' with an oppressive atmosphere.[68] The British left took a similar line, with the *Daily Herald* in the lead. The *Argenta*, in England carrying some of the associations of the penal hulks of ill-fame, was a particular target, described as 'a discarded American wooden cargo hulk... purchased for £3000'. For months the internees, including many public and professional men, had been 'huddled in the bowels of this old tub'. The latrines were only three feet from the beds, and the sanitary conditions were terrible: 'That is how Craig with the "free gift" of British taxpayers' money manages to govern in Northern Ireland.'[69]

The 'floating hell' line was overdone, though it is certain that conditions on board the *Argenta* were far from the pleasant, stress-free near-idyll pictured by Drysdale in his report to the Ministry: it was an improvised prison, penny-pinched, in poor condition, under an administration that struggled to cope, staffed by the ill-chosen and ill-paid. Confinement in such a place could not but entail considerable hardship. A letter to the *Irish Independent* from internees in Belfast Prison put a different spin on conditions, insisting that the *Argenta*'s were far superior to those they were experiencing in Belfast.[70] In response to the various criticisms of the *Argenta*, a crude piece of misinformation was run in the unionist *Belfast Telegraph*. This purported to quote from a letter smuggled off the ship and subsequently captured during a police raid. The unnamed writer reported that the internees were having a good time. The beds were 'splendid', as was the food. Internees did not need to get up at all if they did not wish to. The cages 'are really our bedrooms' since they spent the day from 7 a.m. until 8 p.m. on deck, going below only for meals: 'Except for eating we do nothing but smoke, play cards, make ladies handbags... and rings from 2s. bits.' There were hot baths and everything they wanted, and 'for the unemployed Belfastman it is more of a home than a prison'. For propaganda purposes, the internees had to claim that they were being badly treated, but had his correspondent (notionally a woman friend) been with him he would like to end his days on the *Argenta*.[71] This over-egged pudding can have convinced none but those who wished to believe. It is laced through, moreover, with insinuations about lying, lazy and self-indulgent Roman Catholics.

The release campaign

As the months passed and internment continued, the Roman Catholic community of all shades of republican and nationalist opinion, those who were neutral and some liberal Protestants, became more obviously restive and willing to air objections and concerns. The plight of the internees' families was the key issue – a matter of simple humanity – on which all could agree. Where no other support was available, starvation could be avoided by entering the workhouse: this carried immense stigma and resulted in families being broken up and assigned respectively to the female and children's sections of the institution. Outdoor relief (that is, a dole or food in one's own home) was an entirely discretionary matter for the Board of Guardians in the Poor Law Union in which the applicant lived. Inevitably, sectarian considerations entered into these decisions.[72] Dependants of the internees appealed to Winston Churchill for assistance, one woman pleading for her twelve children. The Northern government was unmoved, stating that it did not think it fit to support the dependants of those suspected of IRA membership.[73]

Some of the Roman Catholic clergy took a line not too far removed from this but drew the conclusion that the internees' first responsibility was to their families and that they were duty-bound to conform and do what was necessary to obtain their freedom. According to an RUC intelligence report, Father H. J. Murray preached such a homily, at evening devotions at St Mary's Church, Belfast, on Sunday 4 November 1923. Teachers and other prominent officials had recognised the Northern government, and Father Murray did not think it any shame for the internees to do so. He urged members of his congregation whose relatives were interned to go to seek their release in a proper manner. A police note accompanying the report concluded that the pronouncement coming from a man such as Father Murray, who had been an ardent supporter of the Sinn Féin movement, was very important.[74]

Not all agreed. Other members of the Roman Catholic community took the view that release conditions were such that few nationalists could conscientiously accept them.[75] Protests began to mount as the months passed. Newry Urban District Council, under nationalist control, asked for releases on the internees signing an undertaking to comply with the existing laws.[76] This suggestion for compromise was rejected, Bates pointing out that 200 men had already been released 'on such conditions as were deemed to be appropriate in each case'. No general release could be undertaken at present.[77]

Father Murray's advice to his flock notwithstanding, by the last months of 1923 he and the Roman Catholic Church were looking for a reciprocal gesture. Just a few days after his sermon, Murray wrote to Sir James Craig, enclosing a resolution adopted at a well-attended Belfast meeting of clergy and laity. The meeting had protested against internment, North and South, as an 'arbitrary abuse of power and a denial of the elementary rights of civil and personal freedom and security'. It noted the hunger strike then under way and called for an inquiry into the 'intolerable conditions' under which some had been held for up to two years. The resolution concluded by noting 'the profound peace' prevailing in Belfast and the six counties for the previous six months 'at which we rejoice'. The men's continued detention was indefensible, and immediate release would produce even better relations among all classes of the population.[78]

Feelings intensified as Christmas and New Year (occasions for possible clemency) passed without movement. Resolutions continued to come in to the Ministry, including one from Armagh which drew special attention to the last remaining female internee, North or South, Miss Nano Aiken.[79] In May 1924, there was a development that the RUC took as a sign that internment was bringing nationalists and republicans together. County-council elections were pending, and, in an atmosphere of growing anger, the nationalist candidate for Armagh City, Hughes, announced that he was stepping down in favour of Mrs Margaret Connelly, the wife of a man two years interned. Hughes asked his supporters to use all their influence to secure Mrs Connelly's election.[80] Connelly's case epitomised the concerns about internment. A draper by occupation, he had been OC of the IRA's 3rd Brigade, 4th Northern Division. He had been interned in 1920, released in 1921 and interned again in June 1922. Undoubtedly he had played a part in the Anglo-Irish War, but that had been brought to an end by the Treaty. Was he forever to be kept in fear of arrest because of his past? Nationalists and republicans duly cooperated in the election campaign, and Mrs Connelly secured 1,158 votes, winning the seat.

Sympathy crossed other political boundaries. In July 1924, a petition from eighty-five Westminster MPs was submitted to the Northern Ireland cabinet. The MPs, nearly all Labour, pointed to the fact that Northern Ireland had enjoyed peace for almost two years: the time had come when internees should be tried or released.[81] Responding to its laity, the Roman Catholic hierarchy had also adopted a firmer position. Local meetings had been held across Northern Ireland (in itself indicating greater confidence on the part of nationalists), and on 23 September 1924 Dr O'Donnell, Co-adjunctor Archbishop of Armagh, expressed his full sympathy with them.[82] There was some pressure on the police to have these gatherings banned, but they could not in themselves be said to be sources of disorder. And the assemblies had their uses. A note from a district inspector, rejecting a proposal that police should suppress a meeting at Newry, pointed out that by allowing it to proceed 'we will be able to see who is actually in sympathy with this business'.[83] The event proceeded in a conciliatory tone, speakers praising the local RUC and emphasising that it was a non-political gathering.[84] In the reports of these meetings there now emerged a clear clerical presence. Addressing a meeting at Omagh, Father Langan attacked internment from a somewhat different angle, but one which doubtless had resonance with his co-religionists. Personal jealousies and business rivalries were entwined with it, he claimed. When the Belfast government was prepared to order releases subject to the approval of local B-Specials, it was known that these releases were vetoed, because of local trade rivalry. England was to blame for this injustice because it financed the Specials. Langan also had hard words for the Free State, which ought to have done more to make it clear to England that there would be no reconciliation in the six counties until Catholics got justice, the first sign of which would be liberation of the prisoners.[85] The ripples were spreading, and there were worrying signs that a hitherto quiescent population was stirring.

Roman Catholics in England (many of whom were of Irish origin) had also begun to show interest in the plight of the internees. The *Catholic Times* (London) ran an editorial on the harsh treatment of internees in Londonderry Prison, based on a personal account. The men spent twenty out of twenty-four hours in cells which were so badly heated that on cold days they had to wrap themselves in blankets. Exercise was taken for four hours a day, in single file, five yards apart. Talking was not allowed, although four months previously the prohibition was eased, to some extent. Internees were not allowed to study, or to have writing materials. Allegations had been made of kicking and beating.[86] This critical editorial was circulated within the Ministry. At this point it was agreed to address the complaint that the Belfast internees were allowed to smoke but those in Derry were not.[87]

Attention was also paid to a Dáil complaint of 2 April 1924 along similar lines.[88] Patrick Baxter questioned Desmond FitzGerald, Minister for External Affairs, about the Derry conditions.[89] These Baxter detailed, as in the *Catholic Times*, with the additional complaint that should a man stop for a rest during exercise he broke the rules and could be punished by three days' bread-and-water diet.[90]

Prior to this, the Ministry of Home Affairs had convened a meeting about the regime for internees. The conclusion was that any loosening of control in prisons was both unnecessary and inadvisable. Free association could not be allowed, 'in the interest of discipline'. Any increase in the four hours of exercise per day would necessitate more staff. The Governor had powers to punish any remand prisoner by three days' close confinement on no. 1 punishment (bread and water), but there was no record of this having been imposed on an internee who had stopped to rest during exercise. With the exception of one tubercular man, none of the Derry prisoners was in bad health.[91]

A similar response was given by Bates to his fellow minister J. M. Andrews, who, in August 1924, had privately expressed concerns about the internees' treatment. There had been only three cases of illness, apart from minor ailments, namely appendicitis, bronchitis and heart trouble, wrote Bates. Of the minor ailments such as colds and digestive troubles, he observed that the majority would not even have been noticed 'were not medical attention provided free'. He also had reassuring words about allegations of bullying by staff. The men had been asked 'out of the hearing of any of the staff of the Camp' if they had any complaints or had heard of any. All had denied knowledge of 'anything of the kind' as had the governor and medical officer.[92]

Yet public concern continued to mount, even in England. The *Yorkshire Observer* ran an article on 1 September 1924 on conditions, based on a pamphlet published by the Internees' Dependants' Committee.[93] The Ministry's response, published via the Ulster Association, was that some of the numbers given in the article were out of date; that internment was a tried expedient against 'organised murder gangs'; that there was an Advisory Committee; and that releases, conditional and unconditional, had been made. As for allegations of ill-treatment, such statements were 'invariably made by prisoners and internees in Ireland for propaganda purposes'. This fact was not so well known in England as it was in the Free State and Northern Ireland and 'by everyone who has had experience of prison life'. Food was an improved version of the diet for untried prisoners and was taken to the cells by well-conducted convicted prisoners. Medical officers' records of internees' weight on reception and release showed that in most cases there had been a gain.[94]

At around the same time, a deputation of Tory and National Liberal Westminster MPs, led by Lord Curzon, visited Northern Ireland. The mothers and relations of the internees petitioned, asking for intercession with the Northern Ireland government. A briefing paper on internment was immediately drawn up for use by members of the Ulster Unionist Council and for the visitors. This followed the usual lines but emphasised the part that internment had played in the reduction of violence and disorder, which two years before had been at truly alarming levels. In the week ending 20 May 1922, there had been thirty-nine murders in Northern Ireland, and in one week in May eighty persons had been wounded. In Belfast during 1922 there had been 188 acts of arson at a total cost of £1,230,000: most of the fires had been set during May and June.[95] But this failed to address the question of why it was necessary to continue internment, when it and other measures had evidently been so successful that the country was now at peace.

The agitation continued. Some of the republican women, who had campaigned so strongly on Free State prisoners, came north, and, on the evening of 28 September 1924, meetings were held at a number of venues, including Belfast, Londonderry, Newry and Omagh. Addressing a meeting chaired by Father H. J. Murray, at Corrigan Park, Belfast, Hanna Sheehy-Skeffington delivered an undiluted Sinn Féin message, proclaiming herself to be 'an unrepentant and convinced Republican'. She repeated the anti-Treaty assertion that the Free State and Northern governments had entered into a thieves' agreement, each finding it convenient to keep certain men in prison; they were glad to help each other.[96] Dorothy Macardle, speaking in Derry, insisted that a government that forced little girls, the daughters of internees, to go out to work to help to maintain the household 'was not a government fit to exercise power in any country'.[97] This type of rhetoric was unlikely to move Craig and his colleagues, but that was not the objective: the intention was to use internment as a bridge between republicans and nationalists, and to rouse both groups. This was the dangerous coalescing of which the RUC had warned.

The prospect of such a unification also concerned the Dublin government, which looked north with much anxiety. Until the Civil War was won and it had emptied out its own camps and prisons, it had been difficult for it to intervene. Even thereafter it had a hard case to make. Craig could point out that if the Free State needed internment to provide for its own security – and the internment not of 500, but of 10,000 – his government was entitled to use the same instrument and was unwilling to accept representations to the contrary. Dublin's second difficulty was that the majority of those interned in the North were pro-Treaty and had a moral entitlement to look to Dublin for assistance. If the Free State could not help its supporters was there not a danger that the republicanism that fired the speeches of Sheehy-Skeffington and Macardle would find new channels in which to run?

From the outset, Dublin had been petitioned by the Northern internees, their clergy, relatives and friends.[98] Collins, of course, had every reason to have an uneasy conscience about the plight of his Northern supporters, given his secret war on the fledgling state. Had he lived, it is possible that the issue of prisoners and internees would have moved further up the agenda. In March 1925,

W. T. Cosgrave, his successor, obliquely confirmed this in a letter to Lord Glenavy: 'One of Collins' last wishes to me was that I should not rest until these men were released.'[99] During his last weeks, Collins had sought releases by every means open to him, including the good offices of the Norwegian Vice-Consul (who arranged that seven men be freed).[100]

But Collins was gone, as was the Lloyd George coalition government, and with it the channels of communication and personal relationships that had grown out of the Treaty negotiations. Embroiled in civil war, the survival of his state far from certain for some months, Cosgrave had to manage as best he could for the Northern prisoners and internees, but they were some way down his list of priorities. Wisely, he preferred oblique approaches to condemnation and confrontation. By far the most liberal and broad-minded member of the Northern cabinet was Lord Londonderry, Minister for Education. Cosgrave wrote to him about the teachers among the internees. There were, he believed, nine primary-school teachers on board the *Argenta*. Their prolonged internment gave rise to special irritation, especially among members of their own profession. In the interest of good relations between the two populations and amity and concord between the two states, he asked Londonderry to help secure their release.[101] Londonderry's response was swift (and probably disingenuous): the teachers should go before the Advisory Committee, but he understood that to date none had done so.[102] Cosgrave agreed that this was the correct course (and one that the Free State required of its own internees) but mentioned that he had heard that those released by the Advisory Committee had been obliged to report frequently to the local police and reasoned that for some teachers this would have been the equivalent to dismissal.[103]

Now Cosgrave was being disingenuous. The teachers were unwilling to recognise the Northern government, and, from time to time, they and colleagues had been encouraged in this by the Free State: this was the principal barrier to their application to the Advisory Committee. Behind this lurked a hope that the Northern state would collapse, join the Free State, be taken over or somehow fade away. This stance had been encouraged among teachers – important leaders of opinion – in the early months of the existence of the Free State, when the Provisional government paid some Northern teachers' salaries and they had recognised the Dublin rather than the Belfast government. A note to Cosgrave from the Free State's Department of Education confirmed that these teachers and others continued to think this way. Some teachers remained obdurate in the hope that the Boundary Commission might rule substantially against Northern Ireland.[104]

The Advisory Committee

The DORA and the ROIA both provided for an Advisory Committee to review internees' cases. Since much of Northern Ireland's Special Powers Act derived from these two measures, an Advisory Committee was embedded in its internment provisions.[105] This body was appointed by the Minister for Home Affairs. The chairman had to have held high judicial office, or to be a recorder, county-court judge, or barrister of at least ten years standing.[106] Before turning to the internees' experience of the Committee, we should note certain of its features. It was, of course, an advisory rather than an adjudicatory entity, and its recommendations were therefore not binding on the Minister – and, as we shall see, it was frequently second-guessed. As from November 1923, moreover, it acquired a new role of recommending to the Minister persons to be interned. It is difficult now to understand how this provision worked, or indeed why it was introduced, and it may simply have been intended as a device to allow the Minister or his designated officials (the 'Civil Authority' of the Act) to obtain the Committee's opinion on a case for internment. The Committee does not appear to have reviewed internees' cases on a systematic basis or to have initiated enquiries. It intervened only on application from an internee or by ministerial request.

The Committee held its first meetings on 1 and 2 August 1922. At that point, forty-one persons had submitted applications, but only twenty-one followed through to an appearance. Drysdale, the Governor of the *Argenta* and Larne Camp, reported that those who had submitted applications had been intimidated by their fellows and this had deterred others from applying. Some prisoners, moreover, believed that the Committee's questions were intended to incriminate others, that it was an investigatory as well as a review body. Drysdale had also obtained a somewhat garbled account of IRA procedures, which he offered as an additional explanation for the low application rate. Any man imprisoned or interned, he claimed, was suspended from the organisation and not reinstated until he had been tried by court martial and acquitted. He concluded that internees feared that to have recognised the committee by making an application would be held against them by the IRA. Despite a reluctance to recognise and countenance the Northern Ireland state by submitting an application, and notwithstanding the operation of the IRA's code of discipline and the moral pressure exerted on waverers (and even a degree of intimidation), 488 of the total of 732 persons interned appeared before the committee, some on more than one occasion.[107]

There were a number of complaints about the Committee's procedures and style of working. Many were reluctant to apply at all; some had no such scruple, or swallowed it. For those who appeared, there seems to have been a standard approach. There were several basic and obvious questions. Was the applicant a member of the IRA? Was he a loyal subject of George V? And so forth. Even to constitutional nationalists the question about loyalty would have been difficult to answer: this was the conscientious basis of their political beliefs. But if they passed this first screening test (and as the months dragged on many were willing at least to mouth the words), other requirements were imposed. Perhaps the easiest of these was willingness to enter into a recognisance for their good behaviour (usually in the sum of £100, a significant amount at the time). The Special Powers Act contained extensive powers to direct or constrain movement, place of residence and the like. The Advisory Committee, in making a favourable recommendation to the Minister, could add a number of these conditions as riders. In July 1923, Kevin O'Shiel listed some of these for Cosgrave. There could be required an undertaking to leave Northern Ireland and to remain away for two years or even, O'Shiel claimed, forever. (The place of banishment was not specified, but for most it probably meant the Free State, purely on the practicalities of finding a place to live, the comparative proximity and support of relatives and finding work.) Severe restrictions could be imposed on those allowed to remain within the territory. Some were directed to live within two miles of their designated home and to report weekly to the local police barracks. Less restrictively, some were required to live in certain counties.[108]

Pro-Treaty internees in September wrote to the Free State Commander-in-Chief, General Richard Mulcahy, noting that some who had been released had such conditions imposed on them, and these were so degrading that no self-respecting man could accept them, even were they offered to the internees as a whole.[109] The hunger strikes of October and November 1923 arose in part from internees' dissatisfaction with these Advisory Committee requirements, which contributed to a sense of despair about the prospects for release and the resumption of normal life. As we have seen, Major A. W. Long, Governor of Belfast Prison, reported to the Minister that the main cause for the hunger strike appeared to be universal dissatisfaction with the Advisory Committee. Several claimed that they had gone before the Committee, agreed to its conditions for release, yet had not been freed.[110] Unknown to the applicants, however, the Committee's recommendation was only a stage in release procedures. This was executive detention, and only the Minister had the power to release or retain – a power he was not shy to exercise. Although not a uniform or obligatory practice, the Ministry would sometimes respond to a committee recommendation for release by asking for a report and comments from the police in the internee's locality. Even here there could be different voices.

James Mayne, a solicitor's managing clerk (and *Argenta* leader) had been a member of pre-Treaty Sinn Féin. The RUC confirmed he had never taken part in violence, or countenanced it. He had been interned because he was said to be a clever propagandist who reported Tyrone police actions to the Dublin press. Despite police disgruntlement at the trouble he had caused them, his RUC district inspector recommended release. The Special Constabulary did not agree, emphasising Mayne's powers of propaganda and his legal advice to people whose houses had been searched by the Specials or by the RUC, to manufacture what police saw as malicious claims. After almost two years in custody, Mayne got his hearing before the Advisory Committee (27 March 1924), answered the standard questions satisfactorily and was recommended for unconditional release. Still the Ministry was uneasy and sought fresh reports. The Intelligence Officer of Tyrone Special Constabulary recommended unconditional release. The local RUC (having picked up the Ministry's unease) was now more guarded than it had been initially but was not definitely opposed. The RUC Inspector-General's office, however, advised against release.[111] After further twists and turns, Mayne was eventually freed in June 1924, but under an order excluding him from Co.

Tyrone and from Magherafelt, Co. Londonderry. This cut him off from his house and means of earning a living. It was not until 31 October 1924, after further representations and having entered into bail on the sum of £100, the restrictions were lifted. Colm Campbell, who analysed the case, concluded that police reports appeared to be more important in the outcome than the Advisory Committee's recommendation and commented that 'the process which led to his release might have been the inspiration for Kafka's *The Trial*'.[112]

As a result of the hunger strikes of October and November 1923, the pressure of the constitutional nationalists, and public comments from the hitherto largely silent Roman Catholic clergy and hierarchy, it was decided that the Advisory Committee could not alone provide a sufficiently speedy and adequate means of winnowing out harmless elements among the internees; nor was it now satisfactory simply to await the internees' applications. Too many among them did not wish to apply to the Committee, even though they might meet its release criteria. In November and December, therefore, all cases were reviewed at a series of meetings chaired by Robert Megaw, the Junior (and fairly hard-line) Minister at Home Affairs. Release was offered to 178 internees on a variety of conditions; this amounted to about two-thirds of those then in custody. In June 1924, another group was recommended for unconditional release. The see-saw had dipped against the ministry side, and the desire was growing to be rid of the burden of internment.

Cases were reviewed by the county of internee domicile. The intention was that local police would attend, providing information on their internees. Since the initial decision to intern was heavily dependent on police advice, this was a sensible approach. As the hearings proceeded there appeared to be an excess of police caution. This provoked an impatient reaction from the Ministry, which, having changed its policy, was now intent on a general but phased release: it wanted favourable decisions. Five men who were thought suitable for release at the review conference were later vetoed by the police. Samuel Watt, Secretary at Home Affairs, wrote somewhat tartly to Sir Charles Wickham, the RUC Inspector-General, on this, and on the broader issues of releases. The Ministry had always given sympathetic and careful consideration to police representations and had never hesitated to take any step to preserve law and order and at the same time to protect the police. It had to be understood, Watt observed, that the power to hold a man in internment for a prolonged period had to be exercised with the greatest circumspection 'as it may be dangerous to press these powers too far'. He ended with an admonition that barely veiled a warning. The Ministry did not wish to be forced into granting 'wholesale and indiscriminate release', and it was for that reason that they preferred carefully to consider cases 'without any pressure from outside authorities'.[113]

Three months later, some differences between the Ministry and the RUC had not been resolved. Bates had directed that all internees with RUC unconditional-release recommendations should be offered their liberty on a personal bail of £10 for six months. He now wished the RUC to consider all remaining cases and to make further recommendations for release on terms, without the men's appearance before the Advisory Committee.[114] Still the RUC held back. At a ministry meeting on 20 June 1924, Megaw asked for views on expediting releases. There had been a further shift in outlook because of the possible recrudescence of agitation on the Boundary issue, with consequent danger in the border counties. Apparently in the face of RUC reservations, the meeting decided to free seventy men who had already been offered and refused release on their own bail of £10.[115] This was evidence that the government and its advisers had concluded that internment had outlived its purpose, becoming burden rather than benefit.

Following this meeting, the pace of releases was gradually increased.[116] By November, the *Irish News* was reporting that only 124 men remained in internment: 107 at Larne Camp, fourteen in Derry and three in Belfast Prison.[117] Two days before Christmas only three remained at Larne Camp, and they were released that morning.[118] Five weeks later, however, the *Irish News* complained that a number of men were still being held in Belfast and Derry prisons and that nobody knew why they had not been freed at the time of the Larne releases.[119] The picture becomes somewhat obscure since later in 1925 there was another small round of arrests and orders of internment.[120] It is probable, but not certain, that the last of the 1922 cohort were cleared in the spring months of 1925. The new batch were held for just under two months, with the final releases apparently on 25 January 1926 from Derry Prison.[121]

Interned government employees

Two groups among the internees received special consideration: imperial civil servants and teachers. The first were mainly minor functionaries, such as clerks and Post Office workers, but, as their employer, the British government felt a special obligation to consider their cases. The Imperial Secretary in Belfast, S. G. Tallents, wrote to Sir John Anderson (now at the Home Office) in February 1923. He proposed that interned Post Office workers should be considered in three categories: (1) established employees; (2) non-established employees who had gone before the Advisory Committee, but who had been refused release; and (3) non-established employees who had refused to go before the Advisory Committee.

For established employees, Tallents proposed that the Free State should be asked if there were employment for them, in exchange perhaps for Southern employees there who wanted to transfer to Northern Ireland. Should there be openings, these men might be freed. Non-established employees who had refused to go before the Advisory Committee were to be told that if they wished to return to their jobs they had a final opportunity to do so by making an application to the Committee. The most controversial proposal, as far as the Northern Ireland government was concerned, was for the non-established employees who had made an application to the Advisory Committee but who had been turned down. In what was an implicit comment on the Committee's capacity and possible bias, Tallents proposed that a senior postal official from London should jointly examine each case with a counterpart from the Ministry of Home Affairs. The two would determine whether a man's post should be declared vacant or held over for further consideration. The officials could also reconsider the cases of those imperial civil servants who had not obtained a favourable recommendation from the Advisory Committee. This proposal to give London an override elicited an ostensibly polite refusal from the Ministry of Home Affairs. Bates and Megaw saw 'great difficulties' with the proposal: 'The main difficulty in – and this constitutes a vital objection – that we could not possibly disclose police reports or other sources of information which have been given to us in strict secrecy.'[122] There was an element of manufactured caution here: the reports seen by the Ministry about the internees were not raw intelligence and information from informers, but were, rather, the opinions and judgements of police officers, based on such material. It was certainly not clear why the trustworthiness of an official of the British government was insufficient for this purpose.

But the refusal to countenance Tallents's proposal was not based on secrecy and security concerns. There had indeed been a deal of fury at Tallents's inter-position, which was taken as yet another example of the tutelage imposed by Whitehall. On 6 February 1923, a colleague – possibly Robert Megaw, now Attorney General – wrote to Bates fulminating against what he saw as an emerging tendency to subject Northern Ireland's administration 'to the inspection of persons appointed by the British authorities'. Tallents's proposal implied that (British) civil servants were entitled to a consideration unavailable to the general public, 'a sort of *droit administrative* – not to be responsive to the ordinary law, or at any rate to have a privileged position – and that just as in Turkey, there are special international tribunals, so there should be in Northern Ireland for the members of the British civil service'.[123] Northern Ireland had statutory authority over its own administration, but proposals such as Tallents's showed there was to be supervision by the British government. The implication was that the Northern Ireland administration was considered to be harsh and oppressive. The protest concluded with some flourishes. Tallents was attempting a serious infringement on Northern Ireland's rights. 'Could you fancy such a proposal being made to the Free State?' What right did Sir John Anderson have 'more than the other people who desire the release of internees?' As for the overall position, 'Are we a government or are we not?'[124]

This was a self-indulgent rant, of a type not unknown in politics. Tallents had no sinister motives in putting forward his proposal; there was no Whitehall plot to dabble. The history of the decades that followed would show that the Whitehall tribe was more than happy to follow Pilate. The idea was simply to deal with the staffing uncertainties of the Post Office and, in the common interest, to tidy up a bit of North–South and therefore Anglo-Irish business. There is no indication in the files of the number of Post Office and other civil servants who had been interned – probably no more than a handful or two. In making his modest proposal, Tallents had poked a stick into a wasp's nest, but, in so doing, had provided an interesting glimpse of some of the tensions between Belfast and London: the issues of security, governance and responsibility. As for the end result, the postmen stayed put.

The other group who received special consideration were the teachers.[125] Here we look back to a very different and more deferential society in which there was not our modern proliferation of professions. They were men of considerable local standing and importance. Within the Catholic community their learning and responsibility for children gave them a level of respect surpassed only by doctors and the clergy. Their position undoubtedly varied from one place to another and reflected their energy, personalities and talents, but their communities would have been especially concerned about their internment: there was something unseemly about their being in custody – and children needed teaching.

As we have seen, nationalist sentiment was strong among some of these teachers – hardly surprising in the light of the Gaelic cultural and sporting revival of the previous forty years. Their prominence in these activities probably contributed to a number being interned. Others, no doubt, had taken a hand in the pre-Civil War Sinn Féin and IRA. An interesting consequence of this, and what seems to have been their generally pro-Treaty views, was their access to Free State officials and ministers. Thus, Frank Gallagher (headmaster of Trillick National School, Co. Tyrone) was able to write, in February 1923, to Frank O'Duffy, Secretary of the Free State Department of Education, reporting that he had been moved from the *Argenta* to Derry Prison. He asked for a position in one of the Free State schools and was willing to join the Free State Army until a vacancy arose.[126] For some at least, an understanding seems to have been reached that if a Free State position were found for them they would be released. This was consistent with at least one of the objectives of the Ministry of Home Affairs: the removal of many of the interned men from Northern Ireland.

In January 1923, Francis Crummey reported to Frank O'Duffy that he had gone before the Advisory Committee. The decision went against him, either in the Advisory Committee or in one of the subsequent consultations with the RUC or Special Constabulary. A Free State post was found for Crummey, and, on 16 April 1923, Cosgrave raised the case with Lord Londonderry, Northern Ireland Minister for Education. Despite Crummey's having his job offer, the Advisory Committee had turned him down. This was most unfortunate and had 'given force to the impression that even those of Nationalist politics and Catholic faith who go out of their way to assist your government and who by so doing incur the hostility of the extreme elements among their neighbours, are treated as dangerous enemies by your institutions'.[127] Londonderry took up the case with Bates, who directed that Crummey should come again before the Committee. With such backing, he was now recommended for conditional release. He accepted these requirements, the principal one, presumably, an agreement to leave Northern Ireland.[128]

Loyalist internees

Although internment netted Roman Catholics almost exclusively, around twenty Protestants were arrested and interned, most for loyalist but four for their IRA and Sinn Féin activities.[129] The four, unremarkably, shared the fate of the other nationalist and republican internees.[130] As early as September 1923, four Protestant rioters were held under the ROIA.[131] There was immediate pressure to release the men. Their supporters denied that the civil disorders were sectarian and instead saw them as political conflicts fundamental to the survival of Northern Ireland. The Ministry of Home Affairs was divided on the issue, with Megaw supporting the Army's arrests and Watt insisting that the extraordinary powers of the ROIA had never been intended for use against those who were loyal to the Crown, for whom ordinary legal powers should be used.[132] The Army resolved the problem in this instance by bringing the four Protestants, and four Catholics arrested at the same time, before the magistrates, who simply bound them over.[133] Using ordinary law to deal with loyalists arrested for rioting and other public-order-related offences reassured the government's supporters and kept to a minimum the number of loyalists who were interned.

The Ulster Protestant Association (UPA), a Protestant terrorist group that used violence and murder against individual Catholics, presented the government with a difficult problem in balancing electoral and security issues. Four members were brought to trial in March 1922. The Association's chairman was convicted on arms charges and sentenced to eleven months' imprisonment (notably *not* penal servitude and flogging). Three other men were acquitted: intimidation of juries was possibly as strong on the loyalist side as it was on the other. In May 1922, with disorders continuing, it appears that some members of the UPA were interned in the first round-ups.[134] Following a series of UPA killings, the police officer in charge of East Belfast, District Inspector R. R. Spears, received permission to arrest and intern two of its leaders. These, however, were released after one month, deported to England and barred from Northern Ireland for two years.[135] In November, Spears was allowed to intern four more leading UPA members.[136] In all of this the sweeping powers of the Special Powers Act were not directed against loyalists, which meant that the police, even where they had good intelligence, could not arrest preventively but instead had to follow the normal judicial processes. This avoided stoking up the ire of the more extreme Protestant and loyalist groups against the government, but at the cost of confirming to Catholics and nationalists the sectarian bias of the Northern state.

Of loyalists' life in internment we know little. There are no memoirs, and it cannot be said for certain where and how they were each accommodated. With such a small number, however, there would have been no difficulty in holding them in Belfast Prison, apart from the Catholic internees. Certainly there are no reports of conflicts between the two groups. A fragment survives in the files to show that, in some cases at least, loyalists and Catholics were mixed. John Williamson of Belfast was interned in Londonderry Prison on 18 November 1922. He had been arrested in September 1922, for possessing five rounds of ammunition, bayonets and two rifles and was then released on his own bail of £100 and two sureties of £50 each to be of good behaviour. As an internee he was held in the normal cellular accommodation and 'mixed along with rebels', as he put it.[137] The common bonds of captivity can be a remarkable solvent. Three months into his internment he assaulted a warder, pleaded guilty and was sentenced to four months' hard labour.[138] The Crown successfully applied to have his earlier bail and sureties estreated.[139] Williamson begged Sir Dawson Bates for leniency, promising to leave the country and make a fresh start. His signature was followed by 'God and Ulster'. Bates was unmoved, and, having served his sentence, Williamson demonstrated a degree of chutzpah (or simplicity) by applying to the Ministry for a cash grant, pointing out that in his seven months in prison he had worn out his clothes. A sum of 15 shillings to purchase new boots, which he had been given on discharge from Londonderry Prison, was insufficient, he pleaded. Oblivious to his own responsibility in the matter, he asked for 'some sort of compensation'.[140] Neither of Williamson's petitions to the Ministry was granted, but his case emphasises how differently loyalist and republican offenders and internees were treated and how they viewed the authorities. His conditional discharge for possessing weapons could not be in greater contrast to the sentences then being imposed on republicans: long prison terms or penal servitude sometimes accompanied by corporal punishment.

Cahir Healy

Cahir Healy's internment from 23 May 1922 until 11 February 1924 was in many ways illustrative of the inherent political weaknesses of detention without trial; also, largely incidentally, it was to establish a parliamentary precedent that would have momentous consequences.[141]

A nationalist member of the Enniskillen Rural District Council, at the time of his arrest Healy earned his living as an insurance agent. He had, according to the Ministry of Home Affairs, been an intelligence officer with the 1st Midland Division, 4th Brigade, of the IRA. Healy always claimed to have been a man of peace in politics – a statement certainly incompatible with membership of the IRA. He had, however, been an open member of Sinn Féin, which may have brought him very close to the IRA organisationally, entailing unqualified support for revolutionary politics.[142] Whatever the quality of the Ministry's intelligence, and whatever early involvement Healy may have had, in his middle and later years – and at the time of his arrest – he was committed to Irish unity and was in peaceful and public opposition to the Northern Ireland State and to the Ulster Unionist Party. He had a strong constituency following, was articulate and intelligent and (within the limits of a cleft community) an effective politician. These qualities of leadership, his unwillingness to accept the legitimacy of the Northern Ireland State, and his past connections with the IRA, led to internment.

The strength of Healy's continuing connection to his Sinn Féin comrades is hard to assess from the files that are available. The term 'Sinn Féin', moreover, was in flux, North and South, with the divisions of the Civil War. The Northern authorities were wont to apply it to anyone who ever had a connection with the IRA, pre- or post-Treaty, and of whatever faction. With the advent of Partition and then civil war, the Sinn Féin organisation in Northern Ireland fractured and rapidly declined. Two months into his confinement, Healy wrote to Kevin O'Shiel, legal adviser to Cosgrave (and, as we have seen, well known to be a door-keeper). This, despite his precautions, was intercepted. Institutions, parties and organisations were in flux, North and South, and Healy sought guidance from someone at the centre of events. Sinn Féin headquarters had given 'no light or leading', he complained. Were he and his comrades to look to the Provisional government for guidance? Was there any probability of a settlement being reached with the British that would include the North?[143]

But Healy was seen as a high security risk, and although, at forty-five, the authorities would scarcely have put him in the tunnelling, wall-scaling or rioting category, they described him as 'a cunning and clever organiser and a leader of disloyal persons in his neighbourhood'.[144] A few weeks after arrest, Healy was transferred to the *Argenta* from which he complained shortly afterwards, applying to be moved onshore to Larne Workhouse, that conditions meant he could have no more than two or three hours' sleep each night: 'mental torture'. With the professional risk-aversion of all gaolers, Drysdale thought it safer to keep him on the water.

Onboard or onshore, Healy would prove to be troublesome. This was not because of an escape attempt or incitement of his comrades but rather because he became a political embarrassment. In the general election of 15 November 1922, he was elected, by a handsome majority, as Westminster MP for Fermanagh-Tyrone.[145] By now the election of imprisoned persons, convicted or interned, had become a well-honed tool for nationalists and republicans: the very fact that one had been imprisoned conferred its own cachet of authenticity, with the bonus that to run a prisoner as candidate created a chance to rally the nationalist community and to harass the government.[146] Another cachet, and one the authorities were immediately urged to consider, was that Healy, now a Westminster MP, had certain privileges and duties. Unlike earlier republicans elected while in custody, Healy did not have the legal disability of conviction and, following procedure, could not be disqualified as a convicted felon.

William Pringle, one of the small rump of the old Liberal Party, raised Healy's case with the Speaker.[147] Members' privileges could not be preserved against the criminal law, nor did they extend to breaches of the peace, but the internment order under which Healy was held did not obviously fall under either of these headings. While Pringle did not question the legality of the internment order, he wished a Committee of the House to examine whether Healy retained an MP's privileges. Jack Jones, a Labour member, seconded Pringle.[148] Healy should not be victimised because of his political opinions. If he were a criminal why had he not been charged? A member of the House should be protected and allowed to attend. Opposing, Captain C. C. Craig, the Ulster Unionist, pointed out that when they voted for him the electors had known that Healy was interned.[149] He was a Sinn Féiner, and other members of that party had declared that, if elected, they would not take their seats. To allow him to take advantage of parliamentary privilege would 'reduce the House to a laughing stock by getting out of detention one who had no intention of taking his seat'.[150]

The Speakers' ruling was the first part of a decision that would have consequences for the next half-century, extending well beyond the comparatively narrow issue at hand. Craig's argument about Healy's possible non-attendance was not a consideration: whether he came to the House or not 'was a matter for the honourable member' (a grand-sounding statement, completely ignoring Healy's circumstances). The sole issue was whether a *prima facie* matter of privilege existed. The internment decision had been taken by the competent Northern Ireland authority, using its powers for the punishment of crime and the maintenance of order. In such cases, privilege had not been allowed by the House, as was shown by 'a little later Parliamentary history'.[151]

Healy's case returned to the Commons five months later when Frank Gray, Liberal MP for Oxford, put down a series of *Argenta* questions for the Home Secretary.[152] A Tory, Sir Malcolm Macnaghten, asked whether it was in order to raise matters that fell within the competence of the Northern Ireland and Free State governments. Lieutenant-Commander Joseph Kenworthy, a Liberal member with a long-standing interest in Ireland, countered. Since one of the *Argenta*'s prisoners was a member of the House, was it not in order simply to ask for information?[153]

The Speaker then gave the ruling that was to close the door on Westminster scrutiny of Northern Ireland affairs. He thought it 'very undesirable' that the Commons should have questions 'on matters which we have delegated by statute to the Irish Governments'. It had escaped his notice, he continued, that Gray's question had appeared on the order paper, but since it had, and he was asking only for information, he would allow it to be put. William Bridgeman, the Home Secretary, gave an answer that would serve as a template for British ministers thereafter: he had no information on the matter, and any questions should be addressed to the Northern Ireland government. Even though the British contribution to the maintenance of Northern Ireland was, as with all such transfers, entirely fungible, he insisted that there had been no British financial contribution to support internment (another possible way into the issue for Westminster MPs). After further exchanges, especially on the contribution made by the British taxpayer to the purchase of the *Argenta* and to the maintenance of the Ulster Special Constabulary, the Speaker, John Whitley, reiterated his ruling, reminding members that he had made a similar decision on South Africa. The Northern Ireland government was responsible for law and order in its own territory. It is quite impossible, he contended, 'once having transferred responsibility to other bodies, that we should deal with matters on the floor of the House'.[154]

Two points are worthy of note before returning to Healy's own story. In terms of their sovereignty, the Speaker equated South Africa and other dominions, including the Irish Free State, to Northern Ireland. After the passing of the Statute of Westminster eight years later, this would have been an impossible equation, but already it was utterly implausible. There could be no practical doubt as to the comparative status of the Free State and of Northern Ireland. The Anglo-Irish War had been fought because nationalists and republicans would not accept Home Rule under Westminster supremacy. After the signing of the Treaty, no one, except as a wilful and perverse semantic exercise, could doubt the independence of the Irish Free State. Northern Ireland was a very different case. In 1912, Ulster Unionists had advanced to the very edge of rebellion to maintain the indissoluble Union: the supremacy of the Crown and Imperial Parliament was the very core of their cause. Law's short-lived but ultra-unionist administration held office at the time of these exchanges, and its assessment of constitutional doctrine was a secondary matter: giving support to Craig and his colleagues, friends and close political colleagues was the priority. It is not difficult to see how John Whitley, the Speaker, would have been influenced by the government's sense of urgency in the matter. It is also fair to recognise that there remained uncertainty and a lack of clarity in the working-out of what were unprecedented relationships within and with the Union. From no part of the House was there a vision in this matter that went beyond the immediate and tactical. Westminster thus imposed a self-denying ordinance that ran counter to its own fundamental doctrines and basic doctrines of administration: the axiom that authority could not be detached from accountability. Where there is a mismatch or disconnection, the consequences are invariably corrosive and usually destructive.

Healy remained on the *Argenta* from mid-June 1922 until 22 November 1923. At that latter point, despite the security concerns that had earlier been thought insuperable, he was allowed on shore. As we have seen, conditions at Larne Workhouse were better than those on the *Argenta* but were still basic. Because he was an MP, Healy had been given certain correspondence privileges. Censorship rules still applied but since by virtue of his office he was allowed to write about topics of political and public concern, it was hard to frame instructions for the prison censor officer. This was all the more difficult when Healy became a candidate in the new general election held on 6 December 1923. The censor was directed that his election address was to be forwarded to the Ministry of Home Affairs, but no guidance or instructions had been given to cover similar political matter.[155]

In consequence of this lapse, Healy managed to send out letters on internment conditions. (He also very likely used clandestine means to communicate.) One of these letters went to Frank Gray, the independent-minded MP who had spoken on his behalf in the Commons. Much to the irritation of the Ministry of Home Affairs, Gray publicised Healy's complaints. Far more serious from their point of view was a longer communication that appeared in Max Beaverbrook's *Sunday*

Express on 6 January 1924.[156] The letter, which described the somewhat squalid conditions in which Healy lived, was damaging enough in itself; far more ominous was the development of Beaverbrook's interest in the case. The *Daily Express* was the world's most widely read English-language newspaper, which gave Beaverbrook immense influence and caused him to be courted by the very top layer of British party politics.

It was already clear that the Conservative Party was entering troubled waters. Following the December general election, a minority Labour government would take office when Parliament reassembled in January 1924. This first advent to power of avowed socialists was an upheaval now difficult to fully appreciate. It was not at all clear who would prevail in the three-party melee that would occupy the time between Labour taking up the reins and yet another general election (the third in less than two years) in search of an administration with a clear parliamentary majority. Healy had again been returned by the electors of Fermanagh-Tyrone, and, given the organic links between the Westminster and Northern Ireland Unionist parties, it was not hard to see that his continued confinement, and internment generally, could become a stick with which Liberals and Labour would beat them. In such times, every vote and every constituency counted, and the now large Irish electorate in a number of British cities could help to tip the balance. Healy could very easily become an electorally consequential cause célèbre.

In anticipation of these difficulties (but before the *Sunday Express* article had fully emphasised them), Stanley Baldwin (who had succeeded the mortally ill Bonar Law in the Conservative leadership) wrote to Craig, the letter marked 'Secret'. Had Craig considered that the question of the internees would be raised when Parliament reassembled? This had been brought to mind by the case of Cahir Healy, recently re-elected: 'I do not know the grounds upon which he is interned, but I understand that he is regarded by the Free State government not as a republican but as a supporter of the constitutional settlement.' He also raised the case of Colonel Woods (a Free State Army officer arrested in Northern Ireland).[157] The policy of internment must be under constant review by the Northern government, he diplomatically observed. 'It occurs to me', he went on, 'that the New Year might offer an opportune moment for releasing any prisoners who you feel are no longer a direct source of danger or embarrassment'. Given that some of the prisoners, North and South, might make trouble if released, he wondered whether Craig and Cosgrave should meet with the intention of agreeing which prisoners might be released 'without danger to the general peace of Ireland'. The situation over the next few months was one of great difficulty, and he was anxious that 'no unnecessary cause of embarrassment either to your Government or to this country should be allowed to continue'.[158] This was a very firm steer indeed, but that it should come so close to the declaration of the general-election results showed that to the leadership of the Conservative Party, Ireland and Irish issues remained as political mines, drifting in unknown currents.

Baldwin received two replies. The first had been drafted by the Northern Ireland Cabinet Office and reflected the concerns of civil servants and ministers, particularly Sir Dawson Bates. A covering personal note from Craig emphasised that the official letter had been written 'in the best interests of everyone concerned'; he hoped that Baldwin would not press further the case of Healy or Woods.[159] The official response ran to four and a half pages and began by referring to the Speaker's ruling of 27 November 1923. Were Healy now to be released it would be seen as a sign of weakness, arising from a fear that 'some Government less friendly than your own may come into power'. Healy had refused to apply to the review tribunal. Should he agree to leave Northern Ireland or provide satisfactory guarantees that he would not involve himself in illegal movements, the government would not oppose his release. No hope was held out for the release of Colonel Woods, who had entered the jurisdiction under a false name and who was behind a series of murders. Although Craig was always willing to meet Cosgrave, he was doubtful as to whether there was any point in a discussion of internees. Cosgrave could, however, 'exercise most useful influence' on Healy by inducing him to agree to the proposed conditions for his release.[160]

The fact that Healy had won a seat at Westminster twice within a short period gave his case particular weight, even within Baldwin's more general observations about the festering impact of internment. Nationalists were not slow to point to the constitutional issues.[161] Baldwin thought it unwise to let matters rest and, setting aside the official response, replied to Craig's personal letter. He did not wish to go into detail about the letter drafted by the civil servants. He could see Craig's problems, and he hoped Craig could see his. The Conservatives were very likely going into opposition, and, as leader, he would have many problems. He did not wish to add Irish issues to them: 'But if Cahir Healy is still in confinement the Labour party is certain to fill the House and the Press with it.' The *Sunday Express* had already begun to campaign for a full inquiry, and he would 'not find it easy to rally our men to support your policy of detaining Healy without trial'. He was, he said, not addressing the merits of the case but was looking ahead and asking Craig whether there was nothing he could now do 'to forestall the troublesome agitation which I foresee'. Woods was a different case, which ought not to be insoluble by the two Irish governments (some mutually acceptable horse-trading, in other words).[162]

This renewed plea was followed a few days later by a cautionary note to Craig from D. D. Reid, an Ulster Unionist MP at Westminster. William Pringle, the Liberal who had first raised Healy's case in the Commons, had given notice that he would again seek a ruling on privilege. Two courses were open, Reid suggested. The first was to stick by the doctrine that the Northern government had responsibility for law and order and that it declined to release Healy. An alternative would be to say that it was satisfied that in any discussion of the issue of privilege, the law-and-order responsibilities of the Northern government had been taken into account and that, in consequence, it would comply were a demand made for Healy's release: 'In other words would we prefer that we should be stiff-necked or that we should be conciliatory.'[163]

In the meantime, Craig was subject to exhortations of a very different kind from his own supporters. G. B. Liddy wrote from Enniskillen, in Healy's constituency. He listed various violent acts of republicans in the district, mentioning Healy's attendance at a Sinn Féin court, and referred to IRA murders, boycotting and burnings, though not asserting Healy's connection to those. The British parliament had no right to interfere, and Craig should stand firm.[164] Predictably, Bates urged the same line. He took some consolation from the fact that even were a House of Commons Privilege Committee to find that internment violated Healy's parliamentary privileges, the decision would affect him alone or any other Westminster MP who claimed exemption from internment.[165] Reid, reporting from London, agreed with this, but took his argument on a different tack. The Northern government could certainly refuse to appear before a House of Commons Committee: it could keep Healy in internment whatever. Alternatively, it could agree to release him, should the Commons so recommend. Reid indicated his own sense of the direction to take: 'On the general grounds of not wishing to raise difficulties with the new Government Sir James may consider Healy's detention not worth fighting about.'[166]

Speaking more directly and authoritatively, Lord Londonderry, the somewhat absent Northern Ireland Minister for Education, wrote on 7 February 1924, asking that Healy be released before Parliament reassembled the following week: 'As you know I have disagreed with the policy of internment in most cases and I was very sorry that the policy was adopted of saying that everybody must come before the Committee and that if they did not do so, they were to remain in internment.' He acknowledged that having made his protest he had not pushed the matter. Alluding to internment, and to the case of Inspector Nixon, Londonderry suggested that as far as it was able to do so the new Labour government was anxious to help Northern Ireland, 'and it is of vital importance that we should not furnish cases to the enemies of the Government which may be difficult to defend'.[167]

Londonderry was pushing at an open door, since the decision had already been taken to release Healy, the announcement being made on 8 February 1924. Craig had still not returned to his duties, and Sir Dawson Bates was deputising for him. This may have been a factor in a mangling of the political benefits of the release. As an expression of reluctance, of having been forced in the matter, of chagrin, or of political spite, Healy's release was made conditional, and the condition was absurd and indefensible. He was not told about this until he had left Larne Workhouse, otherwise he might have refused it.[168] He was forbidden to enter that part of Fermanagh west of a line drawn through Pettigo and Newtownbutler to the border. This denied him entry to more than half of the county of Fermanagh, including Enniskillen, the county town where he lived. The decision was inexplicable, save as a device to separate Healy from a section of his supporters and constituents, or simply and spitefully to make his life more difficult.[169] This was a more difficult position for Belfast to defend than the internment itself had been.

Another scene of political incompetence would follow before the act reached its finale. On being released on 11 February 1924, Healy was handed a rail warrant to allow him to travel home to Enniskillen: this type of warrant was given to all internees who were unconditionally released. At the same time, he was served with Bates's exclusion order under Regulation 23A of the Special Powers Act. Healy assumed, or, more likely, found it convenient to assume, that the rail warrant superseded the prohibition – not an entirely far-fetched interpretation since the only purpose of the warrant was to return him to his home. On the day following his release, Healy was therefore arrested in Enniskillen.[170] Having been held for a further two days in Londonderry Prison, he was then, by direction of the Northern Ireland Attorney General, released and informed that it had been decided not to prosecute him for the breach of his release conditions. Rather than draw a line under the whole affair – by far the wiser course – the order prohibiting his return to his home and to other designated parts of the country remained in force.[171]

The following day, Ramsay MacDonald, now British Prime Minister, wrote to Craig. The decision to release Healy had, 'on a purely legal point', been most welcome. There remained concern about the order excluding Healy from part of his constituency. The legal right of the Northern Ireland government was not in question, but by diminishing the right of electors in that part of the UK to effective representation in the Imperial Parliament, an issue of constitutional privilege might arise between the two parliaments. In that event, the government could be involved in a House of Commons debate 'in which the administration of your Government of the powers assigned to it may become a direct issue'. These were grave and ominous words. Having decided to release Healy, MacDonald asked the Northern Cabinet whether they could not, 'without danger to the peace and order of Northern Ireland', suspend the order that debarred Healy from direct access 'to the greater part of his constituents'.[172] This was an indication, blunt as could be, that things could go badly wrong. Craig knew that there now existed a Commons in which a majority would probably view his government's manner of conducting business with a deal of scepticism and indeed a minority that might be somewhat hostile.

Craig's illness was a handicap to the Northern Ireland government and was indicative of the shallowness and weakness of its cabinet, especially in a matter as delicate for London–Belfast relations as the Healy internment and its aftermath.[173] Craig had the considerable advantage of familiarity with the workings of Westminster and Whitehall; Bates had little concept of either, of how swiftly and how far English politics and public opinion could shift, and how sentiment could suddenly coalesce around a perceived underdog and against bullying. Beaverbrook had taken a campaigning interest in the matter for those reasons; there was a new government, a new and volatile Commons, a political horizon more uncertain than it had been in a generation, yet Bates continued to beat the drum and to march briskly on as before, unaware of the need now to temporise. On his direction, Colonel Wilfrid Spender, the Cabinet Secretary, wrote to Lord

Londonderry, informing him that the *Irish News* had that day reported that Cahir Healy intended to make full use of his information about internment and that Bates expected a press campaign on the issue. There followed an assurance that must have dismayed Londonderry: Bates believed that any such campaign would be greatly discounted because Healy apparently had no intention of attending Westminster.[174] This surely was a moment to be rid of the albatross of internment altogether rather than to be sketching out the lines of its further defence and drawing down yet more political capital. But as far as Healy was concerned, the matter was concluded, and on 18 February 1924, Spender wrote to the Speaker at Westminster, informing him that the Northern Ireland government had withdrawn the order forbidding Cahir Healy from visiting part of his Fermanagh constituency.[175]

Coda

The killing of Patrick Woods by the IRA, in the darkness and fog of the late afternoon on Thursday, 19 November 1925, was the trigger for another bout of internment, targeted and small-scale.[176] This was an IRA execution, sanctioned because Woods, formerly an IRA man, had become a Crown witness in an arms case two months earlier. The Ministry of Home Affairs understandably saw the murder of a witness as a grave challenge to law and order, with the potential for further political trouble because of the imminent publication of the Boundary Commission Report.[177] It was agreed that it was necessary to respond vigorously and that, as a demonstration, a 'moderate' number of IRA militants in Belfast should be rounded up. The RUC Inspector-General was able immediately to supply full dossiers on the men he thought suitable for internment. This was, above all, a warning 'that this Government is determined to maintain its authority'.[178] It was also intended to remind the organisation and its principal figures that they were under close observation and that quite a lot was known about them. Two days later, twenty-nine leading IRA men were arrested, as was a suspect in the Woods case. In announcing the arrests, Bates denied that the action had been undertaken for political reasons.[179] To ease problems of accommodating them in Belfast Prison, where they would have to be kept separate from other categories, the men were transferred to Derry Prison on 25 November 1925.[180] Letters in their files at Home Affairs, then and the following year, purporting to come from Roman Catholics in Belfast and elsewhere (but sent anonymously) gave detailed information on other active republicans. This may have been a genuine expression of war-weariness and a fear that incidents such as the Woods killing would restart the cycle of violence. The letters may also have been opportunistic – simply a settling of personal scores.[181] It is also possible that some came from police officers or from members of the Special Constabulary.

Bates's anxieties may have been somewhat manufactured, for, despite the Woods killing, there was at this point little sign that the Northern IRA was being revived. An RUC intelligence report referred to 'the dying embers of Republicanism'.[182] Finds of documents seemed to confirm this, with complaints about arms dumps that were hard to reach and organisers' unpaid travel expenses, despite reminders to HQ.[183] Yet within a year or two there seemed to be some cause for unease. Arms finds in Northern Ireland and England suggested that efforts were being made to fan the embers, and that to some effect.[184] A series of raids, arrests and arms finds in England coincided with a heated Dáil debate in which the reluctantly constitutional Fianna Fáil restated its objective of an All-Ireland Republic, by means other than parliamentary ones, if necessary.[185]

Some of the arms finds were substantial. On 9 December 1927, police uncovered a Belfast arms dump containing ten rifles, nine revolvers, a Thompson sub-machine gun, ninety-nine Mills grenades and a thousand rounds of ammunition, as well as detonators and explosives. A document was also found that referred to 20,000 rounds of ammunition.[186] It began to appear that the IRA had been recuperating rather than dying, and, to some in Northern Ireland, it seemed possible that the Fianna Fáil–Sinn Féin split might be mended, reanimating violent republicanism. At the end of the Civil War, it was recalled, the IRA had been stood down rather than dissolved; it had cached rather than discarded its *matériel*. This mood of growing alarm was reinforced by a militant statement from the ghostly Second Dáil, part of which referred to Ulster.[187] It was against this background that the debate was conducted on making the Special Powers Act permanent. In his speech to the Northern Ireland Parliament, Bates referred to these various signs of resurgent republicanism, including the acquisition of arms, munitions and explosives, and statements of hostile intent.[188] Wide – virtually unlimited – powers of arrest and executive, court-proof, detention and internment were to become durable features of Northern Ireland's system of policing and politics.

Notes

1 There are no comprehensive histories of the Northern IRA during these years. Both Tim Pat Coogan and J. Bowyer Bell deal almost entirely with developments in the Free State. See Tim Pat Coogan, *The IRA* (London: Fontana, 1980) and successive editions; J. Bowyer Bell, *The Secret Army: The IRA, 1916–1979* (Cambridge, Mass.: MIT Press, 1983). Brian Hanley's excellent study, *The IRA, 1926–36* (Dublin: Four Courts Press, 2002), Chapter 8, provides some pertinent material, as does Michael Farrell in his study, *Northern Ireland and the Orange State* (London: Pluto, 1976), Chapter 6. See also the instructive collection of essays, edited by Alan Parkinson and Eamon Phoenix, *Conflicts in the North of Ireland, 1900–2000* (Dublin: Four Courts Press, 2010), especially Dennis Kennedy's contribution, 'Border Trouble: Unionist Perceptions of and Responses to the Independent Irish State' (pp. 86–97).

2 There is some account of Northern Ireland IRA activities in the Ministry of Home Affairs' file 'Republican Organisations, Seditious Posters, etc.' (PRONI HA/32/1/489). As with many such documents there is an element of chance and haphazardness in its contents.

3 Regulations 23 and 23A. For a discussion of the Special Powers Act, see above, pp. 86–94.

4 Seven women internees were held at Armagh Prison, and there were at least twelve Protestant men interned (*Irish Independent*, 6 April 1923). For a detailed county-by-county nominal list of *Argenta* internees, see PRONI, Cahir Healy Papers, D/2991/E/30/28. The list seems to have been compiled in or around July 1924.

5 As would happen on other occasions when internment sweeps were conducted, there were examples of poor intelligence and police indifference in executing arrest warrants. Cahir Healy, himself arrested and held as an internee for almost twenty months, gave cases: 'Joe Hawkins, an old and infirm man from Belfast, aged sixty-five, was taken because the Specials could not get his son at home. Daniel McPoland, a national school teacher of fifty-eight, was taken in lieu of his boy… The first named spent eighteen months in prison, the second twenty months.' Healy claimed that he could give 'fifty instances' of such arrests (*Irish News*, 18 February 1924, 8f).

6 PRONI HA/32/1/46, Report on Internments, 1922–4.

7 *Ibid*. Healy claimed that barely half those arrested were members of the IRA: 'They made no distinction between those who favoured physical force and the constitutionalists. The talker was considered nearly as dangerous as the actor – they gave each other moral support!' (Healy Papers, D/2991/B/140/10, transcript, 'On a Northern Prison Ship: The Round-up of 1922 – 1924', f. 6).

8 PRONI HA/5/2595, Letter to Lieutenant Colonel M. M. Haldane, Military Advisor, 6 June 1922. Maldwyn Makgill Haldane (1877–?) had been an assistant director of the wartime Special Intelligence Service. For his background, see Christopher Andrew, *The Defence of the Realm: The Authorized History of MI5* (London: Allen Lane, 2009), p. 59. See also Paul McMahon, *British Spies and Irish Rebels: British Intelligence and Ireland, 1916–1945* (Woodbridge: Boydell Press, 2008), pp. 154–7.

9 PRONI HA/5/2595, Henry Toppin to Samuel Watt, 13 June 1922.

10 PRONI HA/5/2595, Henry Toppin to Samuel Watt, 21 July 1922. See also Denise Kleinrichert, *Republican Internment and the Prison Ship Argenta 1922* (Dublin: Irish Academic Press, 2001), pp. 57–8, 350.

11 On Northern Ireland's prison estate and management, see pp. 373–83 below.

12 For the early use of ships as floating prisons, see Seán McConville, *A History of English Prison Administration, Vol. I: 1750–1877* (London: Routledge & Kegan Paul, 1981), pp. 105–7 and 393–6.

13 See *Irish Independent*, 15 May 1923, 9d. Healy Papers, D/2991/E/30/24. Healy calculated the total cost, including the refitting, to be £19,000 (D/2991/B/140/52).

14 This, according to Healy, was because of a near-collision when a Canadian liner failed to see the *Argenta* (Healy Papers, 'On a Northern Prison Ship', *op. cit.*, f. 12).

15 *Irish Independent*, 31 January 1924. Workhouses had been established throughout Britain and Ireland by the ever controversial Poor Law Amendment Act, 1834: 4 & 5 Will. IV, c.76. Unions of parishes were established for rating and relief purposes. They were each administered by a Board of Guardians. Charles Dickens and other nineteenth- and early twentieth-century authors catalogued and condemned their oppressiveness. For a concise and clear account of their history and of several notorious scandals, see Norman Longmate, *The Workhouse* (London: Pimlico, 2003).

16 PRONI HA/5/2595.

17 PRONI HA/32/1/46. In a spirit of cooperation, Dr Thomas Laverty, one of the internees, enquired of the men's elected commandant (Daniel Sheridan, Chairman of Newry's Board of Guardians) whether it was true that the second-hand baths had previously been used by poxy sailors. Sheridan denied the rumour (entirely an invention of Dr Laverty) and claimed that only that morning he had taken a bath in one of the tubs. This transaction took place in front of a small assembly of internees. Healy Papers, D/2991/C/26, *Argenta* journal, f. 90.

18 Looking back over a gap of eighteen years, A. Robinson, Secretary at the Ministry of Home Affairs, recalled that the disciplinary policy on the *Argenta* had been 'broadly, to leave the internees very much to their own devices and provide a very large armed guard to knock blazes out of them if they should get uppish'. PRONI HA/ 32/1/748, A. Robinson to Gravesden (Cabinet Secretary), 7 August 1940.

19 A. D. Drysdale, formerly Governor of Barlinnie Prison, Glasgow, had retired on pension and was appointed as *Argenta* governor on a temporary and non-pensionable basis. He was a former Rugby International for Scotland and had also been a member of the Board of Scottish Prisons: an able and highly experienced man. Drysdale was assisted by a deputy, Captain J. E. Long, who had run an internment camp in Egypt. There was also a chief officer, a Londonderry man called Nelson. He is described in a poem (very likely by Cahir Healy): 'An easy-going lad, but cute as a fox; / He danders around, with a well-sustained smile, / And an eye in his head that could see for a mile'. James Mayne, aged fifty, was Managing Clerk of a solicitor's firm in Cookstown, Co. Tyrone and sometime member of Cookstown Urban District Council. He was arrested on 23 May 1923 and released on grounds of health on 19 June 1924. The grounds for arrest were a rumour that he had taken part in an ambush and that he was an IRA intelligence officer. For Mayne's case, see Colm Campbell, *Emergency Law in Ireland* (Oxford: Clarendon, 1994), pp. 301–7.

20 PRONI HA/32/1/85, Letter to William Grant, MP, signed by nine warders who refused to unload supplies, 12 December 1922.

21 PRONI HA/32/1/85, A. D. Drysdale to Secretary, Ministry of Home Affairs, 6 January 1923.

22 PRONI HA/32/1/85, Colonel F. S. Pountney to Sir Dawson Bates, 6 December 1922. The observations that follow are from this source.

23 PRONI HA/32/1/85, report and file note.

24 PRONI HA/9/2/132, report, 22 September 1922.

25 For some of the background to the Roman Catholic Church's attitude towards the new dispensation in Northern Ireland, see Mary Harris's useful study, *The Catholic Church and the Foundation of the Northern Ireland State* (Cork: Cork University Press, 1993). For a broader canvas, see Marianne Elliott's masterly *The Catholics of Ulster: A History* (London: Allen Lane, 2000), especially Chapter 11. See also above, p. 57, and below, p. 340 and p. 366, n. 65.

26 PRONI HA/9/2/132, report, 30 September 1922.

27 PRONI HA/9/2/132, minute, 10 January 1925.

28 See NAI MS. 8411/13 and 14, Letters to Kate Kelly from Irish political prisoners. These handicrafts were often sold to supporters and sympathisers outside and raised funds for individual and collective use: they also served to keep the internees in the public mind.

29 PRONI HA/32/1/46, 'Report from the Internment Camp Larne, for Secretary, Ministry of Home Affairs, 16 January 1925'.

30 PRONI HA/32/1/46, 'Report from the Internment Camp Larne, for Secretary, Ministry of Home Affairs, 16 January 1925'.

31 Healy recalled that 'half the boys were not up at eleven: they took breakfast in bed... Our jailers left us pretty free within the steel wires to do as we pleased, and some of us pleased, accordingly, to dance until twelve, followed by a game of cards... It was nearly impossible for light sleepers to get "off" much before one or two in the morning' (*Argenta* journal, *op. cit.*).

32 Healy noted that '[o]ut of the 300 men we had not more than forty who cared to read; the distractions were too great, and the place too much crowded to make any sort of concentration possible. Besides, there were cards, chess, etcetera, which formed a stronger "draw"' (*Argenta* journal, *op. cit.*).

33 In his journal, Healy refers to a tussle over parcels. Not knowing that they were prohibited, relatives sent them in. The Governor, probably unable to return them to

relatives and friends, had them locked in one of *Argenta*'s punishment cells. There was a very small hatch in the cell, however, and the internees pushed in one of their number, 'a most diminutive chap, minus coat or vest'. This man passed all the parcels out but had difficulty in getting back through the hatch. One of the warders caught him: 'He was admonished and released, however, there was no place of punishment available!' At a later point (the size of the hatch having been reduced), what Healy describes as 'an ingenious wire sling' was used to remove the parcels (*Argenta* journal, *op. cit.*, f. 39).

34 Some men managed to simulate skin trouble in order to get hospital treatment, Drysdale reported, but after one man was punished and sent back to the ship, such attempts ceased. PRONI HA/32/1/46, 'Report from the Internment Camp Larne, for Secretary, Ministry of Home Affairs, 16 January 1925'.

35 PRONI HA/32/1/748, A. Robinson to R. Gransden, Secretary to Cabinet, 7 August 1940.

36 There were at least two attempts to place a police agent on board the *Argenta*. In one case the ruse failed when the internees questioned the man. He claimed to have been born in Co. Sligo, but when others who knew the locality confronted him he was removed from the vessel. In another instance, a man was escorted on board as an internee. He said that he had come from Armagh but was recognised by some of the men as a Special Constable and was immediately set upon. He was also rescued by the guarding Specials. But, of course, there may have been other, undetected, infiltrators. See Healy, *Argenta* journal, *op. cit.*

37 PRONI HA/32/1/211, Lieutenant Colonel M. M. Haldane, Divisional Commissioner's Office, Belfast, to Colonel Henry Toppin, Ministry of Home Affairs, 29 June 1922.

38 PRONI HA/32/1/211, file note, 30 June 1922.

39 PRONI HA/32/1/211, Henry Toppin to Samuel Watt, 8 September 1922.

40 PRONI HA/32/1/211, Ministry to M. M. Haldane, 27 September 1922.

41 PRONI HA/32/1/279, 'H.H.' to A. D. Drysdale, Larne Camp, 18 January 1923.

42 PRONI HA/32/1/279, A. D. Drysdale to Henry Toppin, Ministry of Home Affairs, 19 January 1923.

43 The Governor merely threatened punishment in most cases. The trouble of transferring a man to Belfast or Londonderry prisons was disproportionate to any administrative gain. Healy recalled that the authorities 'were at their wits end to know how to dispose of those over-energetic lads. As Belfast Prison had been closed to internees, they merely threatened punishment.' But there were exceptions. Healy mentioned the case of a man who had become an effective inmate commandant at Larne Workhouse. He came into conflict with the authorities and was removed to Belfast Prison where he was placed on the same footing as convicted prisoners, with all privileges removed. Healy, *Argenta* journal, *op. cit.*, ff. 39 and 86–7.

44 PRONI HA/32/1/748.

45 Though Healy observed that the men's casualness of dress, the fact that they wore their clothes, and their beards, ragged was to some extent part of the affectations of the young (*Argenta* journal, *op. cit.*, f. 84).

46 *Irish News*, 23 April 1923, 5e.

47 *Irish News*, 23 April 1923, 5e.

48 See, for example, the pro-Treaty repudiation of Count George Noble Plunkett's complaint about Mountjoy conditions: things were much worse on the *Argenta*. Healy Papers, D/2991/E/30/6.

49 Cahir Healy (1877–1970). Born Donegal and, prior to entering politics, worked as a journalist. Member of Sinn Féin; Nationalist MP for Fermanagh-Tyrone in Northern Ireland Parliament (1925–9), Fermanagh South (1929–65), Westminster MP (1922–4, 1950–5). Interned twice: 1922–4 and for eighteen months during Second World

War. Living in England, he had written to a Fermanagh priest commenting, *inter alia*, on a likely German victory. The letter (picked up in the postal censorship) was treated as a serious indication of his subversive intent, and he was interned in Brixton Prison from July 1941 until December 1942. For his correspondence during that time, see Healy Papers, D991/B/141/4–68.

50 Outside activists were not shy about using material relating to the internees for their own partisan purposes. An *Argenta* internee sent a letter to Mary MacSwiney, who gave it publicity to confirm what she saw as Belfast–Dublin collusion: 'Some of our comrades here are being encouraged to break with their fellows and crawl out and go south where they can join the Civic Guard and F.S. Army' (Healy, *Argenta* journal, *op. cit.*).

51 NAI TAOIS/S570/1, Francis Crummey to Frank O'Duffy, 25 January 1924. Francis Crummey had been an intelligence officer with the IRA's 3rd Northern Division. He had advised Collins for Northern policy and had played a part in the Belfast Boycott. A member of the pro-Treaty faction, he was eventually given a teaching position in the Free State (see below, p. 51). Kleinrichert, *Republican Internment, op. cit.*, pp. 48, 53, 341. See also Healy, *Argenta* journal, *op. cit.*, f. 70. For Mayne, see pp. 202–8 above. It is likely that Mayne's committee on the *Argenta* represented neutral nationalists.

52 On O'Shiel, see Eda Sagarra's scholarly and stimulating, posthumously published, *Kevin O'Shiel: Tyrone Nationalist and Irish State-Builder* (Dublin: Irish Academic Press, 2013). (Professor Sagarra was the daughter of Kevin O'Shiel.) See also Fergus Campbell's article, 'The Last Land War? Kevin O'Shiel's Memoir of the Irish Revolution (1916–21)' in *Archivium Hibernicum*, 57 (2003): 155–200.

53 NAI TAOIS/S570/1, memorandum to President Cosgrave from Kevin O'Shiel, 11 July 1923.

54 PRONI HA/32/1/46, Report from the Internment Camp, Larne, for Secretary, Ministry of Home Affairs, 16 January 1925.

55 See above, pp. 203–7; see also *Anglo-Celt*, 14 October 1922, 3f.

56 The *Irish News* (29 October 1923, 5e) insisted that there was no connection between the *Argenta* and Larne Workhouse hunger strikes and 'what is going on in the South and West of Ireland'. The internees had come to believe that they would remain in the vessel for years unless they protested. A joint committee of nationalists and republicans had organised the strike.

57 PRONI HA/32/1/46, Larne Internment Camp Report, *op. cit.*

58 PRONI CAB/8/G/26, summary dated 31 October 1923.

59 There was some truth in this. Of 205 internees who, up to the middle of April 1923, had appeared before the Advisory Committee, only one-third had been released on varying conditions. This was a small proportion considering that the act of applying to the Advisory Committee was in itself a decisive indication that ties with republicanism had not existed, had been passing and circumstantial, or had been broken. See *NIPD*, vol. 3, col. 444, 19 April 1923. By this point a total of 606 internees had been received into custody.

60 PRONI CAB/8/G/26, J. E. Long to Sir Dawson Bates, 1 November 1923. In addition to food, Long reported that the men were refusing medical treatment.

61 *Northern Whig*, 3 November 1923, 7d.

62 The Cat and Mouse Act was the popular term for the measure that had been introduced in 1913 to deal with hunger-striking by Suffragettes, the euphemistically entitled Prisoners (Temporary Discharge for Ill-Health) Act, 1913: 3 & 4 Geo. V, c.4. This allowed the authorities to release a hunger-striker, allow them to make a recovery and then rearrest and return them to prison to resume the sentence against which they had refused food (or the conditions against which they had protested) and so on, until the sentence had been served, slice by painful slice, or the prisoner had submitted and served it as intended.

63 PRONI CAB/8/G/26, Sir Dawson Bates to Sir James Craig, 3 November 1923.

64 PRONI CAB/8/G/26, Sir Dawson Bates to Sir James Craig, 5 November 1923, and accompanying summary table.

65 PRONI CAB/8/G/26, Duke of Abercorn to Sir James Craig, 13 November 1923. Joseph MacRory (1861–1945) had been appointed Bishop of Down and Connor in 1915, later becoming Archbishop of Armagh and Roman Catholic Primate of All Ireland. MacRory, like most of his flock, was an Irish nationalist, opposed to Partition and therefore to the creation of Northern Ireland.

66 NAI TAOIS/S570/5, memos to President W. T. Cosgrave, July 1923.

67 See below, pp. 356–7 and 359–60.

68 *Irish Independent*, c.15 August 1922. For other reports on conditions, see the *Irish Independent*, 16 December 1922, 9b (especially lamenting the want of tobacco on the *Argenta*) and *Freeman's Journal*, 16 October 1922, 5g. The latter (in a letter to the editor) claimed that 'The men must eat their food off the floor, over which the ooze from the night bucket flows, and occasionally the latrines.' In April 1923, Temporary Warder William Comack was dismissed. An internee had informed the Governor that Comack was a regular carrier of letters, including one that provided information for an article in the *Irish News* about conditions in Larne Camp. PRONI HA/32/1/75.

69 *Daily Herald*, 2 November 1922.

70 *Irish Independent*, 6 October 1922.

71 *Belfast Telegraph*, 2 January 1923. In a similar vein, Sir Dawson Bates, in a supply debate, quoted from a letter which 'I came across the other day.' This purported to come from an internee – and may have been genuine or may have been black propaganda – and was intended as reassurance, presumably to friends and family: 'For propaganda purposes we have to describe ourselves as being badly treated, so I don't expect any of you to feel sorry for me when you read the ordinary letters. It is part of the game. You can tell this to my people, and then tell everyone else that the *Argenta* is a floating hell.' *NIPD*, vol. 3, col. 444, 19 April 1923.

72 PRONI HA/32/1/175.

73 PRONI HA/32/1/79.

74 PRONI HA/32/1/76, Report from Inspector-General's Office, RUC, to Secretary of Ministry of Home Affairs, 5 November 1923. For references to Father Murray, see Mary Harris, 'Church, State and Minority Rights', in Dermot Keogh and Michael H. Halzel (eds.), *Northern Ireland and the Politics of Reconciliation* (Cambridge: Cambridge University Press, 1993), pp. 62–83. Murray's support was almost certainly not for the post-Treaty Sinn Féin movement, as the police suggested, but for those who were pro-Treaty and – constitutionally – against Partition.

75 See above, pp. 76–7.

76 PRONI HA/5/2481, Town Clerk, Newry to Sir Dawson Bates, Minister for Home Affairs, 6 November 1923. An almost identical letter had been submitted by Strabane Urban District Council on 5 November 1923.

77 *Belfast Newsletter*, 10 November 1923, 10c.

78 PRONI HA/5/2841, Father H. J. Murray to Sir James Craig, 8 November 1923. Murray pointed out that the Lord Bishop (Dr McRory) agreed with the resolution. This file contains the correspondence concerning several like resolutions, very likely the fruit of a coordinated campaign.

79 *Irish News*, 6 May 1924, 6g. The resolution also pointed to the consequences of internment for dependants: 'In many instances these men were the breadwinners of the family, and their homes were reduced to decay, and the children in those homes once robust, were now suffering from decline in health.'

80 PRONI HA/5/2481, Note to Ministry of Home Affairs from RUC District Inspector, Armagh; *Irish News*, 6 May 1924. See also *Armagh Guardian*, 6 June 1924, 3a.

81 PRONI HA/5/2481, Petition, sent via Home Secretary and Imperial Secretary, to Northern Ireland Cabinet.

82 *Irish News*, 24 September 1924, 5a.

83 PRONI HA/5/2481, District Inspector to Ministry of Home Affairs c. mid-September 1924.

84 *Irish News*, 29 September 1924, 5d. There was one arrest, but this was not connected to the meeting itself (presumably being of a man for whom the police were seeking in another [nationalist] connection).

85 *Irish News*, 29 September 1924, 7e–f. The meeting was chaired by the Very Revd Philip O'Doherty, who pointed out that the internees were being held without charge or trial.

86 *Catholic Times*, 19 January 1924, 11d.

87 PRONI HA/32/1/75, Minute, c.20 March 1924.

88 *Dáil Debates*, vol. 6, col. 2732, 2 April 1924.

89 Patrick Baxter (1891–1959) had a long parliamentary career, representing Cavan (a border constituency) for the Farmers' Party.

90 FitzGerald replied cautiously. The facts as stated by Baxter had appeared in an Irregular (i.e. republican) organ, and he had no other knowledge of the allegations. Were Baxter to provide details of persons detained solely for advocating Irish unity, representations would be made. Baxter's statement of conditions was almost certainly based on a republican leaflet entitled 'Is This Peace?' A draft of this appears in the NAI collection, Irish Political Miscellany, 1916–23 (MS. 5817). FitzGerald was understandably cool about this source, which, *inter alia*, declared that there was little to choose between the "'Six County English Government" and the "Free State English Government"'.

91 PRONI HA/32/1/75 (16 April 1924). The meeting on regime was held on 25 January 1924.

92 PRONI HA/32/1/75, Sir Dawson Bates to J. M. Andrews, 18 August 1924. Bates was either being naive or cynical in drawing such reassurance from the old army question 'Have you any complaints?' Andrews (1871–1956) was Minister for Labour (1921–37) and Finance (1937–40) and Prime Minister (1940–3). He was a founder member of the Ulster Unionist Labour Association. In 1948 he became Grand Master of the Orange Institution. Andrews stood at the heart of unionism, and his concern was therefore particularly significant.

93 *Yorkshire Observer*, 1 September 1924, 8d.

94 PRONI HA/32/1/75, Draft press release, c.8 September 1924. See also *Belfast Telegraph*, 9 September 1924. A much more critical account is given in the nationalist *Irish News* of the same date.

95 PRONI HA/32/1/75, Note on the Petition Regarding Internment, 11 September 1924.

96 *Belfast Newsletter*, 29 September 1924, 8b.

97 *Derry Journal*, 30 September 1924, 5a.

98 See, for example, NAI TAOIS/S570/1, letter to Michael Collins from Revd F. O'Neill regarding the case of John Patton of Eglinton, Co. Derry. There are details of several other cases in this file.

99 NAI TAOIS/S5750/6, W. T. Cosgrave to Glenavy, 21 March 1925. James Henry Campbell, First Baron Glenavy (1851–1931) had a distinguished career in law and politics and managed to straddle the administrations of pre- and post-Independence Ireland. In 1916, he was appointed Chief Justice of Ireland and in 1922 became a member and first Chairman of the Irish Senate. Although he was referring to persons who were serving sentences in Northern Ireland for activities they had undertaken whilst in Free State service, Collins's sentiment would have covered both groups.

100 NAI TAOIS/S5750/6, A. McGann (Collins's secretary) to Norwegian Vice-Consul, 21 August 1922.

101 NAI TAOIS/S5750/2, W. T. Cosgrave to Londonderry, 19 December 1922. The teachers were figures of some standing in their own localities, thus the reference to 'special irritation'.

102 NAI TAOIS/S5750/2, Londonderry to W. T. Cosgrave, telegram, 27 December 1922.

103 NAI TAOIS/S5750/2, W. T. Cosgrave to Londonderry, 9 January 1923.

104 NAI TAOIS/S5750/2, Ministry of Education to W. T. Cosgrave, 17 January 1923.

105 For a useful review of the derivation of the Special Powers Act and its regulations, see Campbell, *Emergency Law in Ireland*, *op. cit.*, Appendix 3; see also PRONI HA/32/1/75, statement on article in *Yorkshire Observer*.

106 Special Powers Act, Regulation 1 (1 June 1922). The first members were John Leech, KC (Chairman) and Lieutenant Colonel Ford Hutchinson, appointed as 'an independent gentleman'. A. P. Henry (described as 'a Roman Catholic Barrister of standing and experience') joined these two after three meetings. See *NIPD*, vol. 3, col. 444, 19 April 1923. Sir Dawson Bates reported that up to that date some 606 internees had been received, and, of those, 401 had refused to go before the Advisory Committee 'on the ground that this would involve recognition of the Northern Government'.

107 PRONI HA/32/1/46, 'Report on Internments in Northern Ireland'. Cahir Healy recorded that such was the feeling against those on the *Argenta* who applied to the Advisory Committee that they had to be segregated. One man (who had not applied) was discovered by his comrades talking to a friend in the shunned group. He was taken by what Healy describes as 'our die-hard group' and bound to the mast, with a cord placed above his head with the message 'A Warning to Traitors'. Healy, who did not apply to the Advisory Committee, had sympathy with those who did. During the Anglo-Irish War some had been interned for two years. With a further spell of custody, indefinite in duration, now before them, they had acute family and financial problems. PRONI D/2991/B/140/52, typescript, 'Life on a Northern Prisonship', f. 4.

108 NAI TAOIS/S570/5, Kevin O'Shiel to W. T. Cosgrave, July 1923.

109 NAI TAOIS/S570/16, letter of 22 September 1923.

110 PRONI HA/32/1/76, Major A. W. Long to Ministry of Home Affairs, 1 November 1923.

111 See Campbell, *Emergency Law in Ireland*, *op. cit.*, pp. 301–7.

112 Campbell, *Emergency Law in Ireland*, *op. cit.*, pp. 306–7.

113 PRONI HA/32/1/39, Samuel Watt to Sir Charles Wickham, 26 November 1923.

114 PRONI HA/32/1/39, Samuel Watt to Sir Charles Wickham, 8 March 1924.

115 PRONI HA/32/1/39, Notes of meeting, 20 June 1924.

116 PRONI HA/32/1/46, 'Report on Internments in Northern Ireland'. On 2 December 1924, the prison population stood thus: convicted, 266; remanded, forty-seven; internees, sixty-nine. Four male internees were in Belfast Prison, seven in Londonderry and fifty-eight in Larne. PRONI HA/9/2/163, 'Statement Showing Strength of Staff and the Number of Prisoners'.

117 *Irish News*, 6 November 1924, 8a.

118 *Irish News*, 24 December 1924, 8a. The last three were P. Maginn of Kilkeel, Co. Down; John O'Rorke, Banbridge, Co. Down, and William O'Kane from Co. Derry.

119 *Irish News*, 2 February 1925, 8b. The *Irish News* correspondent reported that no one outside or inside the Ministry of Home Affairs knew why Belfast and Derry internees had not been released at the same time.

120 See below, pp. 360–61.

121 During the first weeks of January 1926, there remained interned in Belfast and Londonderry prisons a total of twenty-two men. But these were of a later intake,

having been arrested on 22 November 1925 (*Irish Independent*, 13 January 1926, 9f). See also Kleinrichert, *Republican Internment*, *op. cit.*, pp. 250 and 289.

122 PRONI HA/32/1/43, Ministry of Home Affairs to S. G. Tallents, 6 February 1923.

123 Fury had got in the way of perspective here: what was internment if not administrative law allowing the exercise of executive authority?

124 PRONI HA/32/1/43, [indecipherable name] (ministerial colleague) to Sir Dawson Bates, 6 February 1923. The letter went on to complain that the British government's interventions were 'prejudicial' and had the same effect as meddling by politicians in disciplinary matters 'and it subjects our government to such rebuffs as we lately had to suffer in the Cushendall inquiry'. See pp. 79–82 above.

125 Kleinrichert (*Republican Internment*, *op. cit.*, p. 291) lists seventeen national-school teachers among the internees.

126 NAI TAOIS/S570/2, Frank Gallagher to Frank O'Duffy, Secretary, Department of Education, 23 February 1923.

127 NAI TAOIS/S570/2, W. T. Cosgrave to Lord Londonderry, 16 April 1923.

128 NAI TAOIS/S570/2, Sir Dawson Bates to Lord Londonderry, 20 April 1923. Crummey had admitted that he had been an officer in the IRA but ceased to be active following the 31 March 1922 agreement between the Northern Ireland and Provisional governments. He denied any connection with anti-Treaty forces. Crummey took up a teaching post in Dublin. NAI TAOIS/S570/2, Londonderry to Cosgrave, 21 April 1923.

129 Rory Graham was one of the latter, having been active in the IRA's 2nd Northern Division. A Belfast man, after release he moved to Dublin. Kleinrichert, *Republican Internment*, *op. cit.*, pp. 56, 123 and 346.

130 Kleinrichert notes that three *Argenta* Protestants objected that no minister had been provided to meet their spiritual needs. A Church of Ireland chaplain was appointed, but they chose not to see him. *Republican Internment*, *op. cit.*, p. 123. In Cahir Healy's *Argenta* journal there is mention of Charles McWhinny, a Protestant and teacher at the Derry Technical School. Fellow internees elected him as commandant and found him zealous in implementing his orders. The prohibition against smoking below decks was resisted, but, a believer in rules and their enforcement, McWhinny appointed twenty-eight 'policeman' – 'all athletes', Healy noted – to ensure compliance (*Argenta* journal, *op. cit.*).

131 The arrests were made by the Army, which two days later took control of security in the Belfast area, including the direction of the police and the Special Constabulary. Four Catholic rioters were arrested at the same time (PRONI CAB/6/27, memoranda, 28 and 5 October 1921).

132 PRONI CAB/6/27, memorandum, 5 October 1921.

133 PRONI CAB/6/27, minutes of meeting of 20 October 1921 between Sir James Craig, General Sir Nevil Macready (Commander-in-Chief of the British Army in Ireland) and General Cameron (Commanding Officer, Northern Ireland).

134 *NIPD*, vol. 2, cols. 1014–15, 12 October 1922; PRONI CAB/6/30/T/2258, Report of District Inspector R. R. Spears, 7 February 1923.

135 PRONI CAB/6/30/T/2258; Patrick Buckland, *The Factory of Grievances* (Dublin: Gill & Macmillan, 1979), p. 218.

136 Buckland, *The Factory of Grievances*, p. 218.

137 PRONI HA/9/2/190, John Williamson to Ministry of Home Affairs, 23 March 1923.

138 *Belfast Newsletter*, 14 March 1923, 4f; *Belfast Telegraph*, 24 March 1923.

139 *Belfast Newsletter*, 26 March 1923, 8c.

140 PRONI HA/9/2/190, John Williamson to Ministry of Home Affairs, 2 July 1923. This letter referred to his suffering as a loyalist internee and concluded 'Up Ulster'.

141 Healy was arrested on 23 May 1922, but, according to the files, was not served with an internment order until 19 June (PRONI HA/5/956A).

142 On the other side, however, it should be recognised that Healy was an early member of Sinn Féin, representing Fermanagh at the Rotunda (Dublin) meeting in 1905 when the party was launched. He remained active up to 1916 and beyond. During those years the party had not yet made an alliance with the armed republicanism of the Volunteers. See Healy Papers, D/2991/B/140/25, letter to Rory O'Connor, staff of the *Sunday Press* of 7 March 1954 (wrongly dated 1945).

143 PRONI HA/5/956A, Cahir Healy to Kevin O'Shiel, 31 July 1922.

144 PRONI HA/5/956A, Ministry of Home Affairs minute, 18 September 1922.

145 This was a two-seat constituency, and, with Thomas Harbison, his partner on the Nationalist ticket, Healy was returned with a majority of several thousand. The election was conducted under rules of proportional representation. See *Irish Times*, 18 November 1922, 7d; see also Healy, *Argenta* journal, *op. cit.*, ff. 77–9.

146 The first prisoner to be returned in this way was the Fenian Jeremiah O'Donovan Rossa, who narrowly won the Tipperary by-election of November 1869. Two imprisoned republicans, Joseph McGuinness and Éamon de Valera, were returned respectively, in 1917 by-elections in South Longford and East Clare. See Seán McConville, *Irish Political Prisoners, 1848–1922: Theatres of War* (London and New York: Routledge, 2003), pp. 220–1 and 607–8.

147 William Pringle (1874–1928) held seats in Scotland and in the north of England (1910–18 and 1922–4). Educated at the University of Glasgow, barrister (Middle Temple) 1904.

148 John Joseph ('Jack') Jones (1873–1941) was born in Co. Tipperary. Having worked in the building trade, Jones became an organiser for the National Union of General Workers. Elected to Westminster in 1918, for Silvertown, London, he retained his seat until resignation in 1940. See his autobiography, *My Lively Life* (London: John Long, 1928).

149 Captain C. C. Craig was Unionist MP for South Antrim and brother of Colonel (later Sir) James Craig. A gallant soldier, he had been wounded and captured by German forces during the battle of the Somme (1 July 1916). He epitomised the unionist ideal of Ulster heroism.

150 5 *Hansard*, vol. 159, cols. 290–4, 27 November 1922.

151 5 *Hansard*, vol. 159, col. 294, 27 November 1922. This avoided the issue of whether the decision had been taken on party-political grounds, which was what Healy's supporters contended.

152 Frank Gray (1880–1935) was the son of Sir Walter Gray, several times Mayor of Oxford, and spent much of his life in the city. A solicitor, he held various legal appointments in Oxford. He enlisted as a private soldier in 1916 and, after the war, worked as an agricultural labourer; he also lived as a tramp and committed himself to casual wards of the Oxfordshire workhouses. He was elected to Westminster in 1922 and served as a Liberal whip. Pamphleteer, social campaigner and adventurer. See *The Times*, 4 March 1935, 16c.

153 Joseph Kenworthy (1886–1953) was at this time a Liberal, but in 1926 he stood and was elected in the Labour interest. He was an advocate of Indian Independence and was also sympathetic to Irish nationalism.

154 5 *Hansard*, vol. 162, col. 2247, 19 April 1923. John Henry Whitley (1866–1935) came from a prosperous cotton-manufacturing background in Halifax. He was elected MP for his home town in 1900, in the Liberal interest, holding the seat until retirement, in 1928. He was Speaker of the House of Commons from 1921 until 1928. Widely respected, he was a major contributor to debates on industrial relations. A thoughtful man, rather to the left of centre in his party.

155 PRONI HA/5/956A, Inspector-General Sir Charles Wickham to Secretary, Ministry of Home Affairs, 4 January 1924.

156 *Sunday Express*, 6 January 1924, 1d. See also the *Belfast Telegraph*, 7 January 1924, and the *Freeman's Journal*, 7 January 1924, 6g. Healy told *Express* readers that he had been arrested with hundreds of others and that, since being consigned to the *Argenta*, had not been allowed to see relatives. As to conditions, 'I had to eat my food most of the time squatting on the floor like a monkey in a cage. They did not give us fresh blankets for twelve months. They never gave us a pillow case or a sheet. They changed the black shoddy rugs which served for bed covering only once. Our pillows were lifebelts as black as a boot, soiled and greasy.'

157 Woods had been arrested some months previously, as he crossed the border (*Irish Times*, 29 March 1924, 5d).

158 PRONI CAB/9/B/4/1, Stanley Baldwin to Sir James Craig, 19 December 1923.

159 PRONI CAB/9/B/4/1, Sir James Craig to Stanley Baldwin, 27 December 1923. He went on to refer to the British political situation, about which he had not written, 'knowing you would be inundated with sympathy and advice', continuing, 'You well know that my heart is with you all the time and that my confidence is unshaken by the result of the Election. May 1924 see your triumph.'

160 PRONI CAB/9/B/4/1, Sir James Craig to Stanley Baldwin, 27 December 1923.

161 See, for example, the *Irish News*, 22 December 1923, 8a.

162 PRONI CAB/9/B/4/1, Stanley Baldwin to Sir James Craig, 14 January 1924. Woods was released three weeks later, having been acquitted of the murder of W. J. Twaddle, MP (*Irish News*, 18 April 1924, 5c).

163 PRONI CAB/9/B/4/1, D. D. Reid to Sir James Craig, 18 January 1924.

164 PRONI CAB/9/B/4/1, G. B. Liddy to Sir James Craig, 15 January 1924. Liddy was an old-fashioned Carsonite unionist, willing to concede an All-Ireland Parliament, but as part of the UK. He had urged Craig to take steps to that end.

165 PRONI CAB/9/B/4/1, Colonel W. B. Spender (Cabinet Secretary) to D. D. Reid, 21 January 1924, file notes.

166 PRONI CAB/9/B/4/1, D. D. Reid to W. B. Spender, 25 January 1924. There had in the meantime been a very favourable reference to Healy in the *Catholic Times* (London) noting his 'well-known pacificism' (19 January 1924).

167 PRONI CAB/9/B/4/1, Lord Londonderry to W. B. Spender, 7 February 1924. Over the years to come, Londonderry and his wife would establish close political and personal relations with MacDonald. On John William Nixon, see pp. 76–8 above.

168 PRONI CAB/9/B/4/1, A. D. Drysdale to Captain Poynting, Ministry of Home Affairs. Drysdale anticipated that Healy would refuse liberation on the stipulated condition were it made known before release. A copy of the exclusion order is preserved in the Healy Papers (D/2991/B/14/57). When presented outside the workhouse, Healy confirmed that had he known it he would have refused to leave custody.

169 As a condition of release, some internees, including a Co. Down GP, had to agree to expatriation. The doctor's neighbours, including Protestants, had raised a petition for his release, but the decision to exile him from Northern Ireland stood. He went to Glasgow. Healy commented that '[a]nother doctor wanted the dispensary and he had influence' ('Life on a Northern Prisonship', *op. cit.*, f. 4).

170 PRONI HA/D/2991/B/140/52, RUC Report, 13 February 1924. See *Irish News*, 13 February 1924, 4d; *Irish Independent*, 14 February 1924.

171 PRONI CAB/9/B/4/1, W. B. Spender to Speaker, House of Commons, 14 February 1924.

172 PRONI D/2991/B/140/52, Ramsay MacDonald to Sir James Craig, 15 February 1924.

173 For the pressures on Craig at this time, see Patrick Buckland, *James Craig, Lord Craigavon* (Dublin: Gill & Macmillan, 1980). The divisions on internment in the Northern Cabinet were hardly secret. Cahir Healy, on his release from internment, had commented that 'Sir James Craig and Lord Londonderry are credited with good intentions in

this respect. The "bush in the gap" would appear to be Sir Dawson Bates, the Home Minister, a Belfast Attorney, with a rather illiberal mind' (*Irish News*, 18 February 1924, 8f).

174 PRONI CAB/B/4/1, W. B. Spender to Lord Londonderry, 18 February 1924; *Irish News*, 18 February 1924, 8f.

175 PRONI CAB/B/4/1, Speaker (in acknowledgement) to W. B. Spender, 19 February 1924. See also *Fermanagh Times*, 21 February 1924, 2b.

176 *Belfast Telegraph*, 20 November 1925, 10b.

177 PRONI HA/32/1/489, memorandum to Sir Dawson Bates, 20 November 1925.

178 *Ibid.*

179 *Northern Whig*, 23 November 1925, 7e. The *Whig* reported that the men were 'ex-Free State soldiers, ex-internees, and members of the Irish Republican Army'. It stated that twenty men were arrested, but the Ministry of Home Affairs files give the number as twenty-nine. There were extensive exchanges on the arrests in the Northern Ireland Parliament on 14 December 1925. William McMullen, a Nationalist and Northern Ireland Labour member, insisted that the whole political situation had changed since the last internments and clashed with the Speaker when, in that regard, he observed, 'They have even got as Lord Chief Justice now a person who was engaged in gun-running in 1912.' How could people be encouraged along the constitutional path when internment was being used against the government's political opponents? (*NIPD*, vol. 6, col. 1970 *et passim*, 14 December 1926).

180 PRONI HA/32/1/489, Ministry order, confirming verbal instructions, 27 November 1925. One man had been released immediately, on the recommendation of the RUC. Of the twenty-eight remaining, nineteen had previously been interned.

181 PRONI HA/32/1/489, letter of 24 November 1925 from a 'A Nationalist of the Falls Road', 'Those Who Want to Live in Peace', 5 June 1926. But see also the threatening letter to Sir Dawson Bates from 'Nationalists, Socialists, Catholics & Protestants', undated.

182 PRONI HA/32/1/489, RUC to Ministry, 29 November 1926.

183 *Belfast Telegraph*, 7 November 1927. Another document was an IRA HQ form that had to be returned by local units, giving their stock of arms. A month later a considerable quantity of arms and ammunition was discovered in an empty house on the outskirts of Belfast. The find included a machine gun, rifles, revolvers, ammunition and explosives. *Belfast Telegraph*, 10 December 1927.

184 *Belfast Newsletter*, 22 March 1928; *Belfast Newsletter*, 23 March 1928; *The Times*, 23 March 1928; *Irish Times*, 23 March 1928, 7d.

185 *Dáil Debates*, vol. 22, col. 1651, 22 March 1928.

186 *NIPD*, vol. 9, col. 1690, 15 May 1928.

187 PRONI HA/32/1/489, Handbill, 'Dáil Éireann: Do Mhuintir na Poblachta, Beatha agus Sláinte!' These handbills were posted in Derry on 8 April 1928. Another, also purporting to emanate from from Dáil Éireann, was posted in the city on 12 February 1928, calling *inter alia* on young men to train for the defence of the Republic.

188 *NIPD*, vol. 9, cols. 1687–94, 15 May 1928.

8

IMPRISONMENT IN NORTHERN IRELAND

The inter-war years

The process of division

Until the coming into effect of the GOIA in December 1920, Ireland was governed as a single entity. Thereafter, there began a process of separation. Elections were held North and South in May 1921. Those in Northern Ireland led to a Unionist government with an overwhelming majority; in the South a Sinn Féin boycott ensured that the only participating members of the Parliament for Southern Ireland were four Unionists returned by Trinity College. Behind the political drama, a laborious and intricate process of administrative disentanglement was under way. Almost all public services were divided and the administrative work carried out by Sir John Anderson, the Under-Secretary, and his colleagues at Dublin Castle would shape much of the machinery of government that would be taken over by the Provisional and subsequently the Free State governments.

There were insuperable obstacles, administrative, political and legal, to the continued sharing of public services.[1] Most basically, there were two governments to take executive decisions, two very different legislatures to whom they were responsible. Behind this there were two mutually suspicious and, at times, antagonistic electorates. Division on a permanent basis was inevitable. Because of the disparities in size, Northern Ireland just over a third of the area of the Free State, it was to be expected that the majority of public buildings and institutions would be in the South and that the North would have a deficit. Add to this the fact that Dublin had been the civil and military capital of the whole island and that the majority of army barracks and camps were in the South, and the imbalance was accentuated. This was notably so in the penal estate.

The prison system

Obligations and institutions

Whatever its social philosophy and political complexion, no state can exist without the effective exercise of power and authority within its territory. Indeed,

373

the prison, which implies some process of deliberation as opposed to immediate (and usually sanguinary) punishment, may be a mark of the civilisation of a community. During the past decade or so, and notwithstanding the international system and supranational organisations, there have been several examples of states which, through corruption, narco-criminality and terrorism, clan warfare, outside intervention and continuing civil war have gone from failure to collapse.[2] A functional criminal justice system – laws, policy, courts and prisons – is a core component of statehood, offering at least the possibility of reasonable public safety and personal security without which normal life and social development are impossible. Northern Ireland was established as a devolved entity within the UK. It did not require the full apparatus of statehood, since it was not to be a sovereign state but rather a territory in which certain powers, from law-making to law enforcement, would be devolved. It was always, and by choice, subject to the overriding authority of the British Parliament. Defence, external affairs and central taxation remained totally in the hands of Westminster, as indeed did the ultimate guarantee of the existence of Northern Ireland itself. Wrenched out of a united Irish administration, it had to adapt and construct as required in order to meet its responsibilities. The preparation for Northern Ireland's assumption of prison responsibilities began as soon as the GOIA received the Royal Assent, but almost a year would elapse before executive authority was transferred.[3]

On 7 June 1921, Lord FitzAlan, the Lord Lieutenant of Ireland, issued a notice directing that the Northern Ireland Ministry of Home Affairs should take over the administration of law and justice, prisons, reformatories and other various services.[4] An Order in Council was made on 9 November 1921, bringing the Lord Lieutenant's direction in effect. A subsequent letter to Northern prison governors informed them that vesting day would be 1 December 1921, and from that point they would be accountable to the Northern Ireland Ministry of Justice rather than the Under-Secretary or Prisons Board in Dublin.[5]

From 1 December 1921, prisoners who would have been sent to Dundalk or Mountjoy prisons were committed to Belfast.[6] At that point, there were many in Northern prisons who, had the GOIA been brought into operation throughout the island, would not have been sent there. The Ministry of Home Affairs proposed to Dublin Castle (still the seat of British administration) that there should be an exchange of prisoners, North and South.[7] Anderson rejected this proposal. Such an exchange would be complicated and expensive, and a far simpler arrangement would be to leave the two sets of prisoners where they were, and for their respective administrations each to meet the costs for their own prisoners. Anderson added that the two male prisons in Northern Ireland did not have sufficient accommodation to take the numbers who would be transferred there, under the Northern proposals.[8] The Ministry countered that the pressures were largely due to those many prisoners who were being held in Belfast Prison and who ought to be elsewhere. Urgent action was necessary in the light of the impending transfer of the bulk of the prisoners from Dundalk to Northern Ireland.[9]

The issue of North–South transfers was resolved in a conversation in mid-December 1921 between Samuel Watt, Secretary at Home Affairs, and Sir John Anderson.[10] Anderson reversed his earlier position and agreed to the removal of the IRA prisoners. This probably forestalled another Belfast letter (then in draft form) again arguing that the men were London's responsibility. The letter also insisted that Belfast had not granted the ameliorations of regime, and, should the IRA prisoners remain in Northern Ireland prisons, the government would have to consider whether it should restore ordinary discipline for all, 'irrespective of whether they are so called political prisoners or not'. Anderson had indicated that he expected a considerable number of the IRA prisoners shortly to be released. Sir Dawson Bates, Minister for Home Affairs, urged that none should be released directly from Northern Ireland prisons and, as a preliminary to their release, 'if this is decided upon by the Imperial Government' they should be transferred across the border.[11] That transfer had to await the Dáil's ratification of the Treaty on 7 January 1922. A number of steps followed rapidly thereafter, and a week later 137 IRA prisoners were moved from Belfast Prison to Mountjoy in Dublin, preparatory to their release.[12]

The exodus was a boon for the Northern administration. Such a bulk of politically motivated prisoners in Belfast and Derry prisons had reduced management to a coping operation, and barely that. In anticipation of the transfer of 'the so-called Political Prisoners', Watt sought ministerial authority for the issuance of an order requiring the immediate restoration of 'normal prison discipline' and the discontinuance of all concessions and ameliorations for prisoners then in Northern custody, or who were received thereafter. This was agreed, and the scene set for a return to the regime required by the prison rules.[13]

Space was not the whole problem. As we have seen, Ireland had only one convict prison (Maryborough), but the pressures of the Anglo-Irish War meant that Belfast Prison had had to retain fifty-two convicts, sixteen under sentence of death and a further sixteen who had, by the decision of the British government, been granted political status and a special regime; the remaining twenty had not been granted special treatment. Bates repeated his 'strong opinion' that the first two groups should be removed. This was a trifle inconsistent, since some at least would have been sentenced by Northern Ireland courts and under Bates's own proposals should have been retained there. Underlying the argument, however, was the notion that prisoners whose confinement could be attributed to the Anglo-Irish War (convicts, political prisoners and those under sentence of death) were London's responsibility. Whether accommodation was provided in Southern Ireland or elsewhere, it seemed, was not a matter for Belfast. Bates pointed out that Belfast Prison was holding 'a large number' of men awaiting trial before a military court. Some had been in custody for over six months, and he wanted their trials to be expedited. He wished to have removed from Belfast those who were found guilty and sentenced to penal servitude.[14]

Shortly after the setting up of the new Northern government, the issue of the province's defective and inadequate prisons came under urgent consideration. In

January 1921, Sir Ernest Clark, a senior official, drew up a memorandum on the Northern prisons at Belfast, Londonderry and Armagh. Under ordinary circumstances these provided sufficient accommodation. The system was not complete, however, and convicts (those sentenced to penal servitude) were being sent to England, in part because of the pressure on accommodation caused by the influx of political prisoners. Borstal trainees were sent to Clonmel, Co. Tipperary, the only Irish Borstal. The Governor of Belfast Prison thought that these too might be sent to England.[15] Clark seemed unaware that the English authorities, both the Home Office and the Prison Commissioners, with pronounced reluctance, had already agreed to take some Irish convicts, that they might object to receiving Borstal boys and that the prisoners in both categories would suffer a considerable hardship through being so far removed from family and friends.[16] He also made proposals for a Prisons Board and Inspectorate for the Northern prisons – the latter to draw on the expertise of the Home Office.

A few days later, there was a further memorandum, based on a conversation with Max Green, Chairman of the Irish Prisons Board. Again the issue of a Prisons Board for Northern Ireland came up, even though a separate oversight body for only three prisons was, on the face of it, an unnecessary additional layer of administration for such a small system. Green had also raised with Clark a long-nurtured Irish grievance with the British government, going back to 1877, when local prisons in Britain were nationalised. This Act did not extend to Ireland, which had not, therefore, benefited from central government funds to modernise the taken-over prisons. Some contribution to these costs, Green argued, should now be made, since it was wrong that Ireland, North and South, should be operating an antiquated system. Belfast Prison was an example of this unfairness. It had been badly knocked about by the political prisoners, and the Irish Prisons Board had been reluctant to have it reconstructed since it was unsuitable for modern prison discipline. The Board had intended to abandon it, to sell the site and to build a modern prison in a rural area but in a more central position within the province.[17]

Green was anxious to have the Northern Ireland government replace Belfast Prison, and, on 25 January 1921, he walked Clark around the building, pointing out its various defects in condition and design. However, a few days had made a difference to Clark's view of the practicality of providing a new central prison. He was now aware of the extra expense for transportation that an out-of-town site entailed and that prisoners, especially the unconvicted, might become discontented at being some distance from their friends. He had not abandoned the idea of a Northern Ireland Prisons Board but suggested that a technical advisory committee be established before any decision was made on reorganising and rebuilding.[18] Two days later, Clark visited Armagh, which impressed him as being 'admirably run... a very complete contrast to the Belfast Prison'. There were a few political prisoners there, and a guard had been provided, strengthened at night by patrols of Special Constables. He concluded that the prison probably provided sufficient accommodation for all of Northern Ireland's female prisoners. The notion of also closing Armagh and locating the women in a central prison was mooted, since the women could then do the laundry for staff and prisoners, 'work which has to be put out where there are no female prisoners'.[19]

A more comprehensive balance sheet of legal obligations and available institutions was drawn by Andrew Magill, a senior official at the Ministry of Home Affairs, on 27 September 1921, just over two months before Northern Ireland took up its law-and-order obligations.[20] The obligations derived from statutes that had envisaged a much larger jurisdiction than the six counties of Northern Ireland, which was a disproportionately small administrative unit for such an array of responsibilities. In times of peace, moreover, it was a jurisdiction with a low crime rate and small prison and institutional population. To provide for the needs of sub-categories within that number could not but be expensive and perhaps impractical.

Magill identified six penal and related services for which the new government would have responsibility, besides those of the ordinary prison for remands and persons sentenced to imprisonment. The first of those was a Borstal institution for young offenders.[21] The only Borstal institution in Ireland was at Clonmel, and young offenders from the whole of Ireland had been committed at an average annual rate of thirty-eight in the period 1917–19. This committal rate would have made the establishment of a Borstal institution to serve Northern Ireland alone disproportionately expensive. Magill suggested that Northern courts should continue to commit to Clonmel and that the Belfast government pay an annual capitation fee for this service.[22] He did not seem to realise that the imminent creation of the Free State meant that such transfers would necessitate complicated legal and treaty provisions.

The 1908 Prevention of Crime Act had attempted comprehensively to provide a range of penal measures, tailored for various categories of offenders. At the opposite end of the criminal process from Borstal institutions there was the sentence of preventive detention (PD).[23] This was intended to provide special containment for those who had demonstrated, through a career of offending, that they were incorrigible recidivists, largely immune from the effects of ordinary punishment.[24] For these, in addition to sentencing for the offence that immediately brought them before the court, there would be the power to impose an additional, preventive sentence. Incapacitation rather than reform was the objective, and a sentence of PD would be served under a more relaxed penal regime, with ameliorations not available to those sentenced to ordinary imprisonment or penal servitude. Essentially these were places to hold old lags, to keep them out of circulation and to administer only mild penal discipline.

In England, a special PD prison was established at Camp Hill, on the Isle of Wight. Numbers in Ireland were insufficient to require or to justify a separate prison, but part of Maryborough Convict Prison was set aside for this purpose. The Irish courts evidently made little use of PD (and indeed their English counterparts did not warm to the measure), and there was a daily average of only one PD prisoner at Maryborough. As Magill noted, this was not a very serious problem, but some steps would have to be taken to provide against the chance that a Northern court would impose such a sentence.[25]

An earlier English measure which extended to Ireland and which had resource and accommodation implications was the 1898 Inebriates Act.[26] The purpose of this measure was to deal with habitual drunkards by providing for their committal to inebriate reformatories. Drunkenness was perceived as a significant vice in late Victorian England, the source of many social evils, and the Inebriates Act was an attempt to deal with it by means of a hybrid penal and public-health mechanism. Neat and attractive in theory, in England the measure had little impact on the problem it was intended to address. In Ireland the effect was even more negligible. An inebriate reformatory had been established at Ennis, Co. Clare, in 1919, but the daily average population was only eight. The Prisons Board, in 1922, recommended its abolition.[27] There was no point in establishing a separate institution for Northern Ireland, Magill concluded, and, were it necessary to deal with any inebriates by compulsory confinement, a portion of a prison could be assigned for the purpose.[28]

In a similar manner, Magill considered the obligation to provide for reformatories for juveniles. Four Catholic reformatories existed in the South, but neither there nor in the North was there such an institution for Protestant girls. Evidently such girls were exceptionally well behaved and law-abiding, and Magill saw no reason why this happy circumstance might change. He thought that Roman Catholic girls and boys who were committed to a reformatory might be sent South, where both sexes each had two institutions. In any event, the responsibility for providing reformatory accommodation rested with county or borough councils, not with the Northern Ireland government.[29]

Another category of person likely to be committed to custody in Northern Ireland in extremely small numbers was the criminal lunatic. The statute provided that custody and care be delivered in Dundrum, an institution located near Dublin.[30] Magill calculated that at any point there would be no more than twenty to thirty criminal lunatics in Northern Ireland. Since these could be accommodated in a part of Purdysburn Asylum, he concluded, there should be no difficulty in making adequate provision.

Magill brushed over the question of convict provision with surprising nonchalance, possibly because he did not fully understand the distinction between ordinary imprisonment and penal servitude.[31] (He emphasised that his suggestions were only tentative.) The number of convicts in Northern Ireland was likely to be small: the daily average for the whole of Ireland in 1919 was only fifty-seven. Magill thought that it would be sufficient to use statutory powers to designate part of an existing prison as a convict prison. In this, as shall be seen, he (and his colleagues) overlooked the practical and humanitarian problems of holding long-term convicts in accommodation that had been designed and built (and that several decades before) for short-term sentenced and remand prisoners. Continuing discussions and exchanges between officials in Home Affairs led to some clarification and to a realisation that the accommodation of convicts was a pressing and difficult matter.

The state of the prisons

On 1 December 1921, vesting day for the Ministry of Home Affairs, the Belfast Governor, Edward Shewell, submitted yet another report. (He had a few days before briefed the Ministry on his most urgent problems.) His perspective was that of the directly involved prison manager. For some years, he wrote, the proper and orderly management of his and every other Irish prison had been made impossible because of the large number of Sinn Féin prisoners. Ordinary prisoners were treated as individuals with 'no common bond or tie'. Sinn Féin (by which he largely meant the IRA) prisoners grouped themselves together under a commandant. Disciplinary action against any one evoked a response by all. Variously, this would entail a refusal to return to cells, destruction of furniture and windows, attacks on staff 'and in one case the complete destruction of a wing of this Prison'. Unarmed and outnumbered, warders were helpless in the face of concerted violence. The police and the Army had to be summoned in support but by the time they arrived there would be widespread destruction and injury. In addition, any prison officer who incurred the animosity of the IRA prisoners by any marked display of zeal was liable to bring reprisal action on himself or on his family. Since ordinary discipline could not be enforced on the Sinn Féin men, this had the effect of destroying discipline 'to some extent' even with ordinary prisoners. Following the Truce, the government had made numerous concessions to men who, until then, had been presumed to be under the normal rules for convicted prisoners.

It was an unchallengeable truth that the management of the prison was hobbled by the IRA's unceasing and confrontational activities. Another complication was the fact that there were eight classes of prisoners at Belfast, who, in large part, had to be separately located, scheduled and exercised. Prison industries were 'practically non-existent' under the circumstances. There was a little work assisting with the restoration of the destroyed A Wing (which would eventually be used for convicts), some mat-making and boot repairs. Even the make-work of ordinary imprisonment with hard labour (stone-breaking and -cutting and bundling kindling wood) could not be carried out since it was not safe to entrust with hammers and hatchets those IRA men who were willing to work. Like many Victorian prisons built to implement the prevailing separate system of discipline on mainly short-term prisoners, Belfast had very limited space for exercise and workshops: it had not needed it. The separate system had been intended for those serving sentences of days or weeks, who spent most of their time in their cells. Work such as oakum-picking (enforced by quotas and punishments) was performed in cells. There was little, if any, group work and therefore no workshops. Although the system had been modified over the years, and the emphasis had shifted away from separation, to some extent, the footprint of the prison precluded any significant building developments or expansion of facilities. This was now a problem for the governor, who, not being able to put his prisoners to work, had to allow them in over-large numbers into the exercise yards, which became congested. The presence of the IRA men increased what were already worrying security and control problems.

Staffing levels were fixed both with regard to anticipated numbers and the complexity arising from the disciplinary system. Belfast's several subdivisions and the need to manage each of them separately meant a greater amount of work for staff than the supervision of fewer groups, each with very limited entitlements. In 1921, Shewell particularly drew attention to the screening of visits, the searching of parcels and the censoring of letters, in all of which the entitlements of politicals exceeded those of ordinary prisoners. His level of staffing was 'barely sufficient' to cope with these duties and at the same time to provide safe custody. With the exception of the destroyed A Wing, the condition of the buildings was generally satisfactory, but cell equipment was in poor condition. This was partly due to the difficulty of replacing items during the war years and partly because the IRA prisoners caused excessive wear and tear through 'carelessness and want of cleanliness'.

Shewell may have been exaggerating his difficulties as a bureaucratic ploy for increased resources. The substance of his complaints, however, has the ring of truth, especially in the light of what we know about the condition of prisons in the South following their use for political prisoners. When Shewell warned that it would be difficult in the prevailing conditions to contain an outbreak without bloodshed and possible escapes, he may also have been laying a paper trail of record and responsibility, insuring himself against possible future blame. He insisted, somewhat alarmingly, that it was impossible for him to provide an orderly administration or to ensure safe custody. His proposed remedies were close to those of the Ministry: the removal of all men under penal servitude; the trial or release of those detained by military order and a separate place of confinement for IRA prisoners, convicted and unconvicted. (This was a lightly veiled bid to ensure that their custody be passed to the Army.) He was emphatic that there should be an immediate decision on the fate of the capital-sentence men, some of whom had been sentenced five months before.

Londonderry had a much smaller prison, but its problems were very similar to those of Belfast. Of IRA prisoners on 19 December 1921 it had twenty under penal servitude (for which it was completely ill equipped), several serving sentences up to ten years. It also held men serving a range of prison sentences, with and without hard labour. The longest sentence, of twenty years' penal servitude, was being served by Patrick Cassidy; three men, at the opposite extreme were each serving six months' imprisonment, without hard labour. All of these had been sentenced before the signing of the Truce, and one man was on remand, charged with a pre-Truce murder. Offence dates were critical, since it was widely expected that those whose offences had been committed prior to the Truce would be amnestied. In the meantime, Derry prison was under severe pressure.

All of this must be set in the context of a usually low and static number of ordinary prisoners. In 1925, 2,545 persons under sentence of imprisonment were received into Northern Ireland's prisons. The number dropped slightly over the following decade to 2,282 in 1935. Other committals included trial remands and those awaiting sentence as well as persons imprisoned for debt or by civil process (forty-five in 1935) and those imprisoned for want of sureties. Receptions of convicts ranged from fifteen in 1925 to twenty-three in 1935. Committals tell only part of the tale, however, and for administrators and staff the average daily population was probably the more significant figure. This stayed around 350 throughout the decade. However short of resources the prisons might have been (and the whole of the public sector operated in straitened circumstances in those years), the important elements of stability and predictability doubtless eased the administrative task.

Making do

With five months' experience of prison management under the Northern Ireland government, a further review of penal resources was submitted in April 1922 by R. Ronaldson, Assistant Secretary at the Ministry of Home Affairs. Once again the assets and liabilities were surveyed. In addition to Armagh, Belfast and Londonderry prisons, the Ministry had Newry bridewell at its disposal. It could therefore provide for persons on remand, civil prisoners and those serving sentences of imprisonment, male and female, adult and pre-adult. Purely as a bridging measure, arrangements had been made with the English and with the Scottish prison commissioners to accept a limited number of persons sentenced to penal servitude and to Borstal; per-capita payment was being made for this service. It was unlikely that such extra places would be sufficient to meet future demands, and the arrangement had all the inconveniences of distance.[32]

Convicts whose offences were of a political nature were initially excluded from this transfer.[33] The problem of convict facilities was increasing by the day as both penal servitude and ordinary prisoner numbers swelled. The Home Office wanted to know when Ireland would accept back fifteen of its convicts. Some fifty Northern Borstal boys were being held in Clonmel Borstal in the Free State, 'and we may be called upon at any time to take [them] into the Prison Service of Northern Ireland'.[34] The three prisons available to the Northern government were in poor condition. It was a continuing grievance against London that the damage caused by IRA prisoners had not been put right when Britain handed the prisons over. Belfast's A Wing had been substantially damaged and could not be used without major refurbishment.[35] The Free State, Ronaldson noted, had submitted claims to London amounting to 'many thousands' for damage caused to its prisons by the Army whilst it occupied some prisons and by Sinn Féin prisoners whilst in military custody.[36] The supply of prison furniture, bedding and clothing was depleted to the point where all stocks had to be replaced, at a cost of some £4,000. Again, the Free State had done well. Most of the prison clothing, which from 1918 onwards Sinn Féin prisoners had refused to wear, had been sent to the South. Dublin's Mountjoy was the supply depot for all the Irish prisons and had held a large reserve stock; the Northern government was, 'in equity', entitled to a portion of that material. It would have been proper for London to give a grant of £150,000 to meet the various deficiencies. With such a sum, Downpatrick Prison (which had reverted to the local authority) might have been acquired and reconstructed. That could have served as a convict prison, criminal lunatic asylum and inebriate reformatory. The balance of the funding would have been sufficient to acquire more land at Armagh Prison, to repair the damage to Londonderry and Belfast prisons and to restock.

Were this programme to be followed and London to open its purse-strings sufficiently, Northern Ireland would have a prison system adequate for its needs: Belfast for both male and female local prisoners; Londonderry for local prisoners and as an overflow for Belfast; Armagh as a Borstal; and Downpatrick as a convict prison, criminal lunatic asylum and inebriate reformatory. In addition, London should be asked to meet the cost of setting up in Belfast a registry for habitual criminals.[37] An alternative to all of this, of course, would have been a North–South agreement to share prison accommodation, each paying proportionately. This was an island with a low population and, in times of peace, was decidedly law-abiding. But the notion of combining any resources, no matter how pressing a case could be made administratively and economically, was utterly unacceptable to both states and would remain so for many decades to come.

The Free State was in a phoney stage of a full-scale civil war and had not even made a start on repairing the extensive damage arising from the Anglo-Irish War; the North was, in any event, viscerally disinclined to seek cooperation with what it saw as a potential (and indeed actual – in view of the cross-border attacks) enemy. Although distance and expense were considerable disadvantages, there-fore, the only other sources of relief had to be considered: Scotland and England. The former was geographically, and to an appreciable extent culturally, closer. An approach was made to both sets of prison commissioners on 14 January 1922. The Scots agreed fairly promptly to take thirty non-political convicts, maintenance charges to be determined by the Treasury.[38] The English com-missioners, by contrast, having previously been through the experience of hand-ling Irish politicals, pressed the Ministry of Home Affairs to take back some fifty Northern Ireland convicts; there was no question of any more being accepted.[39] By mid-March 1922, thirty men had been transferred to Scotland's convict prison at Peterhead, Aberdeenshire, and the increase in Northern Ireland's convict numbers showed no signs of slowing. It was inexpedient even to broach with the Scots the notion of more being sent, and Belfast had therefore to make do with what it had. Given the prison staffing deficiencies, Sir Dawson Bates asked the Scottish prison commissioners for the secondment for six months of a senior official with special experience of prison administration: 'I would be deeply obliged if you could arrange for him to come over here at once.'[40]

Matters continued in such a desperate state, however, that by year's end another approach had to be made to the less than amenable English prison commissioners. The number of persons in penal servitude in Northern Ireland was thirty-four but by the end of 1923 it was expected to reach 100.[41] Available space was exhausted, and the Scottish commissioners were unable to offer further relief: would the English please accept 100 men? There was a similar problem with Borstal trainees. The English had agreed to accept ten boys, but it was antici- pated that there would be another thirty by the end of 1923: would they expand the agreement to accept a total of forty?[42] This was a bid, and the English were unlikely to accept it in full. They did, however, accept some. These, both Scots and English officials made it clear, were short-term measures, agreed to because of the most pressing need. They remained fretful about the presence of the Northern Ireland convicts and Borstal boys in their system.[43]

Disintegration and restoration

Quite apart from the inadequate penal estate, the damaged and dilapidated state of Belfast Prison and the inability or unwillingness of Home Affairs to replace it, and notwithstanding the shortage of supplies, there were problems of staffing and control that, in the first days and weeks of their assuming responsibility must have seemed even more pressing to the Northern government. Through the aegis of Lloyd Campbell, Northern Ireland MP for North Belfast, a confidential assessment of the state of the prisons was given to the Ministry of Home Affairs.[44]

The Ministry's contact, whose views were strongly anti-Sinn Féin, probably exaggerated the problems of the prisons and certainly looked back to 1911 for comparisons. This was a time just before the political upheavals began in earnest and well before the First World War had its impact. It is true, nevertheless, that this had been a period of stability and order in the Irish prisons. Crime had been low and the penal system was adequate for its task. Indeed, prisons had been closed due to a want of business. (But this, as with other 'golden age' retrospectives, should be viewed with some scepticism.)

The underlying problem, as the contact ('Mr. A') saw it, had been the impact of political prisoners. Privileges had been sought and granted which had eroded discipline and demoralised staff. The prisons had not been designed for the 'elaborate treatment' they had obtained. These allowed them to override the regulations and 'gradually to break down all discipline'.[45] At the heart of this was the impossibility of controlling inmates, who were allowed to congregate together and order their daily routine. Ordinary criminal prisoners took advan- tage of the slackening, had copied Sinn Féin methods and, as 'Mr. A' put it, had made a home for themselves in prison: 'Gaol is no longer a "house of correction" and a terror to evil-doers as in days gone by, which is a serious matter for the great City of Belfast.' In general, the prison service was but a skeleton of what it had been.

His assessment of staff was equally bleak. Many experienced officers had recently retired, and those taken on since 1918 had not been properly trained. The method of recruitment (engagement first as temporary staff and then pro- motion of some to a permanent position) was bad, and some were of 'a most unsuitable class, which never will make reliable prison officers'. The murders and attempted rescue and escapes at Londonderry Prison underlined the point that night duty and thus the whole security of the prison should not have been entrusted to temporary staff, 'men with only one day's pay at stake'.[46] Those prison staff who were loyal and faithful in service had been let down by Dublin Castle officials who, 'Mr. A' contended, had been in sympathy with the Sinn Féin prisoners. Staff had been helpless onlookers while such prisoners, many of whom were murderers, had been pampered and allowed to do as they like: 'Prison treatment contributed very much to the success of Sinn Féin.'

Staff expected the Northern government to put the prisons in order, to bring them up to standard and to manage them in an intelligent manner. With a few exceptions (which 'Mr. A' hoped would soon be cleared out), rank-and-file prison staff would respond and do their duty, were they given wholehearted ministry support. Special privileges should be withdrawn from political prisoners and the rules enforced. If this could not be done, then the ordinary and political prisoners should be kept apart and held in different prisons. 'Mr. A' thought that even this was not enough and that there should be a purge of staff. In a vague statement, which may or may not have been intended to exclude all Catholics from the service, he urged that '[t]he entire staff of the Department should be free from anyone likely to be influenced by Sinn Féin'.

That 'Mr. A' should have been introduced to the Ministry by an MP and was then interviewed by Andrew Magill, the ministry official most directly involved with prisons at that time, indicated that he had things to say that the Minister and his officials, feeling their way through those important new responsibilities, wanted to hear. The prospect of another incident such as the Londonderry murders and attempted escapes (less than a fortnight past) was deeply worrying, as would be any major disturbance or incident short of an escape: the political backlash would have been immediate.[47] Some of the observations and complaints of 'Mr. A' would take time and money to address; others required immediate action. Magill, in an accompanying note, made a number of recommendations to Bates. He urged that the practice of entrusting night duty to temporary warders should cease immediately and that the Ministry review the full service records of all warders. In this he suggested that recommendations for promotions be considered but that such a formative review in setting a baseline for efficiency and loyalty would inevitably require the dismissal of those who had proved to be unsuitable.

It was also apparent to the senior people at Home Affairs that they needed counsel and practical help in getting to grips with prison administration and management: as ordinary civil servants, they were out of their depth. Comments and observations such as those of 'Mr. A' could only go so far to highlight immediate concerns, and, indeed, other judgements and assessments were necessary. (In truth, they were probably incompetent to weigh the worth of incoming advice without getting a range of perspectives.) Magill proposed that an architect or engineer should conduct a survey of the whole prison estate so as to give an idea of how it might best be used 'if things return to a normal state'.

There were some obvious problems, apart from the physical degradation of the prisons. The use of Armagh for all females needed further consideration, and it might be necessary to hold some in Belfast Prison.[48] The opinion of someone with the necessary technical knowledge and experience was necessary on this and other matters. Perhaps because the English prison commissioners had been reluctant again to become involved with their Irish counterparts, Magill suggested that the Scottish commissioners be asked to assist, in effect as consultants. This was agreed by Bates.

As civil disorder diminished, IRA activities wound down, and short-sentence prisoners who had been involved in these events completed their sentences, the lack of a convict prison moved again up the agenda of pressing concerns. Ordinary criminal prisoners sentenced to penal servitude might be slow to object were they subjected to a regime and facilities suitable only for much shorter sentences, but persons with a political background were apt to know their rights and had the ability to make a fuss. This duly happened in June 1924, when John McConville, serving a term of four years' penal servitude, submitted a long and closely argued letter of complaint to the Minister for Home Affairs. Some seven months had elapsed since his conviction, he wrote, but he had yet to be shown the convict rules, despite making application. The respective entitlements of convict and local prisoners to visits differed significantly, and he and his family were suffering as a consequence of his being subjected to the wrong set of rules. McConville also objected to the severe restriction on out-of-cell time on Sundays and holidays and the fact that, with the exception of two hours, he was locked up from 4 p.m. each Saturday until 7 a.m. on Monday – a total of thirty-nine hours in all.[49]

In a ministry memorandum, Ronaldson commented that McConville's letter raised again the problem of keeping convicts in local prisons. It was only partly a matter of physical location. The Criminal Justice Administration Act of 1914 had given power to detain a prisoner in any designated prison and the only issue therefore was the regime.[50] The relevant convict rules in this case concerned dietary, visits and letters, classification and remission of sentence. The convict dietary had not been applied to prisoners such as McConville, but a 'very liberal' one had been substituted (the D diet). The government of Northern Ireland had authority to amend the dietary, and all that was required was the Minister's approval that the D dietary be issued to convicts. In the other matters raised by McConville, the convict rules were being applied. There remained one matter: the appointment of a Board of Visitors, as required by the Prisons Act, 1898.[51] Ronaldson proposed that the Visiting Justices (appointed to Belfast, as a local prison) be asked to act also as a Board of Visitors for the rest of their term. This was agreed, with the proviso that action on the Board should be delayed until the pending reappointment of Visiting Justices was completed.[52]

There was a similar issue at Armagh Prison, which had received a woman under a sentence of four years' penal servitude. The female convict prison for Ireland had in 1917 been designated as Cork, and, while this was now unavailable for Northern use, the precedent was considered to be useful. Orders were prepared, and on 1 August 1924 signed by the Duke of Abercorn, Governor of Northern Ireland, designating Belfast as a convict prison for males and Armagh for females.[53] This was announced in the *Belfast Gazette* on 28 November.[54]

With this legal basis established, and with demand for places in decline, it was proper to consider the repatriation of the convicts from England and Scotland. Apart from the fact that the overflow arrangements could not be considered as other than temporary, there were humanitarian considerations: to hold long-term prisoners at a place remote from their families added significantly to penal hardship. But the principal interest in repatriation seems to have been financial. Northern Ireland paid the English commissioners £94 0s. 8d. annually for each of its seventy-two convicts and the Scots £108 18s. 0d. for each of the forty-six at Peterhead.[55] About half of the charge, as computed by the Treasury, was attributable to staffing, the rest to miscellaneous expenses such as the convicts' board and lodging.

By the summer of 1924, Belfast Prison was being run inefficiently and expensively, with only 220 prisoners. A major element in cost structure was the staff–inmate ratio, and, were inmate numbers increased, per-capita costs could be reduced. The convicts could be brought back with only a small addition of staff. Further economies could be made by converting Derry Prison into a type of bridewell (a short-sentence and remand institution) and transferring some staff to Belfast. The total expenditure for the English and Scottish convicts was about £12,600 annually. Some savings could be made, and, in any case, it would be better if the outgoings went into the Northern Ireland economy; government would also have the benefit of the repatriated convicts' labour. Framing all of this was the tenuousness of the existing arrangements. At Westminster, Labour had formed its first ever administration in January 1924, bringing wide political and administrative uncertainty. Northern Ireland might, at short notice, be obliged to accept repatriation (to 'have the convicts thrown on our hands at very short notice' a Ministry memorandum fretted).[56] Nor was it a matter of simply sending for the men: various practical steps would have to be taken before they could be received.[57] The accommodation for ordinary local prisoners – those sentenced to imprisonment, remanded in custody or imprisoned for debt or contempt of court – was nowhere near as strained as that for convicts. With more settled times returning, and, exceptional outbreaks of civil disorder and criminal behaviour fading away, demand dropped even further.

There were sufficient cells at Belfast and Londonderry prisons for all, even allowing for the fact that Belfast's A Wing, at first unusable, then had to be reserved for convicts. The following year, with prison numbers still falling, and with the Ministry of Finance pressing for economies in public administration, there was discussion of closing Derry. While the closure of a whole institution, on the face of it, suggested a significant reduction in expenditure, it was decided that it would not be politic to proceed. The Ministry was unconvinced by the estimate of savings, since there would be the additional cost of transporting remand prisoners to be produced for trial, from Belfast to Londonderry and to the other courts which the prison served. Staffing costs would indeed be cut by closure, but these would be largely offset by the need for extra staff for escort duty. Although the average daily population of the prison was small, moreover, this concealed the very considerable annual turnover of remands and persons serving short sentences; that in itself had a bearing on expenses. To keep expenditure down, prisoners serving sentences greater than three months were almost invariably transferred to Belfast: this had reduced the Londonderry staff to 'almost skeleton proportions'.[58]

In defending the prison from closure on grounds of economy, the Ministry deployed one further argument, not easily open to rebuttal by mere accountants. The minister had, 'in some respects', based his decision on information which could not be disclosed. This suggested issues of public safety and, short of a cabinet discussion, was probably beyond probing. The reality of the decision may have been quite prosaic and party-political. Even with its 'skeleton' staff, the prison provided a significant disbursement of public money in the Derry area, not merely by means of staff salaries and spending but also through locally let supply contracts and legal work. Turning off this tap, even were it dripping rather than flowing, could disadvantage loyal supporters of the government.[59] A prison indeed had many purposes.

Staffing

Whether for reasons of personal convenience, or political or religious persuasion, an unwillingness to abandon the familiar, the habit of serving the Crown or the desire to cease doing so, there were a number of prison officials who did not wish to serve in the part of Ireland in which they were stationed at the time of the vesting of its prisons in the Northern Ireland government on 1 December 1921. All prison staff were invited, if they wished, to indicate their preference for relocation. These requests were considered by the General Prisons Board in Dublin and by the Civil Service Commission. The hope was that movements North and South would more or less balance and that both staff and the administrations for which they opted would be satisfied. A safety valve of a kind was provided by allowing those who had substantial service behind them to apply somewhat prematurely for a retirement pension.

The arrangement seems to have worked well enough, in prisons as in other branches of public service. In the interregnum when it was in power but not yet in control of the Northern prisons, the Ministry of Home Affairs was under-standably anxious to have some say in the approval of staff to be transferred into its service: they were established civil servants who could expect to remain in post until retirement. The ratio of transfers and the suitability, reliability and loy-alty of the proposed transferees were all factors in these decisions. The Ministry's requests for consultation went unanswered by Dublin (then in the hectic last weeks of preparation for a handover to the Provisional government) even though there had been notification of several South–North transfers and rather fewer moves the other way around.[60]

The processing of requests would probably have proceeded without more than the usual difficulties inherent in attempts to match personal preferences to organisational needs had it not been for the tragic and sensational incident in Londonderry Prison on the Northern vesting day. This is described elsewhere but may helpfully be recapitulated here.[61] The IRA had succeeded in infiltrating or suborning three warders at Londonderry prison. In coordination with outside IRA men, cells were unlocked, Special Constables stationed at the prison overcome and bound, and twelve prisoners had all but escaped.[62] Two warders who had been chloroformed died. Two temporary warders were immediately arrested, the third following shortly thereafter. Since the incident occurred within hours of its takeover of the prisons (the early hours of 2 December), it came as a particular shock to the Northern government. A number of staffing deficiencies emerged in the subsequent inquiry. The Governor, Captain Robeson, was adjudged inadequate for his post. This was easily enough remedied by the appointment of an energetic deputy. The warders and temporary warders, although considered by Watt to be 'a much better class of men' than he had expected, were employed on an unsatisfactory basis. The prison had ten permanent warders and twenty-five temporaries, the latter employed on a day-to-day basis. As far as Watt could determine, no enquiries were made into the antecedents of such temporary men. It did not seem surprising that with such an arrangement 'some undesirables would creep in'. Five of the ten permanent warders were thought by the Governor to be so unsatisfactory that he would not have hired them had he been able to restaff the prison. Watt, who had independently interviewed the staff, agreed with this assessment. The impending handover of control, and turbulent political conditions, may have prevented the resolution of these problems. A month before the escape, Robeson had informed the Prisons Board that his cell doors were so inadequate that they could be opened with a piece of bent wire and that he had found such a lockpick in the prison: no reply had been recorded. Watt found all of this alarming, requiring immediate action. He ordered the five warders to take a week's leave, during which they would be subject to a background enquiry.[63]

The arrest of three temporary warders on a charge of murder and the realisation that half of the permanent staff were possibly unreliable heightened concerns about the transfer, without background checks, into Northern prisons of warders from the South. An official protest was made to Anderson at Dublin Castle, expressing surprise that the transfers had been made without giving the Northern government a chance to express its views. Bates asked that the reassignments be suspended and indicated that although some of the transferred officers were being allowed to remain in place he reserved the right to dissent individual cases.[64] At the heart of this blunt letter was a belief that, as with the RIC, appointments and postings had been made by Dublin Castle without consideration to denomination. Religious affiliation, both in itself and as a denoter of political loyalties, had become a matter of concern to Belfast. This was a pointer to the way that public administration would develop in Northern Ireland.

Anderson, in the midst of the vast upheavals of state formation with which he and his colleagues were struggling, was irritated with what he saw as time-consuming nit-picking. On more recent appointments, he noted, means could doubtless be found 'even at this date' to make the transfers 'accord with the wishes of your Government'.[65] The reply to this rehearsed Northern grievances, in particular the failure of the Prisons Board to respond to correspondence. Escapes which had taken place prior to the vesting of the prison authority in the Northern Ireland government and the shocking events at Londonderry fully justified the Minister's view that 'the closest inquiry should be made into the antecedents of the prison officials'. The Ministry also complained that, prior to the transfer of authority, a number of temporary warders in Armagh, Belfast and Londonderry had been made permanent: 'In none of these cases were the Northern Government consulted in any way.' Where prison officers had already been notified of their promotion (from temporary to permanent status), Bates would not press for a cancellation, but in all other cases special enquiries would be made.[66]

The dispute rumbled on for some weeks. The numbers involved were small but so was the Northern prison service, and the Derry events were a tocsin. The Ministry was not concerned to stop any transfers from North to South, Watt minuting that 'It will be something to get rid of the officers who want to go South!'[67] This was not entirely a boon, however. Two Derry Roman Catholic warders applied to be transferred to the South. The difficulty, Captain Robeson (the Derry Governor) pointed out, was that the prison needed a certain number of Roman Catholic warders.[68] Magill suggested, therefore, that the Ministry might ask the Prisons Board if there were any Roman Catholics who wished to come North: 'we could then have confidential enquiries made and choose two reliable men'.[69]

Anderson was on guard against transfer decisions being made in Northern Ireland on religious grounds or simply on the basis of loose suspicions. He also wished to protect the public service and its staff from unwarranted political meddling. Dublin Castle (now functioning under the authority of the Provisional government) could not agree to the dismissal of any officer concerning whose loyalty there were doubts 'insufficiently supported by evidence to justify any disciplinary action being taken thereon'. No such suspicion existed about any officer transferred North (the inference to be drawn from some statements in the Northern letters). Anderson rejected the complaint that promotions from temporary to permanent status had been made because men were about to be transferred North. Not so, he insisted, the appointments were made in the ordinary course. Since, during their probationary periods on the permanent staff, warders could be dismissed if found unsuitable, Anderson did not see how the Northern prison service had been damaged. He drew attention to what was well-established practice: dismissal was ordered only in cases where evidence against an officer 'while perhaps insufficient for a prosecution, is really substantial'.[70]

As the 1920s advanced, and public administration in Northern Ireland became more settled, prison staffing reverted to what was its normal state in Britain and Ireland. Crime was low, static or declining, and prison populations moved accordingly.[71] As in Britain, a tight control was kept on public expenditure, and there was little by way of innovation or expansion.[72] Bates was able to exert some leverage by approaching the Department of Finance on the basis of anticipated trouble from the IRA; sometimes there were allusions to background information that could not be disclosed. This technique was not always successful, however, and, in 1928, the Ministry of Finance blocked an attempt by Bates to assimilate pay rates for prison staff with those of Great Britain.[73] Likewise, Finance turned down a request that those staff at Belfast Prison who had charge of convicts should be placed on a slightly higher pay scale than colleagues who dealt with ordinary prisoners. The sum involved was small (£10 per annum), and Bates argued that an injustice had been done since this differential had been applied prior to 1921, in the unified Irish administration. There was a clear difference in responsibilities: 'it is beyond dispute that warders in charge of convicts are exposed to a far greater degree of strain and anxiety than warders looking after ordinary prisoners'.[74] This argument of special circumstance failed to carry the day.

By 1936, the Roman Catholic chaplain at Belfast Prison, Father P. McGouran, felt able to comment favourably on staffing by contrasting present and past conditions. Prisoners were being treated humanely, and this was having a good effect on them. In previous years, he wrote, there had been warders 'who treated prisoners brutally and I have unhappy memories of the many occasions when I had to try to settle rows, and cool down the frayed temper of prisoners'. A better type of officer had been employed: able, encouraging and able to act with prudence and tact.[75]

However, Father McGouran was concerned about the much reduced proportion of Catholics among the prison officers. When he had first entered the Prison Service this was about half, he recalled. He doubted if the current proportion was as great as 15 per cent. As a result, there had been occasions when there had been no Catholic staff to collect prisoners from the exercise yards and workshops for escort to confessions. He urged that more Catholic officers should be appointed.[76]

Convicts

The Northern Ireland prison rules had been designed for short- rather than long-term prisoners.[77] As explained above, the new state had no convict prison during its first years and had to adapt as best it could and to send some of its convicts to Scotland, under contract with the Scottish Office.[78] As the men began to return, the anomaly that had allowed long-term prisoners to be confined under the rules for ordinary short-termers became insupportable. The returning convicts complained that they had enjoyed more privileges in British prisons, and senior

Home Office officials acknowledged that they had a case. In May 1926, R. Ronaldson, who, as Assistant Secretary at the Ministry, had special responsibility for prisons, reviewed the rules and made recommendations for their being brought more into line with those in Britain and thus to right an inequity.

The British system was not adopted exactly: Ronaldson did not propose 'going as far' as that. His recommendations were, however, intended to apply the general approach of British penal servitude to the management of convicts in Northern Ireland.[79] Convicts had, from the outset, had certain rewards and advantages set before them, should they be well conducted. These inducements were organised in stages, progress through which was a combination of time served and marks gained. The conditions of confinement were gradually and minutely eased by gaining privileges. These were positive reasons why a convict should conform, and what had been granted could be taken away for breaches of the rules. The privileges themselves might seem trivial when viewed by a free person with no experience of the oppressive tedium of prison and the psychologically draining effects of an unchanging routine endured for months and years on end. Any easement, any increase in comfort or amenity, however small, was hugely valued by convicts, enmeshed as they were in a life of ineluctable conformity, close custody and relentlessly enforced submission. Truly, nothing is trivial in the life of the prisoner, whose world has so shrunk that the commonplace is magnified.

The modified regime set out by Ronaldson and approved by Bates was set out in four stages, each of which, with optimal conformity and marks, would last one year: Probation, Third Class, Second Class and First Class. Having reached the end of his fourth year (First Class), the convict was on a plateau. Thereafter he could continue to earn marks, and thus his maximum statutory remission of sentence, but no further enlargement of privileges. These may briefly be summarised. First, and for many, most importantly, convicts were allowed to smoke, and the tobacco was provided at public expense. During his first year (Probation), the convict (also in distinction to the ordinary prisoner) was allowed to shave, to have his own shaving kit and eating utensils and to attend the prison concerts and lectures. In his second year (Third Class), he became eligible for one further period of association per week, educational classes and, at his own expense, a limited supply of weekly newspapers. Third-year convicts (Second Class) could pay for and receive a limited supply of books and magazines and have 'an improved bed'. The fourth year (First Class) brought meals in association (rather than eating alone in one's cell), evening association on each weekday when there were no classes and permission to associate during exercise (as distinct from the solitary pacing allowed to others). In addition, visits and letters were allowed each month. The First Class convict could also earn 2s. 6d. a month. This could be used to purchase small luxuries such as jam and marmalade. All privileges at each stage were conditional on good conduct and could be forfeited in whole or (more usually) in part for a period as a punishment for breaches of discipline. Demotion to a lower class would follow any misconduct above the trivial.

Visits and letters were also dependent on stage. Probation Class convicts could write a letter in the first week of their sentence and receive a reply to it. Thereafter, they were allowed one letter and one visit every ninety days. The frequency of these privileges was increased to sixty days in the Third and Second Classes and to thirty days in the First Class.[80] These were appreciable and much-cherished gains. The rules on silence were draconian, and convicts could only obtain permission to talk when they had served ten years (seven and a half if they obtained the maximum number of marks). This rule, intended (absurdly) to limit contamination and to discourage subversion, was inhumane and impossible to enforce. In consequence, Ronaldson observed, 'the prison officials, as a matter of commonsense, are not too zealous to enforce silence according to the rule'. The Belfast Governor thought that it would be better to accept reality and to control rather than prohibit talking. The rules were accordingly altered to allow well-behaved prisoners to exercise in pairs and to speak quietly at that time and also when working alongside others. At other times silence would be enforced.

There remained one other aspect of the existing regime, described by Ronaldson as 'indefensible' and which should be discontinued. This was the time spent by convicts locked up in their cells, from 4.30 in the afternoon until 7 a.m. the following morning: fourteen and a half hours. At weekends, lock-up was even earlier, from 12.30 p.m. until 7 a.m. – eighteen and a half hours out of twenty-four. Ronaldson conceded that the men performed some cell tasks during this time and that they had 'a certain amount' of reading material. Even so, he observed, 'the strain imposed by such long periods of confinement [on those] who were incarcerated for long terms may lead to very serious trouble, apart from the inhumanity'. Both the Governor and the Medical Officer had been consulted, and, on the basis of what they had told him, Ronaldson was convinced that 'there would be frequent suicide attempts', 'and we will have great difficulty in maintaining discipline if we continue this system'.[81]

Imprisonment sought to inflict painful deprivations, and penal servitude, its most severe form, was intended to punish, repress and deter, to imprint the experience for life. It is necessary for those unfamiliar with prison life to consider carefully the effect of any prolonged institutional confinement and then add to it the special constraints and minute regulation of every aspect of daily life. Even then, a full appreciation of the nature and effect of imprisonment can only be glimpsed if one attempts the difficult imaginative exercise of projecting that custodial experience over a period of months and years. Modern – even 1920s – imprisonment may be far removed from the sordid and life-threatening 'durance vile' of the eighteenth and earlier centuries, but life as a convict tested mental and physical endurance to an extraordinary degree: none could emerge from it unmarked and unchanged, and some were utterly crushed.

On 9 May 1927, four dangerous convicts escaped from Belfast Prison: three lifers and a twelve-year man.[82] This was one of the most embarrassing incidents in the history of the Northern prisons and prompted further concern about the policy of holding men sentenced to penal servitude – by definition, those convicted of the most serious offences, who for public safety and due punishment had to be incarcerated for lengthy periods – in buildings intended for short-term local prisoners. The anxiety was all the greater because the escape party had managed to obtain the prison keys. The escapers' leader, William Conlon, was recaptured after six days, but the other three remained at large and – ominously – still had the keys. Something had gone seriously wrong with prison procedures; there was also the alarming possibility that the keys could be used again. Modern practice would call for an immediate (and expensive) re-keying of the prison, but that was apparently not how things were done at Belfast Prison in 1927. The outcome instead was a rather forlorn letter to the Prison Commission in London, seeking help and assistance.[83] The subsequent report by Captain F. G. C. M. Morgan, Governor of Dartmoor Prison, revealed much interesting information about the state of Belfast Prison, including its management of convicts.

Set out in spans of years rather than in the months of ordinary imprisonment, sentences of penal servitude, as we have seen, had to be served under somewhat more expansive conditions in order to guard the convicts against gross physical and mental deterioration. Labour was an important part of the regime because it got the convicts out of their cells and gave them some form of occupation. When penal servitude had been devised in the 1840s as an alternative to transportation, labour had been seen as an intensification of the punitive experience: heavy, dirty, crushing and sometimes dangerous toil on public works such as fortification and dockyards. Scandal, and shifts in public and political sensitivity, had gradually wrought a change in thinking about convict labour, though some of it – especially agricultural work at Dartmoor – remained arduous.

Coming from Dartmoor to inspect Belfast Prison in 1927, Morgan found the labour available to prisoners of all categories to be restricted. Ordinary prisoners chopped kindling, made mats and formed the work party for the garden. Convicts made shoes and performed some of the tailoring work. They were insufficient in numbers to have the tailoring to themselves, and the workshop was divided by a partition notionally to separate the convicts from the ordinary prisoners. Morgan had no doubt that the two categories were able to communicate under these circumstances. More importantly, in his view, there was concern that the convicts were not assigned to gardening work. This should be remedied, he proposed, since convicts' 'long confinement in shops is bad mentally and morally'. He proposed that convicts be removed from the mixed-category tailoring workshop and assigned to garden work.[84]

Morgan's recommendation was that convict assignment to the garden party should be conditional on good behaviour. Since not all the convicts would expect to be selected to work outdoors, the knowledge that there was a selection process for such an alternative assignment might be expected to act as an encouragement to conform. Such at least was the thinking at the time (and indeed today). The garden party would not tend the grounds outside the walls and so no substantial security issues arose. Morgan wished to intensify scrutiny and control more generally by placing work parties under the supervision of officers who should have charge of the same prisoners inside the prison. This meant that when a prisoner changed work party he would also shift to another cell. The all-round supervision, Morgan thought, would assist control. Not only would officers learn who to watch but they would 'often gain valuable information from prisoners as to what events are in the air'.[85]

It was inevitable, even allowing for the failure that had led to its commission, that Morgan's report would be received defensively by Major Harris, then the Belfast Governor. Various small changes had been put in train, but Harris was particularly resistant to any amelioration in the convict regime. He rejected the recommendation that convicts should be put to work in the gardens. He already had a plan to expand this work to include market gardening and thus to provide employment for a larger number of ordinary prisoners. They could not work alongside convicts, and convict numbers would be insufficient for them to do gardening on this scale on their own. Harris also objected that gardening was suitable only for country men; 'townmen had been tried and found useless, they do more harm than work'. Harris's trump, however, was security. Once the governor had expressed a concern of this kind, it was unlikely to be overturned further up the chain of officialdom or by a politician. He considered the garden to be 'about the most dangerous part of the Prison, having three outer walls'. It would be necessary to have an armed guard (outside) of at least two warders.'[86] Neither Finance nor Home Affairs was likely to agree to this. Belfast's convicts were thus denied outside work. Instead, they were to be put to one of the most tedious and pointless of all prison tasks: the pure make-work of mailbag-sewing.

The stonewalling in response to the Morgan Report was not entirely reflexive defensiveness by Harris. Located as it was, close to the city centre, with design faults and inadequate physical security, and close to a nationalist population not disinclined to receive and provide shelter to escapers, no sensible governor would want to add further risks to his array of management concerns. This meant that convicts would continue to be held in inappropriate conditions, with little account being taken of the toll on mental and physical health of such long periods of imprisonment in what amounted to close custody and with only minimal opportunities for mental and emotional diversion and healthy physical exertion.

By 1936, it would appear, twenty convicts were employed in the prison laundry. This, at least, was physically taxing for the prisoners, although any such benefits may have been offset by the fact that the work was carried out entirely indoors. Security remained a concern, and, since there had recently been an influx of IRA prisoners, some serving long sentences for treason felony, the parsimoniousness of the Ministry of Finance was overcome sufficiently to allow an extra officer to be appointed so that two rather than one might supervise the laundry.[87]

There had been various reforms in the English convict prisons, with the intention of strengthening the reformatory and reclamatory elements in the regime and easing the deterrent and repressive parts. One of these – a considerable novelty at the time – was the introduction of educational lectures and concerts.[88] The charity Toc H (which had won wide affection among the troops on the Western

Front for its comforting and supportive ministry and social work) had become active in providing these ameliorations and was allowed to carry its activities into Belfast Prison.[89] Another departure was the provision of newspapers to prisoners who had earned them as a privilege. Before this, outside information had been deemed contraband.[90]

Convicts' correspondence and visits continued to be tightly controlled. In addition to the usual censorship of letters to and from prisoners, from 1927 it was stipulated that all communications, including visits, should be 'policed'.[91] This meant that all incoming letters were referred to the chief officer of police in the district in which the correspondent lived. Enquiries were then made on the writer's 'character and history'. The same procedure applied to visitors. Should an unsatisfactory police report come back, the convict was notified that the letter or visit had been refused but that he or she could communicate with somebody else.[92] 'Policing' had been directed mainly at IRA prisoners, although how effectively it was or could be enforced was not always clear.[93] It was decided to discontinue the practice in 1952, since it was then felt that '[t]hings are now back to normal'.[94] It had been a troublesome and time-consuming chore for the police, and an interlude of relative political calm meant that they could be rid of it.

Prisoners had always been restricted in their access to books and other publications: the exclusion of bad influence and the control of means of diversion and enjoyment were seen as part of the penal discipline. A particularly sensitive issue was the availability of material in Irish. Provided there was no subversive political content, the Ministry of Home Affairs was not unduly concerned that this material should be available. Prison staff were more sceptical and tended to view the study and use of Irish as part of the prisoners' unceasing subversion of authority and their continuing self-directed and undesirable political education. It is evident that the prisoners also saw possibilities of this kind in the study and use of Irish. In 1936, the Governor of Belfast Prison, Captain R. W. Stephenson, objected to a Ministry decision to allow prisoners to receive books in Irish. Were a prisoner to become 'efficient' in conversing in Irish, Stephenson contended, prison officers would also have to learn the language in order to know what was going on. His second objection was that detainees and internees were not allowed books in Irish, 'and I don't see why Convicts should be'. He was overruled by the Ministry. As to his first objection, prisoners could, if necessary, be forbidden to speak in Irish. The second point was sidestepped: the convicts were requesting Irish grammars, which could scarcely be considered 'books'.[95]

Following the 1927 Morgan review and a general tightening up at Belfast Prison, there seemed little cause for unease about security, control and safety. Whatever confidence or complacency may have existed was set aside in 1936 in response to a new round of internments. There had, the previous summer, been the fiercest sectarian clashes in a generation, leading to eleven deaths and widespread damage and destruction. The Belfast IRA had played its traditional part as a protective militia. Perhaps emboldened by such action, or anticipating further action, on 27 December 1935, it staged an arms raid on the Officers Training

Corps (OTC) armoury at Belfast's prestigious Campbell College.[96] Vigilance heightened after the related Crown Entry arrests and convictions that spring. The Crown Entry arrests were a major coup for the RUC. The affair originated in raids on the armoury of the OTC at Campbell College (an institution famous in Northern Ireland for the quality of its education) on 27 December 1935. The RUC had advance information, probably from the IRA's Belfast Intelligence Officer, Joseph Hanna, and intercepted the raiding party. The IRA men were unwilling to surrender, and a gunfight ensued. Several were subsequently arrested and brought to court.[97] Anthony Lavery, OC of the IRA in Belfast, issued an order allowing the men to recognise the court and thus to have a chance of mounting a defence. Lavery had thus violated an IRA standing order and was, in consequence, ordered to appear before a court martial. The rules provided that those constituting a court martial must be of equal or superior rank to the accused, and the organisation thus had to assemble a group of its most senior men. On information received (from the IRA's Belfast Intelligence Officer), the police raided the Craobh Ruadh Club at 10 Crown Entry, Belfast, and arrested thirteen men who were preparing to conduct a court martial. The IRA Adjutant General (Jim Killeen) and most of the Northern leadership were taken as was Michael Kelly, also a member of GHQ staff. Charged and convicted of treason felony (a law brought in to deal with the Young Irelanders in 1848), the group were given nearly fifty years of penal servitude between them.[98] Belfast Prison now held a sizeable group of experienced and determined IRA men, serving heavy sentences and with little to lose.

On 4 March 1936, Sir Dawson Bates, already troubled about security and fearing a possible attack on the prison, had personally inspected Belfast Prison and had ordered various changes in procedure and even alterations to the fabric of the building. He sought to restrict the total number of visitors in the prison at one time and directed that no male visitors be allowed to wait inside the main gate while their entitlement to visit was checked. Reviving a concern that had been ventilated at the time of the Morgan Report in 1927, Bates fretted about the key that the Governor took out of the prison with him to facilitate his night-time inspections and also expressed concern about the tunnel between the courthouse and the prison. (The buildings were on opposite sides of the Crumlin Road.) These anxieties were stoked by the laxness with which Bates and his accompanying official had been admitted through the wicket-gate. It is remarkable that Bates felt so strongly about the security of the prison and had such little confidence in its management that he should have inspected it so closely, and more remarkable that he, rather than the staff, came up with so many obvious and apparently sensible suggestions. The last indicates that the prison, functioning comfortably and unremarkably for a decade, had, in the way of all such institutions, settled into a state of complacent confidence.

Action swiftly followed. A rota was drawn up by which a principal warder and three warders were assigned to sleep in the main hall of the prison every night.[99] All who came to see certain prisoners had to submit to a personal search and were turned away should they refuse. Only one person at a time was allowed to visit these high-security prisoners, and they had to use a visiting box equipped with mirrors. This reduced the number of blind spots and made supervision more thorough and reliable. New arrangements were made for key-holding, and the tunnel to the court – previously a potential weakness – was made more secure.[100]

That these various precautions were necessary and timely was confirmed by an incident on 27 April 1936. At afternoon exercise, Sean O'Leary, the IRA prisoners' OC, issued the command 'Volunteers, fall out'. Nine men obeyed and were immediately marched to their cells by staff. Fairly minor punishments were imposed by the Governor, but the incident confirmed that republican prisoners were able and prepared to act together. At the same time, Stephenson reported that the police had requested that some recently received internees (as distinct from sentenced prisoners) be fingerprinted and photographed. The men had refused to cooperate, and 'a certain amount' of force had been used.[101] The Ministry responded immediately, assuring Stephenson that should he at any time consider it necessary in order to deal with an emergency, he could engage additional temporary staff without awaiting ministry approval: 'It is realised that it is essential you should have a free hand to take such measures as you deem necessary to ensure the safe custody of prisoners.'[102]

Bates's anxieties, doubtless based on RUC briefings, continued to run at a high level. On 30 July 1936, Stephenson was asked again if he were satisfied that his staff was 'in all respects sufficient'. The Minister was keenly aware of the character of the Crown Entry and other convicts. Attempts might be made to communicate with these men or to arrange escapes. If Stephenson considered the danger to be greater at the weekends, the Ministry suggested, it might be advisable to arrange for two or three B-Specials to be on guard duty outside the prison. As an urgent matter of public safety, Bates wished Stephenson to assure him that his staff was not under strength and that all precautions had been taken.[103] Stephenson replied, seeking two extra officers and four B-Specials to patrol inside the prison on Sundays – a particularly vulnerable time since most staff were then off duty.[104] Bates immediately had those requests put to the Ministry of Finance. Two years later, in April 1938, there was a repeat of these communications from the Ministry. Captain T. M. Stuart had recently been appointed as Governor of Belfast Prison, and Bates wanted the same under-standing with him. Stuart was directed to take all reasonable precautions and if an emergency arose he should incur whatever expense was necessary and seek authority later.[105]

Mixing with ordinary prisoners

By the mid-1930s, even with the occasional reception of a number of IRA prisoners (and the occasional street agitator), Belfast Prison operated in a manner and at a pace that would have been familiar in any provincial prison in Britain. IRA prisoners brought heightened concerns about security, and their protests some-times tested control. By and large, however, the proportion of these militants in the prison population was insufficiently large seriously to disturb the daily routine for long. There is confirmation of this in the prison journal kept by Anthony Lavery, who was arrested in the RUC's Crown Entry coup. Lavery was sen-tenced to two years' ordinary imprisonment for treason felony and managed to keep his journal for about a month.[106] Much of the journal is taken up with political observations and the protest action that the IRA was then trying to mount in the prison, but there is much about the daily life of the prison, seemingly incidental but both interesting and illuminating.

A key point in the IRA's directive to members who were imprisoned was its insistence that the utmost distinction should be maintained between political and ordinary prisoners. They were warned that the authorities would try to criminalise them. If numbers were small within a class there was no alternative but that the IRA men should mix with the other prisoners. With greater numbers, an attempt could be made to obtain some form of segregation, but, despite hunger-striking and other actions, this was never conceded by the Northern Ireland government.[107] On the other side, there was an attitude of disdain on the part of some IRA prisoners towards their non-political fellows – the social flotsam and jetsam, the habituals whose only true and comfortable home was prison, and the sprinkling of the irredeemably depraved and vicious that together constituted the republic of captivity. Women republicans were generally more sympathetic to their fellow prisoners, as were those relatively rare birds who came from repub-licanism's left wing. But individuals also varied in their attitudes, and Lavery found much to interest him in the ordinary life of the prison.

Those who were part of the revolving door of petty crime and a lifetime of short sentences were apparently known to both prisoners and staff as 'shareholders', and one of these men told tales as the men worked. The tales provided interest and entertainment for Lavery, and it is clear that he looked forward to the next instalment of this unlikely Scheherazade: 'The time in the workshop passed very quickly. Old Tom Coulter, one of the shareholders, kept us going telling us jokes.'[108] Smoking was prohibited in all British prisons at this time for ordinary prisoners, as it was in Belfast Prison, but tobacco still got through. In prisons throughout the world, the flint, striker and a piece of lint – the age-old way of 'striking a light' – were employed, rather than matches. It was a minor revelation to Lavery: 'Saw light being obtained today for the first time by the use of a needle, piece of burnt rag and a piece of flint.' (Deftness of this kind denoted that a prison apprenticeship had been served.) Coulter continued to entertain, Lavery recording that he 'was on the job to-day again telling us of his fight with "Pig McNeilly". We will miss him when he goes out.' These entries also show that, for all the consideration given to the talking rule, prisoners and staff had found a *via media* that allowed conversation – storytelling, indeed – without disrupting order. Certainly the raconteur was not inhibited: 'Old Tom gave us a few examples of slang; other "shareholders" understood him but we could not make out a word he said.' On another day, he was 'full of stories and jokes: we had a lot more new ones to-day'.

But the habituals who provided interest and amusement by lifting the curtain on the *demi-monde* could evoke pity, and also shock. Lavery reported that a non-political prisoner named Steele would be released, having served nine months for larceny:

> He is about 36 years of age but he has very little sense, this is his 3rd term of imprisonment, and I dare say he will be back again before we are released (as the saying here goes). Become shareholders – out today – and in tomorrow – and get No. 3 diet [the most generous allowance] without any trouble.

Habitués such as Steele might pass the time agreeably and might also evoke pity, but they might also shock their fellows: 'The "yarns" one hears in here about the various inmates are terrible alarming and disgusting, if the Governor heard them he would know what "Political Offenders" are forced to associate with, and are classed equal with.'

Diversion through tales and anecdotes that amused or shocked was understandably valued; prison is a device for confiscating time and inflicting tedium by enforcing an unchanging routine. The Friday night concerts (variety performances by outside volunteers) broke the tedium in much the same way as Old Tom. All of the sentenced prisoners (ordinary as well as penal servitude, and no matter what stage they had reached in their sentence) could attend. The audience was not uncritical, if Lavery is representative. He came into Belfast Prison under sentence on a Wednesday, attended the performance on Friday and was somewhat disgruntled: 'very poor, it was over at 8.45 and I went straight to bed'. But the following week it was very good: 'Every item was performed well and there was plenty of variety in the programme – songs, music, dances and recitation… I hope we shall have the same party back again in the near future.'

Another guard against boredom was reading. In the first twenty-eight days of a sentence, this form of relaxation and entertainment was limited by the prison rules, and only works of instruction were supposed to be issued. The rule seems to have been interpreted fairly and included titles such as *Captain Cook's Voyages of Discovery* and *The Life of Queen Elizabeth*.[109] When the twenty-eight days were up, novels were issued from the prison library, including popular works such as Alexander Dumas' *Twenty Years After*. Much more accessible, almost in free circulation, although they were prohibited for sentenced prisoners, were newspapers. These may have been passed on by staff or smuggled over from the remand wing. Lavery regularly received the *Irish News*, only a day old. As with conversation in the workshops, it is probable that provided newspapers were not flaunted the staff tolerated their circulation.

Believer or not (and IRA members were nearly all observant Roman Catholics), religious services allowed time out of one's cell and were in themselves one of the available breaks in routine. Men from other wings could be seen there and, if not spoken to, acknowledged in some form. (To keep the categories apart, penal-servitude prisoners were kept in the chapel's gallery.) As we have seen, IRA men were debarred by the bishops from receiving the sacraments, but individual clergy seem to have taken their own line on this. A visiting priest, Father Crossman, withheld absolution from Lavery because he would not promise to leave the IRA. (The refusal was odd in itself because Lavery had decided to break his IRA ties when he was released.) There is an indication, however, that the regular chaplain, Father McGouran, was inclined to enquire less closely into the matter and to take a more liberal line on the sacraments.

Rumours flourish in prison. Boredom encourages speculation, both of the optimistic and malicious kinds. Close quarters provide all the necessary facilities for dissemination and elaboration. In the summer of 1936, the IRA men in Belfast Prison were as apt as their non-political companions to succumb to hope and to malice. There were persistant rumours that when Edward VIII was crowned the following year (an event that did not take place, of course), there would be ordered, as an act of customary clemency, the release of all political prisoners in Northern Ireland.[110] The story and a newspaper clipping circulated among the various groups of prisoners and no doubt inspired some hopes among the long-term, even were the amnesty to be occasioned by a British coronation. Darker rumours also circulated – dangerous too, when one considers the paramilitary context – that this or that person was a 'stoolie'; accusation and counter-accusation flew. The consequences of this type of storytelling could, with ordinary prisoners, result in an assault on the suspected informant. The IRA man against whom allegations were made could face much worse, and Lavery reported that, in one conversation, it was reported that 'Chuck B' had been deported to Canada by the IRA. ('Deportation' meaning exile on threat of death, no doubt.) But Lavery recognised that a great deal of what he heard was simply malicious tittle-tattle: 'That is all one hears at times, i.e., "So and so is a stool pigeon".' Political and non-political alike, this was an inevitable part of exchanges in a setting from which interest, change and variety had, as a policy, been sucked and which was populated by men to whom subterfuge, for whatever end, was as reflexive as drawing breath and to whom deceit was an instinctive art.

Sedition and social action

Towards the end of 1933 and the beginning of 1934, there were widespread disturbances in Belfast and in other areas. Unemployment had been high since the 1920s, and by 1932, 27 per cent of the registered workforce was on the dole.[111] Public support at the time consisted of a mixture of indoor (workhouse) and outdoor (dole) relief. As we have noted, workhouses had been established throughout Britain and Ireland in 1834, based on the premise that those without work, or a substantial portion of them, were idle, feckless, or both. The notion was to make receipt of payment from the public purse 'less eligible' than the conditions of the most poorly paid employed persons. This was done by a deterrent and substantially penal regime in the workhouse and by stigmatising all who accepted public relief as paupers. The 'workhouse test' was a measure of desperation: are you hungry, cold and sufficiently hopeless to accept relief in the workhouse? In the mid-1830s, outdoor – non-institutional relief – was almost entirely banned, so entry into the workhouse was the test of need. It was a hard-hearted and sometimes brutal way of dealing with the poor, based on a belief that if well-meant but foolish charity were removed or limited, market forces would deal with unemployment by compelling the poorest to accept the lowest rates of payment rather than solicit relief.[112] Capitalism could thus rebalance itself, the hypothesis suggested.

Particularly in the last years of Victoria's reign, pioneering social research and statistics (and an expanding and more questioning type of philanthropy) undermined the notion that poverty and unemployment were due to defective morality, fecklessness and vice. Cyclical movements in the economy and structural changes in industry powerfully affected employment, and this was demonstrated by a number of surveys. Over the years, these insights were grudgingly grafted into policy, and a hybrid system of poor relief emerged, allowing the payment of relief without compelling entry into 'the house'.[113] By the late nineteenth century, outdoor relief was the most usual form of state support for the able-bodied unemployed. The hated workhouse morphed into an asylum for the sick, indigent aged and – with the penal regime of the overnight casual wards – tramps and other itinerants.[114] The means-tested outdoor dole carried the greater part of the stigma of the workhouse, was bitterly resented by many ratepayers (who were the principal funders) and was given under the most demeaning conditions, including home visits in which all possessions were valued to see if the their sale could substitute for public relief.

The fires of sectarian division and suspicion burned steadily in Belfast and elsewhere in Northern Ireland during the 1920s and 1930s and, from time to time, flared into riots, attacks and counter-attacks. To a large extent, these divisions blocked the development of organisations of the militant unemployed. Such organisations had emerged in many areas in Britain with economies based on shipbuilding, textile and other declining industries. It was, however, a measure of desperation and anger that, to some extent, in October 1932, Catholic and Protestant workers and unemployed came together publicly to protest at the miserable doles on which they were expected to live and the humiliating aura that surrounded their administration.[115] These disturbances and their outcome were in some ways more alarming than manifestations of nationalist discontent.[116] South and north of the border, there were warnings about the inroads being made by militant socialism and Communism.[117] The Irish population of all denominations took the warnings of their religious leaders on social and political issues with the utmost seriousness. In the South there had been rifts in the IRA over the left-wing teachings of some influential members, tactics against the Blueshirts and the correct attitude to de Valera's Fianna Fáil government and denunciations from the Roman Catholic hierarchy.[118] The Northern IRA was more conservative and less likely to become involved in labour matters, but nevertheless a number of activists took part in protests and were gathered in.

Militants continued to attempt to organise the unemployed as the marching season passed and sectarian passions ebbed. On Thursday, 11 October 1934, there were arrests, and extra police were deployed when the Irish Unemployed Workers' Movement attempted to hold meetings in defiance of a banning order issued under the Special Powers Act. The demonstrations were intended to mark the second anniversary of the Belfast unemployed protests during which two members of the movement, John Geehan and Samuel Baxter, were shot and killed.[119] The Belfast demonstration, for which there had been advance publicity, was convened close to the city centre and attracted a crowd of some 300 – relatively modest and hardly menacing. Uniformed police and detectives were there in some numbers, and when Thomas Geehan, the Movement's principal organiser, began to speak, he was arrested.[120] Apart from some jeering, the crowd did not interfere. The Movement may have hoped for demonstrations in other parts of Belfast, but either lack of support or the presence of police at key points meant that there were no further attempts at public assemblies.[121] The following day, there was a low-key demonstration in the form of a wreath-laying ceremony at Milltown Cemetery in Belfast. The police attended but did not intervene when a wreath was laid and when Ben Murray, a labour activist, gave an oration on the part played by John Geehan and Samuel Baxter in the fight to have the outdoor relief allowance raised.[122]

Few activists from the Unemployed Workers' Movement or any other organisation of social protest made their way into prison, and, when they did, as far as can be seen from surviving records, they were not a distinctive presence. Their numbers were not sufficient to merit special note or concern by the Ministry of Home Affairs and were certainly too small and inexperienced to attempt to organise in the prison. And it was this that set the IRA apart: the well-established rules by which its members conducted themselves, the fact that imprisonment was anticipated and seen as an extension of the organisation, a repertoire of tactics of protest and disruption and some form of dependants' support. Social-protest movements did not have that tradition (with the exception of the Women's Social and Political Union, the suffragettes), nor was their intent to engage in combat with the state in whatever setting and with whatever means came to hand.

The interlude of Protestant–Catholic working-class solidarity was fleeting, but the possibility of interdenominational subversion was as alarming to the Northern Ireland government as it was beguiling and inspiring to the republican left.[123] It was inevitable that, in such an atmosphere, the authorities would wish to show something of the iron fist, to discourage further ventures in civil disorder and equal-opportunity sedition. Extensive use was made of Regulation 22B of the Special Powers Act to round up suspects against whom there was insufficient evidence to bring a case to court. A number of those gathered in refused to recognise the court, thus conveniently convicting themselves and incurring a short sentence of imprisonment – usually a month. There were others against whom there was enough evidence, often the possession of republican documents such as leaflets, pamphlets or other seditious material. In all, eighty-five persons were arrested, of whom seventy-three were initially detained under the relevant powers of Regulation 23.[124] Thereafter, twenty-three convictions were obtained under Regulation 22B, for refusing to answer a question put by the court, for refusing to recognise the court or for declaring membership of an unlawful association.[125] Twelve convictions were obtained for possession of seditious documents, thirty for drilling or unlawful assembly, five for failing to comply with an exclusion order, one for harbouring an excluded person and two for making a seditious speech. Eleven persons avoided convictions by entering into bail or giving undertakings for future good behaviour, and one fortunate (and innocent) soul was discharged unconditionally.[126] The ten persons who had refused to recognise the court were convicted and sentenced for other offences. Having served their term of imprisonment, they were brought again before the court charged with the Regulation 22B offence. Depending doubtless on temper and demeanour, seven of the ten were allowed to enter into bail to be of good behaviour for twelve months, and three were fined or sentenced to imprisonment.[127]

Such short-term prisoners presented no security or management problems. Their offences rarely rose above what, in another and more tranquil jurisdiction, might be considered to be merely those of public order. A few names appear in these arrests that would reappear later in connection with more serious matters, but, for the most part, the 1933–4 round-up dealt with those on the periphery of the republican movement. Certainly, as the summer of 1934 drew on, and particularly the Orange celebrations of the Twelfth of July, newspaper reports indicated that some of the offences that came before the courts were more in the nature of sectarian provocation than republican or nationalist agitation. Thus, on the Twelfth, there were Portadown convictions (but not prison sentences) for nationalist-sounding remarks shouted at Orange processions or social gatherings.[128] At Armagh, according to the police, a riot was narrowly averted when, on 15 August (Lady Day, a Catholic day of celebration), a contingent of the Ancient Order of Hibernians, returning from their processions, played the Free State national anthem on the edge of a Protestant area.[129] But there were also offences with a more obvious political and paramilitary connection. Thomas Matthews was brought before Armagh Petty Sessions and sent to Quarter Sessions on arms and explosives charges.[130] In May, a group of around eighteen boys in marching formation, and responding to commands, was intercepted outside Newry to Camlough Road. Some were carrying what appeared to be imitation rifles. Given the powers conferred on the police by the Special Powers Act, a surprisingly trivial charge, 'conduct likely to lead to a breach of the peace', was brought.[131] This suggests that the police had decided that the incident was a juvenile masquerade rather than a Fianna or IRA demonstration or training exercise. The incident and several others like it confirm that the summer of 1934 was fraught with sectarian tension and republican stirrings. This was always a concern to the government, but the outdoor relief demonstrations of

1932–3 had shown that public disorder could take on an even more threatening character.

Certainly, as 1934 wore on, the signs remained that the IRA was organising and training, and, as a consequence, a number of men appeared before the courts.[132] Apart from the most serious cases (possession of arms and explosives), conviction did not necessarily lead to imprisonment. The authorities knew that a man who recognised the court had committed a serious breach of IRA discipline and had, in effect, separated himself from it. Conversely, withholding recognition, apart from being an offence in itself, confirmed that a man was an activist, willing to accept a prison sentence rather than to break an IRA edict.[133] This meant that a somewhat more lenient attitude could be taken where the organisation was openly repudiated. In a Derry case on 15 October 1934, Charles McAnena (who had been detained under the Special Powers Act for the previous two weeks) said he had 'cut adrift' from the IRA and promised not to have anything to do with illegal organisations in future. He was charged with the possession of unlawful documents. Magistrates allowed him to enter into bail for £10 to keep the peace for twelve months and released him.[134]

The Belfast hunger strike

By mid-August 1936, there were twenty-three IRA men in Belfast Prison.[135] Because of sentencing and rules on classification within the establishment, they were located in several different parts of the prison. Nine were serving sentences of penal servitude, as Star Class prisoners (meaning that they had been classified as first offenders and otherwise of good character), three were non-star ordinary prisoners, and three were juveniles (under the age of twenty-one). Communication could be difficult but was not impossible since some of the categories worked together (stars and juveniles worked in the wood yard) or met in the chapel or at the weekly concerts. The penal-servitude men were kept apart from the others, occupying the gallery of the chapel during services and for concerts, but notes could, it seems, be passed fairly easily.

Hunger-striking had succeeded in wresting privileges from the British and Irish governments but not from the Northern Ireland government. It was a classic IRA tactic in the battle for political recognition that was in itself generally no more than a staging post in a longer campaign of attrition against officialdom. By the mid-1930s, some consensus seems to have been reached within the organisation that the hunger strike was an extremely unreliable tactic and was to be discouraged. There had been spectacular successes, and these were etched in bold capitals in republican history: Terence MacSwiney, Thomas Ashe and even the arch-apostate himself, Éamon de Valera. But there had been many more failures, and these had been true defeats in the sense that the balance of advantage did not go back to where it had been before the strike commenced but placed the prisoners and their organisation in a worse position than had there been no action at all. They had a sense of deprivation, and of suffering pointlessly undergone, were demoralised and, in some instances, felt ridiculous. Their supporters in the wider movement, who may have mounted sympathy demonstrations, were left dangling.

A number of conditions are necessary for a hunger strike to have even a chance of success, and even where they are present the outcome must always be uncertain. There had to be outside support, ever-widening and reinforced by strong and growing public demonstrations. The government had to be uncertain or torn between objectives – a desire to placate or not to inflame a body of opinion conflicting with the need to appear implacable, for example. Finally, even a vacillating government could not give way to impossible demands such as immediate and unconditional release: politicians always had to be given some form of face-saver. Only a small and exceptionally hardy group, or an individual, could undertake a strike. They had to be carefully selected for the utmost fortitude and, from the outset and throughout, willing to die, and to accept the probability of death. None of these conditions could be met in Belfast in the summer of 1936, and it is likely that all but the most ill-informed and unreflective prisoners knew that.

It was some weeks after the Crown Entry men arrived at the prison under sentence that the decision was made to undertake a hunger strike. The order came from Seán McCool, who was the OC of all the IRA prisoners and, certainly, as Anthony Lavery recounted events, the hunger strike appears to have been undertaken more to satisfy a perceived expectation than with tactical fervour or confidence. Nine demands were put; in comparison to other protests, these were relatively modest. The core IRA demand was always for political status. This was not sought outright but was approached through privileges that would have set the protestors apart from all other prisoners and would thus, if only for administrative reasons, have required them to be treated as a distinct and separate class.

Lavery who had decided by this point to break with the IRA on release, was an unwilling participant in the action, but so too were several others. Three of the nine demands would not be conceded, he thought: the right to wear and regularly replace their own clothes; the use of a razor and toiletries (convicts, penal servitude prisoners, were clipped by the prison barber, rather than shaved) and an hour's Irish class three evenings a week. Most of the remaining six demands, Lavery noted, would be granted anyway, as the prisoners advanced through the various stages.[136] These included the availability of textbooks for study, a monthly letter and half-hour visit, weekly and monthly periodicals and the more generous Class III (convict) diet for all republican prisoners, whatever their class. The last, and the demand that all IRA men could work together in their class, were never likely to be granted because they would have been exceptional privileges and therefore some acknowledgement of IRA prisoners as a special group. Public reaction, if nothing else, made them impossible.

The strike, such as it was, lasted less than a week and that only in a sporadic and unevenly supported fashion. Stephenson reported to the Ministry of Home Affairs that the majority of the men came off it after three days, some renewing it afterwards for two or three days at a time, taking food in between.[137] The preliminaries had got under way on Monday, 10 August 1936, when McCool made an application to see the Governor and presented the nine demands. These were pre-emptorily refused, a decision immediately confirmed by the Ministry of Home Affairs. Several days elapsed, and McCool again saw Stephenson and was told that all prisoners would be treated strictly according to the rules. An order had already been issued that, in this eventuality, the convicts in A Wing would refuse to leave their cells. A strip-strike was not contemplated, and the men would continue to wear prison uniforms until their own clothes were provided. All IRA prisoners, McCool emphasised, were expected to join the strike, 'as it is a struggle for political status'.[138] Those who refused to leave their cells were immediately (Tuesday, 18 August) brought before the Governor and punished with fourteen days' No. 2 punishment diet (bread and potatoes) and loss of all privileges (books, private cash purchases, association, etc.).[139] In response, the men refused to accept the punishment diet.

Thereafter, things spluttered. Two of the convicts took the No. 2 diet but refused to work. Lavery also accepted the punishment diet but not work. All the other ordinary and juvenile prisoners went on hunger strike. Within a day, those in the Star Class decided that they would return to work the following morning (Thursday, 20 August), and the other ordinary prisoners decided that if they could not persuade them to continue with the no-work action they too would start work on the following Monday (24 August). The Star men then rallied and also joined the hunger strike, only to fall in with a general agreement to cease all action on the Monday. There were attempts to communicate between the various groups, with Charles McGlade, a prominent IRA member, deploring the stops and starts and general uncertainties: 'I'm trying to stop a fight from becoming a farce altogether.'[140] But it was indeed a farce and, by the Monday, had come to its end as a collective effort.

Discontent continued, and with it some individual protests. Jimmy Steele, serving five years for treason felony, persisted in his hunger strike for nineteen days, accepting food on Friday, 4 September 1936. According to a newspaper report, his aunt and cousin had visited him and persuaded him to call off his strike, pointing out that he was the only man still on it.[141] On agreeing to come off the strike, he was immediately removed to the prison hospital. Steele's illness as a result of his having refused food was then made the basis of another protest, with some or all of his comrades, convict and ordinary, refusing to attend the Friday-night concerts as a gesture of solidarity.[142] This appears to have been no more than a self-inflicted hardship, but it is possible that it may have caused the authorities at least some inconvenience, since it would have required some extra deployment of staff to cover both the concert and the wing. The IRA men cannot have been popular with their fellows since the Governor announced that in consequence of their action the much valued concerts would be discontinued.

The IRA men were frustrated, but the leaders were realistic enough to recognise that any general re-run of a hunger strike was likely to end in similar disarray. Jim Killeen and Seán McCool decided that they would refuse food for fourteen days from 15 September as a continuing protest against the refusal to grant political status; none of the other prisoners were expected to join them.[143] Six days later, however, Steele joined the protest. All three stuck by the plan and took food again after fourteen days when the period of their punishment, and No. 2 diet, came to an end. This was a demonstration of will more than anything else, an attempt to retrieve some dignity and to assert a modicum of independence.

There was little sign that either the Governor or the Ministry of Home Affairs had been placed under pressure. The on–off nature of the action was one factor, and (despite press reports on the strikes) the absence of any public support was another. It did not seem that any of the men was willing to see the protest through to death. The nature of the protest was summarised, not unfairly, by Governor Stephenson in a report to the Ministry on the various dates of refusing and then accepting food: 'It will be seen that a number of these were merely nominal hunger strikes and in the case of Convict Kennedy, who was undergoing a life sentence for murder, he thought he would strike in sympathy but after being deprived of his dinner went off hunger-strike.'[144]

The RUC took some interest in the prisoners' action, but only in its wider security implications. Steele, whom they described as 'one of the most militant members of the organisation in the Six Counties' had, before going on hunger strike, asked the Roman Catholic chaplain to approach Stephenson on his behalf. Were he to be transferred to the hospital he would not go on strike. The approach was made and the bargain refused. The RUC worried that Steele might have had an ulterior motive in making the request: 'The hospital is used for all classes of prisoners and would be an ideal place to collect and distribute any information that would be of assistance to the IRA prisoners, especially if they contemplated escape.' It would be unwise, the police advised, to grant Steele's request, especially since he might have liaised with outsiders and might have a plan in mind.[145]

In 1936, the IRA in Belfast was in no state to mount or to derive advantage from a hunger strike. Its members outside do not appear to have had a line of communication into the prison, so there could be no discussion or coordination of tactics. But even had there been reliable contacts, it is unclear how helpful they could have been. The self-indulgent organisational embellishment of assembling a high-powered court martial in informer-ridden Belfast, a rodo-montade in perilous times, had been remarkably costly and damaging. The Crown Entry arrests had decapitated the Northern IRA, giving the RUC a bonus of Jim Killeen, Adjutant General of the whole organisation, and Michael Kelly, a member of its GHQ staff.[146] Who, therefore, could have communicated what to whom is not clear. That apart, the men's performance in the prison was distinctly less than impressive: irresolute, fitful and confused. On the other side, there was an administration whose supporters were unlikely to be concerned about an IRA man or two (or more) starving themselves to death. The Northern Ireland government, braced for political and social upheaval, could not but see concessions to its convicted enemies as dangerous and unacceptable weakness. Sir Dawson Bates, as we have seen, had taken a particular and urgent interest in the security of Belfast Prison and, in any event, had a record of dealing strongly with all manifestations of republicanism.[147] Any sensible analysis could not have avoided these facts, but, drawn along by their particular current of republican thought, activists preferred rhetoric and ritual to reality.

A comparison with the force wielded by republican prisoners during the Anglo-Irish War shows how very different the situation was in Northern Ireland a decade and a half later. Max Green, Chairman of the General Prisons Board, wrote to the Under-Secretary in Dublin Castle, as follows: 'A large class of political offenders regard a prison as a stage upon which they can carry out with utmost recklessness, their defiance of authority, and the further they can go, the more they calculate on public sympathy and support.'[148] Such was not true in Belfast Prison in 1936.

First-class misdemeanants

On 25 November 1925, following a jury trial, Samuel Patterson was convicted of sedition and was sentenced by Northern Ireland's Lord Chief Justice to six months' hard labour.[149] He was also required, at the expiration of his sentence, to give bail in the sum of £40 and to provide two sureties of £20 each, to keep the peace for twelve months and to be of good behaviour. In default of these guarantees he was to serve for a further six months. Patterson was an ex-serviceman, evidently of some reputation, and at the time of his offence he was in ill-health. In unionist circles there was an attempt to ease his punishment by having him treated as a first-class misdemeanant, in accordance with s.49 of the General Prisons (Ireland) Act, 1877.[150] The difficulty, however, was that Patterson had been sentenced to hard labour. The Prisons Act, 1898, explicitly precluded a prisoner sentenced to hard labour from being placed in the first or second division (both of which considerably eased penal discipline and restrictions). The Ministry of Home Affairs, faced with a Parliamentary Question, asked the Solicitor General to advise if Patterson were entitled to be treated as a first-class misdemeanant and, if not, whether government had power to transfer him there. As English ministers had found before them, there was no executive authority, short of use of the Royal Prerogative, to make such a transfer.[151]

The issue arose again, in April 1939, when the recently appointed Belfast Governor, Captain Thomas M. Stuart, was questioned by Newton Anderson on first-demeanant status. Stuart referred the matter to the Ministry of Home Affairs, where it was dealt with by the now veteran assistant secretary, R. Ronaldson. The passage of time and changes in practice had largely eroded the difference between hard-labour and non-hard-labour prisoners. The rules specified that if aged less than sixty years of age, a hard-labour prisoner was given no mattress in the first twenty-eight days and was kept in separate confinement, that is, locked in his cell except for exercise and chapel. The rule had ceased to have practical effect because the prison medical officer almost invariably directed that a mattress be issued, and it had become rare for a prisoner to be kept and employed in strict separation. Ronaldson concluded that there was little practical difference between the two categories of prisoner; he also pointed out that the Criminal Justice Bill then before the House of Commons contained a clause that finally abolished the hard-labour element in a prison sentence.[152]

Flogging and birching

The punishment of those convicted of politically related crimes, the imprisonment of Free State soldiers found in Northern Ireland and the question of internment, were topics for frequent exchanges between the three governments. An additional and perhaps more inflammatory issue was the flogging of politically motivated offenders. This power had in part been taken from the Larceny Act of 1916 and expanded by the Special Powers Act, 1922.[153] Within a short space of time (26 April to 17 July 1922) the judges showed their willingness to use it, with no fewer than twenty-one persons being sentenced to corporal punishment by birch or whip, always accompanied by substantial periods of imprisonment.[154] Convictions which qualified for this penalty included offences under the 1883 Explosive Substances Act and the 1920 Firearms Act, as well as firearms offences under the regulations of the Special Powers Act. Whipping could also be imposed for any offence under s.30 of the Larceny Act (demanding money with menaces), for arson, whether charged under common law or statute, and for any offence under the Malicious Damage Act, 1916. Taken together, these offences were likely to include many of the incidents occurring in a country subject to acts of war and civil disorder.

Of the twenty-one persons sentenced to flogging in the three months following the introduction of the Special Powers Act, six had been convicted of ordinary non-political robberies. Coincidentally, three were Catholics and three Protestants. All fifteen sentenced for politically related offences, however, were Catholics convicted of possessing arms and explosives.[155] By 17 July 1922, there had been four floggings: two were Protestants and two Catholics; all were robbers. This prepared the way for the flogging of the arms and explosives offenders. Anticipating nationalist and republican anger, North and South, the Provisional government sought to have the sentences commuted and asked London to intercede.

As a sentence of the court, corporal punishment had been in decline in England since the 1820s. In a society that widely accepted the chastisement of children with cane and strap in school and home and merely raised an eyebrow at severe beatings, there was little objection to retaining corporal punishment for juveniles.[156] Some reformers, including the 1890s Home Secretary, H. H. Asquith, preferred it to a short custodial sentence, which was seen as necessarily contaminating.[157] There was, however, a huge gap between the caning or strapping of a juvenile (unpleasant though that was) and the flogging of an adult. Flogging was inflicted with the cat. This had been modified for use in the English prisons in 1879 and no longer included the barbarous knots on each of its nine strands. These instruments had been intended to tear the skin, to rend the flesh, and to inflict excruciating pain, and were capable of inflicting severe injury and permanent scarring and even maiming. The modified cat also inflicted very considerable pain, equivalent to a significant trauma, and could also leave permanent scarring. The birch – originally a bundle of birch twigs on a handle – had also in 1879 been modified, and a sealed pattern was introduced to prevent pieces of the twigs from breaking off and sticking in the skin and flesh.[158] It is not clear when these new regulations were adopted in Ireland, but it is probably safe to assume that they followed the English reforms, since in most important matters the Irish prisons, prior to Independence and Partition, took this course.

Whipping declined as the use of imprisonment increased, and, where retained, it was intended to mark the special opprobrium attached to a particular offence: the use of violence, the vulnerability of a victim or an exceptional degree of moral depravity. Swimming against this tide of penal reform and the general discontinuance of corporal punishment, Lord Carnarvon's Security from Violence Act, 1863 – sometimes called the Garotters Act – allowed the courts to order up to three whippings for an offence then thought to be particularly despicable and on the increase: street robberies with violence.[159] Section 37 of the 1916 Larceny Act, which empowered the courts to order a flogging, referred to obtaining money by the use of menaces. The offence of pimping, living off immoral earnings, could until 1948 entail a flogging.[160]

Whilst the sentence was available to the courts, a significant section of the public at large apparently approved its use: a flogging was the law's response to cruelty and depravity. By subjecting the offender to a humiliating, degrading and extremely painful punishment, there was appropriate retribution and a fitting and deterrent example was being made. To impose the punishment in addition to a lengthy sentence of imprisonment or penal servitude on offenders whose crimes were politically motivated was an attempt to crush them as persons, to put them in the category of the most despicable and morally abhorrent, as well as to use them as deterrent examples. The sentence, repressive and atavistic, was regarded with particular distaste by the nationalist community in Northern Ireland, by the Free State government and, increasingly, by some British politicians and officials.

The Provisional government reacted strongly to sentences of flogging imposed on its own soldiers who were arrested in Northern Ireland. It is impossible at this distance of time to know which arrests were of Free State soldiers genuinely visiting relatives, taken with the arms they happened to be carrying and had no intention of using against Northern Ireland. It is a fact that in the months during which a section of the IRA was mutating into the National Army, some Free State soldiers were engaging in covert actions against Northern Ireland. The duplicity of Collins's relations with the Northern government is unquestionable. He and close colleagues involved in this deception had every inducement to claim that these soldiers' presence in Northern Ireland could be explained as no more than innocent visits to relatives and friends. It is likely that some may indeed have been innocent; it was equally likely that some were taken on active service, even were that only reconnoitring or liaison. Any army, even one in such a very rapid expansion and transition as the Free State's, attaches the greatest weight to the relationship between the soldier and his weapons. A large part of basic training deals with care of weapons, when they may be used and where they may be taken. Once issued to him, a man has total accountability for his weapons: this is a basic military principle. In virtually all armies at all times the soldier going on leave deposits his arms with his unit. Besides creating a fiction – a face-saver for both sides – to account for the presence of armed soldiers in Northern territory, Collins, as a good commander, wanted, above all, to extricate men from the predicament into which he and the Provisional government's army command had placed them. The Northern Ireland authorities were well aware of the activities of many of those who had been arrested and brought to trial in the jurisdiction. Having subjected the men to the due process of law, Belfast was unwilling, for a number of reasons, to set the convictions and punishments aside at the request of W. T. Cosgrave (as Collins's successor) or on the urgings of London.

Two of the Northern ministers most concerned with criminal justice – Sir Dawson Bates and Richard Best, the Attorney General – also strongly believed in the justice and efficacy of the flogging. The Junior Minister at Home Affairs, Robert Megaw (if anything even more strongly in favour), was able to ensure that many of the sentences were carried out.[161]

The first case raised by the Provisional government was that of Felix O'Byrne of the IRA's Dublin Guards Brigade. This was a unit particularly associated with Collins, trusted and loyal, its sensitivities to be closely regarded in uncertain times. In August 1922, Michael Collins telegraphed Winston Churchill (then Colonial Secretary), insisting that O'Byrne had been at home on furlough, visiting his mother near Banbridge, Co. Down. He had been arrested and brought to trial for the possession of arms and ammunition. A sentence of seven years' penal servitude was imposed, together with fifteen lashes. Collins's warning was stark: 'This raises a question of the greatest gravity. Serious consequences will arise if this sentence is persisted in.'[162] Alfred Cope, the general fixer, who was assisting in the withdrawal of British forces from Ireland, and generally providing liaison between the governments and officials, was enlisted. The political and military ramifications were indeed considerable. The Provisional government, based on a flickering authority, shifting alliances and hope, was struggling for its existence and fighting old comrades, and, should the Dublin Guards falter, the whole edifice might tumble. There were, in circulation and under discussion, appeals from several sections and shades of opinion within the IRA to re-establish unity by openly attacking Northern Ireland. Indeed, something of the kind was happening, scarcely camouflaged. An incident such as the flogging of O'Byrne might pass with simply a strong protest; it could equally provoke an open retaliatory raid into Northern Ireland by his comrades, unleashing a counter-strike and civil disorders. Hostages had already been taken by IRA raiding parties in February and March 1922, and a sizeable number was still being held without too much active intervention from the Free State government. There were numerous possibilities, each bleaker than the other, for those who sought to save and reinforce a fragile peace. Immediate action was required: unlike a prison sentence, a flogging could not be undone. Cope immediately contacted London, Belfast and the Governor General, Lord Fitzalan. The last agreed to use his prerogative powers to delay the flogging.[163] Records are unclear, but it would seem that O'Byrne was eventually released under the general tidying up of those months.

W. T. Cosgrave, Acting Chairman of the Provisional Government, asked Churchill to use his influence to have flogging discontinued altogether. 'In many instances', he wrote, 'sentences of as many as 25 lashes have been inflicted for purely technical offences such as the possession of arms, and it is generally felt that these sentences are unnecessarily harsh and savour of political revenge.' The repeal of the Special Powers Act and the discontinuance of this 'very humiliating' punishment would have a most favourable effect on public opinion in Ireland and would go far to promote more cordial relations between England and Ireland.[164]

Irish ministers evidently received hints from British officials that strong representations were being made to Belfast and that they could hope for a rethink on the issue of flogging. In what was an unfortunate and presumptuous anticipation of this outcome, the *Freeman's Journal* on 17 August 1922 ran a report from its Belfast correspondent claiming 'on excellent authority' that floggings recently ordered by the Belfast City Commission had been indefinitely suspended 'and the general belief is that they will not be carried out'. The prisoners had been reassuring their friends to this effect 'and the news has been received with feelings of relief in this city'.[165] *Freeman's* had got it wrong, and among irate Northern ministers there was agreement that a public repudiation was necessary. On 22 August 1922, this appeared and produced a furious reaction in the Free State press.[166] Floggings continued to be ordered, although 1922 was the peak year, with twenty-seven sentences between April and November. In 1923 there were fifteen floggings, all in the first four months. Thereafter, until 1928, numbers fell to between one and four cases a year.[167]

A few of those sentenced to whipping succeeded in having that part of their sentence set aside. But of the seven sentenced at the Belfast Commission on 17 July 1922 for possession of explosives, all bar one were flogged on 10 October 1922; Anthony Canning, who had been convicted of armed robbery, was also flogged that day.[168] A tabulation of corporal punishment inflicted at Belfast Prison between 22 June 1922 and 5 March 1929, showed that fifty-five men had received the punishment. The majority of sentences were of fifteen strokes, but there were some of twelve, quite a few of ten and, between 1925 and 1929, several punishments of twenty lashes. Almost half the punishments were administered by the birch; the rest by the cat.[169] Liam Burke, an active IRA man in the late 1930s and 1940s, and former OC of prisoners in Belfast Prison, recalled that some of those who had been flogged had described the pain as 'negligible' and that the main intent seems to have been degradation.[170] This may have been the experience of one exceptionally hardy man, however, since quite a different account was given by Anthony Lavery. Three days into his sentence, he recorded the following: 'Pentland and McCready – the two men who were sentenced to 5 years and the cat – received the cat today. I heard them scream.'[171]

Floggings could have traumatic and disturbing effects on other prisoners. Cahir Healy, arrested and interned in May 1922, was told by a friendly member of staff about events at Belfast Prison which took place a couple of days after Healy and others had been transferred to the *Argenta*. Pending floggings were held over until the detainees had been removed. A navy pensioner was then brought in to inflict the punishments. The first to be dealt with was an adult whose back was left in a swollen and livid state, 'upon which the doctor clapped a plaster of iodine and salve. The pain must have been terrible.' The next to be flogged was a teenage boy:

> Having heard the cries of the first man, the boy's own cries could be heard far into the adjacent wing. Pandemonium broke out among the other prisoners. They lost control of themselves, smashed windows, stools, beds and a chorus of yells went up into the night... the whole prison roared like a herd of animals in dread of slaughter.[172]

Even then reeking of atavism, probably all members of Northern Ireland's cabinet favoured the use of corporal punishment or certainly had no great objection to it, and the group most directly involved with criminal justice (Bates, Megaw and Best) were strong advocates. Introducing the second reading of the Special Powers Bill, Megaw condemned the possession of explosives as 'one of the most nefarious means that one can think of in the commission of crimes'. There was no possible reason for a civilian to be in possession of a bomb; it was always intended to injure life or property 'in the most cowardly, sneakish fashion'. The person who was so degraded as to use a bomb 'certainly merits no leniency at the hands of justice'.[173] There was a strong belief, therefore, that the penalty was merited as retribution; it was also seen as an effective deterrent. Whilst agreeing that a precise causal relationship could not be shown, a Ministry of Home Affairs memorandum deduced from a reduction in the number of outrages in 1922 that whipping had had a deterrent effect. It was the almost unanimous opinion of those involved with the administration of justice that the threat of flogging was 'one of the most valuable weapons' against armed robbery, both for its special deterrent effect on those who were punished and as a general deterrent.[174] In January 1933, F. Bowl, a Belfast prison official, wrote to the Ministry of Home Affairs. He had looked into cases of flogging and birching in 1922–3 and had found that in no case had there been a repetition of the offence. Indeed, of the twenty-two men for whom he had full information, fifteen had not been recommitted to prison.[175]

A tabulation of sentences of flogging carried out in Northern Ireland between January 1922 and December 1928 shows, as might be expected, that there was a strong link between the sentences and episodes and periods of social and political conflict. Of the fifty-three floggings during that period, just over half (twenty-seven) were inflicted in 1922. This was the year when Northern Ireland was most under threat from border incursions, when communal tensions were high and episodes of riot and affray occurred with alarming frequency, and when civil war in the Free State induced a general sense of insecurity. A lesser number of floggings (fifteen) the following year were all concentrated in the first four months, coming entirely to a halt when the IRA was defeated in the South. Thereafter, the most significant feature of the infliction of the sentence was its concentration in July, the month in Northern Ireland which is fraught with the greatest tension; only November 1922 (fifteen cases) exceeded July in the frequency of floggings.[176] It would seem that both prosecutors and judges saw in the sentence an effective response to disorder and political violence, a general deterrent as well as justified retribution: authority's megaphone.

Belief in the efficacy of corporal punishment was quite unremarkable; such views have continued to be held by people of broadly conservative outlook into modern times. Demands that the whip be brought back used to be an annual feature of debates at British Conservative Party conferences and still erupt in the popular press following vile and outrageous crimes. The 1920s were, from any perspective, turbulent in Ireland. North and South, there had been sustained (and frequently effective) attempts to undermine law and order by any means to hand.[177] To re-establish law, some ministers argued, a firm hand and consistency of approach was needed. Judges and magistrates should be encouraged to use all the penalties at their disposal and to sentence vigorously. Once sentences had been imposed, attempts to modify them or to set them aside by political intervention should be discouraged. This was the line that Bates, Megaw and Best took with requests from the British and Free State governments for the release of prisoners such as Thomas Hueston and in the flogging cases.[178]

The approach was theoretically sound: it is the classic model of the division of powers in a liberal democracy. It was, however, open to two objections. These were the unruly early days of the creation of two new political entities, and, in seeking to wrest order from chaos, the rules of classic jurisprudence, whilst setting worthy aspirations, could not be a complete or exhaustive guide. Politics and justice had somehow to intersect for the general good, and this on occasion meant inconsistency and fudge. The second basis for doubt was even weightier and raised longer-term considerations. The use of flogging gave additional weight to the accusation that hard-line Unionist ministers were prepared to argue for an independent criminal-justice process (including vigorous sentencing) where Roman Catholic offenders were concerned but took a different line with Protestants. Almost certainly all Unionist MPs deplored Protestant rioting and illegality and the crimes of the paramilitary UPA. Yet electoral considerations and the fact that they needed the backing of the Belfast Protestant working class stayed the hand of justice and meant a more pragmatic approach to Protestant malefactors. This may have had the short-term effect of consolidating and strengthening the new government's position, but the long-term consequences were poisonous for the polity. Summarising his analysis of criminal justice in these formative years, Patrick Buckland observes that they produced a system of law enforcement that differed from that of the rest of the UK and that discriminated in favour of the majority population.[179] In Ireland, as elsewhere, it has repeatedly been shown that law must be impartially made and universally enforced. Should it fail to adhere to these principles, it will be hollowed out and will eventually fragment and disintegrate.

Notes

1 But not all: the Lighthouse Service of Ireland, administered by independent commissioners in Dublin for the whole of the Irish coast, was an exception to the policy of division.

2 Somalia is the prime example of complete collapse. A number of other states such as Sudan, Liberia and Afghanistan have experienced a collapse in large portions of territory.

3 By Order of the Lord Lieutenant, *Dublin Gazette*, 2 December 1921.

4 *Belfast Gazette*, 7 June 1921.

5 PRONI HA/9/2/490, Letter to governors of Belfast, Armagh and Londonderry prisons.

6 By powers derived from the GOIA, 1920; PRONI HA/9/2/126, Ministry of Home Affairs to Clerks of Petty Sessional Divisions, 30 November 1921.

7 PRONI HA/9/2/126, Ministry of Home Affairs to Sir John Anderson, Under-Secretary, Dublin Castle, 16 November 1921.

8 PRONI HA/9/2/126, Sir John Anderson, to Secretary, Ministry of Home Affairs, 21 November 1921.

9 PRONI HA/9/2/126, Ministry of Home Affairs to Sir John Anderson, 29 November 1921.

10 PRONI HA/9/2/126, marginal note by Samuel Watt on draft letter c.17 December 1921.

11 PRONI HA/9/2/126, undated draft (c. 17 December). It is not clear if this was sent. Watt probably did not wish to appear to be pressing the issue too much, since the transfer had already been agreed in principle.

12 PRONI HA/9/2/126, Divisional Commissioner's Office, Royal Irish Constabulary to Ministry of Home Affairs, 16 January 1922. The transfer took place on 14 January.

13 PRONI HA/9/2/126, Samuel Watt to Parliamentary Secretary and Minister, 20 December 1921.

14 PRONI HA/9/2/126, Watt to Bates, 20 December 1921.

15 PRONI HA/9/2/127, Memorandum by Sir Ernest Clark, 17 January 1921. (This had been wrongly dated 1920. The correct date is confirmed by related documents in the file.)

16 The Borstal system in particular placed a deal of emphasis on community ties, on local lay participation in assessing individual progress and on the resettlement of its trainees. All would be very difficult to supply for persons from Northern Ireland at such a remove from their home communities.

17 PRONI HA/9/2/127, Memorandum by Sir Ernest Clark, 21 January 1921. Clark suggested that a new prison be sited in relation to the Lough Neagh drainage and water resources power station. This showed a lack of knowledge of the quality of prison labour and the need to make prisons accessible for visitors and the courts.

18 PRONI HA/9/2/127, Memorandum, 27 January 1921.

19 PRONI HA/9/2/127, Memorandum, 29 January 1921.

20 See Charles W. Magill (ed.), *From Dublin Castle to Stormont: The Memoirs of Andrew Philip Magill, 1913–1925* (Cork: Cork University Press, 2003), for details of Magill's career and experiences.

21 Borstals had been developed out of modified forms of imprisonment and were intended to provide reformatory custody for young offenders. They were innovatory, treating the young as a special and promising category of offender and placing emphasis on individual progress within the institution and on preparation for release. They were given legal footing by the Prevention of Crime Act, 1908.

22 PRONI HA/9/2/121, Magill Memorandum, 27 September 1921.

23 Prevention of Crime Act, 1908, ss.13(2) and 18.

24 See Leon Radzinowicz and Roger Hood, *A History of English Criminal Law and Its Administration from 1750: The Emergence of Penal Policy in Victorian and Edwardian England* (Oxford: Clarendon, 1990).

25 Sections 13(2) and 18 of the 1908 Prevention of Crime Act empowered the lord lieutenant to designate part of a prison for preventive detention.

26 Inebriates Act, 1898: 61 & 62 Vict., c.60. This was associated with the Prisons Act, 1898: 61 & 62 Vict., c.41. The measure authorised the Lord Lieutenant of Ireland (by s.26[b]) to establish inebriate reformatories in Ireland. See also Shane Kilcommins, Ian O'Donnell, Eoin O'Sullivan and Barry Vaughan (eds.), *Crime, Punishment and the Search for Order in Ireland* (Dublin: IPA, 2004), p. 21 and *passim*.

27 *Annual Report of the Prisons Board for Ireland*, 1919–20.

28 Magill Memorandum, *op. cit.* A dedicated ward in an asylum might have been more apt.

29 By s.74(1) of the Children Act, 1908: 8 Edw. VII, c.67. See also ss.74(8, 10, 11 and 15).

30 Central Criminal Lunatic Asylum (Ireland) Act, 1845: 8 & 9 Vict., c.107, Preamble.

31 Persons serving sentences of penal servitude (two years and above) were known as convicts. This term dated back to the eighteenth century when those convicted of felony were either subject to the death penalty or, on commuted sentences, were transported overseas. Gradually, a system of central government prisons emerged, both to hold convicts prior to transportation and for others who, for various reasons, and under changing legislation, it had been decided not to transport. The alternative to transportation was a system of imprisonment and conditional release in the UK. This sentence was known as penal servitude. See Seán McConville, *A History of English Prison Administration, Vol. I: 1750–1877* (London: Routledge & Kegan Paul, 1981), Chapters, 7, 11 and 12. Much older than the convict prisons were the gaols and houses of correction under local-government control, which had existed from time immemorial. These were nationalised in 1878 and brought under the control of central government. To distinguish convicts from ordinary prisoners, the term 'local' was applied to the latter. To avoid confusion here, I have used the terms 'convict' and 'ordinary prisoners'. See also Seán McConville, *English Local Prisons, 1860–1900: Next Only to Death* (London and New York: Routledge, 1995).

32 PRONI HA/9/2/127, R. Ronaldson to Andrew Magill, Ministry of Home Affairs, 18 April 1922.

33 PRONI HA/9/2/121, Secretary for Home Affairs to Under-Secretary for Scotland, 12 December 1921.

34 The Free State was in the run-up to civil war during which the Clonmel Borstal lads would have to be moved in response to military and security concerns. The continued presence of Northern boys at Clonmel was clearly an oversight by a hard-pressed government and may have been of uncertain legality.

35 See *Belfast Telegraph*, 2 October 1920, 3d; 8 October 1920, 4d; 3 May 1921, 5d; for examples of the type and seriousness of disturbances. These and numerous other

pre-Truce offenders were duly sent to Belfast Prison, where disorder and destruction continued.

36 Ronaldson also pointed out that whereas the Northern government had been given a skeleton service, the Free State had received a 'full blooded Prison Service'. The Imperial Government had thus treated Northern Ireland 'very harshly' by not making provision for a full service or supplying the necessary funds.

37 PRONI HA/9/2/127, Ronaldson to Magill, 18 April 1922.

38 PRONI HA/9/2/121, Home Affairs to Scottish Office, 18 January 1922; to Scottish Prison Commissioners, 18 February 1922. The arrangement meant that any expenditure in addition to that covered by the agreement between the two governments became a subject of official correspondence. The Scottish authorities were anxious always to protect the public purse. (See, for example, the exchange regarding the purchase of books in Irish, PRONI HA/9/2/166.)

39 Besides their history of troublesome and refractory behaviour, the Irish convicts were the source of additional paperwork since their petitions and requests had to be forwarded to the Northern Ireland government for decision. See, for example, the request from Hugh Rogers, serving a life sentence at Maidstone, that he might have bound copies of the Northern Ireland Parliamentary Debate: PRONI HA/9/2/166, Petition of November 1923. Rogers was eventually repatriated, and he showed his gratitude on 9 May 1927 by escaping in company of three others (*Weekly Irish Times*, 14 May 1927, 6d); see also p. 129 above for details of the escape. I deal with the 1916–22 transfer to England of Irish prisoners in Seán McConville, *Irish Political Prisoners, 1848–1922: Theatres of War* (London and New York: Routledge, 2003), Chapters 10, 11, 13 and 15.

40 PRONI HA/9/2/121, Sir Dawson Bates to Lord Polworth (Chairman, Scottish Prison Commissioners), 20 March 1922.

41 The Visiting Justices at Belfast Prison found that less than half that number had caused difficulties, due to the limited facilities that the prison had for their segregation from other classes of prisoner. PRONI HA/9/2/50, Report of Visiting Justices to Governor of Northern Ireland, 2 January 1924.

42 PRONI HA/9/2/121, Samuel Watt to Sir Maurice Waller, Chairman, Prison Commission, 19 December 1922. The letter added (somewhat undiplomatically) that the question of building both a convict prison and a Borstal had been 'under consideration' but that it would take 'some years' to build even after the preliminary work of securing a site and preparing it. This was not a wise message to be sending to an agency which had unfortunate experiences with Irish convicts and which might reasonably be averse to being nudged into providing them with long-term accommodation.

43 The days of raucous IRA protests and demonstrations were past, and a large proportion of the transferred convicts and almost all the Borstal boys were ordinary criminals. The arrangement was an untidy one, however, since it meant that persons convicted in one jurisdiction, with its own laws, rules and regulations, and chain of responsibility and decision-making, were being held in other jurisdictions. Decisions on special visits, compassionate parole or other matters had to be made in the originating jurisdiction, according to its rules and precedents.

44 In the files, the confidential contact is identified only as 'Mr. A'. He may have been a Dublin Castle civil servant who dealt with prisoners, or even a former prison officer, such as a chief warder. There are few clues to his identity other than his knowledge of prison affairs and his deep antipathy to Sinn Féin and all its works. Lloyd Campbell took a particular interest in security matters (especially police and prisons) and, at the request of Sir Dawson Bates, chaired a departmental committee on the policing requirements and administration of the new state. See Bryan A. Follis, *A State under Siege: The Establishment of Northern Ireland, 1920–25* (Oxford: Clarendon, 1995), p. 85.

45 This and following quotations are taken from the notes of the meeting with 'Mr. A.' at PRONI HA/2/121, marked 'Secret' and dated 14 December 1921.

46 For the incident at Derry Prison on the 2 December 1921, see PRONI HA/9/2/ 128. Besides the tragedy of two deaths, due to a reckless rather than malicious use of chloroform, the attempted escape shocked the Northern Ireland government because it happened within hours of its assumption of prison powers and involved inside collusion (two temporary warders were arrested) and a well-resourced outside operation to get the prisoners out of the district.

47 See below, pp. 396–97.

48 The conveyance of 'the ordinary Belfast prostitutes' between Belfast and Armagh was costly, and, moreover, 'the public are beginning to object to travelling in the train with them'. There was also a problem with laundering clothes at Belfast Prison. This had been done by female prisoners, but, since they were now all held in Armagh, the work had to be sent out and paid for. Notes on meeting with 'Mr. A.', *op. cit.*

49 PRONI HA/0/2/403, John McConville to Sir Dawson Bates, 19 June 1924.

50 Criminal Justice Administration Act, 1914: 4 & 5 Geo. V, c.58.

51 This was amended by the Criminal Justice Administration Act, 1914, s.17(2).

52 PRONI HA/9/2/403, note of 10 July 1924.

53 The Governor was empowered to make this order by the GOIA and the Irish Free State (Consequential Provisions) Act, 1922: 13 Geo. V, c.2. The relevant prison legislation was the General Prisons (Ireland) Act, 1877, and the Criminal Justice Administration Act, 1914. The Visiting Justices at Belfast Prison did not agree with this arrangement and recommended that part of their prison again be used for females, 'with a view to saving expense and publicity'. PRONI HA/9/2/50, Report of Visiting Justices, Belfast Prison, to Governor of Northern Ireland, 2 January 1924.

54 With a deal of justification, the Belfast Visiting Justices protested at what they saw as presumption and a slight on their office. This had been their first notification of the change, which would have far-reaching effects on the prison. Why had their views not been sought? PRONI HA/9/2/50, Report of Visiting Justices, Belfast Prison, to Governor of Northern Ireland, 7 January 1925.

55 In a note of 7 November 1921, Andrew Magill pointed out that the annual per-capita cost of holding a convict or Borstal prisoner in Scotland was 'much less' than in Ireland. The cost for reformatory places, by contrast, was higher. PRONI HA/9/2/121, Magill Memorandum. These figures were calculated on pre-Treaty and pre-Partition returns.

56 PRONI HA/9/2/121, Memorandum, 18 September 1924.

57 Work and workshops would have to be provided; A Wing, Belfast, would need electric lighting; all building work of refurbishment would need to be completed and new exercise rings laid out; additional quarters had to be provided for married warders and extra sleeping quarters for warders within Belfast Prison. It was suggested that, with a proper modern workshop, the convicts could make uniforms for the RUC. Much of the construction work could also be carried out by prisoners, it was thought.

58 PRONI HA/9/2/276, Ministry of Justice to Comptroller and Auditor General, 13 January 1927.

59 On resistance to prison closures, see McConville, *English Local Prisons, op. cit.*, pp. 195–6.

60 See, for example, PRONI HA/9/2/490, Ministry of Home Affairs to Max Green, Chairman, General Prisons Board to Ministry of Home Affairs, 25 November 1921, etc. A number of individual requests could not be met since there were no vacancies at the prison in question.

61 See above, n. 46.

62 *Freeman's Journal*, 3 December 1921, 5c.

63 PRONI HA/9/2/490, Samuel Watt to Sir Dawson Bates, 6 December 1921.

64 PRONI HA/9/2/490, Samuel Watt to Sir John Anderson, 2 December 1921.

65 PRONI HA/9/2/490, Sir John Anderson to Samuel Watt, 9 December 1921.

66 PRONI HA/9/2/490, Samuel Watt to Sir John Anderson, 12 December 1921; see also Samuel Watt to Sir Ernest Clark, 16 January 1922.

67 PRONI HA/9/2/490, Minute, Andrew Magill to Samuel Watt, 26 January 1922, Watt's annotation.

68 This was, essentially, to supervise Catholic religious services in the prison chapel.

69 PRONI HA/9/2/490.

70 PRONI HA/9/2/490, Sir John Anderson to Samuel Watt, 3 February 1922.

71 Indictable crime (generally more serious offences which could not be dealt with in the magistrates' courts) remained fairly static in Northern Ireland throughout the 1920s and 1930s, averaging around 3,000 cases a year. Looking at the indictable offences reported to the police, there were spikes in 1922 (just over 5,000 cases), 1931 (3,600 cases), 1934 (3,700 cases), 1935 (4,500 cases), 1936 (3,600 cases) and 1937 (3,500 cases). These upward fluctuations coincided with IRA activity and public disorder. Detections (as distinct from reports) averaged around 2,000 cases a year. PRONI HA/32/1/75. Successful prosecutions were in a lower range. The average daily population remained relatively low: around 300 through the 1920s and 1930s. Receptions into custody of ordinary prisoners also remained remarkably constant at an average of around 2,500. By contrast, annual receptions of convicts was tiny: fifteen in 1925, eight in 1933, seven in 1934 and a sharp rise up to twenty-three in 1935. PRONI HA/9/2/140, Annual Report of Prisons, 1935.

72 See Thomas Bartlett, *Ireland: A History* (Cambridge: Cambridge University Press, 2010), p. 439.

73 Pay scales in the Northern Ireland Prison Service were not brought into line with those of Britain until quite recent times. Morgan had made a strong recommendation for assimilation in his 1927 Report, pointing out, in particular, that the RUC had secured parity with its English counterpart.

74 PRONI HA/9/2/78, Ministry of Home Affairs to Ministry of Finance, 14 January 1928. Bates also pointed to the need, which had been emphasised by Morgan, to remove a feeling of injustice among the staff and to revive the *esprit de corps*.

75 PRONI HA/9/2/140, Annual Report of Prisons, 1935.

76 PRONI HA/9/2/140. There may have been an implication in this example of the consequences of a shortage of Catholic staff, that this important penitential and reformatory sacrament of the Church was being neglected.

77 See p. 375 above.

78 See p. 383.

79 PRONI HA/9/2/32, Minute to Minister of Home Affairs, 8 May 1926. All further details of the convict regime are from this source.

80 Ronaldson had asked the Governor of Belfast Prison for his opinions on convict privileges and had incorporated all the suggestions he made in the memorandum to the Minister.

81 PRONI HA/9/2/32, Ronaldson to Minister, 8 May 1926.

82 These were Francis Boyle, William Conlon, Hugh Rogers and Edward Thornton. Boyle, Conlon and Rogers were serving life sentences imposed at court martial in July 1921 for the murder of William McDowell, a garage owner, at Gilford, Co. Down, on 3 September 1920. Edward Thornton was serving twelve years' penal servitude for wounding a girl on a suburban train (see p. 158, n. 95).

83 PRONI HA/9/2/78, George A. Harris, Secretary, Ministry of Home Affairs, to Lieutenant-Colonel H. S. Rogers, Prison Commission, London, 13 June 1927.

84 PRONI HA/9/2/138, Morgan Report, 16 August 1927. Following escapes at Belfast Prison, as we have seen, Captain Morgan, Governor of Dartmoor (then by reputation the most secure of the English prisons), was sent over at the request of the Ministry of Home Affairs to conduct a security review. Most of his recommendations

related to keys and physical security (the prison locks having been shown by the attempted escape to be weak). He also made suggestions about the deployment of staff, particularly for night duty. PRONI HA/32/1/626, Follow-up report, 16 August 1927. The reference to the morally deleterious effects of labour performed only in workshops was probably based on the notion that convicts should, when returned to their cells, be in a tired state and in need of sleep. This would cut off the much lamented and pernicious inclination to engage in criminal or sexual reveries.

85 PRONI HA/9/2/138, Morgan Report, 16 August 1927. Whether the quality and energy of the Belfast officers was at this time equal to such all-round responsibility was not explored by Captain Morgan.

86 PRONI HA/9/2/138, George A. Harris to Ministry of Home Affairs, 12 December 1927.

87 PRONI HA/32/1/626, Captain R. W. Stephenson to Ministry of Justice, 3 August 1936.

88 These extra amenities were introduced with little regard for the need for additional staffing. When Morgan conducted his 1927 security review, he pointed out that most of the staff went off duty at 5 p.m., when the prison was supposedly locked up for the day. On certain evenings, all convicted prisoners who had served more than three months in prison were allowed out of their cells for a lecture or a concert. At such times, only twelve staff were on duty for the entire prison. He recommended that the concerts and lectures be held mid-afternoon, when the prison was fully staffed. This recommendation was rejected since those who provided the concerts and lectures would not be available at that time of day. Afternoon lectures and concerts also interfered with the prisoners' work. PRONI HA/32/1/626, Morgan Report, p. 3, see also follow-up at HA 9/2/138.

89 PRONI HA/9/2/50, Report of Visiting Justices, Belfast Prison, to Governor of Northern Ireland, 5 January 1927.

90 During 1924, several subscriptions to the *Belfast Telegraph* were donated by Sir Robert Baird, a Visiting Justice. PRONI HA/9/2/50, Report of Visiting Justices to Governor of Northern Ireland, 7 January 1925.

91 This requirement arose from a recommendation by Captain Morgan. PRONI HA/32/1/626, Report dated 16 August 1927.

92 PRONI HA/9/2/137, Memorandum, 8 September 1927. Where a prisoner's intended visitor or correspondent lived in the Free State, prison officials were instructed to direct their enquiries to the Inspector-General of the RUC with a request that they be forwarded to the Civic Guard.

93 Thus, Seán McCool wrote (in Irish) to Nora O'Kane of Draperstown, Co. Londonderry, sending a visiting permit. He explained to her that the intended visitors should take the names of persons already on the approved list – herself and McCool's sister-in-law: 'Tell Katie not to forget their new names when they arrive at the Prison... and you might let her know that we are allowed cigs, and sweets, on visits!' (PRONI HA/9/2/137, Intercepted letter, 3 August 1939). The proposed deception suggests that visitors (young women in particular, perhaps) were not too closely questioned at the prison. There was some alarm about this possibility at the Ministry of Home Affairs. There was also legitimate concern about how the letter (which had been discovered by the RUC during a raid on premises at Draperstown) had been smuggled out of prison, and by whom. The Governor was also asked if he was satisfied with the manner in which visits were conducted and whether cigarettes and sweets were not being passed into the prison. PRONI HA/9/2/137, Ministry of Home Affairs, Secret, to Captain T. M. Stuart, Governor, Belfast Prison, 24 September 1939.

94 PRONI HA/9/2/137, Memorandum, 16 September 1952. There is some indication that the change was made at the request of the RUC.

95 PRONI HA/9/2/166, Captain R. W. Stephenson to Ministry of Home Affairs, 14 April 1936, annotations.

96 *Irish Times*, 28 December 1935, 7c. See also J. Bowyer Bell, *The Secret Army: The IRA, 1916–1979* (Cambridge, Mass.: MIT Press, 1983), pp. 123–5.

97 See *Irish Independent*, 30 December 1935, 7d.

98 *Irish Times*, 27 April 1936, 7a.

99 PRONI HA/32/1/626, 'Safety of Belfast Prison', 11 March 1936. The visit had taken place the week before.

100 PRONI HA/32/1/626, Captain R. W. Stephenson to Ministry of Home Affairs, 9 April 1936. Stephenson continued to hold his master-keys when outside the prison. No one knew where he kept them, and, he assured the Ministry, 'they are never far away from a loaded revolver'. The purpose of taking the keys out of the prison was to allow the Governor to enter unannounced during the night-time hours, when laxness by staff might most be expected and the knowledge that a visit was possible would discourage slacking.

101 PRONI HA/32/1/626, Captain R. W. Stephenson to Ministry of Home Affairs, 27 April 1936.

102 PRONI HA/32/1/626, Ministry of Home Affairs to Captain R. W. Stephenson, 28 April 1936. The following day, Stephenson reported to the Ministry that a district inspector of the RUC had called at the prison and had shown him a plan of the prison and two photographs. Stephenson was certain that the person who had drawn the plan had been in the prison before 1928. This material strongly suggested an attack on the prison or that an escape was being planned, or both.

103 PRONI HA/32/1/626, Ministry of Home Affairs to Captain R. W. Stephenson, 30 July 1936. This may have been a political precaution to guard himself against a charge of insufficient diligence should an incident have taken place. Stephenson, unless he were remarkable naive, would have recognised that he was being asked to give something in the nature of a guarantee.

104 PRONI HA/32/1/626, Captain R. W. Stephenson to Ministry of Home Affairs, 3 August 1936.

105 PRONI HA/32/1/626, Ministry of Home Affairs to Captain T. M. Stuart, Governor, Belfast Prison, 20 April 1938.

106 See PRONI HA/32/1/635. The journal may have been discovered in a cell search and left undisturbed to be read, from time to time when Lavery was out of his cell, at work or exercise.

107 Internment, by definition, was for political reasons and did not entail a criminal conviction, and there was no question but that internees should be kept apart from other prisoners. Privileges were conceded by the British government to persons convicted of politically motivated offences, and some of these remained in Northern Ireland's prisons when the new state was formed in 1920. These prisoners were, with few exceptions, released in the Treaty settlement.

108 PRONI HA/32/1/635, Lavery journal. (All following quotations from this source.)

109 C. Lloyd (ed.), *Captain Cook's Voyages of Discovery* (London: Dent, 1920); Agnes Strickland, *The Life of Queen Elizabeth* (London: Dent, 1924). Both were probably the popular Everyman editions.

110 These rumours were not taken up by the press.

111 See K. S. Isles, in Thomas Wilson (ed.), *Ulster under Home Rule* (Oxford: Oxford University Press, 1955), pp. 116–17; see also Norman Cuthbert, *An Economic Survey of Northern Ireland* (Belfast: HMSO, 1957), pp. 566–77; and F. S. L. Lyons, *Ireland since the Famine* (London: Fontana, 1973), p. 710.

112 There is a large literature on poor relief and the workhouse, in particular. Charles Dickens referred to it repeatedly, as did Thomas Hardy, writing three or four

decades later. Many commentators, contemporary and historical, confirmed that it was an institution feared and detested by working people. This was hardly surprising when one considers its origins. One of the early Poor Law commissioners proclaimed that 'our intention is to make the workhouses as like prisons as possible', and another promised to try 'to establish therein a discipline so severe and repulsive as to make them a terror to the poor and prevent them from entering', quoted in E. P. Thompson, *The Making of the English Working Class* (Harmondsworth: Penguin, 1968), p. 295.

113 Workhouses were popularly known as 'the Union' because the institutions were operated by Poor Law unions, which brought several local authorities together for the purpose. On the workhouse generally, see Norman Longmate, *The Workhouse: A Social History* (London: Pimlico, 2003); see also Peter Wood, *Poverty and the Workhouse in Victorian Britain* (Stroud: Allan Sutton, 1991). More locally, see Michael Farrell, *The Poor Law and the Workhouse in Belfast, 1838–1948* (Belfast: Public Record Office of Northern Ireland, 1978). See also R. J. Lawrence, *The Government of Northern Ireland: Public Finance and Public Services, 1921–1964* (Oxford: Oxford University Press, 1965), Chapter 9.

114 Excellent accounts of the casual wards remain in George Orwell's *Down and Out in Paris and London* (London: Victor Gollancz, 1933) and Jack London's *People of the Abyss* (New York: Macmillan & Co., 1903). 'A night in the casual wards' was also a frequent topic for contemporary journalists, making the point that this was an exotic and reassuringly remote world for the middle and established working classes.

115 *Irish Times*, 10 October 1932, 2f. In reporting the disturbances, the newspaper added that '[i]n Roman Catholic churches in Belfast today the congregations were exhorted to take no part in any unemployed demonstrations and to use any influence they possessed to prevent disturbances in the city'. The *Irish Independent* (12 October 1932, 8b) blamed both the authorities and the demonstrators for the troubles. The plan for a mass march, the newspaper contended, 'savours unpleasantly of intimidation', but the attempt to suppress by force all demonstrations by the unemployed 'was singularly ill-advised'. Lyons (*Ireland since the Famine, op. cit.*, p. 713) points out that in some country areas of Northern Ireland the weekly dole for a single person could be as little as 2s. 6d. and in Belfast, 12s. for a married man with one child. Body and soul might be kept together on such sums, but only just – this was existence, not living. A new settlement was announced by the Poor Law Committee on 15 October. Outdoor relief work (short spells of labouring on the roads) had been remunerated at 8s. a week. The work was hard, and many of the men were unsuited to it, so to have such a low payment was intolerable. The Board of Guardians showed how inadequate the rate had been when they announced that thencefoward it would be tripled to 24s. a week for a married man – meagre subsistence instead of near-impossible subsistence. See *Irish Independent*, 14 October 1932, 7f.

116 Both Protestant clergy and Nationalist members of Stormont had (separately) drawn attention to the pressures of unemployment, with 12,000 people in East Belfast alone 'at starvation point'. With 50,000 registered unemployed, 'the storm clouds were gathering in more dangerous volume' (*Irish Independent*, 7 November 1932, 9c).

117 See p. 320, n. 118 above. To take but one example from the period, the Roman Catholic Bishop of Killaloe, Dr Michael Fogarty, contended in a sermon that the 'present awful condition of society was due to the domination of un-Christian principles'. There would be no solution save by a return to the social principle of Christ. He also condemned socialism 'in the true sense it is of its very nature anti-Christian, being opposed to the Divine Order of society'. There was no such thing as Christian socialism: 'A very short time would wear off the Christian gilding from your social structure and leave you only the rusty iron of ghastly Bolshevism' (*Nenagh Guardian*, 5 November 1932, 6a). See also *Irish Times*, 6 October 1932, 6a.

118 Bell, *The Secret Army, op. cit.*, Chapter 6.

119 *Irish News*, 13 October 1934, 7c.

120 Geehan was fined £10 and the following January lost his appeal against this sentence. (*Irish Independent* 18 January 1935, 5f).

121 *Irish News*, 12 October 1934, 7c; *Irish Times*, 17 October 1934, 7d.

122 *Belfast Newsletter*, 13 October 1934; *Irish News*, 13 October 1934. Ben Murray (1895–1938) had been a soldier during the First World War and was an early member of the Communist Party of Ireland and then the Communist Party of Great Britain (CPGB). He later fought on the Republican side in Spain. He was killed on 14 March 1938 in the battle of Aragon. (See *Belfast Telegraph*, 13 December 1938, 15c, for a list of the men from Ulster who fought and died in the International Brigade.) Murray would have been regarded by both Belfast and Dublin as a dangerous figure, confirming fears of subversive influence in the Unemployed Workers' Movement.

123 Thomas Geehan had described the two-week strike by relief workers for better wages as 'the most glorious in the history of the working class in the North' (*Irish Times*, 17 October 1932, 7d). That was ever the hope of the Irish left, that working-class solidarity would transcend religious divisions.

124 This allowed executive detention and had often been (and would again) be used as a prelude to internment.

125 Special Powers Act, 1933, Regulation 22B (8a–c). The Act, which had been renewed annually since 1922, had been extended and made permanent in the spring of 1933. So wide a discretion was conferred on the executive that the Minister for Home Affairs could probably have ordered action against anyone or anything he considered to be seditious, subversive or even distasteful.

126 PRONI HA/32/1/602, Disturbances, 1933–4.

127 PRONI HA/32/1/602, Memorandum of 15 May 1934.

128 *Northern Whig*, 24 July 1934, 8e. There was an offence of a similar kind in Dungannon, Co. Tyrone, which culminated in an assault on the police and a sentence of three months' imprisonment (*Irish News*, 24 July 1924, 6b).

129 *Northern Whig*, 16 August 1934, 7c. The Hibernian contingent came from Portadown, Co. Armagh, an area noted for sectarian tension and for periodic strife. The Ancient Order of Hibernians is a Catholic fraternal order.

130 *Belfast Telegraph*, 27 July 1934, 3c.

131 *Irish News*, 9 August 1934, 5g.

132 The activities amounted to little of substance. Uinseann MacEoin, a well-informed and close observer (and sometime member) of the IRA, was probably close to the truth when he observed that '[t]he outbreak of the Civil War in June 1922 so effectively throttled the Northern IRA that, for sixteen years thereafter, it existed almost solely as a commemorative body'. Uinseann MacEoin, *The IRA in the Twilight Years, 1923–1948* (Dublin: Argenta, 1997), p. 240. This is certainly confirmed contemporaneously, with regard to prisoners' aid, by IRA communications that have survived in the Moss Twomey Papers. On 20 January 1924, Twomey (then Chief of Staff) reported to the Army Council on the state of the organisation in the North. The IRPDF, Twomey noted, did not exist outside some towns. He had tried to impress on Southern OCs the necessity to assist those north of the border: 'Morale is so low up there that if we could treat dependents [*sic*] and others well it would have a good effect of restoring it' (Twomey Papers, P/69/35/168). There was some difficulty indeed in persuading republican prisoners who had been released by the Free State authorities to return to their home areas. The IRPDF was urged to help (P/69/35/197).

133 See the case of John McKenna, who, on 6 December 1933, was convicted of illegally drilling a group of eighteen youths at the McKelvey Hall, Whiterock Road, Belfast (*Belfast Newsletter*, 7 December 1933, 14b). The boys admitted being members of the

Fianna. Those under age were discharged to their parents, and the remainder were fined £10 each. McKenna, who refused to recognise the court, was sentenced to two months' imprisonment. Interestingly, the court does not seem to have regarded it as an aggravating factor that none of the boys were willing to promise to sever connections with the Fianna organisation.

134 *Belfast Newsletter*, 16 October 1934, 14c. McAnena was said to have been a captain in the IRA. For a similar case, see the *Belfast Newsletter*, 1 December 1933. Four men were charged with electioneering in Dungannon, Co. Tyrone, on behalf of Sinn Féin. Three were sent to prison, but one, who recognised the court and promised to sever connections with the IRA, was bound over to keep the peace for two years.

135 This computation was made by Anthony Lavery, who had been imprisoned at least once before, serving a three-month sentence in 1933 for the possession of documents (PRONI HA/32/1/602). As noted, Lavery kept a prison journal from 22 July until 21 August 1936. At some point it and a number of letters between the prisoners were seized, transcribed and filed (see PRONI HA/32/1/635). Despite his resolution to break with the IRA Lavery would be interned during the war years and was one of the last to be released, at Christmas 1945.

136 The prison rules provided for small ameliorations and privileges at various stages of the sentence. Advance to a stage, originally determined by marks recorded each day, was by this time more or less automatic, and came with time served and good – or at least *not bad* – behaviour. The stage system was an inducement to prisoners to conform, and the accrued privileges were available to the authorities for removal, in the event of indiscipline. Lavery's view was apparently confirmed by Captain Stephenson who was reported to have said that had the men made application through the usual channels instead of putting their requests as demands, 'some concessions would have been granted' (*Irish News*, 7 September 1936, 5c).

137 PRONI HA/9/2/180, Captain R. W. Stephenson to Ministry of Home Affairs, c.30 September 1936.

138 PRONI HA/32/1/635, Seán McCool, OC Belfast Prison, to all Section OCs, 15 August 1936.

139 PRONI HA/9/2/180, Captain R. W. Stephenson to Ministry of Home Affairs, 18 August 1936.

140 PRONI HA/9/2/180, Charles McGlade to Anthony Lavery, 22 August 1936. Because it was so short-lived, the strike received little notice outside the prison, but there was a report in the *Irish News* on Saturday, 22 August (7f). At this point, according to the Governor, there were about twenty men refusing food.

141 *Irish News*, 7 September 1936, 7c.

142 *Irish News*, 10 September 1936, 5e.

143 The same procedure was followed. The two men refused work as unfitting to their political status. They were immediately brought before the Governor on a disciplinary charge. He imposed the usual punishment of fourteen days' No. 2 diet and loss of privileges. Killeen and McCool refused to accept the punishment diet and thus embarked on a hunger strike. PRONI HA/9/2/180, Captain R. W. Stephenson to Ministry of Home Affairs, undated, but probably 30 September 1936.

144 PRONI HA/9/2/180, Kennedy announced his hunger strike on 18 August 1936 and came off it the same day.

145 PRONI HA/9/2/180, Inspector-General's Office, RUC, to R. P. Pim, Assistant Secretary, Ministry of Home Affairs, 4 November 1936. RUC suspicions were further increased because of a letter from Jimmy Steele's brother, Daniel. This disingenuously urged Steele's transfer to the hospital to get him away from bad influences in the prison: 'He was always a very good quiet boy as anyone who knows him can testify to this, even Protestant gentlemen can prove this only for his Political opinion,

which his family do not believe in' (PRONI HA/9/2/180, Daniel Steele to Ministry of Home Affairs, 24 October 1936).

146 Bell, *The Secret Army*, *op. cit.*, p. 125.

147 See above, p. 396.

148 NAI JUS/90/16/143, Max S. Green to Sir John Anderson, 7 April 1920.

149 *Belfast Newsletter*, 26 November 1926, 5c.

150 The sedition provision in the Act had, ironically, been inserted at the urging of the Irish Parliamentary Party. See McConville, *English Local Prisons*, *op. cit.*, p. 371.

151 *NIPD*, vol. 6, col. 1955, 14 December 1925; McConville, *English Local Prisons*, *op. cit.*, pp. 369–77. The courts' powers to send an offender to a particular division (form of imprisonment) were discontinued by the 1948 Criminal Justice Act: 11 & 12 Geo. VI, c.58, s.1(3).

152 PRONI HA/9/2/133, Minute by R. Ronaldson, 25 April 1939. Because of the impact upon the parliamentary agenda of the preparations for war, the Bill did not go forward, and the charges referred to by Ronaldson, and many others, had to wait until the sweeping Criminal Justice Act, 1948, was brought in. There had been substantial relaxation in the Northern Ireland convict rules in 1926 and an easing of the silence rule for them and for ordinary prisoners. PRONI HA/9/2/32, minute of 8 May 1926.

153 Larceny Act, 1916, s.37.

154 See *NIPD*, vol. 2, cols. 90–1, 156–7, 23 March 1922. See also PRO CO/739/1, Robert Megaw to Winston Churchill, 6 September 1922 (memo on flogging in Northern Ireland).

155 PRONI HA/9/2/885.

156 See Ian Gibson, *The English Vice: Beating, Sex and Shame in Victorian England and After* (London: Duckworth, 1992), Chapters 2, 3 and 4. See also the anti-flogging work of Henry Stephens Salt, *The Flogging Craze* (London: Allen & Unwin, 1916).

157 See McConville, *English Local Prisons*, *op. cit.*, p. 350, n. 93.

158 McConville, *English Local Prisons*, *op. cit.*, p. 248, n. 49.

159 The whippings (up to 150 strokes for adults and seventy-five for juveniles) could be imposed in three instalments of fifty and twenty-five strokes, respectively, during the first six months of a prison sentence (a maximum of penal servitude for life). See Security from Violence Act, 1863: 26 & 27 Vict., c.44.

160 Criminal Justice Act, 1948, s.2.

161 See Megaw to Churchill memorandum, 6 September 1922, *op. cit.*; PRO CO/739/1, Sir Wilfrid Spender to Lionel Curtis, 14 September 1922; PRONI PM/9/3, Sir Wilfrid Spender to Sir James Craig, 15 and 16 September 1922.

162 NAI TAOIS/S/570/10, Michael Collins to Winston Churchill, 4 August 1922; see also Commandant General Dan Hogan, OC, 5th Northern Division, to Chief of General Staff Eoin O'Duffy initiating complaint and claiming that O'Byrne was 'in Belfast Jail in a dying condition'.

163 NAI TAOIS/S/570/10, W. T. Cosgrave, Acting Chairman of Provisional Government, to Michael Collins, Commander-in-Chief, 9 August 1922.

164 NAI TAOIS/S1443/22, W. T. Cosgrave to Winston Churchill, 15 August 1922.

165 *Freeman's Journal*, 17 August 1922, 5e. The City Commission had imposed eight flogging sentences on 17 July. Seven were for the possession of explosives and one was for armed robbery. In five of the cases, ten lashes were ordered; the remainder were ordered fifteen lashes each.

166 *Irish Independent*, 22 August 1922; *Freeman's Journal*, 22 August 1922; *Northern Whig*, 21 August 1922, 5g.

167 PRONI HA/32/1/75, 'Return of Flogging Ordered and Subsequently Carried Out'. See also HA9/2/885.

168 PRONI HA/32/1/75, 'Return of Persons Who Have Received Corporal Punishment at This Prison'.

169 *Ibid.* The cat was used on the bare back, the birch on the buttocks. A doctor certified the prisoner before punishment commenced and was in attendance throughout, under an obligation to stop the proceedings should medical cause arise.

170 MacEoin, *The IRA in the Twilight Years, op cit.*, p. 458. Brendan Anderson's biography of Joe Cahill draws on the same source with the addition of a tale that seems to suggest that the ordeal was as much moral and mental as physical. One of those birched in the 1940s was visited by his mother, who solicitously enquired about the state of his back. The enquiry was put so frequently that the son eventually expostulated, 'I told you dozens of times, Mother, it was not my back, it was my arse.' Brendan Anderson, *Joe Cahill: A Life in the IRA* (Dublin: The O'Brien Press, 2002), p. 98.

171 Lavery's journal, *op. cit.* The men's offence was apparently non-political and took place at Drumbeg, Newtownbreda, on the night of 11 April 1936. James Pentland and Robert McCready, both of Belfast, were found guilty of assaulting and attempting to rob Mrs Elizabeth Quee, whilst armed with a revolver. All the aggravating factors were present in this case, prompting the judge (Mr Justice Megaw) to consider corporal punishment. See *Irish Times*, 11 July 1936, 9g.

172 PRONI, Cahir Healy Papers, D/2991/B/140/52, f. 3.

173 *NIPD*, vol. 2, col. 90, 21 March 1922. At this point the Nationalist MPs were boycotting the Northern parliament, so there was no counter-argument. Much the same view was taken of firearms. Several years later, some judges were as willing to order corporal punishment. Sentencing seven young men to lengthy terms of imprisonment for firearms and explosives offences, the judge singled out Thomas Byrne, who had fired a shot at a police car (and was the only one actually to use his weapon). Had it not been for the fact that the wounded Byrne was still in hospital, he would have ordered him the flogging 'he so well deserved' (*Irish News*, 23 November 1940). This may have been an IRA fund-raising operation. On 20 September 1940, five post offices and two banks were robbed in Belfast. Seven young men received sentences of fifty-eight years' penal servitude between them; Byrne was given twelve years.

174 PRONI HA/9/2/885, Memorandum on Flogging, prepared at the request of the *Northern Whig*.

175 PRONI HA/9/2/885, F. Bowl to Kirke, Ministry of Home Affairs, 18 January 1933. He did add the caveat that those flogged in 1922–3 were generally not the confirmed type of criminal but were young men aged nineteen to twenty-seven, in many cases first offenders, who had been led astray by disorderly and riotous mobs.

176 PRONI HA/32/1/75, Return of Sentences of Flogging. This tabulation was made in 1932.

177 And, of course, during the Second World War, when the Irish government, anxious above all to protect its neutrality and not to give cause for British (or, indeed, American) intervention, enacted extremely severe penalties against the IRA. Punishments included whipping. On 11 June 1941, a sentence of fourteen years' penal servitude and twelve lashes was imposed on William Stewart for armed bank robbery on behalf of the IRA. Three months later, Patrick Murphy, a member of the same unit, appeared before the Military Tribunal on a range of charges, including armed bank robbery. He received the same sentence. The flogging, which he recalls in Uinseann MacEoin's invaluable *IRA in the Twilight Years (op. cit.*, p. 530), was much more painful than he imagined and left him bedridden for several days. For the court appearance, see *Irish Independent*, 27 September 1941, 8c.

178 See pp. 411–12 above.

179 Patrick Buckland, *The Factory of Grievances: Devolved Government in Northern Ireland, 1921–39* (Dublin: Gill & Macmillan, 1979), p. 220. See also Chapter 9 generally.

9

THE 1939–40 BOMBING CAMPAIGN

Action stations

As we have seen, by the mid-1930s the IRA was in crisis and decay. Against the predictions and dogma of many republicans, Éamon de Valera's Fianna Fáil came peacefully to office in March 1932 and consolidated its position in another general election less than a year later. This siphoned away a deal of the anti-Treaty bitterness that had caused many to adhere to the IRA.[1] The transfer of power challenged the basic assumptions and claims of physical-force politics, whilst the departure from office of the Civil War's victors meant that all but diehard republicans could begin to identify with government and state and to concede credibility to the political process. The territory staked out by the IRA shrank further as de Valera advanced constitutionally towards his realisation of the Republic, his path cleared by the 1931 Statute of Westminster, which confirmed the national sovereignty of all dominions.[2] All the demands of the anti-Treaty side – abolition of the Oath, removal of the Crown from the Irish constitution, the assertion of unfettered sovereignty and the cutting of imperial ties with Britain – had been or would be achieved by de Valera. This was obvious to all who were prepared to cast off the doctrine of the survival of the authority of the Second Dáil.

All republican demands but one: Ireland remained partitioned, and a wide swathe of opinion, nationalist as well as republican, rejected the legitimacy of the Northern Ireland state. It had, they contended, been gerrymandered into existence and continued to exist against the wishes of the majority of the Irish people. In some fashion (never entirely clear in the critiques and so skirted over) it served British imperial interests. Its exclusion of Roman Catholics from power, the partisan operation of state machinery and even the expression of their own national and cultural identity by Protestants and Unionists, confirmed for many nationalists the malignity of Northern Ireland. The grievances, disadvantages and wrongs of the Catholic minority – real, exaggerated or simply imagined – kept the pot of indignation on a rolling boil. The overthrow of the Southern state would remain the long-term goal for a minority of committed republicans, but the more immediate republican objective was the reunification of Ireland by whatever force necessary.

The fissures in thought and perception that in modern times would reshape and reorient the IRA were already there. Activists from the South had little or no idea of the fierce attachment to Ulster and to British identity held by the majority population in Northern Ireland. Those resisting an all-Ireland and republican state were, for the most part, characterised simply as Orangemen or, more usually and reflexively, 'Orange bigots'. The nature of Protestantism – and its diversity – was perceived, if at all, in the most stereotyped terms. Protestant fears of being submerged in a Roman Catholic and republican state were not grasped and were dismissed or represented as a bogus justification for the continued domination of Catholics. For some republicans (and it was probably a majority), the opinions and fears of Northern Protestants were an irrelevance: Ulster had been taken in conquest and could be retaken without a qualm.

Those Southern republicans who held such views generally had the minimum of knowledge of a Northern Ireland they had rarely, if ever, visited. Their visceral irredentist doctrine was essentially similar to the Greek who wept for Constantinople, the Moor who mourned Al-Andalus or the Zionist who demanded in full the patrimony of Abraham. Most or all Northern IRA activists and supporters shared these views with their Southern comrades. There was an additional element in the North, however: the IRA was recognised by its members and supporters, and a wider Catholic group beyond them, as a defence organisation. As many saw it, there was a long, bitter and ultimately tragic history of repressing the minority in Ulster, with pusillanimity or even connivance on the part of the state, and in the resultant vacuum there was a need for a non-state protective and retaliatory organ. Whatever the emphasis republican doctrine gave to inclusiveness, Northern republicans knew from direct experience or community sentiment that the IRA had a key role in the continuing sectarian antagonisms and in episodes of open conflict.

But if the Northern Protestants were not to be seen as having legitimate political and cultural aspirations – only pretensions to hide self-interest – who was the enemy? It could only be the malevolent Britain that had created the Northern Ireland state. The origin of the malignity or its expression in the creation of Northern Ireland was always the least convincing step in the republican analysis. Were Ireland to be reunited, as it must be for the Republic to be realised, then Britain must be removed. British insistence that the majority view must prevail in Northern Ireland pre-empted for several generations at least all hope of reunification through negotiation. Force was both justified and an urgent duty. This answered the question 'What is the IRA for?'[3]

The IRA of the mid-1930s was the merest shadow of the body that had been such a danger at the birth of the Free State. Isolated, enfeebled and uncertain, internal disputes had a ferocity that drove many activists away and, with the very basic business of survival, functioned as a displacement mechanism for those who remained. Inquiries, courts-martial, credentials, military procedures and structures, ranks and all the other apparently satisfying paraphernalia of the military ethos, papered over a dire lack of equipment, manpower, funds, connections, status and support. Chiefs of staff began to come and go. After ten years with the experienced and steady Moss Twomey, Seán MacBride was appointed to the post in May 1936. He held it for less than six months, and was succeeded that November by Tom Barry who, in the spring of 1938, was replaced by Michael Fitzgerald. This turnover reflected and added to the sense of crippling indecision. The status of the post had collapsed. In April 1938, an IRA convention was held in Dublin with the intention of bringing indecisiveness to an end. Strong restoratives were required, and any display of energy or dramatic strategy would be irresistible. Two such elixirs were on offer. These were debated in the belief that one or the other had to be chosen: continued inaction threatened the organisation's existence. It demonstrated that great weakness that the convention's principal questions seem to have been practical rather than strategic: what could be done (rather than why do it); action now (rather than consideration of what the outcome might be). Tom Barry's plan was to take a group of IRA men into Northern Ireland, to attack the RUC and to stage an event that could turn into an uprising or at least be a catalyst to one. Like the romantic hero of Victorian melodrama, he was willing to go that very evening.[4] This derring-do was the stuff and substance of Fenian and IRA legend, but even its strongest advocates could not have claimed much more for it than a leap in the dark – at best an act of faith, at worst a cynical and reckless gamble, with a human price to pay.

The other option had an equal claim to be considered part of the republican tradition. It was fierce, immediate and of Irish-American provenance. For some time, Seán Russell, IRA Quartermaster, had been a close associate of Joseph McGarrity, a leading Irish-American republican of extreme views.[5] Both men were drawn to and sought allies amongst Britain's enemies. In autumn 1936, Russell visited McGarrity in the USA. There, following in Roger Casement's steps of twenty years before, he contacted the German Ambassador, Eduard Hemel, to denounce the Free State government's recent refusal to grant landing rights to German airlines. This, of course, was but the knock on the door. Russell went on to suggest that when they came to power in Ireland, republicans would 'make returns to her friends in Germany for their valued assistance in the early days of the present phase of our fight'.[6] With rare and frequently lamented exceptions, states proceed on interest, not on sentiment, and Nazi Germany would prove even more disappointing to republican suitors than Imperial Germany had done. But the oxygen of revolutionaries is hope, and audacious hope above all: this is not the vocation of health and safety, risk assessment, cost–benefit analysis and balanced books. A possible alliance, or at least German assistance, was a dream that added lustre and plausibility to the projected IRA war against Britain. Neither Russell nor McGarrity applied to their scheme any real knowledge of British political life and reactions, Nazi priorities or European realities. Certainly they had little acquaintance with Nazi ideology or with the sinister and vile events already unfolding in Germany. Their attention fastened only on Germany as a catalyst through which all could be realised: 'my enemy's enemy' was a venerable Fenian doctrine, sealed in blood. With perfervid hope, Russell had become a disciple of this improbable alliance. Although born in Ulster, McGarrity showed little insight or concern for the complexities of religious and cultural divisions in Northern Ireland; if he had concerns, he swept them into the billows of his dreams.

As for the envisaged bombing campaign, the parallels with the dynamitard schemes of the 1880s are striking. The intention was the same: to damage Britain so that it would evacuate Ireland.[7] This time around there was a new and supposedly devastating weapon. In the 1880s this had been the easily manufactured dynamite; now there was a new generation of versatile, compact and especially powerful military explosives. There was the same failure to appreciate both the extent to which a large, extremely wealthy and complex nation could absorb and counter arson and bombs, and the likely popular reaction to such attacks.[8] Another similarity with the 1880s was the lack of support from the Irish community in Britain, made all the more critical by the ability and resources of the Special Branch. This meant a paucity of safe houses and storage places and of British-born or British-sounding operatives who could blend in and move around safely. Just as the Irish-American dynamitards had utterly and wilfully misread the reactions of the Irish at home and in Britain, the IRA fell into the perennial error of activists and mistook its own vision and passion for those of its compatriots. American accents, manners, clothes and footwear cast spotlights on the dynamitards, who became easy targets for the police and, once their campaign got under way, immediate objects of suspicion to the general public. Youthfulness, country clothing, Irish accents, maladroitness, naivety and a propensity to use Irish lodgings did the same for Russell's bombers.[9]

None of these difficulties were seen or given weight at the April Convention, however, and Russell's plan carried. He had been under suspension, but his plan having been accepted he was appointed Chief of Staff to see it through.[10] By August 1938 he was in London where he spoke of the 'S Plan' at a meeting of the staff of the IRA's London unit.[11] Some preparatory work had been done, and the previous year Dan Keating, Jimmy Joe Reynolds and Dickie Goss had been despatched to London by Tom Barry, then Chief of Staff.[12] Their mission was to identify targets and to find safe houses. Keating complained that too many of the IRA men sent over had no knowledge at all of Britain. Some fitted the part more and could blend in, but Special Branch had had advance information that a bombing campaign was planned, and it seems certain that many men and premises were being watched from the outset. By November 1939, Keating, working as a barman in London, realised he was under surveillance ('you get to know the signs') and, eluding capture by a hair's breadth, returned to Dublin. Quite apart from trained manpower, material resources (funds, explosives and arms) were also grossly inadequate for the purpose.[13] A simple shortage of cash would lead to some of the captures.[14]

In autumn 1938, the second echelon of those who had volunteered for the bombing campaign was trained at various locations in and around Dublin.[15] A plan was drawn up for the destruction of power and communications installations, together with military targets. As the weeks passed and preparations for a European war inexorably progressed, the hopes of those involved rose in accordance with the old Fenian formula 'England's difficulty, Ireland's opportunity.' In the last week of 1938, twelve men were ordered to five centres in Britain: Birmingham, Glasgow, Liverpool, London and Manchester. Sufficient Fenian romanticism persisted for the grand gesture, the unfurling of the banner. First, on 8 December 1938, there was a transfer of authority from the ghostly 'Government of the Republic of Ireland' to the Army Council of the IRA.[16] For those for whom the Second Dáil had never ceased to be the legitimate government of Ireland (and de Valera and many of his ministers and Dáil colleagues had for some time been members of that circle of believers), this was a critical step. From then on, the IRA claimed to be the only legitimate ruling body in Ireland (a claim upon which it still insists).

The second part of the grand gesture was the issuance of an ultimatum by the 'Government of the Republic of Ireland' (now the IRA). This gave the British government four days to 'signify its intentions' to withdraw its forces from Ireland. The ultimatum was served on 12 January 1939, with copies to Lord Halifax, the British Foreign Secretary; the government in Northern Ireland; Adolf Hitler; Benito Mussolini; the Chief of British Forces in Northern Ireland and other figures deemed significant by the IRA.[17] In style, substance and format, the document shadowed to parody the 1916 Declaration, down to the layout of its concluding signatures.[18] Four days later, the British government having failed to respond, war was declared. The declaration was immediately blooded by explosions in locations from London to Northumberland, one of which killed Albert Ross, a twenty-four-year-old Manchester fish-porter cycling to his early morning work.[19] The campaign that followed echoed that of the dynamitards of the 1880s and lasted for fifteen months; several more lives were lost and many were injured. The action had been well trailed. Despite this, Russell insisted that it had taken the opposition at home and abroad 'completely by surprise'.[20] They had reason to be satisfied with the number and spread of targets hit and with their coordination and timing. This opening salvo, however, was to be the most impressive and best executed part of the whole operation.[21]

Arrests, seizures and collapse

As Russell had every reason to know, the British and Irish governments had been well forewarned and were prepared. Reports had been received throughout 1937 and 1938, and during the Munich crisis of September 1938, several independent sources indicated that, in anticipation of a European war, IRA plans were well advanced. Munich had further encouraged Russell and his colleagues, who at that point envisaged a Northern Ireland campaign as well as sabotage in Britain. Money was supplied (always a meagre dole), and IRA agents were directed to secure explosives and to arrange for them to be distributed to activists in various cities and towns.[22] Whilst carrying out this work on 19 October 1938, William

Denis O'Connell (twenty-three) and J. McNulty (alias James Joseph O'Toole) (twenty-five) had been arrested. In addition to the explosives in the men's possession, a copy of IRA plans was obtained (how complete they were is not clear). This seizure was deliberately played down during the Central Criminal Court trial the following month. With remarkable leniency, the two were each sentenced to nine months' imprisonment.[23] What the police did not know, however, was exactly when the campaign would start: this had to await the 12 January 1939 ultimatum.

For a conspiratorial organisation, the IRA had an unhappy attachment to all manner of documents, from receipts for purchases to reports, lists, manuals and plans: these were to some extent necessary, but they may also have provided psychological reassurances to members of an army that had no bases, barracks or uniforms. At a later point, the retention of a receipt – merely as a voucher for reimbursable expenditure – would have literally fatal consequences.[24] The IRA failed to ban its active members from carrying or keeping such compromising items. Prudence might have dictated a tightening-up after the arrest of O'Connell and McNulty, but no, and the entire fifteen pages of the 'S Plan', a detailed description of the intended campaign were found when Michael O'Shea was taken in January 1939. O'Shea (who was sentenced at the Old Bailey on 28 March 1939 to five years' penal servitude for explosives, firearms and conspiracy offences) had served as custodian on behalf of the IRA's leadership in Britain for a number of documents besides the 'S Plan'. These included messages between various IRA units and Dublin headquarters. Some of these were in code, but, for farcical convenience, the keys to the codes were kept with them. Other papers detailed the amount and types of explosives stored at various sites in Britain; instructions on the manufacture of explosives and bombs; and (consistent with crass amateurism) lists of members' names and addresses.[25]

This was a devastating find, and, as with the material previously discovered with O'Connell and McNulty, no mention was made of it at trial. The documents reckoned the quantity and type of explosives so precisely that Special Branch could make a number of deductions and calculations. First, and importantly, this was confirmation that earlier information had been correct. The material seized in the various round-ups could then be deducted from the master list and a reasonably accurate estimate made of the amount still held by IRA units. Most of the items listed had been purchased by the IRA including, besides the chemicals, necessities such as pestles and mortars for mixing potassium chlorate and wax, rubber balloons for sulphuric acid (a detonating device), electrical batteries and cheap alarm clocks. Because they had been stolen from collieries and quarries, and therefore did not have to be accounted for on a quartermaster's list of purchases, outstanding stocks of gelignite, other commercial explosives and detonators were impossible to quantify.[26] But that uncertainty apart, by the third month of the IRA's campaign, Special Branch had a very good idea of available ordnance.

Special Branch also reckoned that seizures and arrests had significantly disrupted the IRA's original plans. Despite this, there was no sign that the leadership intended to abandon them.[27] Its HQ was still training and sending over fresh men to replace those arrested or obviously known to the police. Press speculation that the IRA was receiving Italian or German funds was not confirmed by intelligence, but there were indications that a good deal of money was being donated and transmitted by Irish Americans.[28] By 3 March 1939, the Home Secretary Sir Samuel Hoare was able to circulate to relevant departments a version of the 'S Plan', detailing proposed attacks on water, sewage, electricity, transport and other services; he also issued a general alert to all those in charge of public utilities.[29] The threat was not insignificant in itself but it was utterly marginal in the countdown to war with Germany. In frantic haste, Britain was rearming, training and preparing in all possible ways to fight for national survival. In this context, the IRA and its works were seen as well within the province and capabilities of the police – not much more than organised criminality. Colonel Sir Vernon G. W. Kell, head of the Security Service (MI5), had already passed the parcel: 'It seems to me desirable that the responsibility for dealing with these gangsters should be definitely laid at someone's door and I am afraid that we are not in a position to take any responsibility.' Kell was prepared to investigate suspects in the armed services, government departments, armaments firms and places of concern to the police. His rationale for avoiding other involvement was that MI5 had had nothing to do with the IRA for more than twenty years, that work falling to Special Branch and local police: 'the Security Service has no records, no background, nor has it any officer who can be described as having any general knowledge of the problem at all'.[30]

Special Branch, in London and in the provinces, and the local police generally, were indeed up to the job, given their close knowledge of Irish communities and long cultivation of informants. Arrests began even before the campaign got properly under way. Seven men were arrested in London early in January and were charged under the Explosive Substances Act and the Firearms Act.[31] After the first round-ups (the low-hanging fruits), others were gathered in, including a further twelve men on 7 February 1939. Charges of conspiracy to cause explosions and to commit arson followed. Trials were not delayed (the accused helpfully, in most instances, refusing to recognise the courts), and, on 28 March 1939 at the Old Bailey, sentences totalling ninety-one years were passed on nine members of the IRA.[32] The following day, Hammersmith Bridge (beloved of Fenian and IRA bombers), close to the Irish district of Kilburn, was attacked, perhaps as a gesture of defiance in the face of the Old Bailey sentences. Little damage resulted. A second bomb was spotted by a passer-by, who hurled it into the river.[33] Arrests followed, and by mid-April William Browne and Edward John Connell were sent for trial at the Old Bailey.[34] On 3 May 1939 both were found guilty of causing an explosion of a nature to endanger life and to cause serious injury to property. Connell, aged twenty-two, a salesman, was sentenced to twenty years' penal servitude, and Browne, also twenty-two, to ten years.[35] The arrests and rapid progress to trial confirmed a high level of police readiness and should have caused a rethink by the IRA's leaders.

Arrests notwithstanding, the campaign continued at a brisk pace, if at a relatively low level. There was what at first looked like an attempted prison break on

Saturday, 4 February 1939 (weekends always being preferred for such work) when a bomb was placed against the outer wall of Walton Prison, Liverpool, where a number of IRA men were on remand on explosives charges. The device caused some damage to the wall, but there was no sign of what would, of necessity, have been a large operation had an attack on the prison been contemplated.[36] The previous day, bombs had exploded at Leicester Square and Tottenham Court Road tube stations in London. Incendiaries had been left in four stores in Coventry, evidently before the close of business on the Saturday evening, resulting in fires in the early hours of the Sunday. Besides special guards on power stations and fuel storage depots, extra precautions had been taken at Buckingham Palace and Windsor Castle following the discovery of plans in a suspect house in Belfast.[37]

Russell's intention had been to generate momentum with a swarm of such attacks. This would stir up support in Ireland and, more importantly, in the USA. Funding was critical, and the initial allocation to support the various units in Britain soon ran out. Hoping to galvanise Clan na Gael, the IRA's American support organisation, Russell departed Ireland on 8 April 1938 to rouse the Irish-American base and to raise cash. He left Stephen Hayes as Acting Chief of Staff and by June had worked his way across the USA to Los Angeles, supposedly raising £120,000.[38] On the return leg of the trip, still rattling the collection box at large and enthusiastic gatherings, he was arrested in Detroit on a charge of having overstayed his thirty-day visitor's visa.[39] There was an immediate outcry in Congress where Irish-American legislators threatened to boycott a reception for an impending royal visit.[40] This was sufficient for Russell to be released on bond and to resume his fund-raising, apparently to even larger audiences.[41]

The cash Russell sought was vital to continue his bombing, but his departure from Dublin created more uncertainty at the centre. As we have seen, he had been brought back to GHQ to direct the campaign that he had sold to IRA delegates at the 1938 Convention. Edward John Connell, sentenced to twenty years for his attempt to destroy Hammersmith Bridge, recalled that after Russell left Ireland the campaign began to disintegrate: 'Men sent over as replacements disappeared as fast as they arrived.'[42]

By the end of March 1939, twenty men had been convicted. All bar one (sentenced to ordinary imprisonment) had received sentences of penal servitude – up to twenty years. Proceedings were under way against a further seventeen.[43] A Home Office summary, updated throughout 1939, showed the conveyor belt of arrests, charging and committals for trial to be continuous throughout the year. The day after the Manchester explosions (16 January 1939) for example, seven men were arrested and a considerable quantity of explosive material was seized.[44] There was a speculative element in some arrests, and, when tested, the evidence failed to meet the mark. Two of the six who went for trial in Manchester were discharged, but four were convicted and received sentences of between fourteen and twenty years. Similarly, within four days of the first London explosions (also on 16 January 1939), eight men and boys had been taken. Revolvers, automatics and rifles had been seized, together with ammunition, gelignite, detonators, more than three tons of potassium chlorate and iron oxide. Sentences ranged from three years in Borstal to fourteen years' penal servitude; one man had his sentence quashed on appeal.[45]

The criminal process would continue in this way throughout the campaign, with penalties as low as a £10 fine for the possession of a revolver and a number of discharges, acquittals and successful appeals. At the other end, there would be two executions, many long sentences of penal servitude and an array of lesser terms. Large quantities of firearms, explosives, ammunition, detonators, fuses, Mills bombs, grenades and tear-gas bombs were found, together with documents and a number of rubber balloons. (The last used as a basic and sometimes danger-ously unreliable time-delay for the detonation of bombs.[46]) Charges included simple possession of a variety of articles, possession with intent, conspiracy, causing explosions with intent and murder. Arson, bombing and sabotage caused damage from the relatively trivial (the firing of haystacks) to significant destruction of property, severe injuries and loss of life.[47] In all, a total of seventy-seven men and women would be sentenced as a result of the campaign.[48]

Despite the damage caused, the rate of arrests and seizures shows that the IRA had not the remotest chance of forcing British withdrawal from Northern Ireland. The circles within which most of the IRA operatives moved were under close surveillance; information was forthcoming; there was some penetration of the organisation; and the public had been alerted.[49] The more experienced and careful kept out of the net by operating in very small groups, avoiding obvious haunts and associates and moving on promptly when there was the slightest sign of unknown people taking an interest. By the early months of 1940, IRA manpower and resources were so depleted that Dan Keating, who had fled to Ireland because he sensed police interest, was asked to return to England. He recalled his reaction: 'out against the Tans, out again in the Civil War, interned then for two years, and now asked to return to London. There was hardly anyone left active there; they asked me to go back to try and get something going.'[50] It is a measure of the desperation of the IRA leadership at this point that while such demands were being made of the experienced but exhausted Keating, one of Europe's least apt conspirators, the boy bomber Brendan Behan, was despatched to Liverpool with potassium chlorate, sulphuric acid, detonators and the other items of what he would later call his 'Sinn Féin conjurer's outfit'.[51] Behan had previously been used as a courier and had then been spotted by police; he was picked up shortly upon arrival in Liverpool. Because of his age (sixteen and ten months), his court proceedings began in the juvenile courts, where, to his bemusement, he awaited his hearing in the company of truants in short trousers.[52]

The weakness of the IRA campaign (a low impact overall and rapid decline to the level of nuisance) was comprehensively demonstrated by the development of the war with Germany. Even the IRA realised that its occasional acts of arson and explosions were no more than candles at noon. 'Our efforts', Dan Keating recalled, 'would be pinpricks by comparison.' This realisation coincided with the closing of the police net. (Keating bluffed his way past the arresting party on his lodging-house stairs.) For him and his much-diminished and disorganised band of comrades still at large, this war against Britain was over.[53] The final incident appears to have been on 18 March 1940. Somehow, it seemed apt that this was a bomb (seven sticks of gelignite) placed in a litter bin in London's Grosvenor Place: it did not explode.[54] There was no IRA announcement that the bombings had stopped and that the campaign was over, no valedictory address to the activists now in prison or on the run. Just silence. Given de Valera's severe measures against the organisation in Ireland, and with Russell, the campaign's inspiration and director, en route to Germany, the IRA simply did not have the capacity to call off the campaign or to explain to its members what had gone wrong and why so many now sat in British and Irish prisons.[55] The whole formally declared war simply faded away in an utterly demoralising way: a morose and distracted Cheshire Cat. Violent republicanism had suffered a strategic defeat.

Many of the families of those directly connected with republicanism, arrested and imprisoned, or simply subject to suspicion, also paid a heavy penalty at this time. Under the Prevention of Violence (Temporary Provisions) Act, 1939 (a measure rushed through all its stages in just two days), persons who were not born in Britain could be deported to Éire or to Northern Ireland.[56] Deportations started on 3 August 1939, and by the end of the month a hundred had been dealt with under this provision.[57] The government's thinking was that these households provided potential or actual refuge and support for IRA operatives in Britain and that if there were a reasonable suspicion of their involvement then it was in the public interest that they be removed. In consequence, many people long settled in England and with children that knew no other life suffered considerable hardship. Subject to immediate deportation they lost jobs and (in some cases at least) belongings and arrived back in Ireland without funds or prospects. Others, completely without connection to any political organisation whatever, were denied employment and accommodation simply because of their Irish accents and had to leave Britain. The immediate relief of the deportees was undertaken by an IRA front organisation. This was proper, since it had been the organisation's actions that had triggered the Prevention of Violence Act, and the deportations. The arrival of these often destitute families was a considerable challenge to the organisations to which they looked for help.[58] These generally drew their funding from the same pool of sympathisers upon which the IRA relied.[59] A positive side of the deportations for the organisation, however, was that many of the returnees immediately became involved in political activities.[60]

In Britain, damage to property through IRA actions became insignificant as the war took hold. Loss of life and injuries cannot be weighed on the same scale as material destruction, and the placing of bombs in railway stations and crowded thoroughfares showed a callousness and recklessness that the ordinary British citizen found hard to understand or forgive. As we have seen, the campaign started with the loss of life: Albert Ross, killed by a bomb in an under-street duct.[61] London's

Victoria and Kings Cross stations, with their seasonal crowd of holidaymakers, were the targets on 26 July 1939. At the latter, Dr Donald Campbell, a thirty-six-year-old lecturer at Edinburgh University, on his way home from a postponed honeymoon, was killed; his wife and fourteen other people were injured, some severely.[62] Coventry suffered the most serious atrocity. A bomb was left in Broadgate, in the city centre, timed to explode at 2.30 p.m. on Friday, 25 August 1939, when the street was bound to be crowded.[63] Five people died, twelve were gravely injured, and another forty suffered lesser injuries.[64] All eyes had been on the Continent and preparations for war. The country was mobilising, and there were live rehearsals for the evacuation of schoolchildren. The sense of trust betrayed was profound. There was doubtless some public satisfaction when two IRA men were executed on 7 February 1940 for their part in the killings.[65] Perhaps as a reaction and as some form of retaliation, on 22 February a bomb was placed in a litter bin at a bus stop on Oxford Street, London's busiest street. By a fluke, no one was killed, but thirteen people were injured, two seriously.[66] Dunkirk had yet to fall and Hitler to complete his conquest of the Continent, but the British, public and politicians alike, were bitter about such attacks emanating from a people with whom they were so closely intertwined and a neighbouring country with whom they had, after so many tumultuous centuries and bloody conflicts, established a peace. Anti-Irish feeling rose.[67]

This could not but be aggravated as the pattern of bombing continued, and it seemed that the IRA tactics were to target areas where people assembled and were vulnerable. Thus, on Sunday, 27 August 1940, at the height of the summer holiday season, the planting of four bombs in Blackpool, one of the country's most popular holiday and day-tripper resorts, could only be read in one way: that this was a war against ordinary people when they were at their most vulnerable.[68] That same weekend, there were four explosions in Liverpool, one in the shopping area, just as crowds were returning from cinemas and theatres. Another bomb was placed in a letterbox which threw debris over a wide area when it exploded.[69]

The government's response was nevertheless measured, although crowds close to the explosions and to arrests were angry and might have turned violent.[70] In the midst of the bombing (but before Coventry), respect for free speech and the right to demonstrate were tested when on Sunday, 19 June 1939, a Sinn Féin march commemorating Wolfe Tone (the founding figure in Irish republicanism) and demanding the release of IRA prisoners passed through London's West End, protected by constables of the Metropolitan Police. That there had been bombings the day before made the demonstration – about 200 strong – all the more remarkable.[71] In retrospect at least, the event communicated a message quite contrary to the one intended by its organisers: British society was strong and resilient and its tradition of toleration remained intact; the resident Irish population at large, whose contribution to the war effort was so valuable, had nothing to fear. From the point of view of a cynical pragmatist, of course, the demonstration was also a useful Special Branch photo opportunity.

In prison

Classification and location

As we have seen, arrests began even before the bombing campaign started. Preparations had to be made to receive IRA prisoners, who, on the experience of twenty years before, were likely to prove combative and difficult to handle.[72] A Home Office meeting on 20 January 1939 discussed police responses to the bombings. To disrupt IRA communications with prisoners (who might in the early days of their captivity have operational information or warnings to pass on), it was suggested that visitors be prohibited. It was objected that this would have been illegal, and, in any event, useful information could be gathered from visits. When it was pointed out that many visitors' conversations were conducted in Gaelic, it was suggested that Gaelic-speaking prison officers be assigned to supervise visits. (Few, if any, existed, and this proposal never came to fruition.) The Home Office offered concealed microphones so that visitors' conversations in certain prisons could be recorded.[73] Listening in was in many ways the easiest part of such an operation, transcribing, analysing and dissemination being much more skilful and labour-intensive, and it is not surprising that this proposal also failed to bear fruit.

Such possibilities apart, there were important decisions to be made about sentenced IRA prisoners. The first of these was a legal and operational conundrum. Most had no previous convictions. In order to prevent contamination and to facilitate training, Rule 68 of the Prison Rules required such neophytes to be placed with others equally unhardened in crime, in what was called the Star Class.[74] The difficulty was that there were only five convict (as distinct from local) prisons in England, two of which had been set aside for star prisoners: Maidstone and Wakefield. These establishments allowed a greater degree of movement within the walls and operated a looser regime. Neither prison had either the staffing or physical security necessary to cope with a body of men acting together, perhaps calling on outside assistance and determined on disruption, escape or (unlikely but possible) forced entry. Were the Irish prisoners to be sent either to Maidstone or Wakefield, restrictions on movement, tighter supervision and modifications of other aspects of the regime were inevitable: all prisoners would be subject to intensified control. This undermined the reformatory objects of star classification.

It was axiomatic that the congregation of Irish political prisoners in any appreciable numbers led to trouble: disorder, destruction and demonstrations (the last frequently coordinated with outside supporters). The Home Office therefore proposed to the Prison Commission that, the star rule notwithstanding, the IRA prisoners should be broken into small groups and distributed around different prisons. A few could be sent to Maidstone and to Wakefield. Some could be kept in local prisons, for short periods. These last operated very restricted regimes for remands, civil and short-term criminal prisoners and were not intended, either legally or organisationally, for convicts (those sentenced to penal servitude). The use of local prisons for the IRA men could only be on a temporary transfer basis and for small numbers. The remainder could be sent to the three other convict prisons: Chelmsford, Parkhurst and Dartmoor. Here there were no star-class facilities, and they would have to be mixed with recidivist convicts. The IRA prisoners, however, were not a homogeneous group and differed in their offences, culpability, character and antecedents. An element of classification could therefore be retained. Special Branch would be consulted, and those known to be leaders, or who were likely to attract demonstrations by outside supporters or even attempts at rescue, would be sent to these three more secure and tightly controlled institutions.[75] There might be a political reaction to these proposals which could be represented as 'the association of Irishmen of respectable antecedents with ordinary criminals'. Such criticism, should it arise, would have to be endured, since the first consideration was safe custody, for which purpose some departure from Rule 68 seemed inevitable.[76]

Sir Alexander Maxwell, Permanent Under-Secretary, informed Sir Samuel Hoare, the Home Secretary, that he remained unhappy at the prospect of political criticism on this point, some of which would have justification. He wished to avoid sending to Dartmoor men who did not have criminal records, since the public looked on it 'as the establishment reserved for hardened criminals' and such assignments could be regarded 'as a rather vindictive policy'. The Commissioners were therefore asked if there were a way to avoid using Dartmoor.[77] It soon became evident that the limited amount of convict accommodation available, and the need to avoid sizeable concentrations of IRA men, meant that Dartmoor had to be used. Maxwell had no illusions but that the men would cause many difficulties 'mainly because they will cooperate with each other and prepare concerted schemes of action in a way that is foreign to the character of the ordinary criminal'. He reiterated that it would be disastrous to concentrate all in one prison; they should be distributed so that numbers in any one establishment would be only a small proportion of the total population. But even then they would not be allowed to concentrate; they would be dispersed through the various wings and working parties.

As to the prisons themselves, Maxwell considered locals to be unsuitable. He repeated the difficulties of sending the men to Wakefield and Maidstone. Only Chelmsford, Parkhurst and Dartmoor remained. Rule 68 gave sufficient discretionary authority to governors and commissioners to rebut the charge of unjustly withholding star classification. Such a decision did not breach the rule's separation and training requirement, since sending IRA prisoners to Wakefield or Maidstone would adversely affect other star prisoners.[78] Hoare agreed. The IRA and its supporters, in the event, seemed to be unaware of the vulnerability of the commissioners to a legal challenge on the issue of classification and location. Whether, had they known, they would have had the inclination or resources to test the issue in court is doubtful. Some defence on the classification issue was also to be found in the imperfect knowledge of the prisoners' antecedents. A few were thought to have served prison sentences in Éire; several were serving their sentences under an alias, and some of these refused to disclose their true names.[79] There was insufficient cooperation between the police forces of the two countries to provide verification.[80] It is not clear why the Garda Síochána was unwilling to provide information, but it seems reasonable to assume that de Valera's Minister for Justice, P. J. Ruttledge, had issued directions in the matter. By mid-July it seemed clear that the commissioners were in the clear, and, should a challenge be mounted, there would be little public support for it, minimal judicial interest and a reasonable defence for their actions.[81]

The difficulties which had been anticipated regarding Wakefield appeared to have been realised by summer 1939. At first it had been agreed that only two of the IRA men would be placed there, but, as the arrests and trials proceeded, another four places had to be found. This group of six was sufficient reason for a general tightening of control that affected the training regime. Even with these changes, however, the authorities were not satisfied that Wakefield was safe. A proposal was put to relocate the six: two each to Maidstone and Chelmsford and one each to Parkhurst and Dartmoor. It was possible that the Wakefield men would protest at being moved, 'but that cannot be helped, and it is much more important that they should not be allowed to spoil Wakefield'.[82] These transfers were agreed.[83]

Hunger strikes

At an early stage, some of the prisoners refused food, usually demanding political or POW status or protesting at being forced to work or to accept a prison punishment.[84] This was the traditional and venerated IRA posture. How should the authorities react? On 4 July 1939, Courtenay Robinson, Acting Chairman of the Prison Commission; Sir Alexander Maxwell, Permanent Under-Secretary; Alexander Paterson, one of the commissioners; and Dr John Methven, the medical member of the Commission, met to consider the issue. It had been proposed that, as a deterrent, prisoners should be told by governors that hunger-striking would not force release. Such an overt warning, others felt, could be counterproductive and might give the idea of hunger-striking to men not otherwise considering it. Rather, it was agreed, they should be treated like any other prisoner and the normal consequences of misbehaviour, including forcible feeding, should follow 'as a matter of course'. Governors and medical officers might of course give warnings to individual prisoners on the matter.[85]

A second issue was the possibility that forcible feeding would provoke reprisals, either personally against medical officers or by means of bomb attacks. Explosions could be particularly devastating in the Isle of Wight (the location of Parkhurst Prison) during the holiday season. It was mooted therefore that hunger-strikers might be transferred to a London prison such as Wandsworth 'where more adequate police protection w[oul]d be available'. When this possibility was mentioned to the Home Secretary, he saw other dangers and hoped that transfers could be avoided. This effectively blocked the proposal.[86] In January 1940, there was a hunger strike at Parkhurst, but the IRA so lacked capacity and will by this point that no reprisals were possible.

There remained the matter of medical officers' personal liability – civil and criminal – should forcible feeding go wrong. The leading case was *Leigh* v. *Gladstone*, a Suffragette decision. This imposed two obligations on those taking charge of a prisoner. They must do what they reasonably could to keep him or her in health and – still more clearly – save him or her from death. Were this duty neglected and death ensued there could be a manslaughter charge. Second, if in the discharge of the duty to keep a prisoner alive, forcible feeding were deemed necessary, those taking that decision would not be liable should there be a fatal consequence. This immunity held only if the fatal outcome could not reasonably have been foreseen; there would be a defence only if forcible feeding were reasonably likely to have consequences for the prisoner less serious than starvation. Depending on this legal test, there could therefore be legal and illegal forcible feeding. If the feeding were illegal, those who gave the order and those who carried it out would be liable: English law would not accept the defence of superior orders.[87]

The only concerted hunger strike in the war years appears to have been at Parkhurst, under the leadership of Joe Collins. The demands were the familiar ones: recognition as political prisoners and segregation from other inmates. In addition, the IRA group considered that they were being gratuitously victimised and punished. Collins, who had been elected OC, ordered a hunger strike and also refused work. The men were faced with two difficulties: they had, as a precaution against this kind of joint action, been dispersed across the prison. In addition, forcible feeding commenced after five days. This was both painful and effective. Collins realised that, barring an accident during the procedure, the authorities could keep the strikers alive indefinitely; he also had probably concluded that some of his comrades could not see the action through. Whilst the strike was on, there was a change of governor, and an offer was made that sufficiently met the men's demands for the action to be called off.[88]

From the surviving records there seems to have been no other concerted campaign of hunger-striking. Individuals who staged strikes did not persist for long. The caution and anxiety of the Home Office and the Prison Commission was based on their experience of a previous generation of IRA prisoners who had successfully employed the tactic. The men of 1939–40 had neither the popular support nor that circle of sympathisers which gave hunger-striking its essential political bite. The scale and horror of another European war made it virtually impossible to attract any kind of international interest – even from Irish Americans. There is no indication that the IRA prisoners or their supporters would have been prepared to mount a legal challenge to forcible feeding. It may also be that the men, realising that their campaign had utterly failed in its objective (British withdrawal from Northern Ireland) had lost the will to pursue prison protests with the limited means at their disposal, with the small numbers that could be mustered and in political isolation.

Disturbances and demonstrations

Through the summer of 1939, as attacks continued, tensions rose in the prisons. Then, on Friday 25 August, came the Coventry bomb. With that, antagonism intensified: given the face-offs of prison life, more than verbal clashes were inevitable. The worst of these occurred at Dartmoor three days later, at the muster for morning count. Senior staff subsequently confirmed that feelings had been running high for some time: Coventry caused them to boil over.[89] It is difficult to be sure whose was the first hard word, but it is easy to imagine anticipation and barnyard posturing on both sides. It is certain that there were taunts and counter-jeers. At one point, it was claimed, an IRA man shouted, 'Only five killed at Coventry: there should have been fifty. That's nothing to what they will get.' At that point, there was a concerted rush on the eleven IRA men on parade, and a general melee ensued. Such was the confusion (or the balance of staff sympathies) that only two of the attackers could be charged; those assaulted refused to give evidence.

The incident captured the foreground in IRA accounts of imprisonment and became a chapter in the organisation's martyrology. If, as claimed, remarks about Coventry were made, this was an instance of shouting 'fire' in a crowded theatre. It seems, however, to have been a scrum of sound and fury and to have been broken up before serious injury could be inflicted. The medical officer reported various bruises and abrasions to hands, knees and faces. Only one patient gave cause for concern. John Healy (arrested in London) was admitted to hospital with a back injury and shock; there were no signs of internal injuries, and he was later returned to the prison.

Press coverage was immediate: 'The Moor' was, at that time, a perennial object of morbid interest; the IRA men among its most infamous inhabitants. Some editors may have wished to gratify their readers with a tale of rough justice. A month before, the *Daily Express*, fed a line by a newly released convict, had run a largely fanciful story about warring IRA factions at Chelmsford, all the details of which, an embarrassed governor assured the Commissioners, were inventions.[90] Accounts of the Dartmoor incident were generally more accurate and may have come from staff disclosures or an off-the-record briefing. The *Daily Express* was the only newspaper to let the telling of this latest story to get substantially in the way of the facts. It reported that three doctors had been called from Plymouth to save the most seriously injured prisoner (who was not named), that the three were fighting for his life and that the man's injuries were so serious that he could not be moved. The newspaper also claimed that the attack had been organised. All the other newspapers kept to the information they had been given, with only minor flourishes.[91]

These were early and comparatively innocent days in news management and spin. As with many other government departments, and more than most, the Prison Commission was instinctively averse to publicity, which it saw as a hindrance and potential embarrassment in its confidential and delicate work. The

Dartmoor incident confirmed the particular and continuing sensitivity of all matters connected with the IRA. Another such event, moreover, would suggest that discipline in the prisons had somehow slipped and that the Commissioners and their staff were failing in their duties. Ill-treatment of any prisoner was morally and legally unacceptable; it also threatened control and thus security. Ill-treatment of a group could easily lead to an unravelling of authority and to adverse publicity abroad. No general circular seems to have been issued to governors, but all knew what was expected of them. At Dartmoor itself, and as a temporary measure only, all IRA men were relocated to a wing where they would live, work and exercise.[92]

This August clash had thus led the Governor and the Commissioners to break one of their own most important rules: IRA men should never be concentrated in one prison and even less so in one part of that prison. This error was further aggravated by transferring several more men to Dartmoor – doubtless striving to make best use of the accommodation in which they were now segregated and which had to be separately staffed. By March 1940, there were nineteen men in D Wing. They had inevitably taken advantage of their circumstances to constitute a paramilitary unit. There was an OC, a command structure and a desire for action. The perpetual demand was POW status, and a destructive demonstration was to be their opening gambit.

Following the path, albeit unconsciously, of a similar mutiny by IRA men eighteen years before (in July 1921), a Saturday afternoon was chosen. Fewer than half the staff were on duty – the maximum number having been released to enjoy the long Easter weekend. Easter had an added charge for republicans because it marked the 1916 Rising. It is uncertain whether this, or the prior punishment of two IRA men for breaches of discipline, drove the outbreak: perhaps both.[93] There was a more general objective and possibly some coordination in the men's campaign. The goal was removal to another prison set aside exclusively for IRA prisoners. The records show that there had for some time been demonstrative breaches of the rules and demands along those lines. There is no indication of outside commands or influence.

The protest started at mid-afternoon on Saturday, 23 March 1940. The IRA men were being supervised by only two officers, one of whom was seized and locked in a cell. (It is not entirely clear what happened to the other.) Somebody in the prison's production department had stored a quantity of fibre for mat-making in the wing. Discipline staff failed to spot this as a breach of security. Having taken control, the prisoners immediately fired the fibre, which, with the addition of paint and oil, burnt easily, flames swiftly reaching and destroying part of the roof. All staff were called in, as were the Tavistock and Plymouth fire brigades; police attended, but were not required. The blaze was extinguished and order restored within three hours. Canon J. M. Ryan, a Plymouth parochial priest and Roman Catholic chaplain at the prison, acted as intermediary, and the rioters agreed to return to their cells.[94] The officer was released unharmed; damage had been caused to the amount of about £1,000.

There were continuing actions by the IRA men. They refused food for three days (25–8 March 1940) but apparently gave no reason for this and made no demands. The Dartmoor Medical Officer thought it might be a gesture intended to steal the thunder of the adjudicators who were shortly to hear their cases and who would very likely impose dietary punishment. Twelve also refused to wear prison clothes, wrapping themselves in blankets instead: they were not criminals, they said, and would not wear criminals' clothes. Given their isolation and the lack of outside support, the gesture was futile. In the opinion of the Medical Officer, the men were doing it because 'they have to do something, even something unpleasant, to keep their spirits up and the fictions of their immature enthusiasm alive'.[95]

The disturbance was serious enough to merit a top-level Home Office meeting, chaired by the Home Secretary. It was decided not to prosecute the offences at an outside court but instead to remit them to the Dartmoor Board of Visitors. The men's already long sentences and the security risks of producing them in court were decisive in keeping proceedings within the walls. All seventeen who had taken part were to be charged with mutiny, destruction of prison property and any other related matters that could be supported by evidence. These were among the gravest offences a prisoner could commit. The Commissioner responsible for convict prisons, the liberal Alexander Paterson, was despatched to Dartmoor. He was to take soundings on the question of corporal punishment. (Mutiny was one of the few remaining prison offences for which this penalty could be imposed.) It was agreed that he would consult the Governor 'as to the importance or otherwise, from the point of view of the staff and of the other convicts, of corporal punishment being inflicted on at any rate some of the offenders if the Board so recommend'.[96] He was to report to Maxwell for the Home Secretary's immediate information.

Paterson was at Dartmoor on 2 and 3 April 1940. He addressed staff, thanking those who had dealt with the disturbance. The Irish, he emphasised, were to be treated exactly as the English convicts. Visiting the seventeen IRA men in their cells (where they awaited adjudication), he refused to see those (by now eight or nine) 'who had taken off all their clothes and were in a state of nakedness'. Paterson, a kindly man and an inspiring leader who had been at the heart of the progressive development of Borstal and who was a humane influence on penal policy generally, was nevertheless disinclined to temporise.[97] The Governor was told that all had to be properly clothed for the Board of Visitors' hearing: if necessary they were to be dressed by force. Paterson also directed that the men should be handcuffed during the proceedings to prevent them taking off their clothes.[98]

By the time of his visit, the Home Office had come to a decision on the question of corporal punishment as a possible punishment for the riot. Paterson told the Governor, Major Charles Pannall, that should the Board of Visitors ask about an appropriate sentence, he was to let them know that corporal punishment (an order for which had to be submitted to the Home Secretary) would not be confirmed by the Home Secretary. The Chairman of the Board of Visitors did call on Paterson at the prison and was given the information; neither he nor the Governor queried this decision.[99]

At a subsequent review (after the adjudication), Pannall disclosed that he would have had some difficulty with flogging sentences. The mutineers had treated Officer Yetman, whom they locked in a cell, with some consideration. This mitigated the charge of personal violence which four of them faced. Pannall also wished to avoid corporal punishment because it would reinforce the Irish prisoners in their determination not to cooperate.[100] The Board imposed severe punishments short of flogging: the maximum dietary punishments allowed, confinement to punishment cells and loss of privileges. The four who had manhandled the officer lost remission marks equivalent to eighteen months' imprisonment; the others forfeited marks equal to a year's imprisonment. An exception was made for John Martin, aged eighteen, 'ostensibly on account of his youth, in reality to reduce his conceit by showing that he could not be seriously regarded as a dangerous leader'.[101]

There remained the problem of what to do with the Dartmoor men, when, after six weeks, their period in punishment cells was completed. Pannall told the Home Office that prior to the riot the IRA prisoners had frequently refused to comply with prison rules and procedures, repeatedly insisting that they be treated as political prisoners or as POWs. Some would not dress themselves or shave, and others refused exercise. Behind all this was the demand for a prison to be set aside for them in which they would receive special treatment. The men, Pannall believed, were 'quite prepared to undergo any amount of suffering and indeed to sacrifice their lives for what they regard as a holy cause'.[102] The chaplain, Canon Ryan, who at the time of the outbreak had been so helpful in avoiding a violent conclusion and who generally took a clear line in support of prison discipline, strongly believed that a separate prison was the best solution and had let the IRA men know that this was his opinion.[103]

The Home Office begged to differ. It agreed with Pannall that a separate prison, with disciplinary concessions, would produce only short-term peace. The IRA men would always want to run it and, organised under their own leaders, would take action should they dislike a particular order or regulation. A separate prison was therefore not a sensible option. Unless they were prepared to hold the prisoners in what amounted to an internment camp with 'all sorts of privileges and amenities', effective control of a separate prison would require a special and expensive form of administration. It would have to be intensively staffed and run on more rigorous lines than an ordinary prison. Prisoners would be locked in their cells for most of the time and, in order to prevent plotting, given little opportunity for association. Even that degree of sequestration would probably be an insufficient protection. The great difference between them and ordinary prisoners, Pannall pointed out, was that the IRA 'will act as one man and none of their number will give the others away'.[104]

The riot had shown that the Dartmoor arrangements, which had only ever been intended as short term, could not be allowed to continue. Nine or ten of the nineteen would be transferred to local prisons. Although this option had been earlier rejected, it bypassed the severe constraints of the convict estate. It would be impracticable (and inhumane) for the prisoners to serve out long sentences in local prisons, and some form of rotation between local and convict establishments was envisaged. The small group to remain at Dartmoor was to be broken up and mixed with the ordinary convicts around the prison's different wings: force would, if necessary, be used to carry out this dispersal. They would also be divided among the different working parties, and, should they refuse labour, 'as is probable', they would be punished as would any other convict.[105] There were risks in this course. Prisoners could cause disturbances by refusing to join work parties and having to be forced into the workshops; there was also the danger that the ordinary prisoners might attack them again. But, as Sir Alexander Maxwell wrote to the Home Secretary, 'We thought... that these risks must be faced.'[106] The decision paid off, and Dartmoor provided no further opportunity for IRA action.

The August 1939 attack on the Dartmoor IRA men had led to their concentration and segregation, and that in turn had provided the opportunity to riot. This sequence had not been followed elsewhere, although there had been concerted protests. By December 1939, there were twenty IRA men at Parkhurst. Unlike Dartmoor, from the first day the twenty had been dispersed throughout the prison. Laundry, bake house and kitchen had been ruled out as labour assignments, 'owing to the danger of sabotage or tampering with food' reported the Governor.[107] In November and December 1939, the IRA prisoners refused to perform their cell tasks. This was work which had to be carried out in the evenings after the evening meal. The usual task was sewing a quota of mailbags. The sole purpose of this requirement was to extend the day's labour, to restrict rest and recreation and to increase drudgery. The men decided that this form of labour emphasised their criminal status and refused to do it.

For five weeks they were punished by loss of pay and privileges – standard penalties. Those sanctions seemed to have no effect, and the Parkhurst Governor asked the Commissioners' permission to confine the men in punishment cells, sentencing them to periodical bouts of a bread-and-water diet 'until they could be induced to see reason'. The Commissioners demurred. A continuation of the usual punishments, the Governor pointed out, seemed unlikely to produce any better results than before – merely irritation and resentment. Another suggestion, therefore, was the removal of Michael Joseph Mason, deemed to be the ringleader.[108] With Mason gone, he hoped that several men would conform to the rules and perform their cell tasks. To avoid Mason again causing trouble he should be transferred to a local prison where he would have no followers; this was approved by the Commissioners.[109] At Hull Prison, Mason would be sui generis. The governor was instructed in the special arrangements that had to be made for correspondence and visitors.[110]

There was also trouble at Maidstone, which had the most liberal regime of the convict prisons. Again, the men seem to have acted under the order of their

OC, John Gavahan.[111] Having been punished for refusing to obey an order, the men acted together to destroy their cell furniture. The precipitating factor seems to have been the punishment of Thomas Magill for insolence.[112] The incident began with a quarrel between Thomas Magill and a prison officer over water Magill wanted to take to his cell. The IRA men wrongly thought that a baton had been drawn against Magill. Following adjudication he was transferred to Leeds, a local prison. At their Board of Visitors' adjudications, all the men said that they were acting in sympathy with Magill.[113] After the incident, they were separated and further dispersed. A somewhat sensationalised but more complete account of this disturbance was given ten weeks later in the *Sunday Dispatch*. Albert Simons (sometime Warwickshire magistrate, imprisoned for false pretences) told the newspaper that the smashing of the cell furniture had been accompanied by shouts of 'Up the Republic'. Simons also claimed that during a prison count the IRA leader had commanded his men in 'Erse' (Gaelic). The men then left the ranks and marched to a corner of the parade ground, where they drilled for several minutes, in defiance of the orders of the prison officers. The men then marched back to their cells, one waving a green flag. They were immediately locked in (standard procedure pending adjudication). During the staff lunchtime, they smashed their cell furniture. Prison staff then removed them, some forcibly, to the punishment block.[114] Gavahan admitted countermanding the order of the prison officer in charge of the parade by shouting 'Soldiers of the IRA, attention, left turn, quick march.'[115]

Wherever the IRA men were gathered in any number there was likely to be trouble. On 16 January 1941, twenty-two IRA men at Camp Hill (an Isle of Wight prison, originally established to deal with habitual offenders) refused labour. This protest lasted for some ten weeks. Six of the twenty-two were transferred out, but the remainder continued their refusals until the end of March. (It is not clear if the protests were continuous or sporadic.) At that point they appear to have conformed to the regime.[116]

Brendan Behan

Brendan Behan's brief bombing career produced some of the oddest Home Office and Prison Commission exchanges of these years. The cause of much spilt ink and some nicely modulated bureaucratic anger was the interplay between the character and personality of the young Behan and the paternalistic and protective ethos of the Borstal system to which, because of his age, the Court was obliged to consign him. With remarkable and distinctive literary talent, Behan turned his experience of English criminal justice into a witty and shrewd prison memoir, *Borstal Boy*.[117] Besides powers of uncommon perception, he was undoubtedly possessed of great charm and sympathy and a driving sense of fun. Strong socialist beliefs and trade-unionist loyalties, together with a childhood lived amidst Dublin's working and poorer classes, allowed Behan to understand the delinquent youths with whom he found himself and to associate with them easily, and with the staff. No Irish prison memoir since Michael Davitt's so thoroughly discarded the narrow republican disdain for ordinary prisoners and for the errant members of England's working class.[118]

Like Davitt, however, Behan had a commitment to the ideals of extreme Irish republicanism that belied his youth; he had also been found guilty of very serious offences. His family had strong revolutionary beliefs, and several had also been activists.[119] When arrested in Liverpool on 3 December 1939, Behan was two months short of his seventeenth birthday but, according to Special Branch, had already been on courier missions to Britain, delivering incendiary and explosive substances. It was claimed at his trial that early in 1938 he had been sent to London, where he had made up bombs.[120] Behan disputed a great deal of what the police said about his pre-arrest activities, but it is indisputable that he had become known to the police on both sides of the Irish Sea and was arrested the day after he returned to Liverpool with more explosives.

After the usual committal proceedings, which started in the juvenile court, Behan appeared for trial at Liverpool Assizes on 7 February 1940. Evidence was given of his arrest in possession of 20 ounces of potassium chlorate, sulphuric acid, sugar and balloons. The trial was bound to be unusual, given the youth of the defendant, the seriousness of the charges, the destruction and loss of life already caused by the IRA and the general atmosphere arising from wartime conditions. Its oddness was heightened by the prosecution counsel, Eric Errington, MP, appearing in Royal Air Force (RAF) uniform and by Behan's interjections as the trial unfolded.[121] Behan denounced some of the evidence as 'a lot of damned lies' and told the judge that he had no interest in the proceedings.[122] He was reported as smiling and grinning during the trial and upon conviction gave a standard-issue IRA statement, intended mainly for republicans back home.[123]

The judge (Mr Justice Hallett) was understandably incensed by Behan's defiance: this was not the way things should be. Remarks from the dock were irrelevant, he admonished; the court was not a political platform. He lamented his limited powers of punishment. Parliament had recently taken 'an extremely lenient view of what ought to be done with young persons found guilty of offences'. It was not part of his duties to criticise, but, he continued, 'I cannot help thinking that Parliament in passing this legislation must have been thinking of the normal young person.' Sending Behan to Borstal for three years (the maximum allowed), he noted that this was less than he deserved 'and I think you knew this before you started off on this expedition'. He added that he trusted that three years in Borstal 'may curb you of both your precocity and conceit'. Sticking to his IRA-approved lines, Behan, as he was taken from the dock, shouted 'God save Ireland!'[124]

Awaiting trial, Behan had been held in Liverpool's Walton Prison, an austere local establishment run on tough lines, where little had changed since Victoria occupied the throne. Having been convicted and sentenced, on 15 February 1940, he was transferred to the Borstal system. This was a separate and distinctive body, under the charge of the Prison Commission but entrusted with particular social and penal objectives. Its staffing and management style combined elements of the imperial mission, *noblesse oblige*, muscular Christianity, English public-school sensibilities, sports and the notion of encouraging the 'lads' (as they were uniformly called) to take responsibility for themselves and for others. The community at large, or at least a section of the concerned middle class, was involved in all this through the Borstal Association – groups of local volunteers who came into the various Borstals, worked with the boys and helped prepare them for release. It was a formula of social service derived from the high tide of Victorian and Edwardian philanthropy, well suited for its time, but which the war would sweep away.[125]

A Lady Visitor, Mrs C. Cardew, carried out Behan's initial assessment at Feltham Borstal, the institution to which all Borstal 'lads' went first, to be assessed, sorted and assigned. Part of this process was an interview. Cardew was in some ways shrewd in her observations; kindliness drew her to the sentiments and concerns of a family social worker. Behan, she thought, was a revolutionary by training and upbringing, 'but not at all by disposition, though an idealist and enthusiast'. She found him friendly and responsive, 'not conceited about his doings, though convinced he was acting rightly'. He was 'rather temperamental and unstable in emotions, but pretty trustworthy with a sense of honour. A romantic person, but with a small amount of sense of humour.'[126] Behan may have spun a bit of a tale in this interview and was certainly perceptive enough to give his assessor what he thought she wanted to hear. He told her that he had gone to Spain (with the brother that had been killed) but at fourteen and a half was sent back as too young. He also claimed that he had just been taken on at Cammell Laird's shipyard before his arrest.[127] More accurately, he said that he was interested in politics, reading and, as Cardew primly put it, 'discussions of social grievances'. Nor was he lacking in the proper interests of his age group: he was fond of games and swimming 'and can enjoy himself with other boys'. Sadly, this last was not without difficulties since 'His pals are all members of the IRA.'[128]

Behan's Lady Visitor divorced the boy from his offence, the offence from Britain's wartime peril, and Behan from Irish republicanism. She pointed out his poor health record (a bout of pneumonia) and a broken collarbone. The latter she thought he had got whilst playing hockey (confusing this with hurling). She also saw that, serious though his offence and intentions were, he had himself been through an ordeal. A stammer had come on which he attributed to the strain of the previous months during which he 'he had felt responsible for the liberty of his friends'.

Given all the circumstances, Cardew's humanity, maternal concern, perceptions, conclusion and recommendation were remarkable, though perhaps not for the Borstal system as it was then run. In its own way, it was another indication of how and why the IRA bombing campaign was a nuisance rather than any kind of threat to British political stability. 'He seemed to me', she wrote,

> in need of soothing and relaxing, and to live a normal boy's life for a time. He is pretty sensible and open to reason, if tactfully handled…

Really quite a decent simple lad, whose ideas have been put into him ready-made, by his family and associates. He seemed pathetically happy at being decently treated, having apparently expected something very different.

All of this led to the recommendation which would be so important to Behan's Borstal experience. He might respond to the regime of an open Borstal 'if one could be certain that his associates [the IRA] would leave him alone'. The risk was probably too great for that, she concluded, and therefore she recommended his retention at Feltham.[129]

This last would have been very unfortunate for Behan. Feltham, although at the time used as a Borstal, was originally a Victorian convict prison, and the regime and atmosphere matched the surroundings. Lads who knew their Borstal system judged it not as bad as Portland, but it was still one of the least desirable placements. The body and substance of Cardew's report was considered by prison officials, and her favourable impression of Behan was, quite remarkably, found to outweigh the risk of sending an energetic young revolutionary, with outside contacts, to an open Borstal. There was an element of chance in the decision, and it certainly was fairly balanced. By the spring of 1940, however, it seemed safe to assume that most of the IRA's operatives in Britain had been rounded up and that there was little chance of Behan being rescued.

A report by the Feltham Medical Officer, Dr A. P. Lewis, further opened the way to send Behan to an open establishment. Besides the security issue mentioned by Cardew, the principal classification consideration was the lad's level of intellectual and social maturity and his ability to live in open conditions without absconding. This was not simply a matter of trust but a degree of social robustness that would enable a boy to cope with the inevitable pressures of institutional life without seeking a solution by running away. Behan seems to have spoken reasonably frankly to Lewis about his background and political beliefs, although with the inevitable gloss. He claimed to have been connected with the IRA since the age of six and (more plausibly) a courier since 1937. Asked why the IRA had chosen him to do the work at such a young age, he replied 'I was supposed to be above average intelligence for my age and suited for the job.' His justification for the bombing campaign was that if a sufficient amount of property were destroyed the English would 'think us such a nuisance as to return the property to us which they've take from us'.[130]

To Lewis, as to Cardew, Behan was undoubtedly an exotic departure from the usual stream of predictable young thieves, inadequates and tearaways from poor backgrounds who had worked themselves into Borstal. Lewis noted that Behan withheld various details about himself until he realised that they were already known. Although he thought that he had feelings of both inferiority and conceitedness, the overall impression was favourable: 'I would not call him a fanatic: he has good insight and does not carry rationalisation to extremes and has obviously been influenced by older people to take part in political activity.'

Lewis added a prescient sentence in a style not usual in such reports. 'Now that he has been sentenced, I think he feels that like an actor in a play who makes a stage exit early, that he has finished his job and can now wait and simply look on.' It was unlikely that Borstal training would cause him to change his political ideas and outlook, but Lewis concluded that he would respond more satisfactorily at an open Borstal.[131]

Almost the final say in deciding Behan's location fell to Reginald ('Reggie') Bradley, the Assistant Commissioner with Special Responsibility for Borstals. Bradley was a disciple of Alexander Paterson. With Paterson, he saw Borstal as a form of social work. He accepted the logic in the reports of Cardew and Lewis and concluded that Behan should indeed be sent to an open Borstal: either Hollesley Bay Colony or North Sea Camp, and preferably the former. Bradley also partly blocked the way to a closed institution by pointing out that Behan knew Burns and Logue at Feltham and Keneally at Portland.[132] 'If he *must* go to a closed Inst[itutio]n' the choice was one or the other of those. Writing to Maxwell and to Paterson, Bradley asked, 'Do you think we might take a chance on it, & place him in an open inst[itutio]n?'[133] Despite the obvious security and political risks, the answer was 'yes', and on 21 March 1940, just six weeks after his trial, Behan was transferred to Hollesley Bay Colony.

His own chronicle of Hollesley Bay contains a mass of details, anecdotes and impressions and need not be replicated here. A number of matters, such as officials' assessments of his progress, were not part of Behan's memoir, and they are certainly worth attention. Well into his sentence there was an assessment by Gordon Macfarlane, Hollesley Bay's Deputy Governor, who also had charge of St George's House, to which Behan had been assigned. Behan, he wrote, was 'above the average in intelligence and facility of tongue' and very popular with the other 'colonists' (as the inmates of Hollesley Bay were known). And although he did not fit the profile of the 'good prisoner', he was also generally liked by staff. Macfarlane confirms the gist of Behan's own account of his time at Hollesley Bay, noting that he was frequently at the centre of attention: 'He loves the limelight and whilst playing to the gallery he is not unmindful of the stalls.' He enjoyed juggling with words and ideas 'quite undeterred by being snubbed'. The extrovert behaviour, in Macfarlane's view, was a form of compensation for feelings of insecurity, but it was perhaps a saving grace that he had insight into that condition.[134]

As an unrepentant member of the IRA, Behan had been excommunicated from the Roman Catholic Church but nevertheless continued to attend its services, at which he assisted. (Excommunication meant that he was banned from the sacraments.) Given Borstal's understated but definite Christian ethos, attachment to religion and attendance at services went down well with the authorities, and Behan was careful to put a gloss on the development of his political beliefs. He told Macfarlane that he remained passionately committed to his nationalism but that 'his sympathies are all on the side of Britain at the moment, because she is fighting to defend principles in which he wholeheartedly believes'. It had been an error to participate in the bombing campaign, and he would not engage in such activities again: 'The leniency shown... has made a good impression on him.'[135]

This last was undoubtedly true. The treatment at Walton Prison (which, according to his account, included a certain amount of rough handling and bullying by staff – both of himself and others) more fully accorded with the expectations of a boy raised in an unusually political family in which a detestation of all things British would have been taken in with mother's milk. Despite voracious reading, Behan's knowledge of England was rudimentary and stereotyped. Prison memoirs, hunger strikes and brave speeches from the dock laid the foundation for Behan's fears of brutal warders, grim cells and stultifying routines. To meet the kind of people who then staffed the English Borstals at housemaster (assistant governor) and similar levels must have challenged his expectations. From his own account, the emphasis placed on personal responsibility and individual respect and the ease with which he was accepted by inmates and staff alike surprised and then reassured him. He responded well to argument, and the various attempts to understand him and his beliefs were, as his memoir shows, stimulating and encouraging. On their part, staff were taken with his articulateness, intelligence, self-deprecation and charm. Having done his part (as he saw it), he was willing to fit into his new world, which had proved so unexpectedly positive and perhaps even attractive.

As Macfarlane had noted, Behan was neither a model nor a wholly compliant prisoner. That he was not a goody-goody may have raised him further in the estimation of Borstal staff. One of the tactics he used, as did other prisoners, ordinary criminal and political alike, was to write inflammatory letters. He knew that they would be suppressed, but the prison censor and perhaps others would read them. It was a way of cocking a snook and riling the authorities without breaking the rules and being punished. The letter would be suppressed, of course, and the prisoner ordered to rewrite it. By a fluke, a number of the young Behan's suppressed letters have been preserved, so we have an overview of his sly campaign of defiance and provocation.[136]

Two days after arrest, Behan wrote to a family friend, Mrs Fitzsimons, at Cabra, Dublin. Part of the intent of the letter was undoubtedly to communicate with the IRA. A few passages are worth citing: 'I am afraid it didn't work this time as I was pinched 10 hours after I landed. The Broy Harriers [Dublin Special Branch] had sent my age, name, home address full description on 2 weeks beforehand.' Various friends were named and coded regards passed to them. Behan made enquiries about various IRA men in custody in Dublin's Arbour Hill and in English prisons. He made light of his own predicament and asked for preparations to be made for a 1945 reunion: 'I'm expecting 5 years in borstal so have the table laid & a big feed ready.' The veiled and possibly coded communications with his friends would probably in themselves have been enough to cause the letter to be suppressed, but the decisive factor was the criticism of the Walton chaplain, who he said had treated him very badly: 'I cannot go to the altar unless I confess it is a sin to be an Irish Republican.'[137] Behan was instructed to rewrite the letter.

A letter to his brother was pure teenager: 'If I had had a Rod [gun] I would never have been pulled though I was hooked the minute I landed.' At the same time he berated his brother for writing such a short letter: 'By the way for the love of Christ don't waste 2d on about 4 lines of writing nor wait 3 days to answer.' Behan sent his brother £1 10s. – this must have been a substantial portion of his remaining cash. He wanted something to read: the *Kerryman*, the *Irish Press* and the Dublin evening newspapers. He also asked for the Penguin edition of Shakespeare's plays, the Penguin anthology of English poetry and some other titles. There was brotherly sniping: 'In the few lines with which you honoured me you ask do I want anything... *I do*. If you never send the Penguins Jesus help you if you don't.'

This letter would probably have been suppressed because of its profanity, but suppression was made inevitable by detailing the prison routine and also by instructions to give regards to his IRA comrades. Even here Behan endears himself with irony: 'Have I been canonised by Gearóid M. etc. yet?' But still there was the pro-forma statement to the 2nd Battalion of the Dublin IRA: 'For the sake of your comrades held in British jails let every man at home redouble his efforts to secure the complete independence of our country and release of our captured volunteers.'[138]

In a letter to his mother, the day after his conviction and sentencing, seeking to reassure her, Behan had insisted that the English Borstal was 'miles better than any institution of the same sort in Ireland. It has more of a reforming influence "Reward for virtue instead of punishment for vice." That's what made the judge so mad.'[139] Whether or not he believed that at the time of writing, it proved to be true.

In April 1941, however, there came a quarrel with the Roman Catholic chaplain at Hollesley Bay. Behan had canvassed the fifty or so Roman Catholic lads in the Borstal, urging them to take the sacraments at the Easter service. (This requirement for Roman Catholics was known as the 'Easter Duty'.) It had, he wrote to his brother, always been a matter of pride to him that the Catholic boys 'somehow live a little more cleanly than our Protestant mates'. He thought that in Borstal religion had a very healthy influence. Having won over a good-sized group, Behan, to his bitter chagrin (he was at this time an altar server), was himself turned away by the chaplain: he had calculated that the newly arrived priest might not have known about the prohibition on IRA men. In his anger, Behan wished that, when at liberty, should he ever go to church again, the memory of the Liverpool and Hollesley Bay chaplains, and the Bishop of Northampton (in whose diocese Hollesley Bay was located) would trip him upon entering.[140]

As part of his soothing of his mother, Behan told her not to worry about him nor to believe all she had read about prison: 'So long as you don't swim against the current you're alright.'[141] He took his own advice to heart. Although he found Walton Prison grim and Feltham not a lot better, he wrote to a friend that with Hollesley Bay 'it was love at first sight'.[142] To his grandmother he wrote, 'I cannot speak too well of this place. It is at times really very hard to realise that this colony of ours has any connection with Walton Prison, Liverpool. My mother has a photo of it.'[143] To Brian O'Higgins, editor of the then barely legal *Wolfe Tone Weekly*, he wrote that, although prisons and he did not agree, Borstals 'suit me down to the ground'. He had become house captain and, 'in contrast to my first reception in prison am (God forgive me for saying so myself) extremely popular and am pretty well mixed up in anything that's going on'. He did not want to give the impression that he was 'Managing Director' of the place: 'But I am really being very well treated.'[144]

Certainly this impression was conveyed to Behan's family by correspondence to and from Shoemake, Behan's housemaster. On reception at Feltham, the Medical Officer had noted a deflection in Behan's nasal septum that needed attention. In January 1941, he was taken to the East Suffolk Hospital at Ipswich for the necessary corrective operation. On 28 January, the housemaster wrote to his parents. Brendan was making a satisfactory recovery after the operation; a phone call to the hospital had confirmed that he had had a comfortable night. The housemaster hoped to see him within a few days: 'You may rest assured that he is in good hands. The reports from there of our men who have been sent there speak very highly of the care and attention given them and in each case their experience has been a particularly happy one.' Three days later came further reassurance. Behan had been visited, had reported 'the best of attention and... everyone very kind' and had written in this vein to the Governor. It was not certain when he would be returning to Hollesley Bay, but as soon as this was decided, Shoemake would write again. There was no need to worry in any way. Another of the Hollesley Bay lads was in the next bed: 'The ward is a small one and they all seemed very happy and friendly. He was visited on Thursday by another Housemaster and a Matron so you can see we won't allow him to forget us.' It was wartime, and transportation in that out-of-the-way corner of Suffolk was uncertain, but Shoemake ended with a promise: 'If I can get a lift in next week and he is still there, I will certainly pay a visit.'[145]

The staunchly republican Behan family must have been taken aback by such friendly and concerned correspondence from a British official about their bomber son. They immediately replied, but for some reason this letter and others did not reach Hollesley Bay. A letter of 30 March 1941 did get through, thanking Shoemake for his kindness:

> The censorship on this side seems more like suppression as I wrote to you and Brendan after he left hospital (accompanied by no less a personage than the Governor, democracy with a vengeance!!). My wife and I are perfectly satisfied that he could not be better cared for according to his accounts of school, officers & treatment; you will find it hard to get rid of him when the time comes.[146]

This was surely an extraordinary transformation. Here was penal institution, supposedly the sinews, mailed fist and teeth of the detested British state, yet as far removed as one could get from the bathos of Ireland's brave felons in their cold and lonely cells. What makes it the more extraordinary is that both parties to the correspondence – and indeed Behan and the Borstal staff – seem scarcely conscious of the ironies.

The kindness and personal concern went far beyond individual clemency or liking. Behan's needs and welfare were paramount. The telescope was reversed. To the Borstal staff, and those headquarters officials to whom they reported, Behan was a young man who had got into trouble: politics, background and personality traits were seen as part of that picture. The Borstal's underlying philosophy was intensely individualistic, consistent with its Christian and liberal ideas: Behan was not to be defined by what he had done but by his potential; he was an end in himself, and that not fixed but constantly in the process of becoming, like all those who dealt with him. Those abstract ideas, it is certain, were not at the forefront of the minds of staff as they dealt with the daily round of institutional and residential problems, but they were at the heart of the Borstal philosophy, however articulated, and had been powerfully expressed and reconfirmed by William Temple, Archbishop of Canterbury, in his 1934 Clarke Hall lecture, 'The Ethics of Penal Action'.[147]

This concern with the individual, above all, and the duty of the state towards him or her, was evident in Behan's daily life at Hollesley Bay. It was equally manifest at headquarters. Although sentenced to three years' Borstal training, Behan's actual date of release would be decided by the Prison Commissioners, using their powers under s.5 of the 1908 Prevention of Crime Act. The regular reports received from Borstal housemasters, governors and members of the Borstal Association were critical in this judgement. Behaviour and response to institutional life were key factors, as was the view taken of the lad's background, character and prospects. Whilst he would much rather have been free, Behan, as we have seen, found his life at Hollesley Bay full of interest and, apparently, remarkably and oddly satisfying. The institution responded as positively to him as he did to it. With an ordinary inmate, this mutual satisfaction would have secured release at an early point (not long after the six-month minimum had been served), the theory being that freedom should be granted at the optimum moment for post-release success. Behan's case was far from the usual run of things. Despite the determination of staff to treat him as they would any boy entrusted to their care, exceptional political sensitivities could not be overlooked by the Home Office.

In mid-December 1940, a little over a year after Behan's arrest, Reggie Bradley took the first steps to have him released, speaking to Sir Alexander Maxwell. It was agreed to obtain up-to-date reports from Shoemake and from John Cape, the Hollesley Bay Governor.[148] Less than a week later, the reports came back, recommending release. On a recent visit, Bradley himself had spoken to Behan and concluded that he should be freed: 'He is a profound

"Republican" but he assured me he had abandoned all ideas of violence. I consider he was sincere in this assurance.' Behan wanted to be expelled to Ireland, to family and relatives. Would he be willing to go to sea (which had the advantage of removing him from the possibility of being drawn back into the IRA) Bradley had asked. Were this insisted upon as a condition of his release, Behan would agree, 'but says he is always sea-sick'.[149]

It was noted in the Home Office that the other IRA youths (Logue, Burns and Keneally) had all been released after relatively short Borstal terms. The first two, from Northern Ireland, had been freed on condition that they entered the Merchant Marine and did not return to Ulster until the end of the war. Keneally, who came from Éire, had not wanted to go to sea but was nevertheless released and made subject to an expulsion order. Discussion of these cases in relation to Behan's focused on his background, one official insisting that he was

> a revolutionary type coming from a family with similar sentiments. Mr Bradley thinks he has abandoned all ideas of violence, but Behan is clearly an unstable young man & I have no doubt that under family influence he will soon be easily persuaded to take a hand in violence if occasion offer.

At the same time, it had to be agreed that further Borstal time was unlikely to do him any good or change his outlook. The best plan was to expel him to Dublin.[150]

Neither Maxwell nor the Home Office were persuaded, and the file was marked 'No Action'. Terrier-like, Bradley was back again at the end of January 1941. Could the Home Office authorise Behan's release in June, subject to continued satisfactory progress? That would allow him to be told how he stood. C. A. Joyce, the then Hollesley Bay governor, was further consulted as to Behan's reaction to advance notice of release, even were that some months away. He would go on happily enough, Joyce responded, 'if only it could be sort of definite', as Behan had put it.[151] A memo went to the Home Office seeking a July 1941 release, which would have resulted in total time served (including remand) of around twenty months – well above the norm for a lad who had done as well as Behan and who had received such good reports but still a world away from the ten to twenty years' penal servitude of his adult comrades.

Matters still dragged, the Home Office unwilling to make a commitment until there had been further reports later in the year. On 1 June 1941, Hollesley Bay's Deputy Governor, Gordon Macfarlane, reported. Excluding his period of remand, Behan had completed sixteen months and was now Hollesley Bay's longest-serving lad: 'This puts him in a unique position in the eyes of the other colonists, a position strengthened by the fact that he is above the average in intelligence and facility of tongue.' Macfarlane concluded, 'Had this case been an ordinary one I have no doubt Behan would have been recommended for discharge after twelve months.'[152]

Still the Home Office procrastinated, putting the case back to the autumn. It was not until mid-October 1941 that Philip Allen (then a senior official at the Home Office) indicated that Behan's licence and accompanying expulsion order might be prepared.[153] Behind this letter there lay several months of bureaucratic anxieties and exchanges. The inertia was probably broken by Behan himself, in the sense that through misbehaviour he gave evidence that his lengthy confinement with no clear end in sight (short of the three-year maximum) was causing him to 'deteriorate'. Unbeknownst to Behan, perhaps, this fitted exactly with a fundamental theme in Borstal management theory: that there was a right time for release and that could be known through a lad's behaviour.

On the evening of 13 July 1941, Macfarlane reported to the Governor that he had placed Behan in detention on suspicion of extorting money from another lad. Two boys, Lightning and Parkin, had absconded the previous evening. On being recaptured, one had told Housemaster Shoemake that he had had to pay Behan a penny a week ever since finding and handing in a wallet containing tobacco and money. This find had led to Behan being punished for carrying on a money-lending business. This was set in a context that caused particular concern to Macfarlane. Behan had recently been unsettled enough to ask for a transfer to another Borstal. (Given the cardinal importance of personal relations and loyalties, this rejection would in itself been a considerable worry to staff.) In the circumstances, Macfarlane could not dismiss the possibility that Behan would abscond. He had protested that he would not and that it was not right for him to be held in the detention room. 'However that may be', Macfarlane continued, 'I think detention until your investigation expedient because the reputation of the colony would suffer badly if Behan, with his sentence for IRA activity, should abscond.'[154] Shortly after writing this memorandum, Macfarlane went again to see Behan in the detention room. He added a note: 'Protests innocence, but I am sure in my own mind that he is involved somewhere! Says he will hunger-strike… advised at length, but is adamant. Re transfer, I think he must either be transferred or discharged.' Macfarlane opted for discharge 'because of past disappointments'.[155]

Here Macfarlane was merely reiterating the views of his governor, C. A. Joyce, who, five weeks earlier, had written to the Prison Commission: 'In my opinion, Behan is deteriorating as a result of continued detention, and I consider that the best interests of the lad himself would be served by as early a discharge as is possible.'[156] The Prison Commissioners had forwarded this note to the Home Office recommending release as soon as the Borstal Association could make arrangements.

The Home Office had not stonewalled, but it had not been inactive. This was no ordinary case, as Macfarlane had acknowledged: consultations were necessary before the Home Secretary could properly take a decision. Unlike the other three IRA youths, Behan was not going into the merchant navy, nor would he be released to Northern Ireland. He was an Irish citizen, and his government would have to be told about the planned release and asked for its views; this had to be done through the Dominions Office and would necessarily take some time. Special Branch would also provide an opinion as to the likelihood of Behan's resuming IRA activities: were he to be arrested again on similar charges, the Home Secretary could be gravely embarrassed.

On 15 July 1941, Special Branch gave its discouraging assessment. Despite his extreme youth, Behan had worked 'actively and consciously' for the IRA: 'He admitted to the police that he had made bombs which caused explosions in London and Blackpool, and then went back to Dublin to obtain more explosives.' (Behan had denied that he had made any such statement.) The best course would be to persuade him to go to sea, but if that could not be done he should be expelled under the Prevention of Violence Act. This would carry the risk of his again becoming an IRA activist: 'Our experience is, that once a man has been in the IRA, the leaders of the movement usually succeed by persuasion or threats to get him to resume his work.'[157]

Despite this far-from-reassuring letter, it was decided to press ahead. Behan had now been inside for eighteen months, a wholly exceptional time for someone to be at an open Borstal and now halfway to the point at which release would be mandatory on expiration of sentence. A letter was sent to the Dominions Office on 1 August 1941. This outlined the offence, including as fact the police claim that Behan had admitted making bombs used in London and Blackpool. The Borstal view was also put: Behan had been making satisfactory progress but had now been detained far longer than any other youth at Hollesley Bay, including, therefore, those whose progress had not been entirely satisfactory. The Governor concluded that he was unlikely to derive further benefit from the training and would deteriorate if kept longer. Bradley's assessment was quoted: Behan was a passionate nationalist, but in the anti-Axis war his sympathies were with Britain. Most importantly, there was Behan's assurance to Bradley that he had abandoned all ideas of violence. In the normal course of events, Behan's record at Hollesley Bay would have justified his release after about a year. The special circumstances of the case had hitherto fettered the Home Secretary, but, Behan having completed eighteen months of his sentence, Bradley did not feel it justifiable to continue his detention very much longer. Arrangements would be made to expel him to Ireland, where his relatives lived, but the Éire government might protest against receiving a youth who took an active part in the IRA. Lord Cranborne (Secretary for the Dominions) was asked to seek the Éire government's views.[158]

A month passed without a reply. Hollesley Bay continued to fret and worry, and there were further exchanges between the Prison Commissioners and the Home Office. The Home Office sent a reminder to the Dominions Office on 27 August. On 10 September 1941, Bradley wrote to Hollesley Bay explaining that the Dominions Office had been asked to consult the Éire government and that reminders were being sent 'at reasonable intervals'.[159] Behan was summoned and told what was going on; he said that he was satisfied. Weeks passed. On 3 October 1941 came a letter informing the Home Office that the Irish authorities did not object to Behan's return. For some reason, the Home Office then took its time in writing to the Prison Commission.[160] After that, there was fairly rapid movement. A letter (marked 'Secret') was sent to the Liverpool City Chief Constable informing him of the decision to release and expel Behan and setting out the procedure.[161] A week later, Hollesley Bay was asked to obtain from Behan a written undertaking that he would not engage in 'any activities in connection with the IRA': this was to be forwarded to the Home Office.[162] An expulsion order was signed by the Home Secretary on 18 October 1941. This was executed on 1 November 1941, when Behan was escorted on board the *Hibernia* at Holyhead.

In later life, Brendan Behan may have looked back on his nineteen months at Hollesley Bay as a peaceful and positive episode in a stormy and sometimes confusing life in which considerable success as a playwright was marred by excessive drinking and other personal problems. Despite the promises (and possibly sincere intentions), he was, within five months of his release, in very serious trouble again. In the course of a fracas near Dublin's Glasnevin Cemetery on Easter Sunday, 5 April 1942, he fired three shots from a revolver. Although he made off, he was arrested a few days later, tried and sentenced to fourteen years for the attempted murder of two detective officers of the Garda Síochána.[163] The prison conditions into which he now entered as a nineteen-year-old were utterly different to those at Hollesley Bay.[164]

Gone but not forgotten by the Home Office. Special Branch could not resist passing on information about the new and serious Dublin conviction with a dressing of 'I told you so.'[165] Four months after his 1947 release on amnesty from an Irish prison, Behan was arrested again in Britain. He had defied his expulsion order and had entered the country on the identity documents of an RAF deserter. This, unfortunately, was a man known to police to have been a member of the IRA some years previously and whose claim to have lost his documents in Dublin a month earlier had little credibility. It was also worrying that Behan refused to account for his movements during the five days he admitted to being in Britain. On 1 May 1947, he was sentenced to four months' imprisonment for breaching the expulsion order. Having earned full remission he was released and deported on 23 July 1947.[166]

Post-war Dublin was hard for a man with Behan's record, and in February 1948 he wrote to the Home Office, asking for the expulsion order to be lifted. In mitigation, he pointed out that he had been only sixteen when he committed his offence. He offered as a referee C. A. Joyce, his Hollesley Bay governor and even ('given the proper assurances') his arresting officers, Chief Inspector Edward Pierpoint of Manchester CID and Sergeant Hugh Earps of Liverpool CID.[167] The application, he wrote, was being made by 'an honest artisan seeking an opportunity denied him, thru' economic conditions at home, of earning a living in your country, despite that which is now past and, I should hope, forgotten'. The Home Office was not inclined to forget, and its reservoir of sympathy was at a low level: the application was refused on 13 March 1948. Similar applications were turned down in May 1949 and November 1952.[168]

There had been another brush with the law in October 1952, when Behan was arrested at Newhaven Harbour, en route to France. He spent several days in custody while his story was checked, eventually being fined £15 by Lewes magistrates and placed on the Dieppe ferry.[169] He was by now making a living from his writing, his reputation was growing, and it was evident that the dedicated revolutionary was a child of the past: continued exclusion therefore might be represented as vindictiveness and narrow-mindedness. In November 1952, the Home Office invited him to make his case again. Now, in effect, the courted, Behan waited for more than a year before replying on 3 January 1954. He was not now, he insisted, and had not been for many years, a member of the IRA or 'any political body or organisation of any description whatsoever'. He wanted the order lifted that he might travel through Britain to France. His business there was to write articles for the Irish News Agency, the *Irish Times*, the *Irish Press* and Radio Éireann. There was no direct sea route between Ireland and the Continent, except in the summer season, nor did Aer Lingus operate, except through London in conjunction with BEA. He was willing to give the police a week's notice of his intention to travel, were that needed.[170] By now, his bona-fides as a writer were sufficiently established, and enough time had passed. The Home Office revoked the ban, unconditionally, on 25 January 1954.[171]

Individual adaptations

Behan's Borstal experience was utterly different from that of the adult IRA prisoners. The sentences were generally very long and the majority of the men were wholly unfamiliar with English society, let alone English convict prisons. The hardship was considerable. A number of the early letters home were full of formulaic declarations of defiance and reiterations of IRA justifications for the anti-British struggle.[172] As we have seen, the prisoners were spread around the system as far as the limited convict accommodation permitted. The element of solidarity and mutual support was thus missing for many, and it was hard to sustain actions against the regime. There were individual hunger strikes, refusals of labour and other acts of insubordination: all were unavailing, and breaches of the rules were punished by cellular confinement and punishment diet.[173] Some men were quiet and well behaved from the outset, and even the rebellious, with a few notable exceptions, settled down within the first few years.[174] Others appeared to have conformed so thoroughly with prison rules and routine as to have become almost invisible, their files, even after several years, amounting to no more than a sheet or two, each containing an unremarkable few lines.[175]

Reading played a great part in the prisoners' lives, an important means of mental escape and easement of the pains and deprivations of confinement – especially the many hours spent alone in one's cell. From time to time this led to tussles with authority as the men tested the boundaries of censorship by seeking to bring into the prison publications of an Irish republican or, sometimes, a socialist or communist nature. Publications in Gaelic (usually described as 'Erse' in the files) were treated erratically: allowed for quite a long time and then stopped, perhaps when a new member of staff took over the censor's office. As a result, decisions on publications were frequently inconsistent.[176]

Prison chaplains' duties had from time immemorial included the scrutiny of publications. Revd W. R. Lynch, the Parkhurst Roman Catholic chaplain, protested at the Commissioners' decision to allow Patrick McAleer to have the *Irish Weekly*:

> It fosters in the minds of IRA prisoners the very ideas which have led to their conviction. It is critical of the Allied War Effort, and is the means of conveying information of IRA activities, and criminal news. I... suggest that ordinary British newspapers supply news of the right kind, and fair comment.

After some consideration of the chaplain's objection, the Commissioners informed him that they disagreed with his assessment: McAleer was allowed to continue to receive the publication.[177]

Another case illustrates the irrational nature of some decisions on publications, though, in fairness to the prison staff, their usual population of convicts was unlikely to be interested in politically extreme material. Michael Rory Campbell (alias Liam Gaughran) was denied a copy of John Mitchel's *Jail Journal*. The work, which dealt with the aftermath of the Young Irelander insurrection of 1848, was scarcely incendiary and almost entirely an historical curiosity. More defensible was the ban on the republican *Wolfe Tone Weekly* (on which Brendan Behan had cut his author's teeth) and the *Wolfe Tone Annual*. These had been banned from entry into Britain, but, were they to slip through to a prisoner, they were not to be returned to the sender but were to go to the Commissioners, together with any covering letter and the wrapper, for forwarding to Special Branch.[178]

Educational provision was extremely limited at this time, but, using available resources and opportunities, some prisoners studied – either recreational or vocational subjects. Daniel Jordan (alias O'Regan) took up the mandolin, not an easy instrument.[179] Patrick Kelly (alias Michael Griffin) had been an IRA bomb-maker. He turned his mechanical talent in a different direction (perhaps) and enrolled in a course offered to prisoners by the British Institute of Engineering Technology, which body was very impressed by his abilities. It informed the Commissioners that this was 'one of the most promising studentships we have had to administer under the Prison Commission scheme for some time'. It wanted Kelly to undertake more advanced studies. While the Commissioners were impressed with Kelly's programme, they declined to allow a continuation, presumably because they knew his release was imminent.[180]

If the prisoner quietly serving his sentence, doing all he could to avoid the attention of the authorities, could be described as a submarine, there were others who coped with their situation by picking fights with the authorities: the torpedo boats. To the observer, it seems an exhausting and frequently uncomfortable way of serving a sentence, but for some men combative engagement met a political, emotional or psychological need. At its most effective, this form of adaptation was a series of hit-and-run attacks in a war of attrition. This allowed the prisoner, immobilised and neutralised by the state, closely confined, to take some control, to seize some initiative, to demand attention and – at least notionally – to inflict a degree of inconvenience on his captors.

Several prisoners made these choices. Some, as noted, were fractious at the beginning of their sentences, in the first shocking months, while they came to terms with their situation, but then opted for the quiet life.[181] But one who was a constant source of trouble to the authorities, from beginning to end, was Vincent Compton, serving a twenty-year sentence for explosives offences. Unlike most of his comrades, Compton came to prison with a criminal record and having previously heard the slam of the cell door. It might even be that the severity with which he had been dealt as a child contributed to his later extremism and violent political action. His first conviction, in January 1916, at the age of twelve and a half, earned him five years in an approved school. Thereafter he had convictions for a series of petty offences: shop-breaking, theft, loitering, common assault, wounding, wandering and vagrancy. He claimed to have fought in the Spanish Civil War, as a member of the International Brigade. This was certainly the background to embed an aversion to authority.

From the outset, Compton was confrontational. He voiced very strong objections to being forced to associate with criminals, sexual offenders and homosexuals. Between sentence on 27 October 1939 and 22 April 1948, he was placed on report on ninety-five occasions. This would almost certainly have made him one of the very worst behaved prisoners in the English convict system, political or ordinary criminal. His battles were not all on his own behalf, and four months before his release he lodged a protest at the alleged beating up of another prisoner. His behaviour was so turbulent and apparently impervious to disciplinary sanction or control that a medical officer diagnosed him as schizoid with paranoidal tendencies, but not certifiable.[182]

Among Compton's protests were several episodes of hunger-striking. On one occasion he combined this with smashing up his hospital cell, in an apparent frenzy. Ironically, this action was to back demands to be allowed to associate with other IRA men. The outburst appalled the Medical Officer, who reported it in some detail to the Governor. Compton had used all available objects to destroy the cell: religious and other books and his chamber pot included. As the work proceeded, the Medical Officer reported, he kept shouting 'and making filthy remarks'. Everything that could be used for destruction was then removed from the cell. Not to be foiled, Compton managed to extract the bolts from his radiator and to throw them along the corridor, breaking windows. When the doctor tried to reason with him, he spat in his face. A search of the now-destroyed cell uncovered a razor-edged piece of glass, which the doctor speculated might have been intended for a suicide attempt, since Compton had threatened self-harm if all else failed. Further attempts to talk to him provoked further spitting. He was eventually put in a straitjacket. Even then he continued to shout and protest. His chamber pot having been removed, he simply urinated on the floor rather than ask for it. The Medical Officer, obviously shaken, reported that, '[a]t present, it is presumed he is more fanatic than lunatic although his recent conduct almost makes one doubt if the former is the more active mental state'.[183]

Over the rest of Compton's sentence there were more episodes of misbehaviour but not of such manic intensity. There were several hunger strikes: one as a protest at being made to lace up his shoes whilst at exercise, another in solidarity with hunger-strikers at Belfast Prison. In 1946 he spent four and a half of the first five months of the year in the punishment cells. By this point, the authorities seem to have lost all patience and hope of changing his behaviour and may well have been content to leave him locked up and out of the way. Each time he finished a sentence in the punishment cells (stripped-down rooms, bare and bleak and made worse by a highly restricted diet), he would refuse the order to leave, incurring further punishment for disobedience.[184] The Medical Officer reported that Compton considered himself to be the most patriotic of all the IRA prisoners 'although they hold a very different opinion'. He thought that he had an exaggerated idea of his own intelligence and perspicacity and was refusing to cooperate as the only means of asserting his dignity. In May 1946, the Irish Prisoners' Welfare Committee wrote to the Parkhurst Medical Officer about Compton's behaviour. Frank Lee, the Committee Secretary, had been allowed to see Compton and reported that his impression was 'not very favourable'. According to Lee, Compton was of 'a different character [sic] altogether to that of the other Irishmen'. He also reported that many of the other prisoners had asked him to do something for Compton: 'My own impression was that Compton was slightly unbalanced.'[185]

Prison behaviour was of course one of the criteria used to determine the place of the twenty-year prisoners on the list of staggered releases. Compton, because of his 'exceedingly troublesome' behaviour, was recommended for release around November 1949: he was to be the last to go. The Home Secretary took a more compassionate view and ordered his release on 8 November 1948. The boundary between political fanaticism and insanity must in many cases be fluid, and it would seem that Compton crossed it, more than once.[186]

Prisoners as correspondents

Correspondence is extremely important to all in captivity and to political prisoners perhaps more than most. The convict allowance in the 1940s was two letters out and in per month, with an additional one in lieu of a visit. Urgent family matters could be compassionate grounds for an addition to this ration. Sometimes, as we saw with Brendan Behan, letters were written with the intention of criticising, lampooning or provoking the authorities. At other times, there were innocent breaches of the rules: in all such eventualities the letters were suppressed and placed in the prisoner's file and he was ordered to rewrite. We thus have a quantity of material from which to grasp the nature of their concerns and sentiments and even insights into their character. Political sentiments featured most strongly at an early point in the sentence. Gerard Lyons (alias Gerald Anthony Dunlop) had been involved in the Belfast IRA for some years and had served a short sentence there in 1937 under the Special Powers Act. Writing to his stepmother, Anne Lyons, in January 1940, he wanted England to lose the war and thought that the country was not getting the best of it: 'the sooner that she is broken once and for all the better'. He deplored the fact that on St Patrick's Day the prisoners would not be allowed to wear shamrock. The men convicted for the Coventry explosion, James McCormick and Peter Barnes, he considered to have been murdered, not executed.[187] There was much the same in a letter to his sweetheart Brigid. The execution of Barnes and McCormick had been commemorated by the Parkhurst IRA men by a two-minute silence, and a prison mass had been allowed at which prayers were said for the repose of their souls. There was much patriotic rhetoric about Ireland and a declaration that he was more determined than ever 'to carry on in the Old Cause'.[188]

Such correspondence was suppressed for violent sentiments, because other prisoners were mentioned, because it contained phrases in Irish, or all three. Lyons was unrepentant, and the following month he wrote in much the same vein, gloating on Britain's likely defeat: 'Well, I can see now that England has got herself in about the most uncomfortable hole she has ever been in since her existence as a world power.' The war might soon finish with Britain in 'a state of subjugation, unless she is able to make peace terms. I firmly believe that this is the fall of the British Empire, whether another takes her place I don't not [sic] know, but all the signs are pointed in one way.'[189] Eight weeks later, with Dunkirk, many would have shared his views.

Close to the date of their conviction some prisoners focused on their grievances with the police. Peter Campbell, who could write shorthand, was found in possession of a document, very likely intended to be smuggled out of prison, in which he claimed that there had been perjured testimony at his trial. He gave details of some of the things he had himself said in court and of other prisoners.[190] In his first letter to his mother and sister he made further comments on his case. Had he gone into the witness box and denounced the Irish people 'so that the British could make foul propaganda out of it' he could have gone free. He was made of different stuff than the police imagined 'and if I have to forfeit my freedom… I don't mind in the least'. They were not to worry about him: 'you will feel the joy of it all yourselves some time and when the autumn and the long nights come you will have the thrill of it by seeing the glow and the bondfire [sic] on the Border'.[191]

Writing to a woman friend around the same time, Campbell referred to the election of Mrs Tom Clarke as Lord Mayor of Dublin: 'a friend of IRA prisoners'. He referred to the Isle of Wight (the location of Parkhurst Prison) as Tom Clarke's birthplace and to a school in Dungannon in which Clarke had taught and where (many years later) Campbell had been a pupil. Clarke had served fifteen years in an English prison, on a similar charge to Campbell's, 'on identical evidence of prostitutes and the scum and dirt of England'. What the English government could not do by hanging and murder 'without shocking the morals of their own people, who are generous hearted, they achieved by pack [*sic*] juries; by partisan Judges and prepared evidence'. Parkhurst, with its association with periods of Irish history, would serve only one purpose: 'as an inspiration to us to fight, fight on!!'[192]

Later letters to female correspondents included requests for photos, chat about mutual friends and congratulation on engagements, interspersed with anti-British observations. As the battle of Britain raged, Campbell referred to the bombing raids on Portsmouth with a pun: 'We get all the reports and the fun. You get all the lies of the reports and the fun.'[193] Campbell rejoiced in the air raids: 'A thrilling time… our joy was their sorrow.' News of a church being hit by bombs evoked the comment that it was a pity that Cardinal Hinsley (the Roman Catholic Primate of England) 'wasn't among the ashes!'[194] But it was not these sentiments that caused the letter to be suppressed. The offending passages, marked in blue ink by the censor, were Campbell's complaints about the prison's postal arrangements. In particular, the censor objected to what appeared to be a solicitation of cards and letters at Christmas.[195] Post which had been withheld or which had gone astray prompted an outburst about 'the worthlessness of an Englishman's word'.[196]

Two final letter-writers must suffice as samples. The first was John Evans (alias James O'Brien), convicted of conspiracy to cause explosions and sentenced to twenty years' penal servitude.[197] His suppressed letters were much the same as others: social and weather chit-chat ('The air is very nice here and the weather is fairly good'), many requests to be remembered to various friends, mixed with political comment and (sure to attract the censor's eye) observations about prison life.[198] As the months and years went by, a particular element of pathos begins to permeate the letters. Among the group of young men and women with whom Evans had socialised, mentions of marriages become frequent, emphasising his own removal from the normal pattern of life, which continued as before, leaving him behind, missing out on experiences and opportunities which he might never retrieve. On a couple of occasions he had learned of engagements or marriages from third parties, and one supposes that his friends were loath to write to him about their own pleasures and unfolding happiness: such, of course, is the lot of any long-term prisoner. Some of the things Evans missed could not have been imagined by a free person. Mention by Georgina Brady of sitting with family and friends around the fire made him homesick: 'I will be like a child the next fire I see "fall into it if I am not careful!".'[199]

Evans's references to prison life, which were never to pass the prison gate, give interesting insights into how the IRA men lived together. As on the outside, recreational time was passed with storytelling and singing. There was, in many of the letters, a degree of rejoicing about air raids and passages of republican rhetoric. The spirit of the IRA men in Camp Hill, he asserted, could not be broken by sword or iron bars. They were 'all the more determined. Foreign foe and nation [*sic*] traitors have failed to break us "and they done their best", so it is up to us to do the rest.'[200] Britain was elsewhere described as a dying dog, and Evans wrote that there was much more that he could say but that it would not go down well with the censor, so 'I'll have to be good and not hurt their feelings.'[201]

In December 1940, the Camp Hill IRA men went on hunger strike, protesting at what they saw as an unjust punishment of a comrade. A report of this was unlikely to get out via an ordinary letter, since it breached the rule about discussing prison routine. Perhaps Evans realised this, and his letter was intended for the censor's office only. Certainly it was full of protest. Since the men were refusing food they were not allowed to attend mass, 'one of the lowest and meanest & cowardliest things they could have done to us… But God Himself knows we will not be separated from him by freemasonry or paganism which we are the victims of being under.' What they were going through was 'something more than some of our Catholic statesmen would care to think of'.[202] A woman friend had asked Evans if she could send him a pullover. He asked his mother to say that it would not be allowed. 'We would be too comfortable if we were allowed things like that, it would look like as if we were getting treated like Christians.'[203]

In early January 1941, there were several incidents of German bombing in Dublin and elsewhere. The bombs caused a deal of damage to property, many injuries and loss of life.[204] One of the more absurd rumours in Dublin at the time had it that these were unexploded German bombs, retrieved by the British and dropped by them on Dublin. Who would imagine that the British would do things like that, Evans asked with heavy meaning, in a letter to Georgina Brady.[205]

Despite the close censorship (and the IRA prisoners' mail had the extra layer of Special Branch scrutiny), there seemed to be no prohibition on correspondence from other IRA prisoners in Éire. This indulgence may have been an exercise in intelligence-gathering. In February 1941, Evans received a letter from one of the IRA women in Mountjoy Prison, Dublin. He reported enthusiastically on this to Georgina: 'I got a letter yesterday from one of the girls in Mountjoy they are great. They seem to be in the best of spirits and having a good time. They have not heard from the Curragh for some time either.'[206] Standing orders and regulation had the odd effect of allowing Irish prisoners to write whilst enforcing a strict prohibition on corresponding with fellow prisoners in England. Evans was keen to know of the women prisoners at Aylesbury Prison, Buckinghamshire (Mrs Ella Woods and Rita McSweeney).[207] He also asked Georgina to write to Margaret Nolan, then interned at Holloway Prison.[208]

The prisoners were allowed newspapers, but these were also censored, as Evans complained in a letter to Georgina Brady in September 1941. The cut-out sections of a newspaper must have been particularly tantalising and incited much speculation. Some event in Ireland must have been getting great publicity, he wrote, but owing to it being connected to the IRA were not allowed to read it. For a few days the papers were cut up like a 'jig saw' even as far as being stopped altogether. Class distinction is not supposed to exist in here. But Red Tape has got to be extended in the case of IRA 'terrorists'.[209]

As with a number of his comrades, John Evans's ability to express himself in writing improved with the passage of the months and the years. Seven years into his sentence he applied to be excused compulsory attendance at religious services. There was quite a strict rule about this, partly in order to deter prisoners' changes of religion, some of which would have been frivolous or opportunistic, with the attendant administrative inconvenience. A prisoner was asked his religion on reception into the prison and had to adhere to it thereafter, including attendance at all relevant services. Evans made an application to the Governor not to change his religion but to be excused from attending Roman Catholic services. The Governor said that he could not grant the request and suggested that Evans apply to the Camp Hill Visiting Committee: this he did.[210]

His religious ideas had undergone a change whilst he had been in prison, Evans wrote to the Committee. He only attended services under compulsion, and

[t]o have to enter the church for a service and take no part, must to some degree distract other men who wish to worship and take an active part in the service. The alternative of going through the motions is to play the part of a hypocrite which is a position I do not feel inclined to allow myself to be forced into.

His second reason related to a statement by Cardinal Arthur Hinsley at the time of the IRA bombing campaign. This, he recalled, had been worded rather ambiguously but had been taken by the general public and most of the clergy as being a decision to excommunicate the IRA bombers. Evans had been given news of this decision by the Roman Catholic chaplain whilst on remand in Brixton Prison. This meant that he was being forced to attend services in which he no longer had any faith and which, by Cardinal Hinsley's decision he should not be allowed to attend.

The Visiting Committee might think that he should apply for a change of religion, but, Evans stated, 'I do not wish to make a definite change of religion on ideas that have been formed in prison and which prison surroundings may to some extent have contributed.' He wished to wait in order to make a decision about changing his religion 'until I have seen whether my attitude remains the same when I have returned to more normal surroundings when my bias from my present status will not be present'. This was a reasoned, articulate and moderately worded petition, which the Visiting Committee granted.[211] In his years of imprisonment, Evans had indeed come a long way in his ability to express himself, in his self-confidence and reflectiveness. His limited education is always evident in his letters, but behind this he was not lacking in intelligence or in concern about wider issues. It is this quality that gives him, and many of his comrades, a tragic and even pitiable aspect.

Evans was unmarried, as were most of the IRA prisoners. As noted, a particular source of regret for the single would have been the news of engagements and marriages and a sense of exclusion from this very important phase of life. The passages in letters dwelling upon convivial evenings in the houses of their friends' families dealt with a time of commingling, preparatory to pairing off, as many of those to whom they wrote were already doing. For the older, married prisoners there were of course different worries and regrets. Wives and children, intimacy and the close life of the home were deeply missed, and there were worries about how dependants were faring. John Gavahan, married, in his early thirties and with two young children (aged four and five) completes this brief look at prisoners as correspondents.

Gavahan was part of the group of seven sentenced for their part in the Manchester conspiracy.[212] A pipe layer by trade (whose knowledge had doubtless been useful in placing the first electrical-ducting bombs), he came from Belfast and was in employment at the time of his arrest. His family lived with him in Manchester; the police reported him to be sober and industrious. By the end of his sentence, Gavahan had come to be reasonably well regarded by prison officials. The Parkhurst Roman Catholic chaplain wrote just before his release that Gavahan was a determined character and a strong critic of the prison system, by which he had been 'rather affected'. While he was not a man to change his views very easily, the chaplain thought that he was, on the whole, 'a fairly good type'.[213] Like many of the other prisoners, he committed various offences against the rules during the early part of his sentence. The most serious of these was an attempted escape from Leeds Prison, subsequent to which he was placed on the escape list and moved through the system, local as well as convict.[214] By a strange oversight, he was not punished for this attempt.

Gavahan was, however, punished for his other offences, all but three of which were committed during his first year. These were all acts of defiance, none in themselves very serious. They included refusing an order to parade for drill, leaving his work party without permission, refusing to work, refusing to drill, creating a disturbance and causing damage, refusing to accept his gas mask and refusing to draw his blackout curtain. He was variously punished, losing a large number of remission marks. The fact that he then settled down and appeared to change course contributed to the favourable view that the authorities eventually took of him.

Not long after his conviction, Gavahan's wife left Manchester and moved to Charlestown, Co. Mayo, where presumably she had family or other connections. Correspondence thereafter became particularly important to husband and wife alike. As far as can now be seen from the record, his wife was never able to visit him in prison in England, as might be expected for a young mother living in straitened circumstances with her children and with all the difficulties of wartime travel.

A number of Gavahan's letters were suppressed for the usual reasons. Even among this group of extremely anti-British men and women, Gavahan's letters stand out for the extravagance of their statements and for their simple hatred. His complaints about prison were equally unrestrained. On food, he wrote, 'it is like what you would see on a pig's feeding through [*sic*] board, after the pigs walked through it a few times with their dirty feet'. At this point he appeared to have been in a punishment cell, which, he wrote, was 'like being in a cold storage room, and along with this I am on bread and water. This is the treatment we are getting from John Bull and then the[y] talk about the German Camps here.'[215]

The nature of confinement and the personalities of many prisoners make for a deal of self-centredness and selfishness, whatever the times and nature of the offence; this is one of the certainties of prison life. It would not be uncommon for men to make requests for toiletries and other items, seemingly oblivious to the sacrifices that wives or relations might have to endure to provide them.[216] Gavahan did not ask for material items, but, in the early part of his sentence at least, he showed no great concern for his wife's plight. He structured his letters so that the first page was a political rant and instructed his wife to cut it off from the rest of the letter-form and show it around: a type of leaflet. In this early letter (August 1939), his wife was still living in England. Gavahan asked her to burn her gas mask (a criminal offence) as it only served English propaganda. In another letter, he also asked her to have his claims about food and ill-treatment published. There was no indication that he had considered whether she would have had any idea how to go about that, or that, had she done so, she would have been protected from unpleasant consequences.

His wife was evidently a disappointment to John Gavahan, at least as a cor-respondent. Seven months in prison, full of anger and frustration, she bore the brunt of it:

> Your last letter to me was 5 days later than the one before, how do you account for that. Also you write a lot of stuff in your letters which does not interest me in the least. I have asked you in my last letter several things I wished to know of and you have not said one word about it, in fact all the letters I have wrote since I being here [*sic*] has the same tale. Now regards house I don't know what you are talking about, for that matter there is houses in Kiltimagh, Ballandine, Ball, Molina, Coontia and of course not forgetting in the middle of the Big Big Bog.

The letter continued in this manner, incongruously concluding, 'your loving husband Jack xxx'.[217] This was suppressed, not for Gavahan's bullying and gratuitously unpleasant tone but because of the political outburst with which it was prefaced.

However, the marriage developed during the years of Gavahan's confinement – and prison tests all marriages severely – by 1947, it was to his cousin Mary, rather than to his wife, that Gavahan wrote, seeking help with health problems.

He had, he claimed, been brutally beaten by the Manchester police on the night he was arrested. There had been other beatings by prison officers for breaking prison rules. He asked Mary to get in touch with the Northern Ireland MPs Harry Diamond and Cahir Healy and with the Irish lawyer Eoin O'Mahony, on his behalf.[218] Since the letter was suppressed, as surely he must have known it would be, no such contacts were made. But in connection with his health, in another letter he paid the Parkhurst Medical Officer a compliment, favourably contrasting the treatment he had received from him with that at Dartmoor ('Dartmoor Concentration Camp').

Releases

In the criminal and penal fields, as in others, even in the war's slough of despond, British officials and politicians began to turn their attention to peacetime policy. After the victories of El Alamein and Stalingrad (November 1942 and January 1943, respectively) the outcome was scarcely in doubt, and a start had to be made on all aspects of the massive task of reconstruction.[219] The fate of Irish political prisoners was only one item on an immense 'to do' list, and very far down it. Besides, relations between the UK and Éire had comparatively little priority in British foreign policy. Nevertheless, with peace there would be inevitable demands for amnesty, to which ministers had to be prepared to respond. Early Home Office discussions established a number of principles.

The first was that there could be no general amnesty. It was considered repugnant to public sentiment to release men and women who had attacked Britain at the time of its greatest peril. Looking to Germany and its allies, there was a keen appetite for retribution rather than reconciliation; looking to imperial responsibilities alone, many troubles menaced or were in train. A guerrilla war was gathering momentum in the Mandate territory of Palestine; India was on the verge of a troubled and possibly bloody independence; Burma and the Malay Peninsula showed ominous signs of insurrection. Throughout the colonial world a tide of nationalism was rising, with its inevitable attendants: ethnic, religious and linguistic conflicts. At the very least, there was no pressing reason to extend clemency to members of the IRA. Another consideration was the experience of past outcomes. Amnesties had followed the 1916 Rising, in 1918, and in the final settlement of the Anglo-Irish War, yet violent republicanism had regrouped. It could only be an encouragement to future IRA campaigns were yet another general release to confirm the view that no matter how grave their crimes Irish political offenders did not serve their full sentences.

An early stimulus to agree the details of policy and procedure came from enquiries by the Scottish Home Department. The Scots were less concerned with the possibility of amnesty than with the procedure for releasing those who had reached that point in their sentences at which they would be eligible for release on licence. Should they then be freed and could they be expelled from the country?[220] There had been only six IRA prisoners in Scottish prisons. Two had already been liberated on licence and the remaining four would become eligible in 1946 and 1947.[221] Scots' law did not explicitly confer a right to release at the date of licence eligibility. In practical terms, however, there was some difference between the two jurisdictions in the matter. The English customarily released penal prisoners on their reaching licence eligibility, but they had also retained some, on security grounds. Release at this point was viewed as an act of grace, which might therefore be withheld.[222] Although Scots' law agreed in principle that release on licence was an act of executive grace, the Lord Advocate had laid down that it would be 'contrary to the ordinary principles of justice to discriminate in this matter between one convict and another on purely political grounds'. The Scottish Home Department considered this view 'unfortunate', but since it was held by the Lord Advocate did not think there was much point in arguing the case.[223] A month later, still vexed by the forthcoming McSherry release, the Scots returned to the matter, asking the Home Office what legal authority was used to retain on security grounds those who had reached their licence-eligibility date. Possibly Scottish officials hoped that by citing English practice their lord advocate could be persuaded or outflanked in some way.[224]

That remedy was not offered, and, as McSherry's release eventually loomed, the Scots simply sought detailed advice on the procedure for removing him from the country. The Home Office disclosed that it applied pressure on such prisoners. Its 'almost invariable practice' was to inform the prisoner shortly before the release-eligibility date that the Home Secretary was not prepared to authorise release in England but, should the prisoner agree to give an undertaking to go to Éire and not to return, a licence would be issued. This dangled release before the prisoner, provided that he or she signed. (Up to that point, only one man had refused to give the undertaking.) Once release had been authorised, arrangements were made with Special Branch and with the Irish authorities for repatriation.[225]

Days before the war with Japan ended, the Irish High Commission in London began to make discreet enquiries about the release of IRA prisoners. This took the form of an oblique approach from the Irish High Commissioner, John W. Dulanty. Requesting a list of those still imprisoned, he intimated that the Irish government might make representations on behalf of persons sentenced to long terms 'as a result of violent actions prompted by political fanaticism'.[226] Sir Alexander Maxwell, now Home Office Permanent Under-Secretary was immediately suspicious. To provide such information might seem a neutral act, devoid of commitment, but were a response provided, in Maxwell's opinion, it would take on the character of a list of persons prepared by the Home Secretary 'in respect of whom he thought there was a *prima facie* case for representation by the Éire government'. The names were accordingly withheld.[227]

What could not be obtained via an official request could of course be obtained by other means: the information was not a state secret. Once Parliament had reassembled, and with an overwhelming Labour presence in the Commons, it was not too difficult to plant a parliamentary question. On 28 November 1945, George Porter, Labour MP for Leeds Central, asked the Home Secretary to state the total number of Irish citizens detained for political offences; he also wanted to know what prospects there were for their release. The answer was that there were forty-eight such prisoners in England and Wales, including a man about to be released on compassionate grounds.[228] There was no reason to exercise the Royal Prerogative, and it had been decided not to revive the old custom of general amnesty to mark important national occasions (such as the war's victorious conclusion).[229]

Two months later, a group of MPs with a special interest in Ireland (who described themselves as the Friends of Ireland Group), together with William Norton and James Larkin of the Irish Labour Party, were received by the Home Secretary, James Chuter Ede.[230] Norton asked for the IRA prisoners to be released. He did not in any way agree with their aims, but, in retrospect, the sentences looked heavy. All had by now served seven years. Britain's war danger was past, and no harm would come from sending them back home: 'They were not ordinary criminals – their good behaviour in prison would have demonstrated that – but had acted in furtherance of a misconceived political ideal.' Release would be greatly appreciated in Éire and among the Irish electorate in Britain. Larkin said much the same and referred to 'recent treatment of the members of the Indian National Army'.[231] The prisoners, he went on, would give no further trouble: their cause was discredited in Éire. The representations, private, diplomatic, conciliatory and persuasive though they were, failed to shift the Home Office. Chuter Ede replied that the cases of the Irish prisoners would routinely be reviewed but that he could see no reason for a general amnesty.[232]

The Irish Prisoners' Welfare Committee, which had hitherto restricted itself to welfare support for the prisoners, now became more active in lobbying.[233] Its secretary, Frank Lee, was a long-time Labour Party activist. He pushed the prisoners' case through Valentine la Touche (Val) McEntee, Labour MP for West Walthamstow. Faced with what he perceived to be an unyielding Home Office, the tone of Lee's letter to McEntee was bitter. He took three cases as examples of Chuter Ede's refusal to show 'a grain of mercy', a determination to have 'his pound of flesh'. In a letter that wound itself up into a rant, he expostulated that '[t]he common crook, sex maniac and the usual type found in Parkhurst will get plenty of mercy, but our lads will do every day and then be asked to sign some iniquitous document which their conscience won't let them sign'.[234] Lee reminded McEntee of long-standing and active support of the Labour Party at elections and went on to say that rather than being a movement of idealists that might be expected to have some understanding of the Irish struggle, he was beginning to think the Party was 'a bunch of humbugs, opportunists and Thomas's'.[235]

Were Lee intending to persuade the Home Secretary to show leniency, such bombast was absurdly misplaced. For some reason, perhaps laziness, McEntee aggravated Lee's misjudgement. Instead of summarising and recasting it in more acceptable terms, he passed the letter directly to the Home Secretary. Lee's intemperate language stoked Home Office misgivings about his organisation, to which it had accorded privileged access to the IRA prisoners.[236] This was not alluded to in Chuter Ede's reply to McEntee. As he had insisted in his Commons' reply to George Porter on 28 November 1945, and in subsequent private discussions, 'there can be no question of anything in the nature of a general amnesty'. He would from time to time review individual cases on their merits, giving the same attention that other long terms of penal servitude received. There was some flexibility, however. The case of the Conway sisters had been reconsidered, and they would now be released on the same day as Ella Woods.[237]

The more strident tone of the Irish Prisoners' Welfare Committee had been evident in a letter sent directly to the Home Secretary around the same time, demanding that prisoners should not be required to sign an undertaking to quit the country as a condition for release. Thanking Chuter Ede for the cooperation extended by officials in providing welfare contacts, the Committee protested strongly on other issues: 'We learn with disgust that Wm. O'Hanlon recently released from Birmingham has been arrested in the Six Counties & charged with living in his Native Town.' The continued refusal of a general amnesty was 'the knell of all our hopes of a new and better understanding'.[238] Such disappointment may have been increased five weeks later when de Valera publicly indicated that he would not make representations on behalf of the IRA prisoners, although, as we have seen, at some remove, he was doing exactly that.[239]

The Irish Prisoners' Welfare Committee continued its contacts with the Home Office throughout 1946, although Lee's unfortunate language, and suspicions that the rules had been bent or broken during welfare visits, had damaged its credibility. In a more general sense, the organisation had taken on a nationalist rather than welfare hue. Towards the end of the year, the Committee was given permission to send in £2 to each of the Irish prisoners. A note was made on the file, however, that it had recently come under suspicion of being involved in trafficking at Parkhurst. Evidence was sufficiently strong a few weeks later to curtail the 'fairly ready access' of committee members (including Frank Lee): 'Some of these visitors are known to have been smuggling in money for the IRA prisoners.'[240]

The Welfare Committee had lost whatever little influence it might have had, but that did not stop attempts to obtain an amnesty. In December 1946, Cahir Healy and Eoin O'Mahony asked to visit Parkhurst's twenty-nine IRA prisoners. Permission was given, and the visits immediately got under way.[241] O'Mahony spent two weeks visiting twenty-seven men at Parkhurst and at Totworth (later called Leyhill, an open prison in Gloucestershire). Eight of the thirty-five held at the two prisons had refused to see him.[242] Following these contacts and seeking to go over the head of the apparently immovable Chuter Ede, O'Mahony wrote directly to Prime Minister Clement Attlee. All but two of the men were IRA members, O'Mahony acknowledged, contending nevertheless that statements he had taken from five prisoners 'establish their legal innocence'. In one case (Thomas Nelson), O'Mahony had visited the man who actually placed the incendiary device at Madame Tussauds waxworks but who had never been apprehended. The man was willing to admit his guilt by swearing an affidavit but wanted immunity from prosecution before doing so.[243]

No prime minister was remotely likely to challenge the authority of a secretary of state on such an issue, and none less so than the conventional and deliberative Attlee. Replying, he restated Chuter Ede's position, for whom, he added, the matter was entirely reserved.[244] O'Mahony was not deflected, and the following month he addressed the Law Society at Trinity College Dublin on the issue.[245] He followed this up, in late April, by circulating the affidavits he had obtained from prisoners at Parkhurst and Totworth.[246] As a remedy to supposed injustices, this beating of drums outside the walls was totally futile, though for sympathisers it doubtless had the merit of keeping the issue alive.

And, indeed, it was taken up again in the Commons, this time by Henry McGhee, Labour MP for Penistone, who on 24 February 1947 was due to ask for the details of the total number of Irish republican prisoners, their names and expected dates of release.[247] The Home Office preparation of the response raised for internal discussion the matter of the written undertaking. J. P. Martin, serving a ten-year sentence, had been due for release on licence on 3 January 1947. Refusing to sign the undertaking to go to Éire and not to return to Britain, Martin had, accordingly, been retained in custody. He had not objected to the undertaking in principle but would not sign because he was not sure he could honour it – presumably looking to his prospects at home and perhaps the necessity of seeking employment in England, like so many of his countrymen at that time.[248]

Martin's scruples led to second thoughts at the Home Office where closer scrutiny showed the undertaking to be redundant. As soon as a discharged IRA prisoner left the country, an order was made against him or her under the Prevention of Violence Act, and should they return they were liable to be prosecuted. In that event, why require them to sign an undertaking not to return to Britain? All that was needed in Martin's case was an agreement to go to Éire on release. And if that were sufficient for him, it would have to apply to all IRA prisoners. Chuter Ede agreed that the form could be reduced to this one clause. It was also decided that McGhee should be given the number of IRA prisoners but not their names.[249]

Since it had largely forfeited the goodwill of politicians and officials, and realised that it had done so, the Prisoners' Welfare Committee felt free to apply pressure directly on the Labour Party. A by-election was being held in the Liverpool Edge Hill constituency in September 1947. Campaigning for the release of the IRA prisoners, the Committee appealed to the electorate (of which a sizeable portion was Irish by birth or connection) to vote against the Labour candidate. Beverley Baxter, the Conservative MP for Wood Green (North London) intervened by supporting an amnesty, provided those released went to Ireland. A number of sympathisers were induced to send messages of support – a decidedly odd mixture, including the Countess of Antrim, Sir Shane Leslie, Lord Killanin and Seán O'Casey.[250] In the event, the Committee's intervention in the by-election had no discernible effect, as voters showed their general dissatisfaction with government.[251] With a Labour majority in the Commons in excess of

140 seats, there was not the slightest chance of bringing sufficient pressure in this way: the Home Office line remained unchanged.

The focus now shifted to Ireland. An Irish general election was due in January 1948, and de Valera needed to reassure his core supporters following a period during which he had dealt with the IRA with relentless severity. He had also to consider the effect on the chances of those who would enter the election as militant republicans. He therefore considered it advantageous to his party were the IRA prisoners in England to be freed. To this end, on 4 November 1947, during a visit to London, de Valera had rather an extraordinary conversation with the Secretary of State for Commonwealth Affairs, Philip Noel-Baker. He stated that he fully understood the necessity to take action against men who committed such crimes before and during the war; it should be remembered, however, that they had thought they were serving a sacred cause. Without any sense of irony, either in what he was saying and to whom it was being said, de Valera told Noel-Baker that he himself had been obliged to take action against them 'and even order the execution of a few'. He claimed that he 'would rather have resigned from office altogether than do any such thing, but the overriding public interest of maintaining law and order had made it essential'. Even so, he asked Noel-Baker to consider that the men had now been seven or eight years in prison, and, 'when he had been a year in Maidstone himself, he felt that there was no human crime which would not have been expiated by twelve months of such existence. Eight years was an appalling sentence.'[252]

In the light of these observations, the Irish leader asked whether the British government could now consider releasing the men. Irish feeling towards the UK was better than ever before, 'and the old bitterness was passing away'. He then referred to his opponents in the forthcoming election: 'Mr McBride [*sic*] and his friends may use such things as the imprisonment of these IRA men to stir up hostility again.' By releasing the prisoners, 'one more cause of dispute and misunderstanding would be removed'. He hoped that action might be possible in the early future.[253]

De Valera's stock was low in London, and his electoral prospects were of small concern to the British government. The Home Office had already considered a scheme that would accelerate releases but over a time and at a rate that would not assist de Valera electorally. The plan was based on principles which had been adopted in 1944. Fundamental to these was agreement that there could be no general amnesty. It followed that any early releases would have to be staggered. In determining the order in which the men would be freed (and many had sentences of the same length), a second principle would come into play: as far as possible, cases should be considered on individual merits and circumstances.[254] Within these requirements, a scheme for phased release was possible and practical – and politically acceptable. The twenty-year men, it was agreed, would not be kept for longer than about ten years. In turn, this necessitated a completion of releases by the end of 1949.

Miss Turner of the Home Office's Criminal Division had undertaken a detailed review of the cases of all twenty-nine remaining prisoners. From this she drew up a schedule for phased release. This gave weightings for variations in age, degree of culpability, compassionate considerations, family obligations, prison behaviour and present attitude towards the IRA: in essence, this was a re-sentencing exercise. The criteria were applied mainly to the twenty-year men, of whom there were twenty-two. Of the seven with sentences of less than twenty years, some were shortly to be released. Morgan (twelve years) was due to be freed on 7 December 1947, for example, and Turner recommended that Preston (serving the same sentence but not due for release until 30 March 1948 because of mis-conduct) should go out at the same time. Those with fourteen-, fifteen- and seventeen-year sentences would follow.[255]

Differentiating between the twenty-year men required a finer calibration of culpability and careful weighing of mitigating and aggravating factors. Space precludes a case-by-case examination of how Turner applied her criteria, but the official records are interesting and instructive. At the head of the schedule was Patrick McAleer, who had tuberculosis, 'quiescent at present'. Then came John Evans, who had reportedly broken with the IRA whilst in prison. Further down the list, but still recommended for early release, came Pat Dower from Waterford, whose mother was ill. Dower was only twenty-one on conviction and was believed to regret his offence. Some of these distinctions were based on prison behaviour, but this one may have been no more than a chance remark or two overheard and recorded by staff. Jack Gavahan came lower still, the principal consideration in his favour being the fact that he had two young children. Immediately following his name, Turner put Gerard Lyons. In Lyons's favour was his age: twenty-one when convicted; against him were prison reports that showed him to be 'self-opinionated and stubborn'. Timothy Murray had equally balanced qualities. He had been only nineteen when convicted and he had asthma, but weighing against him, he was reported to be a 'Pigheaded youth. Resentful of authority.' J. O'Regan had a widowed mother in Ireland, a huma-nitarian consideration somewhat counterbalanced by the fact that he had, in his early days of imprisonment, planned to escape. Last of all in the order of release was Vincent Compton. Compton's age (thirty-six) was on the negative side of the scale to which was added the fact that he had lost 1,223 days through mis-conduct. Prison reports showed Compton to be 'anti-social, a trouble maker and a schizoid psychopath'. It was further noted that he had several prior convictions for larceny, violence and the like. Turner recommended that he be freed on 30 November 1949. Of all the prisoners, Compton would have benefited most from the early release scheme. Because of his loss of his remission he was otherwise not due to walk through the gates until March 1956.[256]

Turner's schedule had a number of strengths which commended it to senior officials and politicians. Chief of these was its conscientious attempt to achieve equity. Venturing nowhere near a general amnesty, she had managed to make a number of differentiations. Some of her distinctions were hardly more than speculation, but overall they had sufficient substance and logic: these decisions could, if necessary, be defended. For the scheme to work politically and not to provoke a political or public reaction, it was necessary to implement it in an orderly fashion, to start releases almost immediately and to avoid sensation – to avoid, indeed, all notice, were that possible. In particular, the target of completion by the end of 1949 had to be kept within a small circle.

The IRA men's continued imprisonment boiled on as an issue both in Britain and in Ireland. On 23 October 1947, in the Dáil, the opposition Labour Party had pressed de Valera for action.[257] Lord Killanin had put down another question in the Lords.[258] Seán O'Casey (then at the height of his fame) had, in a letter to the *Irish Press*, drawn attention to the prisoners.[259] There was, however, no great weight behind these expressions of concern, much less momentum. The prospect of an end to sixteen years of Fianna Fáil rule and of de Valera's displacement excited the Irish political atmosphere, yet, despite the efforts of sympathisers, IRA prisoners failed to find a place in the election campaign. The Home Office façade remained impenetrable. To all appearances, its policy remained unchanged and, in the sense that each prisoner's case was individually reviewed, this was true. In consequence, the prisoners' fate had not generated a great deal of interest out of Parliament. The main political parties seemed content to keep it thus. In Whitehall, there was, nevertheless, a sense of movement. On 11 December 1947, Chuter Ede issued instructions for the review to be speeded up.[260]

This arose in large part from the representations of the deputation of MPs lobbying as the Friends of Ireland Group. Chuter Ede had received them on 2 December 1947 and was at some pains to explain that the cases were being reviewed in a timely and thorough fashion. Since these were all parliamentary colleagues and members of his own party, he also felt able to unbutton the rather enigmatic official statements that had been issued from time to time. On the assumption that there were no further developments that would make it difficult to give the cases favourable consideration, he said that he could consider all the men for treatment similar to the case of Michael Preston (alias Michael Fleming) whose early release on 7 December 1947 he now announced. There were two cautionary points: an assumption could arise, when long sentences of this type were imposed, that executive action would at some point procure early release. This was a point of some concern since, were there 'a recrudescence of terrorist activities on the part of Jewish extremists' resulting in long sentences, 'it would obviously have the worst possible effect if he at the same time released some of these Irish prisoners'. He hoped, however, that he might be even more generous than had been indicated in the Lord Chancellor's reply to Lord Killanin but insisted that cases could only be dealt with individually: 'there could be no question of the letting out of large numbers of these men at the same time or of anything which could be interpreted as an amnesty'.[261]

A number of subsidiary points were raised by the MPs, and Chuter Ede was pressed to give a more definite commitment. In the time-honoured way of politicians anxious to flatter and to divert whilst giving little away, he then lifted another corner of the curtain, 'for their confidential information'. On the timetable before him, which he hoped might be further compressed, seven of the prisoners would be out before the middle of 1948. In this spirit of mutual confidence, it was agreed that there would be no press statement on what had passed.[262]

The scheme behind the deliberate pace of releases was not yet discernable, and what was known of Home Office policy failed to satisfy all the interested parties. Fianna Fáil had lost office in the Irish general election of January 1948, and William Norton of the Irish Labour Party was now Tánaiste (Deputy Prime Minister) in the new inter-party government.[263] On 18 May 1948, visiting London, he raised the matter with Clement Attlee, James Chuter Ede and Philip Noel-Baker.[264] The policy of staggered releases was rock firm, however, and the British government would not budge. There was an absolute determination to avoid anything that could be construed as a general amnesty, but there also seemed to be little point in changing course now that release was a matter of a few months for the remaining men.

The new government in Dublin was now liable to face questions on the Irish prisoners in Britain and on what was being done to speed releases. This partly accounts for Norton's approach to the British ministers.[265] It is notable, however, that although releases had been accelerated, there had been no general amnesty in Ireland itself. A policy of staged releases was followed there also, and it was not until 9 March 1948 that the last three IRA prisoners were released from Irish prisons.[266] This encouraged Frank Lee to send a telegram to the Home Office asking that the remaining IRA convicts at Parkhurst be freed.[267] The freeing of the IRA prisoners from Portlaoise settled the matter as far as Ireland was concerned but increased pressures from members of the Dáil for further lobbying in London.[268] The phrase 'Irish patriots in English gaols' still aroused strong feelings, even among constitutional nationalists who would have had no truck with the IRA and its works.

Anticipating Dáil difficulties, Seán MacBride (sometime IRA Chief of Staff and now, by a remarkable turn of the political wheel, Minister for External Affairs) broached the matter on 6 April with the UK Representative in Dublin, Lord Rugby.[269] Rugby explained how the Home Office was proceeding, especially the policy of staggered releases. He stressed that 'any procedure which might seem to give a halo to these miscreants would be in the interests, neither of his country or mine'. Suggesting that the change in public sentiment in Ireland may not have been fully grasped in Britain, MacBride persisted: 'The extremist wing had been so weakened that the new government had felt no hesitation in releasing the last of their political détenus.' Had there been any doubt as to the attitude of the Irish government it was no longer a question that they were 'wholly in favour of the release of these prisoners'. Continued imprisonment 'with its propaganda of martyrdom' could be used in Ireland to keep up 'emotional agitation'; the adverse effects of continued detention outweighed any benefits. Rugby acknowledged that the advent of a government of a different complexion from the previous one was something of a new factor and suggested that MacBride's Taoiseach, John Costello, raise the question when he next visited London. He repeated the basic point: no general amnesty and 'clemency adjusted to the circumstances of each individual case'.[270]

On 10 May 1948, James Chuter Ede and Philip Noel-Baker met Clement Attlee to discuss the releases. It was only at this point that Noel-Baker was told of the plan for staged releases and was given the schedule of names and proposed dates. He was cautioned that no details should be communicated to Irish ministers, and a note was prepared of the kind of information which could appropriately be given. In particular, there should be no disclosure of Chuter Ede's wish that all the men be released before the end of the year.[271] A week later, on Noel-Baker's instructions, Lord Rugby called upon Costello and informally told him of the procedure that had been agreed to deal with the remaining prisoners. The date by which the exercise was to be completed was intimated, but not promised. Costello thanked him for the information and said that he would be circumspect in dealing with any related Dáil questions.[272]

The pace of releases continued to cause some friction. On 27 April 1948, Lord Killanin again put a question in the House of Lords, pointing out that all IRA and other political prisoners in Éire had been released. Would the government consider a general amnesty for the remaining prisoners in England? The written answer sidestepped the issue of a general amnesty and pointed out that individual reviews had already allowed the early release of several men.[273] The Home Office continued to fear a political and public backlash were it to become known that a more general act of clemency was under way. The 1939–40 bombings were still lodged in the public mind, viewed with anger and revulsion. This put the government in the curious and uncomfortable (but not wholly unfamiliar) position of actually carrying out the process that the various lobbyists sought, without being able to placate them by acknowledging what was happening. It seems, however, that there were nods, winks and confidential briefings where these were possible.

Morgan Phillips, Secretary of the British Labour Party, warned Chuter Ede that there was a prospect that a resolution urging the release of the prisoners would be put to the forthcoming Labour Party Conference. Herbert Morrison, Lord President of the Council, was also Chairman of the Labour Party, and a copy of the letter which had been sent to Philip Noel-Baker was sent to him. It was again stressed that nothing should be said publicly about the November deadline.[274] As the summer wore on, however, the pace and regularity of the releases disclosed the scope of the plan. At the end of October, Frank Lee realised what was afoot. The release of three of the six remaining men at Parkhurst led him to write a letter in a very different tone from that adopted two and a half years before: 'My Committee desire to acknowledge your very generous gesture in this matter.'[275]

The releases in Éire and Britain were completed in December 1948.[276] Seventy-seven persons – all but a handful or so of them young men – had been sentenced as a result of the campaign. None had been amnestied, but nearly all (bar the few serving short sentences) had been granted a substantial degree of clemency. This act of mercy highlighted the position in Northern Ireland. Although Northern Ireland had not been targeted in the bombing campaign, there were a number of men still in prison there for IRA offences. Five of these had been convicted of the murder of a policeman and their death sentences commuted (though the sixth member of the group had been hanged); four had been sentenced on an explosives charge and one for treason felony. Reporting this to the Home Office at the end of August 1949, the Northern Ireland Cabinet Office lamented the fact that a boycott of British goods had been launched in the USA by the Irish Republican Prisoners' Release Committee. The publicity material of the Committee showed that it did not know that all IRA prisoners had been released in Britain.[277] Given the importance of American goodwill to Britain at this juncture, and the role played by Irish Americans in politics, this indicated a significant diplomatic and consular oversight. Irish political prisoners had had their impact on Anglo-American relations in the past and British interests required that attention be paid to accounts of their treatment.

Repatriation of remains

Apart from the killing of Albert Ross in Manchester on the first day of the bombing campaign, Dr Donald Campbell was killed at Kings Cross station in London on 26 July 1939.[278] Campbell's wife and fourteen others were severely injured. Even worse, as we have seen, was the Coventry bombing a month later, on 25 August 1939. Five were killed and twelve gravely injured; fifty more bore lesser injuries.[279] The Coventry dead could have been chosen by some baneful social survey as a cross-section of the community: James Clay, eighty-two; Elsie Ansell, twenty-one (two weeks from her wedding); Gwilym Rowlands (fifty); Rex Gentle (thirty) and John Arnott (fifteen, a schoolboy). This pitiful list and the wicked callousness of bombing a shopping thoroughfare on a Friday afternoon enraged public opinion.

Pressure on the police for action was intense, and, in December 1939, five people stood trial in Birmingham for their part in the atrocity. Joseph and Mary Hewitt, from whose house the IRA's Midlands Operations Officer had supplied explosives, were acquitted, as was Brigid O'Hara, Mary Hewitt's mother.[280] Two men were convicted and hanged. The first of these was James McCormick, the operations officer, who stood trial and was executed under the name James Richards. Of his direct and immediate guilt there was no doubt. With another (identity unknown) he had prepared the bomb in the room he rented from the Hewitts; he also ordered it to be planted.[281] Peter Barnes was not directly involved in the bombing, but there was sufficient evidence against him to show that he had brought the explosives from London and that he had in his possession receipts linking him to other incriminating items. This was enough under the legal doctrine of common purpose or joint enterprise to hang him.[282] Although he had pleaded not guilty, McCormick declared after the verdict had been reached that, as a soldier of the IRA, he was not afraid, as he was dying in a just cause. Barnes made no such claim, insisting, 'I am sure it will all come out that I had neither hand, act nor part in it.'[283] The view was widespread in Ireland that because of this lesser role Barnes was innocent.[284]

The executions took place on Ash Wednesday, 7 February 1940.[285] The previous day, John Dulanty, the Irish High Commissioner, visited Prime Minister Neville Chamberlain seeking a reprieve. Given the times and the terrible nature of the offence, this was politically impossible.[286] Yet the plight of a condemned man stirred nationalist memories of the Manchester Martyrs and of Roger Casement. In Ireland, flags flew at half mast on the execution day.[287]

It was a prudent regard for those springs of nationalist sentiment that led de Valera to seek mercy for the men. Here was a reprise of a familiar theme in Anglo-Irish perceptions and judgements. Constitutional nationalists, including the Irish government, strong though they were in condemning the IRA, were disposed to see its activists, when brought to bay, as patriots afflicted by an excess of zeal. The fact that Barnes and McCormick had prepared for death by devoutly observing Roman Catholic practices and rites reinforced their martyr status. Those on the receiving end of IRA bombs understandably took quite a different view, seeing those who planted them as common criminals and cowards.[288] Looking back at the Irish pleas for mercy that emanated from so many organisations in Ireland at the time, it is remarkable that nowhere among the resolutions and pleas was there any expression of sympathy for the survivors of those killed in Broadgate in Coventry, for those who were injured, or indeed for the loss of life. None of the victims was mentioned by name, much less by age or occupation. The impression is of a one-sided outpouring of humane sentiment, as though humanity itself depended on nationality.

The IRA, already in disarray, hemmed in on all sides by wartime regulations and heightened security, North and South, and a high chance of internment of those identified as militants, mounted only a limited campaign before and after the executions.[289] On Sunday, 11 February 1940, there were defiant clashes between republican demonstrators and police in the Falls Road area of West Belfast. Police baton-charged protesters who were violating a ban. Armoured cars were deployed: many were injured and thirteen arrested.[290] Other protests were held in Armagh and Derry; posters were put up in various towns and slogans painted on walls. A motion condemning the executions brought before a meeting of the Downpatrick Board of Guardians was ruled out of order by the Chairman.[291]

The preoccupation of the war years, internment and tight security made it difficult to sustain any public campaign among republican and sympathetic nationalists. The retention of the executed men's bodies in Winson Green (Birmingham) Prison provided a possible focus for a return to the cause in more politically propitious times. There were, of course, many precedents for the political use of funerals to revive the movement, and demands for the return of remains had been made almost immediately after the executions.[292] Nor was it all expediency and cynical opportunism. In Ireland, Catholic and Protestant alike had always shown particular respect for the dead. Funeral ceremonies were an important part of the life of the community, occasions when sympathy, ties of kin, friendship and affinities of other kinds could be expressed and reasserted. Such a culture was apt to view with particular horror the notion that remains should lie unmarked in unconsecrated ground. Prison was surely seen as one of the least consecrated of grounds, the furthest that one could be from God's acre. Even the families of those executed for non-political murder must have felt a sense of anguish and continuing punishment of relatives when they reflected on the resting place.

To address humanely and with a degree of compassion the feelings of families to whom the executed was still an object of affection, it had for some time been the practice of the Home Office to allow relatives, on application, and under strict conditions, to pay private visits to the prison grounds in which their kin were interred. The graves were unmarked, but plans of their location were kept and sometimes initials or some other inconspicuous sign on a nearby wall marked the spot.[293] But that was as far as the authorities would go. Law, precedent and political sentiment were against any restoration of remains to families.

Immediately after the war there were approaches from sympathetic MPs, requesting the return to Ireland of the remains of Barnes and McCormick, largely at the prompting of the Casement, Barnes and McCormick Repatriation Committee. William Gallagher, the Clydeside Communist MP, forwarded to Attlee a letter from that committee, asking for a favourable decision, which, he contended, would 'meet with a warm response in many Irish hearts'.[294] The request was passed to the Commonwealth Relations Office (CRO), which fairly quickly turned it down. The CRO referred to the response to de Valera's February 1936, approach to Stanley Baldwin for the repatriation of Casement's remains. There should be a uniform rule: either all bodies should be handed over to relatives, or none; discrimination between cases 'would lead to difficulties'. A second reason for retaining the remains was that in many cases there would be 'unseemly incidents' and perhaps 'a public demonstration of a very undesirable character'. It would be impossible to remove the remains in secret. Even where the family gave an undertaking to avoid publicity, 'crowds would collect and scenes of disorder might in some cases be provoked'. These worries convinced Noel-Baker that the repatriation of the Barnes and McCormick remains 'would result in the exploitation in the Irish Republic of the memory of these men as heroes and martyrs'. This could lead to more bitterness between the two countries than would be caused by a refusal.[295]

The matter stalled for some twenty years, until the advent of a new Labour government, the abolition in Britain of the death penalty and, doubtless, the passage of time, and cooling of anger, permitted both legal and political movement. During Commons debates on the Murder (Abolition of Death Penalty) Act, 1965, Roy Jenkins, the liberal and humane Home Secretary, announced that he would be prepared to consider sympathetically any request for the removal of the remains of an executed person. It became thereafter the usual practice to grant a licence on application from the nearest living relative.[296] The expenses of removal and re-interment were high and had to be met by the applicants, many of whom were from the poorer sections of society; in other cases, family ties or sentiments were not strong. For both sets of reasons, the number of applications was not great. Of six licences over the following four years, two were granted in respect of IRA men. The fact that in those cases procedures were completed, both in England and Ireland, without demonstration or disturbance, cleared the way for Barnes and McCormick.[297]

In May 1969, a memorandum on Barnes and McCormick was put to Roy Jenkins by his officials. The applications had been made by a brother of Peter Barnes and a sister of James McCormick. It was their intention to re-inter the remains in Ballyglass, Mullingar, Co. Westmeath.[298] The government of Northern Ireland had been consulted, but since Barnes and McCormick had no direct links to their jurisdiction they took no stance on the matter. The Irish government had shown no enthusiasm for the proposed repatriation: 'The British Ambassador in Dublin has told us that the authorities there would undoubtedly not wish to admit, if questioned, that they had concurred in the repatriation of the bodies and that they would therefore be embarrassed if we asked them to agree to it.' At the same time, the Irish 'seem to recognise the inevitability of repatriation'. Looking simply to the application, however, the memorandum pointed out that since 1965 such licences had been granted where requests were made by the next of kin, and it would be appropriate to do so in this case.[299] The exhumation took place in the night of 27/8 June 1969. This was to avoid creating any undue curiosity among the Winson Green prisoners, which, since this was a local prison (for short-termers) could easily be communicated to the press by a discharged prisoner. The precaution was fruitless, however. On 20 June, the relatives had been informed by letter of the intended repatriation, and on 23 June the Press Association approached the Home Office for comment. Unlike the earlier transfer of the remains of O'Sullivan and Dunne, this one was orchestrated by an IRA-affiliated committee. The tricolour-draped remains were received at Dublin airport by two Capuchin friars and an eight-man paramilitary honour guard.[300] Additional clergy officiated at the reception of the coffins at a Dublin church. At the Mullingar cemetery on 6 July 1969 there were further ceremonies: pipers, a band and some 5,000 mourners; there was applause for a firing party's volley over the grave.[301] An *Irish Press* article by Des Maguire eulogised the men as 'the stuff that heroes are made of... the last of a long line of Irishmen despised by their enemies because of what they stood for'. The British government was condemned for not trying to find out if they were really guilty. The bomb was described as having exploded 'accidentally'.[302]

In the two wholly differing views of the nature of the men's acts, and the significance of the obsequies, could be seen the dimensions of a chasm that would gape even wider in the years immediately to come. Not for the first time, a republican funeral would be used to transfer something of the political energy of martyrdom and example from one generation to another. The 'Fenian dead' upon whom Padraig Pearse had called more than fifty years before at the funeral of Jeremiah O'Donovan Rossa still had a section of the Irish population in their thrall.

Notes

1 In the March 1932 election, Fianna Fáil was returned as the largest party. Labour's support gave de Valera an additional seven seats to add to his own seventy-two. Facing him, W. T. Cosgrave had fifty-seven seats and his allies seventeen. A majority of five was scarcely overwhelming, but this narrow margin may in itself have helped to calm many fears and anxieties. The January 1933 general election further strengthened Fianna Fáil's position. Many IRA members took a hand in getting out the vote for de Valera, and some took their task to heart, following the old injunction: 'Vote early and vote often.' IRA member Seán O'Neill, arrested in May 1941, recalled the remark of a comrade in the Dublin bridewell: 'Look at me now and in 1932 when de Valera came to power, I voted forty-six times for Fianna Fáil.' Uinseann MacEoin, *The IRA in the Twilight Years, 1923–1948* (Dublin: Argenta, 1997), p. 740.

2 For a concise discussion of these developments, see F. S. L. Lyons, *Ireland since the Famine* (London: Fontana, 1973), pp. 511–23. For the context and legal reach of the Statute of Westminster, see A. W. Bradley and K. D. Ewing, *Constitutional and Administrative Law*, 15th edn (London: Longman, 2011), pp. 321–3.

3 When he volunteered for service in the 1939–40 bombing campaign, Joe Collins (alias Conor McNessa) took the view that 'apart from anything else, without some action, the Army would fade away'. Joe Collins, 'Memoir', unpublished and unpaginated.

4 Tim Pat Coogan, *The IRA* (London: Fontana, 1980), pp. 150 and 156. Tom Barry (1877–1980) was born in Killorglin, Co. Kerry, but is strongly associated with Co. Cork, where in 1920 he became a major and successful IRA leader. Having served in the British Army during the First World War he had acquired military experience and skills, which he used with ruthless determination. Took the anti-Treaty side and was imprisoned. Remained active in the IRA and eventually became Chief of Staff. Was appointed to an important post in the Irish Army in 1940. His wife, Leslie de Barra (née Price) was a senior figure in the Cumann na mBan and later in the Irish Red Cross. See p. 1045, n. 33 below.

5 Seán Russell (1893–1940). Fought in 1916, during the Anglo-Irish War and on the anti-Treaty side in the Civil War. Proposed war against Britain in 1936 and travelled to the USA to gather support for this policy; court-martialled and suspended for three months from the IRA in January 1937 for acting without authority. At the April Convention in 1938, restored to the leadership, became a member of the Army Council and Chief of Staff. In the USA when the Second World War started; travelled to Italy and Germany. Died in August 1940 on a German submarine en route to Ireland. For an account of Russell's death, see the memorandum in NAI JUS/8/802, Seán Russell file. The similarities between Russell's and Casement's German contacts are striking. It is also worth recalling that his journey back to Ireland came within weeks of the Dunkirk evacuation and the capitulation of France: German victory seemed imminent. Joseph McGarrity (1874–1940) was born in Co. Tyrone but emigrated to the USA in 1892. An astute businessman, he became prominent in Irish-American organisations of a revolutionary hue. A close friendship with Roger Casement developed whilst Casement toured America in 1914–15. McGarrity was involved in his departure for Germany. Took the anti-Treaty side in the Civil War and when de Valera entered the Dáil in 1927 denounced what he saw as an 'act of treason'. Prolific fund-raiser for republican causes and a major donor in his own right.

6 NLI, Joseph McGarrity Papers, MS. 17, 455, Seán Russell to Dr Hans Luther, 21 October 1936.

7 This was the point made by Moss Twomey, in discussion with Russell, who preferred to liken his plan to the bombing and arson campaign in early 1921: 'Sean, you have the wrong parallel there; compare instead the last desperate attempts of the Fenian dynamiters under Captain William MacKay Lomasney who blew himself up in 1884

trying to destroy London Bridge. The IRA are too weak and too short of money' (cited in MacEoin, *The IRA in the Twilight Years, op. cit.,* p. 846; see also p. 855).

8 It is only fair to note that even the British government was uncertain as to the effects of air attacks on the civil population or the consequences of the use of poison gas.

9 See Seán McConville, *Irish Political Prisoners, 1848–1922: Theatres of War* (London and New York: Routledge, 2003), Chapter 7, for an account of the dynamitard campaign. The use of Irish lodging houses was in part dictated by the sparseness of funds and in part by a reluctance of English landlords and landladies to accept Irish guests and tenants. Well within living memory, signs of 'No Irish, no coloured' could be seen in lodging-house windows.

10 Veteran republican Dan Keating recalled that Russell 'was taken back solely for the campaign in England' (MacEoin, *The IRA in the Twilight Years, op. cit.,* p. 623).

11 *Empire News,* 7 November 1954; James Michael Lyons (pseudonym), 'I Was an IRA Man', PRO DO/35/4984. For a background account of the early months of the campaign by one of the foot-soldiers, see the series of articles by James Michael Lyons (alias Michael Ferguson) (ghosted, no doubt) in the *Empire News* on successive Sundays: 31 October 1954–28 November 1954. These articles appeared only in the Irish edition of the newspaper and now apparently survive only as clippings in the archives. At this meeting, Russell stated that the bombing campaign in England was to be conducted alongside attacks on British forces in Northern Ireland.

12 On 28 November 1938, Reynolds (by then OC Britain) was killed in Castlefin, Co. Donegal, apparently whilst constructing a bomb to attack a Northern Ireland customs post. John James Kelly and Charles McCafferty died with him. MacEoin, *The IRA in the Twilight Years, op. cit.,* p. 622; PRO HO/144/2/357/196; *Irish News,* 29 November 1938, 5b; 30 November 1938, 5c; *Irish Times,* 29 November 1938, 8d; 30 November 1938, 7f. Patrick Kelly, brother of John, was the tenant of the house. He and his wife survived uninjured, as did their four young children who were asleep in the room off the kitchen, where the explosion occurred. The handling of explosives in such circumstances was utterly beyond recklessness. Pieces of the house were found more than a quarter of a mile away, and, remarkably, some forty sticks of unexploded gelignite were found in the debris. McCafferty survived the explosion and was removed to hospital, where he died. Dan Keating had been working at Mooney's, an Irish-owned chain of public houses. Others in England at the time were Dominic Adams and Maggie Nolan (later married to Adams). Some members of the first group decided to return to Dublin without informing Keating (then OC London). Resources, financial and personnel, were apparently extremely limited (Dan Keating interview).

13 MacEoin, *The IRA in the Twilight Years, op. cit.,* pp. 623–4, 740; Coogan, *The IRA, op. cit.,* p. 157.

14 Joseph Collins (alias Conor McNessa), bomb-maker and operations officer in London and Manchester, describes in an unpublished memoir how he hated going back to his rented room because he feared capture. Despite this he apparently did not have sufficient funds to shift elsewhere (Collins, 'Memoir', *op. cit.*). He was eventually taken in such a staked-out room.

15 McGarrity Papers, MS. 17, 485, Seán Russell to Joseph McGarrity, 21 September 1938. Russell wrote that a third training camp had just been completed. There were three full-time men in Britain. Here was a complete – or even ridiculous – lack of proportion. One of the three may have been Jimmy O'Hanlon, an explosives specialist with the Dublin IRA. MacEoin, *The IRA in the Twilight Years, op. cit.,* p. 773. For a note of some others involved at an early stage, see MacEoin, *The IRA in the Twilight Years, op. cit.,* p. 787 n. 8; see also Collins, 'Memoir', *op. cit.*

16 The transfer was made by the purported 'Executive Council of Dáil Éireann, Government of the Republic' (NAI JUS/8/1063, Lawless Case, Background Information).

17 See *The Times*, 6 February 1939, 12d, for the official disclosure of the ultimatum.

18 See Coogan, *The IRA*, *op. cit.*, pp. 165–7. The six signatories were Stephen Hayes, Patrick Fleming, Peadar O'Flaherty, George Plunkett, Laurence Grogan and Seán Russell (*The Times*, 17 January 1939, 14e). Poster-format copies of the Declaration were posted in many parts of Ireland (*Irish Times*, 17 January 1939, 6g; 18 January, 6c).

19 On 16 January 1939 there were several incidents: explosions at the Central Electricity Board, Southwark, the London Power Company and the North Metropolitan Electric Power Supply Company; pylons damaged in the Midlands, Lancashire and Northumberland; a bomb at Hams Hall Power Station, Warwickshire. Most seriously, there were three separate but almost simultaneous explosions in Manchester, resulting in one killed and two injured (*Irish Times*, 17 January 1939, 7a–b). *The Times* (17 January 1939, 12d and 14e) provided a comprehensive description of the campaign's opening day. See also the *Manchester Guardian*, 17 January 1939, 11a, 13d; 18 January 1939, 9a, 11a; 19 January 1939, 7a; *Daily Telegraph*, 17 January 1939, 15a, 16b; 18 January 1939, 13d, 14a; 19 January 1939, 5f, 13g; *Evening News*, 17 January 1939, 1a; 18 January 1939, 1a, 16c; *Irish News*, 17 January 1939, 5a, 7a; 18 January 1939, 5a, 8c; 19 January 1939, 5f, 7b. Despite numerous and deeply disturbing international reports and destructive gales throughout England, the IRA explosions were, understandably, a major feature in news reporting and comment.

20 McGarrity Papers, MS. 17, 485, Seán Russell to Joseph McGarrity, 25 January 1939. Certainly initial press reports showed uncertainty as to the perpetrators, although the IRA was the leading candidate.

21 Not all the bombs worked. What could have been a particularly devastating attack, had it come off, was directed at electricity pylons crossing the Manchester Ship Canal. Three sacks of explosives, designed to bring down one of the huge structures, failed to detonate when the alarm clock, which would have triggered the explosion at 6 a.m., proved unreliable and stopped. More undetonated bombs were found near an electricity pylon in Birmingham on 17 January 1939 (*Manchester Guardian*, 18 January 1939, 9a–b).

22 To minimise logistical problems, gelignite and other commercial explosives were stolen from English collieries and quarries. Those materials were then used as detonators for various home-made explosive mixtures, this multiplying their destructive powers. Incendiary devices were also assembled and used. From the outset, cash was in chronically short supply. This impeded the accumulation of materials, the rentals of suitable storage and the maintenance of operatives. (See *Empire News*, 14 November 1954, for instances of the shortage of funds, and the consequences.)

23 PRO HO/144/21357/196, Sir Norman Kendal, Special Branch Report of IRA Activities, 13 April 1939; *Irish News*, 19 November 1938, 3c. This leniency would not be repeated.

24 See p. 480.

25 PRO HO/144/211357/196, Special Branch Report, 13 April 1939.

26 Joe Collins, sent over to Britain as an operations officer, was able to obtain gelignite through Irish workers in a quarry that belonged to his employer (Collins, 'Memoir', *op. cit.*).

27 A number of men who had evidently been under police surveillance, or who were living at suspect addresses, were arrested in the immediate aftermath of the first attacks. Seven appeared in court in Manchester on 18 January 1939, and another seven at Bow Street, London. Explosives and arms were taken during the arrests (*Manchester Guardian*, 18 January 1939, 7a–b; *Daily Telegraph*, 19 January 1939, 5f–g). The ages of the men ranged from seventeen to thirty-six. All were remanded in custody.

28 We now know that Hitler's *Ostpolitik* dominated German strategy and that he was supremely anxious to avoid war with Britain, if that could be done, while he made

the necessary preparations to guard his back by defeating or neutralising the western powers. A naked involvement with the IRA (and, given the state of the organisation, *any* involvement would have been naked) would have been a *causus belli*.

29 PRO HO/144/21357.

30 PRO HO/144/21357, Sir Vernon G. W. Kell to Sir Alexander Maxwell, 9 March 1939. There was, some years later, a press report, seemingly well sourced, that British Security Service (MI5) operatives had gone to Dublin in the immediate aftermath of the IRA's Declaration of War, in January 1939. Dermot Brennan, 'When Seán Russell Declared War on England', *Reynold's News*, 22 July 1951. This well-sourced series of articles (24 June, 15 July and 22 July 1951) provides much useful information on the bombing campaign, Russell and his close colleagues. It is significant that nowhere in Christopher Andrew's exhaustive, official history of MI5 is there any mention of the 1939–40 IRA bombing campaign: it was indeed never more than a police matter. Christopher Andrew, *The Defence of the Realm: The Authorized History of MI5* (London: Allen Lane, 2009).

31 PRO HO/144/21356/49; *Daily Telegraph*, 19 January 1939, 5f–g; *Irish News*, 19 January 1939, 5f–g, 6b–c.

32 PRO HO/144/21356/162; *The Times*, 29 March 1939, 4e.

33 *The Times*, 30 March 1939, 11a.

34 PRO HO/144/21357/162; *Irish Times*, 8 April 1939, 10b; 14 April 1939, 5a.

35 *Irish Times*, 4 May 1939, 10d. The men, who had refused to enter a plea, or to defend themselves, made defiant pro-IRA statements when sentenced. Browne said that he regretted nothing he had done and would endeavour to do it all again. Connell struck a more melodramatic note in good metre: 'Come what may, prison or death, I will stand by the proclamation of the Army Council of the IRA.'

36 *The Times*, 6 February 1939, 12d.

37 *Ibid*. There was also thought to be a threat to ministers and senior officials, and firearms were issued to the police who guarded them.

38 *Reynold's News*, 27 July 1951. The sum of £120,000 seems unlikely, the more so since it did not feature in contemporary or later accounts by IRA activists.

39 *Irish Press*, 7 June 1939, 1f. It was suggested that the arrest was prompted by the concurrent visit of King George VI and Queen Elizabeth to Windsor, Ontario, just across the border in Canada, en route to the USA.

40 *Washington Times-Herald*, 8 June 1939.

41 *New York Sun*, 16 June 1939. Russell's remarks to some 1,200 supporters at New York's Transport Hall echoed those of the Fenian and dynamitard Jeremiah O'Donovan Rossa fifty-six years previously in the pages of his *United Irishman*, in pamphlets and newspaper interviews: in essence, 'give me the funds and I will blow the British Empire out of Ireland' (see McConville, *Irish Political Prisoners, op. cit.*, Chapter 7).

42 *Reynold's News*, 22 July 1951.

43 PRO HO/45/23639. These were heavy sentences for the times. An ordinary murderer, were his death sentence commuted, could expect to serve about the same time as a twenty-year convict.

44 Six barrels each containing approximately one hundredweight of powdered charcoal and potassium chlorate and forty sticks of gelignite (PRO HO/144/21357/199, 'Recent Explosions in London and the Provinces').

45 PRO HO/144/21357/199, 'Recent Explosions in London and the Provinces'.

46 Joe Collins commented on the unreliability of the balloon fuse: 'At the start of the campaign we had good quality rubber acid containers, but these had now been exhausted, and we were now using halfpenny balloons which we purchased in Woolworth's. These sometimes had impurities in the rubber, tiny specks of grit or dirt. Whereas it would take three hours for the acid to burn through the rubber, it

would penetrate any of these defects in a matter of minutes' (Collins, 'Memoir', *op. cit.*). This unreliability and the fact that the police had asked stores to be on the lookout for suspicious persons buying balloons led IRA operatives to use condoms instead, 'and these worked very well' (Collins, 'Memoir', *op. cit.*). Condoms were unacceptable to some men, however, despite the dangers of the balloon fuse. In later years, Jim McGuinness, who had been an active IRA man in 1939, recalled that, on Catholic principle, one group of IRA men had refused to handle bombs that contained condoms. Kevin Myers, *Watching the Door: Cheating Death in 1970s Belfast* (London: Atlantic Books, 2006). Myers's ironical note is irresistible: the men of the unit were certainly not going to 'imperil their immortal souls to blow up Londoners' (p. 106).

47 The Home Office summary at PRO HO/144/21357/199 provides a convenient and detailed account of incidents, arrests, seizures, trials and outcomes.

48 PRO HO/45/23639/94, Summary note.

49 Some months into the campaign, recalled Joe Collins, 'an Irishman renting a room, especially when he wasn't working, would be reported to the police in ninety-five per cent of cases' (Collins, 'Memoir', *op. cit.*).

50 MacEoin, *The IRA in the Twilight Years, op. cit.*, p. 623.

51 Brendan Behan, *Borstal Boy* (London: Arrow Books, 1990), p. 1.

52 See below, p. 448.

53 MacEoin, *The IRA in the Twilight Years, op. cit.*, p. 624.

54 *The Times* reported the incident in three lines as an item on its round-up, 'News in Brief' (19 March 1940, 5e).

55 Seán Russell arrived in Genoa, on his way to Germany, in April 1940. He spent several months there in talks with the Foreign Office. It was not until April 1941 that the IRA GHQ learned of Russell's location (*Reynold's News*, 27 July 1951).

56 Prevention of Violence (Temporary Provisions) Act, 1939: 2 & 3 Geo. VI, c.50, s.1 (2). Although the Bill secured an unopposed third reading, there was, even in the last weeks of European peace, disquiet about conferring such extensive powers on the executive rather than the judiciary. Sir Samuel Hoare, the Home Secretary, resisted an opposition attempt to insert a provision allowing deportees to apply to the High Court (see *The Times*, 27 July 1939, 14a). Throughout, it was clear that momentum had been created and scruples overcome by two considerations: the imminence of European war and public revulsion at the IRA bombings. The notion of an enemy within was intolerable. As the Bill was going through its third reading, there were bombs at London's Kings Cross and Victoria railway stations. Whether these were nose-thumbing provocations or the IRA on auto-pilot is hard to know.

57 *Manchester Guardian*, 28 August 1939, 10b.

58 Molly, the sister of Edward Stapleton (sentenced to ten years) and his mother and father were all deported in the wake of his arrest. Deportation was immediate, and they had to leave their belongings behind. The strength of the family connection to the movement was, however, confirmed when Molly went to work at the IRA's training department at 98A Rathgar Road, Dublin (MacEoin, *The IRA in the Twilight Years, op. cit.*, pp. 697–8, 777).

59 The committee set up to relieve the deportees provided small grants in direct relief; it also gave seed-corn money to help them start small businesses (MacEoin, *The IRA in the Twilight Years, op. cit.*, pp. 600–1).

60 MacEoin, *The IRA in the Twilight Years, op. cit.*, p. 791.

61 See n. 19 above. Emphatic instructions had supposedly been given by Russell that no lives were to be endangered. Given that widespread bombing was in preparation, however, this was a ludicrous or simply cynical order (*Empire News*, 7 November 1954). In a fund-raising speech to Clan na Gael and the Irish republican Clubs of Greater New York on 15 June 1939, Russell again ignored the death of Albert Ross.

Through skill and luck no one had been killed, he asserted, but the IRA could not guarantee to 'exercise the same care' were any of its members to be executed in England. Grandly referring to IRA units as an 'expeditionary force', Russell said it would remain there until England ceased to interfere in Irish affairs. Another speaker painted an almost domestic and certainly humdrum picture of the life of an IRA man on active service: 'We are asking men simply to come off the land and learn to wear clothes [sic], and to carry a newspaper and little parcel that anyone would be proud to be seen carrying. He leaves it where he is told and goes home to his English landlady. In the morning she will bring him his newspaper, and he will see how it worked the night before' (*The Times*, 17 June 1939, 11d). The rally, and the hell-raising and simplistic speeches, inevitably recall O'Donovan Rossa's impassioned and extravagant appeals for dollars for dynamitard skirmishes in the 1880s (see McConville, *Irish Political Prisoners, op. cit.*, Chapter 7).

62 *The Times*, 27 July 1939, 14a–b; *Manchester Guardian*, 27 July 1939, 9a–b. A number of people were injured in the Victoria Station explosion but none seriously. Within hours, a post office in Liverpool was wrecked in a gelignite attack, and a canal bridge close to the city was blown up. See also the *Irish News*, 27 July 1939, 5a–b and 7a.

63 In the campaign for the reprieve of the two men sentenced to death for complicity in the bombing, Tom Barry, a major figure in the Anglo-Irish War of 1919–21, IRA Chief of Staff in 1936–7, gave an exculpatory account of the Coventry explosion, alluding to inside information he possessed. The IRA had not intended to kill innocent people, he insisted. The bomb had been intended for an electricity plant two miles away from Broadgate: 'That it went off when it did was due entirely to accidental causes' (*Irish News*, 8 February 1940, 7c). No further details were offered, and, on the face of it, the explanation (and it could not have amounted to an exculpation) failed to account for the presence of the bomb in Broadgate and to explain why, if it went off by accident, the person handling it at the time was not himself blown up.

64 See below, p. 480.

65 The prospect of the executions provoked an upsurge in nationalist and republican sympathy in Ireland. The aftermath, however, as IRA man Derry Kelleher recalled, was 'a damp squib' because of the IRA's impotency and the fact that the organisation had been wrong-footed by de Valera on the question of neutrality. MacEoin, *The IRA in the Twilight Years, op. cit.*, pp. 643–4. See below, p. 481.

66 *The Times*, 23 February 1940, 8; *Evening News*, 23 February 1940, 5b; *Manchester Guardian*, 23 February 1940, 7c.

67 Sensitivities were clearly in the Home Office mind in its announcement on the outbreak of war that prisoners with less than three months to serve would be released. Although this indulgence could not possibly apply to IRA prisoners, the statement provided the assurance that 'no-one sentenced in connection with IRA outrages is among those to be discharged' (*The Times*, 4 September 1939, 5d). In the midst of the campaign, de Valera thought it appropriate to buttress his condemnation of the IRA with a hostile reference to the Protestants of Ulster. They ('the real obstacle') and Partition were the cause of the 'state of turmoil' in Britain. This minority numbered 800,000; 'It would be a good thing to ask them to decide whether they were English [sic] or Irish. They could not have it both ways.' If there were no other way (to resolve the problem of Partition), he thought there could be a scheme for buying them out. Condemning the bombing, de Valera went on to say that the Irish government had no sympathy with such actions although believing that a number of those engaged in it 'were animated by high ideals' (*The Times*, 28 July 1939, 8d). For the full Senate debate that prompted the statement, see *Senate Debates*, vol. 23, cols. 956–1010, 26 July 1939.

68 Only one of the four detonated; the others were made safe. The explosion occurred in the centre of town at 3 a.m. Other devices were found beside the Woolworth's

store, close to the Blackpool Tower (*The Times*, 28 August 1939, 6e; *Manchester Guardian*, 28 August 1939, 10a–b).

69 *Liverpool Daily Post*, 28 August 1939, 4d–e; *Liverpool Echo*, 28 August 1939, 3d, 3g.

70 See, for example, the *Manchester Guardian* report of the aftermath of the Coventry explosion (26 August 1939, 11f).

71 On the evening of the Victoria and Kings Cross bombings, William Curtis, speaking at Hyde Park Corner, under the aegis of the Friends of the Irish Republic, infuriated his listeners by calling for three cheers for imprisoned IRA men. For that, and various taunts and threats of further violence that ignited a melee, he was found guilty of using words likely to cause a breach of the peace and fined ten shillings (*Evening News*, 27 July 1939, 1e). A month later, Curtis appeared in court again for using insulting words, once more provoking the crowd. This time the sentence was decidedly heavier: one month at hard labour (*Daily Telegraph*, 28 August 1939, 4e).

72 See McConville, *Irish Political Prisoners, op. cit.*, Chapters 14 and 15 for a description of IRA imprisonment from 1919 to 1921 and for an account of the political context.

73 PRO HO/144/21356/61, Draft Circular to Police.

74 *Rules and Regulations for the Government of Convict Prisons*, London, HMSO, 1886 (and subsequent editions).

75 PRO HO/45/23639, Courtenay Robinson, Acting Chairman of the Prison Commission, to Sir Alexander Maxwell (Permanent Under-Secretary) and Sir Samuel Hoare (Home Secretary), 30 March 1939. Robinson added, 'We have been warned by Special Branch that there may be such [rescue] attempts but that the risk is likely to diminish as time goes on.'

76 PRO HO/45/23639, Robinson to Maxwell, 30 March 1939. See also the minute of 14 March 1939, on classification and allocation, at PRO P.Com./9/652/19.

77 PRO HO/45/23639, Sir Alexander Maxwell to Sir Samuel Hoare, 3 April 1939.

78 PRO HO/45/23639, Maxwell to Hoare, 3 April 1939. A few IRA prisoners had been sentenced to short terms of ordinary imprisonment, and there was no problem with leaving them in local prisons.

79 This presented a problem for contact with prisoners' families. Both depended on the IRA support organisation to act as a go-between so that the fact of imprisonment became known, as well as the *nom de guerre* used by the prisoner. When Joe Collins was imprisoned, some months passed before his parents knew that he was in Parkhurst (Collins, 'Memoir', *op. cit.*).

80 In February 1939, Scotland Yard communicated with the Deputy Commissioner of the Garda Síochána in Dublin and subsequently reported to the Home Office that 'the Deputy Commissioner is evidently finding a difficulty in giving our people help' (PRO HO/144/21356/123).

81 Prevailing judicial doctrine and custom meant that in practice prison litigation was rare and extremely difficult to mount. This would not change until comparatively recent times.

82 PRO P.Com./9/652. Courtenay Robinson to Sir Alexander Maxwell, 13 July 1939.

83 Francis McGowan and Patrick O'Connell went to Chelmsford; William Browne and George Brendon Kane to Maidstone; John Glenn to Dartmoor and Patrick Deviney to Parkhurst (PRO P.Com./9/652, Movement Order, 19 July 1939). The accommodation problem became even more pressing when, after a heavy German air attack, Parkhurst Prison was substantially cleared of prisoners in July 1942. All the IRA men were then transferred to Dartmoor (Collins, 'Memoir', *op. cit.*).

84 See below, p. 443–47. These were individual rather than IRA-directed actions. It does not appear that the IRA gave its operatives training in counter-interrogation techniques at this time or that it prepared them to continue their activities within the prisons.

85 PRO P.Com./9/652/31.

86 PRO P.Com./9/652/31. He asked to be informed if a transfer were actually proposed. Whereas travel to the Isle of Wight was a major and indeed almost insuperable barrier to the assembly of pro-IRA demonstrations outside Parkhurst, the opposite applied to London prisons. Twenty years before, large crowds had been marshalled at Brixton Prison during the hunger strike of Terence MacSwiney and at Wormwood Scrubs Prison during actions by IRA prisoners (see McConville, *Irish Political Prisoners*, *op. cit.*, pp. 717–55). The Home Secretary most probably had these public order risks in mind, though it is unlikely that London's Irish community would have been as moved to demonstrate as it had been a generation previously.

87 See *Leigh* v. *Gladstone*, 26 *Times Law Reports*, p. 139; Law Officers' Opinion, 11 March 1913.

88 Collins, 'Memoir', *op. cit.* The men were to be located together in a disused wing and allowed to march together to labour each morning. But there was no other segregation, and they had to continue to work alongside other prisoners. Mailbag work in the cells in the evenings was, however, no longer enforced. The arrangement held until the men were moved to Dartmoor in July 1942. Collins claimed that Joe Malone's stomach was so injured during forced feeding that he died the following year.

89 Until that point, according to James Lyons, the prison had been tolerable. On his own arrival from Brixton, for example, a smokers' kit was slipped under his cell door by a Cockney prisoner (*Empire News*, 28 November 1954).

90 *Daily Express*, 1 August 1939, 1b, 2a. Embellishments included the IRA men singing rebel songs in their cells at night (despite the silence rule) and the actions of Robert McCann, who was said to have caught and roasted a sparrow: 'He has an appetite no rations can satisfy. A typical boy straight from the bogs, you would say.' The Governor's report to head office was immediate, denying all the details except that the ordinary prisoners loathed the IRA men (PRO P.Com./9/652/57).

91 *Daily Express*, 30 August 1939, 9e; *Western Morning News*, 30 August 1939, 6d; *News Chronicle*, 30 August 1939, 7a; *Daily Telegraph*, 30 August 1939, 15c; *The Times*, 30 August 1939, 7e.

92 PRO P.Com./9/652/57, Courtenay Robinson to Sir Alexander Maxwell, 29 August 1939. This was a disused wing, and the men were told by the Governor that they would have to make it habitable (James Lyons, in *Empire News*, 28 November 1954).

93 The two were punished for refusing to work on RAF uniforms, which was being made in the prison workshops (*Empire News*, 28 November 1954). Refusal of war work at Dartmoor is mentioned also in Collins, 'Memoir', *op. cit.*

94 Punishments followed: restricted dietary and confinement to their cells. According to James Lyons, the outbreak eased relations with other prisoners: 'anyone who defies authority in a prison is a hero to the other prisoners' (*Empire News*, 28 November 1954). There was a brief blood-and-thunder (and largely inaccurate) account of the riot in the *United Irishman* (December 1953, 5c–d). Canon J. M. Ryan, who helped end the riot, was given a sour mention in Joe Collins's memoir. A Corkman, Ryan was a strong supporter of the excommunication edict and apparently had minimal contact with the Irish prisoners, seeing them only when they applied to do so (Collins, 'Memoir', *op. cit.*).

95 PRO P.Com./9/652/86, Report of Dr W. L. Roper, Medical Officer, 28 March 1940.

96 PRO P.Com./9/652/85. Those present at the meeting included Sir John Anderson, a remarkable civil servant, who was shortly to become Home Secretary in Churchill's government. Anderson had been closely involved in Irish affairs during the Anglo-Irish War and immediately thereafter. Others attending were Courtenay Robinson (Acting Chairman of the Prison Commission) and Sir Alexander Maxwell (Permanent Under-Secretary).

97 Alexander Henry Paterson (1884–1947), an Oxford graduate, was a major figure in penal reform in Britain and, through his innovations and charismatic leadership,

gained widespread respect and influence. He came into prison work through his experience in the Bermondsey-based Oxford Medical Mission. He chose to enlist for service in the First World War, in order to be with the young men of Bermondsey, but rapidly was selected for promotion, later winning the Military Cross. He became a Prison Commissioner in 1922 and was particularly associated with the imaginative and humane development of Borstal and, through the migration of its staff to adult institutions, the system as a whole. The Borstal that Brendan Behan found so remarkable (and indeed sympathetic) was of Paterson's creation (see pp. 451–55 below).

98 Joe Collins insisted that a 'reign of terror' existed at Dartmoor, with disciplinary charges being brought for the most trivial reasons and with brutal handling in the segregation block. The Governor (as was almost universal practice) would always accept the staff account of an incident (Collins, 'Memoir', *op. cit.*).

99 PRO P.Com./9/652/85, Alexander Paterson to Sir Alexander Maxwell, 9 April 1940.

100 PRO P.Com./9/652/85, Minute of Meeting, Sir Alexander Maxwell, 9 April 1940.

101 PRO P.Com./9/652/85, Paterson to Maxwell, 9 April 1940. John Percival Martin was the pseudonym of Pearse McLaughlin, arrested in March 1939, convicted of possessing potassium chlorate and sentenced to ten years' penal servitude.

102 PRO P.Com./9/652/85, Sir Alexander Maxwell to Sir John Anderson, 9 April 1940. In 1942, the Dartmoor Governor, Major Charles Pannall, avoided another confrontation with his IRA prisoners (including some transferred to Dartmoor from Parkhurst) by an informal deal that if they would agree to perform their cell task of sewing a quota of mailbags, he would not require them to do war work (Collins, 'Memoir', *op. cit.*).

103 PRO P.Com./9/652/85, Paterson to Maxwell, 9 April 1940. Ryan's view may have been dictated by his pastoral relationship with the men, and he may have thought it better for their moral welfare that they be removed from association with the recidivist prisoners who made up the Dartmoor population.

104 PRO P.Com./9/652/85, Maxwell to Home Secretary, 9 April 1940.

105 *Ibid.*

106 *Ibid.*

107 PRO P.Com./9/652/76, Governor to Commissioners, 22 December 1939.

108 At the age of twenty-nine, in February 1939, Michael Joseph Mason had been arrested in London and was serving seventeen years' penal servitude (PRO HO/244/21357/199). He was considered by Special Branch to be one of the most important IRA figures then in custody (PRO P.Com./9/652, Special Branch to Home Office, 13 March 1939).

109 PRO P.Com./9/652/76, Governor, Parkhurst, to Commissioners, 22 December 1939; reply 30 December 1939.

110 To conform to convict entitlement and to meet Special Branch requirements.

111 Aged thirty-two. Arrested in Manchester in February 1939, serving twenty years for the unlawful possession of explosives.

112 Aged twenty-one. Arrested in Birmingham in February 1939, serving seven years for possession of a home-made bomb.

113 PRO P.Com./9/652/79, Governor, Maidstone, to Commissioners, 2 January 1940.

114 *Sunday Dispatch*, 17 March 1940, 7b. Simons also told the newspaper that it was wrong that the Irishmen should be confined alongside other young convicts (this younger and unhardened age-group being a Maidstone speciality): 'Almost the sole topic of their conversation is sedition. But the prisoners at Maidstone are loyal to Britain. Many of them have applied to join the army since the war began.'

115 PRO P.Com./9/652/79, Governor, Maidstone, to Commissioners, 2 January 1940.

116 PRO P.Com./9/652/94. The local prison option was used for the six transferees. Dennis Duggan was sent to Durham, Edward John Connell to Birmingham, John

McCabe to Pentonville, George Brendon Kane to Stafford, Michael Rory Campbell to Wandsworth and George Whittaker to Gloucester. Joe Collins, writing of the period after July 1942 and his transfer to Dartmoor, noted that although the IRA men had staged various protests in their desire to be segregated, 'we either had to accept association with criminal prisoners or else serve out our sentence in the punishment cells in solitary confinement, on a diet of bread and water, and a beating up at intervals' (Collins, 'Memoir', *op. cit.*).

117 Brendan Behan, *Borstal Boy* (London: Arrow Books, 1990).

118 See Behan, *Borstal Boy, op. cit.*; Michael Davitt, *Leaves for a Prison Diary; or, Lectures to a 'Solitary Audience'*, 2 vols. (London: Chapman & Hall, 1885).

119 Behan's father had served in the British Army but had subsequently become a member of the IRA during the Anglo-Irish War, had taken the anti-Treaty side in the Civil War and had been imprisoned. A brother had been killed in Spain whilst soldiering in the Spanish republican cause. Two other brothers were interned in Ireland during the Second World War.

120 *The Times*, 8 February 1940, 5c.

121 Eric Errington (1900–73), Conservative politician, was educated at Oxford University and was called to the Bar in 1923. He became an MP (Bootle) in 1935 and had strong Liverpool connections, including a spell on the City Council. He held his Bootle seat until 1945 when he lost it in the sweeping Labour victory. He became MP for Aldershot (Hampshire) in 1954, holding the safe Tory seat until retirement in 1970. Knighted in 1952 and created baronet in 1963. He served in the RAF, 1939–45.

122 The statement to which Behan objected was a product of the police practice known as 'verballing' – not uncommon until recent times and impossible wholly to eliminate, despite legislative and regulatory safeguards. Detective Sergeant Earps testified that Behan had said, 'I have been sent over to take the places of Chris Keneally, Nick Lynch and the others who have been arrested. I was to organize further operations in Liverpool. I intended to put bombs in big stores, Lewis's and Hughes's I think they call it. I was making up some to put in letter-boxes to-night. I am only sixteen, and they can't do much with me' (*The Times*, 8 February 1940, 5c). Brendan felt so strongly about the remarks attributed to him by the police and was so worried that he would be in trouble with the IRA for disobeying the general order not to participate in proceedings that in his first letters out of prison (suppressed, in any case) he denied saying anything. Writing to his brother Seán, he began, 'The first thing I want to say is this: I didn't at any time make any verbal statement to the police… tell everyone back home… The police made it up out of their heads.' PRO P.Com./9/1907, enclosures, Brendan Behan to Seán Behan, 13 December 1939. The following day he wrote to someone who could be trusted to pass it on to the IRA, asking that everyone be told that he had not said the ridiculous things stated in court. He had made a written statement, itself against IRA instructions, 'as they had pinched my landlady and I wanted to get her out'. PRO P.Com./9/1907, enclosures, Brendan Behan to Mrs Fitzsimons, 14 December 1939. According to Behan's memoir, a constable accompanying Sergeant Earps had, when arresting him, given him several punches in the face, 'though not very damaging ones'. Earps had called the man off. Behan, *Borstal Boy, op. cit.*, p. 1.

123 'It is my proud privilege and honour to stand in an English court to testify to the unyielding determination of the Irish people to regain every inch of our national territory and to give expression to the noble aspirations for which so much Irish blood has been shed and so many hearts have been broken, and for which so many friends and comrades are languishing in English gaols' (*News Chronicle*, 8 February 1940, 5d). Given his wicked wit and sense of the ridiculous, this was a particularly unimaginative speech, which could have been stencilled by the IRA's publicity department. See also *Irish News*, 8 February 1940, 1f–g.

124 *News Chronicle*, 8 February 1940, 5c; PRO P.Com./9/1907, Brendan Behan to his mother (suppressed letter), 8 or 9 February 1940. See also the *Evening News*, 8 February 1940, which gave Behan the fanciful (but possibly apt) name 'Behan Defan'; *Daily Telegraph*, 8 February 1940, 8c; *The Times*, 8 February 1940, 5c.

125 See Roger Hood, *Borstal Re-assessed* (London: Heinemann, 1965), Chapters 1–3, for further historical background; see also Rupert Cross, *Punishment, Prison and the Public: An Assessment of Penal Reform in Twentieth Century England by an Armchair Penologist* (London: Stevens, 1971), especially pp. 16–37. As noted, Alexander Paterson was a major figure in the development of this progressive institution (see p. 491, n. 97 above).

126 PRO P.Com./9/1907, Report of Lady Visitor, 18 February 1940.

127 PRO P.Com./9/1907, Report of Lady Visitor. Both stories seem unlikely.

128 He confirmed that he knew Christopher Keneally, another boy bomber, then at Portland Borstal.

129 PRO P.Com./9/1907/9.

130 PRO P.Com./9/1907/2, Medical Officer's Report, 29 February 1940.

131 PRO P.Com./9/1907/2, Medical Officer's Report.

132 The three had been also sentenced for IRA activities.

133 PRO P.Com./9/1907.

134 PRO P.Com./9/1907/8, Gordon Macfarlane to Governor, Hollesley Bay Colony, 1 June 1941.

135 PRO P.Com./9/1907/8, Macfarlane to Governor.

136 The letters were kept in Brendan's Borstal (as distinct from Prison Commission or Home Office) file. In July 1964, John Gilder, then Governor of Hollesley Bay, wrote to the Home Office. A circular had been received ordering the pulping of such records. Did the order apply to Behan's suppressed letters? Gilder referred to 'the late Brendan Behan's fame as an author and playwriter' and suggested 'it may be felt that certain parts of the record, particularly the suppressed letters, ought to be preserved'. By quick reply came the order to forward the material to the Home Office (PRO P.Com./9/1907, John Gilder to Home Office, 6 July 1964).

137 PRO P.Com./9/1907, enclosures, Brendan Behan to Mrs Fitzsimons, 14 December 1939.

138 PRO P.Com./9/1907, Brendan Behan to Seán Behan, 13 December 1939. Seán was also asked to reassure Gearóid M. that Brendan had not said the things the police attributed to him, but 'Don't say I let H M Prisons see his Holy Name in writing.' This letter included a hammer and sickle drawing; another had the broad arrow by the signature of the convict.

139 PRO P.Com./9/1907, Brendan Behan to Kathleen Behan, 8 or 9 February 1940.

140 PRO P.Com./9/1907, Brendan Behan to Seán Behan, 26 April 1941. The letter was suppressed because it criticised the clergy. (It was striking how the handwriting had matured and improved over the eighteen months that Brendan has served and how much more developed and confident his style had become.) The rulings of the English Roman Catholic bishops were not uniform. Joe Collins recalled that, whilst in Manchester and Dartmoor, he was under an order of excommunication, but that Dr William Cotter, Bishop of the Diocese of Portsmouth, took a different view, and the IRA men in Parkhurst (and Camp Hill, the other Isle of Wight prison) were not under an order of excommunication (Collins, 'Memoir', *op. cit.*).

141 PRO P.Com./9/1907, enclosures: Brendan Behan to mother, 8 or 9 February 1940.

142 PRO P.Com./9/1907, Brendan Behan to Edward Regan, 21 June 1941.

143 PRO P.Com./9/1907, Brendan Behan to Christine English, 10 November 1940.

144 PRO P.Com./9/1907, Brendan Behan to Brian O'Higgins, 14 April 1941. Behan had, as a fourteen-year-old, contributed to the *Wolfe Tone Weekly*.

145 PRO P.Com./9/1907, 31 January 1941.

146 PRO P.Com./9/1907, Stephen Behan to Shoemake, 30 March 1941.
147 London, Clarke Hall Fellowship, 1934.
148 PRO P.Com./9/1907/8.
149 PRO P.Com./9/1907/8, Minute, 30 December 1940. Two other IRA youths, Logue and Burns, had agreed to join the merchant navy. For obvious reasons, the armed services and the merchant navy were regarded by prison and Borstal authorities as particularly suitable employment for young men who had been in trouble.
150 PRO HO/144/23212, Minute, 2 January 1941.
151 PRO HO/144/23212, Minute, 4 February 1941.
152 PRO P.Com./9/1907/8, Housemaster's report, 1 June 1941.
153 Philip Allen (later Lord Allen) (1912–2007) had a successful and influential career at the Home Office and became Permanent Under-Secretary in 1966. Although involved in several controversial decisions, in some of which (such as the 1950 execution of the undoubtedly innocent Timothy Evans, an event which he profoundly regretted), Allen took the line of positive steps in social reform. Borstal and its approach were very much in line with this general social philosophy.
154 PRO P.Com./9/1907, Gordon Macfarlane to C. A. Joyce, 13 July 1941.
155 PRO P.Com./9/1907, addendum.
156 PRO P.Com./9/1907, C. A. Joyce to Commissioners, 5 June 1941. Macfarlane had continued, 'He is quite clearly worried about the future, and, in spite of his constant quips and jests about religion, he is more perturbed than he would have us know about his excommunication. Whatever leniency may be possible would be appreciated by him.'
157 PRO HO/144/23212, Special Branch to Home Office, 15 July 1941. Should it be decided to expel him, the Garda Síochána in Dublin should be given plenty of notice and the details of his travel, the advice continued.
158 PRO HO/144/2321, Philip Allen to Sir Eric Machtig, Under-Secretary of State, Dominions Office, 1 August 1941.
159 PRO HO/144/2321, Reginald Bradley to C. A. Joyce, 10 September 1941.
160 PRO HO/144/2321, letters of 25 September, 3 October, 4 October and 13 October 1941.
161 PRO HO/144/23212, Home Office to Chief Constable, Liverpool City Police, 16 October 1941. Behan was to be collected from Hollesley Bay and kept in custody until placed on board ship. The Garda Síochána were to be informed of his arrival in Dublin.
162 PRO HO/144/23212, Home Office to C. A. Joyce, 22 October 1941. The undertaking was signed on 24 October 1941. In giving the undertaking, Behan had committed what the IRA condemned as a grave offence and, had it become known, would have incurred the stigma of 'signing out'.
163 The two were Detectives Hanrahan and Kirwan. See *Irish Times*, 25 April 1942, 1g, for a full report. The *Irish News* briefly noted the sentence (25 April 1942, 1b).
164 See below, pp. 721–22.
165 PRO HO/144/23212, Special Branch to Home Office, 1 May 1942.
166 PRO HO/45/25068, Special Branch to Home Office, 4 March 1948. Behan had told the magistrate that he had come to Britain to seek employment. This was probably a true explanation for his breach of the order, and his unwillingness to account for his movements arose from a desire to protect friends.
167 PRO HO/45/25068, Brendan Behan to Home Secretary, 17 February 1948.
168 PRO HO/144/23212.
169 PRO HO/45/25068, East Sussex Constabulary to Home Office, 10 November 1952. When arrested on 26 October 1952, Behan had said, 'I will explain everything but not now as I am suffering from a hangover.' He had broken the order in August 1950 on the same route to France but had left the country before he could be

arrested. A watch was then kept for his return but it was thought he had gone from France to Ireland on a cargo boat.

170 PRO HO/45/25068, Behan to Home Secretary, 3 January 1954.

171 His letter had concluded with a bit of the charm that had probably worked well for him at Hollesley Bay: 'In the event of you revoking the expulsion order against me or varying it, in the way that I request, I do undertake to, in no way abuse your indulgence, and if you cannot, well, sure you cannot, and there's an end on't, and will still remain yours sincerely, Brendan Behan.' He may have been poking a little fun here. The full (anonymous) rhyme runs thus: 'Where is the man who has the power and skill / To stem the torrent of a woman's will? / For if she will, she will, you may depend on't; / And if she won't, she won't so there's an end on't.'

172 A number of these letters were suppressed, which is why they are still to be found in the files.

173 See, for example, Daniel Jordan (alias Daniel O'Regan), PRO P.Com./9/866; Patrick Dower (from Waterford), PRO P.Com./9/855; Lawrence Dunlea (Cork), PRO P.Com./9/858 and Michael Rory Campbell, PRO P.Com./9/1501, for examples of short-term hunger-striking, refusal of labour and punishment.

174 Thus Daniel Jordan's prison file remains virtually unnoted after his initial protests in 1940, up to his release in August 1948. This was a common pattern.

175 As with Joseph McGillicuddy, who served a sentence of ten years' penal servitude. PRO P.Com./9/981.

176 Thomas Nelson (alias O'Neill) was for seven years allowed to receive the *Gaelic Messenger*. It was then prohibited as a Gaelic publication, despite the intervention of Jack Beattie, the Northern Ireland Labour Party Stormont MP. He was, however, allowed two religious booklets in Gaelic, after they had been checked by Special Branch. Texts from Edinburgh University were also allowed, the Prison Commission having been advised that they were standard works of poetry and prose (PRO P.Com./9/862).

177 PRO P.Com./9/852, 21 June 1943. Joe Collins had bitter memories of Father W. R. Lynch on several counts, including his sweeping censorship of books sent in for the Irish prisoners, such as the *Capuchin Annual* and the *Catholic Digest*. The prisoners managed to get news of this out, and the *Irish Democrat* condemned Lynch's zeal in an article (Collins, 'Memoir', *op. cit.*).

178 PRO P.Com./9/1501.

179 PRO P.Com./9/866.

180 The Institute wrote to the Commissioners on 13 May 1947; Kelly was released and sent back to Ireland (he came from Co. Kerry) on 24 August 1947 (PRO P.Com./9/853).

181 Some displayed astonishing stubbornness. Shortly after arriving at Parkhurst, Joe Collins was denied a letter from his mother because it contained news of arrests in Éire. Infuriated, Collins warned the Governor that if he did not get his mother's letter he would never write again from prison. His adherence to the promise was an embarrassment to the authorities, since his family were anxious to know about him. The Governor subsequently asked him to write out, but he refused (Collins, 'Memoir', *op. cit.*). This denial of what must have been a longing to give and receive news was, according to Collins, maintained throughout his sentence: heavy self-punishment, somehow to punish the authorities. Collins and Jack McCabe were the last two men to be released in Britain, on 15 December 1948, having refused to sign any and all undertakings.

182 PRO HO/45/22290, 22 January 1947. One indication of the degree of risk posed by prisoners, or the amount of trouble they caused, was whether they had a Home Office as well as a prison file: Compton achieved that distinction.

183 PRO P.Com./9/2023, 15 September 1941. This volcanic urge to destroy all around him signalled an extraordinary level of anger and frustration.

184 PRO P.Com./9/2023, 30 May 1946. This hardly seems a humane or even responsible way of dealing with a man so evidently unbalanced. Other prisoners, criminal and political alike, had been talked out of the punitive bunker into which they had retreated.

185 PRO P.Com./9/2023, Frank Lee to Parkhurst Medical Officer, 30 May 1946.

186 As might be expected, his life after release failed to mend. In 1950, he received a number of sentences in Dublin for wounding with intent. Convictions for theft in Edinburgh and London followed, with others arising from vagrancy and homelessness: a sad and lost life.

187 PRO P.Com./9/849, Gerard Lyons to Anne Lyons, 20 February 1940.

188 PRO P.Com./9/849, Gerard Lyons to Brigid, c.20 February 1940.

189 PRO P.Com./9/849, Gerard Lyons to Anne Lyons, 15 March 1940. There was much the same in his letter to Brigid. He thought that Russia and Germany would form a bloc with all the neutral countries as allies. They would then give England 'a last chance for peace, which, if she fails to accept, they may be apt to open up on her'. Such was the strength of their anti-British feeling that a number of republicans – perhaps even the majority of the activists – hoped for Soviet or Nazi domination of Europe. See Humphreys Papers, P/106/889–90, Paddy McGrath to Jim Killeen, 3 December 1939; Jim Killeen to Sighle Humphreys, 1 January 1940.

190 PRO P.Com./9/851, 19–22 May 1939. Police established that Campbell, who refused to give any information about himself, had been in New York. His parents had returned to Ireland in 1922, taking him with them to Ballybeg, Stewartstown, Co. Tyrone. Campbell had, in 1935, been employed as a shorthand writer by the *Irish Press*. He was said to have served a short term of imprisonment in Dublin the following year for an IRA-related offence and also to have served on the republican side in the Spanish Civil War, where he was wounded in the hip (Special Branch Report, 24 May 1939). On 19 May 1939, Campbell had been sentenced to ten years' penal servitude for possessing explosives with intent.

191 PRO P.Com./9/851, Peter Campbell to his mother and sister, 19 July 1939. With other IRA prisoners he gave his address as 'Irish Prisoners, Parkhurst Prison'. Others preferred 'Irish Political Prisoners' or 'Irish Republican Prisoners'. The IRA campaign against the border areas of Northern Ireland, about which Campbell so broadly hinted, did not materialise. Had he and the other republican prisoners placed any great hopes in this, its failure to come off must have been demoralising for them.

192 PRO P.Com./9/851, Peter Campbell to Eibhlís, 18 July 1939. He asked her not to send him books since they were not given to him. A subsequent letter (10 August 1940) to Brigid was suppressed because it contained two lines in Gaelic. These amounted to little more than greetings and a request that she should write to him, but the rule on foreign languages was rigid.

193 PRO P.Com./9/851, Peter Campbell to Eibhlís, 10 August 1940.

194 PRO P.Com./9/851, 7 November 1940.

195 PRO P.Com./9/851. 'By the way, for your information, I am allowed to receive as many letters and Post Cards at Christmas that arrive for me from anyone.'

196 PRO P.Com./9/851.

197 *Daily Telegraph*, 18 October 1939, 8b. It should be noted that although many men were tried under false names, most seem to have dropped the pretence once in prison and corresponding with friends. The prison standing orders, however, insisted that a man would be known officially by the name under which he was convicted. In a letter to a friend, Evans mentioned this: 'Take no notion of the printed side of this letter, or the name, as this is the name I was sentenced under. They call me

Evans in here, but most of them know me by O'Brien. Its [*sic*] important of course to remember my no. 45 otherwise the letter is libel [*sic*] to be sent back.'

198 Evans, who had no previous convictions, came from Loughrea, Co. Galway. He left school at fourteen and worked as a labourer. Special Branch commented, 'The prisoner, who appears to be an illiterate type of Irishman, has undoubtedly been an active member of the Irish Republican Army.' His correspondence, however, while occasionally ungrammatical and misspelt, was far from illiterate, challenging a chaplain's comment, 'Labouring type. Ignorant and arrogant' (PRO P.Com./9/865, 20 August 1940). Two years later, he noted, '[f]ull of resentments and imaginary injustices', and, the following year, 'cunning and secretive. Not a hopeful case, I fear.' This antipathy continued for four or five years. When Evans was transferred to the neighbouring Parkhurst, the chaplain there found him to be '[a] quiet well-behaved man', although one that might be easily influenced by others.

199 PRO P.Com./9/865, John Evans to Georgina Brady, 6 February 1941.

200 PRO P.Com./9/865, John Evans to Joe, 28 July 1940.

201 PRO P.Com./9/865, John Evans to Georgina Brady, 10 November 1940.

202 PRO P.Com./9/865, John Evans to Lillie (sometimes Lily) Timmins, 2 December 1940. Evans referred elsewhere to Freemasons, whose days were numbered (PRO P. Com./9/865, John Evans to mother, 20 January 1941).

203 PRO P.Com./9/865, John Evans to mother, 20 January 1941. This was suppressed for mentioning prison routine. In what looks like an act of petty tyranny, so was the next one, for not starting on the first page of the form.

204 There was little discussion in the heavily censored Irish press of these attacks. The *Irish News* (Belfast based) carried the news on its front page but (possibly fearing confiscation in Éire) initially confined reporting to the terse statements of Dublin's Government Information Bureau (see the issues on 2 January 1941, 1b–d; 3 January 1941, 1a–c, 5a; 4 January 1941, 1a–c). *The Times* (London) reported the first bombings in the briefest fashion (2 January 1941, 4e; 3 January 1941, 4b). A less abbreviated report was carried on 4 January 1941 (4e), including Dublin's protest to Berlin (see also *Manchester Guardian*, 3 January 1941, 6b). However shocking the bombings were to the Irish government, they scarcely merited report in the welter of war news from North Africa and the Aegean, and blitz and counter-blitz. The *Irish Times* showed clear signs of censorship and directions as to page placement, captioning, content and tone in its first reports (2 January 1941, 5d). As the bombing continued, the reports became more expansive but still controlled in tone, emphasising what positive elements there were: rescue, fire-brigade efficiency and the like (3 January 1941, 5a–c, 6c–d). It might of course be argued that, apart from the bombings' political ramifications, the incidents were indeed minor. On 1 January 1941, three bombs fell in the area of Drogheda. The next night, three people were killed by a German bomb at Boris, Co. Carlow. At the same time, four bombs were dropped in Dublin and three each at Wexford and the Curragh. These injured more than twenty people and destroyed a number of homes. The Irish government protested to Berlin and privately wondered whether Hitler was signalling that it should be wary of any cooperation with Britain. See Clair Wills, *That Neutral Island* (Cambridge, Mass.: Harvard University Press, 2007), pp. 208–9. A far more serious bombing in North Strand, Dublin, on 30 May 1941 killed thirty-four people, injured several hundred and destroyed some 300 homes.

205 PRO P.Com./9/365, 6 February 1941. Four months later, after a devastating air raid on Belfast, he had abandoned the British conspiracy theory of the Dublin bombing but asked his correspondent 'what would it have [been like] if the "union Jack" had been floating over Dublin. It would be another Belfast or perhaps worse' (John Evans to Lily Timmins, 28 June 1941).

206 PRO P.Com./9/365. This was one of his longest letters, with many 'do you remember?' lines, including this one evocative of the social life of young men and women of the time, based around simple and inexpensive activities: 'Do you remember ever the night I was going home from [a social gathering] and nearly got [killed] of the bicycle. Do you know the mark is gone off my forehead now. I often think of my poor mother that night. She did not know who I was till I told her.' The remembrance of past and happy times was a necessity for those whose world had shrunk to the width of a cell. In another letter (April 1941), he wrote, 'we pass endless hours in telling one [an]other of our wild enterprises'.

207 Rita McSweeney was sentenced to five years' imprisonment for possessing explosives with intent; she served three years and nine months and was released in mid-March 1943.

208 PRO P.Com./9/365, April 1941.

209 PRO P.Com./9/365, John Evans to Georgina Brady, 28 September 1941. Because it mentioned a prison event, this letter was itself suppressed. Evans probably sealed the letter's fate by observing that while the British shouted about Nazi persecution of the French for listening to the BBC they did not say much about Irishmen not being allowed to have news of their own country.

210 PRO P.Com./9/365. The date of the application cannot now be ascertained precisely from the records, but from comments by the Roman Catholic chaplain it appears to have been September 1946.

211 PRO P.Com./9/365, Petition to Camp Hill Visiting, c. June or July 1946. The petition may have in part been driven by a personality conflict with Father Lynch. On 20 July 1940, he recorded his first impressions of Evans: 'An active member of the IRA. Labouring type. Ignorant and arrogant.'

212 See the *Manchester Guardian*, 11 March 1939, 13d, 16a. Many features of a convicted person's character and circumstances are open to alternative readings at the point of sentencing, depending on the intent of the judge or magistrate. Gavahan's position as a husband and a father of young children was seen as a form of aggravation of his culpability. Sentencing him at Manchester Assizes, Mr Justice Stable said, 'It passes human belief that a man of 32 years of age, married, with two children, one aged five, the other four, should have taken part in a conspiracy that reached such a point that explosions were actually brought about in this city.' The five who received sentences of twenty years' penal servitude before this court were Michael Rory Campbell (twenty-one), John Glenn (thirty-three), Dennis Duggan (thirty-three), Patrick O'Connell (thirty-three) and John Gavahan. Patrick Deviney (twenty-five) was sentenced to fourteen years and Mary Glenn (twenty-two) to seven years. Patrick Walsh was found not guilty on all charges, and two others had been discharged without the cases going to the jury. After sentence there were shouts of 'God Save Ireland' and 'Up the Republic' from the men. Campbell, who, despite his comparatively young age, was thought to be the ringleader, shouted, 'Well, it was for a good cause, and I would do it again. God save Ireland.' Such remarks frequently (but not invariably) found their way into prison records and could have serious consequences when release reviews were conducted.

213 PRO P.Com./9/840.

214 His attempt was made on 16 October 1940. He managed somehow to get over the twenty-foot outer wall but fractured his ankle and was unable to make his escape.

215 PRO P.Com./9/840, John Gavahan to wife, 21 November 1939.

216 Irish political prisoners were not immune from a tendency to this unpleasant thoughtlessness. This apart, even the provision of basic comforts told heavily on families and supporters. Thus, Ernie O'Malley's comment on internment in 1923–4: 'The Staters by keeping us interned were endeavouring, consciously or unconsciously, to make us waste time, to impoverish families and dependants, to use up the money

of individuals as well as that of organizations.' Ernie O'Malley, *The Singing Flame* (Dublin: Anvil Books, 1992), p. 289.

217 PRO P.Com./9/840, John Gavahan to wife, August 1939, writing from Maidstone Prison. Whatever the cause of delays in the post, this file shows that prison censorship was only one factor. All Gavahan's outgoing and incoming letters went to Special Branch and had a fairly rapid three- or four-day turnaround.

218 PRO P.Com./9/840, John Gavahan to his cousin, Mary, 21 April 1947.

219 Much of the case for the post-1945 welfare state was set out in the 1942 Beveridge Report: *Report of the Inter-Departmental Committee on Social Insurance and Allied Services* (London: Stationery Office, 1942), Cmd. 6404. So also was the Education Act, 1944: 7 & 8 Geo. VI, c.31 (Butler Act), which laid the foundation for post-war secondary-school education. The comprehensive Criminal Justice Act of 1948, originally brought forward in 1938, abandoned in 1939, was before war's end down for a post-war revival.

220 PRO HO/45/23639, Scottish Home Department to Home Office, 19 September 1944. Amnesty was mentioned as a possibility.

221 Francis McNeese (seven years' penal servitude, for an offence under the Explosive Substances Act, 1883, s.4[1]) had been licensed on 1 February 1944. Samuel Kennedy had been given a five-year sentence for the same offence and was released on 10 October 1942. There remained four men. Terence McSherry had been dealt with at Stirling High Court with the two already released, but, viewed as the ringleader and with a ten-year sentence, would not be eligible for release on licence until 2 February 1946. The three others, all ten-year men, were John Carson (possessing explosives), Edward Gill and Michael James O'Harr. They had varying licence-eligibility dates because of prison misconduct, ranging from April 1946 to April 1947.

222 *Morris* v. *Winter* ([1930] 1 KB 243); Penal Servitude Act, 1853: 16 & 17 Vict., c.99, s.9.

223 PRO HO/45/23639. The Scottish Home Department particularly regretted that it would oblige them to release Terence McSherry in March 1946. He was 'a man whom it is most undesirable to have released in this country'.

224 PRO HO/45/23639, Scottish Home Department to Home Office, 24 October 1944.

225 PRO HO/45/23639, Scottish Home Department to Home Office, 22 January 1946; reply, 4 February 1946. After the prisoner left the country, the Security Division of the Home Office made a prohibition order under the Prevention of Violence Act. Because of continuing travel restrictions a travel permit card had to be obtained from the Irish High Commission.

226 PRO HO/45/23639, John W. Dulanty to Sir Alexander Maxwell, 10 July 1945.

227 PRO HO/45/23639, Maxwell memorandum.

228 This was William Browne, real name William (Willie) Gaughran, who was in the advanced stages of tuberculosis. He died shortly after release.

229 5 *Hansard*, vol. 416, cols. 1507–8 (W), 28 November 1945.

230 The delegation consisted of Val McEntee, Labour MP for West Walthamstow (a constituency with a substantial Irish population); F. Longden, Labour MP for Deritend; and Captain H. J. Delargy, Labour MP for Platting. William Norton was the Secretary of the Irish Labour Party. James Larkin was a veteran Irish Labour Party member and prominent trade unionist.

231 The Indian National Army had initially been formed of Indian POWs captured by the Japanese in 1942. Reformed in 1943 and reaching a strength of 43,000, it fought alongside Japanese forces, mainly in Burma. At war's end, many of these soldiers were returned to India. Some leaders stood trial for waging war on the Crown and other serious offences, but the rank and file, equally traitorous but not equally culpable, were not prosecuted. It was this latter group to which Norton referred.

232 PRO HO/45/23639/17, Home Office notes of meeting of 25 January 1946.

233 The Connolly Association, closely associated with the CPGB, also ran a release campaign. Besides public meetings (including one addressed by Hewlett Johnson, Dean of Canterbury – known as the 'Red Dean' – an improbable but faithful fellow traveller), members of the Prisoner Release Committee of the Association were also able to visit the Irish prisoners. The Connolly Association's newspaper, *The Irish Democrat*, closely followed the CPGB line and demanded immediate and unconditional release for the prisoners. On several occasions, the *Irish Democrat* was smuggled into Parkhurst Prison (see Collins, 'Memoir', *op. cit.*, *passim*).

234 PRO HO/45/23639, Frank Lee to Val McEntee, 16 April 1946. Lee picked out the cases of Patrick Dowler, '[a] mere boy', who was in a state of depression in Parkhurst and Patrick McBrian, 'an aged man of seventy', semi-invalid and only partially sighted. He also referred to the Conway sisters and to Ella Woods at Aylesbury female convict prison. Because the sisters had forfeited seven days' remission through misconduct, Ella Woods would be released before them: 'This will be a terrific hardship on them, as these three have lived in such close association for the past eight years.' Would anyone suffer were the seven days' remission restored, he demanded.

235 PRO HO/45/23639, Frank Lee to Val McEntee, 16 April 1946.

236 See below, p. 473.

237 PRO HO/45/23639/19, James Chuter Ede to Val McEntee, 14 May 1946. The IRA prisoners had been treated in exactly the same way as other long-termers. He rejected the suggestion 'that they have in any way been singled out for harsh or unusual treatment'.

238 PRO HO/45/23639/18, Irish Prisoners' Welfare Committee to Home Secretary, 8 April 1946.

239 *Manchester Guardian*, 16 May 1946, 6b. See p. 471.

240 PRO HO/45/23639/28, 35.

241 For biographical details of Cahir Healy, see above, pp. 352–60. Eoin O'Mahony (1904–70) had been active in Fianna Fáil in the 1930s and took a part in Catholic lay activities and organisations. He had studied medicine at University College Dublin and law at Trinity. Something of a maverick, he was an eloquent orator who repeatedly failed to secure a political platform. His *Irish Times* obituary carried the sub-heading, 'Genealogist, raconteur, defender of lost causes'. He acquired a nickname, 'The Pope', supposedly because of his schoolboy aspirations, and held it throughout his life.

242 One of those was Joe Collins. Collins resented the activities of the Irish Prisoners' Welfare Committee: 'To my mind, they were agents of compromise.' He also claimed that they were hostile to men who refused their visits (Collins, 'Memoir', *op. cit.*). He took a different view of the Connolly Association, which arranged a celebratory dinner in London on the evening of his release and provided some immediate financial assistance.

243 PRO HO/45/23639/38, Eoin O'Mahony to Clement Attlee, 21 January 1946. This offer was meaningless in judicial terms and completely empty politically. If accepted, it would have opened the door for several other men, provided each could find his own shill.

244 PRO HO/45/23639/38, Francis Graham-Harrison (Attlee's Private Secretary) to Eoin O'Mahony, 16 February 1947.

245 *Irish Press*, 12 March 1947, 5e.

246 PRO HO/45/23639/42.

247 *Hansard*, vol. 433, cols. 251–2 (W), 24 February 1947.

248 Joe Collins also refused to sign any undertaking because he took the view that it conflicted with his duty of obedience to the IRA; he also considered that a signature

would compromise the general order not to recognise an enemy court (Collins, 'Memoir', *op. cit.*).

249 PRO HO/45/23639/61.

250 PRO HO/45/23639/61.

251 The by-election had been caused by the death of the Labour incumbent. The Labour candidate, Arthur Irvine, was elected with a reduced majority and an adverse swing of 10 per cent. Most of the switch went to the Conservative candidate.

252 PRO HO/45/23639/66, Memorandum of conversation between Éamon de Valera, Irish Taoiseach, and Philip Noel-Baker, Secretary of State for Commonwealth Relations, 4 November 1947. De Valera had of course seen such sentences imposed during his years in office in Ireland for both politically motivated and ordinary crime and had clearly approved of them, apparently suffering little of the anguish to which he referred. His government, moreover, continued to hold several long-term prisoners in Portlaoise. Philip Noel-Baker (1889–1982) had a strong Quaker and pacifist background (he would win the Nobel Prize in 1959), and it is likely that de Valera tailored his remarks accordingly, emphasising the prospects for reconciliation.

253 PRO HO/45/23639/66. His reference was to Seán MacBride and a group drawn mainly from republicans who had broken with the IRA and who, turning to constitutional politics, sought to blend republican with social objectives. This party, Clann na Poblachta, was bound to erode support for de Valera's Fianna Fáil.

254 PRO HO/45/23639/67, Memorandum to Sir Alexander Maxwell, 12 November 1947.

255 PRO HO/45/23639/67, undated Turner memorandum, most likely October or early November 1947. Turner also considered the judge's views, where these were available. This enabled her to show that one judge had sentenced two men differently, whom he considered to be equally culpable. His reason, completely indefensible, for giving one man (Mason) seventeen years and another, his accomplice (Stuart), a lesser sentence was that he wanted to avoid their simultaneous release.

256 PRO HO/45/23639/67. One man (J. L. Duignan) had already reached the release point in his ten-year sentence but since he had refused to sign the undertaking to return to Ireland had been retained in prison. If he did not relent, it had been decided 'in the last resort' to keep him until the expiration of his full sentence on 16 May 1949. He persisted and was indeed kept to the end.

257 *Dáil Debates*, vol. 108, cols. 842–3, 23 October 1947.

258 5 *Hansard* (Lords), vol. 152, col. 704, 18 November 1947.

259 *Irish Press*, 16 December 1947, 5c.

260 PRO HO/45/23639/74.

261 PRO HO/45/23639/69, Memorandum of meeting of 2 December 1947.

262 PRO HO/45/23639/69. The subsidiary points concerned repatriation requirements and the nature of the undertaking that prisoners would be required to sign. Two prisoners who had lived in Britain for years were raised as hardship cases. Chuter Ede insisted that were there any prisoners who claimed to have no remaining ties in Ireland and whose connections were in Britain, they must establish that fact to Home Office satisfaction: the implication was that for such prisoners deportation might be waived. He also assured the deputation that (such cases apart) if on release these prisoners agreed to go to Éire, no further undertaking would be required from them.

263 In the election, Fine Gael had secured thirty-one seats, Labour nineteen, Clann na Poblachta ten, Clann na Talmhan seven and the Independents twelve. Fianna Fáil was still far and away the largest party with sixty-eight seats, but the desire for change prevailed. John Costello, leader of Fine Gael, was Taoiseach and Seán MacEoin his Minister for Justice.

264 PRO HO/45/23639/74.

265 *Dáil Debates*, vol. 110, cols. 994–5, 4 May 1948.

266 *Irish Press*, 9 March 1948, 1e; 10 March 1948, 1b and 1d; 15 April 1948, 5d. See also Dáil statement on the prisoners in England (*Dáil Debates*, vol. 110, cols. 623–4, 14 April 1948).

267 PRO HO/45/23639/83. This communication (which has not survived) seems to have been expressed in a proper way.

268 See, for example, James Larkin's persistent question on the issue (*Dáil Debates*, vol. 110, col. 1991, 25 May 1948).

269 John Loader Maffey (later Lord Rugby) was a significant presence in Dublin throughout the war years, serving from 1939 until 1949. His high rank prior to taking up the post of UK Representative (Permanent Under-Secretary for the Colonies) indicated the importance that Britain attached to the appointment – if for no other reason than wishing to avert trouble with a close neighbour which at times seemed so uneasily at peace. For a biographical note see below, p. 736, n. 6.

270 PRO HO/45/23639/74, Lord Rugby to Sir Eric Machtig, Permanent Under-Secretary, Commonwealth Office, 6 April 1948. Rugby was well aware of the irony in those issues being represented to the British government by MacBride: 'Parenthetically I should perhaps point out that Mr MacBride was at one time a leading figure in the IRA but resigned from them in 1938 before the policy of outrage in England was adopted.' On this and others of his official duties, MacBride himself must have reflected on the curious fortunes of politics.

271 PRO HO/45/23639/87, Draft letter, James Chuter Ede to Philip Noel-Baker, 11 May 1948. The accompanying table showed that the last four to be released in November would be Donaghy, Glenn, Compton and Duignan. The case of Duignan, already mentioned, was curious and rather sad. His stubbornness was misguided, perhaps based on the principle that he would have no truck with the British government. It is all the harder to understand as his comrades signed, their political consciences apparently undisturbed.

272 PRO HO/45/23639/87, Lord Rugby to Sir Eric Machtig, 19 May 1948. Rugby's comment on the interview is interesting and indicative of the new Irish government's position: 'You will… understand that there is little interest here in the clemency side of the question. What Mr Norton is out for is to show that the new Government is able to do more for these men than the de Valera Government could do.' He concluded, 'In fact the interest in the question is a "headline" interest. We offer clemency without headlines. I do not think we shall have much more trouble over this question.'

273 5 *Hansard* (Lords), vol. 155, cols. 456–8W, 27 April 1948.

274 PRO HO/45/23639/87, A. W. Peterson (Private Secretary to James Chuter Ede) to Miss E. M. Donald (Labour Party), 12 May 1948.

275 PRO HO/45/23639/83, Frank Lee to James Chuter Ede, 28 October 1948.

276 The last two were Jack McCabe and Joe Collins, who were released on 15 December 1948. Both refused to accept the convict licence which was served on men released before the expiration of sentence. Collins was outraged when, on 15 November 1951, in a debate on the Expiring Laws Continuance Bill, Chuter Ede claimed (without mentioning names) that Collins and McCabe had given undertakings prior to their release (5 *Hansard*, vol. 493, col. 1198). He immediately wrote to the Irish newspapers to denounce what he saw as a deliberate lie. See *Evening Mail*, 23/4 November 1951, 4e. In his letter, McCabe argued that 'neither of us gave any undertaking whatsoever. We walked out together through the gates of Parkhurst freer and happier in our conscience than Mr Ede, who I now challenge to prove his statement.' McCabe's fellow prisoner, Joe Collins, had written to the *Mail* on the matter a few days earlier (see *Evening Mail*, 20 November 1951, 4f). Collins called Chuter Ede's statement 'deliberate, calculated and planned to ignore militant Republicanism here and degrade members of the Irish Republican Army who stood up to the inhuman treatment meted out to them in English jails'.

277 PRO HO/45/23639/107, Northern Ireland Cabinet Office to Home Office, 30 August 1949.

278 This was a second attack: two bombs had exploded at the station on 9 February 1939. For the 9 February explosions, see *The Times*, 10 February 1939, 11a. Two bombs were placed in the coal bays at Camley Street, Kings Cross, but only damaged a pillar; another bomb exploded in a timber merchant's yard in Harrow Road – again there were no injuries. For the 26 July 1939 bombs, see *The Times*, 27 July 1939, 14a–b; *Manchester Guardian*, 27 July 1939, 9a, 13a; *Daily Telegraph*, 27 July 1939, 1a, 15a, 16c; *Irish News*, 27 July 1939, 5a, 5f and 7a, 7f. For the 25 August 1939 bomb at Coventry, see *Midland Daily Telegraph*, 26 August 1939, 1a–f. For the execution of Richards and Barnes, see *Midland Daily Telegraph*, 7 February 1940, 1c–e, 5a–d, 8d. On the previous day, Tuesday, 6 February 1940, three explosions in mailbags (two in London and one in Birmingham) occurred, which, *The Times* reported, 'All are regarded as reprisals by members of the IRA for the refusal to reprieve the two Irishmen who are due to be executed in Birmingham this morning.' See *The Times*, 7 February 1940, 5e.

279 See above, p. 437 and n. 63.

280 *Irish News*, 15 December 1939, 1a–b; 16 December 1939, 4g.

281 McCormick denied this. He admitted his membership of the IRA and that he had taken part in the bombing. He told the court that it had been a mistake that the device went off in the middle of the day and that IRA instructions were that no lives should be endangered. His part in the operation was limited, he claimed, to assisting another man to get the bicycle used in the attack. He had nothing to do with the making of the bomb, he insisted: 'All I had to do was to give them the chlorate' (*Irish News*, 14 December 1939, 5c).

282 Letitia Fairfield, 'Introduction', in Letitia Fairfield (ed.), *Trial of Peter Barnes and Others* (London: William Hodges & Co., 1953). The receipts had been retained, no doubt, to verify expenditure, in accordance with the IRA's accounting procedures.

283 *Irish News*, 15 December 1939, 1a. In his final words after sentence had been passed, McCormick evoked the Manchester Martyrs: 'I say, in conclusion, God bless Ireland and God bless the men who have fought and died for her.' The defence made an application for Barnes's fiancée to see him in the court cells before he was removed, and this was granted.

284 In 1969, the Insight team of the *Sunday Times* published a convincing article on the bombing in which the journalists claimed to have met the man who planted the bomb, who had managed to escape undetected to Ireland (6 July 1969, 24a–c). This did not affect the culpability and legal liability of those who took part in the enterprise, though the critical question, then and always, was the degree of foreknowledge of what was planned.

285 *The Times*, 8 February 1940, 8f. Hundreds of people congregated outside Winson Green Prison. There was no demonstration, but, at 9 a.m., as the execution took place, those present bared their heads. After the notice of execution had been posted on the prison gates, and with a strong police presence, the crowd was permitted to file past it, before dispersing.

286 PRO HO/282/51. There had also been speculation by the prosecution (certainly no evidence was offered to support it) that there was German finance behind the Coventry (and presumably other) bombings: 'Investigation of the paymaster in this case might take us not only to Dublin, but further afield, perhaps in another direction' (*Irish News*, 15 December 1939, 1b). Republicans saw the shades of the venerated Manchester Martyrs, Allen, Larkin and O'Brien; the British government the shadows of Roger Casement and his German allies. The last may have been reinforced by German comment on the executions, which Berlin described as 'merely a

continuation of the suppression of Ireland by Britain during the past centuries'. Barnes and McCormick were described as 'fighters for Irish liberty' (*Irish News*, 8 February 1940, 1f; 9 February 1940, 5d).

287 See *Irish News*, 8 February 1940, 1e, 7b; 9 February 1940, 1f, 5c. There were demonstrations in Dublin, Cork and Belfast, the last consisting of groups of apparently unorganised girls who paraded in city-centre streets singing rebel songs. Across Éire, sports fixtures were cancelled and cinemas were closed. IRA slogans were painted on walls in Belfast. During one such incident, police arrived at the corner of the Falls Road and Derby Street, and, following a scuffle, a constable fired a shot (*Irish News*, 9 February 1940, 5c).

288 The *Irish News* reported that the men had made 'most edifying preparations for death and faced the scaffold happy and resigned to God's will'. During their six weeks at Winson Green Prison (Birmingham) under sentence of death, they had attended mass twice a week. An hour and a half before their execution, mass had been conducted in each man's cell and special blessings were given to them (*Irish News*, 9 February 1940, 5c).

289 On the evening of Thursday, 14 December 1939, hours after Barnes and McCormick were sentenced, small incendiary devices caused limited damage at two Birmingham city-centre cinemas. The technical resources of the IRA at this stage of the campaign may be inferred from the primitive construction of the bombs: boxes of matches with balloon fuses (*Irish News*, 15 December 1939, 1g).

290 *Irish News*, 12 February 1940, 1d and 5c. One poster claimed that Barnes and McCormick 'had been murdered in cold blood because they refused to stand by and see their country looted and ravaged by a merciless monster' (PRONI HA/32/1/478).

291 PRONI HA/32/1/478. See also *Irish News*, 12 February 1940, 5e.

292 James McCormick came from Mullingar, Co. Westmeath, where there were particular marks of respect following his execution. A meeting of the Mullingar Mental Hospital Board, held on the day of the execution, asked the Irish government to request the return of the remains of both men 'to be buried in the sacred soil of their native land' (*Irish News*, 9 February 1940, 5d). For an account of protests and gestures of respect, see the *Irish Times* (8 February 1940, 5f–g). These included a demand at a Dublin public meeting that the remains be returned 'to their native land, for which they died'.

293 The relatives of Roger Casement were allowed to visit his resting place in Pentonville Prison (see McConville, *Irish Political Prisoners, op. cit.*, p. 599, n. 168).

294 PRO HO/144/23448, William Gallagher to Clement Attlee, 19 May 1949. A Barnes and McCormick Repatriation Committee had earlier been formed in Mullingar and Tullamore to assist the relatives in their efforts to bring home the remains (NLI, MS. 17879, Flyer).

295 PRO HO/144/23448, Patricia Llewelyn-Davis (Private Secretary to Philip Noel-Baker) to S. P. Osmond (Private Secretary to Clement Attlee), 3 June 1949.

296 PRO HO/282/51.

297 The two were Joseph O'Sullivan and Reginald Dunne who, on 22 June 1922, had shot Sir Henry Wilson on the steps of his home in London's Eaton Place and who had been hanged for that offence. Because Wilson had been a stalwart Ulster unionist, and was regarded as a martyr in the unionist cause, the Home Office consulted the Northern Ireland government about the removal of the bodies. Both Belfast and Dublin were unenthusiastic about repatriation. The Northern authorities were concerned that, were the issue of the Home Secretary's licence made public, it could lead to disturbances. Dublin had been well satisfied by the 1965 return of the remains of Roger Casement and apparently did not wish to detract from the unique character of that transfer. In the event, the July 1967 transfer and re-interments passed off quietly with the minimum of publicity.

298 PRO HO/282/51.
299 PRO HO/282/51. There was a practical problem in that another body had been buried on top of the two men. This was C. M. Roberts, who had been executed in 1955 for the murder of his wife. The usual practice was to consult the next of kin, but the Home Secretary was not obliged to do so. In this case, it was suggested, it might be inappropriate to do so because '[s]hortly before he was executed, Roberts wrote an abusive letter to his daughter in which he wished upon her the same fate as had overtaken his wife'. It was decided not to contact the daughter, especially as the disturbance of the grave would only be temporary.
300 The honour guard was dressed in what would, in the years immediately ahead, become a familiar uniform: black berets, black gloves and black sweaters. The hearse was followed by some 200 members of the repatriation committee and the National Graves Association.
301 *Guardian*, 7 July 1969.
302 *Irish Press*, 5 July 1969, 4c. Maguire repeated the claim made by Tom Barry during the reprieve campaign in February 1940 that Broadgate had not been the target and that the explosion had been an accident (see n. 63 above). An impressively researched *Sunday Times* article published the following day exculpated Peter Barnes from having a direct part in the explosion but left no doubt that the blast was intended to explode when and where it did (*Sunday Times*, 6 July 1969, 24b).

10

INTERNEES IN NORTHERN IRELAND, 1939–45

The IRA in Northern Ireland

The petering out of its bombing campaign in Britain left the IRA with one target: the state and government of Northern Ireland. Any move against the de Valera administration would provoke a counterstroke of further repressive measures. Furthermore, there now existed in the South little or no popular base from which to organise. The organisation took some time to learn these lessons fully, as we have seen.[1] To the IRA leadership, fortified by its ideology and supported by a lattice of wishful thinking, prospects inevitably seemed more hopeful. The greater part of Northern Ireland's Catholic minority remained unreconciled, and sections of it were indifferent or unsympathetic to the British war effort. The trial of three men and two women charged with involvement in the Coventry explosion of 25 August 1939, played out through the autumn into the execution of James McCormick and Peter Barnes on 7 February 1940.[2] The reprieve campaign stirred nationalist, republican, labour and sections of liberal opinion and made the political mood and degree of receptiveness seem to be more sympathetic to the IRA than it actually was.[3] Even so, the possibility of members of the Catholic community in Northern working-class areas declining to give at least some comfort or shelter was remote. Yet, while few gave information to the police, some clearly did, and this, combined with local knowledge and effective surveillance, kept RUC intelligence abreast with many developments and provided extensive lists of names of activists and associates, as well as suspicious addresses and haunts. Northern republicans knew that they lived under heavy surveillance.

As we have seen, the British campaign had been well trailed in 1938 and was in itself reason for heightened alarm and security concern in Northern Ireland – a base for recruitment and supply, as well as a target. And at a low level, with periods of intensification, the Northern state had never ceased to be subject to attacks, ranging from frequent nocturnal burnings and bombings of customs huts to more determined forays against RUC targets and associated premises and installations.[4] Rarely did these rise above nuisance level in the damage inflicted, but, even as pinpricks, they served to remind Belfast of the potential of irreconcilable republicanism.

The British campaign suggested that something more might be on the IRA agenda which would intensify attacks in the North. Intelligence reports of the 1936 and 1938 Army Conventions, an aborted attack on a British Army barracks in Armagh, the assassinations of Daniel Turley, a former OC of the Belfast IRA on 4 December 1936, and Joseph Hanna, a former intelligence officer, also of Belfast, on 26 January 1937 (both for treachery) had shown that the organisation's resolve, if not its capacity, remained strong.[5] That it was also readying itself for operations in Northern Ireland was the seemingly unavoidable significance of a number of incidents in the lead-up to the British campaign. The explosion at Castlefin, Co. Donegal, on 28 November 1938, could only be an accident during preparations for a cross-border attack.[6] The following day this was confirmed, with attacks at opposite ends of the border, in Co. Down and Co. Fermanagh.[7] This was not unduly alarming in itself. Customs huts were residual targets – probably training missions for IRA neophytes – but, with other information to hand, Stormont and the RUC had reason to suppose that the bombings of 29 November were a warming-up exercise.[8]

The bombings in Britain inevitably increased alarm in both Belfast and in Dublin. A Treason Act was thought necessary by the latter to extend the reach of the Offences Against the State Act (OASA), 1939.[9] While some legislators could not stomach the proposed increased recourse to the death penalty, the majority saw the severity of the measures as a justified response to the peril of the state.[10] The government of Northern Ireland had made a similar statement of intent in response to the IRA's declaration of war in January, promising 'prompt and drastic action' and, if necessary, legislation to confer further powers on the executive to stamp out 'outrage and murder as means to achieve political ends'.[11]

There were worrying signs on both sides of the border that the tensions caused by the IRA's campaign in Britain and by attacks along the border could spill into popular discontent and perhaps even communal action. Days after the IRA's declaration of war on Britain, there was a third attack on a large Celtic cross, the focal point of the republican burial plot in Milltown Cemetery, Belfast. This took place even though the cemetery and the republican plot had been placed under special police guard and while late buses from the city centre were setting down their passengers.[12] The identity of the attackers was not disclosed, and, no doubt sensitive to the dire possibilities of sectarian violence, the newspapers were careful not to speculate.

In the South, there was little possibility of communal violence, but de Valera's government had to be alert to a nationalist head of steam that might be raised by the events in England. This at least is one reading of de Valera's remarks, delivered only six weeks before the outbreak of war, emphasising that his government had 'no sympathy' with the IRA's campaign in England. Conspicuously stopping short of outright and simple condemnation, he recognised that some of those involved were 'animated by high ideals'. Again ambiguously, he declared his intention to take necessary action to deal with political violence (the term 'IRA' was always avoided by Fianna Fáil in order to deny the organisation historical legitimacy) while at the same time declaring that the root of the problem was Partition and 'the minority of 800,000 people in the North East of Ireland'.[13] This was but one more demonstration of de Valera's unceasing effort to draw to himself as much republican sentiment as possible – a venture in which he was immensely successful.[14]

The times were fraught with tragedy. The most violent and destructive war in history was unleashed in September 1939 and developed with hideous fury. Governments everywhere tightened security, and the liberty of citizens (as well as their property) was everywhere circumscribed by state necessity. The rule of law was preserved in both parts of Ireland, but this was law for extraordinary times.[15] Any organisation that threatened security and stability to almost any degree was deemed a fundamental threat to the state and would become subject to an amount of coercion and suppression beyond any contemplated in times of peace. This would extend to capital and corporal punishment for politically motivated offences of violence or preparation for violence. These sanctions were not frequently invoked but were nevertheless indicative of the willingness of the state to use its repressive power to whatever degree was thought necessary.

An execution in Belfast

There would be six executions of IRA men in Éire during the war, but only one in Northern Ireland. This last arose out of a badly planned, poorly conducted and wholly unnecessary IRA operation, part of a basically peaceful protest, intended to lift republican morale. A type of stalemate had set in by the war's third year. There had been widespread round-ups, and hundreds were interned, with a smaller number serving sentences of imprisonment. The IRA structure and most of its equipment (such as it was) remained intact.[16] The organisation did not, however, have the capacity to mount sustained attacks on the police or army, or extended action in rural areas, and was restricted to occasional fund-raising raids on payrolls and banks and a few shoot-and-run confrontations.[17] In the spring of 1942, what would turn out to be a disastrous decision was made. A public ceremony to commemorate the Easter Rising – the paramount republican event – was to be held in Belfast on Sunday, 5 April. This would necessarily have to be a surprise and rapidly concluded demonstration. Catholic areas were compact, and police would quickly be on the scene. A diversion was needed to give the demonstration a bit more time and to allow for dispersal. This secondary operation was not planned in any detail and was foolishly executed; there was no fallback agreed. A unit of six men (none older than twenty-two) would open fire on a police car and flee. Two young women and a further man (Patrick Simpson) would be on hand to take the guns away. The assumption was that police reinforcements would then be rushed to the scene, allowing the IRA commemoration – the principal objective – to proceed elsewhere. The ambush was duly staged at the junction of Kashmir Road and Clonard Gardens, in the heart of Catholic West Belfast. Rather than driving off to summon assistance, however, the three well-armed constables got out of their car and returned fire. In what was a brave but unwise decision they then took up the pursuit. The chase terminated with the IRA party trapped in a house.[18] In the subsequent exchange of fire, the leader, Tom Williams, was badly wounded and Constable Patrick Murphy was shot dead.[19] All members of the IRA party were arrested and brought to trial. The men were sentenced to death, and the young women were dealt with on lesser charges.[20] The law of joint enterprise (and the malice aforethought that permeated the attack) meant that several men could be executed for an act of murder by one or more of them.

The execution date was set for 18 August 1942, but this was vacated when an appeal was lodged. There was an immediate and widespread reprieve campaign. A reprieve committee in the South, under the leadership of Seán MacBride (who had stood down as IRA Chief of Staff not long before) collected more than 200,000 signatures.[21] As with the Coventry campaign, a wide swathe of nationalist and republican opinion, including members of Fianna Fáil, together with trade unionists and others who were politically uninvolved, sought mercy. A section of British opinion was convinced that the executions would be counterproductive.[22] Attempts were made to influence the British government by means of American representation.[23]

In Belfast, as might be expected, things looked rather different, certainly to the Protestant majority. A police patrol had been ambushed and fired on without provocation and a constable subsequently killed. At any time one of the gravest crimes, this wartime murder of a police officer had to be viewed as an attack on the state itself. The men had stood their trial before a regular court and jury: in Éire, they would have faced a military court and would have had short shrift. They did not elect for separate representation, and only some made statements. All had been convicted, and the recommendation of mercy for one (Patrick Simpson, aged eighteen) had, if anything, undermined the lack of such a recommendation for the others.[24] An appeal had been lodged and dismissed.[25] Constable Murphy had been struck by five bullets, fired by two revolvers. Convinced that he was dying of his wounds, to take blame upon himself and to save his comrades, Williams had disregarded an IRA standing order that no statement should be made to the police. He admitted firing three of the shots, but the Crown did not identify the gun from which the other two had come. Adhering to IRA orders, none of the men had chosen to give evidence at trial. In law, all were equally guilty, despite Williams's attempt to exculpate the others.

The question of reprieve was of such importance that it had to be considered by the Northern Ireland cabinet as a whole. John C. MacDermott, Minister for Public Security, was asked to comment.[26] In his view, the trial had been fair and the conviction sound in law. He noted that although the jury's verdict was justified it did not bear with equal weight against all the men. MacDermott attempted to draw those distinctions in culpability that defence lawyers might have made, had there been separate representations. For Tom Williams there was no hope. He had fired five shots, including the three that had hit Constable

Murphy; he admitted to being the leader of the group and had volunteered his overriding culpability. Patrick Simpson (one of the three who were to take the firearms away) did not appear to have been armed, and, had he given evidence on his own account and been separately represented, he might well have avoided conviction. The jury had entered a recommendation for mercy in his case, and the Attorney General regarded him as the least culpable. Henry ('Dixie') Cordner was armed with a defective weapon and had not fired, and he was in much the same category. William (Jimmy) Perry admitted to firing a shot but did not hit Constable Murphy and had not fired at the car. His culpability, on balance, did not seem to be the heaviest. Between the two remaining men, John Oliver and Joseph Cahill, little distinction could be drawn. It appeared that both had fired at the car, and one had also fired at Constable Murphy.[27] The trial judge arrived at somewhat the same conclusions, supporting the jury's recommendation for mercy in the case of Simpson, putting a major share of the blame on Williams but leaving the fate of the others to be settled by the politicians. He insisted that all six were morally as well as legally guilty and commented unfavourably on the demeanour in the dock of Cordner, Perry, Oliver and Cahill. All, apart from Simpson, were over the age of nineteen. Youth might be a factor in their favour, though he could not see this as the sole ground for exercising mercy.[28]

The Northern Ireland Cabinet met on 26 August 1942, and papers went to the Duke of Abercorn the following day with recommendations for mercy in only two of the cases. The Cabinet considered that Patrick Simpson's sentence should be commuted to fifteen years' penal servitude and that of Henry Cordner to twenty years. The remaining four – Thomas Williams, William Perry, Joseph Cahill and John Oliver – should be executed.[29] The Governor appears to have consulted the British government at this point, despite his ministers' assurances (questionable without a doubt) that no imperial considerations were involved. On the evening of 29 August 1942, the Home Secretary telegraphed to the Northern Ireland government: they were to take no action until they heard from him.[30] The Governor summoned John Andrews, the Northern Ireland Prime Minister, and expressed his strong opinion that only Tom Williams should hang. Simpson should be sent to penal servitude for twenty years and the others for life. Andrews had no option but to reassemble his cabinet. There was prolonged and evidently divided discussion of the Governor's use of the Prerogative, including an assurance from Andrews that, notwithstanding the view he had expressed, the Governor would now endorse whatever decision Cabinet made on a reconsideration of the case. The consequence was clear: the Governor would act in accordance with the advice of the ministers, as constitutional convention required, but, having expressed his own opinion (with the implication that it carried London's backing), responsibility would then be the Cabinet's alone. Andrews strongly urged a reprieve for all except Williams, in accordance with the Governor's opinion.[31] The Cabinet accordingly backed him, and the revised opinion now went to the Governor, who exercised the Prerogative accordingly. Cahill, Cordner, Oliver and Perry had their sentences commuted to life at penal servitude; Simpson's was reduced to fifteen years. Williams's sentence was to stand, and he was executed on 2 September 1942.[32]

There had also been secret approaches from the Roman Catholic Church.[33] Cardinal Joseph MacRory, the Catholic Primate, approached the British government via Cardinal Arthur Hinsley, his counterpart in England. Taking a wider view of the possible effects – especially in Irish America and therefore on Anglo-American relations – Churchill had ensured that his judgement that only one of the six be executed was made clear to Belfast, both through the Home Secretary and the Governor. Mindful of the constitutional relationship between London and Belfast, he was careful to keep the approach at this indirect level, confident that Andrews would do the right thing. On the day of Williams's execution, Churchill wrote to Cardinal Hinsley about the Northern Ireland government's decision.[34] Two days later, a letter went to Andrews. The War Cabinet had been clear that this was a case on which they did not need to make representations; 'I may, however, express my personal and private opinion that the course you took was both right and humane.' He gave the decision its wider context with the next and seemingly disconnected sentence: 'We are steadily forging ahead in this war, but I see no reason to expect a speedy conclusion.'[35]

Had the Northern Ireland government stuck by its original decision and hanged all but Simpson, there could have been violent repercussions and public disorder. As it was, vigils, petitions, appeals and protests continued to the end and were followed by various acts of IRA retaliation.[36] It is difficult now to say what turn the public temper had taken in the Catholic community following the execution, but it was probably not as the IRA had hoped. A police officer had been shot dead, and the man most directly responsible had been tried and executed. Hanging was the usual penalty for murder at the time. No gloss could conceal the fact that the shooting had been intentional. Even among sympathisers it would have been hard to stir more than passing indignation at this outcome, though there certainly would have been sorrow and sympathy for Williams's family. The IRA had, it appeared, launched yet another campaign, and its activity was sufficient and police apprehensions such that a curfew was declared in West Belfast on 10 October 1942, prohibiting movement on the streets between the hours of 8.30 p.m. and 6 a.m.[37]

This flurry of IRA activity concealed a strategic vacuum. The optimum aim was to keep the organisation intact and in some kind of fighting trim and to hope that the war, even in that summer of 1942 still in doubt, would take a favourable turn against the Allies.[38] The comprehensive and total defeat of Field Marshal Erwin Rommel at El Alamein on 4 November 1942 put paid to that.[39] In retrospect (and a trifle inaccurately) Churchill noted, 'Before Alamein we never had a victory. After Alamein we never had a defeat.'[40] Unfolding events, not least the mobilisation of American might and resources, would have made clear to all but the most blinkered Axis supporter that there could now only be one outcome. Armed robberies, sporadic bombings and shootings were serious for those involved, but with all of Northern Ireland an armed camp, there was not the remotest possibility that these activities would rise above the level of nuisance. Between September and December 1942 the organisation staged sixty-odd armed attacks.[41] None achieved a notable success, and the only definite outcome was a further tightening of the screw, by both Belfast and Dublin. In Éire, garda pressure increased, as the Irish government, even more concerned about its neutral status now that the USA had joined the war, reacted to the IRA upsurge in the North as well as incidents in the South. Whatever IRA hopes there may have been that the Axis would prevail, and therefore open a new chapter of possibilities, were finally laid to rest by the German surrender at Stalingrad on 31 January 1943. By the spring of 1943, IRA activity had virtually ceased. Those still at large did what they could to avoid attracting attention, tried not to move around or even to meet each other. There would be occasional incidents, but what remained of the IRA was now in its winter quarters – and it looked like being a long winter.[42] North and South, recalled Liam Burke, 'there was not a kick left in the organisation'.[43]

Flogging and birching

Corporal punishment had greatly declined in use in Britain and was generally imposed for offences involving violence or, occasionally, for crimes of moral turpitude, such as pimping.[44] It continued to be used in Northern Ireland, although, again, relatively rarely. We have seen how it was included in the Special Powers Acts, attracting particular criticism since the Acts were intended to deal with politically motivated offences.[45] Two instruments were used to inflict the punishment: the cat o' nine tails for those aged over eighteen and the birch for those under that age. The whip was applied to the bared upper back, the offender being strapped to an apparatus. Those who were birched were made to bend over and the instrument was used on their bared buttocks. The whip inflicted by far the heavier punishment.

An indirect account of corporal punishment at Belfast Prison survives in Liam Burke's interview with Uinseann MacEoin.[46] Burke was OC of A Wing (the long-termers' wing) and spoke to James Mooney, Joe Doyle and Arthur Steele, the men who were subject to the punishment. They had been sentenced by Lord Justice Murphy at Belfast City Commission on 4 August 1943 for illegal drilling and the possession of arms and ammunition. All had been sentenced to twelve years' penal servitude and to twelve strokes of the cat.[47]

There was a considerable interval, from August to mid-December, before the corporal punishment was inflicted. As in Britain, there was a process of ministerial review before such sentences were confirmed.[48] Most of the IRA prisoners in A Wing had, by this time, come to believe that the sentences had been forgotten or cancelled. On what Burke recalled as a cold night close to Christmas, preparations for the punishments began. The men were taken from their own cell to an empty cell in C Wing and were locked in, together with prison staff. They were ordered to strip off their shirts and to await their turn for the punishment.[49]

Each was eventually escorted through ranks of watching officers to the boilerhouse. There they were, Burke stated, 'suspended by rings, hands and feet, inches above the ground'. A hooded prison officer then administered the whipping or birching. Each stroke was counted off by the Governor while the prison medical officer checked the man's heart. After punishment, the man was taken down and escorted back to his cell, the only treatment being a gauze bandage over the bleeding parts.

Burke examined the men the following morning and found each to be bleeding. He protested to Captain Thomas M. Stuart, the Governor, about the barbarity of the punishment, the unnecessary attendance of so many warders and the lack of proper medical attention. To this Stuart gave the only reply he could, that he had acted in compliance with instructions from the Ministry and had carried out the sentence of the court.[50] The men apparently did not suffer any long-term physical or emotional after-effects, and Patrick McCotter and others, who had been whipped at an earlier point, told Burke that the physical pain was negligible and that the punishment demeaned those who inflicted it more than it did its recipients.[51]

Internment

Corporal punishment had more of a symbolic than an immediate and direct role in the Northern state's response to the IRA. It was a statement that the authorities were willing to act with whatever vigour was necessary. Imprisonment was, however, the dominant feature in what became a prospect of desolated republican hopes. During the preceding years the authorities had taken preventive action. Internment had been revived, criminal charges had been pressed wherever possible, and several hundred IRA men and women and their associates were caught in the firm embrace of Armagh, Belfast and Londonderry prisons. To understand this sequence of events we must take a step backward.

By the spring of 1939, the inevitability of a conflict between Germany, France and Britain was incontestable. In accordance with the doctrines of violent republicanism, the wider war would sound reveille. Writing to E. W. Scales, Assistant Secretary at the Ministry of Home Affairs, Lieutenant Colonel Sir C. G. Wickham, RUC Inspector-General, was emphatic. Whether or not conscription was enforced, the IRA would act: 'It is their opportunity, which they must use or disappear.'[52] There was some uncertainty about the security effects of conscription. Enforced in Northern Ireland, it would place actual and potential IRA men under military control: they would either serve or be imprisoned as refusers. Yet an anti-conscription campaign could invigorate their organisation and standing with the nationalist community: this had happened twenty-one years previously. The British government's conclusion that the conscription of the unwilling in Northern Ireland would be counterproductive and impractical removed the issue from the portfolio of immediate war worries.[53]

That internment would be necessary there seemed no doubt in political or official circles. Nowhere in the Northern government's papers is the case against it raised, nor are its unavoidable difficulties and disadvantages considered. Such had been its use since the formation of the state that it was now a reflexive prophylactic. Yet, as we shall see, the IRA was by 1939 under close surveillance, apparently well penetrated, and overt illegality could almost certainly have been crushed sufficiently by the normal processes of law. Internment is always prone to overreach; it is inconsistent and sometimes capricious; it is expensive and politically troublesome; it generates sympathy for the incarcerated and can be an effective recruiting sergeant. These may from time to time be costs which the state decides it must bear, but they were not properly considered or cast onto the scales in 1939. A more positive view was taken. Internment was seen as preventive, incapacitatory, deterrent and, for the Unionist government looking to its constituency, had undoubted political advantages.

One of the major places of internment during the Anglo-Irish War had been the military camp at Ballykinlar, Co. Down. It was proposed (another indication that the old template had been dusted off) to re-establish a compound on the site for the internment of aliens 'and also local disloyal men'.[54] The RUC had its own views on aliens, who it thought should be encouraged to leave the country. It was likely that on the outbreak of war, therefore, that the numbers of enemy aliens would be small: police took the view that 100 was probably 'an extravagant estimate'. As to IRA members and sympathisers ('disloyal men'), it was more difficult to gauge: Wickham could only refer back to 1922 and considered that a total of 700 places would be adequate, 'if not excessive'.[55] This was not a properly researched or closely calculated estimate by any means and was made without allowing for the extremely disturbed conditions prevailing throughout Ireland, North and South, in 1922. A recurrent difficulty (though it is not a constant) in prison administration is that if places are made available they display a tendency under certain conditions to suck in persons to fill them, a capillary effect arising from judges', magistrates' and officials' antipathy to risk. The tendency to expand to available capacity is even more likely to occur where incarceration is a purely executive and preventive process. In such circumstances if doubts are raised about an individual, internment must seem a compelling and indeed responsible precaution.

One consequence of exempting Northern Ireland from conscription was to remove the military from the process of internment: there was no demonstrable connection between army priorities and the containment of militant republicans. Manpower would have to be provided and charges met locally. Rather than a revival of a Westminster measure akin to the ROIA (which parliamentary time would not allow), internees would be dealt with by the devolved civil powers, using the Special Powers Act. E. W. Scales, at Home Affairs, seemed reasonably confident that the Northern Ireland government could cope with the 'republican element' and that a by-product of the presence in Northern Ireland of large numbers of troops under training would be a smothering of IRA activities.[56] Apart from an armed insurrection, which would have to be dealt with in whatever way necessary, the activities of the 'disloyal element' would be a matter for the

Northern government. As of May 1939, moreover, there was so much available space in the prisons that it would be difficult to justify the expense of constructing new accommodation which might never be required.[57]

The Army had rapidly distanced itself from these developments. The responsibility for enemy aliens was clearly for Westminster rather than Stormont, and they should be removed from Northern Ireland and 'sent to the United Kingdom' for internment. As for republicans, 'Disloyal Irishmen will not be dealt with by the military after mobilization, provided accommodation is available in H.M. Prisons.'[58] A similar line was taken by the Home Office. It would be better, Sir Ernest Holderness (Assistant Secretary at the Home Office) contended, were internment to be handled under 'your Special Powers Acts'. This would avoid the necessity of delegating Westminster powers under the Defence Regulations. Delegation could present difficulties in the exercise of powers, the hearing of appeals and the responsibility for looking after the internees.[59]

All well and good, but, as a Home Affairs memo swiftly contended, this meant that Northern Ireland would be applying different regulations from those of Great Britain. More importantly, the cost of internment under the Special Powers Act would fall on Northern Ireland; Defence Regulations internment, by contrast, would be an imperial charge. At this point it seemed that there could be no question of the military running an internment camp for persons held under a Northern Ireland Act, though, the writer added with a deal of hopeless optimism, 'it might be possible to arrange for this'.[60] Rather late in the day, Sir Dawson Bates, Minister of Home Affairs, attempted to pass the parcel back to London. The Special Defence Regulations and the Special Powers Acts were designed for different purposes, he argued, and it would be unwise to rely solely on the Northern Ireland Acts for an emergency such as the outbreak of war. He therefore tried again for delegated powers under the Defence Regulations, using the Northern Ireland legislation as a supplement.[61]

At this point, conducted though it was in a veiled and elliptical manner, with each side carefully ignoring or sidestepping the basic issues, the argument could have gone either way. Northern Ireland was a curious creation – a subordinate government within the UK. Save as an element in the resolution of Anglo-Irish relations, it is doubtful that Westminster had fully fathomed its nature and the consequences of introducing such an entity into the British constitution and political and administrative processes. The delineation of imperial and local responsibility was a moving point, affected by political, contingent and, in some instances, subjective factors. During the confusing and frantic opening weeks of the war, the matter of internment took another turn, when the War Office temporarily and inexplicably reversed itself, accepting responsibility for providing an internment camp for persons held under the Special Powers Act. The Ministry of Home Affairs delightedly seized the moment, writing on 14 October 1939 to Major-General R. V. Pollock, the GOC in Northern Ireland. Some seventy internees were being held in Belfast Prison, of whom at least sixty should be held for the duration. There was a risk in holding the men in Belfast – not only for their own safe custody, but because they increased the threat to the prison itself and were very disruptive. The Ministry wanted to hand them over to the Army 'with the minimum delay'.[62]

Pollock, like other high-ranking soldiers, had not acquired his red tabs without learning how to deal with civil servants and politicians. Moreover, he held some very high trump cards. The war effort was everything, and he and his staff were the best judges and, in Northern Ireland, the only judges of its priorities. The construction and running of an internment camp for only seventy detainees could not claim a position anywhere close to the front of the queue, especially when there was sufficient accommodation in the civil prisons, when there existed an efficient and well equipped constabulary and when there was no immediate threat to order, supplies and security. Faced with what was undoubtedly an incontrovertible statement of the facts, the Ministry's hopes that the Army would take charge, and that HM Treasury would foot the bill, withered. The Northern Ireland government had to get on with the job, unaided.[63] It was agreed that the best way of doing this, addressing security concerns about Belfast Prison, was to remove the criminal lunatics from Londonderry Prison, replacing them with internees.[64]

In one form or another internment had run almost continuously throughout the state's short history. The most recent instalment had begun in January 1939, spurred not by the darkening European scene but by the IRA's bombing campaign in Britain and intelligence of a similar plan for Northern Ireland. Thirty-four men had been rounded up under the Special Powers Act; on the outbreak of war, a further forty-eight were lifted. A number had been taken because of faulty or out-of-date intelligence – a failing that was reflected in immediate and successful appeals to the Advisory Committee.[65] Three men were released from the January batch, and a further fourteen appealed and were released in September. This left sixty-five internees in Belfast Prison at the close of the year. In their unwillingness to appeal to the Advisory Committee, these men implicitly confirmed that they were committed supporters or active republicans. They were a difficult group to handle. The prison was a relatively small building on a constricted site, meanly built, intended to enforce the separate and silent penal system of Victorian prison legislation.[66] Silence had been enforced by strict discipline rather than design or construction, and sound carried between floors and even wings. Internees could not be dealt with as sternly as persons under sentence, whether convict or local prisoners.[67] The justification for their incarceration was prevention rather than punishment. They had and were fully entitled to much the same status as those remanded for trial. In theory, apart from the deprivations and restrictions inseparable from custody, they should enjoy all the amenities of purely civil detention. Certainly internees could not be deprived of prison privileges, be given dietary punishments or forfeit remission. Largely immune from official sanction, to vent frustration, to amuse themselves, to pass the time, to wage a little war of attrition and to repulse subjugation with jollity, the internees sang songs and created a merry din into the small hours.

Since the prison was on a war footing and lighting was reduced to a glimmer, staff could not easily detect those who were making the noise and, even if they had, could do little to them.[68]

As we have noted, Northern Ireland was a small and (politics and religion apart) law-abiding jurisdiction, with small need of custodial capacity. Belfast had therefore to function as a multi-purpose prison, holding several categories of inmates, each with their own regime and routine. Propinquity provided extra opportunities for the internees to bait the administration. It was unrealistic to imagine that a sizeable group of men, frustrated, disgruntled and defiant, by definition at the extreme end of political disaffection, would meekly submit to their captivity. This was even more unlikely in the first months, when energy and morale were at their peak and with all the uncertainties and chances of world war fanning hopes. A British defeat, another Munich, could throw open the prison gates and hand over the prize of a united republican Ireland – or so they could dream.

Alongside the problems of moral authority and control at Belfast, there were various administrative problems, with staff having to juggle yet another set of privileges and allowances in addition to their existing mixture of convict and local, remand and civil – the complicated lot of the multi-purpose prison. Among the several good managerial reasons why categories of prisoners are kept apart is that pervasive gall of institutional life – the minute comparison invariably undertaken between one inmate and another of position, possessions and advantages. Grievance, truculence, misbehaviour and complaint, always finding fertile soil in covetousness in the wider world, flourish and multiply within prison walls. So little means so much in this singular setting and bizarre economy. Bringing into contact those with more and those with fewer privileges and goods, moreover, is a strong stimulus to trafficking and becomes a constant pressure on staff. It was with the thought that these difficulties were packed up and going with them that Captain Stuart bade a relieved farewell to his sixty-five internees as they boarded their buses for Londonderry.[69]

The Londonderry mutiny

In short order, Captain Stuart had even greater reason to thank his good fortune. The majority of the internees were from Belfast and eastern parts of Northern Ireland, and, mile by mile, as they travelled north-west, an already considerable discontent and frustration intensified into rage. The sudden and necessarily unannounced move disrupted imminent visits, delayed parcels and post and meant significant extra travel and expense for families and friends – all adding up to fewer visits and fewer domestic comforts. Distance was only one reason for the reduction in the all-important visits, however. Despite the assumptions of senior officials, Londonderry prison was ill prepared for the influx. Crucially, it lacked Belfast's facilities, and visits, not long after the internees' arrival, were first restricted and then suspended.[70] News from home, a friendly face, clean linen and extra food and tobacco were all of understandable importance to the internees, yet little regard seems to have been paid to the consequences of choking these off.

At first, despite the mutterings, all appeared to have gone well; certainly the transfer itself was flawless. Sir Dawson Bates was so impressed by its smoothness that he sent a letter of appreciation to Captain A. Fryer, the Derry Governor, and to his staff.[71] But putting prisoners on buses and making sure that none escaped, whilst crucially important, was no more than the first stage in a complicated operation. Within days of receiving his new charges, Fryer submitted an order for basic equipment: 200 extra blankets, water cans for cells and tea mugs. This requisition, so tardily submitted, was a worrying indication that preparations had not been as thorough as Bates's congratulations suggested. The shortfall in equipment was in part due to an incomplete inventory at Derry and partly also to the dilapidated state of existing stock: threadbare blankets that Fryer now said should have been condemned years before (but which were, presumably, thought adequate for the criminal lunatics, who had been evicted) together with other defective items.[72] It was also significant and added to these fairly basic deficiencies that Fryer was an inexperienced governor, having been in post only since September 1939.[73]

It was to these depressing and straitened conditions that the internees arrived, most of them furious about their enforced flit. They immediately vented feelings by smashing cell windows. Given the time of year, the dampness of the climate and the indifferent heating system in the prison, window-breaking may not have been the wisest form of protest, especially as Fryer refused to authorise repairs. The outpouring of anger and the increased ease of communicating more easily between cells after lock-up may, however, have been some compensation for the draughts, chilly cells and threadbare blankets – but those who shivered in the small hours of the night must have wondered about this.

Despite their ill-tempered arrival, the men agreed to continue to carry out domestic duties. This was a key element in the IRA's prison strategy of obtaining as much control over the daily routine as possible. Two internees would be assigned to cook for all the others and three to work the laundry. These duties were presumably assumed by rota, but it was agreed that the laundry party would not have to do the washing of fifteen men who had applied to the Advisory Committee and who had thus become pariahs within the little community. Fryer arranged for two of the appellants to wash for their comrades each Saturday. Agreement was also reached on a gardening party and on cleaning for the chapel.[74] An uneasy equilibrium seemed to have been reached.

It would later become known that the internees had added to their domestic toil by starting on an escape tunnel. Planning for this, if not the work itself, may have begun as soon as the internees had settled in. The chilly and sullen peace was intruded upon by a loyalist demonstration outside the prison on Sunday 10 December. A woman, carrying a Union flag, began to parade up and down outside the prison, inventively barracking the internees. She was joined by children and a number of teenage girls, some also carrying small flags. A number of residents of adjoining houses joined in, from their back doors. A constable was despatched to disperse the demonstrators, but by that point the internees were engaged with the crowd, shouting counter-slogans, singing republican songs and breaking several more panes in their windows. The police promised to prevent a recurrence of the street theatre, but the internees had become even more truculent. There was an element of extra humiliation in being jeered at by an assembly of disorderly women and children and randomly abusive neighbours.

By mid-December the Governor was reporting his charges to be 'unsettled and sullen'. There was continual shouting, hammering and singing between cells, and when in association the men engaged in intense and private consultations. Fryer reported that the subject of these discussions had not leaked out but that all staff were 'prepared for anything and continually on the alert'.[75] This was an empty boast and an unnecessary hostage to fortune, but Fryer gave an even greater one the following week. Consultations had continued between the internees, he told the Ministry, 'but I don't believe anything is likely to happen of any importance'.[76]

This complacency would be utterly confounded. The prison was thinly staffed at the best of times and was even more stretched over Christmas 1939 as staff were given as much time off as the routine of the prison allowed to be with their families on that first worrying wartime break. An obvious weak point in control was the movement of the internees from their cells to exercise. This had not been spotted by the inexperienced Fryer but was well marked by his charges. On Christmas morning the five staff supervising the movement were easily overwhelmed by the forty-five internees who were exercising. Keys, batons, belts and whistles were seized, and the five officers were bundled into cells. Barricades were then thrown up to prevent reinforcements getting access to the top tier of cells. The unfortunate officers were released within minutes by their colleagues, but the barriers at each end of the tier could not be breached.[77] Two Irish tricolours and a placard were pushed through the cell windows and were visible to the crowd (some of whom were walking to a football match) that began to gather.

At this point Fryer seems to have panicked, at least for a while. Despite the country being at war, no one was on duty at Home Affairs and so he had to phone Sir Dawson Bates at home. Police and Special Constabulary help was mobilised, and a party of twenty soldiers was also brought into the prison and kept in reserve in a covered lorry. Reinforcements notwithstanding, the barricades and locked doors could not be breached. The internees, having armed themselves with chair and table legs and officers' batons, stood ready to repel invaders. Fryer decided to cut the doors down with an acetylene torch and then to run a high-pressure hosepipe into the tier to soak the men into submission. All was made ready, but, farcically, the prison's hose failed to stretch to the top landing. The fire brigade was called and ran their hoses up to the top tier. By 4.30 p.m., the doors and barricades were down and the hosepipes were in action.[78] Resistance (and bits of the building) crumbled, and by 5 p.m. all were locked in their cells. The riot had lasted for some seven hours.[79] The curious crowd outside the prison, passive, but largely sympathetic to the internees, was dispersed by police.

The official papers are conspicuously silent on how the prisoners were returned to their cells. According to Liam Burke, the men had signified their surrender by hanging out a white flag. Once the door to the top tier was opened, he claimed, the internees were assaulted by soldiers, Specials and the RUC. This involved being made to run the gauntlet whilst being beaten with batons. There were later attacks, he also claimed, with bits of lead piping torn from the ceiling (presumably gas fittings), boots and the butts of rifles. Seán McArdle, the OC, was taken to the exercise yard for further beating.[80] In general terms, this is a plausible account, consonant with what is likely to happen when a riot is suppressed without sufficient control or supervision by superior officials. That Captain Fryer, giving many other details, does not report to the Ministry on how the prisoners were dealt with immediately after their barricades were broken down is somewhat suggestive. Equally, it must be said, Liam Burke is curiously silent on the internees' resistance: meek submission would most certainly not have been on offer.[81] The men sent out a statement emphasising that they had no quarrel with the Governor but were protesting because the married men among them had been denied visits.[82]

During the time the men were behind their barricades they had started a fire in one of the top-floor cells. They also did much other damage, ranging from yet more smashing of windows to the destruction of doors, wiring, telephones and cell equipment. It was also a matter of some seriousness that, despite a thorough search, a cell key remained missing (it was recovered a day later). Fresh kit was brought to the prison from Belfast, the internees were restricted to minimum out-of-cell movement, and all visits, letters and parcels were stopped. They were put on ordinary prison diet.[83]

The riot had understandably shocked Dawson Bates and his officials, as well as his cabinet colleagues. It was more of a worry than a consolation that there could have been a far worse outcome. It was, for example, not clear what might have happened had the internees rushed the main gate instead of barricading themselves on the top floor – had the object been escape rather than protest. The possibility of coordination between an uprising inside the prison and an IRA attack on the perimeter was a constant concern to the RUC and to the Ministry. Short of that, the internees could have set fire to the entire prison or otherwise damaged it beyond use. Quite apart from security considerations, there would have been a considerable political and popular reaction had this happened. Feelings would have been ratcheted up were lives lost in retaking the prison or in preventing escapes. The gravity of all this was underlined by Sir Dawson Bates himself, heading a two-day inquiry that opened in Londonderry on 1 January 1940. Bates was accompanied by his permanent secretary, Adrian Robinson, Assistant Secretary E. W. Scales and other senior officials. Internees' spokesmen were interviewed as well as members of staff.[84]

In the aftermath, a number of weaknesses were identified, including Fryer's weak grasp of the security routine and his poor management ability. It also emerged from a police report that Fryer lacked confidence in his staff and relied on the Special Constabulary for extra security, a squad of whom he had managed, by some unofficial means, to have stationed outside the prison nightly. One Special was even on duty inside the prison (armed with a baton rather than his usual firearm).[85] Since the Ministry had received the information from the police rather than directly from Fryer, there was initially some reluctance to confront him about it. It had been strongly represented to Robinson that it was improper to have non-prison staff on duty inside a prison, '[a]part altogether from the fact that "B" Specials have a somewhat brighter political hue than the average Prison Officer'.[86]

Officials agreed that Specials should not be deployed in this way and that only prison officers should have contact with prisoners, and especially with internees. In the event of another outbreak, it was decided the Special Constabulary would remain outside, guarding against external attack, lest the disorder inside was merely a ruse to draw defenders away from their positions. Should it prove that Fryer and his staff could not cope with trouble inside, reinforcements would be rushed up from the nearby RUC barracks.[87]

As a result of these deliberations, a detailed letter was sent to Fryer by the Ministry; the advice and micro-management scarcely veiled criticism. Fryer was not to draw on the external guard for any other duty since they were needed outside the prison twenty-four hours a day. The danger of an uprising or other sudden move was at its greatest when internees were moving en masse and so restrictions were to be placed on numbers at such times, reducing them to groups of six at a time, the total number at this point being forty-five.[88] Once locked in the exercise yard there was a limit to the amount of damage the refractory could accomplish. Similarly, once in the chapel, the internees could refuse to leave but they would then become their own captors and would not be able to access other parts of the prison. Fryer was advised, therefore, that there was little point in placing a number of officers into such assemblies of men, and, indeed, the fewer the better since there was a chance of their being overpowered. With fifteen or sixteen prison officers at his disposal during the day, Fryer was urged to keep them out of large groups of prisoners, as far as possible. They were not sufficiently numerous to overcome the forty-five internees and could themselves be taken hostage. Likewise, he was to ensure that keys were more tightly controlled so that even were an officer taken by the internees they would only get hold of a key with limited capabilities. In effect, this meant that staff would be let into a tier or other division of the prison by a colleague who would remain outside the locked gate. This was all elementary gaol-craft and must have been set out by Robinson and others at the Ministry with a deal of irritation.[89]

Fryer remained uneasy. He wanted Specials to remain inside the prison or to be available to be brought in, and he fretted to Home Affairs about the danger of his staff being 'exterminated'. Robinson was unmoved and again insisted on a clear division of labour. Armed Specials outside as a guard against external attack, prison staff inside and the RUC to be an emergency reserve for both. Were prisoners to seize control of some 'small and unimportant' part of the prison, it would be purely temporary: 'If this is the most they can do and if the consequences of such an attempt are what they should be, I think you have little to fear.'[90]

Steps were taken to restore the normal routine of the prison. As an interim measure, time outside cells was restricted to the hours between 9.30 a.m. and 5 p.m. This curtailment was doubtless tolerable, at least in the short term. As a result of the representations that had been made to Dawson Bates and his officials, the Ministry belatedly recognised that internees' anger had been fuelled by inadequate visiting arrangements. With a view to their resumption, an urgent request was placed for wire screens to be fitted to the visiting room's two tables.[91] By the end of January 1940, Home Affairs had approved Fryer's proposal to resume visits and the supply of daily newspapers and periodicals. An order, applied at the end of November, which debarred certain internees from any visits, was rescinded, but all visits were to be restricted to close family members. One visit a week was to be permitted to each internee by two close relatives, and if a visit by someone outside that category were sought a special application had to be made. A full programme of visits would be resumed from 12 February 1940, but this was dependent on the screens being installed in the visiting room. All identities were to be checked carefully; there was to be no physical contact between internees and visitors; and 'the most careful supervision' was to be exercised.[92]

The men were far from reconciled to their lot: 'sullen, and far from being subdued' was Fryer's description of their temper in mid-January. Kitchen and laundry work was continuing 'although in a very slovenly manner'. He had withdrawn recognition from the internees' leaders, 'because of their conduct in organising the revolt'. To go on as before 'would undermine discipline and good order'. Individual prisoners were making applications to him for special letters and visits.[93] Since the riot had not spilled beyond the prison and the damage, extensive though it was, had been confined to one part of the building, there was, at least, an element of comfort in the incident.

But the internees had shown that, for the most part anyway, they were committed republicans, willing to resort to violence. A declaration pinned to the door of the lavatory that had served as pound for a captive prison officer confirmed this. Other than venting anger and frustration, it is hard to see what the writer hoped to achieve. With a pointed use of quotation marks, it was addressed to '"The Minister of Home Affairs, Northern Ireland"' and demanded immediate and unconditional release. The takeover of part of the prison was intended to attract public attention, and 'any regrettable consequences' were the responsibility of Bates, 'the Six County Junta of which you are a member and the British Government'.[94] The writer referred to the British war aims: democracy, self-determination, individual liberty and the 'sweeping away of the era of the concentration camps'. So long as Irish unity and independence were denied and while internment continued, 'those ideals will stink in the nostrils of all lovers of truth and justice as hypocrisy of the most disgusting kind'. The letter ended with a slogan: 'An Phoblact Abú'. Officials and the Minister made no comment in the files. None was necessary: this was self-incrimination. Given that internment would last until the end of 1945, and that its continuance – especially in the months after the Allied victory – would depend on official and ministerial assuaging misgivings about releases, this was not a good document to have in the files when clemency petitioners came knocking on the door.

All aboard: *Al Rawdah*

With the German sweep through the Low Countries and the final British evacuation from Dunkirk in the first days of June 1940, the Empire's very survival looked uncertain. Located a handful of miles from the border with an insistently neutral Éire and with a much-depleted military to defend the area, Londonderry Prison no longer looked so secure. The GOC Northern Ireland, now General Hubert Huddleston, told Home Affairs that he wanted the Derry internees removed.[95] This was not fear of an attack by the Irish Army across the border, or of a German invasion through Éire. In either improbable eventuality, the fate of a relatively small number of internees would be chaff in the wind. The threat – not entirely unfounded, as it turned out – was of the internees creating an opportunity for an IRA operation and a mass escape across the always-permeable frontier.

In July 1940, Lord Craigavon, Sir Dawson Bates and Minister of Public Security John MacDermott met to consider options for moving the internees.[96] These had been narrowed to four: use existing premises, build an internment camp, transfer the internees to Great Britain or acquire and adapt a ship. The first foundered on the fact that no suitable premises existed or were thought to be available. Dublin had, as the administrative capital of the island under British rule, concentrated a great collection of military and other public premises, and even the Southern provinces were comparatively well provided with barracks, depots and the like. No such plentitude existed north of the border, the most pro-British part of a sometimes restive island, and the wartime armed forces necessarily had the pick of what was available. The option of an internment camp had been exhaustively explored with the Army and was emphatically not on the table. The Prison Commissioners for England and Wales had been approached, but, having had prior and unhappy experience of the many difficulties attending Irish political prisoners, nothing short of a cabinet direction would have induced them to open another chapter in that painful history. They replied to the Stormont request with the evasion that they had no suitable reserve accommodation.[97] A process of elimination thus led to the prison ship.

Even before Londonderry was deemed unsuitable, Home Affairs, because of the increased number of internees on its hands, had decided to seek additional accommodation. The GOC's objections to the use of any border area meant that more space and flexibility were urgently required. At a meeting of the Defence Executive Committee, the idea of a prison ship was mooted. There was no legal obstacle, since under both ordinary law and the Special Powers Acts the Minister had extensive powers to designate any place of confinement as a prison. The Committee's military representative thought that General Huddleston would prefer this to any other option. One can see why. To an appreciable extent a prison ship moored offshore provides its own security, and there would at most be only a limited call for a military guard on shore and certainly nothing approaching the scale of deployment of an internment camp.[98]

A ship would be expensive, but bearing in mind the Army's strong preference and recalling 1922, when the number of internees had reached some 700, the Ministry decided to see what might be available. The immediate requirement was for an additional 400 places, with a maximum of around 700. Staff of around 150 would also require accommodation. After a final, half-hearted, consciously hopeless and futile attempt to persuade the Army to agree to a camp, ship-finding began in earnest. Only weeks later, a request for a vessel on which to confine civil internees in the UK would have met with a dusty and probably incredulous response from the Ministry of Shipping.[99] The battle of the Atlantic, with its terrible losses of shipping – 160,000 tons in September alone – had yet to get fully under way. With the fall of France, moreover, and the signing of the Armistice, much of the French fleet had been seized, destroyed and disabled by Britain, and available French merchant shipping taken over.[100]

It was from this last category that the prison ship – the second in Northern Ireland's short history – would come. The Egyptian-owned *Al Rawdah* was mainly employed in the Mediterranean trade of transporting Muslim pilgrims to Saudi Arabia. Unfortunately for its owners, it had been registered in France and sailed under the French flag, which was the basis of its seizure by the British in the summer of 1940. Complete with crew, the *Al Rawdah* was then based at Liverpool, where at first it returned to something like its old trade, interned aliens and POWs substituting for pilgrims. It was then refitted as a troop ship. This had just been completed when, somewhat surprisingly, the Ministry of Shipping agreed to hand it over to the Northern Ireland government.[101]

A troop ship seemed ideal for Belfast's needs, with a capacity for several hundred men in fore and aft converted holds. Water, ventilation and other support systems such as galleys, lavatories, showers, ventilation and refrigeration were already installed. Fitted for a little over a thousand troops, the ship slept about 300 on deck and the rest below in hammocks. Internees obviously could not sleep on deck, and security and control barriers would have to be installed to ensure that numbers in each division did not exceed 100. After these alterations, there was space for about 500. Accommodation was of a good standard and had the advantage, should the internees or their supporters complain, of allowing the riposte that what had been intended for troops should be satisfactory for internees. In reporting this, Adrian Robinson, Secretary of Home Affairs, observed that one of the reasons why a prison ship had until then been resisted by the Ministry of Home Affairs had been memories of the *Argenta*, whose conditions had been 'not at all good' – so bad, in fact that 'it would be difficult to stand over them now'.[102]

The two vessels differed in another and – for the time- and resource-pressed Ministry – critical way: the *Al Rawdah* came as a fully equipped package, including crew. The *Argenta* had been bought outright by the Northern Ireland government and, Robinson recalled, 'fitted up in a rather amateurish way and in the crudest possible style'. The *Al Rawdah* came with all necessary facilities, down to eating utensils and an option to contract with the British India Steam Navigation Company for messing. Whatever dietary the Ministry chose could be provided, using the existing and lowly paid Levantine crew to prepare and serve. Some alterations would be necessary: extra physical security for the holds and Lewis guns for anti-aircraft protection. An armed guard would be on duty against external threat, but actual custody would be handled by prison officers. The aim was to keep a tight grip on discipline rather than to follow the *Argenta* precedent which, Robinson recalled, was 'broadly, to leave the internees very much to their own devices and provide a very large guard to knock blazes out of them if they should get uppish'.[103] As for the staff, even distinctions of rank could be accommodated. Prison officers and the armed guard would use the second-class quarters, while the Governor, Deputy Governor and ship's officers would have the first-class cabins and public rooms.[104]

Because of the possibility of bombing or machine-gunning by enemy aircraft (trawlers and coasters were regular Luftwaffe targets), it was decided to moor the ship well away from Belfast, which offered many attractive targets in its industry, transport and population (and little in the way of anti-aircraft protection). A mooring off Killyleagh in Strangford Lough was chosen. *Al Rawdah*'s captain, J. T. Harvey, had impressed Robinson and those colleagues who had gone with him to Liverpool to inspect the ship. Another one of the *Argenta*'s defects, Robinson recalled, had been the division of control between the ship's company and Mr Drysdale, the largely shore-based governor. The possibility of Harvey holding the joint position of governor and captain was therefore attractive: there would be a clear line of responsibility, authority and accountability and no basis for managerial squabbling. He was brought over to Belfast for interview by Sir Dawson Bates, who confirmed his appointment. Gaol-craft would be provided by Taylor, chief officer at Belfast Prison, who was appointed as his deputy.[105] On the night of Sunday, 25 August 1940, *Al Rawdah* sailed from Liverpool and by the following morning lay at its Strangford moorings. The reception of internees began a week later. By 2 September 1940, forty-five were on board, rising to what would be a maximum of 207 over the following week.[106]

At this point, the tale metamorphoses into a chapter in *Men at Arms*, Evelyn Waugh's satiric account of Second World War military life and operations.[107] In reply to a Stormont MP's questioning of the safety of a prison ship under war-time conditions, Sir Dawson Bates expressed himself 'quite satisfied' with all safety precautions.[108] The problem, it almost immediately transpired, was that the military did not agree. They may have reflected that the Luftwaffe sent out patrols precisely for the purpose of destroying British shipping. This thought had not occurred to Home Affairs as its officials busied themselves with contract details. In his chronicle of the *Al Rawdah* affair, Robinson noted that no sooner were the internees on board than a Home Office thunderbolt struck: on urgent army advice, all were to be disembarked immediately. To complete the *opéra bouffe*, it was announced that military objections to Derry prison had been dropped.[109] This abrupt démarche led to recriminatory exchanges between officials extending over a period of several months. Taken completely aback, the Ministry – probably Dawson Bates himself – took its own plunge into the improbable and fanciful. Since the military wanted the ship evacuated because of a possible air attack, why not evacuate the ship itself and all on it? *Al Rawdah* could be sailed to an unquestionably safe haven which, at the same time, would place the internees out of sight, out of mind and utterly unable to engage in mischief against Northern Ireland: why not pack the whole lot off to a Canadian mooring?[110]

London's response was urgent, abrupt and final, lest even a whiff of the notion should survive: 'Afraid your suggestion impracticable. Essential in order to avoid serious embarrassment His Britannic Majesty's Government that these persons should be housed on land locally. Understand GOC will cooperate if required.'[111] Craig was immediately informed and, as Robinson's memorandum put it, 'told us that we would have to haul down the flag and submit as quietly and quickly as possible. I rather thought he would as I imagine that when they talk about H.B.M. Government it is a polite hint that they mean business.'[112] Now beached, the Ministry listlessly and hopelessly asked the Army again to provide an internment camp. This produced a nil result, even though the Home Office had said that the GOC would cooperate. The Army would act as advisers in the construction of a camp, if that were to be the Ministry's chosen form of accommodation, but internees would continue in every respect to be a responsibility for the civil authority.[113]

Dismay, irritation, embarrassment and disarray coursed around the Ministry.[114] In a note to the Northern Ireland Cabinet Secretary, Robert Gransden, Robinson insisted that either the *Al Rawdah* was likely to be bombed or that it was not: he did not specify how that useful determination might be made. Home Affairs had proceeded on the basis that the ship would not be attacked; the Army now said otherwise. Until alternative accommodation could be made ready, there must be adequate air-raid protection. If London did not give this, it could only be because an attack was not likely. What then was the justification for evacuating?[115]

But this was mere fuming and foot-stamping – a trifle unseemly and certainly unproductive. Steps were already being taken to abandon ship. A batch of internees on the point of despatch was held back, and a few appellants were returned to Belfast Prison.[116] There was an attempt to extract some advantage from the Home Office by insisting that until the Army provided a camp the ship could not be entirely evacuated. Various expensive arrangements were about to be made to cope with winter conditions, and the Ministry did not wish to put these in hand were the ship not to be used: 'You will see, therefore, that apart from our anxiety to do as we are bid in the matter, from a purely administrative point of view we have every inducement to shift the internees on to land as soon as possible.'[117]

It was inevitable that the chorus would now make its entry: the internees did not want to leave the *Al Rawdah*, 'a place where at least we have the status of political prisoners'. They had no wish to go to an ordinary prison where there were no suitable amenities.[118] At the same time, various belated comments in the Irish press deplored the danger in which the internees had been placed.[119] Robinson, in a peppery internal memorandum, suggested that since the Éire government claimed jurisdiction over all Irishmen it should ask Germany for immunity for the ship.[120] The Ministry at this point was at the centre of a host of competing demands and pressures: the Home Office, Army and Irish press all wanted the internees removed; the inmates wanting to stay; the police reported that they had another 150 candidates for immediate internment; and the assessment was that all the combined prison places available on shore could not meet this demand. The stage was crowded and confused.

There was a fleeting alliance born of mutual inconvenience between the Ministry and the *Al Rawdah* internees.[121] The *Sunday Express* delightedly reported the inmates' petition to stay put. This was not entirely helpful public relations since the story described meals which, for enforced confinement of any kind, were lavish: the catering contract with the East India Line had been amply honoured. The comparison was made with prison fare, and indeed with the population at large, now subject to strict food rationing. The internees, the *Express* reported, had heard rumours that the authorities had been staggered by the catering account. The headline was an irritation in itself: '180 Plead to Stay in Prison Ship.'[122]

But embarrassing press coverage was little more than froth. The Ministry had no accommodation for the 199 shipmates now to be cast on shore, and any premises of a suitable size with potential for conversion had already been commandeered by the Army. The only solution, it appeared, was a purpose-built camp. The tussle with the Army returned to its opening round.[123] In that relieved and thoughtful mood of the autumn of 1940, when it had become clear that a respite had been won and that a German invasion would not be attempted before the spring, the civil authorities had no leverage. Providence had been kind, but none could be certain what national ordeal lay ahead. The fate of a few hundred internees in Northern Ireland was less than the merest tiny feather in this grand balance. The Ministry of Home Affairs was not alone in being at the receiving end of some baffling and seemingly arbitrary military decisions, but, after all recrimination had run its course, it alone was holding the baby.

Faced with this unshakeable and unshiftable fact, officials took another and more imaginative look at their existing estate: it was make-do and mend time. In this spirit, Londonderry Prison was reappraised by Robinson, accompanied by other Home Affairs officials and by the government's Chief Architect, Thomas F. O. Rippingham. Even with so few options open to them, all agreed that the old female prison, disused for some time, was fit for storage only. The male prison offered accommodation and exercise space for 150 internees. Various relatively minor works such as repainting and repairs to ventilation and windows were necessary, but these could be swiftly completed. A small exercise yard, previously used by the criminal lunatics, could be covered over, and, using hammocks, an additional fifty men could be accommodated. With hammocks rolled up during the day, this space could also be used to serve meals instead of taking them to cells. A Nissen hut could be obtained from the Army to provide for exercise in inclement weather. Other building works were necessary to improve quarters and facilities for staff, but 150 cells could be available within weeks and an additional fifty beds upon the roofing-in of the small exercise yard.[124]

Belfast Prison was also reappraised, and officials concluded that it could also be more intensively used, with the whole of D Wing reserved for internees. Using hammocks, workshops could provide space for another 100 men, making a total of 258 places. Alterations had to be made to separate the internees from other categories and to replace the workshops that were being taken over. With a comparatively small outlay, however, the two prisons could thus provide at least 450 places with the possibility of another thirty at Derry, were the Protestant chapel ('which is scarcely ever used now and which would not be used if Londonderry were exclusively used as a place of internment') taken over.[125] When looked at more closely, it seemed, Home Affairs could comparatively easily provide for all the internees presently in custody or anticipated. Some in Whitehall (and perhaps at Stormont) must have wondered what the fuss and bother had been about and why the venture into shipping had been necessary.

All that remained was to put the proposals into effect. Evelyn Waugh's army made its genial but no doubt infuriating reappearance. Nissen huts were essential to the Derry and Belfast expansion plans. After alternate pleading and pressuring, the Army agreed to hand some over. But there was small print: collection and delivery. Robinson wearied himself with telephone calls, 'about those blasted huts' and was, in the time-honoured manner, passed from one official to another: even bureaucrats can be caught in the toils of officialdom. There was no let-up in the pressure to evacuate the *Al Rawdah*: 'we are being badgered, and badgered, and badgered to move these confounded internees'. The huts were the key, but,

> [h]aving regard to the difficulty that one has in getting the Transport Board to pick up a simple thing like a barrel from a pub, I tremble to think of the complications that would ensue if they were told to go to some military camp… and pick up things like Nissen huts.

If the Army could somehow be induced to deliver the huts, a great deal of bother would be saved.[126] But for secondary, and civilian, projects, wartime inefficiencies and delays were inevitable. Home Affairs had to wait and fret for its Nissen huts.

The fiasco provided abundant blame for all involved to hurl and receive.[127] By mid-January 1941, an increasingly acrimonious correspondence between Finance and Home Affairs had reached its futile climax. Most of the internees were still on board the *Al Rawdah* despite the virtual completion of works at Belfast Prison. Absurdly, the final obstacle was that there were missing domestic articles, and there was much penny-pinching dithering about whether they could be procured locally by the Supplies Branch or removed from the *Al Rawdah*.[128]

Robinson, run ragged and exasperated with delays and buck-passing, offered a solution by borrowing from local institutions any articles that Supplies and the *Al Rawdah* between them could not deliver. This would allow the internees to be removed and the ship surrendered at the end of January.[129] Improvisation oiled the hinges, and within a week the shipping authorities were informed that, weather permitting, the *Al Rawdah* would be evacuated on 28 and 29 January 1941.[130] In keeping with the spirit of the multi-act play, the very elements refused to cooperate, thus holding back completion until 13 February.[131] The ship was immediately recalled to the Ministry of Shipping and, having served its five months of custody, immediately sailed out of Irish waters and penal history.[132]

Decidedly unhappy with their impending removal, several internees had decided to abandon ship in the early hours of 27 January 1941: knowledge that better weather would see everyone back in Belfast Prison provided the spur. The opportunity came when the *Stanley Bridge*, a coaling tender, was alongside. A number of men (thought to be five) in No. 3 mess managed to break locks securing the doors between their ablutions area and a coal chute into the lower hold. The attempt was detected and the alarm raised. All but one of the men managed to return unidentified to their quarters.[133]

The would-be escapers and all their shipmates who woke up in Belfast's Crumlin Road prison on St Valentine's Day 1941 must have had mixed feelings as they contemplated their cramped and dismal Victorian surroundings.[134] *Al Rawdah* had been very different from the *Argenta* and even more different from Crumlin Road, and its loss was indeed something to lament. Though institutional, the food had been markedly superior to the usual prison fare, and it had the inestimable advantage of not being served in Belfast Prison.[135] The difference in food was partly a matter of the quantity (and perhaps quality) of provisions, partly the skill and standards of the cooks and partly the low expectations of a prison kitchen. And food was not the least of the losses. Strangford Lough was certainly a location with a greater sense of tranquillity and beauty than many ordinary civilian locations could offer, much less a prison; even the changes in weather and the seasons provided interest to erase the tedium of confinement. Nor had life on board been dragooned and squeezed. Days had been fairly relaxed, commencing at 7 a.m. and ending with lights out at 10 p.m. Ablutions, rolling up of hammocks, tidying quarters and breakfasting took the men in a leisurely fashion to governor's inspection at 9.30 a.m. Thereafter they had recreation until the midday meal, eaten below deck. From 2.15 until 5 p.m. they again had access to the deck. After more washing-up and tidying they had recreation until 10 p.m. and lights out. So long as they kept to the rules and regulations they were left much to their own devices. There was organised deck exercise, led by the internees' officers. Evenings were passed with sing-songs, accompanied by uilleann pipes, accordions, concertinas and mouth organs.[136] Internees were allowed newspapers and could have visitors once a month. Visits took place on board, visitors coming out by launch.[137] There had of course been a number of restrictions. All outgoing post (one letter and two postcards per week) was censored, as were incoming items.[138]

From an intercepted smuggled letter (turned up in routine civilian postal censorship), we know that the latitude given to the internees extended to overt military activity. On 18 November 1940, John Gaffney died as a result of a cerebral haemorrhage.[139] Permission was given for the internees to pay tribute by mustering on deck in military fashion. The chaplain, Father Enda Elliott, recited the rosary as the coffin was brought on deck. Internees fell in as companies, based on the ship's four messes. All were called to attention as the coffin was lowered over the side. The ship's OC and the mess OCs then gave the salute. All remained at attention until the launch was out of sight.[140]

Despite the internees' embarrassment when their reluctance to leave the ship was first revealed in the press, there was no doubt that some (how many is unclear) were so keen to remain on board that they decided to forgo an appeal to the Advisory Committee. On 6 February 1941, RUC County Inspector Ewing Gilfillan wrote to H. C. Montgomery, Assistant Secretary at Home Affairs, passing on information from confidential sources. Internees who lodged appeals got poorer food, and, in consequence, some not previously connected to or active in the organisation, on the poorer diet, went in with the IRA. Gilfillan evidently could not believe his informant, as a postscript to the letter indicated, 'I imagine all are on the same diet.'[141] But the story was true. Upon submitting an appeal, men were at once removed to Belfast Prison, where they could be segregated from erstwhile comrades. Internees on the ship, Montgomery conceded, were on 'rather a special dietary which is much better than that which could be given in the prison'. Attempts were being made to improve prison food. The results would still not be as good as the ship's dietary, but much better, he hoped.[142]

As in earlier episodes of republican internment, sympathetic (and perhaps romantically inclined) young women seem to have made a special effort to visit.[143] Writing to a female friend, an internee asked her to contact another young woman who happened to work only six or seven miles from the ship and ask her if she would visit him: 'Anyone nearby, particularly girls will be approved for visit[s] now. That is, of course, if they aren't sympathetic to us politically.'[144]

The *Al Rawdah* affair throws a deal of light on the working of important sections of the Northern Ireland government. It is also instructive regarding the policy of internment more broadly viewed. As we have noted, the round-ups began in January 1939, in response to the bombing campaign in Britain. Those arrests, detentions and internments were based on information about known or suspected IRA involvement. The September 1939 arrests cut a second swathe of those who were active, but less prominent. This left 207 persons in internment. But there was a feeling – and it amounted to little more – that two or three times that number would have to be rounded up – an extrapolation from the experience of 1922. There was no coherent analysis of the comparative strength of the IRA in the two very different periods. It had undergone a deal of reorganisation by the end of the 1930s but was far removed from its 1922 pre-Civil War strength and levels of support. Internment projections were therefore much more of a guess than a realistic and verifiable assessment of need, and the guess was a poor one. This was confirmed by the gap between those estimates and the actual amount of accommodation with which the Ministry of Home Affairs made do, when it lost the *Al Rawdah*. Had the Army been able and willing to open a camp for 600 or 700 men, would it have been filled? Very possibly. With the severe competition for accommodation from the military and other services, the number interned at a given time in Northern Ireland never rose much above 425.[145] At the same time, during those wartime years, the IRA was effectively crushed. As far as internment played a part in this (and a variety of causes might be listed), necessity bred parsimony, which seems to have resulted in a more selective and possibly more effective use of the measure.

On shore

Accommodation returned as a pressing issue in September 1942, when there were sixty-seven further arrests of suspects as a consequence of an upsurge in IRA activity.[146] The campaign – and it was hardly that – soon faltered, but the accumulation of *matériel*, the recruitment and deployment of men and the success of some initial operations greatly alarmed both Irish governments.[147] The Northern arrests were made under the Special Powers Act under which it had been decided that detention should be no longer than twenty-eight days. Within this period, charges had to be brought or the internment order made.[148] In the eighteen months or so since the evacuation of the *Al Rawdah*, a number of internees had been released.[149] Even with this influx, therefore, both Belfast and Derry prisons could cope. The Belfast Governor, Captain Stuart, did ask Home Affairs to delay the issuance of internment orders for as long as the law permitted. This was to keep the men in their initial detention status within the prison and to help reduce internee movements to exercise and recreation.[150] With these new arrests, all spare capacity for internees was brought into use. Belfast's D Wing had places for 300 men, but on 21 September 1942 was holding 425, placing such a strain on space and services that transfers to Derry again became necessary.[151] Nissen huts were once more on the agenda. Londonderry had insufficient space for the extended periods of recreation to which internees were entitled. One hut, provided in January 1941 (and following the bureaucratic saga we have described) had helped, but another was urgently needed – so urgently that Sir Dawson Bates himself approached Northern Ireland GOC for assistance: only the top brass, it seemed, could dispense these valuable structures.[152]

By the end of September 1942, the Ministry had identified 100 internees for transfer to Derry. Before finalising the list, Special Branch was consulted and on 12 October 1942 indicated those it thought should be transferred. It is not now clear what criteria were applied, but, given the earlier army concerns about the proximity of the prison to the border, it is likely that most of those recommended for transfer were the lesser security risks. Perversely, from the point of view of welfare and amenity, family contacts in Derry also disqualified some. Sir Dawson Bates issued the necessary order on 15 October 1942, and the transfer took place the following day.[153] Such was the secrecy and the Ministry's unwillingness to brief the press, even after the event, that both Northern and Southern newspapers speculated that more than 250 men had been transferred – a number not only inaccurate but then well beyond the capacity of Londonderry Prison.[154] That capacity was reached, however, with all space and facilities fully used, when a second transfer took place on 13 November 1942.

Removal to Derry when one's family and friends were in the Belfast area was a hardship for all concerned. The expense of making the journey across the province was prohibitive for those on restricted incomes – and almost by definition many internee families were in this category. The men used various ploys to get back to Belfast. One stratagem, successful, at least for a time, was to report sick repeatedly. The Derry Medical Officer, either because he did not have the facilities to cope with so many patients or because he was disinclined to take on extra work, recommended that the persistently unwell be returned to Belfast.[155] There was also some suggestion that internees might be prepared to assault staff with the intention of being prosecuted and for that purpose returned to Belfast Prison. Unlikely though this may at first appear, it would have made at least initial sense to internees. Provided the assault were not of a serious character, any sentence would be in months, and they were in custody anyway and likely to remain there.[156] A certain amount of more or less continuous juggling with available spaces was necessary, since the two prisons were operating so close to capacity and were, in effect, being treated as one resource. To minimise the effects of genuine ailments and of malingering, good health was added to the criteria for eligibility for transfer to Derry, the others being no previous residence in the city and not currently having an appeal before the Committee.[157] By 15 August 1944, there had been a sufficient number of releases for the Ministry to charter four buses and to return ninety-two Derry internees to Belfast, much to the relief of families from Belfast and districts beyond.[158]

Prisoner-support organisations

As in all phases of imprisonment and internment, the IRA raised relief funds for its members and their families. Political and humanitarian purposes mingled in this compact. Support groups helped maintain morale, connecting the organisation with wider circles of sympathisers and supporters, and renewing and maintaining links. The groups were also useful in campaigns on prison conditions, particularly the core demand for political status for convicted prisoners. A number of individuals, such as Nationalist MPs and members of the Roman Catholic hierarchy, completely opposed to the IRA and all its works, were nevertheless willing to be associated with support groups, provided that they were sufficiently distanced from the IRA. For these constitutional nationalists the political and the humanitarian also intertwined. To show sympathy with those who had carried their nationalist aspirations too far helped to divert and drain more extreme opinions. The Irish Prisoners' Aid Society and similar bodies were recognised as IRA fronts and functioned mainly with close supporters of the organisation.[159] Constitutional politicians and clergy were careful to keep a conspicuous distance.

There were strong and urgent reasons for bringing whatever relief could be provided to dependants. No great effort was required to muster compassion for these innocents. The internees themselves were untried and were detained by executive action, and if a political case could not be made, a moral case might for extending some public support to their families. For party-political and public-economy reasons and out of concern for the reaction of supporters, the government refused to give it support directly or to encourage the local Poor Law administrators, the Boards of Guardians, to do so.[160] Families were thus cast upon the charity of relatives, friends and the wider Catholic community. To organise this, a new organisation with an old name, Green Cross, was established in January 1941.[161] Initially the sole objective was relief for internees' families, thus distancing the organisation from the families of persons tried and convicted of IRA-related offences. This distinction, morally obscure and impractical in the face of need, was soon dropped, however, and relief was extended to convicted prisoners' dependants. The organisation also sent parcels of food and other comforts to the internees, though this appears to be a less publicised part of its work.[162] The veteran republican, twice internee and prisoner and now Nationalist MP Cahir Healy gave his support, as did Patrick Maxwell, MP.[163] Cardinal Joseph MacRory, Roman Catholic Primate of Ireland, gave a conclusive stamp of respectability with his donation of £10; bishops, clergy and laity comfortably followed this lead. There was no suggestion that the organisation was a republican front or conduit. A Home Affairs intelligence review confirmed that the Green Cross was receiving 'the support of the semi-moderate type of Roman Catholic in Northern Ireland'. With this backing and what evidently was a deal of Catholic dissatisfaction with internment, branches were rapidly established across Northern Ireland. By June 1941, it was reported that the fund had received about £800 in Co. Tyrone alone.[164] Within a year, it was claimed that £9,500 had been raised in Northern Ireland and another £500 in Éire and in Scotland.[165] Branches were also established in centres of Irish population in the USA.

The Irish government, many of whose members had, and not so long before, insider knowledge of prisoners' support organisations – and may indeed have been beneficiaries – had been equally suspicious. Katharine Moloney, a trustee of the Dublin branch of the organisation (perhaps more accurately a franchise than a branch) secured an interview with the Minister for Justice, Gerald Boland, on 12 October 1940, to explain the aims of the organisation and to seek permission to publicise its activities. She left documents with the minister, and these were passed to Stephen Roche, Secretary of the Department of Justice, for comment.[166] A few days later, he gave his views to Boland.

Roche objected to the description of the fund's activities: 'to raise money for relief of distress among dependants of Republican prisoners'. Such a formula was objectionable because they suggested 'that there is a recognised Republican Army at war with the Government, the Government itself being, of course, by implication, anti-Republican'. Although ostensibly humanitarian, any appeal to the public for the relief of families' distress was essentially based on the notion that those in custody at Mountjoy, Arbour Hill and the Curragh were 'patriots suffering undeserved punishment'. The basis of the organisation was not the relief of poverty and suffering but the support of republican militants by guaranteeing a certain security for their families. The honest title for the proposed fund would be 'The Irish Republican Army Dependants' Fund'. Some of the Fund's promoters might deny this, and believe their denial to be honest, but they were only deceiving themselves. The immediate priority, Roche contended, was to get the IRA and its friends and supporters, whether in or out of prison, to recognise that their campaign was foolish and to stop it. This stricture applied equally to friends and supporters who were 'half-in, half-out, ladies and gentlemen'. If the fund supporters were willing to take a stand on the principle that the IRA campaign should cease, then it would be possible to consider a 'better atmosphere' for the relief of the distress that the IRA's activities had caused among its own supporters.[167]

In the light of this advice, and the government's great concern about national security, Boland could not allow free rein to the Green Cross. He did, however, decide not to suppress the organisation but to keep it tightly constrained. Press-censorship instructions would not allow it to get publicity, but, provided the fund did not break the law, it would be allowed to operate as an auxiliary to the official body for the relief of distress, National Aid.[168]

A different view was taken of the organisation operating in Northern Ireland, and the endorsement by Cardinal MacRory and the Northern bishops carried great weight, as did the support of Nationalist MPs and senators at Stormont. This became apparent when the Belfast organising committee of the Green Cross applied for permission to broadcast an appeal for funds on Radio Éireann in 1941. This was initially shelved, but, when another application was made some months later, the senior official at the Department of Posts & Telegraphs recommended 'sympathetic consideration', assuring the Minister that the personnel of the Belfast committee was not the same as in Dublin. A carefully worded appeal should be allowed on humanitarian grounds: 'Our people in the North are forced into extremist organisations by the treatment they receive, and men who are not in any such organisations are in prison.' Should permission to make a broadcast appeal be refused, 'We will be accused of showing no interest in the people of the North.'[169]

Despite reassurance from its own intelligence sources, Home Affairs continued to be suspicious of the Northern Ireland organisation. Respectable credentials were critical to its success. Prior experience showed that such relief organisations were almost always set up by, infiltrated by, authorised or manipulated by the IRA. Months and then years passed, and the closest scrutiny failed to produce evidence of any of these things. Eventually, the Ministry of Finance raised a mundane but crucial concern that, in a way, signified acceptance of the bona fides of the organisation. Was the Green Cross a genuine charity and thus exempt from entertainment duty in respect of its dances and other functions?

Audited accounts were submitted to show that, apart from reasonable administrative expenses, the funds that were raised were indeed disbursed to the dependants of internees and political prisoners. In 1941, the Attorney General had been consulted on the matter, and he had in turn sought police advice. The RUC still had suspicions, but no evidence to suggest that the fund had been administered for any improper purpose.[170]

Further investigations turned up nothing new. Whether the IRA had decided it would be unwise and counterproductive to infiltrate the Green Cross Fund or lacked the personnel to do so, or had been rebuffed, or concealed its intervention – or a combination of all of these, is not clear. The police watch continued. An anonymous letter alerted them to the activities of a schoolteacher at Rocktown School in Maghera, Co. Londonderry, who had been producing plays in aid of the fund. The subsequent inquiry showed that the teacher (Michael Morgan) had indeed produced plays, one *The Croppy Boy*, dealing with the 1798 Rising. The profits had either gone to Catholic parochial funds or to the Green Cross. The only query against his name was that the drama group he had founded and led in those productions was known as the 'Padraig Pearse Amateur Dramatic Club'. The police, however, knew nothing unfavourable against him, against any member of his family or against any of the players. Indeed, his brother, a priest, had denounced IRA activities from the altar of his church at Cranagh, Co. Tyrone. The suspicion attached to the troupe's name must moreover have been somewhat dissipated by the fact that at one performance chairs had been borrowed from the Orange Hall, Maghera, and thanks for this had been offered from the stage by Michael Morgan.[171]

The Catholic hierarchy did not falter in its support – a strong indication that there had been no infiltration or manipulation. There was among Northern Catholics a widespread feeling that internment had been unfair. In particular, it was contended that many of those interned, or even detained for a short time, had lost their employment and that they were then branded and consequently had little chance of working again in the foreseeable future. This had dire and long-lasting effects on families. A message from Cardinal MacRory to a conference of Green Cross representatives in Northern Ireland stressed that dependants could not be held responsible for internees' views or actions.[172] Despite such august support, the task was a difficult one. The central office reported that even their collectors were experiencing great difficulties. Many had been arrested and detained and when released frequently found that they too had lost their employment and were deprived of the dole or other public relief. To meet all the demands upon it, the fund needed about £500 weekly. The total coming in from collections was only about £125, and the fund was disbursing some £300 per week.[173] In its appeals, the fund always gave prominence to the bishops' strong support, particularly the Lenten Pastoral of Dr Daniel Mageean, Bishop of Down and Connor, which had referred to 'the helpless dependants of the internees, from whom the government of the Six Counties has seen fit to withdraw the dole' and who were in want of the actual necessities of life.[174] The fund was careful to draw a distinction between Northern and Southern internment. Catholics in the Six Counties had to live 'under a bigoted dictatorial system that regards our religion as a crime'.[175] Although this was a tilt against the Northern government, it was also an indirect criticism of the IRA, implying that internment in Éire might be justified.

The Advisory Committee

As noted, an Advisory Committee had been established to advise the Minister for Home Affairs on release applications. This was placed under the chairmanship of Judge Marcus Dill Begley, KC; the two lay members were R. B. Alexander and W. H. Scott, both Justices of the Peace.[176] The committee had its own secretary and shorthand note-taker. The process consisted of interviews with prisoners and a study of police intelligence. Meetings were held both at Londonderry and Belfast prisons.

As with its predecessor and successor bodies, this committee was an attempt to introduce a semblance of due process into a system of executive detention that, at times, had the appearance of the *lettres de cachet* of pre-Revolutionary France. The committee, whose origins may be traced back to the DORA of the First World War, had several irremediable defects.[177] The most basic was that it could only make recommendations and, although set up as a quasi-judicial forum, had no judicial powers. It had no established procedures to test evidence, either by inquisitorial investigation or by adversarial confrontation. It could receive intelligence from the RUC but was obliged, even should it press a point, to take it at face value. The basic questions as to reliability of sources were put (an invariable part of a normal application for a warrant by the police or other agency) but could not be probed. The inequity of withdrawing liberty from the citizen without giving him or her a chance to hear and challenge the evidence was thus never addressed, even indirectly. The internment process was deemed to be illegitimate by, as far as now can be seen, virtually the whole nationalist community. To add the pretence of judicial review merely increased that alienation and dissatisfaction by lending credibility to accusations of cynicism. The outcome was to strengthen rather than to weaken anti-state sentiment and subversion, both in the short and the long term.[178]

Over the course of the war years, 827 persons were interned. The vast majority appealed to the Advisory Committee, and of these 559 were released on entering into bail to be of good behaviour; thirty-seven were freed on compassionate grounds. The high proportion of releases indicated that so widely had the net of internment been cast that many with no connections with the IRA had been gathered in, as well as a number of minnows of no significance. Reviewing internment in 1946, however, the Ministry took a different view. Those released after review by the Advisory Committee were persons who 'after a short experience of internment realised the folly of their actions' and appealed.[179] This was a new and retrospective rationale for internment. What had originally been announced as a preventive was now was being justified as deterrent and, indeed, as retribution. The revised version was also at odds with the way in which the Advisory Committee had worked, since it looked less to a repudiation of past follies than to the strength of present IRA connections.

Any significant and continuing association with the republican organisations was taken as justification for continued internment. A few examples will show how cases were handled. Denis Kelly, an insurance agent from Lurgan, Co. Armagh, had been interned on six grounds: (1) that in 1940 he had been one of the Co. Armagh delegates of the Prisoners' Defence Fund; (2) that he had attended IRA commemorations at Bodenstown and similar meetings elsewhere; (3) that he had taken part in a presentation to Seán Fox in 1936;[180] (4) that he had collected funds for Sinn Féin in the 1936 Westminster general election; (5) that in March 1940 he had attended the Irish Prisoners' Committee Convention; and (6) that he was suspected of carrying out IRA propaganda in the course of his work as an insurance agent. When interviewed by the Advisory Committee, Kelly admitted to IRA membership for seven years, up to Easter 1939, and stated that he had then resigned because of disagreements with IRA methods. He denied that he had held office in the Prisoners' Aid Society. Unconvinced, the Advisory Committee recommended that his detention be continued, and the Minister agreed.[181]

Other cases had similar features. Association with known republicans and with the Prisoners' Aid Society were sufficient justifications for internment, as was involvement in IRA commemorative activities. Sometimes the RUC offered more specific intelligence, such as IRA rank or function, or activities and associates in prison. One man, Frank McCann of Bessbrook, Co. Armagh, was said to have conferred in Belfast Prison with William Mulholland, known to be the internees' OC. The RUC assumed that the IRA had agreed to McCann's application because it had plans for him when he was again at liberty.[182]

Another man admitted past active membership of the IRA in Lurgan, attendance at a training camp near Dundalk and participating in an assault on a man suspected of being an informant. Ironically, he then went on to offer information himself, in an attempt to procure his release. When the police looked into what he told them, they found it inconclusive and so general as to be of little value and already known to them. He was also refused release.[183]

On five days in November 1940, the Committee considered thirty-nine cases. Four of these were resubmissions – applications for which further RUC information had been sought. Twenty-nine were second appeals, and five were fresh appeals. Of the cases considered, twenty-two were recommended for release, twelve were turned down, and in five cases more police information was requested.[184] Oddly and indeed indefensibly, given its preventive rationale, some applicants were approved for release but with the delay of a month or two. The committee cannot have believed that the men would be less of a threat several weeks off, so the decisions must have been retributive or deterrent – a belief perhaps they would not be found guilty at law but deserved some punishment that a longer spell of internment would be a more effective deterrent against future misbehaviour.

The committee was strongly criticised by the Northern Ireland Labour Party MP, Jack Beattie, in Stormont on 10 March 1942.[185] This left the Ministry of Home Affairs unmoved, but Scott and Alexander, the committee's two lay members, were deeply upset and had to be reassured by Judge Begley.[186] Beattie had stated that he knew all three members of the Advisory Committee, had spoken to them about its work and had been told that despite their recommendations certain people remained in internment. He also called for the committee to be scrapped, arguing that it was unfair for the treasurer and chairman of a unionist association to be members.[187] This public attack on the body caused offence and concern, and Scott and Alexander appear to have felt that Beattie had made their role unduly controversial, with a personal undertow; there was also the implication that information had been leaked to Beattie by one or the other of them.

Many releases were accompanied by the requirement that the applicant entered into bail, either himself, or through surety given by another person such as a priest.[188] Occasionally the decision was effectively handed over to the police. In one case, release on bail was recommended '[i]f police are satisfied that their original report is incorrect'.[189] It was rare for the Minister to disagree with the Advisory Committee's recommendations, but this sometimes happened. Since this was presumably based on political considerations or secret information, not made available to the committee, the files, not surprisingly, are not enlightening.[190] Even more rarely the Minister ordered release when the Advisory Committee had recommended retention. Such cases were probably due to private political approaches, perhaps by the internee's MP or by a member of the clergy or hierarchy.[191]

By the end of 1943, possibilities for a general release became stronger. The draining attrition of the years of captivity, the deterrent effect of possible rearrest and the decay of the organisation outside all greatly reduced the chances of men returning to IRA active service – if they had indeed been involved in the first place. The pace of releases speeded up with favourable recommendations considerably outnumbering unfavourable ones in most Advisory Committee sittings. As general international, political and security conditions improved, the comparative risk of releases diminished. In late November 1943, this mood of confidence had created a mood of anticipation within the prisons. Captain Fryer, the Governor of Londonderry Prison, wrote to Montgomery asking if the Advisory Committee could meet at the prison in time to allow those granted release to be home for Christmas: 'I understand several of them hope to be married then, and their speedy release would have a marked effect on many internees who are wavering at this moment.'[192]

By the following year, numbers had dwindled, and it was evident that all except those thought to be leaders would soon be freed. Meeting in March 1944, the Advisory Committee heard twenty-nine cases and made twenty release recommendations. In May it reviewed forty-five appeals and freed thirty-one – a ratio the more remarkable since, as the population declined, those left were, by definition, regarded as the harder cases.[193] Between 1 August 1943 and 31 July 1944, 110 men from Derry Prison appealed to the Advisory Committee, and eighty-two were released. The ratio at Belfast was not so generous (eighty-eight out of 194 applications) – in some measure, presumably, reflecting the policy of holding at Derry those thought to be lesser security risks.[194] A Green Cross Fund delegation led by the Nationalist Senator Joseph Maguire (former Speaker of the Northern Ireland Senate) met the Minister for Home Affairs on 19 December 1944. The Minister rebuffed pleas for the release of the remaining internees. His view was that the men's release was in their own hands. A means of appeal had been provided to them, and, with one exception, all who had applied had now been released. Application was 'a very clear indication' that internees were prepared to sever their IRA connections. The delegation asked him to release without requiring a bond since a number of the men were very strong-willed and felt that since they had done nothing wrong they should not have been interned. The Minister was unmoved: he would not throw open the prison gates.[195]

General release

Internees

As the Allies swept into Germany in the spring of 1945, the certainty grew that the war in Europe was in its last weeks. On 10 March, a reconstituted but tiny and stricken IRA formally declared a ceasefire.[196] The pace of releases by the Advisory Committee confirmed that the RUC was confident that the threat posed by militant republicanism was now slight. Within the nationalist community and inside the prisons the expectation grew of a general release. It was not, however, to be undertaken without hesitation and some delay. The government did not wish to be seen as giving way to nationalist pressure; there also remained a genuine concern that the release of the remaining internees, thought to include the most militant and committed, and all of whom had refused to apply to the Advisory Committee, could reignite republicanism. The RUC, always heavily influential, if not decisive, in such matters, remained opposed to a general release. More generally, officialdom followed the path furthest from risk.

Responding in a supply debate in mid-March, the Minister for Home Affairs, now Edmond Warnock, seemed equally uncompromising. Nationalist MPs had complained about postal censorship, the existence of a secret service and continued internment. The duty of the government was to defend the Constitution, Warnock insisted. It was not the existence of these security measures that was regrettable but the fact that they were necessary. Nobody had been interned or imprisoned for their political faith but because they were suspected of or convicted for supporting violence. Any internee could go before the Advisory Committee, and, as far as he was aware, its advice to the Minister had never been rejected. (He would later correct this claim.) Northern Ireland's measures were far less rigorous than those of Éire. Warnock had no desire to intern anyone, 'but I am not prepared to release any man so long as that man remains a danger to the security of Northern Ireland'.[197]

On 8 May 1945, the day that the German military leadership signed an unconditional surrender, a party of Nationalist politicians lobbied the Prime Minister, Sir Basil Brooke. Led by T. J. Campbell, the group argued that a general release was both expedient and humane. When internment had been introduced, Lord Craigavon, then Prime Minister, had indicated that it was an emergency measure that would last for the duration of the war. The emergency having passed, the government should make 'a generous gesture'. Others made similar points. The republican movement was now dead, and with police and army released from wartime duties it would be easy to exercise surveillance over released internees. Internment could not continue indefinitely, and this was an opportune time to end it.[198]

In response, Sir Basil noted that internment had existed long before the war, and nothing but 'grave necessity' would induce him to agree to it. The war danger was over, but these young men believed that the constitution could be overthrown by force, and the government could not take the responsibility of releasing them 'without being quite certain that they would behave themselves in future'. Warnock added that all who had appealed, with one or two exceptions, had now been released. He had himself recently examined all internees' papers and had ordered releases where possible. He did not agree that the republican movement was dead; it was, indeed, very active. He referred to 'certain people' who had gone to work 'wearing mourning for Hitler'.[199]

Promises were given to look again at certain individual cases (including the Armagh female internees), and Sir Basil said that he would talk the matter over further with Warnock. He cautioned, however, that it would be very difficult to agree to a general release. Much as everyone disliked the idea of internment, it was the policy of the organisation to which the men belonged to make ordinary trial impossible, through the intimidation of witnesses. All would like to see peace and good feeling, but the government had its responsibilities.[200]

This remained the gist of Brooke's subsequent letter to Campbell. Campbell responded, politically, angrily and probably counterproductively. Some 400 citizens had been cast into prison 'simply of a scrap of paper signed by a Minister or his deputy'. Some 140 were still retained, 'including a score or so of refined cultured ladies'. Britain had recognised the end of the war in Europe by unconditionally releasing its internees. Brooke's letter suggested that there would be 'an indefinite prolongation of dictatorial powers'. These were without parallel in any part of the British dominions and bore the hallmarks of a dictatorship 'deemed necessary after twenty-four years of "resolute government"'. The internees, persons of 'unblemished character', were being held because their offence was to be 'unbending opponents' of the Northern Ireland government. He was going to the press with the correspondence.[201]

Home Affairs had received information from the police and prisons on the internees' state of mind following this public exchange. This had duly been passed on to ministers and was part of the background to their deliberations, particularly on the issue of showing good faith by applying to the Advisory Committee. The RUC informed the Ministry that Senator James Lennon, a Nationalist politician, had told the mother of internee Francis McGeough, that her son and all other internees would be released unconditionally within a few days.[202] Lennon's assurances were only part of the reason why the number of appeals to the Advisory Committee had dried up. Some, described as 'the more uncompromising republican internees', had insisted that the government could not hold them after the cessation of hostilities. So convinced were they that many had already packed their personal property 'expecting to be turned out of the gaol at any moment'. The RUC had no doubt that but for the extremist pressures at least half the remaining internees would already have applied for release. It was also convinced that, were internment to continue for another two or three months, the wavering half would go to the Committee 'and willingly accept conditional release'.[203]

The police view was that the militants wanted, at all costs, to save face by holding out for unconditional release. There was some truth in this notion, since, as we have noted, to militant republicans, 'signing out' carried a great stigma and was a sign of submission to what they regarded as an illegitimate and indeed unlawful authority. Should they avoid this act of submission, the argument continued, their cause would be bolstered, and, once freed, they would immediately attempt to revive the IRA 'with the assistance of the nucleus now existing in the seven companies comprising the Belfast Battalion'. It would be a mistake to assume that the organisation had been suppressed. Internment had subdued it, but an outbreak of sectarian trouble or even industrial unrest would revive it overnight.[204] Some of the internees had indeed completed a very long term of imprisonment.[205] Were they to show themselves willing 'to play our rules' by applying for release, they would be strongly recommended by the RUC. They would not do so, however: 'they are too comfortable in Belfast Prison – and they have too many friends seeing them from inside and outside the Prison'. If perhaps 100 men were transferred back to Derry, 'I believe you would see a great many more applications for release as they do not see or hear from their friends so much.' A police list of potential transferees had been prepared.[206]

Information also came from within the prisons. Captain Stuart wrote that the exchange between Sir Basil Brooke and T. J. Campbell (which the Belfast internees had presumably read in the *Irish News*) had made about half of them sullen and defiant. The other half regarded Brooke's statement as 'a political stunt', not to be taken seriously, believing that they would be released unconditionally after the forthcoming general election. The Advisory Committee was, in consequence, being ignored by both groups.[207]

The report from A. Ronald Booth, new governor of Armagh Prison (succeeding Major G. H. Brush) came in the form of a selection of internees' letters. Una MacDowell wrote a chatty letter to a friend in the course of which she dismissed rumours of impending release. Were all such tales heeded, 'we would have been in the nuthouse long ago'. She did not expect release 'for a long time yet, because you see the "democratic" British government that was fighting for the freedom of small nations daren't risk letting 9 Irish girls out of jail in peace-time'. Continued detention was 'the biggest compliment I was ever paid in my life when I think that the forces who "conquered" Germany can't conquer a handful of girls and I am one of them'.[208]

Another woman referred to 'Dictator Brooke's answer to Mr Campbell'. It had not surprised the internees, but if the government imagined that they were going to keep people in a place like Armagh indefinitely, 'they have another thought coming to them for there will be trouble and bad trouble'.[209] Writing to 'Nonie' (possibly Annie Ward) she denounced the Advisory Committee as the 'tail end' of the G Division (Special Branch). It functioned as an information bureau, seeking information from those 'weakened in spirit by the misery of imprisonment'. This was not a figment of her imagination since those who had appeared before it had reported on the Committee's questions. Knowing that because of their time in prison the women had lost touch with outside affairs they questioned them about other women internees, 'And it is to this iniquitous tribunal no decent person would ever think of going.'[210]

Knowing that all outgoing mail was censored, such letters were written at least in part with the intention of riling the authorities. In this they succeeded since in forwarding them to Home Affairs Booth drew attention to their bitterness, commenting (predictably), 'Verily the Female of the species is more deadly than the Male.'[211] Since releases were almost certain to be staged in batches, bitter and uncompromising expressions could have delayed them, had it not been for the view in Home Affairs that the women were not as deadly as the men and, probably, that such emotional outpourings could be expected.

It seemed as though a stand-off had been reached. A large section of the remaining internees refused to show their good faith – as the government saw it – by submitting to the appeals process. On their part, a section of the internees felt strongly that having been subjected to the indignity and deprivations of internment for several years they were being pressured to acknowledge the legality, even justice, of what they had been put through by participating in and thereby legitimising an instrument of oppression and deception. And, indeed, it is not too hard to see that, having held out so far, an internee would, at the stroke of a pen, render worthless the years of deprivation that lay behind them. There remained for these a sense of betrayal, contamination even, in the whole ritual and rigmarole of 'signing out'. At the same time, it was clear that, whatever Brooke said, internment could not last indefinitely. In this tussle, therefore, the internees now occupied the most advantageous ground, provided they were willing to continue to sit in prison.

The wider domestic and international situation also favoured the hold-outs. Most generally, although Brooke was correct in stating that the duration of internment would not be fixed by the war, it was a time affected by powerful sentiments, of homecoming, thanksgiving and rejoicing, of mourning and of new beginnings.

Churchill was yet to introduce Marsh's epigram into his multi-volume history of the Second World War, but its spirit was abroad: 'In war: resolution; in defeat: defiance; in victory: magnanimity; in peace: goodwill.'[212] The deep-seated desire for a new start was demonstrated by Labour's unexpected and overwhelming victory in the general election announced at the end of July: 393 seats against 210 for the Conservatives and National Liberals. The political balance, anchored in sectarian bedrock, had not perceptibly budged in Northern Ireland, but Belfast had to do business with a new, unknown, possibly radical and certainly reforming government in London.[213] Labour, the party of the working-class and city constituencies, had traditionally been sympathetic to the nationalist community. Better not to add to the uncertainties of the Stormont–Westminster relationship by appearing obdurate or vindictive over internment; best indeed not to draw too much attention to oneself. The Japanese declaration of capitulation on 14 August 1945 and the worldwide publicity given to formal surrender on board the USS *Missouri* on 2 September confirmed beyond all doubt that this was a time for repair, renewal and the restoration of civic rights and comforts.

That the IRA had allied itself with the defeated enemy, and had done its best to give practical expression to that alliance, in a paradoxical way increased rather than decreased the case for magnanimity. It was far less a matter of humane sentiment than a recognition that the organisation had failed in every campaign to which it turned its hand, and allying itself with an utterly ignoble – and, as a horrified world was daily learning, utterly vile and evil – force had done so on an international as well as domestic level. It was difficult to accept the RUC assessment that such a discredited and spent force could regenerate itself, no matter who now came out of captivity and in whatever frame of mind they came.

Such evidently were the lines along which Sir Basil Brooke and Edmond Warnock were thinking. At a cabinet meeting on 5 July 1945, the Prime Minister referred to a discussion the two had had about the issue. Despite Dublin's having had to return to custody some men it had released, Brooke thought the time had come to begin a general release in Northern Ireland.[214] The impending royal visit would be a suitable occasion to make an announcement. This was a shrewd move since the connection of mercy to royalty would, at once, deflect criticisms that might come from his own hardliners while at the same time be a reminder to republicans that the institutions and symbols of the Union were robustly intact.[215] Warnock would make the announcement before the royal visit, but the releases would not begin until afterwards. A further timing consideration was the heightened unionist feeling connected with the Twelfth of July holiday, and so it was not until the evening of 13 July that Warnock released the news that releases of the 'great majority' would begin before the end of the month.[216]

This was still not a general release, and the principle of releasing the 'great majority' meant that those thought to be hardliners would be retained. The RUC was asked to provide a list of these; full reasons were to be given in each case, and it was cautioned that only a 'small number' of retentions was contemplated. Unless the police made special representations regarding any individual, it was proposed to release all the female internees within a week or so. The male internees would be released in batches of thirty or forty on a first in, first out basis.[217]

A week later, the RUC supplied its list of fifty men for continued detention. Of these, eleven had, according to police intelligence, at some point been implicated in murders or attempted murders. With those men the outlook was bleak: 'as their antecedents and political characters generally are of the most bitter Republican outlook, there is no hope that they will amend their ways and cease their illegal activities'.[218] Home Affairs was now able to proceed with the general releases. On 26 July 1945, Warnock agreed the first thirty-six names. These were to be freed during the following week, but all nine Armagh women were to go at once. The men were internees who had been held from 1939 (sixteen) and 1940 (fifteen), together with five men for whom there were special reasons for release (unspecified but likely to be compassionate).[219] Another thirty-three men from 1940 were to be freed during the week ending 11 August 1945. Other batches, according to year of internment, were to follow in successive weeks, with all releases, except for the fifty named by the RUC, to be completed by 1 September. The largest group was thirty-six and the smallest the Armagh women.[220]

The women, of course, had had no intimation of their release, and, as we have seen, some had braced themselves for a long stay. They had not been told about the government's announcement of 13 July. On the morning of their release they were teasingly asked by the Matron if they would like to go home immediately: within a few hours they were indeed on their way. All were delighted to be free but expressed sorrow that they had left one of their number behind. She, being a convicted prisoner, had another ten months to serve.[221]

The programme of releases proceeded smoothly enough, but, on Monday, 30 July 1945, there was a small demonstration by men not yet due for release. As those being discharged were leaving the prison, men appeared at the cell windows of the top floor of D Wing (which overlooked the Crumlin Road). Slogans such as 'Up the Republic' were shouted, and the prisoners waved to passers-by. Staff ordered the demonstrators out of their cells. The men refused to leave and increased their shouting. Matters then appear to have got out of hand. Staff drew batons, and cells were cleared by force, one demonstrator being slightly injured. Sixteen men were identified as ringleaders, of whom four were on the RUC's special list. It was decided as a punishment that those who had various release dates over the following month would all be held back to the last batch.[222]

Of the group of fifty, seven had been interned following completion of a prison sentence. The Governor reported on these cases. Their original offences ranged from withholding information (eighteen months' imprisonment) to illegal drilling (two years' hard labour) to six years for possessing explosives. Only two of the seven were recommended by Stuart for release, but the Ministry took a more liberal view, and by 9 October 1945 all but two had been freed. One of those retained had previously escaped from internment (the mass exodus from Derry on 20 March 1943) and had been at large for some seventeen months. His continued detention would have been hard to justify since he had already served a sentence of twelve months' hard labour for escaping. His escape, however, was sufficient to put him into the suspiciously round number of fifty to be retained. The other man, who had served four and a half years for his 1939 explosives offence, fell into the same category.[223]

Nationalist politicians continued to press for the completion of releases, linking the internees to those convicted of political offences, for whom they wanted an amnesty. Warnock was not to be rushed on either, as was shown in an ill-tempered and finger-pointing adjournment debate at the end of July. There were strong – perhaps intentionally provocative – speeches by Thomas Campbell, Nationalist MP for Belfast Central and Harry Diamond, Socialist Republican MP for Belfast Falls, citing the condemnation of the Special Powers Act by Professor Harold Laski, Chairman of the Labour Party in Great Britain – now the governing party. There would be a phased release of 'the great majority' of internees, Warnock maintained. He denied that there were any political prisoners, but, in so far as he affected to understand what was being asked, he firmly stated that there would be no general amnesty: all cases would be considered individually.[224] Despite a deal of foot-dragging by police and politicians, however, as the autumn of 1945 wore on, there was a greater willingness to contemplate further releases. Once again, Christmas emerged as a target date. If indeed those men on the special list were to be freed, Christmas provided a convenient peg for mercy and humanitarianism and a modest harvest of sentiment for politicians. Should prolonged detention be decided, conversely, there would need to be a strong defence of a stand which would provoke protest and resentment across the nationalist community.

Towards the end of November, Montgomery submitted a list of twelve names to Warnock. This was the first bite at the core of incorrigibles: 'I cannot say that these men are harmless or likely to be harmless', he wrote, but he considered them to be 'the least harmful of the remaining internees'.[225] By December, only thirty-six internees remained at Belfast Prison. In a Stormont statement, Warnock confirmed that in view of the 'reasonably peaceful' situation he had hoped to release this remnant. At a rally in Londonderry the previous weekend, however, a statement had been made by Eddie McAteer, then a prominent Nationalist MP, which, on Warnock's reading, suggested that the IRA could in certain circumstances be used to subjugate Ulster. He had asked for more details, and, until that information had been received and considered, he had no further statement to make about releases.[226]

Warnock's speech was party-political window-dressing, a shot across nationalist bows to show his own party and supporters that there was no lack of steel. He recognised that internment had become increasingly difficult to sustain, and its final cessation was now a matter of timing. At a meeting on the same day that he had apparently backtracked in Stormont because of McAteer's speech, he told cabinet colleagues that he had discussed the matter with the Inspector-General, whose opinion was that, although the element of danger 'was not entirely absent', the remaining internees could be freed without serious risk. Brooke concurred. Some men, it was obvious, would never appeal, and they could not be held indefinitely. The Cabinet then endorsed Warnock's proposal that all the remaining internees be released in batches before Christmas; any final decision would be subject to the report on the Londonderry speeches.[227] Nine days later, he ordered the release of all remaining men. Fifteen were freed on 14 December, another nine the following day, and the remainder by 21 December.[228]

Finale

Even though the last of the internees was home for Christmas, there had been doubts about the status of John O'Doherty, who had escaped from Belfast Prison on 6 June 1941, and also of the ten men of the Derry escape on 20 March 1943. All were liable to rearrest. The matter was raised with the RUC in August 1945 since there was a problem of public perception as well as legal mechanics. Was it feasible to charge persons with escaping from internment, when internment had been discontinued? And how would it look to have them serving sentences for the offence long afterwards? Since most of the Derry escapers had been interned in the Curragh, would rearrest and a further spell of custody not seem like mere vindictiveness? Such concerns may have prompted officials to ask for RUC guidance. The answer may not have been entirely welcome to a Ministry now intent on tidying the whole episode away. The RUC Inspector-General thought that the risk of re-internment 'hangs over their head' and was deterring the escapers from returning to Northern Ireland. There was no information as to whether the escapers had undergone a change of heart. A decision on the internment orders against them should therefore be deferred for a further six months.[229]

With internment definitely in its last stages, officials again raised the issue with Warnock in mid-December. The eleven men were listed in a memorandum which Montgomery simply annotated, 'I think the Internment Order in all these cases might now be cancelled.' A few days later, Warnock gave his five-word assent.[230] Some men remained to be released, but they would be home in time for Christmas. The second large recourse to internment in Northern Ireland's quarter-century history thus sidled to its close.

Reviewing the outcome of wartime internment, Home Affairs struck a confident and justificatory note. In all, 827 persons had been interned, which had 'effectively stifled' the IRA's activities. This outcome had the approval of the vast majority of the general population. Nor did the Ministry doubt that the right people had been netted. Conveniently disregarding the large proportion of the 827 who had been released by the Advisory Committee, it insisted that internees – presumably meaning all of them – had been prepared to identify themselves with the IRA's objectives and methods. This had been a grave matter, since the IRA had 'openly boasted of its readiness to join forces with the enemies of the country' and was 'a positive menace'.[231]

Sentenced prisoners

Those sentenced for politically motivated offences continued to serve their sentences, being released as these expired and also by commutation of sentence.[232] A number remained, still facing many years inside. By late August 1949, there remained ten men in this category, and Home Affairs decided that the time was right for their phased early releases.[233] On 19 October 1949, Cahill, Cordner, Oliver, Perry and Simpson, whose death sentences for the murder of Constable Patrick Murphy had been commuted to long periods of penal servitude, were freed.[234] As we saw at the beginning of this chapter, this had been an offence of particular political sensitivity to the authorities, a cause of great anger to the unionist population, necessarily requiring great care in its handling, even after the lapse of many years. With such men freed, those who remained in prison began to feel hopeful, but it was not until August 1950 that Hugh McAteer (brother of the Nationalist politician Eddie McAteer and former Chief of Staff of the IRA who, in January 1943, escaped from Belfast Prison) and Liam Burke were released, with Jimmy Steele (a fellow escaper) following a few weeks later. Another page had been turned.

Notes

1 See above, pp. 431–34.

2 See above, pp. 480–81. Co-defendants Joseph and Mary Hewitt were acquitted, as was Brigid O'Hara. Joseph Hewitt was then tried on explosives charges but, on 6 February 1940, was also acquitted when the Crown offered no evidence. *Irish Independent*, 7 February 1940, 8b.

3 The law of murder, reformed by the Homicide Act, 1957: 5 & 6 Eliz. II, c.11, s.1, made those who undertook a felony (such as planting of a bomb) liable to the substantive charge of murder, even though they had not taken a direct part in the killing itself. Constructive malice aforethought (as the doctrine was called) could bring various partners in an enterprise into the net. One leading authority, reflecting on the pre-1957 law, notes that it was 'capable of operating very harshly'. Richard Card, *Criminal Law* (London: Butterworths, 1995), p. 205. For the formative post-1957 case, see *R.* v. *Vickers* (1957) 2 QB 664 Court of Criminal Appeal. It is difficult to be certain, but McCormick and Barnes would probably still have been convicted under the law as amended in 1957; they would, however, have stood more chance of acquittal than under earlier law. The public at large and, in this case, the Catholic population of Ireland, had difficulty in understanding the doctrine and were, at the very least, uneasy about its application. The indirect part played by Barnes and McCormick in the explosion and five deaths made it easier to mount a campaign for their reprieve.

4 See, for example, J. Bowyer Bell, *The Secret Army: The IRA, 1916–1979* (Cambridge, Mass.: MIT Press, 1983), Chapter 7.

5 *Irish News*, 5 December 1936, 5f–g; 27 January 1937, 5a–c.

6 James Joseph Reynolds and Charles McCafferty were killed instantaneously whilst preparing bombs for use against customs huts at Clady and Strabane, Co. Tyrone; John James Kelly was mortally injured and died several days later (see above, p. 485, n. 12). *Irish News*, 29 November 1938, 5b–c; 30 November 1938, 5c.

7 Carrickarnon and Ferry Hill in the southern part of Co. Down and Belleek and Newtown Butler in Co. Fermanagh. *Irish News*, 30 November 1938, 5a–b.

8 The visit of the King and Queen to Northern Ireland on 28 July 1937 was the occasion for a considerable destruction of customs huts (more than thirty, newspapers estimated) on both sides of the border, including Carrickcarnon (Co. Armagh), Middletown (Co. Armagh), Crossmaglen (Co. Armagh), Carnagh (Co. Armagh), Tullydonnell (Co. Down), Swanlinbar (Co. Cavan), Blacklion (Co. Cavan), Belleek (Co. Fermanagh), Pettigo (Co. Donegal), Clones (Co. Monaghan), Tyholland (Co. Monaghan) and Clontivern (Co. Fermanagh). There were also attempts on 28 July 1937 to destroy the Belfast-to-Dublin railway line in several places. *Irish Times*, 29 July 1937, 7a and 8d; *Irish Press*, 29 July 1937, 1b–c and 7c–e; *Irish News*, 30 November 1938, 5b.

9 See below, pp. 612–16 for background.

10 See, for example, the debates and discussions on the Treason Act and the Offences Against the State Act: *Irish Times*, 4 May 1939, 10a–b; *Dáil Debates*, vol. 74, cols. 87–90, 8 February 1939 (and successive stages).

11 *Irish Times*, 17 January 1940, 7c. Dublin, as it turned out, would enact and use more draconian measures than those deemed necessary by the Stormont government.

12 *Irish News*, 19 January 1939, 5a–b, 7g; *The Times*, 20 January 1939, 12e; *Daily Telegraph*, 19 January 1939, 13g.

13 *The Times*, 28 July 1939, 8d; *Manchester Guardian*, 27 July 1939, 13a–b; *Daily Telegraph*, 27 July 1939, 6c.

14 A further manifestation of this strategy was the encouragement of lawful anti-Partition organisations on both sides of the border, preferably with the active participation of Roman Catholic clergy. See, for example, *Irish News*, 17 January 1939, 7a.

15 And, it must have seemed, an extraordinary challenge. Although ultimately a failure, the audacious IRA raid of 23 December 1939 on the Magazine Fort in Dublin's Phoenix Park netted most of Éire's small-arms ammunition reserve – this in the fourth month of the unfolding European war. Fear must have mixed with fury in the Government's reaction. See Bell, *Secret Army*, *op. cit.*, pp. 172–3, for a graphic and informed account of the incident.

16 Although its one-time Chief of Staff, Stephen Hayes, had been arrested by IRA leaders, ill-treated and forced to sign a confession of treachery (*Irish Times*, 20 June 1942, 1d–e). This revelation split the organisation and dealt a major blow to morale. See pp. 607–8, n. 122.

17 The organisation was also alleged to be in receipt of at least some German funding (see *Irish Times*, 8 June 1940, 7f).

18 The hopeless amateurism of the action was confirmed by the fact that, although pursued, the firing party and arms couriers felt unable to refuse a pressing invitation from the owner of the house to have a glass of lemonade. Then, according to Joe Cahill's recollection, 'As quickly as it takes to tell, the house was surrounded by RUC.' Brendan Anderson, *Joe Cahill: A Life in the IRA* (Dublin: The O'Brien Press, 2002), p. 48.

19 Constable Patrick Murphy, stationed at Springfield Road barracks, was a Roman Catholic. He lived in the Beechmount district and was apparently personally known to some of those involved in the shooting (Anderson, *Joe Cahill*, *op. cit.*, p. 48).

20 *Irish Press*, 29 April 1942, 1b; 31 July 1942, 1f. The two women were dealt with leniently. Madge Burns (aged nineteen) was released without charge but was immediately interned. Margaret Nolan (aged seventeen) pleaded guilty to being an accessory after the fact and was released with a recorded sentence of one year and on bail to be of good behaviour for three years.

21 *Irish Times*, 17 August 1942, 1d; 1 September 1942, 1g–h; *Irish Independent*, 3 August 1942, 3e.

22 See *Manchester Guardian*, 1 September 1942, 2f.

23 See Ronan Fanning, Michael Kennedy, Dermot Keogh and Eunan O'Halpin (eds.), *Documents on Irish Foreign Policy* (Dublin: Royal Irish Academy, 1998–), vol. VII, pp. 245–6, 331–2. See also David Gray (US Ambassador to Ireland) to US Department of State, 11 October 1942, at FDR Presidential Library, Albany, New York, PSF Box 52.

24 See *Irish Independent*, 29 July 1942, 3g; 30 July 1942, 3e–f.

25 *Irish Independent*, 8 August 1942, 3h; 22 August 1942, 2g. The Attorney General refused a petition from the prisoners to appeal to the House of Lords.

26 John Clarke MacDermott (1896–1976) was educated at Campbell College and at Queen's University, Belfast. He served with distinction during the First World War and was called to the bar in 1921. He took silk in 1936 and, between 1938 and 1944, was one of the Queen's University MPs at Stormont. Serving for a time as Minister for Public Security, he was appointed Attorney General in 1941 and to the High Court in 1944. In 1947 he became a Lord of Appeal and returned to Northern Ireland as Lord Chief Justice in 1951. He was liberal in his judicial outlook and an early advocate of human rights in legal doctrine.

27 PRONI CAB/4/522, Report to Cabinet, 22 August 1942.

28 PRONI CAB/4/522, Judge E. S. Murphy to Cabinet, undated.

29 PRONI CAB/4/522, John M. Andrews, Prime Minister of Northern Ireland to the Duke of Abercorn, Governor of Northern Ireland, 27 August 1942.

30 PRONI CAB/4/522/23P. See also PRO CAB/65/31/17, ff. 100–1, 105, 190–1.

31 *Ibid.*, Memorandum signed by Robert Gransden, Cabinet Secretary, and John M. Andrews, Prime Minister, 29 August 1942.

32 *Irish News*, 31 August 1942, 1a–b; *Irish Press*, 31 August 1942, 1b; *Irish Times*, 3 September 1942, 1e.

33 All the men were devout Catholics and had been preparing for their deaths under the guidance of the chaplain, Father Paddy McAlister. The men's spiritual seriousness would have impressed the church authorities.

34 Churchill Archives Centre, Winston Churchill Papers, Char. 20/54A/71, 2 September 1942.

35 Churchill Papers, Char. 20/54A/72, 4 September 1942.

36 Police patrols were fired on in Belfast immediately following the execution, and on 5 September 1942, Constable James Laird and Special Constable Samuel Hamilton were shot and killed at Clady, Co. Tyrone (*Irish Times*, 7 September 1942, 1d). There had been firefights in Belfast the previous day, resulting in the wounding of a man and a child (*Irish Times*, 5 September 1942, 1c).

37 On 11 October 1942 there was an attack on the RUC barracks in the Donegall Pass in Belfast. A bomb was thrown. Special Constable James Lyons was fatally injured and a number of others at the scene, police and civilians, were less seriously hurt (*Irish Times*, 12 October 1942, 1f). A large quantity of arms and munitions had been moved across the border and men prepared for action. The first phase was to stage attacks in the aftermath of the Williams execution. A police car and its crew were captured after a firefight at Culloville, Co. Armagh. A constable and a sergeant had surrendered when faced by a much larger armed group. Apart from one man wounded in the exchanges there was little injury. The police appear to have been disarmed (*Irish Times*, 3 September 1942, 1c).

38 On 20 April 1942, the IRA Army Council met and stated its preliminary conditions for cooperation with the Nazi government (Bell, *Secret Army*, *op. cit.*, p. 223). In his recollections of the time, Cahill remembers the prisoners' delight at German victories (Anderson, *Joe Cahill*, *op. cit.*, pp. 81–2). This had long antedated Cahill's arrival in the prison, of course. Particularly bitter relations had been stimulated between prisoners and staff by the exuberant rejoicing by the former on the sinking

of HMS *Hood* (the Navy's largest ship) by the pocket battleship *Bismarck* on 24 May 1941. The *Bismarck* itself was sunk, but the prisoners' reaction to this is unrecorded.

39 A week later, Allied troops commanded by General Dwight D. Eisenhower landed in Algeria and Morocco.

40 Winston S. Churchill, *The Second World War: The Hinge of Fate* (Harmondsworth: Penguin Books, 1985), p. 541.

41 Bell, *Secret Army, op. cit.*, p. 229.

42 There were flourishes, but they were no more than that. On Easter Saturday, 24 April 1943, the IRA seized the Broadway Cinema on the Falls Road. In the interval between films, an IRA statement was read to the audience, together with the 1916 Proclamation (*Irish News*, 26 April 1943, 1g–h). A triumphant element was added to the event by the fact that the readers were, respectively, Hugh McAteer, IRA Chief of Staff, and Jimmy Steele, the most prominent of Belfast republicans. Both had escaped from Belfast Prison on 15 January 1942 (*Irish News*, 16 January 1943, 1a). See below, pp. 589–90.

43 Uinseann MacEoin, *The IRA in the Twilight Years, 1923–1948* (Dublin: Argenta, 1997), p. 450.

44 It would be abolished (as a sentence of the court) in 1948.

45 See above, pp. 90–91.

46 MacEoin, *The IRA in the Twilight Years, op. cit.*, pp. 456–9.

47 *Irish Times*, 4 August 1943, 2g. During the same sitting of the Commission, heavy sentences of penal servitude were imposed on several other men (William Doyle, William Burke, Alphonsus White, John Joseph Doyle, Lewis Duffin, Joseph Lunney and Francis Notarantonio) but none other of corporal punishment.

48 See Seán McConville, *English Local Prisons, 1860–1900: Next Only to Death* (London and New York: Routledge, 1995), pp. 245–8. See also above, pp. 444–45. The administration of corporal punishment is dealt with in correspondence between the Ministry of Home Affairs and the Home Office and others at PRONI HA/8/1913. This showed, *inter alia*, that between 1938 and 1943, fourteen sentences of corporal punishment were passed: twelve of flogging and two of birching. Two sentences of flogging and one of birching were remitted on medical grounds. J. B. O'Neill, Assistant Secretary, Ministry of Home Affairs to Cicily Craven, Hon. Secretary, Howard League, 22 March 1950. Remission, where granted, seems therefore to have been for medical reasons rather than because of review by senior officials.

49 Burke recalled that the men told him after that on a cold night without their shirts they were anxious not to shiver, lest the prison officers should subsequently boast that they had been afraid (MacEoin, *The IRA in the Twilight Years, op. cit.*, p. 458). This fear of being thought fearful recalls the last concerns of Charles I before his execution in Whitehall.

50 MacEoin, *The IRA in the Twilight Years, op. cit.*, p. 459.

51 MacEoin, *The IRA in the Twilight Years, op. cit.*, p. 458. At least four other men besides Mooney, Doyle and Steele were subjected to corporal punishment during these years. They were Patrick MacCotter, Patrick Donnelly, John McMahon and Edward Tennyson.

52 PRONI HA/32/1/748, C. G. Wickham to E. W. Scales, Assistant Secretary, Ministry of Home Affairs, 11 May 1939. Lieutenant Colonel Sir Charles Wickham (1879–1971) fought with distinction in both the Boer War and the First World War. He became Inspector-General of the RUC in June 1922, retaining the post until his retirement in August 1945.

53 See Fanning et al., *Documents on Irish Foreign Policy, op. cit.*, vol. V, pp. 445–51; vol. VII, pp. 74–7; PRO CAB/65/18/32, ff. 47, 51. There had been an earlier decision on similar lines when Winston Churchill, then First Lord of the Admiralty,

had failed to convince his cabinet colleagues to take action on the Treaty Ports, Anthony Eden observing that it would be impossible for de Valera to grant the facilities since at least 80 per cent of the Irish people favoured neutrality. Roy Jenkins, *Churchill* (London: Pan, 2002), pp. 654–5. The conscription issue reappeared in May 1941, but, after a deal of discussion within government, Churchill announced that Northern Ireland would continue to be exempt (5 *Hansard*, vol. 371, cols. 1718–19, 27 May 1941). See also PRO CAB/65/18/33, f. 51.

54 PRONI HA/32/1/748, Major-General R. V. Pollock, GOC Northern Ireland District, to Commander R. B. Pim, Assistant Secretary, Ministry of Home Affairs, 11 April 1939. Pollock pointed out that the military had no accommodation suitable for internees and asked if the Northern Ireland government had suitable premises.

55 PRONI HA/32/1/748, C. G. Wickham to E. W. Scales, 18 April 1939. Wickham cautioned against internment being used as a device to escape conscription, then still a possibility.

56 PRONI HA/32/1/748, E. W. Scales to John C. Davidson, KC, Parliamentary Secretary for Home Affairs, 8 May 1939.

57 PRONI HA/32/1/748, E. W. Scales to C. G. Wickham, 10 May 1939. Wickham largely agreed but suggested that the location of an internment camp at Ballykinlar be agreed in principle, although it would not be constructed until an emergency demand for accommodation made that necessary. By February 1942, the population of Belfast Prison, in round numbers, was as follows: 300 internees, 160 ordinary prisoners and 90 convicts. The greater portion of the latter were politically related. PRONI CAB/9/B/156/1, Captain C. H. Petherick, Ministry of Finance, to John I. Cook, HM Treasury, 26 February 1942.

58 PRONI HA/32/1/748, Major W. H. Grant, Staff Captain, Northern Ireland District, to R. B. Pim, Assistant Secretary, Ministry of Home Affairs, 3 July 1939.

59 PRONI HA/32/1/748, Sir Ernest Holderness to E. W. Scales, 12 August 1939. The last point referred to decisions on regime and management.

60 PRONI HA/32/1/748, Sir Ernest Holderness to E. W. Scales, 14 August 1939. To imagine that an army straining every sinew in preparation for war could be cajoled into taking over a responsibility of the civil power was indeed naive.

61 PRONI HA/32/1/748, E. W. Scales to Sir Ernest Holderness, 24 August 1939. Bates, the letter went on, would be glad to offer such supplementary assistance as might be required. This was disingenuousness in scarlet ink, stealth with ankle bells.

62 PRONI HA/32/1/748, E. W. Scales to Major-General R. V. Pollock, 14 October 1939.

63 These exchanges were essentially about resources. Once that issue had been resolved and internment was confirmed as a Northern Ireland rather than an imperial responsibility, it became possible to examine in more detached terms the respective responsibilities with regard to persons thought to be subversive. An interesting exchange arose in late October 1940 concerning the case of Charles Robert Short (alias O'Donald), who was the subject of a Security Service (MI5) file. That file is not now accessible, but since the Security Service had no responsibility for investigating Irish republicans, it seems likely that Short was suspect because of pro-German views or activities. In his case, detention under Defence Regulation 18B was deemed appropriate rather than the Special Powers Act, 1933, under which he was initially detained. Short had not been brought into association with the republican internees and detainees, and there was no intention of doing so. Authority had therefore to be obtained for an 18B detention in Northern Ireland. This necessitated action on the part of the Governor of Northern Ireland, who designated the Government of Northern Ireland as a Regional Commissioner under the Statutory Regulations and Order 1940, No. 1536. The order of detention was then apparently made (PRONI HA/41/7).

64 PRONI HA/32/1/748, Summary letter, Adrian Robinson, Secretary, Ministry of Home Affairs, to Captain G. H. Petherick, 25 October 1940.

65 One man helpfully decided to remove all doubt by giving the Nazi salute when arrested (PRONI HA/32/1/176, Internment Advisory Committee, Miscellaneous papers, 4 and 6 December 1941).

66 For an interesting recent account of the prison, see Patrick Greg, *The Crum: Inside the Crumlin Road Prison* (Dublin: Gill & Macmillan, 2007), especially pp. 15–35.

67 The term 'local prisoner' referred to anyone sentenced to imprisonment, usually with hard labour, but sometimes without, as distinct from the convict, who had been sentenced to penal servitude (three years and more).

68 PRONI HA/32/1/748, E. W. Scales to Commander Oscar Henderson, Private Secretary to Governor, 17 November 1939.

69 PRONI HA/32/1/748, 'I understand they have settled down there quite comfortably and are comparatively well-behaved' (Captain T. M. Stuart to Home Affairs, 12 November 1939). Thomas Moore Stuart (1888–1959) had served and been wounded in the First World War. He joined Belfast Prison as Deputy Governor in 1922, transferring to Londonderry as Governor in 1938, then back to Belfast, where he served until retirement in 1953.

70 Surviving records do not give exact dates but that visits had been suspended in late November is confirmed in Ministry correspondence. PRONI HA/9/2/192, Captain A. Fryer to Home Affairs, 16 December 1939; Adrian Robinson to L. J. Mason, Ministry of Finance, 8 January 1940.

71 PRONI HA/9/2/192, Sir Dawson Bates to Captain A. Fryer, 16 November 1939.

72 Following the First World War, the prison had been used for the confinement of criminal lunatics (see *Derry Standard*, 23 August 1944, 9e).

73 Fryer would go on to serve as Governor of Malone Borstal and Reformatory School.

74 PRONI HA/9/2/192.

75 PRONI HA/9/2/192, Captain A. Fryer to Ministry of Home Affairs, 16 December 1939. With some understatement he noted that 'on the whole, the conduct of Internees in only "Fair"'.

76 PRONI HA/9/2/192, Fryer to Ministry, 23 December 1939. Beside the last comment, an unknown ministry hand had scribbled 'Oh Yeah' – retrospectively presumably. The general misbehaviour was carrying on but, ever optimistic, Fryer observed 'the conduct of Internees is slightly improved'.

77 PRONI HA/9/2/192, Fryer to Ministry, 26 December 1939.

78 Liam Burke recalled the pressure of the water jets being so intense that it took plaster off the walls and drenched the prisoners: high pressure indeed.

79 Details are given in Fryer's report to Home Affairs the following day, together with some statements from staff (PRONI HA/9/2/192, Fryer to Ministry, 26 December 1939). See also the *Irish Independent* (26 December 1939, 7d) and the *Glasgow Herald* (27 December 1939, 8b) for accounts of the riot.

80 MacEoin, *The IRA in the Twilight Years, op. cit.*, p. 443.

81 The *Irish Independent* reported that the internees had thrown bottles and that three RUC men had been slightly injured (26 December 1939, 7d).

82 *Irish Independent*, 26 December 1939, 7d.

83 *Derry Journal*, 27 December 1939, 4d.

84 *Daily Express*, 1 January 1940, 7c; *Irish Press*, 28 December 1939, 7c.

85 Fryer should have been cautious about the presence of a B-Special in the prison since, less than twenty years before, staff had been infiltrated to effect an escape, with tragic consequences (see above, p. 136). As it happened, the IRA had, around this time, directed at least one of its members, Desmond Hedley Wright, a Protestant, to join the Special Constabulary. Although Wright was unmasked in 1942, this ploy

showed what might be done within an organisation by this time open to those with the correct background. See obituary of Wright, 'IRA Member Who Infiltrated B-Specials', *Irish Times*, 7 March, 2009, 12c.

86 PRONI HA/9/2/192, Green (Home Affairs) to Adrian Robinson, 16 January 1940.

87 PRONI HA/9/2/192, Green to Adrian Robinson, 16 January 1940; and Adrian Robinson to Captain A. Fryer, 24 January 1940.

88 This figure excluded the fifteen men who had applied to the Advisory Committee and been ostracised by the remainder and who could be expected to behave well. Five others had been released by order of the Advisory Committee since the transfer to Derry had been effected: the protesting group therefore was reduced to forty-five.

89 PRONI HA/9/2/192, Adrian Robinson to Captain A. Fryer, 24 and 30 January 1940.

90 PRONI HA/9/2/192, Robinson to Fryer, 24 January 1940. Robinson had emphasised that if the prisoners could not get into a part of the prison where they could stand a siege, 'they can be taught such a salutary lesson without publicity or fuss as will discourage any further attempt'. This can only be read as a contemplation (and thus approval) of rough, even brutal, handling. Such summary (and illegal) punishment, we know from various sources, was not unknown in the police stations and prisons of the time.

91 PRONI HA/9/2/192, Adrian Robinson to L. J. Mason, 8 January 1940. It is noteworthy that a request for this very modest alteration and expenditure had to be made at such a high official level.

92 PRONI HA/9/2/192, E. W. Scales to Captain A. Fryer, 16 January 1940. All newspapers and journals were subject to strict inspection.

93 PRONI HA/9/2/192, Captain A. Fryer to Ministry of Home Affairs, 13 January 1940. This must have been permitted by Seán McArdle, the OC, whose stand until then was, in compliance with IRA procedure, that all contacts with staff went through him.

94 PRONI HA/9/2/192, Internees to Minister for Home Affairs, 25 December 1939. The original is in block capitals. The letter is annotated 'Submitted – found attached to Lavatory in which Officer Magill was locked in.' Liam Burke gave a different account of the letter, which, he recalled, was given to the Governor on Christmas morning by McArdle (MacEoin, *The IRA in the Twilight Years, op. cit.*, p. 443). The text of the copy that Burke had preserved is identical with that in the Home Affairs file (p. 461).

95 His concern, understandably, did not extend to ordinary prisoners, and arrangements were therefore made to transfer men serving sentences of three months and more from Belfast to Derry (PRONI HA/9/2/164, Home Affairs to Finance, 5 August 1941).

96 PRONI HA/32/1/176, Internment Advisory Committee, Miscellaneous papers, Summary memorandum, 10 September 1940.

97 The Commissioners did in fact have sufficient accommodation available but slipped out of the Northern Ireland request with the qualification that none of it was likely to be of use.

98 PRONI HA/32/1/176, Summary Memorandum, Adrian Robinson to Captain G. H. Petherick, 25 October 1940.

99 By December, Churchill was writing to Roosevelt about the fatal prospects should British shipping losses in the Atlantic continue at their existing rate. Even in September 1940 (the figures probably becoming available several weeks later), the dangerous shortfall was all too clear. Martin Gilbert (ed.), *The Churchill War Papers: Never Surrender, May 1940–December 1940* (London: Heinemann, 1993–4), vol. II, pp. 1189–97.

100 On 3 July 1940, the Royal Navy attacked and sank the French fleet at Mers-el-Kébir, Algeria. Protracted negotiations had failed, and the British feared that the fleet

would fall into German hands. Just under 1,300 French sailors died in the action. Vichy French merchantmen were seized as opportunity allowed.

101 PRONI HA/32/1/748, Adrian Robinson to R. Gransden, 7 August 1940.

102 PRONI HA/32/1/748. On the *Argenta*, see p. 328 above.

103 PRONI HA/32/1/748, Robinson to Gransden, 7 August 1940.

104 It is not clear how many of the ship's crew came to Strangford Lough. This had originally been around 100 men, with a number of European officers and supervisors. Robinson observed at the time that although they were paid a very low wage, 'and their upkeep is very small', a crew of 100 seemed very large for an idle ship (PRONI HA/32/1/176, Internment Advisory Committee, Miscellaneous papers, Summary memorandum, 10 September 1940).

105 PRONI HA/32/1/748, Adrian Robinson to J. T. Harvey, 2 August 1940. The remaining custodial staff consisted of a chief, and three principal and forty-three basic grade officers. Arrangements were put in hand for a permanent or visiting medical officer and chaplain (PRONI HA/32/1/176, Internment Advisory Committee, Miscellaneous papers, Summary Memorandum, 10 September 1940). The chaplain, Father Enda Elliott, was subsequently praised by Sir Dawson Bates and by the Ministry, who were 'very pleased indeed with the way in which he has carried out his somewhat difficult duties and, particularly, with the splendid influences he has had on the internees' (PRONI HA/9/2/115, Home Office to Roman Catholic Bishop of Down and Connor, 11 February 1941).

106 PRONI HA/9/2/402, Ration Certificate, 15 November 1940; *Sunday Express*, 6 October 1940.

107 Waugh must be credited with supplementing the sombre notion of 'fog of war' with the equally evocative and opposite 'farce of war'. This is brilliantly and hilariously explored in his *Men at Arms* trilogy (London: Chapman & Hall, 1952–65).

108 *NIPD*, vol. 23, col. 1994, 17 September 1940. It was, he declared, 'essential that accommodation be found for the internment of disloyal citizens of Northern Ireland'. He was 'quite satisfied with the precautions which have been taken to ensure the safety of those on board'.

109 PRONI HA/32/1/748, Adrian Robinson to Captain G. H. Petherick, 25 October 1940.

110 The actual communication in which the proposal was made has not survived in the file, but references to the 'Canadian wire' in connection with the British response leave little doubt as to what was suggested, while obscuring by whom. It would seem, from the arrangement and sequence of papers, that the proposal arose from a private discussion at Stormont between Sir James Craig (who was only weeks away from death), Dawson Bates and John MacDermott, then Attorney General. Robinson was not present at the discussion (PRONI HA/32/1/748, Cabinet Secretariat memo, 26 September 1940).

111 PRONI HA/32/1/748, Coded telegram, 27 September 1940. There had that day been a report in *Truth*, the Roman Catholic journal published in London, deploring the vulnerability of the *Al Rawdah* to air attack. If the reports were true, this was 'a first class scandal', which should be investigated immediately both on grounds of humanity and because Britain should never give Goebbels the opportunity of returning 'a *tu quoque* when we inveigh against Nazi concentration camps' (*Truth*, Friday, 27 September 1940, vol. 128, p. 276). See also a rehearsal of this argument in the Northern Ireland Senate a few weeks later (*Irish Press*, 23 October 1940, 1h).

112 PRONI HA/32/1/748, Adrian Robinson to W. B. Spender, Ministry of Finance, 30 September 1940.

113 PRONI HA/32/1/748, Colonel C. J. N. Greenwood, I/C Administration to Adrian Robinson, 1 October 1940. Waspishly, Robinson wrote back on 3 October, grateful

for the offer of advice on how to construct a camp, offering Home Affairs' advice any time the Army was perplexed about the best way 'in which to repel an invasion or storm a redoubt'. Absolutely free of charge, the Ministry, the Public Health and the Derating Section would also be at the Army's disposal: 'We cannot allow ourselves to be outbid in helpfulness' (PRONI HA/32/1/748, Robinson to Greenwood, 3 October 1940).

114 The mood was not helped when T. J. Campbell, the Nationalist MP, got hold of a version of the debacle and raised it in Stormont on 15 October 1940, implying that Belfast had misled the British government (*NIPD*, vol. 23, cols. 2350–1; see also *Irish News*, 16 October 1940, 1f).

115 PRONI HA/32/1/748, Adrian Robinson to Cabinet Secretary Robert Gransden, 2 October 1940.

116 PRONI HA/32/1/748, Robinson to Gransden, 2 October 1940. The *Irish News* (7 October 1940, 4f) reported that at first seven and then a further twenty were taken on shore. This was inaccurate. During October, only nine men were transferred to Belfast, and one was released (PRONI HA/9/2/402, Ration Certificate, 15 November 1940).

117 PRONI HA/32/1/748, Robinson to Gransden, 2 October 1940.

118 PRONI HA/32/1/748, Neil Gillespie, on behalf of *Al Rawdah* internees, to Minister for Home Affairs, 4 October 1940. See also *Irish News*, 16 October 1940, 5e.

119 See *Irish Independent*, 29 October 1940, 5f.

120 PRONI HA/9/2/402, Memorandum, 3 October 1940.

121 This embarrassed both parties. The internees, through wives, sought to counter the impression that they had petitioned to stay on the *Al Rawdah*, which would have been the revolutionaries' equivalent to lese-majesty. It was a matter of indifference to them where they were confined, 'provided that their political status is unimpaired' (see *Irish News*, 17 October 1940, 5d–f).

122 *Sunday Express*, 6 October 1940; see also *Irish News*, 16 October 1940, 5e. Prison officers (or at least forty-four of them) had sent a round robin to the Ministry, expressing satisfaction with their *Al Rawdah* posting. They disavowed complaints that had been made by the newly recognised Prison Officers Association (PRONI HA/9/2/406, Note to Ministry of Home Affairs, 14 November 1940).

123 PRONI HA/32/1/748, Adrian Robinson to GOC, 10 October 1940.

124 PRONI HA/32/1/748, J. B. O'Neill, Ministry of Public Security, Memorandum, 18 October 1940.

125 PRONI HA/32/1/748. These figures have to be set against an average daily population at Derry of no more than thirty-five in the years between 1927 and 1937 (PRONI HA/9/2/59, Population Table, 1927–47).

126 PRONI HA/32/1/748, Adrian Robinson to Major L. E. Curran, 22 October 1940.

127 The Northern Ireland government was at least spared the embarrassment of revealing the cost of the episode, pleading the public interest – particularly convincing in time of war (*NIPD*, vol. 23, col. 1994, 17 September 1940). Some notion of the additional cost emerged when supplementary estimates were published on 25 February 1941. An extra £5,800 was required for the *Al Rawdah* and an extra £15,890 for the prisons' vote as a whole (*Belfast Newsletter*, 26 February 1941, 5d–e; Supplementary Estimates, 25 February 1941).

128 PRONI HA/32/1/748. There were hints that the latter may have entailed extra expense. W. B. Spender to Robert Gransden, 8 January 1941; W. B. Spender to Adrian Robinson, 11 January 1941; Adrian Robinson to W. B. Spender, 14 January 1941.

129 PRONI HA/32/1/748, Robinson to Spender, 14 January 1941.

130 PRONI HA/32/1/748, Ministry to Divisional Sea Transport Officer, 23 January 1941.

131 Ninety-two of the remaining 178 men were transferred on 11 February and the remainder on 13 February (PRONI HA/9/2/402, Ration Certificate, 15 February 1941).

132 See p. 554, n. 99 above.

133 PRONI HA/9/2/405, Governor, *Al Rawdah*, to Secretary, Ministry of Home Affairs, 28 January 1941. The report was accompanied by a sketch of the escape route, but the captured escaper (who was held in close confinement) was not named.

134 They were held at the prison entirely separately from the other prisoners, not mixing even for religious services. PRONI HA/9/2/115, Dr Daniel Mageehan, Bishop of Down and Connor to Ministry of Home Affairs, 31 January 1941.

135 This was reflected in costs. The Ministry of Home Affairs had originally budgeted for the victualling of internees in the sum of £5,350 but in February 1941 had to bring in a revised estimate of £9,950 – not far short of a doubling of anticipated costs (*Belfast Newsletter*, 26 February 1941, 5d–e; Supplementary estimates, 25 February 1941).

136 For a journalistic description of the *Al Rawdah* dietary and routine, see the *Sunday Express*, 6 October 1940.

137 There is no record of an internee at this point seeking compassionate parole, but the issue was raised more generally by a spokesman two years later. The Ministry decided that a general rule would be inappropriate and that it would continue to make decisions case by case (PRONI HA/9/2/176, Minute, 16 August 1943).

138 Visitors seem, at least on occasion, to have smuggled letters off the ship. It was presumably no more difficult to take them on board. See PRONI HA/32/1/740, Letter to Nora O'Kane, Draperstown, c.20 November 1940. This was taken off the ship by M. McNamee who had visited her brother of 19 November 1940 and who then posted the letter to Nora. It was picked up in the general interception of post then in force (see above, pp. 94–97).

139 See *Irish News*, 19 November 1940, 1d; 20 November 1940, 1e–f.

140 PRONI HA/32/1/740, Letter to Nora O'Kane, Draperstown, Co. Londonderry, c.20 November 1940. The writer, who signed himself only as 'A7' was greatly moved: 'The scream of the gulls the only sound, the lovely sunset and his comrades carrying him on his last journey. It was most impressive.'

141 PRONI HA/32/1/740, County Inspector E. Gilfillan, Inspector-General's Office to H. C. Montgomery, Assistant Secretary, Ministry of Home Affairs, 6 February 1941.

142 PRONI HA/32/1/740, H. C. Montgomery to E. Gilfillan, 11 February 1941.

143 See Seán McConville, *Irish Political Prisoners, 1848–1922: Theatres of War* (London and New York: Routledge, 2003), p. 461.

144 PRONI HA/32/1/740, Letter to Nora O'Kane. He continued, 'Patsy Peter has been turned down [for visits] and another chum of Patsy's McGookin approved. Maybe on account of her job Peggy wouldn't care to come. Find out as soon as you can and let me know.' Applications for visiting orders were assessed by the RUC and reports were made to the Ministry. These examined both the claimed relationship to the internee and the would-be visitor's political affiliations, both grounds for turning down an application. The former was to thwart political contacts who were not kin or long-standing friends from visiting to conduct IRA business. On 18 October 1940, for example, three persons who had applied to visit were reported as suitable, but two others were considered suspect. Both were thought to have links to Cumann na mBan and were reported as 'very hostile and bitterly opposed towards the police' (PRONI HA/32/1/678, Inspector-General's Office, RUC, to Secretary, Home Affairs, 18 October 1940). The Army was also interested in any of its personnel who applied to visit internees. It requested the Ministry for information on conversations between army personnel and internees and other prisoners whom they might visit (PRONI HA/32/1/680, Army HQ to Ministry of Justice, 8 July 1943).

145 See PRONI HA/32/1/748, Sir Dawson Bates to Major-General V. N. N. Majendie, GOC, Northern Ireland District, 21 September 1942.

146 By this point, Captain Stuart estimated that some 85 per cent of his charges were members of the IRA (*Irish News*, 16 April 1942, 3b–c).

147 An outline of the campaign is provided by J. Bowyer Bell in his *Secret Army, op. cit.*, pp. 225–6. An audacious cross-border raid on 1 September 1942 in which an RUC patrol car and its occupants were captured was followed eight days later in the South by the murder of a Special Branch detective at his Rathfarnham, Co. Dublin, home.

148 Special Powers Act, 1922, Regulation 23, *Regulations and Orders* (Belfast: HM Stationery Office, 1934).

149 As before, an Advisory Committee examined applications for release, following the provisions of the Special Powers Act. The *Irish News* reported in October 1940 that approximately forty men had applied for release. All denied IRA connections, were willing to enter into bail and to abide by any condition that might be required. All these applications were refused, and, in consequence, seven went on hunger strike (*Irish News*, 14 October 1940, 1e).

150 PRONI HA/32/1/748, Captain T. M. Stuart to H. C. Montgomery, 6 September 1942.

151 There had been complaints by the Nationalist Party politician, Thomas McLaughlin, in the Northern Ireland Senate about the work of the Advisory Committee at this time. The Dominions Office was sufficiently concerned about McLaughlin's claim that the conditions were 'shocking' that it asked Home Affairs for rebuttal material to be used by its press attaché in Dublin (PRONI HA/32/1/726, Home Office to Ministry of Home Affairs, 26 October 1942). The Dominions Office had only noticed McLaughlin's claim when it was referred to some months later by the *Irish Independent* (20 October 1942, 2g). McLaughlin had then called for an investigation by the ICRC, and this had presumably alarmed London. Ignorance of prison conditions was at this time not entirely the Ministry's fault, reflexively secretive though it was. Elementary security precautions had necessitated the unannounced move of the internees. Following complaints in the Northern Ireland Senate by the Nationalist Senators Thomas McLaughlin and Thomas McAllister in October 1942, Dawson Bates invited them and other Nationalist members of the Northern Ireland Parliament to visit Belfast Prison and see conditions for themselves. The Nationalist politicians – reflexive in their own way – declined to take up the offer (PRONI HA/32/1/726, Home Affairs to Home Office, 28 October 1942). See also *NIPD*, vol. 24, col. 2310, 25 November 1941. The offer of a visit was made several times – and refused.

152 PRONI HA/32/1/748, Dawson Bates to GOC, c.20 September 1942. The request was agreed at once, and a few days later the Ministry was in touch with the Army's Chief Engineer about the details of delivery and erection.

153 PRONI HA/32/1/726. For reasons of security neither internees nor relatives were given advance warning. This caused some inconvenience in the supply of clean laundry, and there were some sad domestic tales of the consequences of missed visits (see *Irish News*, 19 October 1942, 1a–b).

154 *Irish Independent*, 20 October 1942, 2g; *Irish News*, 19 October 1942, 1a.

155 PRONI HA/32/1/726, Report by Prison Officer Johnston to Governor, Londonderry Prison, 1 January 1943.

156 PRONI HA/9/2/190, Captain A. Fryer, to Ministry of Home Affairs, 9 August 1943. Internment did not confer total immunity, however, since an offender could either be transferred to the more stringent conditions of the ordinary prison, or, alternatively, might be held back to serve the sentence when other internees were eventually released.

157 PRONI HA/9/2/190, Ministry memorandum, 1 March 1943. The 'no previous residence in the city' rule reflected the Ministry's concern that in such a small town

there would be childhood and other links between staff and prisoners (PRONI HA/32/1/860, Committee of Inquiry into Escape of 20 March 1943, f. 26).

158 PRONI HA/9/2/190, Orders of 15 and 21 August 1944; PRONI HA/9/2/154, R. G. Ronaldson (Prisons' Section, Ministry of Home Affairs) to Captain A. Fryer, 12 August 1944. Most transferees had Belfast addresses. Following this, Derry Prison was again used for ordinary prisoners (*Derry Standard*, 23 August 1944, 9e; *Belfast Newsletter*, 22 August 1944, 2g).

159 Agnes Ryan, an organiser of the Irish Prisoners' Aid Society in Derry, was arrested at a meeting of the group, in possession of IRA documents. She refused to recognise the court during subsequent proceedings and was sentenced to a total of twelve months' imprisonment. While she was in custody her shop was searched and a magazine for a Thompson sub-machine gun was found. For this offence she received a further sentence of three years penal servitude (PRONI HA/41/31).

160 *NIPD*, vol. 23, cols. 1993–4, 17 September 1940. The emphatic refusal to give assistance was given by Sir Dawson Bates in response to a question from Northern Ireland Labour Party MPs Paddy Agnew and Jack Beattie. See also *NIPD*, vol. 23, col. 1408, 11 June 1940.

161 For the Green Cross, see below, pp. 728–30.

162 PRONI HA/9/2/402, Governor, Armagh Prison to Home Affairs, 7 December 1943.

163 By 1944, the Green Cross letterhead showed five Nationalist MPs and three Nationalist Senators in various positions of sponsorship and responsibility. For Healy's Second World War detention in England, see the succinct and informative article by Eamon Phoenix, 'Cahir Healy (1877–1970): Northern Nationalist Leader', *Clogher Record*, 18 (1): 32–52.

164 PRONI HA/32/1/828, Monthly Intelligence Summary, 1941.

165 *Irish Freedom*, June 1942.

166 Stephen Anselm Roche (1890–1949), a Trinity College Dublin graduate (1914, BA and LLB). Joined the Department of Home Affairs (later renamed Department of Justice) in 1922. He drafted the Offences Against the State Acts but was cautious about the extension of police powers and of internment.

167 NAI JUS/8/869, Stephen Roche to Gerald Boland, 17 October 1940.

168 This message was passed to Katharine Moloney by William Norton, leader of the Labour Party and confirmed by Boland in a telephone call (NAI JUS/8/869, Katharine Moloney to Gerald Boland, 28 October 1940). A few days before, Roche had written to Kathleen Barry stating that the Minister had decided that 'in the existing circumstances' it would not be in the public interest to permit a collection 'along the lines indicated' (the last referring to advertisements and other publicity) (NAI JUS/8/869, Stephen Roche to Kathleen Barry, 23 October 1940).

169 NAI JUS/8/869, Secretary General, Department of Posts & Telegraphs to Department of the Taoiseach, 11 August 1941. Caution ruled, and, following a government (Cabinet) discussion on 3 September, it was agreed that the broadcast should not be permitted. NAI JUS/8/869, M. O'Muimhneachair (Department of the Taoiseach) to Secretary General, Posts & Telegraphs, 4 September 1941.

170 PRONI HA/32/1/828, Ministry of Finance to Ministry of Home Affairs, 21 July 1942.

171 PRONI HA/82/1/828, Inspector-General's Office, RUC, to Secretary, Home Affairs, 22 March 1945. The Ministry remained dissatisfied, particularly by the evocation of Pearse. Officials thought that the Ministry of Education should be told about Morgan's activities.

172 *Irish News*, 5 December 1942, 3c.

173 PRONI HA/32/1/828, Circular notice, undated, but probably 1942. The balance in the sum collected and funds disbursed was presumably met by monies remitted from outside Northern Ireland.

174 *Irish Times*, 8 March 1943, 1d–f. Eamon Donnelly (1877–1944), republican abstentionist MP for the Falls, contended that outside Belfast no outdoor (i.e. non-workhouse) relief was granted to dependants. In Belfast it was granted, but only on the production of a medical certificate (*Irish News*, 5 December 1942, 3c). Donnelly was very active in the Green Cross and was credited with raising the then very considerable sum of £45,000. Daniel Mageean (1907–62) was strong in his condemnation of what he saw as anti-Catholic discrimination in Northern Ireland.

175 PRONI HA/32/1/828. The implication was not entirely clear, but the suggestion that some were interned only because of their religious affiliation, which was untrue.

176 By mid-1943, Begley had been replaced as chairman by Judge Davison.

177 Both the substantive Act and the Regulations were amended many times. A number of key provisions made their way into related legislation in the Irish Free State and in Northern Ireland.

178 This dilemma of security versus the rule of law, immediate security gains (often wrapping up party-political necessities) versus a subversion of the rule of law remains contentious. In an age of mass murder by international terrorists, some politicians would point out, it is easier to state the dilemmas than to resolve them.

179 PRONI HA/32/1/676, Ministry of Home Affairs, Minute, c.1946.

180 This probably refers to John Fox who had been a member of the IRA Army Council and who, among other spells in custody, had been sentenced to two years' hard labour following his arrest and trial in the Crown Entry affair (see pp. 395–96). See MacEoin, *The IRA in the Twilight Years, op. cit.*, pp. 129 and 381.

181 PRONI HA/32/1/176, Internment Advisory Committee, miscellaneous papers, 15 October 1940. The minute of the decision noted that Kelly also was a hunger-striker.

182 PRONI HA/32/1/176. McCann admitted that he had collected funds for the Prisoners' Aid Association but denied ever having been a member of the IRA. Police intelligence claimed that he had been Transport Officer of the IRA and OC of the Newry area. His appeal was rejected.

183 PRONI HA/32/1/176. This man was also marked as a hunger-striker.

184 PRONI HA/32/1/176, Advisory Committee to Parliamentary Secretary, Ministry of Home Affairs, 14 November 1940. In time, some men resubmitted their appeals as many as seven times (PRONI HA/32/1/175, Internment Advisory Committee meetings, 4–6 November 1941).

185 *NIPD*, vol. 25, cols. 515–18, 10 March 1942. Jack Beattie (1886–1960) was a maverick socialist who had various Labour affiliations during his career. He was a consistent campaigner on unemployment and public relief issues. A Protestant, he supported Irish unification, differing on this from the majority of the Northern Ireland Labour Party.

186 PRONI HA/32/1/176, Internment Advisory Committee, Miscellaneous papers, 11 March 1942.

187 *NIPD*, vol. 25, cols. 517–18, 10 March 1942.

188 See, for example, the case of Patrick Hughes, considered on 16 April 1941 (PRONI HA/32/1/175, Internment Advisory Committee Meetings).

189 PRONI HA/32/1/175, 18 September 1941.

190 See the cases of Samuel Francis McNellis (fourth appeal, 8 December 1943) and Patrick Murray (third appeal, 13 December 1943) (PRONI HA/32/1/175).

191 PRONI HA/32/1/175. See the case of Joseph Patrick McKinney, 10 February 1944.

192 PRONI HA/32/1/175, Captain A. Fryer to H. C. Montgomery, 23 November 1943.

193 PRONI HA/32/1/175, Meetings of 28–30 March and 9 May 1944.

194 PRONI HA/32/1/175, Summary of cases handled.

195 PRONI HA/32/1/828, Minute, 20 December 1944. The delegation also told the Minister that the Green Cross Fund was not in a healthy state and that they could not support dependants indefinitely.

196 Bell, *Secret Army*, *op. cit.*, p. 240.

197 *NIPD*, vol. 28, col. 427, 14 March 1945. Warnock agreed with Beattie that prison conditions were not as they should be. As soon as the Government could do better it would. He pointed out that 477 persons were interned in Éire compared with 282 in Northern Ireland and that Éire conditions were 'vastly more rigorous than they were in Northern Ireland' (col. 424). A month later, Warnock reiterated these views in an interview with the *Empire News*, responding to the question as to whether he was prepared to follow Herbert Morrison (Home Secretary) and release all internees (15 April 1945).

198 PRONI HA/32/1/892, Note of Deputation to Prime Minister and Minister for Home Affairs, 8 May 1945. The plight of families and the risk of embittering a section of the community were also raised.

199 PRONI HA/32/1/892.

200 PRONI HA/32/1/892.

201 PRONI HA/32/1/892, T. J. Campbell to Sir Basil Brooke, 3 June 1945. The correspondence appeared in the *Irish News* (7 June 1945, 1a–b). Apart from the general unwillingness to acknowledge that there had been anything like a threat from the IRA, Campbell was wrong on two points: a police recommendation was necessary for internment, not a 'scrap of paper', and the number of women interned at this point was nine rather than twenty.

202 PRONI HA/32/1/892, Inspector-General's Office to H. C. Montgomery, 23 May 1945. The reported conversation had taken place on 17 May. The letter was annotated 'Shown to Minister'.

203 PRONI HA/32/1/892. At the time of writing there were 136 internees and two detainees in Belfast Prison, six Belfast and three Derry women in Armagh Prison. Some eighty-two men convicted of IRA offences were also serving sentences in Belfast Prison.

204 PRONI HA/32/1/892. With demobilisation and the winding down of war industries and rising unemployment there was some expectation of industrial unrest by the end of 1946. (See interview with Edmond Warnock, *Empire News*, 15 April 1945.)

205 Those who had been interned in 1939 and who remained in custody in 1945 had completed the equivalent of a nine-year prison sentence (one-third remission being granted as standard). A sentence of this length would have been imposed for a serious criminal offence such as rape, grievous bodily harm or aggravated robbery.

206 PRONI HA/32/1/892, Inspector-General's Office to H. C. Montgomery, 23 May 1945. The Inspector-General had already discussed the transfer idea with the Minister.

207 PRONI HA/32/1/892, Captain T. M. Stuart to H. C. Montgomery, 11 June 1945. Stuart cautioned that the mood of the internees was unsettled and that the internal police guard should not be withdrawn from the prison.

208 PRONI HA/32/1/892, Agnes Patricia (Una) MacDowell to Mrs Creen, 9 June 1945. She also referred to the '"Atrocity"' camps that the British had found in Germany and compared them to Belfast Prison 'where an Internee was stripped naked and kicked a few weeks ago'. This crass and repulsive comment can only have arisen from her ignorance of the enormities at Belsen and the other camps, or a refusal to believe reports. The letter was, of course, composed with the knowledge that it would be seen by the prison censor and that its contents would be noted – as indeed they were.

209 PRONI HA/32/1/892, Nora (Nancy) Ward to Maur(een), 11 June 1945. The letter continued, without a perceptible change of gear, to discuss knitting and embroidery and concluded with a request for wool and soap.

210 PRONI HA/32/1/892, 'Nonie' (Annie Ward?) to Jack, 10 June 1945. The letter ended with a threat that 'the time is soon coming when we'll put into practice the Motto "God helps those etc."'.

211 PRONI HA/32/1/892, A. Ronald Booth to H. C. Montgomery, 11 June 1945.

212 The epigram was composed by Sir Edward Marsh after the First World War. Sir Edward Marsh, *A Number of People: A Book of Reminiscences* (London: Heinemann, 1939), p. 152. Churchill used it in each of his volumes of *The Second World War* (London: Cassell, 1948). The line 'In war: resolution' was perhaps the sentiment that bound the irreconcilable internees. This would have resonated with the now venerable and revered republican doctrine that victory came to those who could most endure.

213 The results were: Unionist Party, thirty-three; Nationalist Party, ten; Northern Ireland Labour Party, two; Independent Unionists, two; Commonwealth Labour Party, one; Independent Labour Party, one; Socialist Republican, one. Twenty candidates were elected unopposed: thirteen Unionist; six Nationalist; one Independent Unionist.

214 On the Dublin arrests, see Bell, *Secret Army, op. cit.*, p. 241.

215 PRONI HA/32/1/892, Cabinet Meeting, 5 July 1945. The only dissent came from William Grant, Minister for Health and Local Government, who remained concerned about timing. He wanted the announcement made sooner rather than later lest there be an appearance of yielding to the Nationalist pressures that could be expected when Stormont reconvened.

216 That this timing was a decision of Brooke and Warnock and not the officials, is confirmed in a letter to the RUC Inspector-General from H. C. Montgomery at Home Affairs: 'the official intimation… only reached me on the 13th instant and it now only remains to implement the Government decision' (PRONI HA/32/1/892, Home Affairs to RUC, 16 July 1945).

217 PRONI HA/32/1/892.

218 PRONI HA/32/1/892, RUC Inspector-General's Office to Home Affairs, 23 July 1945. The eleven men had allegedly variously and severally been involved in the attempted murders of Raymond Moore, C. Costello, Head Constable William Fannin, Special Constable Armstrong, and R. J. Hyndman. Three of the men had been involved in the attempt on Fannin. For an interview with Fannin, long after the event, see Tim Pat Coogan, *The IRA* (London: Fontana, 1980), pp. 236–7. Two were thought to have had a part in the murder of Constable Patrick McCarthy during a robbery at the Clonard Mill in the Falls Road district on 1 October 1943 (*Irish Times*, 2 October 1943, 1d). One had allegedly been implicated in the murder of prison officer Thomas Walker on 6 February 1942. Two others were thought to have been involved in the murder of Daniel Connolly.

219 PRONI HA/32/1/892, Informal note of Minister's decision, dated 26 July 1945. One man was added to the second wave of releases before his time because he had given information to the Governor of Belfast Prison.

220 The women were as follows: Mary (Molly) Helena Craig, Catherine O'Hara, Nora (Nancy) Ward, Annie Teresa Ward, Agnes Patricia (Una) McDowell, Teresa Donnelly, Alice Ashton, Rosaleen McCotter and Mary Ann McDonald. Three were from Derry and six from Belfast. PRONI HA/32/1/892, H. C. Montgomery to Inspector-General, RUC, 26 July 1945; see also *Irish News*, 28 July 1945, 1b. Mary Craig had been held since 1941.

221 *Irish News*, 28 July 1945, 1b.

222 PRONI HA/32/1/892, Captain T. M. Stuart, Belfast Prison, to Secretary, Home Affairs, 30 July 1945, with annotated list. One of the internees, not involved in the

demonstration, wrote to reassure his mother. The incident had been 'a bit of a scuffle but nothing like what the papers had it'. One man had been struck 'but is running around to-day as if nothing had happened there never was even need for as much as bandage'. He had been in the exercise yard at the time but regarded the incident as little more than 'a bit of a send off' for the released men (PRONI HA/ 32/1/892, Frank Ross to Mrs W. Ross, Dungannon, 1 August 1945). On 31 July 1945, Warnock told Stormont that 184 internees remained (*NIPD*, vol. 29, col. 234); see also *Irish News*, 31 July 1945, 3e. Six of the thirty-three released on 31 July had been in custody since December 1938, a period of more than six and a half years – the equivalent (with remission) of a ten-year sentence.

223 PRONI HA/32/1/892, annotated list, July or August 1945.
224 *NIPD*, vol. 29, col. 303, 31 July 1945.
225 PRONI HA/32/1/892, H. C. Montgomery to Minister, 22 November 1945.
226 *NIPD*, vol. 29, col. 1603, 4 December 1945; *Northern Whig*, 5 December 1945, 3e; *Irish News*, 5 December 1945, 3c. In a subsequent letter to the *Derry Journal*, Eddie McAteer denied that he had been preaching revolutionary action. He had said that if British forces withdrew, 'the Irish people could solve their problems quickly'. Warnock had deliberately misinterpreted this speech, using it as an IRA threat and therefore as an obstacle to the release of the remaining internees. This 'malignant result' had compelled McAteer to write his first letter to a newspaper, 'to do what I can to undermine this latest excuse for internment'. See biographical note below, p. 929, n. 35.
227 PRONI HA/32/1/892, Cabinet meeting, 4 December 1945.
228 PRONI HA/32/1/892, Lists of 14 and 15 December.
229 PRONI HA/32/1/892, Inspector-General, RUC, to Secretary, Ministry of Home Affairs, 8 September 1945.
230 PRONI HA/32/1/892, Minute, 11 December 1945.
231 PRONI HA/32/1/677, Ministry of Home Affairs, minute early 1946.
232 The *Irish Times* (27 August 1949, 1f) reported a Lords speech by the Labour Peer, Lord Calverley, in which it was asserted that, since 1945, the Northern Ireland government had recommended the release of more than 100 persons convicted of serious politically related offences.
233 *Irish Times*, 27 August 1949, 1f.
234 This appears to have been a last-minute decision since Cahill's parents had only that morning been informed by the Labour MP Harry Diamond that the Minister for Home Affairs expected all the men to serve out their sentences. Anderson, *Joe Cahill*, *op. cit.*, p. 105; PRONI CAB/9/B/32/5.

11

IMPRISONMENT IN NORTHERN IRELAND, 1939–48

Cohabitation, conflict and complaisance

IRA prisoners, whatever their legal status, entered into captivity with a well-established repertoire of resistance techniques. The command structure which they invariably established, and on which they insisted, was in itself an act of defiance. The notion of an inmate entity with its own processes was emphatically rejected by the authorities, both at ministry and at prison levels. More practically, however, the closer officials were to day-to-day custodial routine the more convenient it would be to use the mechanisms upon which the prisoners insisted. There were various ways in which this could be done, far short of formal recognition, and the degree of tacit recognition accordingly varied over time and between the prisons and their governors. Captain Thomas Stuart, Governor at Belfast, seems to have resisted most strongly any notion of collective representation. He had to deal with a considerable body of hardened and experienced activists under sentence, and Belfast was a town in which news travelled easily. Stuart was well aware that the Ministry constantly looked over his shoulder. He could not afford to give way on any issue that would attract press or political attention, yet excusal from labour or the wearing of uniform were key demands of those convicted prisoners who sought political or POW status. Over the years, they would pursue these objectives vigorously and would, with equal determination, be resisted by the government. Short of such headline IRA demands, however, and while enforcing the regulations in all their essentials, Stuart, and even more his subordinate officers, worked with the prisoners' command structure to a considerable extent in the domestic routine of the prison. Little of this, understandably, found its way into records or official papers.

At Londonderry and Armagh prisons there was a different tale. For most of the wartime years, as we have seen, the former was used for internees only and the latter held women, only one of whom among the republicans was sentenced.[1] Captain A. Fryer at Derry could allow his internees a deal of latitude. As we shall see, he was not closely supervised or directed by the Ministry – though perhaps he should have been. He was as inexperienced as his charges were devious and calculating. He granted permission to the internees to organise a number of different recreational and educational activities, for the purpose of which cells and association rooms were provided. Signs in Irish were made and displayed about the cell house which, because of their political significance, Stuart could not have tolerated at Belfast. Fryer also acknowledged the internees' OC, and when – after the mass escape of March 1943 – this unauthorised concession emerged, and he was asked to account for himself, he pointed to precedent, going back to 1922.[2] Little more was said about this by the Ministry, probably because a formal rebuke was not justified on such a secondary issue and because it was not a matter of great importance in an internee-only prison, where there was no chance of recognition of the prisoners' command reinforcing pressures from convicted prisoners or stimulating press or political objections that the criminal process was being diminished by a gradual bestowal of political status.

The Armagh Governor, Major G. H. Brush, adopted a similar approach. As far as can now be seen, only one of the republican women held there during the war years was a convicted person, and all the rest were internees. Numbers were very small, and the women adapted themselves easily and quietly to a domestic routine and constructive recreational activities; there was little day-to-day confrontation. Their leader, Catherine (Cassie) O'Hara, was an educated and forceful woman, and there was no point in attempting to pretend that she did not have the respect of her comrades and spoke for them. When three of the women broke away from the main group following a quarrel (the details of which are now lost) and were accommodated in a different part of the prison, the situation was dealt with by Major Brush by acknowledging that there were now two leaders. He was subsequently rebuked for making promises in order to end the women's protests – but not for having contacts with their leaders.[3]

Although it resisted strongly the use of terms such as 'political prisoner', the Ministry recognised that internees were in a very different position from those who had been tried and sentenced. Political views were only part of their reason for internment, associations and supposed activities being the determining factors. This was difficult territory, it was acknowledged that, in times of peace and national security, internment, even where associations were known and worrying, would have been impossible to justify without overt and definite actions. A deal of latitude had therefore to be extended to internees, but not to the extent that concessions should embarrass the government.

For all the differences between penal and preventive detention, internees saw themselves as prisoners. That they had not been subjected to due process – allowed to know what was alleged against them, much less to confront their accusers – added to their frustrations; that no term was fixed to their confinement added yet more. They could apply to the Advisory Committee – a type of ritual purging of guilt by submission – but, as we have seen, many were reluctant to do this, and for a variety of reasons. In the early period of internment, moreover, it was uncertain how the Advisory Committee would receive and process appeals. For those whose politics, affiliations, scruples or dignity barred the Advisory Committee route out of prison, there remained the satisfaction of battles of attrition. In this respect, they and the convicted prisoners occupied similar ground with similar intent.

Little latitude would be extended to convicted prisoners, either those in penal servitude or in ordinary imprisonment. The regimes for both had been devised and consolidated during Victoria's reign and, although modified over the years, were still, by the 1940s, substantially unchanged. A minutely regulated day, limited periods out of cell, tightly controlled movements, obligatory labour, institutional food of a fairly low standard, limited visits and correspondence, and unquestioning submission to all this in a penal, impersonal and comfortless environment made for a harsh experience. Personal possessions were minimal, as were cell comforts, and all under sentence were required to wear a prison uniform. The punitive purposes of the regime included the obvious elements of containment, retribution and deterrence, served by the fact of custody and the disciplinary and psychological pressures to accept shame and to see one's imprisonment as justified exclusion from decent society. A battery of sanctions, from loss of privileges to dietary and corporal punishment, awaited the refractory. Complete and consistent compliance was rewarded by tiny increments of slight but, to the prisoner, highly valued privileges. In every respect, except perhaps custody on the lines of civil or military detention, these objectives and methods were anathema to the IRA. Its traditions, now strong and clear in members' minds, were to resist by whatever means were available and, wherever possible, to take the fight to the enemy. As we shall see, during the wartime years, opportunities for the latter were so scant as to be almost non-existent.

Both imprisonment and penal servitude are discussed above.[4] Joe Cahill's account of his years in Belfast Prison includes a description of daily life, confirming its Victorian austerity.[5] In one respect, however, there had been a departure from the model: prisoners were permitted to receive parcels of food and tobacco three times a year: at Christmas, Easter and Halloween. This privilege dated back to the early years of the imprisonment of republican offenders in Northern Ireland. It would not have been countenanced in Britain, but in Northern Ireland it was to be extended in the later years of the 1940s imprisonment. A few other ameliorations were eventually conceded: a dining room for A Wing (instead of eating all meals in cells), longer periods of out-of-cell association, classes and a wider range of reading material.[6] Some of these easements had been won by the republican prisoners but in the main they were granted because of the gradual and general liberalisation in prison policy and management then under way.

None of the IRA's cardinal demands (the right to wear one's own clothes, free association with comrades and excusal from penal labour) were won. A number of hunger strikes and other forms of protest were attempted. None succeeded, and, after the last of them, in 1944, sentenced republican prisoners resigned themselves to serve out their time in prison uniform and to work in the shoe, tailoring and mat shops – traditional prison trades. As Uinseann MacEoin, a republican historian and former prisoner noted, 'In effect the Northern authorities never conceded political treatment until the great hunger strike of 1981 in which ten men died.'[7]

Hunger-striking

There was to be no repeat of the mass hunger strikes of the 1920s, but individuals and small groups of internees did refuse food from time to time. These protests were uniformly unsuccessful. Given wartime conditions, tightly controlled information about prison conditions and incidents, suppression of the IRA and harassment of its support organisations and sympathisers, as well as the determined stance of the Northern Ireland government, it was obvious that self-starvation could not become a key to the prison gates. Strikes were undertaken not with the prospect of release but as short-term protests, to vent frustration or perhaps even to break the monotony. They usually lasted for only a few days and caused little concern to the authorities. Cases were sometimes taken up by Nationalist politicians at Stormont, but there seems to have been little other response from the nationalist community.[8]

The IRA had much experience of hunger-striking. With few exceptions, these actions were unsuccessful, but for there to be even a glimmer of hope strikers had to be few in number, if possible well known, physically and mentally fit and willing to die an awful death. There also had to be strong political support outside, expressed by demonstrations and petitions, and a wide coalition of humanitarian and religious sympathy. If all these conditions could be met, then, by death or near-death, hunger-striking could produce a very considerable gain for the organisation and for the republican cause. At their most successful, these actions could achieve international renown, as with Thomas Ashe (1917) and Terence MacSwiney (1920). Death by starvation or botched force-feeding would invariably embarrass the government and would give rise to domestic concern and Irish-American outrage and lobbying. But such outcomes were rare. Where, as was almost always the case, the strikes were impulsive, ill prepared, general and not coordinated with outside support, they collapsed and damaged IRA morale, credibility and organisation. By 1941, the leadership recognised the very great difficulty of bringing off strikes and issued a general army order forbidding them.[9]

This order had not prevented the internees – not all of whom were subject to IRA discipline – from staging hunger strikes. Wartime conditions meant that almost any open community support was out of the question. Censorship would muffle it, and association with a republican protest was a gilt-edged ticket to internment. But even had outside conditions been more favourable, the issue on which some strikes were called hardly had weight in the wider world. To prevent contraband being passed, *Al Rawdah* visits had taken place in a cabin divided by a wire screen. In response to internees' requests, a portion of the screen was cut out to allow handshakes; some internees climbed on the table and managed to kiss or embrace their visitors.[10] Internees understandably preferred this arrangement to the intimidating and forbidding double-mesh visiting box and close supervision at Belfast Prison. They were, moreover, civil detainees, not criminal prisoners. The issue was taken up with the Governor even before the general transfer from *Al Rawdah* took place on 11 and 13 February 1941. A protest was mounted in support of the open, unscreened visits. On the morning of 8 February, the internees (all held in D Wing) protested by shouting and by refusing to clean cells and empty slops. Determined to stamp out any sign of trouble, Stuart called all available staff to the wing and also asked for RUC help. Unless order were restored, he warned, force would be used. At this, the demonstration collapsed.[11]

When, a few days later, all the *Al Rawdah* men had arrived at Belfast Prison, the internees decided to try another protest about visiting conditions, this time by refusing all visits. At this point, Belfast Prison held 550 men, of whom Stuart thought 458 to be either 'closely allied' with the IRA or sympathisers.[12] The intention was to get publicity for their protest, since baulked and disappointed visitors could be counted on to go to the press and community organisations. This entailed short-term pain since it meant that relatives, some of whom had travelled a distance with parcels of hard-wrought comforts and necessities, were put to useless expense and left the prison inconvenienced and worried. The protest had the advantage, however, of allowing Nationalist politicians at Stormont to raise the matter both in private and in the chamber.[13] Stuart would not shift on the issue, and the Ministry backed him. On 24 March 1941, forty-six men refused food. This was not a general strike and was not supported by the IRA's leadership (such as it was at this point). The forty-six amounted to rather less than one-sixth of the total of 299 persons (men and women) then interned. With only minority support inside the prison, and apparently none outside, the strike was utterly futile and was called off.[14]

Eight months later there was another attempt at a concerted hunger strike in Belfast Prison. The issue was even more difficult to explain to outsiders. Internee workers who prepared the meals for D Wing refused to do so unless they were allowed to cut up the meat in the stores. Since these were outside the kitchen and adjoined the visiting area, the request was refused on security grounds. The following day, the kitchen party refused to work and so no food at all was served. Having missed several meals the men approached Stuart again. Their request was repeated and once more rejected, this time with the warning that they would have to forgo not only food but also all letters and parcels.[15] After urgent discussion, the men agreed to resume kitchen duties.[16] This seems to have been a high point in the internees' desire and capacity to assert themselves; it also demonstrates the isolated and powerless state to which they had been reduced. Apart from families, friends and the vestiges that remained of the IRA support organisation, the men and women were on their own.

On 15 January 1942, there was another hunger strike. The intention was to enlist all inmates: internees, local prisoners and convicts. The issue was the punishment of John McMahon (serving eighteen months' hard labour) for refusing to obey an order. The following day, Friday, 16 January, another local prisoner (E. J. Anderson) refused work as a protest.[17] Over the weekend there were communications between divisions, and attempts were made to spread the protest to sixteen short-term convicted IRA men and eight juvenile adults in the B and

C wings. By Tuesday, 20 January, fifty-four penal-servitude men were refusing labour and, in consequence, were locked in their cells. That evening, these men staged a demonstration, shouting to each other and singing republican songs. Since the noise carried into the other wings, the probable intention was to cause a general tumult. Stuart threatened force if the noise and disorder continued, and staff entered a number of cells and removed men from windows from which they were shouting. There were some scuffles but apparently no injuries. The internees in D Wing did not become involved in the protest.[18]

The following day, the fifty-four convicts were charged with refusing to work, and a number were additionally accused of creating a disturbance. Found guilty (the inevitable outcome of such hearings) they were confined to their cells on bread-and-water punishment diet; all items, apart from the most basic, were removed from them. The cells were opened in turn by a party of staff. The men were strip-searched, and any foodstuffs and tobacco remaining from their Christmas parcels were confiscated and their beds were removed for the day. According to an IRA report, this was accompanied by threats and ill-treatment. That evening, the IRA men, under orders, stood at their cell windows singing. Cells were again entered by staff and the demonstrators pulled down: again there were IRA accusations of threats and assaults.[19] The following morning two men refused to put out their beds and were then, according to the IRA report, beaten up by staff. When taken before the Governor for adjudication, the men, either acting on orders or on their own initiative, would not stand to attention and, during the hearing, were held up by staff.[20] The men who had refused work were sentenced to cellular confinement on a punishment diet; those involved in the disturbance forfeited all privileges (letters, visits, etc.) for between three and four months. These were severe punishments but within the tariff of the times.

On release from close confinement and punishment diet, forty-two of the men declared a hunger strike and were again locked down. Starting a hunger strike from having been on bread and water, and in an underheated prison in mid-winter, was a foolish decision, and by the morning of 28 January those refusing food had dropped to twenty-seven. None of the other divisions participated. On 31 January, Jimmy Steele, one of the strike leaders and a senior IRA figure, was admitted to the prison hospital with abdominal pains and vomiting. All the strikers then accepted food.[21] A note was intercepted in which the convicts' OC regretted having had to submit to the Governor's orders but that he could not do otherwise since he had no backing from the men and he could not therefore risk staging a physical confrontation.[22] Their own ranks divided, the convicts had no hope of mounting an effective protest and certainly could not lead internees and local prisoners into one.

It was possibly in reaction to this frustrating and humiliating episode, and with the realisation that unless they could convince the Advisory Committee to recommend their release they would sit out the war in prison, that three internees attempted an escape on St Patrick's Day, 1942. They had smuggled a hacksaw blade into the prison with, the Governor suspected, the collusion of temporary staff. A section of cell bars was cut, and the men had just commenced their escape attempt when a prison officer and special constable on patrol inside the boundary wall of the prison heard noises and spotted a dangling sheet-rope. The three, fully dressed and with their escape equipment, were then discovered in the cell. Punishment duly followed.[23]

A more serious hunger strike was undertaken by convicts in the spring of 1944. These men were of a different calibre to the internees who, by definition, spanned a range of engagements with republicanism and levels of commitment and militancy. All the strikers were serving substantial terms of penal servitude for treason felony, murder, firearms, explosives and similar offences. They were led by Hugh McAteer, former IRA Chief of Staff and one of the few men to have successfully escaped from Belfast Prison.[24] Three who joined the strike had been flogged. The action began with nine men on 27 February 1944. The demand was for political rather than criminal treatment and to stop what was claimed to be their continued victimisation in the prison.[25] There were promises of support from the internees and from local prisoners. A note, from one or the other of these groups some ten days after the strike began, promised McAteer and his men that 'we will be joining you in a few days & we shall be prepared for the battle'.[26] Another cheer from the sidelines promised that preparations were being made for the second front.[27]

Despite these encouraging shouts from the trenches, the strike did not spread beyond the convicts. Even within that group it had little momentum. By 8 March 1944, the numbers had grown from the original nine to twenty-six. This was the peak, however, and from the following day there was a falling away. The first to go was a late joiner, hungry for two days only. There seemed to be a rally on 10 March when three more men joined, but the falling-off continued thereafter. By the morning of 15 March, twenty men were still refusing food. On 19 March, the leader Hugh McAteer refused hot milk but agreed to take some brandy to counter severe abdominal pains. Whether there was then a joint agreement to abandon the action or whether men decided individually is not clear, but by 23 March, the prison medical officer was able to report to the Ministry that it was all over.[28] Prisoners' letters which mentioned the strike confirmed that it had been a demoralising affair. One man, who had joined for four days, wrote that during that time he had seen its futility. Through his 'lack of foresight and foolhardiness', he lamented, he had lost the extra pint of milk which he had been given each day, 'and of course any Easter parcel'. Another man wrote, 'This great strike is now over, a complete fiasco from beginning to end.'[29]

The episode was curious for several reasons. The organisers were experienced men and must have known by heart all the prerequisites for even a hope of success. None of these was present, and the men additionally knew that no hunger strike had succeeded in a Northern prison since the foundation of the state. It was perhaps the action of those in near despair for whom any chance, even the most remote, was worth taking. The aim, indeed, may have been no more than to show each other that they could act. Nevertheless, the lesson had been learned, and there were no further concerted hunger strikes for many years.[30]

Female internees

Female internees, of whom there were at least nineteen, were held at Armagh – Northern Ireland's only prison for women.[31] Under the leadership of Catherine O'Hara, sixteen women went on hunger strike on 20 November 1943.[32] The reasons seem to have been general dissatisfaction with Armagh. A number of demands were made, ranging from removal to a more modern wing of the prison with improved amenities, to total relocation. The Governor, Major G. H. Brush was inclined to temporise, moving the women to another wing and adapting some rooms to give them a kitchen and a sitting room.[33] This brought a stiff rebuke from H. C. Montgomery, Assistant Secretary at Home Affairs, regretting in particular that the women had been given the idea that they would be provided with a dining hall 'with oil stoves'. The Ministry, Montgomery emphasised, 'is determined not to allow the internees to run the gaol, and I thought I had made the Ministry's attitude in regard to dealing with these people quite clear'. Brush was asked not to make any more promises to O'Hara.[34]

Despite its remonstration, Home Affairs was far from indifferent to the hunger strike, requiring regular reports on the women's condition and instructing Brush that their part of the building had to be kept warm.[35] The death or serious illness of a female internee would have inflamed nationalist opinion, North and South, and could have raised concerns in wider liberal and humanitarian circles. The Governor, the Roman Catholic chaplain and the Medical Officer all urged O'Hara to give up, the Governor in particular still looking for a compromise on accommodation and facilities. Nine days into the strike (which was not complete, since the women were taking a mix of milk and water), a wholly misleading report about its causes appeared in the *Irish News*. The demand, the newspaper stated, was that the sixteen on strike should not have to associate with three internees from Derry – as well as other objections to the prison routine.[36] This caused further upset, since the Derry women and the others had been kept in separate parts of the prison for some months. The Derry three were very concerned that they were being represented as republican apostates. One of the three, Nora Ward, contemplated legal action and wrote to the *Belfast Telegraph* demanding a correction.[37] The letter was handed to the Governor and was not posted. Feelings simmered throughout December 1943, and on 19 January 1944, Nora Ward and her two comrades went on hunger strike 'until Miss O'Hara and her associates publicly withdraw their lying accusations'.[38]

Although numbers had dropped off, Catherine O'Hara's strike continued for several weeks. She insisted that there was only one objective: 'to be removed from Armagh Gaol to some place more suitable for human beings. Another winter here would finish us.'[39] Caught between his concern for the well-being of the women and the unbending attitude of the Ministry, Brush repeatedly asked O'Hara to give up 'this senseless strike'. This plea had an important outcome since O'Hara did speak to the Governor for the first time since 30 August 1943 and in doing so agreed to free the other women from their hunger-strike pact. The Governor thought that a gesture towards the women at this point would have a beneficial effect, but the Ministry again demurred. The strike began to disintegrate, with O'Hara herself coming off it on 12 December 1943.[40]

Neither strike lasted long enough for the women's health to be seriously threatened. None of their objectives had been achieved, and they had generated no outside support. The Ministry had not given way, and the only positive outcome, very likely, was a venting of feelings of anger and frustration.

Their numbers were low in any event, and some of the women, because of their youth and inexperience, were good release prospects. As 1944 advanced and as the political and international situations became ever more stable, the Advisory Committee made positive recommendations in most cases. At an otherwise fruitless meeting with the Minister for Home Affairs in December 1944, the few remaining female internees were discussed with lobbyists for a general release. The number of women in internment had been more than halved over the course of the year.[41] Hugh Corvin of the Green Cross Fund argued that the rest could be released without threatening public security. Although he made no direct reply, the Minister asked the RUC Inspector-General to look at these cases especially. This request was given no great priority. Eight weeks passed without RUC comment, and the Ministry wrote again on 19 February 1945.[42] It was not until 26 July 1945 that the last of the women were freed – their numbers by then reduced to only nine.[43]

Other protests

Disorder

One of the first internee protests took place at Londonderry Prison on Christmas Day, 1939. This took the form of a confrontation with staff, refusals to obey orders and general insubordination. The word 'riot' was not used in the Governor's reports, but the incident appears to have been not far short of that.[44] The defective design of the prison (a horseshoe form), and a holiday deployment of staff that was demonstrably inadequate, gave the incident possibilities that alarmed Home Affairs.[45] In its aftermath, the authorities had to deal with four groups: (1) the main body of internees who had rioted, (2) internees who had not taken part in the Christmas Day protest, (3) internees who had appeared before the Advisory Committee and (4) untried prisoners. The Governor was obliged to keep these apart, because each was on 'unfriendly' terms with the others – the four men who had submitted appeals being regarded by all the others as renegades. Extra staffing was required to ensure that order could be maintained in the event of another challenge.[46]

The Governor of Londonderry Prison, Captain A. Fryer, remained apprehensive about a repeat of the disorder, recognising that the Christmas Day protest could have had a more serious outcome. Six months later, he received an RUC warning that an outside attack would be coordinated with an uprising inside. The likely time was again a weekend, always advantageous for riot and disturbance. Fryer responded by calling in all available staff and cancelling rest days. Following a discussion of the respective responsibilities of the prison staff and the RUC, it was agreed that the former's duty was to ensure that internees could not mutiny when out of their cells and to prevent escapes. The RUC was there to prevent external attacks and threats.[47] The outside attack, unlikely anyway because of the insufficiency of IRA resources, as well as the disadvantage of long hours of daylight, did not materialise. The warning could have had a number of sources and reasons, but neither the police nor the Governor could have neglected to respond – if they valued their careers.

A different type of action was mounted in Belfast in November 1941. A trap was baited for a temporary officer supervising internees during the afternoon association period. An internee asked several times to use the lavatory and was permitted each time to do so. Finally, the officer became suspicious and followed the man. As he reached the lavatory door, the internee rushed out and attacked him; three other men joined in and threw the officer to the floor, beating him with his own baton. The men made a grab for the keys, but the officer had hidden them, and, when he got the chance, he threw them out the window to a colleague. The alarm was raised and the men were subdued.[48]

On the face of it, this might have been little more than an opportunistic attack on an officer, seizing the moment in the hope of escape. The luring of the officer and the participation of a number of men in the attack convinced Governor Stuart that a more considered and subtle plan had been put into operation. One of the men involved was J. S. O'Hagan, said to be an IRA quartermaster and suspected by Stuart of having previously organised trouble between staff and internees while himself remaining in the background. Because of the numbers of officers in the immediate vicinity, Stuart dismissed the possibility of an escape attempt. Rather, he thought, the intention was to breach the strict separation between internees and sentenced men, convict and local. If the four were brought before the court, tried and sentenced, they would spend some months among sentenced prisoners and be returned to internment on the expiration of sentence, having had many opportunities for communication with IRA men in the local division of the prison. A deal of organisation and coordination could be accomplished in that time. The Ministry agreed with Stuart's assessment, and it was decided to deal with the four by means of governor's punishment (necessarily much milder) instead of mounting a prosecution before the courts.[49]

The parcels skirmish

Although penal servitude entailed a regime set out in minute and apparently inflexible detail in rules and standing orders, local usage had blunted some of its sharper edges. One such amelioration – unknown in Britain and in Éire – was to allow convicts to receive parcels of extra food, tobacco and other comforts at Christmas and Easter. It is not clear when this privilege was granted, but it seems to have been during Captain Stephenson's governorship. Its terms were imprecise, and, as the convicts and their friends and relatives tested the boundaries of the definition of 'parcel', a conflict was bound to arise. When Stuart took over Belfast Prison in 1938, he was surprised to learn about the parcels and queried the issue with Home Affairs. Commander R. P. Pim, then the Ministry's most senior prison official, decided not to stop the privilege but directed that contents should be restricted to approved food items and a small number of cigarettes or an equivalent amount of tobacco. The prisoners responded with a declaration that until these limitations were lifted they would not work. The Governor forthwith punished the forty-nine protestors by the forfeiture of forty-eight remission marks each and the loss of all privileges.[50]

Once again, little thought had been given to the consequences of a confrontation or the *casus belli*. In times when all civilians were suffering the shortages and considerable privations of war, there was unlikely to be much sympathy for convicts protesting that their comfort parcels were not large enough. Some relatives did feel aggrieved on behalf of the men, but theirs was an emphatically partisan and personal view, unlikely to command attention or wider support. James Brogan, serving ten years for unlawful imprisonment, smuggled a letter out to his mother. (His letter-writing privileges had been withdrawn as part of his punishment for refusing labour.) Indifferent to the fact that she was disclosing receipt of a contraband letter, she wrote indignantly to Stuart: her son was a political prisoner serving a long sentence, and at the very least he should receive moderate treatment. The prisoners' ill-treatment was being talked of throughout the country: nine days' bread and water and the denial of parcels. The men had little enough and should receive that to which they were entitled. Her son was a young man, not an animal: 'I hope that you are aware of the fact that Almighty God will hold you responsible for these men and I may tell you I would not fancy your chances.'[51]

The outcome of this admonitory letter was not what Mrs Brogan and her son might have wished. Brogan had not been put on bread and water punishment, but he had been punished for a breach of discipline by forfeiting his privileges, and this decision stood. In addition, as we have seen, Stuart questioned the whole rationale of allowing the holiday parcels and addressed the Ministry on the issue. The upshot was that Captain Stephenson's original decision was queried: there was no statutory authority to allow convicts to receive parcels, and the practice – of which the Ministry now said it had no prior knowledge – must either stop or a rule would have to be brought in under the Prison Act and approved by the Governor of Northern Ireland.[52] Perhaps it was decided not to take official notice of the practice rather than to venture down this bureaucratic path, with all the tiresome risks of publicity and partisan public debate. However it came about, the privilege survived, and the men who continued to receive these home comforts had little idea how close they had come to losing them altogether.

Internees, not having been tried, should have enjoyed much the same privileges regarding parcels as remand prisoners. Following the spectacular escape of twenty-one internees from Londonderry Prison on 20 March 1943, Home Affairs imposed a number of additional restrictions.[53] The most important of these was that food could no longer be included in internees' parcels. William Lowry, then Minister for Home Affairs (a position he held from May 1943 until November 1944), denied that this was a punishment for the March escape; rather, it was a belated recognition that the wartime food controls and regulations precluded such gifts.[54] The new restriction did not extend to confectionery, and much ingenuity was subsequently employed in stretching the meaning of the term 'confectionery'.

In December 1943, Major G. H. Brush, the Governor of Armagh Prison, reported to the Ministry that parcels sent in by relatives, friends and the Green Cross had become 'a positive menace'. In addition to cakes, pastry and other items that could be classified as confectionery, cigarettes and chocolate came in such quantities that 'from eating & too much smoking' the women were constantly refusing the prison food that was prepared from what was allowed by the general rationing regulations. Brush, irritated no doubt that what had been a quiet life in a true backwater of public administration had become rather more challenging because of the republican women, requested that parcels be restricted to confectionery narrowly defined. To any outsider, this was a petty institutional grumble, and the Ministry, unwilling to give mileage to what would have been almost certain complaints and protests, declined to impose further limitations.[55]

Nakedness

Like certain sea creatures, revolutionary organisations must be in constant motion: they need action if they are to survive. At a loss how to pursue their perennial campaign for political status, well aware that under existing conditions hunger-striking was futile and a refusal to labour counterproductive, a different form of action was decided upon by a group serving penal servitude. From 16 June 1943, twelve IRA convicts, nearly all from Belfast, refused to wear prison uniform.[56] For a hundred years or more, convict garb had denoted for Irish revolutionists a criminal and shameful status which they utterly repudiated; this was at the very heart of republican doctrine, practice and history. For this reason, it was possibly thought that the protest would generate support outside as well as within the prison. The refusal to don the uniform was seen by Governor Stuart as a particularly defiant breach of discipline. Immediately confined to their cells, the men were deprived of all amenities.[57] This harsh line was endorsed by the Minister for Home Affairs, as was Stuart's subsequent rejection of the Roman Catholic chaplain's request that the men each be issued a blanket to cover their nakedness.[58] By 5 July 1943, twenty convicts had joined the protest. They had been locked in their cells for nineteen days, without exercise. A dispute between the Medical Officer and Stuart then came to a head. The former, fearing for the men's health, wanted them to be allowed to exercise naked, in a yard not overlooked from the outside. Stuart reported this to Home Affairs, arguing that exercise should be withheld until the men had submitted: even in the yard in question they could be seen by other inmates. And in any event, overlooked or not, Stuart considered it indecent for twenty convicts to exercise in the nude. He may have also been conscious that such naked parading would be an expression of mocking defiance and contempt by the prisoners. Should the Ministry decide to grant exercise, nevertheless, Stuart was adamant that it be taken in prison uniform or else 'without covering of any description'. The convicts must not be allowed to turn the tables on the prison authorities: 'On that point I must take a firm stand.'[59]

The following day, Jack Beattie, the Labour MP for the Pottinger constituency, raised the issue at Stormont. He pointed out that the regulations required the men be permitted to exercise and that they be given work likely to keep them in a healthy state. Minister William Lowry defended the Governor's decision, mixing firmness with a certain amount of fun-poking about nakedness. Clothes were placed in the men's cells, and they could don them and go to exercise if they wished, but they would not be allowed to perambulate naked around the exercise yard; he did not propose to direct the prison officers to dress the men 'as if they were children'; nor did he intend to ask the Governor to search for fig leaves in the prison garden.[60]

Imaginative though their naked protest had been, Stuart's decision and the government's adamantine backing left the men in a difficult and ultimately hopeless position. They were in total lock-up, in bare and utterly comfortless cells. Other than the uniform (left in the cell), every item of furniture and clothing and all cloth (including blankets, towels, blackout blinds and the mattress) was removed from the cell from 8 a.m. until 8 p.m. each day. Reading and writing materials were also withdrawn, and the men's only source of comfort and diversion was the arrival and consumption of their food – the standard prison dietary. Mid-June had been chosen to commence the protest, presumably on the basis that nakedness and other deprivations could more easily be borne in clement weather. If this had indeed been the calculation, it was flawed, since the heating system was turned off during the summer months and the building was still cold to those on protest.[61] The protest therefore was no small ordeal: pervasive chilly discomfort, the oppressiveness of isolation and the lack of any pastime – altogether a considerable psychological strain.[62] The strikers capitulated on 16 September 1943, when all, with the exception of Jimmy Steele, put on prison clothes and returned to work.[63] The ostensible reason was to allow one of the men to receive treatment for a swollen knee, but even the most determined would have found it hugely daunting to continue to endure such a state of lonely seclusion and gnawing discomfort, passing into autumn and winter. The armoury of prisoners is small. Endurance and self-sacrifice, highly praised among those imprisoned in the republican cause, have few opportunities for display. The strip strike did not achieve its objectives, but would be tried again some thirty-five years later.

Suborning, subverting and scaring staff

Menaces

As we have seen, by 1941 the IRA had largely lost its ability to take the initiative. Many of its leaders had been picked up, and it was clear that police intelligence was good and often effectively used. Their organisation's increasingly inert condition affected prisoners in all classes, remand, convicted and internees. Morale was bound to decay as prisoners underwent a metamorphosis. From being an army in waiting in 1939 and 1940, they had by the following year become a crowd of prisoners peering hopelessly into the dark tunnel of protracted captivity. It was the task of the prison OC and other senior figures to do what they could to counter despondency and a permeating sense of defeat, of lost time and of the decay of youth. A cache of IRA documents captured in Belfast in March 1943 shed an interesting light on the relationship between the inside and outside organisation, the prisoners' priorities and the methods used to subvert imprisonment and staff confidence. The letters were in the handwriting of Jimmy Steele, OC of Belfast prisoners and internees, and were written between January 1941 and mid-February the following year.[64] Most were addressed to the Adjutant General of the Northern Command.[65] The courier for what was obviously an extensive and frequent correspondence was a member of staff referred to by Steele as an 'inside linesman'. (This was an officer whose identity the RUC believed they knew but which evidently they could not prove.) Only a part of the correspondence was found, and from the relaxed, almost chatty tone, it is clear that Steele had complete confidence that his linesman would deliver as required and that the frequency, reliability and security of correspondence allowed him the luxury of sometimes leisurely and discursive exchanges. The linesman also gave Steele a deal of information about members of staff and occurrences in the prison, which he passed on to his outside correspondent.

Reports of the ill-treatment of prisoners by named members of staff formed a large part of Steele's correspondence. He provided details of these officers' addresses, leisure habits and haunts, with the wish that something be done about them – that something being a warning or even violence or death.[66] Having given the name and the address of a café frequented by an officer whom the convicts regarded as one of their principal enemies, Steele complained, 'we were expecting good news at the beginning of the week but were disappointed and I need not tell you how much we felt that failure'.[67] A few weeks later, he again berated Northern Command. The prisoners were very loyal and remained disciplined despite the violence and ill-treatment they had endured and despite the organisation's failure to protect them. This, Steele emphasised, could not go on: 'unless something is done and done quickly to show that the Army is in earnest about the promises of the past year morale will be completely shattered'.[68] Eleven days later, Steele gave more information about movements and addresses. Several named officers had threatened and beaten men. In two cases, 'a good warning is all that is necessary', but in the case of Chief Officer G. D. Crowe, held by Steele to be most responsible for the prisoners' plight, murder was obviously intended: 'It would be good enough seeing him any morning.' Once again Steele urged the Northern Command to do something soon. It was, he wrote, 'terrible to see such spirited lads having to suffer'.[69]

It was not only prison staff that Steele targeted. He gave the address of R. G. Ronaldson, the Inspector of Prisons. He appeared to Steele to be 'a man of peace whose only aim is that the prisoners will not escape'. Were Ronaldson, thought by Steele to have a violent dislike of Crowe, to be visited 'or kidnapped quietly', the situation in the prison explained to him and a warning issued, there might be a favourable outcome, especially if action were also taken against the 'culprits' already named by Steele.[70] Successive letters carried the same message. Individuals were named, with their addresses and off-duty movements, coupled with demands for action, especially against those who were 'disheartening the younger lads amongst us'. Repeatedly Steele asked when those he had denounced would be attended to. On 6 February 1942, his demands were apparently met when prison officer Thomas Richard Walker was shot.[71] The killing did not have the effect that Steele had predicted.[72] (In fact, the wrong officer had been shot.[73]) It did not have 'any particular effect' other than the resignation of three temporary officers. As for the prisoners, there was a difference of opinion. As Steele nonchalantly recorded, 'Some few deplored the fact that it was the wrong man but soon got over it.'[74]

Not all the references to staff were hostile, but it seems clear that relationships had deteriorated during 1941 in particular. At the beginning of the year, Steele reported on Christmas Day 1940 in the prison to Northern Command. There had been no special breakfast on the day 'but we had a splendid dinner'. On Boxing Day evening, three officers had volunteered to come into the prison, unpaid, so that the men in A Wing could have an extra hour out of their cells: 'Taken all round we had a very pleasant Xmas.'[75]

Such amiability was the exception in prison life. As in any institution, individual relations varied, and there were ebbs and flows in general staff–inmate relations. In the early months of 1944 there was a marked deterioration in these relations. On 25 January 1944, there was an unsuccessful attempt on the life of twenty-seven-year-old officer Nathaniel Robinson, on Alliance Avenue, Belfast.[76] Within forty-eight hours, Robinson and twelve other members of staff at Belfast Prison had submitted a request for firearms for their own protection.[77] The RUC was consulted, and they supplied a list of twenty-four members of staff of Belfast Prison they knew had been 'marked' by the IRA. The list was in order of importance – presumably the degree of opprobrium attached to each by the IRA, as calculated by the police. At the top was Chief Officer G. D. Crowe, followed by Principal Officer Thompson. The police had no objection to supplying weapons to anyone on the list.[78]

The Ministry was also supplied with copies of a number of threatening letters sent to staff by the IRA. Nathaniel Robinson had received one at home, warning him not to identify one of the men who shot him:

> A Chara, you state you know one of the men who shot you. I think you have made a mistake, just watch your step, the second time always proves fatal. It is bad to ride around in patrol cars. If your brother continues to talk and threaten he might meet with an accident.

The letter was signed 'I/O N/C'.[79] Another letter, addressed to four other officers at their homes, in similar terms, was also sent to the Ministry. Officer J. Riordan (a Roman Catholic) was warned that he had become 'very prominent' in activities against republican prisoners. These prisoners, the warning continued, 'have a certain status to maintain'. Since all other means of redress were closed to them, 'the Army Authority in Belfast will surely see that they do not suffer at the hands of petty tyrants'.[80] Riordan received a follow-up letter on 23 February 1944, in even more threatening tones: 'You still persist in your attitude to Republican Prisoners. The police may guarantee your protection. I hope they succeed.'[81]

These letters and the issuance of revolvers were most certainly discussed by prison officers, and inevitably raised tensions. A number of men not on the list then applied for revolvers, and Montgomery approached the RUC on their behalf. The RUC baulked at this, foreseeing trouble arising were some members of prison staff to be issued with revolvers and others not. This appears to have headed off what may have become a move to arm all staff at Belfast Prison. A total of thirty-five revolvers were eventually loaned to Belfast Prison by the RUC. A number of these were held in the prison armoury, and it seems that only those officers on the threat list, with perhaps a few more, were issued with revolvers.[82]

Trafficking

The overt struggle for control of the prison, as recounted by Steele and others, flaring up from time to time into open confrontations and protests, was but one side of a continuing trial of strength: concurrently, and seemingly uninterrupted by open hostilities, the age-old practice of trafficking ebbed and flowed – as venerable and as ineradicable as imprisonment itself. Trafficking had been identified as a problem at Belfast Prison even before the 1939 influx of internees and sentenced IRA men. There was an unpleasant and murky incident in 1938, which included an apparent conspiracy to frame a workshop officer by planting a revolver. This affair went back over several years and seems to have originated in the type of grudge-bearing and bad blood which so easily arises and persists in a closed institution with minimal staff turnover. The principal grudge against the targeted officer was the belief that he had republican sympathies and that he trafficked with IRA prisoners.[83] There was an official (but secret) inquiry, as a result of which the victimised officer was moved to Derry, entailing a wage cut. Home Affairs was alarmed by the affair, which reflected badly on the administration of the prison and the atmosphere within which staff operated. Had details become public there would have been much ammunition for the government's critics.[84]

A similarly obscure and worrying sequence occurred between 1939 and 1944. An ex-prisoner, Frederick William Willis, made a number of claims about trafficking prison officers and produced hard evidence in the form of smuggled letters to back up at least some of his allegations. Willis had been in Belfast Prison from 14 March 1939 until 2 February 1940, serving a sentence of fourteen months for manslaughter, arising out of a motoring accident. Some contraband letters were of an ordinary personal nature, from and to prisoners who simply wished to avoid the prison censor's eye and blue pencil or whose correspondence entitlement was insufficient for their needs. Others, however, were from IRA members on the business of the organisation. On 15 July 1939, for example, Seamus Walker, then OC of the IRA prisoners, wrote to Peter Donnelly, a remand. Walker, a sentenced man, told Donnelly that the Belfast Battalion suspected that Donnelly's arrest had been due to an informer. Should he wish to comment on this to GHQ, or anyone outside, Walker would send a letter for him. Donnelly replied that he was also sure that his arrest had been due to an informer, but he could not say who.[85]

Willis contended that such communications were possible not simply because of lax and inefficient supervision but also because of staff corruption and connivance. While in the prison hospital, recovering from his accident injuries, he had himself seen copies of the illegal IRA publication *War News* being given to IRA prisoner Jim Killeen. There was scepticism about the story among officials, although Special Branch thought it possible that a Dublin edition of the paper may have been in circulation at a time when Willis might have seen it. His claims, however, and those of Robert Carson, the prisoner who had provided Willis with copies of the contraband documents, were to be treated with some caution, according to the detective to whom Willis had initially complained.[86]

Another of Willis's claims was that fire-raising materials had been smuggled into the prison by visitors and staff, in toothpaste tubes. This was merely an alarmist description of the flints which were an essential part of the ubiquitous tinderbox lighters.[87] More worryingly, he also named five members of staff as being untrustworthy. A subsequent RUC report was hardly reassuring. One man's morals gave ground for misgiving, the report said, but he was otherwise regarded as loyal and trustworthy. Of two others, nothing adverse was known. Another had been under suspicion for a considerable time. Information had been received that arms were concealed at his house, which had then been searched, without result. The last of the five was suspected of being complicit in the notorious and deeply embarrassing May 1927 escape of three IRA men, Conlon, Rogers and Boyle (as well as the ordinary convict Thornton) but nothing had been proved.[88] The five officers named by Willis were variously alleged to have been involved in the passing on of contraband; carried letters within the prison, from one wing to another; provided facilities for IRA men to meet; contacted republicans outside the prison, passing on messages; recommended a suspect person for a temporary post in the prison; permitted IRA drilling in the prison yard; and, in a number of other ways, damaged security and procured degrees of latitude for IRA prisoners. A particularly damaging claim was that during Willis's time in the prison hospital, almost every day a small group of political prisoners was brought in and put into a room with Jim Killeen where they could talk freely and without supervision.[89]

These were allegations of such an alarming nature that E. W. Scales, Assistant Secretary at Home Affairs, investigated them personally. He made an unannounced visit on a day when Governor Stuart was on leave from the prison. It is hard to know what he expected to find, but all was clean and orderly, with the usual activities proceeding as normal. There was an undue accumulation of property in convicts' cells (a perennial complaint of gaol-keepers), and he gave directions on this. Willis was invited to the Ministry of Home Affairs, to discuss his allegations in the presence of Stuart. He came, but would speak only to Scales. When the Governor withdrew from the room, Willis made a number of additional complaints, mainly about the Medical Officer and hospital staff. Scales recognised that it would be difficult to evaluate these allegations. Willis and Carson, his fellow informant, each had an agenda: the lifting of a twelve-year driving ban and early release, respectively. To this end, they had undoubtedly noted the occasional 'peccadilloes' of prison staff. Beyond that, Scales felt 'considerable anxiety' that Willis, now a free man, had been able to tell him in detail about his (Scales') visit to the prison and to hand him a six-page, closely written letter from Carson, still a prisoner. This proved conclusively that there existed a channel of clandestine communication involving at least one member of staff and that prisoners were sufficiently free of supervision to be able to write such a lengthy letter. Scales backed away from a formal inquiry: much evidence would have to be taken from prisoners, whose veracity must always be questionable. Even staff would have a direct interest in transferring blame to superiors or colleagues. Instead, Scales proposed that the papers be passed to the police for investigation, and prosecution if possible. In the meantime, Stuart had allowed a certain laxness with the convicts to arise, which would be corrected.[90] In this decision to concentrate on individuals rather than on the management, procedures and culture of the institution, there was a prudent recognition that many facts of an undesirable nature might better be left undisturbed.

Scales also wrote to Arthur Black, the Attorney General. Trafficking was 'the bane of prison administration', and he wanted an example to be made of the officer who had been Carson's courier. The Special Powers Act conferred powers of interrogation which should be used to force Willis to disclose the officer's name. This was an 'excellent opportunity', and, were the guilty person not held to account, effective administration would suffer.[91] Not long after, Carson, who had served his sentence (without managing to persuade the Ministry to reduce it) named the officer who had carried letters between himself and Willis in an unctuous and self-serving statement.[92] Now that definite action was possible, Scales and his colleagues began to have second and indeed third thoughts: lifting the lid of this particular box might not be wise. A further review of the allegations and corroboration (or lack of it) curbed enthusiasm for a day in court ('an unsavoury and unsatisfactory case'). Carson's courier was interviewed and warned, and various arrangements in the prison, including the conduct of visits, were tightened up. The police were asked to keep an eye on the officers against whom allegations of disloyalty had been made.[93] This was a near total climbdown, but the overriding concern was to avoid a deeply damaging public scandal. Scales and Sir Dawson Bates agreed that discretion was the wiser course.

One immediate outcome was that convicts and other prisoners faced more severe restrictions during visits, which now took place through a wire-mesh screen in a completely partitioned room. Cell-searching was intensified, and prisoners were allowed no unnecessary accumulation of items (always a good camouflage for contraband). Stuart was told to take more care in his appointment of the library assistant, to guard against this privileged prisoner carrying messages between wings and landings.[94] A particular watch was to be kept for collusion between those serving longer sentences and those among the short-termers who (on their release) might transmit letters. Having eschewed legal action, the Ministry could now only mutter that it was 'not entirely satisfied' that the allegations of Willis and Carson were 'quite devoid of foundation'. Stuart, in effect, was instructed to take a tighter grip on the reins.[95]

Incidents of trafficking may have dipped briefly, but, after a period of caution, it was almost certainly business as usual again. The general postal interception in operation in Northern Ireland during the war years turned up some prisoners' letters which had been smuggled out and then posted in the normal way. A meeting was convened on 5 February 1941 at Belfast Prison. County Inspector Richard Harrison of the RUC stated that he was 'absolutely satisfied' that two Belfast Prison officers were involved. Unfortunately he could not disclose the source of his information, nor was he in a position to bring charges. The problem had been discussed with Bates, Lowry (his Parliamentary Secretary at the time) and the RUC Inspector-General Sir Charles Wickham. Bates refused to dismiss the two officers – not so much because of the doubts about the evidence against them, but for electoral and party reasons. Harrison asked whether the pair could be kept out of contact with the political prisoners, but Stuart insisted that this was not practical. Staff had access to all parts of the prison, and it would be impossible to arrange things in any other way. (He might have added, though it should have been obvious, that the minute such a limitation were ordered it would be common and troublesome knowledge throughout the prison, promoting endless speculation and making the affected officers' position untenable.) To transfer the suspect officers to Londonderry was out of the question since 200 internees would shortly be moved there, and the corrupt pair would then have a feast of opportunities. The male staff at Armagh female prison was so small that room could not be made for them there. The other option, Malone Training School (for young offenders) was also ruled out since the two were unsuitable for that work. Options thus exhausted, the RUC recommended that the men be dismissed, but, since they were established civil servants, this could only be done with the authority of the Governor General of Northern Ireland, and this could not be obtained without producing the evidence in full. The only option, it was lamely concluded, was to have the two officers carefully watched within the prison.[96]

The precautions, general and particular, evidently had little effect on contraband mail, as, from time to time, the general postal interception showed.[97] In the summer of 1941, the matter was reopened. One man was shortly to retire, but the other would remain. H. C. Montgomery, now Secretary at Home Affairs, wanted rid of both as soon as possible. Having been foiled on the weight of evidence against the two, and the difficulties of any kind of formal proceeding, Montgomery tried a different and more effective tack. The Superannuation Act provided that on reaching the age of fifty-five civil servants could be called upon to retire by their head of department.[98] In such an eventuality, pension payments would be affected. Obviously, the closer a man was to the normal retirement age of sixty the smaller the impact on his pension of early retirement. Montgomery had all this in mind when he observed that it was practically impossible to catch traffickers. At the same time, he had wholly justified concerns about the bad influence of some of the older men over the younger ones and, thus, the continuation of the cycle of corruption; the process had to be interrupted. If the Minister agreed, Montgomery would order the two to be removed from the prison immediately they were served with their retirement notifications; they would be fully paid for any period of notice to which they were entitled. Lowry agreed, and the men were retired as from 1 September 1941. Writing to County Inspector Ewing Gilfillan, Montgomery anticipated that the event would have 'the most beneficial results generally'.[99]

Whatever the short-term effects, the old trade would revive: demand would ensure supply. In the spring of 1943, another case of alleged trafficking came to light, this time reported by a convict. The details confirm that one of the main-springs of the trade was the prison officers' low salaries and allowances (and poor prospects for advancement). One of the alleged inducements was as slight as allowing the dishonest officer to wear a pair of internee boots while his own were being repaired. For this service the officer gave the convict (Barr) a packet of cigarettes and also posted a letter. Once hooked by this initial breach of the rules, as is almost invariably the case, the corrupt relationship developed. The officer met a friend of Barr's outside and brought in letters. Having been read, these were handed back to be destroyed, lest they were turned up in a search. The only payment mentioned was a £1 note, which came with one of the letters. The traffic supposedly continued for some months until Barr and the officer quarrelled. The officer put Barr on report, and Barr retaliated by disclosing what had been going on.[100] Barr was a chronic recidivist who had been coming into prison since 1910, and the officer had a good service record. The Governor, in the absence of any corroborating evidence, chose to believe that this was a baseless accusation, payback for being put on report. The officer was informed that the Ministry considered him entirely blameless. He asked for this to be confirmed in writing.[101]

Barr was an habitual criminal, and his allegations, true or not, were of little lasting consequence. A good deal more serious was the possibility that the IRA had good and regular communications with their incarcerated comrades. This required channels into and out of the prison and between the various divisions.[102] A search of the Belfast Prison chapel in December 1942, after a Roman Catholic service, turned up three copies of *War News*, together with a message in numerical code. The latter was handed over to Special Branch, who managed to decipher all of it, except for the signature. Used by all the various classes of prisoners, the chapel was an obvious junction and ideal for passing material to and fro between the classes, which were otherwise strictly separated. The authorities knew this to be a weak point, and searches were regularly conducted, usually without result. On 5 January 1944, however, following the convicts' attendance at confession, a packet was found, tucked under the altar rails. This was addressed to Richard Magowan, an ex-civil servant serving two years' hard labour for IRA activities. It contained five copies of the December 1943 issue of *War News* and some notes. The letters were deemed to be unimportant, with the exception of one from IRA GHQ Belfast to the Adjutant, IRA prisoners, A Wing. This referred to the recent killing of Constable Patrick McCarthy and was therefore handed over to Special Branch.[103]

Despite these finds, and the caution that must have accrued during his years of service, Stuart told Home Affairs that he was satisfied that visits and authorised letters were being scrutinised efficiently and that illegal communications were being stifled – a curious offering to the fickle god of fortune. Careful searching of prisoners, cells, workshops, the chapel and other places, and a special watch on suspect prisoners had, Stuart claimed, 'almost completely severed the internal connecting link which the IRA in the respective Divisions had hoped to be able to maintain'.[104] An occasional note might get through, but this caused him no alarm. The chief danger was not internal prison communications but contact with the IRA outside, using a corrupt officer. Such a link could be maintained indefinitely without the evidence to back charges against suspects. Stuart offered the Ministry a fresh list of three doubtful officers. There were circumstantial grounds for suspecting each, but this was insufficient. Stuart had, therefore, asked Special Branch for a report, recognising that his suspects might not be the only ones engaged in the traffic.[105]

A few weeks later, Special Branch reported on fairly reliable information that one of the three suspects, a temporary officer, was indeed in collusion with the IRA prisoners and that he had taken in copies of *War News* and, on one occasion, a bottle of whiskey.[106] The man was watched (by whom is not clear) and assigned to duties that did not allow him easy and unsupervised access to prisoners. Stuart thought him a poor officer, in any case, apt to be intimidated by prisoners. He wished to remove him and another suspect temporary officer. The third suspect, however, was an established civil servant with all the problems that dismissal entailed. 'Why take unnecessary risks?' Stuart asked.[107]

Shortly afterwards, the RUC supplied a fuller report to the Ministry on the three, and on three others who had recently come under suspicion. All were Protestants. One had served in the Great War, and the police had previously learned that he had carried IRA letters in and out of the prison for the 'occasional' £1. A second man was Scottish, and the police had heard that he had trafficked newspapers into the convict division. Again, no hard evidence, but it was said that 'he goes about town a good deal and spends money beyond his income'. A third officer was also an ex-soldier, who had served in Palestine. Nothing was known against him other than a suspicion arising from his intimacy with the friends and relatives of political prisoners who visited the prison. He addressed some by their Christian names, and they him. The fourth (also an ex-serviceman) had recently been carrying things in and out of the prison for internees. Nor was this all. Reliable sources had reported that a fifth officer, an orderly in the prison hospital, had carried letters. A sixth was reported as being 'very doubtful, and suspected of trafficking'. There was a coda of little cheer: 'This is as far as we can go, and I hope it will be of some use to you.'[108]

Despite Stuart's sanguine report, therefore, control over illicit communications was as weak as it had ever been. Access to even modest funds and its organisation had enabled the IRA to recruit a useful stable of corrupt staff. The RUC could not disclose their sources, and without a strong and verifiable case it was hard to dismiss even temporary officers. The matter was made even more difficult because there had recently been exchanges at Stormont about six prison officers who had been dismissed.[109] In the circumstances it would hardly be advisable to stir the pot and dismiss on suspicion alone. Reporting to Lowry, Montgomery recommended that no more be done than to instruct the principal officers (the first line of management) that they should pay particular attention to the six suspects. Lowry was even more cautious: 'I am not inclined to recommend the dismissal of any P[rison] O[fficer] on mere suspicion – no matter how strong.' He agreed that the principal officers should strengthen their supervision but did not want the Governor's directions to be more than general: the six men were not to be named.[110]

None of the suspects, as far as can be seen from the records, was at any time a likely IRA sympathiser: they trafficked in return for small but apparently regular sums of money.[111] Wages were low; a prison officer earned the wage of the semi-skilled, though he did have a high level of job security, allowances and significant pension rights (and overtime was available). In an economy with restricted opportunities for men without craft, skills or advanced training, this was a good position, much sought. But a family lived frugally to get by on such wages. Many former soldiers were used to having virtually all living expenses found by the Army, with their wages, though hardly handsome, theirs to spend.

'Goes about town a deal' was a euphemism for regular and maybe heavy use of public houses. Police intelligence was frequently picked up in drinking places: pubs and clubs. They were equally useful for the IRA: a hard-drinking prison officer was not hard to spot and, in an atmosphere of relaxed and inebriated camaraderie, was easily sounded out. Alcohol was not cheap in relation to income, and the offer of a drink was an easy and accepted way of opening a social encounter.

On their part, the corrupted officers may have minimised the significance of their trafficking: what harm could there be in carrying information to and from men who were securely locked up for the duration of the war? Even *War News* had scarcely the aspect of danger – the mimeographed newsletter of an outcast and defeated band. The smuggling of occasional comforts would hardly have registered with men who had been regular soldiers and who had learned to adapt to hard and testing circumstances.

Quite apart from these corrupt officers, on one occasion at least the IRA men got more than spiritual comfort and notice from visiting clergy. In an undated note to the IRA's Northern Command, Jimmy Steele described the celebration of mass by Father Hilary, a Passionist priest of the Ardoyne parish. Hilary had concluded his mass with prayers in Gaelic and finished these by saying 'God Save Ireland'. What the prison officers supervising the service made of this is not recorded, but Steele was enthusiastic: 'The boys went wild and it has been the means of even making Hughie Kerr learn Gaelic.'[112] In private conversation, the priest had told Steele that the prison authorities were checking his own political record but that 'it would do the church good if they threw a lot of priests in jail'. This was a welcome gift of support from an unexpected source, as chaplains generally seem either to have been reluctant to express any political opinions at all or to have condemned violence and secret organisations. Steele was delighted: 'It was certainly a tonic to us', he continued in his note to HQ, 'and it would be worth your while to have a talk with him.'[113]

Escapes

Just like imprisoned soldiers of regular armies, the IRA men, whether remand, convicted or internee, regarded themselves as POWs, still in service and under an obligation to harass the enemy whenever and however opportunity allowed. For a prisoner, this duty included campaigns of sabotage, confrontation, attrition and, of course, escape. All of these activities were distinguished from the normal refractoriness of prisoners by being subject to the authority of the IRA's prison command. No action was supposed to be taken without permission, and all, of course, were strengthened if taken in concert and as part of a plan. Besides all this, young men in custody, wrapped about with its irksome physical and emotional deprivations and pains, were instinctive (and almost certainly unknowing) disciples of Rousseau: 'L'homme est né libre, et partout il est dans les fers.'[114] Prison, despite all the activities that the IRA command could organise to maintain morale, was an experience of waiting and deteriorating. The chance to act, to gain freedom, to be again with family, friends and comrades was an immensely attractive prospect to some. Others (the majority) were apparently content to hunker down and to endure.

For the IRA, a successful escape was an enormous fillip, both for its activists and close supporters and for its reputation in the wider nationalist community. A foiled escape or an early recapture, by the same token, was likely to cause disappointment in the ranks and a distancing from would-be sympathisers. Escape was also dangerous to the outside organisation because it provoked police raids and roadblocks, leading to, in some instances, further arrests and the uncovering of literature and *matériel*. For those reasons not all escapes were welcome. There was a standing order that escapes had to be authorised and, where possible, coordinated with the outside organisation. Internees, however, were more loosely involved in the IRA's disciplinary structure, even though most accepted it, and it was from their ranks that the first escapers from Belfast Prison, in mid-1941, stepped forward.

De l'audace

Gerry Doherty, an internee from Londonderry city, had noted weakness in both physical security and control. From the top windows in D Wing (where the internees were held) he could look into the C-Wing yard, and he saw that the ordinary local prisoners were brought in from their work in the wood yard at 12.15 p.m. and again when the afternoon session finished, at 4.15 p.m. The internees came in from exercise at 12.30 p.m. and 4.30 p.m., and, in the two fifteen-minute overlaps, it might be possible for internees to gain access to the empty wood yard and from there to the prison wall. The only obstacle was a corrugated partition, separating the wood yard from the exercise yard. Were this breached, escape was possible. Equipment was gathered and prepared: a spanner for opening the partition, a rope made from sheets and a grappling hook. This last, made from plywood, broke when one of the would-be escapers (Patrick Gallagher) put his weight on it and tried to pull himself up the wall.[115] The three men – Eddie Keenan and Gerry Doherty as well as Gallagher – managed to get back to the exercise yard unobserved, just as their comrades were going in for their midday meal.

In the weeks that followed, three more men joined in preparations for another attempt, and Patrick Gallagher dropped out.[116] The hook that had failed in the first attempt was replaced by one made from metal bars taken from the collapsible tables in the D-Wing dining hall. On Friday, 6 June 1941, the five made another attempt. The hook caught on the wall successfully, and all five ascended. Doherty, the last to ascend, and the originator of the plan, was tackled by two prison officers, who had seen what was going on. Two other internees, not involved in the escape, wrestled with the officers, giving Doherty his chance to climb the wall and get away.[117] Once over the main wall, the men climbed a smaller one that separated the playing fields of the adjoining St Malachy's College and the nearby convent from the prison grounds. From this smaller wall, the men entered the grounds of the convent. Their appearance caused some consternation among the nuns, but the Mother Superior came on the scene and led them to the main door. Although the account of Eddie Keenan, one of the escapers, is coy at this point, it would seem that the Mother Superior also summoned Dr John Harrington, a Catholic doctor with a 1920s republican background. Harrington drove three of the men to a house in the Falls Road area. By good luck, the other two men also made their way to sympathetic households. It is worth noting that there was no organised IRA involvement in the escape itself. Once the men were over the wall, however, the organisation was able to draw on the resources of sympathisers to shelter the escapers and, eventually, to get them across the border.[118] An inquiry was of course inevitable: this was a major embarrassment to the government.

Apart from the fleeting opportunity of exceptional circumstances, escapes require a set of skills, and a set of vices: audacity, determination, preparation, concealment and systematic and protracted observation on the part of the prisoner; slackness, disengagement, unthinking routine and complacency in management. The June 1941 escape is an almost perfect demonstration of this formula.[119] It was established that although two men had failed to escape, the break was made possible by a lack of staff vigilance before and during the escape and by their indecisiveness immediately afterwards. In the best tradition of prison escapes, the five had made a ladder from torn sheets, fitted with four iron bars bent into large hooks. The sheets were not those issued individually, the disappearance of which would (or should) immediately have been noticed. The metal strips had been removed from tables in the recreation and mess rooms. Staff had not thoroughly checked these and thus had failed to see what was missing.[120] In their constant observation of staff and routines, the internees noted that exercise-yard supervision was slack. Sometimes only one officer was left in charge of the 226 internees, and his duty station had restricted visibility. The Governor and Chief Officer (who had visited the yard only minutes before the escape) had not noticed this defective deployment. As we have seen, a corrugated iron fence separated the exercise yard from the wood yard and from that there was access to the wall. This insecure partition should have been spotted, together with the prisoners' efforts to weaken it further. It was a well-prepared and cleverly executed action, with mirror-image staff and management incompetence.

Ministry officials were acerbic in their report of the incident. Many staff, they noted, gave the impression of 'merely putting in time while on duty instead of watching the activities of their prisoners'. Some were evasive and gave unbelievable explanations; the majority seemed to lack intelligence. Staff shortages were not the problem, but if there was a lack of anything it was of quality rather than quantity. Management was strongly criticised, and, as recommended, the Minister severely censured the Governor, the Chief Officer and a principal officer. Six other recommendations were made, touching on security, control and management, including the incorporation of the internee division into the prison's general staffing structure and procedure.[121]

Such a successful and dashing escape boosted IRA morale, a stimulus particularly needed for the rank and file and for supporters and sympathisers. The organisation had been decimated by internment and imprisonment, North and South, and was especially lacking in experienced operatives and leaders. The Stephen Hayes affair had dealt a near-mortal wound and had undoubtedly alienated many members and supporters, so the escape was a kiss of life to a body that had all but expired.[122]

All republican individuals and connections were under close surveillance. The organisation itself was in hibernation, and, by the third year of the war, those in captivity could expect little by way of outside assistance. Once over the wall, however, they had ready access to nearby working-class Catholic areas where shelter could easily be obtained and where the likelihood of information being given to the authorities was slim – at least in the short term. Once the immediate hue and cry had died down, they could remain under reasonably secure cover or make their way to the border.

Et encore de l'audace

The next escape was even more devastating. As we have seen, on 9 October 1942, the IRA Chief of Staff (such was the attrition rate for this post by this point that one must add *pro tem*) Hugh McAteer and Gerald O'Reilly, his director of intelligence, were arrested in an RUC sting operation in Derry.[123] Sentenced on 25 November 1942 to fifteen years' penal servitude for treason felony, McAteer seemed to have many years ahead of him in which to repent his folly at walking so easily into captivity.[124] His organisation needed him; he needed an action to redeem his reputation; and the escape of another high-profile IRA leader would be a powerful restorative.

By careful observation (and presumably analysis and discussion), a flaw in the physical security of the prison was identified, and in late December a small group began to plan an escape from A Wing, the convict division.[125] Four were involved: Hugh McAteer, Patrick Donnelly, Edward (Ned) Maguire and Jimmy Steele.[126] They had the perspicacity of dedicated revolutionaries and the obsessive feline energy of long-term prisoners who would never be reconciled to their lot; they also had a shrewd idea of the prison routine's strengths and weaknesses. The convict and local divisions were run much more strictly and with more vigilance than D Wing (the internees' section). The censuring of the Governor and senior staff for the June 1941 break and the consequent general tightening up had made a re-run more difficult. Boldness and imagination were needed rather than the exploitation of mere slackness or the hope that opportunity might present itself. There was a further difficulty. The wing had three landings, and the escapers were distributed between all three. On their side was the fact that Ned Maguire, an orderly, was released from his cell early in the morning and had a great deal of freedom within the wing.

Again ladders were prepared from sheets and grappling irons from metal taken from beds and an extending pole from broom handles. During the early morning of 15 January 1943 (midwinter and therefore dark), the men – possibly with the assistance of an officer – assembled on the top floor.[127] The four gained access to the roof space through a ceiling trapdoor in the third-floor lavatory. From there they carefully broke through the slates (Maguire, conveniently, was a slater by trade), tied a rope ladder to a rafter and let themselves down into the prison yard. They then used another rope, also partly fitted with rungs, to scale the perimeter wall. A blanket was thrown over the barbed wire on top of the wall, and the four dropped down on the other side. McAteer injured his leg, but all got away.

News of the escape came as a thunderbolt, a devastating blow to the credibility of the forces of law and order and, inevitably, the political leadership of Northern Ireland.[128] For a polity not much larger than an English provincial city, this was a crisis indeed. It also made the most adverse comment possible on the general state of Belfast Prison.[129] What aggravated the matter in every way was the widespread public knowledge that McAteer was the IRA Chief of Staff.[130] An intensive search immediately commenced employing every available policeman. Pedestrians, cars, vans and commercial vehicles were stopped, and a £3,000 reward was offered for the men's recapture.[131]

Such a level of activity and concern was worth more to the IRA than a string of bridges blown up and pylons blown down; the status and supposed reach and competence of the organisation were vastly (if temporarily) inflated. The RUC investigation produced an indignant and scathing report: they had caught the men, and somebody else had let them get away. It was possible that there had been staff connivance in obtaining and preparing the escape material, 'or there was no attempt at supervision to [sic] the convicts at all'. Two of the items used – leather and sheets – could have been obtained in the workshops to which the men were assigned. District Inspector W. H. Moffatt, in charge of the investigation, concluded that 'if nothing worse, there is at least an entire lack of anything resembling discipline or efficiency in the supervision of these political convicts'. So soon after the 1941 (internees') escape, Moffatt found it barely conceivable that men of the escapers' character had been assigned to the leather shop and the laundry since these were the places from which the materials had been obtained for the earlier gaol break. He expressed strong doubts about the morale and even the loyalty of some staff.[132] In an addendum to the report, Richard Harrison, Belfast RUC Commissioner, commented, 'I was at the prison on the night of the 18th instant. There is an obvious lack of discipline. No matter what the warders say someone must have opened McAteer's cell.'[133]

To back up allegations of laxness and possible subornation, the RUC submitted a number of documents to Home Affairs. One was certainly an odd take on events which cannot have carried great weight with the Ministry and probably raised more than one eyebrow. It consisted of a selection of comments by 'ordinary decent criminals', three English and one from Co. Antrim. These concerned citizens were serving sentences of penal servitude of between three and ten years, in the same wing as the escapers. The gist of what they had to say was that IRA prisoners were treated with undue laxness, that some staff showed them favours and that they exploited these advantages.[134] More serious was a set of IRA documents captured by the RUC, just nine weeks after the escape. These contained many observations on prison staff, including suggestions that some could be and were being bribed. The very fact that such an extensive correspondence could be maintained proved that staff had indeed been suborned.[135]

The RUC inquiry was only the first stage in the Ministry investigation. A three-man commission, chaired by J. J. Campbell, was appointed to look into the escape and related matters and to make recommendations.[136] The committee held its first meeting at the prison on 28 January 1943, and its preliminary findings confirmed the initial RUC assessment. In the weeks that followed, blame was apportioned and findings communicated to the Ministry. After due consideration, six officers who had been immediately in charge of the escapers were summarily dismissed, without a period of notice.[137] A decision on the fate of the Governor, who had previously been censured over the escape of the five internees in June 1941, was delayed for some months. Finally, on 12 October 1943, the Ministry wrote. In the usual officialese and terse understatement, Captain Stuart was told that the report had shown that the management of the convict wing of the prison 'left much to be desired'. Discipline had been allowed to deteriorate 'to a very low standard', and Stuart, as Governor, could not escape blame. The Ministry drew particular attention to the fact that, contrary to the regulations, two convicts had not bathed since their reception. Apart from the hygiene implications (which apparently were not a great issue), this meant that the two had not had to surrender their soiled sheets, which was the routine at the time of bathing. These evasions allowed the men to accumulate sheets. Without a supply of sheets, the ropes necessary for the escape could not have been woven, so the bathing oversight – trivial at first sight – was, in fact, a serious breach of security. Another very obvious failure concerned a table and small stepladder being used by prisoners who were whitewashing A Wing. These were used to gain access to the roof space, as anyone seriously considering their potential for breaching security should have realised. There were empty cells available in which the items could have been secured when not being used, and 'elementary precautions' had not been taken. As a consequence, some convicts had been able to spend 'considerable time' in the roof space. As required, the Governor had visited all the divisions of the prison each day. This made it all the more remarkable that he had failed to observe the various deficiencies and irregularities enumerated in the letter and had failed to issue corrective orders. In the light of these shortcomings, the Minister had decided that Stuart be reprimanded and that the increment in salary which would have come due on 12 March 1943 be withheld for six months.[138] This was an unmistakable final warning and, considering that subordinate staff had been dismissed and would suffer considerable hardship, a relatively lenient punishment for the most senior member of an establishment that had failed so conspicuously.

The cases of two of the six dismissed officers were raised by the Prison Officers' Association (which had recently extended its operations from Britain into

Northern Ireland). The two officers were not long in the Prison Service and, as befitted newcomers, had been assigned to the local division of the prison, dealing with the short-sentence men. On the morning of the escape, they had been detailed to A Wing, substituting for more experienced officers who normally worked with the convicts. In view of this extenuating circumstance, the Association asked for their reinstatement.[139] The Minister refused, and the cases of all six were taken up by the maverick MP John Nixon, former police inspector, militant Protestant, populist and ultra-loyalist Independent Unionist member of Stormont. Nixon's was an important voice, and he had a significant working-class following in his Woodvale constituency and beyond. Determined that the dismissals would not be forgotten, several months later Nixon introduced a motion condemning them as 'a violation of the rights of free and loyal men', which tended to 'discourage loyal Protestants from taking service in H.M. Prison'. The motion also called for a judicial inquiry into the 'recurring escapes'.[140] William Lowry, though a new incumbent as Minister for Home Affairs, responded robustly. He may, however, have carried forward some doubts but that there was justice in the Prison Officers' Association plea, or that officials had involved him in a decision he did not fully understand. When pressed subsequently to dismiss other officers strongly suspected of trafficking, he refused absolutely to do so without clear evidence: strong suspicion was not enough.[141]

A striking feature of the escape and its aftermath was the failure of the Campbell inquiry, the Ministry's own assessment, or the police investigation, to address the issue of staff brutality. The RUC had an extensive set of captured IRA communications, mostly between Jimmy Steele and the IRA's Northern Command. These letters, urging the organisation to take reprisals, alleged numerous instances of staff brutality and named the officers involved. The RUC and the authorities clearly accepted the accuracy of Steele's references to staff who had been suborned. There was a conspicuous and wholly inconsistent unwillingness to take any step to investigate the allegations of assaults and ill-treatment. Brutal staff were breaking rules, regulations and the criminal law just as much as those who trafficked were doing. The ill-treatment of prisoners and clearly illegal use of force were further indications that Stuart was not in full control of his prison.

While investigations and recriminations continued for many months and were at the very least a distraction to the Northern government and an unsettling influence for officials and prison staff, the IRA continued to draw on the audacity and derring-do of the January escape. The organisation also benefited more directly since, on St Valentine's Day 1943, McAteer was reappointed as Chief of Staff. Another of the escapees, Jimmy Steele, was appointed as Adjutant to the Northern Command; Ned Maguire became Quartermaster. All had been highly respected within the organisation but now carried the additional and confidence-inspiring cachet of the famous escape.[142]

Within the prison, as might be expected, there was a considerable tightening in discipline. New staff came in to A Wing to replace those who had been dismissed. Previously, a certain latitude had been extended when the prisoners wished to commemorate one of their comrades who had been killed on active service or for special occasions such as Easter. This was now stopped, and any attempt to address prisoners or to command them, military fashion, was punished. Joe Cahill recalled a new type of anti-republican officer in the wing: 'None of them, of course, were pro-republican, but some were fair and were just doing a job. These [new] boys were in it to try to break republican prisoners.'[143]

Et toujours de l'audace!

In a matter of weeks, however, republican prisoners had another cause for celebration. Although it did not involve major IRA figures, the escape this time was on a spectacular scale. A tunnel, some forty feet in length, was run under the wall of Londonderry Prison. Its construction had been under way for some time.[144] The *Irish News* claimed that it had been intended to get eighty men away, and though this number was not achieved, the size of the escape group was a major embarrassment for the Northern government.[145] Again, the timing was careful, if obvious. On the morning of Saturday, 20 March 1943, the tunnel broke out into the garden of a house in the adjacent Harding Street.[146] Twenty-one internees then passed through the house like a stage army: fifteen made their way to a hijacked furniture-removal van, parked nearby.[147] The journey across the border, three miles away, was easily completed, despite a rapid deployment by the police, according to existing contingency plans.[148] This was a large group to disperse and hide, and, once over the border, arrangements broke down, possibly because the organisers had not fully anticipated such a quick and vigorous response by the Éire authorities. Money was available to help their dispersal, but (always the IRA's jinx) not a promised lorry. Five men from the van escaped, but by mid-afternoon the Irish army and police had captured a group of eleven, also from the van.[149] Because of the sensitivity (indeed deformity might be a more apt description) of North–South relations, the escapers were not handed over to the Northern authorities but were interned for the duration.[150] Of those who evaded capture in Éire, two were subsequently recaptured in Northern Ireland. One was re-interned and the other imprisoned on further charges. By the end of April, only three of the twenty-one remained at large.

Coming so closely together, the two escapes lifted republican morale and stirred nationalist sentiment. On such occasions, of course, sympathisers and supporters tend to overlook the limited nature of the accomplishment: the escape is merely a step towards the status-quo ante, in arithmetical terms. The uplift comes from the delightful piquancy of embarrassing the forces of law and order: the repressive strength and deterrent sternness of the prison are challenged and made to look ridiculous. For their part, prison management and staff must learn the lessons of each escape: heads would roll were the same methods to be used successfully again. Following the Derry escape, and because the tunnel had been dug from a cell, the internees were immediately locked out of their cells during the daytime and passed the time in the covered exercise and recreation yard.

Minister Lowry denied that this was a collective punishment but rather the withdrawal of a privilege that had been abused.[151]

The Ministry now had a deal of experience in commissioning prison escape inquiries, and a special meeting of the Northern Ireland Cabinet was convened three days after the escape. Despite the reservations of Lowry (then Parliamentary Secretary for Home Affairs and on the cusp of promotion), majority opinion favoured an independent rather than a departmental inquiry.[152] The Prime Minister (now John Andrews) insisted that the earlier Belfast inquiry had set a precedent and were the Ministry now to depart from it, the public would feel that the government wished to shield individuals and to prevent a full discourse of the facts.[153] Lowry, though in the minority in the discussion, put his views on record, that 'the wrong type of Governor and Deputy Governor had been appointed in the past' – a fairly explicit criticism of his own ministry.[154] Another three-man panel was appointed, under the chairmanship of a barrister, R. J. Jackson.[155] Doubtless with a view to reassuring the politicians, the initial police report emphasised that the RUC had reacted swiftly and that contingency plans existed and were immediately implemented. The report also revealed that the police had known about escape rumours, which had been circulating since December, but that they had not anticipated a tunnel and therefore had taken no precautions against digging. (A hit-and-run attack on the prison, the liberation of captives, and a swift getaway across the border were the possibilities against which they had prepared.) To ensure that the prison was not covertly captured by armed raiders, there was a standing arrangement for a prison officer to call Victoria Street RUC barracks every hour on the hour, from midnight until 9 a.m. Had the call not been received, the police would have activated their plans. At this early point in their enquiries, the RUC mentioned that William Agnew, a prison officer, had been on duty on the ground floor on the morning of the escape. Subsequent reports also referred to Agnew, who, according to intelligence, was the IRA's conduit 'to get any despatch they wanted to the internees'. The police considered him to be shrewd and intelligent and quite capable of acting as a courier without arousing suspicion. Two other prison officers had also caused concerns and were discussed with the Governor a few weeks before.[156]

The Jackson inquiry described a regime that allowed freedom of movement, much of it unsupervised, from morning unlocking until 9 p.m. lock-up. For more than twelve hours each weekday, most of the men were in association in the exercise yard or in the prison. There was, moreover, fairly uncontrolled movement between the recreational areas and the cells. It is the alpha and omega of prison security and management that movement be restricted and closely monitored. Various regulations were supposed to check and supervise daytime access to cells, but Jackson and his colleagues concluded that in practice there were few if any impediments and that the internees had 'what might be described as "the free run of the place"'. This was crucial, since the tunnel had been dug from a ground-floor cell and the escapers had managed to gain entry to it although nine of the twenty-one had been housed on the second and third tiers.[157]

On the morning of the escape there was the normal melee, and various rules were, as usual, ignored. Giving evidence to the inquiry, a number of officers contradicted each other, were suspiciously vague, or restricted themselves to giving an outline of what usually happened. One admitted that he had unlocked Cell 11 (where the tunnel started) to allow an internee to enter, while having no idea whether or not the man was the cell's occupant. This in itself was an alarming confession.

In addition to unhampered movement, there was other evidence of the internees' dominance in the prison. Much was made of the fact that a ground-floor cell was used for the teaching of Irish, and there were signs in Irish on cell doors throughout the prison. More directly relating to control and management, the internees had elected a leader (Paddy Adams, of Abercorn Street, Belfast), openly called him OC, and the Governor recognised his authority. When pressed, Captain Fryer said that the principle of recognition of the OC had been accepted since 1922.[158] A possible breach of security was read into the fact that two musical groups were allowed to have practice sessions in the evenings in a ground-floor dormitory. It was implied that this could have been related to the escape since the bands – mainly drums and pipes – would have synchronised with and masked the sounds of digging. More generally, the Governor had no idea that the internees were subject to the same regime as remand prisoners, he had never received instructions on the matter, and he had never been supplied with the relevant rules and regulations.

A deal of information was uncovered about the escape itself, and there were also some informed guesses. Belated searches had shown that there were two tunnels. One, which the Committee determined had been dug in 1940, during the previous use of the prison for internees, was only six feet below ground and had been discontinued when it came to the prison wall, the foundations of which were twelve feet deep. The later tunnel diggers had disposed of the soil by the traditional means of flushing some down the toilets and also distributing some over the exercise yard. The sewers had blocked four times in one week, and, taking this as a warning, the tunnellers changed their methods of disposal. Astonishingly, neither the Governor nor his staff had queried the repeated blockages. Most of the digging was done at night by the three occupants of Cell 11 – 'all small men' – but some may also have been done during the day. The ready communication achieved between the internees and the outside organisation was confirmed by the ordering of the furniture van. This had been booked on a provisional basis, with final confirmation and precise timing to be given on the day before the escape. There were police suspicions as to who had carried the messages, but no evidence.[159] Attention focused on officers William Agnew and Robert Doherty, about whose loyalties there were long-standing doubts.[160] To curtail Doherty's contacts with prisoners as much as possible, he had some time previously been appointed to an office job, as the Chief Officer's clerk. This fulfilled its prime purpose but did allow Doherty to make up the duty roster for staff. He had assigned Agnew to Tier 1 of the cell block on the morning of 20 March. It seemed more than coincidence that this was the first time in four months that

Agnew had performed that duty. Jackson had no hard evidence that Agnew had colluded in the escape but took him to be complaisant, at the very least. He claimed that although responsible for the supervision of the immediate area Agnew had failed to notice twenty men enter Cell 11 and also the return to the prison of two failed escapers who had been scared back by a constable at the tunnel exit.[161]

Had the IRA had access to the report, it would have confirmed to the organisation that the escape was another cleverly conceived operation, executed with great care and discipline. Whichever prison officers were used, they were handled subtly and in a manner that protected them from criminal charges. Even the RUC informant who had identified Doherty as attending planning and preparation meetings could not be used, since for obvious reasons he could not be put in a witness box. While arrangements at the prison end had been an unqualified success, preparations thereafter were haphazard, with the bulk of the escapers apparently being left to find their own way to safety once they had crossed the border. This was the only morsel of consolation that the authorities could pick from an otherwise bitter dish.

A number of recommendations were made by the Jackson Committee, most worryingly predictable and obvious: an instance of sprucing up the belatedly closed stable door. Officers were to be better instructed in their duties. This was particularly needful since 75 per cent of the staff at Derry were temporary officers.[162] The Committee recommended various restrictions to be placed on internees' movements within the prison, together with access to their cells and property. A few recommendations were also given about physical security.[163] It was recognised that it would not have been possible to deal with the internees as though they were remand prisoners, although this was the supposed basis of their regime. 'What is startling', the Committee observed, 'is to find that the prison officers in immediate charge… have allowed… a freedom of action far beyond anything that the Governor regards as admissible… In fact, the subordinate staff, as a body, has exercised little or no control.' Jackson and his colleagues regretted the overwhelming proportion of temporary officers in the Londonderry establishment. They could not be sure if they were scared, simply inexperienced or inadequately instructed, but they did seem 'to be suffering from an inferiority complex in dealing with the internees'. Captain Fryer had dismissed seven officers in five months for getting too friendly with their charges.

Jackson claimed that there was no evidence of intimidation, but then, somewhat contradictorily, went on to instance how internees would gather around when an officer reprimanded an internee in the yard, 'which would certainly tend to have an intimidating effect'. Fryer and his chief officer seem to have been unaware of all the laxities that had developed, which indicated a lack of basic supervisory skills. The two had 'suffered from a complacency which was not justified, as was exemplified by their lack of involvement in the examinations that had been undertaken against tunnelling'.[164]

This was a scathing report, and its strictures were no doubt well merited. The disciplinary outcome was inevitable and much the same as at Belfast. On

9 June 1943, Fryer was informed that William Agnew was to be dismissed forthwith. The supervisory and ordinary staff could not be absolved from responsibility and were therefore censured 'for neglect of primary precautions in carrying out their day-to-day duty and for general slackness in looking after the internees under their charge'.[165] On 12 October 1943, Captain Fryer himself received what must have been an expected and weighty rebuke. It came in a format identical to that used in the censure of Captain Stuart, the Belfast Governor. Fryer's shortcomings were listed and detailed in relation to the facts set out by the Committee of Inquiry. He also was reprimanded, and the increment of salary which would have been due to him on 25 April 1943 was withheld for six months.[166]

Coda

Just ten weeks after he received this formal reprimand, Captain Fryer's capabilities were again called into question. In the small hours of Thursday, 30 December 1943, nine internees made another break for freedom.[167] They were discovered only in the final stages of their attempt, within ten yards of the main gate. Four officers of the external patrol raised the alarm and covered the men with their fire-arms until they could be taken back inside the prison and locked in cells.[168] Since the escape had been foiled, the authorities hoped to keep it secret. A report – probably from an informant in the police or prison service – was nevertheless leaked to the press.[169] Even though the escape had been thwarted, this was no triumph, and the authorities were reluctant to unveil yet another indication of lax security.

That the attempt reflected very badly on the running of the prison there could be no doubt. This was no opportunistic event but rather the product of careful planning and preparation. In many ways this was a tribute performance, following the Belfast escape of 15 January. Once again sheets had been knotted and twisted into a rope; grappling hooks had been prepared from pieces of metal removed from furniture; there was also an extending pole device to allow the sheet-rope to be hooked onto the wall – a more effective method of securing a grip than throwing rope and hook. More worrying to the authorities than any of this, however, was the fact that the escapers had managed to obtain or to make, two keys. One released prisoners from their cells. Adrian Robinson, Secretary of the Ministry of Home Affairs, pointed out to his minister, William Lowry, that once the prisoners had been shut in for the night, the double-action lock on each cell door could only be opened by a cell master-key; the ordinary cell key would not be sufficient. Clearly, therefore, the internees had got hold of this master-key, as well as the pass-gate key that allowed them to leave their corridor and the cell building. A lead copy of this last key had been discovered under the sand of a fire-bucket on the top floor. It was supposed that one of the escapers had brought the key back into the building and had shoved it into the bucket when being marched back to his cell.

A prison depends on locks and keys as the first line of physical security. The discovery of this key and the knowledge that keys had been obtained either to trace or to take an impression led on very obviously to other questions. If the key had not been copied outside and brought into the prison, then metal-working tools had been introduced. In either case, it was almost certain that there had been staff collusion. William Agnew, recently dismissed from the prison for suspected sympathy with the IRA, was the prime suspect, especially since, as the Chief Officer's clerk, he normally worked in the room in which the prison's keys were kept locked in a safe. It was suspected, moreover, that the lead copy of the key was merely a model and that the internees had duplicate keys which had not been discovered.

Between the cell block and the perimeter wall there was an exit gate, which, in addition to the usual integral lock, was fitted with a padlock. The escapers had managed to break the padlock, supposedly because of a flaw in the metal. It seemed improbable that such a well-planned operation would have relied on being able to break a padlock, and Robinson suspected that the 'flaw', far from being a natural one, had been made in advance.

There was much suspicion and little hard evidence in all of this, and Robinson advised the Minister against a formal inquiry. It was not, after all, a successful escape but merely an escape from one part of the prison to another. A formal inquiry was unlikely to produce any evidence that could be used against staff. A police report had been requested, and any decision should await its conclusions. Were the police unable to come up with further information, the prison itself should seek to discover how the escape materials had been made and secreted. Other steps should be taken to augment the existing locks; the night patrols inside the prison should also be strengthened.[170]

As expected, the police report took the matter very little further. Three months later, another reprimand was sent to Captain Fryer. The possession of keys and the concealment of pieces of wood six feet long could only have been possible because of prison officers' negligence in searching cells. The 'general laxity' that permitted this neglect of duty 'must ultimately be held to be the responsibility of the Governor'. No further enquiries would be made, but the new Minister, John Warnock, had made clear that he was 'gravely perturbed' that such an incident should have occurred so soon after the previous escape. He trusted that there would be no recurrence.[171]

Match tied

These events showed that the IRA and the Northern Ireland prisons were well matched. A relatively small group of men among the internees and prisoners showed great determination and skill in escapes, rather less in subverting the prison and confronting authority. They were successful in suborning staff, and the layers of prison management were always, it seems, one step behind. But their outside organisation was incapable of providing support of a quality and volume to take full advantage of the ingenuity and audacity of the leading prisoners and internees. The IRA's weakness and inability to build upon prison and internment issues showed its isolation. Its shortage of talent was shown by the speed with which escapees were redeployed on operations.

This pallid performance was matched in the prisons. Skill and diligence in matters of security and control fell far short of what was required and what was possible. The disproportionate employment of temporary staff was both a cause and a symptom of an ill-adapted management. An alert leadership would have evaluated the consequences of shifting from a fairly torpid and ordinary criminal population – only occasionally spiced up with small influxes of IRA detainees or sentenced prisoners – to one that posed a significantly greater challenge to control and security. To evaluate the changed risks and to provide operational plans, procedures, training and motivation to an essentially complacent (and partly corrupt) staff was beyond the capacity of the managers of the three prisons. And, it must be observed, there was little encouragement from officials and politicians to take the necessary steps. The perennial prison–politician pact was attended to only when it failed: 'Keep it quiet and get on with it.'

Notes

1 Derry occasionally received non-political remand prisoners, but these were few in number and were kept apart from the internees.

2 See below, p. 593.

3 See below, pp. 571 and 595.

4 See pp. 377–78.

5 Brendan Anderson, *Joe Cahill: A Life in the IRA* (Dublin: The O'Brien Press, 2002), pp. 75–8.

6 Anderson, *Joe Cahill, op. cit.*, pp. 99–100.

7 Uinseann MacEoin, *The IRA in the Twilight Years, 1923–1948* (Dublin: Argenta, 1997), p. 457.

8 See, for example, the question put by T. J. Campbell to the Minister for Home Affairs on 22 October 1940 about the case of three internees who had been on hunger strike for a week. One of the three, Bennett, was said to be in a state of extreme exhaustion. Not so, replied Sir Dawson Bates (*NIPD*, vol. 23, col. 2400, 22 October 1940). See also *Irish News*, 23 October 1940, 4d.

9 A copy of this order was obtained by the authorities when a search was made of Jimmy Steele in April 1941. Steele was a leading figure in the Belfast IRA. In June 1935 he had been sentenced to five years' penal servitude for treason felony in connection with the Crown Entry court martial (see pp. 395–96). Released in May 1940 he was soon rearrested. At the Belfast City Commission on 19 July 1940 he was sentenced to ten years' penal servitude for the possession of arms and explosives. He was one of five men who escaped from Belfast Prison on 15 January 1943. He then served for three months as Adjutant of the IRA's Northern Command. Recaptured in May, he returned to prison to serve out his full sentence. A document obtained from such a high-ranking member of the organisation carried the stamp of authenticity and authority. See PRONI HA/3/1/768, T. M. Stuart, Governor, Belfast Prison, to A. Robinson, 9 April 1941. During the first year of his penal-servitude sentence, Steele had himself staged a hunger strike of nineteen days (*Irish News*, 7 September 1936,

5c; 10 September 1936, 5e). A copy of General Order No. 4 (still in force more than three decades later) is reproduced in Brendan O'Brien, *The Long War: The IRA and Sinn Féin* (Dublin: The O'Brien Press, 1995), Appendix 2, p. 407. These General Orders had been amended and reconfirmed by the Army Council in October 1973.

10 PRONI HA/32/1/763, T. M. Stuart to Ministry of Home Affairs, 14 March 1941.

11 PRONI HA/32/1/763, T. M. Stuart to Ministry of Home Affairs, 8 February 1941.

12 PRONI HA/9/2/59, Home Affairs to Finance, 19 February 1942.

13 Nationalist Senator Thomas McLaughlin wrote privately to Home Affairs expressing his abhorrence at the visiting arrangements and asked that the men be treated as internees and not convicted criminals (**PRONI HA/32/1/763**, Thomas McLaughlin to Ministry of Home Affairs, 4 March 1941). Thomas J. Campbell, Nationalist MP for the Belfast Central Division, openly questioned the Minister about the matter (*NIPD*, vol. 24, cols. 592–3, 27 March 1941). Neither intervention was successful.

14 PRONI HA/32/1/763, Belfast Prison to Ministry of Home Affairs, 26 March 1941; H. J. Campbell, Ministry of Home Affairs, to Home Office, 8 April 1941.

15 PRONI HA/32/1/757, T. M. Stuart to Ministry of Home Affairs, 25 November 1941.

16 PRONI HA/32/1/757, annotation. Weekends were frequently chosen for protests and attempted escapes since generally only a reduced staff was on duty. In facing down the protest, Stuart had thought it prudent to keep a full staff on duty rather than the normal weekend and much reduced rota. He got little credit for the successful outcome, however, a ministry official grumbling that his decision had entailed 'a considerable amount of overtime that will have to be paid for'.

17 PRONI HA/9/2/59.

18 PRONI HA/9/2/180, T. M. Stuart to A. Robinson, 28 January 1942.

19 These details are of course one-sided, and it is likely that at least some of the prisoners resisted. It is equally likely, however, that staff handled roughly those who failed to obey orders. See the captured IRA letter, undated (but probably late January 1942) addressed from inside the prison to the IRA's Northern Command (**PRONI HA/32/1/856**).

20 PRONI HA/9/2/180, T. M. Stuart to A. Robinson, 28 January 1942.

21 PRONI HA/9/2/180, S. W. McComb, Medical Officer, to A. Robinson, 31 January 1942.

22 PRONI HA/32/1/856, T. M. Stuart to A. Robinson, 1 February 1942, copying intercepted note.

23 PRONI HA/32/1/832, T. M. Stuart to Home Affairs, 20 March 1942.

24 See p. 589 below.

25 *NIPD*, vol. 27, cols. 777–8, 22 March 1944. Parliamentary question by Thomas Campbell, Belfast Central Division.

26 PRONI HA/9/2/933, Note found on Patrick J. Mulgrew, dated 3 March 1944. The writer ('Huck') gave encouraging (and inventive) news of outside developments: 'masses were being said for the strikers every morning at St Mary's and the army outside is ready for anything & the publicity is growing'.

27 PRONI HA/9/2/180, No date. The second front, in the months before D-Day, was a much discussed topic.

28 PRONI HA/9/2/180, Note forwarded by the Governor.

29 PRONI HA/9/2/180, Extracts from convicts' letters, forwarded to Ministry, 3 April 1944. Liam Burke blamed the wartime restrictions on publicity for the failure of the strike. His recollection that it lasted for forty-three days is incorrect: the correct figure is twenty-five days (MacEoin, *The IRA in the Twilight Years, op. cit.*, p. 457).

30 Some individuals refused food again in the 1950s, to protest at their internment arising out of the IRA's border campaign but there was no concerted hunger striking.

31 John McGuffin (an internee of a later period) claimed that altogether eighteen women were interned during the war years. He did not provide a list but stated that twelve women were from Belfast with three from Derry and three from Tyrone. John McGuffin, *Internment* (Tralee: Anvil Books, 1973). Surviving records do not provide a single definitive list of interned women. On 23 November 1943, the following were being held in Armagh's B1 ward: Margaret Agnew (aka Toland), Margaret Burns, Mary H. Craig, Mary J. Dempsey, Teresa Donnelly, Rosaleen McCotter, Mary A. McDonald, Agnes P. McDowell, Nora McDowell, Norah McKearney, Bernadette T. Masterson, Agnes Moore, Catherine O'Hara, Josephine O'Neill, Christina P. Rafferty, Josephine Rafferty. It is likely that some had been released before the date of this list. Others submitted multiple appeals and were rejected because of police reports on their republican involvement and activities. See PRONI HA/9/2/933, G. H. Brush to Ministry of Home Affairs, 23 November 1943. For appeal hearings the women were taken to Belfast Prison for the day. In addition, Armagh held three Derry internees who did not associate with the others. There had been a falling out (possibly a clash of personalities) between these three and the rest of the women on 31 August 1943, and it was thought necessary to separate them. The dissident group was led by Nora (Nancy) Ward; the other two being Alice Ashton and Annie T. Ward (PRONI HA/9/2/933). Ages on internment ranged from nineteen to forty-seven years, most being under thirty.

32 Hugh Corvin of the Green Cross Fund described Catherine O'Hara as 'a very strong-minded woman'. Some years before, she had given up her teaching post rather than swear the Oath of Allegiance. Corvin thought that 'she would probably continue that attitude until the end'. PRONI HA/32/1/828, Minute of meeting between Green Cross Fund delegation and Minister for Home Affairs, 20 December 1944.

33 In a subsequent letter to the Ministry on the subject of the excessively large parcels of sweet and fancy foods and cigarettes sent to the women, Brush sourly observed that, with excessive eating and smoking, 'I fancy their livers went wrong, hence all this trouble' (PRONI HA/9/2/402, G. H. Brush to R. G. Ronaldson, 1 December 1943).

34 PRONI HA/9/2/402, H. C. Montgomery, Assistant Secretary, Ministry of Home Affairs, to G. H. Brush, 7 December 1943.

35 The Attorney General was also asked whether the Prisoners (Temporary Discharge for Ill-Health) Act, 1913 (better known as the 'Cat and Mouse' Act) could be used to release women on hunger strike – and to return them to custody when they regained health. He responded that the Act did not apply to internees and that, in any event, the Minister already had sufficient discretionary powers to release and to re-intern (PRONI HA/9/2/122, Attorney General's minute, 8 December 1943).

36 *Irish News*, 30 November 1943, 3f; *Belfast Telegraph*, 29 November 1943, 3f.

37 PRONI HA/9/3/933, Nora Ward to Editor, *Belfast Telegraph*, 1 December 1943.

38 PRONI HA/9/3/933, Nora Ward to G. H. Brush, 19 January 1944. See also the despondent letter from Nora Ward to a woman friend, 23 December 1943: 'We have been publicly maligned in the Press over things that have happened in here.'

39 PRONI HA/9/3/933, Catherine O'Hara to G. H. Brush, 4 December 1943. Recorded cell temperatures were low (certainly by modern standards), ranging from 8.9°C to 14.4°C.

40 PRONI HA/9/3/933, G. H. Brush to Ministry of Home Affairs, 11 December 1943. In the last few days, only Josephine O'Neill continued on strike with Catherine.

41 On 1 April 1944, there were sixteen female internees, on 1 July ten, and on 1 October nine. PRONI HA/9/2/164, Ministry of Finance to Ministry of Home Affairs, 5 February 1945.

42 PRONI HA/32/1/828, Minute, 20 December 1944 and annotations.

43 See above, p. 545.

44 See above, pp. 520–21.

45 PRONI HA/9/2/164, Captain A. Fryer, Governor, Londonderry Prison, to A. Robinson, 4 January 1940. The report of the disturbance itself has not been discovered in the files, but this correspondence refers to it.

46 PRONI HA/9/2/164, Ministry of Home Affairs to Ministry of Finance, 6 January 1940.

47 PRONI HA/9/2/164, Ministry of Home Affairs to Major J. K. Gorman, County Inspector, Londonderry, 3 June 1940.

48 PRONI HA/9/2/190, T. M. Stuart to Ministry of Home Affairs, 17 November 1941.

49 PRONI HA/9/2/190. It is not now possible to say whether or not Stuart was correct. Another advantage of prosecution to the four men, he reasoned, was the opportunity for publicity it would give them when they were produced in court. J. B. O'Hagan would, after release, participate in the IRA's 'border campaign' of 1956–62 and, in November 1957, was elected to the Army Council. See J. Bowyer Bell, *The Secret Army: The IRA, 1916–1979* (Cambridge, Mass.: MIT Press, 1983), Chapters 14 and 15, *passim*. Even in the early 1940s, he was an experienced IRA operative.

50 PRONI HA/9/2/190. Loss of privileges, of course, meant no parcels at all.

51 PRONI HA/9/2/190, Mrs Brogan to T. M. Stuart, 11 April 1941.

52 PRONI HA/9/2/190, Ministry memorandum, 21 April 1941. The convict regime was regulated by statute, in part to establish the prisoners' entitlements, as well as the obligations and liabilities. A change in regime, even an ameliorative one, could therefore be deemed illegal. Short of that, it might expose the administration to political criticism. The Ministry was bound to act once Stuart had raised the matter: it may, however, have wished that he had turned a blind eye.

53 See below, p. 593.

54 *NIPD*, vol. 26, cols. 1376–7, 8 July 1943. William Lowry (1884–1949) was educated at Foyle College, Londonderry. Called to the Irish bar in 1907; Reid Professor of Constitutional and Criminal Law at Trinity College Dublin; silk in 1913. Stormont MP for Londonderry in 1939; Minister for Home Affairs, 1943–4; Attorney General, 1944–7; appointed Judge, 1947. His son (Robert Erskine Lowry) would become Lord Chief Justice of Northern Ireland (1971–8).

55 PRONI HA/9/2/402, G. H. Brush to Ministry of Home Affairs, 7 December 1943.

56 Only sentenced prisoners were required to wear uniforms, so the issue was moot for remand prisoners and internees. See *Irish News*, 6 July 1943, 1d.

57 This included the removal of tables and chairs so that the naked men either had to sit or stand on the stone floor all day (Anderson, *Joe Cahill, op. cit.*, p. 95).

58 PRONI HA/9/2/933, T. M. Stuart to H. C. Montgomery, 16 and 18 June 1943.

59 PRONI HA/9/2/933, T. M. Stuart to H. C. Montgomery, 5 July 1943. The last sentence could be read as a resignation threat. The importance of an official such as the Governor of Belfast Prison within Northern Ireland's small and certainly compact system of public administration was considerable, and so sensitive to the government and its supporters was any matter concerning IRA prisoners, that this was a threat of some weight.

60 *NIPD*, vol. 26, cols. 1339–41, 6 July 1943. Lowry was emphatic. These were convicted prisoners, 'and they will not coerce the prison authorities or this Ministry into according them political treatment by simply refusing to put their clothes on'. See also *Irish News*, 7 July 1943, 1b–c.

61 Even late into the summer of 1943, for example, the Advisory Committee meeting (fully clothed) at Belfast Prison was keen to emphasise that a room 'suitably heated' if necessary be put at its disposal (PRONI HA/32/1/175, Internment Advisory Committee Meetings, 26 July 1943).

62 This was described by Jimmy Steele in his journal *Resurgent Ulster* (Belfast: Republican Publicity Bureau, 1952). This frank, evocative and grim piece of prison writing is reproduced in Tim Pat Coogan, *The IRA* (London: Fontana, 1980), pp. 242–6, together with the names of the twenty-two men who took part in the strike. Joe Cahill lasted only one day before collapsing from the cold. When he regained consciousness he was fully clothed and a medical orderly was giving him spoonfuls of restorative whiskey: 'As far as I was concerned, that was the finish of the strike for me' (Anderson, *Joe Cahill, op. cit.*, p. 95).

63 PRONI HA/9/2/933, Deputy Governor, Belfast Prison to Ministry of Home Affairs, 16 September 1943. The Deputy Governor (temporarily in charge of the prison) wanted to have the men brought before him on disciplinary charges. He would find them guilty and sentence them to three days' bread and water. Montgomery at Home Affairs, evidently uneasy, put the proposal to the Minister, who commented that he did not think it worth risking a renewal of the trouble 'in order to impose a trivial punishment of this kind'. He did agree that the 'Nudists' (as Montgomery called them) should forfeit remission marks (PRONI HA/9/2/933, H. C. Montgomery to Secretary, with annotations, 21 and 23 September 1943). See also the short letter to the *Irish News* (23 September 1943, 2g) from Hugh McAteer on the strip strike. McAteer had escaped from Belfast Prison on 15 January 1943 and had been reinstated the following month as IRA Chief of Staff, a position he held when writing the letter. Nine months later, on 20 November 1943, McAteer was again arrested. *Belfast Telegraph*, 20 November 1943, 3d–e; *Irish News*, 22 November 1943, 1d–f.

64 All the divisions of Belfast Prison – local, juvenile adult, internee and convict, were constituted as a battalion of the IRA. Each division constituted a company and had an OC, with Steele in overall command as Battalion OC. The battalion was either designated as Belfast No. 3 or No. 2 (both appear in the correspondence) – doubtless more as a morale booster than an indication that they were operational, or indeed that the IRA had a number of functioning battalions in Belfast.

65 The letters (found in an unoccupied safe house in Belfast) accompanied by an explanatory note, marked 'Most Secret', were sent by the RUC to A. Robinson, 26 March 1943 (PRONI HA/32/1/356).

66 Thus, on 21 December 1941, Steele wrote about four officers, including Chief Officer G. D. Crowe, who, he said, 'practically run this place'; he also named five others, 'their willing tools', and observed 'your I/O [Intelligence Officer] has been supplied with the addresses of all these men and the habits etc of most of them'. He did not wish the Adjutant General, Northern Command, to think he was dictating, but he (Steele) had a responsibility to his men and must see that they had 'adequate protection against the enemy whenever that protection can be given'. Steele would not allow them 'to suffer punishment and tyranny without striking back at those responsible'. He expected his superiors to do the same for him. He had previously called for help, 'but unfortunately up to the present that help has not been forthcoming except in verbal promises'. PRONI HA/32/1/356, Jimmy Steele to OC Northern Command, 21 December 1941. Crowe was the man that Steele most frequently identified for retaliatory and deterrent action.

67 PRONI HA/32/1/356, Jimmy Steele to OC Northern Command, 11 December 1941.

68 PRONI HA/32/1/356, Jimmy Steele to OC Northern Command, 15 January 1942.

69 PRONI HA/32/1/356, Jimmy Steele to OC Northern Command, 26 January 1942. At this point, prison staff were being advised to be careful in their movements outside the prison (*Irish News*, 16 April 1942, 3b–c).

70 PRONI HA/32/1/856, Jimmy Steele to OC Northern Command, 27 January 1942. Steele also named another officer who had been 'terrorising' the prisoners: 'an immediate visit to this hypocrite is necessary'.

71 Walker was a temporary officer who had joined the Prison Service only eighteen months before; he had been married for about a year, and his wife was nearing the end of her pregnancy. He was on his way back to the prison after his midday meal. At a hearing in the Belfast Recorders' Court in April 1942, his widow Jane was awarded compensation of £1,500 (PRONI HA/9/2/274; *Belfast Telegraph*, 7 February 1942, 3e). Coogan (*The IRA, op. cit.*, p. 241), drawing on his interviews with some of the leading IRA men of the time, claims that Walker was 'the most popular warder in the prison' and killed by mistake. Steele was unmoved by the mistaken killing. He reported to Northern Command that conditions in the prison were unchanged. He concluded that they would persist until those officers he had identified as ringleaders were 'removed' (PRONI HA/32/1/356, Jimmy Steele to OC Northern Command, 19 February 1942). Several of the internees had reportedly complained to the IRA about the killing: Walker had been one of the 'half-decent screws' and should have been left alone. According to Joe Cahill, the IRA then carried out an inquiry into the mistaken shooting (Anderson, *Joe Cahill, op. cit.*, p. 75).

72 PRONI HA/32/1/356, Jimmy Steele to OC Northern Command, 3 February 1942: 'they honestly believe they can get away with such things'.

73 According to the RUC, the target had been Officer Nicholl. He was said to have been so intimidated by the shooting that an informant reported that he was 'slavering' on the IRA prisoners (PRONI HA/32/1/860, Inspector-General's Office, RUC, to Ministry of Home Affairs, 29 September 1943).

74 PRONI HA/32/1/856, Jimmy Steele to OC Northern Command, 2 March 1943. Although Coogan does not name the intended victim, he refers to him as 'a particularly bullying warder', which, from the Steele correspondence would probably have been Chief Officer Crowe. Coogan refers to the bullying of prisoners but attributes it to the escape of January 1943. As we have seen, however, Steele complained of bullying and beatings two years before the escape. The January hunger strike and the murder of Thomas Walker were given as instances of the particular stresses to which Belfast prison officers were subject when twelve days later Home Affairs sought for them a special duty allowance of 3 shillings per week. PRONI HA/0/2/59, Home Affairs to Finance, 19 February 1942.

75 PRONI HA/32/1/856, Jimmy Steele to OC Northern Command, 30 January 1941. The RUC was interested in another of Steele's references to a prison officer: 'I asked Anna [Steele's wife] to send in some [tobacco] at Xmas for old Fletcher. I wanted to give him some for doing cards for me.' This may have referred to the illicit posting of Christmas cards from Steele by Fletcher. The authorities would also have been disturbed at the ease with which Steele referred to the smuggling in of tobacco.

76 *Belfast Telegraph*, 25 January 1944, 3d–e.

77 PRONI HA/32/1/880, Joint letter to T. M. Stuart and A. Robinson, 27 January 1944.

78 PRONI HA/32/1/880, RUC Inspector-General's Office, to H. C. Montgomery, 9 February 1944. Both Crowe and Thompson already had revolvers.

79 PRONI HA/32/1/880, undated letter, Intelligence Officer, Northern Command, Óglaigh na hÉireann, to Officer Nathaniel Robinson.

80 PRONI HA/32/1/880, undated letter, Intelligence Officer, Northern Command, Óglaigh na hÉireann to Officer J. Riordan. The note concluded, 'These men are doing no one any harm so why treat them like criminals. Pay attention to this.'

81 PRONI HA/32/1/880, Intelligence Officer, Northern Command, Óglaigh na hÉireann to Officer J. Riordan, 23 February 1944.

82 PRONI HA/32/1/880, RUC to Ministry, 7 March 1944; T. M. Stuart to Ministry, 4 February 1947.

83 There was no explicit sectarian element in this incident, though the Ministry took a close interest in the religious affiliations and general political attitudes of its employees. See the exchanges on the appointment of a new clerk at Belfast Prison in 1938–9 (PRONI HA/32/1/676).

84 The details of the affair are difficult to summarise but may be found at PRONI HA/32/1/656. There was no evidence that trafficking had occurred in this case, and it did seem that the officer had been victimised. The principal reason why he was moved was that he had apparently kept a detailed log of prison disagreements, slights and conversations, going back for several years. Note-taking made him an unreliable employee with unpredictable but possibly volatile effects on the staff chemistry. There was concern that at some point he could publicise his grievances, drawing on his considerable back-up material.

85 PRONI HA/32/1/74, Copy of intercepted letter, Seamus Walker to Peter Donnelly, 15 July 1939; and reply, 21 July 1939. This, of course, was a potentially lethal exchange, since had Donnelly named someone as an informer retribution would certainly have followed.

86 PRONI HA/32/1/74, Special Branch Memorandum, 9 May 1940.

87 Prisoners were issued with cigarettes or the equivalent amount of tobacco, but not with matches or lighters. The official arrangement was that a single cigarette or pipe would be smoked at the designated smoking time, a light being provided by an officer. This did not satisfy the cravings of a generation heavily addicted to tobacco, and much ingenuity was exercised on the double problem of securing and lighting extra supplies. See Anderson, *Joe Cahill, op. cit.*, pp. 78–80.

88 PRONI HA/32/1/74. See above p. 129. A police officer noted that, besides his sentence of imprisonment, Willis had been disqualified from driving for twelve years and that his desire to 'help the authorities' may have been driven by a desire to regain his driving licence.

89 PRONI HA/32/1/74. Memorandum by Frederick William Willis, 6 May 1940.

90 PRONI HA/32/1/74, E. W. Scales to Sir Dawson Bates, 29 May 1940.

91 PRONI HA/32/1/74, E. W. Scales to Arthur Black, Attorney General, 4 June 1940. Scales had two reservations. Irish prison law was unclear on trafficking. Whereas English legislation (Prison Act, 1865: 28 & 29 Vict., c.126, s.39) made it an offence to convey letters in or out of prison, the comparable Irish legislation made it an offence only to bring items into prison but not to take them out. Prisons (Ireland) Act, 1826, 7 Geo. IV, c.74, s.110; and Prisons (Ireland) Act, 1856: 19 & 20 Vict., c.68, s.34. He also recognised the difficulty of proceeding on prisoners' evidence 'particularly such a low type' (referring to Carson).

92 PRONI HA/32/1/74, Statement by Robert Carson, witnessed by Governor and Deputy Governor, 15 June 1940. An investigation by R. Ronaldson of the Ministry's Prison Branch described Carson as 'the most despicable type of stool pigeon using his status as assistant in the Library to carry messages all around the Prison, and to betray any confidence reposed in him either by prisoners or the Authorities' (PRONI HA/32/1/74, Memorandum, 2 July 1940).

93 PRONI HA/32/1/74, Ronaldson Memorandum, 2 July 1940. It is not clear what 'keeping an eye on' entailed.

94 This was an utterly futile direction, showing little knowledge of how prisons worked. If prison staff could be bribed and intimidated, what hope was there that a prisoner could or would resist the demands, threats and inducements of his fellows, with whom he lived and worked?

95 PRONI HA/32/1/74, Inspector of Prisons to T. M. Stuart, 15 July 1940. Further clarification was given regarding visits. The special room was not to be used for 'respectable and well-conducted prisoners' and the old 'cage' visiting boxes were not

to be brought back into use, except in special circumstances: 'It is agreed that their use has a degrading effect upon all involved' (PRONI HA/32/1/74, E. W. Scales to T. M. Stuart, 19 August 1940).

96 PRONI HA/32/1/740, Memorandum of 5 February 1941. It is not clear why the Governor of Northern Ireland and his staff could not have been apprised of the RUC case against the men, on a confidential basis.

97 PRO HO/144/21530 and CJ/4/30. See, for example, a letter from Hugh McAteer to Mrs B. McAteer, 13 April 1941. This was apparently stopped, opened and copied at the Derry post office, probably because the address was on a watch list. It had been posted in Belfast, and the Derry police asked that it be reposted from there (PRONI HA/32/1/740). Hugh McAteer was serving a sentence of fifteen years' penal servitude for treason felony. He had been a leading figure in the planned September 1942 campaign against the North, was OC Northern Command and then (from July 1942) IRA Chief of Staff. He had been picked up in an RUC sting operation in October 1942. On 15 January 1943, he was one of four men who escaped from Belfast Prison. He was reappointed Chief of Staff the following month, but was rearrested in October 1943. It was astonishing naivety on McAteer's part to imagine that the post of the family of a high-profile IRA man would not be intercepted.

98 Prison (Officers Superannuation) Act, 1878: 41 & 42 Vict., c.63; see also General Prisons (Ireland) Act, 1877: 40 & 41 Vict., c.49, s.32.

99 PRONI HA/32/1/740, Memoranda of 2 August and 20 August 1941. One man was a basic grade officer, the other a principal. Their removal, Montgomery particularly hoped, would have a deterrent effect.

100 PRONI HA/32/1/740, Statement of D. J. Barr, 8 March 1943.

101 PRONI HA/32/1/740, Memoranda, 13 March and 6 August 1943.

102 Cahill recalled the difficulties that arose when a regular courier was retired or transferred. An attempt to enlist a replacement backfired, though the offence did not seem to be viewed as hugely serious, entailing a punishment of twenty-one days' confinement to cell on punishment diet (Anderson, *Joe Cahill, op. cit.*, pp. 84–5).

103 PRONI HA/32/1/740, T. M. Stuart to Secretary, Ministry of Home Affairs, 7 January 1944. Constable McCarthy was shot dead while protecting a wages delivery at Ross's Flax Mills, Odessa Street, Belfast, on 1 October 1943. See *Irish News*, 2 October 1943, 1e–f. He was within months of retirement and left a wife and four children. The incident and the subsequent manhunt provided the material for F. L. Green's novel *Odd Man Out* (London: Michael Joseph, 1945) and the subsequent film (dir. Carol Reed, 1947).

104 He was an experienced enough gaoler to recognise that he had little chance of controlling contacts – including the passing of smuggled newspapers and other items *within* the wings. By using weighted lines held outside the cell windows, packages could be passed from one floor to another and swung sideways. Short of placing a constant watch on the outside of the block, and lighting the exterior at night, this could not be stopped (see Anderson, *Joe Cahill, op. cit.*, pp. 82–3).

105 PRONI HA/32/1/740.

106 PRONI HA/32/1/740, Inspector-General's Office to H. C. Montgomery, 3 February 1944.

107 PRONI HA/32/1/740, T. M. Stuart to H. C. Montgomery, 10 February 1944.

108 PRONI HA/32/1/740, Inspector-General's Office to H. C. Montgomery, 16 February 1944.

109 *NIPD*, vol. 26, cols. 1494–7, 26 August 1943. Charges against prison officers were sensitive on a number of grounds, not least because a substantial proportion of them were ex-servicemen.

110 PRONI HA/32/1/740, H. C. Montgomery to William Lowry, 16 March 1944; Lowry's annotated instructions, 18 March 1944. His concern, clearly, was that there should be no grounds for claiming victimisation.

111 Cahill reported that occasionally a friendly officer would carry a letter out for no charge, were he convinced that it was on purely family business (Anderson, *Joe Cahill*, *op. cit.*, pp. 84–5).

112 See PRONI HA/32/1/856, set of letters captured at premises at Devonshire Street, Belfast on 6 March 1943. 'God Save Ireland' would have been familiar to the IRA men as the last words of the Manchester Martyrs, members of the IRB. William Allen, Michael Larkin and Michael O'Brien were executed on 23 November 1867 before a crowd of between 8,000 and 10,000, for the murder of Sergeant Charles Brett. See Seán McConville, *Irish Political Prisoners, 1848–1922: Theatres of War* (London and New York: Routledge, 2003), pp. 131–4.

113 PRONI HA/32/1/856. Father Hilary told Steele that he had prepared Seán McCaughey (sometime IRA Chief of Staff of the IRA's Northern Command) for death and that he had taken a letter to Éamon de Valera from Cardinal Joseph MacRory, asking for McCaughey's reprieve. McCaughey had been the key mover in the arrest and 'trial' of Stephen Hayes, IRA Chief of Staff, in June and July of 1941 (see pp. 607–8, n. 122). He was arrested on 2 September 1941 and sentenced to death by the Special Criminal Court. McCaughey's sentence was commuted to life imprisonment. He died on 11 May 1944 in Portlaoise Prison as a consequence of his hunger and thirst strike for unconditional release. See pp. 630–6 below.

114 Jean-Jacques Rousseau, *Du contrat social* (Paris, 1762), Chapter 1. Usually translated as 'Man was born free, and everywhere he is in chains.'

115 MacEoin, *The IRA in the Twilight Years*, *op. cit.*, p. 694.

116 The three additions were Liam Burke, Phil McTaggart and William ('Bildo') Watson. MacEoin, *The IRA in the Twilight Years*, *op. cit.*, p. 694.

117 MacEoin, *The IRA in the Twilight Years*, *op. cit.*, p. 695. Keenan recalled that, although most of the men approved of the escape attempts, there were some who did not. One, a well-known Belfast republican, rebuked Keenan, saying that the group, who had been in for only a few months, had no right to escape and that, by doing so, they could perhaps cause all the internees to lose their privileges. MacEoin, *The IRA in the Twilight Years*, *op. cit.*, p. 694.

118 See also Liam Burke's account in MacEoin, *The IRA in the Twilight Years*, *op. cit.*, pp. 444–5.

119 The five were noted in the records as Liam Burke (thirty-eight), Eddie Keenan (twenty), Billy Watson, Philip J. McTaggart (twenty-five) and John Gerard O'Doherty (thirty-one). All but O'Doherty were from Belfast. See MacEoin, *The IRA in the Twilight Years*, *op. cit.*, p. 444; *Belfast Telegraph*, 6 June 1941, 5b–c; *Irish News*, 7 June 1941, 1f–g.

120 Details of the escape are taken from the report to the Minister for Home Affairs by the officials H. C. Montgomery and John Dunlop, 1 July 1941 (PRONI HA/32/1/769). The other side, which is somewhat more complete since it gives details of the preparations, and the getaway via safe houses, is given by Liam Burke in MacEoin, *The IRA in the Twilight Years*, *op. cit.*, pp. 444–5.

121 The Minister accepted all the recommendations except this last one. PRONI HA/32/1/769, H. C. Montgomery to T. M. Stuart, 8 July 1941.

122 Stephen Hayes had been the IRA Chief of Staff. A number of Northern leaders, principally Seán McCaughey, OC Northern Command, and Charles McGlade, his adjutant, suspected that Hayes was a traitor. On 30 June 1941, Hayes was arrested for treachery by McCaughey and other men of the Northern Command. All were convinced that the IRA's many setbacks could be explained only by the presence of a

traitor at the highest levels. Following several weeks of ill-treatment and bouts of torture, Hayes, after condemnation by an IRA court-martial and then trial, in the manner of Scheherazade, offered to write a comprehensive 'confession'. This delayed his execution by several weeks, not only in the writing but in his captors' attempts to evaluate what he claimed. On 8 September 1941, Hayes escaped from the Dublin house in which he had been held and sought refuge with the Gardaí. He claimed that the 'confession' had been his life raft. The ill-considered decision by the IRA GHQ to publish the document had devastating effects and contributed to the near destruction of the organisation. Most IRA members and supporters could not judge the truth of the allegations of the confession, of course, but many reasoned that, either way, it made continued association with the organisation impossible and dangerous. Either the IRA had permitted a traitor to worm his way into its highest levels or it had tortured a false confession out of an innocent comrade. The matter has never been resolved to the satisfaction of historians, but it seems unlikely that the Irish government had been so successful in manipulating the IRA to destruction. See Bell, *The Secret Army, op. cit.*, Chapter 10, for an account of the episode. Bell is highly sceptical about the allegations.

123 *Irish News*, 10 October 1942, 1h.

124 *Irish News*, 26 November 1942, 1g–h.

125 The escape is recalled, from the IRA side, by Joe Cahill, albeit with a retrospect of nearly sixty years (Anderson, *Joe Cahill, op. cit.*, pp. 87–91); see also MacEoin, *The IRA in the Twilight Years, op. cit.*, pp. 450–2. The last account reveals that the IRA controlled the Auxiliary Fire Service on the Falls Road and was able to make use of this to issue uniforms and identity cards at this time.

126 McAteer was described as a bookkeeper from Derry. Patrick Donnelly had been sentenced to twelve years' penal servitude on 23 November 1940 following a gunfight between a group of five men and the police. *Irish News*, 25 November 1940, 5d–e; 27 November 1940, 5c–d. In addition to penal servitude, Donnelly was sentenced to ten strokes of the cat. Edward (Ned) Maguire had been sentenced to six years on 29 August 1940 for stealing a soldier's rifle, and Jimmy Steele, who had been arrested in the Crown Entry raid, was sentenced to five years for that offence. Released, he had been sentenced to a further ten years on 26 February 1941 for possession of a revolver and documents (*Irish News*, 27 February 1941, 5b–c).

127 An RUC inquiry into the escape concluded that all the officers on duty and directly responsible for the men were lying. Even the time of the escape, therefore, could not be stated with any confidence. The police could only say that it had taken place between 6 a.m. and 8.15 a.m. Later accounts given by the IRA to authors such as Bell (*The Secret Army, op. cit.*, pp. 230–2) claimed that the escape was timed for between 8.30 and 9 p.m. However, even twenty-five years after the event, this may have been a bluff to protect a suborned prison officer.

128 It could have been worse. A second team was waiting to take its turn once it was certain that the first group had got away. They remained locked in their cells until it was too late, however, and the escape was discovered and the whole prison locked down (Anderson, *Joe Cahill, op. cit.*, pp. 90–1).

129 News of the escape reached as far as Berlin where it featured in a propaganda item broadcast by the Rundfunkhaus's *Germany Calling* the following day. The Catholic *Irish News* castigated Berlin for manufacturing a crisis out of 'a comparatively minor incident' (18 January 1943), but William Joyce (the renegade presenter of *Germany Calling*) and his associates needed to do little to sensationalise the story. The government most certainly did not treat it as a minor incident.

130 In accordance with IRA procedure, McAteer had been replaced from the moment of his arrest. In this instance, his deputy Charlie Kerins had taken over (Bell, *The Secret Army, op. cit.*, p. 229).

131 *Irish News*, 16 January 1943, 1a–c; *Northern Whig*, 16 January 1943, 1g–h, 4a–c.

132 PRONI HA/32/1/856, District Inspector W. H. Moffatt to Commissioner, 26 January 1943. Moffatt noted that when he visited Steele's cell on the morning of the escape he saw on the walls several photographs of rebel leaders such as Liam Mellows and Joe McKelvey. He saw this as further evidence of the unsatisfactory state of discipline and staffing at the prison.

133 PRONI HA/32/1/856. Cahill is silent on the matter, but the fact that McAteer managed to get out of his cell is suggestive of staff collusion.

134 Nineteen prisoners had been interviewed, but only five had offered comments. Some of the complaints were extraordinarily petty, but doubtless significant in prison life, where the most minute of comparisons are made, such as the question of who carved the meat on Christmas Day. PRONI HA/32/1/856, attachment no. 16.

135 These documents, captured during a raid on 6 March 1943, are discussed above, p. 577.

136 J. J. Campbell, KC, was a retired judge of the High Court of the Central Provinces of India, born and educated in Ulster. The other members were Captain W. J. Fyffe, Crown Solicitor, Co. Tyrone, and W. F. Martin, Crown Solicitor, Co. Down. *Belfast Newsletter*, 19 January 1943, 4e; *Irish News*, 19 January 1943, 1g–h; *Northern Whig*, 19 January 1943, 4f.

137 Stuart was informed of the decision on 9 June 1943. The six were to be dismissed immediately and paid up to and including 8 June. They comprised one principal, four established basic grade officers and one temporary officer (PRONI HA/32/1/856, H. C. Montgomery to T. M. Stuart, 9 June 1943). They lost their pensions as well as their places. See also *NIPD*, vol. 26, col. 1496, 26 August 1943.

138 PRONI HA/32/1/856, Ministry to T. M. Stuart, 12 October 1943.

139 PRONI HA/32/1/856, Prison Officers' Association to William Lowry, 29 November 1943.

140 *NIPD*, vol. 27, cols. 327–30, 29 February 1944. In a fiery and angry speech he also condemned the change of incumbent as Minister for Home Affairs during the period when the men's case was being considered. Nixon's motion was lost. See also vol. 26, col. 1490, 26 August 1943.

141 See above, pp. 582–83.

142 Bell, *The Secret Army, op. cit.*, p. 231. Since all the men remained active, their time at liberty was not prolonged. Patrick Donnelly saw out the war years in freedom. Ned Maguire was arrested in Donegal in June 1943. (He had assisted in the Derry escape.) Jimmy Steele remained free until May 1943 and returned to prison with an additional twelve-year sentence for the possession of arms and ammunition. The IRA Chief of Staff, Hugh McAteer, was arrested on 21 November 1943 (*Irish News*, 22 November 1943, 1d–f). In theory, recaptures and rearrests should have given the government a degree of success and triumph to compensate for the original loss of face – but in practice this never happened.

143 Anderson, *Joe Cahill, op. cit.*, p. 94. See also Coogan, *The IRA, op. cit.*, p. 241.

144 Cahill recalled that it was five months in the making (Anderson, *Joe Cahill, op. cit.*, p. 92). Liam Burke named the tunnellers as Billy Graham, Eddie Steele, Harry O'Rawe and Jimmy O'Hagan (MacEoin, *The IRA in the Twilight Years, op. cit.*, p. 453). Tim Pat Coogan mentions John McGreevy as being among the initiators of the escape (*The IRA, op. cit.*, p. 239).

145 *Irish News*, 22 March 1943, 1f–h. The Committee of Inquiry gave a different account. The alarm came from outside the prison, and it was at first thought that the escape had been over the wall. It took some time to discover the entrance to the tunnel. It seems unlikely, therefore, that it had been intended to get eighty men away, since there had been time to do so.

146 The men surfaced, according to Burke, in the coal shed of the Logue family, who were understandably surprised: 'Pat Scullion, all black and with a long beard, floored

them; "Holy St Patrick," cried the father, "Daddy it's the devil," cried the daughter' (MacEoin, *The IRA in the Twilight Years, op. cit.*, p. 453). True or not, an extra sheen for a memorable tale.

147 Adding flavour to their publicity coup, the IRA sent Curran Brothers, the removals firm whose van had been hijacked, payment of £9. A covering note, headed 'Military Headquarters, Ministry of Finance', apologised for the rough treatment meted out to the van driver and hoped he was none the worse (*Irish News*, 25 March 1943, 1f). A Press Association report in the same news item claimed that the eleven internees captured by the Irish authorities wished to return to Derry Prison 'because they do not relish the prospect of going to the Curragh'.

148 A few minutes before 9 a.m., the Derry RUC received an anonymous telephone call reporting the escape. Contingency plans were immediately implemented, armed police blocking all main roads out of the city. These roadblocks continued to operate until the late hours. Had the escapers delayed by even a few minutes to take more men with them, their route to the border would have been blocked (PRONI HA/32/1/860, Report by County Inspector, Londonderry, 23 March 1943).

149 *Irish News*, 22 March 1943, 1f–h; *Northern Whig*, 22 March 1943, 1a–b; see also same newspapers following day, 1d–e and 3d, respectively. By 9 April 1943, all but four had been recaptured, sixteen in Éire and one in Northern Ireland. Liam Burke had been one of the organisers and supplies more interesting detail, although there are contradictions between the various accounts on numbers. Six men did not make it to the furniture van. One stayed in Derry and was arrested thirty-six hours later. Five others made their way on foot across the border.

150 *Irish News*, 22 March 1943, 1f–h. This was one of the few incidents to be photographed – not the escape itself, but the round-up by the Irish Army in Co. Donegal. The photograph is reproduced in Coogan, *The IRA, op. cit.*, after p. 158.

151 *Irish News*, 9 July 1943, 3c; *NIPD*, vol. 26, cols. 1375–6, 8 July 1943.

152 Sir Dawson Bates, in the last weeks of his long tenure as Minister for Home Affairs, did not attend the meeting, probably because he was out of the country.

153 PRONI HA/32/1/860, Draft conclusions of cabinet meeting, 23 March 1943. John Andrews (1871–1956) had taken over as Prime Minister from James Craig in 1940. He held strong Protestant views and was a leading member of the Orange Order. Rumours of favouritism and cronyism within the prisons were current, and he may have wished to set these at rest with an independent inquiry. He was to be displaced as Prime Minister two months later.

154 PRONI HA/32/1/860. He also hinted at an over-cosy relationship between politicians and prison governors and other staff by arguing that MPs should not also be visiting justices at the prison. The Cabinet agreed. It is not clear what Lowry meant by the 'wrong type' of person having been appointed, but it seems probable that he would have preferred persons with appreciably more prison experience rather than former army officers; it may also be that he was objecting to cronyism, in general terms.

155 The other members were Captain W. H. Fyffe, Crown Solicitor, Co. Tyrone, and William Currie, Crown Solicitor, Co. Antrim.

156 PRONI HA/32/1/860, Inspector-General's Office, RUC to Ministry of Home Affairs, 26 March 1943. Subsequently, an IRA informant was able to describe and then identify Robert Doherty (one of the two other officers) as the person who had been the link between the escape organiser (Liam Burke) and the internees. The police had suspected Doherty for some years. After the Christmas disturbances at Londonderry Prison in 1939, he had been transferred to Belfast but had subsequently been reassigned there. PRONI HA/32/1/860, Inspector-General's Office to Ministry, 13 July 1943.

157 PRONI HA/32/1/860, Report on escape of 20 March 1943, ff. 6 and 7.

158 PRONI HA/32/1/860, Report on escape, f. 7. Adams had been one of the escapers. He was an uncle of Gerry Adams, republican leader in the modern Troubles.
159 PRONI HA/32/1/860, Report on escape, ff. 26–7.
160 These went back to the Derry riot on Christmas Day, 1939. Then Fryer reported
that Doherty had 'a reputation for talk' both inside and outside the prison. Both
RUC and Specials had said that 'he would sell his Maker for a pint'. Fryer had no
proof of this but implied that he had leaked information to the *Belfast Telegraph*. Fryer
thought Doherty 'decent in many ways' but from a medical point of view was 'not
really fit' (PRONI HA/9/2/192, A. Fryer to Ministry, 30 December 1939).
161 PRONI HA/32/1/860, Report on escape, f. 31. Doherty had entered the service in
March 1921. The fact that he had been appointed before the Northern Ireland
government had been vested with police and prison powers, including appointments,
was another factor weighed against him. There was a widespread belief among
Unionists that Dublin Castle, especially in the last years of British administration,
had been unduly lax in requiring evidence of loyalty when making civil-service
appointments. This was not, however, explicitly mentioned in the letter to the Governor of Northern Ireland, but the precise date of appointment was given and the
inference would have been readily understood. PRONI HA/32/1/860, Ministry of
Home Affairs to Private Secretary, Governor of Northern Ireland, 17 July 1943.
162 This was a bind to which the Committee offered no solution (presumably because it
was beyond their remit). Established prison officers had life tenure in their posts and,
as we have seen, could be removed only for cause, such as serious misconduct, and
that only with the consent of the Governor of Northern Ireland. The Ministry of
Home Affairs could not afford to have an establishment bloated beyond its normal
peacetime requirements. Temporary officers, with all their limitations, were therefore
the only way in which internment could be manned.
163 PRONI HA/32/1/860, Report on escape of 20 March 1943, ff. 31–2.
164 PRONI HA/32/1/860, Report on escape, f. 30.
165 PRONI HA/32/1/860, H. C. Montgomery to A. Fryer, 9 June 1943.
166 PRONI HA/32/1/860, A. Robinson to A. Fryer, 12 October 1943.
167 The nine were J. McGlone, Q. McNeill, F. Connolly, J. J. McGouran, John Magea,
T. Monaghan, A. Catherwood, J. J. McAllister and J. Loughran. The men were
located in closely adjacent cells on the top floor.
168 PRONI HA/32/1/877, A. Fryer to A. Robinson, 30 December 1943. Fryer reported
that, as a result of information received, he had, since 17 December, been taking extra
precautions during the hours of darkness. He was satisfied that another escape attempt
was being planned but that it might be delayed as a result of that morning's events.
169 The *Belfast Telegraph* reported the escape, 'nipped in the bud by the vigilance of
warder', but could get no comment from the RUC or from the prison (31 December
1943, 5d–e).
170 PRONI HA/32/1/877, A. Robinson to William Lowry, Minister for Home Affairs,
10 January 1944.
171 PRONI HA/32/1/877, A. Robinson to A. Fryer, 21 March 1944.

12

A WORLD AT WAR

Guarding the Irish state

In preparing to take special powers to protect the state as a European war became every more likely in the months after Munich, there were numerous confidential exchanges between senior civil servants in the Department of Justice, the Department of the Taoiseach, and the Attorney General's Office. These, and ministerial comments, were conducted at a high level of legal and constitutional awareness, exploring possible conflicts between the necessities of state, civil rights and movements in public sentiment. The need to protect the state was paramount in these exchanges, but they were certainly not closed, one-sided or predetermined. As the terrible landscape of world war became discernible, moreover, it was surely proper that the preparation of the state should be given priority: all else depended upon it and public duty could be defined by it.

There was no question of the Irish following the lead of the Continental countries, totalitarian or democratic. Writing in December 1938, Stephen Roche, Secretary of the Ministry of Justice, pointed out that such countries had taken an approach far more drastic than anything contemplated by the Irish government. The common-law tradition and constitutional jurisprudence would not be abandoned, but they did not fit current needs precisely or completely. Giving credit to the old adversary, Roche pointed out that

> The marked tendency in this State has been to follow the English practice in these matters. That practice… is, no doubt, admirable in its scrupulous respect for the liberty of the citizen and its dislike of 'extra-ordinary courts', but is based on, and dependent for its success on, a large tradition of internal security and of cooperation between the public and the police, a tradition which does not exist here.[1]

Roche acknowledged that where it was deemed necessary the English legislature had acted with vigour, and he instanced the communist–fascist street confrontations that had led to the 1936 Public Order Act.[2] Referring to Northern Ireland, Roche observed that '[t]he Six-Counties Government, notwithstanding in respect for English institutions, has not hesitated to adopt very strong remedies against its internal armies'.[3]

Against the background of the IRA's declaration of war and bombing campaign in England, Roche went on to examine what measures needed to be taken to promote the security of Éire. As the conduct of the campaign of violence passed into the hands of a younger IRA generation, police intelligence, 'never very copious', tended to dry up. Without such information, and without special powers, the police would be under pressure. Frustration could take them in unsatisfactory directions. They might decide that political crime was something that lay quite outside their control, and, unless attacked, they would not concern themselves with it. And if they were attacked they might resort to 'secret and unauthorised reprisals'. This was the counter-argument to those who argued that it was 'illiberal, reactionary or unnecessary' for the courts or the police to be given some new powers. It was preferable to confer 'the most drastic powers' and exercise them within the law than to take the risk that the police would ignore political crime or, 'if sufficiently goaded will retaliate by counter-crime'. In these circumstances government might have to tolerate such police illegality because the alternative could be 'even worse anarchy'.[4]

The Irish position was a difficult one. Roche did not allude directly to the short period in which the Irish state had been in existence, nor to the manner of its establishment, but his reference was clear enough. One of the weakest parts of the Irish legal system, 'considered as a really effective assessment for the suppression and detection of crime' was that, unlike English law enforcement, it lacked 'a general willingness to help the police'. Nor was it equipped, as were the Continental systems, with a machinery 'capable of dealing with people who obstruct or simply refuse to help the officers of the law'.[5]

This was an honest and perceptive account of the underlying social forces and attitudes affecting security in a state not long formed, living with the fresh and bitter memories of civil war and founded on a tradition of insurrectionary violence. And there was another dimension to these difficulties:

> In times of international friction, war, and rumours of war, a small country cannot afford to invite attack from without by a seeming inability to keep order within its own territory. The danger in this case becomes acute when the unlawful organisations extend their activities into other States, whilst using this country as a base.[6]

To put this in plainer language: the UK's restraint in the face of IRA provocations could not be tested too far in the tumultuous times upon which all were entering.

Discussions and exchanges on the special powers that would be required continued into the spring of 1939. The yardstick was Article 2A of the now defunct Free State Constitution. Article 2A had been repealed when de Valera's Constitution had come into effect on 29 December 1937. It became obvious that existing powers fell short of the old in several regards. One of these was the status and autonomy of the new court being contemplated: the Special Criminal Court. A joint submission to the government (Cabinet) by the Department of

Justice and the Attorney General's Office argued for the new body to have extensive powers and high standing: 'It is essential that the Court should be respected and even feared.' As long as the government retained overriding powers of remission of sentence and of pardon there was no reason to apprehend excessive severity from the Court.

The issue of appeal from the Special Criminal Court was of particular importance. This had not been allowed under Article 2A of the Free State Constitution. Should an appeal mechanism be provided, the consequences might limit or even paralyse the Court. The thinking in 1931 (when Article 2A was introduced) and now, the Department submitted, must be consistent, based on a recognition that to ask the new court to do its work effectively but to do it 'with the same attention to forms of procedure and the law of evidence as is required of an ordinary Court is to ask an impossibility'. The basic reason for introducing a Special Court under Article 2A had been that since the ordinary courts were unable to cope with the activities of an unlawful organisation, a quite different type of body was necessary: 'A Commission chosen not as lawyers but as men of known courage, patriotism, and ability, who were not fettered by any legal rules, and who constituted, in reality, not a Court but a Committee of Public Safety.'[7] To harness such an extraordinary body to the ordinary rules of evidence and procedure would certainly lessen its effectiveness, and, moreover, 'the kind of man who is best fitted to sit on such a Court is just the kind of man who will not undertake that duty unless he has a free hand'.[8]

The legal culture and reflexes that Justice was anxious to step away from were, not surprisingly, viewed differently by the Attorney General. He pointed out that normal sentencing powers, extending to long terms of penal servitude, were adequate, and the only effect of granting unfettered discretion to the Special Court would be to invite unfavourable criticism from the High Court, the public and the legislature. This could give rise to a measure of sympathy for those brought before the Court. The same argument held in the opposite direction for a right of appeal which, if provided, would increase confidence in the Special Court. He also pointed out that few, if any, of the decisions of the Article 2A Tribunal would have been reversed by the Court of Criminal Appeal on questions of fact. Overall, the Attorney General considered that it would be better for the Special Court to be respected by the public than simply to overawe it. So also the judiciary: 'The fiercer and more direct' the contemplated legislation, the more likely it would provoke constitutional review. There was a danger that the Supreme Court 'might be tempted to invoke principles of natural justice, as they would be called, as animating the judicial provisions in the Constitution'. It would be better to graft the new body on to the existing courts, 'though not necessarily as an ordinary court'.[9]

The comments of the Attorney General's Office showed that an important section of the government's legal establishment thought that the reach of special powers should be relatively modest and that security by extraordinary means might lose public consent. The Department of Justice, less committed to the tenets of legal culture and doctrine, took a more robust view. In times of crisis, governments are wont to look more to outcomes than procedures and to prefer expedition to deliberation. This is the natural inclination of any group of individuals upon whom decisions are forced. It was inevitable, therefore, that the government would prefer the Department of Justice's reasoning and, with few misgivings, set aside the wishes of the Attorney General's Office: dangerous times require drastic measures.

The Irish Bar was particularly cohesive; the size of the country and the Bar and a relatively small volume of business ensured that. The sentiments of the judiciary therefore were probably not much out of line with those expressed in the Attorney General's memorandum. This raised a further issue: who was to sit on the new court? Here was another matter touching on perceived legitimacy and public acceptance. It had been addressed in a somewhat exasperated note from Stephen Roche to his minister at the end of 1938. High Court judges had been approached in 1931 with a request that they serve on the Tribunal. They refused, pointing out that the duty had not been contemplated when they had accepted office and that to press it on them now would be a breach of faith.[10]

There was little that could be done about this, Roche lamented. There was, he noted, 'a lot to be said for having a Judge of the High Court as President of such Special Court', and the opportunity should be taken, when appointing new judges, to add to their duties the possibility of sitting in a special court.[11] Roche, wisely, did not seek to press the issue with those already in office. To try to renegotiate their terms of appointment would have been the extremely fraught and possibly inflammatory course, touching on a constitutional nerve centre, to be avoided most of all in uncertain times. With the cachet of the higher judiciary unavailable, the panel and its chairman would have to be recruited elsewhere. For several reasons, including standing and personal safety, this could only be the military.

This was the reasoning and the course of debate within the executive that led to the establishment of the Special Criminal Court by an order under the Emergency Powers Act, 1939.[12] Members of the panel were appointed, and the first case came before it on 16 October 1939.[13] It is worth considering both the differentiating features of the Court as well as those it shared with other courts. It was special in the sense that, although summary (operating without a jury) it had at its disposal the full range of sentences from short periods of ordinary imprisonment to extended terms of penal servitude. It was free from any practical prospect of intimidation both by its avoidance of a jury of vulnerable laymen and by the fact that its judges included serving army officers. In other respects it was like other courts, implementing the principles of natural justice. Charges had to be brought and evidence offered. The defendant had a chance to rebut the charges and to have legal advice. In practice these rights were waived by members (or close sympathisers) of the IRA when they refused to recognise the jurisdiction of the Court. The rules of evidence were followed – again a safeguard of little use when defendants refused to contest charges. There was a right of appeal, but the IRA's General

Order forbidding its members to acknowledge the legitimacy of proceedings to the extent of entering into proceedings, nullified these protections. The Court's deliberations were further streamlined by the nature of the charges brought before it, particularly refusal to answer questions and to account for one's movements, as well as more tangible matters such as the possession of documents, articles and weapons.[14]

The Court had the power to sentence for any offence as though it were the court before which such an offence would normally be brought. It was 'special' in the nature of its rules of procedure and in its personnel and absence of a jury. As far as possible, it was to adhere to the practice and procedure of the Central Criminal Court.[15] Unlike the Military Court, there was a right of appeal from the Special Criminal Court, provided the Court certified that the case was fit for appeal or, should it not so certify, the Court of Criminal Appeal granted leave.[16]

In practice, the Special Criminal Court operated in a way not very different from the ordinary courts, especially given the IRA's apparent determination to ensure its members who were accused would be convicted. But the lack of a jury was important, as was the speed with which it processed cases. The prosecution did not get a blank cheque, despite the fact that the judges, as serving soldiers, came under the control of the executive branch of the government. In the course of its operations from late 1939 until mid-1946, the Special Criminal Court heard 1,013 cases and acquitted 105.[17] This rate of acquittal (rather below one in ten) may seem to confirm that the Court was merely a fig leaf for executive detention, but when it is remembered that most defendants refused to participate in the proceedings, in effect acting as their own prosecutors, the acquittal rate might seem rather more respectable.

During the war years the government came to believe that the state was faced with such dangers from without and within that its survival was imperilled and that an instrument even more formidable than the Special Criminal Court was necessary to deliver retributive and deterrent counter-blows of a sufficient strength, with certainty and speed – truly a Committee of Public Safety. That story will be told when we come to it.

In terrorem

At the Curragh, in Mountjoy and in Arbour Hill, the emphasis during the war years was on prevention rather than on repression. Months and years of captivity, with no certain date of release, certainly had deterrent and repressive properties, but these were by-products of the primary function of these institutions, which was to take republican activists out of circulation for as long as the necessities of state required. The regimes, accordingly, could be comparatively lax, if unavoidably institutional, restrictive and Spartan. There was no need to confront internees and sentenced prisoners on core issues signifying submission, such as labour, prison uniform and association. Equally, those who did not conform to the loose rules of confinement placed themselves in the same position as those who refused to recognise the courts: they justified their exclusion from remission of sentence, prolonged their confinement and, of course, removed all doubts about IRA membership, or close association.

But there were other prisoners, little more than a handful, the gravity of whose offences and records justified to ministers and senior officials their subjection to a more active form of repressive and exemplary punishment. The criteria for allocation to this group included the use of violence against the police or the Army or the direction of others in such acts, notoriety and particular gravity of an offence and disruptive behaviour in custody – especially an attempted or successful escape. Not all who met these criteria, however, were assigned to this select group. Processes within the Irish Cabinet and Department of Justice, some of which remain opaque, also played their part. The three exemplary punishments were assignment to Portlaoise Prison, flogging and capital punishment. In examining how these were used it is necessary to bear in mind that there was no neat flow chart for sentencing or executive review: politics, bureaucracy and unfolding events all intermingled.

Portlaoise

In the latter years of British administration, Maryborough was Ireland's principal convict prison. Under the Free State government, its name was changed to Portlaoise. As we have seen, there was a certain amount of change in function of the various prisons over the years, especially during the Civil War and its aftermath.[18] By the 1940s, however, Portlaoise held penal-servitude prisoners, traditionally known as convicts. These were long-term prisoners, serving sentences of three years and more, making up an average population of around 200 men. During the wartime years, few IRA men received such long sentences. Most were dealt with under the OASA and given sentences of up to twenty-four months' imprisonment. Rearrested at the moment of discharge from Mountjoy and served with internment orders, nearly all sat out the war years in the Curragh, the last man being released on 21 June 1945.[19]

The place of detention of persons sentenced by the Special Criminal Court was determined by the Minister for Justice, using his powers under the OASA.[20] In general, prisoners serving such sentences were, as an extra measure of security, sent to military detention barracks (Arbour Hill and the Glasshouse at the Curragh), where they were in the custody of the Army. There was within this group, however, a subset for whom it had been decided that ordinary penal servitude, with the same regime as that for non-political criminals would be imposed. Gerald Boland, Minister for Justice, set out the type of offender for whom this treatment had been prescribed. They were cases of 'murder, attempted murder, kidnapping with great violence and threats of murder, armed robbery, or treachery by State servants'.[21]

Another category of offender was brought before the Military Court (established under the 1939 Emergency Powers Act) which could either acquit or find guilty and sentence to death.[22] Thirteen men were subject to this process, of whom nine received the death penalty; four others were acquitted.[23] Four sentences were commuted to life at penal servitude. Of cases in which mercy was bestowed, the most notable were Tomás MacCurtáin and Seán McCaughey. For MacCurtáin, commutation came a few hours before sentence was to be carried out; for McCaughey, it came a week after his original sentence was imposed. During the wartime years, one death sentence was also imposed by the Special Criminal Court. This was Charlie Kerins, convicted of the murder of Special Branch Detective Sergeant Dennis O'Brien at his home in Rathfarnham, Co. Dublin, on 9 November 1942.[24]

The general rule was that those sentenced by the Special Criminal Court would, by order of the Minister for Justice, be transferred to military custody, either at Arbour Hill or the Curragh. The period under sentence was almost invariably followed by internment, with the regime in both cases being almost identical. But a select group did not follow this path. During the wartime years and (in the case of Harry White) those immediately following, ten men served sentences at Portlaoise. In addition, Richard Goss and George Plant were transferred to the prison for their executions – on 9 August 1941 and 5 March 1942 respectively.[25] By 1945 eight IRA men remained at Portlaoise, serving long determinate sentences or, where the death sentence had been commuted, life at penal servitude.[26] Of the six death sentences carried out, five were by firing squad. Charlie Kerins, having been convicted by the Special Criminal Court rather than the Military Court, was hanged at Mountjoy prison.[27]

Assignment to Portlaoise was by political and administrative decision rather than a requirement of the penal regulations or court direction. A number of men serving long sentences were held in Mountjoy and then were transferred to the Curragh in 1943 where they enjoyed the same conditions as the internees.[28] The men transferred to Portlaoise were all serious offenders, but some no more so than comrades who had gone to the Curragh. In a few instances, the threat to the state of their escape justified custody at what today would be called maximum- or super-maximum-security levels. Others were not in this category, although committed and resourceful IRA men.

Tomás MacCurtáin had been sentenced to death and, as we shall see, was given a late reprieve. At the time of his arrest in Cork, on 2 January 1940, Detective John Roche had been shot dead in an exchange of fire, and it was probably only the standing of MacCurtáin's famous father, a venerated martyr in the wider republican ranks, that led to his reprieve.[29] Seán McCaughey, briefly IRA Chief of Staff (June to September 1941), had been arrested following Stephen Hayes's escape. Charged with assault upon and the unlawful detention of Hayes, McCaughey was brought before the Special Military Court on 18 September 1941, found guilty and sentenced to death. His reprieve apparently came because the offences of which he had been found guilty were not grave enough and would not have resulted in the death penalty, had he been brought before another court.[30] The escape of either of these men would have been a major embarrassment to the government.

There were two men at Portlaoise with a record of escaping; another escape would have seriously undermined the authority and credibility of the government. Frank Kerrigan and Jim Smith (alias Brennan) had escaped from Mountjoy Prison on the night of 31 October/1 November 1942, together with Michael and Mort Lucey and Peter Martin. (Another escaper, Jackie Griffith, remained at large – unluckily for him.)[31] All the men were recaptured in April 1943 and transferred to Portlaoise.

Jim Crofton, another maximum-security prisoner, had served in the Special Branch. Switching allegiance, he had for a time passed information to the IRA GHQ. Such was the shortage of experienced men, however, that Crofton – an invaluable and utterly irreplaceable source – was used on an IRA operation. This was a fantastical scheme to smuggle Hermann Görtz, an Abwehr agent, out of Ireland and across the heavily patrolled seas separating Ireland from occupied France. In February 1941, Crofton travelled down to Fenit, Co. Kerry, to make preparations to purchase a small fishing boat which he himself would captain. Always a place in which strangers were noticed, it was under particularly close surveillance because of the war. Only extraordinary care or luck would have ensured the men's safety. They did not exercise one and did not have the other, and so Crofton, and his assistant Johnny O'Connor, were arrested. Crofton was brought before the Special Criminal Court and sentenced to five years' penal servitude. He was transferred to Portlaoise on the orders of Gerald Boland; there was much bitterness in the state's most sensitive agency about Crofton's renegade activities.[32]

Patrick Murphy and William Stewart had been involved in IRA bank raids. Stewart was arrested in a farmhouse, a joint Special Branch and army operation. Shots were exchanged (there were claims about crossfire between soldiers and police), and two soldiers were wounded. Murphy was arrested at another safe house on the same day.[33] Both men were sentenced by the Special Criminal Court to fourteen years' penal servitude and twelve strokes of the cat. After the whipping had been inflicted they were transferred to Portlaoise. The apparatus for flogging was kept at Mountjoy, where there was also a warder with the necessary skill and experience.[34]

Two other men were transferred to Portlaoise. One case was clear. Michael Walshe was one of three sentenced to death for his part in the killing of Michael Devereux, a suspected informer.[35] George Plant was convicted and a reprieve refused. Walshe's sentence and that of an accomplice in the affair, Patrick Davern (alias Brown), was commuted to life at penal servitude. For some reason, not now clear, Davern was not sent to Portlaoise but to Mountjoy. Walshe, having had a death sentence commuted, was in the same category as McCaughey, but since Davern was not sent to Portlaoise it seems that other factors were considered. It may be, for example, that the Department of Justice did not wish to have both survivors of the Devereux sentences in the prison at the same time.[36]

The final member of the Portlaoise group was Joby O'Sullivan. He arrived in the prison in 1942 under the alias of Jack Kehoe. He was another escaper, having done so while undergoing treatment at the Dental Hospital in Lincoln Place, Dublin; he had also acted under the direction of Seán McCaughey as one of Stephen Hayes's guards.[37] After some months it became evident that O'Sullivan's mental condition had deteriorated, and he was declared insane and transferred to the Dundrum Asylum.[38] Joe O'Callaghan was in the prison from 1941, but MacEoin, who records this, provides no information other than that he was young and came from Dundalk.[39] He does not feature in such official records that have survived, and it may be that his Portlaoise stay was brief. George Plant, who was considered to be the principal in the Michael Devereux murder, was in Portlaoise only a matter of hours. He had been brought down from Arbour Hill to be executed by firing squad. The sentence was carried out very shortly after his arrival on the morning of 5 March 1942.[40]

Speaking in Cork on 26 May 1946, de Valera said, 'We cannot segregate crimes of violence into two categories – one shameful and punishable and the other to be recognised by the government as not really so blameworthy.'[41] This virtuous insistence on uniformity in the administration of punishment was awkward. How did de Valera justify the differential treatment meted out to McCaughey and the others were it not a form of selective punishment? An arrangement whereby the executive was allowed to re-sentence by deciding levels of punishment was certainly not compatible with the rule of law and the constitutional doctrine of the separation of powers. The Minister for Justice had made the transfers to military custody in the vast majority of the 412 cases between 1939 and the end of 1943 in which sentence was passed by the Special Criminal Court: why had the Portlaoise men been treated differently?[42]

Managing Portlaoise

Major W. R. Barrows, a long-serving governor and hold-over from the days of the General Prisons Board, had charge of Portlaoise. He had served in the British Army and was in Dundalk on the outbreak of the Civil War when the town was captured by republicans under the command of Frank Aiken (who, by a turn of the wheel of political fortune, had become Minister for Defensive Measures).[43] Barrows liked to recall that he had been locked in his own prison for some days, released only when anti-Treaty forces evacuated the town.[44] After service at various prisons he had been appointed to Portlaoise in 1929.[45] According to the recollections of the republican prisoners, Barrows ran the prison strictly, according to the rules; there were no accusations of overzealousness or personal unpleasantness.[46] His chief officer at this time was Blennerhassett, also a long-time prison official. Both these men, and their staff, were used to the ordinary criminal prisoner who, caught in the inflexible routine ordained for prisoners under penal servitude, frequently isolated and demoralised, gave little trouble. They generally preferred to make the best of things and to work with the system rather than confront it: 'head down and do your time' was the attitude approved by staff and prisoners alike. Having charge of a group of political prisoners, and those of such importance to the state, was, for Barrows and Blennerhassett, almost certainly a greater worry than the responsibility for the other 200 in their charge.

This IRA group, as we have seen, included men who had demonstrated audacity and a willingness to both face and use force, and who, far from renouncing or even regretting it, treated violence as their lodestone. Deeply committed to the IRA, all of them would do whatever possible to further its interests. The government believed that they should not be allowed to manipulate the system, and that determination, most crucially, meant that they would not be granted political status at Portlaoise. This was an apparent inconsistency, since a considerable degree of latitude was extended to IRA men at Mountjoy and Arbour Hill, and the bringing together of internees and convicted prisoners at the Curragh in 1943 would obliterate the distinction between the two, admitting the latter to the civil-detention regime of the camp. Republicans referred to the personal 'lusting after vengeance' of the Secretary of the Department of Justice (now Peter Berry), the Minister for Justice Gerald Boland and Taoiseach Éamon de Valera.[47] It might be argued that the Portlaoise men had to be held under conditions of maximum security, but that close custody did not necessarily affect other aspects of the regime. Why these men, serious threats that they were, should be singled out from the hundreds of others under sentence or in internment in the mode of their custody is not at all clear. The most obvious explanation is that Portlaoise was seen as part of the redoubt of the state in which no breach would be tolerated. Retreat here would mean a dangerous loss of credibility; taking a stance of severity at Portlaoise would ensure that all other IRA members and supporters in custody understood that the government would not be moved by any pleas of hardship or by appeals to traditional republican sentiment. This would be a contest of wills. To use a different but perhaps more apt image, Portlaoise was an arena.

It was a combat which the small group of IRA men were willing to join. In their years at the prison, almost all showed that they had the strength of mind and physical stamina to endure the closest conditions of confinement, isolation and extreme discomfort. In an asymmetric contest, the weaker party must generally, as artfully as possible, adopt tactics that give it parity or advantage. The Portlaoise prisoners simply charged headlong at authority, seemingly driven by fury. For them it was a struggle of principle, and tactics featured hardly at all in such calculations as they made, almost as though they obscured or even besmirched the cause. This left them with no chance of success. The group was minute and unable to inflict any significant physical damage on the prison. A few cells might be smashed up, had they chosen, but Barrows had abundant accommodation available, and offenders could be transferred to stripped-down punishment cells. They could and did stage demonstrations, but by definition a demonstration needs an audience, and wartime conditions meant that there would be none other than the distinctly unencouraging one made up of the officials of the Department and the staff of the prison. Even if news did seep under the front gate (and by their actions prisoners would forswear both visits and letters), there was no IRA or Sinn Féin organisation to amplify it; even had there been, the general population was largely indifferent. De Valera was in office and control, and the opposition Fine Gael supported his anti-IRA stance, and was perhaps the least likely of Irish political parties to seek ameliorations for republican prisoners. There were in the Dáil some sympathetic figures (including the Independent TD for Portlaoise, Oliver J. Flanagan) but national peril in a world at war eliminated any leverage or suasion they might have.[48]

The fact that Tomás MacCurtáin had embarked on his campaign for political status eighteen months before anyone else joined him in Portlaoise, and had, in consequence, endured considerable hardship, pre-empted any discussion among new arrivals. None was likely to ask for a reassessment, negating what MacCurtáin had gone through, casting him as a fool. Once embarked upon, moreover, confrontation involving extreme hardship became progressively difficult to abandon for the same reason: all that suffering, and for nothing. There was something of the moral quicksand about such an enterprise. Defiance and endurance also led in quick order to the more banal and ordinary considerations: aversion to a loss of face and humiliation.

Flinty determination on both sides meant that the Portlaoise IRA men would serve extremely hard time and for a longer period than any others in such circumstances. Their demands were utterly familiar and their argument well rehearsed: as political rather than criminal offenders, they would not submit to penal discipline. Refusing to wear the prison uniform or to perform prison labour, they insisted on collective representation, their own chain of command and freedom of association. They had been conceded one traditional demand forthwith: segregation from other prisoners. Whether, had they agreed to conform, they would have been mixed with the general population, one can only speculate, but it is difficult to see how this could have been avoided or justified. With opportunities to correspond, receive visitors, move about the prison and agitate, access to the general population could have given them more opportunity to make mischief, to lodge complaints and requests and to exploit whatever limited opportunities there might have been to harass the authorities. But this was not in the IRA repertoire, or in the temper of the times.

MacCurtáin established the line at the outset. On arrival he had been presented with the prison uniform and told to change into it; he claimed political status and refused. Patrick Murphy had the same experience. He was received by a hostile prison officer who took him to Major Barrows's office for the customary reception interview. There he was read the convict rules and regulations in which the prospect of remission for good behaviour was emphasised: 'I said I was not interested in convict regulations; I was a political prisoner and that was that.' Murphy was then escorted to the cellhouse where he was left in a cell and told to change into the prison uniform. When staff returned, his civilian clothes were forcibly removed.[49]

As others arrived, they took the same stand. Seán McCaughey was held at Mountjoy on remand, and the issue of prison clothing did not arise since remands wore their own clothes. This exemption continued while he was held at Arbour Hill for trial by the Military Court and after he had been sentenced to death. On his sentence being commuted to life at penal servitude he was immediately transferred to Portlaoise, where he also refused the prison uniform. Consequences inexorably followed. By refusing to clothe himself he was in a state of continuous offending and confined to his cell with all privileges forfeit: no correspondence in or out, no visits, no religious services, no exercise, no association, no library books. The only time a uniform-refuser left his cell was for a weekly bath.[50] This was a state of confinement that made the most severe demands on mind and body, a testing isolation almost impossible to imagine. MacCurtáin endured these conditions from July 1940 until June 1943, when limited association was permitted. Seán McCaughey was in this close confinement from his reception on 27 September 1941 until June 1943.[51]

In the implementation of this regime it could plausibly be argued that the minister and prison officials were acting illegally. Portlaoise was conducted under the authority of the Convict Prisons (Ireland) Act, 1854, which provided that the period of confinement to a cell could not exceed one month, that this punishment could only be imposed for a major or repeated offences against prison rules, and that it could be ordered only after a sworn hearing by the Board of Directors of the prison.[52] This position had been further defined by Convict Rules made in 1894 by the General Prisons Board. This directed that persons in separate confinement should be permitted such open-air exercise as was deemed necessary for their health.[53] Nor was the matter governed only by laws and rules inherited from the British. Rules made in 1925 restricted the maximum period of solitary confinement to fourteen days, and that could be imposed only after an investigation by the Visiting Committee, taking sworn evidence.[54] The prison authorities and Boland pointed out, of course, that McCaughey and the others had been punished for repeated individual acts of disobedience, each entailing its own punishment: continuing disobedience meant continuing punishment. To most people, however, this was mere casuistry verging on cynical disingenuousness. The rules had been broken by failing to hold separate adjudications each time, almost certainly in the letter as well as in the spirit.[55]

Isolation was not quite complete since the men (spaced out on E5 landing, each with an empty cell on either side – a tactic pioneered at Arbour Hill) could communicate by holding their tin mugs to the hot-water pipes that ran through the cells, the mugs acting as microphones and receivers and the whole constituting a primitive telephone system.[56] And some prisoners, such as Patrick Murphy, managed to focus on small mercies. He recalled that prisoners could choose two books a week from the prison library list: this helped to ease the deadly monotony of cellular confinement. Murphy also commented that the food was 'not bad'. Breakfast was a canteen tin of porridge, tea without milk and bread ('a wee square loaf'). Dinner (served late morning) was 'good': soup followed by stew or, on Friday, fish; this was accompanied by tea and bread and margarine. The so-called supper or evening meal was served at 4.40 p.m. and consisted of tea and bread.

An hour later, Murphy remembered, 'your last crumb was eaten and lights went out at eight o'clock'.[57] Unlike IRA men in other prisons, those at Portlaoise could not supplement prison rations with parcels sent in from outside: this was one of several privileges they had forfeited.

The Portlaoise cells were heated by pipes rather than by Sir Joshua Jebb's ineffective hot-air flue system which was usual in other Victorian prisons. This meant that the men who refused to wear prison uniform were not as cold and uncomfortable as their comrades taking the same action in Belfast Prison.[58] The Portlaoise men were also allowed to cut a hole in one of the four army blankets supplied to each cell. The blanket was then pulled over the head and worn as a poncho. A strip of the blanket was cut off and worn around the waist to hold the garment together. This sounds more cosy than it was: Liam Rice (who was OC) remembered that the blankets were not of the domestic type and provided inadequate warmth.[59] Patrick Murphy also pointed out that, by using one of the blankets as a garment, the men had only three for their beds.[60]

In accordance with the regulations, the Governor inspected the prison each morning and spoke to the men. Little of substance could pass in these exchanges since they gave only one response to his enquiry as to complaints and needs: they wanted political status. The same answer was given to the enquiries of F. C. Connolly, an official of the Department of Justice, who visited monthly. The exchanges had become routine, with nothing expected on either side when, in June 1943, immediately following one of Connolly's visits, the prisoners were informed that thenceforward they would have association twice a day. Open-air exercise was still withheld while they refused to conform, but the chance to leave their cells twice a day was an immeasurable improvement over the once-a-week solo walk to take a bath. A long room, formerly a workshop, was set aside for association; the men christened it *An Caidreamh* (The Social).[61] Here, during their periods of association, they were permitted to talk and to play board games. Equally importantly, at this time, limited rights of correspondence (but not visits) were restored: the men could write and receive one letter a month. For MacCurtáin, the longest serving among them, this would be the first correspondence in three years.

We examine below the protracted process of reviewing and releasing the last IRA convicted prisoners in Éire.[62] Eleven months after the war ended in Europe, there remained in Irish custody thirty-four men convicted of IRA-connected offences. Two of these were in Mountjoy, eight in Portlaoise and twenty-four in the Curragh Military Detention Barracks (the Glasshouse).[63] Rather less than half of these had been recommitted (having been released in 1945) as a result of their attempt to revive the IRA at the Ardee Bar meeting on 9 March 1946.[64] Deducting this number, we can see that a score or so of men had been in close detention for a considerable period. Largely because they chose not to obey the rules but partly also because of the stern response of the authorities and the punitive design of the rules of penal servitude, that select group of IRA men who had been consigned to Portlaoise during the war years underwent an unprecedented level of custodial deprivation.

To balance the picture, we must acknowledge that, when the men chose to conform, the regime – especially after June 1943 – was not crushingly onerous and indeed, because of the association room, was less punitive than that which was the lot of ordinary criminal prisoners. In his May 1946 remarks to the Dáil, Gerald Boland pointed out that the men were by that time being housed in a modern (1901) portion of the prison, 'very bright and airy'. The cells (fourteen and a half feet by twelve, and ten to twelve feet in height) were relatively spacious. The prison had a thirty-acre farm that provided produce and work. (However, even had they conformed to the prison rules, the latter would almost certainly have been denied to maximum-security prisoners such as Tomás MacCurtáin.)

The Portlaoise day began at 6.45 a.m. when the prisoners rose, washed and emptied slops. Cleaning of cells began at 7 a.m. and breakfast was at 8.40. The working day was a little over five hours, with the midday meal (the main one) at 12.40 and the evening meal at 4.40. By 1946, the regime had been loosened, and the former lock-up time of 4.30 had been extended to 7.45, when the last meal of the day was taken in cells. For two hours, from 5.30 to 7.30 p.m., there was recreation, which included board games and listening to the radio. Lights were turned off at 8.30 p.m. In 1946, Boland admitted that the dinner was not 'what one will get in the Gresham Hotel' but was 'plain and wholesome'. The same was true of the other meals, the total being estimated at 3,400 calories per day.[65] As to uniform, Boland confessed himself somewhat dissatisfied. It was certainly comfortable and warm, but 'there is something depressing about them which I do not like'. For a long time he had been trying to get a better type of uniform 'that will not have such a depressing effect on a prisoner'.[66]

The pudding was probably over-egged in Boland's description of Portlaoise. It is hard to interpret his attitude towards the prisoners, and, having been in prison himself, he was probably ambivalent. Ordinary prisoners qualified for more compassion than republicans, and, among republicans, there were most likely further divisions and subdivisions, with the small group at Portlaoise being a particular target for Boland's pugnaciousness and determination.[67] His defensiveness about Portlaoise found expression in his claims for it, asserting that 'some think that Portlaoise is about the best [prison] in the world'. He quoted favourable comments that had been made by James Dillon (formerly Fine Gael but, in 1946, sitting as an Independent member in the Dáil). He also referred to a visit by the Warden of San Quentin to Portlaoise in 1937, following which the visitor said that it was 'one of the best and best kept of the small prisons he had seen in the course of an inspection of the major prisons in Great Britain and Europe'.[68] The rosiness of the picture was such that Boland exposed himself to the interjection of Michael Donnellan (Clann na Talmhan TD for Galway East): 'It is nicer to be there than in the Dáil.'[69]

And, indeed, despite all his claims for Portlaoise and his expressions of concern about ordinary prisoners, Boland must have known that the treatment of the small group of political prisoners at Portlaoise could not but cause unease – and he was probably aware that it had been a bleak chapter in the short prison history of the state. The prisoners' own responsibility apart, there was a deal of stubbornness or even brutality, not reflecting well upon or fitting for those exercising authority, in the extended barring of correspondence. Little reflection is required to grasp what a relief it must have been for wives, parents, families and friends to hear from their men. In a statement made after his release, Jim Crofton referred to being incommunicado for so long: 'One of the children died while I was in prison. To all intents and purposes I was dead.' Political status was not in the hands of the Governor or Visiting Committee, both said, adding that all that happened to Crofton in the prison was in accordance with the rules.[70]

Seán McCaughey's hunger strike

Politics and tactics

The IRA had always been ambivalent about hunger-striking. Whilst serving penal servitude in 1916–17, de Valera had waged his own battle against the authorities at Dartmoor, Lewes and Maidstone convict prisons. His tactics included a hunger strike, a move he subsequently condemned.[71] Terence MacSwiney, Lord Mayor of Cork, died on the seventy-fourth day of a hunger strike that became a sensation and received worldwide publicity. By his determination and suffering, MacSwiney's hunger strike aided the republican campaign in Ireland as much as it harmed the British administration there, as well as Britain's image throughout the world.[72] These were successful actions, and there were others, both in the closing days of British administration in Ireland and also under the Free State.[73] But there were also failed hunger strikes.[74] Hunger-striking required huge reserves of determination, approaching fanaticism, together with moral certainty, physical endurance and true courage to be prepared – fully prepared – to starve oneself through to an agonising death. Such qualities and such men and women are rare indeed.

A hunger strike is the defiant threat of the weak to die and to bring shame and opprobrium upon the strong. Once embarked upon, it must be carried though to a credible victory (obtaining all or most of the objectives) or to death. Commenced and abandoned, with little or nothing to show, it were better not to have undertaken the strike at all since the moral capital of the striker was diminished. The striker's organisation invests moral and political capital by supporting and publicising the protest, and he or she comes to exemplify, for activists and supporters, idealism, courage, self-sacrifice and all that is best about the cause and its followers. Should the striker dissemble, falter or fail, the organisation also stumbles, having backed the rhetoric and (sometimes) bluster of a grave but empty gesture, an activist who assumes the garb and graces of martyrdom but who cannot pay the commensurate and final price. Since most people are blessedly deficient in the qualities of heroic martyrdom, direct-action organisations, for reasons of practical politics and agitation, learn to be wary of the hunger strike. This is particularly true, as we have seen, of any kind of mass or group strike, where the entire enterprise stands or falls on its weakest participants.[75] In consequence, the IRA has long forbidden its members in prison to hunger strike without express GHQ approval.[76]

The least satisfactory state of mind in which to start a hunger strike must be despair. Anger, militancy, confidence or (best of all) tactical calculation can stoke up the necessary psychological reserves and may blend qualities of tenacity and flexibility. Despair has a linear logic which, once read by the authorities, gives them space for manoeuvre. Most critically, despair cuts a man or woman off from any assessment of the reaction of politicians and the public. The hunger strike, above all, must cast shame upon the target and therefore requires arena and audience. Since it is a lack of faith in the indifferent community that is the usual basis for despair, the hunger strike in such circumstances from the outset defines itself as a lost cause and is embarked upon because it is such; it must therefore be an act of self-destruction. Aside from death, its resolution is not in the hands of the striker but lies instead with politicians and officials and with their willingness to extend a humane hand to draw the striker back from despair and folly. These benign qualities and possibilities were starkly absent in 1946.

The death of Thomas Ashe in 1917 was a core element in nationalist and republican consciousness, as was the fact that he had died as a result of being force-fed.[77] This, and the understanding that the leading English case defining the duty of a prison administration towards hunger strikes apparently did not apply in the Free State, meant that it was policy not to force-feed.[78] Besides the unfavourable historical connotations, this made sense politically and legally. Forcible feeding was a primitive operation, requiring the pinioning of the subject so that a tube could be inserted up the nose (or into the mouth, which was held open by a clamp), down the throat and into the stomach, allowing liquid nutrients to be introduced. If a prisoner resisted and struggled, and sometimes if he or she did not, there could be a dangerous diversion of the feed-tube into the breathing passages and lungs, gravely injuring or killing the patient. Even when successful, it was an acutely uncomfortable, and often painful, operation. Embarking on his hunger strike, Seán McCaughey could be sure that he would not be force-fed. Short of that, the medical officer might decide, should McCaughey lose consciousness, to feed a little liquid food by mouth.

The reason, above all, why Terence MacSwiney had died was that his objective – unconditional release – was impossible for the government to concede. Had it done so, no republican prisoner could have been held in a British prison who was able to endure starvation sufficiently to convince the authorities of his seriousness: there was no room for fudge or manoeuvre, even had the government wished to seek a compromise. McCaughey commenced his action on the same inflexible and impossible basis as MacSwiney. In 1946, the Irish government could not be seen to give way to moral threat, perhaps even less than the British three decades earlier. It would be held against it that it had needlessly caused the deaths of Tony D'Arcy and Seán McNeela in April 1940 in Mountjoy.[79] De Valera and his colleagues had, at that juncture, realised that the government itself was imperilled were it unable to meet the challenge of the hunger-striker; there was no going back.

The years in Portlaoise had fragmented the small IRA group, which, by May 1946, was reduced to a core of eight.[80] Their outlook was grim. The outside organisation was close to extinction: internment and imprisonment, and the threat of both, had ground it into fine particles, and the storms of world war had largely blown those away. Life in captivity had split rather than united the ranks. The public was almost totally indifferent to the plight of the prisoners and internees and not remotely in a mood to receive the IRA message. Some or all of this was known to the handful in Portlaoise. They continued to serve long or indeterminate sentences, months after their Curragh comrades had gone home.

At bay

Seán McCaughey had sought some relief from the suffocation of his cell by writing to Dr Thomas Keogh, Bishop of Kildare and Leighlin, in whose diocese the prison was located.[81] He was excluded from religious services because he would not wear the uniform and was therefore deemed to be improperly dressed. He had made the usual poncho from a blanket and, thus attired, declared himself prepared to attend mass. He had also asked that the prison chaplain (Father Harris) if he would bring communion to him in his cell, but this had been refused: 'having been pronounced a "protestant" by the parish priest I now appeal to you My Lord'.[82] The Governor refused to forward the letter. Dr Keogh was a busy man, and his chaplain agreed that if McCaughey had any grievance concerning his religion his first recourse was the prison chaplain. It was a hopeless outcome for McCaughey, since part of his reason for writing to the bishop was his dissatisfaction with Father Harris. The decision to hold back McCaughey's letter, however, was the Minister's – not the bishop's chaplain's.

With relief withheld by both secular and religious authority, in February 1944 McCaughey donned the prison uniform and was allowed to leave his cell to attend mass. Correspondence, parcels and visitors continued to be withheld. The two and a half years' cellular confinement had taken their toll on McCaughey's mental as well as physical health. For reasons not now clear, he decided, a month after his release from his cell, that he would no longer attend mass.[83] At first, however, this was not understood as a new retreat from the very limited world he had briefly rejoined. Indeed, McCaughey seemed to have an awakening interest in that world. He applied for a book on Irish prose composition, and Barrows put in a special order with a Dublin bookseller, even though, according to the Rules and Directives, McCaughey and the others were not entitled to have such material.[84]

His comrades began to express concerns that had been forming for some time.[85] On 25 January 1944, Liam Rice, who at that time was the prisoners' OC (albeit not recognised as such by the authorities) asked to see the Governor. The previous night, Tomás MacCurtáin had contacted him on the hot-water pipes. He had asked Rice, who as a protest had been refusing to come out of his cell for the association period, to call a truce and to opt for association the following day. MacCurtáin's reason for making this request was that he and the others were convinced that McCaughey was becoming mentally ill ('going off his head'), and they wanted Rice's comments. Responding to this information, Barrows appeared to be indifferent: whether or not Rice availed himself of association was a matter for himself; he made no comment on McCaughey. The indifference was feigned, since McCaughey's possible insanity was disturbing news. Barrows immediately informed Dr Thomas Duane, the Medical Officer. As a cover, Duane visited all the IRA men, but he paid special attention to McCaughey. He could see no obvious signs of mental disorder, but McCaughey complained that for several nights he had been unable to sleep. Duane offered a sleeping mixture. To this McCaughey responded that trouble such as his could not be cured by a doctor. For some time past, the other prisoners told Duane, McCaughey had suspected them of disloyalty to the IRA and of being government agents. This fitted with reports from members of staff about McCaughey's aloofness from the group. Barrows himself had noticed McCaughey's 'dejected attitude' and was now sufficiently concerned to order a special watch. Reporting all this to the Department of Justice, he promised Peter Berry that he would be kept in touch with developments.[86] Should McCaughey become insane and have to be removed from Portlaoise, embarrassing questions would be inevitable – and not only from the now thin ranks of militant republicanism.

There is no further reference in the records to the possibility that McCaughey had become mentally ill, and, if he had, his condition and symptoms were not unmanageable. In the two years that followed, however, it became evident that mutual suspicions and recriminations had been vented. By March 1946, Barrows reported to the Department that the tiny IRA group had openly split into three, a division that had existed *de facto* for some months. One faction consisted of Seán McCaughey, Tomás MacCurtáin, Liam Rice and Jim Smith. William Stewart and Eamon Smullen comprised another; Paddy Murphy and Frank Kerrigan the third.[87] According to Barrows, there were some differences between the two smaller factions, but these were minor in comparison to the 'definite break' between them and the McCaughey-led group.[88]

On 15 March 1944, the differences erupted. This, as much as anything, the Governor commented, was a release of the tensions to be expected in a group of young men 'cooped up in close association over such a long period'. Verbal exchanges followed McCaughey's being hit by a handball played by Murphy, and a general melee rapidly developed. Liam Rice broke free from the man he was fighting (William Stewart) and smashed a leg from a cell table, intending to use it as a weapon. Stewart did the same, and, had blows been struck, serious injury would have been inevitable. The men pulled back, and the incident finished in ineffectual grappling and an exchange of words; McCaughey was heard to say that the fight had been brewing for some time. Barrows reported all this in fairly low-key terms to the Department of Justice. Until the men had time to cool down he was releasing them for exercise in two groups, the McCaughey faction having association in the morning and the other two groups in the afternoon.[89] Over the weeks that followed, Barrows reasoned with all of them. Conciliation was not achieved, the men insisting that their differences were such that they could not promise to avoid a violent replay should they come together again. In consequence, the arrangement for staggered and segregated association continued.[90] The fight was certainly more serious than chance ill-temper and bitter words, a tantrum in the continuing tedium of confinement.

This outbreak may have been the final straw for McCaughey. The European war had been over for almost a year, and there was no sign that the government was contemplating an amnesty for those still serving sentences, or that Gerald Boland would give way on the issue of political status and ease the Portlaoise regime. McCaughey's despair and frustration seem also to have prompted him into a more general review and reassessment of his life as a revolutionary. The struggle to which he had given his young manhood had ended in utter defeat – more than defeat, indeed: a void had been created. But had the lost years been a futile sacrifice? He perhaps reasoned that he had one chance left to salvage something. Alternatively, he may have decided that he could take no more of Portlaoise and wished to end it, one way or another. Indeed, he may not have been at all clear on his objective.

On Tuesday, 16 April 1946, McCaughey handed a note to Barrows: 'This is to notify you that unless I am released before Friday, the 19th inst. I will be compelled to go on hunger strike until I am.'[91] It was to be a relatively short hunger strike, lasting only until the small hours of 11 May 1946.[92] For the last fourteen days, McCaughey had also refused liquids and so died in a particularly horrible way, even by the measure of a hunger strike.[93] As the strike progressed he had passed several urgent messages to the Department of Justice, via the Governor. The essence of these was that he wanted to capitulate and if released would cause no more trouble. He did not want to sign a declaration to that effect, but he would give his word. He seemed unaware that he had little with which to bargain. He was a particularly notorious prisoner, and the only inducement to the government to release him was probably repentance and a public renunciation of violence, both of which he had ruled out. If McCaughey could be seen to walk free because of a hunger strike, who then could be held?

Six days into the strike Dr Duane reported that McCaughey seemed 'not quite normal mentally'. This was also the implication of the Governor's report of his conversation with McCaughey on the same day. It was quite a long talk, and, while McCaughey's appearance was 'wild looking', he spoke quite normally, 'finishing up by saying "Oh I want to tell you that from today I am taking no water."'[94] This bizarre disjunction of affect and inappropriate manner in delivering such a grave message indicated considerable mental instability.

In the days that followed, the tragedy of McCaughey's unnecessary and painful death took shape. A number of options were available to move away from confrontation but they were either ignored or rejected by both the government and by McCaughey. The formula that Barrows used in telling McCaughey that the government had rejected his message was closely contrived but did provide some room for manoeuvre, had McCaughey seen it: 'The Minister for Justice had carefully considered his note submitted with my report of the 16th instance and that under no circumstances would McCaughey be released by virtue of his hunger and thirst strike.'[95] There was a hint here that means other than a hunger and thirst strike might offer a way to release. Certainly there was no declaration that McCaughey must accept that release from his life sentence lay well into the future. McCaughey was in no state, mentally or physically, to perceive such nuances and evidently trusted no one to advise him.

On its part, the government (but not, it seems, the prison officials) had lost sight of the fact that it was dealing with a broken and isolated man, a lost soul indeed, suspicious of his comrades and without the resources of intelligence, education and emotion necessary to withdraw himself from the impasse he had created. And whatever resources of person he brought into Portlaoise, prolonged cellular confinement had severely tested and diminished him. However wicked his offence (and the prolonged imprisonment, ill-treatment, torture and intended murder of Hayes were crimes meriting heavy punishment), the state had a duty of care for all prisoners, McCaughey not a whit less than the others. It might, for example, have been appropriate to use a psychiatric evaluation to consider whether he ought to be removed from Portlaoise or to allow a sympathetic intermediary such as Seán MacBride to point out to him how, within the government's constraints, and his own expressed desire to leave the life that he had led, a way out other than death or ignominious backdown might be found.

By the afternoon of 26 April 1946, Barrows was sufficiently concerned by McCaughey's condition to send a telegram to his sister Mrs Annie McCluskey in Belfast, saying that her brother was seriously ill and that she might visit if she wished. This type of compassionate visit was granted only when a prisoner was in a grave or terminal condition. It would be the first time that Annie had seen her brother since his imprisonment in September 1941, and probably (since he was on the run) for some time before that. Annie, her sister and her brother-in-law came immediately. The prison clerk who supervised the visit reported that the unnamed sister had tried to persuade her brother to desist. He told her to stop talking like that and insisted he was in the fight to the finish; he also told his visitors not to send in some family snaps that he had mentioned since he would soon see them outside.[96]

Patrick McCaughey visited five days later, and he also reasoned with his brother, asking him to accept food and liquids: the family, he said, considered that the strike had gone far enough. Seán insisted that he was prepared to die but did not think it would be necessary since his request would be granted. Patrick passed on greetings from various friends and told him that a petition had been submitted to de Valera by seventeen deputies and three senators, but no reply had yet been given.[97] Two days later, McCaughey was still optimistic and told the Chairman of the Visiting Committee that he would soon be free.[98]

Divisions in the family became apparent two days later when two of McCaughey's sisters, Mrs J. McCluskey and Mrs P. O'Hara visited, the latter with her husband.

They urged him to continue his action, saying that the entire family was behind him in that except for Patrick – and he had no authority from the family. McCaughey replied that he was willing to die but had a feeling that it would not be necessary. Asked if priests had visited him, McCaughey said that several had come but that they would not give him absolution while he remained in the IRA.[99]

It was a mark of the deterioration in McCaughey's condition that his sister Annie was allowed to visit again the following day. The clerk who supervised noted that McCaughey's mind seemed to be wandering, that he had difficulty in sticking to the point and was 'rambling and incoherent'. His sister said that all the family were proud of him. He replied that he knew that and was going to force the issue 'even if I have to go into eternity to do it'. Later, he pointed to his head, observing that he knew they all thought 'I am going here'. He insisted that his sister swear on a crucifix that he was not 'mentally queer'.[100]

The next day, Sunday, 5 May 1946, McCaughey made his offer to the government. His conduit was an unlikely one: Thomas Bracken, a temporary officer and trained nurse, on night watch. Bracken set down the remarks as close to verbatim as he could:

> All this could be ended if my request was granted. I am prepared to be quite reasonable. All that is necessary is to put a paragraph in the papers stating that Seán McCaughey has been transferred to a Nursing Home where he is recuperating. It is my intention if that happens to have a holiday in the Gaeltacht, and meanwhile to consider the problem of my future means of livelihood. My political career up to the present time would, in my opinion, be detrimental to national well being if dwelt upon and would not be dwelt upon by me in the future. I am not prepared to sign any contract in this connection as I consider it a matter of honour. I consider it most unfair that I have not been given any idea as to what the Government would consider to be a reasonable conclusion to this.

McCaughey asked Bracken what he thought of his proposition. Bracken replied that he was not allowed to give his personal opinion and asked if McCaughey had made such remarks to the Governor. McCaughey, who was in an excited state throughout, said that he had not, and Bracken asked if he wanted him to pass the message on. McCaughey agreed, and Bracken, despite the hour, immediately contacted Barrows, who came into the prison and, at about midnight, spoke to McCaughey. McCaughey asked if he were going to be released. Barrows replied that he had no authority to do so and repeated the Department's affirmation that under no circumstances would McCaughey be released as a result of his hunger strike. The Governor was joined by Dr Duane, and the two remained with McCaughey until 3 a.m. Some time after they left, McCaughey got back into bed.[101] At 6 a.m., he asked Bracken if a reply had been received, and Bracken told him the matter was now in the Governor's hands.[102] Following this exchange, McCaughey's behaviour became somewhat irrational, and he got out of bed and lay on the floor with only one blanket covering him.

On the morning of Monday, 6 May 1946, Barrows reported the night's events by telephone to the Department of Justice, following which he returned to McCaughey's cell. He told him that he had spoken to the Department and that the final answer was that under no circumstances would the Minister release him as a result of the hunger strike. He asked McCaughey if he understood, and received the testy reply, 'Yes, you've told me this three times.' That day, the Governor received from the Department notice of a question that had been put down in the Dáil by Patrick Finucane. This asked about McCaughey's condition and whether the Minister and relatives had been kept informed by the prison authorities. A full draft answer was submitted by Barrows to the Department. All the possibilities set out by Finucane had been covered. Barrows also confirmed that McCaughey was now in imminent danger of death.[103] The question appeared on the order paper and was answered in the Dáil on 8 May.[104]

McCaughey seems to have tried to accelerate his deterioration, in order to force the issue. Since he was already refusing both food and liquids, there was little more he could do other than to insist on throwing off his bed-covering and clothes, lying naked on the bed. On the morning of Tuesday, 7 May 1946, Tomás MacCurtáin, whose cell was adjacent to McCaughey's, managed to rush past the staff and spoke to him, asking what was wrong with him. He several times asked McCaughey, who was naked, to cover himself, but he refused to do so. He said that the authorities were trying to get him to conserve his energy, stating enigmatically, 'You know what for and so does Liam [Rice].' He assured MacCurtáin that he was not being ill-treated and then asked him to return to his cell.[105]

At midnight that day, Barrows visited again and, at McCaughey's request, asked the hospital officer to leave them alone. Composed and coherent, McCaughey then discussed his position for about an hour. He made another offer to the government, which he wished Barrows to pass on. Were he released, he would cause no further trouble. He would guarantee this in writing but would require a counter-guarantee that the government would not publish his undertaking, though it would have a sanction to hold over him should he fail to honour his promise. It was a vain hope that this was an inducement sufficiently strong to obtain his release, and Barrows told him so. Notwithstanding this discouragement, Barrows left McCaughey's cell 'on the most friendly terms'.[106]

There followed an episode that must have reawakened substantial doubts about McCaughey's mental state and capacity. Barrows would have been well within his rights as governor to set these out for the government but chose not to do so, explicitly at least. He had, as he recorded, 'barely got back to bed at about 1.20 a.m.', when Bracken called from the prison, to tell him that McCaughey had agreed to take liquid food. The Governor told Bracken to prepare some and that he would come over to the prison later. A few minutes later, there was another call: McCaughey wanted a witness from his own side. Barrows refused to agree to this – why is not clear, but, concerned lest he overstep his authority, he may have wished to stick closely to the rules in what was a case of great political significance and volatility. He immediately dressed and returned to McCaughey's cell, where he found him lying on his bed naked. McCaughey said, 'You are too late now. I won't take it.' He then stood up and attempted to leave the cell and was held back by the two warders in attendance. McCaughey appeared to be agitated by the Governor being in his cell, and so Barrows waited outside for about half an hour while the warders attempted to resettle McCaughey in his bed and to cover him with blankets. Some two hours later, McCaughey again asked to see Barrows. Sitting in his bed, he said, 'What's your government's answer?' Barrows replied that he would not be released, and McCaughey 'became excited and had to be restrained'. Barrows waited for a short time and again left the prison.[107]

Barrows evidently had second thoughts about allowing McCaughey to speak to one of his comrades, for later on 7 May he obtained permission from the Department of Justice to allow Liam Rice to spend half an hour with him on the condition that Rice would try to persuade McCaughey to end his hunger strike. Barrow told Rice that he believed that McCaughey wished to come off the strike and asked Rice to assure him that if he did so the others would support him.[108] Rice, who shared the general concerns about McCaughey's mental state, agreed to do this and, according to the supervising officer, made every effort. McCaughey, however, was now adamant that he would continue.[109] He reproached Rice for not supporting him in the hunger strike and, in response to a question, said that he no longer had faith in him: some time previously he had told Rice that it was to be death or release and that still held. Rice demurred, saying that surely he had suffered enough; he also urged him to cover himself up: McCaughey refused. That his grasp of reality had seriously slipped was confirmed when he claimed that the authorities were trying to keep him alive with 'some sort of oxygen' and that he could not find where it was coming from. After some further remarks, he reiterated his claim about oxygen and then, in the words of the attending warder, 'could speak no more'. Rice, troubled and distressed, left the cell in tears.[110]

The following day, McCaughey refused to see his sisters; their request was put to him three times but he would not relent. They were nevertheless asked if they wanted to go to his cell but declined, saying that they would call later in the day when perhaps he might be in a better mood.[111] This they did at about 10 p.m., and it must have been clear by then that the end was approaching. McCaughey told them that he felt happy and asked if they were worrying about him. When they assured him that they were not worrying, he asked them to remain with him to the end and to allow nobody but themselves to touch his body after death. The women promised but evidently without sufficient force or conviction to satisfy him. He then kissed a crucifix and asked them to do the same. All then joined hands on the crucifix and, at his request, repeated the words, 'I swear to remain with you, Seán, until the end.' The sisters then prayed silently until 10.25 p.m. McCaughey told them to go, saying that if he wanted to see them again he would send for them.[112]

One of the sisters (Mrs P. O'Hara) had attempted to leave a handkerchief with McCaughey during a visit on Tuesday, 7 May. Principal Warder Frawley insisted that the rules forbade this and would not allow it. McCaughey himself said that he did not need the handkerchief. Even so, it was a punctiliousness that seemed callous, unnecessary and at the very least inappropriate: a sister was reaching out to her dying brother. On leaving the prison, Mrs O'Hara spoke to a reporter, and the incident received immediate coverage.[113] There was evidently some difference of opinion in the family over this, or there had been second thoughts. Visiting the next day, Annie McCluskey asked to see the Governor and apologised for the press coverage, which, she said, was due to a remark that had been twisted. The officer had done his duty in stopping the handkerchief, and the Governor and all his staff had been most kind. They were grateful to all and repudiated the charges that had been made in the Dáil about the matter.[114]

What the handkerchief incident had shown was not the callousness of the attending warder, who, with all the staff, seems to have treated the McCaughey family politely and with kindness and consideration, as Annie's remarks confirmed. Rather it showed how acutely aware staff were that they might make an error of judgement in what was bound to be a highly fraught and unpredictable political situation. Quite properly, without closer direction from above, they protected themselves by adhering to the regulations. If there was fault, it lay, perhaps, with the Department and with the Minister, who appear to have failed to ensure the correct degree and pace of consultation and intervention. Some form of crisis management was required but was not provided.

By this point, McCaughey was in a shocking condition. Nineteen days into the strike Rice had found him to be 'no more than a skeleton covered by a parchment of skin'. Were he to touch him, Rice felt, the skin would break: 'His eyes were dried holes, his sight gone. His tongue was no more than a shrivelled piece of skin between his jaws, while his body and hands, from what I could discern, were those of a skeleton.' When he spoke, Rice had to lean close to hear what he was saying.[115] Whether, from such a condition, he could have recovered, or recovered fully, must be doubtful.

But this appalling ordeal was drawing to a close. McCaughey's sisters visited on the evening of Friday, 10 May, but he did not speak to them and appeared not to be interested in their presence. When, at 9.40 p.m., they left, he was drifting in and out of consciousness; at one point the hospital warder was unable to find a pulse. According to the narrative report, McCaughey was unable or unwilling to speak and communicated by gestures and nods. He was restless and evidently uncomfortable, shifting his position in the bed and alternately throwing off and assenting to the restoration of the bedding. Barrows and Duane arrived at 11.30 p.m. and spent a quarter of an hour in the cell. When they left, McCaughey started to moan and found it difficult to breathe. The Governor and Medical Officer returned at 12.45 a.m. on Saturday, 11 May, having been called by Hospital Warder Bracken. It was decided that the family and the priest (Father Harris) be summoned. They arrived about twenty minutes later, and at around 1 a.m. McCaughey died. The pathos of it all was captured by Warder Bracken:

> Assisted by Warder Murray I uncovered the corpse at 1.40 and laid it out in a Christian manner. Assisted by Warder Humphries I shaved the corpse at 4 a.m. and washed it at 5 a.m. We tidied the cell and left the holy candles burning on the table beside the bed with the Crucifix. At 7.10 a.m. I went off duty.[116]

Aftermath

A week before the end came, the Department informed Barrows that, in the event of McCaughey's death, his remains were to be handed over to his relatives, should they so request.[117] This was duly done, and the body was transported to Belfast and buried on 13 May. The inquest was held in the prison on the same day as McCaughey's death; the Deputy Coroner, Dr T. J. McCormack, presided. In the course of the examination of the medical officer, the conditions under which the IRA men had been held were brought out. Seán MacBride, appearing for the family, and using a well-tried advocates' tactic of offering words, asked Dr Duane if he would keep a dog in the way that McCaughey, MacCurtáin and others had been held, and Duane replied that he would not.[118] The jury's verdict was straightforward but narrow, attributing death to cardiac failure arising for 'inanition and dehydration following lack of food and fluid intake'. The sting came, as it had in similar circumstances in the past, in the rider: 'The Jury would like to add unanimously that the conditions existing in the prison are not all to be desired according to the evidence furnished. No reflection on the Governor, Medical Officer of Staff intended.'[119]

Whether the jury had intended it or not, the fact that there was no mention, never mind exculpation, of the Visiting Committee – supposedly the conscience, eyes and ears of the broader community – caused it a deal of offence. On the Monday following McCaughey's death, an emergency meeting of the Visiting Committee was held at the prison to express its unhappiness with the rider, 'the result no doubt of the statements made by Counsel in regard to the treatment of convicts in this prison'. The Committee went on to insist that its members 'jointly and severally' had the prisoners' welfare constantly in mind; they had frequently been interrogated, and no justifiable complaint had been made regarding conditions or ill-treatment. The resolution went on to praise the accommodation as 'excellent' and the food: 'whilst plain [it] is good and ample'. The prison staff 'always acted with humanity when carrying out their difficult duties'. They had no objection to their views being published if the Minister thought fit, 'in view of the reflection cast upon the Visiting Committee by the Jury's Rider'. They went on unanimously to pass a vote of sympathy with McCaughey's relatives.[120] A statement outlining the satisfactory conditions at Portlaoise was drafted for the Editor of the *Irish Times*.[121]

There was fury in the Department of Justice at the inquest jury's rider, and on 15 May an instruction was drafted for the Government Information Bureau. What particularly rankled was MacBride's question to the Medical Officer and his agreement that he would not treat his dog in the way the prisoners had been treated. The really serious point, insisted Peter Berry, was that 'a small group of prisoners *are* living under conditions which are not natural even in a prison – not getting any exercise in the open air'. This was admitted by the Department, 'the only question being whether the result follows inevitably from their own mis-conduct or is a vindictive and unnecessary punishment'. It followed that the 'dialectical victory' by Counsel for the McCaughey family should not have been left unchallenged. Berry went on to sketch out the re-examination that should have followed MacBride's question to Duane and the answer it elicited. The doctor should have been asked how he would have treated a dog that had become a killer. The doctor would then agree that such a dog should be destroyed, and, were that legally impossible, it should be kept in the 'closest restraint', even if that involved its living in unnatural conditions.[122]

Berry's anger and resentment impeded his judgement on this occasion. Gerald Boland had a truer instinct for what would play with public sentiment and what might influence it. Comparing McCaughey to a killer dog was both provocative and demeaning, and disrespectful to his family. When he saw Berry's draft to the Infor-mation Bureau, with the strong hint that the canine comparison be planted in the press ('I think that somebody should say this'), Boland immediately intervened, directing that there should be no such statement but that the Visiting Committee should communicate with the press, if they wished.[123] The Government Information Bureau was instructed accordingly, and the Visiting Committee's bland and over-defensive statement, which conspicuously failed to address the conditions of the IRA men, was issued instead.[124] In the Dáil, Boland then threw the blame for the remark onto Seán MacBride, whom he had previously seen in action with juries.[125]

The aftermath to McCaughey's death showed that despite the huge contraction in the IRA's base, emotions ran high. There were obsequies in Dublin, attended or watched by a considerable number of people, but the crowd was measured in hundreds rather than thousands, and there was nothing approaching a mass demonstration.[126] There was abudent sympathy, but it seems to have derived more from pity for the loss of a young and what some saw as an idealistic life, rather than political identification or engagement; the prolonged and terrible mode of death could not fail to move. The government was implacable in its response to demands for a change in the Portlaoise regime. It could hardly be otherwise since any change would have been an admission of neglect or wrongdoing in administration. On 29 May 1946 there was a move in the Dáil, in an alliance of Labour and Clann na Talmhan, for a select committee to enquire into all the circumstances of McCaughey's death. This was rejected by Boland and by de Valera, in strong, confident and combative speeches.[127]

Portlaoise went on as before. The men remained in their blanket ponchos, excluded from all but a minimum of privileges and with no more than the easing in cellular confinement that had already been granted. The choice was unchanged: conform to the penal regime or forfeit all but the most slender connections with the outside world and endure the monotony, unremitting strain and corrosiveness of close confinement.[128]

Opinion far beyond republican ranks had been dismayed by McCaughey's death and by what it had disclosed. Half in or half out, as Boland observed, Seán MacBride was making his transition from a background of violent republicanism to civil- and human-rights advocate, and there was a small but growing interest in this approach. Owen Sheehy-Skeffington rejected a letter of condolence on his mother Hanna's death sent by the Rory O'Connor Cumann (branch) of Fianna Fáil:

> I received your letter of sympathy on the morning that the papers carried the account of McCaughey's inquest. I can accept no official sympathy from Fianna Fáil, nor would my mother want me to. She had nothing but contempt for the party who so assiduously carried on the British tradition in the treatment of prisoners, and so consistently betrayed the ideals for which it was founded.[129]

There was a heated public debate when Noel Hartnett, a lawyer who had assisted in the representation of the family at the McCaughey inquest was removed from his position as compère of the popular *Question Time* on Radio Éireann for subsequent remarks.[130] The removal was effected simply by the ukase of P. J. Little, Minister for Posts and Telegraphs, who informed Radio Éireann that Hartnett would not be allowed to broadcast.[131] This was a self-inflicted wound on the government and helped to inflame already uneasy liberal opinion.[132]

More generally, the death of McCaughey and the conditions it uncovered revealed how deep the division had grown between constitutional and violent republicanism. On his accession to office in 1932, as we have seen, de Valera adopted the strategy for which he had once bitterly denounced his opponents – especially Michael Collins. This was to use the settlement with Britain as a stepping stone to other objectives. The form, style and source of authority of the state were significantly changed by the 1937 Constitution. De Valera considered that he had taken risks in achieving what he saw as a basic change in the substance of the state. With the process more or less complete it followed that any attacks which were made were on what was a virtual republic, a worthy entity deriving directly from the Rising of 1916. In the manner of all such conflicts, those closest to each other became the subject of mutual anathema and deepest contempt: the IRA and Fianna Fáil (embodied in de Valera) grappled with abandoned anger. The war years intensified pressures and distilled bitterness; Portlaoise became the fulcrum of the struggle. McCaughey's hunger strike was not planned by his IRA comrades in prison, and the fragments of the outside organisation (which had ceased to exist in any substantive sense) certainly had no hand in it. Rice and MacCurtáin tried to dissuade him from embarking on his action and then encouraged him to cease it: they knew, with absolute certainty, what the outcome would be, and they had – at the very least – reservations about his mental health and capacity to take such a grave decision.[133]

Yet his death had an impact, albeit quite other than the one he might have contemplated and desired. Immediate republican circles were indeed moved to anger and public indignation, but there was little or no accession in their cause: this most definitely was not a re-run of the great republican hunger strikes of the past. There was a predictable response to the Portlaoise regime and the death of McCaughey from republican supporters in Ireland, the USA and elsewhere.[134] There was, however, in sections of respectable society, among people whose politics were worn lightly, an unease, and perhaps revulsion, that the penal logic that had governed the lives of the small group at Portlaoise had been followed so remorselessly and with a relentlessness that excluded broader humanitarian concerns. People would have agreed that the Portlaoise men were by their records and disposition wicked and dangerous, and, at a time of unprecedented international strife, a threat to the stability and even the survival of the state. Some would have reflected, however, that notwithstanding all this, the state had an obligation to act in accordance with the high principles enshrined in its constitution, even to the least deserving – perhaps especially to such. In modern terms, it had a duty of care even to its most wayward citizens.

The times were apt for such reflections. Ireland had survived world conflagration intact: the override of state survival no longer held. More expansively, the end of the war revealed the horrors of totalitarianism and the hitherto-inconceivable cruelties committed in prisons and camps from the Aegean to the Arctic. Stalin's atrocities remained largely concealed and disputed, but Hitler's were delineated and dissected in the detached and measured language and dispassionately terrifying proceedings of the war-crimes trials. Atrocity and horror were brought home to all in the images of the cinema newsreels. For all its insularity, it would have been amazing if these perversions of human capacities had not caused some self-reflection in Ireland, especially in legal and official circles. And indeed, Ireland, with the special status of a non-belligerent, began to participate in the discussions that would lead to the European Convention on Human Rights. It would be foolish to put McCaughey's death and Portlaoise conditions centre-stage in any of this, but they were somewhere on the stage. One of the first acts of the incoming coalition government in February 1948, in which Seán MacBride held a senior portfolio (External Affairs), was to release the remaining Portlaoise men and the other sentenced IRA prisoners.[135] A line had been drawn not only politically but also administratively: within the Department of Justice a consensus emerged that it would never again engage IRA prisoners on issues such as prison clothing, labour and association because the logic (and history) of such encounters led inexorably to the hunger strike. Safe custody, prevention and punishment were the core issues on which the state could not retreat; the traditional IRA demands were almost entirely peripheral. Worse, they were politically inflammatory, given the origins and history of the Irish state. IRA tacticians used such contests as kedge anchors allowing their campaign to be drawn forward.

The Portlaoise regime for the selected group of IRA men during the wartime years, and the death of the mentally unstable Seán McCaughey, did not redound to the credit of a government that, within its doctrine and strategy, had steered a small, politically divided and barely established state through many complications and great dangers. Beyond the politicians, senior officials and some otherwise in the service of the state may have contemplated the events at Portlaoise with unease – not only in themselves but as a telling comment on the relations between ministers and those whose services they commanded.

Political implications

Had McCaughey's death occurred during the wartime years, with all their weight of censorship, comment would have been all but stifled. Even apart from formal controls, there was, certainly until the Allied supremacy became evident from 1943 onward, an existential fear that laid its own hand of restraint on most members of the Dáil, an effective type of self-censorship. Fianna Fáil and de Valera still dominated the political scene after 1945, but, by mid-1946, international peace had revived political energies, as had the prospect of a general election. Expectations of new things, restiveness and resentments were in the air. The Fianna Fáil administration would be held to account for its wartime record, including law and order and public security. It would also – perhaps unfairly – pay a price for austerity and restraint: party politics has its seasons.

Oliver J. Flanagan, the independent and pro-rebel (in its loosest sense) TD was a particular goad to the government on Portlaoise during this period. His grip on the subject was undoubtedly helped by having the prison in his constituency and by – it may be speculated – a flow of information from within and about it. Flanagan was the instigator of the petition that attracted a number of Dáil signatures calling for McCaughey's release.[136] In an adjournment debate, he remarkably argued that McCaughey could not even be classed as a criminal since he had been convicted only of common assault, an offence that should be punished with, at most, only a few months' imprisonment and most definitely not the death penalty. Flanagan dismissed the argument that the hunger strike was self-inflicted suffering and mortal peril, contending that it was the only way that McCaughey could draw his plight to the country's attention. Were he to continue being held in the same conditions, Flanagan asked, 'would he not be as well dead as having to exist in a Southern Ireland Belsen Camp?' McCaughey was 'a good Irishman to go on hunger-strike. Not only is he carrying on the tradition of his fellow-republicans, but he is the cream of the republicans in this country to-day.'[137]

In the same adjournment debate, Daniel Spring alluded to a rumour that was evidently going the rounds: that McCaughey had been immured and might be done to death to prevent his disclosing information that was deeply damaging to the government.[138] This presumably was based on the belief that the confession that McCaughey and his comrades had tortured and beaten out of Stephen Hayes was true in part, or in its entirety. The allegation was of truly monstrous conduct, a dishonourable and wicked conspiracy:

> I believe that what is behind this is that government want to put Seán McCaughey to death because he knows too much, because he may be able to give information that would implicate members of this House… he is a man who knows something that would terrify the members of the Government.[139]

Earlier that day, Flanagan and Spring had launched a joint attack on Gerald Boland, alleging that McCaughey, now weakened by his hunger strike, was being treated with extreme and calculated callousness and, as death approached, was being kept in conditions deliberately made squalid. Spring raised the question of the handkerchief. McCaughey's sister found, when she visited, that he was using 'a very dirty rag' to wipe his mouth, and when she gave him a handkerchief, it was taken from him.[140] This statement was made early in the Dáil's business day, in time to be taken up by Dublin's evening newspapers and by the morning nationals the following day. Flanagan, appearing to want to go a stage further than his colleague, asked if Boland were aware that McCaughey was 'lying on a piece of dirty sack'. Was this, he demanded, the way that any citizen should be treated under a Christian government?[141]

Boland responded with the now familiar official version of events. We know from the file, which was compiled by a number of prison officials, sometimes on an hourly basis, as McCaughey progressed in his terrible strike, that the Minister's statements were truthful. Conspiracy would have been all but impossible in such circumstances. Staff in Portlaoise had been horrified when, on 8 May 1946, the Dublin evening newspapers reached them. Quite apart from indignation at having being traduced, they were doubtless concerned about the reaction of the community at large and, no doubt, their neighbours, to such accusations. Boland that evening condemned what he characterised as Flanagan's vilification of Portlaoise staff, and, he insisted, 'from the governor down to the humblest', they tried to ease McCaughey's suffering; he also insisted that McCaughey was being kept in decent and humane conditions.[142] Detailing these, he noted that McCaughey's relatives had visited him several times, and were there that evening, and if any should say that things were not as he described, they were not being truthful.[143]

The following day, the McCaughey family were again the subject of a Dáil statement, but on this occasion to exculpate the staff. As noted, Annie had, with members of her family, visited the prison to see her brother and, on her own and their behalf, had apologised for the story about the handkerchief incident, which, through the newspapers and Daniel Spring's remarks in the Dáil, had been exaggerated and distorted. Annie then made a brief statement to the Governor which, while no doubt authentic, had a deal of formality about it that suggested careful drafting, possibly by a press officer or the like. The statement thanked Barrows, the Governor, and his staff, and repudiated the allegations that had been made in the Dáil.[144]

North–South relations were brought into the hunger strike around this time. David Fleming, who had been arrested in Belfast in 1942 following an exchange of shots with the RUC, was on hunger strike in Belfast Prison.[145] Using some odd political algebra, it was suggested by Oliver Flanagan that if Dublin were to release McCaughey in response to his hunger strike, Belfast might respond by freeing Fleming.[146] Why de Valera and Boland would want to aid Fleming in any way was not clear; even more obscure was the benefit to the Northern Ireland government. The notion, however, was abroad, and, on 8 May, de Valera confirmed that he had received a letter from Harry Diamond, the Socialist Republican MP for the Falls constituency in Belfast. Flanagan and others evidently thought that Diamond has asked de Valera to release McCaughey to give an example to the Northern Ireland government. This, de Valera revealed, had not been the line taken by Diamond, who instead simply asked for McCaughey's release.

This was de Valera's cue to reiterate the position he had set out in July 1943 and December 1944.[147] The issue remained one of state and public security, the protection of lives and property. In this, imprisonment was a key tool, and the question was one of purpose and will: 'Whether we are to endeavour intelligently to preserve the means of maintaining public order or revert to primitive anarchy by foolishly permitting to be taken from our hands the only method, short of capital punishment, known to civilised man for the restraint of the wrongdoer, namely that of imprisonment.'[148] In making this statement, de Valera knew that McCaughey was approaching death. This was the afternoon of Wednesday, 8 May; McCaughey would die some sixty hours later, an hour or so after midnight on the night of 10/11 May. The reports that were being received by Boland at the Department of Justice would leave little doubt but that the point of no return had been reached, if not actually passed. All such speeches were grave but in the minds of de Valera and his minister for justice, this had the extra significance of justifying a policy in the face of this imminent death, and of any others that might come. The logic was unanswerable: allow hunger-striking to be fashioned into a master-key, and imprisonment ceased to be a mainstay of the state. The political calculation was altogether more difficult: which course was best in these circumstances and at this time? Would a fudge be better than a death in this season of politics?[149]

By conviction, and perhaps hedged in by past unequivocal statements (though stepping around such is commonplace – and necessary – in politics), the government, led by de Valera and Boland, decided not to alter course. The government's decision, de Valera told the Dáil, 'in the definite terms I have announced, stands, and is irrevocable'. Rather than attempting to weaken the government in the matter and thus, following the logic of de Valera's argument, causing further loss of life, those who were appealing for McCaughey's release would be better to address the prisoner himself or 'those groups who order or incite him to [continue his strike]'.[150]

The Dáil rose on Thursday, 9 May 1946, and did not reconvene until Wednesday, 15 May, four clear days after McCaughey's death. The story had featured in national and regional newspapers on Monday, 13 May, and none could doubt that it was a matter of some national importance.[151] It was not until Tuesday, 21 May, ten days after the death, that the matter was raised in the Dáil. This came from one of the government's persistent opponents on issues concerning republican prisoners: Michael Donnellan, the Clann na Talmhan Deputy for Galway East.[152] In his question, he managed to encapsulate the whole unhappy McCaughey story: prolonged cellular confinement without exercise outside, and the comment that MacBride elicited from the prison Medical Officer. Would the Minister for Justice order a public inquiry into prison conditions?

In his reply, Boland repeated a number of well-aired points. The refusal by the Portlaoise group to wear uniform had led to their wearing blanket-clothes of their own devising. This, in turn, for disciplinary reasons, led to their being denied outdoor exercise and exempted from work. But it was not true to say that the men were being held in solitary confinement: they had frequent cell visits from prison officials and, for three hours a day, associated 'in a large and well-ventilated room, the windows of which look out on the prison farm'. (He neglected to say that this easement had been available only since mid-1943.) The men had correspondence, letters and books, and the ordinary prison dietary. All the restrictions they faced arose from their unwillingness to wear the prison uniform. It had not been to protest about prison conditions that McCaughey had gone on hunger strike but to force his release. Boland also brushed aside the comments of the Medical Officer at the inquest.[153] Donnellan protested at the answer (Boland had gone on to reiterate the points made a number of times before about imprisonment and national security) and asked permission from the Ceann Comhairle (the Speaker) to raise the matter more fully on Adjournment. This was refused, since another Deputy had already been granted permission to raise an Adjournment issue.

Inconclusive sniping and skirmishing continued over the following weeks. Oliver Flanagan asked de Valera whether he knew that, in Belfast, the tricolour had been forcibly removed from Seán McCaughey's coffin on Sunday, 12 May, and whether he would take up with the Northern Ireland authorities this insult to the national flag, 'with a view to obtaining an apology for the incident'. In his capacity of Minister for External Affairs, de Valera responded somewhat dryly that he did not think that 'any good purpose would be served by engaging in futilities'.[154]

Several days later, Flanagan returned to Portlaoise Prison issues by asking about staffing, inspection and the health of Tomás MacCurtáin and Liam Rice. Responding, Boland gave details of the previous service and qualifications of Major Barrows and referred Flanagan to the Estimates for details of his salary. He also paid tribute to Barrows: 'I take this opportunity to acknowledge the diligence, humanity and courtesy which this officer has shown throughout his service and particularly in the recent very trying circumstances.'[155] As for a recent visit of inspection by Deputies, this had been requested by the Labour Party. Boland had agreed, provided all were members of the Oireachtas (Dáil and Senate), and the Labour Party nominations had been submitted accordingly, and approved.

Michael Donnellan got his Dáil opportunity at the end of May. The political temperature was kept up by de Valera in a speech delivered in Cork on Saturday, 25 May, referring to Donnellan's motion for a Select Committee on McCaughey's conditions of confinement and death and making the more general observation that the government was again being challenged by armed forces.[156] Donnellan referred to de Valera's remarks when he proposed his motion in the Dáil: de Valera, he insisted, was following his usual scare tactics.[157]

In calling for an inquiry, Donnellan emphasised that he and his party stood for law and order. The issue was not one of the past conduct of McCaughey and others: prisons were a necessary part of the state, and it would sometimes be necessary to imprison political offenders.[158] But the inquest verdict on McCaughey was recognised by every honest citizen as a vote of censure on the government. He pointed to the irony of Fianna Fáil's background: 'they are the people who climbed into power in 1932… by talking about the way in which Republican prisoners were ill-treated at the time'. Citing the Coroner's juries in three cases besides that of McCaughey, Donnellan insisted that, by failing to respond to these findings, either by changing conditions or ordering further enquiry, the government had, in effect, placed itself above the law.[159]

There was a deal of repetition in Donnellan's speech, but he identified the cardinal weakness in the government's position. As we have seen above, not all those sentenced to penal servitude were sent to Portlaoise; and, at a certain point, sentenced men, including those serving penal servitude as well as ordinary imprisonment at Mountjoy and Arbour Hill, were gathered together at the Curragh, where they had the same regime as internees. This included extensive freedom of association and involvement within the perimeter. Those subject to the regime were allowed to wear their own clothes. That being so, why were McCaughey and his companions held to such a strict regime in Portlaoise? The question was all the more critical because the government had thought it so serious that it was willing to see a man starve himself to death for it.[160] Donnellan asked whether the Taoiseach or the Minister for Justice could deny that the Portlaoise Governor and Chaplain had informed them McCaughey was willing to give up his hunger strike were he transferred to the Curragh?[161] Citing statute and rules going back to 1826 that limited periods of separate confinement and directed that such prisoners should be allowed such exercise as was necessary for their health, Donnellan asked by what authority McCaughey had been kept in solitary confinement for three years.[162]

These were all important questions, though some were based either on exaggeration or on false information. Donnellan then strayed into the fantastical: McCaughey as the Irish Man in the Iron Mask. The reason why McCaughey was kept for four and a half years 'without being allowed to associate with any human being' was the fear that he would reveal an important government secret. This Donnellan then revealed: three weeks before his arrest, McCaughey had been brought to Government Buildings by a high-ranking police officer named O'Carroll and by Sergeant Cahill 'of Carrickmacross'. The offer of a salary was put to McCaughey, provided he acted as a secret agent for the government.[163] At a later point, after McCaughey had been arrested and was in the bridewell, he was approached again and offered his freedom, 'provided he prevented the publication of a certain document'.[164] At this point, Oliver Flanagan interjected in support: 'He [McCaughey] was put away to keep his mouth shut.' McCaughey was brought to see Seán O'Grady (TD and Parliamentary Secretary to Gerland Boland), Donnellan insisted. Working from the rough dates given, this would have been in early August 1941. How the two detectives managed to bring McCaughey into Government Buildings was not stated. Donnellan's evidence was that these were things 'the people throughout the country are talking about'.[165] There were two immediate problems with the allegation: McCaughey had never been held incommunicado and Deputy O'Grady immediately and unequivocally declared that he had never in his life met the late Seán McCaughey.[166] Against this, the historian of the IRA, J. Bowyer Bell, narrates a tale that he collected from his sources in the 1960s. This was that the Irish government contacted the IRA's Northern Command to obtain information on British military activities in Northern Ireland. McCaughey, with the approval of Northern Command, went to Dublin where he met Garda Assistant Superintendent Carroll of Special Branch and Seán O'Grady, 'a Clare TD close to de Valera'. Bell notes that nothing came of this meeting.[167] It is impossible to assess the credibility of the story. There may have been a contact along the lines described by Bell, or he may have been told a story that went the rounds at the time. Nowhere in his messages passed through Barrows to the Irish government during his hunger strike does McCaughey refer to any past meeting with authority. On the other hand, the fact that he thought that he could pass such messages may indicate a confidence based on past experience.

Boland's version of McCaughey's contacts with authority had a more plausible ring than the series of allegations of conspiracy mounted by Donnellan and Flanagan. It more directly corresponded with the organisational state of the IRA and the drift of its politics. In late 1939 or early 1940, Seán O'Grady, a Clare TD, had indeed contacted Boland, saying that McCaughey had asked, through an intermediary, if he could see a member of the government. The answer was no, but Boland agreed that, if McCaughey wished, he could see a high-ranking police officer. When this meeting took place, a proposition was put: there would be no more IRA attacks in Éire if the IRA were left alone by the police to prepare attacks on Northern Ireland. Similarly, there was an approach via the police in the border area, and a meeting was agreed. There was an interesting variation on the proposition this time. The gist was the same: no attacks in the South in return for being allowed to use the territory for preparation and as a launching place. The emissary told the police officer that 'the IRA were dissatisfied with the policy carried on by their headquarters in Dublin'. They wanted a change by proposing mutual toleration in the South.[168]

Offensive and outrageous though it was in places, Donnellan's excursion into conspiracy was undoubtedly useful to the government, both as a distraction and as a means of discrediting Donnellan and Flanagan. Other deputies put a more reasoned case and more convincingly called the government to account. Patrick Cogan, another member of Clann na Talmhan (and a Co. Wicklow farmer), seconding the motion, made the point that, since the Coroner's jury had passed a critical verdict, the response of the Minister for Justice should have been to institute an inquiry. Boland had said that, for various reasons, he did not want to comply with the motion for a sworn inquiry, but surely he should offer an alternative, such as a judicial inquiry. The government should steer a course between excluding enquiry into its actions and the opposite danger of being seen as irresolute and weak.[169]

The debate proceeded along fairly predictable party lines. Gerald Boland described conditions at Portlaoise and then turned to the IRA activities as a threat to the government and the perils of the wartime years.[170] He spent a deal of time on Seán McCaughey's character and the nature of his crimes, including the imprisonment and torture of Hayes.[171] When arrested, McCaughey was in possession of maps, reports and plans setting out the disposition of the Irish Army and also of the British Army in Northern Ireland; he also had plans of airfields and points of strategic importance. Boland laid particular emphasis on McCaughey's contacts with Hermann Görtz, notes of a meeting with whom McCaughey had on him when arrested. More conclusive in terms of a conviction was McCaughey's possession of the keys of the chains and padlocks with which Hayes had been fettered.[172] Boland prefaced his long recital of McCaughey's crimes with the observation that Flanagan had claimed that a fine of one shilling would have been an appropriate sentence.[173] The disparity between the deeds and the proposed punishment was incontestable.[174]

On the issue on which the government was most vulnerable, Boland was least convincing. He outlined the particular seriousness of the crimes of the Portlaoise men – and indeed they were grave offences. But on the question of why they were sent to Portlaoise rather than the Curragh he was vague and discursive. Mountjoy had become overcrowded as a result of the general increase in crime, and the IRA prisoners could not be kept there: 'There were riots and the governor said that they could hardly manage the prison.' The Minister for Defence agreed 'to house them in one of his prisons'. This was for the generality of the IRA prisoners, but those who had committed crimes 'such as murder, armed robbery, kidnapping and so forth' were sent to Portlaoise to serve their sentences, 'as any criminals sentenced by the ordinary courts for like offences'. There were men in the Curragh 'who committed rather serious crimes', but there was no truth in the claim that there were Curragh prisoners who had committed more serious crimes than had the men at Portlaoise.[175]

It was the question of if and why McCaughey had been given special treatment that was the pivot of John Costello's response, on behalf of Fine Gael, to the debate. As a former Attorney General, his remarks carried particular weight. He dismissed much of what had been said by both Donnellan and Boland as mere party-political manoeuvring. The history of the IRA was an irrelevance, as were its misdeeds, in considering the merits of the motion.[176] Law and regulations and how they were carried out was what Costello had hoped to hear from Boland: 'Are the prison regulations in accordance with law, were they carried out in practice in connection with Mr. McCaughey in the same manner as they would have been in connection with every other prisoner acting in the same way?'

Quite before the matter of McCaughey, and long before Costello had heard of it, conditions at Portlaoise had been drawn to his attention by a non-political friend, speaking entirely on grounds of humanitarianism, morality and religion. It was a matter for urgent consideration whether prison conditions in general accorded with 'modern humanitarian and Christian standards'. The case of McCaughey should be dealt with as an individual matter, looking to the law and its application: 'If the Minister has given us an assurance that in no respect was this man treated differently from any other prisoner in the prison, then I think we would have been satisfied and the public would have been satisfied.'[177]

On behalf of the Labour Party, William Norton supported the motion for a Select Committee. He homed in on the question of why some men had been sent to Portlaoise but not others. Between 1939 and 1943, 412 prisoners were transferred from civil prisons to military custody.[178] If that number could be moved, why not all? There was also a particular consideration in the case of McCaughey: 'Everyone knew there was a political issue red-hot there, as to whether they would wear prison garb.' McCaughey had been sent to a place where this dispute was already under way, 'where he had virtually no chance except to do what other people were doing'. This was 'a challenge to our intelligence, a monument to our stubbornness'. He hoped that the enquiry proposed by the motion would lead to a policy for those whose offences were connected with political activities, 'without having periodical crises on the question… as in the past'.[179]

Dealing with the circumstances of McCaughey's imprisonment, Norton observed that there was considerable disquiet 'putting it no higher than that lest I exaggerate' that a prisoner had been held in solitary confinement for three years and was without normal clothes for four and a half years. It had been said that McCaughey had, by his own actions, denied himself access to open-air exercise, but even if this were true, 'those considerations do not weigh heavily in the scales if there is a human life on the other side'.[180] Norton again asked the key question: what was the principle on which a person could be sentenced by a court and sent to the Curragh where he could wear his own clothes or to Portlaoise where he must wear a prison uniform: 'Is it because some are specially selected to go to Portlaoighise owing to the nature of their offences, or is it because of some personal dislike of their activities?'[181]

The substantive debate concluded with an extensive contribution from de Valera. This rehearsed a number of themes that he had set out before, in the Dáil and in other places, and in large part either repeated or amplified points made by Boland. We shall return to de Valera's reflections on political prisoners below, but in this speech must note that he mentioned again his own hopes and expectations on coming into office in 1932, his policy of conciliating the IRA and his disappointment that it did not work. He also referred to the perils of the war years and to the necessity for special measures against the IRA in order to safeguard the state. Without going into the detail that Boland had given, de Valera mentioned the violence and wickedness of many of the offences committed by the IRA and the determination of its members to defy prison regulations when they found themselves inside. It was not an impressive speech, though it had many interesting passages. Most crucially, it failed adequately to address the central points: why Portlaoise for certain offenders, was the regime there legal and, as some had asked, what was the moral justification for its imposition.[182]

There was also a deal of irony in de Valera's remarks, in particular his determination not to distinguish between politically motivated and ordinary crime. He and other members of the Dáil had had the experience of imprisonment under British administration; some (de Valera included) had further spells of custody during the Civil War. In all of this time, de Valera and his comrades had insisted that theirs was not individual crime, emanating from greed, a propensity to violence or moral turpitude. That being so, they would not submit to being treated as criminals in prison. In his speech to the Dáil on this occasion, however, de Valera, as he had in other places and at other times, rejected the distinction between ordinary and political criminals: 'Is there', he asked, referring to political murder, 'any single Deputy in this house who can honestly say that such a distinction should be made?'[183]

There was further irony in de Valera's references to campaigns by republican prisoners for special treatment. These were people who had shot policemen and witnesses and who had intimidated judges (the IRA had certainly done this when he was a member); they kidnapped and tortured their own members and when they confessed, shot them (also a practice of the Old IRA). Whilst de Valera may not himself been involved in these activities, he certainly cannot have been unaware of them and, to that extent, was complicit in them. This applied across the Dáil, to all who had been engaged in the Anglo-Irish and Civil wars, yet de Valera asked if the ministers had not been right to hold the line on Portlaoise (which he had done with the support of his government colleagues): 'Was he to give way? We know that if he gave way in this [the wearing of the prison uniform], that would not be the only plea alone.'[184]

Yet more irony followed in de Valera's description of the IRA's ladder of demands. Giving ground on one demand simply cleared the way for further demands (as had shown himself when in Dartmoor, Lewes and Maidstone prisons in England in 1916–17).[185] He well understood, both intellectually and by direct experience on both sides of the wall, the tactics of prison battles: 'The moment you conceded that [demand] you were met with further demand and when you had conceded that… you were met with another.'[186] These tactics had been such an important part of the War of Independence, in which republican prisoners had, by example, morale-raising, propaganda value and attrition, played such an important part that few members of the Dáil would have failed to recognise the truth in de Valera's observations. He underlined the point himself: 'I do not think there is in the wide world today a legislative assembly whose members have such a wide knowledge, such a wide personal knowledge of prison conditions as we have.' He disclosed (with some pride, it seemed) his own remarkable qualifications: 'I have been in about 14 prisons'.[187]

Boland and de Valera were not allowed a free ride in their protestations about law and order and the need to deal sternly with the IRA. For Dr Thomas O'Higgins, a Leix-Offaly Deputy, unconscious irony had tipped into hypocrisy. He had been born and raised not far from Portlaoise Prison and had spent part of his life as a medical practitioner in the town. He was, he claimed, as familiar with the prison as any other member of the Dáil, except perhaps the Minister for Justice. As for the staff of Portlaoise, he was emphatic that 'there never was any brutality, inhumanity or ill-treatment of prisoners'. He was satisfied, as far as anyone could be, that there was no officer of the prison, high or low in rank, who would not give whatever benefit he could to the prisoners, within the rules: 'They would never dream of exceeding the regulations in order to punish any of their prisoners.' He did not know why the government had not made that case and published the regulations. He answered his own implied question by accusing de Valera and Boland, as others had, earlier in the debate, of using the McCaughey case and talk of an IRA revival as a pre-election scare.

That, O'Higgins may have felt, was an inevitable, if distasteful and irritating, part of normal party politics. What particularly irked him was de Valera's assumption of the character and stature of saviour of the nation from 'complete anarchy and chaos'. Making his own party point, O'Higgins reminded the government benches that there was a time when it was difficult to gain respect for the institutions of state and to 'grapple with organised crime' (a reference to the IRA) and to gain acceptance for law and order: 'When those on these benches were endeavouring to do that, in vain could we look to the Taoiseach and his colleagues for any assistance to the state in that direction.'[188]

This was a provocation, and the debate slipped away into exchanges of insults and interjections. 'What about the Board of Works contract?' was answered by 'Shut up. You are only a sucking bottle', and O'Higgins himself referred to 'people' (members of the Dáil, one assumes) 'of glib tongues and empty heads who produce that kind of prattle'. There were allegations that the debate was being stifled and challenges to the Chair's authority. First, Dominick Cafferky (of Clann na Talmhan) and then Oliver Flanagan were ordered out of the House (the latter by resolution of Members).[189] Disorder continued, with another Clann na Talmhan member, Bernard Commons, also being ejected by resolution.[190] It was getting late, and, amidst unruly and bad-tempered exchanges, the debate lost all coherence (and a deal of dignity) and stumbled on to a vote. The Clann na Talmhan motion for a Select Committee of Inquiry was lost, Fine Gael deputies abstaining.

This was the end of the McCaughey case in the Dáil. It had, perhaps inevitably, become a party-political matter, and this had inevitably buried it. An election was in the air (and would be called within fifteen months), and issues of law and order would inevitably be at the centre of that contest. There appeared to be a division between de Valera and his minister for justice on the possibility of a general inquiry into the penal system – though this may have been no more than a few words going astray in the heat of debate. Irish prisons were, in Boland's view, generally satisfactory or better. There were shortcomings, of course, but these could be addressed as resources permitted. De Valera concurred and asserted that the Irish prison system would compare 'very favourably' with that of any other civilised country. He did observe, however, that if 'in other circumstances' an inquiry were proposed into the prison system as a whole, 'neither I nor the Minister for Justice would object very strongly'.[191] The temper of the times, governed as it was by the electoral cycle, did not allow this approach, which would have stood a reasonable chance of being constructive.

Instead, there was, within a fortnight, a re-run of the Dáil debate on McCaughey and Portlaoise, this time in the Senate. Unease and anger about the treatment of McCaughey had not been dissipated by the Dáil debate. The peg this time was solitary confinement. On a motion of Senator Luke Duffy, Secretary of the Labour Party and a member of the Industrial and Commercial Panel of the Senate, the government was invited to submit proposals for restricting the use of solitary confinement.[192] An amendment was proposed by James Douglas, which would have had the effect of asking for an inquiry into prison treatment generally.[193] This amendment was accepted at the outset by Duffy. The debate lasted for several hours and since there emerged few, if any, points that had not been raised in the earlier Dáil debate, it is unnecessary to provide another detailed analysis.

Despite the attempts of several senators to broaden the discussion to penal policy generally, this was also a party-political debate. While the temper of the Senate was more restrained than the Dáil had been, the underlying dynamic was the same. Speaking late in the debate, James Tunney (Labour) observed that had it not been for the death of Seán McCaughey there would not have been a debate.[194] Gerald Boland (who, as the relevant minister was present and could speak, but not vote) largely agreed: 'I know that the public mind is upset.' But the reason why the public was disturbed was the reason why he would agree neither to the motion nor the amendment: 'Decent and kind people in the country are very much upset by these lying statements, especially from lawyers who ought to know better.'[195]

This last was a reference to Seán MacBride and others. Boland saw MacBride as a conscious agent of the IRA rather than a dupe; others he may have seen as honest men (and women) who were being used and misled. During the Dáil debate, Boland had referred to IRA documents that had come into his possession that showed that the IRA was working up campaigns on prisons and that they fully expected MacBride to play an important part in these.[196] From the tone of his remarks, it was clear that he thought the move in the Senate was part of a move against the government in what was becoming a distinctly pre-election period.[197] When, during the debate, it was suggested that if the appointment of a commission of inquiry be delayed for six months, the government might take a more benign view of the amended proposal, Boland emphatically rejected the notion. It is not difficult to see why: the appointment of an inquiry was in itself an implied criticism of the government, and there was no saying what such a committee might find or recommend that would be explicitly critical; and all this in the run-up to an election. It mattered little how the debate developed: there would be no inquiry.

Boland noted that the proposal for a prison inquiry had been made in 1943, so why had the motion not been put down then? Answering his own question, he said that it was because the IRA's campaign, to which he had referred in the Dáil, 'was not ready for launching'. While he was not accusing any senator of being a knowing participant in a campaign, 'the campaign is here, lined up and well planned'.[198] Were he to agree to a commission of inquiry, he knew well what the result would be: a vehicle for propaganda.

Expanding on the last point, Boland cast his mind back to earlier times and the use that the Old IRA had made of imprisonment. He had seen propaganda: 'if not lies, gross exaggeration amounting to lies'. And he revealed that this tactic went back at least thirty years:

> I am pleased to be able to say today that I was one of the few in Frongoch who refused to sign an exaggerated statement, the publication of which would alarm our relatives at home... I understand this thing inside out. It is not a question of asking for ordinary treatment.[199]

While he had the interests of ordinary prisoners at heart ('I read O'Donovan Rossa and Oscar Wilde'), his attitude to the IRA prisoners was very different: 'I am not going to let that particular crowd run the country, unless they go to the Irish people as we did and get the right to do so.'[200]

In the course of the debate there were several references to the long periods of solitary confinement served by the eight Portlaoise men. Duffy referred to the matter as he opened his remarks. He pointed out (without giving the prisoner's name) that Tomás MacCurtáin, when his death sentence had been commuted, had been in Mountjoy. Now under a sentence of penal servitude, he had nevertheless been kept in solitary confinement, which continued from 24 July 1940 until 2 June 1943 (two years, eleven months and four days, Duffy said). Rehearsing all the statutes, going back to the Prisons (Ireland) Act, 1826, Duffy pointed out the restrictions that had been placed on the use of solitary confinement, both by law and regulation, British and Irish.[201] He took MacCurtáin as his example, but his point applied no less to the other Portlaoise men who, as a consequence of refusing to wear the prison uniform, had been kept to their cells: 'If solitary confinement has been ordered for these charges, there must be some statutory authority for that Act. I would like to know that authority. I have been unable to find any.'[202]

This line of criticism was followed by others, notably by Senator T. C. Kingsmill Moore (a senior counsel). He made two telling points. The Act most central to and governing prison matters, the General Prisons (Ireland) Act, 1877, s.12, provided that no rule made by the General Prisons Board could be inconsistent with the Prisons (Ireland) Act, 1826. Section 109 of the 1826 Act directed that, whether in solitary confinement or not, every prisoner should have two hours' exercise daily. More than that, in researching prison law, Kingsmill Moore had found it 'altogether impossible' to get hold of the regulations. There was a serious question about legal authority, but also one about consistency. When Boland had eased the custody of the eight men in June 1943, it was because he rejected a regime that in 1940 he had deemed to be suitable.[203]

Boland's response to these and other observations was personal and heated. He declared that he would not run away from his responsibilities and was not going to apologise. He had never thought that he would have the position of Minister for Justice and be responsible for keeping people in prison: 'I cannot say the amount of personal pain which that gives me.' But he had evidently been irked by the debate: 'I object to being spoken to from an eminence by Senator Kingsmill Moore.'[204] This bluster aside, he was unable to refute Kingsmill Moore and to give authority for the extended use of solitary confinement:

> About the legal position, this is no place to argue law. Those Senators who doubt we are acting within our rights can test the matter for themselves... They can seek an injunction against me and have the matter thrashed out, but I say that the law has not been broken and we are not going to allow people out [of their cells] dressed in that condition.[205]

He was slightly more conciliatory about the rules, which Kingsmill Moore had found so hard to obtain. They were being consolidated and would be published soon, as would a report to cover the wartime years, when the annual reports on prisons were not published. With these documents before them, senators might send him suggestions or put down a motion which he 'could consider' and 'might find possible to accept'.[206] There would also be a consolidating Bill brought in the following year, preceded by an amending Bill, Boland told the House, but on this he was noticeably vague.[207]

It had not been as heated a debate as in the Dáil, and if there were at times party and personal sniping, these had been counterbalanced by thoughtfulness, compassion and erudition. Boland, believing that the motion and debate were part of a campaign – if not by the IRA then by others acting in the vein of republicanism, and with IRA connivance and encouragement – was in turns heated, defensive, bombastic and sentimental. It is impossible from the written record alone to judge the moral balance in the Senate that evening but, although the government won the vote, it did not appear to win the argument.

That, of course, is far from uncommon in parliamentary politics and the working of democracy.

Corporal and capital punishment

Flogging

During the wartime years two sentences of flogging were imposed on politically motivated prisoners in Éire. In the British penal tradition, from which the Irish code was derived, flogging was added to a prison sentence to mark a heinous, aggravating or infamous feature of an offence, usually involving violence or extreme moral turpitude: it was reserved for offences such as pimping, robbery with violence and assault on the weak. It was the *lex talionis* of Mosaic doctrine – with the express purpose of humiliating, degrading and delivering salutary personal deterrence through pain. The spectacle and (when whipping was removed from the public gaze) notion of an offender writhing in pain became increasingly archaic and unacceptable in Western societies, especially as democracy advanced: its British connotations lent an additional unease to its use in the Irish Free State, and in the two decades following independence it was rarely ordered. It was used twice during the wartime years on IRA offenders: on Patrick Murphy and William Stewart. In both cases their offences included firing on the police and the Army and bank and post-office raids. The prison sentences were heavy, a permutation of consecutive and concurrent terms amounting to terms of fourteen years each. In addition, twelve strokes of the cat were ordered.[208] Had they been charged with shooting with intent they would have been liable for trial before the Military Court and consequently for the death penalty.[209]

A number of accounts of flogging are available in the penological literature, but Patrick Murphy's may be the only one from a republican source of a Southern flogging.[210] Most popular perceptions come from cinema versions in which a hero stoically endures a lightly lacerating whip, shrugs manfully or winces and then, with little more ado, goes about his business as soldier, sailor or cowboy.[211] The reality was very different. In Murphy's case there was a gap of four weeks between the imposition of sentence and its execution, adding uncertainty and anticipation to the punishment. He had been in Arbour Hill awaiting trial before the Special Criminal Court. This took place on Friday, 26 September 1941, and he was afterwards removed to Mountjoy, where he was held in D Wing. As the weeks went by, he recalled, 'I commenced to think that, maybe, they had forgotten about the cat; that I would not have to suffer it.'[212] But the sentence had been under review at the Department of Justice, and on Monday, 20 October, Murphy was summoned to the office of Seán Kavanagh, Mountjoy's veteran governor, who informed him that he had received notification that the flogging was to be carried out; this was to be done forthwith.[213] The prison medical officer and a doctor from the nearby Mater Hospital were in attendance, and Kavanagh offered Murphy spirits, which he refused. The group then went to a basement cell. Murphy was asked to strip to the waist, and he was strapped to the flogging triangle and blindfolded. The warder who was to conduct the flogging then entered the cell, and the punishment commenced. The lashes 'curled around the exposed body and were much more painful that I had imagined'. The strokes were counted off by Kavanagh, and after the ninth he asked Murphy if he could take any more. Refusing to make any sign of submission, Murphy replied, 'go ahead; finish it'.[214]

The whipping itself was obviously traumatic, and the aftermath was prolonged and extremely painful. Wrapped in a sheet that had been soaked in iced water, Murphy was put on a stretcher and taken to the prison infirmary. His punctured and bleeding skin was treated and dressed, and he was again offered brandy. One of the doctors, forestalling another bravado response, accepted on his behalf. At this point Murphy remembered that he fell into 'a deep and dreamless sleep' – perhaps more aptly described as unconsciousness following severe trauma. On awaking, the pain was intense. 'I was the most miserable man alive. I was in pain all over.' He was allowed to remain in bed for two days, and on the third Kavanagh visited the cell, asking how he was feeling: 'I had to say that the soreness was still shooting through me.' The following day he was told to dress and was taken to the Governor's office where an escort of four Special Branch men awaited him. He was immediately and in silence taken from Mountjoy to Portlaoise.[215]

Given the determination and sternness with which the government repressed the IRA during these years, it is an interesting question as to why whipping was not more frequently imposed. It was not a matter of judicial independence, since sentencing at the Special Criminal Court was in the hands of a military panel that would certainly have carried out a new order extending the use of the whip. It may simply have been a pragmatic judgement. Murphy's demeanour during his flogging – stoical and unsubmissive, as he reports it – would probably have been the norm for the IRA men. There was always the risk that a flogged man could become something of a martyr, though this was a society that was unmoved by the liberal use of strap and cane on its schoolchildren. Certainly neither of the IRA men who were flogged became a republican notable because of it. As a vehement expression of the will of the state, flogging could scarcely have been bettered, but were it widely or unselectively used, the government ran the risk of seeming brutal and sadistic rather than resolute. The topic receives little mention in the official papers, as far as can be seen, and the sparing use of the whip may have been due to no more than the sentencing panel's disinclination or to distaste on the part of the prison officials charged with its administration. Irish official and military circles were sufficiently compact for such feelings and reservations to be communicated discreetly and without fuss.

Executions

Consideration of the death penalty for IRA-linked offences during the Second World War must be given two contexts. We have already examined the general political and international situation.[216] The other must be the general political and popular attitude toward capital punishment. Viewing this from a time when all European democracies have abolished the death penalty, and when a state's membership of the Council of Europe and the European Union is contingent on abolition, we need to remind ourselves that, several decades ago, both politicians and the public viewed matters rather differently. Independent Ireland, once past the Civil War, was fairly parsimonious in its use of the death penalty. From 29 November 1923 to 20 April 1954 there were thirty-five executions.[217] There were three or four executions a year in the 1920s, with a decline in the 1930s: none at all in 1930, 1933, 1935–6 and 1938, and one in each of the other years. From the executions of Patrick McGrath and Francis Harte on 6 September 1940 until that of James Lehman on 19 March 1945, there were twelve deaths, variously by hanging or shooting. Half of these were for IRA-related offences.[218]

In general, therefore, there was little use of the ultimate penalty in the Free State and Éire. An execution was certainly newsworthy because of this infrequency of occurrence (and also because of the usual morbid interest in the circumstances surrounding murders). At the same time, this was an accepted penalty, resisting calls for abolition from the 1930s onward.[219] Even when partially abolished in 1964, the death penalty remained available for offences such as treason (including conspiracy) and murder of police and prison officers or certain politically motivated murders. Such offences were thereafter committed, and where convictions were obtained (as they were in ten cases between September 1975 and June 1985) the death penalty was commuted to life imprisonment. Well into the era of abolition, therefore, Ireland, with its special experience of politically motivated murder and high feelings of revulsion about the murder of its unarmed gardaí, retained an attachment at least to the concept of capital murder and its condign penalty.

This is the broad context in which we must consider the six death sentences which were carried out during the war years. Convinced as it was that national survival was at stake during the Second World War, the de Valera government was willing to inflict the ultimate penalty on IRA men and thus to expose itself to the opprobrium it had not spared its opponents when they were in government. It remained steadfast in this decision, despite pleas from sympathisers, supporters, political and personal intimates and insiders, and others, that the crimes for which the men had been condemned were political in nature. Being free from personal gain, malice or moral turpitude, the argument went, they should not be subject to the maximum penalty of death. There were inconsistencies in the use of the death penalty, but in these cases they were mainly seen at the review stage, when the decision was taken on commutation.[220] Yet some decisions were marked by expediency. Tomás MacCurtáin, were his offence judged alongside those whose sentences were carried through, should certainly have been executed, but he was saved by the memory of his father and the political cost that would attach to his death.[221] Seán McCaughey probably did not merit the death penalty. His crimes were serious, but not as serious as he wished and intended. No one had been killed, even though the murder of Stephen Hayes, McCaughey's ill-treated and tortured captive, had been agreed and was only a matter of days away. The commutation of McCaughey's sentence was not as clear-cut as some of his apologists have argued, but it did reflect some application of the principle of proportionality.[222]

Any execution came as a shock to the republican movement, and certainly to a swathe of Fianna Fáil, drilled as it was in the iniquities of its hated opponent in the Civil War, when the Free State executed seventy-seven men: the number itself became infused with meaning and was used as a taunt, a term of denunciation and abuse in political exchanges.[223] The opprobrium, in republican eyes, attached to the pro-Treaty section of what had been Sinn Féin and its descendant party, Fine Gael. De Valera, for all their bitter disagreements with him, and their denunciations of his apostasy, came from the anti-Treaty side. With the wartime executions, a new, bitter and seemingly unbridgeable gulf was opened. It was a great and continuing shock for those who had hoped that differences could be fudged away and the republican family restored.

The first two to be executed were Patrick McGrath and Thomas Harte, who went before a firing squad in Mountjoy Prison on Friday, 6 September 1940.[224] Both men had been arrested after the firefight at 98A Rathgar Road, Dublin. This was the IRA's Training Department HQ from 1938 onward and was operated behind a bogus shop; there was also an arms dump on the premises. It appears to have been well known to Special Branch, who no doubt found it a useful source of intelligence. Its usefulness came to an end, however, and detectives staged an early morning raid on Friday, 16 August 1940. Someone on the premises opened fire with a Thompson gun, and others used handguns as they tried to escape. Three detectives were hit. Detective Richard Hyland died on arrival in hospital; Detective Sergeant Patrick McKeown died the following day; and Detective Michael Brady was wounded but recovered.[225] Thomas Harte, one of the IRA party, was also wounded as he made his break. Patrick McGrath was arrested as he returned to help his comrade.[226] Another of the IRA men, Thomas Hunt, got away but was arrested in Dublin five days later.[227]

As soon as the government received the report of the incident, wounding and fatalities, it decided on a stern and exemplary response. Using its powers under the Emergency Powers (Amendment No. 2) Act, it made an order on the evening of 18 August establishing a Military Court.[228] As noted, this body was given power to try certain offences, including murder, which were attacks on the state.[229] As with the Special Criminal Court, the new tribunal was summary in nature, acting without a jury. It was composed of commissioned officers of the armed forces. Unlike the Special Criminal Court, however, the Military Court was restricted to one sentence only: a guilty verdict entailed a mandatory death sentence. The possibility of delay and uncertainty in the superior courts was cut out by removing all rights of appeal, and protecting this celerity by acting under cover of the government's emergency duties and powers. In place of appeal, it was provided that every sentence would be subject to automatic executive review, at which stage the sentence could be let stand, commuted or set aside.[230] Execution was to be by firing squad.

The decision on whether to remit a case to the Military Court was made by the government, advised by the Attorney General. Patrick McGrath and Thomas Hunt were duly brought before the Court on Tuesday, 20 August – only four days after their offence. They had been caught in flagrante delicto, the evidence against them incontestable, and after a fifteen-minute deliberation the two were convicted and sentenced to death.[231] Thomas Harte was arrested on 21 August, brought before the Court, found guilty and automatically sentenced to death. Execution was delayed whilst the conformity of the new court with the Constitution was tested before the High Court on a writ of habeas corpus, lodged by Seán MacBride. On 26 August, Mr Justice Gavan Duffy, sitting in the High Court, rejected the application; this decision was confirmed on 4 September by the Supreme Court.[232] The government then reviewed the sentences and denied a commutation for Harte and McGrath. The execution took place two days later. McGrath had fought during Easter Week and reportedly still had a British bullet lodged in his body. This record of gallantry and service failed to persuade the government. Of the three, only Hunt was spared, his sentence commuted to penal servitude for life. In asking Special Branch men to risk their lives in the pursuit of armed and dangerous IRA men, the government entered into a compact to use all means – including severe penalties in law – to protect them. To fail to have carried the executions through, it was doubtless calculated, would have adversely affected Special Branch motivation and might perhaps encourage IRA gunmen – quite apart from any consideration of the enormous seriousness of killing policemen in a time of war; and of course any notion of just deserts. It is noteworthy that only three weeks elapsed between the killings and the men's execution: this was a much shorter period than usual in ordinary criminal cases and extraordinarily short considering that there had been a major legal review. The swiftness and certainty of proceedings contained its own message about the government's determination to confront the IRA challenges.[233] Six years later, in a Dáil debate, the Minister for Justice, Gerald Boland, responded to the charge that the Military Court had been a terror court: 'That is exactly what it was. It was a terror court – a court set up to meet terror in a drastic and summary manner in order to save this nation from the perils which threatened it at the time.'[234]

Grave and important though the cases of Harte, Hunt and McGrath were, the consequences of the Rathgar Road shootings and the government's response went beyond the men and their victims. The government, charged supremely with the preservation of the state, wielded an instrument of enormous reach, flexibility and simplicity of operation. The Military Court was not wholly a court in the legal sense of judicial independence. Its members were serving officers, ultimately responsible to the government, through the Minister for Defence. Review of each case in which a guilty finding was made was automatic, and this provided an element of checking and an opportunity for reflection, but this by the same executive that commanded the officers on the panel. But if the Court lacked independence it could not be said that it was arbitrary or that its findings were prejudged. Evidence had to be produced, and defendants were entitled to representation and counsel of their choice and had a full opportunity to rebut the case against them, including the cross-examination of state witnesses and the calling of their own. The proceedings were not secret, and the press was admitted and allowed to report. In the course of its operation, moreover, the Court did acquit in four of the thirteen cases brought before it.[235] This was indeed an emergency response to an armed conspiracy, but while it was not arbitrary or without basic elements of natural justice, it was, as Gerald Boland admitted, *in terrorum*.

In assessing the Court, one must look beyond the firefight in the streets of Dublin and the killing of police officers – capital offences then in almost all democracies. The face of Europe had changed that summer. The German armies had completed their conquest of the western European land mass and had forced France to accept an armistice, occupation of much of its territory and subordination of the rest. The remnants of the British Army and Free French forces had been gathered up at Dunkirk, and a German invasion of Britain seemed imminent. The battle of Britain had yet to be fought and won. Any political and strategic observer would have had to conclude that the Nazi New Order was about to triumph. The fate of small and neutral states was uncertain, and their outlook was grim in a world now ruled by force and the will of dictators. There could not be a juncture less appropriate for an uncertain response to an underground army that asserted its supremacy and sole legitimacy over territory, and each and every individual thereon. There are no indications in the interviews of IRA survivors of the period or records of their deliberations, policies and actions, that anything of the wider context occurred to any in the leadership, or that it would in any way have affected their stance. Indeed, their actions prior to and in the early years of the war showed that in chaos they discerned and sought opportunity. Certainly the position of some who were close to them was that the only guarantee for the survival of the Irish state was to throw open the state armouries and deploy the IRA alongside the regular army and auxiliary forces. The unreality of this notion for a state established for only two decades and still carrying the lesions of civil war scarcely needs comment. The wider reality of such a state surviving British (and later, American) preventive intervention requires but a moment's thought. In this all constitutional politicians were agreed.

The speed with which the government acted in the case of the murders of Detective Sergeant McKeown and Detective Hyland elicited another type of complaint: that it was contrary to natural justice to try the three IRA men and to execute two of them under a system of justice which had not been established at the time they committed their offence. This was scarcely a conclusive objection. The offences with which they were charged were grave offences – the gravest – under existing law. The new procedure did not alter that law but did provide a new mode of trial. That in itself continued to provide the essentials of natural justice, as we have seen. The difference was in the constitution of the panel, executive rather than judicial review and a mandatory death penalty were guilt proved. Those elements came from the well-founded decision by the government that an emergency existed and that it had to exercise extraordinary powers. That power of government was provided for by the Irish Constitution and had been affirmed both by the legislature and by the higher courts.

There was in fact some indication that the government was willing to go beyond the type of procedure embodied in the Military Court. On 7 May 1940, there had been another direct challenge to the Irish state, which, like all others in the community of civilised nations, had a fundamental obligation to protect foreign diplomats personally and in all matters connected with their duties. IRA GHQ decided to stage an armed interception on the British diplomatic bag as it was transferred from the port of Dublin to the British Embassy in Merrion Square in the heart of the city. The notion was that the diplomatic post might contain matter to the discredit of the de Valera government, touching on his cooperation with the British in suppressing the IRA. The raid was duly mounted and failed. The two Special Branch men carrying the mail refused to surrender it and returned fire: both were wounded.[236]

In an angry statement on the incident, and in the context of an assertive and emboldened IRA, de Valera seemed to contemplate a reaction beyond emergency legislation, perhaps executive action based on the necessities of state alone:

> I warn these now planning new crimes against the nation that they will not be allowed to continue their policy of sabotage. They have set the law as defiance. The law will be enforced against them. If the present law is not sufficient it will be strengthened: and in the last resort, if no other law will suffice, then the Government will invoke the ultimate law – the safety of the people.[237]

The Emergency Powers Act and its various amendments and extensions, conferred draconian powers, but it is clear that had these not sufficed, martial law, in some form or another, would have followed. Fine Gael, the principal opposition party, indicated that a stern exercise of repressive powers had its full support.[238] The signs could not have been clearer. This was no time to call de Valera's bluff. But revolutionary organisations cannot hibernate, and it is possible that even had it wished to do so the IRA leadership could not have ensured a cessation of activities by its units. And so the executions would continue.

Richard Goss's death sentence also arose from a shoot-out. Goss had been involved in post-office and bank robberies in 1941, including a raid on the Hibernian Bank, Castlepollard, Co. Westmeath, on 9 June (netting £636). He and his group travelled about by bicycle and staying in the houses of sympathisers. Five weeks after the Castlepollard raid, they were at the house of the Casey family at Oghill, Drumlish, Co. Longford.[239] The group had been tracked, and available refuges were limited. On Wednesday, 16 July 1941, there was a joint Special Branch and army raid. There was an exchange of fire, republicans subsequently arguing that it was difficult to know who had fired at whom in the confusion. Richard Goss and Joe O'Callaghan were charged with shooting at members of the Defence Forces and the Garda Síochána with intent to evade arrest and were brought before the Military Court. Goss was found guilty and condemned to death but Joe O'Callaghan was found not guilty and discharged.[240]

It may be that O'Callaghan's age (eighteen) was a factor in the Court's decision (though a death sentence would almost certainly have been commuted).[241] No such consideration applied to Goss, and he was executed by firing squad at Portlaoise Prison on Saturday, 9 August 1941 – again just over three weeks from arrest to the end.[242] Since there had been no injury or loss of life, the proportionality part of Goss's sentence was not as clear as it had been for those of McGrath and Harte, but retribution was not the only purpose of the emergency laws. Deterrence was also intended, and the government was content to allow the death sentence to be carried out in accordance with the law's deterrent purpose.[243]

There was no such noise or confusion to provide even the semblance of a defence in the case of George Plant, and he went before the firing squad at Portlaoise on 5 March 1942. His crime was a cold-blooded killing, though he would himself have claimed it to be an authorised execution. Michael Devereux had been arrested by Special Branch at IRA premises at 22 Lansdowne Road, Dublin, on 22 August 1941. Jim Crofton, the renegade Special Branch man, informed Stephen Hayes, then IRA Acting Chief of Staff, that Devereux had talked under interrogation and had then been released. According to Bell, Crofton 'despised informers and insisted that something had to be done'. Hayes, without convening a court martial, then directed the Wexford battalion to do something about Devereux.[244] There was an ambiguity, possibly deliberate, in the instruction, but the outcome was deadly. Devereux was lured to a meeting, and Plant killed him. On 23 September 1941, police, acting on information, found the body under a pile of stones at Slievenamon, Co. Tipperary. A few weeks later, George Plant and Joe O'Connor (an IRA man attached to GHQ) were brought before the Special Criminal Court on a charge of murder. The Devereux case was of great legal importance. Patrick Davern and Michael Walshe, who had been identified as accomplices, were offered as state witnesses.[245] After the arrests of the suspects, Walshe and Davern gave statements to the police. When the case opened before the Special Criminal Court, both men withdrew their statements, claiming that they had made them as a result of being beaten. The state then entered a *nolle prosequi*. The case was transferred to the Military Court, which, authorised by the Emergency Powers (Amendment No. 2) Act, 1940, had power to accept into evidence any statement that had been taken down and acknowledged by the person who made it. This allowed the withdrawn statements of Davern and Walshe to be considered by the Court.[246] An appeal was mounted by Seán MacBride but rejected by the Supreme Court.

Plant was immediately rearrested, and he, together with the two reneging witnesses, Michael Walshe and Patrick Davern, was brought before the Military Court, charged with Devereux's murder. This body had powers and procedures to deal with the withdrawal of evidence by witnesses. These powers were challenged on the grounds that the common-law legal tradition, from the time of the reign of Charles II, required the taking of oral evidence by the Court. To deal with a situation where, through intimidation or second thoughts, statements were withdrawn, the Military Court was permitted to consider such evidence if it considered it originally to have been given lawfully and voluntarily.[247] The basis of the rather hopeless appeal, asking for an order to nullify the Military Court's powers, was simply legal custom, adhered to in Ireland in times of peace and rebellion alike. An additional argument, also claiming a tradition going back to Charles II, was that once a *nolle prosequi* had been entered an Attorney General should not prosecute on the same charge. The Supreme Court took the view that the Emergency Powers legislation and its derivative orders were compliant to the Constitution and it was not for the judiciary, in such circumstances, to set themselves against the legislature.[248] It also took no notice of the speculative (and desperate) argument that it was obliged to consider law more fundamental than that of the Constitution. The application for a direction to stay the proceedings of the Military Court was accordingly refused.[249]

The way was cleared for the case to proceed to the Military Court, where, on 26 February 1942, all defendants were found guilty and sentenced to death. Walshe and Davern's sentences were commuted on review, but Plant's was confirmed, the government taking the view that he was the leading figure in the affair. That the killing of Devereux had none of the arguably mitigating features of the panic and confusion of an exchange of fire certainly justified Plant's execution on the scale of deserts then being applied: it did not hinder his name being entered in the republican roll of honour.[250]

Maurice O'Neill was executed in Mountjoy some eight months later, on Thursday, 12 November 1942. Once again there was a firefight at the bottom of his offence. Together with Harry White, O'Neill had been in one of the few IRA safe houses left in Dublin, Kelly's at 14 Holly Road, Donnycarney. 'Safe house' is an undoubted misnomer, for at this point Dublin's Special Branch clearly had comprehensive knowledge of IRA premises and hideouts and adequate manpower to deal with them. Some they kept under observation with the intention of gathering intelligence, others they raided and turned into traps, occupying them quietly and arresting all visitors. On Monday, 19 October 1942, word came to O'Neill and White that their refuge was known to the police, and, as the night came on, they attempted to escape. The house had indeed been surrounded, and the two opened fire as they fled. White, still recovering from the wounds of an earlier engagement, managed to get away, but O'Neill was arrested. Detective George Mordaunt had been hit in the exchange of fire, and there were the now familiar republican arguments that such had been the confusion at the time that O'Neill's culpability could not be certain.[251] That type of pinpoint evidence, however, was not necessary for the Military Court, which found O'Neill guilty of shooting with intent and, on 10 November 1942, sentenced him to death.[252]

Manner of execution is, at first sight, a fine point, but it is desperately important to some condemned persons and to their sympathisers. It is hard to dispute that mode of execution has both political and moral significance, and that is has had such from time immemorial. Death by shooting was seen as an acknowledgement that one was a combatant, a soldier, albeit an irregular.[253] Hanging, over several centuries, was seen as a death appropriate to the infamous, the criminally and morally dissolute. The image of the gallows, the hangman, the drop, the body jerking at rope's end, with bodily functions dissolving, was associated with shame, degradation and the sordid crimes of murderers.[254] The firing squad, like swordsman, axeman and block before it, was, by contrast, given none of these associations and was seen as a fit and clean end for an honourable enemy, a soldier. Such a death had some dignity and granted a moment when bravery and composure could be displayed and perhaps later recalled. In times of peace, and in an era when most civilised states have abolished the death penalty, these may seem to be recondite concerns, but they were far from being so in the Ireland of the 1940s. The status and myths of martyrdom, resolution and fidelity in the face of death were key to the state's founding narrative and remained a vital thread in the weft and weave of Irish political consciousness. In any event, the connotations of the two modes of execution – one adding degradation to death, the other offering a final opportunity for dignity – were well understood by the general population. It may have been more in accordance with the desires of some in de Valera's government, therefore, that all those condemned to death in the wartime years be denied the indulgence of a firing squad, but having opted for a dual mode of trial – the Special Criminal Court, an essentially civilian process, albeit with military judges, and the resolutely non-civilian Military Court – it had to abide by the forms. Those condemned by the Special Criminal Court were, therefore, hanged, and those whose sentences issued from the Military Court were shot.[255]

The last one of the six to be executed in the wartime years was Charlie Kerins, sometime IRA Chief of Staff. By 1943, the IRA, north and south of the Border, had been reduced to a handful of fugitive leaders and units that were either out of touch or wholly inactive. Kerins and the other leading figures were familiar to Special Branch and much hunted. Only by staying deep and still could such a man expect to remain out of custody – a condition so constrained that it could scarcely be described as freedom. Kerins found refuge at the house of Dr Kathleen Farrell, the veteran republican and oppositionist, at 50 Upper Rathmines Road, Dublin. Her sympathies were well known, and she was under at least casual surveillance. Kerins did not show himself and was not discovered. Not wishing to exhaust his luck he eventually left his refuge and returned to Kerry, leaving papers and weapons to be collected later. Such was the rate of attrition, however, that no one was available to remove these items, and so, on 16 June 1944, Kerins returned to the house with a pony and trap to collect them. The state of the organisation was encapsulated in this scene: its Chief of Staff as a removal man, a hired pony and trap as his vehicle and the remaining papers of IRA GHQ and a handful of weapons as his cargo. Capture also confirmed the ineptitude of Kerins and his comrades, senior and junior alike. All rules of conspiracy had been violated: the use of a house long known to the police, the accumulation there of weapons and documents and then his personal return. Two more elementary errors made Kerins's capture inevitable: he telephoned the house to announce that he would be arriving that evening, and, when he did so, he dallied.[256]

The offence for which Kerins was wanted – and as head of the IRA the state had its choice of Emergency Powers counts against him – was the murder on 9 September 1942 of Detective Sergeant Denis O'Brien. This was a man whose vigorous pursuit of the IRA and numerous captures had given him a prime position in the organisation's demonology. Despite a policy of not attacking Southern police and army, it was decided to kill O'Brien, and Kerins, as Chief of Staff, was presumed to have issued or at least approved the order.[257] The decision can only have been based on revenge; pragmatically it was disastrous, increasing Special Branch activity and zeal, putting Kerins on every policeman's most wanted list and giving a personal edge to anti-IRA duties. Short of leaving the country, his netting was only a matter of time. The circumstances of the killing (O'Brien was shot down outside his home in Ballyboden, Rathfarnham, Co. Dublin) also removed the IRA even further from public sympathy. His place in republican myth, 'Charlie Kerins, the Boy from Tralee', was, however, assured.

The government, not surprisingly, took precisely the opposite view. Gerald Boland's son Kevin recalled (from his father's remarks) that the Irish Cabinet was 'incensed in a personal way' at the killing of Sergeant O'Brien. By June 1944, ministers had the lowest opinion of the IRA, concluding that 'it was an organisation which had been taken over by unscrupulous gangster types from Belfast'.[258] Kerins, once arrested, was marked for speedy execution. His execution was indeed achieved, but not in a speedy fashion. By June 1944, war's end was in sight, and the country may have recovered something of its nerve and civic robustness. Of all those arrested and tried on capital charges during the war years, Kerins's legal proceedings were the most prolonged – some six and a half months from arrest to execution. Republicans were especially embittered and enraged when the government engaged the British hangman, Albert Pierrepoint, to conduct the execution. It took place on Friday, 1 December 1944.[259]

When, in 1868, public executions had ceased in what was then the UK, the statute had decreed that the bodies of the executed should be interred within the precincts of the prison.[260] In a strongly religious and family-oriented country such as Ireland, a special horror attached to the body of an executed relative being buried in unconsecrated and distinctly unholy grounds. The practice before this legislation was to hand the body over to relatives, friends or to Surgeons' Hall for dissection. The 1868 Act was greatly concerned with the decorum of what it wanted to be a terrible and solemn state action and was intended in part to suppress a ghoulish interest in the bodies of hanged persons, which extended to gross superstition and necromancy.[261] The burial of bodies within the grounds of the prison was intended to put an end to all this. It was also found, however, that it increased the dreadfulness of the capital sentence to which it could even be seen as a form of aggravation. It was indeed a harking back to an era when denial of Christian burial was seen as an additional and heavy penalty.[262]

Conditions in wartime Ireland, more than seventy years after the passage of the Capital Punishment Amendment Act, were substantially, but not entirely, different from those which had led to the legislation. In particular, the IRA and its predecessor organisations, and immediate circles of supporters and sympathisers, had shown themselves expert in mounting funerals as political spectacle. In the circumstances then prevailing, this was not going to be allowed, and the rule of prison interment was enforced. In the easier post-war years, with the IRA seemingly devastated and former IRA men in the coalition government, a different course was possible. In September 1948, the bodies of the six men executed during the war years were released to their families and quietly buried.[263]

There is a reductionism in considering and writing about politicians which is never content or secure unless some seam of base motivation is discovered in an utterance or deed. Far too many examples in all ages, locales and situations make it imprudent to abandon this somewhat depressing approach. Yet, to stick to it exclusively is as much a mistake as naivety. There is little doubt that de Valera, Boland and their colleagues sought to present themselves as saviours of the state, sea defences against a deadly flood tide of subversion, disorder and war. That they may have ramped up these perils for electoral purposes is surely beyond remark: for the practitioners of their trade this was a reflex as natural as breathing. But the dangers did exist, and the state, not long and fractiously established, needed defending. A strong state can be sparing in its defensive measures; a weak one shows elements of desperation. Whether Éire needed all the draconian powers that it took after 1939 may be a subject for speculation and debate, but that, it should be recognised, is conducted in hindsight and in some comfort and security.

The severe prison sentences and the executions during the Second World War deeply affected de Valera and Boland; the two floggings were of little or no importance to them, the country or their IRA opponents. Repeatedly, in speeches in the Dáil and elsewhere, de Valera and Boland set forth a narrative of constitutional reform, attempted conciliation and violent rejection. Both had fought in 1916 and in the Civil War; both had condemned British and then Free State repression, as they saw it. Here they nevertheless were, faced with an armed conspiracy, acting on the venerable adage, 'England's peril, Ireland's opportunity'. They defended the state with the same instruments as their predecessors: a political detective branch, informers, rewards, stern and repressive laws, special courts of pre-emptory despatch and condign punishments, severely retributive and deterrent. In many of their speeches it is impossible to deny genuine indications of personal grief and frustration. This was not how it was supposed to be; here were political careers of great disappointment.

It is not surprising that this mixture of public duty, party-political posturing and private frustration erupted in baffled anger from time to time. De Valera and his colleagues in Fianna Fáil had sought, and largely succeeded, in advancing the republican project and in unifying its family. But in the IRA they found a group of very close relatives who despised the extended hand. It is probable that both de Valera and Boland were irritated by and certainly determined to subdue the IRA rank and file. But in the statements about internees there rarely surfaces the anger that the Portlaoise men evoked. This, to them, was a malignity within republicanism requiring drastic treatment.

We turn below to a further episode of IRA internment and imprisonment, during the Border Campaign of 1956–62.[264] For part of this time de Valera was out of office, and when he returned he was in the twilight of his parliamentary career. The times were vastly different; the world was at peace (albeit uneasily), and the IRA was no more than a policing problem. The heat and passion had died, and there were no more life-and-death decisions. But it is safe to assume that memories of those earlier and terrible times were never far away.

Notes

1 NAI JUS/90/8/140, Antisocial Organisations Bill, General Observations.
2 *Ibid.* The Public Order Act, 1936: 1 Edw. VIII & 1 Geo. VI, c.6, forbade the wearing of political uniforms, regulated demonstrations and confirmed the police in their public-order powers. More generally, it prohibited the creation of associations 'for the purpose of enabling them to be employed in usurping the functions of the police or the armed forces of the Crown'. The Act blocked the street-bruiser tactics of Sir Oswald Mosley's British Union of Fascists (imitative of Mussolini and Hitler). It laid a catch-all prohibition on 'the use or display of physical force in promoting any political object'. This wording was notionally comprehensive enough to embrace traditional events such as the Miners' Gala (hardly a threat to the state) but had the effect of conferring on the Home Secretary (and therefore his officials) wide discretionary powers, the exercise of which would be tempered by common sense and a respect for traditional events and long-established organisations. (The uniformed and public-processing Salvation Army, for example, never fell foul of the law.)
3 NAI JUS/90/8/140, Antisocial Organisations Bill, General Observations.
4 *Ibid.*
5 *Ibid.*
6 NAI JUS/90/8/140, Antisocial Organisations Bill, General Observations, revised draft.
7 *Ibid.* The phrase, although it certainly conveyed the grave purposes and powers of the body, was ill chosen, evoking as it did the blind, bloody and forever infamous activities of the body of the same name that bestrode the Terror phase of the French Revolution. See Stanley Loomis's classic, *Paris in the Terror* (Philadelphia, Pa.: J. B. Lippincott, 1964), for a vivid account of the activities of the Committee.
8 NAI JUS/90/8/140, Antisocial Organisations Bill, General Observations. These comments came from the Department of Justice although the submission to the Government was a joint document with the Attorney General's Office.
9 *Ibid.* There was the somewhat non-consequential rider: 'After all there would be no necessity for any Special Court if Juries could be absolutely relied upon to act on evidence.'
10 Relating this to Minister for Justice Gerald Boland, Stephen Roche commented: 'There is no record of this, nor have I any personal recollection of it: whatever was done was done very confidentially, but I believe that the facts are as stated' (NAI

JUS/90/8/140, Antisocial Organisations Bill, Stephen Roche to Gerald Boland, 17 December 1938). No account has survived of the judiciary's private view of the new tribunal, but there must have been concern about the effect that membership would have on long-term reputation, especially the crucial element of independence. A special court would inevitably blur the boundaries of the executive and judicial branches of government. It could not, moreover, be separated from the immediate political context.

11 *Ibid.*

12 As permitted by Article 38.5.1. Membership of the court was announced on 25 August 1939: Colonel Francis Bennett, Colonel Daniel McKenna, Major John Vincent Joyce, Major Cornelius Whelan and Major Patrick Tuite. Commandant Richard Feely was appointed Court Registrar.

13 The first case was of Myles Heffernan, a thirty-two-year-old insurance clerk from Rathgar (*Irish Times*, 26 August 1939, 11f). The case came before the court on 16 October 1939, and Heffernan was convicted and sentenced to three months' imprisonment (*Irish Independent*, 17 October 1939, 5c–d; *Weekly Irish Times*, 21 October 1939, 17a).

14 Offences within the jurisdiction of the Court included the following: usurpation of the functions of government and obstruction of government (both catch-alls), illegal drilling or other military exercises, formation or maintenance of illegal societies in the Army or police force, administering unlawful oaths, publication of treasonable or seditious material and membership of an illegal organisation (*Irish Independent*, 28 February 1939; *Irish Times*, 28 February 1939, 7a–b, 8d–e).

15 OASA, ss.41(1–4).

16 OASA, ss.44(1 and 2).

17 *Dáil Debates*, vol. 102, written answer, 11 July 1946.

18 See above, pp. 168–73.

19 See below, pp. 734–35.

20 See Section 50 of the Act.

21 *Dáil Debates*, vol. 100, cols. 2509–10, 9 May 1946. This was in response to a question from James Larkin, Jr., asking why persons convicted before the Special Criminal Court for like offences connected with unlawful organisations served their sentences under differing prison conditions.

22 See Emergency Orders Nos. 41A and 139 and Emergency Powers (Amendment No. 2) Act, 1940, s.3.

23 NAI JUS/8/944, Statistics, Internment, etc. (1946): Table of Sentences. Two executions were carried out in 1940 and in 1942 and one each in 1941 and 1944.

24 See below, n. 27.

25 Plant had been found guilty of the murder of Michael Devereux. Richard Goss was one of a party that carried out post-office and bank robberies in 1941, and was charged with firing on the police and army.

26 The eight were Tomás MacCurtáin, Seán McCaughey, Liam Rice, Jim Smith (alias Brennan), William Stewart, Eamon Smullen, Patrick Murphy and Frank Kerrigan. MacCurtáin was the longest-serving prisoner, having been transferred to Portlaoise in July 1942. He remained there until released in March 1948, along with the remaining prisoners, Rice, Smith, Smullen and Harry White. (The last had been at Portlaoise for thirteen months only, arriving in February 1947.) MacEoin (*The IRA in the Twilight Years*, *op. cit.*, pp. 533–41) provides much valuable detail on Portlaoise in the war years.

27 The English hangman, Albert Pierrepoint, came over to Dublin to perform the execution. This aroused especial ire in republican circles because of Pierrepoint's nationality and because hanging was seen as a degrading form of the death penalty. The firing squad would, in their view, have been more appropriate for someone who

claimed to be acting under military colour – albeit that of a clandestine army. The de Valera cabinet was not at all inclined to grant this indulgence. Kevin Boland, son of Gerald Boland, who had been Minister for Justice at the time, recalled that the Cabinet 'were incensed in a personal way at the killing of [Sergeant] Dinny O'Brien. At this time, in June 1944, their opinion of the IRA was at its lowest; that it was an organisation which had been taken over by unscrupulous gangster types from Belfast.' Kevin Boland also noted that it was de Valera's view that since he had encouraged young men to join the police and army he had to protect them (MacEoin, *The IRA in the Twilight Years, op. cit.*, p. 897). MacEoin is unclear (p. 823, n. 2) as to how sentences of death were differentiated between hanging and shooting and notes that Tomás MacCurtáin (whose sentence had not been carried out) had also been sentenced to hang. The distinction came from the court that imposed the sentence. The Special Criminal Court was a civilian body, staffed by military men; the Military Court was entirely that, and its penalty was therefore the customary military one. Four of the executions were carried out at Mountjoy Prison, of which three were by firing squad and one by hanging. Two executions were conducted at Portlaoise, both by firing squad.

28 See below, pp. 722–24.
29 See NAI TAOIS/3/S11931/B and PRES 1/P/1743. Writers sympathetic to the IRA or those who drew heavily in IRA interviews (MacEoin and Bell, respectively) are wont to explain the killing of police officers in IRA shoot-outs as a result of confusion or even crossfire, with armed police shooting each other. Such exculpatory accounts ignore a basic fact; IRA men involved in those incidents opened fire with the intention of wounding or killing. They had the option of surrender but chose to try to shoot their way to freedom.
30 NAI TAOIS/S11136.
31 *Irish Press*, 4 November 1942, 3d; *Irish Independent*, 4 November 1942, 3d. Griffith was killed on 4 July 1943 in Holles Street, Dublin. Republicans claimed that Special Branch shot him without warning. See *Irish Press*, 5 July 1943, 1e–f; *Irish Times*, 5 July 1943, 1h–i.
32 Crofton appeared before the Special Criminal Court on 11 March 1941 (*Irish Times*, 12 March 1941, 8a; 13 March 1941, 8f; *Irish Press*, 12 March 1941, 8c). See also NAI TAOIS/3/S12365. In early 1945, Crofton was transferred from Portlaoise to the Curragh and was released the following year, having served his full five-year sentence (MacEoin, *The IRA in the Twilight Years, op. cit.*, p. 536).
33 MacEoin, *The IRA in the Twilight Years, op. cit.*, pp. 528–9.
34 For an account of flogging, see below, pp. 653–54.
35 Formerly Quartermaster of the Wexford Battalion, Devereux was said to have broken under Special Branch pressure whilst in custody. Stephen Hayes (himself shortly afterwards deposed, tried and condemned to death by the IRA as a traitor) ordered that Devereux be dealt with. No IRA court was convened, and Plant carried out what he thought was Hayes's order. For an account of the Devereux murder and its aftermath, see J. Bowyer Bell, *The Secret Army: The IRA, 1916–1979* (Cambridge, Mass.: MIT Press, 1983), pp. 187–8.
36 See NAI TAOIS/S12682 (trial) and S12741 (death sentence and reprieve petitions).
37 MacEoin, *The IRA in the Twilight Years, op. cit.*, p. 445. There had been a number of visits to the Dental Hospital by detained IRA male and female internees, and Dublin's Special Branch, without knowing the details, were concerned that something was afoot, possibly involving members of staff at the hospital (NAI JUS/8/879, Political Prisoners Visiting Dental Hospital, April 1941).
38 Humphreys Papers, P/106/1365/1–2, 11 June 1943. See also leaflet (same source) 'Political Prisoners Held by Fianna Fáil'.

39 MacEoin, *The IRA in the Twilight Years*, op. cit., pp. 529–33, *passim*.

40 MacEoin, *The IRA in the Twilight Years*, op. cit., pp. 532–3. *Irish Times*, 6 March 1942, 1g; *Connacht Tribune*, 7 March 1942, 3b; *Irish Press*, 6 March 1942, 1f. See also Michael Moroney, 'George Plant and the Rule of Law: The Devereux Affair, 1941–42', *Tipperary Historical Journal*, 1 (1988): 1–12.

41 *Irish Times*, 27 May 1946, 1d–e; *Irish Press*, 27 May 1946, 1a–c. For a comprehensive table on the numbers transferred to military custody, 1940–5, see table in NAI 8/944, Statistics, Internment, etc. (1946).

42 See below, pp. 722–4.

43 Barrows had been Deputy Governor at Derry and then Belfast prisons. The IRA men at Portlaoise Gaelicised his name with the satiric but erroneous 'McTockle' (MacEoin, *The IRA in the Twilight Years*, op. cit., p. 532). They thought it meant 'son of the wheelbarrow' but *tochail* means 'to burrow' and *tochailt* 'excavation'. Barrows came from a family with strong prison connections. His father had been Governor of Belfast Prison and was described by Gerald Boland (who had been an inmate there in 1916) as 'a kind, decent man'. *Seanad Debates*, vol. 31, col. 2174, 12 June 1946.

44 There is no direct documentary evidence on the circumstances of this, but see *Freeman's Journal*, 31 January 1923, 5e; *Irish Times*, 31 January 1923, 6a–b.

45 See tribute of Oliver J. Flanagan, Portlaoise TD, on 21 April 1959 (*Dáil Debates*, vol. 174, col. 719).

46 Patrick Murphy remembered that Barrows 'would speak conversationally to you in the cell. He would give you what you deserved, no more and no less' (MacEoin, *The IRA in the Twilight Years*, op. cit., p. 534).

47 MacEoin, *The IRA in the Twilight Years*, op. cit., p. 536.

48 Oliver J. Flanagan (1920–87) quite properly spoke on issues related to the large prison in his constituency. Although sympathetic to some of the inmates' concerns, he also made a point of referring favourably to staff. He was a constant presence in the Dáil from his election in June 1943, holding his seat through two later IRA campaigns until he decided not to contest the February 1987 election.

49 MacEoin, *The IRA in the Twilight Years*, op. cit., p. 531. Because he had been flogged only a few days before, Murphy's back was lacerated and covered in sores. The Medical Officer intervened to ensure that he did not receive unduly rough treatment during the tussle over clothes lest his condition be aggravated.

50 MacEoin, *The IRA in the Twilight Years*, op. cit., p. 537. Post was withheld because neither the prisoners nor their correspondents were willing to use convict numbers in addressing letters. During a visit to Portlaoise by Senator Luke Duffy on 8 June 1946, the Governor was questioned about this. This visit, of Duffy and three Labour Deputies (William Davin, TD for Leix-Offaly; James Larkin, Jr., Dublin South; and Martin O'Sullivan, Dublin North-West) was arranged with the assistance of the Labour Party. See Larkin's preliminary question, *Dáil Debates*, vol. 99, cols. 1532–3, 27 February 1946.

51 For a few weeks, from 13 February 1944, McCaughey agreed to put on the uniform to attend mass. After a month or so he returned to his original stance. See below, p. 628.

52 Convict Prisons (Ireland) Act, 1854: 17 & 18 Vict., c.76, s.16.

53 It seems extraordinary that the Portlaoise Medical Officer did not intervene on grounds of prisoners' health, for which he was responsible, or indeed that the chaplain did not express concern on moral grounds.

54 SI 03/06/1925, Prisons (Visiting Committees) Order, 1925, 16(a).

55 In 1946, these and others issues concerning the Portlaoise prisoners were skilfully presented and blended into a campaigning programme by Seán MacBride. He and other former IRA men had decided to take the constitutional path in a new republican grouping, Clann na Poblachta, inaugurated in July 1946. After some twenty

months, the Clann was able to take ten seats in the general election of February 1948 and thus – great paradox – entered into power in coalition with John Costello's Fine Gael. The following month the five remaining Portlaoise republicans were released.

56 There was no attempt to stop this communication. When he first arrived at Portlaoise, Patrick Murphy did not know that the system was in operation. A prison officer told him after his first night that Seán McCaughey had been trying to talk to him and apparently instructed him how to use the pipes, which, he remembered, worked 'tolerably well'. When a man wanted to make contact, he knocked on the pipe as a signal that the mug should be placed on it. MacEoin, *The IRA in the Twilight Years, op. cit.*, pp. 531–2.

57 MacEoin, *The IRA in the Twilight Years, op. cit.*, p. 534. There was some disagreement in subsequent accounts, but it appears that lights were put out at 8.30 p.m., not 8 p.m., as Murphy recalled. Prisoners complained that security checks throughout the night (including switching the lights on and off every fifteen minutes) affected their sleep. See Senator Luke Duffy, *Seanad Debates*, vol. 31, col. 2129, 12 June 1946, and also the reply by Gerald Boland, Minister for Justice, at col. 2178.

58 See above, pp. 575–7.

59 MacEoin, *The IRA in the Twilight Years, op. cit.*, p. 537.

60 MacEoin, *The IRA in the Twilight Years, op. cit.*, p. 531. He described the outfit: 'You wore a blanket… with a hole cut in it through which your head passed; and a strip of blanket formed a belt for the waist. You had shorts and a pair of rough carpet slippers and no other clothes' (p. 532).

61 MacEoin, *The IRA in the Twilight Years, op. cit.*, p. 534. This room was the largest available in the prison. In a Dáil speech, de Valera described it: '60 feet by 15 feet by 10 feet, or whatever the height is. There are eight windows looking out on the best prospect that could be got, namely the prison farm' (*Dáil Debates*, vol. 101, col. 1162, 29 May 1946).

62 See below, pp. 731–5.

63 *Dáil Debates*, vol. 100, col. 948, 2 April 1946.

64 See below, p. 778; see also Tim Pat Coogan, *The IRA* (London: Fontana, 1980), pp. 325–6. There appear to have been fourteen committals, and sentences ranged from three to twelve months (see *Irish Times*, 5 April 1946, 2c–e; *Irish Press*, 5 April 1946, 5a–c).

65 Breakfast was a pint of stirabout, three-quarters of a pint of milk, four ounces of bread, half a pint of tea with sugar and three-eighths of an ounce of butter. Dinner (served as a midday meal) varied. On two days a week, it was Irish (mutton) stew; on other days various forms of meat and vegetables (always including potatoes). Supper was almost identical to breakfast, and there was a special supper of bread, butter and cocoa.

66 *Dáil Debates*, vol. 101, cols. 1113–15, 29 May 1946.

67 Speaking of ordinary prisoners, Boland referred to Wilde's *De Profundis* and asserted that he had never had anything 'but the greatest sympathy for any person who has had to be kept in custody for the protection of the public' (*Dáil Debates*, vol. 101, col. 1112, 29 May 1946).

68 *Dáil Debates*, vol. 101, col. 1113, 29 May 1946.

69 *Dáil Debates*, vol. 101, col. 1114, 29 May 1946.

70 MacEoin, *The IRA in the Twilight Years, op. cit.*, p. 535.

71 See Seán McConville, *Irish Political Prisoners, 1848–1922: Theatres of War* (London and New York: Routledge, 2003), pp. 518–21.

72 McConville, *Irish Political Prisoners, op. cit.*, pp. 735–50.

73 McConville, *Irish Political Prisoners, op. cit.*, pp. 722–30; see below, pp. 693–7.

74 See McConville, *Irish Political Prisoners, op. cit.*, pp. 754–5 for a failed hunger strike at Cork in 1920; see above, pp. 203–6 for the collapse of an IRA hunger strike during the Civil War.

75 See above, pp. 202–8, for example.

76 General Order No. 4 is emphatic: 'Volunteers are forbidden to undertake hunger strikes without the express sanction of General Headquarters.' Cited in Brendan O'Brien, *The Long War: The IRA and Sinn Féin* (Dublin: The O'Brien Press, 1995), Appendix 2, p. 407.

77 See McConville, *Irish Political Prisoners, op. cit.*, pp. 610–12.

78 *Leigh* v. *Gladstone and Others* (1909) (26 *Times Law Reports*, 139) set out the obligations of the authorities. Responsibility for a decision on forcible feeding was shifted from officials and politicians to the prison medical officer. See McConville, *Irish Political Prisoners, op. cit.*, pp. 739–40.

79 See below, pp. 695–6.

80 Three persons who had been sentenced to death by the Military Court and whose sentences had been commuted had been released. Tom Hunt was arrested in the Rathgar Road raid by Special Branch. His confederates in the firefight and deaths that followed – McGrath and Harte – were tried and executed. Hunt had been reprieved on grounds of youth and his subordinate part. Gerald Boland recalled Hunt as 'the sort of young fellow who got landed in it more by accident than anything else'. He was transferred from Portlaoise to the Curragh and then released as part of the general exodus. The Devereux case had similarly resulted in three death sentences: George Plant, Patrick Davern and Michael Walshe. Only Plant had been executed. Boland took the view that the others, though capitally culpable, had been accessories. They followed Hunt's path to eventual release. See *Dáil Debates*, vol. 101, cols. 1131–2, 29 May 1946. Those who remained at Portlaoise (besides McCaughey) were Tomás MacCurtáin (life); James Smith (fourteen years' penal servitude); Liam Rice (twenty years); Eamon Smullen (fourteen years); William Stewart (fourteen years and twelve strokes of the cat); Patrick Murphy (fourteen years); Frank Kerrigan (ten years). See *Dáil Debates*, vol. 101, cols. 1131–2, cols. 1134–6, 29 May 1946.

81 Before limited correspondence was granted, McCaughey had few outside contacts. Seán MacBride and Con Lehane, lawyers and both former IRA men, had visited him early in his sentence. An English convent of the reclusive order of Poor Clares had sent him a devotional letter which the Department of Justice allowed him to receive (Department of Justice, McCaughey file).

82 Department of Justice, McCaughey file, 19 March 1943. He pointed out that he had been in his cell for a year and a half. Father Harris was not as unfeeling as McCaughey's letter suggested, since he probably acted on superior instruction. Liam Rice, sometime OC of the Portlaoise men, recalled Harris as 'a noble Christian priest whom we all remember with respect and gratitude. He was a faithful and constant friend to Sean in the last days' (MacEoin, *The IRA in the Twilight Years, op. cit.*, p. 538).

83 This must have reflected a spiritual crisis of some kind since, from the tone and wording of his appeal to the bishop, McCaughey was devoted to the observances of the Roman Catholic Church.

84 Department of Justice, McCaughey file, 12 March 1944. In late May 1944, McCaughey also asked for a ruler and compass 'for the purpose of studying geometry'.

85 Concern about McCaughey's capacity went some way back in the IRA. Moss Twomey, whose tenure as IRA Chief of Staff (1926–36) was the longest in the history of the organisation, considered McCaughey to be 'devoted but not particularly clever'. Twomey had also advised McCaughey not to publish the confession of Stephen Hayes, a document which was to have a cataclysmic effect on the organisation (MacEoin, *The IRA in the Twilight Years, op. cit.*, p. 848). See pp. 607–8, n. 122.

86 Department of Justice, McCaughey file, 25 January 1944.

87 Decades after the event, none of the Portlaoise men interviewed by Uinseann MacEoin mentioned the splits and divisions into factions.

88 Department of Justice, McCaughey file: W. R. Barrows to Peter Berry, Secretary General, Department of Justice, 18 March 1946.

89 *Ibid.*

90 Department of Justice, McCaughey file: W. R. Barrows to Peter Berry, 23 April 1946.

91 Department of Justice, McCaughey file: Chronology of McCaughey's imprisonment, Report of 16 April 1946. Liam Rice recalled that McCaughey's action totally surprised his comrades. The men were all in the *Caidreamh* at 3.30 p.m., when the Governor and Chief Officer walked through as part of the daily inspection. McCaughey (who at that time was OC) overtook them as they left the room and spoke briefly to Barrows. On his return to the group, he told them about the note. His comrades were 'stunned and shocked'. They had no idea this was in his mind and thought that the authorities would let him die (MacEoin, *The IRA in the Twilight Years*, *op. cit.*, p. 537). They were right: this was an ultimatum to which no government could give way.

92 He died at 1.10 a.m. on the morning of 11 May.

93 McCaughey could not have lived for fourteen days without any liquid at all, but he had consented to wash his mouth out twice a day, and this was probably sufficient to ingest some liquid. Enormous strength of will would have been required not to swallow the mouth rinse.

94 Department of Justice, McCaughey file, Report of Medical Officer and Governor, 24 April 1946.

95 Department of Justice, McCaughey file, W. R. Barrows to Peter Berry, 26 April 1946.

96 Department of Justice, McCaughey file, Report of visit, Saturday, 27 April 1946. The rendering of McCaughy's sisters' names varies in the various reports (including McCloskey instead of McCluskey). I have used the most commonly adopted spellings, but there is some uncertainty.

97 Department of Justice, McCaughey file, Report of visit, Thursday, 2 May 1946. On the petition, see Oliver J. Flanagan's speech in the Adjournment Debate on 8 May 1946 (*Dáil Debates*, vol. 100, col. 2490, *et seq.*).

98 Department of Justice, McCaughey file: Chairman of Visiting Committee, Entry in Minute Book, Saturday, 4 May 1946.

99 Department of Justice, McCaughey file, Report of visit, Sunday, 5 May 1946. McCaughey also told his sister that conditions at Portlaoise were 'all right'.

100 Department of Justice, McCaughey file, Report of visit, Saturday, 4 May 1946. The brother-in-law said little during these exchanges.

101 Department of Justice, McCaughey file, Report of Temporary Warder Thomas Bracken, Monday, 6 May 1946.

102 Department of Justice, McCaughey file, W. R. Barrows to Department of Justice, 6 May 1946.

103 Barrows to Department of Justice, 6 May 1946.

104 *Dáil Debates*, vol. 100, cols. 2338–40, 8 May 1946; *Irish Independent*, 9 May 1946, 5g–h.

105 Department of Justice, McCaughey file, Reports to Governor, 7 May 1946. Liam Rice's account of the incident does not differ significantly other than to note that it was McCaughey crying out – apparently in delirium – that prompted MacCurtáin to shout out to him. McCaughey, in this account, assured him that he was not being ill-treated (MacEoin, *The IRA in the Twilight Years*, *op. cit.*, p. 538).

106 Department of Justice, McCaughey file, Further report, 7 May 1946. The strain on Barrows himself, at this point, though not recorded, must have been considerable.

107 Department of Justice, McCaughey file, Further report, 7 May 1946.

108 MacEoin, *The IRA in the Twilight Years*, *op. cit.*, p. 538.

109 Department of Justice, McCaughey file, Third report from Governor to Department of Justice, Tuesday, 7 May 1946.

110 Department of Justice, McCaughey file, Warder J. Humphries to Governor W. R. Barrows, 7 May 1946. Liam Rice confirmed this account. He had told McCaughey that if he wanted to come off the strike the others would stand by him. McCaughey, barely able to talk and horribly emaciated, replied that he never thought that Rice would talk to him like that. The strike would go on: 'It must be death or honourable release.' MacEoin, *The IRA in the Twilight Years, op. cit.*, p. 538.

111 Department of Justice, McCaughey file, Chief Warder E. J. Kelly to Governor W. R. Barrows, Wednesday, 8 May 1946.

112 Department of Justice, McCaughey file, Principal Warder J. Frawley to Governor W. R. Barrows, 9 May 1946.

113 *Dáil Debates*, vol. 100, cols. 2497–8, 8 May 1946.

114 Department of Justice, McCaughey file, W. R. Barrows to Peter Berry, 9 May 1946. *Irish Press*, 9 May 1946, 1g–h. It is recorded in the file that Barrows visited McCaughey again on the afternoon of that day and pleaded with him to end the hunger strike. He 'emphatically' told him three times that the government would not release him as a result of the strike. He asked if McCaughey understood. McCaughey replied that he did, adding, 'I don't want any more of that talk.' Department of Justice, McCaughey file, Note, Chief Warder E. J. Kelly, 9 May 1946.

115 MacEoin, *The IRA in the Twilight Years, op. cit.*, p. 538.

116 Department of Justice, McCaughey file, Temporary Warder T. Bracken to Governor W. R. Barrows, 11 May 1946.

117 Department of Justice, McCaughey file, F. C. Connolly, Department of Justice to W. R. Barrows, 3 May 1946.

118 This response was probably true in both the literal and the moral sense. Even in 1946 it would have been deeply reprehensible to keep a dog in virtual solitary confinement for three years; it may, in fact, have been illegal. Seán MacBride, as we have noted, had been IRA Chief of Staff for a short time in 1936. When arrested in 1940, he had signed an undertaking: 'I do solemnly and sincerely promise that I will not engage in or encourage any activity prejudicial to the peace, order or security of the State' (*Dáil Debates*, vol. 101, col. 1130, 29 May 1946). This had been sufficient to secure his release, since the promise itself was magnified in credibility by the fact that it broke the taboo on signing out. Gerald Boland insisted that MacBride had not kept his promise and, in May 1946, commented on MacBride's relationship with the IRA: 'He is about half out of it now, if he is half out of it' (col. 1127).

119 Department of Justice, McCaughey file, W. B. Barrows to Peter Berry, 14 May 1946. The Deputy Coroner had closed off the possibility of a general examination of conditions at Portlaoise by announcing that he would take no evidence on events prior to 19 April, the day on which McCaughey commenced his strike. This made the verdict inevitable, but the jury's rider could not be prevented. See *Irish Independent*, 13 May 1946, 1h and 7c–h

120 Department of Justice, McCaughey file, Visiting Committee to Minister for Justice, undated (cover note shows it to have been 17 May 1946).

121 Department of Justice, McCaughey file, Visiting Committee to Gerald Boland.

122 NAI 90/16/10, Portlaoise Prison, Minutes of Visiting Committee. Note by Peter Berry to Frank Gallagher, Director, Government Information Bureau, 15 May 1946.

123 Department of Justice, McCaughey file, Boland's annotation, 15 May 1946.

124 *Sunday Independent*, 19 May 1946, 1c–d; *Irish Times*, 20 May 1946, 6e; *Irish Independent*, 20 May 1946, 2a–b. One consequence of the Visiting Committee's action was that Liam Rice demanded that its members should stop visiting the IRA men and made unspecified threats about what would happen if they continued to come. The other

men apparently did not back him in this (Department of Justice, McCaughey file, Principal Warder J. Frawley to W. R. Barrows, 17 June 1946).

125 *Dáil Debates*, vol. 101, cols. 1128–9, 29 May 1946. Boland referred to the 'unfortunate' doctor who had been led and trapped by MacBride into making a remark 'which was not quite correct'. He went on to recall that he had seen MacBride in action with jurors on another occasion, 'and I must say my feeling was one of pity for the jurors'.

126 The remains lay overnight at the Franciscan church on Merchants Quay. On Sunday, 12 May it was taken by stages to Belfast for a service at Holy Cross Church, Ardoyne. Crowds assembled at places on the northward route. On the outskirts of Dublin the 'Last Post' and 'Reville' were sounded and three revolver shots were fired. *Irish News*, 13 May 1946, 1b–c; *Northern Whig*, 13 May 1946, 1b–c; *Evening Herald*, 13 May 1946, 3c.

127 *Dáil Debates*, vol. 101, cols. 1087–174, 29 May 1946.

128 Boland recalled Fianna Fáil's policy of leniency, which had not worked, and insisted that the Portlaoise men were 'not going to get out now until they have served their time or until the Government feel that they have been in prison long enough and review their sentences. But they are not going to be released by this means [hunger-striking]. That is final' (*Dáil Debates*, vol. 101, col. 1127, 29 May 1946).

129 MacEoin, *The IRA in the Twilight Years, op. cit.*, p. 541.

130 The reason given was that, at a political meeting, Hartnett had called the government 'Belsen Camp Gaolers', which the Minister deemed to be 'defamatory and subversive' (*Dáil Debates*, vol. 101, cols. 1311–12, 5 June 1946). The programme was sponsored by the semi-state Irish Tourist Board. Patrick Little informed Radio Éireann that should Hartnett compère the show the broadcasting permission of the Department for Posts and Telegraphs would be withdrawn. Hartnett was accordingly dismissed. Ironically, Little was also a lawyer and journalist.

131 *Dáil Debates*, vol. 101, cols. 1310–11, 5 June 1946.

132 See, for example, the trenchant letter by author Seán Ó Faoláin in the *Dublin Evening Mail*, 8 June 1946, 2e–f; see also NAI JUS/8/939, Noel Hartnett.

133 See above, p. 634.

134 A pamphlet by Gerald O'Reilly was published in 1947 under the auspices of the Connelly Commemoration Committee of New York. Dealing with Portlaoise, its content may be discerned from its title, 'They Are Innocent! The Story of the Irish Republican Prisoners'. Such was the irritation with the pamphlet in the Department of Justice that the Secretary General proposed that the Washington Legation publish a rebuttal. Boland thought it 'not worth while' to answer O'Reilly (NAI JUS/8/964, Political Prisoners in Éire, A reply to malicious propaganda in America, memo, 17 February 1947).

135 The remaining three Portlaoise prisoners were released on 9 March 1948. Party-political ambitions and necessity were major factors in the formation of the unlikely Fine Gael–Clann na Poblachta government in 1948. But, whether as rationalisation or genuine belief, it was asserted by John Costello, the new Taoiseach, that the span of the parties in the new government was in itself conducive to the removal of violence from Irish politics and that the coming together of the right-of-centre and conservative Fine Gael with the republican and decidedly left-of-centre Clann na Poblachta was a grand gesture of political conciliation: 'The chief of my reasons for becoming head of this Government was that I held and sincerely believed, as I do sincerely believe now, that in consequence of the coming together of these Parties, and particularly the Clann na Poblachta Party, we would see in this country the end of the gun as an instrument for furthering political theories or wishes' (*Dáil Debates*, vol. 110, col. 931, 15 April 1948). *Irish Independent*, 10 March 1948, 3c and 5c–d.

136 *Dáil Debates*, vol. 101, cols. 2490, *et seq.*, 8 May 1946.

137 *Dáil Debates*, vol. 101, cols. 2493–4, *passim*.

138 Daniel Spring (1910–88) was a National Labour TD for Kerry North and a trade-union official. He would remain in the Dáil for this constituency (with the Labour Party from 1951) until 1981 when he retired. In 1956–7, he was Parliamentary Secretary to the Minister for Local Government.

139 *Dáil Debates*, vol. 100, col. 2495, 8 May 1946. He added, 'He must be a good Irishman when he is willing to lay down his life for his country.'

140 See above, p. 635, for another view of this incident.

141 *Dáil Debates*, vol. 100, col. 2340, 8 May 1946. Spring also alleged that McCaughey was without a shirt; *Irish Independent*, 9 May 1946, 5e–g; *Irish Times*, 9 May 1946, 7d–f.

142 These included the provision of a spring hospital bed and mattress, three pillows, two air-cushions, eight woollen blankets, two hot-water bottles and an electric heater. In addition to attending staff, the Chaplain, Governor and a visiting justice had been at the bedside.

143 *Dáil Debates*, vol. 100, col. 2497, 8 May 1946.

144 'I want to apologise to you, Governor, and all your staff. You have been most kind to us and have done your best for Seán. We are very grateful to all the prison officials and repudiate entirely all the charges made in the Dáil against the prison officials' (*Dáil Debates*, vol. 100, col. 2513, 9 May 1946; *Irish Times*, 10 May 1946, 7a; *Irish Press*, 10 May 1946, 1c–d; *Irish Independent*, 10 May 1946, 7f). Oliver Flanagan somewhat mystifyingly addressed Boland immediately after this statement had been relayed to the Dáil: 'I am sure the Minister is satisfied that I made no charge against the prison officials.' This prompted a tart response from Boland: 'I am anything but satisfied.'

145 David Fleming (c.1920–61), a native of Killarney, Co. Kerry, had been sent north by the IRA. He was arrested on 10 September 1942 when police raided the publicity office of the Northern Command. Charged with several serious offences, he was given twelve years' penal servitude (*Irish Times*, 27 November 1942, 2g; *Irish Press*, 27 November 1942, 1a). When first arrested, Fleming used two aliases: John E. Allen and Henry McCormick (*Irish Times*, 3 October 1942, 1d).

146 *Dáil Debates*, vol. 100, col. 2323, 8 May 1946.

147 *Dáil Debates*, vol. 91, cols. 600–6, 9 July 1943; vol. 95, cols. 1456–62, 1 December 1944.

148 *Dáil Debates*, vol. 100, col. 2322, 8 May 1946.

149 McCaughey's mental state, noted above, would have opened a reasonably defensible exit. Confinement in a secure hospital, moreover, could have been represented as (and was) a continuing form of custody. Neither on the side of McCaughey's family (to whom his state of mind must have been obvious), nor on the side of those who sought release, nor on the part of the state was this course considered. It may well be that psychiatric doctrine in Ireland in 1946 could not entertain, or would not have been comfortable with, such an approach. The substantive issue apart, doctors would certainly have been wary about being drawn into such an episode.

150 *Dáil Debates*, vol. 100, cols. 2322–3, 8 May 1946.

151 *Irish Independent*, 13 May 1946, 2c–f; *Irish Times*, 13 May 1946, 1f and 7c–h; *Irish News*, 13 May 1946, 3e.

152 Michael Donnellan (1900–64) was a Galway farmer. In the periods when Fianna Fáil was out of power in 1948–51 and 1954–7 he became Parliamentary Secretary to the Minister for Finance. A member of Sinn Féin and then of Fianna Fáil, he became increasingly unhappy with the latter's policies when in power in the 1930s. For an Irish politician, he had the huge advantage of having been an All-Ireland footballer. Fittingly, he died in Dublin's Croke Park in 1964, after the All-Ireland final. (The Galway team, captained by his son, were the victors.)

153 *Dáil Debates*, vol. 101, cols. 367–8: 'The replies given by a single witness under the type of cross-examination to which he was subjected do not give any true picture of the real situation.'

154 *Dáil Debates*, vol. 101, col. 503, 22 May 1946; *Irish Independent*, 13 May 1946, 2c–f.

155 *Dáil Debates*, vol. 101, cols. 880–1, 28 May 1946. Flanagan obviously had information on the health of Rice and MacCurtáin, but this, as Boland reported, was no more than a slight swelling of the glands, in the case of the latter, and a complaint by Rice of indigestion, for which a light diet was prescribed. All the prisoners, excepting MacCurtáin, had gained weight: his loss was slight and 'he is in good form'.

156 See above, p. 620.

157 Donnellan claimed that de Valera had gone further in his claims than had been reported, alleging that a conspiracy to overthrow the Government by force was under way between certain army officers, teachers and republicans. Donnellan dismissed these claims (*Dáil Debates*, vol. 101, cols. 1088–9; 29 May 1946). See *Cork Examiner*, 27 May 1946, 5a–c.

158 Donnellan focused his motion on McCaughey's treatment and called for a Select Committee, with power to summon witnesses, to call for papers and to take evidence on oath. The principal headings for the Committee would be McCaughey's detention in solitary confinement for three years; confinement for four and a half years without clothes or open-air exercise; refusal of visits for the same period; why prison clothing was insisted on for him but not for others sentenced by the Special Criminal Court and Military Court; and why others sentenced to penal servitude were allowed to serve their sentences at prisons other than Portlaoise (*Dáil Debates*, vol. 101, col. 1088). These were all valid and worrying concerns, and had such a committee been authorised, it would have caused the government a deal of trouble.

159 The inquests to which Donnellan referred were those on Seán Glynn (22 September 1936), Tony D'Arcy (17 April 1940) and Seán McNeela (22 April 1940). The juries' riders in each case were critical or suggested changes in policy (*Dáil Debates*, vol. 101, cols. 1090–1).

160 Donnellan made the additional point that the men in Portlaoise had been convicted of less serious offences than those at the Curragh. As we have seen, this was not true, unless an impossibly lenient view were taken of McCaughey's offence.

161 There is no mention of such an offer in the extremely detailed file that was kept of McCaughey's last days. Had it been made, it is inconceivable that Barrows would not have reported it. See pp. 630–6 above.

162 *Dáil Debates*, vol. 101, cols. 1100–1, 29 May 1946. Would the government have fallen to pieces had McCaughey been allowed to wear his own clothes or sent to the Curragh?

163 *Dáil Debates*, vol. 101, cols. 1102–3, 29 May 1946.

164 The allusion, of course, was to Stephen Hayes's 'confession'.

165 *Dáil Debates*, vol. 101, cols. 1103–4, 29 May 1946.

166 *Dáil Debates*, vol. 101, col. 1105, 29 May 1946.

167 Bell, *The Secret Army, op. cit.*, pp. 194–5.

168 *Dáil Debates*, vol. 101, cols. 1137–8, 29 May 1946. Boland was equivocal on the allegation that McCaughey had been offered money: 'I never heard anything about McCaughey being offered money', but as to the offer, there was no equivocation: 'The police officer simply laughed at the suggestion.' Since the entire strategy of the Irish government was to keep out of the war, the IRA proposition was preposterous.

169 *Dáil Debates*, vol. 101, cols. 1106–8. Cogan also criticised de Valera for his Cork speech. This was a tactic used before in a pre-election period. He also denied that Clann na Talmhan had any sympathy for an illegal organisation and pledged, whether in opposition or in power, to fight any such body. The best way to combat the illegal organisation making its appeal to young men (the IRA, in other words) was to reduce the ground on which it made its appeal, and that could be done by a thorough investigation of the prison system.

170 See above, pp. 612–3.

171 Ill-treatment and torture had included striking Hayes on the head with revolvers, stamping on his bare feet with boots and kicking his shins and thighs – all while tied to a chair and blindfolded. Boland could not, however, say what part McCaughey had taken in these attacks.

172 *Dáil Debates*, vol. 101, cols. 1120, *et seq.*

173 *Dáil Debates*, vol. 101, col. 1120. There had been several assertions that McCaughey had been guilty of no more than common assault.

174 McCaughey had undoubtedly participated in the ill-treatment and torture of Hayes, but Boland could not leave culpability there. He detailed a case dating back thirteen years, to April 1933, in which McCaughey had no part. This involved brutal torture of an IRA member suspected of passing information. The man was held prisoner, beaten, kicked, and struck with guns and chairs. Pincers were forced into his mouth to pull teeth, lips and tongue. The case was revolting. See *Irish Times*, 21 September 1945, 1h–i. Boland was allowed to put this into debate to show that the IRA used torture and imprisonment. The effect (and intention) was to blacken McCaughey by association (*Dáil Debates*, vol. 101, cols. 1122–4, 29 May 1946). See also *Irish News*, 21 September 1946, 4d–e.

175 *Dáil Debates*, vol. 101, cols. 1136–7, 29 May 1946.

176 'I thought that all Parties were agreed that the law must be enforced and that no political party outside this Parliament has the right to dictate to this Parliament or to use force. I thought we all took our stand on that ground' (*Dáil Debates*, vol. 101, col. 1144). Costello also objected to extensive and disparaging references to Seán MacBride: 'So far as I know him, I know nothing of his political associations. He is a loyal colleague at the Bar and a man of honour and integrity, so far as my association with him is concerned. What has that to do with the motion?' (col. 1142).

177 *Dáil Debates*, vol. 101, cols. 1144–5, 29 May 1946.

178 *Dáil Debates*, vol. 101, col. 1148, 29 May 1946, citing the *Statistical Abstract* published by the Department of Industry and Commerce.

179 *Dáil Debates*, vol. 101, col. 1149, 29 May 1946. He also observed that, while the Taoiseach and members of the Government could make their assertions, it had to be recognised that, from 1922 until relatively recently, it had been accepted that political status was granted to prisoners.

180 *Dáil Debates*, vol. 101, col. 1147, 29 May 1946. At this point, Seán MacEntee (Minister for Local Government and Health) interjected, 'What about the dozen lives on the other side?'

181 *Dáil Debates*, vol. 101, col. 1148, 29 May 1946.

182 *Dáil Debates*, vol. 101, cols. 1150–67, 29 May 1946, *passim.*

183 *Dáil Debates*, vol. 101, col. 1155, 29 May 1946.

184 *Dáil Debates*, vol. 101, col. 1160, 29 May 1946.

185 See McConville, *Irish Political Prisoners, op. cit.*, pp. 512–37. During this period, de Valera resorted to various forms of protest to wring concessions from the authorities. Each victory enabled the republican prisoners to move on to the next.

186 *Dáil Debates*, vol. 101, col. 1160, 29 May 1946. And when the demands were met, the prisoners would have numbers enough 'to burn your camp or break down your prison'.

187 *Dáil Debates*, vol. 101, col. 1152, 29 May 1946. Whilst in the USA, moreover, he had investigated prison conditions there. De Valera never forgot his own imprisonment. The late Garret FitzGerald told me that, in 1973, when, in his capacity as Minister for Foreign Affairs, he met President de Valera, the matter of imprisonment came up. Whilst imprisoned in England, de Valera had been transferred from Dartmoor Prison to Maidstone. During the journey, he had been handcuffed to Desmond FitzGerald (Garret's father). He asked, on more than one occasion, on which side Desmond had been shackled to him. The detail seemed to be important to him.

188 *Dáil Debates*, vol. 101, col. 1169, 29 May 1946.

189 The vote being sixty-four to fourteen.

190 By fifty-seven to thirteen votes.

191 *Dáil Debates*, vol. 101, col. 1152, 29 May 1946.

192 *Seanad Debates*, vol. 31, col. 2120, 12 June 1946.

193 James Green Douglas (1887–1964), a member of the Senate from 1922 to 1936, and again, when it was restored, in 1938. He was defeated in the Seanad election of 1943 and, from 1944, sat as a member of the Industrial and Commercial Panel.

194 *Seanad Debates*, vol. 31, col. 2195, 12 June 1946.

195 *Seanad Debates*, vol. 31, cols. 2175–6, 12 June 1946.

196 *Dáil Debates*, vol. 101, col. 1131, 29 May 1946. The letters did not, however, refer to any part he might be playing in the current campaign on McCaughey.

197 *Seanad Debates*, vol. 31, col. 2173, 12 June 1946.

198 *Ibid.*

199 *Seanad Debates*, vol. 31, col. 2174, 12 June 1946. He also implied that in 1916 there had been similar propaganda about Belfast Prison, where he had also been an inmate: 'the governor there was a kind, decent man, the father of the present governor of Portlaoighise'. Frongoch was an internment camp in North Wales, used after the 1916 Easter Rising to hold the rank and file of the rebels, between Easter and Christmas, when they were released (see McConville, *Irish Political Prisoners, op. cit.*, Chapter 10).

200 *Seanad Debates*, vol. 31, col. 2175, 12 June 1946. 'That crowd' was a term not just of condemnation, but of contempt.

201 Prisons (Ireland) Act, 1826. *Seanad Debates*, vol. 31, cols. 2121–4, 12 June 1946.

202 *Seanad Debates*, vol. 31, cols. 2122–3, 12 June 1946.

203 *Seanad Debates*, vol. 31, cols. 2161–6, *passim.*

204 *Seanad Debates*, vol. 31, cols. 2172–3, 12 June 1946.

205 *Seanad Debates*, vol. 31, cols. 2176–7, 12 June 1946.

206 *Seanad Debates*, vol. 31, col. 2178, 12 June 1946.

207 *Seanad Debates*, vol. 31, col. 2187, 12 June 1946.

208 William Stewart appeared before the Special Criminal Court and was sentenced on 11 June 1941 (*Irish Press*, 12 June 1941, 5c–e). Patrick Murphy was dealt with on 25 September 1941 (*Irish Times*, 26 September 1941, 1c).

209 See above, p. 612.

210 For corporal punishment in Northern Ireland, see pp. 90–91, above.

211 The exception was the 2004 film, directed by Mel Gibson, *The Passion of the Christ*, which shows gouts of blood and flesh during the whipping of Christ. Significantly, there were numerous complaints about excessive and gratuitous violence in various scenes.

212 MacEoin, *The IRA in the Twilight Years, op. cit.*, p. 530.

213 See NAI TAOIS/S12606, S12633 and, particularly, S12393.

214 MacEoin, *The IRA in the Twilight Years, op. cit.*, p. 530. The question was no doubt put with merciful intent, but it was inappropriate. If the punishment was to be stopped on medical grounds, it was for the two doctors to intervene: Kavanagh had no formal power in the matter and may simply have been repulsed by the process.

215 MacEoin, *The IRA in the Twilight Years, op. cit.*, p. 531. Murphy's defiance continued at Portlaoise where he brushed aside the Governor's summary of the rules. The Medical Officer treated him humanely, but, he claimed, a warder named MacBride from Dundalk (he describes him as Chief Warder) was abusive and, when escorting him up the five flights of steps to E5, hit him with a leather strap on every step. After that he slept for two days.

216 See pp. 612–3. See also p. 737, n.21

217 *Dáil Debates*, vol. 552, Written Answers, 23 April, 2002.

218 *Ibid.*, my calculations.

219 For a fairly typical exchange, see the question put by James Larkin, Jr., on the matter of abolition in 1948 (*Dáil Debates*, vol. 110, cols. 1186–7, 5 May 1948). It was partly

abolished by the Criminal Justice Act, 1964, and then for all remaining offences (including treason, military offences and the murder of a police or prison officer) by the Criminal Justice Act, 1990.

220 One of the arguments against the death penalty is that inconsistencies in its use are even more unacceptable than with secondary punishments. Yet in every jurisdiction, it is safe to assert, there have been inconsistencies in its application, some gross and inexplicable, both at the sentencing and at the review stages. For an historical account that illustrates this unavoidable flaw in the capital sentence, see Leon Radzinowicz, *A History of the English Criminal Law and Its Administration from 1750* (London: Stevens & Sons, 1948), especially Part V.

221 For MacCurtáin's reprieve, see NAI TAOIS/3/S11931/B; PRES 1/P/1743.

222 See NAI TAOIS/S11136 for consideration of McCaughey's case and his reprieve. MacEoin (*The IRA in the Twilight Years, op. cit.*, p. 536) contended that the decision to reprieve was one of political calculation: 'Could the Belfast man be executed following conviction on a mere charge of assault and unlawful detention?' MacEoin concluded that 'wiser and more influential voices prevailed' (p. 536). It should also be noted that desert, governed by the calculation of proportionality is, like other principles of justice and sentencing, extremely hard to apply. The notion of harm, for example, is highly susceptible to political interpretation, varies with broad as well as narrow circumstances and can be seen to shift considerably over time. Offences committed during times of war, civil unrest or natural calamity have always been viewed with particular concern and subject to an increased tariff of punishment. For a comprehensive discussion of this and other aspects of sentencing, see D. A. Thomas's *Principles of Sentencing*, 2nd edn (London: Heinemann Educational, 1979). See also Brian P. Block, *An Introduction to Judicial Decision-Making* (Chichester: Barry Rose, 1998).

223 See, for example, Brendan Behan's tirade of abuse to a Curragh officer (p. 722). For a list of those executed during the Civil War, together with dates and places of execution, see Dorothy Macardle, *The Irish Republic* (London: Victor Gollancz, 1937), Appendix 34, pp. 1022–3. Modern tallies add another four deaths, making a total of eighty-one executions.

224 They had been held at Arbour Hill Prison until 9 p.m. the previous night and were then transferred to Mountjoy for execution (MA, Weekly Reports, Arbour Hill, 7 September 1940).

225 See *Irish Times*, 19 August 1940, 3f. The proceedings were made more arbitrary by the IRA's standing order (later modified) that those brought before a court, Irish or British, should not defend themselves, since this was a form of recognition of what, to the IRA, was an illegitimate body. None of the three men appearing before the Military Court chose to defend themselves. Considering the circumstances, it probably would have made little difference to the verdict had they done so, but representation may have affected the Government's conclusions when the review process was under way. See *Dáil Debates*, vol. 102, cols. 844–5, 16 July 1946, for further observations on the case.

226 See p. 689. There was the usual defence of uncertainty of culpability because of cross-fire.

227 Hunt was also brought before the Military Court, convicted and sentenced to death. On review his sentence was commuted to life at penal servitude. See his reprieve papers at NAI TAOIS/3 S12065.

228 Emergency Powers (Amendment No. 2) Act, 1940, s.3.

229 Emergency Powers Orders Nos. 41 and 41A, 1940; *Irish Times*, 17 August 1940, 8a. The scheduled offences falling within the jurisdiction of the new court were as follows: treason, attempting or conspiring to procure the forcible overthrow of the state; obtaining, recording or communicating information likely to prejudice the safety of

the state; impeding work on any vessel, aircraft, vehicle or machinery used by the Defence Forces; unlawfully wounding or shooting at with intent or to resist arrest; assault and unlawful imprisonment; unlawfully causing an explosion; reasonable suspicion of possessing explosives for an unlawful purpose; and possession or control of ammunition or firearms with intent to injure life or property (*Irish Times*, 26 August 1940, 6f).

230 As any criminal lawyer would affirm, the course of a criminal prosecution may often be determined by what a suspect says to police after detention. Legal advice at that stage may affect conviction, but even for persons for whom conviction is inevitable, legal counsel may be beneficial and affect sentence or the review of a sentence. It was significant, therefore, that persons arrested under the OASA were liable, by ss.30 and 52, to be kept incommunicado for up to forty-eight hours. See *Dáil Debates*, vol. 100, cols. 947–8, 2 April 1946, for a defence of this procedure, and cols. 1210–12 for a further expression of concern by John Costello. IRA men were, of course, in a double bind: these restrictive government rules and police practice, and their own organisation's instruction that they were not to defend themselves before a court.

231 *Irish Times*, 21 August 1940, 3b–d.

232 *Irish Times*, 5 September 1940, 3b. Harte, who had been wounded in the leg, was brought into court on a stretcher. The Court adjourned to the Meath Hospital, where evidence was taken from the wounded Detective Michael Brady. Six years later, the justice of this decision was challenged in the Dáil. Seán Brady, a Fianna Fáil TD for Dublin County, referred Boland to a question put some months previously to John Costello, a Fine Gael TD and former Attorney General. This had suggested that Harte and McGrath had improperly suffered the death penalty since Emergency Powers Order No. 41 (1940) had not been in effect at the time the two men committed their crime. Boland rejected the suggestion. The Order prescribed mode of trial and manner of execution: 'I need hardly say that the offence of murder was not created by any Government Order, or that the penalty for their offence has always been death' (see *Dáil Debates*, vol. 102, cols. 844–5, 16 July 1946; see also vol. 99, cols. 2401–2, 13 March 1946, and vol. 101, cols. 2605–8, 27 June 1946).

233 In this, instinctively but almost certainly unknowingly, the government was applying the dictum of the Italian jurist, Cesare Beccaria, that 'Crimes are more effectually prevented by *certainty*, rather than the *severity* of punishment.' But he also set a difficult test in his general approach: 'Every act of authority of one man over another, for which there is not an absolute necessity, is tyrannical'. Cesare Beccaria, *An Essay on Crimes and Punishment*, 5th revised English translation (London: E. Newbery, 1801), pp. 95 and 97.

234 *Dáil Debates*, vol. 101, col. 1116, 29 May 1946. Boland pointed out that when the Emergency Powers (Amendment No. 2) Bill was being enacted, it went through the legislature with complete unanimity.

235 NAI JUS/8/944, Statistics, Internment, etc. (1946). This is not wildly out of line with the acquittal rate of about 40 per cent before judge and jury.

236 *Irish Times*, 8 May 1940, 7e–f. For an account of the incident from an IRA perspective, see MacEoin, *The IRA in the Twilight Years, op. cit.*, pp. 889–90. This had followed by less than a fortnight a bomb attack on Special Branch offices in Dublin Castle in reprisal for the deaths on hunger strike of Tony D'Arcy and Seán McNeela (see above, pp. 695–6). Five detectives and a caretaker were injured in the attack and extensive damage was caused to buildings (*Irish Times*, 26 April 1940, 5a–b).

237 Cited NAI JUS/8/938, Special Criminal Court; *Irish Times*, 9 May 1940, 8c.

238 Both in public statements and by declaring that it would not contest the vacant West Galway by-election. See Cosgrave's statement and de Valera's response in *Dáil Debates*, vol. 80, cols. 211–12 and 285–6, 9 May 1940.

239 It showed how difficult it had become for IRA men to find safe houses that they had to stay at the home of a nationally known republican family, almost certainly under

surveillance and likely to be raided. Barney Casey, a son of the family, had been shot dead in the Curragh on 16 December 1940, and the Caseys were well known to be committed republicans.

240 O'Callaghan was then charged with a Dundalk Post Office raid, tried, sentenced to fourteen years' penal servitude and removed to Portlaoise.

241 For an account of the bank and post-office raids and Goss's arrest, see Patrick Murphy's interview in MacEoin, *The IRA in the Twilight Years*, *op. cit.*, pp. 529–30. O'Callaghan's executive would have evoked memories of the British execution of Kevin Barry, an eighteen-year-old student, twenty years previously (see McConville, *Irish Political Prisoners*, *op. cit.*, pp. 697–8).

242 *Irish Press*, 11 August 1941, 3g; *Sunday Independent*, 10 August 1941, 1d.

243 For one of Goss's letters, written shortly before execution, see MacEoin, *The IRA in the Twilight Years*, *op. cit.*, p. 530.

244 Bell, *The Secret Army*, *op. cit.*, pp. 187–8.

245 *Irish Times*, 11 December 1941, 1g–h; 12 December 1941, 4f.

246 See *Irish Press*, 3 January 1942, 3a–c.

247 Emergency Order No. 139, 30 December 1941 (made under Emergency Powers Act, 1939, s.2[1]) provided (with retroactive effect) that where it was proved that 'a statement relevant to the charge was made by any person including the accused and that such statement… was made voluntarily and lawfully… taken down in writing and was acknowledged by the person who made it, then at any stage of the trial the prosecution may read such a statement as evidence and may cross-examine the person who made it'. The order also allowed the Court, at any time during a trial, to disregard any rule of evidence, military or common law. Intimidation, it must be noted, cut both ways. Police could intimidate during interrogation (either verbally or physically), and the IRA could threaten injury or death after the statement had been made.

248 The Dáil had another opportunity to consider the matter when, on 28 and 29 January 1942, it debated a Labour Party motion to annual Emergency Powers Order No. 139. This was a wide-ranging and, at times, heated debate, but at its conclusion the motion was comprehensively defeated, seventy-one votes to twenty (see *Dáil Debates*, vol. 85, col. 1451, *et seq.*, 28 January 1942; col. 1579, *et seq.*, 29 January 1942).

249 *Irish Times*, 23 January 1942, 6g; 28 January 1942, 2e–f.

250 Patrick Murphy gives a description of Plant's demeanour immediately before his execution at Portlaoise in MacEoin, *The IRA in the Twilight Years*, *op. cit.*, p. 532. For Plant at Arbour Hill (from which he was brought to be executed), see Pierce Fennell's recollections (p. 572).

251 MacEoin, who describes Mordaunt as 'a 1922 Free State man' (one who in 1922 took the pro-Treaty side in the Civil War) goes further than mere confusion and is emphatic that he 'was killed by fellow Branch men, in a shoot-out at Donnycarney on October 24, 1942' (*The IRA in the Twilight Years*, *op. cit.*, p. 180 n.).

252 *Irish Press*, 13 November 1942, 1c; *Irish Times*, 13 November 1942, 1e; NAI PRES/ 1/P/3005; TSCH/3 S12996; TSCH/3 S13004; MacEoin, *The IRA in the Twilight Years*, *op. cit.*, p. 742.

253 Thus, Roger Casement, having been convicted of treason in 1916, asked to share the fate of the leaders of the 1916 Rising and to be executed by firing squad. The British government was unwilling to lift the opprobrium of what it saw as a betrayal in time of war and insisted that he be hanged. See McConville, *Irish Political Prisoners*, *op. cit.*, Chapter 12 for an account of Casement's trial and execution.

254 Opinions about the mode of execution have of course varied over time and from one country to another. That hanging was seen to have particularly degrading and therefore aggravating properties may be confirmed by an improbable witness: Adolf Hitler. In the aftermath of the burning of the Reichstag (27 February 1933), Hitler

sought to bring in a special law retrospectively to punish the supposed arsonist, Marinus van der Lubbe, and wanted the culprit to be hanged in order to give him an ignominious death. He was thwarted in this by the fact that this mode of execution had not been used in Germany since the eighteenth century (axe and guillotine were preferred) and was not authorised by any law. See Richard J. Evans, *Rituals of Retribution: Capital Punishment in Germany, 1600–1987* (London: Penguin, 1997), pp. 618–20.

255 Of the six persons executed in Éire during the war years, only one – Charlie Kerins – was hanged. He had been condemned by the Special Criminal Court. The other five, sentenced by the Military Court, were shot.

256 This account is taken from Bell, *The Secret Army, op. cit.*, p. 234.

257 There is nothing to qualify or contradict this in the description that Bell gives of the events. He reports, however, that the IRA GHQ, then located in Belfast, considered a court martial for Kerins for authorising the assassination. Evidence given at Kerins's trial included fingerprints, documents and circumstantial matters.

258 MacEoin, *The IRA in the Twilight Years, op. cit.*, p. 897.

259 *Irish Times*, 2 December 1944, 1d; *Irish Press*, 2 December 1944, 1a–e, h. See also NAI PRES/1/P/2457; TSCH/3 S13567/1, S13567/1A. These papers cover the death sentence, appeals and petitions.

260 Capital Punishment Amendment Act, 1868: 31 & 32 Vict., c.24, s.6. For a discussion of this legislation (which extended to Ireland), see Seán McConville, *English Local Prisons, 1860–1900: Next Only to Death* (London and New York: Routledge, 1995), pp. 409–31.

261 See, for example, Thomas Hardy's evocative tale of the supposedly curative properties of the corpse of the condemned. This was taken, as was much of his work, from childhood memories (and the lore of those who then were adults): 'The Withered Arm', *Wessex Tales* (London: Macmillan, 1888).

262 See Radzinowicz, *History of the English Criminal Law, op. cit.*, pp. 196–7 on the burial of suicides, and pp. 199–200 on the practice of gibbeting the bodies of the executed. Richard J. Evans provides much of interest on the dishonourable disposal of the bodies of executed persons in eighteenth-century Germany (*Rituals of Retribution, op. cit.*, pp. 86–98).

263 The decision to release the bodies was made in late August 1948 and was reported in the newspapers over the following days (see *Irish Independent*, 1 September 1948, 5g; *Irish Times*, 4 September 1948, 1c; *Irish Times*, 7 September 1948, 5d). Charlie Kerins was reinterred on 19 September 1948 (*Irish Times*, 20 September 1948, 1e).

264 See below, Chapters 18 and 19.

13

IMPRISONMENT AND
INTERNMENT IN ÉIRE, 1939–48

The porcupine posture

Revolutionaries thrive amidst uncertainty and disorder. The Second World War offered an abundance of such elements. The IRA, long shifting on its anchor, now had a certain course: to exploit the opportunity.[1] Custodians of the Irish state, not yet eighteen years old, and with a persisting current of violence in its politics, knew its vulnerabilities. Ireland was on the geographical periphery of the immediate conflicts. Its strategic position between Europe and North America, however, betokened other possibilities, in addition to its historically fateful position on Britain's western flank. What these might be was demonstrated by the cynicism, brutality and speed with which the Munich agreement was discarded and when, in accordance with the Anglo-Soviet agreement, Poland was crushed and dismembered by the totalitarian powers. Further alarm bells rang with the precautionary seizure of bases in Iceland by British forces on 10 May 1940.[2] The Treaty Ports, a keystone of the Anglo-Irish Treaty, had been surrendered by Chamberlain's cabinet and evacuated by the British on 9 and 10 July 1938, only fourteen months before the outbreak of war.[3] Churchill had vehemently opposed withdrawal, which, he insisted, damaged British national interests; many of his countrymen considered the decision to be perverse. Back at the Admiralty, Churchill could provide an impetus for action.[4] A forced occupation of the ports could bring renewed war between Ireland and its old adversary; reoccupation by agreement meant certain war with the Axis powers.

The gall had not drained from Anglo-Irish relations, but popular opinion favoured the Allies. Ties of kinship, of shared history (only some of which was acrimonious), relatives in the British forces, the fate of Czechoslovakia and Poland, the wickedness of German ambitions and the indisputable evil of Nazi methods meant that all but a minority of Irish citizens wished London, Paris and their allies and supporters to prevail.[5] In an interview with Sir John Maffey, the British Representative in Dublin, Éamon de Valera estimated that two-thirds of the Irish public were pro-British or at least anti-German.[6] There was, however, he warned Maffey, a very active minority, which took a different view. To this group de Valera was a malign apostate, with all that entailed, and, he told

Maffey, his administration was threatened by the IRA and by its wider circles of supporters and sympathisers. These would represent any comfort given to Britain as a return to British rule.[7] For internal and external security reasons, and probably because de Valera was viscerally unable to contemplate an overt alliance with the British Commonwealth, the Irish government, hours after Britain and France declared war on Germany, proclaimed its neutrality.[8] This was in line with de Valera's Dáil statement the previous spring.[9] There seems little doubt that the stand was popular: the majority of Irish citizens almost certainly willed Hitler's defeat but equally wished their country to remain out of the fray.[10] Legislative provision was made for the perilous times to come. The Constitution was amended to broaden the definition of the phrase 'time of war' to include a state of war to which the country was not a party.[11] The Dáil then resolved that within the meaning of the amendment a state of national emergency existed, affecting the vital interests of the state.[12]

Confident in his mandate, and armed with formidable legal instruments, de Valera and his colleagues ordered steps to be taken to suppress any domestic threat to Irish neutrality. Remaining a non-belligerent was an objective of vital national importance and would be pursued with commensurate determination. Some legislation was already on the books in response to the bombing campaign in England. The OASA passed through the Dáil in the spring of 1939 and came into operation on 14 June 1939, allowing detention without trial. It also authorised a Special Criminal Court, and this was activated on 22 August 1939.[13] In June, the IRA had been declared 'an unlawful organisation'.[14] By 25 September, there were sixty-six men in Arbour Hill; a total of seventy-three would be interned in 1939.[15] The authority for internment under the OASA was successfully challenged on 1 December 1939 when Justice George Gavan Duffy granted a writ of habeas corpus to Seamus Burke, interned in Arbour Hill.[16] The government then ordered the release of the fifty-three Arbour Hill internees.[17] The passage of the Emergency Powers Acts in 1939 and 1940, based as they were on the overriding duty of the executive branch to defend and preserve the state in time of war, effectively freed internment from judicial review. Thereafter, and for the duration of the war, apart from escape, the only door to freedom was for a detainee to convince the authorities that he had broken with the IRA. Once again, IRA inflexibility worked against it. Any application for release (save by prior permission from the Camp Council on compassionate or tactical grounds) rendered a member liable to IRA court martial, a lifelong breach with comrades and stigma in wider republican circles. The internee was, in effect, in double custody.[18]

The reins of power

On the outbreak of war, the government had assumed extensive control of the nation's economic activity and took further extensive powers for security.[19] The determination to crack down on any unlawful challenge was emphasised by a cabinet reshuffle in which P. J. Ruttledge was, on 8 September, replaced at Justice by Gerald Boland, who in 1936 had dealt sternly with extreme republicanism.[20] Special Branch was reorganised, and Military Intelligence given extra resources to deal with internal subversion and the activities of foreign spies.[21] A list of prospective internees was updated.[22] This was not confined to extreme republicans and included many of the militant left.[23] There commenced a series of raids on known IRA premises. GHQ men, ammunition, many deeply incriminating documents and most of the IRA's available cash (US$8,265) were picked up in a small house in Rathmines, Dublin, on 9 September 1939.[24] Other arrests took place throughout the country.[25] On 15 September 1939, internment began with the arrest of sixty-four persons under warrants issued by the Minister for Justice.[26] As noted, on 1 December the warrants were found to be unconstitutional and therefore invalid. The following day all these who had been arrested on the authority of Part VI of the OASA were released. Internments proceeded under the Emergency Powers Act throughout 1940.[27]

The IRA leadership had failed to understand the sea change in politics and to take protective steps, and they continued to operate in the same manner as before.[28] Harried, beleaguered, wilfully blinkered in political judgements and led by young, inexperienced men, the organisation made two wholly counterproductive decisions that enraged the already jumpy Irish government and alarmed an equally nervous population. Practising revolution by rote, the IRA leadership fell back on the formula of 'my enemy's enemy' and opened communications with German intelligence. De Valera and his colleagues viewed this as an extremely dangerous step: should events take a certain turn, German activity in Ireland could become a British *casus belli*. Conversely, should the Axis prevail, it would have a shadow government in waiting in Dublin. In either event, the foundations of the Irish state would be swept away: these were deeply worrying possibilities. The second IRA move was an audacious and immediate challenge. It required a large amount of arms and ammunition for a planned large-scale assault on Northern Ireland. The Irish Army's principal store of ammunition was at the Magazine Fort armoury in Dublin's Phoenix Park. Inside information revealed an astonishingly lax and complacent set-up, and a successful IRA raid was mounted at 8.30 p.m. on the evening of 23 December 1939, pre-holiday torpor further reducing the alertness of the small, bored, unmotivated and wholly unprepared guard.[29] On this occasion, transportation had been well organised, and four lorry-loads of ammunition, amounting to well over a million rounds, most of the Irish Army's reserve, were removed in less than two hours.[30] This *matériel*, in itself, was all but useless in the IRA. A simultaneous raid had been planned on Islandbridge Barracks, to obtain the rifles to fire the stolen ammunition. This operation was cancelled at the last moment because the raiders could not get into the premises. The organisation therefore had lorry-loads of ammunition but no more weapons with which to use it.

The Army and the Gardaí reacted with roadblocks, raids, searches and arrests. A reward of £1,000 was offered for information leading to the recovery of the ammunition. IRA logistics, used to dribs and drabs of *matériel*, was overwhelmed. Security, poor management and perhaps a disbelief that they would pull it off meant that local units had been ill prepared and did not have enough hiding places. Galvanised and enraged, with careers to be made and lost, the police knew where to look and for whom; cash was not stinted on informers.[31] Vigorous police and army activity uncovered many long-established IRA dumps and gathered up supplies wholly unconnected with the Magazine Fort. Operations eventually recovered all, and then some more, ammunition. Raids also netted a number of IRA men of various ranks, several of whom were each sentenced to twelve years' penal servitude.[32] Under emergency legislation it was an offence (as it was in Northern Ireland) to refuse to answer questions. Helpfully for the police and the Army, the IRA had an inflexible standing order on the matter. Denied even the simplest tools of deception, the arrested men consigned themselves to prison, wilful silence putting a quality-control stamp on their detention.

The IRA had again poked an unprotected hand into a hornets' nest. Government anger – a compound of acute embarrassment, genuine fear and a helping of panic – was not to be assuaged by the full recovery of the *matériel*, even when this was garnished with many arrests and a deal of extra IRA equipment.[33] In times of complete tranquillity, such an episode would have been seen as a calculated challenge, an outrage requiring the strongest of responses. Doing it because it could be done rather than as part of a medium- or long-term strategy, the IRA had committed a grave error, for which it would pay a heavy price. Meeting in emergency session on 3 January 1940, a worried Dáil was more than ready to agree with Gerald Boland that further protective powers were urgently required.[34] The public mood appears to have been more than favourable. All residual complacency was dispelled, as Eunan O'Halpin observes, and a flood of information came in to the authorities.[35] The following day, the Emergency Powers (Amendment) Act, 1940, received Seanad approval.[36] The Offences Against the State (Amendment) Act (OAS[A]A) was passed by the Dáil on 5 January 1940. A number of constitutional objections were raised, pending resolution of which the measure could not come fully into operation.[37] That it would, or some version very close to it would, was beyond doubt; the government already had internment powers under the Emergency Powers Act, since the legislature had, the previous September, recognised and proclaimed the existence of an emergency. Belatedly, those IRA activists still at large took what precautions they could against the inevitable stepping up of mass internment. The mechanism now in the Minister's hands operated in the manner of a combine harvester. Men were brought before the Special Criminal Court and received short sentences – usually for refusing to answer questions. All that was necessary for conviction was a statement from the arresting officer.[38] On expiration of sentence, usually having taken no more than a few notionally free steps, the man was rearrested and interned.[39] IRA inflexibility and the comprehensiveness of the law were complementary and completed the job.[40] Thereafter, the only issue was to provide sufficient prison and camp places.[41]

Action and reaction

Prisoners were divided into internees and those convicted before a court, civil or military, even though the ultimate destination of a man sentenced was (with very few exceptions) an internment camp. Dublin was intensively policed, Special Branch eager and well resourced, and provided with many persons evidently willing to provide information. The country was small, and the domain of revolutionaries and Special Branch was even smaller. This was not Northern Ireland, where the IRA had a Catholic defence role, and where a nationalist minority, largely alienated from the state, could at least provide silence, cover and often sanctuary. De Valera and all other Southern politicians contested republican legitimacy with the IRA and made their own appeal to nationalist sentiment. It is hard now to be definite, but it is more than likely that many members of the public were worried about the threat posed to the state by international developments, which grew ever more alarming. Information was indeed forthcoming from police contacts and from members of the public, but a number of arrests arose from street and public transport surveillance and from intensive patrolling. As noted several times above, the IRA was fixated on Dublin, treating it as its indispensable administrative centre, acquiring a succession of offices and safe houses and regularly drawing in activists from all parts of the country for meetings and conferences – and for easy arrest.[42]

The IRA's political ineptitude and trajectory of seemingly purposeless confrontation helped the government to rally public opinion. In an attempted gaol break on 22 October 1939, explosives had been used against the perimeter wall at Mountjoy Prison.[43] There were no injuries, but this was an alarming event, in an urban area with a hospital and many dwellings in the vicinity: it also indicated a fierceness of intent that overrode public safety. Most of the IRA's available cash was apparently seized in the Rathmines raid of 9 September 1939, and the organisation urgently needed to replace it. Wartime postal censorship and restrictions on travel had already begun to close off American sources of funds, and robbery became a practical necessity. The sums were large; £5,000 was taken from the Amiens Street Post Office (Dublin) on 18 November 1939.[44] A bank raid followed on 23 November. Just over a week later, a bread van was stopped on Dublin's North Strand. The driver was seriously wounded and some £469 stolen.[45] An elaborate tale needed to be spun to convince the public that this was more than mere banditry.

Worse followed. On 3 January 1940, Detective Officer John Roche was gravely wounded as he attempted to arrest Tomás MacCurtáin in Cork; Roche died the following day.[46] This put much wind in the government's sails as it secured Dáil passage of the Emergency Powers (Amendment) Bill the same day. Speaking to the Seanad on 5 January 1940 as the Offences Against the State (Amendment) Bill proceeded there, Boland contended that a lot of his old republican comrades 'had unconsciously become criminals'. He rejected the argument that they should be called something other than criminals: 'A man who commits a crime is a criminal. I don't care whether he has been a friend or comrade of mine in the past or not, it is all the same to me – if he commits a crime he should be made amenable for it.'[47]

Even after the emergency legislation passed, the IRA offered continued and undiminished enthusiasm to press on government reasons for suppressing it. On 10 February 1940, four armed men raided the British Army camp at Ballykinlar, Co. Down, taking more than 100 new rifles. This was another mindless episode.[48] Perhaps the idea was to provoke trouble between Northern Ireland and the South, or with the British government; more likely, no consideration was given to the aftermath, which was heightened urgency in Dublin's actions against the IRA. According to Tim Pat Coogan, who interviewed men active at the time, the raid did not even have a logistical purpose, since the organisation did not have ammunition to fit the rifles.[49] It is likely that during this period, besides the fractured political vision of the IRA, its leadership was misled by a surge in morale following the Magazine Fort raid and then the widespread sympathy for Barnes and McCormick. As we have seen, the two men had been sentenced to death on 14 December 1939 for their part in the Coventry bomb of 25 August. Their appeals ran their course, reprieve was refused, and they were executed in Birmingham on 7 February 1940.[50] Far outside the IRA, Irish opinion condemned the British government's decision. Cinemas and other entertainment venues in Dublin and Cork were closed on that day. Since militant republicans were central to the demonstrations and to demands for clemency, it was all too easy (especially if one lived within tight IRA circles and had poorly functioning political antennae) to mistake a single-issue upsurge in sentiment for more general sympathy and incipient support.

The folly of summoning activists to Dublin was, it seems, beyond the IRA's calculations, and on 17 February 1940 a joint police and army raid on the Meath Hotel netted staff officers of the IRA's Western Brigade and several of the GHQ, including Belfast man Michael Traynor, the IRA's Adjutant General. Money and an inventory of arms and ammunition held by certain western units were also captured. Two days later, fifteen men appeared before the Special Criminal Court and were given sentences of between three and six months: all were destined for internment until war's end.[51] Bravado was undiminished, and on 31 March another army and police operation rounded up twenty-three men illegally drilling in the grounds of St Anne's in the Dublin suburb of Raheny. Sentences ranged between six months and two years.[52] Threats were issued to Dublin's newspapers on 8 April, and four days later Radio Éireann's Cork studio was raided by three men, and a five-minute broadcast was made, largely comprising of IRA threats against the government.[53] Over the following weeks there were other incidents: a spectacular bomb attack on Special Branch which injured several people at Dublin Castle on 25 April 1940 and, on 7 May, a raid on mail being carried to the Department of External Affairs.[54] Two detectives (William MacSweeney and William Shanahan), who refused to surrender the mail, were wounded.[55]

After the mail raid, de Valera broadcast. At the moment when small nations throughout Europe were strengthening their unity in defence of their independence, a group had chosen to try to destroy the country's 'organised life'. Over the previous few years, every obstacle that could possibly be used to justify political violence had been removed. The government had, for many years, shown extraordinary patience, 'I am afraid that I must say, now, an excessive patience towards these people. Putting our hope in patience, we punished mildly and with reluctance, and we forgave easily.' This policy had failed. The government would do its part in ridding the country of the deadly conspiracy and armed menace. The people should assist: 'If they value what has been won for them they will now, as in the days of the Black and Tans, be the eyes and ears of the national defence.'[56]

There was immediate support from Fine Gael, the largest opposition party. W. T. Cosgrave, its leader (and former head of government) had been due to issue a writ for a by-election in West Galway (arising from the death ten months previously of Seán Tubridy, a Fianna Fáil deputy). He announced that in a show of unity, at a time when armed attempts were being made on the authority of the government, his party would not contest the election. Further, he would not move the writ for a by-election in Co. Kilkenny, where one of his own party had been the incumbent. Nothing would be done until the Taoiseach was able to confirm that the danger of civil disturbance had passed, lest this might then be interpreted as a lack of support for the policies that it had taken in recent months to defend the state.[57] The ranks of constitutional politicians further closed up on 28 May 1940 when, to the backdrop of Belgian surrender to German forces, de Valera announced the formation of an inter-party National Defence Council. Senior politicians from Fine Gael and the Labour Party joined ministers in this largely symbolic body.[58] Two weeks later, the leaders of the three main parties appeared together on the platform at a mass meeting in Dublin's College Green. Calling for national unity, they urged all those eligible to join one of the various national-defence services.[59]

Such unprecedented accord was the background to the government's most determined steps to suppress the IRA. On 3 June 1940, Boland issued some 400 detention orders.[60] If internment were mainly a preventive measure, an addition to the Emergency Powers Act was its deterrent counterpart. This was introduced two days after the mass round-up of 3 June and passed all parliamentary stages within three weeks. Far more drastic than anything available to the UK authorities, the new power underscored the deep alarm within political and other influential circles about the security and very existence of the state. The Emergency Powers (Amendment No. 2) Act, 1940, Section 3, gave the government the authority to make an order for the summary trial by military court of anyone accused of an offence specified in the order. Upon conviction, there would be a sentence of death – 'and no appeal shall lie in respect of such conviction and sentence'. The Military Court, in other words, was limited to two courses: acquittal or the death sentence.[61] The Minister for Justice promised that the powers, which amounted to executive legislation, trial and sentence, would be used only in the most extreme of cases and that the death sentence would be carried out speedily should the government not decide to commute or remit the sentence. The measure would meet existing conditions of a state of war.[62]

Quite apart from the continuing activities of the IRA, Europe's conflagration fed the sense of profound alarm in Dublin. In May 1940, the phoney war ended with a German sweep through the Low Countries. Dunkirk was evacuated, Norway surrendered, Italy entered the war, and on 22 June 1940 in France, Marsal Philippe Pétain signed an armistice with Germany. The battle of Britain began in July, and Hitler began the preparations for an invasion of Britain, his last functioning military opposition in Europe. This was a summer that promised a terrible autumn and relentless winter.

The IRA sailed on. Apart from endlessly pronouncing anathema on the Irish state, it had never really factored that entity's reality into its strategic and political thinking. To overthrow it would mean a return to civil war, disregarding all electoral expressions, inviting outside intervention and, in all of this, massive loss of life and destruction. Through the two major political parties and a host of other organisations, the roots of the state had reach and grip, and only cataclysmic upheaval could hope to sweep them away. As the IRA had pursued its course throughout the preceding years, illegalities were apt to be widely and at times indulgently regarded as an excess of patriotic zeal. If prosecuted, egregious breaches of the law had generally attracted fairly light penalties and, no doubt, a blind eye here and there – or mild admonition from various minor officials and local figures. Had the European war not erupted there probably would have been a longer lead-in to the inevitable confrontation with de Valera, but it had been in the making since Fianna Fáil came to power. Without the appalling and urgent dangers of the summer of 1940 it is doubtful that de Valera would have needed or wanted the draconian measures that he had taken: equally doubtful that the Dáil, the Church and the judiciary would have been so compliant. But now the scene was clear to all: Ireland was a lifeboat cast on darkening, stormy and uncertain seas, and there could be but one captain if it were to survive.[63]

IRA men continued to resist arrest by firing at police, to collect and distribute large quantities of arms, to make explosives, to organise prison escapes, to kill and to drill and train.[64] As noted, on 16 August 1940, there was a determined attempt to escape a Special Branch raid on IRA training and storage premises at 98A Rathgar Road, Dublin. Patrick McGrath, IRA Director of Training, Francis Harte (alias Thomas Green) and Thomas Hunt, opened fire with revolvers and a Thompson gun. Detective Richard Hyland was killed instantly, Sergeant Patrick McKeown died next day of his wounds and Detective Michael Brady was severely injured. Francis Harte was wounded in the leg as he escaped and Patrick McGrath returned to help him.[65] Both men were then arrested. The following day they appeared before the Military Court and were remanded until 20 August. Following trial and a guilty verdict, a death sentence was passed, but execution was delayed by a conditional order of habeas corpus, granted on 23 August. On 25 August, the same judge (Mr Justice Gavan Duffy) heard full arguments and rejected the application. Seán MacBride (former IRA Chief of Staff but now practising law) applied to the Supreme Court.[66] After a three-day hearing that court unanimously rejected the appeal. Patrick McGrath and Francis Harte were executed by firing squad in Mountjoy Prison on the morning of Friday, 6 September 1940.[67] With these first executions of IRA men since the Civil War, several lines of profound political, psychological and cultural significance were crossed. The new powers had been thoroughly tested and found compliant with the Constitution, and the two men had been tried and executed within three weeks of their crime.[68] No less tested was the will of de Valera and his government. All doubts and hesitations had been set aside.

Cinemas in Cork received threats from the IRA should they not close on 9 September as a mark of respect for Patrick McGrath and Francis Harte ('murdered in Mountjoy prison'). Forty-four known republicans were immediately rounded up.[69] No cinemas closed, and all performances were held without incident. Arms raids were frequent and often fruitful. Sentences for the possession of arms now increased significantly. On 17 October 1940, in the case of Patrick Conway, the Special Criminal Court handed down four years' penal servitude for his possession of a radio transmitter. Unlike a Miss O'Connor (who avoided her two-year sentence by entering into a recognisance to keep the peace), those in possession were given heavy sentences of penal servitude. Two men who had opened fire on gardaí on 8 November 1940, without causing injury, were sent down for fourteen years by the Special Criminal Court a fortnight or so later.[70] By the end of 1940, 'Times already bad grew worse', noted J. Bowyer Bell.[71] Three years later, observes Uinseann MacEoin, a chronicler with direct and intimate knowledge of these men and women and of events, 'one could say that north and south there was not a kick left in the organisation'.[72]

Hitler's invasion of the Soviet Union in June 1941 extinguished all hopes of Germany overwhelming Britain. And then bile and rottenness began to spew out of the IRA itself. The accusations against its Chief of Staff, Stephen Hayes, were devastating. One youthful new recruit described his feelings as the denunciation was read out to his unit: 'That we were dumbfounded would be an understatement... We felt utterly demoralised... My heart felt chopped in two as I left the darkened mill at the Liffey-side that night.'[73] To rally the ranks and show defiance in the face of the devastating round-ups, the Dublin IRA decided on a bizarre gesture of defiance and on Easter Sunday 1942 marched en masse to the republican graves at Glasnevin Cemetery.[74] As an identity parade the event could not have been bettered, and Special Branch was out in force. Numerous arrests followed.[75] In the years 1939–45, a total of 463 were received under sentence and 1,196 as internees.[76]

Military custody

Some optimism apparently prevailed at this point, even as large numbers of IRA men entered captivity. It would be better by far to have men free and available for action, but past experience taught that imprisonment, for those whose nerve and commitment held, gave many opportunities to take the struggle in other directions, to harass the authorities, to train and regroup and to harvest public sympathy. The difficulty, of course, in drawing on such a counsel of comfort is that history never repeats itself exactly.

From the outset, little distinction was made in the matter of regime between most convicted prisoners and the internees. While this benefited the convicted, it imposed more restrictions on internees than would have been justified were standards taken, as they should have been, from those appropriate to civil detention. This approach arose more from the staffing resources available than from any considered evaluation of internee status in equity or in the recent usages of imprisonment. At a meeting of the Cabinet Subcommittee on Internal Security on 19 February 1940, it was decided that persons sentenced by the Special Criminal Court to penal servitude should be confined in Mountjoy Prison. A number of proposals were put to the Minister for Justice for the rules that would govern the treatment of these prisoners. They were to have the same dietary scale as convicts but the allowance of visits and letters applicable to non-penal servitude prisoners; all visits were to be conducted in the 'cage', a heavily screened visiting box. Newspapers would not be allowed, and the usual Mountjoy arrangements regarding smoking by convicted prisoners would apply. Those not engaged in outdoor work would be permitted two one-hour periods of outdoor exercise daily. In one significant and potentially troublesome respect a distinction would be drawn between these Special Criminal Court men and the generality of prisoners: they were to be allowed to wear their own clothes rather than prison uniforms.[77]

Early in March 1940, the Department of Defence submitted a memorandum to the Cabinet on internees and non-penal-servitude convicted prisoners. The impetus for the submission was the Army's need to staff the regime and the manpower demands of what it saw as its more expansive provisions.[78] The Department took particular exception to visiting and correspondence privileges and to the provision that various articles might be purchased for internees and prisoners by the governor of the prison. There was an allowance of one visit per month from relatives, with convicted prisoners being permitted an additional visit every three months from an unspecified person.[79] Such access, the Department noted, enabled internees and prisoners to keep in close touch with their friends outside – IRA and republican contacts, in other words. Visits also 'furnish an opportunity for certain internees and prisoners to make lying statements to visitors as regards their treatment'. More to the point, one suspects, there was the objection that the supervision of visits imposed additional work on prison staff.[80]

The provisions for correspondence and the purchase of items from outside were also queried, on staffing grounds. The work of censoring correspondence was 'considerable'. Under the Directions and Regulations, the governor of a prison could purchase various goods for his charges. These items included clothes, books, fruit and other food, stationery, tobacco and cigarettes. With some justification, the Department noted that the provision of this shopping service involved a deal of accountancy.

The curtailment of these obligations and the saving of manpower required some loss of amenity for internees and prisoners. The most drastic proposal was to prohibit all regular visits, allowing them 'only in exceptional circumstances and at the discretion of the Attorney General'. The proposals for correspondence and for supplies were modest: cutting the entitlement to outward correspondence to one letter per week and the deletion of some food items from the list of permitted purchases. The last would impose little hardship, the Department argued, since the rations for internees and prisoners were similar to those provided for soldiers.[81]

The government was not willing to go as far as Defence desired. The proposal for visits, in particular, offended against widely and strongly held beliefs about family ties and loyalties. With a substantial number of persons in custody politicians might be apprehensive about the representations they would face from constituents. There was also the traditional republican attitude to politically motivated prisoners to be considered: many in the legislature and even in government had in the past campaigned inside and outside prison on precisely this issue.

Yet even with these changes the regime for internees and prisoners in military custody remained basic but not punitive.[82] Allowing for differences in layout and facilities, much the same routine was followed at the Curragh and at Arbour Hill. The day began at 7 a.m. with reveille, bed-making and cell-cleaning. Arbour Hill prisoners then left their cells to cast out their slops and to collect fresh water. Breakfast was collected by orderlies at 8 a.m., delivered to cells and eaten by 8.30 a.m. Inspection followed at 8.45, and at 9 a.m. came a general unlocking for exercise, which continued until 12.30. Lunch was collected at 12.45 and eaten by 1.20. Exercise and classes took the afternoon to 5 p.m. Thirty minutes was allowed for tea, followed by more exercise and association, until 9 p.m. when supper was served. Lights out was at 10 p.m.[83]

A comprehensive set of rules detailed offences against discipline. As would be expected, prisoners and internees were obliged to obey the orders of staff and were forbidden to show disrespect. Idleness, bad language, indecency, making excessive noise or giving 'unnecessary trouble' were prohibited, as was the possession of any unauthorised article or leaving one's cell or other appointed location without permission. Escapes were, of course, against the rules, as was any connivance in such. There were catch-all clauses: attempts were treated the same as substantive breaches, and there was the gaoler's standby, prohibiting acts that offended 'against good order and discipline' in any way.[84]

Personal obligations and privileges were also governed by rules. Prisoners had to keep themselves, their clothing and their cells clean and their hair cut and had to comply with orders concerning all of these. Legal visits were restricted as to purpose.[85] No limit was placed on incoming mail, but all correspondence was subject to censorship. Recreation was permitted in the form of classes, handicrafts and hobbies, all subject to the governor's permission. A member of staff had to be present during all classes. Prisoners were not allowed to hold cash personally, but funds could be held on their behalf by the prison. From these, again subject to the governor's approval, clothes, books, stationery, fruit, tobacco and cigarettes could be purchased.[86]

Protests

The fuel rod of the protest engine was always the demand for political status: the term itself was elastic as were the conditions it justified. It was invariably affirmed that patriots were not criminals and that only criminals treated them as such. This axiom precipitated protests, inside and outside, and usually a hunger strike; in propitious times, humanitarian or sentimental sympathy or political solidarity could be generated across a swathe of the otherwise uncommitted. Should political status be granted, four important points of leverage were gained: an element of moral ascendancy over the authorities; a progressive cowing and marginalisation of staff; the opportunity to turn the prison into a revolutionary training academy; and the consolidation of a platform from which other demands could be made, never intended to be satisfied. The Cosgrave government, many of whose members had themselves pursued such tactics against the British, had been prepared to sit out hunger strikes and had broken the mass strike in 1923. The de Valera administration, equally acquainted with the revolutionary potential of imprisonment but drawing support from an electorate particularly volatile on political prisoner issues, had previously proved unwilling to let a striker die. Despite these releases under duress it was adamant that political status would not be conceded, in part because to do so would be an explicit acceptance of IRA accusations of Fianna Fáil apostasy. A conflict of particular bitterness seemed inevitable.

There were preliminary skirmishes over relatively minor matters. One such was the screen dividing internees from their visitors. This was three feet high, running from one side of the counter at which visits were conducted to the other and was intended to stop contraband being passed. It comprised double mesh with a gap of about six inches between the two. Internees arrested in the 15 September round-ups had had their first visits at Arbour Hill on 15 October, in accordance with the regulations. They protested about the screens, which, they said, humiliated them and their visitors. They were internees, not convicted criminals, and refused to accept any further visits under such conditions that made them seem 'little better than animals housed in some Zoological Institution'. Commandant Michael Lennon, the Governor of Arbour Hill, seemed to agree, at least to some extent. He wrote to the Provost Marshal, pointing out that the screen had been 'a constant source of trouble' with the internees: with the second set of visits coming up on 15 November, could the screen be modified? He proposed that the barrier be reduced from thirty-six to twelve inches. This would allow visitors and internees to see each other but would remain an effective guard against contraband being passed. The proposal was agreed by the Provost Marshal but vetoed by the Adjutant General. The screen remained in place.[87]

Wills were tested over more central issues in those first months of wartime conditions. Charlie McCarthy, an Arbour Hill prisoner, refused food from 16 September until 12 October 1939 and was then released.[88] Hard on the heels of this clemency came a strong warning that other hunger-striking prisoners would not be released.[89] Three Cork men (Jeremiah Daly, Richard McCarthy and John Lynch) refused food on 15 October 1939.[90] They were individually warned of the government's determination not to release them but, equally, had before them the example of Charlie McCarthy and also of Con Lehane. The latter had taken the very grave step of refusing liquids as well as food on 12 October. Death would follow very quickly. A week later, his case was raised in the Dáil by William Norton, the Labour deputy leader.[91] Some back-room understanding was then seemingly reached, and Lehane (who had broken with the IRA the previous year) took sustenance at some point before 24 October and was released on 2 December 1939, in consequence of the Burke habeas corpus decision.[92]

It seemed that the government was prepared to issue dire warnings but then to fudge rather than see a man die. Its credibility was under threat, and evidence of a failure of nerve would certainly have more general and long-term consequences. The cases of Daly, Lynch and Richard McCarthy were raised by Labour, the Parliamentary Group of which adopted a resolution, on 8 November 1939, asking for the release of all hunger-striking prisoners. De Valera confirmed his 'no release' position in a Dáil statement the following day.[93] Despite this, another deal was done. Jeremiah Daly accepted food two days later and was released on 14 November. The other two men had been sufficiently weakened that on 18 November they were removed to St Bricin's Military Hospital from which, after treatment, they were freed.[94] Patrick McGrath (who would be executed the following year) had a similar history. He was arrested on 22 October 1939, remanded and went on hunger strike on that same day, averring that he would have his freedom or die. By 15 November he had supposedly so deteriorated that he was removed to Jervis Street Hospital, even though a three-week fast would not normally be life-threatening. He was released as part of the Burke decision exodus. He left hospital on 4 December, and three days later a *nolle prosequi* was entered at the Special Criminal Court.[95] The government's credibility was crumbling to the point where, as de Valera had forecast, nobody could be held for a political offence were he willing to accept the privations of a hunger strike for a few weeks: much of the point of the emergency legislation, enacted and in prospect, was in doubt.[96]

During the course of a debate on the Offences Against the State (Amendment) Bill, 1940, the Minister for Justice Gerald Boland was pressed by Senator Desmond FitzGerald about a series of unequivocal statements that had been made by de Valera only to be followed – more or less immediately – by backdowns and releases. On the surface, it did look bad, Boland conceded. To make a statement and then to go back on it conveyed weakness. Patience and conciliation had been overstretched. But this was now going to stop: 'There is no question of ruthlessness or rigour, but I am sure that there is going to be insistence that everybody in this country will obey the law.'[97]

As Boland was speaking, he must surely have been aware of an emptiness in his rhetoric: who in Ireland thought that patience and conciliation would have affected the IRA's goals and commitment to action. Would the release of a few hunger-strikers reconcile their comrades to the state? Who would now believe that determination proclaimed by the government? Still carrying a note of desperation and openness to deals, the statements of de Valera and Boland would be probed by a group of prominent IRA men. There was some indication that this next action was not, as other strikes had seemed to be, a spontaneous action. The group's demand was not for release but for free association.[98] Freedom of movement would transform the nature of confinement, give substantial control of their lives inside and allow them to implement well-tried routines and programmes to serve their revolutionary cause. In the event of a future confrontation with the authorities – and one would certainly be engineered – they would be in a more advantageous position to counter attempts to control and subdue them. This was like a textbook infantry assault: fire, probe the flanks, dig in, fire again. To reinforce their new campaign, they also demanded the transfer to Arbour Hill (and thus military custody) of two men (John Dwyer and Nicholas Doherty) serving sentences of penal servitude in Mountjoy.

There were some individual hunger strikes, but none lasted or was able to secure concessions. Only a collective effort with outside support stood any chance of success.[99] A major test of wills commenced on 25 February 1940, when seven leading IRA men refused food at Mountjoy Prison, demanding political status.[100] By this time, a tense and troubled atmosphere had developed at Mountjoy. On occasions, there had been quite serious hand-to-hand fighting with prison staff and police reinforcements.[101] The prisoners particularly objected to the fact that men sentenced to penal servitude were being obliged to submit to convict rules and to don prison uniform. Given the circumstances and nature of their offences, they demanded that all sentenced by the Special Criminal Court be held in military custody 'and get the same treatment as is being meted out to the men in Arbour Hill Military Prison at present'.[102] The focus for conflict was the penal-servitude (convict) wing of Mountjoy and not the wing for those sentenced to ordinary imprisonment.

The seven hunger-strikers were Tony D'Arcy; Thomas Grogan, facing charges in connection with the Magazine Fort raid; John Lyons, who dropped out of the strike after nine days; Tomás MacCurtáin, charged with murder; Seán McNeela; Jack Plunkett, involved in running the IRA's radio station; and Michael Traynor, imprisoned for refusing to answer questions.[103] They were facing a variety of charges and were at different stages in their proceedings, but all commenced the action together. Eventually they were transferred to Arbour Hill (though only after violent resistance from their comrades in the case of McNeela and MacCurtáin). The strike was to last well into April, despite attempts by clergy, friends, sympathetic politicians and other intermediaries to resolve it. A decisive factor, strengthening the hand of the government, was the extent and severity of press censorship. Very brief and simple reporting was allowed, commentary and feature articles were not. Without a chance to rouse public opinion, there was little prospect of success.[104] The government was now determined not to give in; the men, all experienced and deeply committed, were willing to see matters through. Tony D'Arcy died at St Bricin's Military Hospital in the early hours of 16 April 1940, after a strike of fifty-one days. The strike ended on the evening of 19 April, but this was too late to save Seán McNeela who died just under three hours later, having refused food for fifty-five days.[105] As the strike was entering its concluding phases there had been a flurry of visits from parents and other members of the close family, as well as from clergy and solicitors.[106] Jack Plunkett and Michael Traynor then remained for some time in hospital, recovering. Grogan and MacCurtáin made swifter recoveries.

The Arbour Hill prisoners, assembled for evening association, had staged a brief protest on 19 April 1940. Referring to the death of Tony D'Arcy, Larry Grogan, the OC, promised that the remaining five would continue. To show their defiance, six more, himself included, would go on hunger strike that night: they were fighting for the same concessions that Thomas Ashe had died for in 1917, and several others since.[107] In the light of what was to happen forty years later, when Maze prisoners embarked on serial hunger-striking, it is possible (but far from certain) that Grogan and his comrades might, had they begun to die one by one, have wrung some concessions. No account has survived of the prisoners' discussions after McNeela's death, but, however arrived at, the conclusion was that de Valera and Boland would not give in. The six did not begin a new strike, and the four survivors of the existing strike accepted food.[108] De Valera's will was not tested further.[109]

The immediate political fallout for the government was mixed and, in any event, masked by the all-pervasive censorship. Fine Gael, which had fretted that the government had shown insufficient resolve in dealing with earlier episodes of hunger-striking, demonstrated its support and relief by not fielding a candidate in the Galway by-election. This was particularly important since Tony D'Arcy came from Headford, Co. Galway, and, if a protest vote was going to materialise anywhere, it would be there. In the event, the Fianna Fáil victory in the by-election was substantial and offered no comfort to those who wished it to be a response to the death of D'Arcy.[110]

Both de Valera and Boland paid a more immediate personal price for their hunger-strike firmness. At the annual Easter commemoration at Arbour Hill, when wreaths are laid on the graves of the 1916 leaders shot by the British, Philomena Plunkett, sister of Joseph Mary Plunkett (one of those being remembered and honoured) and of Jack Plunkett, then on hunger strike, shouted at de Valera, denouncing him as a traitor. In themselves, Philomena's connections would not greatly have discountenanced de Valera, since other relatives of leading republican figures had done much the same. But to see and hear such naked anger at the most solemn moment in the republican year, and in such a sacred place, could not but have been shocking to all present, including de Valera.[111]

At the inquests on D'Arcy and McNeela, Gerald Boland was shouted at and taunted by IRA sympathisers in the public gallery, and Seán MacBride, now appearing as barrister for the relatives of the dead men, mounted a penetrating cross-examination. In later years, Boland recalled his appearance at the inquest as 'one of the worst experiences I have ever had'. Unpleasant though it was, Boland was not afraid to tell the inquest jury what he had told the Dáil and the Seanad: that the government would retreat no further from the hunger-strikers, having already been too willing to do so.[112] Time and the chance to reflect away from the pressure of events did not alter Boland's views. The Mountjoy hunger strike had been a climacteric in the life of the nation. Had the government given way and conceded to the strikers, its authority would have evaporated, and resignation was inevitable. This, Boland believed, would have allowed chaos to destroy the country. So emotive and emblematic had hunger-striking been in the birth and life of the young nation that Boland's claim cannot be dismissed. A running flank attack by the IRA on the core institutions of state, using the hunger-strikers as cover, could well have precipitated a deeply destructive, possibly fatal, series of events.[113]

In the late spring of 1943, there was another hunger strike, at the Curragh, this time for unconditional release. On 23 May 1943, eight men submitted a letter to the government stating that they would refuse food until they were freed. By early July, only three were maintaining the strike. At this point, the men (Seán McCool, John G. O'Doherty and Terence McLoughlin) had been without food for forty-four days. Entering the dangerous and possibly fatal stage of hunger-striking, the death zone, their case was raised in the Dáil by William Norton, Labour leader.[114] Boland's response was unequivocal and unyielding: the men would not be freed.

Much of Boland's argument was a repeat of what he had said three years before. No one in the Dáil had objected to internment, and it was his judgement, on police advice, that the men were a menace to public safety and could not be released. Norton pressed the matter in a subsequent adjournment debate, with much the same results. He was concerned about the adverse effects of the men's death, should that occur. There would be damage to national unity at a critical time, and, moreover, since the men were now weakened – were invalids – as a result of their strike, they could not be a danger to the state.[115] Three other deputies expressed their agreement, each adding his particular gloss.

Boland was in no mood to give way, and, besides the general argument in favour of internment, he had specific points to make about the hunger-strikers. One of the men (Seán McCool) had previously been released, against strong police advice. Boland had decided to give McCool 'a fair chance' and ruefully reported the results of his leniency: 'inside three months we found that he was acting as Chief of Staff of the IRA'. All of the hunger-strikers' cases had been reviewed carefully, and he was not prepared to release them. Were he to give way to the hunger-strikers, it would mean that thereafter they could hold nobody. He would not give way: if the men died, 'the responsibility is on themselves'.[116] Faced with this determination the Curragh hunger strike collapsed.

Tony D'Arcy and Seán McNeela had died convinced that they were wielding a weapon which an Irish government, itself a beneficiary of the earlier generation's republican endurance and sacrifice, could not resist. Indifferent to the boundlessly threatening international context in which de Valera and his ministers now had to operate, and which changed by the day, this was a fatal miscalculation. That there existed a degree of humanitarian sympathy for the two was shown in the proceedings of the inquests, but no one suggested that this sadness and regret cleared the way for an IRA victory. From the government's point of view, the two deaths had finally affirmed and proclaimed its willingness fully to enforce the emergency legislation. Breaking down in the face of a strike thereafter would carry the additional opprobrium of having needlessly wrought the deaths of D'Arcy and McNeela. But, apart from the notable hunger strike of Jeremiah Daly and fifteen other men against the Curragh Camp Council in March 1942, there was little danger of organised hunger-striking.[117] Individuals did threaten it, and some did embark upon it, but usually as a personal protest against decisions by the authorities.[118] Throughout the period 1939–46 there were a total of sixty-six hunger strikes but only seven in the years 1944–6.[119] Since in the Curragh political status had been given in full to men who were, by definition, political prisoners, there were few grounds on which to gather support for a strike.

Short of hunger-striking, there were individual protests at various points, though these seem generally to have been self-defeating or self-damaging. In February 1940, for example, Michael Dowling, serving a sentence at Arbour Hill, refused to accept a visit (from a friend who had travelled all the way from Tralee) as a protest against the wire barrier that had been installed in the visits hut. Other men refused to see relatives and friends for the same reason.[120]

Arbour Hill

Arbour Hill Military Prison (officially, Arbour Hill Detention Barracks), well sited amidst the barracks and other British-built military premises spread out along the Liffey, played an important part in both internment and in imprisonment throughout the war. Although internees and those sentenced by the Special Criminal Court were civilians, Arbour Hill remained under military control. In the autumn of 1939 it held a slightly fluctuating population of around sixty internees. As we have seen, following the Burke decision, the Department of Justice was obliged to release all internees on 2 December 1939.[121] By New Year, however, Arbour Hill was again holding civilian prisoners, though now men under sentence. A total of eighty-three were serving time by mid-February 1940, with numbers fluctuating throughout the year, again averaging around sixty.[122] Personnel of the German armed forces were also held at Arbour Hill, generally for short periods pending transfer to the Curragh.[123]

Remarkably for a Victorian prison, Arbour Hill had no cell heating. Since the system of warm-air heating via flues was standard in all British prisons constructed from the mid-nineteenth century onward, the omission was presumably intended as an additional punitive element.[124] Whilst this hardship could be endured by healthy young soldiers serving short sentences, spending only limited time in their cells and subject to the vigorous and physically demanding regime imposed by armies on recalcitrants, it would have quite a different effect on long-term civilian prisoners, many of whom were unfit for reception into such custody or who were past their physical prime.

Commandant Michael Lennon, Governor of Arbour Hill when the first civil prisoners arrived in 1939, realised the degree of hardship entailed in prolonged close confinement. At that point, internees were locked in their cells for eighteen hours daily, from 4.30 p.m. to 9 a.m. and from 12.30 to 2 p.m. With the onset of the winter months, the period out of cell was due to be reduced further (because of security concerns during extended hours of darkness). Captain Lennon recommended against this curtailment of out-of-cell association.[125] The Provost General decided against him. The following month, the internees, putting their case in a reasonable and non-confrontational manner, made application for an extension of hours of association. Robert (Bob) Clements, their spokesman, asked for an additional two hours out each evening. Lennon did not go that far, but in his report to the Provost Marshal he urged that an additional thirty minutes each day would be beneficial to both prisoners and staff. This was approved 'on the understanding that it will not interfere with the safe custody of the Internees'.[126] The following spring when, as a wartime daylight-saving measure, clocks were advanced earlier in the year, Lennon secured yet more out-of-cell time, arguing that this would aid discipline since men locked in for protracted periods shouted from cell to cell, breaking the glass in their windows the better to communicate.[127]

The regime itself was not penal, apart from the prolonged cellular confinement. After 1940, prisoners had longer periods of association out of cells, in practice from morning unlocking until late evening. Classes were organised and generally held every day, the most consistently popular being Irish.[128] In his weekly despatches to the Provost Marshal the Governor was able, for the most part, to report a quiet and orderly prison. There were occasional lapses but very few acts of concerted defiance. The rare occasions stand out on which a man was punished for a prison offence or where he staged a protest.[129] We can reasonably infer that prisoners did not find the discipline irksome beyond the fact of custody itself. Indeed, the Governor and his staff took an active interest in the welfare of their charges. Parole was granted for grave and urgent family matters, and, on one occasion, Lennon went to some trouble to get replacement boots for his prisoners from army stocks, twice reporting that several men's footwear was unfit.[130]

Conditions at Arbour Hill appear to have been satisfactory for most prisoners. In late 1943, notes taken of a conversation between a prisoner (Seán Hamill) and his visitor (Ann McBride) illustrated this point. Conditions were good in 'the

Hill', Hamill said, so good that the prisoners 'had no grumble against the prison, food or staff' and, as a result, were inclined to turn against each other.[131]

More sombrely, it was to Arbour Hill that Francis Harte and Patrick McGrath were taken after sentence of death had been passed by the Military Court on 10 August 1940.[132] They stayed at the prison during subsequent legal challenges to the sentence but were removed to Mountjoy on the evening of 5 September and executed there the following morning.[133] Seán McCaughey was another of those under sentence of death received at the prison. In his case, the sentence was commuted, a week after the judgment, to life at penal servitude.[134]

Cork Prison

The smaller provincial prisons were occasionally used to hold IRA men, but this, almost invariably, was a temporary matter, pending transfer to Mountjoy or to the Curragh. In the summer of 1940, both Limerick and Cork prisons were used in this way, particularly following the big round-up of 3 June 1940. Within a few days, the Limerick men were moved to Cork. The regime was fairly relaxed, with free daytime movement between the cells. Various escape attempts were made, and a tunnel was dug from the condemned cell to the perimeter wall. A tunnel to meet it was dug from the grounds of the adjoining La Retraite Convent. This unintentionally broke cover on 8 July 1940, and the military police opened fire, killing John Joe Kavanagh.[135]

Derry Kelleher, a student when caught up in the 3 June arrests, remembered the 'benign control' of the prison's military governor, Commandant MacHenry, who allowed him to have textbooks sent in and apparently held out the prospect of parole to allow him to sit examinations. Internees had been collected from all over Munster, the majority located in the north wing of the prison. The Cork City men were mainly assigned to the formerly female south wing. As was customary, each wing had its own IRA command structure. The internees and military knew that this was an interlude and that long-term accommodation was going to be elsewhere. Arrangements accordingly, were of a temporary nature and rather informal. Kelleher remembered 'a period of tranquillity' broken only by the shooting of John Joe Kavanagh.[136]

The Mother Superior of La Retraite was horrified by her new neighbours, and, writing to the Minister for Defence, she explained her distress. Parts of the prison overlooked the convent, and, following the arrival of the internees, there emanated from it 'incessant and most raucous shoutings and yells, a well-nigh unceasing racket and unnerving din'. The disturbance was greatest at night and on Sunday was added to by the 'still more objectionable and intolerable din from abettors'. The latter came into the convent grounds and climbed onto out-buildings in order to make contact with the internees. 'Sleep', the Mother Superior lamented, 'has become impossible.' Indeed, the new arrivals had wrought such a change that 'life has become well-nigh impossible'. Several students had given notice that they would not return in the autumn if the conditions persisted, and retreats that had been booked for the summer months would have to be cancelled. Could not the Minister do something to end the 'misery' in which the convent was living?[137]

Cork police then acted. The Superintendent in charge concurred with the facts stated by the Mother Superior. For the first week or so after the arrival of the internees, 'a large crowd of unruly persons' assembled in the vicinity of the prison. The prisoners were boisterous, and there was much shouting, to and fro. 'Strenuous' police action had reduced the level of nuisance, but, since the prison was in an area of heavy pedestrian traffic, shouting to passers-by had continued; it was not a suitable place in which to hold political prisoners.[138]

Conditions were so relaxed that, until there was an attack on some of their number, the military police guarding the prisoners would play cards with them in their cells. Even following this incident, internee Pierce Fennell recalled, 'there was a bit of friction, but otherwise no hassle'. So amiable were relations and so inexperienced the guard that an elementary part of gaol-craft, the searching of prisoners, was overlooked. Even as the men were marshalled to leave the prison, this precaution was neglected.[139]

The internees remained at Cork Prison for ten weeks before transfer to the Curragh. Altogether there were about 170 men in the convoy, fifteen to a lorry, all handcuffed. There was heavy security along the route, and the convoy itself included a large military contingent and Bren gun carrier. Despite some trouble from the internees, including stone-throwing and damage to the army lorries, all arrived safely at the Curragh. Pierce Fennell did what he could to be disruptive and destructive en route, which one of his comrades objected to, threatening him with an IRA court martial for ripping the canvas cover of the lorry with a knife. When he asked what offence there was in damaging Free State property, he said that he would 'get our death of cold'. This produced an outbreak of derisive merriment from Fennell, with comments on the hardiness and soldierly qualities of the complainer.[140]

Mountjoy

Mountjoy Prison remained under civil control and was administered by the long-serving Seán Kavanagh.[141] The rules of engagement between staff and IRA prisoners, remand and sentenced alike, were well established, and there was little disposition on either side to change them. The prisoners refused to work and to wear prison uniform, and these points of discipline were conceded, with no fuss.[142] They were held initially in B Wing, separated from the ordinary prisoners, but denied the free association that they desired. The nature of the relationship between Kavanagh and his charges, and the general atmosphere, may be gleaned from an exchange he had with newly sentenced Christy Quearney and Seamus Murphy on their return from their Special Criminal Court hearing. The government had begun to warn of the prospect of imposing the death penalty for the possession of arms. Kavanagh greeted the pair and asked them how they had got on. Quearney replied that he had been sentenced to ten years' penal servitude and Murphy to seven. 'Thank God', Kavanagh exclaimed, 'it could have been worse.'[143]

The placid relationship between the IRA men and the administration was not ruffled by the B-Wing IRA OC, Denis Griffin, who in the main took his lead from Kavanagh. Another example of Kavanagh's relaxed style of management came in 1941 when several German prisoners, who had been convicted of spying and sentenced to penal servitude, were assigned to B Wing. Kavanagh approached Griffin with the proposition that, provided they did not associate with or become too friendly with the newcomers, extra privileges were on offer.[144]

In order to preserve this arrangement of mutual accommodation from being disturbed, it was decided that the men sentenced to penal servitude following the Curragh fire in December 1940 should be kept apart from those already in Mountjoy. The new arrivals were, accordingly, held in D Wing, separated from the main body of IRA prisoners. Kavanagh and his colleagues regarded the Curragh men as probable troublemakers and were anxious not to provide scope for their skills at Mountjoy. Segregation was maintained for two years, but early in 1943 the authorities felt sufficiently confident to move the erstwhile trouble-makers to B Wing.[145] Within a short time, however, Kavanagh got wind of an escape plan and moved all to D Wing, which housed the condemned cell, and which was in a more secure part of the prison.

On 31 October 1942, six men had escaped from B Wing. For some time, hacksaws had been smuggled into the prison. Under the cover of a German class, several men had been allowed to gather in a cell; their real business, however, was to saw through the cell bars. The night before the planned breakout, another group jumped the gun and got away. According to Christy Quearney, none of those who had first planned the escape were among the esca-pers – it appears to have been purely opportunistic, what in the gold-diggings would have been called claim-jumping.[146]

The mix at Mountjoy had become too rich, and it was inevitable that there would be further trouble in the form of a disturbance or even an escape. Either would have been an embarrassment to the authorities and to the government, profoundly unwelcome and distracting at a time of acute national and international tension. The prison itself and its civilian staff failed to provide sufficiently reassuring levels of security, and in June 1943, just a few weeks after they had been moved to D Wing, all the IRA prisoners were moved again – this time to Arbour Hill.

The Curragh

Ground down by catch-all legislation, faced by the relentless and white-knuckled determination of an anxious government living in dangerous times, a solid con-sensus between the political parties and a public which had apparently cast away its last dregs of sympathy, the detainees settled down to wait out the war. The camp population was hugely expanded by the round-ups that had started in June 1940, growing from around sixty to more than 450 a few weeks later.[147] This number remained stable for several months, and fluctuations were not great.[148] By 31 March 1943, 543 men and eighteen women were interned. A year later, the number had dropped to 240 men, and all women had been released.[149] The rent and much diminished nature of their organisation was bound to be reflected by IRA members inside the prisons and camps.[150] The Stephen Hayes affair, which became public knowledge in the autumn of 1941, was at least as devastating as the government's repressive measures, adding bewilderment, cynicism and disillusionment to a surreal mix. It would have required inspired and far-sighted leadership within and outside the camp to prevent a slide into what Bell describes as monotony, boredom, schism and dispute.[151] Nothing remotely akin to that quality of leadership now existed. Men enduring the loss of freedom, family, occupation and prospects, who had given unconditional trust, staking everything on the integrity, probity and judgement of their leaders, now faced the questionable value of their sacrifices. Without credible and convincing direction and some form of strategy to match, it was only a matter of time before those in captivity turned on each other. A remarkably foolish decision by the Curragh OC provided the catalyst.

Unlike conventional military organisations, the IRA elected its officers and had an elaborate constitution that preserved this electoral mandate to the highest level.[152] This ingenious blend of the military chain of command and democratic control from within made for unity and gave the IRA a degree of protection from the fissiparous tendencies endemic in revolutionary organisations. Whatever the organisation, its members understandably make a stronger commitment when they can see that the body they have joined or to which they have submitted themselves is itself accountable and under membership control. This organisational doctrine held both when at large and in captivity. Entering custody, IRA members crossed a line which, whilst it did not remove the overriding authority of the outside leadership, placed them under the operational control of an elected prison or camp leadership. The thinking was sensible: only those enduring prison and camp life were in a position to assume day-to-day command, to address privations, to encourage and exhort, to assess personal qualities, to resolve and mediate conflicts, to maintain discipline and to exploit opportunities. As with any military structure, the moral authority of those in command entailed commensurate responsibility for the consequences of decisions and orders. Because of the enforced closeness of living, domestic and immediate, the prison or camp leader carried that responsibility in a way that no commander beyond walls or wire could assume or was required to have. This was wrapped around with a formal arrangement followed so closely that it became instinctive. An IRA man was only partly jesting when he claimed that if two IRA men found themselves in prison one would be elected OC.

A corollary of this structure meant that, once captured, rank was forfeit and previous function forgone. This had two substantial benefits. The position of the captive could immediately be filled and role and responsibilities could be passed on with minimum disruption – priorities for a revolutionary organisation. A further advantage was that prison leadership was not constantly kept in flux by the arrival of men who, whilst at liberty, held a rank higher than the incumbent OC and who therefore had a claim or even the obligation to displace him. In choosing prison and camp leaders, it was, of course, likely that men would have regard to previous command experience and reputation and that those senior in the organisation outside would generally be chosen to command inside. But the rule of automatic loss of rank on imprisonment was key to making these arrangements work.

This was the background to a departure from the conventions in late 1940. Larry Grogan was one of the GHQ men arrested in a raid on the Rathmines safe house on 9 September 1939.[153] Grogan had appeared with his fellow cap-tives before the Special Criminal Court on 24 October 1939. He was sentenced to eighteen months for refusing to give his name and address and served his time at the Curragh Military Detention Barracks ('Glasshouse') and at Arbour Hill.[154] On 28 October 1940, having completed his sentence (less remission and time served on remand), he was made subject to an internment order and transferred to the Curragh. Close on his arrival, Grogan, who, as a signatory to the 1939 declaration of war, had been part of the collective supposedly invested with the authority of the Second Dáil, insisted that he take over the camp leadership.[155] A group of men, including Peadar O'Flaherty, considered that Grogan would provide an effective focus and means to displace the existing camp leadership, which they considered to be too lax. In line with this, Grogan (who seems to have been a figurehead for the disciplinarians) stated that his first priority was to restore morale and military discipline.[156] To this end he pushed forward a list of demands which the prisoners had already submitted and which were being stonewalled by the authorities. An immediate set of goals, supported by con-frontational action, would stimulate militancy and promote unity.

There had already been a rehearsal for this. Shortly after arrival at the Glasshouse in January 1940, Grogan had submitted demands to the Governor. His objective then was recognition for the prisoners' command structure, for their OC and staff to be accepted by the Governor and for all orders to be transmitted through them. Still convinced of the efficacy of ultimatums, seven days were given for the authorities to signify its agreement.[157] Skirmishing and minor altercations then took place. Prison staff issued lists of men detailed to orderly duties for the day – to clean, to draw rations, to stoke the boilers and the like. The prisoners refused to accept the assignments because they had not come from their own officers. In consequence, prisoners had to draw rations individually, no cleaning was done, fires and boilers went unstoked, and the building was left unheated and without hot water. In the middle of a cold winter, this affected the prisoners far more than it did the staff, since the latter had warm homes and barracks to go to when their shifts were over. It was hard to see where Grogan thought he was exerting leverage.

Grogan's hold on the protest was unsure, and the prisoners were far from united. Some drew rations individually; others refused food. Nine of the forty-six, apparently all from Cork, adhered to prison regulations. Two of them were then appointed as orderlies for the dissident group and carried out the daily tasks of collective housekeeping. In reaction to this defiance of his authority, Grogan told the other prisoners that the group of nine were suspended from the IRA, pending court martial.[158] But even among those who had obeyed Grogan's orders there was a deal of dissatisfaction, one man telling prison staff that he did not agree with the action 'at all' and would draw his rations. Another expressed disagreement but indicated that he would carry on with the policy of non-cooperation out of loyalty to those who, with him, were the first to arrive at the Glasshouse.[159] Four days into the protest, only thirty-one men were fully participating and on 2 February 1940 it ceased.[160]

The fire

By mid-1940, no one could doubt that the government would stand firm on all prison issues. The Curragh military guard was deployed, and although arguably undermanned, it was well armed, confident of political support and supposedly capable of suppressing rioting or attempts at mass breakout.[161] There seemed to be few options for protest. Histories of the IRA assume that it was Grogan's decision to resort to arson, but secret Irish Army documents show that as early as 4 September 1940, Commandant P. J. Whelan, Command Adjutant at the Curragh, sought guidance from the Adjutant General at the Department of Defence as to the level of force he could use should the internees seek to burn the camp's huts 'or otherwise destroy them'.[162] This suggests that the authorities had got wind of an intention to destroy portions of the camp, and this pre-dated Grogan's arrival. It was, however, under the leadership of Grogan and his group that intention became action.[163]

Internees were given the same rations as private soldiers in the Irish Army.[164] In line with this, on the afternoon of 13 December 1940, they were informed that from the following day their daily butter allowance would be reduced by half an ounce (from 2 to 1½ ounce) in line with the reduction that would apply to the Army.[165] Here was the spark for an event, the repercussions of which would last and corrode. That the butter allowance, of all things, was taken as a sufficient cause for riot and destruction showed an almost complete indifference to political realities. Inevitably, the public and their politicians would conclude that since soldiers were getting less, why not the internees? Indeed, was the population at large not having to adapt to wartime shortages? Because of a drastic contraction in external grain and other food supplies, the government would have to direct a major reduction in pasturage and increase in tillage. This and export needs meant that the Irish civilian butter ration for adults was tightly constrained in December 1940.[166] It was inconceivable that there would be sympathy for prisoners engaged in a tantrum-like outbreak on this issue: ridicule and incredulity certainly, but not sympathy.[167] The government was never remotely likely to concede. The choice of issue was all the more inexplicable because it was not a genuine grievance. The new camp leadership, recalled Séamus Ó Goilidhe, wanted 'a mere excuse' to promote an active struggle in the camp.[168]

The internees' Camp Council took some hours to consider what to do and, on the morning of Saturday, 14 December 1940, presented a ten-point list for the improvement of conditions. The spokesman also warned Camp Commandant M. J. Cummins that were the butter allowance not restored the men would not accept any rations at all and would not be responsible for what might happen.[169] Tragedy and farce followed. Two and a half hours later, fire was seen in the huts, some of which were not in use. The internees equipped themselves with weapons of wood and metal (some pointed and sharpened) and made for the main gate, at that stage guarded by military policemen armed only with batons. Bricks, stones, trestle stands and fire buckets were thrown. The Curragh garrison (as distinct from the camp) was alerted. Additional military police (who had earlier been stood to) then interposed themselves, brandishing revolvers, which they showed every willingness to use. Any attempted breakout would have entailed bloodshed and loss of life.[170] The internees retreated, the military police apparently using their batons freely. Since their huts were on fire, they had no place to shelter and were driven towards the sports ground. According to Colonel T. McNally, OC, Curragh Command, the rioters were menacing, truculent and persistent in their attempts to spread the conflagration. The order to open fire was given with the intention of re-establishing control. Two military policemen were seriously injured in the melee, and two internees were wounded; there were other, less serious, injuries on both sides.[171]

Pierce Fennell was one of those ordered to set fires. He recalled that there had been no intention to fire the adjacent building and that the huts chosen for burning had no tunnels. His was a thorough job, using paper packed between the sheet lining of the hut and the outer boarding and with a plastic wood preparation (used by the internees in hobbycraft) as an accelerant. In order to surprise the guards there was no attempt to clear the huts, and in Fennell's hut (C12) there was at least one person sleeping. Fennell, having set the fire, displayed a foolish and near-fatal bravado. Determined not to appear rushed, he packed his belongings into a suitcase in a deliberate way. When he was finished, he made for the exit 'down a tunnel of smoke and flames each side of me inside the hut'. Unsurprisingly, he lost consciousness and came to outside, having been rescued by comrades.[172]

The immediate aftermath was almost equally disastrous. Larry Grogan maintained that he had not intended to burn the entire camp.[173] But controlled arson needs considerable expertise and equipment, neither of which the internees had. There was a strong wind on the day, the creosoted wooden huts were relatively close together, and the internees hampered attempts at firefighting. Fire extinguishers were pointlessly discharged, fire buckets emptied and hydrants damaged – all of which pointed to an attempt to maximise the conflagration.

And, indeed, it worked: six huts were destroyed, together with beds, bedding and many of the necessities of camp life. The loss of personal property was considerable: books, arts and crafts, gifts received and in the making, clothing and musical instruments. 'When the contents of seven huts that contained 400 men go up much will be lost', Joe Dolan remembered, 'much that is of sentimental value and irreplaceable'.[174] Other huts were damaged to varying degrees. More devastating still for the men was the uncovering of tunnels which had been dug under the huts, one of which had almost reached the perimeter fence. The discovery was a body blow to prisoner morale and a jolt to a torpid camp administration.[175] The tunnels were blocked forthwith and searches begun to uncover any others: careers must suddenly have seemed not quite so secure.[176] The Army's review of the incident was unimpressive, paying little attention to intelligence and control, focusing instead on firefighting equipment.[177]

The authorities had only narrowly avoided a mass breakout; the camp had been virtually destroyed (to the cost, it was later calculated, of £9,083 10s. 3d.); there had been a number of injuries; the military guard had been shown to be complacent and inefficient (Magazine Fort syndrome). There was a loss of face, compounded by the shock of the events. The burning of the camp was bad enough in itself, but, had there been better inmate planning and a mass breakout, not impossible in the circumstances, the government itself would have suffered a heavy blow. The incident necessarily cast a critical light on the Army more widely, on the Department of Defence, and on the energy and preparedness with which this aspect of national security had been addressed. With so much blame swirling about, a storm of recrimination perceptively gathering, neither camp command nor rank-and-file guards were likely to be sympathetic to the prisoners' plight. In mid-December weather, some form of shelter had immediately to be given, but it was going to be rudimentary. The men were searched and confined to two unburnt huts; these had neither beds nor bedding. The official reason for this deprivation was that bedding had been used to spread the fires and that what had remained had been damaged or destroyed by water and broken glass.[178] Although details were glossed over, there also seems to have been few stoves in the huts into which the men were now crammed.[179]

Understandably partisan, Pierce Fennell's account of the consequences for those whom the authorities suspected of leading or participating in the firing of the huts nevertheless rings true. Immediately following the melee, and with some random firing of shots, the men were driven onto the football field. There they were warned by their own officers to remain in military formation lest the guards fire on them. They remained in that position for three hours, in the rain, until the remaining huts were searched. Fennell insists that this was accompanied by considerable and wanton destruction of personal property. When the search was completed, the men were crowded into the remaining huts: 'no bed boards, no clothes; nothing only water'. That night, they slept in rings around the stove, trying to keep warm.[180] Over the following days, the men were moved from hut to hut as washing and searching proceeded. The bed boards burnt in the conflagration were not replaced, and so, for the two years following, the men's palliasses rested on the hut floors.[181] This unhealthy practice, soiled blankets, a shortage of sheets, poor personal hygiene and the men's run-down state contributed to infestation by lice.[182]

The cold comfort of this confinement to huts, including one with a concrete floor, a disused mess hall known as the 'Ice Box', was part necessity and part collective punishment.[183] It lasted for two days, only cookhouse orderlies being allowed out to collect the rations. These were readily accepted – except for the butter: a protest that had begun ostensibly because of a reduction in the butter ration thus comically came full circle.[184] Part of the justification for cramming the men into the unheated huts was because, following the fire and the melee, it could not be established if any had escaped. Chagrined by their situation, the men refused to cooperate in the count; armed parties were then sent into each hut. When numbers had finally been tallied, the men were allowed to go to the mess hut. As they emerged to line up, no doubt somewhat bewildered and in no tranquil state, some apparently began to crowd too near the armed, apprehensive and still shaken guard. Fearing another concerted rush, some opened fire. Bernard Casey was gravely wounded and subsequently died; two others were hit, and one narrowly escaped when a bullet lodged in his shoe.[185] Following this confrontation and the reintroduction of basic amenities, there was a clampdown. Every night now the men were locked in the huts in which the lights were kept on. Occasional shots warned what would happen were there any defiance.[186]

Around fifty suspected ringleaders (including Grogan) were removed to the Glasshouse, where, according to some accounts, they were beaten and kept in solitary confinement.[187] (The number removed from the camp may have been dictated by the space available in the Glasshouse.) Forty-nine men – actual and suspected ringleaders, including Michael Traynor – were taken before the Special Criminal Court and received sentences of between one and ten years.[188] This had a paradoxical result. All the internees were going to sit out the war, so being a sentenced offender was scarcely a punishment. Traynor claimed to be delighted to be taken from the camp to much better conditions at Mountjoy. Above all, he viewed his transfer to a civil prison, away from the custody of the military police, as a positive boon, 'as if I was in heaven'.[189]

This sense of relief was due to the harsh treatment that, according to several accounts, the men experienced whilst at the Glasshouse. There had been casual ill-handling of the group that was facing charges, and, according to Pierce Fennell's recollections and those of Bertie McCormack, a deal of more deliberate brutality. On arrival at the Glasshouse, various prisoner accounts insist, the men were beaten up in their cells. Each morning they were asked if they had any complaints. If, in response, they refused to say 'Sir', they were punched or kicked. No great injury appears to have been caused, but Pierce Fennell remembered being 'sore all over'. It is probable that there was some exaggeration in internee reminiscences, but, even allowing for this, the willingness of the guards to use casual violence and rough handling to cow and deter seems plausible. Besides intimidation, there were elements of pre-emptive punishment in the routine doling out of punches, kicks and baton strikes.[190]

Joe Dolan, one of the internees, concluded that nothing at all was gained in the burning of the camp. Besides the loss of the tunnels and valued personal property and the considerable hardship in the weeks immediately following the fire, the camp administration was subsequently much less tolerant of the military trappings and posturing of the internees. Before the fire there had been no roll-call; afterwards there was one inside the locked huts each night. Parading in military formation was forbidden, and hut lights were left on all night.[191] Much of the give and take, the implicit bargain that had eased the prisoners' lot and the camp authorities' work burden, had evaporated. Privileges, suspended for many weeks after the fire, were restored after the trials of those accused of involvement, and internees were again allowed to purchase tobacco, cigarettes and newspapers. Correspondence resumed, but the length of outgoing letters was curtailed.[192]

For some internees, the burning of the huts was a test too far in their already over-tested loyalty to the camp leadership and the organisation beyond. The men in Hut C1 had been ostracised for drawing coal for their hut stoves. The argument here was similar to that concerning the butter allowance. The coal ration for each hut had been reduced so the new OC, Liam Leddy (who replaced the imprisoned Grogan), directed that the internees should draw none at all.[193] By any reckoning, this was a completely pointless privation to bring on oneself, and the C1 men ignored the order. Behind their decision to break with Leddy's leadership lay an even deeper dissatisfaction, centring on the decision to burn the huts. Tadhg Lynch had approached Grogan and the other camp leaders and had offered to burn the unoccupied huts rather than those which were in use and under which the tunnels had been dug. For some reason this offer had been refused. With others, Derry Kelleher decided that 'after this debacle… we were done with the IRA'.[194]

The picture was certainly bleak and prospects grim for the period of detention stretching indefinitely ahead. As the war reached equilibrium and then, in the spring of 1943, swung to the Allies, all thoughts of an Axis *deus ex machina* evaporated. However, the strong national tradition of respect for family obligations did soften if not the nature and duration of incarceration then the context. Parole was granted fairly liberally for bereavements and for serious family crises.[195] There was little concern about security issues (at least in the narrower sense) in these temporary releases. The internees could not flee the jurisdiction (Northern Ireland was scarcely a haven) and were subject to the discipline of their own organisation as well as the authorities, should they violate their parole, since a violation could have consequences for other prisoners and internees.[196] The giving of a parole undertaking to an authority that the IRA contended was usurping and illegal and which it refused to recognise on arrest or in court was clearly an inconsistency if not a contradiction. To have ordered its men to refuse to give parole, in circumstances only likely to arise in conditions of family distress and hardship, would have pushed loyalty and discipline well beyond breaking. There was always the historical precedent, moreover, in that the Old IRA had allowed parole to be given to the British.

Classes and recreation

Classes were the traditional and usually effective means of countering some of the debilitating effects of imprisonment; they could also be used as a cover for military instruction. Yet, from the outset, attendance was uneven, as the authorities were careful to note.[197] Gaelteacht (Irish-speaking) huts and parts of huts were established, and classes in the language were offered by the gifted Máirtín Ó Cadhain and others; these were so successful that they were still referred to many years later.[198] In a retrospective article in the *Irish Independent*, Pearse Kelly claimed that at least 70 per cent of those who passed through the Curragh left with at least some ability to speak the language.[199] Other classes and courses were conducted by internees who could teach foreign languages or who had special skills and interests. It is not clear to what extent military instruction continued or was possible, but there are some reports of a secret bomb-making class.[200] The camp had a reasonably good sports ground, and the Secretary of the GAA stimulated interest and competition by providing both equipment and medals.[201] Outside sympathisers sent in books and other items for common use. The Society of Friends sent books – 'good readable books' – and games.[202]

Among the internees there were a number of educated, intelligent and committed men. These taught classes, attended others' classes and helped to support an educational ethos which would later, with a deal of misty hindsight, be described as 'Tintown University'. It seems likely that only a minority became involved in sustained educational activity, but these promoted a respect for study and helped to integrate it into republican thinking. Matty O'Neill remembered the Curragh as 'a place where men could (and many did) advance themselves educationally'. Besides Irish classes, O'Neill mentioned mathematics, English and even Latin. At a later point, the Leddy faction allowed classes to be held in economics and sociology. The intention of such study was to explore and promote Roman Catholic social doctrine, drawing on the 1891 Papal Encyclical *Rerum novarum*. These classes and discussions, O'Neill remembers, 'would have been anti-Marxist, not just non-Marxist'.[203] There was, indeed, a tight control kept on classes through an education committee, An Coiste Oideachais, which reported to the Camp Council. Neil Goold-Verschoyle, a communist, left the Leddy side of the camp after the big split and moved to the more tolerant Kelly side, where most of the left-thinking internees had pitched up. Before this, he had applied to the Camp Council for a blackboard for his Russian language classes and was refused.[204]

In general, this was education in only a narrow sense of the word: instruction rather than exploration. Discussion was confined within the limits of IRA tradition, current policy and the parameters of Roman Catholic teaching. There was no attempt to strengthen, much less modify, the mainstream IRA beliefs by opening them to examination, however constructive. The task of the teacher was to convey the detail of orthodoxy at the political level, to show how the world fitted into it and to dwell upon the classics of Gaelic culture. 'Tintown University' was far closer to the fundamentalist religious foundations in some parts of the USA than to the ethos and objectives of a true university. The only target of critical thinking, it would seem, was any institution or approach seen as anti- or even non-republican. Matty O'Neill, whose interview in Uinseann MacEoin's book confirms his continued adherence to IRA orthodoxy, remembered that 'too much of what we had been getting there was propaganda; IRA propaganda'. There was also a fear that some of those who held socialistic or communistic views would be foxes to the helpless chickens. O'Neill again: 'When you recollect the type of people we had in the Curragh, you will agree that some of them were wide open to manipulation. Perhaps indeed they already were manipulated in other directions.'[205]

Conditions varied with the seasons, with winter darkness bringing long hours locked in the huts, for reasons of security. In December and January, morning unlocking could be as late as 9.30 a.m. Then, according to Seamus O'Donovan, came breakfast, dinner and tea 'in all too quick succession', with lock-up as early as 4.45 p.m. In summer, the huts were unlocked at about 8 a.m., and evening lock-up was put back to 9.30 p.m.[206] Radio broadcasts were relayed to the various compounds, although the sound quality was not good.[207] Besides classes, sports and organised activities, personal and domestic routines filled up the time. Clothes and bedding had to be washed by hand and daily hygiene met by a cold wash in a central washroom. Razor blades being in extremely short supply, men shaved only twice a week, and by mid-1942, owing to fuel shortages, baths were restricted and taken only fortnightly. Irrespective of status or reputation, all internees were allocated domestic duties (fatigues). O'Donovan, prominent in the War of Independence, took charge of his hut's stove and had to carry the latrine buckets daily for eight months, as well as sweeping the floor.

As the months and years passed, two contradictory influences were at work. Prolonged and indefinite incarceration drained energy, hope and moral reserves.[208] Yet, as selective releases began to gather pace, those remaining inside increasingly comprised the hard core of the IRA's activists and leaders. This change in the composition of the ranks of the prisoners and internees contributed to the re-emergence of a more purposeful life in captivity. Writing to a supporter in the spring of 1944, Seán McCool described an evidently successful day of entertainments for Easter. He also gave some details of his busy life as Chairman of Curragh Camp's Education Committee, as well as teacher of history, economics, arithmetic and English. (The last, he half-apologised, helped the men with their Gaelic.[209])

Young men eat a lot of food, but this was wartime, and the Curragh was a camp, and so there was a deal of hunger, or at least of feeling underfed. Worse, at certain points there appeared to be some pilferage in the cookhouse, which was staffed by internees. Tony McInerney recalled that the bread allowance was unevenly cut by the cookhouse staff, who kept extra slices for themselves and for friends. One day, entering the cookhouse between meals, McInerney found a cookhouse crony eating a meal of bacon and eggs, 'something the rest of us never saw from one end of the year to the other'.[210] For some reason, the Camp Council allowed this petty corruption to continue.

Splits

Unity and a sense of purpose, not strong at the outset, became even more elusive as time passed. The men quarrelled about a range of issues. There were divisions based on locality and personalities and those who lined up behind one or the other; most gravitated to groups from their home area. Another fissure opened in December 1941, between the new OC Liam Leddy, a Corkman (who had taken Larry Grogan's place when Grogan was removed from the camp) and a Northern-oriented group, led by Pearse Kelly.[211]

As we have seen, the men of Hut C1, under the leadership of Tadhg Lynch, disobeyed the Camp Council's directions and were then ostracised.[212] Around December 1941, Pearse Kelly circulated a document which proposed new council elections and the termination of the split.[213] This led to further rancour and another Leddy ostracisation order, followed by the defection to the side of the excluded of about 150 men. A cold war ensued. Relations were hostile and bitter; anathema was generously pronounced, and fraternisation between the two groups was strictly prohibited and punished by instant expulsion from the Leddy faction. However, the Kelly group prevailed, and by war's end claimed the allegiance of all but a handful.

All places of confinement have elements of the pressure cooker. The hostility between the two groups was a daily and hourly matter, enforced by mutual supervision; it was intensely personal and direct; and it was driven by a constantly replenished supply of malign energy. Joe Dolan was fully behind the ostracisation of Hut C1. He believed its occupants had obtained supposedly exceptional concessions by way of beds and fuel in the bleak period after the fire, and well ahead of the rest of the camp. Their exclusion was justified, Dolan reasoned 'because… they had cooperated with the enemy'. It was more difficult for him when it came to the much larger Pearse Kelly group. To have any dealings with these men required express permission from the Leddy Camp Council, Dolan recalled.

> But it was hard passing men you had known all your life and yet never exchanging a word with them. If they had been playing football and, as sometimes happened, the ball travelled in my direction, I would kick it back, yet I saw fellows who would not look at the ball. I could not do that.[214]

The ostracisation process assumed the characteristics of the biblical practice of shunning, still relished and practised by the most fanatical of fundamentalist sects. The other side were seen as doctrinally unclean, vile and contaminating, utterly unworthy and unknowable, to be cast out.[215] In a world torn apart by slaughter, suffering and destruction on a scale never previously seen, the spectacle of this small tribe – the Legion of the Lost as some called themselves – encamped on the windy plains of Kildare, divided into grouplets fanatically ignoring each other as they moved within their claustrophobic parish of wires and huts, was a truly remarkable illustration of the folly of doctrine, power and personality.[216] A wider view may have been hard to achieve, but some took a personal and local view to see beyond the shunning. Tom Doran joined the Kelly faction because he and a comrade were friendly with the Dundalk men and they were in a Kelly hut. In Doran's experience, moreover, the relaxed rule of the Kelly faction Camp Council was easier to live with.[217] He was not willing to ignore men on the other side, and, although a greeting to one of their leaders was met with an earthy expletive, another man met him behind one of the huts and gave him news of friends in the Leddy huts. The meeting was furtive because the Leddy penalty for speaking to anyone on the opposing side was to join them in internal exile.

There was a deal of localism connected with the huts. Pierce Fennell had had a peripatetic childhood as the family followed his lighthouse-keeper father around the Irish coast. He had thus established a connection with Limerick, and this was the affiliation he chose at the camp. The Limerick group occupied Hut C12 and was led by Joe Crowe ('a good clean military man') who had little regard for the Camp Council. Returning to the camp in mid-1941, having served a sentence in Arbour Hill for his part in the burning of the camp, Fennell found that discipline had broken down. At this point, his thinking had become more communistic, and he opted to join the Pearse Kelly faction, which included those inclined to a socialist or communist thinking, influenced by the thought of James Connolly. This group was within the Kelly faction, led by Neil Goold-Verschoyle, who was particularly anathematised by the IRA leadership because of their fear of being tarnished by any association with communists.

As a congenial, if unlikely, Cerberus, Commandant James Guiney used to deliver a satiric speech to some newcomers to his realm. The remarks reflected the bemusement (and certain amount of satisfaction) of the camp administration in the face of the splits and shunnings. As reported by George Fluke, the welcome went as follows: 'What part of this open university would you like to go into?' When Fluke said he did not know, Guiney outlined his options:

> You can go in and join Mr Leddy who is totally republican; republican flag and republican to the backbone. If you don't like his side of the Camp, you can go and join Pearse Kelly who is a little bit more liberal with his northern republicanism; there is more give and take and he is not as dogmatic. Then if you don't like that, you can go and join Mr O'Donovan's group; the ones that believe in Hitler all the way through. If you are still not satisfied you can join Mr Goold, who marches under the banner, workers of the world unite.[218]

The necessities of war had for two years made unlikely allies of Stalin and Churchill, but in the Curragh orthodox IRA men were so outraged by the existence of a supposedly communist bloc in their midst that Pearse Kelly had Goold-Verschoyle removed by appealing to Cardinal MacRory, Archbishop of Armagh, a figure of immense importance in Catholic Ireland and a stern defender of Roman Catholic orthodoxy.[219] He in turn approached de Valera, and Goold-Verschoyle was removed to Mountjoy.[220] Men tried to stand apart from the quarrelling and mutual recriminations, but neutrality generally did little more than expose them to the scorn and hostility of all the others. The camp seemed to be enacting a cautionary moral fable or vision of Dystopia or a laboratory demonstration of the critical mass and chain reaction of dogmatism and paranoia.

The cult of discipline

As we have noted before, internment carries the special torment of uncertainty. Tried and sentenced prisoners have a date, a horizon on which to fix their gaze which, even if distant, is a comfort.[221] The Curragh internees knew that release was hitched to the great uncertainties of the war and, when peace eventually came, to the public mood and the temper of the government. The last seemed unlikely to be benign since the IRA had so emphatically been defined as the enemy within, and had embraced the role with enthusiasm. With an intact organisation and adequate support from outside bodies, it would have been a task of great difficulty to sustain morale and commitment. Without such sustenance, the internees' leaders' options were few, and they were driven back to the notion that cult-like controls could substitute for allegiance freely given.

On 17 September 1940, Commandant M. McHugh, Army Provost Marshal, sent a secret memo to Commandant Cummins. Certain internees, he had learned, had put together an organisation to prevent men from taking advantage of the liberties and privileges available to them through compliance with the rules and regulations. Among other steps, this clandestine body was censoring internees' letters, controlling their visits and preventing them from communicating with the camp authorities. The camp commandant was directed to take every step within reason to 'smash and break up' the conspiracy, clearing the way for those who wished to accept and benefit by the camp regulations. Since internees were divided into two factions, he was also asked to consider separating them. Those suspected of involvement in counter-control activities he was to remove to the Glasshouse.[222]

The Provost Marshal's information was confirmed by Lieutenant Ryan of the Intelligence Branch of the Chief of Staff's Office. Visiting the camp for another purpose (possibly to see an informant), Ryan had confirmed that the internees were running a comprehensive parallel system of control. Outgoing letters could not be put directly into the camp mailbox but had first to be handed to the hut leader (by whom incoming post was also distributed) for censorship. The rule was strictly enforced:

Any letter put into the box is regarded as an application for release and the individual is ostracised. The internees are paraded in the compound – the 'offender' is called out by the O.C. while the parade stands to attention. The parade is informed that the individual is ostracised and give the order 'about turn'. The 'offender' is then marched away by two 'policemen' who are internees.[223]

The supposed rationale was that no one outside should receive information on how the internees were faring other than a message approved by the IRA command. This was a riposte, of some kind, to the government's minute censorship of all reports relating to the IRA. On the same plane, the IRA leadership evidently believed that discussions of splits, demoralisation, weariness and the like could affect the organisation as a whole and its supporters and sympathisers. Likewise, bad news or negative views coming into the camp had to be filtered out or suppressed. Contacts with non-republicans and with those hostile to the organisation could be minimised.

The internee was subject to double duress. Within the barbed-wire fence and with all the restrictions of official confinement, he was in another prison of moral and psychological sanction. In addition to controls over his post, he had to obtain his hut leader's approval to set up a visit or interview. Even camp staff who wished to see an internee submitted to this procedure. These rules were effective obstacles to men who wished to submit an application for release ('signing out').[224] But were he discovered to have submitted an appeal, the miscreant could be subjected to the daunting, wounding and deeply unpleasant ostracisation ceremony. And even when that was over there was the long, drawn-out burden of living in but simultaneously being cast out of a community. Release might then be a matter of weeks or even months, during which time he would, at best, be an outcast. The application might indeed be unsuccessful, creating the prospect of indefinite confinement, ground between official and unofficial regimes, reviled and with none of the comforts of fellowship and communal life but rather a daily diet of hostility, humiliation and ostentatious rejection. For some, this must have been a traumatic experience, with lifelong consequences. Bullying and childish cruelty lurked behind all of this, and, beyond the cruelties of shunning, more active steps were taken to punish backsliders. It was reported that one ostracised prisoner was prevented from getting his food and had to go without for five days. Another applicant had to wait so long for a decision, during which time his life was made unbearable for him, that he resubmitted to the internees' command system.[225]

The near-absolute and all-pervasive nature of the internees' disciplinary structure in itself challenged government. The ceremony of degradation was a particularly efflorescent manifestation of a process that framed and determined much of daily life. These ceremonies and similar activities would have been criminal offences (criminal threats, assault, conspiracy, affray) if undertaken outside the camp. It seemed to Major Dan Bryan of military intelligence that the legal position was not altered in the slightest because the participants were internees. The Minister for Justice, he noted, would not be pleased to learn that persons interned to prevent their breaking the law were still able to exercise illegal authority within their camp. There was a practical question of sanctions, of course. A man at liberty could be punished for an illegal act, but what could be done to a man already in captivity? Major Bryan wanted the Camp Commandant to have the power to punish severely persons who refused to obey camp regulations.[226]

The camp authorities responded defensively to these observations, which they took as criticisms. Commandant Cummins thought that the internees were satisfied that their correspondence was not being interfered with by the inmate organisation. The other incidents mentioned by Ryan and Bryan were either exaggerated or based on unreliable information, he insisted. A shunning ceremony had indeed taken place, but the disgraced man had not been marched off by inmate police, and the internees' commander had given his word that such a demonstration would not be repeated. It was true that an applicant for release was shunned by his comrades, 'but we cannot prevent this'. The reason why men were unwilling to apply for release was that having maintained their silence whilst detained they now found it difficult to state that they did not belong to an illegal organisation.[227]

There were further exchanges between Cummins and the Provost Marshal's office, with Cummins insisting that no changes were necessary in his administration, and G2 Branch (Military Intelligence) insisting that their information was reliable and deeply worrying.[228] The matter was eventually brought to a head by the OC Curragh Command, Colonel T. McNally, concluding that the prisoners were indeed not under 'the strict disciplinary control that is desirable'. He demanded responses to a series of concerns: the prisoners' censorship of letters and control over visits, the procedure at roll-call, the cleanliness of food areas and lavatories, the hanging of washing on the barbed-wire fences, the damage to public property, to clothing and to the defences of the camp.[229] Unfortunately for Commandant Cummins's credibility, some of the exchanges took place against the background of a suspected escape on the night of 15 October 1940, the murky circumstances of which indicated, at the very least, a deplorable slackness.[230]

Being a professional soldier in a small and poorly resourced neutral country was, for the most part, an experience over-rich with inactivity and waiting. To be a prison guard in such an army at such a time was an even more dismal experience, with fear of failure rather than hope of success being the principal spur to duty. It became evident that the camp command had entered into a state of near paralysis, masked by a complacent routine and the calculation that it was better not to confront the internees, or, indeed, to stir them up in any way. It was the age-old bargain that a weak prison administration makes with its inmate groups: laxity, concession and the blind eye in return for an implied promise of no visible trouble, a quiet life and no attempt to escape. This cannot ever be a good-faith agreement, compatible with the rule of law and duty to the state. The failure to understand or accept this axiom had consequences for camp security as well as control, since an evasion or disregard of the rules combined with an unwillingness to enforce them allowed escapes to be prepared. It also sets aside, as we have noted, all concern for any but the physical welfare of inmates, fairly narrowly defined.

Even after detailed investigation, the events of the night of 15/16 October 1940 – what had happened and in what sequence – remained unclear. It was established that on three occasions, over a period of two hours, the camp lights had failed. Such outages were unusual and thus might be the result of sabotage, but this was not confirmed. It did emerge, however, that the circuit for the perimeter lights included the supply to the huts, giving internees the ability to fuse the fence lights. With some understatement, the investigating committee concluded that this was definitely an oversight. During the first power failure, the internees gathered at a particular spot, near which the inner barbed wires of the camp fence were later found to be cut. The guard responded relatively quickly, however, and a mobile patrol went to the point where the attempted escape – if that was what it was – was taking place. At the same time, the prisoners were milling about, and when a tally was ordered, this was obstructed by some moving from hut to hut; others hid between or under beds.[231] None of this could have happened without orders from the IRA command.

The incident demonstrated beyond question that control had slipped perilously. The most basic disciplinary requirement of any prisoner is to be counted; the prison-keepers' equally indispensable duty is to count. Seeking to avoid friction, staff no longer undertook the minimum necessary routine. Men were not required to stand by their beds when a check was made and were allowed to change bed space and even hut without permission. This had the most obvious security implications, but even after the attempted escape the investigating committee reported that the camp staff saw 'no remedy for this'. The other allegations, which a few weeks earlier had been so vigorously contested by Commandant Cummins, were now shown to be wholly or substantially true. Camp staff had not attempted to challenge, much less dismantle, the parallel system of authority. The duality of control was emphasised every time that group movements took place. Without an order from their own officers, the men would not return to their huts in the evening. This was a matter of considerable consequence since at this point there were about 460 men in the camp, and to have them assembled in one place and under their own military command was a danger.[232] Staff morale, which seems to have subsided into hapless resignation, was further damaged when cat-calling, jeering and generally derisive shouting went wholly unpunished. Officers evidently did not think that they had a duty other than physically to protect the soldiers of their command.

Colonel McNally and his colleagues catalogued and deplored the loss of control. This was, they recognised, a tacit stand-off. All was exemplified by a police visit to fingerprint and photograph the internees. Garda Superintendent O'Reilly and two of his officers came to start the work. The internees refused to cooperate, and Milligan, one of their leaders, was so outraged at what he saw as the pre-sumptuousness of the Gardaí that he attacked O'Reilly and had to be restrained by two military policemen. He then broke free and jumped into the camp cookhouse through the window, protected by his jeering comrades. Super-intendent O'Reilly offered to make another attempt at the work, but the Camp Commandant asked him to desist 'as he did not want any trouble or disturbance in the Camp as a result'.[233]

Critical though he was, Colonel McNally also took the view that a tightening of discipline could be met by 'rowdyism, prison breaking and even hunger striking', and more. His proposal was therefore truly anticlimatic: a conference at Army GHQ 'at which the whole situation could be discussed fully and frankly'.[234] This unwillingness to make firm proposals was, however, a recognition that little could be done without a commitment at the most senior military and political levels – and here McNally was making a fair point. There may also have been a prag-matic judgement that the internees were largely without purpose and were sliding into demoralised impotence. To provide them with galvanising issues could therefore be counterproductive. In the meantime, a number of improvements in the physical security of the camp were ordered, together with some very clearly necessary changes in the deployment of the guard. All of these skirted the issue of internal control, subversion and anti-discipline, though they improved camp security.[235] It seemed that the Camp Commandant was not alone in seeking the quiet life. And beyond the Army, it is far from clear that politicians – even the feisty Gerald Boland – wanted or saw any advantage in escalating a sequence of Curragh skirmishes. Better, they probably reasoned, to leave the internees in their fractured and mutually recriminatory state than to provide a cause to unite them against the government: they were in a stewpot, and they would gradually render themselves down.

Turning inwards: discord and disintegration

Fracturing

If, indeed, this was the government's and army's view, they had good reason for holding it. Derry Kelleher had been drawn into the IRA by an unconditional admiration for fellow Corkman, Tomás MacCurtáin. He had been devastated by the decision to fire the huts, and by the aftermath. The removal of the camp leaders to Mountjoy to serve their sentences increased a sense of drift, and by the beginning of 1941, Kelleher remembered, 'demoralisation reigned supreme'. The men tried to occupy themselves with the traditional prison crafts: matchstick crosses, embroidered linen, silver and (occasionally) gold rings made out of coins, as well as the ubiquitous leather wallets. In early autumn came appalling news of the 'arrest' of Stephen Hayes, the IRA Chief of Staff, of his prolonged inter-rogation and trial and his escape of 8 September 1941. Completely alienated from the organisation, Kelleher took the extreme step of signing out of the camp and breaking his IRA contacts.[236] Others lived without hope of any IRA success or even revival and remained in the camp because of personal loyalties, pride and a visceral horror of signing out and desertion.

A fractured and demoralised body of internees had its own dangers for the camp administration, different from the threat posed by a united and disciplined inmate body but pregnant with unhappy possibilities nonetheless. In the autumn of 1941 and the months that followed there were piecemeal attempts to improve control and discipline. There was also some attempt to clamp down at Arbour Hill, which was, for most men, the portal to the Curragh; expectations set there for sentenced men would be carried on into internment.[237] Men who were insolent to staff on arrival at the Curragh now began to be reported for indiscipline. As inmate morale began to slump, factions to flourish and inter-group relations became ever more acidic, the authorities had an easier job.[238] In the spring of 1942 there were quarrels between new arrivals from 'The Hill' and men already at the Curragh. Sometimes fist-fights erupted, which the camp staff surmised arose from disputes over seniority and precedence.[239]

Close attention was paid to internees' visits as a means of gauging the state of inmate morale. In reporting these overheard conversations, there would have been some temptation to give senior officers, officials and the politicians beyond them a ration of good news. A report of a visit to Seán Hamill by Miss Ann McBride at Arbour Hill in December 1943, nevertheless bears a stamp of authenticity. Hamill spoke to McBride about the split and said that a small minority of the prisoners were 'the worst type of filth he had ever met – the scum of the earth who had no religion and openly cursed the Pope, his Church and anything attached to it'. This group were enough to make anyone sign out, but Hamill did not like to use them as an excuse. If, however, he could only get his freedom, he said, 'I would never touch any organisation again. The so called IRA, here are a bad mob.'[240]

By late 1943, there were the reports of sharp divisions among the Arbour Hill men. Commandant Michael Lennon noted that since the arrival of prisoners from Mountjoy 'they have been by no means a happy family'. (This contingent was made up of those sentenced for their part in the December 1940 Curragh fire, removed to Mountjoy to serve sentences, and now back again.) Blows had been exchanged in the Arbour Hill exercise yard, and a generally bad atmosphere had developed into a definitive split. The majority group, about thirty men, was headed by Peadar O'Flaherty. Whilst the minority did not appear to have any particular leader, it included the more important men such as Larry Grogan, William McGuinness, Michael Traynor and Sean O'Brien, as well as three or four men 'who are the Communist element'.[241] Matters did not improve over the weeks that followed. On 4 January 1944, a fist-fight between two men from the different factions led to further confrontations the following day, culminating in a general melee that required staff intervention to quell it. All prisoners were then confined to their cells for the rest of the day.[242]

These divisions were a final assurance that there would be no republican rallying over the issue of internment. Men at odds with each other could not hope to claim sympathy beyond relatives and their close supporters. Fights and confrontations, and the fact that the participants were careless as to whether staff witnessed them, showed that internee cohesion and solidarity had dissolved and that deeply cherished military dignity had been discarded. Decline led to further decline by feeding rank-and-file disillusionment and withdrawal. This, after all, was a body that represented itself as the army of a living Republic, that comprised volunteers who had submitted themselves to military discipline in a noble cause. This claim was incompatible with brawling and scuffling in front of the enemy.[243] Eventually, relations between the feuding groups became so bitter and volatile that, for reasons of good order and discipline, they had to be segregated as far as possible and assigned to different recreation rooms.[244] This, had they not abandoned self-perception, would have been the ultimate humiliation. By late 1943, Colonel F. J. Henry, Provost Marshal, was reporting a complete dissolution at the Curragh. There were at least four distinct groups, all operating against one another, 'and it is felt that the seeds of complete disintegration have been sown which will remain during internment'. Arbour Hill was nearly as bad: 'two distinct groups – one not recognising the other and having nothing in common with every sign of future disintegration'.[245]

The unique hunger strike

That energy and enmity had been absorbed in matters internecine was bizarrely illustrated in March 1942 when sixteen, mainly Cork men, under the leadership of Jeremiah Daly, staged a hunger strike against the Camp Council, emphasising that their protest was in no way directed against staff and officials. The strike began on 11 March and was called off on the evening of the 19th. It transpired that the sixteen had been ostracised by the Leddy Camp Council. Their shunning had lasted a full fifteen months, with neither side backing down; the hunger strike was intended to bring matters to a head. Interviewed by the Camp Commandant, Daly refused to answer detailed questions lest he and the other strikers be represented as informers. He did say that 'as our life in the Camp has been made impossible we decided to go on hunger-strike and are determined to see it through'.[246]

Even while this unprecedented (and probably unique) hunger strike against the IRA leadership was taking place, Leddy insisted that ten new arrivals from Arbour Hill, whom he knew to have been under an order of ostracisation there, be segregated from other camp inmates. He asked Commandant Guiney to send the men to Daly's hut. Guiney was non-committal, but put it to Daly. 'As a special request', Daly asked not to have them, presumably because he and his followers wished to concentrate on the hunger strike. All of this indicated yet further dimensions of strife, Guiney reporting to the Provost Marshal that 'matters are not what you could call happy' since the new arrivals.[247]

Army headquarters was perplexed by the Daly group's strike and ordered Guiney to check that it was a genuine action (rather than an IRA manoeuvre), directing that daily reports be sent to Dublin by ration vans or by whatever other vehicle was available.[248] Further information trickled out from observation and informants. Leddy issued terms for the ending of the ostracisation, requiring Daly to apologise to the Camp Council. Climbdown and flask of humiliation were refused. It also appeared that Daly and his group had a deal of general support from Cork and Kerry internees, who were not themselves on hunger strike.[249] Guiney had no doubt that the strike was genuine. He had a careful watch kept and the striking men had stored no food, nor was any being smuggled in to them. Until a few days previously, Leddy's order placing their hut out of bounds had been obeyed, but by 18 March 1942 a number of internees visited them, and it appeared that they were gathering quite a few supporters. Still in denial, Leddy appealed to Guiney to do what he could to get the sixteen to call off their strike, observing that it would be a terrible thing if anything were to happen to any of them: all bans had been called off, and the men were no longer subject to ostracisation. It appeared to Guiney – and he reported it with evident satisfaction – that 'Leddy has a fear in him that if the hunger-strike will be persisted in the consequences would be serious to himself and his Camp Council'.[250]

On 19 March 1942 there was, according to Guiney, 'a general air of uneasiness in the Camp all day', with groups of men milling about, in large and small groups, discussing the strike. Leddy and his colleagues held several meetings with the hunger-strikers' emissaries. Adding to the unreality, there was a rumour that up to half the general population of the camp were about to go on hunger strike in sympathy with the strikers. Staff overhead remarks to the effect that Daly was a good man who had already been on hunger strike at Arbour Hill and that Tom Barry of Cork looked upon him as an outstanding man.[251] Faced with this threatening coalescence of sympathy, the Leddy group unconditionally rescinded their ostracisation order. The sixteen agreed to take food and were, as a precautionary measure, removed to the camp hospital. They stayed there for four days, when all but Daly and Thomas Murphy were returned to the general population.

Holding on to shreds

Apart from strife based on questions of rank, procedure and personality, and all the contrived issues of principle adopted to adorn vanity and pettiness with fig leaves, violent republicanism was being challenged at the doctrinal and political levels. De Valera's steadfast neutrality had succeeded in one of its strategic objectives: undercutting extremism. There is significance in a report by Guiney on 23 March 1944, that many internees had expressed 'whole-hearted' approval for some government policies.[252] Resistance to incarceration slipped from premeditated and concerted actions on matters of practical and symbolic significance to individual surliness and sometimes foul-mouthed abuse. An incident involving Brendan Behan and others was sparked by this combination of frustration, despondent truculence, lack of self-control and the imminent execution of Charlie Kerins. This incident occurred on 30 November 1944 in Hut C2. A party of military police led by Captain Connolly entered the hut for the evening tally and called on the men to muster. One (Cathal Holland) remained by the stove with a pack of playing cards. When asked again, he said that he was not going to line up, whereupon the men who had done so broke rank. Only one man answered the roll-call, but a head count was taken. As this was going on, Brendan Behan called Connolly a 'fucking shite hawk' and a 'fucking murdering 1922 bastard and I'll say the same if ye take me to the fucking glass house... fuck you'. Patrick Martin joined in and called the officer and his sergeant and corporal 'fucking murdering 1922 bastards'[253] Doubtless alarmed that the remaining rags of discipline were shredding, Pearse Kelly, of whose loose left-inclined faction Behan and the others were members, summoned Cathal Holland (who had initiated the incident) the following day before a disciplinary court. It is not clear whether a punishment was imposed, but guards overheard fragments of an admonition later directed by Kelly to the residents of Hut C2: 'I do not want any trouble and I won't stand for it.'[254]

Omnium gatherum

As we have noted, the term 'prisoner' is generic, embracing all forms of captivity. There are numerous categories and distinctions within it. The different classes must always be kept apart because of the need to administer the appropriate regime with its restrictions and privileges and to do so without confusion or undue friction. The substantive distinction between IRA men tried and sentenced for catch-all offences, such as refusing to answer questions, and those simply interned, to say the least, was slim. Almost without exception, as we have seen, sentenced men were automatically rearrested on release and interned; there were no great differences in regime and in the type and general character of the men, in whichever category they were held.

This was the basis for a February 1942 decision to bring internees and sentenced prisoners together. It arose from an urgent request from the considerably expanded Irish Army for accommodation for soldiers under punishment.[255] Because Arbour Hill had been taken over for those sentenced under the OASA and the Emergency Powers Act, soldiers who were delinquents and deserters, and who had been sentenced under military law, were being held in guard rooms.[256] This was obviously unsatisfactory. They could not be subjected to a rigorous and punitive regime, and their detention – scarcely onerous – could not serve as a deterrent example to reinforce discipline. Idle days in the guard room, accompanied by a deal of socialising, were not wholly unattractive to an idle or unwilling soldier on manoeuvres, soaking on a wet mountainside or bog, or bored and freezing on guard duty. Various options within the available prison estate had been considered, some involving turf skirmishes between the powerful departments of Justice and Defence. After a deal of toing and froing, it appeared that the only acceptable solution was to move all civilian prisoners out of Arbour Hill. Thought had been given to using the Curragh No. 2 camp exclusively for this group, but the expense of preparing and opening yet another place of detention decided against this. It would offer little practical advantage, moreover, since it would be impossible to prevent communications between No. 2 and No. 1 camps.[257] Holding prisoners and internees together therefore appeared to be a sensible and indeed inevitable solution. In addition to their common character, the certainty of internment on completion of sentence (with only one exception to date, it was noted) and the similarity of conditions, the mixing of the two categories in this way would permit the efficient use of an experienced staff. The proposal was submitted to the cabinet on 23 February 1942 by the Minister for Defence, without objection from Justice, and was agreed the following day.[258]

Three days later, the Adjutant General's Office issued the necessary transfer order for the fifty-three men then at Arbour Hill.[259] The move itself was completed smoothly on 7 March 1942, although the insertion of such a substantial group, with its own loyalties, into what had become a settled, introspective, depressed and tense community was fraught with difficulties.[260] Throughout the remaining war years, the pressure on accommodation was acute because of the competing demands of the enlarged military, internees and prisoners. The Army, divided into regional commands, was insistent that the expense of transporting military detainees (public transport was severely restricted at the time because of fuel shortages) prevented a national use of available accommodation; it also strenuously resisted any civilian encroachment on its estate.[261] Despite these objections, civil prisoners were returned to Arbour Hill in their former numbers by the summer of 1943, remaining there until 12 June 1944, when all were removed again to the Curragh.

It had been decided that sentenced and interned IRA men might be mixed at the Curragh, but there remained another group for whom especially secure accommodation was necessary. These were men held in Mountjoy who were serving long sentences imposed by civil courts for serious offences. In April 1942, it was agreed that these should also be handed over to the Army.[262] Since space had been made available at Arbour Hill by transferring the short-sentence civilian prisoners to the Curragh, the possibility was raised of using some of the vacated accommodation for these special prisoners. This was stoutly resisted by the Provost Marshal, who insisted that the space had already been allocated to meet army needs nationally and that to add another civilian category to Arbour Hill's four categories of military prisoners would cause great difficulty.[263]

Superintendent Eamon Broy, eponymous head of the Broy Harriers (Special Branch), had taken a great deal of trouble to get the small group of special prisoners into custody on long sentences and saw their continued safe confinement as a matter of state security. Giving the Army responsibility for these men was, to Broy and his colleagues, the best guarantee that they would not escape or foment disorder in prison. On 24 April 1942, Frank Aiken, Minister for Defence, agreed that they should indeed be taken into army custody and, if necessary, held at Arbour Hill until other arrangements could be made for them.[264] By the end of the year, it was decided that all but a handful of persons serving sentences, imprisonment as well as penal servitude, for political offences should be held in military custody. The Provost Marshal's department was at this point appreciably under strength, and Colonel Henry sought permission to augment it, if necessary by recruiting directly instead of the usual method of selecting military police from serving soldiers. As an alternative, he proposed that recruits might be drawn from eligible candidates waiting for an opening in the Garda Síochána.[265] The issue was the more acute since it had been decided that room would have to be found for the transferees at Waterford or Cork.[266]

It is not clear from the records what transpired with these various proposals, other than that there were tussles between officials at Justice and Defence; it is also likely that shortages of material and equipment got in the way of plans. It seems that in the end it was easier to expand Curragh accommodation by opening another compound, known as 1A; a small overflow internment camp was also opened at Athlone.[267] By January 1946, this had been reduced to only ten inmates.[268]

Divisions and units within bureaucracies are always, to some extent, in competition for resources and consequently have a tendency to function defensively against each other. It emerged that some at least of the Army's arguments about the dire shortage of space for its disciplinary purposes were questionable. Arbour Hill was being underused, and in the summer of 1943 it was decided again to make it available for civil prisoners sentenced to military custody under the OASA. Fifty-seven men were accordingly transferred from Mountjoy on 15 July 1943. The military underuse of the prison is shown by the fact that there were at the time only nine ex-military prisoners at Arbour Hill. These were kept strictly separate from the civil prisoners and employed in cleaning and military fatigues.[269]

Latter days in the Curragh

Divina comedia

By the war's fifth year, any pretence at the Curragh of living by military standards of order and cleanliness had been discarded. Arriving from Arbour Hill in June 1944 as one of the clear-out of about fifty men, Tom Doran was astonished by Curragh conditions. The arrivals were greeted by men who had in the outside world dressed smartly but who were now much altered. Some had beards, and others had shaved their heads; their Martin Henry (government issue) suits were crumpled and shabby. By contrast, Doran thought the Arbour Hill men looked like 'a visiting delegation'. Conditions inside the huts were 'indescribable'. Beds were just six inches off the floor and were provided with army blankets, but no sheets. Old coats and pieces of blanket were fixed to the hut walls to keep out draughts and drying clothes were strung overhead: 'Mugs, half washed, and other utensils lay on the floor… It was all very depressing.' Food was served in a hut 'dubbed the dining hall' in which Doran thought hygiene was non-existent: 'a terrible looking dive'.[270]

Demoralisation, depression, despair and consequent abandonment of self-respect were thus writ large; the Curragh experience distilled. Hope, as demonstrated at least by personal hygiene, deportment, dress and purpose, had indeed been rendered down in the camp pressure cooker. Splits, the passage and attrition of time and the intrinsically inadequate facilities of the camp were only parts of the story. The men had lost almost all sense of who they were and why they were there, and the camp authorities – themselves only partly grasping the significance of the gradual slide in standards – were content to have a docile population on their hands.[271] By this point, moreover, releases had started, and such aspirations as remained were focused on the day of release. There was no animating thought beyond the gate and, for the vast majority, apparently not the remotest notion of a resumption of IRA activity. Little purpose remained in the rituals and duties of military life and, indeed, to have undertaken them would have entailed self-mockery or an exquisite sense of irony. The camp was a dismal waiting room inhabited by characters that Samuel Beckett would make familiar to the world of literature, a tragic parody rather than any kind of preparation for life. Deliverance was the arrival of release papers and a ticket home.

By this time, alcohol was being produced, apparently in some quantities, both fermented and distilled. Yeast was freely available from the cookhouse, and fruit and vegetable wines were easy to make. In addition, a still had been contrived, which, according to Tom Doran's recollection, provided 'first class clear run poteen'. Since there were no reports of alcohol poisoning, the quality of this spirit was clearly adequate, and its consumption (in moderation) was safe. This was to be expected since the distiller, Eddie Joe Gallagher, 'was one of the best poteen makers that Co. Mayo produced'.[272] The availability of alcohol in any quantity may have dulled the pains of purposeless and indefinite captivity and soothed the rawness of the daily round, but it surely added to the very torpor and dissoluteness that fuelled the regrets.

It was not, of course, a Hogarthian debauch, and the extent of tipsiness and drunkenness was far removed from Gin Lane. Even at this point, although they were not remotely military in purpose, there were other collective activities, such as impromptu music-making, play-acting, kite-flying, a band and football. In at least some of the huts, men would gather around the stoves in the evenings for sessions of gossip and storytelling. Casting his mind back almost fifty years, Tom Doran claimed of the last months at the Curragh that while numbers were dwindling 'there was no crack up in the morale'.[273] Yet morale, if defined in any way by the activities of an underground army, had long since evaporated. What his recollection told him was that men remained loyal to each other, to whatever faction they belonged, and that they were willing to sit it out rather than to sign out. Endurance had become the test and measure of all, perhaps the only effective antidote for self-disgust.[274]

Nor, it must be noted, had organised and disciplined resistance among the internees entirely ceased in the middle years. In 1943, the Leddy faction began work on a new tunnel. The plan was ambitious and involved taking a long route – less obvious and therefore not easily discovered – to the fence. Entries were forced into the old uncovered and abandoned tunnels, which were back-filled with the waste from the new one. Liam Leddy, Tony Magan and others took charge, drawing up rotas and devising a general plan of work. A huge amount of digging was entailed because of the length of the tunnel which worked its way to the wire under other huts and also dropped shafts on both sides of the 10-foot security ditch that surrounded the camp. It cannot now be established at what precise point the authorities got to know about the tunnel, but digging had been efficiently organised and proceeded at a good pace. One morning, the camp staff arrived in force and uncovered and blocked the diggings. 'And that', Mick Fitzgibbon (one of the tunnellers) recalled, 'was the end of our tunnel and the last effort to burrow out from the Curragh'.[275] There were rumours that the project had been betrayed by a certain internee, placed in the camp in order to gather information.[276] Equally, the fact that the entire stock of chocolate had been purchased from the camp shop might have been something of a giveaway.[277]

The official files attribute the discovery to a far more mundane cause. There had for some time been a fortnightly check by camp staff on the old and uncovered tunnels. This had been neglected on one occasion, and there was an interval of three weeks between inspections, according to Commandant Guiney. On looking into the D11 hut tunnel, it was discovered that it had been backfilled with fresh clay. Guiney immediately had the hut cleared and searched, and the entrance to the new tunnel was discovered. This ran parallel to the old working, was some eighty-two feet long and extended to the outer wire. Another tunnel, like a spur, linked the new tunnel to the old one, permitting access for spoil disposal. The work had progressed so far, Guiney estimated, that had it not been discovered an escape could have taken place within forty-eight hours.[278] The police report was more specific and alarming than that of Guiney: the tunnel extended beyond the wire, had successfully passed under the anti-tunnel ditch and was within a few feet of the surface.[279] The speculations of former internees to the contrary, it would seem that the tunnel was discovered through routine, albeit delayed, inspection and came as an alarming surprise to the camp command. Had its existence been disclosed by an informer, it would certainly not have been allowed to come to within a few feet of completion. But the consequences were clear: the D11 tunnel was the last to be attempted, and its discovery removed another possibility for rallying and uniting the camp and – had it been successful – for rebuilding morale and cohesion.

From 1943 onwards, there was a steady thinning of the ranks with the release of those considered to be low-risk followers rather than leaders. This helped to ease tensions among the remaining internees. The prospect of indefinite detention was for many the hardest part of their predicament. With war's end in sight, there was a more general lifting of gloom and an easing of cats-in-a-bag fighting. The inmates staged an entertainment for Easter 1944 that indicated a measure of resilience. It included a concert, a parade, a historical pageant and a fancy-dress céilí. Seán McCool described the event in enthusiastic terms. The internees processed around the camp, led by the Tintown Hard Core Band before the céilí:

> All the 'ladies' and gents in costume paraded and I can assure you it was some sight… there were South Sea maidens, nurses, cave men, the 'holder of the key', pirates, film stars, oriental chiefs, a 'horse' and the 'last internees, 1960'! I myself was one of the boys from Portadown [an Orangeman]. It was the most enjoyable day I have spent in prison so far.[280]

The event showed that with the prospect of release becoming more tangible, spirits were beginning to recover; it also demonstrated that relations with the staff had improved immeasurably in the three and a half years since the burning of the camp.

Women prisoners and internees

The number of women interned and sentenced to imprisonment for IRA-related activities during the war years was not great. Up to 31 December 1940, three or four were brought before the Special Criminal Court.[281] Failing to account for movements, possession of arms and ammunition, conspiracy and possession of incriminating documents brought sentences of between six months' and two years' imprisonment. No women were interned in 1939, but there were sixteen or seventeen (out of a total of 662) during 1940.[282] Uinseann MacEoin, whose efforts to record the details of the wartime years of imprisonment and internment were painstaking and conscientious, compiled a list ('regretfully imprecise') of thirty-eight women who had been held in Mountjoy from mid-1940 onwards.[283] A women prisoners' reunion, organised in January 1944, listed forty-seven names, but this included a few who had been imprisoned in England.[284] In a Dáil debate in July 1943, Oliver J. Flanagan named seven women then interned in Mountjoy 'without any charge or crime in the wide world'. It would appear, but it cannot be said with certainty, that these were the only female internees at that point.[285] Although records now do not allow complete certainty as to totals, it is beyond doubt that women comprised a very small proportion of those sentenced and interned during wartime years. All were held in the female wing at Mountjoy, where, irrespective of legal status, they were subject to a common and non-penal regime.[286]

Most were released in 1943. In March of that year, there were eighteen female internees with only seven women remaining by July.[287] They came out to what one former internee, Miriam James, described as 'hardship, disillusionment, cynicism and bitterness. Everywhere was a sense of hopeless despondency, and the feeling of nothing being worthwhile.' Despite this gloom, the experience of imprisonment, and of membership of such a small group, led to strong post-release ties. Miriam James went on to affirm that while some in Mountjoy met as strangers, they parted as comrades, 'in spite of the very lively differences of opinion which animated us while we were there'. She thought that none of them regretted the days in prison, and she herself thanked God for the comradeship, 'for the bad times as well as the good'.[288] Some allowance must be made for rose-tinting, since this was an upbeat message to a reunion, but it would seem that the women prisoners, as a group, were not as divided and fractured by their experience as were the men.

Cumann na mBan organised support for the women prisoners (as they did for the men), and on 28 January 1943 noted that conditions in the women's wing had improved as a result of representations made by the Red Cross.[289] Wool and materials were supplied to the women prisoners, to be worked into garments that could be sold.[290]

Prisoner-support organisations

It was well known to the government that prisoner-support organisations were controlled by the IRA and operated in accordance with its policies and with the wishes of its leaders. Under wartime conditions, the usual fictions of a front organisation would not be tolerated, and anyone involved in such a body was at high risk of internment. It was not until the war's end and the repeal or easing of emergency legislation that the IRA was again able to take an open hand in campaigning for prisoners.[291] During the war years, therefore, an organisation more plausibly distanced from the IRA had to be established. Before this could take place, an agreement had to be negotiated with the Minister for Justice and the police. These had to be convinced that funds would be disbursed only to the dependants of internees and prisoners and would not be used to support the IRA.

It was necessary to break with previous support organisations and to enrol the assistance of persons who were politically respectable and whose integrity and motives of humane involvement could not be questioned. The Green Cross Fund was set up in January 1940, and Mrs Katharine Moloney had an interview with Minister Boland to explain the purposes of the organisation and to give an undertaking that its funds would be applied only to dependants' relief.[292] The Commissioner of the Garda Síochána, Michael Kinnane, indicated that if the funds were used only for the purposes set out, the body would be a legal charity, 'subject to reasonable checks', and it would be difficult to prevent it operating.[293]

As we have noted, Stephen Roche, Secretary General of the Department of Justice, took a very different view. The very term 'Republican Prisoners' in the organisation's statement of objectives implied, he contended, 'that there is a recognised Republican Army at war with the Government, the Government itself being, of course, by implication anti-Republican'. Even were the terminology remedied, the organisation's activity would implicitly suggest that those in prison and at the Curragh were 'patriots suffering undeserved punishment'. The basic idea was not the relief of poverty and suffering in themselves but rather to support militants 'by guaranteeing for the "Army" activists certain security for their families'. The real title of the organisation ought to be 'The Irish Republican Army Dependants Fund'. The government's obligation was to bring a stop to the IRA's foolish and wicked campaign, and only if the promoters of the Green Cross took an honest line on that would it be possible to consider 'in a better atmosphere' the relief of the distress which the IRA's campaign had caused among its own supporters.[294]

Boland largely agreed but looked for a compromise. This was attained through the mediation of William Norton, leader of the Labour Party in the Dáil. The Green Cross Fund would not be allowed to operate independently as a public body. The founding committee would, however, not be subject to government action provided that it did not break the law. Press censorship on its activities would not be lifted, and it would have to operate within the auspices of National Aid (an approved charitable body). All this was restrictive, but the government remained anxious that the IRA should not find an easy means for raising funds. Thanking Boland for the compromise, Katharine Maloney hoped that the committee's activities might in time persuade him to lift press censorship about it.[295] And, indeed, that appears to have happened. In March 1942, permission was given to hold a Green Cross Week in Dublin. Proceeds, however, were intended for the dependants of prisoners and internees in Northern Ireland.[296]

Internment in Northern Ireland is considered elsewhere, but a note is appropriate here on the attitude of Boland to Green Cross activities in the neighbouring jurisdiction.[297] In the summer of 1941, the Department of Justice sought further information on the activities of a Green Cross Committee seeking to raise funds in Castleblaney, Co. Monaghan – a border district. The Department's concerns appear to have been set to rest when the organiser confirmed that he was acting on behalf of the Belfast-based organisation, which was supported by the Roman Catholic bishops and clergy and by Cardinal MacRory. The funds were intended for and solely controlled by this Northern Ireland body.[298] The tone of this statement and other material from the organisation was that the relief was required because of the discrimination practised against Catholics in the North. Even in wartime conditions, and at the height of Dublin's concern about the IRA, this was persuasive, and in August 1941 an official from the Department of Posts and Telegraphs submitted a memorandum in favour of the Green Cross being allowed a Radio Éireann slot to appeal for funds:

> Our people in the North are forced into extremist organisations by the treatment they receive and men who are not in any organisations are in prison. We will be accused of showing no interest in the people in the North if we decline to allow this radio appeal on behalf of the dependants of the men in prison.[299]

Going back to the days and conditions of their foundation, the Society of Friends had an interest in the relief of prisoners and in penal affairs generally. When, in the mid-1930s, criminal and penal policy was being considered by the Free State, they submitted various observations and proposals to P. J. Ruttledge, then Minister for Justice.[300] They attempted to apply the approach and practical work of the notable penal reformer Margery Fry to Irish prisons. In numerous ways, but most of all in its use and justification of violence, the IRA had objectives and employed means which were directly counter to Quaker beliefs. The Society has, however, always insisted on the value of Christian example and appeals to individuals and was therefore likely to be interested in what it may have seen as this group of lost and forlorn men and women. This small organisation (particularly so in Ireland) applied themselves to relief work at the Curragh. They were not admitted into the camp but after the fire visited regularly and were able to meet the men's OC in the administration building. They asked what they might send to assist the prisoners and internees. A former internee described them as 'the only body of people who ever gave us any practical help'.[301]

Releases and amnesty

Both the OASA and the 1940 amending Act provided for the establishment of a Commission to hear appeals against internment orders.[302] The Commission comprised two lawyers and an officer of the Irish Army. Any internee was entitled to have his or her case reviewed. Should the Commission determine that no reasonable ground existed for continued detention the internee had to be released. This was a stronger power than that provided in Northern Ireland, where the equivalent body could only make recommendations to the Minister for Home Affairs who made the ultimate decision on release or retention.[303] Despite its power to override Éire's Minister for Justice, however, few cases were referred to the Commission.[304] Whether actively involved in the IRA, a past member or merely a supporter, such an appeal was seen as an act of repudiation and desertion as well as acceptance of the authority of the state. Because of the strength of this feeling, a submission to the Commission was of itself a fairly fail-safe indication that the applicant had either not possessed or had decisively severed links with the IRA.

Parole, a more routine exercise of executive discretion, was applied for and liberally granted throughout the duration of internment. By 1944, the proportion of internees on parole had risen to 26 per cent.[305] This well-established practice extended back to the days of British administration. There may have been instances when a parolee failed to return, but none is recorded. It was too much a matter of common benefit and interest that parole be preserved for delinquency to be tolerated; persons accepting parole were sensible of the obligations they owed their comrades. Return to camp, moreover, was in many ways seen as a return to the republican ranks. Parole was granted for several reasons, including personal illness so serious as to require surgery at an outside hospital, or the grave illness or death of an immediate relative; it was also allowed for extended periods (sometimes in excess of three months) where the labour of an internee was vital for the survival of a family farm.

Peace came to Europe and then to Japan, and with the general public relief there came a number of pressures to release the internees. The overriding national interest that had justified detention without trial had passed; Ireland's neutrality and the state's survival were no longer in doubt. It was also apparent to all who had any knowledge that the IRA had been wrecked and could no longer function as a paramilitary body. Its leadership had been rounded up or neutralised; imprisonment and prolonged internment had destroyed the revolutionary aspirations and pretensions of most of its followers, and without centre or strategy its units and support organisations had withered and lost purpose and contact.[306] Although Ireland had not been a belligerent country, its population was party to the general desire to return as swiftly as possible to the pace and promises of peacetime. There was also the pressing matter of public expenditure. Internment was a significant cost to a country with a shallow public purse. At an organisational level, the pool of staff from which that of the camps was drawn was shrinking. The small internment camp at Athlone, for example, was due to lose three experienced officers on their retirement on 31 March 1946 (part of a more general wave of retirements among junior officers and NCOs), and there was no obvious way of replacing them. In raising the matter with the Provost Marshal, the Athlone Commandant put forward three possibilities, the first one of which was to release the entire group of ten internees. This was described as 'the ideal solution' since it would mean that no replacements would be required and that Athlone staff could be assigned elsewhere.[307] This was merely one expression of an army preparing itself for peacetime duties with a much reduced strength.

Releases had been in progress as far back as late 1943 and early 1944.[308] By the spring of 1944, Seán McCool was writing to Sighle Humphreys about the exodus: 'Our family here is now "sadly" depleted. Less than half the number we had this time last year and they're still dribbling out. Hope I am not the last of the Mohicans!'[309] On 4 May 1944, McCool reported that 80 per cent of the Kerry men had been released.[310] The problems of those who were freed were the same as all prisoners re-entering a society from which they had become estranged. A man who was arrested in 1940, served a sentence of several months and was then interned would have been in custody for four years, and there were many in this category. Such a lengthy imprisonment was the equivalent of a six-year sentence of penal servitude. The world had moved on – change accelerated by war – and they had not. They had memories of prison and camp and very intensive experiences, but, like soldiers returning from a war, they found that these memories, feelings and attachments were alien and almost unimaginable to the civilian population, to the extent that it was at all interested. Joe Dolan recalled his first full day of freedom and of meeting children going to school: 'I had not seen a child for four years and thought I had not seen anything so small in all my life. Women's voices too; I could not bear to listen as they seemed so sharp; eventually, I got used to them.'[311] This sensation of being an outsider would lose its intensity, but a residue of alienation would always linger in the fading shadows of lost years.[312]

Throughout the early months of 1945 many of the 160 or so men who remained in prison viewed with apprehension any IRA actions in the outside world that were likely to persuade the government that the organisation retained the will and capacity to threaten state security.[313] They need not have worried: no one had will, means or reason to act. Although there were warnings of an IRA recrudescence, the decision to begin releasing the last and hard-core internees was taken on 11 May 1945. The last forty were released by Midsummer's Day, 1945.[314] The sentenced prisoners raised more difficult issues.[315] These had been convicted of serious offences for which they had received heavy punishments. In the ordinary course, with full remission for good conduct, a number would not be eligible for release for several years – one man as late as 1953.[316] It was a weighty matter of political and public concern to set aside a sentence of penal servitude for life, especially were that sentence already commuted from death.[317] These were notorious offenders, and further clemency could, even now, signal government weakness or ambivalence, both of which might assist an IRA revival. There were also electoral factors involved. After sixteen years in office, Fianna Fáil would face a difficult election in 1948 and would need to head off Fine Gael accusations of being lukewarm in handling subversion. On the other hand, with the war ended, there was likely to be a favourable popular response to the tidying away of the detritus. It was a fine, and always shifting, political judgement.

Things looked very different on the other side of the wire. Conflict had finished, the Allies were triumphant, and everywhere armies were being demobilised and captured combatants released; whole populations were returning home. (Though millions, of course, found they had no homes – in some cases no countries – to which to return.) Looking back to the Civil War, when men had been imprisoned for equally grave offences, amnesty had been granted shortly after the cessation of hostilities which to a far greater extent had challenged the survival of the state. There had been delays then, but the state of disorder in 1923 and 1924 may have justified these; now the country was at peace, secure and wholly intact. There was also an equitable consideration. One of the consequences of locating convicted political prisoners at the Curragh Camp, and mixing them with internees, was an implicit acknowledgement that the men were of the same character and background as the internees, and that their culpability was equal. Why, otherwise, some might argue, were both categories permitted to share the same regime?

Therefore, with the release of the internees, expectations intensified among the sentenced, nine of whom were released from the Curragh Detention Barracks (the Glasshouse) on 9 July 1945. In August 1945, the remaining twenty or so were transferred to the Glasshouse from what Tom Doran remembered as 'the vast, near empty, camp'.[318] Hopes were further heightened when Peadar O'Flaherty, Sean O'Brien and Thomas Hunt were released.[319] These were well-known leaders, and those who saw themselves as followers and lesser figures had good reason to take such cases as a sign that they too would soon be on their way. Commandant Guiney reported that for some time the Glasshouse prisoners, now down to twenty-four, anticipated a Christmas release. Staff noted that prisoners were completing outstanding handicraft tasks and that they had largely withdrawn from the general routine of pastimes and games. They were over-heard to say such things as 'It won't be long now' and 'Did you hear any news?' There was also a change in their attitude towards staff, becoming markedly more familiar.[320]

Those who still took an interest in Dáil proceedings and politics outside the wire would have recalled the unpromising announcement by de Valera some months before. On 4 July 1945, he had set out his intentions regarding wartime emergency legislation. At the second reading of the Emergency Powers (Continuance and Amendment) Bill, 1945, he told deputies that powers of postal and telegraphic censorship were being dropped, together with what were now comparatively marginal provisions affecting arrest without warrant and the summary trial of civilians by army officers. With these exceptions, he wanted to retain Emergency Powers provisions until 2 September 1946. This was necessary because as soon as hard-core internees had been released they had recommenced plotting. The murder of police officers had been discussed, and at a public meeting, a former IRA Chief of Staff had urged enlistment in the IRA. (In consequence he had been re-interned.) It continued to be necessary, for public safety, to retain internment powers.[321] This statement was critically received by James Dillon and John Costello of Fine Gael, both concerned that with only a few exceptions the broad swathe of wartime powers were being retained. For those in the Curragh, however, this opposition was cold comfort since a general election was not due until 1948. De Valera had a strong enough majority to deliver his legislative programme and to stand by his politics in the interim, and might, in any event, be able to form another government after the election. Extended internment was a distinct possibility, especially were some life to be coaxed into the all but cold embers of armed republicanism.[322]

The men's general anxiety put pressure on their leadership to provide information, and Seán Hamill, the Glasshouse OC, sought an interview with Commandant Guiney almost every day, 'on the slightest pretext', asking his opinion on the chances of a Christmas release. When, on 21 December 1945, the Northern Ireland government released its last eleven internees, Hamill told Guiney that he and the men were now convinced that they would be released. Following an IRA action at Dundalk, it became evident that there was not to be a Christmas release, and the remaining prisoners blamed the Dundalk men. Hamill told Guiney that his men were very angry and warned that those involved in the incident should not be sent to the Curragh: he would not be responsible for what might happen to them.[323]

Commandant James Guiney had charge of the Curragh Camp from the fire of December 1940, and this had given him a perspective on the prisoners' thinking and morale. The denial of a Christmas release had been a bitter disappointment, causing even more resentment to focus on those who had held leadership positions yet who had been freed nevertheless. The Brugha family was mentioned, particularly the fact that Rory had been able to do his sentence on parole 'while the fools had to suffer on'.[324] Others who had been released were returning to substantial accumulated pension arrears and to employment: to those still in captivity this was galling.

The prisoners, either spontaneously or as a somewhat desperate tactic to improve release chances, broke completely with past confrontational attitudes and became more friendly towards staff. At the Christmas dinner, Seán Hamill came forward and gave Christmas and New Year greetings to Guiney on behalf of all the prisoners; he also expressed warm appreciation for the manner in which they had been treated. In reporting this, Guiney noted that the incident might be said to characterise their general demeanour. He pointed out that this was the first time in six Christmases that the prisoners had adopted such an attitude, 'which to my mind portrayed a changed mental outlook'.[325]

Impressed by those changes, Guiney began to intercede more actively. The few prisoners who had visits from relatives and friends around the Christmas period were heard, he reported, to express disapproval of their former associates, particularly those who had been released. It was his 'unbiased opinion' that those remaining at the Curragh had 'lost all enthusiasm for the IRA and what it stands for'.[326] There was nothing now that they would cherish more than their liberty; they realised with despondency that their best years were passing, leaving them without prospects. The majority had indicated that if freed they would emigrate. Looking back over the preceding five years, Guiney contended that 'even the very toughest of them show a marked degree of improvement in their general conduct, manners and behaviour'. He went so far as to suggest, albeit obliquely, that they had some grounds for a sense of grievance in that they thought they had not been treated impartially, not understanding why one sentenced man should be released and another retained, considering that all their offences had sprung from the same political code.[327]

These views were shared by Guiney's superiors. The twenty-four remaining Glasshouse prisoners had release dates ranging from April 1946 to 1953. There were ten prisoners at Athlone, and the combined demands of providing custody was clearly unwelcome to the Army. There were, moreover, problems in providing sufficiently experienced staff to carry out what were always sensitive and sometimes difficult duties. Using Guiney's letter and other material, on 23 January 1946, Colonel James Flynn, Adjutant General, wrote to Minister Boland. The gist of his letter was that there had been a very considerable shift in the attitudes of the men, that those who could be released might be freed sooner rather than later and that in any event the groups could be consolidated and transferred to civil custody 'in the light of the satisfactory internal situation in the Country and the ending of War conditions abroad'.[328]

In April 1946, there were, at the very least, mixed feelings when ten leading figures and hard-core IRA men reinforced what had been a dwindling Glasshouse band. These arrivals were the fruit of an attempt to revive the IRA. A meeting, intended to be held at the Ardee Bar in Dublin on the evening of 9 March 1946, provided Special Branch with a useful opportunity to stamp on the embers.[329] Tom Doran recalled that the thoughts of the prisoners immediately turned to their own plight: 'how does a reorganisation meeting at this stage affect our chances of getting out?'[330] There was further consternation when Pat Shannon, an IRA veteran, who had been released early in 1945, arrived back with a five-year sentence for shooting at a Special Branch detective.[331] So strong was the feeling that such actions were prolonging their imprisonment that, ahead of Shannon's arrival, some of the leading figures among the Glasshouse group proposed that he be ostracised. After some debate, the proposal was defeated.[332]

Those were troubling incidents, but the government nevertheless took the view that the substantive threat had passed and that these events did not presage any significant IRA revival. As noted above, the earliest possible release dates extended as far into the future as September 1953, with many occurring in 1947, 1948 and 1949.[333] During October 1946, a further six were released from the Glasshouse. Christmas still retained a sentimental connection with prisoners' releases, and a week prior to the holiday in 1946 most of the men serving sentences for IRA activities were released. Shannon, just lately arrived at the Glasshouse, was kept, as were four of the seven Portlaoise prisoners. Sixteen were freed on 18 December and five men who were on parole were informed that they did not need to return.[334] There remained in Portlaoise Tomás MacCurtáin and James Brennan (alias Smith), serving life at penal servitude; Eamon Smullen (fourteen years) and Liam Rice (twenty years). Harry White, sometime Chief of Staff, joined the four in December 1946. He was sentenced to death by the Special Criminal Court on 13 December 1946 for his part in the April 1942 killing of Detective Mordaunt. This delayed sentence was reduced to twelve years' penal servitude.

The next releases were in February 1948, an early decision of the incoming coalition government. Rice, sentenced in April 1941 for the attempted murder of a police officer, and Smullen, sentenced in 1943, were freed on 26 February. MacCurtáin, Brennan (Smith) and White remained, but for less than two weeks more, being freed on 9 March 1948. MacCurtáin, who of all the long-term prisoners had come closest to death, had been in prison since July 1940 and served the longest sentence of any of the wartime IRA men.[335]

Notes

1 Seán Russell, IRA Chief of Staff, was in the USA seeking financial support and arms. He was reported in the *New York Times* (20 August 1939, 5e) as planning to take over the whole of Ireland by revolutionary action. A European war would provide the opportunity to do so.

2 British occupation led to an agreement between the USA, Britain and Iceland for British forces to be succeeded by Americans, based at Keflavik. This occupation began in February 1942 and lasted until September 2006. By March 1943, the British Representative in Dublin was telling his American counterpart that the British military was no longer concerned about the Irish ports, Northern Ireland, Iceland and other locations allowing necessary protection for the Atlantic convoys. See Brian Girvin, *The Emergency: Neutral Ireland, 1939–45* (London: Macmillan, 2006), p. 300. The Portuguese dictator António de Oliveira Salazar agreed in 1943 to provide

bases in the Azores for US forces, a concession that was viewed with alarm and displeasure by de Valera's government.

3 Some reassurance had been given by de Valera's speech (made before the Treaty Ports were handed over) indicating that the Free State (as it was called at that point) would not be allowed to become a base for an attack on Britain and that his government would do everything in its power 'to see that no foreign country would get a footing here on our soil' (*Dáil Debates*, vol. 67, col. 721, 19 May 1937). This pledge fell far short of that which Winston Churchill and others wanted: that in times of dire necessity the southern and western Irish ports would be open to British vessels and aircraft.

4 With the terrible losses in the North Atlantic dragging down the British war effort and showing no signs of abating, Churchill (now Prime Minister) spoke to the Commons on 5 November 1940. Denial of facilities for ships and planes on the south and west coasts of Ireland was 'a most heavy and grievous burden and one which should never have been placed on our shoulders'. These facilities protected Irish as well as British trade (5 *Hansard*, vol. 365, col. 1243, 5 November 1940). Two days later, de Valera replied in the Dáil. The ports would not be handed over as long as Ireland remained neutral, and any attempt to take them by any of the belligerents, including Britain, would lead to bloodshed (*Dáil Debates*, vol. 81, col. 585, 7 November 1940).

5 Including some members of the IRA, particularly those with left-leaning politics. For others, the subjugation of Britain by whomsoever was the overriding objective. Recalling the increasingly beleaguered state of the IRA in early 1940, Christy Quearney, a member of the Dublin Brigade, found solace in the fact that 'Germany was crawling all over Europe, and we had hope that they would crawl over England also.' Uinseann MacEoin, *The IRA in the Twilight Years, 1923–1948* (Dublin: Argenta, 1997), p. 775.

6 John Loader Maffey (1877–1969), educated at Rugby and Christ Church, Oxford. Served with distinction in the Indian Civil Service and, in 1933, became Permanent Under-Secretary for the Colonies. Appointed first British Representative to Ireland in 1939 and served there until his retirement in 1949. Created Lord Rugby in 1947. Had good working relationship with de Valera and with Costello, his successor. For a full account of Maffey's first interview with de Valera, see Robert Fisk's excellent *In Time of War: Ireland, Ulster and the Price of Neutrality, 1939–45* (London: André Deutsch, 1983), p. 91 *et seq.* On de Valera's remarks, see Girvin, *The Emergency, op. cit.*, pp. 63–4.

7 Joseph T. Carroll, *Ireland in the War Years, 1939–1945* (Newton Abbot: David & Charles, 1975), p. 18. Séamus Ó Goilidhe, then a socially sheltered and politically inexperienced recruit to the IRA, recalled the outlook he shared with his colleagues: 'Most of us, while not pro-German, hoped nonetheless that England would be trounced. We were ignorant of the Nazi philosophy as, indeed, was everyone, until the war had ended' (MacEoin, *The IRA in the Twilight Years, op. cit.*, p. 712). ('Everyone' presumably referred to Ó Goilidhe's IRA comrades.)

8 See Brian Girvin's thoughtful and well-informed analysis in *The Emergency, op. cit.*, Chapters 2 and 3, for a description of the lead-up to the adoption of a neutral stance and its operation as war commenced. Clair Wills deftly and imaginatively combines cultural, social and political analysis to cover the same ground, providing more of the non-political (in its formal sense) hinterland cultural and civic context in *That Neutral Island: A Cultural History of Ireland during the Second World War* (Cambridge, Mass.: Harvard University Press, 2007), Chapters 1 and 2.

9 *Dáil Debates*, vol. 75, col. 1160, 27 April 1939. He had insisted that 'there is no reason for any nation to think that our attitude would be other than that of neutrality'.

10 There were no opinion polls, so all assessments were subjective judgements. Writing to the British Foreign Secretary on 23 October 1939, Maffey insisted that neutrality

'commands widespread approval among all classes and interests in Éire'. Even men who had served in the British armed forces and would do so again, and whose sons were at the front, 'loyalists in the old sense of the word' generally supported the neutrality policy; see PRO CAB/66, WP (39) 34. See also Wills, *That Neutral Island*, *op. cit.*, p. 44. The British government was provided with regular secret reports on conditions in Éire (presumably through the British Representative's Office in Dublin). These reports, entitled 'Irish Affairs', dealt with events, social and economic conditions, and public and political opinion. Certainly the secret British reports from Éire during the war repeatedly emphasised the popular support for neutrality. PRO DO/121/85, 'Irish Affairs' (marked 'Most Secret') bulletin of 1 May 1942 and successive bulletins.

11 First Amendment of the Constitution Act, 1939. This amended Article 28 of the Constitution. It was from this amendment that the term 'national emergency' was derived and used throughout the years of the Second World War instead of the term 'war'. On 2 September 1939, the Dáil resolved that a state of emergency existed, in accordance with Article 28.3.3.

12 *Dáil Debates*, vol. 77, col. 19, 2 September 1939.

13 See *Dáil Debates*, vol. 74, col. 87, 8 February 1939 (first stage of passage of Treasonable Offences Bill); col. 89, 8 February 1939 (first stage of Offences Against the State Bill). The Court was activated under Part V (35[2]) of the OASA and internment under Part VI (54[2]). Both parts were activated and the appointment of the five members of the Court announced (*Iris Oifigiúil*, 22 August 1939). By 1946, a total of 429 people had been convicted by this court. NAI JUS/8/944, Statistics, Internment, etc. (1946).

14 *Iris Oifigiúil*, 23 June 1939. This designation has never been lifted.

15 MA, BMH, CP 16, Weekly Reports, Arbour Hill, 25 September 1939.

16 Judge Gavan Duffy held that Part VI of the OASA conflicted with the Constitution and was therefore invalid (1940 Irish Law Reports, 141–57). The judgment is also published in full in Gerald Hogan, *The Origins of the Irish Constitution, 1928–1941* (Dublin: Royal Irish Academy, 2012), pp. 717–32; see also pp. 668–95.

17 MA CP 16, Weekly Reports, Arbour Hill, 25 September 1939. Interestingly, one man, Patrick McSweeney, was at large on parole the following week. See also UCDA, P/104/3712, Office of the Minister for Justice, Department Notes on Events, from 1 January 1931 to 31 December 1940 (hereafter 'Department Notes'), Appendix M.

18 See Chapter 19 below.

19 See the sweeping Emergency Powers Act, 1939. This is informatively discussed in Seosamh Ó Longaigh, 'Emergency Law in Action, 1939–45', in Dermot Keogh and Mervyn O'Driscoll (eds.), *Ireland in World War II: Diplomacy and Survival* (Cork: Mercier, 2004), pp. 63–80; and in Seosamh Ó Longaigh, *Emergency Law in Independent Ireland* (Dublin: Four Courts Press, 2006). See also the extensive adjournment debate on 28 September 1939, reflecting some of the many consequences of the war for Éire (*Dáil Debates*, vol. 77, cols. 375–517).

20 See above, pp. 308–11.

21 For a clear and comprehensive account of Irish defence and security concerns and provisions at this juncture, see Eunan O'Halpin, *Defending Ireland: The Irish State and Its Enemies since 1922* (Oxford: Oxford University Press, 1999), Chapters 5 and 6. The eminent Irish-American republican Joseph McGarrity, leading member of Clan na Gael, an associate of Roger Casement and, importantly, involved in Casement's First World War mission to Germany, visited Ireland during the summer of 1939. On 14 August, he departed for Hamburg. This pattern of consultation and travel was noted with concern by the Irish government. See 'Departmental Notes', *op. cit.*

22 But not without some friction between Military Intelligence (G2 Branch) and the Garda Síochána. The former subsequently indicated that the Gardaí were unable,

through pressure of work, to provide the detail the Army had requested (MA PM 663, Colonel L. Archer to Provost Marshal, 28 October 1940). Some names on the list showed a detailed knowledge of the innermost meetings of the IRA, going well beyond the high-profile or locally known leaders. Although he was not detained in the first batch and had avoided known contacts and republican meetings, Seamus O'Donovan was arrested in September 1941. He had been on Michael Collins's staff as Director of Chemicals (Explosives) from the start of the War of Independence. He was, nevertheless, on the anti-Treaty side in the Civil War. After his release from prison in 1924 he took no further part in republican activities until in 1936 or 1937 he was asked for assistance in preparing the bombing campaign against Britain. See NLI, James L. O'Donovan Papers, MS. 22, 307; J. Bowyer Bell, *The Secret Army: The IRA, 1916–1979* (Cambridge, Mass.: MIT Press, 1983), p. 146. See also David O'Donoghue, *The Devil's Deal: The IRA, Nazi Germany and the Double Life of Jim O'Donoghue* (Dublin: New Island, 2010).

23 See NAI TAOIS/S11436.

24 The arrested men were Larry Grogan, Patrick McGrath, William McGuinness and Peadar O'Flaherty. Three of the men received sentences of eighteen months before the Special Criminal Court. McGrath successfully delayed his case for months by hunger-striking and eventually a *nolle prosequi* was entered in his case. See *Dáil Debates*, vol. 78, cols. 1311–13, 3 January 1940, for further details.

25 Bell, *The Secret Army, op. cit.*, pp. 169–70.

26 The warrants were authorised by Part VI of the OASA. Dublin, Tralee and Co. Tipperary were the principal centres of arrest. See *Southern Star*, 9 September 1939, 9b–c; *Irish Independent*, 16 September 1939, 8a–b; *Irish Press*, 23 September 1939, 7b. Fifty-eight were received at Arbour Hill on 15 September 1939. Within a week three had been discharged, presumably because they had been arrested in error. Although other arrests followed, the total in the autumn of 1939 probably did not exceed seventy (MA, Civilian Prisoners, Admissions to Arbour Hill, 15 September 1939). Patrick McGrath, in private correspondence with another IRA member, noted that perhaps many of the internees were 'not members of our organisation' (Humphreys Papers, P/106/889, Patrick McGrath to Jim Killeen, 3 December 1939). Christy Quearney, a technical specialist and sometime Director of Training of the IRA, was arrested at this time. He estimated that about 40 per cent of those in Arbour Hill with him were not active IRA members but had been arrested because police lists were out of date (MacEoin, *The IRA in the Twilight Years, op. cit.*, p. 774).

27 *Irish Press*, 2 December 1939, 6b–e; 4 December 1939, 3e; *Irish Independent*, 4 December 1939, 5f–g. This first group of internees under the OASA were held in Arbour Hill Military Prison. By 25 September sixty-six men were being held. (MA CP 16, Weekly Reports, Arbour Hill, 25 September 1939). See also Mick McCarthy on this brief episode. He recalled favourably the Arbour Hill Governor, Commandant Michael Lennon: 'A Kilkenny man, whom most of us found reasonable and not overbearing' (MacEoin, *The IRA in the Twilight Years, op. cit.*, p. 656).

28 Thus the Recruits' Company of the IRA's Dublin Battalion, just under thirty strong, was taken to a disused estate at Clontarf, no more than five miles from Dublin city centre, for training in field tactics. The entire group was then arrested in a joint police and army operation. Brought before the Special Criminal Court, most were given one-year sentences, with Mick Dunne, the OC, receiving twice that. Having served their sentences in Arbour Hill, almost all then spent the rest of the war years in internment. It had been completely irresponsible to muster so many young men in this manner. (Some were aged only seventeen.) See Séamus Ó Goilidhe in MacEoin, *The IRA in the Twilight Years, op. cit.*, p. 710.

29 The guards' state of intent may be gauged by the ease by which entry was allegedly obtained: one of the raiders knocked on the front door and asked to borrow a bicycle pump (private information to author). As was customary, a military court of inquiry was conducted. Despite legitimate political and public interest in the raid – it had rocked the nation – the government refused to publish its findings (see *Dáil Debates*, vol. 78, cols. 1677–8, 21 February 1940). Two months later, faced with a motion to appoint a select committee of the Dáil, Oscar Traynor, Minister for Defence, gave a detailed and, in places, scathing account of the raid and its aftermath. This explanation proved sufficient, and the motion for a Dáil inquiry was defeated by fifty votes to thirty-one (*Dáil Debates*, vol. 79, cols. 1879 *et seq.*, 30 April 1940).

30 The government admitted to the loss of 472,111 rounds of .303 rifle ammunition and 612,297 rounds of .45 Thompson sub-machine gun ammunition. Some of the arms and equipment of the fort guard were also taken, including four Lee Enfield rifles, a Webley revolver and three bayonets (*Dáil Debates*, vol. 79, col. 1986, 30 April 1940). Within a week, 1,021,751 rounds in almost 650 boxes were recovered.

31 In one of his last reports to the US State Department from Dublin, John Cudahy, the US Minister, noted de Valera's private admission to him that the Irish government had been humiliated by the Magazine Fort raid. Those responsible he characterised as 'vindictive, vehement, venomous, violent Irishmen' (NAUSA, 841 DOO/1237, Cudahy to State Department, 19 January 1940). John Cudahy (1887–1943), of Irish extraction, was a wealthy Democrat from Milwaukee, Wisc., who had seen action in 1919 as part of the anti-Bolshevik Allied force of intervention in northern Russia. Prior to his 1937 Dublin posting, he had served as US Ambassador to Poland. From Dublin he went on to Belgium and Luxembourg, leaving when those countries were invaded by German forces in May 1940.

32 *Irish Press*, 13 March 1940, 2d–c; 4 July 1940, 2a–b.

33 The raids had also netted the IRA's pirate radio station which started broadcasting the previous April. A broadcast was under way when the Gardaí struck. Four men were arrested and brought before the Special Criminal Court where they received sentences of eighteen months and two years. *Irish Times*, 11 January 1940, 5b; 2 March 1940, 7a–b; *Irish Independent*, 2 March 1940, 7a–b; *Irish Press*, 2 March 1940, 7f–g. One of the four, Seán McNeela, went on hunger strike and died at St Bricin's Military Hospital on 19 April 1940 (see below, p. 696). See *Irish Times*, 27 February 1940, 5f; 20 April 1940, 8b–c; *Irish Independent*, 20 April 1940, 7a–b; *Irish Press*, 20 April 1940, 7c–d.

34 Details of the raid itself were withheld because of a number of civilian arrests and the hearing of charges by the military courts in respect of the Magazine Fort raid. Gerald Boland, Minister for Justice, was pressed on this but insisted that, since the matters were *sub judice*, he could go no further. He did, however, catalogue a number of IRA activities that had come to light as a result of raids and painted a picture of a high level of IRA training and preparation (*Dáil Debates*, vol. 78, cols. 1312–16). Despite the obvious unwillingness of Boland and de Valera to discuss the raid, a number of details as to the quantity of ammunition lost and recovered had to be given.

35 See O'Halpin, *Defending Ireland, op. cit.*, pp. 247–8.

36 *Seanad Debates*, vol. 24, col. 561, 4 January 1940.

37 The President referred the legislation to the Council of State, an advisory body set up under the 1937 Constitution. After consultation, the President referred the Offences Against the State (Amendment) Bill to the Supreme Court, under Article 26 of the Constitution, for a decision on the Bill's compliance with the Constitution. The Supreme Court heard arguments between 24 and 30 January 1940, reserving judgment. On 9 February the Court announced that the Bill was constitutionally valid. *Irish Times*, 10 February 1940, 8c–d; *Limerick Leader*, 10 February 1940, 7a–b; *Irish Independent*, 10 February 1940, 10a e. See also Hogan, *The Origins of the Irish*

Constitution, op. cit., pp. 668–95. A Commission had been established on 3 February 1940 under the Emergency Powers Act to consider internees' applications for release. Its members were Mr Justice William Black, Major Michael Tuohy and Commandant John Wall, BL. This Commission remained in operation until 7 June 1940 when the Minister for Justice was given powers to consider representations. By removing an independent element (albeit one that had included two army officers), Éire retained for the executive greater powers than the government had in Northern Ireland.

38 Emergency Powers Act, 1939, as amended by the Emergency Powers (Amendment) Act, 1940: the latter brought Irish citizens under the powers of detention previously restricted to non-citizens. The offence of refusing to answer questions or to give information was created by the OASA, s.52(1) and (2).

39 Prisoners, local or penal servitude, whether in military or civil custody, were entitled to a remission of sentence for good behaviour. Remission for good behaviour during penal servitude (sentences of three years and more) was up to a quarter. (This was less generous than the English scale, on which it was based, which allowed remission of between a quarter and a third, on a sliding scale, according to the length of sentence.) Ordinary imprisonment attracted remission of between a sixth and a quarter. Good behaviour was recorded in marks, and awards were made solely at the discretion of the commandant or civil governor (see MA CP 1236, Minute on Remission of Sentence, 22 December 1939). All of this was a formal exercise, however, since internment followed release, whenever it was granted.

40 The annual total of persons sentenced to imprisonment for offences against the state, 1939–45, were as follows: 1939 (twenty-five persons), 1940 (198), 1941 (136), 1942 (sixty-five), 1943 (thirty-three), 1944 (two), 1945 (four). The total was 463. The declining annual numbers track the suppression of the organisation. NAI JUS/8/944, Statistics, Internment, etc. (1946).

41 The combine-harvester effect also applied to persons released from prison in Northern Ireland. Seán McCool was sentenced on 21 July 1936 to five years' penal servitude for his part in the Crown Entry affair (see above, p. 396). With remission, he was released on 4 May 1940 and served with a deportation order. After some weeks at home he visited Sligo, where he was arrested at the home of an IRA comrade. Local gardaí sent him to Dublin, and, on 1 June 1940, he was served with an internment order and removed to the Curragh, having been free for less than a month. The critical factor in this case seems to have been the resumption of old associations. See O'Donovan Papers, MS. 22, 307, Statement of Seán McCool, 27 October 1941.

42 Part of this self-destructive method of work was the organisation's insistence, going back to its origins, that it was the country's legitimate government and thus entitled (or obliged) to have in miniature the appurtenances of a state. In turn, this entailed offices for its various departments and functions. All of these premises and patterns of association would in time become known (with few exceptions) and thus become funnels for arrests and convenient depositories for documents of all kinds, which were duly scooped up. Special Branch watched comings and goings, made identifications and followed subjects to yet other premises. When a raid was eventually made, there would be arrests and seizures of documents, arms and other items. Sometimes a raid would be conducted discreetly and police would then wait on the premises, spiderlike, for further callers. For a photographic portfolio of the numerous premises used by the IRA at this time, see MacEoin, *The IRA in the Twilight Years*, *op. cit.*, pp. 411–20 (under the revealing heading 'The IRA, a State within a State').

43 *Irish Times*, 23 October 1939, 7c; 24 October 1939, 5d; *Irish Press*, 23 October 1939, 1g; *Irish Independent*, 23 October 1939, 5d. That only a small quantity of gelignite had been used and that little damage resulted (some broken glass) did not reduce the

anger caused by the explosion. In particular, the prison authorities were deeply concerned to know how three or four sticks of gelignite had come into the prison.

44 *Irish Times*, 18 November 1939, 7e; 21 November 1939, 8d; *Limerick Leader*, 18 November 1939, 7a–b; *Irish Independent*, 18 November 1939, 10b–c.

45 *Irish Independent*, 24 November 1939, 9c; *Irish Press*, 24 November 1939, 1a–b; *Irish Times*, 24 November 1939, 7c. For a chronological list of these incidents, see 'Departmental Notes', *op. cit.*

46 *Irish Press*, 4 January 1940, 1c–d; *Irish Times*, 4 January 1940, 7e; *Leitrim Observer*, 6 January 1940, 1f. Tomás (Óg) MacCurtáin (1915–94) was a leading republican who had served on the IRA Executive. Following his release from the penal servitude to which his death sentence had been commuted, MacCurtáin resumed IRA activity, including another period as a member of the Executive. The commutation apparently caused a deal of police dissatisfaction, somewhat offset by a surrender of IRA arms. The government had spread the word that it expected a quid pro quo for sparing MacCurtáin and that any illegal arms surrendered within a week of the reprieve would be spared prosecution. See Fisk, *In Time of War*, *op. cit.*, pp. 299–300; PRONI PREM/3/129/2, RUC Report, 20 July 1940.

47 *Seanad Debates*, vol. 24, col. 643 (*passim*), 5 January 1940. 'Our patience has been tried, our policy of conciliation has been given an over-trial… we have tried it *ad nauseam* – went too far, I thought… we are going to insist that everybody in the country will obey the law… There is going to be no question of ruthlessness, but there is going to be insistence on that.'

48 *Irish Times*, 12 February 1940, 5a–b; *Irish Press*, 12 February 1940, 1e–f.

49 Tim Pat Coogan, *The IRA* (London: Fontana, 1980), p. 181; Bell, *The Secret Army*, *op. cit.*, p. 177. Ballykinlar showed an unconscious appetite for symmetry. The Magazine Fort raid had netted ammunition without guns; here were guns without ammunition.

50 See above, p. 437.

51 *Irish Independent*, 20 February 1940, 10d; *Irish Press*, 20 February 1940, 1d–e.

52 *Irish Times*, 6 April 1940, 10b; 19 April 1940, 10a; 23 April 1940, 2d. Two men, having indicated contrition, had their sentences commuted on condition that they entered into recognisances in the sum of £10. A year later the lesson remained unlearned: twenty-eight officers and men were arrested at Crumlin brickworks at 10 p.m., on Friday, 2 May 1941. The catch on this occasion comprised a large part of the Dublin activists (MacEoin, *The IRA in the Twilight Years*, *op. cit.*, p. 740).

53 *Irish Press*, 13 April 1940, 1b; *Irish Times*, 13 April 1940, 8d.

54 The bombing at Dublin Castle was organised by Jim Crofton, a renegade member of Special Branch and IRA agent (Girvin, *The Emergency*, *op. cit.*, p. 79).

55 Six shots were fired by the raiders before their Thompson gun jammed. Garda William McSweeney was hit in the lung, William Shanahan in the spine, back and hand. One of the raiders was wounded. *Irish Times*, 8 May 1940, 7e–f; *Irish Press*, 8 May 1940, 1a–c; *Irish Independent*, 8 May 1940, 9f–g. An especially serious view was taken of the attempt to seize this confidential post, which undoubtedly contained items of vital importance to the government and the state. A reward of £5,000 was immediately offered for information leading to the arrest of the raiders. De Valera visited the two wounded detectives in hospital (both had immediately been promoted to sergeant) and on 8 May broadcast to the country. For an IRA account of the incident, see MacEoin, *The IRA in the Twilight Years*, *op. cit.*, pp. 888–9.

56 *Irish Independent*, 9 May 1940, 9e; *Irish Times*, 9 May 1940, 1a–c. German attacks on the Netherlands, Belgium and Yugoslavia were imminently expected, and Britain's Norwegian expedition had failed.

57 *Dáil Debates*, vol. 80, cols. 211, 285–6, 9 May 1940.

58 *Irish Times*, 29 May 1940, 5a–b; *Irish Press*, 29 May 1940, 1a–c. *Dáil Debates*, vol. 80, cols. 1169–70, *et seq.*, 28 May 1940.

59 *Irish Independent*, 17 June 1940, 7f–g, 9a–c; *Irish Press*, 17 June 1940, 1a–c. At this point France had effectively ceased to be a combatant and Marshal Pétain formed his first government in Bordeaux; Dunkirk was finally evacuated on 4 June 1940.

60 *Irish Press*, 5 June 1940, 8b; *Irish Times*, 5 June 1940, 5c; *Irish Independent*, 5 June 1940, 7c. During the wartime years a total of 1,196 IRA men (and a small number of women in associated organisations) were interned. NAI JUS/8/944, Statistics, Internment, etc. (1946).

61 Convictions before this court were as follows: 1940 (three convictions), 1941 (two), 1942 (four). There were none thereafter. Of the nine death sentences passed, six were carried out. NAI JUS/8/944, Statistics, Internment, etc. (1946).

62 *Dáil Debates*, vol. 80, col. 1741, 19 June 1940; *Seanad Debates*, vol. 24, col. 1991, *et seq.*, 26 June 1940. The three trial officers would be selected from the panel of five that currently comprised the Special Criminal Court. On the working of the policy of repression and maximum deterrence, see pp. 656–7, above.

63 The arrival and arrest of a number of German agents, equipped with explosives and British currency, heightened the sense of danger (*Irish Times*, 17 August 1940, 7g). On 16 August 1940, the Luftwaffe bombed London for the first time, and the battle of Britain intensified. It was not known at the time how many German agents had slipped the net and what German objectives were in Ireland. See 'Departmental Notes', *op. cit.*, pp. 86b, 86c and 86d. The most important of the German agents was Hermann Görtz, who arrived by parachute on 5 May 1940. He would remain at large and in close contact with the IRA until the summer of 1941. Eunan O'Halpin paints a convincing and detailed picture of Éire in the year that followed the collapse of France (May 1940–June 1941) in *Spying on Ireland* (Oxford: Oxford University Press, 2008), Chapter 3.

64 In 1940, the IRA killed one civilian and three gardaí; in 1942, three gardaí. NAI JUS/8/944, Statistics, Internment, etc. (1946).

65 *Irish Times*, 17 August 1940, 7f–g; *Irish Independent*, 17 August 1940, 7b–c; *Irish Press*, 17 August 1940, 1b–c.

66 MacBride never sought payment for his legal services to republicans. Liam Burke interview in MacEoin, *The IRA in the Twilight Years*, *op. cit.*, p. 449.

67 They had been held at Arbour Hill until 9 p.m. the previous night and were then transferred to Mountjoy for execution the following morning. MA CP 16, Weekly Reports, Arbour Hill, 7 September 1940. See above, pp. 302–1.

68 'Departmental Notes', *op. cit.*, pp. 86g and 86h. The third man, Thomas Hunt, was lucky. He had succeeded in getting away from the scene but was arrested six days later. The Military Court imposed the death sentence on 23 September 1940, but two days later this was commuted to life at penal servitude. His youth was one reason for mercy as was the fact that his two companions had already been executed. NAI TAOIS/2, Cabinet minutes series.

69 Fifteen of these were subsequently interned, and a Miss O'Connor was sentenced to two years' imprisonment for the possession of arms. A return of civil servants and persons in public employment interned and convicted for IRA offences (no date, but probably 1941) shows twenty-four men and four women convicted. Occupations ranged from a foreman with University College Dublin, to postmen and van-drivers to teachers, unspecified civil servants and a former garda. Sentences were short, with the exception of Bridget Cunningham (a twenty-six-year-old teacher) and Maureen Cullinane (a civil servant) who had received sentences of between six months and two years. A smaller number of civil servants were interned: sixteen, including one woman. Again, most held minor posts, teachers and mental-hospital attendants

predominantly. NAI JUS/8/968; *Irish Times*, 28 March 1941, 8h; *Anglo-Celt*, 29 March 1941, 8b.

70 *Irish Times*, 23 November 1940, 9c. The men were James Brennan of Derry and Patrick McGlynn of Dublin. They shot at Gardaí Leo Flanagan and Matthew Wilson.

71 Bell, *The Secret Army*, *op. cit.*, p. 191.

72 MacEoin, *The IRA in the Twilight Years*, *op. cit.*

73 Tom Doran in MacEoin, *The IRA in the Twilight Years*, *op. cit.*, p. 499.

74 For a guerrilla army, this parade went utterly against the most basic doctrine of elusiveness, mobility and saving oneself to fight another day, articulated many times and summed up in Mao's doctrine that when the enemy advance, we retreat; when the enemy retreat, we advance. See *Quotations from Chairman Mao Tse Tung* (Peking: Foreign Languages Press, 1972), pp. 95–8, for a fuller statement of the principles of asymmetrical and guerrilla warfare. It also violated elementary common sense.

75 'I knew it was madness', Doran recalled, 'and that any of us, not known, would be on their lists for rounding up later on.' He attended against his better judgement because 'not for all the world would I let the lads down' (MacEoin, *The IRA in the Twilight Years*, *op. cit.*, p. 500). It was at the end of this parade that Brendan Behan fired shots, committing the offence for which he was sentenced to fourteen years' penal servitude ('extremely lucky, in view of the times that we were in it, to receive a sentence and not the rope').

76 There is a deal of overlap in these numbers, since virtually all who were sentenced to imprisonment were subsequently interned. The yearly figures were as follows (sentenced and interned, respectively): 1939 (25, 75), 1940 (198, 669), 1941 (136, 152), 1942 (65, 191), 1943 (33, 86), 1944 (2, 19), 1945 (4, 4). NAI JUS/8/944, Statistics, Internment, etc. (1946). Seosamh Ó Longaigh gives slightly different figures: 'Emergency Law in Action, 1939–45', *op. cit.*

77 NAI JUS/8/1144, Regulations for Prisoners Sentenced to Penal Servitude by the Special Criminal Court, P. Chinnéide, Deputy Secretary of Justice, 20 February 1940.

78 The regulations for internees were set out in the Emergency Powers (No. 20) Order, 1940, Detention Directions, and those for convicted persons in the OASA (Military Custody) Regulations, 1939 (Statutory Rules and Orders No. 288/1939). The Directions regarding internees were issued by the Minister for Defence under Article 3(1) of the Order and were identical to those issued earlier under the OASA (Part VI) (Detention) Regulations, 1939 (Statutory Rules and Orders No. 249/1939). The Regulations for convicted persons were issued at Statutory Rules and Orders No. 249/1939 and 288/1939 and were approved by the Cabinet Subcommittee on Internal Security on 18 and 30 September 1939.

79 No more than three persons could visit at once.

80 NAI JUS/8/1144, Regulations for Prisoners Sentenced to Penal Servitude, Memorandum for Government, Department of Defence, 5 March 1940.

81 NAI JUS/8/1144, Regulations for Prisoners Sentenced to Penal Servitude.

82 The status of such prisoners was made clear under the Emergency Powers (No. 28) Order of 1940. They were persons 'detained' under the Emergency Powers (No. 20) Order of 1940, or under s.4 of the OASA. A person 'in military custody' was one sentenced to penal servitude or to imprisonment by the Special Criminal Court and transferred to military custody by the Minister for Justice under s.50 of the OASA.

83 MA CP 97, Standing Orders No. 1 Internment Camp and Arbour Hill Barracks, Daily Routine. Because of its high level of security and layout, Arbour Hill was able to cope with much longer hours of unlocking than the Curragh, where the short days of winter raised pressing issues of security, entailing a considerable curtailment of unlocking time. Pierce Fennell recalled Arbour Hill conditions as generally good: 'we had recreation outside, basketball and handball; playing cards in the shed, and of

course trying to figure out how to break out' (MacEoin, *The IRA in the Twilight Years*, *op. cit.*, p. 571).

84 Standing Orders, *op. cit.*, 'Abstract of Rules'. The last is a fairly standard provision in prison rules. Fennell and two others attempted to escape from Arbour Hill. Part of the plan was to knock down one of the guards. This was duly done, but, under fire, the escape had to be abandoned. The punishment for this, including the assault on the guard, was a not-excessive three days confined to cells on bread and water. The three refused the bread (MacEoin, *The IRA in the Twilight Years*, *op. cit.*, pp. 571–2). 'Good order and discipline' (often abbreviated to GOAD) is used in most prison systems to encapsulate the residual discretionary authority of the administration.

85 Legal representatives were required to give an undertaking on their 'professional honour' that the interview with their client would deal only with the legal business for which it had been authorised.

86 MA CP 97, *op. cit.*, Abstract of Rules Made by the Minister for Defence. As noted, the 'no cash' rule is maintained by almost all prison systems as a guard against the bribery of staff, a resource for escape and a means of at least curtailing the effects of gambling.

87 MA CP 159, Commandant Michael Lennon to Provost Marshal, 9 November 1939 (and annotations). In other ways, the regime at Arbour Hill during this first short period of internment was quite relaxed. After morning inspection the men were released from their cells and had free association. MacEoin, *The IRA in the Twilight Years*, *op. cit.*, p. 656. Commandant Lennon had a good reputation with the IRA men. Seán O'Neill described him as 'fair and upright' (p. 741).

88 *Irish Press*, 16 October 1939, 2g; *Irish Independent*, 16 October 1939, 8g.

89 The Government issued a statement following a cabinet meeting on 31 October 1939. Since the hunger-strikers' arrest and detention had been in accord with the powers conferred by Parliament – 'the only means available for the maintenance of public order and security' – they could not allow state authorities to be deprived of those powers by means of hunger strikes: 'The prisoners on hunger strike will, accordingly, not be released.' *Irish Independent*, 1 November 1939, 7e; *Irish Press*, 1 November 1939, 1g.

90 *Irish Press*, 1 November 1939, 1g. Mick McCarthy, who was in the prison at the time added Charlie McCarthy to the trio. He did not think that the men were acting in concert. MacEoin, *The IRA in the Twilight Years*, *op. cit.*, p. 656.

91 *Dáil Debates*, vol. 77, cols. 830–1, 19 October 1939.

92 See above, p. 683; *Irish Press*, 4 December 1939, 3e. Daly and Lynch were reported to be persisting in their strike on 10 November (*Irish Independent*, 10 November 1939, 8a). Daly accepted food the following day and was released on 14 November 1939. *Dáil Debates*, vol. 77, cols. 1342–3, 15 November 1939.

93 *Dáil Debates*, vol. 77, cols. 1208–11, 9 November 1939. Pointing to the general situation in which 'comparatively large nations had lost their freedom, and government's duty to protect the state', de Valera cast the hunger strikes in the form of a dilemma: 'two evils, one to see men die that we do not want to see die if we can save them, the other, to permit them to bring the state and the community as a whole to disaster'. Government had chosen the lesser evil and had prayed that the strikers and their leaders might change their minds. If, however, the strikers were released, the remaining prisoners would go on strike 'and not merely would we be abdicating as a Government, but we would be making it impossible for any other Government to govern'.

94 *Irish Independent*, 20 November 1939, 8c; *Irish Times*, 20 November 1939, 6d.

95 *Irish Times*, 8 December 1939, 7d; *Irish Independent*, 8 December 1939, 10e; *Irish Press*, 8 December 1939, 11d. The Dáil rose on 7 December 1939 for the Christmas break, but there were no questions or statements on McGrath or other hunger-strikers before the recess. McGrath was a well-known and venerated republican who had

been out in 1916 and who still carried a British bullet in his body. His death would have been a particular embarrassment to the de Valera administration at this time. Nine months later Patrick McGrath would become involved in one of the most notorious shoot-outs of the wartime years in Ireland when he was one of three men involved in the murder of Detective Richard Hyland and Sergeant Patrick McKeown and the wounding of Detective Brady. Speaking in the Dáil on 8 July 1943, de Valera described McGrath's release from internment in November 1939 as 'one of the biggest mistakes I made in my life'. Instead of causing one death, i.e. through hunger-striking, McGrath's release was responsible for six deaths. De Valera computed the six deaths as the two detectives, McGrath and Thomas Harte (both executed for the offences) and two hunger-strikers, D'Arcy and McNeela, who had been emboldened by McGrath's release. With what reads as heat and emotion, de Valera told the Dáil that '[i]t has been one of the great regrets of my whole life and will remain until my death' that, having made that statement in the Dáil in November 1939 that no hunger-striker would be released, he had allowed any consideration to retract from that. *Dáil Debates*, vol. 91, cols. 604–5, 8 July 1943.

96 Jim Killeen, serving seven years' penal servitude in Belfast, watched the hunger strikes at some remove and, despite the releases, thought that an opportunity had been missed: 'It is a great pity no attempt was made since then to organise the people' (Humphreys Papers, P/106/890, Jim Killeen to Sighle Humphreys, 1 January 1940).

97 *Seanad Debates*, vol. 24, col. 643, 5 January 1940. The extended debates on this legislation in both the Dáil and the Seanad provide an excellent insight into the range of political and constitutional concerns with which the country's security problems were being addressed.

98 The men were Tony D'Arcy, Thomas Grogan, John Lyons, Tomás MacCurtáin, Seán McNeela, Jack Plunkett and Michael Traynor. MacCurtáin's participation in the hunger strike delayed by some months his trial for murdering Detective John Roche on 3 January 1940 (see above, pp. 686–7).

99 See, for example, the hunger strike of Patrick Maloney who refused food for four and a half days in late October 1940. MA Weekly Report, Arbour Hill, 2 November 1940.

100 See Fisk, *In Time of War, op. cit.*, p. 297.

101 For an account of these, see Séamus Ó Mongáin's recollections in MacEoin, *The IRA in the Twilight Years, op. cit.*, pp. 884–5.

102 Statement handed to Father O'Hare (an intermediary) by the hunger-strikers on 11 April 1940, quoted in Boland's statement to the Dáil a week later, after the death of Tony D'Arcy (*Dáil Debates*, vol. 79, col. 1639, 18 April 1940). Boland summarised the men's demands, which could never be acceptable to the government: all IRA prisoners, 'no matter what offence they commit, should be held in military custody and recognised as members of a military force entitled to be treated as men engaged in legitimate warfare' (col. 1640).

103 Seán McNeela volunteered for the strike, even though he did not approve of the tactic (MacEoin, *The IRA in the Twilight Years, op. cit.*, p. 886).

104 Girvin points out (*The Emergency, op. cit.*, pp. 93–4) that by this stage censorship was being implemented for political (as distinct from national-security) purposes. Newspaper editors had been brought to heel by the censorship authorities and knew that penalties for transgression were severe. By the middle of the year, the Editor of the *Cork Examiner* was privately complaining that 'nothing that *is* news is allowed into the papers'. Relaying this in a secret report to London, the author Elizabeth Bowen commented that she had herself been struck by the silence of Irish papers on the subject of Irish affairs. Elizabeth Bowen, *Notes on Éire* (Aubane: Aubane Historical Society, 2009), p. 25. Irish journalism had indeed been hollowed out.

105 MA CP 16, Weekly Reports, Arbour Hill, 19 April 1940; NAI TAOIS/2, Cabinet minutes. Stephen Hayes, the IRA Chief of Staff, was said to have informed the four surviving strikers that their demands had been met. This was untrue but it cannot now be known on what information Hayes was working. Seven days before D'Arcy's death, Dr Andy Cooney, a leader in the Old IRA, was persuaded to contact de Valera on the men's behalf. Unless the men gave up their hunger strike, de Valera insisted, he would not intervene (MacEoin, *The IRA in the Twilight Years, op. cit.*, p. 479). For the progress of the strike, see the *Irish Times*, 27 February 1940, 5f; 20 April 1940, 8b–c; *Irish Independent*, 20 April 1940, 7a–b; *Irish Press*, 20 April 1940, 7c–d. The inquest on McNeela, which terminated with mildly critical riders from the jury, is reported in the *Weekly Irish Times*, 27 April 1940, 3c–d.

106 Coogan, who was able to interview one of the survivors (Michael Traynor) gives an eye-witness account of the two men's death in St Bricin's Hospital (*The IRA, op. cit.*, pp. 188–9).

107 MA CP 225, Reports of Acting Corporal John Gallagher and Sergeant P. Pollock, to Governor, Arbour Hill, 19 April 1940. The Governor announced that he did not wish to see any further IRA parades in the prison, and Grogan said that he did not think there would be any.

108 A key part was played in the settling of the strike by Father O'Hare. After a private meeting with the prisoners on 19 April 1940, authorised by the Adjutant General, Father O'Hare announced an end to the strike (MA CP 16, Commandant Michael Lennon, Governor, Arbour Hill, to Provost Marshal, 20 April 1940). Aided by an impenetrable press censorship, public anxiety and the all-but-exhausted funds of sympathy on which the IRA customarily drew, the political dimension of the strike was a complete failure. The Thomas Ashe Memorial Committee had held support meetings and issued duplicated leaflets. Participation was confined to immediate supporters, and the leaders were familiar republican stalwarts: Countess Plunkett, Maud Gonne MacBride, Mrs Austin Stack. The audience at a public meeting in Dublin on 10 April 1940 largely comprised numbers of Cumann na mBan, the Fianna and other children's organisations – about 100 in all (NAI JUS/8/786, Thomas Ashe Memorial Committee, Special Branch report).

109 In 1946, statistics on wartime hunger-striking showed the following numbers (numbers of hunger-strikers, and deaths respectively): 1939 (6), 1940 (15, †2), 1942 (23), 1943 (15), 1944 (5), 1945 (1), 1946 (1). The last was Seán McCaughey (see above, pp. 630–6). NAI JUS/8/944, Statistics, Internment, etc. (1946).

110 There were two candidates: John J. Keane for Fianna Fáil and Michael Donnellan for Clann na Talmhan. Keane secured 72 per cent of the first-preference votes; Donnellan 28 per cent. The turnout was 48 per cent.

111 Enno Stephan, *Spies in Ireland* (London: Four Square, 1965), p. 96.

112 *Irish Press*, 23 April 1940, 1f–g, 9a–g; *Irish Times*, 27 April 1940, 3c–d.

113 The British government saw the IRA threat in terms of the European struggle and the impossibility of allowing Germany to gain a foothold in Ireland. At a time when many influential persons were calling for pre-emptive intervention, a collapse of authority and control in Dublin would almost certainly have provoked military intervention. From there it is impossible to say what might have followed.

114 *Dáil Debates*, vol. 91, col. 231, 7 July 1943.

115 *Dáil Debates*, vol. 91, cols. 364–5, 7 July 1943.

116 *Dáil Debates*, vol. 91, col. 370, 7 July 1943. He reflected that the last time a man ('He was a friend of my own') had been released because of his hunger strike, the result had been tragic: 'he [Patrick McGrath] and a comrade shot two of our Gardaí in Rathgar, and he and his comrade had to be executed for that'.

117 See above, p. 117.

118 See, for example, the threatened hunger strike of Seán McCool in February 1943. This arose from his dissatisfaction at being discharged from the camp hospital when he claimed to be in an unfit condition (MA CP 204, Provost Marshal to OC, Curragh Command, 10 February 1943). In September 1940, John Byrne refused food for seventeen days; the following month Patrick Maloney staged a four-day strike. It is not clear from the papers why the men made these protests, but it seems likely that they arose from individual grievances. MA CP 16, Arbour Hill, weekly reports of 5 October and 2 November 1940.

119 See above, note 109.

120 MA CP 16, Commandant Michael Lennon, Governor, Arbour Hill, to Provost General, February 1940.

121 See above, p. 683.

122 See MA CP 16, Weekly Reports, Arbour Hill, 1940, *passim*.

123 MA CP 16, Weekly Reports, Arbour Hill, 18 April 1941, refers to Sergeant-Major Max Hohans and to Second Lieutenant Hans Marshner without providing information as to the circumstances of their detention. Hohans was in Arbour Hill custody but was actually a patient in St Bricin's. By late 1941, the Abwehr agent Hermann Görtz was also in Arbour Hill, arrested at Blackheath Park, Clontarf, on 27 November, in the trap house that also captured Pearse Kelly. Those convicted of espionage received sentences of imprisonment, but airmen and sailors, German and British, who had ended up on Irish soil, were interned under very relaxed conditions at the Curragh. Day parole was allowed, and internees of both sides were able to travel to Dublin and to dine there. As the fortunes of war shifted decisively in 1944, the Allied personnel were released. The Germans were held until the end of the war. See T. Ryle Dwyer, 'The Mad Escape', *An Cosantóir*, August 1979, pp. 223–7.

124 On prison construction under the Surveyor General Sir Joshua Jebb and thereafter, see Seán McConville, *A History of English Prison Administration, Vol. I: 1750–1877* (London: Routledge & Kegan Paul, 1981), particularly Chapter 11, for an account of the improved design of local prisons after 1850. In summary, however, it might be said that the hot-air system worked (fittingly) better in theory than in practice – but it was still better than Arbour Hill's nothing. The prison was indeed designed for military prisoners by Jebb and Frederick Clarendon and was opened in 1848. It became part of the civil prison system in 1975. A tunnel connected it to St Bricin's Military Hospital. An adjacent burial plot contains the remains of the executed leaders of the 1916 Rising. Lieutenant Colonel Sir Joshua Jebb had enormous influence on prison design, in Britain and in many other countries. Frederick Clarendon was one of the architects responsible for Dublin's Natural History Museum and the Dundrum Asylum (now the Central Mental Hospital).

125 MA CP 108, Commandant Michael Lennon to Provost Marshal, 27 October 1939.

126 MA CP 108, Commandant Michael Lennon to Provost Marshal, 20 November 1939 and annotations.

127 MA CP 108, Commandant Michael Lennon to Provost Marshal, 28 February 1940 and annotations.

128 By the spring of 1941, for example, with the prison population in excess of sixty men, an average of eighteen attended the daily Irish class, which lasted for an hour. At other times, French, Spanish and shorthand were offered but for a lesser period each week (and there were weeks when no classes at all were offered). Smaller numbers participated in the non-Irish classes. MA CP 108, Commandant Michael Lennon to Provost Marshal, 8 March 1941, 17 May 1941, 27 September 1941, 13 December 1941.

129 Thus, on 30 July 1941, Martin Calligan was deprived of privileges for interfering with the lock of his cell. A month later, for damaging his cell and being disrespectful

to staff, Sean Kilroy was deprived of letters for a month. We then wait until 4 February 1942 for another reported offence, when Cathal Goulding, J. J. Martin and John Joe McGill assaulted P. McGuinness. Another long period of untroubled discipline was broken on 16 December 1943 by Brendan Behan, who was confined to his cell for three days for destroying two blankets. This was a remarkably low rate of prison offending and points to a general atmosphere of live and let live. MA CP 108, Weekly Reports, Arbour Hill, 2 August 1941, 7 February 1942, 18 December 1943.

130 MA CP 108, Weekly Reports, Arbour Hill, 17 February 1940, 24 February 1940. He requested part-worn boots from army stocks since the men were serving such short sentences. Repaired boots were supplied from stock at Collins Barracks. Family emergencies extended to the death of a brother-in-law. MA CP 108, Weekly Reports, Arbour Hill, 20 June 1941.

131 MA CP 724, Acting Corporal Francis Cosgrave to Governor, Arbour Hill, 12 December 1943.

132 See above, pp. 656–7.

133 MA CP 108, Weekly Reports, Arbour Hill, 24 August 1940 and 7 September 1940. Again, there were numerous visits from family members, clergy and solicitors. The names and addresses of these and all visitors to prisoners were noted in the weekly reports.

134 MA CP 108, Weekly Reports, Arbour Hill, 27 September 1941. He was almost immediately transferred to Portlaoise. See pp. 618–9.

135 Pierce Fennell in MacEoin, *The IRA in the Twilight Years*, *op. cit.*, pp. 559–60. The other members of the group were Roger Ryan, Connie Byrd and Jobie Sullivan. Republicans asserted that the Special Branch man in charge, Inspector Jim Moore, later boasted that Kavanagh's shooting was in reprisal for the killing of Detective John Roche by Tomás MacCurtáin (p. 645). For an account of one of the IRA men involved in the project (but not in the tunnel itself), see Jim Savage's interview (pp. 814–16). The readiness to open fire may well have been one of the legacies of the Magazine Fort raid and the sharp and continuing criticism of complacent soldiers on guard duty.

136 Derry Kelleher in MacEoin, *The IRA in the Twilight Years*, *op. cit.*, p. 645. Seamus Ronayne remembered his stay there almost fondly, mixing with those of his own cultural background and inclinations and improving his Irish: 'a sociable, relaxed place'. For twelve hours, from unlocking at 8 a.m., each day was filled with 'chat, amusement or classes'. In the evenings, after lock-up, the men could read or relax in their cells: 'it was like college or the religious life' (MacEoin, *The IRA in the Twilight Years*, *op. cit.*, pp. 801–2).

137 NAI JUS/8/837, Mother Superior to Minister for Defence, 10 June 1940. The Mother Superior recalled that a similar situation had arisen in 1923 but had immediately been resolved by the removal of the prisoners. The Gardaí were doing what they could, but a regiment of them would be insufficient to keep sympathisers at bay because of the busy roads in the area of the convent and the prison.

138 NAI JUS/8/837, Superintendent's Office, Cork City South, 24 July 1940.

139 MacEoin, *The IRA in the Twilight Years*, *op. cit.*, p. 560.

140 MacEoin, *The IRA in the Twilight Years*, *op. cit.*, p. 561. It was probably one of the Cork party who hurled a pair of handcuffs from a lorry, breaking a glass sign. The Gardaí were understandably unable to identify the culprit. NAI JUS/8/856, Superintendent's Office, Kildare, to Commissioner, 7 September 1940.

141 See above, pp. 185–6 for Mountjoy's early governance.

142 There was a short-lived flare-up on Friday, 1 March 1940, when Jack Plunkett and Seán McNeela (two of the four arrested when the IRA's pirate radio was raided) resisted attempts to escort them to the Special Criminal Court for their hearing.

Gardaí were called in to assist prison staff. *Irish Times*, 2 March 1940, 7a–c; *Irish Independent*, 2 March 1940, 7a–b. The incident had no lasting repercussions.

143 MacEoin, *The IRA in the Twilight Years*, *op. cit.*, p. 780.

144 MacEoin, *The IRA in the Twilight Years*, *op. cit.*, p. 781.

145 MacEoin, *The IRA in the Twilight Years*, *op. cit.*, p. 782.

146 The six were Jackie Griffith and Peter Martin (Dublin), Frank Kerrigan, Michael Lucey and Mart Lucey (Cork) and James Smith (Oldcastle, Co. Meath). According to Tom Doran, the escape was 'an unwished for success' and put great pressure on safe house accommodation (MacEoin, *The IRA in the Twilight Years*, *op. cit.*, p. 501).

147 NAI JUS/8/970, Superintendent J. O'Sullivan to Commissioner, Garda Síochána, 16 October 1940.

148 At the beginning of November 1940, there were 462 men interned at the Curragh (*Dáil Debates*, vol. 81, col. 513, 7 November 1940).

149 NAI JUS/8/944, Statistics, Internment, etc. (1946).

150 And, indeed, many entered into internment from conditions of some deprivation and likely demoralisation. In February 1940, it was decided to issue some men with part-worn army boots, since their own footwear was unfit (MA Weekly Reports, Arbour Hill, February 1940).

151 Bell, *The Secret Army*, *op. cit.*, p. 179. Though the rancour can be overdone. At a deeper level, the Curragh gives more an impression of Dante's *Purgatorio*: 'A place there is below not sad with torments, / But darkness only, where the lamentations / Have not the sound of wailing, but are sighs'. Dante Alighieri, *The Divine Comedy*, trans. Henry Wadsworth Longfellow (London: George Routledge & Sons, 1886), *Purgatory*, Canto VII.

152 See above, pp. 430, 777–8.

153 *Irish Times*, 11 September 1939, 4a; *Irish Independent*, 11 September 1939, 10b. Larry Grogan (1899–1979) joined the Volunteers in 1917. During the Civil War he took the anti-Treaty side. Imprisoned in Mountjoy in 1922 and later interned at the Curragh. Elected to the Army Council in 1938 and supported the bombing campaign in Britain. He was a signatory to the IRA's ultimatum to Britain on 12 January 1939.

154 Grogan was one of a group of six prison leaders who went on hunger strike, demanding political status and an improvement in conditions. According to Michael O'Riordan (also in the Glasshouse in the spring of 1940), the IRA men were held on the ground floor and soldiers of the Irish Army under punishment were held on the floor above them; the soldiers had a worse time than the IRA men (MacEoin, *The IRA in the Twilight Years*, *op. cit.*, p. 760).

155 Veteran IRA man Dan Keating, who served on the Camp Council, recalled that Grogan had been appointed OC on the orders of the IRA GHQ (MacEoin, *The IRA in the Twilight Years*, *op. cit.*, p. 26).

156 MacEoin, *The IRA in the Twilight Years*, *op. cit.*, pp. 710–11.

157 MA CP 146, Larry Grogan to Captain M. J. Cummins, Governor, Military Detention Barracks, Curragh, 20 January 1940.

158 MA CP 146, Corporal William Deegan to Captain M. J. Cummins, 29 January 1940.

159 MA CP 146, Captain C. P. Barry to Captain M. J. Cummins, 29 January 1940.

160 MA CP 146, Captain M. J. Cummins to Provost Marshal, Department of Defence, 2 February 1940.

161 But see pp. 499–50, n. 162, above.

162 MA PM 644, Defence of No. 1 Internment Camp, Curragh; Whelan to Adjutant General, 4 September 1940. He was informed of the well-established legal principle that only proportionate and reasonable force would be legal. This was probably a follow-up to intelligence that indicated an escape was being contemplated and that raised the broader concerns in Whelan's mind. The report that seems to have

prompted the enquiry did not refer to fire, however, but to some collusion on the part of tradesmen and labourers employed at the camp. NAI JUS/8/858, Cork Special Branch to Commissioners Office, 31 August 1940. The police report was vague but would undoubtedly have alarmed the Curragh Camp authorities. The total staff establishment at the camp was small, and the pressures of work were considerable. Before the fire, the establishment, for a notional 400 internees, was set at seven officers, twenty NCOs and fifty-six privates. Of the last, only thirty-eight were assigned to guard duties. Allowing for twenty-four-hour coverage, sickness and leave, this was barely adequate for a camp proceeding on the basis of unchallenged routine, and certainly not for crisis (MA PM 598, Staff, Internment Camp Curragh, undated but probably July 1940). Towards the end of 1941, Commandant James Guiney wrote that his establishment was 'only barely sufficient' and had been strained further by his having to assign guards to the hospital when internees were admitted. This meant that he had available only one man to cover two gates and an insufficient number for compound-supervision duties: 'This is a serious position and it is only right that you should be made aware of it' (MA PM 598, Commandant J. Guiney to Provost Marshal, 4 November 1941).

163 Larry Grogan had been one of a group of three (with Peadar O'Flaherty and William McGuinness) who had taken over the Camp Council from Billy Mulligan (OC), Seán McCool and Pearse Kelly. The change, O'Flaherty announced, was because the Council had become too left-wing. MacEoin, *The IRA in the Twilight Years, op. cit.*, p. 663.

164 Those who had resources or whose family were supportive could supplement them. Although food parcels could not be sent in, items such as tobacco, cigarettes, stationery and fruit could be purchased at the camp canteen. Relatives and friends could send clothing and stationery as well as approved books and journals (*Dáil Debates*, vol. 81, col. 513, 7 November 1940).

165 Some of the internees found the rations generally inadequate. Liam Burke, a Belfast man (interned under the alias of Sean Maguire) was in the Curragh for the first half of 1942. His abiding memories were the incessant wind and severity of the hunger: 'I was always hungry; I can recall fellows hanging around outside the cookhouse kitchen ready to grab bones being thrown out' (MacEoin, *The IRA in the Twilight Years, op. cit.*, p. 448).

166 During the wartime years it varied between two and six ounces per week for adults. In Britain at this time it was also a few ounces. For those who had money, however, almost everything continued to be available except fuel. But the internees (and few were well-off) were not able to benefit from wealthy friends' and relatives' largesse, since food parcels were not allowed. (On food, and the means to purchase it in Éire, see Wills, *That Neutral Island, op. cit.*, pp. 244–5.) In reality, food (a continual grouse in all residential institutions) was simply the issue of choice for a contrived confrontation with the camp authorities. Writing clandestinely to his wife two and a half years later, when wartime restrictions had become even tighter, Seamus O'Donovan (well accustomed to comfortable standards of living) reported that 'Life here is o.k. on the whole. The food is tolerable tho' I'm afraid you couldn't take it.' He did, however, complain about poor bedding and 'hopeless' medical attention. O'Donovan Papers, MS. 22, 307, O'Donovan to his wife (smuggled letter), n.d. but probably mid-1942.

167 Even allowing for wartime censorship rules and the newspaper's traditional editorial stance, the *Irish Times* item heading show how Curragh events would be received: 'Internees Cause Trouble' (16 December 1940, 6b). Dan Keating recalled that the IRA had a good line of communication out of the camp (a medical orderly), but this was of little use for publicity purposes, given the strength of the censorship. The orderly was overused and was discovered and brought before a military court

towards the end of 1944 (interview with Dan Keating). At the time of his death, Keating (1902–2007) was the last survivor of the War of Independence. A lifelong uncompromising republican, he refused to recognise any of the versions of the modern Irish state. Taking the anti-Treaty side in the Civil War, he served several periods of imprisonment in the 1920s and 1930s. He was a significant operative in the 1939–40 bombing campaign in Britain and was interned shortly after his return to Éire. He was removed from the IRA in a clear-out of the old guard but remained an active supporter of whichever faction remained true to what he saw as republicanism (see *The Times*, 26 October 2007, 77a–e).

168 MacEoin, *The IRA in the Twilight Years*, *op. cit.*, p. 711. We heard an alternative version from John L. McCormack, who was an internee at the time of the fire. According to this recollection, Commandant Cummins, the Military Governor of the camp, had agreed with the Camp Council that the reduction in the butter ration would be compensated by an issue of jam. This agreement was abandoned when an issue of the Dublin *Evening Herald* came in, reporting that the Irish government was exporting a large quantity of butter to England. The camp leadership took the view that this was helping the British war effort and therefore repudiated the jam-for-butter agreement. It was decided to burn four huts, but the wind spread the flames to the others (interview with Séamus Ó Goilidhe). Butter export figures were not published from 1939 onward, but in 1938 under half (327,636 of 766,460 hundredweight) was exported. *Dáil Debates*, vol. 81, col. 1815, 5 February 1941. Any reduction in the domestic supply would have had immediate effects.

169 Both the military records and the 'Departmental Notes' refer to the inmates' spokesman without naming him. It is possible that Grogan concealed his function and entrusted communications with the authorities to somebody else.

170 Earlier in the year, the Attorney General had been consulted on a number of issues relating to police and army powers under the Emergency Powers Act, 1939, and Orders arising therefrom. In his opinion, it would have been legally difficult to justify the use of firearms to prevent an escape attempt by internees. An attempt to escape was an offence under Article 4 of the Emergency Powers Order, 1939, and under 5.5(1) of the Act itself (NAI JUS/8/781, Emergency Powers Act, 1939, Memorandum to Government, Department of Defence, 22 February 1940).

171 MA PM O 2/67598, 'Outbreak of Fire at No. 1 Internment Camp, Curragh, 14/12/40': Colonel T. McNally to Chief of Staff, 15 December 1940. 'Departmental Notes', *op. cit.*, pp. 86O–86N. See also Pierce Fennell's recollections in MacEoin, *The IRA in the Twilight Years*, *op. cit.*, pp. 563 7. From this it is clear that one of the military policemen, Sergeant Matthews, escaped likely death only because an internee intervened when a comrade was going to deliver a second blow with an iron bar. Regimental Sergeant Major Gus Cronin, who served as a military policeman at the Curragh, recalled his concern that the camp authorities had agreed to issue hurleys to the internees. He recalled one incident in which he was threatened with a hurley by an inmate and a member of the IRA command structure intervened. In general, the inmates who came from Northern Ireland were more hostile towards camp staff than were Southerners (interview with Gus Cronin).

172 MacEoin, *The IRA in the Twilight Years*, *op. cit.*, pp. 563–4.

173 Bell, *The Secret Army*, *op. cit.*, p. 179, n. 13. A former internee (seemingly providing cover for what had been a foolish and ill-considered action) insisted that the decision had been to burn 'a carefully selected number of huts' and that the 'greatest care' had been taken to avoid those over the tunnels. The general conflagration was due to 'a sudden change in the wind' ('"Tintown, 1940–45", by "An Ex-Internee"', *United Irishman*, June 1951, 8b). This runs contrary to Pierce Fennell's account, and he was one of the fire-setters, acting under orders.

174 MacEoin, *The IRA in the Twilight Years*, *op. cit.*, p. 487.

175 Arriving at the camp shortly after the fires, Bob Clements saw the maze of tunnels: 'I thought, what madness, to burn down seven huts and expose them. Nearly everyone else thought it and also, including some who had helped to burn them!' (MacEoin, *The IRA in the Twilight Years*, *op. cit.*, p. 468).

176 Commandant Cummins was immediately relieved of his command, being replaced by Commandant Guiney, who held the position until the last releases. He was well known to some of the internees from North Kerry and, Derry Kelleher hints, was favourably disposed to Tadhg Lynch, who headed his own breakaway hut (MacEoin, *The IRA in the Twilight Years*, *op. cit.*, p. 648). Regimental Sergeant Major Gus Cronin recalled that Commandant Cummins never entered the compound itself and that, when Guiney took his place, staff were pleased because 'we all knew then there would be someone to back us up' (Cronin interview). Guiney was equally well liked by the internees. Dan Keating recalled that when Guiney took over from Cummins he changed everything for the better, including clothing and food (interview).

177 MA PM O Files, 2/67598, Colonel McNally to Commander-in-Chief, late December 1940, *op. cit.* Accidental deaths attributable to poor fire precautions would perhaps have created public disquiet and sympathy.

178 According to Guiney's account, fires had been spread by throwing burning blankets and mattresses onto felted hut roofs. Internees also tried to push flaming mattresses into the huts through broken windows (MA, 'Outbreak of Fire at No. 1 Internment Camp: Curragh 14/12/40'). Guiney's report was written hours after the outbreak. It seems unlikely, however, that all the camp's bedding had been destroyed, as indeed the later cost estimates of damage confirmed.

179 'Outbreak of Fire', *op. cit.* There were no WCs in the huts, and sanitary needs had to be met with buckets. An ex-internee recalled that even when there were only thirty men in a hut, at night the atmosphere was 'stifling' ('"Tintown, 1940–45", by "An Ex-Internee"', *United Irishman*, August 1951, 8b).

180 In Fennell's recollection, one of the guards came into the hut the following night and threw a bucket of water over the stove, causing a near explosion, with ash and steam all over the hut (MacEoin, *The IRA in the Twilight Years*, *op. cit.*, p. 567).

181 MacEoin, *The IRA in the Twilight Years*, *op. cit.*, p. 567.

182 Tony McInerney recalled the lice. He also remembered his first sight of his comrades-to-be in the camp when he arrived in the autumn of 1940: 'Awful clothing, torn and shabby boots, heavy grey shirts and long beards.' He thought it terrible that human beings could sink to such a level 'not realising that I must soon join them myself' (MacEoin, *The IRA in the Twilight Years*, *op. cit.*, p. 671). Séamus Ó Goilidhe's recollection was almost exactly the same. The contrast with Arbour Hill life ('compact, neatly attired, almost collegiate') was a shock. There was the 'windswept desert' of Kildare, but the internees made even more of an impact. Shuffling around they were dressed in 'mis-shapen Martin Henry suits, grey and frequently unbuttoned army shirts, tie-less... bearded, and with clogs of boots that they seemed to drag around, shuffle, shuffle; I hated to admit it but I knew I would soon be joining them' (MacEoin, *The IRA in the Twilight Years*, *op. cit.*, p. 711). See also '"Tintown, 1940–45", by "An Ex-Internee"', *United Irishman*, August 1951, 8b. The author claimed that blankets were not changed or washed during the years of the camp's operation. Even before the fire, Commandant Cummins was driven to complain about the long delays in exchanging bedlinen (MA PM 651, Captain M. J. Cummins to Provost Marshal, 29 June 1940). By 1945, no sheets were being issued 'on the ground of inadequate supplies' (MA PM 335, Commandant J. Guiney to OC Curragh Command, 16 January 1945).

183 For recollections of the Ice-Box interval, see *United Irishman*, June 1951, 9a. Former Sergeant-Major Michael Fahey, who served in the Glasshouse from 1940, recalled

that following the fire the camp authorities realised that they had to break the internees' new leadership, thus the tough regime in the Glasshouse, to which the supposed ringleaders of the fire and riot were removed. As to the first nights after the fire, 'the nights spent with no clothing subdued the internees. The cold… nearly killed them' (MacEoin, *The IRA in the Twilight Years, op. cit.*, p. 917).

184 MacEoin, *The IRA in the Twilight Years, op. cit.*, p. 917. Earlier in the year there had been a similarly absurd outcome to the internees' dissatisfaction with food. On 16 July 1940, there was a supply problem with potatoes, and the men were issued with 5 ounces of bread in lieu. William Mulligan, the OC of the Curragh internees, informed the Governor that unless an allowance of 8 ounces of bread were issued the men would refuse to eat their dinner. Since the authorities did not give way, no dinner was eaten that day (MA CP 126, Captain M. J. Cummins to Provost Marshal, 17 July 1940). Such actions closely resembled those of the parent-punishing child – and were as ineffective.

185 The *Irish Times* was consistent in its heading of the Government Information Bureau's announcement: 'More Curragh Trouble: Internee Dies from Wounds' (19 December 1940, 6g). At the subsequent inquest, the Coroner, acting on the direction of the Minister for Justice, narrowed the focus of the hearing. He took evidence only on identification, date and cause of death. Medical evidence showed that death was due to shock and haemorrhage, due to gunshot. The circumstances of Casey's having been shot were excluded from consideration, but when it was established that the point of entry for the wound was the back, Seán MacBride, appearing for the next of kin, caused uproar by demanding to know why (see *Irish Times*, 18 December 1940, 2g, a censored report from which MacBride's question was omitted; see also MacEoin, *The IRA in the Twilight Years, op. cit.*, p. 479). One of our interviewees (who required anonymity at this point) hinted that it was not a military policeman who opened fire. He would not be drawn, but the inference was that it was someone from another branch of the security forces.

186 Coogan, *The IRA, op. cit.*, p. 253; MacEoin, *The IRA in the Twilight Years, op. cit.*, p. 487. The government account differs slightly. There is no mention of the mess-hut incident, but reference was made to the concern raised by Grogan going from hut to hut, which the authorities took as an indication of preparation for another organised outburst. ('Departmental Notes', *op. cit.*, p. 86N). This firing of apparently random warning shots is reminiscent of what happened in Mountjoy Prison as the Civil War got under way (see above, p. 187).

187 Bell, *The Secret Army, op. cit.*, p. 179. The lack of detail at this point in Bell's narrative suggests somewhat hazy recollections and second-hand reports by his interviewees. Joe Dolan recalled the men being removed but did not mention their ill-treatment (MacEoin, *The IRA in the Twilight Years, op. cit.*, p. 487). Bertie McCormack, on the other hand spoke of the ringleaders being beaten up the hill from the camp to the Glasshouse (p. 663). An anonymous former internee, writing in the *United Irishman* more than a decade later, insisted that there was concerted and gratuitous violence as the men were removed to the Glasshouse and also later in the Glasshouse cells. He was not one of those directly involved but claimed to have seen brutality in his own hut (*United Irishman*, July 1951, 8a–b).

188 MA Department of Defence, Provost Marshal Office, 2/67598, J. K. Ryan, Quartermaster, Curragh Command to Staff Officer, Q1, 29 May 1942.

189 Coogan, *The IRA, op. cit.*, p. 254. At around this time, when there was a change both on the Camp Council and in the governance of the camp (Leddy took over from Grogan and Commandant James Guiney from Commandant Cummins) the internees decided to renew their demands for improvements in conditions. Dan Keating recalled that rather than being sent to the Glasshouse for his temerity, the internees'

spokesman's 'demands' (probably submitted as requests) were well received and conditions immediately improved. A different set of internees took over the running of the cookhouse and 'did a wonderful job' (MacEoin, *The IRA in the Twilight Years, op. cit.*, p. 627).

190 The command staff of the prison were obliged to control their men but seem to have tolerated staff violence provided it did not take place in front of them. According to Pierce Fennell, Captain Guiney left the cell of Thomas Sheeran, who had given a lot of trouble and who had knocked down two guards. While he was out of the cell, the guards did not attack Sheeran, but they made a move towards him when Guiney returned. They were stopped by Guiney, who said they had not the guts to do it when they had the chance (MacEoin, *The IRA in the Twilight Years, op. cit.*, p. 569). See also Bertie McCormack's account of these events in which he describes the 'reign of terror' to which the men were subject during their five week stay in the Glasshouse (p. 663).

191 MacEoin, *The IRA in the Twilight Years, op. cit.*, p. 487. See also the comment of Seamus Ronayne who remembered being surprised at the decision to burn the huts, especially after all the work that had been put into the network of tunnels. The cut in the butter ration 'seemed such a silly excuse' (p. 802).

192 "'Tintown, 1940–45", by "An Ex-Internee"', *United Irishman*, July 1951, 9a–b. Before the fire the weekly outgoing letter could be of any length. When letter-writing was reinstated, internees were limited to three pages. The denial of cigarettes and tobacco for several weeks would have been a harsh ordeal for many. But in other ways, Guiney improved conditions, according to Dan Keating (see p. 734).

193 Again, there was a lack of judgement. Coal imports from Britain had come under acute pressure, both in quantity and quality, the start of a contraction in fuel supplies that would progressively curtail economic activity throughout the war years (see Wills, *That Neutral Island, op. cit.*, pp. 238–9).

194 MacEoin, *The IRA in the Twilight Years, op. cit.*, p. 649. He added, 'For my part this decision has been strictly adhered to.'

195 In answer to a Dáil question in November 1943, Gerald Boland, Minister for Justice, reported that on 1 June 1943, 529 men were held in the Curragh Internment Camp. Between that date and 9 November 1943, 249 men had applied for parole and 188 had secured it (*Dáil Debates*, vol. 91, col. 1956, 11 November 1943). Roughly speaking, half of the population of the camp may have applied for parole, and just under one-third were successful. It is hard to be certain about these proportions since some men may have applied more than once. Urgent family business or a crisis could include a farming matter (itself important in wartime). One interviewee told us that he was released on parole when his father was granted more productive land by the Land Commission. Of four sons, three were interned, and it was agreed to release one brother on parole to assist with the move from one farm to the other. He returned to the Curragh after about one month working on the farm (interview).

196 Sentenced prisoner C. Connors was, for example, granted four days' release on parole from Arbour Hill in April 1940 because of the death of his brother (MA CP 16, Captain M. Lennon, Governor, Arbour Hill to Provost Marshal, 19 April 1940). See also the case of T. McDonagh, who was allowed parole for seven days because of the serious illness of his brother; this was extended by another four days when his brother died (MA CP 16, Captain M. Lennon, Governor, Arbour Hill to Provost Marshal, 1 November 1940). A number of such releases confirm that this was a customary privilege.

197 In February 1940, between sixteen and twenty men out of sixty-two at Arbour Hill attended daily classes. The Irish language seems to have been the most popular subject for study (MA Weekly Reports, Arbour Hill, February 1940).

198 There are differing memories of the Irish-speaking huts. Mick Fitzgibbon recalled that almost half the huts were Irish-speaking; other accounts mention only one such

hut. Probably the number varied over the years of the camp's operation (see MacEoin, *The IRA in the Twilight Years, op. cit.*, p. 590). Dan Keating recounted a tale of Máirtín Ó Cadhain. He was asked by another Irish-language teacher in the camp how the men's interest in learning the language might be stimulated and replied, 'Teach them first the curses, and if you see they are learning them… you will know that they are making progress' (p. 627). But in interview, Keating expressed some doubt about the 'Gaeltacht' huts: 'they were more or less regarded as upper class, which was wrong'.

199 According to Kelly, several hundred men were at least up to a *Fáinne* standard. Besides Ó Cadhain, Kelly also mentions Seán Óg Ó Tuama and Rory O'Driscoll of Cork (*Irish Independent*, 24 January 1969, 6f–h).

200 MacEoin, *The IRA in the Twilight Years, op. cit.*, p. 646; Keating interview. G2 Branch, the Irish Army's loose equivalent to Britain's MI5, kept the supply of books going into the camp under review, and made recommendations: 'In addition to literature of a Communist, Facist [*sic*] or Nazi propaganda nature, books on chemistry which might be of use for instructional in the manufacture of explosives have been withheld' (MA Major Dan Bryan to Adjutant General, 1 August 1940). In withholding this material, the authorities were acting outside the Regulations promulgated under the Emergency Powers Act. To avoid trouble, incoming correspondence that referred to books which had been withheld was censored. An expanded regulation was provided in the Regulations by way of amendment. This brought G2's recommendations for withholding books again within the letter of the law.

201 This was Padraig O'Caoimh, a former member of the IRA. Pearse Kelly recalled that Gaelic football was the mainstay of the Curragh sports programme and that the standard was consistently high. This was assisted in large part by the presence in the camp and on the field of several well-known All-Ireland and county players, including John Joe Sheehy, Dan Ryan and Purty Landers. Medals were awarded in the football competitions, and this stimulated rivalry (*Irish Independent*, 23 January 1969, 3a–b).

202 Memoir by Pearse Kelly, *Irish Independent*, 24 January 1962, 6f–h. Kelly added, 'I still have a lovely little chess set they sent us.'

203 MacEoin, *The IRA in the Twilight Years, op. cit.*, p. 725. *Rerum novarum* dealt with the social, economic and moral consequences of the development of capitalism: 'Rights and Duties of Capital and Labour'.

204 MacEoin, *The IRA in the Twilight Years, op. cit.*, p. 726.

205 MacEoin, *The IRA in the Twilight Years, op. cit.*, pp. 726–7.

206 O'Donovan Papers, MS. 22, 307, smuggled letter, O'Donovan to his wife, n.d. (but probably mid-1942).

207 MA PM 335, Commandant J. Guiney to Provost Marshal, 27 April 1944. Guiney sought permission to have a radio for each factional compound. G2 Branch opposed the concession.

208 Máirtín Ó Cadhain's novel, *Cré na Cille* (Dublin: Sáirséal & Dill, 1949) is a distillation of the crippling boredom and isolation of rural life in Ireland in the 1940s and the equivalent quality of life in the Curragh. The novel is set in a graveyard in which the dead communicate with each other but not with the living: the central metaphor is undeniably apt, and though imagery and allusion may seem contrived, they are evocative and telling, the whole being particularly penetrating. The newly dead bring news from the world, in which respect they provide the same one-way links as the newly arrived internee or sentenced prisoner. The novel contains sly references to the Curragh splits and various factions. Clair Wills makes such points in her thoughtful discussion of *Cré na Cille* (*That Neutral Island, op. cit.*, pp. 337–43); she also provides a valuable summary guide to the novel for the non-Irish speaking reader. It is instructive in itself that there were no Curragh memoirs, apart from Ó Cadhain's imaginative recreation, and MacEoin's collection of interviews (*The IRA in the Twilight*

Years, op. cit.). Who would wish to revisit such an experience unless prompted by an interviewer of the standing and persuasive charm of MacEoin? Given this paucity of material, there surely is a case to make available in the English language Ó Cadhain's letters from prison: *As an nGéibheann: Litreacha chuig Tamás Bairéad* (Dublin: Sáirséal & Dill, 1973). Máirtín Ó Cadhain (1905–70) was born in Cois Fharraige, Connemeara. Active in the IRA, he became a member of the Army Council in 1938 and supported Russell's bombing campaign in Britain. Interned for a short period in 1939, he was re-interned in April 1940 and released in July 1944. He had been dismissed from his position as a schoolteacher for his IRA activities.

209 Humphreys Papers, P/106/893/1, Seán McCool to Sighle Humphreys, 28 March 1944. One must allow, however, for the fact that McCool was an exceptionally committed republican and that he was writing to a kindred spirit who would wish to hear of activity and determination. For McCool's background, see n. 280, below.

210 MacEoin, *The IRA in the Twilight Years, op. cit.*, p. 672. Some of the men, inevitably, felt the pangs of hunger to an exceptional extent. Cathal Goulding (who would become prominent in the IRA of the late 1940s, 1950s and early 1960s) used to collect scraps and in the evenings would cook them on the hut stove (p. 734).

211 The three leaders of the group were Pearse Kelly (the longest-serving Curragh OC), Eoin MacNamee (sometime IRA Chief of Staff) and Tom Cullimore. Pearse Kelly had also been Chief of Staff of the IRA for a short time and was a member of the IRA's Northern Command.

212 Taking in a reduced ration of fuel for the hut stoves was deemed to be acquiescence in the manner in which the camp was being run and was therefore forbidden – this in the middle of bitterly cold weather. Hut C1 decided for warmth rather than military, and took in fuel. Shunning followed, and all new arrivals at the camp were informed by Leddy group members that the C1 men had drawn coal (MacEoin, *The IRA in the Twilight Years, op. cit.*, p. 803).

213 Recollection of Bob Clements in MacEoin, *The IRA in the Twilight Years, op. cit.*, p. 469. The Hayes confession, then circulating in the camp, was another source of conflict. It was not the confession alone that drove about half the prisoners into the Kelly group but their own concern to end what Clements describes as the 'ugly practice' of ostracism.

214 Interview in MacEoin, *The IRA in the Twilight Years, op. cit.*, pp. 487–8.

215 More than once, Kelly recalled, GHQ attempted to establish an inquiry into the split (presumably hoping to heal it), but nothing came of these instructions. Most of the time, he continued, the internees attempted to ignore the split, 'but the positions had become entrenched and the problems magnified by the enforced confinement in one place, so little progress could be made' (*Irish Independent*, 24 January 1969, 6f–h). As men were released and others were received at the camp, there was some easing of tensions, Kelly remembered, but the division could not be healed as long as any of the original protagonists remained.

216 Dan Keating described the practice as 'dirty' although he had himself, under the orders of the Camp OC, taken part in the shunning ceremony of a married man who had decided that he could not neglect his wife and children: 'The man, I stayed in his house, Jesus I didn't agree with it at the time, but you could say nothing' (Keating interview).

217 'There was no great point of principle involved; we just had more friends on this side' (MacEoin, *The IRA in the Twilight Years, op. cit.*, p. 509).

218 MacEoin, *The IRA in the Twilight Years, op. cit.*, p. 573. Guiney was described by former Sergeant-Major Mick Fahey as 'friendly and talkative to everyone; a real Kerryman with no regard for rank' (MacEoin, *The IRA in the Twilight Years, op. cit.*, p. 915). The British government kept an eye on the Curragh and noted (presumably

through official sources) the international outlook of the factions: 'The left-wingers, probably about 140 in number, though remaining anti-British are wholeheartedly in favour of an Axis defeat by Soviet Russia. The opposing faction, numbering about 220, are in favour of collaboration with the Axis and are hoping steadfastly for the defeat of the United Nations. The remaining minority are diehard republicans who are neutral as regards the split of the larger groups' (PRO DO/121/85, 'Irish Affairs', 1 September 1942).

219 Bell, *The Secret Army, op. cit.*, p. 180; see also *Irish Independent*, 24 January 1969, 6f (a memoir by Pearse Kelly). In addition to his abhorrence of Marx and his works, Cardinal Joseph MacRory (1861–1945) was a fierce opponent of the Northern Ireland government and its discriminatory politics against Catholics (see p. 366, n. 65). There may have been some basis for Kelly's fear since Goold-Verschoyle was evidently a persuasive lecturer. Pierce Fennell kept detailed notes of these talks and recalled that in each of the huts there were one or two men who were spreading the doctrine (MacEoin, *The IRA in the Twilight Years, op. cit.*, p. 575).

220 The young Michael O'Riordan, a future leader of the Communist Party in Ireland and a veteran of the International Brigade in the Spanish Civil War, was also in the Curragh at this time. Whether because his proselytising was conducted with discretion or because he was under the linguistic wing of Máirtín Ó Cadhain, or for some other reason, he was not reported to Cardinal MacRory (see obituary, *Irish Times*, 20 May, 2006, 14a–e).

221 Christy Quearney, serving ten years' penal servitude, recalled his arrival in the Curragh in 1944 (when the remaining internees and the convicted prisoners were brought together). Even though he had another four years to serve, internees told him that he was all right because he knew when he was getting out. He was amazed by their apathy: 'I can remember looking into their eyes and they were dead; there was no life there; as if all hope had been abandoned… I will never forget the bleakness of their eyes' (MacEoin, *The IRA in the Twilight Years, op. cit.*, p. 784).

222 MA PM 651, No. 1 Internment Camp, Curragh, Administration, Commandant M. McHugh, Provost Marshal to Camp Commandant, 17 September 1940.

223 MA PM 651, Lieutenant C. C. Ryan memorandum, 13 September 1940. This account is confirmed by that of the combative and left-leaning Pierce Fennell: 'All the huts would come out, march down and form a square; they would then march this poor sod down; put him in the middle, and we would all turn our backs on him.' No one would speak to the victim for the remainder of the time at the camp. Fennell thought this procedure to be 'too much of the Fascist German type' and claimed that it ceased after the December 1940 fire. IRA censorship of members' letters may have dated back to 1937 when Tom Barry, as Chief of Staff, ruled that letters could not be sent to prisoners without his approval. This order was resented, not least by the veteran Patrick McGrath (later executed) who recalled that he had 'a decided objection to his censorship' (Humphreys Papers, P/106/889, Patrick McGrath to Jim Killeen, 3 December 1939).

224 Seamus O'Donovan, who had been interned as a result of his reinvolvement with the IRA after a gap of some twelve years, attempted to get around the ban on correspondence by smuggling letters out. He had had a good position in the Electricity Supply Board (a semi-state enterprise) and the usual middle-class financial obligations. Six months on full-time sick pay and another six on half pay helped him to bridge the gap, but he was understandably desperate to be released. He was not willing, however, to sign an undertaking and relied on his status as a former member of the IRA GHQ in the War of Independence to obtain special treatment, writing clandestinely to an outside contact whom he had asked to see a member of the government. He contended that 'a lot of respect' was due to him because of his

service and standing in the War of Independence. There could be 'no question' of being asked to sign an undertaking, he wrote (O'Donovan Papers, MS. 22, 307, letter, circa July 1942, no addressee). The government was apparently unmoved, having earlier turned down a parole request to allow O'Donovan to put his affairs in order.

225 MA PM 651, Major Dan Bryan to G2 Branch, Department of Defence, 18 September 1940. In submitting, the man presumably accepted whatever punishment was ordered for the purging of earlier disobedience and attempted apostasy.

226 Bryan to G2 Branch, 18 September 1940, *op. cit.* There was also the question, not addressed by Bryan, of the conditioning of camp staff, including its command. The degradation ceremony was apparently accepted as part of the camp order, yet it was a defiant bid for control of daily life. It was also a moral assault on a camp inmate and the opening page in what all knew would be a chapter of bullying and humiliation. The camp command, and the Irish Army generally, evidently accepted no responsibility in the matter, apparently accepting a minimal definition of safe custody and a concept of inmate welfare that embraced little beyond physical sustenance, sanitation and shelter. The moral, social and psychological aspects of camp life were ceded to the IRA and its various factions. Quite apart from what might be seen as a failing in humane duty, the shortcomings of this policy precluded all consideration of life beyond the camp – of resettlement and the avoidance of lasting harm. To all of this the authorities would have replied 'sign out', but this, as we have seen, was a taboo of such strength as to create another set of equally long-lasting problems.

227 MA PM 651, Commandant M. J. Cummins to Provost Marshal, 3 October 1940. By this time, Minister Boland had been made aware of the extent of IRA control over the internees. On 17 September 1940, the Adjutant General wrote to the Provost Marshal in fairly sharp terms, informing him that the Minister had expressed his concern 'that conditions in the internment camp are far from being satisfactory'. He noted that IRA leaders in the camp had formed an organisation that 'directs its attention towards the censoring of letters, control of visits and preventing the more amicable section from conveying their desires to the Curragh Command' (MA PM 651, Adjutant General to Provost Marshal, 17 September 1940). In turn, the Provost Marshal directed Cummins to 'make every effort, within reason, to smash and break up this organisation' (MA PM 651, Provost Marshal's Office to Commandant, No. 1 Camp, Curragh, 17 September 1940; reminder sent on 27 September 1940).

228 MA PM 651, letters of 27 and 28 September 1940; 11, 19, 20, 21 and 22 October 1940. The exchanges deteriorated into a fairly acrimonious stand-off.

229 MA PM 651, Colonel T. McNally to Commandant M. J. Cummins, 22 October 1940.

230 MA PM 651, Colonel T. McNally to Adjutant General, 22 October 1940.

231 The military authorities summoned the police but would not let Superintendent J. O'Sullivan of Special Branch enter the camp 'for reasons best known to themselves', he subsequently noted. At first the camp reported that two internees were missing. One was then found, and, on 18 October 1940, three days after the initial report, the Commandant informed O'Sullivan that he was satisfied that there had been no escape. O'Sullivan was frustrated by the lack of cooperation and concluded that 'there was undoubtedly a move on foot on the night of the 15/16.10.40 to effect escapes'. He did not think that outside assistance had been part of the plan. NAI JUS/8/870, Superintendent J. O'Sullivan to Commissioner, Garda Síochána, 16 and 18 October 1940.

232 NAI JUS/8/870, O'Sullivan to Commissioner, 16 October 1940.

233 NAI JUS/8/870, O'Sullivan to Commissioner, 16 October 1940.

234 NAI JUS/8/870.

235 That the camp had been poorly and indeed negligently managed was shown by the need (for the first time) to order such an obvious precaution as relieving perimeter guards who were taken off patrol to assist in the count; that all vehicles and persons entering the compound be searched; that only known and reliable civilians be allowed into the compound; and that military police be assigned to specific huts and areas so that they should get to know their prisoners.

236 MacEoin, *The IRA in the Twilight Years, op. cit.*, pp. 649–51. Derry Kelleher, whose politics were left-leaning, had also come to see the Nazi conquest of Europe as the supreme issue for the times. With others in C1, the hut of heretics, he was pro-Soviet, a stance that was unacceptable to the orthodox Catholic leadership of the IRA for whom the boundless iniquity of Britain remained the defining circumstance of international politics and their own lodestone.

237 MA CP 724, Discipline of Prisoners and Internees: Adjutant General memorandum, 5 February 1941.

238 MA CP 724, Commandant J. Guiney to Provost Marshal, 3 March 1941. Two men, Samuel G. Flake and Norman Clarke, were reported for incidents and sarcastic language and for failing to cooperate. The lack of unity and the attention devoted to internal disputes seems to have closed down concerted escape attempts. Writing (probably) in mid-1942, Seamus O'Donovan noted that plans that had some months previously been under consideration were now impossible (O'Donovan Papers, MS. 22, 307, undated letter).

239 MA CP 724, Commandant J. Guiney to Provost Marshal, 11 March 1942.

240 MA CP 724, Provost Marshal, Discipline Prisoners and Internees, Acting Corporal Francis Cosgrave to Governor, 12 December 1945. Possibly unbeknownst to Hamill and others, the IRA had experimented with a very limited form of signing out. So great was the attrition from arrests after September 1941 that Harry White (later by default to become Chief of Staff of a non-existent IRA) signed out, in April 1942. Francis Duffy and Liam Burke followed – the last because he knew the location of the arms dumps in the south-east. These men immediately returned to active service with the IRA (MacEoin, *The IRA in the Twilight Years, op. cit.*, p. 448). It seems remarkable that the authorities should accept undertakings from senior figures not to become involved in subversive activities again. Such was the abhorrence with which signing-out was regarded, it was probably reasoned that in giving any undertaking the men had cut themselves off from the republican movement.

241 MA CP 724, Commandant M. Lennon, Governor, Arbour Hill, to Provost Marshal, Department of Defence, 17 December 1943.

242 MA CP 724, Commandant M. Lennon, Governor, Arbour Hill, to Provost Marshal, Department of Defence, 6 January 1944.

243 See, for example, official reports of fisticuffs between Michael Traynor and Peadar O'Flaherty (both IRA GHQ men) on 5 December 1943 (MA CP 724, reports by Sergeant P. Pollick and Commandant Michael Lennon, 5 December 1943).

244 MA CP 724, Provost Marshal, Discipline Prisoners and Internees, Lennon to Provost Marshal, 6 January 1944.

245 MA PM 1217, Colonel F. J. Henry to Adjutant General, n.d. (December 1943/early 1944). There had been only one new reception at Arbour Hill since 14 October 1943.

246 MA CP 204, Commandant J. Guiney to Provost Marshal, 12 March 1942.

247 MA CP 204, Commandant J. Guiney to Provost Marshal, 12 March 1942.

248 MA CP 204, Adjutant General's Office to Commandant J. Guiney, 18 March 1942.

249 MA CP 204, Report, Sergeant William Callaghan to Commandant J. Guiney, 17 March 1942. In forwarding the report to Headquarters, Guiney cautioned that

Sergeant Callaghan's informant, M. Falvey, was a 'half wit'. While much of what Falvey had said might be authentic, 'a big lot of reliance cannot be placed on his story'.

250 MA CP 204, Commandant J. Guiney to Provost Marshal, 18 March 1942.

251 MA CP 204, Commandant J. Guiney to Provost Marshal, 20 March 1942. On Daly's hunger strike, see above, pp. 720–1.

252 MA CP 204, Commandant J. Guiney to Provost Marshal, 23 March 1944. There was some obvious over-egging, in references to 'praise for An Taoiseach for his capable and determined stand in preserving our neutrality'.

253 MA CP 204, reports of 30 November 1944, 1 December 1944 and 2 December 1944. In view of the circumstances, it was decided not to take action against Behan, Martin and Holland, who were described as, at the very least, irresponsible. For Behan's equally irresponsible – and unhygienic – stay at Mountjoy, where he was awarded the sobriquet 'Filth' by his companions, see MacEoin, *The IRA in the Twilight Years, op. cit.*, pp. 505–6. Charlie Kerins (1918–44) had also been IRA Chief of Staff in 1942–3 and for a few months in 1944. Arrested on 15 June 1944, he was brought before the Military Tribunal charged with the murder of Special Branch Sergeant Dennis O'Brien at Rathfarnham, Co. Dublin, on 9 September 1942. Found guilty by the Military Court on 9 October 1944, he was sentenced to death and hanged on 1 December 1944 (see above, p. 617).

254 Kelly had been IRA Chief of Staff for a few months in 1941 and was arrested on 27 November of that year, when, attempting to warn Abwehr agent Hermann Görtz of his impending arrest, he was himself captured. On the afternoon of the day of Kerins's execution, Kelly assembled internees and prisoners of all factions to observe two minutes' silence and to recite prayers. Following this, the men dispersed quietly. This was a dignified and disciplined type of action that once would have been automatic.

255 In September 1939, Éire's armed forces numbered fewer than 20,000. By May 1941, numbers had more than doubled.

256 All those convicted under the OASA were removed from the Military Detention Barracks at the Curragh (known as the Glasshouse) to Arbour Hill Detention Barracks in February 1940 (NAI JUS/8/169, Committals of Convicted Prisoners).

257 In February 1942, correspondence and exchanges were detected between No. 1 (Internment) Camp and No. 2 (Army) Camp. It seemed clear that a customised ring had been ordered by a soldier and an attempt had been made to deliver it. More worrying than this low-level illicit commerce was a series of questions in the letter that accompanied the ring – both thrown in a matchbox. The letter asked a series of questions, the gist of which was directed to escape: how easy would it be to get out of No. 2 Camp were it possible to pass therein from No. 1 Camp? A soldier whose name matched that on the customised ring was arrested and interrogated by G2 Branch. Commandant Guiney ordered a special search of No. 1 Camp, and further brooch and ring orders and correspondence was turned up (MA PM 335, Commandant J. Guiney to Provost Marshal, 18 February 1942).

258 MA PM 362, Transfers: Civilian Prisoners and Internees, Memorandum Submitted to Government, 23 February 1942. See NAI TAOIS/2, Cabinet minutes.

259 MA PM 362, Transfers, Adjutant General to Colonel McNally, OC Curragh Command, 27 February 1942.

260 See above, p. 722.

261 Transport difficulties became a major theme in national life, and the unreliability of the turf-burning trains a thing of wonder. In some provincial areas, enterprising souls offered stagecoach services (Wills, *That Neutral Island, op. cit.*, p. 251).

262 NAI TAOIS/2, Cabinet Minutes.

263 MA PM 362, Colonel F. J. Henry, Provost Marshal, to Adjutant General, 23 April 1942.

264 MA PM 946, Minute, 24 April 1942. The ministerial portfolio had been expanded and renamed on 8 December 1939 as Minister for Co-ordination of Defensive Measures. The short form is used here for convenience.

265 MA PM 1217, Colonel F. J. Henry to Provost Marshal, 29 December 1942. In January 1943, it was decided to reactivate Waterford as a prison, removing a marine depot and stores then installed in the building.

266 Cork Prison was taken into use for internees in June 1940 but was discontinued for this purpose just two months later, when the men were transferred to the Curragh (MA CP 332, Colonel M. J. Costello, OC, Southern Command to Adjutant General, 7 June 1940; Commandant M. McHugh to Commandant, Cork Prison, 6 August 1940). A comprehensive set of standing orders survives in this file. See also MA PM 362, Colonel F. J. Henry to OC Curragh Command, 9 February 1943; PM 1217, Colonel F. J. Henry to Provost Marshal, 29 December 1942.

267 This was the Army's response to the search for accommodation in 1942 and the agreed undesirability of lodging the special political prisoners in a wing of the female prison at Mountjoy. See MA PM 312, Colonel F. J. Henry, Provost Marshal, to Adjutant General, 30 March 1942.

268 MA PM 1217, Colonel James Flynn, Adjutant General, to Minister, 23 January 1946.

269 MA CP 16, Weekly Report, Governor of Arbour Hill to Provost Marshal, 30 July 1943; see also Weekly Report, 4 March 1944. The term 'ex-military' applied to those whom it had been decided to discharge from the Army but who were first undergoing punishment for their offences.

270 MacEoin, *The IRA in the Twilight Years*, op. cit., p. 508.

271 There is at least one plausible account of an informer at work in the camp. Whether this person was recruited in the camp or before going in is unclear, but he apparently continued his activities on release (see MacEoin, *The IRA in the Twilight Years*, op. cit., pp. 577–8).

272 MacEoin, *The IRA in the Twilight Years*, op. cit., p. 509. And that, doubtless, was an accolade.

273 MacEoin, *The IRA in the Twilight Years*, op. cit., p. 511. Doran's earliest release date on his five-year sentence was 21 October 1947. NAI JUS/8/944, Statistics, Internment, etc. (1946). List of prisoners in Curragh No. 1 Internment Camp.

274 It is not clear how the factions fared as the camp emptied and whether there came a point where numbers were so reduced that shunning had to cease.

275 See Mick Fitzgibbon's detailed account of the tunnel in MacEoin, *The IRA in the Twilight Years*, op. cit., pp. 590–1.

276 MacEoin, *The IRA in the Twilight Years*, op. cit., p. 627.

277 MacEoin, *The IRA in the Twilight Years*, op. cit., p. 744.

278 He confessed himself surprised with the progress that had been made, which suggests that more than three weeks (the interval he claimed) had elapsed since the old tunnel had last been inspected. The usual range of tunnel-making tools had been scrounged or adapted from items available in the camp, including wax candles from the altar of the camp chapel. NAI JUS/8/910 x 1943, Commandant J. Guiney to OC Curragh Command, 29 April 1943.

279 NAI JUS/8/910 x 1943, Superintendent P. J. Gaffney to Chief Superintendent, Naas, 4 May 1943.

280 Humphreys Papers, P/106/893, Seán McCool to Sighle Humphreys, 4 May 1944. McCool indicated that he and the others were nevertheless looking for signs of war's end. 'I suppose everyone outside is waiting these days to hear that the much heralded Second Front has been opened at last.' McCool was a long-serving and

prominent IRA man. He had been arrested in connection with the Crown Entry court-martial and then served a sentence of six years' penal servitude in Belfast Prison. He went to Dublin on release and then served briefly as IRA Chief of Staff (at a time when the average tenure was measured in weeks). Subsequently arrested and interned, he was clearly destined to be one of the last releases.

281 'Departmental Notes', *op. cit.*, Appendix K. Uncertainty as to the exact number arises from one name which was probably but not certainly feminine.

282 'Departmental Notes', *op. cit.*, Appendix M.

283 MacEoin, *The IRA in the Twilight Years, op. cit.*, p. 945.

284 Humphreys Papers, P/106/1285/39, Prisoners' Reunion, 30 January 1944.

285 *Dáil Debates*, vol. 91, col. 366, 7 July 1943. The seven women were Maire O'Sullivan (interned August 1940); Eileen O'Kelly (February 1942); Mollie and Pat Gallagher (September 1942); Maggie O'Halloran (October 1942); Maggie Doyle (November 1942) and Patricia Kelly (March 1943). Oliver J. Flanagan (1920–87) was a Monetary Reform member of the Dáil. Since the new (Eleventh) Dáil had assembled on 1 July 1943, this may well have been his first Dáil speech. In the 1948–51 and 1951–4 Dáils he sat as an Independent, thereafter as Fine Gael, but always for Leix-Offaly (renamed Laoighis-Offaly in 1961).

286 Humphreys Papers, P/106/1285/39. Fiona Plunkett, writing to Sighle Humphreys on 26 September 1940, reported all the women in her wing singing that day.

287 NAI JUS/8/944, Statistics, Internment, etc. (1946); Humphreys Papers, P/106/1321, Political Prisoners' Committee, leaflet distributed to delegates at Fianna Fáil Ard Fheis, 27 September 1943.

288 Humphreys Papers, P/106/894, Miriam James to First Reunion of Women Prisoners, 27 January 1944. MacEoin lists six women as having been imprisoned in England, with sentences of between two and seven years. Another woman, Mary Duggan, failed to answer her bail (MacEoin, *The IRA in the Twilight Years, op. cit.*, p. 946). Sadly, there is no woman amongst the thirty-three veterans interviewed by MacEoin, although references to republican women abound.

289 Humphreys Papers, P/106/1125, Cumann na mBan Executive minutes. This was the Irish Red Cross rather than the International Committee of the Red Cross.

290 Humphreys Papers, Minutes of Cumann na mBan, 30 September 1943.

291 See, for example, the police report on a meeting in Swinford, Co. Mayo, held to establish a branch of the Republican Prisoners' Release Committee. Kevin Campbell, who was the principal speaker at the meeting, was explicit in his political message and condemned prison staff by name. This type of speech would undoubtedly have resulted in imprisonment and internment during the war years. NAI JUS/8/943, Kevin Campbell speech, 19 May 1946.

292 NAI JUS/8/869, The Green Cross Committee, 8 October 1940. See above, pp. 534–5.

293 NAI JUS/8/869, Secretary General's Minute of 17 October 1940. The control of funds in such organisations is always likely to present difficulties. In November and December 1943, British intelligence received information that there had been resignations from the IRA of senior figures because of alleged misappropriation of funds intended for dependants (PRO DO/121/85, 'Irish Affairs', 1 January 1944).

294 NAI JUS/8/869, Green Cross Committee, 8 October 1940.

295 Maloney expressed disappointment that Boland had been unable to meet all her requests but thanked him for his courtesy 'and for your friendly suggestions and sympathetic attitude to the work of our Committee'. If this was more than mere politeness, it would seem that Boland had a less fierce attitude than that of his senior civil servant, at least on the matter of prisoners' dependants. In 1942, Commandant James Guiney, who commanded No. 1 Camp, raised with the Provost Marshal the

matter of handicrafts being gifted to the Irish Prisoners National Aid Society. In response, the Provost Marshal alluded to the tacit acceptance of the Society by the government. It had for years past been well known to the authorities that collections had been made on behalf of prisoners' dependants 'and no objections have been raised (presumably on humanitarian grounds, and official Government policy) and such collections have not been viewed as supporting an illegal organisation' (MA PM 335, Provost Marshal to Commandant J. Guiney, 23 February 1942).

296 'Irish Affairs', the secret reports from Ireland to the British government, wryly noted that 'it appears that Church and State differentiate between acts of the IRA in Northern Ireland and similar acts of the same organisation in Eire' (PRO DO/121/85, 'Irish Affairs', 1 May 1943).

297 See p. 534.

298 NAI JUS/8/869, Statement of Edward McMahon, 6 June 1941.

299 NAI JUS/8/869, Memorandum, 11 August 1941.

300 NAI JUS/8/81, Penal system: Society of Friends to Minister Patrick J. Ruttledge, 12 September 1935.

301 '"Tintown 1940–45" by "An Ex-Internee"', *United Irishman*, August 1951, 8b: 'Their presents to us from this [first visit] to the time when the Camp closed were far too numerous to list here.'

302 OASA (Part VI) (Detention) Regulations 1939 (Statutory Rules and Orders No. 249/1939); OAS(A)A. The latter legislation, before being enacted, was referred to the Supreme Court by the President, under power conferred by Article 26 of the Constitution. The Supreme Court found that the Act was not repugnant to the Constitution. In Re. Article 26 of the Constitution and the Offences Against the State (Amendment) Bill, 1940 (1940 IR 470). The transcript of the Supreme Court hearing may be found at NAI 90/8/164, Supreme Court Hearing Re. Offences Against the State Bill, 1940.

303 See above, pp. 537–40.

304 OASA, s.59; NAI TAOIS/S11436. The Commission announced on 17 September 1939 consisted of Chairman Hugh J. McCann (a barrister), Major Michael Tuohy and Major Felix Devlin. The Burke decision terminated that commission. On 3 February 1940, another Detention Commission was established under Article 6 of the Emergency Powers (Detention Commission) Order, 1940. William Black, a judge of the High Court, chaired the Commission. Major Michael Tuohy was carried over from the previous body and was joined by Commandant John R. Wall, who was a barrister as well as an officer. See NAI TAOIS/1/G3/4, ff. 25–7.

305 Applications for parole were received daily on grounds of illness, family bereavement, tilling and harvesting of crops and the like. Each case was considered personally by the Minister for Justice. On 31 March 1943, sixty-six internees were on parole – almost 12 per cent of the total interned. Four convicted prisoners were also paroled on that date. By 20 March 1944, the number of paroled internees was twenty-seven, amounting to 26 per cent on the internee population on that date. NAI JUS/8/944, Statistics, Internment, etc. (1946). In September 1942, the British 'Irish Affairs' report noted that the Minister for Justice (Gerald Boland) had increased the number of internees who had been granted parole and enigmatically observed, 'So far it is understood this policy has proved itself justified.' Whether this meant that parolees had obeyed the conditions imposed on them and had returned in time to the Curragh, or some other criterion of success, is not clear. It is possible that by this time parole was being granted as a means of testing those individuals who were released and that if they did not renew their activities and connections they could with more confidence be considered for release. See PRO DO/121/85, 'Irish Affairs', 1 September 1942. This document was designated 'Most Secret'.

306 Bell, *The Secret Army*, *op. cit.*, pp. 234–5.

307 MA PM 312, Commandant, Athlone Internment Camp, to Provost Marshal, c. December 1945. Other possibilities were to transfer the men to the Curragh or to Arbour Hill.

308 Séamus Ó Goilidhe was released without notice in September 1943. About a week after his release, he was visited at home by gardaí who asked him to sign an undertaking. He refused, and that was the last he heard of the matter. (MacEoin, *The IRA in the Twilight Years*, *op. cit.*, p. 713.)

309 Humphreys Papers, P/106/893, Seán McCool to Sighle Humphreys, 28 March 1944. On 3 March 1943 there were 543 men and eighteen women interned. By 20 March 1944, this number had indeed more than halved, to 240 men and no women. NAI JUS/8/944, Statistics, Internment, etc. (1946). Given his IRA record and standing McCool was indeed destined to be one of a very small band of last-stand Mohicans.

310 Humphreys Papers, P/106/893, Seán McCool to Sighle Humphreys, 4 May 1944.

311 Interview in MacEoin, *The IRA in the Twilight Years*, *op. cit.*, p. 489.

312 In March 1944, British intelligence in Ireland reported that about half the Curragh internees had been released over the previous year, 'and the majority have shown no inclination to interest themselves further in IRA affairs' (PRO DO/121/85, 'Irish Affairs', 1 March 1944).

313 On 31 March 1945, there were 104 IRA internees at the Curragh and fifty-nine serving sentences imposed by the Special Criminal Court and the Military Court (NAI JUS/8/944, Statistics, Internment, etc. [1946]).

314 MA CP 110, P. Ó Cinnéide, Assistant Secretary to Government, to Provost Marshal, 14 May 1945. Speaking in the Dáil on 4 July 1945, de Valera said that the decision to release the internees had been taken 'with a certain amount of misgiving' (*Dáil Debates*, vol. 97, col. 1881). On last releases, see the *Irish Times*, 22 June 1945, 1h. By 1944, Ireland's transportation difficulties were so acute that the exact day of release had to be determined by the availability of a bus or train to take a man home. It was agreed between the departments of Justice and Defence that internees would be freed to fit with the availability of transport and that the release of convicted persons might be brought forward by some days for the same reason. NAI JUS/8/926, Prisoners and Internees, letter of 9 and 20 May 1944.

315 The government's 11 May release decision was that the remaining seventy-two who were internees and the four men serving sentences for their part in hut-burning would be released in small batches, the operation to be completed by 1 June or 1 July 1945. Apart from the hut-burners, no decision was taken at this point with regard to those under sentence.

316 MA PM 312, Colonel James Flynn, Adjutant General, to Minister for Defence, 23 January 1946.

317 These cases were Thomas Hunt, convicted of the murder of Detective Officer Hyland on 16 August 1940. His accomplices, Francis Harte and Patrick McGrath, had been executed on 6 September 1940. Thomas Hunt had, on 23 September 1940, been sentenced to death, but his sentence was commuted two days later. Seán McCaughey had been sentenced to death for imprisoning Stephen Hayes but also had his sentence reduced to life at penal servitude. Others in the group of long-term and problematical prisoners were Patrick Davern and Michael Walshe, both convicted of murdering Michael Devereux, and whose accomplice, George Plant, had been executed.

318 MacEoin, *The IRA in the Twilight Years*, *op. cit.*, p. 511. At this point, the number was down to twenty or twenty-two; the records are contradictory.

319 O'Flaherty's earliest release date had been August 1948. His was a significant case because he had been a member of the IRA Army Council and one of the signatories

of the declaration of war on Britain. He was arrested with other members of the GHQ in the Rathmines raid on 9 September 1939 and sentenced to eighteen months. That sentence had expired, but he was then sentenced to ten years following another conviction. Sean O'Brien had also been on the Army Council as Director of Intelligence and was sentenced to seven years' penal servitude. NAI JUS/8/944, Statistics, Internment, etc. (1946).

320 MA PM 312, Commandant J. Guiney to OC, Curragh Command, 18 January 1946.

321 *Dáil Debates*, vol. 97, col. 1881, 4 July 1945; *Irish Independent*, 5 July 1945, 3a–b; *Times Pictorial*, 14 July 1945, 10c–d. See also NAI TAOIS/S13706.

322 Pearse Kelly, a former IRA Chief of Staff, was one of those kept at the Curragh until the very end. He remembered that its indeterminacy was the principal depressing feature of internment: 'With a jail sentence you knew by the calendar when it would end, but with internment it just kept going on and on unless you took the easy way out – via parole or signing out' (*Irish Independent*, 23 January 1969, 3a–b).

323 MA PM 312, Commandant J. Guiney to OC, Curragh Command, 18 January 1946. The prisoners were worried about IRA activities generally and the effect they might have on release prospects.

324 Guiney to OC, Curragh Command, 18 January 1946, *op. cit.* The Brugha family were the survivors of the unreconciled Cathal who had died a defiant death in O'Connell Street when cornered by Free State forces in the early clashes of the Civil War. As an irreconcilable fighting man, Brugha was held in particularly high regard by the IRA for this heroic death and for his service as Dáil Minister for Defence during the Anglo-Irish War. His widow Caitlín and at least three of her children Nóinín, Neasa and Ruairí were bitter opponents of the Free State and then of de Valera. They were particularly active in providing courier and safe-house services but do not seem to have been part of the formal structure of the IRA. This, and their middle-class background, fed resentment in some IRA members.

325 Six months later, Hamill resigned as OC because his authority was not being respected. Certain prisoners had gone to the Staters, he complained, to ask for privileges, instead of putting their requests through him. Attempts to persuade him to stay in post failed, and Seán Ryan was elected in his stead. (MA PM 335, Sergeant J. Dollard to Commandant J. Guiney, 9 July 1946).

326 Among some of the survivors of this period we were able to interview, there was broad agreement that, at the end of the Curragh years, the IRA was a broken organisation.

327 MA PM 312, Commandant J. Guiney to OC, Curragh Command, 18 January 1946.

328 MA PM 312, Colonel James Flynn, Adjutant General, to Gerald Boland, Minister for Justice, 23 January 1946.

329 See Bell, *The Secret Army, op. cit.*, p. 241.

330 MacEoin, *The IRA in the Twilight Years, op. cit.*, p. 512.

331 Shannon had fired at John F. O'Brien in Westmoreland Street, Dublin, on the evening of 8 June 1946. He was brought before the Special Criminal Court (which he refused to recognise) on 21 June 1946 and sentenced to five years' penal servitude for shooting with intent (*Irish Times*, 22 June 1946, 7h). This was a comparatively light sentence: Brendan Behan had received fourteen years for the same offence.

332 MacEoin, *The IRA in the Twilight Years, op. cit.*, p. 512.

333 NAI JUS/8/944, Statistics, Internment, etc. (1946).

334 The three released from Portlaoise were William Stewart and Patrick Murphy (sentenced for IRA-inspired robberies in Dundalk) and Frank Kerrigan, a Mountjoy escapee who had fired on gardaí attempting to rearrest him (*Irish Times*, 19 December 1946, 1g–h).

335 *Irish Times*, 27 February 1948, 1b; 10 March 1948, 2f. Rice and Smullen had been released before the others on health grounds. In a press interview, Taoiseach John Costello said that both were 'in very bad health', and their release was entirely justified on that ground. The remaining three were freed because their continued detention 'would only result in the perpetuation of resentment and unrest'. He was at pains to deny that the releases had been part of the Fine Gael/Clann na Poblachta coalition pact. The decision had to be taken by the Minister for Justice and himself. This was a carefully worded statement that few commentators took at face value.

14

THE BORDER CAMPAIGN, 1953–62

Anglo-Irish relations

In the post-war years, Anglo-Irish relations ossified. Within Ireland, the two states reached their respective quarter-centuries with significant problems remaining unresolved between them. With their politicians, the communities seemed incapable of advancing towards what, in the Cold War era, might be called the normalisation of relations: energy, will and imagination were all lacking; no one wanted to step out of line, and the finger-pointing of party politics mandated minimum risk policies. Suspicion and disdain prevented all but minimal and necessary contacts between North and South; and even these were constrained, at both official and political levels, by anxieties concerning popular perceptions. Only Britain could be the honest broker, yet in Westminster and Whitehall alike there was a fervent wish to remain uninvolved and that all matters Irish should remain undisturbed. This wariness was reinforced by the many preoccupations of a country exhausted and economically prostrated by a war only barely survived, the multifarious demands of an empire on the point of dissolution and the uncertainty of national identity undergoing reformation. In the official files and correspondence there is a further, more intimate and personal note: the Irish (and de Valera in particular) were perceived as not being easy people with whom to do business. Best therefore to do nothing.

The view from Dublin was different. Consumed by his own notions of Irish identity and national unity, de Valera had done nothing practical to achieve the latter. A skilled and determined party politician, he must have been somewhat aware of the contradictions he embodied. He constantly proclaimed the imperatives of Irish unity while moving decisively and with scant regard away from Northern Ireland's majority population. His 1937 Constitution, with its many nationalistic and religious tones, asserted Dublin's *de jure* authority over the Northern state and, at the same time, defined and entrenched a special position for the Roman Catholic Church. Divorce had been forbidden in the 1920s (in a political consensus), not as a matter of ordinary law but by the Irish Constitution itself. The state thrust its way into the bedroom by banning all access to contraception.[1] Links to the Commonwealth had been cut to a minimum, and the goodwill of countries such as Canada and South Africa, usefully built up in the 1920s, was thoughtlessly squandered. De Valera and his supporters consistently dismissed the claims of Northern Protestants (and some Catholics) to a British identity. A ditch had always lain between the two groups that populated the island: by 1945, it had become a moat.

Ireland was not on the losing side in the world conflagration, but it had emphatically declined to be on the winning one. In 1945, de Valera sat among the ruins of Irish foreign policy, epitomised by his signing the German Embassy's Book of Condolence on the death of Adolf Hitler.[2] He had leverage neither with London nor Washington. A broad swathe of the British public opinion, and most politicians, recalled with bitterness Ireland's denial of the ports in times of Britain's mortal struggle. With its own losses and sacrifices Washington had been just as incensed by Irish neutrality. The old fires of the Irish-American community had appreciably cooled: too many of Irish extraction had died or suffered in the Second World War for the usual sentiment towards 'The Old Country' to come to de Valera's aid. The League of Nations, which had given the Irish, and de Valera in particular, an international pulpit, had collapsed in pusillanimous ignominy and irrelevance. As part of the wider East–West stand-off, Ireland had been blackballed by the Soviets in its application for UN member-ship. With little influence and few friends on the international scene, de Valera's principal domestic project as he entered the last phase of his career (the ending of Partition) had not the slightest prospect of moving forward. Ireland remained an inward-looking country, both self-righteous and with a marked lack of self-confidence. A temporary wartime prosperity as a supplier of labour and food had given way to much leaner times and rising unemployment. As ever, emi-gration siphoned off the young, energetic, questing and talented, and a life of economic exile again became a common expectation.[3]

The distinction between the removal of Partition and promoting Irish unity was never contemplated. The former was envisaged by de Valera and nationalist politicians of his generation as a territorial deal between London and Dublin. It was an article of faith that they had been bilked by the Treaty and the Boundary Commission, and they believed just as strongly that this injustice could be put right by bypassing Ulster's Protestants and Unionists. To Irish unity they paid little attention. This was necessarily a much more complicated project, involving an enlargement of Irish nationality and identity, making it fully inclusive of both Protestant and Catholic traditions, the British dimension in Northern identities and abandoning the Fenian romanticism of Pearse: 'Not free merely but Gaelic as well; not Gaelic merely but free as well.'[4] Unable to make the leap of imagination and incapable of the necessary generosity, de Valera hoped that those Ulster men and women unwilling to accept a London–Dublin démarche would be removed or would leave the island. Looking into his own heart, he had con-cluded that such were not, and never could be, his compatriots. To some extent this was a mirror image of exclusionary and equally fervent Unionism in Northern Ireland.

Driven by these convictions, possibly by an abiding guilt and a need to justify his pivotal role in the Civil War, certainly aware that his democratic accession to office had confirmed Michael Collins's argument that to accept the Treaty was but to stand on a stepping stone, de Valera's principal project was a new representation – largely by means of style, symbol and rhetoric – of the state against which he had taken arms. His constituency was nationalist Ireland, living and dead, and he was determined not to be outflanked: the 1937 Constitution was the consequent product. Commonwealth ties were stretched to breaking, and in all essentials a republic was established. Rejecting the Constitution of the Free State, the new document asserted authority independent of the Treaty, vesting it in the Irish people.[5] This allowed the redefined state to make a provocative claim to Northern Ireland, while recognising that, pending what it described as 'the reintegration of the national territory', the Dáil's executive authority would extend only to the twenty-six counties. To mark its new status, the name of the country was changed from the Irish Free State to Éire.[6] Although the Constitution's territorial claims were aspirational only, such language was offensive and disturbing for the unionist majority in Northern Ireland.[7] The assertion of rightful title also created a situation in which the Dublin government shared with the IRA a *de jure* claim to Northern Ireland, which the IRA sought to turn into *de facto* subjugation. Consequently, there were dangerous uncertainties, ambiguities and contradictions in public and political perceptions of the relations between the two states and of highly volatile elements within them. Over the two following decades these would coalesce in several forms, including armed force.

Despite its proposed status as fundamental and entrenched legislation, de Valera sought no more than a simple majority when he submitted his Constitution to a referendum on 1 July 1937. The majority was clear, but well short of the two-thirds required in many other states for such basic law: 685,105 votes in favour of adoption and 526,945 against.[8] The new constitution came into effect on 29 December 1937. There was British disapproval but no willingness to assert in arms or even by political and economic sanctions the inviolability of the Treaty. The conviction of an earlier generation of British politicians that any departure from the Treaty, never mind its abandonment, should trigger hostilities between the two countries had faded away with little fuss. There was no doubt, moreover, that the battlefields and cemeteries of Europe were again being prepared. Ireland was peripheral to these dreadful anticipations. Whatever raiment and rhetoric Dublin chose for its adornment, London noted, there was little practical outcome: the 1937 Constitution was a cosmetic rather than a surgical transformation.[9]

During the wartime years, as we have seen, de Valera was less concerned with the reunification of Ireland than with the survival of the Irish state; Irish unity was nowhere on the agenda. Behind the scenes, in conversation with the British Representative, there was much said about Partition as the root of all evil, but in public only murmurs of anti-Partitionism. Activities of the IRA, asserting its all-Ireland authority, were visited with an unrelenting campaign of suppression.

Attempting to rematerialise after its pulverisation by de Valera and Gerald Boland (his Minister for Justice), the IRA after 1945 was, very wisely, *sotto voce* in its intention to displace what its fundamental doctrine held to be a usurping Southern legislature: rhetoric and activities were now sedulously directed to the liberation of Northern Ireland. With the anti-Partition sentiments of the conventional parties legitimising such pronouncements, and apparently meeting with electoral approval, a degree of complicity won enough headroom for the IRA to reorganise and prepare a new campaign – at least up to the point at which the bare-bones Anglo-Irish relations were threatened. Sabre-rattling was useful to the mainstream politicians in several ways, but action was quite another matter.

Towards the end of the war, with an Allied victory within months inevitable, Sir John Maffey, the UK Representative in Dublin, had an informal conversation with de Valera. The meeting lasted for two hours, three-quarters of which was devoted to the issue of Partition. Maffey contended that the only way in which trouble could start would be through acts of violence by Catholic nationalists in the North or armed attacks from the South. De Valera maintained that the North was held by force and that London could resolve the situation. If there were insuperable popular difficulties with this, there should be a transfer of population out of the North to resolve them. This proposal was ignored by Maffey, who mildly suggested that Dublin should strive to make itself more attractive to Northerners. Short of large-scale – possibly forced – population transfers to Britain, which seemed to be his preferred solution, de Valera obliquely suggested that a redrawing of the border might ease the situation. Another means of advancing the relationship between the two islands, he observed (with a prescience that would have gratified had he lived to see it) was 'a regional system of powers'.[10]

On his part, though he certainly did not let de Valera catch even a glimpse of it, Maffey was pessimistic about Northern Ireland's prospects, referring to it (in a memorandum to the Dominions Office) as 'a ramshackle and somewhat discreditable structure'. He favoured excising Fermanagh and Tyrone, scrapping Stormont and making the four remaining counties part of Scotland 'thereby absorbing the Catholic minority in the North in the general community of the United Kingdom'. This would end the gerrymandering which Stormont, in order to preserve itself, had to impose on the Catholic population. Partition could not continue without trouble – perhaps a 'blood sacrifice' (a reference to the Easter Rising) – on which de Valera and other patriots would be bound to act.[11]

Maffey's reflections were not well received in London (and would have had inflammatory consequences, had any part of them leaked). Sir Eric Machtig, Permanent Under-Secretary of State for the Dominions, agreed that Maffey's was a possible reading, but it was not the only one. He judged that de Valera knew that violence would not resolve Partition, and that, should trouble break out, he would do his best to control it. The problem, nevertheless, was very much one of de Valera's own making.[12] London had no reason to raise the issue. Were de Valera willing to put forward proposals to provide safeguards for

Ulster, and to satisfy Britain's strategic needs, it was open to him to make the approach – but Maffey must be careful not to give the impression that he was inviting this.[13]

Eight months later, de Valera probably hoped that the new and apparently radical Labour government, strong in Parliament and in the country, and with an unquestionable mandate for change, would put Partition on the table once again. Labour, or at least a section of the movement, had long been sympathetic to Irish grievances. In a number of city constituencies, Irish voters were a significant element. The replacement of the imperialist Churchill, a signatory to the Treaty, by the reforming Clement Attlee, was doubly encouraging. A remarkable visit by Herbert Morrison, Lord President of the Council, and a major Labour Party figure, may have reinforced optimism.[14] This was the first such contact in a generation. Following a private visit to Co. Cork, Morrison spent three days in Dublin in September 1945. This was choreographed by Maffey to provide opportunities to meet major political figures. In such encounters Morrison had the advantage of being a member of Cabinet, but without the powers and responsibilities of heading a department of government, and he could use his lack of executive authority to deflect questions. He got on well with de Valera, members of his government, the Irish President (Seán T. O'Kelly), and W. T. Cosgrave, leader of Fine Gael. Various international topics provided the hors d'oeuvres before de Valera and Morrison turned to Ireland, via India. De Valera asserted that Partition was the principal barrier to better Anglo-Irish relations. Morrison took the line that time was a great healer: were the issue to be raised in any precipitate manner, there could be first-class trouble. Here he was drawing on background knowledge of Northern Ireland gained during his time as Home Secretary. Restricted and certainly one-sided though this may have been, he was probably as well informed as de Valera.[15]

De Valera wanted the British to act as the proper imperialists he believed them to be: to change by fiat rather than by consent. Insisting that reunification was thus a practical prospect, he said that he would preserve Stormont's existing powers provided that they were exercised within the framework of an all-Ireland government. With such an agreement, Ireland's foreign policy would, he intimated, change dramatically. It would resume membership of the Commonwealth and assume appropriate obligations for military cooperation. Unimpressed, Morrison again cautioned that any attempt to rush the issue would be harmful. A change of view on the part of Northern Ireland would be another matter altogether, 'but to expect us to coerce Ulster was expecting too much, especially in view of the troubled state of the world in which we all live'. According to Morrison, de Valera was not cross at the rebuff but indicated that in that case the difficulties in Anglo-Irish relationships would have to continue.[16] In a bid to counter this abiding but low-key hostility, Morrison proposed to Cabinet that in a quiet way much good could come from the encouragement by ministers and officials of visits and other contacts with their opposite numbers in Dublin, in a spirit of friendliness and cooperation.[17]

Viscount Addison, Secretary of State for Dominion Affairs, confirmed Morrison's assertion that de Valera and his colleagues would raise Partition and its problems on all occasions when they met British politicians. The British government should have a clear position from which to respond. The wishes of the majority in Northern Ireland were against any form of union with Éire: 'The roots of this feeling go deep. Religion, loyalty to the Crown and the British connection and material interests are all factors which govern their attitude.' The war and Éire's neutrality had strengthened those feelings: 'It is unthinkable that we could or should persuade or force them against their will.' A second consideration was the strategic importance of Northern Ireland's ports and bases. Their value had been demonstrated during the war, and it would be folly to throw away such an asset 'unless on terms which will secure its continued availability and the availability of bases also in Éire'. De Valera, invited to join Britain in the war on the fall of France, on the understanding that London would do its best to bring about union with Northern Ireland, had replied that he could only contemplate a united Ireland on the basis of the whole country being neutral. It was, as Morrison had observed, for de Valera to give as well as to take. The wisest course, given the strong feelings on both sides, was to avoid any suggestion that the British government was willing to give the matter serious consideration.[18]

Partition was now de Valera's dominant leitmotif. This effectively precluded many opportunities to improve Anglo-Irish relations on other matters and blocked any development of relations of substance with Northern Ireland. Maffey, now ennobled as Lord Rugby, met de Valera in the summer of 1947 and, *inter alia*, suggested that technical cooperation between the two governments would generally improve the atmosphere. This, he reported to the Dominions Office, 'led to the usual harangue about partition'. It would be most helpful, de Valera contended, were a responsible minister to make a statement that the UK was not bent on maintaining Partition for its own sake, that it was not in principle opposed to a settlement if the parties could come together. There was a view that England was intent on preserving Partition, whatever the parties might agree. If only the Partition question were dealt with, relations between the two islands would be smooth.[19]

But, after sixteen years of Fianna Fáil, there was a mood for change. Electoral considerations and a desire to revive the fortunes of what was now an understandably tired and wrung-out administration by a *coup de théâtre* had probably lent some urgency to the conversations with the British Representative. De Valera lost office in the general election of February 1948, replaced by a coalition of Fine Gael (under John Costello), Labour (under William Norton) and Clann na Poblachta (under Seán MacBride, leader of the party which he had founded two years before). It was an unlikely combination: a party distinctly right of centre with one more centrist and another just as distinctly to the left. Clann na Poblachta would provide a relatively short-lived parliamentary platform for former IRA men, fellow travellers and supporters. The common ground was not much more than a desire to end Fianna Fáil's ascendancy and to curb de

Valera's dominance in public life. Anglo-Irish relations were unlikely to improve, or to receive any boost from the new government, if only because the troika was so ill-matched and flimsily yoked. MacBride was well down a path that would take him from IRA Chief of Staff to human-rights campaigner and (in 1976) the Nobel Peace Prize, but, because of his record and narrow vision, he was nevertheless incapable of nuancing relations with London or Belfast: his tenure as Minister for External Affairs was unlikely to move things along with his country's two closest neighbours.[20] When, on 18 April 1949, the coalition government repealed the Executive Authority (External Relations) Act, 1936, and declared the Republic of Ireland, little changed in terms of the Constitution and system of administration. An immediate consequence, however, was the passing of the Ireland Act by Westminster.[21] This provided that there could be no change in the status of Northern Ireland within the UK without the consent of its population.[22] Mindful of Morrison's warning of 'first-class trouble', Westminster had notionally and ostentatiously tied its own hands (although British constitutional doctrine is clear that Parliament is supreme and that any statute may be repealed): Partition was more firmly established than ever.

The coalition government fell in June 1951, and de Valera returned to office. Partition continued to frame his talks with the British representative. (Since the declaration of the Republic, this representative had been given the rank and title of ambassador.) This was such a usual occurrence that it did not merit any special report to London. In his first meeting with Sir Walter Hankinson, the new ambassador, on 19 December 1952, a review of the rather gloomy world situation (on which de Valera was well informed) led back, inevitably, to Partition. This time, the journey was via Europe (de Valera was an anti-federalist) rather than India. He was baffled, Hankinson reported, 'how any Englishman could not see that the solving of Partition was the most important problem for England just as it was the most important problem for the twenty six Counties'. This was true obsessiveness, solipsism indeed, considering that the conversation had ranged from Korea, Indo-China, Malaya, Persia, Egypt, the arms talks and relations between the western European nations.[23] To imagine that, with its empire in dissolution, Europe struggling with reconstruction and Communist subversion, and a third world war a distinct possibility, with all the scarcely imaginable destruction that could be wrought by nuclear weapons, that in the face of all of that, the status of Northern Ireland was Britain's greatest problem, was an impressive feat.

The issue of Partition was dealt with outside government, during these years, its removal being a defining article of faith for the Southern political class and many associations and civic bodies. The Anti-Partition League, founded in 1945, gained membership, took subscriptions, published leaflets, held meetings, generated indignation and passed resolutions.[24] When he left office in mid-February 1948, de Valera highlighted the anti-Partition cause in tours of the USA, Australia and Britain. Speaking to audiences of Irish immigrants and their descendants in these countries, he received rapturous approval when he castigated the division of Ireland.[25] But when the pamphlets were all sold, the leaflets distributed, the resolutions passed and the audiences had gone to their homes, what then? Three parties were needed for this debate, and neither London nor Belfast was listening. All negotiations need points of mutual advantage or leverage, and none existed. The Costello government initiated a tactic as inane as it was futile by instructing its officials to raise Irish Partition on all possible occasions at international meetings. The only outcome was bewilderment and bemusement (and eventually boredom) among those exposed to this dull government propaganda: here too, no one was listening.[26]

A second coalition government took office at the beginning of June 1954, again led by John Costello and with Labour leader William Norton as Tánaiste (Deputy Taoiseach). Weaker than the previous one, this alliance had not secured an overall working majority and governed only with the uncertain support or neutrality of the smaller parties and independents. The Irish policy of protectionism and high taxes, combined with cuts in public expenditure, had been disastrous. Economic problems therefore dominated the new government's agenda (as they had that of the outgoing one), and there was little room or energy for any development in Anglo-Irish relations. They nevertheless forced their way onto the agenda in quite an urgent way when, just over a week after assuming office, Costello and his colleagues had to deal with the consequences of the IRA raid on Gough Barracks, Co. Armagh.[27] While he and de Valera had been fretting and nagging London, and musing on improbable scenarios to settle Partition, the IRA had been preparing for an offensive intended to force British withdrawal from Northern Ireland.

The IRA revival

The war years had reduced the IRA to the remnant of a remnant, but its reputation, myth and aura could not so easily be extinguished. Intelligence, informers, searches, surveillance, arrests, prosecutions, prison sentences, executions and internment had crushed the organisation to a husk, North and South. Conspicuous, unwavering and aggressive vigilance exerted a powerful deterring influence. The IRA was relentlessly and drastically thinned and could not replenish itself. By 1945, only one member of its GHQ, Harry White, remained at large: captivity and six executions had swallowed up the others.[28] Such was the pressure on all IRA connections and communications that White had to remain still and hidden, unable to risk any but the most limited of contacts. Earning his living by playing in a Derry dance band, his sole IRA activity seems to have been to keep open a line into Belfast Prison. The purpose of this is unclear since White had no organisation to make use of information and no orders to issue.[29] This was necessarily a highly restricted operation – hermetically sealed – involving no more than a handful of people, all experienced, careful and highly trusted but also unable to make contact outside their tiny circle. Perhaps the justification for this minimal activity, risky and while resistant to penetration always liable to discovery through surveillance, was the obligation to support the prisoners' morale, though such was the wraithlike existence of the IRA, captive and free, that even were that achieved it could have no practical outcome or possibilities. Help to the prisoners' families – itself a source of intelligence to the authorities – had dwindled away to sporadic and minimal money grants.[30]

Those emerging from internment from 1944 onward, and the sentenced prisoners who followed, generally had little desire or will to continue in revolutionary activity. And for the few who had, the shattered organisation was of little use. GHQ had ceased to exist: there was no strategy and therefore no tactical objectives for which to train. Some units around the country had survived more or less intact – but only in the sense that by remaining quiescent they had escaped notice, searches and arrests: stilled and silent submarines on the ocean floor. Since GHQ had held the threads of communication between units, organisational isolation was more or less complete, except for haphazard personal ties. Yet a certain amount of *matériel* had been preserved. Republican circles were small, as was the country, and former activists were still in touch, were neighbours or friends, or otherwise knew how to revive contacts. But without objectives, orders and working links, these were simply networks of old comrades, overgrown foundations showing the outline of the edifice that once had stood.

There was little to suggest that the IRA could be restored as a functioning organisation. Over a twenty-year period it had been defeated in a civil war, suppressed alike by the victorious party and then by former republican comrades. It clung to an old Fenian doctrine of the virtual existence of a pure, unsullied and uncompromised Republic to which alone fealty was due. Abstractions, organisational formalities, traditions, structures and hopes – an idealistic and romantic trajectory – determined tactics rather than a cold eye and an assessment of the possible. It had squandered resources on a wholly fanciful and ineffective bombing campaign against Britain. Politically rigid and unresponsive, it floundered from passages of glory in the 1919–21 war against the British, through a quarter-century of defeats, becoming ever more isolated from the pressing problems of fellow citizens. During the Second World War years it had been comprehensively suppressed by the security organs of the Irish state, as were its support bodies and connections. This devastation had been compounded by the Hayes affair – a bizarre and scandalous series of events that in themselves would have broken the back of organisations far healthier and operating in a less hostile environment.[31] This, and the prolonged bitter conflicts and schisms of the prisons and camps, months and years of festering grievances, of carefully and venomously chosen hard words and cruel slights, had injected a virus that, it seemed, would never be suppressed. It was not a matter of a vanquished organisation regrouping and rebuilding but of a body that had rejected its own vital organs whilst impossibly retaining some disconnected sinews and muscles. All revolutionary organisations face seemingly insuperable problems, but at this point any dispassionate assessment would have led to but one conclusion: this group could not, in any foreseeable future, pose a challenge to the much reinforced Northern and Southern states: all hope was gone.

Accommodation, acceptance, repudiation, regret, repentance, obedience, discretion and at least outward conformity, together with the aid of respectable and respected friends and contacts could open doors to productive lives and create chances of redeeming something from lost years and vanished opportunities. Given the origins of the Irish state, a tradition had developed of incorporating those who stepped off the anti-constitutional path, and this helped to reduce the potency of the blacklist. But work was hard to find, educational opportunities were restricted, and emigration beckoned to the irreconcilable and disheartened alike. These were the experiences of the great majority of the 1939 membership of the IRA, whether they came from internment camp, prison or the frozen existence of those who had managed to remain at large. But there remained, after all the repeated winnowing, a small group for whom there could be no other life but that of the IRA, no other law but its necessities. Some lived by their convictions and could find no other endurable purpose in life; others defined themselves by their friends and activities, and, for them, personal freedom was but movement in a void without life's previous rounds and shared hopes. Some had already thrown so much on the table that a further gamble was inevitable.

And if its blunders since the Civil War and the thoroughness of suppression during the Second World War years had withered popular support for the IRA, that was no lasting handicap to an organisation that had always preferred principles to ballot boxes. For reasons which in Catholic Ireland stretched back some hundreds of years, moreover, defeat had its own allure. Authority, by whomsoever exercised, was never wholly embraced and republican violence never wholly rejected. This ambivalence was more likely to be dissolved when action was directed against the Irish state, was more likely to persist when the target was foreign, or supposedly foreign, bodies, proxies and persons within the country. It could crystallise into sympathy when the target was Britain and its creation, Northern Ireland.

Only the most fanatical and disconnected of revolutionaries in the post-war period could have envisaged a new civil war and overthrow of the Southern state. For the great majority, that would remain as a long-term objective, venerated in the tabernacle of their faith. An opening that could provide room for immediate and resuscitating action was to be found in the campaign against Partition. With varying degrees of enthusiasm and commitment, constitutional republicanism, Northern nationalism and the mass of overseas Irish here found common cause. Indeed, no Southern politician could have plied his trade had he not paid fulsome lip service to the anti-Partition cause. As we have seen, the Free State had become ever more Catholic since independence, both in the numerical decline in the non-Catholic fraction of the population and in the penetration of the Church into all spheres of public life. Nationalism and republicanism were wholly entwined with Catholicism, and, to the law-abiding and revolutionary alike, the fate of their countrymen and co-religionists in Northern Ireland was a constant theme in agitation on the issue (though it is fair to note that, outside the border area, few had direct knowledge of their neighbour). The reunification of Ireland by force of arms, therefore, was likely to make the most of the reflexive alliances in Irish life. There was, of course, a proviso that attaches to most such generalised sympathy with the use of force: it should not affect the benignly acquiescent onlooker.

A Northern campaign was also predictable as the IRA's reanimator because there was no other. Life could not begin again for the organisation without an objective, and an objective was meaningless without the means to obtain it. This was a circle of perplexity, but it could be broken. The first step was to restore the framework. This had two elements: legitimacy and the chain of command. The chain of authority was central to IRA thought. It claimed direct descent from the Republic proclaimed by Pearse and his comrades in 1916 and legitimacy through the Second (and never dissolved) Dáil. The line was preserved by a supposed transfer of the Second Dáil authority to the IRA in 1938. From this apostolic succession came legal and moral authority for IRA actions. All states are entitled to defend themselves, and, when the IRA ordered the taking of life or the destruction or confiscation of property, it was essential in a devoutly Catholic country – to its members' satisfaction at the very least – to be able to rebut accusations of murder, vandalism or robbery. These, the organisation insisted, were the measured and justified acts of a republic with as much right to self-defence as any existing state.[32] The chain of command was equally vital. Orders were issued only by leaders and officers who had been appointed by proper procedures, themselves conforming to standing and superior orders, all traceable to the fountainhead of legitimacy.

This was the background. The first stirrings of revival were inevitably at local level as those still committed to the organisation were released from camp and prison. Those who had the inclination knew whom to contact and to trust. For those whom it had not disillusioned or turned into bitter foes, a remembrance of the years of confinement, camaraderie and shared hardships might in any case have exerted a gravitational pull, providing justification and comfort: old comrades' reunions the world over show this to be true. Meetings sometimes ventured nowhere beyond the glow of reunion, the tale told and remembered, or the satisfaction of having survived; others led to a formal assembly under military command, the parade for duty. The order to stand to attention was living, energising proof of continuity, a type of communion. Officers were elected and a potential created. Without a centre, however, the local parades – and there were evidently not many – were rituals of commemoration and consolation or, at best, declarations of availability for service. The next step was for men from various parts of the country to get together, representing local groups, and to reconstitute a GHQ. That necessitated rather more than a declaration. The rules required that a representative Army Convention be summoned. From this was elected the Army Executive. This in turn appointed the seven-man Army Council, which then installed one of its number as Chief of Staff.

The Army Convention was not a routine or annual meeting but was summoned at strategic junctures. The last one had met in April 1938, when the English bombing campaign had been sanctioned and Seán Russell was transfigured from suspended member to Chief of Staff. Without a functioning organisation there could be no new convention, and, without that, no new executive and army council. The impasse was not total, however. Five willing and reputable men remained of the 1938 executive.[33] They agreed to co-opt new members, enlarging and strengthening the Executive with more active elements. A new army council was then elected, and this appointed Patrick Fleming as Chief of Staff. Continuity was restored and the IRA's constitutional proprieties observed.[34]

In the autumn of 1945 there was a move to bring together representatives from each reactivated area. This seems in large part to have been a move against Fleming, who almost immediately was found unsatisfactory by the more militant elements. Once again, as it had back to the years of the Fenians, Dublin proved to be a fatal rendezvous. Special Branch knew that the embers were being fanned and put a watch on Cathal Goulding, who had been travelling around the country contacting local leaders.[35] Private transport was still uncommon. Dublin had a limited number of points of ingress, easily watched.[36] As a result of surveillance (and, probably, information), twelve men who had turned up to the meeting at the Ardee Bar in central Dublin were arrested on 9 March 1946 and brought before the courts. Sentences of between three and twelve months were imposed on various charges.[37]

This was a setback, but not a disaster. Indeed, the prosecutions were a form of advertisement to militants that the game was afoot once more. With the key men inside, there was, however, another lull. Early in 1947, the various leaders were again at liberty, and the augmented executive met and appointed a new army council. William McGuinness became Chief of Staff, Seán O'Neill his Adjutant General and Jack Finlay a full-time organiser. By September 1948, sufficient contact had been established with reactivated units for an army convention to be summoned. Quite remarkably, considering its recent and prolonged devastation, there was a strong demand for action from those assembled, and an executive was elected which was of that mind. From this came an army council of militant and determined men. Tony Magan was elected Chief of Staff, choosing Gerry McCarthy as his Adjutant General.[38] The Convention had, in a general way, agreed on a military campaign against Northern Ireland – republican motherhood and apple pie. No one questioned whether that was a practical, good or necessary idea: anti-Partitionism had, as we have noted, become the overwhelming dogma of national life. Seeking to preserve a sanctuary and hinterland, and mindful no doubt of the wrath that had descended on the IRA during de Valera's war years, the Convention directed that there were to be no attacks in the South. It was agreed that an active political wing was desirable, and members were ordered to participate in Sinn Féin, which, for the first time in a decade, managed to publish its own newspaper.[39] The first issue of the *United Irishman* appeared in May 1948, offering an opening into militant republicanism for those dissatisfied with conventional politics and further evidence to the faithful that things were indeed stirring again.[40]

Within two years, Special Branch was sufficiently concerned to brief senior officials and politicians that it would be wise to prepare for renewed IRA violence. Seán MacEoin, a veteran republican of formidable reputation, and now Minister for Justice, on 18 October 1950 approached his colleague at Defence, Thomas O'Higgins, to initiate discussions on preparing for internment.[41] 'It is not possible at present to give an estimate of the number of persons who may have to be interned, but it may be taken that the number is not likely to exceed 500.'[42] This was not well received, and Defence pondered its reply for more than three months. It was not usual in countries with a similar legal system to Ireland's for civilians to be detained in military custody, it eventually proffered. The special conditions of the 1939–45 period no longer existed. There were additionally 'very strong reasons' against having internees in the midst of the military establishment at the Curragh. Finally, civilians being placed in military custody would look bad internationally: Justice should take charge of internment.[43] This provoked a counter-argument but no movement from Defence. A year later, a Department of Justice internal memorandum proposed that the issue be shelved. If an emergency did arise, there was little doubt that Defence could be persuaded to undertake all internment work. In any event, 'in view of the present position of subversive organisations, there is unlikely to be any need to intern big numbers immediately on the occurrence of an emergency'.[44] The memorialist had good reason for both judgements: the Army would indeed do what the government required, and, whatever its ambitions, IRA strength was not likely to grow beyond a few hundred activists.

Numbers were indeed still pitifully small. Dublin, notionally, had two dozen men, but barely half of those could be mustered for parades.[45] In the provinces there was a haphazard distribution of small units. Some had survived the war years; others had blossomed and just as quickly withered in the post-war months. Leading figures were convinced that the IRA had prospects but recognised that it remained in organisational limbo. It could attract volunteers but laboured to retain and develop them at a time when training (and that was of a rudimentary nature) was the only dish on the menu. A range of types was drawn to the IRA, but most shared a desire for military action (though few had any notion of what that entailed). Denied this in the South and still distant from action in the North, the IRA had little to offer and so most recruits drifted away just as easily and lightly as they had come forward.

Activities in Britain

The IRA in Britain had always functioned as an auxiliary, and the crushing of its parent organisation in Ireland made any activities it might have been able to sustain quite purposeless during the wartime years.[46] The same was true of Sinn Féin, though not of the several cultural, sporting and social organisations, completely legal and peaceable, which the IRA regarded as gateways and from which, when possible, it took protective colouration. Regular surveillance was comparatively easy in bodies that functioned so openly, and new arrivals or changes of routine or mood were duly noted; it seems likely that there were several long-time informers. Special Branch in 1951 thus became aware that IRA contacts had appeared in hitherto dormant republican circles, and that these were interested in the location of armouries.[47] It is not clear when an IRA unit was reactivated in London, but it was probably within a few years of the first signs of a more general revival in republican activities. The unit was run under the usual conditions of secrecy (which, however, failed to avoid police attention).[48] Regular meetings included lectures on arms and military matters. Members were tasked with the collection of information and were instructed on what was required and how to obtain it. Matters of interest included friendly organisations, persons willing to assist, likely safe houses, plans of prisons and their immediate area, possibly sympathetic prison officers, locations of army units, police stations, drill halls and, inevitably, armouries. Information was also required on the purchase of explosives, camping equipment and ex-army items.[49] All this had to be undertaken with great care, since any obvious enquiries or the appearance of a systematic collection of information by persons with obvious Irish connections would stimulate public alarm and police action. How conscious IRA GHQ was of police penetration is hard to say, but when operations were eventually undertaken against British targets, local activists were prudently bypassed.

If the British unit was a double-edged weapon, much the same applied to Sinn Féin. This also revived in the 1950s, with a London-based executive committee and five branches. Legal and ostensibly functioning openly, it had a number of objectives centred around Irish cultural and political values and the propagation of the republican case for a united Ireland. Implicitly, it functioned as an IRA support body, principally through the collection of funds. It also acted as a useful means of engaging young men, assessing their suitability and loyalty and steering a few of the more promising to the IRA. Some trusted members, who, for a variety of reasons, would not become members of the IRA, could be useful in the collection of information and in providing accommodation when required.[50] But, unlike the 1938–9 campaign and the attacks that would be mounted from the 1970s onward, Britain itself was not an IRA target.

The arms raids

It was not until the middle of 1951 that a strategic plan could be put together. This was approved by the Army Council, and the first steps were taken towards implementation. Heading the list was arms procurement. In the immediate post-war period, Europe had been awash with *matériel* of all kinds, some available from dealers who were willing to sell from the back door as well as the front. But the IRA had then been little more than an idea; such dealers needed to be sure of their customers, agonised about bona fides and required cash in advance and were not above betraying a would-be client for money or police favours – the security risks and logistical challenges were formidable. In the USA, Clan na Gael, a support organisation of extreme republicanism from the time of the Fenians onward, had long since lost its strength, focus, unity and ability to send funds and weapons. Locally, arms might be acquired in dribs and drabs from disaffected, hard-up or avaricious British soldiers, but such paltry, mixed and uncertain lots, whilst useful for training, could not possibly support a campaign of any substance. Each deal, moreover, carried disproportionate risks. Attacks on British forces in Northern Ireland, therefore, were out of the question until an arsenal had been acquired by the only means available: a series of arms thefts and raids. With the Republic of Ireland completely off limits, these actions could only be in Northern Ireland and Britain.

The first (more larceny than raid) used good intelligence and both took advantage of and confounded the consensus that, apart from chatter, the IRA had gone out of business. On Sunday, 3 June 1951, a raiding party, completely undetected, carried off a small but useful haul of guns and ammunition from the Ebrington Territorial Army armoury, near Londonderry.[51] Within a short time these weapons were in the hands of units. Training with new and effective weapons – and even the knowledge that they had been obtained by raiders – boosted morale, dissolved ennui and raised confidence that something could be done.

This was a walk-in theft; it was also a harbinger of a republican spring. A raised state of alertness closed off a repeat opportunity in Northern Ireland. Future raids, however stealthy, necessarily risked confrontation, firefights, deaths, arrests and a further ratcheting up of police and army preparedness. This trajectory was indeed followed, but first, there was to be another Ebrington, this time in a sleepy part of Essex, about 30 miles north of London, where the OTC of Felsted School held a cache of weapons.[52] The 400-year-old school, set in 80 acres of park and playing fields, was in the middle of its long summer break and largely deserted. It housed its cadet armoury in one of its many outbuildings (as did many other English public schools); security was minimal. The Army Council decided to mount an operation, sending the required men over from Ireland (with one exception).[53] The burglary went off without difficulty on the night of Saturday, 25 July 1953, far exceeding its planners' hopes. In what would become a trademark weakness, transportation had been neglected. Shortage of cash, stinginess or simple ill-preparedness meant that an elderly van had been procured for the job. Such was the cornucopia that this poor beast could not cope with the weight. Part of the haul had to be offloaded before it could be persuaded to move.[54] In the early hours of a Sunday morning the still-overloaded vehicle, its back windows obscured, was a beacon for bored traffic police. The van was stopped, and its three occupants – Manus Canning, Cathal Goulding and Sean Stephenson – were arrested. This was an instance where the masked robber with a bag labelled 'swag' was caught in a spotlight. With almost 100 rifles in the van, there were minimal formalities before the gaoler's welcome. A number of Bren and Sten and other automatic weapons and a mortar launcher simply added to the comprehensiveness of the collection. The three were duly charged, committed for trial and, having being convicted on 7 October 1953 at Hertfordshire Assizes, were each sentenced to eight years' imprisonment.[55]

Still the authorities were unwilling to order and maintain a state of heightened alert entailing as it would both expense and inconvenience. It became known that Gough Barracks in Armagh, home depot of the Royal Irish Fusiliers, did not mount an armed guard.[56] The front-gate sentry carried a Sten gun without a magazine. The fact that it had not even been thought necessary to employ the subterfuge of an empty magazine advertised a generally low level of security.[57] Seán Garland enlisted in the Fusiliers and commenced basic training at the barracks, sending out information on layout, guard rotas and routines.[58] In early June 1954, Garland reported that all arms were to be collected and checked by the armourer. The raid had been planned for Saturday, 12 June, so this gathering in of weaponry was great good luck. Under the command of Charlie Murphy, nineteen took part in a daylight operation, netting 340 rifles, fifty Sten and twelve Bren guns and other weapons. All got safely into the Republic, and the arms were cached in prearranged dumps. This more than made up for the Felsted fiasco – within the ranks of the IRA, of course, but also among nationalists and republicans more generally. It also stimulated funding from support groups in the USA. In bars and clubs, a ballad swiftly celebrated, 'The Night that They Raided Gough Barracks, Armagh'.[59]

No doubt remained but that the IRA, back in business, was preparing a new campaign. A week later, during the customary annual statement at the Wolfe Tone commemoration at Bodenstown, Co. Kildare, the IRA spokesman promised that the arms would be used against British forces in Northern Ireland.[60] In mid-July, Lord Brookeborough, Northern Ireland Prime Minister, crossed to London for consultations.[61] The Home Office agreed that there was cause for alarm. IRA training was intensifying and becoming more purposeful, and visitors (probably agents) had reported drilling in border areas of the Republic. Documents confirmed that attacks on Northern Ireland military targets were being planned. The Armagh raid had, of course, been trumpeted by the IRA, but, more worryingly for the Home Office, 'it had been received with public or silent approbation by many individuals and a number of public bodies in the Republic'.[62] The Garda Síochána were apparently hesitant to act, partly, it seemed, because of fear of the IRA and partly because of uncertainty as to ministerial support.[63] There was a substantial risk of further raids, injury and loss of life. This increased the danger of loyalist reaction and even 'widespread bloodshed' and a return to the disorders of 1922.[64] The dynamics of insurrection also had to be considered. Once the IRA had been brought to a state of readiness, its leadership might be compelled by the momentum of expectations to engage in armed actions.[65] We consider the impact of the campaign on Anglo-Irish and London–Belfast relations at greater length below.[66] For the moment it is sufficient to note that both London and Belfast thought that the Irish government was dragging its feet.

Oblivious to these exchanges (and it would have cared little had it known about them), the IRA continued with its preparations. Its leadership, whatever its inclinations – and it certainly wanted action – was riding a tiger. It well understood that action begat action, inaction atrophy. Successful raids provided increased armaments for further raids and ultimately for a campaign of attacks on the British Army. This creation of momentum was a key chapter in the handbook of guerrilla doctrine. Raids strengthened the commitment and experience of members, created heroes and martyrs and energised supporters. From the guerrilla's point of view, this is the benign spiral. A useful by-product might be insensitive and counterproductive policing by the RUC, the British Army and, above all, the B-Specials. But, more immediately, Gough Barracks' arms were rushed to training camps in the Dublin mountains. Handling weapons with such a provenance was doubtless electrifying to recruits, since they would have been seen as having been taken by brave and resourceful men to whose comradeship recruits aspired. More generally, the guns emphasised that the organisation wanted to do business and could do it.

It could not have been known at that stage, but Armagh had been the high point. Omagh, Co. Tyrone, the base of a distinguished and renowned battalion, the Royal Inniskilling Fusiliers, was the next target. The Army was now on high alert, and a frontal attack was impossible. It was known, however, that there was a clandestine route into the camp, used by soldiers late for curfew. Another ostensible recruit was put into the barracks, information was collated and checked, and a plan drawn up.[67] Again, a weekend was chosen: Saturdays and Sundays always entailed a fall-off in vigilance and tempo in a peacetime army, and, despite the alert against raids, there was no general stand-to. The action took place on the night of Saturday 16 October 1954.[68] Stealth was everything, but it was not maintained, and the garrison was alerted. In the ensuing firefight four soldiers and two of the raiders were wounded, with another injured. In a panicked departure, eight men – almost half the strength of the party – were left behind. Blacked-up and boiler-suited, they were variously arrested as they straggled towards the border.[69] After some deliberation, the Attorney General decided to prosecute for treason felony. This marked the Northern Ireland government's assessment of seriousness and rendered the raiders liable to longer sentences. The eight refused to recognise the court, but having been taken in flagrante delicto, defence was irrelevant. Found guilty, they participated in proceedings to the extent of questioning witnesses and, before sentence, making the traditional defiant speeches from the dock. Each was sentenced to ten years' imprisonment, with their leader, Eamonn Boyce, receiving an extra two years.[70]

This was the first raid in which there had been an exchange of fire, and the IRA men had shown themselves to be poorly prepared and inept combatants. There had been a lack of ruthlessness and decisiveness which had allowed the first soldiers captured in the barracks to raise the alarm. After that, the lack of a fallback had turned raid into rout. Plans for evacuation were muddled, and the transport had, in any case, prematurely sped off. This was pondered by an immediate IRA court of inquiry, but the extent of the debacle was kept from the rank and file and from supporters. Without knowledge of the details, and taken only at face value, the raid played reasonably well. An IRA unit had gone north, penetrated a British camp, exchanged fire with soldiers and had managed to get a substantial portion of its strength back across the border. Even the fact that men had been captured and put on trial could be turned to advantage. The flow of funds into the Prisoners' Dependants' Fund increased from a few hundred pounds to some £30,000 in a matter of six months. There was also a marked quickening in the pace of recruiting.[71]

The campaign was now all but declared. On 30 November 1954, a manifesto was published. This took the form of a three-page leaflet which was delivered to addresses in Dublin (including the house of a member of the British Embassy staff).[72] It ponderously set out the IRA's case, following the *United Irishman*'s org-speak house style. Northern Ireland was a British creation. Despite its constitutional changes, the Republic of Ireland had simply confused the national issue, 'only to lull the youth of the country into a false sense of national well-being'. Styling itself after the 1916 Easter Proclamation, the manifesto affirmed that in the present generation young men were 'pledged to wrest freedom from the enemy by force of arms'. Those 'under the heel of British tyranny were not willing to wait twenty, thirty or forty years' for Orangemen to ask for a united Ireland. Such hopes were for professional politicians. Despite the reference to Orange intransigence, it called for unionists of 'every class and creed', whether civilians or members of the RUC or the B-Specials, to stand aside from a conflict between 'the foreign forces of oppression and the volunteer soldiers of the Irish Republican Army'. None need fear the IRA as long as they gave allegiance 'to our common fatherland'.[73]

An arms raid, possibly enthusiastic opportunism by a local unit of the IRA, or (more likely) by freelance supporters, was mounted in Liverpool on 9 December 1954. Defence establishments were on watch, but precautions had not extended to inactive units. Such was the 16th battalion of the Liverpool Home Guard, a remnant of Dad's Army. An anti-tank weapon was seized (of no use without munitions), together with two rifles without bolts and two small calibre rifles. No ammunition was taken. The anti-tank weapon was found by police in a nearby field, too cumbersome to be carried away. Police were puzzled that other arms and ammunition were left undisturbed. The incident bore all the indications of poor planning or of two or three inexperienced raiders having been interrupted and frightened away.[74] The IRA issued a press statement denying that it had been involved.[75]

On a different level altogether, IRA GHQ was considering other raids, including return visits to Omagh and Armagh. When the latter was eventually mounted, however, on the night of 5 March 1955 (again a Saturday), the scouting party encountered widespread RUC and B-Special border-patrolling, and the raid was cancelled.[76] The prospects for another successful raid in Northern Ireland were now bleak. England, however, was sufficiently far removed from the apparent point of danger to make it worthwhile to try again there.[77] These were the days of National Service in Britain, and all young Irishmen, North or South, resident in the country, had to submit to conscription. The IRA had previously obtained information from disaffected servicemen and now acted on a tip received from Frank Skuse, who, while on leave in Cork, had contacted the IRA via the *United Irishman*. The target this time was the Arborfield Depot of the Royal Electrical and Mechanical Engineers (REME), near Reading in Berkshire. The weekends were the invariable preference, and the raid took place in the early hours of 13/ 14 August 1955. There was little expectation of a raid, and opposition was easily and silently overcome. Two vanloads of ammunition and weapons were driven away. A rearguard waited for new sentries coming on duty, then subdued and tied them up: extra time had been gained for a getaway.

Arborfield appeared to be a well-conceived and smoothly conducted operation that had learned from previous errors. In reality, it was permeated with sloppy planning and with equally poor execution. Moreover, since there was no reliable IRA network in England, the final phase (caching the arms) had been poorly prepared. It was a re-run of Felsted: a lack of caution combined with sparse traffic in the very early hours of a Sunday brought disaster. Traffic police noticed a van breaking the speed limit for commercial vehicles and pulled it over. The cargo of ammunition spoke for itself, and Joe Doyle and Donal Murphy (who decided not to resist arrest with the revolvers they carried) were taken to Ascot police station.[78] The second van got through to London. The cargo was deposited at a rented shop in the then rather seedy Caledonian Road. One of the men who had organised the raid, James Andrew Mary Murphy, had, helpfully for the police, hired the vans in his own very distinctive name and had left the receipt in the captured van.[79] There was a quick arrest. The raid was widely reported in the newspapers, and the shop's landlord reported his suspicions about the Irishmen to whom he had rented. The premises were staked out in the hope of further arrests. When, after a time, no one appeared, the arms and ammunition were removed from the shop, watched by the public, press and television.[80]

Donal and James Murphy (who were not related), together with Joe Doyle, were tried at Berkshire Assizes on 5 October 1955.[81] In conformity with IRA instructions, they refused to plead or to recognise the court. As was customary in such cases, a not-guilty plea was entered on their behalf, but the almost instantaneous finding of the jury was inevitable. A much more serious view was taken of the offence than of the earlier Felsted burglary. A raid under arms on a British Army camp was of a different order to the removal of weapons from an unguarded school OTC armoury, and this kind of thing could not be allowed to become a fashion. Life sentences were imposed on all three.[82]

At this point, the IRA leadership might have thought it prudent to reconsider their position. There had been two completely successful operations: Ebrington and Armagh; there had also been three failures: Felsted, Omagh and Arborfield.[83] Neither success produced the *matériel* with which to wage a campaign against one of the world's best-equipped and most effective armies, operating in a territory with excellent communications and majority civilian support. False comfort was no doubt taken in a 'what if' form. Had it not been for transport problems Felsted and Arborfield might have been successful; had it not been for an untoward alarm, Omagh might have been another Armagh. However, sober and professional assessment might have concluded that the successes were the flukes, not the failures. Equally misleading was the reading of the rate of IRA expansion, the assessment of momentum and the nature of nominal strength. Because the organisation had been effectively suppressed by 1945, any sign of revival was likely to be given far greater weight than it objectively deserved. To come from torpor, despair, isolation and hopelessness to any arms raids at all, and to mount any firefight with British troops, must have been heady stuff indeed in that small and mutually reinforcing circle that was the IRA leadership.

There was also more tangible encouragement. RUC Special Branch noted that after every arms raid there had been an increase in IRA recruitment. It was claimed (with what accuracy it is now difficult to gauge) that after Arborfield there were between 200 and 300 enlistments in the organisation. As before, the raids also stimulated fund-raising. The United Irish Counties Association in New York remitted funds, as did the branches of Sinn Féin.[84] Action, the optimists would have argued, was demonstrably self-sustaining: determination and audacity might still win the day.

The dissident groups

There were other reasons why momentum had to be maintained, even if it meant disregarding realities. One was the eruption of dissension in IRA ranks. An active, educated, self-confident and relatively new recruit, Joe Christle, had begun to force the pace. This began to trouble the IRA leadership as either calculated indiscipline or, at the very least, excessive independence; and the IRA was inclined to be obsessive – fetishistic even – about structure and procedures. Such freelance enthusiasm and energy encouraged suggestions of leadership pusillanimity. Christle, a keen cyclist, had numerous contacts throughout the country and a substantial following in the Dublin IRA, which magnified the threat.[85] In June 1956, after a series of mutually irritating incidents, Christle was expelled for a trivial and technical breach of the rules.[86] Such an obvious set-up rankled, and about half of the Dublin activists left with him, setting up their own organisation. Some able members outside Dublin also transferred to the new body, which adopted a prospectus of serious action in the North within three months.[87] The IRA in the South no longer had a monopoly: militants had a choice.

That monopoly had already been broken in Northern Ireland. Ulster nationalists and some militant republicans took a rather pragmatic view of the Dublin government and certainly one which was at odds with that of absolutists within Sinn Féin and the IRA. Those who were thoroughly opposed to the Northern Ireland state, suffering the disabilities and disadvantages of an irreconcilable minority, saw Dublin as an alternative, consoling and hopeful source of authority: their people, Catholic and Gaelic-minded, held power and were developing their state within a short distance of any part of Northern Ireland. The doctrine of shunning the Dáil and the Southern state was puzzling and unattractive to those who, in the gerrymandered North, seemingly had no hope at all of political power or cultural parity.

This, and the inevitable conflict of personalities that is in the DNA of small organisations, was the background to the emergence of Saor Uladh (Free Ulster). A Co. Tyrone activist, Liam Kelly, was dismissed from the IRA in October 1951 for planning an operation in another unit's area, without consultation or permission. As far back as the Anglo-Irish War, localism had been a feature of the IRA, and members of Kelly's unit deemed themselves excluded with him.[88] The group came from a rebellious part of Co. Tyrone and had a strong sense of that rebel identity. IRA GHQ offered to negotiate for reinstatement, but Kelly had neither the inclination nor the personality to come to heel, to apologise and to give undertakings as to future behaviour. In October 1952, the IRA issued a statement of repudiation.[89] Undeterred by this public rebuke, Kelly and his associates undertook at least four actions in the following months.[90] In October 1953, he stood as an abstentionist candidate in Mid-Tyrone and, in a poll of 7,600, was elected with a majority of 800.[91] At around this time, the group began to put its activities on a more formal organisational footing. Kelly recognised the legitimacy of the Southern state and also the need for a political dimension for republican activity.[92] His subsequent arrest on a sedition charge and one-year sentence enhanced his public stature and reputation.[93] During his imprisonment, an open political organisation, Fianna Uladh, was launched in Pomeroy, Co. Tyrone, and Kelly was elected Chairman. RUC Special Branch estimated a local membership of about 200.[94] On release in August 1954, Kelly began to build up an armed group, mainly in his local base. He appears to have had a following of about fifty men, some arms and a limited supply of explosives.[95]

Never more than a marginal threat to the security of Northern Ireland, Kelly was a significant worry to the IRA. On 26 November 1955, a Saor Uladh party, fifteen-strong and led by Kelly himself, attacked the Rosslea RUC barracks on the border of Co. Fermanagh. Following the tactics of the Anglo-Irish War, the building was bombed to make a breach and was then raked with automatic weapons. A constable was wounded, a raider (Connie Green) fatally wounded and a comrade (Gordon Knowles) injured, and the building was severely damaged.[96] Despite their loss, the Kelly group was prepared to continue.[97] As long as he operated from within or near his Tyrone base, Kelly was invulnerable to IRA pressures. As with Joe Christle's break away, his militant posture was a standing rebuke to the IRA.[98] By the end of 1955, Saor Uladh was claiming more than 100 members in counties Fermanagh, Derry and Tyrone and had a small following in Belfast. In addition, there were supporters (and possibly members) in the Republic. Training exercises were conducted, and there could be no doubt that the organisation had arms, money and determination, which was what young militants wanted. IRA leaders suffered the frustration of being in the final stages of preparing a campaign which had a weight and a strategic structure and which would have a far greater impact than Saor Uladh's succession of pinpricks. That very fact required that they remain silent and preserve the element of surprise.[99] This made them seem overcautious and dithering to their younger and more impatient members and increased the risk of further splinters.[100] A further fracture in republican unity would have been crippling, and, although the small breakaway groups that had thus far emerged had been dealt with (with the exception of Christle and Saor Uladh), the tensions arising from an appearance of inaction could not long be diffused. Equally threatening was Dublin's warning that further attacks in Northern Ireland would lead to preventive action in the Republic.[101]

Saor Uladh's activities (training, raids and the acquisition of cash and arms) thus brought great pressure on the IRA leadership, and it was obvious that this was not going to lessen in any way. In the view of RUC Special Branch, this realisation led to the launching of the IRA Border Campaign (known as Operation Harvest) on 12 December 1956, 'long before the IRA Army Council could be adequately prepared for it. It is impossible to estimate what might have been the result had the IRA leaders been allowed to prepare and consolidate, as they had wished, for another two years.'[102] Once Operation Harvest had been launched, Kelly lost some of his allure for the more militant elements, who had been willing to support him when he alone was carrying out armed actions. His share of the incidents carried out in the six months after 12 December 1956 was, in the opinion of the RUC, 'comparatively insignificant'.[103] Despite the retrieval of its support, Kelly further infuriated the IRA when, in October 1957, he undertook an extensive tour of the USA, speaking to sympathisers and raising funds. At this point the IRA's outlay for its active servicemen and their dependants was about £325 a week, and funds were low. This ungenerous budget was the minimum needed to continue the campaign, and the organisation must have been somewhat chagrined to hear of Kelly's barnstorming. According to RUC intelligence, he had been very successful, bringing in between £50,000 and £80,000. This, in large part, was a sum now denied to the IRA. On Kelly's return from the USA, Saor Uladh began to revive. Modern weapons were purchased and training camps were held. Recruits began to come in, persons who, for various reasons, were still disaffected with the IRA.[104] Kelly remained, therefore, a tactical and strategic worry to the IRA GHQ – always likely to complicate its plans, always a threat on its militant flank.

Operation Harvest

Another ingredient was added to the mixture that would propel the IRA into a Northern Ireland campaign. Seán Cronin had served as an officer in the Irish Army and then as a journalist in New York, where he had been active in republican circles.[105] He decided to return to Ireland with the intention of participating in armed action, arriving back in Dublin in October 1955. This was a welcome boon to the IRA, which, after a much-compressed period of formal induction and evaluation, attached him to GHQ in charge of training matters. Such was his knowledge, application and personal impact that he was shortly thereafter appointed as Director of Operations. Working to the broad outline of the plan of action already adopted by the Executive, Cronin undertook the detailed staff work.[106] He also introduced some elementary infantry tactics, straight from the textbook but apparently previously unknown to that generation of the IRA.

Cronin's presence in the upper ranks had the effect of increasing and distorting the leadership's sense of confidence in the abilities of their ill-trained and very part-time soldiers. It also reinforced the tendency, already pronounced in IRA thinking and implicit in its campaign plan, to divorce armed action from its social and political setting. In world affairs, the ten post-war years were marked by anti-colonial struggle, some of it violent, from India to Indonesia, Cyprus, Kenya and Vietnam. A great deal of this was reported and analysed in the press and in a slew of books. Guerrilla organisation and tactics had mired and then astonishingly defeated the French Army at Dien Bien Phu; the British had been tested from Haifa to Kuala Lumpur and others of their more volatile colonial possessions and mandates. Combining guerrilla and conventional warfare with political organisation and local activism, the Chinese Communists had driven out the seemingly invincible Nationalists. War histories and memoirs lauded the part played by partisans in the Nazi defeat in the Balkans, Italy, Greece, Russia and other occupied territories. Conventional armies, British, American and Russian, had established highly successful irregular forces.[107] Under General Georgios Grivas, EOKA (Ethniki Organosis Kyprion Agoniston, the National Organisation of Cypriot Fighters and the military arm of the Cypriot movement for unity with Greece) waged an intense urban guerrilla struggle which for some years coincided with the Border Campaign.[108] The IRA dwelt on its own glory days, only a generation past, when, at its most intense, the anti-British campaign denied swathes of the Irish countryside to its enemies, when bombing and assassination terrorised and immobilised its opponents in towns and cities, and when its invisible writ ran stronger and deeper than that of Dublin Castle.[109] It was all too easy to imagine a glorious rebirth of this effective form of warfare, the working out of a new style, adapting it to the pursuit of unchanged objectives in changing times.

Much of the IRA's hit-and-hide rural warfare in 1919–21 had been conducted in the rebel south-west. Conditions in Northern Ireland could hardly have differed more, yet were wilfully disregarded in IRA planning. This, by ignorance, determined optimism or ideological self-deception conjured up images of a civil population shading from a hostile minority, or a largely neutral mass, or a benign population of nationalists.[110] It also painted and embellished a picture of poor enemy resources and communications and of vacillation in London, Belfast and Dublin: Pollyanna was more influential than the ghost of Michael Collins. There was to be preliminary training and intelligence work by Southern IRA men operating from various safe houses north of the border. Given that outside the border areas comparatively few people from the Republic travelled to or knew much about Northern Ireland, this was a further source of distortion. When the campaign opened, these Southerners would form a leadership cadre, selecting the most able and committed of those local men they had got to know during training. A subordinate role was assigned to existing Northern units who would provide intelligence and logistical support to flying columns drawn solely from the South.[111] Belfast, the area with the greatest IRA strength and resources, was excluded entirely from the operation because it was feared that the organisation there had been penetrated by an informer.[112] There was little realism about the replenishment of strength. It was accepted that some who passed through preparatory training might then decide that actual fighting was not for them. This was supposedly to be offset by new recruits stirred and drawn in by the achievements of the campaign. Again, a number of wilful assumptions, not least of which was a degree of benign indifference on the part of the Irish government, police and army. The basic, abiding and greatest flaw, however, was to confuse Munster with Ulster. Much of the population of Cork, Kerry, Clare and Tipperary was inclined to the republican cause during the Anglo-Irish War and perhaps even during the Civil War. Two-thirds of the Northern population was Protestant, nearly all were strongly anti-republican and pro-unionist. IRA attacks on police, army and public utilities would be seen as an attempt to destroy the security and way of life of this majority and would heighten feelings of hostility and encourage alertness. If the model behind the campaign was Mao's guerrilla, swimming in the sea of sympathisers, Northern Ireland offered, at best, some isolated and vulnerable tidal pools.[113]

Even at a basic technical level there was carelessness. Intelligence is decisive in guerrilla action, yet some objectives were chosen simply from maps rather than from reconnaissance – and the maps were out of date. This was confirmed when portions of Operation Harvest were read out in open court in December 1956.[114] One of the target bridges supposedly crossed the Bann at Newferry, Co. Antrim. The name alone should have been a giveaway, and, as one of the leaders of the Special Constabulary gleefully pointed out, there was no bridge, and the ferry had stopped running twenty years before.[115] Intelligence must reveal as much as possible about actual conditions; if it merely explores the landscape of heart's desire it is devastatingly and dangerously counterproductive. The whole of the conceptual and planning process of Operation Harvest suggested that, apart from border areas, Northern Ireland was as remote from the experience and knowledge of the IRA planners as some part of the Caucasus.

The training officers were deployed in the early autumn of 1956. Four columns were envisaged, attacking in designated zones from Armagh to Fermanagh. These areas had two advantages: proximity to the border and a concentration of Catholics – and therefore a greater chance of sympathy or at least neutrality and silence. A document obtained by the *Irish Times* set out textbook guerrilla objectives of cutting communications, concentrating on enemy strong points and administration centres, attack and withdrawal. The objective was to compel the evacuation of enemy forces and the liberation of areas, which, as more territory was freed, would link up.[116] This was a romantic fantasy, little more than cribbing from one of the guerrilla-warfare cookbooks then in circulation.

Operation Harvest opened on the night of Tuesday, 11 December 1956. Despite considerable intelligence that it was in the offing, the RUC did not have the launch date; nor did the authorities in the Republic.[117] It was an inclement night, which favoured surreptitious movements and discouraged all but those with urgent business from being out and about.[118] A BBC transmitter, Magherafelt courthouse and police and army buildings were attacked successfully. Operations to destroy strategically significant bridges in Fermanagh were botched.

There was an attempt to revisit the scene of earlier success, Gough Barracks. Yet again the operation foundered on inadequate transport, in this case a cattle truck without either a silencer or a functioning exhaust: an exuberant marching band would have been a shade less conspicuous. Even had utmost silence prevailed, however, the raiding party was in for a shock. Quite remarkably (and with scant regard for the lives of those despatched on the mission), there had been no attempt to reconnoitre or to refresh intelligence. Gough Barracks expected an attack, even if the timing was unknown. Physical security had been hugely improved, the guard was alert, and a rapid-reaction patrol was deployed. The mine intended to blow the front gate had to be uselessly detonated as the sentry fired warning shots, and an alarm siren destroyed all chances of pressing on.[119]

The IRA repeatedly failed to observe another one of the cardinal rules of all warfare (and a *sine qua non* for guerrillas): intelligence always precedes action. The revamped security precautions and routines of Gough Barracks had gone unnoticed but so also had a new watchtower, which gave a clear field of vision – and fire – over the most obvious path of attack. Had the runes been read, the first night would have revealed all that needed to be said about a campaign that would drag on for six years. To set the scene of tragedy and force combined, there was the customary proclamation the next day, partly a lazy pastiche of the Pearse–Connolly declaration of 1916 and partly grandiose promises of liberation to a people, the majority of whom considered themselves to be liberated already and who were quite happy as they were.[120]

In the fortnight before Christmas there were several other attacks. On 13 December 1956, Lisnaskea and Derrylin RUC barracks in Co. Fermanagh were attacked with firearms and explosives. Despite extensive damage, no one was killed or seriously injured.[121] After a Christmas break, during which the IRA men returned to their homes, attacks resumed. A persistent curiosity of GHQ thinking was that a return to earlier targets would not be expected. This completely misread police and army procedures and, indeed, showed a great ignorance of career paths. A commanding officer who coped with a surprise attack, even were his performance just passable, could expect support and commendation. He, who, after the first attack, failed to take every possible precaution against a second, could count on an unhappy and possibly truncated career. The return visit to Derrylin barracks on 1 January 1957 was greeted by a well-prepared and determined guard, which, despite a heavy assault with explosives and automatic fire, held the attackers at bay. Constable John Scully was killed in the firefight. Although the IRA party made it back across the border, eight men were then arrested by the Gardaí near Ballyconnell, Co. Cavan.

Brookeborough attackers were not so lucky. It was a particularly ill-judged target, seemingly based on little more than the existence of the barracks, and executed without skill. The mines which were intended to clear the way into the building failed to explode, the attackers took up unfavourable firing positions, and the RUC men resisted effectively. There were no police casualties, but two attackers were gravely wounded and three others injured, one seriously but not mortally. With great difficulty the party got away in their damaged lorry, closely pursued by RUC patrols. The two mortally wounded men, Feargal O'Hanlon and Seán South, were left in a shed, and local people were told to summon medical and spiritual help.[122] Twelve men got across the border, cached their arms and were arrested by gardaí and soldiers. They received what were seen in Northern Ireland as derisory sentences of six months' imprisonment under the OASA for refusing to answer questions.

Reaction in the Republic showed the ambivalence of a sizeable section of the population and gave comfort to the IRA leaders and members. Many ordinary citizens believed that Northern Ireland belonged to and in the Republic and that the IRA were trying to right a historic injustice to the nation and to redress the wrongs of the Northern Catholics.[123] Seán South came from Limerick, and his cortège, on its way home, stimulated enormous public attention. Twenty thousand waited into the small hours to greet the coffin as it arrived in Limerick on 4 January; an estimated 50,000 followed it to the grave the next day. The Mayor of Limerick, several councillors, a senator and other local figures attended, and several priests took part in the obsequies.[124] A number of county councils and other public bodies passed resolutions of sympathy for the families. This upsurge in feeling was a greater boost to the IRA than a successful attack at Brookeborough and the survival of South would have been.[125]

These outpourings carried a warning which no government could ignore. Over possible sectarian disorder in Northern Ireland and British sanctions of various kinds loomed a more direct challenge to stability in the Republic. The IRA leadership had counted on a longer period of equivocation by Dublin, on weeks of progressively serious warnings and threats, heralding round-ups and giving ample time for key men to go underground. The Seán South obsequies short-circuited all that, and most of a wholly unprepared leadership was rounded up under the always-useful OASA.[126] That the Special Branch had such up-to-date and detailed information on names, functions and locations was warning in itself, had there been anyone in the IRA leadership willing to consider it.[127] This, however, was not the time for hesitation – or so it surely seemed to the stand-in leadership that now took over.[128] The hiatus was partly covered by the operational autonomy and momentum of the IRA units already in place. There was an attack on Dungannon Territorial Army barracks, Co. Tyrone, on 18 January 1957, and on 2 March 1957 an empty train was run at speed into Londonderry goods yard, wrecking itself and causing substantial damage.[129]

The short sentences of months rather than years imposed in Dublin under the OASA meant that the established Army Council was able to take up the reins again in April. By then, momentum had largely been lost. The RUC and Special Constabulary had gone from a state of alert to a semi-war footing. Barracks were heavily sandbagged, armoured Land Rovers conducted reinforced patrols, communication systems were improved, and nearly all minor and unauthorised border roads were blocked. Operatives were forced to concentrate on evading capture and had certainly lost the initiative and element of surprise of their early operations. A combination of police and army pressure and the lengthening hours of daylight reduced scope for action to comparatively minor acts of sabotage.[130]

The IRA leadership could, nevertheless, draw comfort and encouragement from what they had managed to accomplish. Between the opening night of the campaign on 11/12 December and the beginning of March 1957, there had been eighty-one incidents. The targets ranged from an RAF radar station to army and RUC barracks to bridges, roads and telegraph equipment. Such a level of activity in a matter of three months demonstrated a degree of capability and determination and an amount of *matériel* well beyond the previous estimations of the authorities, North and South.[131]

Two major impediments were cast in the path of the campaign, one more serious than the other. On Saturday, 19 January 1957, the Standing Committee of the Roman Catholic hierarchy issued a statement, to be read to all worshippers after mass the following day. This declared membership of any secret organisation that armed its members and allowed these arms to be used against its own or any other state to be a mortal sin.[132] Northern Ireland's Special Branch considered that, despite the organisation's attempt to counter it, the pastoral warning had dealt the IRA a 'severe blow'.[133] Much more serious was the return of Nemesis. The Republic held a general election on 5 March 1957. Sinn Féin secured a substantial bag of 65,640 first-preference votes, and four of its abstentionist candidates were elected to the Dáil. This masked a highly unfavourable outcome. Replacing Costello's fragile coalition, Fianna Fáil returned to government with seventy-eight seats, an ample working majority.[134] De Valera had, on several occasions, taught the painful lesson that in his house there could be only one master. His resoluteness, republican credentials, popular following and Dáil majority meant a much more decisive response to challenges to the state than that offered by the outgoing creaking coalition.[135]

Despite this portentous change, the IRA mounted an ambush on an RUC patrol on 4 July 1957 near the nationalist redoubt of Forkhill, Co. Armagh. One constable was killed and another wounded.[136] Within days there was a major and well-directed round-up in the Republic.[137] The combine harvester of imprisonment followed by internment again began its devastating work. The parallel world in which most of the IRA leadership had been living was demonstrated by the fact that they utterly failed to anticipate Dublin's reaction to Forkhill. As with Fenianism, ninety and more years before, a curious sense of ethereal immunity allowed the leadership to pursue its conspiratorial life while living more or less openly and (to repeat history) to hold a meeting of the Army Council in a known office of the movement – in this instance Sinn Féin HQ. The authorities duly decapitated the leadership with one powerful blow.[138] The Northern Ireland campaign would continue for another four years and eight months, but the flickering flame of success had been extinguished.[139]

This would take some time to become obvious. The IRA had a number of experienced men deployed, and, despite the disadvantage of the long days, they were able to stage thirty-three attacks between 26 July and 10 August 1957. These were all acts of sabotage, indicating that, at least for the time being, it had been decided to avoid contact with police and army patrols. Sectarian tensions, always on a hair-trigger in Northern Ireland during much of the summer, were given a dangerous twist, when, on Saturday, 17 August 1957, RUC Sergeant Arthur Ovens was killed in a booby-trap explosion at a derelict farmhouse near Coalisland, Co. Tyrone; a constable and two members of the accompanying army unit were wounded.[140] Anticipating a tactic that would be favoured twenty years later, police had been lured to the building by a bogus tip-off.[141] This carefully planned assassination was seen by the majority population as a particularly wicked and callous crime – different in kind from the loss of life resulting from the tumult of a firefight – and greatly hardened feelings. It is difficult to remember, when considering this incident, that the IRA's prime objective was the reunification of Ireland. On the night of 2/3 September 1957, there was an attack of sorts when a joint army–police patrol in the area of Clogher, Co. Tyrone, was fired on from across the border and one policeman was wounded.[142] Three weeks later, Colonel Walter Topping, Minister of Home Affairs, reported that since December 1956 there had been about 200 major and 200 minor incidents in Northern Ireland.[143] On the IRA's scoreboard this must have looked encouraging.

The RUC put IRA strength at this point at 455 men in the Dublin area and some 500 elsewhere. These were distributed throughout the country, with concentrations in Dundalk, Drogheda, Wexford, Cork, Limerick, Cavan and Leitrim. This was very likely a considerable overestimate, since the same briefing claimed that there were eight columns, each of fifteen men, operating in Northern Ireland. It also reported rumours of training in amphibious tactics and of limpet mines promised from the USA; the possibility of another campaign in England was also said to be under consideration. Far from being able to sustain such levels of deployment and to introduce new weapons, equipment was basic and operations largely opportunistic. Action was, of course, essential to keep the pot of militancy on the boil for the autumn campaign proper.[144]

The IRA command decided to concentrate on the RUC armoured patrols since only if these were countered would it be possible to gain mobility and to develop other forms of attack. The patrols, and the roadblocks they mounted, made hit-and-run attacks on barracks and bases almost impossible and constantly hampered the movement of IRA parties and even individuals.[145] A number of ambushes were laid, but none was more than marginally successful. The RUC followed well-tried procedures and, if engaged, easily outgunned the IRA. Their armoured vehicles were largely immune to the IRA's light weapons, and it was rare for injury of any kind to be inflicted.[146] The flying-column formation showed its utter impracticality. Its objective had been degraded, and the mission now was simply to exist; its principal activity therefore was evasion of detection and arrest. There was another and more practical model, but this was not considered. A concentration of local men for swift actions, followed by an immediate return to the normal round of their lives would have limited the number and type of actions undertaken, and carried some risk of arrest, but it would have avoided the concealment and supply problems of a disconnected group operating in a hostile environment. Given RUC and B-Special effectiveness, and the reluctance of the nationalist population to expose themselves to the dangers of supporting an implausible campaign, safe houses were difficult and sometimes impossible to find. As an alternative, the units had to resort to the dugout, an expedient developed during the Anglo-Irish War. These varied in the manner of their construction, and in the skill of their builders, but rarely rose above the most basic covered excavation in a bank or ditch. Living in them for several weeks at a stretch took a considerable toll on health and mental well-being. These hides were also vulnerable to aerial reconnaissance – particularly in winter.

Intelligence and police activity south of the border resulted in arms finds and arrests, which, given the shortage of both men and equipment, were damaging blows. On 2 October 1957, arms and ammunition were discovered near the border in Donegal, and the owner of a nearby cottage was arrested. There was a similar find and arrest in Co. Monaghan the following month; six men were arrested in a border area on 30 November, together with a large quantity of arms and ammunition. The biggest loss was on 18/19 December at Ballintra, Co. Donegal, when twenty rifles, six Thompson and six Sten guns, twelve revolvers and a large quantity of ammunition and explosives were seized by gardaí. More serious than any of these occurred at Carrickcarnon, Co. Louth, on 11 November 1957. Five men died when the bomb they were assembling exploded, completely demolishing the cottage in which they were working. The fierceness of the explosion and fragments in the debris indicated that a large quantity of *matériel* had been stored at the cottage, together with arms and ammunition.[147] Altogether, this was a heavy loss and also raised doubts about the safety of IRA training, a matter of understandable concern to potential recruits.

Counter-insurgency

Floggings?

The bare-bones issue of Partition and its removal by force was not going to generate the interest and support the IRA needed to get its campaign off the ground, to create momentum and to make the enterprise self-sustaining. The guerrilla needs to provoke the security authorities into overreaction, to overreach themselves in the onerousness of security restrictions on the civil population or to behave in a brutal manner.[148] The hope is that hitherto-uncommitted sections of the population will become disaffected and thus will be drawn into the circle of sympathy, support and action. In the autumn and winter of 1957–8, two possibilities arose that, had they come to fruition, might have opened that path of accelerating alienation and anger. One did not pass beyond confidential exchanges between senior civil servants and ministers; the other came to widespread national and international attention. Topping explored the possibility of bringing in legislation to provide for mandatory corporal punishment in arms and explosives cases. This punishment had been used during border incursions and civil disturbances in 1922–3 and had then seemed effective as a deterrent. A review of the files appeared to confirm this impression, showing that during that period whipping had been ordered in twenty-two cases for arms and explosive offences. Up to 1933, there had been no repetition of the offence by any of the men who had been thus punished.[149] No special legislation was necessary in Northern Ireland to reactivate the penalty. It had been abolished as a court sentence (in 1948) in Great Britain, but Northern Ireland courts could continue to use relevant sections of the Special Powers Act or of the Larceny Act of 1916.[150]

Civil servants were cautious about the notion of mandatory whipping, birching or caning, and the judiciary disliked any kind of mandatory sentence. It was true, a briefing note observed, that many coming before the courts for arms and explosives offences were men in their early twenties, and it was possible that a few sentences of birching 'would have a salutary effect'. Against that, the punishment had a controversial character. Judges already had adequate powers to order a whipping in arms and explosives cases, but 'it would attract considerable unfavourable publicity to Northern Ireland if we were to amend the Acts to make whipping a mandatory punishment'. Unless the situation 'deteriorated considerably', therefore, new legislation was not recommended.[151] The Minister pondered the advice, and the proposal was shelved. Not mentioned in the review, and perhaps not considered, was the strong possibility that, however such punishments had been viewed thirty years before, their use now on men convicted of politically motivated offences, albeit of a violent and threatening nature, would run the risk of garnering sympathy for them in the nationalist community, in the Republic, in Britain and abroad. Mandatory whipping of all those convicted in the Border Campaign might, indeed, have given the IRA some of the political fuel that it so clearly lacked: 'flogged for Ireland' might have created currents of indignation all too clearly lacking in the summer and autumn of 1957. The wider European context of human rights, beginning to have an appreciable impact through the Strasbourg judgments, was not considered at all, but might well have had an impact on the reputation of Westminster as well as Stormont had the whipping or birching of politically motivated offenders come under review.[152]

Torture

That an international and reasonably widespread campaign could be got under way on allegations of ill-treatment of IRA prisoners seemed unlikely at that point. Out of nowhere, the perspective changed over allegations of serious police ill-treatment of two men suspected of involvement in the murder of Sergeant Ovens.[153] The two, Kevin Mallon and Francis Patrick Talbot, both aged twenty-one and known to the police as IRA activists, were brought in for questioning three months later – seemingly as part of a general round-up rather than on information received. The allegation against them was that they had together made the telephone call that resulted in the police going to the abandoned house where Sergeant Ovens was killed by the booby-trap. (The ruse required that someone with a local accent should make the call; it was thought by the police that persons from outside the district had planned and executed the plot.)

Two matters attracted attention well beyond the usual circles of IRA supporters and sympathisers. The length of the proceedings, extending for nine months, was the basis for one set of criticisms. There was a deal of weight in the argument that it was unconscionable to keep so long under the strain of a charge of capital murder two young, poorly educated working-class men. The Ministry of Home Affairs readily agreed that the delay was unfortunate but, with some justification, insisted that the prosecution was not entirely to blame.[154] This criticism, however, merely provided a backdrop for a far more serious one: that both men had been tortured. Quite apart from the charge of criminal misconduct itself, the issue was central to the trial since virtually the only evidence against the two came from their admissions to the police.

Standards of investigation and interrogation were very different six decades ago, in both parts of Ireland and in Britain. Even so, there might have been objection to the fact that facing a charge of this, the very gravest kind, the two were questioned without access to a solicitor, that they had been interrogated well into the small hours and that relays of interrogators had been used. A blind eye might have been turned to strong language, a threatening demeanour and even a certain amount of menace and casual rough handling, improper though all these were. Customary practice and some public sentiment may have tolerated these as acceptable ways of putting pressure on suspects in a case of such seriousness. What was utterly beyond the pale was beating bogus confessions out of suspects, and this is what Mallon and Talbot claimed had happened.[155]

Neither man denied that he had signed admissions, but both denied that the statements were true or that they had signed them voluntarily. Their narratives conform to what we know about extreme interrogation and torture. Kevin Mallon claimed that on the evening of his arrest he was beaten over a period of several hours, from 6.30 or 7 p.m. until midnight. The two policemen who beat him (a district inspector and a head constable), he added, also abused him and made threats of death including blowing him up with a booby-trap. Following this, Mallon said, he was put in a car to be taken to Belfast. A short distance out of Dungannon, Co. Tyrone, the car stopped, and he was taken out and prodded about the body with rifles by two policemen who had been on patrol. There was another stop, where he was again punched and choked and told to confess. He claimed to have been hit so hard in the solar plexus that he became semi-conscious. He arrived in Belfast at about 2 a.m. and was further questioned for thirty or forty minutes. Mallon contended that at this point he was covered with blood from his nose and mouth. Questioning was resumed by a new police officer at 3 p.m. the following day and continued with one short break until 11 p.m. After another short break, the interrogation went on until 6 a.m. the following morning. His ordeal, Mallon alleged, included being stripped naked, choked, burned in the mouth with a cigarette and hit in the stomach with a window pole. At some point, one of the interrogators trod on his bare feet. At a late point in these events, one of the policemen began to crawl all over him, clawing him and behaving 'like a maniac'. As this was happening, Mallon said, the policeman was shouting that he was Ovens, the murdered police sergeant.[156] A noxious liquid was poured on a rag and forced into Mallon's mouth, making him vomit.[157] He was taken back to his cell where later, from another cell, he heard the sounds of beating, kicking and shouts. Concluding that Talbot was also being tortured, Mallon said that he decided to provide the police with the confession they required and, on being brought into his cell, signalled to Talbot to do likewise.

Patrick Talbot also claimed to have been ill-treated, though not to the same extent. There were no beatings at Coalisland (where he was arrested) or at Dungannon, but shortly after arrival in Belfast, the same head constable identified by Mallon had attacked him. In addition to punches in the head and stomach, a handkerchief had been tied around his neck and tightened and loosened, choking and releasing breath as questioning went on.[158] Later in the night, after the questioning had ceased, someone came into his cell and began to bang Talbot's head against the wall. Throughout the police had called him a murderer. Talbot confirmed Mallon's account of the final confrontation in his cell, when the two men had agreed to confess.

Through the agency of Seán MacBride, the two men were ably represented by the talented and highly respected Welsh barrister, Elwyn Jones, whose trial strategy had to be to negate the confessions by laying the story of gross ill-treatment before the court.[159] The RUC indignantly and utterly denied these claims, denouncing them as a smear. Brian Maginess, who led for the Crown, ridiculed the very notion of ill-treatment by members of the RUC. Could the jury believe that three police officers, including a district inspector, would torture and ill-treat the men? All three had gone into the witness box and denied the allegations under oath.[160]

Lord Justice Black, before whom the trial was conducted, directed the jury on two points.[161] It had not been claimed that the two men were central to the plot, but if the jury was convinced that they had acted, even as mere catspaws, they were guilty of murder. He also pointed out that virtually the whole crown case was based on the men's admissions. The jury had to be satisfied that these had been given voluntarily 'without compulsion, threats, duress or violence'. If they were not so convinced, the confessions should be disregarded. Just over two hours after they retired, the jurors came back with a not-guilty verdict: they had not accepted police claims that the confessions had been made voluntarily. The trial had attracted enormous attention in Ireland and beyond. This sensational outcome was a major opportunity for the IRA, its supporters and sympathisers; it was also a blow to the reputation and standing of the police.[162]

The RUC, and Special Branch in particular, was in equal parts devastated and outraged. Writing to the Secretary of Home Affairs, R. F. R. Dunbar, County Inspector J. G. T. Nelson, head of Special Branch, lamented 'What a vile opportunity this trial has given our enemies: just look at the pages of "The United Irishman" and "The Irish Democrat". And they have not nearly finished writing and shouting about it yet.'[163] The damage had gone a deal further than that, however. Liberal circles in England were disturbed by what had emerged at the trial, and there were calls for an independent inquiry from a number of respectable people, including members of the clergy. Such concerns became more widespread still when the *New Statesman* on 16 August published a letter from J. Hostettler (the Connolly Association's *soi-disant* 'independent observer' at the trial).[164] Topping's approach was simply to deny the charges, to refuse an independent inquiry and to rely on the evidence of Dr S. W. McComb, Medical Officer at Belfast Prison, and on an inquiry conducted by RUC headquarters. These had found Mallon's and Talbot's allegations to be unfounded. The difficulty, of course, was that these were not seen as independent or impartial authorities. There was also a clumsy attempt to create a countercurrent of opinion.[165]

The allegations of torture were given weight not only by their plausibility, the fact that the police had been unable for three months to bring to account the murderers of a colleague, their wholly understandable anger and outrage at the calculated and atrocious nature of the crime and their reliance on the confessions alone to secure a conviction. While there may not have been a general public awareness of the willingness of a minority of police officers to 'fit up' men who they believed to be guilty but against whom they had no evidence, those with an experience of criminal cases – solicitors, barristers, journalists and habitual criminals – knew that it happened. More generally, educated people had noted with concern accusations of torture by British forces in Kenya, Cyprus and Malaya and by the French in Algeria. A book by a victim of French torture had just been published in English and had been widely reviewed.[166] John Stewart, a senior civil servant in Gibraltar, had read the book and wrote to Topping. The evidence of Mallon, as published, was convincing because it was so full of detail 'as to be beyond the limited powers of invention of a 21-year-old Irishman of working class education'. *The Question*, banned in France but just published in England, 'confirms – (and from cast-iron authority) – that torturers work exactly as Mallon described'.[167]

In Ireland there was a slew of resolutions from local-government bodies; in England, the Connolly Association and kindred bodies held meetings, orchestrated telegrams and letters of protest and circulated a petition calling for an independent inquiry. So much was predictable and fairly easily discounted. Not so readily set aside, however, were letters from branches of the Labour Party and the visit of Paul Johnson, a senior *New Statesman* journalist, to Dublin to interview a spokesman for the IRA. This resulted in a letter to the *New Statesman* from 'J. McGarrity' (denoting authorised IRA spokesmen) making further allegations of torture despite '[t]he strict instructions on the use of torture which Paul Johnson suspects were issued by RUC headquarters after the Mallon-Talbot exposures'.[168] Whatever the truth of the new accusations, a deal of credence would be given to them. It showed the appalling slippage in Stormont's standing that a journal of the authority and reputation of the *New Statesman* would be prepared to interview and to give column space to a spokesman for the IRA.

As would also be expected, there were protests from Irish-American organisations. A Boston Mallon–Talbot defence committee was established, and there were signs that a more general interest might be taken in the condition of prisoners in Northern Ireland. Much of this was naive and uninformed, but the British Embassy in Washington had begun to detect a change in possibilities. They would not normally bring to the attention of the Foreign Office the protests they received from Irish-American organisations, but those referring to Mallon and Talbot were different since

> there seems to be a possibility that the alleged mistreatment of these two men is going to become a frequent charge against us over here. Generally speaking the wrongs of Ireland are losing their force as a rallying-cry in the USA, but a specific accusation of this kind might still be troublesome. We should therefore be glad if you could arm us with the facts.[169]

British politicians and senior civil servants no doubt shared these concerns.

In the Republic there was sufficient concern in political and official circles for Thomas J. Coyne, Secretary of the Department of Justice, to write to Commissioner D. Costigan of the Garda Síochána to ask if he had particular information about torture and ill-treatment in the six counties. The reply was carefully balanced, and, indeed, gardaí generally must have looked at the murder of a sergeant of the RUC, a fellow police officer, irrespective of the border, with deep concern. As to the allegations of torture, the Commissioner had no information available to him, other than newspaper reports and the allegations of the 'Republican Publicity Bureau'.[170] There were resolutions on the matter by local bodies, including Leitrim County Council.[171] But such concern and agitation as there was did not extend much beyond the usual groupings and failed to ignite indignation in the Republic.

There were three reasons why the IRA could not take full advantage of the Mallon–Talbot scandal. The first was that while the men had been found not guilty of the murder of Sergeant Ovens, they were guilty of other serious offences.[172]

Arrested immediately after their acquittal, they appeared before a Special Court in Belfast on explosives and arms charges. On 21 October 1958, they were sentenced to three terms of fourteen years (concurrent) for possessing explosives and conspiracy to cause explosions.[173] Victims of torture and ill-treatment they almost certainly were, but they could not be presented as innocent bystanders.

By mid-1958, moreover, the IRA had been completely hollowed out. It simply did not have the necessary manpower, resources, talents or connections to develop a campaign on the back of the Mallon–Talbot abuses. The Dublin government would certainly have thrown obstacles in their way. The handling of funds and access to office facilities and telephones by front organisations all required a degree of toleration which de Valera was not willing to grant, no matter what view his government took of the torture allegations. Finally, agitation, pressure, lobbying and related activities require certain journalistic skills and networks of contacts, as well as an acceptable cover organisation. The IRA could not conduct such activities itself, and Sinn Féin, abstentionist, single-issue, also skeletal in organisation and with little talent or political capital, was in no position to act on its behalf. Realisation by the IRA that it needed effective political cover was several decades off. The Mallon–Talbot affair was certainly not forgotten by Northern Ireland's nationalists. It has remained a prominent item in the display cabinet where the iniquities and injustices of the state were stored and contemplated. But grotesque and suggestive though the episode was, it did not remotely provide motivation for those not previously activists to become involved in a violent confrontation with the government of Northern Ireland. Few, outside core IRA members, now believed that this offered any prospects for success.

The Lawless case

The IRA's myopia and political isolation was also confirmed by the Lawless case. Because Gerry Lawless was not a member of the organisation, and because it scorned all legal processes, the IRA decided to ignore what could have been a useful device for broadening its appeal and range of sympathisers.[174] This case, the first to be heard by the newly established European Court of Human Rights, was brought through the agency of Seán MacBride. IRA Chief of Staff in 1936–8, MacBride had metamorphosed into the leader of Clann na Poblachta, which, as we have seen, had taken its place in the 1948–51 coalition government. In that capacity, he had been appointed Minister for External Affairs, holding that office at a time when new supra-national bodies were being mooted and carried forward in Europe.[175] That experience, and his legal focus on defence work in the 1940s made MacBride particularly sensitive to the emerging jurisprudence of human rights. With other Irish lawyers of his generation he had begun to combine English common law, in which he was trained, with the jurisprudence of an entrenched constitution and civil rights enforceable through the courts. His final break with the IRA had come, in large part, from his response to de Valera's

1937 Constitution, which, he argued, completed the republican legal and institutional agenda.[176] In January 1957, MacBride had brought down Costello's second coalition government on the issue of the Republic's policy to the IRA. A human-rights challenge to the de Valera administration was timely for MacBride for several reasons and was in line with his curiously coherent combination of republicanism, liberalism and legalism.

MacBride and Lawless were brought together through Lawless's contacts with the Dublin solicitor, Ciarán Mac An Alí.[177] Mac An Alí and MacBride knew that it was essential if internment were to be challenged that there should be a party who would see the matter through. It was a doctrinal impossibility for the IRA, except in matters of the death penalty, to allow its members to acknowledge the legitimacy of any but its own courts in Ireland.[178] To gain a hearing in Europe, all domestic remedies had to be exhausted, and that meant the submission of pleas to the Irish courts. It followed that an internee had to be found who was not a member of the IRA.

Gerry Lawless fitted the bill exactly. As a juvenile he had been convicted of damaging a plate-glass window in order to destroy an image of Queen Elizabeth. Two years later, in 1955, he became a member of the IRA, in which he soon developed a reputation for impatience for militancy and some expertise with the tools of the trade.[179] He was one of the young men who, unaware of the methodical but slow steps being taken by the IRA leadership to put together the Border Campaign, chafed for immediate action and began to constitute an opposition of sorts within the organisation. When Joe Christle was expelled in 1955, Lawless was one of many youthful activists who joined him in the splinter body. As we have seen, this agreed to act with Liam Kelly's Saor Uladh and, much to the chagrin of the IRA, began to set the pace. The police were also paying attention. Lawless, who, in November 1956, had a lucky escape when he appeared before Dublin Circuit Criminal Court on firearms charges, was given a priority spot on the list of prospective internees prepared by Special Branch. He appeared again in court in May 1957, charged with membership of an illegal organisation and the possession of seditious documents. After a trial during which he alleged that he had been beaten up by gardaí, he was convicted and sentenced to imprisonment for one month.

Lawless was one of those released from Mountjoy in the period before internment was brought in, and, as news of the first wave of arrests spread, he decided to flee. Northern Ireland was out of the question, the USA impossible to arrange at such short notice, and so he attempted to get to England. Special Branch was on the lookout for fugitives, and Lawless was arrested at the Dun Laoghaire mail boat terminal on the evening of 11 July 1957. Two days later he was taken to the Curragh and served with an internment notice. With others, Lawless was first held in the Glasshouse (the military detention barracks) before being transferred to the newly opened internment camp. There, Tomás MacCurtáin, the IRA OC, who knew him well as part of the ginger group, refused to accept him in the common accommodation on the grounds that he was not an IRA man.

Lawless was accordingly allocated a hut of his own (the split had not at that time developed at the Curragh) and was ostracised by the IRA men.[180] This background showed that, whatever else, Lawless was his own man, pragmatic and tough, willing to see the legal process through and unlikely to object to any tactics that MacBride thought might be effective.

Europe, with its restrictive and protracted procedures, was never likely to be Lawless's deliverer. On 10 December, with the case still in its first stages, he gave a verbal undertaking before the Detention Commission, sitting at the Curragh. This outcome had been negotiated to avoid Lawless incurring the stigma of 'signing out', and the hearing was attended by the Attorney General and supporting lawyers. Lawless was represented by MacBride and another senior counsel, again with instructing solicitors. Having heard the undertaking, the Attorney General stated his intention to advise the government to release Lawless, and he was set at liberty the following day.[181]

Lawless's release did not end proceedings, which continued on their complicated way until July 1961, when the European Court of Human Rights concluded that his human rights had not been violated and that he was therefore not entitled to compensation.[182] The Irish government's arguments had prevailed: in introducing internment it had acted within the Convention procedurally (notifying the Secretary-General of the Council of Europe of its derogation regarding Article 5); proportionately (a state of armed emergency existed in the country which was beyond the scope of the normal criminal process); and humanely (in the administration of internment).[183] The Lawless case had nevertheless shown the willingness of the European Court to consider such matters, to require states to justify their actions and, in some regards, to accept that in this international forum the state was on the same footing as its citizens.

The Lawless case became increasingly moot as the IRA campaign appeared to dwindle away in the months and years that followed. De Valera's government had authorised releases, closing the Curragh on 15 March 1959.[184] As we have seen, violence returned in the spring of 1961, with the killing of two constables of the RUC and with explosions and ambushes.[185] With the possibilities of Lawless-type litigation in the background, and unwilling again to resort to internment, in November 1961 the Republic's government reactivated the Special Criminal Court under the provisions of the OASA.[186]

Hope and peace gone

But this lay ahead when, in the spring of 1958, amidst gathering gloom among activists, the Northern Ireland campaign drifted on. The depletion of IRA resources and the organisation's general lack of depth were shown by two events. As noted, in an attempt to obtain rocket launchers with which to counter RUC armoured patrols, B-Specials and the Army, a raid was organised at the REME camp at Blandford in Dorset on 15 February 1958.[187] It was essentially repetitive, speculative and under-resourced, and, predictably, it failed, telling all that suitable men were so scarce that Cronin (now risen to Chief of Staff, itself an indication of the dire shortage of talent; he had been a member for less than two and a half years) led the raiders.[188] Another indication of how attenuated the organisation had become was its willingness to cooperate in Northern Ireland with Saor Uladh. As we have seen, Kelly mounted his own operations quite independently of the IRA, which, insisting that it was the sole and legitimate republican government of Ireland, had claimed a monopoly in what it deemed to be the legitimate use of political force.[189] It was a climbdown indeed to accept assistance and explosives from a maverick and previously excoriated rival, but there was hardly a range of choices.[190]

Plans for the 1958–9 season were almost completely nullified when, on 30 September 1958, most of the members of the Army Council still at large were arrested in a raid on an IRA safe house on the Serpentine Avenue in Dublin.[191] No amount of past experience had modified the organisation's obsession with using Dublin as its command centre or deterred the concentration of the bulk of the Army Council in one building: these were patterns of failure. As Chief of Staff, Cronin had been under such pressure that he had been unable to make sufficient time to share plans, contacts and operational information with his colleagues, and manpower was too stretched to provide him with aides and direct-report deputies. The ad-hoc council that stood in for the arrested men therefore had little knowledge of current operations and few contact details.[192] A largely unsuccessful attempt was made to retrieve and reconstruct details of what had been planned.[193] Therefore, few attacks were mounted during the vital winter months. Energy, already dwindling, faded still further, and Northern units were left without a sense of direction or command. The IRA command still refused to recognise the utter impossibility of success and would not stand its members down. It may well have been that, with its leaders in prison, no one had sufficient standing and authority to dare to make the proposal and carry it through; bunker mentality and the obstinacy of an essentially sequestered group made continuing an easier choice than stopping. Now very sensitive to the domestic political drag of internment, and with its own very good information on the state of the IRA, the Irish government had no doubt that the campaign had irrecoverably declined to the level of nuisance. On 17 February 1959, it felt able to begin staggered releases of the Curragh internees.[194] Belfast was understandably less sanguine and held onto its prisoners and internees but eventually began a graduated programme of releases, completing them on 25 April 1961.[195]

The small band of activists had shown endurance and determination and, indeed, had retained some scope for initiative. Much against the declining trend, in the month of July 1958 there were seventeen incidents.[196] The intention was to show that the organisation was alive and could still mount sustained and coordinated attacks. These were mainly small explosions and the destruction of customs posts, but five of the incidents were rated as major by the RUC. Constable Henry Ross, aged twenty-six, on solitary bicycle patrol near the border at Forkhill, Co. Armagh, on 16 July 1958, was fatally wounded by a mine.[197] This was the fourth RUC fatality since December 1956. This may have been an act of retaliation, since a fortnight previously a party of Saor Uladh men had been intercepted near Newtownbutler, Co. Fermanagh. When challenged, the party had opened fire, and in the exchange one of its number was killed and another wounded and arrested. Six Thompson guns and some ammunition were seized as the raiders retreated back across the border.[198] Also on 16 July 1958, four raiders crossed the border from the Irish Republic and attacked the Killeen, Co. Armagh, customs post – with little doubt the IRA's top target – on the main Dublin–Belfast road. Holding customs officers and some civilians at gunpoint, bombs were placed and considerable damage was caused to the building.[199] The IRA party then recrossed the border, a few hundred yards away.

The following day, three IRA men placed a large bomb inside the sandbag emplacement at the front of the RUC station in Irish Street, Armagh. The bomb's command wire was insufficiently long and broke as the spool was run out, foiling the attack. With the police alerted and in pursuit, the three commandeered a taxi and were taken to the Roman Catholic cathedral. They were spotted, surrounded and arrested. The RUC claimed that they had prepared a temporary hiding place for themselves in the cathedral vault, entered through an underground passage by way of a manhole in the cathedral grounds.[200]

In the Republic, the campaign also suffered several setbacks. As part of the mid-July attacks, Patrick McManus described by Tim Pat Coogan as ('the principal IRA leader at liberty in the North') tried to retrieve a bomb from a cache in a ditch near Swanlinbar, Co. Cavan. The device exploded, killing him and injuring two companions. An IRA statement described the dead man as the OC of the South Fermanagh active-service unit.[201] A renegade Irish Army officer who had made contact with the IRA with the intention of supplying ammunition and perhaps other materials was arrested, court-martialled and sentenced to two years' imprisonment and discharge with ignominy.[202] Speaking in a Dáil debate adjournment on 17 July 1958, de Valera made clear his government's reaction to the upsurge in Northern Ireland. The IRA was seeking to drag the Republic into war, and he would if necessary seek further powers to deal with this threat.[203]

On 11 March 1959, the last detainees were released from the Curragh internment camp.[204] Reaction in Northern Ireland and in Britain was unfavourable since the IRA campaign, although spluttering, had not been called off. The British Ambassador, on instruction from Commonwealth Relations, immediately expressed concern to the Irish government.[205] Indeed, the IRA had ambushed an RUC patrol on 13 March 1959, injuring four constables. De Valera's motives in closing the Curragh had been linked by some commentators to the impending general election in the Republic, and to his own desire to become president. He was anxious to dispel the notion that he had been courting or placating the more extreme nationalists and republicans among the voters and made a strong statement about the ambush: 'We sympathise', he said, 'with the men who have been injured and thank God that there has been no loss of life.' He also issued a warning: if the IRA 'usurpations' continued, the Irish government would use every means at its disposal to prevent them.[206] De Valera was on very familiar ground here. He was not displeased, one imagines, to be criticised by Northern Ireland's Minister for Home Affairs, Brian Faulkner, or by the British premier Harold Macmillan. In a pre-election period, and in their very different ways, the IRA, Ulster Unionists and British Prime Minister were all helping him. But none of his nationalist manoeuvring signalled any disinclination to deal firmly with the IRA.

And still the campaign ground on, albeit at a very low level – minor acts of sabotage, some mere vandalism. An Army Convention met in June 1959. Instead of revitalising the campaign and restoring morale, a vast amount of time and much emotional energy was expended on the bitter recriminations that had followed the released internees from the Curragh.[207] A new army council was elected, dominated by men who had conceived and initiated the Border Campaign.[208] Despite the reduction and decay of the structure in the North, the lack of arms, resignations, the drifting away of members and an ever more averse and alarmed nationalist population in the border areas, it was decided to resuscitate the enterprise. Money, arms and men were lacking, and, while some may have had a sense of urgency in procuring them, the organisation did not. Little was done during the winter of 1959–60. Men released from the Curragh and still adhering to the organisation were directed to lie low and to await retraining and regrouping. Orders were issued to resume recruiting. Training camps were held in various parts of the country during July. Two sites preparing to receive a considerable number of men were raided by the Gardaí. Camping equipment was seized, and eight men charged with firearms offences were each sentenced to six months' imprisonment. The RUC received information that a total of eighteen training camps had been held, of various sizes and durations. Following these events, men were regrouped in areas along the border. It also claimed that an IRA leadership meeting in April 1959 had been informed that 170 men were fully trained.[209] Orders had been issued to conserve ammunition during the training camps so that more rounds would be available for attacks in the North.[210]

Mick Ryan, actively involved in the campaign from the outset, recalled the state of mind of the most militant of his comrades at this point. Some, including himself, had realised six months or so into Operation Harvest that there was little chance of victory. They continued to press their attacks, drawing inspiration from the much venerated republican notion of Terence MacSwiney of demonstrating superiority through endurance. This doctrine had of course been sealed in MacSwiney's death on hunger strike in Brixton Prison in October 1920; it also had many resonances with Roman Catholic teaching. It was this notion of the ultimate triumph of sacrifice that led Ryan and others to make another attempt: 'to reopen this failed campaign in the coming winter (1959–60) with no real improvements in conditions or equipment was a particularly hard decision to make. But some of us agreed to reopen it.'[211]

A number of IRA intelligence officers, sometimes accompanied by their families, were sent across the border on ostensibly innocent day trips. These excursions did not go unnoticed, and the RUC reported that army and police movements were being observed and that the Nutts Corner airport near Belfast had also received attention. That such a method of collecting information was necessary underlined the effects of persistent IRA suspicions that its Northern membership had been penetrated or had been immobilised by surveillance. This was confirmed, according to the RUC, by the fact that none of the intelligence officers contacted local people. In their belief that what remained of its Northern network was, for various reasons, insecure and compromised, the IRA leadership were probably correct. This realisation and numerous arrests undoubtedly had an effect on Northern members and supporters and further excluded them from activities; it also stifled the wish of anyone to become involved. The thin fiction that the IRA men from the South were acting in support of their Northern comrades was believed by no one: this had been and remained an almost exclusively Southern campaign.

The release of men from the Curragh had been something of a blood trans-fusion.[212] It was presented as a government backdown in the face of public pressure, and it certainly allowed a number of experienced men to get back into circulation. The extent to which the Irish government had responded to direct public pressure is debatable, but it seems clear that there was unease about the policy of detention without trial.[213] As we have seen, the Lawless case had raised more general and somewhat imponderable legal difficulties.[214] With its constant denunciation of Partition and its *de jure* claims over the territory of Northern Ireland, the Dublin government would always be put on the back foot when justifying action against those who were doing something more than talking. The IRA leadership may also have been encouraged by de Valera's stepping down as Taoiseach in June 1959. With the man who, for decades, had contested IRA claims to republican legitimacy most bitterly, tenaciously and effectively no longer the chief executive of the state, hopes for some form of accommodation with the Southern authorities revived.

The lull in activities in 1959 was brought about by several factors. There was a concern not to reverse the Curragh releases or to extinguish the possibility that Stormont might follow Dublin in opening the gates. With internees returning to the senior ranks, it was inevitable that there would be a review and a reconsideration of the campaign. This was diverted to some extent by the fierce row which had begun in the Curragh and which was forced on the Convention held in June 1959 for resolution. The quarrel, which drew in some of the most respected and experienced members, had similar effects to the Hayes affair, laying down the footing for a feud, spreading the poison of denunciation and widely forcing the taking of sides throughout the various levels of activists.[215] Resignations and disengagement by men of unquestionable standing who had given years of ser-vice increased the sense of confusion and meltdown. As on previous turning points, some were simply tired of a struggle that had drained their lives and laid waste to the years: they wanted to retrieve what they could or simply to hunker down. Others were driven away by the small-minded passions, backbiting and personal feuding.

Cathal Goulding and Manus Canning, imprisoned in England for their part in the Felsted raid, had returned to Dublin on completion of their sentences.[216] Neither had been involved in the Curragh faction-fighting, and both continued to support the campaign.[217] Despite RUC intelligence that the two had sought to persuade the Convention to adopt EOKA-style terrorist tactics, which would have included urban warfare and targeted assassinations, there was no significant shift from the aims and tactics outlined by Cronin in Operation Harvest: a rural setting for operations, attacks on army and police, disrupting communications and attempting to rouse the Catholic population in border areas.[218] Another Army Convention was held in June 1960. Once more there was a failure to make a realistic assessment of prospects. Renewed activity was approved for the long nights of 1960–1. Cronin was arrested immediately afterwards and given six months under the OASA. Whilst inside, charges were made against him by the US-based Irish Freedom Committee. These suggested, with a suspicious comprehensiveness, that Cronin was both an agent of the Irish government and a Communist. Although no evidence supported the accusations, and an IRA Court of Inquiry exonerated him, Cronin's lustre had gone and his commitment was blunted; he resigned from the Army Council.[219]

By this time, the campaign was truly dead, but no one was willing to conduct the obsequies. Mick Ryan had spoken at the 1960 Convention, briefly arguing in favour of continuing the campaign. Ruairí Ó Brádaigh had been appointed Chief of Staff, and he in turn appointed twenty-four-year-old Ryan as Director of Operations, a post he held until the campaign was formally ended. The Army Council included five other members, but they were not greatly involved in GHQ activities, being scattered around the country. All pointed to the chimerical character of a campaign rebirth. Ryan had no experience 'except the little bit of battle experience… and a good bit of common sense'. He recognised that the campaign could not extend beyond 'little acts of sabotage, blowing up bridges or an odd ambush, that couldn't do much damage'. All travel was done on foot, and at night. For a time in North Antrim, and in brutal winter weather, he operated with just one other man. Lack of supporters inevitably multiplied the hardships: 'We were sleeping in barns, caves, dugouts and less and less in homes because so few were safe. We had no proper clothes… no light military outfits that were warm, waterproof and could dry fast.'[220] These were impossible conditions, and the sequence of hopeless actions continued only because no other course seemed possible.

There was to be a final flare-up. On 27 January 1961, Constable Norman Anderson, aged twenty-six, was killed near Rosslea, Co. Fermanagh. There was a particularly strong reaction, North and South, since Anderson had apparently been taken shortly after parting from his girlfriend. He was marched up a lane and shot in the back thirty-four times. Any murder is appalling, but these circumstances singled the deed out in callousness and pitiless cruelty.[221] This atrocity was followed by a number of incidents in March and April – mainly attacks on transportation and customs posts, but including, on 28 March 1961, an attack on an

RUC patrol at Killea, Co. Derry.[222] None of this amounted to much, and, despite prisoner and internee releases, IRA resources were not replenished. North and south of the border, security forces continued to bear down hard. There was talk on the Army Council of a purely terrorist attack (along EOKA lines) such as the machine-gunning of a dance hall attended by off-duty soldiers.[223] This went no further than talk, but it was significant that it was raised at all. From its traditional forms of military action, an honour-limited campaign, conducted in a manner to resemble as closely as possible the actions of a conventional army in the field, extreme republicanism had been driven by utter failure to contemplate unadorned terrorism.[224]

Another killing sounded the tocsin for the campaign. In October 1961, the Army Council was already discussing a stand-down, even while hoping – like a desperate and deluded gambler – for a transforming turn of the wheel.[225] As we have seen, on 4 October 1961, the Irish electorate showed that its ambivalence had been resolved, at least for the time being. Sinn Féin received only 36,393 first-preference votes, less than 3 per cent of those cast.[226] It was more the IRA's indifference to politics than a belief that a successful action in Northern Ireland could stem the move away from militant republicanism that allowed the killing of yet another RUC man – twenty-eight-year-old Constable William Hunter – near Jonesborough, Co. Armagh. The attack, which wounded three others, took place on 12 November. There were strong protests from the Northern Ireland government, and the British Ambassador, Sir Ian Maclennan, called on Taoiseach Seán Lemass.[227] A strong government statement was made in the Dáil.[228] Ten days later, the Irish government reactivated the Special Criminal Court.[229] Leading IRA figures were rounded up in Dublin in the early hours of 27 November 1961, in what was the biggest Special Branch raid in three years.[230] The first sitting of the Tribunal took place in Collins Barracks, Dublin, on 28 November, and nine men were remanded in custody for further proceedings. Once the trials got under way, the Court began to sentence in years for offences previously punished by months.[231] Punishment was on an ascending trajectory, and there was talk, possibly inspired by government briefing, that death sentences might be imposed.[232]

Perhaps the IRA wanted to show that it was not intimidated or, more likely, its active units proceeded without direction. Four days later after the first sitting of the Tribunal, a mine was detonated 400 yards from the border, under an RUC Land Rover, slightly injuring three constables.[233] The death penalty remained in the statute books in the UK for certain types of murder (including the use of firearms), and Faulkner threatened to extend its use.[234] On 18 January 1962, the Army Council finally concluded it needed to end the campaign. Despite every effort and expenditure of men and money, failure had been comprehensive. Armed action had generated little support among Northern nationalists and even less in the South. Both Irish governments (and successive administrations) showed no sign of wearying or reducing the pressure; the British were not an atom closer to considering, much less announcing, a withdrawal from Northern Ireland. The IRA had drained every last reserve of its resources – human, *matériel* and cash – while its reputation and standing among republicans and nationalist sympathisers had been squandered. Its ideology, stripped out, had been shown to be devoid of strategic intelligence. On 26 February 1962, the public announcement came that the campaign was over. True to the underlying and tragic myopia of the five preceding years, there was no hint of self-criticism or contrition. Reflecting a venerable and elitist strand in republican thinking, the communiqué blamed the general public 'whose minds have been deliberately distracted from the supreme issue facing the Irish people – the unity and freedom of Ireland'. The door was left open with a grandiloquent reference to the 'final and victorious phase of the struggle for the full freedom of Ireland'.[235] The people had failed, not the IRA.

The destructive purity of will

As with the 1939–40 bombing campaign in England, and its posture on the outbreak of war, the IRA had corralled and isolated itself. It is a commonplace that generals have a tendency to fight the last war; the IRA leadership seemed unable to do anything else. The organisation was trapped on a historical treadmill, ever wont to confuse movement with progress and its cage with the wider world. The Border Campaign was the last flourish of a style of armed struggle that had succeeded against the British in 1919–21 to an extent that transfixed and obsessed a minority of republicans for two generations thereafter. Despite the vast changes that had been carried through in the intervening years, North and South, the IRA's analysis was fixed in amber: the need to rid Ireland of its colonial power. That there existed in the South a form of government and institutions supported by the overwhelming majority of the population was ignored, as was the fact that that mandate was periodically renewed in open and fair elections. That the maximum goal of the majority of Northern nationalists was probably to join that political entity rather than a new revolutionary order counted for nothing. The fact that two-thirds of the population of Northern Ireland did not want to leave the UK was most wilfully and energetically ignored. And there were other material realities that only the greatest effort of will could disregard: the determination of the two Irish governments, and the British, to defend themselves and their ample means to do so.

The overriding importance of will is at the heart of almost all revolutionary doctrine, of whatever complexion. For revolutionaries, self-appointed custodians of national, class or some other honour and interest, the ballot box had little significance beyond the tactical. The IRA saw politics, with its deals and compromises, its shading of differences, as a destructive contagion. Public opinion was ignored except when an increase in the Sinn Féin vote could be produced as evidence of approval of IRA policies. As for politics in general, let accommodation and manoeuvre into the organisation and it would inevitably sicken and succumb as to a deadly virus; only the armed struggle, its disciplines and sacrifices, was pure and immune from careerism, corruption and betrayal. Had not Collins, de

Valera, MacBride and a host of others wrecked themselves and the Republic on the rocks of politics? At every turn, the IRA had taken decisions, or had simply acted, with a deliberate, even perverse indifference to the political consequences, in what it saw as an honourable contrariness – justification through purity of intent. The formulaic anti-colonial analysis, the unwillingness to accept the authority of the electorate, the attempted reprise of the organisation's years of success and glory and the insistence that only force would resolve Ireland's problems had, by February 1962, taken the IRA to an empty and desolate place from which it seemed there could be no return.

Hundreds of its supporters had paid a price, from police raids, broken families and lost employment to prison and disrupted lives. Ten IRA and two Saor Uladh men had been killed; two republican non-combatants had also died. Six members of the RUC had lost their lives, and thirty-two police and soldiers had been injured.[236] Although the campaign had never amounted to a national emergency and had been countered without severe disruption in the North, even in border areas, there had been many adverse effects on the lives of ordinary people. Significant damage had been done to the existing and prospective economies of Northern Ireland and the Republic. Both were sickly, and several years of armed strife gave them both stereotypical images, damaged domestic and inward investment and, thus diminished employment and the life chances of ordinary people. Sectarian suspicions and hostilities in the North had been reinforced, and the scope for man-oeuvre of constitutional politicians of all complexions had been greatly limited. The losses and costs could be calculated. Damages in Northern Ireland amounted to more than £1 million; increased security expenditure £500,000 per annum throughout the campaign.[237] The Republic incurred charges of an extra £350,000 per annum on increased deployment of gardaí and soldiers.[238] The costs to the British government were harder to quantify since the Army was already garrisoned in Northern Ireland and deployment costs were submerged in more general expenses.

And there was the price paid in internment and imprisonment, to which we now turn. One hundred and sixty-one men had been interned in Northern Ireland and a similar number in the Republic. Their lives had been interrupted, some for three or four years, and their prospects blighted. Up to mid-July 1959, ninety-five men had been sentenced to a total of 553 years in Northern Ireland. By the final ceasefire in both jurisdictions, perhaps 200 had been convicted and sentenced for periods ranging from a few months to several years. At the conclusion of the campaign, forty-three men were serving sentences of between four and fifteen years in Belfast Prison; forty-two were held in Dublin's Mountjoy. Two men, Joe Doyle and Donal Murphy remained in England, serving life sentences for their part in the Arborfield raid.[239] This had been a shoestring campaign, and the funds for the dependants of men on the run, on active service or in captivity had been meagre. For these families, there had been sentences of another kind: material and emotional privations and the absence of a breadwinner, husband, son or father. In damage, lost lives, grief, anger, distrust and community polarisation, the Border Campaign cast a long shadow.

Notes

1 The Fifth Amendment to the Constitution (enacted 5 January 1973) removed the Article conferring special status on the Roman Catholic Church and recognised various other religious denominations. Divorce became possible by the Fifteenth Amendment (17 June 1996). This Amendment was carried by a margin of about 0.6 per cent, and deleted Article 41.3.2, replacing it with a permissive Article 41.3.2. It should be noted that the original prohibitory Article, expressing Roman Catholic doctrine, had been supported also by the Anglican Church of Ireland.

2 This was on 2 May 1945, and was followed (doubtless on de Valera's advice) by a similar visit from Douglas Hyde, President of Ireland. The background to these gestures, which caused indignation throughout the victorious Allied countries, is ably described by Brian Girvin in *The Emergency: Neutral Ireland, 1939–45* (London: Macmillan, 2006), Chapter 1. Of particular interest is Girvin's assessment of the knowledge that de Valera and his colleagues had at this point (May 1945) of the monstrous and evil deeds of Nazi Germany, led and inspired by Hitler.

3 And worse was to come. Once wartime restrictions allowed, the pace of emigration from Ireland increased, reaching one in eight of the population. (More than that proportion were children and the elderly excluded from the calculation.) Economic opportunities were only part of the reason for this huge movement in population, one suspects, cultural claustrophobia and inertia providing additional spurs. This was a rate of haemorrhage that brought the population of the Republic of Ireland to its lowest recorded level of 2.8 million. See Dermot Keogh, Finbarr O'Shea and Carmel Quinlan (eds.), *Ireland in the 1950s: The Lost Decade* (Cork: Mercier Press, 2004). For a contemporaneous analysis and expression of concern, see John A. O'Brien, *The Vanishing Irish: The Enigma of the Modern World* (London: W. H. Allen, 1955). See also Mary Daly, *The Slow Failure: Population Decline and Independent Ireland, 1920–1973* (Madison, Wisc.: University of Wisconsin Press, 2006), pp. 160–221.

4 Padraig Pearse, *Collected Works of Patrick Pearse: Political Writings and Speeches* (Dublin, Talbot Press, 1922), p. 135.

5 Prefaced by a religious declaration: 'In the Name of the Most Holy Trinity, from Whom is all authority and to Whom, as our final end, all actions both of men and States must be referred.'

6 Bunreacht na hÉireann (Constitution of Ireland), Articles 2, 3 and 4. Éire is translated simply as Ireland.

7 See *Irish Independent*, 7 May 1937, 8c–e. Lord Creighton, the Northern Ireland Prime Minister, called a snap election and won the usual overwhelming vote in favour of the Union. Speaking to an Orange Order meeting in north Antrim, he observed that 'the North and South are as far apart as the respective poles. So long as we are Ulstermen so long will we say we are British also' (*Northern Whig*, 5 July 1937, 7f–g). This was the theme of many Twelfth of July speeches. See, for example, *Northern Whig*, 13 July 1937, 9c and 10e–f; *Irish News*, 13 July 1937, 2d. At the last, Sir Basil Brooke (a future prime minister) warned, 'If Ulster ever gave in, it would be the beginning of the disintegration of the Empire.'

8 Votes in favour of the Constitution, therefore, amounted to 56.5 per cent of all votes cast. In the general election, held at the same time, Fianna Fáil secured 72,095 more votes than those cast in favour of the Constitution. This points to uncertainty about the new constitution among perhaps one-eighth of those willing to support de Valera in other ways.

9 See *Irish Independent*, 30 December 1937, 9a–b; NAI TAOIS/S10463, copy of statement of British government, 30 December 1937 and Irish response. The British Cabinet discussed the new Irish Constitution on 25 January 1937. The consensus was that the position of the Free State was unaltered by the Constitution. Concern was expressed

about Commonwealth relations and the Crown as symbol of the free association of nations in the Commonwealth. In this regard, the Cabinet concluded that, '[t]he position of the Crown was very inadequately and unsatisfactorily expressed in the new Irish Free State legislation' (PRO CAB/23/87, Meeting of the Cabinet, 25 January 1937).

10 PRO DO/35/2081, Memorandum reporting conversation between Sir John Maffey and Éamon de Valera, 10 November 1944. De Valera, according to Maffey, twice repeated his proposal that those opposing Irish reunification should be 'physically transferred to the country to which they wished to adhere'. Such conversations had occurred at various junctures during the war years, Maffey noting in respect of each that almost invariably de Valera turned the topic under discussion into a tour of the manifold iniquities and injustices of Partition.

11 PRO DO/35/2081.

12 PRO DO/35/2081, Minutes of meeting held on 15 December 1944. Had de Valera not 'with such complete obstinacy' resisted joining the Allies in the war 'the position might well have been very different'. This was an understandable reading of the situation by an official who had for several years assessed everything by the needs and progress of the war. De Valera's problem, however, went far beyond the diplomatic: he had promulgated a definition of nationality in which political and religious affiliations were dominant, and would be most bitterly contested, possibly in a civil war.

13 PRO D035/2081, Sir Eric Machtig to Sir John Maffey, 23 December 1944. Machtig, in a separate memorandum to the Secretary of State, was critical of Maffey for appearing to encourage de Valera or at least for not having been more assertive when the topic of Partition had been raised. Whether it was important to resolve the issue or not, 'we should under no circumstances divulge this to Mr de Valera or the Eire Govt. They would only put up their price' (11 December 1944). Others in the senior policy-making circle agreed with this analysis.

14 Herbert Morrison (1888–1965) had been Minister for Transport in Ramsay MacDonald's second Labour government. In the wartime coalition, he was, successively, Minister for Supply, Secretary of State for the Home Office and Home Security and, from 1942 to 1945, a member of the War Cabinet. In Attlee's first and short second administrations he was Lord President and then, briefly, Foreign Secretary. He was created a Life Peer in 1959.

15 During his tenure as wartime Home Secretary, Morrison had visited Northern Ireland, where he met only members of the government and the Unionist Party. Asked at a press conference why he had met no representatives of the nationalist community, he retorted that the fault lay with them since they had not asked to meet him. See James Kelly, *Bonfires on the Hillside* (Belfast: Fountain Publishing, 1995), p. 83.

16 PRO DO/35/2099, Éire and Northern Ireland: Memorandum by the Lord President of the Council. Morrison noted that de Valera had previously been lucky in his dealings with the British, instancing the Treaty Ports in particular. In any future negotiations it would be well to indicate that he had to give as well as take 'and that the giving cannot be a vague anticipation of the future'.

17 PRO DO/35/2099, Cabinet Paper (46) 381, 16 October 1946. The strategic importance of Northern Ireland's air and naval facilities was already a part of Cold War thinking and would grow as the critical importance of long-distance submarine patrols (including missile carriers) drew attention to the 'Iceland Gap' through which Soviet submarines could enter the North Atlantic.

18 PRO DO/35/2099, Éire and Northern Ireland: Draft Memorandum by the Secretary of State for Dominion Affairs.

19 PRO DO/35/3996, Lord Rugby to Dominions Office, 14 June 1947. De Valera also raised the issue of the Lane Collection (not resolved until 1959) and asked if in

the course of his summer holiday on board an Irish corvette he might call in at Rathlin Island, a Gaelic-speaking community off the north Antrim coast. Apprehensive about publicity and an adverse reception in Northern Ireland, the Dominions Office consulted the Home Office and advised against such a visit.

20 MacBride's views on Northern Ireland were of such a nature that when Costello's second coalition government (June 1954–February 1957) introduced internment in response to the IRA's border campaign, he withdrew his support and the government fell. John Costello, his erstwhile coalition partner, noted that MacBride's support had been withdrawn, 'to put it quite bluntly because of Government action against the unlawful use of force' (*Irish Independent*, 7 February 1957, 9b–c). But Costello should not have been surprised by this turn. During the first coalition government – indeed, only two weeks into that administration – MacBride's ambivalent attitude to the IRA became a matter of contention. Gerald Boland, former Minister for Justice, raised the matter of MacBride's attendance at an Easter commemoration at which the IRA made an open appeal for recruits. John Costello, now Taoiseach, professed himself 'profoundly disgusted' by Boland's raising the issue and contended that 'very great damage' had been done by it. Intimating that MacBride had become a bridge between constitutional and physical-force republicanism, Costello told the Dáil that '[t]he chief of my reasons for becoming head of this government was that I held and sincerely believed that in consequence of the coming together of these Parties, and particularly the Clann na Poblachta Party, we should see in this country the end of the gun as an instrument for furthering political theories or wishes' (*Dáil Debates*, vol. 110, col. 931, 15 April 1948).

21 The Republic of Ireland was established by means of a 1948 Act of the same name, introduced by John Costello's coalition government. The Act came into force on Easter Monday, 1949. London responded by passing the Ireland Act, 1949: 12 & 13 Geo. VI, c.41. This excluded the Republic of Ireland ('that part of Ireland heretofore known as Éire') from the British Commonwealth and confirmed that Northern Ireland would not be detached from the UK without the consent of the Northern Ireland Parliament.

22 The Executive Authority (External Relations) Act was passed by the Dáil in 1936 when de Valera took the opportunity presented by the abdication of Edward VIII to redefine the relationship of the Free State to the Crown in internal and external matters. The Ireland Act acknowledged Ireland's departure from the Commonwealth and reaffirmed the status of Northern Ireland within the UK. The decision to declare a republic was not discussed fully by the Irish government nor was the matter, which touched on the Constitution as well as on external relations, put to a referendum. See F. J. McEvoy, 'Canada, Ireland and the Commonwealth: The Declaration of the Irish Republic, 1948–49', *Irish Historical Studies*, 24 (1985): 506–27.

23 PRO DO/35/3996, Sir Walter Hankinson, British Ambassador to the Republic of Ireland, to Sir Percivale Liesching, Permanent Under-Secretary, Commonwealth Relations Office, 2 January 1952.

24 The Anti-Partition League was formed by nationalist members of Stormont at a meeting in Dungannon, Co. Tyrone, in November 1945. A Southern counterpart, the Anti-Partition Association, was duly inaugurated, which mobilised a wide swathe of social and political support in Éire. The apotheosis of the combined organisations seems to have been a mass gathering in Dublin, in May 1949, to protest against the British government's legislative response to the declaration of the Republic of Ireland.

25 See *Irish Press*, 14 May 1949, 1a–e, 7a–d; *Times Pictorial*, 14 May 1949, 10a–c.

26 See Conor Cruise O'Brien's comments on this campaign in which, as an official, he was involved: Conor Cruise O'Brien, 'The Embers of Easter', in O. Dudley Edwards and Fergus Pyle (eds.), *1916: The Easter Rising* (London: MacGibbon & Kee, 1968),

p. 233. Costello clung to this policy but took no practical steps to advance it. In the run-up to the 1957 election, he announced a study group to look into 'all practical problems relating to Partition'. That was to be followed by another group which would make recommendations to the government 'for consideration as a basis for discussion in connection with the ending of partition'. This age-old device of appointing an advisory body with grand and vague terms of reference was an implicit acknowledgement of tactical stalemate and strategic vacuity (*Irish Independent*, 7 February 1957, 9b–c).

27 See pp. 783–4.

28 See Uinseann MacEoin's *Harry: The Story of Harry White of Belfast* (Dublin: Argenta, 1985), pp. 148–54.

29 J. Bowyer Bell, *The Secret Army: The IRA, 1916–1979* (Cambridge, Mass.: MIT Press, 1983), p. 239. White remained at large until arrested by the RUC in October 1945. He was sought by the Éire government for his part in the shooting of Detective George Mordaunt on 19 October 1942, while escaping a Special Branch raid on an IRA house in Holly Road, Donnycarney, Dublin. On 31 October 1942, a 'Wanted for Murder' notice had been issued to the press, with a photo of White (*Evening Mail*, 2c). Maurice O'Neill, his accomplice in the incident, had been arrested and brought before the Military Court. His appeal failed, and he was executed on 2 November 1942 (see Dublin *Evening Herald*, 2 November 1942, 1a–b, 2c; 3 November 1942, 1b–c; 5 November 1942, 1f–g). Had the Military Court still been in existence, this would also have been White's fate when the RUC handed him over to the Irish authorities. He was brought to trial before the civil courts in December 1946, found guilty and sentenced to death. On appeal, Seán MacBride succeeded in getting his conviction reduced to manslaughter; a sentence of twelve years' penal servitude was substituted for the death penalty (*Irish Press*, 4 December 1946, 5d–e, 6e–f; *Anglo-Celt*, 14 December 1946). See the *Donegal News* (8 February 1947, 2f) for a concise account of the reduction of White's conviction from murder to manslaughter.

30 Such activities could be undertaken only on a strictly humanitarian basis by persons whose respectability and antecedents were beyond question and who were thus themselves safe from criminal proceedings or internment. The Roman Catholic hierarchy usually provided the necessary guarantees of probity. In October 1945, nevertheless, the Republican Prisoners' Release Association was formed. In a letter to the *Irish Times* (31 May 1946, 6b), a representative (Domhnall O Donnchadha) insisted that the sole purpose of the organisation was to secure the release of republican prisoners and to create a fund 'which would assist their rehabilitation in normal life on release'. This was certainly not the full story. For further details on the activities of the Republican Prisoners' Release Association, see NAI JUS/8/1138. It was an unabashedly republican organisation. While claiming that it was not connected with any political party, it appealed to 'all freedom-loving men and women who believe in the right of Ireland to be free from foreign aggression in any form' (Republican Prisoners' Release Association, *Constitution*, Dublin, 1946). This was another instance where prisoners provided an energising link between republican activists and wider circles of supporters and sympathisers – to the advantage of both the IRA and those tasked with their surveillance.

31 See above, pp. 607–8, n. 122.

32 This doctrine was repeatedly publicised by the IRA. In May 1952, as the organisation was undergoing the process of rebuilding, its organ, the *United Irishman*, denounced both the Southern and Northern states as 'two puppet statelets'. They were instruments in an English plot to divide Ireland and to hoodwink the Irish people (*United Irishman*, May 1952, 1a–b).

33 Bell, *The Secret Army, op. cit.*, p. 240. These were Ned Carrigan (Tipperary), Charlie Dolan (Sligo), Larry Grogan (Drogheda), Ted Moore (Kilkenny) and Peadar O'Flaherty

(Enniscorthy). Harry White, still at large and, notionally at least, still Chief of Staff, was not contacted (MacEoin, *Harry, op. cit.*, p. 152).

34 Constitutional punctiliousness extended to a formal termination of the state of war with Britain. On 10 March 1945, a ceasefire was declared.

35 Cathal Goulding (1923–98) was born in Dublin. Joined Na Fianna Éireann (a militant republican youth organisation under IRA control) and then the IRA. Took part in the initially successful Magazine Fort raid (see pp. 684–5) and, in November 1941, was imprisoned for membership of an illegal organisation. Subsequently interned at the Curragh. Arrested and sentenced to eight years' imprisonment for his part in the Felsted arms raid. On release, resumed IRA activities, first as Quartermaster, then (in 1962) as Chief of Staff, remaining in that position when the Provisional IRA broke away in December 1969. Developed a Marxist perspective on the Irish troubles and was central in developing the Workers' Party of Ireland.

36 As were certain key streets, junctions and meeting points in the city. Eamonn Boyce recalled of the early 1950s that as an active IRA man he wished to avoid Special Branch surveillance and therefore never attended a parade or the annual republican gathering at Wolfe Tone's grave at Bodenstown, Co. Kildare: 'And you never walked through O'Connell Street, you got a bus if you were going through the centre, they [Special Branch] were always around O'Connell Street' (interview). See also Eamonn Boyce, 'Question and Answer Session', in Eamonn Boyce, *The Insider: The Belfast Prison Diaries of Eamonn Boyce, 1956–1962*, ed. Anna Bryson (Dublin: Lilliput Press, 2007), pp. 432–3. Boyce was the leader of the Omagh raid and had also taken part in, but had not been convicted in connection with, the successful Armagh raid. He subsequently changed the spelling of his first name to 'Eamonn', but I have decided to adhere to the later form.

37 See Boyce, *The Insider, op. cit*, p. 10 n. 55, for details of the abortive meeting and its aftermath.

38 Boyce saw the organisational structures more simply: 'Tony Magan was a veteran in the 1940s. He had been interned in the Curragh Camp and had suffered ill-health as a result of his treatment there. And he was the boss-man. There was a thing called the Army Council, but it was really Tony Magan was running things' (interview). Tony Magan (1911–81) became a dominant figure after his release following the Ardee round-up. Appointed Chief of Staff in September 1948. Served, with one three-month absence (whilst serving a short sentence) until July 1957 when he was interned. On release in March 1959, became involved in a protracted and bitter dispute about events in the Curragh. See pp. 1082–3.

39 Bell, *The Secret Army, op. cit.*, p. 246. Sinn Féin had always provided a measure of political cover and agitational flexibility for the IRA; it was also a useful mustering place for auxiliaries. The mechanism is instructive. Here Clausewitz was turned on his head: politics was seen as the continuation of armed force by other means. This had been and would long remain a genetic flaw within republicanism.

40 The journal was edited by Seán G. O'Kelly. It could hardly be said to be an inspiring publication, but it reflected the claustrophobic nostalgia which was so representative of life within the IRA and of the leadership at that time. Issues had little news but were strong on historical pieces, patriotic verse and (eventually) appeals to support prisoners. See, for example, the front pages of the *United Irishman*, May 1948 (vol. 1, no. 1), May 1952 and April 1954, as well as the feature on the Dartmoor mutiny in the December 1953 issue (5c–d). With few exceptions (and there were exceptions), this was tired, unreflective and unengaging stuff. Going through the motions in order to bring out an issue seems often to have been the objective: simply appearing was enough. This conclusion is in line with IRA discussions in May 1947, preparatory to re-launching a newspaper. (This discussion was recorded

in detail by a Special Branch source.) Seán McCool observed that 'The function of a republican paper was, above all, to keep itself from being destroyed' (NAI JUS/8/953, Proposal to Re-issue Papers, 18 May 1947). It should also be noted that, however much it attempts to keep its operation at arms' length, a clandestine organisation that publishes a journal firmly grasps an Ariadne thread at the other end of which are the security and intelligence origins of the state. For further discussion of the *United Irishman* and its function within republicanism, see Brian Hanley and Scott Millar, *Lost Revolution: The Story of the Official IRA and the Workers' Party* (Dublin: Penguin Ireland, 2009).

41 Seán MacEoin (1894–1973) rose to the rank of General in the IRA during the Anglo-Irish War, notably defeating a Black and Tan force at Ballinalee, Co. Longford. He was later captured by British forces and sentenced to death but released as a condition for Truce discussions. He supported the Treaty and became an officer in the Free State Army, in June 1922 being appointed GOC Western Command. In 1929, he was appointed Chief of Staff of the Free State Army. Entering the Dáil, he represented constituencies in counties Sligo and Longford (1929–65) and served in two inter-party governments (as Minister for Justice, February 1948–March 1951, and Minister for Defence, 1954–7). Despite his willingness in 1950 to contemplate internment and his party's current support for it, in 1957 MacEoin argued against it. Offenders should be tried and punished, '[b]ut arrest and internment never ended anything – and everyone knows that' (*Longford Leader*, 3 August 1957, 1e–f).

42 NAI JUS/8/993, Secretary, Department of Justice to Secretary, Department of Defence, 18 October 1950. Thomas F. O'Higgins (1890–1953) was the brother of the assassinated Kevin. He was a founder of the Army Comrades Association (Blueshirts) and, in 1944, became leader of Fine Gael. He entered government in 1948 as Minister for Defence.

43 NAI JUS/8/993, Secretary, Department of Defence to Secretary, Department of Justice, 30 January 1951.

44 NAI JUS/8/993, Department of Justice memorandum, 14 February 1952.

45 Bell claims that there were forty men in the unit (*The Secret Army*, *op. cit.*, p. 250), but Eamonn Boyce, an activist of the time, put the figure at twenty-two, with a maximum turnout of twelve.

46 See above, pp. 430–1. The 1939 Prevention of Violence Act had had a drastic effect on support activities. Organisations could be proscribed, and membership became an arrestable offence, as was any action in support of such an organisation. The Act also allowed for orders of expulsion from the UK and for orders of prohibition of entry into Britain from the Republic or Northern Ireland. In addition, regulations required registration with the police, regular reporting to police stations and other restrictions. This Act (with amendments brought in in 1940) was actively enforced during wartime and remained in effect (though not much in use) until 1954.

47 PRO NIO CJ/4/843, Memorandum on IRA, 14 March 1957 (unsigned but probably RUC Special Branch). Following his conviction for the raid on Felsted School Armoury in October 1953, the police told the press that Sean Stephenson had been Chairman of the London branch of Sinn Féin and that '[h]e has been seeking sources of supply of arms and ammunition for the IRA since 1951' (*Irish Times*, 8 October 1953, 7c).

48 As long as the unit was incapable of mounting attacks, it was useful (and safe) for the police to allow it to function, with surveillance of various kinds providing an ever-expanding list of members, contacts and locations. If it had not existed, police work would have been more difficult.

49 PRO NIO CJ/4/843, Memorandum on IRA, 14 March 1957, pp. 4–5. In the post-war years, a vast amount of military clothing and equipment (excluding arms) was available for purchase at army-surplus stores on high streets throughout Britain.

50 There were other republican-related organisations, to varying degrees under IRA control or influence. Special Branch listed these as the Republican Aid Committee (An Cumann Cabhrach), a welfare support organisation founded in 1953 and shortly thereafter supporting the families of nineteen prisoners in England. The United Irishmen was an organisation of openly republican views which operated from 1948 until disbanded in 1955. It was succeeded by the Irish National Union. Under both identities it was well known for its weekly meetings at Hyde Park's Speakers' Corner. Constitutional organisations such as the Anti-Partition League and a range of sporting and cultural organisations played no part in IRA support activities, but they did bring young Irish men and women together and therefore were of almost equal interest to the IRA and the Special Branch. For the same reason, the congregations at certain Roman Catholic churches also held some interest to these opposing bodies (PRO NIO CJ/4/843, Memorandum on IRA, 14 March 1957, pp. 5–6).

51 *Northern Whig*, 6 June 1951, 1b–d; *Derry Journal*, 6 June 1951, 1a–b. The *United Irishman* carried a front-page report on the raid which it said had been planned as a protest against 'the visit of English royalty to Ireland' (June 1951, 1a–c). The booty consisted of twenty Lee Enfield mark IV rifles (better than the then standard issue for the Irish Army), twenty Sten, two Bren and other machine guns with a deal of ammunition.

52 The name 'Officers' Training Corps' is misleading to those unfamiliar with the scheme. Intended to provide a relatively modest amount of basic military training to teenage school pupils, the organisation was a junior division of a broader scheme that operated in universities. Only a small proportion of those who participated in the scheme went on to seek commissions in the regular or territorial armies. A school armoury in the early 1950s would contain a reasonable stock of older-model rifles, ammunition and a small stock of other weapons for instructional purposes. Armoury security was generally little more than stout locks and barred windows.

53 The one local man was London-born John (then Seán) Stephenson (later to become IRA Chief of Staff under the Gaelicised name of Seán Mac Stíofáin). He had served in the RAF and was thought to be a trustworthy, serious and reliable man.

54 Bell, *The Secret Army*, op. cit., p. 257.

55 See the *Irish Times*, 8 October 1953, 7a–c; *Irish Independent*, 8 October 1953, 7d–e. The judge (Mr Justice Streatfield) rather mildly – more in sorrow than anger – rebuked the three. It was 'regrettable', he said, that they had allowed their political views to govern their activities to the extent of breaking the law (*Irish Times*, 8 October 1953, 7b). For a different reaction, see *United Irishman*, November 1953, 1. By modern (and wartime) standards, these were lenient sentences. There was, however, no general alarm about IRA activities in England to which the prosecution could point, and the three had not resisted arrest. The sentencing judge probably took the view that the three were posturing adventurers.

56 Boyce, 'Question and Answer Session', op. cit., p. 431.

57 The Gough Barracks raid was an IRA success, but its execution was indicative of a basic flaw in the organisation and its relationship to supporters. The fact that the front-gate sentry was carrying an unloaded weapon was noticed by Leo McCormick, an unemployed Dublin man sent north to scout opportunities by Tony Magan, the IRA Chief of Staff. Eamonn Boyce did follow-up observations over several weekends. Boyce, 'Question and Answer Session', op. cit.

58 There was only a gradual realisation that the IRA was planting men in British Army units and enlisting the aid of others, both regular and national servicemen. Around the middle of 1957, security was stepped up and men known to be IRA sympathisers or suspected of membership were watched more closely. Action (presumably discharge) was taken in twenty cases (PRO NIO CJ/4/843, Special Branch intelligence briefing, October 1957). The subterfuge had two benefits, since, besides the information

gathered, the false recruits received military training. Seán Garland (1934–). A life-long activist. Joined the IRA at the age of nineteen and, on its instructions, became a British Army recruit preparatory to the Gough Barracks raid. Deserted and resumed IRA activities. Led and was wounded in the raid on Brookborough Barracks on 1 January 1957. Escaped after hospital treatment in the Republic but was subsequently rearrested and interned. Resumed IRA activities north of the border after his release and was arrested, tried and imprisoned. Embraced Marxist thought and took the Official side when the IRA split and became a leading figure in that organisation. President of the Workers' Party (formerly Official Sinn Féin), 2000–8.

59 In the aftermath of the raid there was extensive questioning of the usual republican suspects in Northern Ireland, but the police became convinced (correctly) that the raid was a 'southern job' (see *Connacht Sentinel*, 15 June 1954, 1d). There remained a chronic need for recruits. We have noted that in Dublin only a dozen members of the city's IRA unit turned out for parades. The Cork unit was half a dozen strong, and there were various veterans scattered around the country. The Belfast unit seems also to have been tiny: Jimmy Steele, Joe Cahill and perhaps another handful (Boyce interview). For a report of the raid, see the *Sunday Independent*, 13 June 1954, 1a–c.

60 *Sunday Independent*, 13 June 1954, 1c.

61 PRO DO/35/4984, A. F. Morley, Permanent Secretary CRO to Sir Walter Han-kinson, British Ambassador, Dublin, 11 August 1954. Basil Brooke, 1st Viscount Brookborough (1868–1974). Educated at Winchester, he passed into Sandhurst and served on the Western Front, 1914–18. Played a leading part in the formation of the Special Constabulary and held various posts in the Northern Ireland government before becoming Prime Minister (1943–63). Lifelong member of the Orange Institution. Made a number of public statements offensive to Roman Catholics, readily recited within their community. See the extended entry in *Dictionary of Irish Biography* (Cambridge: Cambridge University Press, 2009).

62 PRO DO/35/4984, Extracts from Home Office Note of Discussion on IRA Activities, 30 July 1954. The concerns about wavering or uncertain ministerial support were, as we shall see, well founded.

63 There was even some sympathy for the raids within the Gardaí (though certainly not in Special Branch). Eamonn Boyce, who took part in the successful Gough Barracks action (and was arrested following its unsuccessful Omagh follow-up) recalled that on the journey south after the Gough Barracks, gardaí in Balbriggan, Co. Dublin, stopped one of the lorries and told the occupants "'Yous should have told us you were coming. We'd have cleared the way for you.'" The lorry was then allowed to go on its way. (Interview.)

64 The sectarian clashes of the 1920s were not so distant, much less so those of the 1930s. The possibility of recurrences was not at all far-fetched, especially should an atrocity result in loss of police or civilian lives. Even the IRA seems to have been conscious of this dire possibility and initially issued strict instructions to avoid conflict with police or civilians (see Boyce, *The Insider, op. cit*, p. 439). For a history of com-munal violence in Belfast, see Andrew Boyd's depressingly instructive *Holy War in Belfast* (Tralee: Anvil Books, 1969). More than forty years after publication, as these words are being written, there are reports of violent street confrontations between republicans and loyalists.

65 PRO DO/35/4984, Extracts from Home Office Note of Discussion on IRA Activities.

66 See Chapter 17.

67 The Trojan horse on this occasion was Paddy Webster. Following the raid, he returned to the Republic, where, in January 1955, he was arrested and sentenced to three months' imprisonment.

68 There had been another attack by a splinter republican group in the early hours of 11 October 1954. The target was the home of General Sir John Woodall, General OC in Northern Ireland. The bomb consisted of forty-eight sticks of gelignite of which only four detonated. Had the whole bundle exploded, Woodall's house would have been destroyed. No report of the attack made its way into the press (PRO DO/ 35/4984, British Embassy, Dublin, to CRO, 12 October 1954). The following year, Woodall was moved to the pre-retirement post of Governor and Commander-in-Chief of Bermuda.

69 Eamonn Boyce, under direct and dire instructions from Tony Magan, could not use his weapon to coerce a civilian to give him shelter or take him across the border. 'I found myself in Omagh that night, armed. I was the only one that knew where I was and I knew the way back. I could have knocked on any door. I could have threatened any person to drive me to the border. The thought never struck me. Tony Magan would have killed me if I had come back that way' (interview). The lack of local support was the price of excluding Northern IRA units, but this had been thought necessary for security reasons. An essential element of the doctrine of guerrilla warfare (that combatants could hit and run and hide within a sympathetic, or intimidated, population) had thus been discarded. The guerrilla doctrine had been neglected in another important way. Magan's instruction that no civilian should be coerced showed a punctiliousness that no true revolutionary would have contemplated. It was well meant, no doubt, but a long way from the thinking of those Leninist omelette-makers who cracked their eggs with indifference and sometimes with perverse relish.

70 In passing sentence, Lord MacDermott, Northern Ireland's Lord Chief Justice, warned that the leaders and teachers of Church and State throughout Ireland must act if the country were not to be plunged into chaos. It was tragic that young men from the South were unconscious of wrongdoing in embarking on a campaign of violence (*The Times*, 16 December 1954, 5f; *United Irishman*, January 1955, 1a–d; *Northern Whig*, 16 December 1954, 1a–c). In the eight weeks between the Omagh raid and the sentencing of the eight captured men, there was a lull in IRA activities. Both Dublin and London thought that this was intended to avoid an element of heavier, deterrent sentencing on the Omagh group and that, once the case had been disposed of, a spectacular operation might be attempted (see PRO DO/35/4985, Record of Liesching–Boland conversation, 15 December 1954; Sir Walter Hankinson to Sir Percivale Liesching, 21 December 1954).

71 Bell, *The Secret Army*, *op. cit.*, p. 266. Armoury keys captured in the Armagh raid were displayed to supporters and a training film was made. Eamonn Boyce thought that the 'bit of gunfire' had excited a lot of publicity (interview). He also noted that the republican movement was not able to cope with the influx: 'it got out of control in some places' (Boyce, 'Question and Answer Session', *op. cit.*, p. 434).

72 PRO DO/35/4984, British Embassy, Dublin, to CRO, 3 December 1954. The fact that at least some of the houses of embassy staff were known was of course being underlined.

73 *Irish Resistance to British Aggression* (Dublin: Army Council, Óglaigh an hÉireann, November 1954). The cover was laid out with the initial letters of 'Irish', 'Resistance' and 'Aggression' in bold type. Instructions subsequently given to the armed groups sent across the border emphasised that under no circumstances were they to engage any civilian, RUC or B-Special constable. The target was the British Armed Forces only (Boyce interview). This restraint would not last.

74 *The Times*, 10 December 1954, 6f.

75 In conversation with Sir Percivale Liesching at the Commonwealth Relations Office, F. H. Boland, the Irish Ambassador, indicated that his government accepted the IRA's denial of involvement in the Liverpool raid (PRO DO/35/4958, Conversation

of 15 December 1954). Liesching, during this exchange, told Boland that 'I found no comfort at all in what he had told me and that still less comfort would come if the IRA were left to judge the time when they next indulged in violence and bloodshed.'

76 That the state of alert had been raised to a point of jumpiness by the B-Specials was demonstrated by a fatal shooting that night. One wholly innocent teenager (Arthur Leonard) was shot and killed and two other persons were injured when Specials fired on their van at a road junction on the Augher–Aughnacloy road, Co. Tyrone (*Northern Whig*, 7 March 1955, 1a–d). For the aftermath, including a rowdy scene at Stormont when Seán Dunne, a Labour member of the Dáil, was ejected from the distinguished strangers' gallery for heckling the Minister for Home Affairs, see *Northern Whig* (9 March 1955, 1a–d). See also *Belfast Newsletter*, 7 March 1955, 5a–c; 8 March 1955, 5a–c; 9 March 1955, 7a–c.

77 British intelligence at this point lacked operational forewarning, with little evidence of penetration of the main IRA organisation, either in Ireland or in Britain. The RUC, however, had sufficiently strong sources for Brian Maginess, the Minister for Justice to ask (via the Home and Commonwealth Relations offices) that Dublin take action against an IRA training operation, involving small arms and open range practice, in the townland of Doogery, near Scotstown, Co. Monaghan. The spot was a well-chosen Southern salient, allowing access to the counties of Fermanagh, Tyrone and Armagh. It was about five miles from the Northern Ireland border at Rosslea (PRO DO/35/4984, Brian Maginess to Gwilym Lloyd-George, Home Secretary, 14 February 1955).

78 Tim Pat Coogan claims that the men did not use their weapons lest a failure of the police patrol to report in sparked a general alarm. He also gives Wokingham rather than Ascot as the police station to which the men were taken. Tim Pat Coogan, *The IRA* (London: Fontana, 1980), p. 344. But see Norman Lucas, *The CID* (London: Barker, 1967); see also *Belfast Newsletter*, 15 August 1955, 5a–b; *Irish News*, 15 August 1955, 1a–c.

79 Coogan states that it was through the hiring itself that Murphy was traced. In either event, the slip was rank amateurism, for which Murphy paid a high price.

80 *Irish News*, 16 August 1955, 3c–f and 5b; 17 August 1955, 1a–c.

81 James Andrew Mary Murphy (1935–) would escape from Wakefield Prison on 12 February 1959 in a joint EOKA–Saor Uladh operation. Donal Murphy (1932–), brother of Charlie Murphy (see pp. 868–70 below), remained in prison until October 1962. Doyle was a thirty-year-old shopkeeper from Bray.

82 *Irish News*, 6 October 1955, 1b–c and 2d–e.

83 There had been two smaller raids at Bristol and Kinmel Park (a military camp in North Wales) (*Belfast Newsletter*, 16 August 1955, 5a–b; *Irish News*, 16 August 1955, 1a–b). These were not claimed by the IRA, and the British Embassy in Dublin considered them to be 'pieces of clumsy amateur freelancing set off by Arborfield'. The Embassy also recognised that even in Northern Ireland defence establishments could not be kept permanently on what it described as a 'permanent Palestine footing' (PRO DO/35/4984, British Embassy to CRO, 16 August 1955).

84 Memorandum on the IRA, 11 March 1957, *op. cit.*, f. 5.

85 Cycling was both a recreation and a widely used mode of transport at the time. Contemporary photos of central Dublin during rush hour show it crammed with bicycles. At the weekends, cycling-club events (speed, endurance and touring) took hundreds of young men (and some young women) to destinations around the country.

86 RUC Special Branch reported that when Christle left the organisation he took about seventy-five members with him. This was a sizeable fraction of the activists then available. Joe Christle (1928–98) was educated at University College Dublin, where he was prominent in the National Students' Council. Involved in a number of athletic activities and organisations. Trade-union activist. Served short prison sentence

in 1957. Called to the Bar. Became lecturer and eventually vice-principal of a technical school, the Rathmines School of Commerce, in Dublin.

87 Bell, *The Secret Army, op. cit.*, pp. 277–80. Two months later, Christle and his group reached an agreement with Liam Kelly of Saor Uladh to conduct joint operations. Their combined forces amounted to about seventy men (Coogan, *The IRA, op. cit.*, p. 375).

88 Liam Kelly (1922–2011) came from a family with formidable republican antecedents, which added to his own standing. His grandfather, William John Kelly, was an associate of Thomas Clarke (who was executed for his part in the 1916 Rising); his father had been an officer in the IRA during the 1916–21 period. According to RUC Special Branch, Kelly had joined the IRA in 1940, rising within a year to become an intelligence officer. In September 1941, he was arrested, charged and sentenced to two years' imprisonment for possession of IRA documents. On expiration of his sentence (with remission for good behaviour) in May 1943, he was interned. He was released in September 1945 under general amnesty.

89 PRONI HA/32/1/955, Special Branch briefing: 'Convinced as the Army Council is that it is dealing with an erratic individual whose actions are unpredictable and who might, for his own purposes, attempt to carry out these threats [of unofficial armed action] and thus endanger the liberty of loyal volunteers in Co. Tyrone and bring the Army in general into disrepute, the Army council hereby repudiates Kelly and warns the few individuals adhering to him of the possible consequences of their misguided alliance.'

90 According to the RUC, in January 1953, Saor Uladh staged an armed hold-up at Dungannon Labour Exchange, netting £1,225. Three months later, they attempted to destroy customs posts at Culmore, Mclennan and Galliagh Cross, Co. Derry. These were thought to be training operations (PRONI HA/32/1/955, Special Branch briefing).

91 *Irish News*, 24 October 1953, 1b–d. The election contest unseated a nationalist member and was conducted amidst many recriminations. The RUC considered that Kelly had ventured into politics 'possibly as an end in itself, but more probably to enhance his stock and to cover up his illegal activities' (PRONI HA/32/1/955, Special Branch briefing).

92 In 1958, Kelly reflected on Saor Uladh's policy of recognising the Dáil and the 1937 Constitution. It was, he wrote, 'dictated by reason and conscience'. And even if these did not compel recognition, 'we should feel constrained to respect them on tactical grounds since non-recognition of the institutions of government is the stock excuse availed of by unscrupulous Southern politicians in their efforts to coerce and crush the republican movement. Our attitude does not, however, preclude us from viewing with horror and abhorrence the anti-national and undemocratic policies of the present Government and its predecessors since the Great Betrayal of 1921.' (Pamphlet written by Liam Kelly and published in March 1958: PRONI HA/32/1/955, Special Branch briefing on Liam Kelly, July 1958, Appendix).

93 *Irish Independent*, 21 November 1953, 4f–g; *Irish Times*, 21 November 1953, 1e–f.

94 The new body proclaimed Kelly's 'self-sacrificing example'. It upheld the 1937 Constitution, 'which the people of Unoccupied Ireland adopted by referendum in July 1937' and demanded that Nationalist MPs should cease to attend Stormont and Westminster (PRONI HA/32/1/955).

95 PRONI HA/32/1/955, HA 9/2/753; PRO NIO CJ/4/843, Special Branch intelligence briefing, October 1957. There evidently was some police penetration.

96 *Irish News*, 28 November 1955, 1b–c, 6h; *Northern Whig*, 28 November 1955, 1a–d, 6c–d; PRONI HA/32/1/971, HA/32/1/955. Connie Green, was Saor Uladh's first loss in action and was commemorated on at least two occasions in 1956 (*Irish Press*, 16 January 1956, 5a; *Anglo-Celt*, 7 April 1956, 3b). The month before, Kelly had held a public meeting in Dublin under the auspices of his open organisation, Fianna Uladh. He was sharply heckled by members of the IRA. Even at this point, however,

he was able openly to proclaim that he was a member of an armed force and always had been. Although this was reported, gardaí took no action (PRO DO/35/4984, British Embassy, Dublin, fortnightly summary, 7 October 1955).

97 There was a sharp and adverse reaction from most of the principal newspapers in the Irish Republic. The Taoiseach, John Costello, issued a long statement, condemning Partition and excoriating the British government for a 'cynical disregard of principle and consistency' for upholding it. With this pious preamble, he threatened that his government would take action were the attacks to continue (*Dáil Debates*, vol. 153, cols. 1336–9, 30 November 1955; see also *Irish Times*, 28 November 1955, 1a–c; 29 November 1955, 1a–d; 30 November 1955, 1a–d).

98 By mid-1957, however, because of increased RUC pressure, Kelly moved across the border to Co. Monaghan (PRO NIO CJ/4/843, Special Branch intelligence briefing, October 1957).

99 Such was the strength of IRA concern that in July 1956 it reissued its October 1952 statement repudiating Kelly and, according to RUC intelligence, 'seriously considered having him shot' (PRONI HA/32/1/955, Special Branch briefing on Liam Kelly, July 1958).

100 A number of small offshoots had already appeared. One was led by Brendan O'Boyle, who had escaped from Londonderry Prison in March 1943 (see above, p. 593). Using contacts and funds arising from his time as a fugitive in the USA, O'Boyle prepared his own campaign against Northern Ireland. On 2 July 1955, he blew himself up while attempting to bomb the Stormont telephone exchange (*Northern Whig*, 4 July 1955, 1a–c). Bell (*The Secret Army*, *op. cit.*, pp. 256–7) details others of these groups, none of which had any significant strength or effect.

101 In his statement on 30 November 1955, Costello warned that, should the unlawful activities continue, 'we are resolved to use… all the powers and forces at our disposal to bring such activities to an end'. Speaking from the opposition benches, de Valera urged that Costello's appeal be heeded 'and that those who can influence public opinion will realise fully the direction in which we have been drifting' (*Dáil Debates*, vol. 153, col. 1350). Seán MacBride (now out of government) made an equivocal statement. He did not believe that any act of violence unsupported by the resources of the state could achieve reunification and argued that, in certain circumstances, such armed force might be legitimate. The 'situation' (of sporadic IRA activity) was Britain's responsibility. He seemed to urge toleration of IRA activity as long as it remained north of the border: 'We must throughout be careful not to place ourselves here in the position of acting as instrument of British policy in Ireland' (*Dáil Debates*, vol. 153, cols. 1351–3, *passim*). See also *Irish News*, 1 December 1955, 1b–c and 6g–h; *Northern Whig*, 1 December 1955, 1a–d.

102 PRONI HA/32/1/955, Special Branch briefing on Liam Kelly, July 1958. The December 1956 issue of the *United Irishman* published a statement emphasising that neither Joe Christle nor Liam Kelly had 'any connection with the Irish Republican Movement'. There was also what could have been deadly innuendo: 'Somewhere among these dissidents, but always difficult to find, are the paid agents of the enemy' (*United Irishman*, December 1956, 1c–e).

103 *United Irishman*, December 1956, 1c–e.

104 PRO NIO CJ/4/843, RUC Special Branch intelligence briefing, March 1958.

105 Seán Cronin (1920–2011). Man of action and of letters. Served in the Irish Army from 1941 until 1948. He emigrated to the USA but returned in 1955. He had developed his career in journalism and obtained a position in Dublin's *Evening Press*. Cronin joined the IRA in late 1955 and was given express promotion to Director of Operations early in 1956. In this capacity, and with the assistance of Charlie Murphy, he drew up the staff plan for 'Operation Harvest'. Briefly imprisoned in the

Republic of Ireland in January 1957. Led raid on Blandford depot (Dorset) on 16 February 1958. Interned at the Curragh in October 1958, released in March 1959. Sentenced by Dublin District Court to six months' imprisonment in June 1960 and again in December 1961. Resigned from the IRA upon release and secured employment with the *Irish Independent*. Later returned to the USA, serving as Washington correspondent for the *Irish Times*. Published several books on Irish history and politics. His short length of service with the IRA was disproportionate to the impact he had on the organisation.

106 This included calculations of the required arms, munitions, supplies, logistics, funding, training and accommodation. Given the severe material and intelligence limitations within which he had to work, much of this planning seems to have been based on the most optimistic assessments and a hope that it would all come right on the day.

107 Britain's Long Range Desert Force had morphed into the highly regarded Special Air Service from such roots. See Fitzroy Maclean's *Eastern Approaches* (London: Cape, 1949). The guerrilla exploits of Major-General Orde Wingate and his Chindits in the Burma war against Japanese forces were much discussed in memoirs and news features. And there were many other such tales. Had Cronin and his comrades encountered this and similar literature? Almost certainly, since no one reading the serious press and reviews (and indeed some of the more sensationalist newspapers) could have avoided doing so.

108 General Grivas's memoirs point to a range of resemblances in the two campaigns. EOKA, however, was far more willing to countenance urban guerrilla warfare, assassinations and terror. General Georgios Grivas, *Memoirs*, ed. Charles Foley (London: Longmans, 1964).

109 Confirmation of this may be taken from many of the organisation's key public statements and from almost every issue of the *United Irishman*. Past and present blended and were hardly distinguishable.

110 Mick Ryan had attended IRA lectures on guerrilla warfare but later realised that the various experiences on which these were based were almost totally irrelevant to Northern Ireland in the 1950s and 1960s 'because everything had changed and also you had the sectarian situation up there that you hadn't got in the South or the other theatres dealt with'. Nor did the Catholic population support the IRA campaign: 'They didn't condemn it but they didn't want to know – they wanted it quietly to go away. Because they didn't want to bring retaliation on themselves, particularly in some areas where they'd be isolated… You can't blame for that. I can understand that as we would not have been able to defend them' (interview). It seems highly doubtful that Seán Cronin had spent any appreciable time in Northern Ireland, if any at all.

111 The notion of a flying column, a highly mobile, low-maintenance group operating in the countryside, attacking and then moving on and concealing itself, was also a harking back to the middle and final stages of the Anglo-Irish War (and, of course, the tactic had been used at other places and in other times). It was dependent entirely on a largely sympathetic or at least benignly or fearfully neutral population to provide shelter and food, withholding information from the enemy while giving it to the flying column. The tactic is crucially dependent on the column being more mobile than the enemy. Even a cursory evaluation by a person of little experience would show that none of these preconditions existed in Northern Ireland. By March 1957, Mick Ryan realised that the flying column was an outdated tactic: 'You could see that people were being picked up everywhere – support was minimal and it was getting increasingly difficult to billet large groups of men on the run with any degree of safety and the population at large, North and South, didn't support us – so you'd break up into smaller groups of two or three' (interview).

112 See Brendan Anderson, *Joe Cahill: A Life in the IRA* (Dublin: The O'Brien Press, 2002), Chapter 6. Belfast was so thoroughly cut out that Joe Cahill, then Belfast Battalion OC, heard about Operation Harvest's commencement only when police raided his house on the morning of 13 December 1956 (pp. 136–7). A consequence of their being kept in ignorance was that the Belfast IRA could not prepare for the arrests and internment that would inevitably follow the initial actions. That lack of preparation and the activities of informers meant that internment immobilised much of the Northern IRA leadership.

113 Mick Ryan recalled his own restricted view, with the focus of the armed campaign on separated brethren in the North, 'not realising that there were a million Protestants; none of us thought of that… the word "sectarianism" – I don't believe I had ever heard it up to that, not until after that time'. There was a complete unwillingness to face realities: 'to talk, as we did in our propaganda – in the *United Irishman*… that the Unionists and the RUC should put up their arms and join with us in the struggle… it was pure romanticism and idealism, overboard' (interview).

114 *Irish News*, 15 December 1954, 5d. A set of seven training documents had been found in the possession of Leo James McCormick. These related to the objectives of the campaign as well as practical instructions for handling arms and explosives. One of the documents was headed 'Volunteers in Prison'.

115 Wallace Clark, *Guns in Ulster* (Upperlands: Wallace Clark Booksales, 2002), p. 101.

116 *Irish Times*, 18 January 1957, 1e–g.

117 Six weeks into the IRA campaign and in private conversation, the Irish Chief of Staff, General Patrick Mulcahy, told his British opposite number in Northern Ireland (General Sir Brian Kimmins) that the Irish Army, the Gardaí and the government had been taken 'completely by surprise'. Like the Northern security forces, they had background intelligence and knew that something was in the offing, but they believed that action was some time away. See PRO DO/35/4987, Sir Alexander Clutterbuck (British Ambassador in Dublin) to H. J. B. Lintott, Under-Secretary of State, CRO, 28 January 1957.

118 *Irish News*, 12 December 1956, 1a–b; *Irish Times*, 12 December 1956, 1a–c.

119 *Connacht Tribune*, 15 December 1956, 9b–c; *Irish News*, 12 December 1956, 1a–b; Clark, *Guns in Ulster*, *op. cit.*, p. 99.

120 The proclamation was issued on 12 December 1956 and echoed in the January 1957 issue of the *United Irishman*, 1a–d. Some current phrases had crept in: 'freedom fighters' and 'national liberation struggle'. These already carried their own Orwellian charge of doublespeak, cynicism and betrayal. This was evident also in the effrontery of the claims that were made: 'Our people in the South are not aware of the wave of enthusiasm passing through the North. And our people in the North are apt to blame their kindred in the South for not backing more strongly the fight for freedom… The enemy's bridgehead is weakening. We hope that in the months to come it will crumble completely' (*United Irishman*, January 1957, 1d).

121 *Irish News*, 14 December 1956, 1g–h; *Donegal News*, 15 December 1956, 1g–h.

122 There were allegations that, when captured, the wounded had been shot by the RUC. Coogan, who interviewed one of the IRA men involved in the attack and retreat, was convinced that they had died of their original wounds (*The IRA, op. cit.*, p. 399). Allegations of RUC murder circulated for some years, generating anger and bitterness. Quite apart from opening themselves to a charge of murder, of course (however improbable that might have been in the circumstances), the two men would have been of much greater police value were they captured and interrogated. Seán South (1929–57) was an enthusiast for the Irish language which he combined with devout Roman Catholicism, publishing a journal (*An Gath*) for Gaelic-speaking members of the Catholic lay organisation, the Legion of Mary. Feargal O'Hanlon

(1936–57) was an employee of Monaghan County Council and a Gaelic football player.

123 See, for example, Seán MacBride's Dáil speech of 30 November 1955 (n. 950, below).

124 *Evening Herald*, 4 January 1957, 1c–d; 5 January 1957, 1c–d. See also report from British Embassy at PRO DO/35/7811, 3–17 January 1957.

125 South's death also stimulated great enthusiasm in republican-minded circles in the USA. Reporting in the early spring of 1957, Special Branch noted that some £9,000 had been collected in New York by the United Irish Counties Association (PRO NIO CJ/4/843, Memorandum on IRA, 11 March 57, p. 5). This was one of several organisations then collecting, so we may multiply that sum several times to form an estimate of the total stimulated by the Brookeborough raid.

126 Arrests commenced on the night of 8 January 1957 and continued over the next two weeks (*Irish Independent*, 8 January 1957, 7d; 11 January 1957, 7g–h; 19 January 1957, 9d).

127 It was also significant that, despite preparatory work involving the identification of Special Branch officers, following them and collecting information about them, the IRA had apparently not succeeded in getting an agent inside the Branch. This left them at a disadvantage. More importantly, the leadership, never mind the rank and file, seems to have had little notion of operational security, or, if they had, to have failed to practise it.

128 Another indication of wishful thinking overwhelming reality was the failure to prepare and brief a stand-in leadership. A temporary Army Council was put together after the round-ups, but it was crippled by its ad-hoc character and unpreparedness (Bell, *The Secret Army, op. cit.*, p. 301).

129 *Evening Herald*, 19 January 1957, 1a–d; *Northern Whig*, 19 January 1957, 1a–d. Two-thirds of the new barracks was demolished. The railway attack was less effective than might have been hoped because an alert signalman had switched the track, preventing even more damage (*Evening Herald*, 2 March 1957, 1a–d; *Northern Whig*, 4 March 1957, 1h).

130 See *Irish Independent*, 7 March 1957, 13c; 19 March 1957, 3f. There were some unimpressive copycat operations such as the unsuccessful attack on the war memorial at Islandbridge, Dublin, which took place during the Christmas holidays. This commemorated Irishmen who had lost their lives in British service in the two world wars. Even to staunch republicans the attack may have carried a whiff of desecration. The IRA repudiated the action.

131 See PRO NIO CJ/4/843, Memorandum on IRA, 11 March 1957, p. 7.

132 It also declared sinful any expression of approval, assistance or cooperation with such an organisation, and 'if the cooperation or assistance be notable, the sin committed is mortal' (*Irish Independent*, 19 January 1957, 9d). In Roman Catholic teaching, a mortal sin condemned the miscreant to eternal damnation, should he or she die unshriven. Absolution and divine forgiveness could be obtained by the sacrament of confession, but this was expressly forbidden to the impenitent – such as those who continued in IRA service.

133 PRO NIO CJ/4/843, Memorandum on IRA, 11 March 1957, p. 8. There was an ingenious attempt by the Christle splinter group and its supporters to deflect Church condemnation. In June 1957, Dublin Corporation adopted a resolution asking the government to make arrangements for Roman Catholic detainees at Dublin's bridewell to attend mass on Sundays and 'Holidays of Obligation' (certain saints' days and other Church celebrations). This was dismissed by the Gardaí as propaganda on behalf of the splinter group, twenty-eight members of which had been arrested in the course of a supposed walking tour in the Wicklow mountains. All had been released since they had no documents and no names, and the tour was described as a 'stunt' to provoke the police. It had not been possible to process all the men on the morning of Sunday, 2 June, and therefore some had been unable to attend mass. No further

action was recommended (NAI JUS/8/1049, Memorandum, 27 June 1957; *Irish Times*, 3 June 1957, 1a; 4 June 1957, 3e–f).

134 The results were (1954 figures in parentheses) Fianna Fáil 78 (65), Fine Gael 40 (50), Labour 12 (19), Clann na Talmhan 3 (5), Clann na Poblachta 1 (3), Sinn Féin 4 (0), Independent 9 (5) (*Irish Independent*, 8 March 1957, 9a–g).

135 The role of the Costello government – or parts of it – in the secret and highly irregular inquest on Connie Green, one of the Rosslea attack party, showed the difference in temper of the two administrations (see above, p. 787).

136 *Irish News*, 5 July 1957, 1a–e; *Northern Whig*, 5 July 1957, 1a–c. There followed a heavy police and army deployment in border areas.

137 A total of sixty-three people were detained in raids in Dublin, Cork, Dundalk, Drogheda, Wexford, Ennis and other locations (*Irish News*, 8 July 1957, 1a–c; *Northern Whig*, 8 July 1957, 1b–c). Special Branch reported that the Irish authorities had completely disorganised IRA plans for the winter campaign. It also noted that the new staff for the IRA's Dublin battalion were interned as soon as they were appointed (PRO NIO CJ/4/843, Special Branch briefing, October 1957).

138 *Irish News*, 8 July 1957, 1a–c. Mrs Margaret Buckley, Sinn Féin Vice-President, the only woman attending the meeting, was not detained. The following day, those arrested were moved to the Curragh (*Irish News*, 9 July 1957, 1b).

139 Mick Ryan, on active service from the opening of the campaign, recalled that by June 1957, 'anyone that had a bit of sense knew… six months into the campaign, that it was finished' (interview).

140 Sergeant Ovens (forty-four) was a married man with two daughters (*Irish News*, 19 August 1957, 1b–c).

141 *Northern Whig*, 19 August 1957, 1a–c. This incident led to the controversial Mallon and Talbot case (see below, pp. 797–81).

142 *Northern Whig*, 4 September 1957, 1d–e.

143 *Irish Independent*, 26 September 1957, 7b–c. On 22 October 1957, Topping informed Stormont that, in the previous twelve months, there had been over 200 incidents, causing in excess of £600,000 worth of damage. During the same period, forty-one persons had been convicted and sentences totalling 217 years imposed. Thirty-three cases were pending. *NIPD*, vol. 41, col. 2029, 22 October 1957.

144 The circulation of the *United Irishman* was also estimated at 120,000 copies per issue – an impossibly large figure.

145 Units of the British Army with experience of the anti-EOKA campaign in Greece were now being rotated through Northern Ireland. The Duke of Wellington's regiment was one such, and, as B-Special officer Wallace Clark records, 'had much to tell us' (*Guns in Ulster, op. cit.*, p. 111).

146 See, for example, reports of such encounters in the autumn of 1957: *Irish News*, 11 October 1957, 1e; 17 October 1957, 1f–g; 2 December 1957, 1a–b.

147 PRO NIO CJ/4/843, RUC Special Branch intelligence briefing, March 1958. Bell confirms that explosives were being prepared by an active service unit of four men (*The Secret Army, op. cit.*, p. 314). Initially only three bodies were found at the one-storey farmhouse at Carrickcarnon, Co. Louth, approximately 300 yards south of the border, in secluded country, yet close to the Dundalk–Newry Road. A fourth body was discovered in a field, 70 yards from the cottage, and the fifth body was found even later. Body parts and fragments were blown across nearby hedges and fields (see *Irish News*, 13 November 1957, 1b–c; *Northern Whig*, 12 November 1957, 1a–c). The owner of the cottage was Michael Watters (fifty-four), a supporter but not a member of the IRA. The men were Oliver Craven (twenty-one) of Newry, George Keenan (twenty-nine) of Enniscorthy, Patrick Parle (twenty-seven) of Wexford and Paul Smith (thirty-two) of Bessbrooke. See *United Irishman*, January 1958, 7c–d and 12a–c;

Irish News, 12 November 1957, 1b–c, 6a. Bell notes that this was the greatest single IRA loss since the Civil War (p. 313).

148 This element in guerrilla warfare has been analysed in numerous articles and books. In 1963, Sir Fitzroy Maclean provided a succinct overview in an essay for the Royal United Services Institute. This has been republished in the *Journal of the Royal United Services Institute*, vol. 156, no. 1, February/March 2011, pp. 90–6. It provided particularly interesting insights, addressing counter-insurgency as well as the imperatives of irregular warfare. Coming from an author experienced both in soldiering and politics, the short piece has a particularly apt quality.

149 PRONI HA/9/2/885, Memorandum to Minister, 20 September 1957.

150 Special Powers Act, 1922, s.5. The Special Powers Acts were withdrawn after the war but reintroduced in December 1956, following the first wave of attacks. Powers to flog were also provided by the Larceny Act, 1916, s.37(6), amended in part by the Prison Act (Northern Ireland), 1953 (1 Eliz. II, c.18, s.4[2]). The latter placed more controls on the punishment, prescribing the maximum number of strokes and specifying the instrument to be used.

151 PRONI HA/9/2/885, Memorandum to Minister, 20 September 1957. The birch continued to be used (but very infrequently) in ordinary criminal cases. In 1961, birching was inflicted on three prisoners convicted of robbery with violence (PRONI HA/9/2/885, Ministry of Home Affairs to Governor, Belfast Prison, 17 January 1967).

152 See below, pp. 801–3, for more on the European Commission and Court, and events in Ireland.

153 The police made no headway in the investigation, and, five weeks after the killing, the Northern Ireland government offered a reward of £5,000 for information leading to the arrest and conviction of those responsible. This was an unusual course for the Ministry of Home Affairs, and the reward was, for the time, a large sum (*Irish Independent*, 26 September 1957, 7b–c).

154 There was an interval of several weeks between arrest on 19 November 1957 and committal proceedings on 9 January 1958. On a defence application the trial was then adjourned to the next sitting of the Belfast Commission in April. The trial commenced on 22 April but had to be abandoned on the second day because of the illness of a juror. A further adjournment meant that it did not commence until 28 July 1958 – eight and a half months after the two had been arrested.

155 The accounts that follow are taken from the report of the trial in the *Irish Times* (30 July 1958, 7g). The Connolly Association (a CPGB front organisation) also published an account of the trial by an English lawyer, John Hostettler: *Torture Trial in Belfast* (London: Connolly Association, 1958). This is certainly not the independent version of events it purported to be, but it does provide a useful narrative of the Mallon and Talbot case.

156 One of the effects of prolonged sleep deprivation, combined with high-pressure interrogation, can be hallucination. In these circumstances, pretending to be a resurrected murder victim could be terrifying. An experienced interrogator might be aware of this mechanism. Civil litigation in which I was involved in the USA (the aftermath of a wrongful conviction) included such an allegation arising out of prolonged interrogation.

157 Pollution in various forms is a frequently mentioned abuse of interrogation procedures, and of torture. Forcing a person to eat polluted food or to drink tainted water, or otherwise contaminating them, induces a sense of degradation and hopelessness, and makes the victim more willing to submit to the demands of the interrogator. One of the abuses of suspected terrorist prisoners in Iraq has combined pollution with sexual humiliation by smearing menstrual blood on male Muslim prisoners and forcing them to wear women's underwear on their heads. See, for example,

Karen J. Greenberg, 'The Rule of Law Finds Its Golem', in Karen J. Greenberg (ed.), *The Torture Debate in America* (Cambridge: Cambridge University Press, 2006), pp. 1–9, at p. 5.

158 This form of torture has been used widely over the past few years (with White House authority) in the form of 'waterboarding'. Manual choking is notoriously dangerous, as the regular fatalities from auto-erotic strangulation demonstrate. Choking or simulated drowning cause the victim great distress and a fear of imminent death.

159 Elwyn Jones (1909–89) was a distinguished and experienced barrister. Born in the Welsh heartland of Llanelli, he was educated at the University of Wales, Aberystwyth, and the University of Cambridge. He was a participant in the Nuremberg Trials (Junior Counsel) and, in 1945, was returned as an MP in the Labour interest. He became Attorney General in the Labour government of 1964 and served until 1970. With the return of another Labour administration in 1974, he was appointed Lord Chancellor (until 1979). An outstanding legal and political career was in the making when he represented Mallon and Talbot.

160 Those were not, by any means, the first allegations of police misbehaviour during interrogations. The previous November, the Nationalist MP for South Down had raised at Stormont allegations of an interrogation so severe that his constituent, Seamus O'Hare, subsequently suffered a mental collapse. While in RUC custody, he had become distressed and had been released. William Topping had simply dismissed the complaint, stating that the young man (who was not connected with paramilitary activities) was 'of a nervous disposition'. It was his disposition rather than any police action that had caused his distress. This answer was denounced by the MP who raised it, Joseph Connellan (Nationalist Party), and by Murtagh Morgan (Irish Labour Party), MP for Belfast Dock (see *NIPD*, vol. 41, cols. 2391–2 and 2448–9, 12 November 1957).

161 Arthur Black (1888–1968) had been educated in Belfast and Cambridge, called to the English Bar in 1915 and appointed King's Counsel fourteen years later. A Unionist, he was returned to Stormont in 1925 (South Belfast). Attorney General, 1939–41. Retired from politics in November 1941 on being appointed Recorder of Belfast and a County Court judge. Northern Ireland Supreme Court, 1943–40 and Lord Justice of Appeal, 1949–64.

162 *Belfast Newsletter*, 6 August 1958, 5g–h; *Evening Herald*, 5 August 1958, 1f–g; 6 August, 4c–d; *Irish News*, 6 August 1958, 1a–c.

163 PRONI HA/32/1/11337, County Inspector J. G. T. Nelson to R. F. R. Dunbar, 20 October 1958. See *United Irishman*, January 1958, 1d–e ('British Terror in Ireland') and 2c–d ('British Torture in Ireland').

164 *New Statesman*, 16 August 1958. The *New Statesman* was a much respected Labour-leaning journal and, at that time, under the long-time editorship of Kingsley Martin, a distinguished journalist, widely influential in left and liberal circles.

165 The Ministry of Home Affairs put together a rebuttal letter which appeared in the *Manchester Guardian* on 19 August 1958, over the signature of Professor Sir Douglas Savory. A draft of this letter is to be found in the Mallon and Talbot file (PRONI HA/32/1/11337). The *New Statesman* (23 August 1958) published a letter from Lieutenant General Sir Brian Kimmins, formerly GOC Britain forces in Northern Ireland. In essence, this simply stated that he had worked closely with the RUC, found them to be at all levels to be considerate, reasonable and humane men. The torture charges against them were 'fantastic'. More than somewhat naively, the general claimed that as a result of his eighteen months in Northern Ireland 'I feel I can speak impartially.'

166 Henri Alleg, *The Question* (London: John Calder, 1958). This received much notice as part of a growing international awareness of the bitter war being waged in Algeria

between the Front de Libération Nationale and the French Army and security authorities. Jean-Paul Sartre provided a preface. After similar types of allegations, a major inquiry had been launched into the torture and ill-treatment of Mau Mau suspects in Kenya. See *Record of Proceedings and Evidence into the Deaths of Eleven Mau Mau Detainees at Hola Camp in Kenya*, Parliamentary Papers, Cmd. 795 (London: HMSO, 1959).

167 PRONI HA/32/1/1337, John D. Stewart to Colonel Topping, 22 August 1958.

168 *New Statesman*, 4 October 1958. The new allegations concerned some of a group of thirty-five men arrested in south Co. Londonderry, following IRA attacks.

169 PRONI HA/32/1/1337, British Embassy, Washington, DC, to American Department, Foreign Office, 14 June 1958. The Embassy's concern may have been increased by a stirring of interest within of the United Nations.

170 NAI JUS/8/1085, letters of 27 and 29 January 1958. Coyne passed on to the Taoiseach's office the Commissioner's confirmation that he had no further information. The Irish Republican Publicity Bureau in December 1957 published a four-page leaflet on the Talbot and Mallon case. With a degree of coyness, it summarised the murder: 'Near Coalisland, Co. Tyrone, an RUC Sergeant named Ovens was killed in an explosion in a disused house at Brackaville, in August 1957.' The blame for the incident, it implied, lay with the Stormont authorities who had offered 'rewards for information leading to the capture of Irish freedom fighters'. *British Torture in Ireland* (Dublin: Irish Republican Publicity Bureau, 1957).

171 The County Council adopted a resolution protesting at 'the cruel and unjust treatment' meted out in 'Britain Occupied Ireland'. It also condemned internment in the twenty-six counties and called for the immediate release of those interned (*Kerryman*, 8 February 1958, 15e–f).

172 Before the explosives' and arms' charges were brought, however, a question was put in the Dáil by Michael Donnellan (Clann na Talmhan, Deputy for Galway North). This may doubtless have afforded Donnellan the satisfaction of vituperative language, such as 'Republicans are tortured day and night by members of the RUC and of British military forces' and 'a torture mill has been established in Occupied Ireland by the Stormont Junta'. It is less clear whether he was able to attract support in this way (NAI JUS/8/1085, Notice of Question; see also *Dáil Debates*, vol. 165, col. 2, 12 February 1958).

173 Within the general framework of Northern Ireland's sentencing tariffs, these were heavy sentences.

174 See pp. 801–3. See also John Maguire, 'Internment, the IRA and the Lawless Case in Ireland, 1957–61', *Journal of the Oxford History Society*, 2004.

175 The European Convention on Human Rights, drawing on the 1948 United Nations' Universal Declaration of Human Rights, was agreed by the Council of Europe in 1950. It was ratified by the Republic of Ireland in 1953. MacBride was involved in these developments, as a lawyer and a politician, both in the Council of Europe and in Ireland. To give effect to the Convention, two bodies were established. The Commission comprised a member from each state of the Council of Europe, elected by the Council of Europe's Committee of Ministers. The European Court of Human Rights consisted of judges of the member states, selected in the same way. The Commission's function was to review cases, to decide if they fell within its remit and to assess whether a friendly settlement were possible. Only if a settlement were not possible would a case be submitted to the Court. The procedure, inevitably, was protracted, but this was a body intended to be of last rather than first resort.

176 MacBride's remarkable life and character are dealt with in Anthony J. Jordan's instructive *Sean MacBride: A Biography* (Dublin: Blackwater Press, 1993). This evolution in his political outlook and legal thinking and practice eventually led, in 1961, to his becoming a founding member of Amnesty International, the bestowal of the Nobel

Prize (1976) and, bizarrely, to acceptance of the Soviet Union's Lenin Peace Prize (1977).

177 Coogan, *The IRA, op. cit.*, p. 411.

178 See General Orders 1 and 2. All General Orders were brought together, with some explanatory material, in *An tÓglach*, September 1958. (This mimeographed journal was for the internal use of members of the IRA.) A transcribed copy may be found at NAI JUS/8/1078, Lawless Case, papers.

179 NAI DFA/93/3/127, Part VI, Misc. Papers, Garda Memorandum, 15 December 1958. Lawless, while still a teenager, had assembled a youth group, the Irish National Brotherhood, which was later absorbed into the IRA's youth movement, Na Fianna Éireann.

180 Sean Edmunds, *The Gun, the Law and the Irish People: From 1912 to the Aftermath of the Arms Trial 1970* (Tralee: Anvil Books, 1970), p. 204.

181 *Irish Independent*, 11 December 1957, 10d–e; *Evening Herald*, 11 December 1957, 1f.

182 *Irish Times*, 3 July 1961, 6a–b.

183 Its rebuttal brief may be found at NAI JUS/8/1063 and 1078.

184 The last internees left on 11 March 1959 (*Kerryman*, 14 March 1959, 19d; *Irish Independent*, 12 March 1959, 12c–d).

185 See above, pp. 808–9.

186 *Dáil Debates*, vol. 192, cols. 838–42, 23 November 1961. Seán Lemass (now Taoiseach, de Valera having resigned in June 1959) referred to 'the widespread condemnation of the acts of violence on the Border and the emphatic repudiation of those who supported them at the recent General Election'. Notwithstanding this, the government had confidential information indicating that further IRA activity was being prepared. Everything that could be done within the normal law had been done, but the need to suppress the campaign of violence speedily meant that the Special Criminal Court should be reactivated (see below, p. 809). The government (and constitutional parties) were, moreover, able to use the outcome of the general election on 4 October 1961 as a pointer to the political and moral isolation of the IRA. Running twenty-one candidates, Sinn Féin garnered only 36,393 first-preference votes in a total turnout of 688,691 – a proportion of less than 3 per cent; two-thirds of their candidates lost their deposits (*Irish Independent*, 6 October 1961, 13d–e).

187 A sergeant and seven soldiers were overpowered by five masked and armed men. One of the soldiers was shot in the stomach, and two others, returning from a late dance, were hit on the head with revolver butts. Two soldiers, who had been tied up, freed themselves and sounded the alarm, and the three raiders fled. There were similarities with earlier raids. The REME Training Battalion may have been thought a safer target than an infantry regiment. It is probable that a soldier, Corporal Frank Skuse, had provided the information necessary to mount the raid. Skuse went absent without leave the day before the raid and had been at Arborfield two and a half years before when that REME camp had been raided (*Irish Times*, 17 February 1958, 1a–c). Skuse made it back to Dublin, where he received a six-month sentence under the OASA. An attempt to rescue him from Mountjoy by means of a ruse failed (*The Times*, 14 May 1958, 9a).

188 Coogan, *The IRA, op. cit.*, p. 382. Coogan states that nine men altogether were involved in the operation. There was a raid on a Nottingham gunsmith on 20 February 1958, which the RUC attributed to the IRA. Other accounts based on interviews with IRA members do not, however, claim this raid (see PRO NIO, RUC Special Branch intelligence briefing, March 1958). The same briefing noted that a REME deserter had provided the information for the Blandford raid and that he may even have taken part himself. For the IRA account of the raid, which provides a number of details, see the *United Irishman*, March 1958, 1a–e and 12b: 'British Military Camp Seized, Held: Full Story'.

189 Saor Uladh continued to mount fairly ambitious operations. On 13 May 1957, it used explosives to destroy lock-gates on the Newry Canal (*Examiner* [Dundalk], 18 May 1957, 3g). Coogan reports that younger IRA members were more willing to have contact with Kelly and Saor Uladh (*The IRA, op. cit.*, pp. 361–2). On one occasion, Kelly was said to have handed over a large quantity of ammunition but a senior figure in the IRA ordered its return. Another young IRA man on the run found Kelly's organisation more efficient than this own.

190 Saor Uladh did not abide by the IRA Standing Order no. 8, forbidding actions in the Republic. Its raids for explosives ran counter to the IRA's repeated and rather desperate assurances to the Irish government and population that IRA force was directed entirely at Northern Ireland.

191 Almost the whole GHQ staff appear to have been netted: Seán Cronin (Chief of Staff), Mick McCarthy, Seamus Graham, Seán Hennessy and Hugh Heaney (*Irish Independent*, 1 October 1958, 9d; Bell, *The Secret Army, op. cit.*, p. 322).

192 Bell states that there were twenty-seven incidents in 1959 and twenty-six in 1960; this compares with 341 in 1957 (*The Secret Army, op. cit.*, pp. 328–9).

193 Bell, *The Secret Army, op. cit.*, pp. 322–3.

194 NAI TAOIS/CAB/19, Meeting of the Cabinet, 17 February 1959.

195 Sentenced men were not released nor were they given partial amnesty. All served their full sentences less the usual remission.

196 Two of these were attributed by the RUC to Saor Uladh; the rest were carried out by the IRA (PRO NIO CJ/4/843, RUC, Security Intelligence Review, July 1958). In the first action of the month, organised by Saor Uladh, twenty-year-old Aloysius Hand was shot by RUC officers (*Belfast Telegraph*, 3 July 1958, 11a–c; 4 July 1958, 1b–c; PRONI HA/32/1/955).

197 *Evening Herald*, 16 July 1958, 1a–d, 11c–d; *Irish News*, 17 July 1958, 1f–h; *Belfast Newsletter*, 17 July 1958, 5f–g; 18 July 1958, 2g–h. Constable Ross's revolver and ammunition were taken by his killers, who escaped across the nearby border. He managed, despite his injuries, to walk to a nearby house but, having been taken to hospital, died there the following day. He left a wife and child.

198 PRO NIO CJ/4/843, RUC Intelligence Review, July 1958.

199 *Belfast Newsletter*, 17 July 1958, 5f–g. Customs posts had been destroyed so many times that it was decided that at some locations business would be conducted from caravans, towed away from the site each evening.

200 PRO NIO CJ/4/843, RUC Intelligence Review, July 1958. Bell gives a different account of the men's escape (*The Secret Army, op. cit.*, pp. 320–1). In particular, his informants said that the three had been arrested in the cathedral's confessional booths. There was no mention of a hideout in the vault. It is now difficult to judge which account is the more accurate, but, since the creation of a hideout in the cathedral would have hugely angered the Catholic hierarchy and clergy and scandalised the laity as akin to sacrilege, it seems unlikely that the IRA would have taken that risk. On the other hand, the confidential RUC report is unequivocal and emphasises that the hideout showed evidence of use. All parties may have considered it wiser not to make the full details known, lest they inflamed sectarian feeling.

201 PRO NIO CJ/4/843, RUC Intelligence Review, July 1958; *Irish News*, 17 July 1958, 1f–h; Coogan, *The IRA, op. cit.*, p. 416.

202 *Irish Press*, 2 July 1958, 3b–c.

203 *Dáil Debates*, vol. 170, cols. 1072 *et seq.*, 17 July 1958.

204 See below, p. 1088. See also *Irish Times*, 16 March 1959, 1a–c.

205 5 *Hansard*, vol. 602, col. 65(w), 19 March 1959.

206 *Irish Times*, 16 March 1959, 1a–c.

207 See below, pp. 1082–3.

208 The new council consisted of Seán Cronin (again Chief of Staff), Ruairí Ó Brádaigh (Adjutant General) and Cathal Goulding (Quartermaster General). The other members were Frank McCarry, John Joe McGirl, Seán O'Dowd and J. B. O'Hagan.

209 Here the estimates were wildly off. The IRA leadership had managed to get only a couple of dozen volunteers to agree to reopen the campaign, according to Mick Ryan, who was one of them. These men attended a special training camp in the summer of 1959. The intention was that they would operate as one unit. In two subsequent training camps, half of the men were arrested by the Gardaí. If that recollection is correct, only about a dozen men were then available for action in Northern Ireland. (Interview.) This was a tiny fraction of RUC estimates.

210 PRO NIO CJ/4/843, Terrorist Campaign against Northern Ireland by IRA and Saor Uladh, 31 July 1959.

211 Ryan interview.

212 *United Irishman*, March 1959, 5c.

213 See, for example, NAI JUS/8/1099, 1100, 1101 and 1103.

214 See above, pp. 801–3.

215 See below, pp. 1082–3.

216 See above, pp. 781–2.

217 See below, pp. 1082–3.

218 The RUC intelligence assessment was very precise that the older methods had been rejected in favour of EOKA tactics, introduced by Goulding and Canning as a result of their close prison contacts with Greek Cypriots. RUC members had already been selected for murder, the assessment insisted, and the methods by which they were to be killed were agreed. Yet again this was unreliable intelligence, poorly assessed, as the following months demonstrated (PRO NIO CJ/4/843, Terrorist Campaign against Northern Ireland by IRA and Saor Uladh). IRA–EOKA cooperation was certainly mooted, but came to nothing of a practical nature. The ending of the EOKA campaign in 1959 and Cypriot independence the following year wrote *finis* to what must always have been an improbable alliance. Archbishop Makarios, the EOKA political leader, made statements against Partition which were carried by the *United Irishman* (see, for example, April 1958, 1d–e).

219 See Coogan, *The IRA*, *op. cit.*, p. 415. On his release, Cronin resigned altogether from the IRA and resumed his career as a journalist.

220 Interview. That there had been a catastrophic falling away in sympathy and support was shown by *United Irishman* sales and distribution. Mick Ryan recalled that it was very hard to get it out because IRA members were demoralised about selling it, and they were the only ones that were buying and reading it (interview). This meant that the IRA's press frontage was very small indeed. In the early autumn of 1967, Curragh camp censors noted that internees appeared to believe that the only provincial newspapers that gave Sinn Féin a break were the *Kerryman* and the *Longford Leader* (MA, PM/I/ADM/12, report of 8 September 1957).

221 *Northern Whig*, 26 January 1961, 1a–h. The IRA tried to justify the killing by claiming that Anderson was a spy.

222 *Derry Journal*, 31 March 1961, 1b–c.

223 Bell, *The Secret Army*, *op. cit.*, pp. 331–2. Some intimation of this proposal may have been the foundation of the RUC's predictions of a terrorist campaign. There had been contacts and discussions with the Felsted raiders and the ill-fated Nikos Sampson in Wakefield Prison, and the IRA saw many common features and drew encouragement from the EOKA struggle. Sampson had been sentenced to death for the killing of a serviceman in Cyprus, reprieved and transferred to Wakefield Prison. In 1974, he played front man in the Greek junta's coup in Cyprus, was president for eight days and was later sentenced to twenty years' imprisonment. For background

to the contacts between Irish and Cypriot prisoners in British prisons in the 1950s, see Vias Livades, *Cypriot and Irish Political Prisoners Held in British Prisons, 1956–1959* (Nicosia: Power Publishing, 2008). This is passionately partisan but gives interesting detail and recollections. For all the warmth between the groups, there was virtually no possibility of joint military action or cooperation. They did, however, work together in a partly successful escape plan on 12 February 1959 (see below, pp. 868–70).

224 An attack on a dance hall would almost inevitably have involved inflicting injury or death on young civilians, many of them girls, which, added to the notion of machine-gunning off-duty soldiers, would have produced the deepest revulsion in feeling. In little more than a decade, however, there would be reservoirs of feelings so bitter that even such a deed would fail to affect them.

225 The first Army Council meeting, in October 1961, was beset by bad weather, and only Ó Brádaigh (Chief of Staff) and Ryan (Director of Operations) turned up (interview).

226 *Irish Independent*, 6 October 1961, 13d–e.

227 *Irish News*, 13 November 1961, 1a–c; *Northern Whig*, 13 November 1961, 1a–h.

228 *Dáil Debates*, vol. 192, cols. 838–42, 23 November 1961.

229 The Special Military Tribunal had never gone out of existence but had not been used since the wartime years. Only two officers (Colonels John Joyce and Frank Bennett) remained on the panel, and three new appointments were made to bring it up to its full complement of five (*Irish Times*, 23 November 1961, 1a–d; NAI TAOIS G3/27). Authority for the court came from Part V of the OASA. The government had extensive powers to declare certain offences or categories of offences as scheduled and subject to the jurisdiction of the Special Criminal Court. Cases were referred to the Court by the Attorney General. The officers deliberated without a jury. Appeals could be made to the Court of Criminal Appeal, with leave from the Special Criminal Court, or by means of a preliminary appeal for a hearing.

230 *Evening Press*, 27 November 1961, 1f–h.

231 There were twenty-five sentences imposed by the end of December 1961.

232 *Evening Herald*, 24 November 1961, 3e–f.

233 The three were treated for facial injuries and returned to duty (*Evening Press*, 27 November 1961, 1f–h).

234 *NIPD*, vol. 52, col. 564, 28 November 1962. There had been a mixed response from Stormont politicians to the reactivation of the Special Criminal Court. Brian Faulkner firmly welcomed the announcement, saying that the Court had been helpful in stopping terrorist activities across the border (*NIPD*, vol. 52, col. 1785, 4 December 1962). The former Northern Ireland Attorney General, J. Edmund Warnock, said that Lemass's announcement was 'not worth a damn until the Éire authorities arrest the man responsible for the murder of Constable Hunter' (*Irish Times*, 23 November 1961, 1a).

235 *United Irishman*, March 1962, 1a–c; *Irish Times*, 27 February 1962, 1a–c. Ryan, who was Director of Operations at the time (a positively Ruritanian flourish, since the army had shrunk to a dozen or two activists) recalled that some supporters reacted badly 'because it was made to appear that the IRA had given up the struggle for freedom. And we had to talk to people and make it clear in the statement that it was this "phase" that was over.' There was a reference to reorganisation: 'a cheeky statement in a sense, because we were broken and defeated, totally' (interview).

236 See *United Irishman*, March 1962, 1c. The IRA stated that it had lost nine in total, two in action and seven accidentally. In addition, a Sinn Féin organiser had been killed, it claimed, by crown forces near Swanlinbar. See also Chris Ryder, *The RUC, 1922–2000: A Force under Fire* (London: Arrow Books, 2000), pp. 94–5.

237 Ryder, *The RUC, op. cit.*, p. 94.

238 Bell, *The Secret Army, op. cit.*, p. 334.

239 See above, p. 785.

15

CONVICTED PRISONERS IN NORTHERN IRELAND AND ENGLAND, 1954–62

Accommodation

Largely because, politics apart, Northern Ireland was a law-abiding part of the world, diligently observant in its religions, social control stiffened by family, community and locality, there was relatively little demand for prison services. Even while Britain experienced an upswing in crime statistics in the post-war period, Northern Ireland retained its gratifying respectability. In the early 1950s, its prisons held an average daily population of around 350.[1] As we have seen, Belfast Prison had never been intended to hold long-term prisoners, but, because after the 1922 division of the country there were no convict prisons in the new Northern state, Belfast had eventually been adapted.[2] A wing was then set aside for long-term men (three years and over), who, until 1953, served sentences of penal servitude and were usually referred to as convicts. The design of the prison, as others of its mid-Victoria vintage, allowed each wing to be adminis-tered independently and allowed for the principal categories of prisoners to be separated from each other.

Within A Wing there were several different types of long-term offenders. Most republican prisoners were held on A2 landing; the ground floor was occupied by other 'star' (first-time) prisoners. Unlike many prisons in Britain at the time, it was not deemed necessary to hold sex offenders separately to protect them from attack by other prisoners. There were also in the wing some prisoners who had been found by the courts to be habitual offenders and who were serving long sentences of preventive detention.[3] In a larger prison system, some of these sub-categories would have been held in separate wings or prisons, but this was not possible in Northern Ireland, and the men simply had to be managed and had to accept that they had to get on together. This mixture probably lessened the possibility of any direct conflict between the republican prisoners and the authorities since, in any action, protestors could not expect solidarity from this range of fellow inmates. It also meant that the IRA and Saor Uladh men had to be careful in conducting any activity that ran counter to the rules. Strict though the convict culture was in its prohibition of informing, and draconian though the retaliation was when 'snitches' were uncovered (or even suspected), some among the ordinary criminal prisoners would have passed on information to obtain favours were the opportunity to arise.

While Northern Ireland had not experienced the rapid rise in criminal offences and consequent committals of other parts of the UK, there had been a gradual increase between 1940 and 1951, and this, together with the limitations of its prison estate, created difficulties. A multi-purpose establishment, such as Belfast, because of the need to keep separate at least the principal categories of prisoner, is always more constrained in its accommodation and complex in its administration than the total number of cells might suggest. With the influx of internees after December 1956 (discussed in Chapter 16), the limit to the prison's capabilities seemed to have been reached. The need to find space for more long-term prisoners brought a crisis, of sorts, in the autumn of 1958. The Governor, Major Lance Thompson, and the Ministry of Home Affairs agreed that it was not desirable to hold long-termers two to a cell and began to cast around for means to make more space for them in Belfast Prison. Armagh, hitherto reserved for Northern Ireland's tiny population of female prisoners, seemed to offer a solution.[4] Its security fell far short of that needed for more serious offenders, but it could be used with reasonable confidence for short-term and largely petty offenders. Since there was nowhere else to hold the women and there was an overriding requirement to keep them completely separate from the men, not all the available space could be used. Separation and the configuration of the prison limited the total to be transferred from Belfast to fifty-eight. No political prisoners were among this number, but the relocation freed the required space in Belfast for long-termers.[5]

Liam Kelly

None of the IRA prisoners of the later 1950s attempted to confront the authorities with the customary republican demands: exemption from labour, the right to wear civilian clothes, freedom of association and all business to be conducted through their OC. The state of public opinion, their small numbers, the implacable determination of the prison management and the Northern Ireland government and, possibly, the example of the painful and fruitless efforts of their predecessors in the 1940s, all in various proportions and ways affected this decision. There had also been a very short-lived attempt to win political status, in November 1953. This was well publicised but almost immediately abandoned and may also have been a factor in these considerations.

Morally, Liam Kelly had reasonable grounds for claiming political or at least non-criminal status, were English practice followed. He had been convicted of sedition, and, largely on the urging of Irish members, Westminster had in 1879 decided that these offenders should be subject to a special regime.[6] It is true that Kelly's seditious statements had all but crossed over into incitement, but that was not the charge on which he had been convicted. In October 1953, he had been elected to Stormont for Mid-Tyrone, defeating the sitting Nationalist member by an 800 majority in a poll of 7,600. Until that point, Kelly, who had for a decade or more been associated with violent republicanism and who had been imprisoned and interned for it, had been cautious – noticeably guarded in his public speaking and conduct. Perhaps he counted on a degree of immunity as a result of his election victory, or maybe he was swept away by the spark of victory and the enthusiasm of his supporters, but, for whatever reason, on 21 and 23 October he made rash statements during victory speeches at Carrickmore, Co. Tyrone and his home village of Pomeroy, as a result of which he was arrested and charged with sedition.[7] At the Northern Ireland Winter Assizes on 4 December 1953, he was convicted and ordered to enter into recognisances to keep the peace for five years or, alternatively, to be imprisoned for a year.[8] Having refused to recognise the authority of the court, Kelly could hardly backtrack and enter into a recognisance, and he was duly sent to prison. The whole incident was an uncharacteristic, unnecessary and unproductive confrontation. Normally his tactics were a great deal more pragmatic and flexible than those of the IRA.[9]

During his pre-trial remand at Belfast Prison, Kelly told his wife that were he convicted and sentenced he would refuse to wear prison uniform.[10] This remark was duly noted and reported by the officer supervising the visit. Major Thompson decided to follow the policy adopted to deal with republican prisoners who, ten years before, had made the same protest.[11] Kelly would be deprived of all privileges (including letters and visits), locked in a cell from which everything would be removed, except for a blanket and the prison uniform: 'This is the only way to force him to put on prison garb as if we make him too comfortable by leaving his bedding he would be content to lie in bed.' (Bed and bedding would be removed each morning and returned at night.) Asking for the Ministry's comments, Major Thompson observed, apropos the blanket that '[t]he last lot who refused to wear clothes were left absolutely naked, but I don't think that would be wise at this time of the year'.[12]

A few days later, Kelly confirmed his intentions. In a memorandum to the Governor and the Ministry he declared that, 'I shall not submit to the indignity of wearing the garb of a convicted criminal. I shall offer no resistance if any of my own apparel is removed, but will don no other.' But not all was meekness. The 'charge' against him was political, and, in the event of 'conviction' (his quotation marks) were prison officers to use violence against him to enforce the donning of the uniform, 'inevitably such action must have decidedly unpleasant repercussions'.[13] Yet, in the accompanying note, he assured Major Thompson that his decision had been taken 'in no spirit of rancour'. Indeed, he continued, he had been 'most favourably impressed by the improvements effected here under your administration, and desire to express any appreciation of the courtesy shown me whilst awaiting "trial"'.[14]

After sentencing on 4 December 1953, and on Kelly's return from court, Major Thompson told him what would happen should he refuse to wear the prison uniform. There was no backing down, and Kelly insisted that, having given the matter careful thought (and having nailed his colours to the mast in public state-ments), he was prepared to accept the consequences. Thompson then asked if he would take off his civilian clothes or if it would be necessary to use prison staff; Kelly replied that he would undress himself. Thompson advised Kelly to think about the matter overnight and sent him to his cell in civilian clothing; he also asked the Roman Catholic chaplain, Father Patrick McAlister, to intervene. Having seen Kelly, on Saturday, 5 December 1953, the chaplain reported his belief that Kelly might see reason and suggested a further short period of grace. Reinforcements were brought in on the Sunday afternoon, in the form of Kelly's parish priest from Pomeroy, and, after further conversation, Kelly agreed to put on the uniform.[15]

Having marched himself to the top of the hill and down again without even a skirmish, Kelly, the republican firebrand, scorner of Stormont and con-temptuous of IRA GHQ, was in an awkward position: credibility as well as face had to be saved. His protest would harm nobody but himself and had little hope of landing a political punch. A way out was found, probably through the parish priest. A report appeared in the Monday newspapers that Kelly had spent the earlier part of the weekend in his cell with only a blanket wrapped around him. This was untrue, a ploy to make him look defiant: at no point had he been without clothes. The newspapers were further informed that his newly formed political party, Fianna Uladh, had instructed him to wear prison clothes 'for the sake of his health'. A clever spin was given to the tale in the suggestion that an effort would be made to persuade him to give his recognisances, so that he might be released.[16] Although he had agreed to put on prison clothing, despite his defiant statement in open court and letter to the Governor, Kelly could still assume an heroic stance, sitting in his cell as a man of principle instead of accepting conditional release. He was, indeed, far more pragmatic than the older generation of republican leaders, from whom he had split, and probably regretted painting himself into such a corner. But, whilst his acceptance of the uniform could be represented as a tactical matter, were he to enter into a recognisance he would assuredly lose all credibility, as a 'signer'. He had no option but to remain in prison.

During the months that followed Kelly continued to conform, performing the required labour in prison uniform. There was a minor spat with Major Thompson when he and nineteen others (out of 313 prisoners) were locked in their cells during a concert arranged by the Presbyterian chaplain. The prisoners had been told that the British national anthem would be sung at the end of the concert and that they would be expected to stand. They were given the option of remaining in their cells. Kelly, certainly not willing to rise for 'God Save the Queen', protested that he had been unfairly denied his evening association, since the concert was in lieu of that time; he threatened to have the issue raised in Parliament.[17] He must have realised, however, that this was petty nit-picking, with no little political mileage.

But his months in prison were not wasted. Underlining his importance to non-IRA republicans, and on the initiative of Seán MacBride, Kelly was appointed to the Irish Senate in July 1954, sitting on the Labour Panel.[18] The Ministry of Home Affairs, probably sensing that a political trap had been laid, made no objection to his formally accepting the appointment by signing the Senate roll-book, nor was there a problem when it was further requested that Seán MacBride and two Senators attend Belfast Prison to witness the signing and to speak to Kelly.[19] However, the ceremony was conducted on 14 August 1954, with only the Assistant Clerk to the Senate, Kelly's solicitor (A. B. Agnew) and a prison officer attending.

Having earned maximum remission for good conduct, Kelly was released a few days later, on 19 August: the signing of the Senate Roll had been useful political theatre. That his term in prison had enhanced his standing with republicans and militant nationalists was confirmed that evening when a crowd of several hundred supporters, led by two bands, welcomed him home to Pomeroy. The police had warned that the parade would not be allowed to proceed were the Irish tricolour carried. The prohibition was ignored, and the demonstrators attempted to breach a police cordon. A pitched battle followed, and around forty marchers and twelve RUC men were injured.[20] But nothing in Kelly's experience provided hope or a template for those IRA men, convicted of arms, explosives and kindred offences, who began to trickle into the prison in the months that followed Kelly's release. They faced years of captivity with few hopes of glory and every expectation of protracted hardship.

Regime for long-term prisoners

In his eight years in A Wing, Eamonn Boyce, leader of the Omagh raiders, left it only twice, other than for religious services: once for a hospital visit and again for a dental appointment.[21] Since the IRA men were of previous good character, they were, despite the gravity of their offences, classified as 'Star Class' prisoners.[22] This gave certain benefits, particularly additional time out of cell when they could socialise with others in the Star Class – the original notion being that those unhardened in crime were less likely to corrupt each other. It is doubtful if this optimistic logic applied to highly committed Irish republicans, whose conversations centred around their common identity and thus provided both mutual support and reinforcement of their beliefs. But the men were well behaved and no trouble to staff; they followed the rules and were civil: they wore the prison uniform and carried out the work to which they were assigned.[23] Notionally, though almost never in practice, labour had to be performed for up to eight hours a day, either in workshops or at tasks connected to the running of the prison.[24]

Following the principles established by Victorian prison administrators, the passage of time (accompanied by good behaviour) brought ameliorations in discipline. Association (the chance to mix and socialise after work) was highly prized. It released the prisoner from the debilitating tedium and oppressive loneliness of his cell and provided the diversion of approved games (chess, draughts and the like) and quiet conversation. For the first six months of a long-term prison sentence a man was locked in his cell at 6 p.m.; thereafter, lock-up was 7 p.m., allowing two hours of evening association. Morning unlocking was at 7 a.m., when the men emptied their chamber pots into the slops' sink ('slopping out'). At 7.30 a.m. they could leave their cells for breakfast. This was followed by another half-hour lock-up before being taken to the workshops. After early lunch they were locked up for a further hour, while staff had their meal. A man who was entitled to the maximum time out of cell was therefore locked up for fourteen hours a day and some twenty hours on Sundays.[25] Convicted men, unlike those on remand, or the internees, ate only prison food, a subject for perennial and bitter complaint.[26] This was eased to a minor extent by the parcels which all prisoners were allowed to receive at Christmas time.[27]

The long haul

As we have repeatedly seen, the IRA's procedures were as firmly established as the official regulations and could be paraphrased: 'Wherever in prison two shall meet, one shall be the OC.' Although kept strictly separated from them, the internees of the December 1956 round-up and subsequent arrests were able to make contact with those serving long sentences for various arms-raids offences. The convicted men had made no escape attempts, and their general approach was that one should settle down and serve the sentence. This reinforced itself since staff knew that they need fear little trouble and so left the men alone. GHQ also gave little priority to organising an escape, and the sentenced men did not wish to divert IRA resources.[28] Dublin's suspicions about the Belfast Battalion, the possibility of entrapment and of an escape being turned inside out, were significant considerations. It is doubtful, in any event, that the organisation had the ability or means to organise a break. Moreover, Belfast Prison was a difficult place from which to escape. During the Border Campaign's five and a half years, only one man managed to get away, and he was not part of the IRA organisation at the prison.

Tom Mitchell, sentenced for his part in the Omagh raid of October 1956, eventually became OC of the convicted men.[29] Under his leadership (and he was regularly re-elected), the prisoners continued to live the quiet life, with only minor bickering between themselves and no stand-offs with staff.[30] Since the sentenced men had the status conferred by their actions when on active service, this approach to their imprisonment set the tone for all the IRA men, sentenced and interned alike.

Labour and uniform, as we have seen in earlier periods, were core issues for IRA prisoners. Another point of contention was collective representation: where possible, they tried to get the authorities to deal with their OC rather than with individuals. This was simply not possible at Belfast in the 1950s and was not pursued by the IRA group. Major Thompson used a heavy hand when dealing with staff and prisoners alike. If a prisoner used 'we' in the course of an interview (and all prisoners were entitled to see the Governor), he was immediately checked by

Thompson and told that he represented himself alone. There was, however, some blurring of this position. A prisoner, provided he did not explicitly claim to be a spokesman, could raise a matter of general importance. There was an element of practicality here since the time-wasting alternative would have been for Thompson to hear a dozen or more identical applications. The rules conferred the right upon each prisoner to make a personal application to the governor, and those who so applied had to be seen in person by the governor himself. As the years passed, and the IRA prisoners showed themselves compliant, there was a further easing in relations, and, according to Boyce's recollection, staff were willing to 'overlook little things, and they would unofficially recognise you as a spokesman for the rest, but never admit to it'.[31]

There was even some overt, if tangential, acknowledgement of collective identity. Adhering to the doctrine of the GAA, the IRA men viewed soccer as a foreign game and would not play it. Brahmin-like, they regarded those who had participated in foreign football as contaminated and deserving of exclusion. Arrangements were therefore made, quite amicably it seems, for the small cinder-surfaced football pitch to be made available on alternative nights for soccer and Gaelic football.[32]

The IRA sentenced prisoners during the 1950s differed from earlier groups not only in their compliance with the regime but also in their willingness to mix with non-politicals without expressing synthetic horror or affecting an attitude of moral superiority. Hugh Cunningham, who joined the prison as a basic grade officer in 1955, remembered that A-Wing IRA men were 'willing to talk [to staff] they didn't appear to be as bitter [as later prisoners] in their outlook'.[33] They certainly did not regard themselves as criminals, and they did maintain their collective identity, but, at the same time, 'you come to terms with the fact that everybody is in the same boat'.[34] Another difference with some IRA prisoner groups was their assuming the characteristics of a collective rather than the usual IRA military hierarchy. This was partly due to their small number but also reflected the closeness of their relationships and, perhaps, their personalities. When the Omagh raiders first began to serve their sentences, there were two other IRA men in the prison.[35] The group of ten chose not to have an OC, and it was only some years later that Tom Mitchell was elected to the position. Since the men had decided against confrontation and disruption, the post seems to have been more titular than substantive. The IRA doctrine was that captives lost rank, function and priority, and, although Boyce had secured a very good line out of the prison, there was little for the group to communicate and little that the IRA could have done as a consequence. This was a long way from the 1940s, when a group of angry prisoners, smarting at perceived ill-treatment, sent out requests to have named prison officers threatened or killed.[36]

A complication in the normally neat IRA command chart was the presence, from March 1957, of men who were members of Saor Uladh. Dessie O'Hagan was the first of these (remanded, then sentenced), and a few others followed.[37] They took a pragmatic approach, recognised the IRA structure and acted with but did not subordinate themselves to it. Inevitably there was wariness and occasionally mutual irritation, but no conflicts, and when general issues arose there was consultation. More directly, Saor Uladh prisoners did not have to seek IRA permission before making an application to the authorities for a concession or facility.[38] Where a problem arose concerning all prisoners, the Saor Uladh group appear to have been content to let Tom Mitchell make the representations.[39]

Because the Belfast prison officers generally favoured a 'get-along-together' approach, and because Major Thompson was, by contrast, a textbook martinet, there was no ill-treatment of IRA prisoners – apart from the incidents that occurred in March 1958, when a party of RUC and Special Constabulary men was brought into the prison to search the internees in the wake of an escape attempt.[40] Boyce saw Thompson's management style as a protection for all: 'The rules of the prison, and they were strictly enforced, the very rules of the prison protected us.'[41] Prison officers were, for the times, reasonably paid, and could make overtime earnings, thanks to the Border Campaign and the greater number of prisoners to be accommodated. In the Belfast of the 1950s, such employment, secure and pensionable, was scarce, and the prospect of losing it was a great constraint. Although they benefited in important ways from Thompson's firmness, the prisoners, sensibly, avoided him if possible. If they needed to make a governor's application they would choose a day when Thompson was away and the Deputy Governor, Alec Taylor, was on duty.[42]

Relations between the IRA men and ordinary A-Wing staff were, by contrast, quite good and relatively relaxed. This was confirmed by both prisoners and staff in interview and throughout Boyce's diary.[43] In this long-term section, there was a low rate of turnover of prisoners, and both they and staff knew that they were fated to work and live alongside each other for years to come. This stability of inmate population was matched on the staff side. Unlike their colleagues, A-Wing staff did not rotate around the prison or through a range of duties; nor did they work nights. (A-Wing night duty was performed by a special night guard.[44]) This meant that they avoided the more complex duty rotas that shift work required. With the same staff on duty every day, both prisoners and officers got to know each other. In terms of security and control, this had two sides. The character and behaviour of prisoners became very familiar to staff, and, as in any settled domestic existence, anything the slightest way out of the ordinary was likely to be noticed. Prisoners could, of course, make exactly the same observations of staff and, because they had no outside distractions, could concentrate their attention and were perhaps better able to elicit information and predict reactions. An unvarying routine, combined with few new faces and the presumptive ease of relationships, inevitably led to a degree of staff complacency and therefore a vulnerability that could be exploited by prisoners for a range of activities, from small breaches of discipline and minor instances of subordination to the preparation of an escape.[45]

One of the prisoners contended that there was no need to bribe, intimidate or persuade staff over minor items of contraband. Boyce noted in his diary that a prison officer had done him a favour by posting a letter in an outside letterbox: 'I'm very grateful to him. Of course, he's a PO [principal officer] but he's good enough to us.'[46] Relations were such that on one occasion a prison officer agreed that on coming off duty he would go and check on the state of a prisoner's father, thought to be perilously unwell.[47] A high degree of trust was involved on both sides, since the officer, from a Protestant area of Belfast, was going into a strongly nationalist area. Quite apart from political and religious issues, however, there was a degree of personal consideration and kindness involved in the incident that was indicative of relations between A-Wing staff and prisoners. It seems to have fallen as much into the category of foremen and shop-floor workers as of captive and captor.

Prisoners and some staff found common ground in a shared dislike of Major Thompson's disciplinarianism. According to one prisoner's recollection, even his deputy (Alec Taylor) supposedly hated Thompson: 'he was a wee bastard'. In more measured terms, an officer of the period remembered him as 'a tough wee guy. He really was.'[48] Rebuking a popular officer in front of his prisoners (akin, of course, to a teacher rebuked in front of his or her class) confirmed feelings of dislike and fear, and one prison officer (in charge of the laundry) was seen to walk behind Thompson with his fist raised.[49] Yet Hugh Cunningham, feeling that he had been unjustly admonished by Thompson for the way in which he was conducting a visit, spoke to him privately and said so. Certainly the demurral must have been expressed respectfully and in proper form, because Thompson accepted it, and the incident did not affect Cunningham's standing in the prison.[50]

Tobacco constantly led to minor breaches of discipline, even though some staff would, occasionally, give cigarettes to the prisoners.[51] It was a near obsession for some and a concern for many more: how to get more of it and how to eke out allowances. In the first year of sentence a man was entitled to a third of an ounce a week, two-thirds in the second year and one ounce a week in the third year. For many, that amount, even on the top scale, proved insufficient. The prison chapel was a convenient place for leaving contraband messages and packages since both sentenced men and internees used it. The latter had food, clothing and tobacco sent in, and, since their service was held before that of the sentenced men, they would leave tobacco concealed in various places. With this supplement, the sentenced men were able to continue smoking on Thursday and Fridays (the allowance was issued on Saturday) without, apparently, arousing staff suspicion – or perhaps staff simply did not want to know or to speculate.[52]

Food also caused dissatisfaction, both because of its quantity and its quality. In the first months of sentence, Boyce concluded that some of his comrades were suffering from malnutrition. He reasoned that the dietary allowance was the minimum required to keep a man in good health but that it had been so finely calculated that should a man not eat all he was given, however unappetising it might be, he would sicken. Potatoes were of poor quality, but 'I ate the skins, and I ate the other fellows' skins. If you got a banana or an orange, I ate the skin, and I was always proud of the fact that I was the only one that never had a hospitalisation period.'[53] Dessie O'Hagan remembered the food as being bad, with one fried egg a year, on Christmas Day; there was a weekly hard-boiled egg. The morning porridge had a skin on it, having been cooked the night before. There were forty-eight undeclared hunger strikes in protest but the food did not improve.[54]

The food caused the long-term men to come as close as they were to get to a confrontation with Major Thompson. Like many residential institutions, prisons operate a periodic menu, and stew was one of the meals provided each week. One serving, however, contained a whole mouse. Whether it had been put there deliberately, or because of poor hygiene and infestation in the kitchen, is unclear. In either event (and both were possible in prison), the men were understandably revolted, and the image of such contamination would be hard to dispel. For peace of mind, the matter had to be ventilated, and a man was selected to lodge a complaint. On hearing of the incident, Thompson, it was said, provocatively replied (in a version of the 'fly in my soup, waiter' joke), 'Well, it will put a bit more meat in the stew.' This jocularity, real or invented, as much as the mouse itself, led to a passive revolt and, for several weeks, a boycott of the stew. This was a genuine sacrifice since it was the one meal that everyone liked. The protest came to an end when one of the IRA group broke ranks. The issue became moot when the menu was altered and another item was substituted for the stew.[55]

Not everyone reacted in the same way, and presumably the food varied over time – and one grew accustomed to it. Boyce noted in his diary on 2 July 1957 that 'Dinner very good today – almost as good as what I got outside, but I don't suppose that too many of the new people will be satisfied. I don't know what's wrong with them.'[56] Since Boyce had already determined that, in order to preserve his health, he would eat everything he was offered, his views probably tended to the non-fastidious side of the spectrum.

As the Border Campaign itself (as distinct from the preceding arms raids) got under way, more men arrived in A Wing. Numbers remained small, however, and they were absorbed into what had become an established community. Relationships had an intense quality, which Boyce recalled: 'It is very difficult to put in words… but you had a camaraderie there that was… unique.'[57] Living in close quarters, substantially cut off from the outside world and with years of confinement in prospect, the men had scarcely any emotional shelter from each other. For life to be endurable, solidarity had to be tempered by a respect for privacy and a willingness to stand back. Bouts of depression were common: they are an inevitable part of the lot of many, perhaps most, long-term prisoners. A number of the men were former cyclists, and they used the term that they had applied to that feeling of exhaustion and being drained that long-distance cyclists sometimes get: 'the bonk'. When a bout of depression came on, a man would tell the others that he was 'getting the bonk'. Rather than impose a black mood on comrades (and to cope the better himself), he would keep to his cell as much as possible, refusing association.[58] The prisoners seem to have been successful in keeping their state of mind from the staff, and Hugh Cunningham, an observant officer, could not remember any showing signs of depression.[59]

But sometimes depression could be extreme. Introspection, longing and frustration are inevitable features of prison life, but with some these could occasionally intensify a sense of the weight and implacability of confinement, of futility, loss and panic: there seems to have descended a consciousness of existential loss and displacement. All of these (and more) made a volatile mixture that came from nowhere to grab and overpower. One prisoner recalled such an experience, towards the end of his sentence: 'I remember one night, I don't know what it was, I suddenly felt like – as if I was going to start screaming, and I knew if I started to scream… you used to hear people.' This was the only occasion when he thought that he was going to 'flip his lid'. The attack continued for some time: 'I grabbed the bed-rail and held on. And it must have lasted, I don't know what, the sweat rolled off me. Gradually I quietened down again, but that was the only time.'[60] Such an experience could never be forgotten.

Within the IRA group it could not be all camaraderie, emotional deference and sharing. Prisons are pressure cookers of emotions and flare-ups, and long-term grudges are unavoidable. And, indeed, there are irritating, recriminatory (and worse) intervals even in the most intimate and supportive of relationships in the free world. For adults brought together almost by chance – certainly by the exigencies of their activities and the working of the legal system – the challenges are inevitably greater than those of kin or domesticity. And the IRA men, mixing with all but associating with each other, were doubly confined, with emotions doubly concentrated. Membership of a group such as that existing in A Wing must at times have resembled a yoke rather than the uplift and security of comradeship. A tiff, a slight or an irritating personal habit had to be endured with the prospect of little relief for thousands of days and countless twists and turns of interaction: anger and other emotions had to be masked and civility maintained; one could not easily walk away and cell respite was limited. Words spoken or gestures made were picked over and analysed, entering into daily life in an almost corporeal way – a new, unpredictable and certainly wearing tension on the wing.[61]

No matter the lapidified face they turn to the world, long-term prisoners are inevitably worn down by the passage of time and the relentless and eroding monotony of the years. Boyce put it frankly: 'I'll tell you what prison is like… you're all bravado and all the rest of it [at the start] but, after the third or fourth year, you begin becoming institutionalised and it's like, you take three steps forward and you fall back two. You're constantly trying to keep the same ideas that you had, and to keep your morale up, you know… it does get into you.'[62]

Education and recreation

Belfast Prison in the mid-1950s, like most prisons in Britain and in the Republic, was minimally equipped for education, either self-directed or tutored courses.[63] The A-Wing library was skeletal, with a preponderance of pulp novels. Through quiet, persistent and non-confrontational lobbying, the IRA men managed to get the stock increased and the range and quality improved. The prison management would have said, with some (but not conclusive) justification, that the library stock reflected the educational level and interests of prisoners. In those years, however, the regime for long-term prisoners at British prisons such as Maidstone was being rethought and restructured, emphasising the need to make available to adult prisoners the opportunity for appropriate education and to create a more positive atmosphere within the walls.[64] Even though Major Thompson may have been unaware or out of sympathy with this new approach, officials at the Ministry of Home Affairs were more open to it.[65] From a more substantial library with at least some serious books, the next step was permission to study.

For those unfamiliar with its routines and dynamics, many would imagine that a prison's elements of monastic seclusion would provide an environment conducive to study. But whatever the resemblances (and there are some), the monastic life is structured to encourage prayer, reflection and study: prison life is stressful, depleting rather than augmenting inner strengths and resources, and prisoners are not volunteers or aspirants.[66] Even when expanded, there were no textbooks in the A-Wing library, and much depended on the goodwill of the prison-officer librarian, who would sometimes obtain a necessary book from the public library.[67] Oddly, the other problem was lack of available time. The convicted men were in workshops from morning until their evening meal at 4.30. As noted, on the completion of three years of sentence a man was allowed an extended evening association, from 5 to 7 p.m. With its opportunities for conversation and company, it is understandable that this time was much valued, and few chose to remain in their cells.[68] For study, there remained the two hours before lights out, between 7 and 9 p.m. For men without reasonably well-developed study habits and experience, this period at the end of the day, when various other tasks had to be performed in their cells, was inadequate.[69] Even for the motivated, it was a challenge to fit in and persist with study.

Since the Anglo-Irish War, republican prisoners, sentenced and interned alike, had tried to learn or to improve their Irish, and this was the only subject in which the sentenced men at Belfast were able to organise classes.[70] Whilst the Irish language was part of the Republic's school curriculum, teaching in Northern Ireland was much more patchy. But from whichever jurisdiction and no matter what progress they had made, many men felt that the language was a core part of their national and republican identity and therefore deserved priority in the allocation of available time. For the most part they relied on their own resources, since some activists had already achieved a good grasp or even fluency in the language. This was the path taken by Boyce, who had left school at age fourteen, had entered Belfast Prison without any knowledge of the Irish language (despite the Republic's curriculum) and had achieved a degree of fluency by the end of his sentence. During the earlier years he walked around the exercise yard with Tom Mitchell but then began to pair with Seán O'Hegarty, who was fluent in the language.[71] O'Hegarty conversed in Irish, and Boyce soon began to pick up words and phrases. Four of the men subsequently decided to set themselves the target of becoming fluent by a certain date.[72] To do this they needed to take a correspondence course. This caused problems.

In 1958, eighteen months into a twelve-year sentence for possession of explosives, Patrick A. (Tony) Cooney applied to enrol in an Irish-language course offered by a Dublin tutorial college, with a view to taking a London University General Certificate of Education (GCE).[73] This request went to the Ministry of Home Affairs, which consulted the RUC (meaning Special Branch), which recommended refusal. It was a matter of resources, they said. They did not have the manpower to censor the correspondence and course material, which would not stop with Cooney: a number of similar applications would follow were this one granted. Irish was only one of a number of GCE subjects offered by London University, and Cooney could quite easily select another if he wished. To allow course material from Dublin to pass without police censorship 'would no doubt be a great risk to the security of Northern Ireland. It is imperative that this application should be refused.'[74]

The RUC's reaction was overstated (certainly in language). Behind it lay a more rational assessment that a correspondence course might be used as a channel into the prison: neither it nor the Ministry took exception to the study of Irish nor to the taking of examinations in the subject. In July 1959, Tom Mitchell, self-taught, was granted permission to sit for his GCE in Irish, and various facilities were provided, including the appointment of an invigilator from the adjacent St Malachy's College.[75] Mitchell did sufficiently well to be granted permission in February 1961 to study for the London University external Bachelor of Laws. This also involved a correspondence course, but since communications were conducted directly with the university the Ministry had no objections.[76] Boyce and others were granted permission to take the same examination.[77]

The chaplaincy

When at liberty, the IRA prisoners were conscientious in their religious duties to varying degrees, no doubt.[78] But now, in the camp of their enemies, they were more than ever in need of spiritual consolations. Their relationship with the prison chaplain was bound to be stormy. He had intersecting loyalties and worked within two lines of subordinacy and accountability. He was an employee of the Stormont government and an officer of the prison: he was also licensed by the bishop. In the wake of the bishops' pastoral letter of 19 January 1957, the ecclesiastical line of reporting was perhaps more damning in the eyes of the men than the secular one. The chaplain was seen as a representative of the Bishop of Down and Connor whom the men saw as a hostile figure. The pastoral duties of any prison chaplain are onerous and full of conflicts that are hard to resolve. As in any pastoral relationship, it is essential that he be open and available to his flock, yet he works within and must, at all times, uphold the prison rules. It is inevitable that he becomes a lightning conductor for the many turbulent emotions that surge within the walls.[79] For all their devoutness (which easily shaded into pietism), Father Patrick McAlister's work in ministering to the convicted IRA men and, later, to the internees, was fraught with challenges.[80] Nor did they have a monopoly of his time. There were many troubled and troublesome men among the ordinary criminal prisoners. In his captive congregation, republicans stood out as stalwarts: serious law-breakers indeed, but generally untainted by many of the moral and personal failings of their non-political comrades. Yet to the IRA men he was compromised as an agent of the prison authorities and the Northern Ireland government, as well as a hostile hierarchy; in particular, he was the representative of the malign temporal and spiritual powers that promised freedom and consolation to those who renounced violent republicanism. His acceptance of the status quo was seen as an abuse of his position of trust, since his priestly authority applied pressure to the men in their extremity and at their most vulnerable.

This was therefore destined to be a difficult ministry. But, unlike some other chaplains encountered by republicans over the years, there seemed to be no personal dislike for McAlister. He disappointed and frustrated, no doubt, but he did not bully, and none of the recollections refer to the patronising, offensive or haughty manner which was alleged against some other chaplains. As far as was known, none abandoned the IRA because of him, and, as the years passed, some prisoners found a way of observing their religion that gave them ease of conscience. Some were so bitterly hurt by the bishops' edict and McAlister's faithful implementation that they departed the Roman Catholic Church permanently.[81]

Ireland has long been one of the countries where religion and politics so fatefully intermingle and where there is no protective membrane of separation. This, and the willingness of prisoners always to seize a space where they can exercise autonomy meant that there had to be limits on the men's conduct of their own religious affairs. On 12 November 1957, an incident occurred in the chapel that confirmed the Ministry in the view that the chaplain should keep a tighter rein. Tom Mitchell applied to Father McAlister to use the chapel that evening to say prayers, and the priest wisely refused. Mitchell then approached the principal officer on duty and asked if, immediately after the evening meal, the IRA prisoners could have sole use of one end of the recreation room for fifteen minutes, to recite the rosary. Such group prayer had been allowed on other occasions without problems, and the request, on being referred to Major Thompson, was granted. Following prayers, and to underline the solemnity of the event, the IRA men asked to return to their cells, forgoing further participation in evening association.[82]

Thompson had been duped, a rare but particularly embarrassing event: he had cleared the way for an IRA memorial service. He was unaware or failed to regard it as significant the death the previous night of four of the men's comrades in Carrickcarnon, Co. Louth, largest single IRA loss since the Civil War.[83] Thompson had also failed to consult the chaplain whom Tom Mitchell had earlier requested to see. Father McAlister had spent some time in discussion with the IRA men. They asked him to lead prayers for the dead bombers and their host, and he had refused. Mitchell's subsequent approach to the discipline staff – ultimately the governor – had succeeded, but it was to come at a price.

News inevitably leaked out of the prison, and the Ministry asked for a report. Thompson took full responsibility for what had happened and, indeed, could not do otherwise. It was accepted that he had acted for the best, but he was left in no doubt as to the Minister's unhappiness. Neither in Parliament nor on a public platform could Topping defend this kind of concession to republican violence: many in the unionist community would have seen it as sentimental coddling. In what was a form of rebuke, he was directed that any similar matter should be referred to the Ministry: 'It must have been known that the request was linked in some way to the five men who were blown up, and no facilities should have been granted for any form of memorial service to them.' All requests of such a nature were to be channelled through the chaplain and had to be referred to the Ministry were there any doubt about their propriety.[84]

This was one side of the balancing act that the chaplain had to attempt daily. He could not allow himself to be manipulated by any prisoner. The pastoral care of his paramilitary charges was especially susceptible to such attempts.

At another point, he was faced with a boycott. One of the attackers of Rosslea RUC barracks, Connie Green was wounded in the raid and later died in Tydavnet, Co. Monaghan (in a Saor Uladh safe house). Gordon Knowles, a twenty-five-year-old constable, was badly wounded during the incident.[85] The Bishops' standing committee had already denounced membership of the IRA as a mortal sin. It followed that the absolution of the confessional could not be granted unless there were a sincere indication of repentance and an abandonment of the path of this grave sin.[86] These pronouncements were repeated. This could only mean a decisive and complete renunciation of IRA membership. The prisoners would not do this and were consequently denied the sacraments of confession and communion. Father McAlister attempted to get an exemption from the episcopal edict, possibly on the grounds that, whatever they wished, his prisoners could not further IRA activities in any practical sense. No such dispensation was granted. Subject to ecclesiastical discipline, Father McAlister had to refuse the sacraments to all who were impenitent. Tom Mitchell and Boyce were altar servers at the time. The chaplain, who valued the republicans' exemplary devoutness, wished them to continue to serve, even though they were, in effect, excommunicated. After initially declining, they agreed to do so, but, according to Boyce, only because they did not want to lose the opportunity that the position gave them to collect the tobacco being left by the internees for the sentenced men.[87]

There was no question of boycotting religious services. Quite apart from the religious directions on obligatory church attendance, most of the prisoners found spiritual consolation in the mass and other services. Even the sceptical minority found reason to attend. Faced with a twenty-hour Sunday lock-up, chapel gave a welcome break from the cell.[88] The men of A Wing, as Father McAlister doubtless anticipated, were, as far as we know, steadfast in their IRA allegiance and, in consequence, were denied the sacraments for two and a half years. In Roman Catholic teaching, confession and communion (and especially the former) are critical sacraments, and exclusion from them is inimical if not a complete bar to eternal salvation. Their denial was therefore a matter of considerable importance to believers, even those lukewarm in the faith. It was only when Father McAlister went on a trip to Rome and Father Timothy O'Regan, a Redemptionist priest from the Clonard Monastery in Belfast, came in to conduct services that the ban was disregarded and the men were allowed to attend confession and to receive communion. As all the IRA group were observant Catholics, this act of grace and charity by this 'great little man' was a boon, gratefully received.[89] On McAlister's return from Rome, the men were careful not to mention his colleague's breach of ecclesiastical discipline.[90]

Prisoners' welfare

Support for dependants was an important part of the IRA's compact with those who went on active service.[91] The capacity and vitality of support associations closely followed the strength of the organisation and its campaigns. Notionally, they were independent and humanitarian bodies, but in reality they were either controlled directly by the IRA or influenced by it, directly or through proxies. During the 1950s, the support organisations were the Green Cross in Northern Ireland and An Cumann Cabhrach in the Republic.[92] Tom Doyle, a major IRA activist during the wartime years, long-term prisoner and then internee and eventually Vice-President of Sinn Féin, one of those arrested on 6 July 1957, also found time to be Secretary of An Cumann Cabhrach.

Nationalist politicians were unequivocal in their condemnation of the IRA campaign.[93] Their attitude towards the prisoners was more complicated. They regarded the Northern Ireland government and administration as intrinsically unjust and discriminatory towards nationalist-minded people: this was their own *raison d'être*. IRA prisoners were opposed to constitutional politics but came from the nationalist hinterland, and a duty of care existed and had to be met. The MPs therefore reflected the ambivalence of their constituents: no support for the IRA's actions but some sympathy for their plight. MPs felt safe and comfortable in focusing on prison conditions and on the problems of dependants.[94] That type of intervention, however, seems to have dwindled as the Border Campaign – as distinct from the arms raids – got under way.[95] Dessie O'Hagan, who came into prison in the early months of the Border Campaign, recalled that neither nationalist politicians in the North nor opposition TDs in the South were interested in prison issues.[96] Once the IRA campaign had finished, nevertheless, the Nationalist MPs pressed the issue of the release of those convicted men who remained in prison. They met Lord Brookeborough, the Northern Ireland Prime Minister, and Brian Faulkner, his Minister for Home Affairs, on 5 July 1962 and urged releases on the grounds that the conflict was over and unlikely to recur, especially if the remaining prisoners were freed.[97] The timing was poor: a week before the

Twelfth of July celebrations and a period when Brookeborough's followers were likely to be angered and displeased should leniency be displayed towards those who had committed serious offences under colour of the IRA, beaten or not. Brookeborough predictably indicated that he could not interfere with court sentences.[98] The Nationalist MPs were not at all surprised, but they had ventilated what they saw as a concern and sentiment of their constituents.

Prison security

By the mid-1960s, even the most formidable of Britain's prisons would be found wanting in security when faced with the resources of professional criminals, audacious and flush with funds, or with the ideological leverage and resources of the Cold War and with possible access to outside assistance.[99] This seemed exactly the mixture that Belfast Prison (Northern Ireland's most secure institution) faced when it received the eight Omagh raiders at the end of 1954. It had held many IRA men since the foundation of the state, but after the border incursions of 1922 they were, with a few notable exceptions, remanded or convicted of rather 'passive' (through still serious) offences such as possession of arms and explosives, conspiracy and conducting the business of the IRA through documents or meetings. The Omagh raiders came in at a time when the Border Campaign was yet to be launched. But with the IRA having declared its purposes and methods in its manifesto of 30 November 1954, even the most sanguine of officials could see that the prison had to be fortified and its security upgraded. Improvements were needed to the buildings themselves, armed guards would have to be brought in for the perimeter and – most difficult of all – staff alertness would have to be raised and maintained, changes made to deployment and all the routines of the prison reviewed. As we shall see, only some of these measures were successfully carried through.

When, on 26 November 1955, Liam Kelly's Saor Uladh attacked the RUC barracks at Rosslea, Co. Fermanagh, the raiders used a technique which had been a favourite in the Anglo-Irish War.[100] A mine was placed against one of the walls of the building. (The gable end, if there was one, was preferred since it was not usually overlooked.) A successful explosion tore a hole, through which attackers threw more bombs, fired and then entered. The occupants of the building were likely to be disoriented were they not killed or injured. This type of raid was also suitable for a prison break and had a pedigree going back to the devastating and bloody Clerkenwell House of Correction explosion of December 1867.[101] Whether historical precedents were known to them is uncertain, but the Rosslea attack and other information led the RUC to believe that the IRA had plans, and the means, to mount a similar operation against Belfast Prison. There was an urgent review of the physical security of the prison itself, and of that of the adjoining courthouse. The latter, on the opposite side of the Crumlin Road, linked to the prison by an underground tunnel, was an obvious weak point, potentially a Trojan-horse pathway. It was decided to reinforce the prison's perimeter with a wall-top inward-curving barbed-wire extension. This was to foil an escape during exercise periods, which might take the form of a mass rush on the wall with a rope ladder and grappling-hooks while staff were kept at bay. The RUC noted that prisoners had in the past managed to get over Belfast's wall.[102] They also recommended that a concealed alarm be fitted in the underground tunnel. In order to prevent penetration of the prison from the courthouse, various reinforcements were necessary in its basement ground-floor windows and doors. In the face of a strong, specific and urgent police warning, based on firm intelligence, these recommendations encountered little official foot-dragging or political indecisiveness. A meeting of police, the Ministry and prison officials on 7 December 1955 approved the various strengthenings. The Ministry turned down an RUC proposal for watch towers, to be sited on the corners of the prison perimeter, equipped with searchlights and alarms and sufficiently high to allow guards to have a view of both sides of the wall.[103] As a measure of the level of concern at the possibility of an attack or breakout, it was, however, agreed that guards overlooking the exercise yard should be equipped with Sten guns.[104] By the early part of 1956, there was also a police guard assigned to the prison.

Operation Harvest and the introduction of internment were almost a year off. The Omagh raiders in particular, although their operation had failed, were a cause for concern. They were committed, bold and resourceful men whose escape – even were it only one of them – would embarrass the government and reinforce the IRA. Later, the RUC warned that a prison break 'would do more to re-unite the splinters in the ranks of the IRA and Sinn Féin movement than anything else'. There had been a great deal of grumbling in the IRA that the prisoners had been allowed to languish so long and the leadership needed an answer 'badly'.[105] This was largely police guesswork, but it was plausible and politically alarming.

By the end of 1956, the prison buildings had been heavily reinforced and provided with a number of armed posts and with a siren. Three static posts within the prison were manned by armed guards during the day. Revolvers were carried by these officers, who, for obvious reasons, did not come into contact with prisoners at any point. Another guard post, overlooking the main entrance gate, was provided with a Sten gun. There were armed night patrols, directed to pay particular attention to that part of A Wing in which the IRA men were held. Against all previously accepted conventions, a Sten gun was even held inside the cell house on Saturday and Sunday nights (the times of minimum staffing levels). A police patrol car attended the front gate at morning unlocking and on the handover to evening staff. Hospital staff were provided with revolvers in the evening, and an officer with a concealed revolver was placed in the hall where visits to IRA men were conducted. The staff rota and deployment had been expanded, a costly measure since both had to be funded at overtime rates.[106]

Despite the activities of Seán MacBride, the IRA was utterly indifferent to the laws of what it saw as an alien state. But had it paused to lift its eye from the rifle-sight it might have wrung advantage from a set of concerns that greatly perplexed the Ministry. The use of firearms by prison staff or by police acting in their support was a grave matter since, if in certain circumstances injury or death resulted, the person who had opened fire could face serious charges, including murder. The law had been set out in a directive to the governor of Belfast Prison more than three decades before, in May 1927. The intentional infliction of death or injury was not a crime when it was done to prevent a felony or when it was reasonably believed that force might be imminent to commit the felony. It was also lawful to use lethal force to arrest, recapture or keep in lawful custody a felon who had escaped or who was about to escape. In these instances, there was a requirement that before opening fire it had been reasonably concluded that the objective could not be accomplished by other means. The law also covered any attempt to rescue a felon from lawful custody since that in itself was a felony.[107]

The law had one major drawback for those obliged to make the on-the-spot and immediate decision to open fire. Spur-of-the-moment decision-making might merit some latitude from the courts, but immunity was available only for actions relating to felony and felons. Persons convicted of a misdemeanour fell into quite a different category, and it was not lawful, in the event of an escape attempt, to open fire on them or on those intent on assisting them. Since both felons and misdemeanants (as well as remands and, eventually, internees) were held in Belfast Prison, a member of staff or a police officer would need to be very sure of the legal status of their target – escaper or helper – before opening fire. The Ministry was emphatic: shooting at a person other than a felon 'would involve most serious consequences and [where death occurred] would render the person responsible legally guilty of murder'.[108] In 1959, the law was restated for the staff of Belfast Prison, with the order that on no account should a Sten gun be used on prisoners or internees in the prison.[109]

As noted, the RUC had pressed for protective watchtowers, but the Ministry had baulked, probably on the grounds of the expense of manning them, as well as their significance in denoting a state of emergency. In early 1957, with Operation Harvest upon them, the RUC resurrected its earlier proposal. Improvements in security already undertaken had, they acknowledged, much improved the prison's capabilities. The earlier decision not to proceed with the watchtowers may well have been correct, but '[t]imes had changed... and the most vital thing at the moment was to keep these IRA leaders where they were. There was trouble catching them, and it would be fatal if they, by any means, got out.' Pointing again to the IRA's method of attacking police barracks, the RUC advised that the prison's exterior had to be under constant observation to prevent explosives being placed, and only watchtowers would serve for that purpose. These would need to be constantly manned by police.[110] It was possibly this last point that cleared the way for accepting the RUC proposal alongside the fact that a specific and urgent warning had been given (and a paper trail established) which no prudent official or politician could disregard. Approval was given immediately to construct the watchtowers.

In its first months, the Border Campaign was pressed vigorously, and, given the patchiness of intelligence on both sides of the border, there was every reason to suppose it would be progressively intensified after reinforcement, regrouping and resupply. Concern remained that a spectacular prison rescue would be attempted, especially under cover of darkness. At the end of August 1957, with a season of longer nights ahead, the police asked for improved searchlights.[111] With these improvements they were satisfied that all points of physical security had been addressed and that the IRA must conclude that an assault on the prison would be repulsed. A direct attack on the lines of Rosslea, using a mine to blow the walls and following up with rifles and automatic weapons, also seemed unlikely because of the very great problems of moving an armed group into the vicinity of the prison and the even greater problems of getting it (and the rescued prisoners) away after an engagement. As a practical proposition, therefore, the police concluded that escape tactics would be adapted to practicalities and cautioned that the topic was continuously raised in IRA discussions. Physical security being so formidable, escape was more likely to be effected by trick or ruse, old or new.

At this point, someone at RUC HQ seems to have swallowed an extremely fanciful line from an informant or to have embarked on an imaginative course of speculation. Two new possibilities, the RUC warned, had now come to notice. The first was an unlikely item of James Bond gadgetry: pistols disguised as fountain pens.[112] These supposedly fired a gas pellet capable of knocking out a number of guards for several minutes. A scenario was presented in which a party of visitors might use the gas pens and seize a number of key points, clearing the way for a mass escape. (How they would do so without themselves or those they would rescue being overcome by the fumes in an enclosed area was not explained.) The other device was less exotic: packets of pepper to be flung into the eyes of police and staff, disabling them in the same way as the gas. 'These might be thought to be fantastic methods', County Inspector Nelson cautioned, 'but we know that the IRA have been in training in how to employ them. In fact we have captured men with these articles in their possession.'[113] Nelson concluded his warning with a declaration of institutional piety: 'I am quite sure it is only necessary for us to mention these matters to make certain that they will never succeed at Belfast Prison.'[114]

At Home Affairs, J. G. Hill passed the advice on, sardonically noting Nelson's 'touching confidence in the Prison authorities'.[115] Satire may have seemed misplaced when, a few weeks later, on 27 December 1960, Dónal Donnelly escaped.[116] The subsequent inquiry showed that the floodlights with which two towers had been provided had not been cleaned or properly maintained. Complacency and carelessness, the constant foes of prison administrators, had exacted their inevitable price. Luminosity had dropped by a third or more because both reflectors and lenses had been allowed to become very dirty. Cleaning and replacement was at once undertaken, and two additional lights were installed to cover poorly lit areas.[117] But this particular stable door was off the hinges.

The driver of this considerable expenditure on physical security and staffing was a small group of sentenced men in A Wing; internees, far more numerous, were seen as a lesser threat by far. In January 1957, there were fourteen sentenced IRA men at Belfast Prison. Two were serving only three months.[118] Besides the eight Omagh raiders, there were three others convicted of explosives offences and one of an offence under the Special Powers Acts.[119] Apart from the three-month men, sentences ranged from three to twelve years. Seven of the Omagh raiders were serving ten-year sentences, with Boyce, who had been punished as their leader, serving twelve. In the period before the introduction of parole, increased rates of remission and a general lengthening of nominal terms, these were substantial sentences.[120] Nine of the fourteen came from the Republic of Ireland: six from Dublin and three from Cork. Of the long-sentence men, the earliest date of release, with maximum time off for good behaviour, was merely a couple of months away (for a man serving three years who had been sentenced in January 1955). The Omagh raiders would not be freed until the middle of 1962 (the end of 1963 in Boyce's case). Therefore, apart from their political motivation and desire to rejoin the struggle, the long-termers had ostensibly strong reasons for escape.[121] But, as we shall see, neither the prisoners nor their comrades outside gave priority to the matter.

Escape

As a matter of course, the A-Wing IRA unit established an escape committee, led by Seán Garland.[122] Little seems to have been expected of the committee, and, after several years in prison, it seems to have been assumed that the men would have to sit out their time. Boyce and others had concluded that in view of the prison's enhanced security and the deployment of armed guards, escape would be impossible without outside assistance: 'You would have had to impose this on somebody else outside, so that was one thing you didn't do.'[123] But this was thinking of escape as a break of all or most of the IRA group. A smaller and more opportunistic attempt was another matter.

And this, in the last few days of 1960, was the basis of the only successful Northern escape of the Border Campaign. The Campaign had by then dwindled to a halting trickle of acts of minor sabotage and disruption. The state of the IRA may partly be measured against the escape: it played no part in it, the man who got away was no longer a member, and the organisation was unable to use the break to re-energise its supporters; indeed, the escape caused irritation and some consternation among comrades left behind. At no point during the Border Campaign was escape an item on the IRA agenda, despite the RUC's insistence that it had information that the rescue of the Omagh raiders was a priority for the organisation. Certainly it would have benefited from a return to its ranks of such a group, as well as the general lift in spirits that would ensue, but there is no record that an operation was ever planned.[124]

The escape attempt was made on Boxing Day 1960.[125] The two men involved were twenty-one-year-old Dónal Donnelly, serving ten years for being a member of an unlawful organisation, and John Kelly (aged twenty-four) serving eight years for possessing explosives and also for being a member of an unlawful organisation.[126] Escape material was minimal (a few hacksaw blades), and Kelly may have had Belfast contacts who arranged to have these smuggled into the prison.[127] The break was made possible by a number of factors. The first was the intelligence, powers of observation, timing and mettle of the two men; the second was a still inadequate level of control and security in the prison, combined with the torpor of the festive season.[128] The perimeter was fairly secure, particularly against outside attack, but staff alertness inside was low, and, during the Christmas period, the hierarchy of time-entitled privileges meant that manning relied heavily on temporary staff.[129]

The plan was simple, as traditional as the season, to the point of cliché. A sufficiently large portion of the metalwork of a cell window was cut out, and the two men levered and wriggled through the gap and lowered themselves to the ground. On a night of murk, wind, heavy rain and occasional sleet, they managed to throw their improvised rope and grapple onto an internal wall, about 23 feet high. This abutted the external wall, and they crawled along it, without being noticed by the armed RUC guard. Donnelly then lowered himself down the perimeter wall, but when the improvised rope parted he fell heavily on the other side. Kelly, hearing him groan, decided that he had been badly injured and pressed the bell, summoning staff to admit him from the yard into the prison. Staff (at least according to accounts that they gave later) had by then noticed that the two men were missing. Kelly was taken back into the cellhouse where he revealed that Donnelly had fallen from the wall and was lying injured on the other side. There was an immediate rush, but Donnelly, despite his injured ankle, had managed in the meantime to hobble off to Kelly's house, assisted by two off-duty nurses from the nearby (Catholic) Mater Hospital who had chanced upon him in the street. Knowing that a swift police visit was certain, the Kelly family rapidly passed him on.[130] After some days being sheltered in Belfast, Donnelly made his way first to Tyrone (he was from Omagh) and then, disguised as a priest, across the border. He resurfaced in Cork.[131]

Like most successful prison escapes, this one had depended on close observation of how staff worked, their vigilance and general disposition, the timetable of the prison and an assessment of how staff might react under certain circumstances; it was also a skilful exploitation of a rare opportunity. Electrical contractors had been in the prison for more than two years, carrying out major rewiring. This involved the removal of old conduits and cable. Hacksaws and other cutting equipment had, at least in theory, been tightly controlled, as had obsolete and discarded materials. Having contractors on the premises for such a long time inevitably led to a relaxation in vigilance. The escape showed that security procedures had not been followed or had been insufficient. Kelly obtained electrical cable which he wove together with strips of blankets to make the escape rope. The prison, strongly denying any possibility of staff collusion, was baffled by the hacksaw blades. The Trades' Officer reported that they were not prison issue but did not go so far as to deny that they were of a type used by the contractor. Notionally, there had been a safeguard in that the blades were issued to workers on a strict one-for-one exchange basis. The blankets had been easier. It was established procedure that, when they were deemed to be worn out, blankets were cut up for use as floor cloths. Lacking imagination, and seeing parsimony thus served, the prison management had seen little need to control such material.

Kelly had used an awl handle into which he embedded the hacksaw blades, or portions of them, in order to cut the metal of his window frame and a central bar. The frames themselves were mild steel rather than the hardened steel of modern prisons. The Trades' Officer subsequently carried out an experiment in cutting out a frame and window and estimated that a total of just over three hours' uninterrupted work would complete the task. This must be multiplied many times over for the occasional few minutes that could be snatched when Kelly and Donnelly were reasonably certain that they could avoid detection. The task was also prolonged because after each session the bar and window frame had to be made good by filling with putty and colouring.[132]

The men's target date was the few days over Christmas.[133] Calculating backwards, they had to be careful not to make too much progress (window bars were regularly and frequently, if not thoroughly, tested) and yet sufficient to enable the breakout to take place. During those weeks, Kelly carried the hacksaw blades in a little pouch which he wore on his thigh. In another indication that Belfast Prison fell short of the standards of necessary security, personal searching routines were so lax that Kelly was able to pass the pouch to other men, as necessary. Seventy-three feet of cable was used in making the escape rope. Again, by post-hoc experiment, it was concluded that this quantity could be compressed into a roll about six inches in diameter and three inches wide – not too hard to conceal. The woven rope itself would have been more bulky, and the device was probably assembled at the last possible moment, which might have contributed to its failure. The weaving and plaiting, it was calculated, would have taken about three hours of uninterrupted work, assuming that the blanket had previously been cut and prepared.

Equipment alone was not enough: timing had to be exact. The principal problem was to get both men into Kelly's cell, from which the escape was to be made. The Christmas Day routine provided the answer. After the special evening meal at 5 p.m., men were allowed to return to their cells with portions of cake and other items which they had received in their Christmas parcels. Everyone was then supposed to return immediately to the dining hall on the ground floor for evening association. Kelly and Donnelly held back. A check was made by the landings officer (Rampf) and the pair were found in Kelly's cell. They said that they were waiting there for an Irish-language class, but, since no classes were being held on Christmas evening, they were told that they must either be locked in their respective cells or return to the recreation hall.

This spelt failure for their plan. Were they to go to association they would be unable to return together to Kelly's cell. Either improvising, or because it was their fallback plan, they opted to be locked in their cells. Twenty-five minutes later, Kelly rang his bell and said that he had changed his mind and now wanted to go to recreation. The supervising officer unlocked Kelly and told him to make his own way to the dining hall; he did not relock the cell door. Immediately afterwards, Donnelly's bell rang, and the officer made his way up to the floor above. At this point, he lost sight of Kelly and compounded his errors by directing Donnelly, who also said he had changed his mind, to make his own way to recreation. The men had correctly and cleverly calculated that Officer Rampf would not wish to escort Kelly from his first-floor cell to recreation on the ground floor and return to do the same for Donnelly.

According to subsequent accounts, at least ten minutes elapsed before the landings officer checked whether the two men had arrived in the association area. A count showed that the group was two short. A search was ordered of the first- and second-floor landings, and a visual check was made on the exercise yard. No one could be seen. By this time, Donnelly was over the wall, and Kelly had summoned help, bringing his escape attempt to an end. Standing orders then took over. All prisoners were ordered back to their cells and locked in. The alarm was given (a siren), and a search was started of all areas immediately adjacent to the prison. Many staff who lived nearby in Prison Service quarters and those who had heard the siren immediately reported for duty. Searches inside and outside the prison continued for several hours.[134]

The IRA had played no part in this escape and, beleaguered as it was, lacked the resources to turn it to advantage. The method and timing precluded a mass escape, but it is possible that another two men might have got away had the IRA unit in the prison been involved. It was, however, a freelance effort not in any way involving Garland's escape committee. Donnelly was not a member of the IRA group in the prison and therefore was not an IRA member at all; he had been excluded. All these circumstances show the state of the IRA at the time, inside and outside the prison. After an interval of four days, Donnelly appeared in Cork but, being something of an embarrassment to the rule-bound organisation, was not made the focus of a publicity campaign.[135] It was not until 8 January 1961 – nearly a fortnight after the event – that the IRA's Irish Republican Publicity Bureau issued a rather tight-lipped, begrudging and factual statement.[136] The public mood in the Republic at this time was unfavourable to IRA activities, and, although de Valera no longer headed the government, his successor, Seán Lemass, was apt to react just as strongly where he thought Dublin's authority was being directly challenged.[137] There was, nevertheless, some scope for promoting the escape as an act of republican derring-do, but this could not be imagined or grasped by the now hollowed-out IRA, which continued to be concerned that Donnelly was not one of its members.

The Ministry of Home Affairs was also embarrassed; politicians were enraged. Donnelly and Kelly were top-security prisoners whose escape was, by definition, an affront and a blow to the security of the state. They had also posed a substantial extra risk over ordinary prisoners by, theoretically at least, having available to them the resources of an outside organisation to aid their escape, concealment and transportation to a safe haven in the Republic. Despite these undeniable and blindingly obvious facts, they had been treated in the same manner as ordinary long-term prisoners. But, even if judged by that more limited and inappropriate standard, procedures, staffing and management were inadequate. The history of escapes and disorders showed beyond all doubt that weekends and holidays were periods of high risk because of staff depletion and laxness. Yet, with all this knowledge and experience, no stiffening had been provided by the Governor to cope with the high-risk IRA men during the Christmas wind-down. If temporary staff were predominant in the prison over the holiday, there was an obvious and pressing need to have them closely supervised and supported.

There was the usual inquest and the usual result: a junior member of staff, the temporary officer who had been on duty on the landings of A Wing (and alone in that duty) and who had fallen for the men's ploy, was charged with an offence under the prison rules and was severely reprimanded.[138] Kelly pleaded guilty to the charge of trying to escape and was sentenced to six months' forfeiture of remission (in effect an extra nine months' imprisonment) and loss of evening association for six months (a severe punishment since, as we have seen, this period of recreation was so highly valued). There were also financial penalties. He lost earnings for twenty-eight days and also had to pay almost £11 for the repair of the damaged window.[139] Kelly could have been tried before an outside court and would in that event have been liable to a heavier penalty. The Northern Ireland Attorney General, no doubt with an eye to cost and unfavourable publicity, decided that an internal disciplinary proceeding was preferable.[140]

And there were political reverberations. Some months later, the Minister for Home Affairs (now Brian Faulkner) was questioned in Stormont. Nat Minford, Unionist MP for Antrim, was incensed by the article that a few days previously had appeared in the *Sunday Review* in which Donnelly had given details of his escape and had 'actually boasted about it'.[141] It was incredible, Minford contended, that Donnelly could have escaped so easily, that the window bars should be filed through without detection, that two men should creep across the tops of walls and not be picked up by the searchlights and that Donnelly should escape and four days later be in Cork. The question was expressed in moderate terms, but Minford's incredulity could be read as implying staff collusion, information about which Faulkner was concealing.[142]

The escape, Faulkner insisted, had been possible simply because of a 'temporary lapse' from the prison's normally high standards, and the weather on the night (sleet, rain and gusts of wind) had greatly helped. Prison officers and police had been under extreme strain for four years, on alert against the possibility of attack from outside as well as from within. This one incident could not justify a wholesale condemnation of the security system or those whose job it was to enforce it. He addressed Minford's real question and gave an 'absolute and convinced' assurance that there was no question of staff collusion or disloyalty.

It would not be in the public interest, however, to give further details of the security review that had been carried out.[143]

The government was not the only body unhappy with the escape. The IRA needed to function as a disciplined organisation in captivity as much as outside. The organisation had little option but to embrace Donnelly – but it was at arm's length – once he had reached safe quarters, and it would have looked odd had he not been produced for the press. But the Kelly–Donnelly escape attempt had not been authorised, and that created difficulties. Common sense might suggest that, if the organisation were unable to assist in an escape it should not stand in the way of those who had the daring and resources to make an attempt. The counter-argument was that the organisation may have needed forewarning. Perhaps an operation was being mounted, or a meeting (or arms) were being held at a house that was likely to be raided in the aftermath of an escape. There would almost certainly be roadblocks in areas where IRA operatives might be in transit. As it happened, these ill consequences did not arise, but they might have, and could arise on another occasion, so the principle did matter. Against all of that was the enduring tendency of the IRA to make a fetish of procedures and to brush pragmatic judgements aside.

Inside the prison there was irritation in the IRA group rather than jubilation. Boyce knew nothing of the escape until the siren sounded. There were consequences of a completely predictable kind, particularly a general search. All prisoners at almost all times have unauthorised items in their possession; some have contraband of various kinds. Having advance warning of an escape attempt would have allowed prisoners in the know to take precautions, to dispose or more adequately to conceal things that were important to them. Boyce fretted over the post-escape clampdown and worried that he might lose his diaries – a serious matter since they were contraband in themselves, the fruit of a forbidden activity, and a danger to the IRA group in the prison.[144] Besides this, the tightening-up meant the removal of many little comforts and blind-eye indulgences that had softened prison life. Until final lock-up and count each evening, for example, it was decreed that all cell doors had to be left open. Belfast Prison was poorly heated, and the draughts made it more miserable still. Whether this strictness was truly and exclusively precautionary and not in part a dose of collective punishment cannot be said. The effect was well captured in Boyce's diary entry for New Year's Day 1961 (a Sunday): 'A bad start to the New Year – our whole world upset here because of the escape. The cell is cold and bare because the tablecloths, etc. are gone. I've no interest in anything here anymore.'[145]

In the days that followed, prison life grew even more uncomfortable. Searches turned up tobacco and other items, newspapers were delayed, and letters were severely censored. Existing divisions among the prisoners intensified. By this time, Boyce and others had been inside for several years, and their priorities had shifted. Some had come to the conclusion that the IRA campaign had been a failure and that the organisation was devastated. Institutionalisation had set in, and it must have seemed reasonable to wonder what had been the point of their venture and the punishment they were enduring, and which now was intensifying. Others, perhaps shorter term, or of a different disposition, got cheer and encouragement from the escape and the discomfiture of the authorities. A fortnight after Donnelly got over the wall, the divisions persisted, as Boyce noted: 'All of his friends here are boasting and laughing… but there are a few… myself included, who are angry.'[146]

A degree of freedom

Had the Ministry decided on a proper inquiry instead of entrusting the task to Major Thompson, an interested party, it might have discovered that security procedures were fundamentally flawed and that the prison was generally inadequate for the task it had been given. To take but one example, Boyce, a top-security prisoner, was able to evade searching procedures to a remarkable degree, keeping a diary for six years and, when he chose, getting them safely out of prison. Even more remarkably, he had smuggled one of the first transistor radios to be available in Ireland into the prison and had used it for six years. This he also managed to get out of the prison just before he was released.[147] These two feats of concealment eluded spot searches as well as the more regular routine of cell searches. He was able to anticipate any special attention from staff and to pass the radio on. With the IRA in a different and more effectively aggressive mode, of course, a weapon, escape tools, money, disguises and other items, rather than just a transistor radio, might have been smuggled in.[148]

The IRA men also closely observed and engaged with staff. This did not become as systematic or self-conscious a form of conditioning as it would for a later generation in the Maze and Whitemoor prisons, but it did help men to evade some restrictions. On the basis of ostensibly innocent banter with his workshop officer, Boyce (and doubtless others) was able to anticipate who would supervise certain visits. And, he observed, there were some officers who, whilst not amenable, were 'weak in their own way'. When a talkative officer was on duty, Boyce would aim to get two or perhaps three family members to visit. One would then engage the attention of the officer, and Boyce would be able to pass on a message for the IRA: 'You cannot talk to somebody and listen at the same time.' As an alternative, an urgent message would be passed in, in the form of a code word.[149]

Understandably, there was a deal of social tension, embarrassment and anxiety on both sides during family visits. Apart from special visits, authorised by the Governor to discuss family emergencies or other pressing matters, a prisoner was entitled to one visit a month.[150] These brief and constrained occasions were eagerly anticipated, much mulled over and fraught with feelings. Intimacies and endearments had to be constrained or suppressed – worry, longing, insecurity, resentment and happiness could create an almost unbearable intensity; detachment and a lack of news or interest on the prisoners' side made for regret and disappointment. The visitors brought news and the variety of even humdrum experiences in the free world. The prisoner was prohibited by the rules from talking about his life in prison: conversation was bound to be difficult and unable to carry its burden of expectations. This frustration and emotional intensity could be difficult for a member of staff to handle, and any opportunity, such as the officer conversing with a child, might be used to create some degree – even if it were illusory – of privacy for the married couple or for other family members. It was an additional feature of their unnatural air and awkwardness that these visits were taken in a small cubicle, a square of four or five feet – not much more than the size of a dining table – and with a prison officer sitting between the prisoner and visitor, only a foot or two away from them. No physical contact was allowed between man and his wife – or his mother or his children. Hugh Cunningham recalled, 'it wasn't a pleasant duty' – an understatement indeed. These could be emotional and occasionally heart-breaking occasions: 'I suppose in a way it was demeaning to a prisoner to be in there with his wife… they didn't want to discuss private things in front of us.'[151] An additional consideration for visitors and families was that most families had to travel from Dublin, Cork or other places in the Republic. Yet, despite their challenges and anticlimactic aftermath, these contacts were immensely important to both parties, and the possibility of their forfeiture was an additional inducement to conform to the rules.[152]

Visits, past, present and future, disturbed the inertia and penetrated the insulation of institutional life. They engendered weeks, days and hours of thought and concerned expectation. The encounters themselves can scarcely have become easier. As the years passed, the contrast became more marked between those outside whose circumstances changed and lives developed, and those inside who existed through the unchanging days, trapped in penal amber. Boyce was emphatic:

> I hated visits – most of us did – because you usually had to fight against depression afterwards. You could picture them going out the gate, going down the road, going down to the station, that sort of thing, and you had to keep putting it out of your mind all the time… and of course my mother thought I was living in a lovely place, and I had everything… you'd give her the spiel.[153]

As in the Republic, there were firms of solicitors who were suspected of being conduits for the IRA, using the privileges of legal visits. These meetings were, according to the rules, conducted within the sight of a prison officer but out of hearing. Some solicitors were searched on entry and exit to ensure that IRA documents were not being passed. Hugh Cunningham recalled one rather inept legal courier who, on being searched after his visit, was found to have an illicit letter that he had forgotten to hand over.[154] The IRA men, their families and supporters, consulted only a handful of solicitors, whom they thought trustworthy. The possibilities of passing verbal messages were reasonably high, provided the solicitor cooperated; documents were altogether more difficult, and their discovery could have serious professional and even criminal repercussions.

Correspondence was in the main restricted to families and legal advisers, and, in content and tone, this was bound to be as constrained as visits since prisoners and their correspondents knew all would pass before the eyes of the prison censor and possibly Special Branch. This caution had been driven home at the trial of the Omagh raiders. A letter written by Boyce to a relative was produced in court and used as evidence against him. Another letter, from Tom Mitchell to his mother, was released to the press by the RUC.[155] These incidents show the naivety of the young men at the time of their arrest and the failure, or inability, of the IRA to prepare them for imprisonment.

Publicity

There were well-tested techniques to publicise the plight of prisoners which had been proved effective as far back as the imprisonment of de Valera in 1917 and, indeed, long before that, in the times of the Fenians.[156] Contesting a parliamentary election from behind bars was a proven device for gathering support, commanding attention and cocking a snook at the powers that be. In February 1957, the Ministry of Home Affairs decided to block prisoners from receiving nomination papers, which, on both sides of the border, a prospective candidate had to sign in order to allow the nomination process to go forward. In September 1961, the issue came up again when there was an attempt to nominate David O'Connell (Dáithí Ó Conaill) as the Sinn Féin candidate for Cork City. This was foiled by the ban on election papers.[157]

Very little sympathy was generated in wider nationalist circles for the plight of the sentenced men. Boyce considered that prisoners were not a big asset to the IRA during the 1956–62 campaign, although the organisation drew attention to their plight as much as possible by selling cards with the caption 'In Jail for Ireland' and similar messages.[158] Another prisoner was even more dismissive and considered that he and the others were not at all important during the 1950s campaign.[159] But this was not a wholly accurate view. Boyce recalled that in the wake of the Omagh raiders' treason-felony trial there was an increase in IRA recruitment. The wording of the charge, he thought, referring to the defendants' supposed duty of allegiance to the Crown, combined with the tone of the speeches from the dock, struck a militant chord among national-minded young men in the South.[160]

Release

For sentenced prisoners, legal freedom came in three possible ways: (1) temporary release (parole), often linked to urgent family matters but also granted to well-behaved long-termers as a reward and resettlement aid; (2) early release by exercise of executive prerogative; and (3) release on expiration of sentence. The last need not detain us, since the 1950s IRA men had decided not to confront the authorities and, consequently, almost all earned the maximum remission of one-third for good behaviour.[161] Nor need much time be spent on early release. Provided he were willing to renounce former beliefs and associations, petition the Crown and undertake to have no further contact with the IRA, a prisoner stood a good chance of being granted early release. Only three of the 1950s men took this course.

Paddy McGrogan, Philip Clarke and Patrick (Paddy) Kearney all successfully petitioned for release.[162] Clarke had been elected as Stormont MP for Fermanagh and South Tyrone in the UK General Election in 1955. This had been a massive nationalist and republican victory, backed by more than 30,000 votes. Until this election was overturned by the High Court of Northern Ireland, Clarke, at twenty-two, was the youngest MP on the Westminster Roll. He was an exceptionally well-known republican, and his signing out was bitterly resented by others in the IRA group, as was the defection of Kearney. Paddy Kearney was the son of nurse Kathleen Kearney, who had been in the GPO during the Easter Rising and therefore trailed more than a little republican glory in his name.[163] The procedure for seeking early release required a prisoner to submit a petition to the Queen. Quite apart from the actual appeal, the archaic language of the petition, with its emphasis on humility and pleading – 'you had to grovel', one of the prisoners commented – was anathema to IRA activists. An interview with County Inspector William Fannin, head of the RUC Special Branch, followed. He was, noted Boyce, 'A policeman, but a very smart man.' After four years in prison, the men would have no operational information of value, but they could still provide useful background intelligence. On all matters of release the RUC risk assessment was critical, so the interview with Fannin was not only obligatory but decisive.[164]

There were no prospects of a general release. The number of sentenced prisoners was too small, and there was a lack of support or even interest from what might have been the expected quarters: the minority population in Northern Ireland, Southern politicians and trade unionists and liberal figures and organisations in Britain. In addition, the stuttering continuation of the IRA's bombing and shooting campaign made it difficult for anyone who might be sympathetic to know when to start lobbying. This was a factor that added greatly to internees' uncertainties. But the sentenced prisoners also hoped for early release when it became clear that the campaign's downward trajectory could not be reversed. Each new and futile raid or explosion was a hammer blow to early release. A sentenced prisoner recalled the mood: 'And then there was a couple came [into the prison] in 1959 for a stupid raid that they did. I'll tell you they weren't terribly welcomed by the prisoners who were doing long-terms.'[165]

A few of the arms raiders who completed shorter sentences were, as in the Republic, served with internment orders and stayed on in a new status, transferred from A to D Wing. Since internment did not end in Northern Ireland until 25 April 1961, some internees had served more than four years, the equivalent, with remission for good behaviour, of what was then a fairly heavy sentence of six years. Those still under sentence at the time of the general releases of internees were not freed and, less the usual remission, served out their time in full.

Parole

Sleepy backwater though it may have been in matters of penal reform, Northern Ireland was ahead of the rest of the UK in one respect: the availability of short-term non-emergency home leave. This scheme started in 1948 and reflected key characteristics of Northern Ireland's social structure: the strong emphasis on family and community, localism and the fact that it would be extremely difficult for an absconding prisoner to remain at large. The level of crime was low as, for the greater part, was the gravity of offences.[166] Temporary release met two distinct types of needs: family emergencies or bereavement or practical preparations for release. It was also a highly valued carrot: home leave at Christmas, or, indeed, any other time, was a powerful inducement to be well behaved. Prison privileges all have this element: that which is granted can be taken away or refused.[167] They are, therefore, an integral part of the disciplinary system, and no prison operating within a democracy can do without them.

A number of considerations arose when the applicant for parole was an internee or a convicted political prisoner. IRA men could at that time consider themselves safe from Northern Ireland's justice system once they got to the Republic.[168] So far as can be ascertained, none domiciled in the Republic at the time of conviction was granted short-term parole. A time would come when the IRA itself, in order to safeguard the parole scheme, would insist that its members returned promptly. That degree of discipline and ability to enforce it was, in the 1950s, well beyond the IRA.[169] Implicitly or explicitly to rely upon the guarantees of a paramilitary organisation when deciding upon parole would have been completely unacceptable for a number of reasons. There was also a concern that an IRA man would, during home leave, be in contact with or indeed act on the orders of the organisation. Therefore, to obtain parole, applicants had to show that they had severed all connections with violent republicanism. An internee who made such a case would almost certainly be released.[170]

For sentenced prisoners, a stronger case had to be made. Hugh McCrory's 1958 application shows some of the difficulties. With four others, he had been sentenced on 7 August 1958, receiving five years' imprisonment for his part in damaging a transformer at Ballymena, Co. Antrim.[171] He had strong community ties, and there was some doubt that he had ever been a member of the IRA: the sabotage was probably a freelance copycat action. Police, exceptionally in such cases, did not oppose bail for the McCrory brothers. They had subsequently surrendered to the court as required, knowing that a prison sentence was inevi-table. In October 1958, Hugh McCrory applied for short-term parole to enable his father to carry out a rush job; this was particularly pressing because of the precarious state of the family printing business. McCrory's application was sup-ported by a letter in which he abjectly repented his offence: 'the most sinful and very disgraceful act which I did'. He promised never to associate with republicans again and pointed out that he had not done so in prison.[172]

McCrory was supported by Major Thompson, and his plea was favourably reviewed by J. B. O'Neill, Assistant Secretary at the Ministry. With a non-political offender, the application would have been granted with a little more ado, but, before taking it to the Minister, O'Neill sought RUC background information and comment.[173] A. H. Kennedy, RUC Deputy Inspector-General, responded swiftly and strongly: 'Mr McCrory, Senr., is a decent law-abiding man, and he really does require the services of his son to carry out the rush printing job described. The police would be glad to see him facilitated as far as possible.'[174] Parole was duly granted. That was not the end of the story, however, and local reaction underlined some of the difficulties the Ministry faced in making decisions. Robert Simpson, Unionist MP for Mid-Antrim at Stormont and a family doctor in Ballymena (where he was a well-known figure, going by the affectionate sobriquet 'Dr Bob'), expressed his dissatisfaction. With Christmas approaching, he advised that no further parole be given to the McCrory brothers. Altogether, five men had been sentenced in the case, and he had been approached in the street by one of the wives who asked for help in getting parole for her husband. As their family doctor he knew that all the families were hoping for Christmas home leave for their men, and McCrory's recent parole had encouraged them. He counselled against any further leniency: 'I am convinced that even limited parole to any of these five men would result in bitter comment from the loyalists of the town.'[175]

Despite such local considerations, the Ministry continued to process applications for parole on compassionate or other compelling grounds. Writing to Deputy Inspector-General Kennedy, seeking comment on a case similar to McCrory's, J. B. O'Neill indicated that the Ministry was prepared to grant the application. They were not, however, willing to make it a general rule to grant applications where and because the Governor of Belfast Prison was satisfied that IRA links had been severed.[176] Not enough can be gleaned from the papers for us to know if this humane case-by-case approach was sustained in the face of local objections such as those voiced by Dr Simpson, anxious as he was to avoid stirring up local unionist discontent.

The last few

By late July 1963, eight men remained under sentence for IRA activities.[177] Internment had a Damoclean quality for those in Northern Ireland who became too active in matters associated with republicanism, but there was, nevertheless, a certain amount of campaigning for leniency and early release. Mainstream politicians in the Republic were willing to lobby on behalf of the IRA men in English prisons – long an emotive caption for Irish nationalism – but were distinctly wary about doing the same for the Belfast prisoners. There was, in addition, a lack of contact with the Northern Ireland government. For some forty years, the Southern doctrine had been that if one did not acknowledge that Stormont existed it might at least be imagined, if not actually conjured, to go away. In consequence, before 1963 there were relatively few contacts, even at the informal and social levels, between the politicians and officials of the two parts of the island.[178] Dublin's thinking was that Stormont was simply the creature of London, so why talk to anyone but the organ-grinder? This was a narrow view to take and could be counterproductive. Stormont's subordinacy was unquestionable in the broader constitutional sense, but authority had been devolved and across a wide swathe (including law and order) much had been reserved to the Northern Ireland government. This was a basic in any textbook that dealt with public administration in the UK. When approaches were made to the British Embassy in Dublin about the Belfast prisoners, the CRO was obliged to point out that matters concerning Northern Ireland's law and legal administration were solely within Stormont's competence, to whom it inevitably passed the correspondence.[179]

As a result of this unwillingness by public bodies in the South to acknowledge even the *de facto* nature of Northern Ireland's government and administration, the representations that were made in the Republic generally emanated from the more strident republican groups and were declamatory and admonitory rather than persuasive. Pickets at the British Embassy epitomised the tone: a series of futile 'We Demand' placards, the purpose of which can only have been to raise the spirits of the faithful and to keep some semblance of militancy alive. The chutzpah prize in this type of agitation must surely go to the Political Prisoners' Release Campaign. Writing in June 1963, it cited the fact that some prisoners had already been released in acts of clemency as evidence that the British government was not applying standards of justice but was rather acting on grounds of political expediency.[180] Damned if you do; damned if you don't.

Two events stimulated efforts to secure releases. The first was the IRA statement of 26 February 1962, ending the Border Campaign. Drawing an inappropriate but convenient parallel with relations between states, some activists and sympathisers took the view that, since the war was over, all those who had taken a part should forthwith be released.[181] This was not an opinion shared by the Northern Ireland government, which regarded the 'war' as a series of criminal acts, whose perpetrators, when caught, had been fairly tried and, where found guilty, properly punished: having had their day in court, the IRA men should expect to serve their sentences. These were in a completely different position from the internees, who had not been tried. The justification for holding them was preventive, and it would have been improper and indefensible to prolong their detention once the threat had passed.[182] The argument that the 'war' was over and that those serving sentences should be released overlooked two vital points, Belfast insisted. The Border Campaign's termination was due entirely to the inability of the IRA to continue: there had been no armistice. Had the IRA been able to secure an advantage, it would have done so. It was, moreover, a key part of its ceasefire statement that it would return to the path of violence when conditions allowed.[183] Second, the men serving time in Belfast Prison had been punished as retribution and deterrence, and there was no reason to interfere with those proper and appropriate sentencing objectives.

Sixteen months after the IRA statement of cessation there was a second stimulus to the hopes of sympathisers. This was the four-day visit to Ireland of the first Roman Catholic President of the United States of America, John F. Kennedy. The visit (26–9 June 1963) was intended to celebrate the Irish origins of Kennedy's family and was of historic importance, considerable pride and great public celebration in the Republic of Ireland.[184] There was some thought that this auspicious occasion could be an opportunity to resolve Irish problems and, at the very least, that it constituted a jubilee, to be marked by the customary release of prisoners.[185] This desire to add another element to the Kennedy visit, and one very out of kilter with the joyous theme the event carried, had no effect in Belfast or London, and it was a foolish whim to imagine that, either on the part of the USA or the UK, there was the slightest wish it should do so. It is doubtful if many politicians in Dublin thought otherwise.

As time passed and sentences expired, the released men were welcomed home with ceremonies, demonstrations and even dances. The prisoner-support bodies in the three jurisdictions continued their activities. From time to time, town or even county councils in the Republic adopted resolutions calling for the release of the remaining prisoners. But, in the autumn of 1962, six months after the IRA ceasefire, thirty-two sentenced prisoners remained in Belfast Prison.[186] The pages of the *United Irishman* (already shifting its orientation to the social agenda of the IRA's new leadership) indisputably show that the heart had gone even from the issue of prisoner release. The activities that were reported were those of the faithful and others to whom vaguely nationalist and humanitarian concerns were appealing and entailed no cost. There is a strong sense of a limited number of actors being moved around to make a crowd. The soldiers of a defeated army find little solace and that, for the greater part, comes from within their own ranks.

The last English prisoners

IRA operations had continued in Northern Ireland until as late as 26 November 1961, but several years had elapsed since the English arms raids. Two men remained in prison as a result of the raid on the REME depot in Arborfield in August 1955.[187] For a range of offences, including robbery under arms, three had been sentenced to life imprisonment, with concurrent sentences of fourteen years and lesser periods. James Andrew Mary Murphy had escaped from Wakefield prison on 12 February 1959, in an operation organised by the live wire and dissident republican Joe Christle.[188] Back in Ireland, Murphy opted for left-wing rather than republican politics.[189]

Decisions on life-sentence releases were taken by Home Office officials, in all but a very few cases without political intervention: process, precedent and demonstrable principle were crucial. There was a regular and well-established structure of review and consultation as part of which periodic reports were submitted to Whitehall by the prison authorities. The prison reports of Donal Murphy (no relation to James) had been sufficiently encouraging to justify his release on licence in October 1962. Only Joe Doyle remained, and sympathisers' energies were concentrated on him, in a campaign with support from politicians across the spectrum.

Representations addressed to the British Embassy in Dublin were passed to the CRO and thence to the Home Office. As with the picketing outside the Embassy, one group of correspondents seemed largely indifferent as to the outcome. Their letters were combative, strident and stereotypical: none was abusive, but many were hectoring; their purpose was to make a protest rather than a case. These included resolutions from some town councils, the Society of Friends of the Irish Language, the Irish Workers' Party (as the Embassy explained, 'the name under which the Communists find it safer to travel here'[190]), a branch of the GAA, the National Civil Liberties League, a militant cumann (branch) of Fianna Fáil, the Student Representative Council (Galway) and the Republican Prisoners' Release Association.[191] None of these carried the slightest weight in Anglo-Irish relations or within Irish politics. As the core of their expertise, mainstream politicians knew the elastic properties of appearance and substance and the tactics and idiom with which they could be manoeuvred. Seventy-three members of the Dáil and Senate supported a carefully worded petition for Doyle's release. Labour signed en masse, but there was also significant support from members of both principal parties and from independents.

Disagreement and even a degree of friction developed between the Embassy in Dublin and the Home Office as to the manner of handling these approaches from the respectable and established end of the Irish political spectrum. The Home Office, led by its formidable permanent under-secretary, Sir Charles Cunningham – a guardian of long-established practice – ploughed on like a dreadnought, its course set entirely by the weight and momentum of its own rules and procedures. Cunningham fiercely resisted, as wholly improper, anything that could be construed as political interference in what amounted to quasi-judicial processes. Life-sentence prisoners were subject to executive release, but, within the standards of the times, cases were considered closely and carefully – which is not to deny the subjective elements in decisions. The process was controlled by senior civil servants and proceeded on the basis that all prisoners in a category (such as lifers) be treated alike. Detailed reports and recommendations were regularly submitted by staff, based on the prisoner's disciplinary record and their observations of his associations and notes of conversations overheard or passed on. These were considered by the lifers' section of the Home Office, which in turn developed a brief and submitted a recommendation to the Home Secretary. All such contacts went through Cunningham, who checked his subordinates' work – as they knew he would. Donal Murphy was reported to have responded favourably to his imprisonment, which essentially meant that he was compliant to the rules and temperate in his conversations and correspondence. In July 1962, he was told that he was to be released on 2 October.[192] Doyle was kept back because he was considered still to be 'a fairly militant IRA supporter', but it nevertheless had been decided by the Home Office that 'if all went well' – that is, if his behaviour remained good – he could be released in 1963.[193]

The Home Office's reasoning and even its procedures for reviewing lifers were confidential and left the British Embassy awkwardly placed when it was lobbied by groups of respectable politicians, members of the Dáil and Senate and former and current aldermen and lord mayors of Dublin and Cork. An impressive delegation was received at the Embassy on 21 November 1962. In these transactions, to encourage a favourable outcome, petitioners must tactfully suggest a way in which their requests can be accommodated without challenging the handling of the case to that point, without creating an inconvenient precedent and without giving rise to unfavourable publicity. In this case, the delegation spokesman was the Independent Labour deputy, Seán Dunne. He pointed out that, apart from his one grave offence in 1955, Doyle had no police record, and his life sentence had at the time seemed excessive. While it might have been justified as a deterrent in 1955, the situation was now very different; Doyle had, in any event, served seven years. What eventually became the strongest point was then put. Doyle's mother was over seventy-nine, and it was hard on her not to know whether she could ever hope to see her son again.[194]

The Ambassador and senior officials knew but could not disclose that a probable release date had been set. The Christmas season was a time when clemency had been customarily sought (and sometimes obtained) for republican prisoners. The Ambassador, treading carefully, so as not to ruffle interdepartmental feathers (Sir Charles Cunningham's plumage in particular), noted in his report of the meeting that he could not say whether or not it was fitting to release Doyle, but, were there any prospect of doing so it would help Anglo-Irish relations to make an imaginative gesture and let him go before Christmas: 'If he is released some time in the middle of next year we shall get no credit for it any more than we got any credit for releasing Murphy in the middle of 1962.'[195]

Cunningham's heavily armoured craft refused to deviate by an inch: Anglo-Irish relations were an irrelevance. In the following months, Doyle's mother's condition deteriorated. Christopher Bonass, an Irish trade unionist with good contacts with the *Sunday Times* management, travelled to London in mid-February 1963 for a meeting with Cunningham, to present, he emphasised, 'a purely compassionate case'. Bonass had known Doyle's family for many years and lived not far from their home. He told Cunningham that Mrs Doyle was deteriorating mentally and physically and had no will to live. She was no longer fit to travel to visit her son, even were he moved to a closer prison, such as Liverpool. A daughter had come home from Scotland to care for her but might not be able to stay indefinitely. The case had been reviewed the previous December, Cunningham noted, but he accepted Bonass's offer of a report on Mrs Doyle's health. He promised to put to the Home Secretary the representations that had been made. Immediate release was unlikely, he thought, but it might be possible to fix a prospective date, and he hoped that this would do something to comfort Mrs Doyle.[196]

Agitation continued in Ireland. There were more pickets on the British Embassy and on the Ambassador's car. There was a peaceful demonstration outside the CRO in London. It would be hard to point to a direct impact on official or political deliberations, but these events probably did serve to keep the issue alive. Lamenting the lost opportunity of a Christmas release, the Ambassador continued to urge a compassionate approach, emphasising Mrs Doyle's poor health. Were she to die before her son was released, there would be 'a very bad press indeed' in Ireland. He would not mind this were any useful purpose being served, but (in an uncharacteristic flash) he would be sorry if it arose 'merely because of a wooden adherence by the Home Office to rules and regulations'.[197]

Con Cremin, the Irish Ambassador in London, also lobbied the Home Secretary but was told that no decision was possible ahead of the scheduled March review. The same line was taken in a brief prepared for the March 1963 visit of Taoiseach Seán Lemass and Irish Minister for External Affairs Frank Aiken.[198] Later than month, at the end of a meeting with British officials on other matters, Aiken again urged Doyle's release. He worried that during the forthcoming Easter commemorations Doyle would provide a focus for republican demonstrations. In British Ambassador Sir Ian Maclennan's view, Aiken's continued interest in Doyle's case arose from his calculation that 'a lot of undesirable people (Sinn Féin, IRA, etc) are getting a great deal of kudos by organising these demonstrations and he would like to see the wind taken out of their sails by Doyle's release'.[199] A month later, having adhered to its own review timetable (and made something of a point in Whitehall), the Home Office announced that Doyle would be freed on 2 July. No public announcement would be made, but Lord Longford and one or two other people who had taken an interest in the case had as a courtesy been informed. Maclennan should feel free to inform the Irish government and anyone else he thought should know.[200]

There was another twist. Mrs Doyle died on 30 April 1963, and Seán Dunne, the TD who had taken a leading part in the discreet lobbying, asked the British Embassy to request Doyle's immediate release. This was not agreed, but exceptionally (since it meant he would leave the UK), Doyle was granted temporary release to attend the funeral.[201] Although only weeks remained, the Home Office insisted that Doyle honour his undertaking and return to Wakefield Prison, to await permanent release on 2 July.[202] Doyle complied, much to his credit. On 25 June, the Embassy in Dublin was informed that to avoid publicity it had been agreed that Christoper Bonass could collect Doyle from Wakefield on 1 July.[203]

The Home Office's wish that there be no publicity when Doyle was freed was unlikely to be fulfilled, given the time and effort invested by Sinn Féin, the Political Prisoners' Release Committee and similar republican bodies. His release was their moment to bask in largely undeserved credit. Doyle arrived back in Dublin on the evening of Monday, 1 July. A weekday was inconvenient for getting a good turnout, so demonstrations were postponed until the Saturday following, when a three-band parade and a public meeting at the Town Hall welcomed him back to Bray.[204]

The campaign for Doyle's release displayed much that had previously marked such campaigns – and would continue to do so. There remained a fund of sympathy in Ireland, well beyond republican circles, for young Irishmen who ended up in English prisons. The words in themselves triggered perceptions and emotions going back beyond the Easter Rising to the Fenians. Even mainstream political parties and politicians responded to such currents and would have faced questions had they not. At the same time, mainstream politicians were aware of how campaigns could be hijacked by republican outriders and consequently sought to deny them the opportunity to garner support for their own causes and organisations. For its part, the British government was anxious not to create a precedent and open itself to pressures of a similar nature on a future occasion. In Doyle's case there had been some disagreement between the Dublin Embassy and London on how best to proceed: immediate political yield versus the integrity of a quasi-judicial procedure. And, through the whole episode, there could be discerned a familiar transfiguration, from IRA activist to victim, with the original offence either justified, attributed to youth and an excess of patriotism or simply not mentioned.

To be free

All long-term prisoners, political and ordinary criminals alike, face significant problems on release. These include the obvious difficulties, such as accommodation and employment, but, hard though these are to surmount, psychological and social adjustment can be even more intractable. The political prisoners of the 1950s faced several difficulties picking up the pieces. Their campaign had failed miserably, the IRA had run into the sand, and the general political and economic situation was very different in the early 1960s from that which they had known when they went into prison. The first waves of the great tides of social change had begun to reach Ireland. All of this was bound to lead the released men to an appraisal of their time in prison, the unbridgeable gap in their lives, the discontinuities and the losses they had incurred. For many of the men, such issues would be revisited again and again throughout their lives, never satisfactorily resolved.[205]

Much immediate adjustment of a practical kind was required for re-entering everyday life. Apart from visitors, the men had been in exclusively male company for several years. Mixing with women and children again, and observing the conventional courtesies and civilities, was testing, requiring thought and a profound series of adjustments; it also drove home in a very stark way what the lost years had meant. Boyce was typical in finding his first year of freedom particularly challenging. As a survival technique, the psycho-sexual impulses had been secured as tidily as possible during the years of captivity. The locks and bolts now had to be undone, and that, especially in working-class Catholic Ireland, was not to be spoken of or shared. No counselling was offered or, apparently, sought. It was a matter of self-help – or no help. Everyday and relatively superficial social interactions could so easily trip one up. If in prison a man said something that others found stupid or unacceptable, there would be an immediate and blunt reaction. The intensity of the relationships within the IRA unit in Belfast Prison and the male ethos made this type of interaction natural, supportable and even supportive. Outside, it came across as intolerant and aggressive; there was little doubt such a way of conducting oneself carried a lot of barely recognised, much less understood, anger.[206] This was only one of the barriers to integration. Some men were able to analyse and adjust, others continually struggled, finding understanding, shared memories, support and a degree of comfort only with comrades.

One man who served two and three-quarter years of a four-year sentence commented, '[i]t definitely leaves a mark on you, I don't care who you are'. This was a comparatively short sentence, he noted, and those who served longer ones were more severely affected. The emotional and sexual strains on young men were considerable and left their enduring mark:

> I was in A2, I was on the Crumlin Road side, and you have never had anything more disturbing than, late at night, on a bright winter's night, particularly on a Saturday night, to hear fellows and girls coming up the road, laughing and talking, and I remember the click of their high heels. I can still hear that, going up the road.[207]

Notes

1 See *NIPD*, vol. 33, col. 129, 8 March 1949; vol. 38, col. 2131, 18 May 1954.

2 See above, pp. 372–83. Control over law and order was handed over to the Northern Ireland government shortly after the establishment of the new state.

3 In interviews, both republican and loyalist prisoners mentioned these men, whose heavy sentences were so disproportionate to the crimes they had committed. Dessie O'Hagan remembered a man who was sentenced under this provision to five years' imprisonment for stealing five Woodbine cigarettes. Preventive detention was introduced by the Prevention of Crime Act, 1908 (ss.10[1 and 2]). In essence, this was a system under which an offender was sentenced twice: once for the offence before the court and again, if he met the criteria, for being an habitual offender. For a succinct account of the origins of preventive detention see Sir Leon Radzinowicz and Roger Hood, 'Incapacitating the Habitual Criminal: The English Experience', *Michigan Law Review*, 78 (8): 1305–89, especially pp. 1363–70. See also, Sir Leon Radzinowicz and Roger Hood, *A History of the English Criminal Law and Its Administration*, 5 vols. (London: Stevens & Sons, 1986), vol. V: *The Emergence of Penal Policy*, pp. 268–78 and *passim*.

4 These women, Hugh Cunningham (a former governor) recalled, 'Wouldn't have gone out if you had opened the gate – maybe up to ten prisoners, old wine victims and people like that… they used to have… parties for them on their birthday' (interview).

5 The use of Armagh for males was made possible by a 1955 change in the Prison Rules. Until then it was a legal requirement for men and women each to be

accommodated in prisons reserved exclusively for their sex. The 1955 change addressed a long-standing problem by allowing women undergoing trial in Belfast to remain there overnight in a special unit. This cut the expense of bringing them from Armagh each day. The rule change also permitted male prisoners to be used for repair and maintenance work in Armagh, holding them there as necessary. These changes worked smoothly and cleared the way for the larger and more permanent transfers of 1958. See Prison (Amendment) Rules (Northern Ireland) 1955; *Belfast Newsletter*, 13 July 1955, 5f; PRONI HA/9/2/953.

6 See the Prison Act, 1877: 40 & 41 Vict., c.21, ss.40 and 41. This continued a policy that can be traced through successive statutes going back to an Act of 1840 (Prisons Act, 1840: 3 & 4 Vict., c.25, s.2). Parliament was reluctant to submit to criminal infamy and penal discipline persons who had not committed an offence of violence or moral turpitude. See Seán McConville, *English Local Prisons, 1860–1900: Next Only to Death* (London and New York: Routledge, 1995), pp. 369–77. The Northern Ireland legislature, however, had had no such qualms.

7 As reported by the RUC, he said, 'I believe in the use of force, the more the better, the sooner the better.' He also said, '[t]he time has come when we must oppose force with force' and 'England does not understand what we mean by force but we will make them. We will make them understand by the strong-arm method' (PRONI HA/32/1/955, Special Branch Memorandum, 'Liam Kelly and Saor Uladh', July 1958). See also *Irish News*, 5 December 1953, 1d–e.

8 *Irish News*, 21 November 1953, 1c–d; 23 November 1953, 1h; *Northern Whig*, 5 December 1953, 1a–c.

9 See below, pp. 841–2; 901.

10 PRONI HA/9/2/753, L. F. Thompson to Ministry of Home Affairs, 26 November 1953. As a remand prisoner, Kelly was entitled to wear his own clothing. The obligation to don prison uniform came with conviction and sentence.

11 See above, pp. 575–7. Thompson had served in the Ulster Special Constabulary and in the Royal Inniskilling Fusiliers before joining the Northern Ireland Prison Service. An interviewee who had served under him described Thompson as 'a tough wee man'.

12 Although not dwelt upon by Thompson, it would have been politically incendiary to leave naked in his cell a man who, whatever his views, had been elected to Stormont. Besides, times, and sensibilities, had changed.

13 There is some menace in this statement. It is difficult to say whether Kelly meant his threat to imply physical retaliation on staff by persons outside the prison (such as happened in the 1940s) or legal action. If the former, it is doubtful that he or his associates had the means to inflict it; if the latter, no Northern Ireland court would have provided redress.

14 PRONI HA/9/2/753, Kelly letter and memorandum, 30 November 1953. Kelly was thoroughly familiar with past conditions in the prison. In September 1941, he had been sentenced to two years' imprisonment. On the expiration of that sentence (with time off for good behaviour) in May 1943, he was served with an internment order and remained in Belfast Prison until September 1945. He had thus served the equivalent of a six-year sentence (less the usual one-third remission).

15 PRONI HA/9/2/753, Thompson to Ministry, 6 December 1953.

16 *Belfast Telegraph*, 7 December 1953, 11b; *Irish News*, 7 December 1953, 5d.

17 PRONI HA/9/2/753, Thompson to Ministry, 22 February 1954. Eleven of the twenty refusers, Thompson estimated, were IRA sympathisers.

18 *Irish News*, 23 July 1954, 2g. Kelly, like MacBride, had broken with the IRA on the issue of recognising the Constitution of the Southern state, the validity of its electoral process and the legitimacy of its government. No longer himself involved in political violence, MacBride was at the very least ambivalent towards it. Kelly's

political organisation, Fianna Uladh, put its spin on the election: 'We are glad to realise that the people of the Twenty-Six Counties have endorsed Liam Kelly's stand… of abstention from a foreign-controlled Parliament' (*Irish News*, 16 July 1954, 5d). Kelly received eighty-nine votes from the Dáil to secure the appointment – mainly from Labour and Fianna Fáil TDs (see *Ulster Herald*, 24 July 1954, 3c; *Irish Independent*, 16 July 1954, 7f–g).

19 PRONI HA/9/2/753, P. J. Agnew & Sons (Solicitors, Maghera) to Ministry of Home Affairs, 2 and 7 August 1954; *Irish News*, 16 August 1954, 3c.

20 *Irish News*, 20 August 1954, 1b–c; *Northern Whig*, 20 August 1954, 1a–c.

21 Interview.

22 Prison Rules (Northern Ireland), 1954 (Statutory Rules and Orders of Northern Ireland, 1954, 7), Rule 4 (3). Star Class men were held together on the same floor, but (defeating the original purpose for designating neophytes as Star Class, the prevention of corruption and contamination) mixed with the ordinary prisoners. Over the years, IRA prisoners got to know all on their wing.

23 O'Hagan was emphatic: 'We all wore a uniform. There was a strike on that years ago, in the forties, it never worked. And the authorities were never going to concede it' (interview).

24 Prison Rules (Northern Ireland), *op. cit.*, Rule 44. As far as possible, labour was intended to be productive and to have a training element. For security reasons, the IRA men were not appointed as orderlies – a position of some trust. Orderlies cleaned the cell block, but Hugh Cunningham, then a prison officer, observed, 'We couldn't afford to have them [IRA men] wandering about' (interview).

25 O'Hagan interview. The details of prison routine were governed by rules and standing orders, within the broad limits of the prison regulations. There was a general requirement, for example, that all convicted prisoners should 'so far as practicable' work for at least eight hours a day outside his cell, with a maximum of ten hours (Prison Rules [Northern Ireland], *op. cit.*, Rule 44). For a variety of administrative staffing and security reasons, few prisons managed to work inmates for the maximum number of hours, even in housekeeping duties.

26 See below, pp. 843–4.

27 See above, pp. 574–5. A list was published of the items that could be included in the parcels. Hugh Cunningham remembered that very few of the ordinary prisoners got anything from their friends and families. The IRA men sometimes exceeded their allowance and agreed that any surplus should be made up into parcels for those who had none. The parcels had to come from relatives and were searched before being handed over (interview).

28 Eamonn Boyce interview.

29 Tom Mitchell (1931–). Joined the IRA at age nineteen and was arrested following the October 1954 Omagh raid. Sentenced to ten years' imprisonment. Despite his imprisonment, elected Westminster MP for Mid-Ulster in May and again in August 1955. (He was, as a convicted man, debarred from the position.) OC for long-term prisoners in Belfast Prison from June 1957 until October 1960.

30 Hugh Cunningham, a basic grade officer at the time (later rising to governor) recalled the men's attitude. They certainly felt that they should not have been in prison, but they nevertheless got on with the other prisoners: 'And all the staff in A Wing, we were there all the time, every day, day after day, you knew everybody, you talked to them, and life wasn't all that bad in those days' (interview).

31 Boyce interview. It was also possible to make a complaint outside the formal structure.

32 O'Hagan interview.

33 Cunningham interview. There were some, 'like every other crowd you get', who were not all that friendly, but 'in the main you were able to talk to them'. And there

certainly was give and take. Boyce recalled that the nightly whistling of a police officer who was on guard duty outside the prison was irritating to him, and he complained to a prison officer who said he'd have a word with the whistler. Eamonn Boyce, *The Insider: The Belfast Prison Diaries of Eamonn Boyce, 1956–1962*, ed. Anna Bryson (Dublin: Lilliput Press, 2007), p. 119.

34 Cunningham interview. The same sentiments were expressed by one of the prisoners: 'You don't ask what a man is in for, or anything like that, and I often said to chaplains, "I found more charity, Christian charity, in that place than I ever found in the world outside."' The feeling of being different disappeared, he recalled. (Boyce interview.) Contradicting that, somewhat, is a recollection by Hugh Cunningham of a sectarian undercurrent. The IRA men and other Catholic prisoners played Gaelic football during their allotted evening yard time. A Catholic prisoner played soccer one evening, violating – in all probability without thought – the GAA injunction. The man appeared thereafter to have been excluded from the Catholic choir, which he had previously trained (Cunningham interview).

35 Joe Campbell (Newry, Co. Down) was sentenced for explosives offences on 6 July 1953 (*Newry Reporter*, 9 July 1953, 1a–b; for pre-trial proceedings, see *Newry Reporter*, 25 June 1953, 3e–f; 2 July, 2c–d). Kevin O'Rourke (Banbridge, Co. Down) had been found guilty on explosives charges (*Newry Reporter*, 19 August 1954, 1d–e; 9 December 1954, 6d; *Irish Press*, 8 December 1954, 6a–c).

36 See above, pp. 577–9. Boyce gave an instance to illustrate the lack of connection between the prisoners and the IRA outside. The prisoners believed that corrupt staff were pilfering food from the prison. 'It was coming in the gate and being transferred to cars... and we sent out a lot of information but they [the IRA] never did anything about it' (Boyce, *The Insider, op. cit.*, p. 444).

37 O'Hagan was sentenced to four years for his part in a failed armed rescue of a wounded comrade from Belfast City Hospital (*Belfast Telegraph*, 12 March 1957, 1a–b; 3 May 1957, 1h; *Irish News*, 3 May 1957, 5g–h; *Irish Press*, 3 May 1957, 8c–d). His companion in this venture had been Patrick Pearse McGrogan. O'Hagan came from the (Catholic) Divis Street area of Belfast, which corrected those who claimed that Saor Uladh membership was restricted to Tyrone and adjacent areas. He remained an active republican after his release from prison and was interned in the August 1971 round-up.

38 Dessie O'Hagan wished to get Advanced and Ordinary Level qualifications in the GCE. This involved submitting a written request to the authorities. There was a certain political stigma attached to this since it implied a degree of recognition. Whereas an IRA man had, in consequence, to get permission from GHQ O'Hagan did not need this, and he obtained permission from the authorities for his study. A number of IRA men subsequently followed his lead, having obtained IRA permission. Boyce was opposed to seeking permission from a Northern Ireland minister, since this implied recognition (*The Insider, op. cit.*, p. 117).

39 O'Hagan interview.

40 See below, pp. 903–12. The search was confined to D Wing. O'Hagan emphasised that he and the others in A Wing were properly treated: 'There was no ill-treatment [in the wing] and no ill-treatment in the prison itself either. None whatsoever' (interview).

41 Once the prisoners discovered that staff were 'terrified' of losing their positions they felt more secure from possible ill-treatment. Occasionally, Boyce recalled, and provided there were no witnesses, a prison officer might insult or try to rile one of the IRA men (interview). This seems to have been a relatively rare occurrence.

42 Boyce interview.

43 Boyce, Cunningham, O'Hagan interviews; Boyce, *The Insider, op. cit.*

44 An officer on night guard in one of the other wings would be off duty on the afternoon before the duty and on the following day. This made for irregularity in his daytime contacts.

45 See, for example, pp. 591–2; 855–7. Because the men conformed to the prison discipline, Cunningham commented, '[y]ou began to think these were just ordinary guys'.

46 Boyce, *The Insider, op. cit.*, p. 163. Had Boyce's diary been discovered, the prison officer (who he named) would have been, at the very least, severely reprimanded, more probably dismissed. The prison officer, in taking the letter out of the prison, had additionally trusted Boyce's assurance that its contents were purely personal.

47 O'Hagan interview. O'Hagan's father had been reported as being gravely ill, and a member of a Catholic charitable society came to the prison to advise him to make an application for compassionate parole. O'Hagan said that he would consider the matter overnight and the following morning spoke to Bertie Noble, one of the senior prison officers. He said, 'Look, I know this is difficult for you, but can you go over to our house and see to what extent my da is seriously ill, if he's dying?' Noble was hesitant, but he did go and told O'Hagan that his father was not as ill as it had been supposed. O'Hagan commented, 'He was decent, I found him a decent fellow personally.'

48 Cunningham interview.

49 The officer rebuked in front of his prisoners was Tommy Kearns, who was a trades officer in charge of the boot workshop. This officer (basically a tradesman rather than a discipline officer) frequently did not know how many men were supposed to be in his charge (a fundamental part of gaol-craft) and would be warned that the Governor was on his rounds. Frantic counting would then follow. The number in the workshop was supposed to be written up on a blackboard, and, on the day in question, Kearns in error counted two more than he was supposed to have (O'Hagan interview).

50 Cunningham interview. It helped that Cunningham had served in the Royal Navy for many years and knew how to put his case firmly but respectfully. The Navy, he observed 'taught you to stand on your own feet'.

51 One officer would bring in cigarettes 'out of badness' (presumably resentment of some kind against the prison management) and others 'would have been throwing a couple of smokes here and there' (O'Hagan interview).

52 O'Hagan interview. It is also probable that unless the breach of rules was flagrant and without a decent attempt at concealment, staff simply did not care.

53 Boyce interview. Modern dieticians have long encouraged the consumption of skins with the rest of the potato when method of cooking allows.

54 O'Hagan interview.

55 Boyce interview. The man who broke the strike was thereafter excluded from the IRA unit. His former comrades were not overtly hostile, but 'he wasn't included, and it was markedly so, he wasn't included.' Such was the feeling about this incident that Boyce recalled it as the one major disagreement that the IRA unit had during those years. Hugh Cunningham recalled neither the mouse incident nor the boycott, and Thompson's alleged remarks have a suspicious ring of the apocryphal about them.

56 Boyce, *The Insider, op. cit.*, p. 104. But the successful despatch of the letter seems to have turned thoughts to home: 'I'm sick of the whole thing and my life in this place. I'd like to go home.'

57 Boyce interview. He continued, 'I'm married over forty years but I shared a thing with these men that nobody else could have a part of, even my wife.'

58 Boyce interview. See also Boyce, *The Insider, op. cit.*, pp. 148–9, 151, 162, 179, etc. These bouts, which everyone got, lasted only a day or two. 'But fellows had great consideration for each other, without realising it.' Boyce returned to the intensity of the relationship: '[y]ou were climbing out of a pit, you were trying to keep your head above water. You took three steps up, and you slipped back one, and the longer it

went, the more that you were aware of the fact that you were going under. But the only thing that kept you alive was the comradeship... so unique that you would have to be in that position before you could realise it.' When former comrades meet, 'It all comes back, it all comes alive again. You could almost say a worthwhile experience' (interview).

59 Cunningham interview.

60 O'Hagan interview. He remembered another prisoner, Tommy Ferron, who did give way after a long time in prison. 'They found him in the corner of the cell, rolled up in a ball like. He was the only one I ever heard.' O'Hagan also confirmed that when a man felt the onset of depression he would keep to his cell as much as possible. See also Boyce, *The Insider, op. cit.*, pp. 212–13. Visits were always full of emotion and had both positive and negative effects. Following a visit from his mother and a friend, Boyce lost control: 'Tonight – and for the first time since I came here – I was so sad that I began to cry' (*The Insider, op. cit.*, p. 162).

61 Boyce, *The Insider, op. cit.*, p. 143. On 16 January 1958, Boyce noted the culmination of what clearly had been a long-distance grudge: 'Great surprise this evening. Having eaten at our table for three years, Paddy [Kearney] left. I'm being uncharitable but I'm glad we haven't exchanged a word since 1954.'

62 Boyce interview.

63 Because the IRA men had to mix with ordinary prisoners and did not regard them with traditional IRA disdain, they were able sometimes to help the less fortunate. Boyce recalled such a case: 'There was one poor fellow there, I don't know what he was in for, but he used to come along to us and ask for any magazines – magazines with pictures.' They discovered that the man was illiterate (not uncommon among prisoners). 'Paddy Kearney took an interest in him, tutored him during association periods and taught him to read and write' (interview).

64 See John Vidler, *If Freedom Fail* (London: Macmillan & Co., 1964), especially Chapters 6 and 7, for an account of the development of a positive and educational regime at Maidstone prison. This was an influential establishment within the English penal estate, and Vidler was an evangelist for the humane and constructive in prison life.

65 Boyce recalled, 'You gradually wore them down in a very quiet kind of a way, with a little persistence. They'd have to think about it for a long time before they would say OK and you wore them down' (interview). He also contended that Thompson refused to allow one of the men, enrolled in a BSc course, to take his examinations in prison because he did not want anyone to graduate out of his prison.

66 For a discussion of the similarities, and differences, between what Erving Goffman calls 'total institutions', see his seminal collection of essays, *Asylums* (New York: Anchor Books, 1961).

67 Provided they were approved by the prison authorities, the men were allowed personally to receive a certain number of books; how many and the criteria for approval is not now clear. Dessie O'Hagan had no difficulty in obtaining a wide range of literature, from James Joyce to Karl Marx; he also received *The Economist*. The practice in Britain at the time was that any books sent in would be added to the prison library when the prisoner to whom they had been sent had finished with them. One of the prisoners, later a priest, apparently made it his task to censor this material, O'Hagan recalled. 'He would try and get to the books, and go through them, and if there was any sexual material explicitly, he would tear the pages out in case people enjoyed themselves' (interview).

68 'You needed that [out of cell time] to keep you sane. We used to sit down on our backsides and solve the problems of the world' (Boyce interview).

69 At one point, with long summer days giving more natural light, some of the men requested that the night-duty officer should bang on their cell doors to wake them at

5 a.m. so that they could do extra studying. Thompson, reluctant to set a precedent which would impose an extra duty on staff and necessitate the keeping of yet another roster, refused the request (Boyce interview).

70 O'Hagan interview.

71 Seán O'Hegarty (later he appears to have preferred Ó hÉigeartaigh) (1933–2002), born in Cork, had been an engineer with the Post Office and, since the 1940s, an IRA member. He was one of those arrested following the Omagh raid. Given a ten-year sentence, he was released in July 1961, having gained maximum remission.

72 Boyce interview.

73 Tony Cooney (1936–), born in Cork, was arrested following an exchange of fire at Torr Head radar station, Co. Antrim, on the opening night of Operation Harvest, 12 December 1956.

74 PRONI HA/9/2/783, RUC to Ministry of Home Affairs, 3 July 1958. The police anticipated that internees, a much larger group, as well as sentenced men would avail themselves of the privilege, were the initial request granted.

75 PRONI HA/9/2/770, Mitchell to Ministry of Home Affairs, 19 July 1959. The RUC approved the invigilator, who had been recommended by Father McAlister, the Roman Catholic chaplain.

76 PRONI HA/9/2/770, Ministry of Home Affairs to Governor, Belfast Prison, 15 February 1961. The course was taken at Mitchell's own expense. It probably assisted a favourable outcome that Mitchell, in six years at Belfast Prison, had never been charged with a disciplinary offence. At the time of the application, Mitchell had about fifteen months of his ten-year sentence left to serve, having been granted full remission.

77 Casting his mind back, Boyce speculated that permission to enrol in a London University course had been granted because application had been made during a spell when Governor Thompson was off duty and Deputy Governor Alec Taylor was in charge. While this shows what a naysayer the men considered Thompson to be, the reality was that no matter of importance could be dealt with in the prison (especially correspondence with Home Affairs) without passing through Thompson's hands. The IRA unit in the prison had initially disapproved of external tutorial courses, presumably on the basis that it implied some kind of recognition of British authority. See Dónal Donnelly, *Prisoner 1082: Escape from Crumlin Road, Europe's Alcatraz* (Cork: Collins Press, 2010), pp. 80–1.

78 One of the Omagh raiders, Seán O'Callaghan, before sentence was passed at his trial, told the Lord Chief Justice that it was 'a great load off my shoulders to know that I will be rewarded by God for service to my country' (*Northern Whig*, 16 December 1954, 1b).

79 For a searching account of the sometimes impossible conflicts in the work of prison chaplains, see Alan Duce, 'A Christian Approach to Punishment', in Seán McConville (ed.), *The Use of Punishment* (Cullompton: Willan, 2003), pp. 23–54. Duce was a full-time chaplain for twenty-eight years and writes perceptively and movingly about the work.

80 Canon Patrick McAlister (1914–2000) was educated at St Malachy's College and Queen's University, Belfast. Trained for priesthood at Pontifical Irish College and Luteran University, Rome. Bursar at St Malachy's College and chaplain to Belfast Prison, 1941–65. Thereafter, assigned to parish, diocesan and other duties. A well-educated, socially secure and prominently connected member of the clergy.

81 'Not that any of us were saints or anything like that, but it was a terrible thing to happen, the most demoralising thing of the whole lot to happen, and we resented McAlister for it – not realising of course that McAlister was only a pawn in the thing – he did his best, the bishop was the bishop, and that was that' (Boyce, *The Insider, op. cit.*, p. 442).

82 PRONI HA/32/1/1338, L. T. Thompson to Secretary, Ministry of Home Affairs, 18 November 1957.

83 See above, p. 795.

84 PRONI HA/32/1/1338, Ministry of Home Affairs to Governor, Belfast Prison, 26 November 1957.

85 The raid took place in the early hours of 26 November 1957. See *Northern Standard*, 2 December 1955, 1a–e; 9 December 1955, 1a–b.

86 For the Lenten Pastorals, see, earlier in the year, *Northern Star*, 26 February 1955, 2f–g (Revd Dr C. Lucey, Bishop of Cork); *Connacht Sentinel*, 22 February 1955, 2c–d (Revd Dr Browne, Bishop of Galway). Lucey warned that secret societies (a reference to the IRA) 'are of their very nature evil'. He was emphatic in his condemnation. 'It is a sin to organise such a society, to join it, or to subscribe to its funds.' Browne noted that Christ had blessed the peacemakers but 'promised death to those who have recourse to the weapons of war'. See also *Meath Chronicle*, 26 February 1955, 2a (Revd Dr Quinn, Bishop of Kilmore).

87 Boyce interview; O'Hagan interview. One wonders how much of a blind eye was turned to this activity. Many skilled in gaol-craft like the ballast of a harmless but supposedly secret activity.

88 O'Hagan interview: 'I knew that you were trapped in the situation. If you stayed in your cell one of the screws, one of the Catholic screws, would have told the priest that you weren't going to church… you would have had hassle… But for most people, it did get them out of their cells.'

89 All but one of the IRA men resumed chapel attendance, but it is not clear that they again became observant Catholics.

90 Boyce interview. Boyce remembered the withdrawal of the sacraments as 'a very hard blow… when your religion was your only consolation, and it was your only consolation… a lot of the fellows never went back to their Church after it. They got very hostile.' As for Father O'Regan of Clonard: 'He's dead now, but he was one of the best. The most human priest I ever [knew].' He had smuggled an Irish-language book, *B'fhiú an Braon Fola*, by Séamus O'Maoileoin in for Boyce. Boyce lent it to another man, and it was discovered in a cell search. There was considerable alarm in the prison, and the private visits of another priest (not at all involved) were stopped.

91 Circumstances varied a great deal. Boyce had supported his widowed mother. He worked at CIÉ (the nationalised transportation body), where his politics and membership of the IRA were unknown. Two weeks after his trial, workmates at Donnybrook Garage, Dublin, began to collect funds, each contributing 6d. (nominally 2½ pence in modern currency; closer to 20p in purchasing power) and handed over to Boyce's mother the equivalent of a week's wages. This continued for the eight years of Boyce's imprisonment. When he was released, an additional sum of £200 was given to Boyce (interview). After a few weeks' rest, Boyce resumed his work for CIÉ. In August 1957, there had been a sharp reaction from workmates when it had been rumoured that two other employees, Patrick Carney and Hugh Boyle, would be dismissed. It is not clear if management had indeed taken that decision, but there was serious talk of a strike (MA, PM/I/ADM/12, Extracts from Internees' Correspondence: Remarks Passed During Visit to T. Doyle, 31 August 1957). Since there was no strike it would appear that assurances were given.

92 For the Green Cross, see above, pp. 533–6; for An Cumann Cabhrach see pp. 912–3.

93 See, for example, the remarks of Harry Diamond, Republican Labour Stormont MP for Belfast Falls. In a Stormont speech he rejected the 'unconstitutional action of a self-appointed association of gunmen to override and subvert the sovereignty of the people of Dáil Éireann and the Government of the Republic as the custodian of the Irish people's mandate for the direction of national policy' (*NIPD*, vol. 41, col. 51,

6 February 1957). Other Nationalist MPs took a similar line, as republicans often reminded the nationalist community.

94 See, for example, *NIPD*, vol. 40, col. 2532, 30 October 1956; vol. 41, cols. 772–3, 2 April 1957.

95 Boyce interview.

96 O'Hagan interview.

97 PRONI HA/32/1/1339, A. J. Kelly, Secretary to the Cabinet to W. F. Stout, Home Affairs, 6 July 1962.

98 *Belfast Telegraph*, 6 July 1962, 13f.

99 A succession of escapes in Britain in 1966 created a crisis in confidence in the prison system. Charles Wilson and Ronald Biggs, two of the Great Train Robbers, escaped from maximum-security prisons in 1964 and 1965 respectively. Peace activists rescued George Blake, one of the most damaging of Soviet double agents, from Wormwood Scrubs on 22 October 1966. Frank Mitchell (the 'Mad Axe Man') was sprung from Dartmoor on 12 December 1966 by the notorious Kray brothers (London gangsters). There was widespread public alarm. It suddenly seemed that British prisons could keep no one in custody who had the determination and resources to escape. A fundamental reappraisal of security and control followed. See *Report of the Inquiry into Prison Escapes and Security* (Mountbatten Report) (London: HMSO, 1966, Cmd. 3175) and its corrective, *The Regime for Long-Term Prisoners in Conditions of Maximum Security* (Radzinowicz Report) (London: HMSO, 1968). There are two accounts of the Blake escape, an event of seismic importance for prison administration: Michael Randle and Pat Pottle, *The Blake Escape* (London: Harrap, 1989) and Seán Bourke, *The Springing of George Blake* (London: Cassells, 1970). On the springing of Mitchell (more an absconding than escape), see Chapter 13 of John Pearson's excellent *The Profession of Violence* (London: Panther, 1973). There is no wholly reliable account of the Great Train Robbers' escapes.

100 Tim Pat Coogan provides a deal of colourful detail on the raid: Tim Pat Coogan, *The IRA* (London: Fontana, 1980), pp. 360–3. See also PRONI HA/32/1/971 and p. 787 above.

101 See Seán McConville, *Irish Political Prisoners, 1848–1922* (London and New York: Routledge, 2003), pp. 136–8.

102 PRONI HA/32/1/626, County Inspector Nelson to R. F. R. Dunbar, Home Affairs, 2 December 1955. See above, for example, pp. 587–8.

103 PRONI HA/32/1/626, Minutes of 7 December 1955 meeting. There may well have been political as well as financial considerations in this decision. Such a prominent security display at a location so near the city centre could have alarmed rather than reassured public opinion.

104 PRONI HA/32/1/626, Minutes of 7 December 1955 meeting. Any investigation of the practice in jurisdictions in which firearms were used for custodial purposes would have confirmed that sub-machine guns were not suitable for prison use and were certainly incompatible with the common-law doctrine of reasonable force. They fired too many lethal rounds too rapidly to justify use on a milling crowd and were insufficiently accurate to use against a lone escaper on the wall. The Sten gun, in particular, was notorious for its inaccuracy. Rifles and shotguns were more suitable weapons. There was also a greater risk of accidental discharge of a Sten gun. This happened on the night of 5 January 1957 when an officer ignored standing orders that a magazine should be inserted only in the event of an emergency. Taking a toilet break, he handed the weapon to another officer, who, deciding to remove the magazine, fumbled and accidentally fired off all rounds. By a mercy the gun was pointing at a wall at the time, and masonry was the only casualty. What other staff and the prisoners thought of the sound of a burst of gunfire within the prison was not

recorded (PRONI HA/32/1/626, L. F. Thompson, Governor, Belfast Prison, to Ministry of Home Affairs, 6 January 1957).

105 PRONI HA/32/1/626, County Inspector J. G. T. Nelson to J. B. O'Neill, Ministry of Home Affairs, 20 September 1956. At this point, the RUC was more concerned about an escape being mounted by means of a trick or ruse than the use of armed force from outside and wanted to explore with prison staff what precautions might be taken.

106 PRONI HA/32/1/626, L. F. Thompson to Ministry of Home Affairs, 14 December 1956. The Ministry, anticipating that the emergency would blow over, was reluctant to take on permanent staff. Overtime was expensive in the short term but was less costly and more flexible than increasing the number of established prison-officer positions.

107 PRONI HA/9/2/847, W. A. Magill, Assistant Secretary, Ministry of Home Affairs, to Governor, Belfast Prison, 13 May 1957.

108 PRONI HA/9/2/847, Magill to Governor, Belfast Prison, 13 May 1957.

109 PRONI HA/9/2/847, 'Orders for Use of Firearms', 25 June 1959.

110 PRONI HA/9/2/847, Minute of meeting of 17 January 1957.

111 PRONI HA/9/2/847, note of 30 August 1957. Existing searchlights were cumbersome to move and required the guard to use both hands, thus putting down his weapon. The police also wanted battery-powered emergency floodlights, which would cut in immediately in the event of a power cut.

112 Ian Fleming's first Bond novel, *Casino Royale*, reached the bookshops in 1953.

113 PRONI HA/9/2/847, J. G. T. Nelson to J. B. O'Neill, Ministry of Home Affairs, 28 November 1957. None of the many memoirs of IRA men or other accounts of the period confirms or even hints at the existence of such devices, nor were any men brought to trial for the possession of gas or pepper weapons.

114 PRONI HA/9/2/847, County Inspector J. G. T. Nelson to J. B. O'Neil, Ministry of Home Affairs, 28 November 1957.

115 PRONI HA/9/2/847, J. G. Hill, Principal Secretary to the Minister for Home Affairs, to L. F. Thompson, Governor of Belfast Prison, 2 December 1957.

116 See below, pp. 855–6.

117 PRONI HA/32/1/1365, RUC to Secretary, Ministry of Home Affairs, 7 January 1961.

118 Both had been found guilty of possessing IRA documents and one of the additional offence of possessing drawings of explosive devices and of recording the movements of police and other vehicles.

119 PRONI HA/32/1/991, County Inspector J. G. T. Nelson to R. F. R. Dunbar, Secretary, Ministry of Home Affairs, 22 January 1957 (attachment). It is some indication of the impact of physical-force Irish nationalism and republicanism that all of the Acts under which the men had been sentenced had been introduced to deal with their previous campaigns of violence, actual or anticipated. The Special Powers Act went back to the establishment of Northern Ireland, the Treason Felony Act to John Mitchel of the 1848 Young Irelanders, and the Explosive Substances Act, 1883, to the Dynamitards (see McConville, *Irish Political Prisoners, op. cit.*, pp. 30–3). The Omagh men were at first uncertain as to how they should react to the treason-felony charges. Major Thompson was anxious to discover if they intended to defend themselves. This would have entailed recognising the court, and the group did not know if the IRA would permit this. They delayed their decision until a sympathetic barrister was able to obtain a legal visit. This, as the rules provided, was conducted in the sight but not the hearing of the supervising officer. The barrister was able to read the GHQ orders to the men (Boyce interview).

120 During the currency of the Omagh raiders' sentences, the proportion of remission granted was raised from a quarter to a third (see Boyce, *The Insider, op. cit.*, p. 113: August 1957).

121 Another stimulus was the prospect of internment once their sentence had been served. The RUC kept an up-to-date list of all IRA prisoners, and, by an arrangement with the Ministry of Justice, were given at least one week's notice of any impending release. This allowed time for a decision on internment and to obtain the necessary order (PRONI HA/32/1/991, County Inspector J. G. T. Nelson to R. F. R. Dunbar, Home Affairs, 22 January 1957).

122 It is not clear if this committee had existed from the beginning, but, given the informal way the unit conducted business, it seems unlikely. The term 'committee' seems grandiose. More likely, Garland agreed to receive and to give consideration to escape suggestions and to consult the others. Boyce notes that John Joseph Kelly was a member of the escape committee, but there is little information on its level of activity (see Boyce, *The Insider, op. cit.*, p. 326). Garland was one of the more spectacular and effective IRA activists. He had been the 'insider' in the Omagh raid, joining the British Army at the barracks, providing the information that enabled the raid to take place and remaining in post, undetected, for some time thereafter. During the Border Campaign, Garland led several raids, including the disastrous attack on Brookeborough RUC barracks in which Feargal O'Hanlon and Seán South were mortally wounded. Garland himself was wounded but managed to escape across the border and recover. He was arrested in Belfast on 4 November 1959. For a biographical note on Garland, see above, pp. 818–9, n. 58.

123 Boyce interview.

124 Bell makes only one reference to escape plans: J. Bowyer Bell, *The Secret Army: The IRA, 1916–1979* (Cambridge, Mass.: MIT Press, 1983), p. 326. Work rotas of staff and floor plans of Belfast Prison were smuggled out, but it became clear that IRA GHQ was not going to help.

125 Dessie O'Hagan recalled that three men had initially been involved in the escape, but that the third man could not squeeze through the gap cleared by cutting the bars (interview). Donnelly's detailed recollection of the escape and surrounding events, *Prisoner 1082* is instructive and necessary reading. The 'third man' to whom O'Hagan refers may have been Séamus McRory of Ballymena. According to Donnelly, McRory was standing by as the breakout was made. His task was to drop out the men's coats (which could not be worn as they squeezed through the bars). Because of the need to distract a prison officer, however, he was unable to do so. Both men therefore found themselves out of doors in freezing weather, wearing only light clothing and footwear (Donnelly, *Prisoner 1082, op. cit.*, p. 2).

126 John Kelly had led a flying column and had been arrested in the aftermath of an abortive attack at Dungannon, Co. Tyrone. Donnelly had never been a member of the IRA unit in the prison. This was because his solicitor had entered a plea of mitigation in an earlier case of putting up illegal posters. By doing so (and Donnelly insists that it was without his prior knowledge), he had broken the IRA's general prohibition on recognising British or Irish courts and thereby incurred automatic and seemingly permanent dismissal (Donnelly, *Prisoner 1082, op. cit.*, pp. 78–9).

127 This was Bell's information, but there was another possible way in which the two men may have obtained the necessary material, as we shall see. There was, in 1953, an almost identical escape attempt by a non-political prisoner serving a sentence of seven years. All the elements were the same: hacksaw blades, surreptitiously cut cell bars and a rope. In this earlier instance, the police acquired information about an officer who was trafficking and the planned escape. A cell search and check of the bars foiled the escape. The corrupt officer was dismissed. (PRONI HA/32/1/951, Ministry and prison memoranda, July 1953.)

128 This despite the fact that earlier in the year the prison had held the notorious English prison escaper and litigant in person Alfred Hinds (*alias* William Bishop). An

exceptionally large police presence, uniformed and plain clothes, was deemed necessary when Hinds was moved. The level of alert in Belfast Prison should at least have matched the escape threat of Hinds (see *Belfast Telegraph*, 9 March 1960, 1f–g; PRONI HA/9/2/840). Hinds had confided in one of the IRA men that he could not escape from Belfast Prison because of the security (Boyce interview).

129 Dessie O'Hagan had, at an earlier point, occupied the cell from which the two escaped and had noticed that from his window he could not see either of the two watchtowers; it followed that they could not see him. He had told Donnelly and Kelly about this (interview).

130 Boyce interview.

131 Many details of the escape are taken from the official inquiry that took place immediately in its wake. There was both an incompleteness of information and a desire to deflect or minimise blame, so the official account cannot be assumed to be wholly accurate (PRONI HA/32/1/1365). The account of Donnelly's movements is taken from his book *Prisoner 1082* and from the interview of his brother-in-law, Boyce. It was not until the mid-1990s that Donnelly was informed that he could, without fear of arrest, return to Northern Ireland. His had been the first IRA escape in eighteen years. The previous one had been in April 1943, when Hugh McAteer and Jimmy Steele had also got over the perimeter wall.

132 The escape had shown the weakness of the existing window frames and bars and, subsequently, a second, outer set of bars was installed on each window (Cunningham interview).

133 Cunningham was insistent that, generally, 'there definitely was no drunkenness or anything' and that no officer would come on duty with drink on his breath (interview). Whether this rule was as scrupulously observed over Christmas is now hard to say.

134 This chronology and all details are taken from the report by Major Thompson to the Ministry (PRONI HA/32/1/1365). The timings cannot be entirely relied upon, since they were given after the escape, and some may have been intended to minimise any appearance of sloth or neglect of duty: all staff had an interest in this. Yet there is some verification, from an unexpected source. Donnelly consulted the official papers when compiling his recollections and was much impressed: 'The exceptionally detailed and truthful report sent by Governor Lance Thompson to the Minister for Home Affairs in Stormont is probably reflective of the innate honesty of the underlying Presbyterian ethic' (*Prisoner 1082, op. cit.*, p. 13).

135 *Cork Examiner*, 29 December 1960, 3c; *Irish Press*, 31 December 1960, 1f. The *United Irishman* (January 1961, 1b–c) gave five and a half column inches on its front page to Donnelly's escape, describing him as a 'republican prisoner' rather than a 'volunteer' (the term for a member of the IRA). Only one inch of the report dealt with Donnelly, the rest describing Belfast Prison. It was not until 7 May 1961 that an article appeared in the *Sunday Review* (5a–d) in which Donnelly gave details of his escape. A short factual mention was also carried in the *Sunday Independent* of 7 May 1961 (5f), as a result of the *Review* piece. By this time, it would appear, Donnelly wished to keep a low profile and to get on with his life, having found employment in Cork as a clerk.

136 *Irish Independent*, 9 January 1961, 6e.

137 De Valera had resigned as Taoiseach on 17 June 1959 and was succeeded six days later by Lemass.

138 From this flowed other consequences. He had hoped to advance himself to the permanent staff, with its considerable advantage of job security, salary improvement and pensioning, but was told that all such hopes must be suspended for a year and even at the end of that time there could be no promise as to the outcome (PRONI HA/32/1/1365, Ministry memorandum, 31 January 1961).

139 PRONI HA/32/1/1365, Ministry memorandum, 31 January 1961. The forfeiture of remission was the maximum allowed under prison rules as was the loss of evening

association and earnings. Kelly could, in addition, have been subject to dietary punishment and confinement to his cell, but these were usually reserved for improper language or behaviour or the threat of violence. See Statutory Rules and Orders of Northern Ireland, 1954, 7: Prison Rules (Northern Ireland) 1954, *op. cit.*

140 PRONI HA/32/1/1365, Ministry of Home Affairs to RUC, 16 February 1961. Other favourable factors were Kelly's youth, together with the fact that he had surrendered peacefully and had not been able to leave the prison grounds (PRONI HA/9/2/784).

141 *Sunday Review*, 7 May 1961, 5a–d.

142 *NIPD*, vol. 48, cols. 1890–1, 10 May 1961. It may have been that Minford was hinting at collusion specifically by Roman Catholic prison officers since in 1959 he had linked security to religious background by proposing that civil servants be security-checked and that the percentage of Catholics in the Civil Service be published. See Marc Mulholland, 'Why Did Unionists Discriminate?', in Sabine Wichert (ed.), *From the United Irishmen to Twentieth-Century Unionism: A Festschrift for A. T. Q. Stewart* (Dublin: Four Courts Press, 2004), p. 198. Minford had a history of erratic statements on religion, having been censured by the Ulster Unionist Party for an anti-Catholic statement and by the Orange Institution for attending a Roman Catholic service.

143 *NIPD*, vol. 48, cols. 1892–3, 10 May 1961.

144 As noted, diary-keeping was forbidden by both his masters: the prison and the IRA. The latter had a point, of course, since diaries can often disclose valuable and damaging information. The counter-arguments to forewarning any or some other prisoners of an impending escape attempt are obvious. Staff might notice changes in habits; some hint of what was in train might get out; and those not included in the plan (including ordinary prisoners) might demand a place.

145 Boyce, *The Insider, op. cit.*, p. 324. His entry the previous day had been equally unhappy. The cell was 'like a morgue, cold and icy'. Conditions were as bad as they had been in 1954, 'but I've only got two years to do and that won't disturb me too much'. His general outlook and hopes had been blighted: 'I suppose that the Volunteers are broken as an organisation but maybe some good will come from that – some time.' On that last evening of the year, he wanted to reflect on friends and family, 'but I'm too sad, too tired and too cold' (*The Insider, op. cit.*, p. 323).

146 Boyce, *The Insider, op. cit.*, p. 326.

147 Boyce interview. The radio reached him from Japan, via New York and Dublin. He kept is as a souvenir after his release. When given an item of breaking news by a friendly member of staff, he would feign surprise.

148 In dimensions or weight, it might be noted, a radio is not dissimilar to a small handgun or other weapon, or a metal-cutting tool.

149 Boyce interview. These verbal messages would necessarily be brief but might check, for example, whether an earlier written communication had got through.

150 Rule 105(1) Prison Rules (Northern Ireland) 1954: Statutory Rules and Orders of Northern Ireland, 1954, no. 7.

151 Cunningham interview. Some of the women were more hostile to staff under these circumstances than were the prisoners. Staff were obliged to report on anything out of the ordinary that transpired – particularly anything relating to republicanism. Prisoners and their visitors knew this, but sometimes forgot. Cunningham remembered one wife who 'tended to rattle on about things that he didn't want us to hear. He would keep saying, "We will pass no remarks." He shut her up.'

152 Though not all did so. Dáithí Ó Conaill (sentenced to eight years on 24 March 1960) strongly objected to a prison officer's attempt to prevent him embracing his girlfriend during a visit in October 1961. Ó Conaill lashed out at the officer, thereby terminating the visit and enhancing his standing with some prisoners.

153 Boyce, *The Insider, op. cit.*, p. 438.
154 Cunningham interview.
155 *Irish News*, 18 November 1954, 1g–h; 15 December 1954, 6f. See also MA PM/I/ ADM/12, Extracts Internees' Correspondence, copy of letter from Seán O'Rian to Father G. M. Keane, SJ, 20 April 1958.
156 See McConville, *Irish Political Prisoners, op. cit.*, Chapter 11.
157 PRONI HA/9/2/841, Ministry of Home Affairs to Governor, Belfast Prison, 19 September 1961. Dáithí Ó Conaill (1938–91) had been wounded and captured in an RUC ambush near Ardboe, Co. Tyrone, on 10 November 1959, and was serving an eight-year sentence. Born in Cork, he had joined the IRA in 1955 and was in command of the attack on Brookeborough Barracks on 1 January 1957. Arrested in Monaghan shortly afterwards, he served a short prison sentence before being interned in the Curragh. When released, in September 1963, Ó Conaill obtained a teaching position in Co. Donegal. He became a major figure during the modern Troubles and was a founding member of the Provisional IRA's Army Council. Arrested and imprisoned in the Republic in 1975. On hunger strike for forty-seven days in 1977, he was released in August of that year. Broke with Provisional Sinn Féin over the abandonment of the abstentionist policy (in Republic of Ireland elections) and became a leading member of the breakaway organisation, Republican Sinn Féin. See *Cork Examiner*, 25 March 1960, 7e–f; 25 September 1961, 7f; *Irish Independent*, 7 October 1961, 13d.
158 Boyce interview.
159 O'Hagan interview.
160 Boyce interview. He reasoned that many young men from Dublin and Cork and elsewhere, seeing Boyce as an Irish citizen, asked how he could be charged with treason against a British monarch. It is entirely possible, however, that some of these militant youths were attracted because the Omagh, Armagh and other raids showed that the IRA was able and willing to act.
161 There had been a change in 1957 when the rate of remission had changed from one-quarter to one-third. Those who had been sentenced before the rule change benefited from the point at which the change was introduced: Rule 25 Prison Rules (Northern Ireland), 1954: Statutory Rules and Orders of Northern Ireland, 1954, 7. Amended by Statutory Rules and Orders, 1957, 157.
162 There had been considerable division within the small IRA group. By October 1957, five of the sentenced men had withdrawn their allegiance. Kearney ceased to eat at the IRA table in the mess hall in January 1958. By the end of the year (18 December 1958), their 'signing out' and receipt of a pardon came as a shock and an unpleasant surprise to the remaining IRA men. The news was widely carried by newspapers the next day. Boyce recorded the defections and attendant publicity as 'the worst week we ever had here' (*The Insider, op. cit.*, p. 43). The *Irish News* (the principal newspaper for Northern Catholics) carried a particularly damaging report on the releases, noting that the two had 'severed their connection with the IRA following the condemnation of violence by the Catholic hierarchy' (19 December 1958, 1b–c). The Government Press Office release added that both Clarke and Kearney had 'expressed their firm intention not to have any further dealings with any illegal organisations or to be associated in any way with any person or body seeking to subvert the established lawful government of Northern Ireland' (*Irish News*, 19 December 1958, 1c and 8a–b).
163 Kathleen Kearney (1889–1960), born in Kilkenny, was a member of Cumann na mBan and served in support of the Citizen Army in 1916.
164 These defections affected the morale of the IRA group so much so that fifty years later, when the topic was raised in interview, the response was immediate and

showed that the wound had been deep and of lasting effect. The process had been kept confidential within the prison, so much so that wing staff did not know about it: 'He just disappeared. He was there one day and the next day he wasn't there' (Cunningham interview). Boyce, at least in retrospect, was more willing to acknowledge the pressures on the men and, in later years, when people condemned them, would comment, 'when you do four years, come back and tell me' (interview). Nevertheless, a man who signed out irrevocably put himself outside the republican movement.

165 O'Hagan interview.
166 There was, between 1940 and 1951, a steady rise in the number of offences recorded by the RUC and then a fall in 1952–3. The crime rate remained low despite the post-war rise (*NIPD*, vol. 38, col. 2129, 18 May 1954).
167 See the comments, along these lines, of the Board of Visitors of Belfast Prison: PRONI HA/9/940, Reports of 1953 and 1961. Christmas parole was introduced in 1948. Well-behaved prisoners who had served at least twelve months of a three-year sentence could apply. In 1955, this scheme was extended, allowing seven days' release in the summer. See Prison (Amendment) Rules (Northern Ireland) 1948 and 1955; *Belfast Newsletter*, 13 July 1955, 5f.
168 Escapers from Derry Prison who had made it across the border in March 1943 had, it is true, then been interned by the Irish authorities, operating under wartime conditions. Even though the men had exchanged one prison for another, this was an uncertain and certainly unsatisfactory outcome to the Northern Ireland authorities. See above, p. 593.
169 See below, pp. 1076–80.
170 Apart from occasional instances of youthful offending, or trivial offences when adults, all but a handful of IRA personnel had good character (in the legal sense) up to the point of paramilitary offending. For reasons both of reputation and security (vulnerability to police pressure), persons of criminal character were not accepted into the IRA. Ordinary criminal careers, moreover, although surprisingly heterogeneous, rarely show political interest or commitment.
171 *Northern Whig*, 7 August 1958, 5d–e. The others involved were James McKernan, Seamus Loughran, Brian Loughran and Séamus McRory.
172 PRONI HA/32/1/1247, Hugh McCrory to Ministry of Home Affairs, October 1958.
173 PRONI HA/32/1/1247, J. B. O'Neill, Ministry of Justice, to A. H. Kennedy, Deputy Inspector-General, RUC, 3 November 1958.
174 PRONI HA/32/1/1247, A. H. Kennedy to J. B. O'Neill, 7 November 1959.
175 PRONI HA/32/1/1247, Dr Robert Simpson, MP, to W. W. B. Topping, Minister for Home Affairs, 2 December 1958. Robert Simpson (1923–97) was a liberal unionist and eventual supporter of the O'Neill–Chichester–Clarke leadership succession.
176 PRONI HA/32/1/1247, J. B. O'Neill to A. H. Kennedy, 14 November 1958.
177 PRO DO/130/128, CRO to British Embassy, Dublin, 5 August 1963.
178 But there was more regular contact at lower levels of officialdom on practical matters of cross-border concern. These connections were permitted because they were necessary and hidden from public and political attention. We know very little of cross-border contacts between police officers, but, on more recent experience, it seems likely that, on matters of ordinary criminality, there were instances of cooperation (particularly in the exchange of information) between local officers in adjoining districts.
179 Thus, when Tralee Urban District Council forwarded a resolution concerning republican prisoners in England and Northern Ireland, the Embassy was able to

respond on behalf of the Home Office regarding persons imprisoned in England but made it clear that comment on the Belfast prisoners had to come from the Northern Ireland government (PRO DO/130/128, British Embassy, Dublin, to Acting Town Clerk, Tralee Urban District Council, 9 January 1963).

180 PRO DO/130/128, Political Prisoners' Release Campaign to British Embassy, Dublin, 26 June 1963. The Campaign's decision to write to the British Embassy, Dublin, even though it was writing from a Belfast office, was indicative of the utter unwillingness of republicans to communicate with the Northern Ireland government, even on an ostensibly humanitarian matter. It is also fair to note, however, that Northern Ireland politicians and officials had a history of forwarding such communications to Special Branch and refusing to acknowledge them.

181 This was the gist of a letter from the National Civil Liberties League to the British Embassy. The wording thereafter was slightly unfortunate: 'Having regard to Mr Doyle's motives (*which cannot be questioned*) and the circumstances leading to his imprisonment we would urge most strongly on humanitarian grounds, his immediate and unconditional arrest' (PRO DO/130/128, National Civil Liberties League to British Embassy, Dublin [undated but probably February 1963]; my italics).

182 Internment was explicitly preventive and implicitly deterrent. Even on the latter ground, however, its continuance could not be justified once the Border Campaign terminated.

183 The final words of the cessation statement referred to 'a period of consolidation, expansion and preparation for the final and victorious phase of the struggle for the full freedom of Ireland' (*United Irishman*, March 1962, 1c).

184 There had of course been many previous presidents of Irish origin, but they were not Catholics. W. F. Marshall, in his campaigning *Ulster Sails West* (Belfast: Northern Whig, 1950, p. 46) claimed that very nearly half of US presidents up to 1940 had been of Ulster Protestant stock.

185 On the visit, see Ryan Tubridy, *Four Days That Changed a President* (London: Collins, 2011); see also James Carroll, *One of Ourselves: John Fitzgerald Kennedy in Ireland* (Lancaster: Gazelle, 2003).

186 *United Irishman*, September 1962, 2e.

187 See pp. 784–5.

188 *Irish News*, 13 February 1959, 1f–g; *Northern Whig*, 13 February 1959, 1b–c.

189 Murphy had good reason for keeping his head down in Dublin. As long as he did not provoke or embarrass the government he would be left alone. The escape had been organised in conjunction with prisoners who were members of EOKA, the Greek Cypriot organisation, which wanted to rescue its chief operative, Nikos Sampson. Sampson, however, failed to get over the wall. Christle had also offered a place on the escape team to Klaus Fuchs, the atom spy. Fuchs, within months of completing his fourteen-year sentence, wisely decided to stay put. It had been intended to release another Arborfield man, Joe Doyle, but his health (he suffered from tuberculosis) prevented his participation in the escape. See Bell, *The Secret Army*, *op. cit.*, p. 317, for a brief outline (though he erred in the date, giving 19 rather than 12 February); for a more detailed account, see Vias Livades, *Cypriot and Irish Political Prisoners Held in British Prisons, 1956–1959* (Nicosia: Power Publishing, 2008), pp. 143–58.

190 PRO DO/130/128, British Embassy, Dublin, to CRO, 27 February 1963.

191 These may be seen at PRO DO/130/128. There were also letters to the Queen from apparently unaffiliated individuals. One began 'Dear Queen' and, *inter alia*, commented on the weather in Ireland. Another hoped the letter would find everyone (at Buckingham Palace) 'real well'.

192 Representations had also been made confidentially by Lord Longford and Seán MacBride.

193 PRO DO/130/128, CRO to G. E. Crombie, Counsellor, British Embassy, Dublin, 27 July 1962.

194 PRO DO/130/128, Memorandum of meeting, 21 November 1962. Various ages would be given, but all agreed she was nearing eighty.

195 PRO DO/130/128, Sir Ian Maclennan, British Ambassador, to G. W. St J. Chadwick (Permanent Under-Secretary, CRO), 21 November 1962. He also argued that keeping Doyle was more likely to intensify his IRA sympathies. He pointed out that Doyle would find the Ireland to which he returned very different to that which he left eight years before, implying that a return to the IRA was much less likely. In addition, persons who had petitioned for his release would seek to influence him, out of a sense of responsibility.

196 PRO DO/130/128, Memorandum, 20 February 1963. Compassionate release would have fitted into one of the Home Office's acceptable categories for consideration. Vicarious compassion was less straightforward.

197 PRO DO/130/128, Sir Ian Maclennan to CRO, 27 February 1963.

198 PRO DO/130/128, Brief, March 1963.

199 He added that, while he had thought that everything that could be said about Doyle's case had been said, perhaps this was a new point of substance (PRO DO/130/128, Sir Ian Maclennan to CRO, 27 March 1963).

200 PRO DO/130/128, Home Office to CRO, 25 April 1963.

201 PRO DO/130/128, Sir Ian Maclennan to Seán Dunne, 2 May 1963.

202 PRO DO/130/128, Sir Ian Maclennan to CRO, 3 May 1963.

203 PRO DO/130/128, Telegram to British Embassy, 25 June 1963.

204 *Irish Press*, 1 July 1963, 5c; 8 July 1963, 4e; *United Irishman*, August 1963, 12a–b.

205 Dessie O'Hagan was scornful of what he called the 'cult of prisoners' and emphatic that his years in prison were a waste of time. Nor was this his experience only, he insisted. Tom Doyle, IRA Adjutant General in the 1940s, had told him that on returning home after five years' internment in the Curragh, a neighbour had asked him how he was remarking that he had not seen him for 'these past few weeks'. (Interview.)

206 Boyce remembered that he was completely intolerant in the immediate post-release period. There was also a period of even more basic adjustment. Because freedom came long after it was granted to the other Omagh raiders, and through a misunderstanding about release arrangements, on the morning of his release Boyce found himself outside the prison gate with no one to meet him: and Belfast was a city that he did not know. As he walked away, he thought that everyone was looking at him. There was a long hesitation before he could bring himself to cross the road. Being able to walk on the grass of a public park, after so many years exercising by walking around a patch of forbidden turf, was an immediate and memorable sensation. A playground made such an impression that he stayed, fascinated, for a prolonged period, watching the children. (Interview.)

207 O'Hagan interview.

16

NORTHERN IRELAND

Internment, December 1956–April 1961

Arrests

Both Northern Ireland and the Republic were well provided with powers for internment, and not very much dust had accumulated on the files since its last use. The Stormont Cabinet agreed to reintroduce internment, the first arrests taking place on Saturday, 15 December 1956.[1] By the end of the following month, ninety-nine men were held in Belfast Prison under the detention and internment provisions of the Special Powers Act.[2] In accordance with this measure, the initial period following arrest was known as detention.[3] During this time, interrogations were conducted and decisions were made as to whether there were grounds to support prosecution, internment or release.[4] Should the police fail to initiate either prosecution or internment within two weeks, the Northern Ireland Attorney General had to order release.[5]

The arrests were conducted without any marked degree of ill-treatment. Some rough handling did occur, but this was not systemic, and those we interviewed took it as a matter of course.[6] Breandán O Rahallaí did not experience brutality 'worth talking about', either from the police or prison staff but did remember 'a thing or two' being done, just to show who was boss. There were also threats to take him into a back room and beat him for information, 'but it didn't materialise, this was all a trial and error to see how it would affect different people'.[7]

Accommodation

As with the two earlier exercises in large-scale internment, the issue immediately arose of where the internees could most conveniently be held. Considerations of security and the need to separate internees from other prisoners were factors in the decision, as well as available space. Belfast Prison, already fortified to hold the sentenced IRA men more securely, had been used for the first arrests, but in early January 1957 it was anticipated that space for between 200 and 300 would shortly be required. An assessment concluded that Armagh Prison, 'if we were to remove the ladies', could not accommodate more than 100. Londonderry Prison had for some time past been used only as a store, and it was doubtful if even 100 places could be made available there without considerable renovation. Both prisons were accordingly ruled out.[8]

It was twelve and a half years since the end of the Second World War, and military installations abounded. A number of wartime Army and RAF stations, mothballed or simply disused, were therefore considered as places of detention. The RAF station at Bishopscourt, Co. Down, was rejected for security reasons and because of plans to reactivate it as a base for a new RAF squadron. The station was, moreover, accessible from the sea, and the station commander thought that recent activities by motorboats from the Republic might have been a rehearsal for something more sinister. Unwilling to give up Bishopscourt, the RAF proposed instead Langford Lodge, a site on a peninsula in Lough Neagh. There were several possibilities for readily available accommodation in that area, including a former American Forces camp. Despite having being disused for an appreciable period, all its huts remained weatherproof, and water and electricity were laid on. This site had ample accommodation for up to 300, and the RAF, which doubtless saw an opportunity to drop from its budget a camp for which it had no use, was willing to hand it over. The huts would be easily secured with barbed-wire fences, and there were vague hints that the Army would provide a guard. Apart from a perimeter guard, up to thirty prison officers would be required.

There were drawbacks, not least with staffing. The camp would have to be subdivided into various compounds, each holding forty to fifty men. These would have to be mustered together at various times, the aggregate then necessitating a large staff presence. In addition to that, staff would have to be available to supervise visits and to enforce discipline. The last would not be as onerous as the fairly tight custody for ordinary prisoners but would entail supervising the internees in the chores and routine of the everyday life of the camp as well as conducting special and general searches and controlling movements. Another difficulty was the remoteness of the site, 10 miles from the nearest town. At a time when private vehicles were not widely available – certainly not for prison officers – this meant that accommodation would have to be provided for staff and a house for the governor. Some prison staff could be released from other establishments for camp duties, but nowhere near enough; it was also doubtful if potential secondees could be compelled to serve in an internment camp.

At this point, the district RUC objected to the prospect of having a new neighbour. The character of the area's population was unsuitable. To the north-east, west and south of the peninsula there was 'a strong nationalist element'. The site could easily be reached by water from these areas. The terrain, with timber, scrub and a lack of dwellings, might aid escape. Langford Lodge was also comparatively remote from any RUC station, the nearest one at Crumlin being 4 miles distant and without transport.[9] Far better a camp in the centre of a unionist population, a place such as Ballyclare, Co. Antrim, 'and in an open position in which there were Unionists' houses around it and in sight of the perimeter'.

As discussions continued, it became clear that all locations other than Belfast Prison posed problems: finance, security and state of readiness being the main ones. Belfast's D Wing had room for 103 internees, and, by putting two bunks in each cell, this could be expanded to 200. (At a later point, C Wing was also taken into use for internees.) Little, if any, initial expense would be incurred. There was good news also about running costs, since Major Lance Thompson, the gung-ho governor, thought he could manage this expansion with little addition to his staff. In this calculation, no consideration was given to the type of regime that he could provide for men who were, after all, civil detainees. Belfast was an old, poorly conceived and meanly built prison, previously condemned by the Prisons Board and certainly showing the wear and tear of its century of use. In the end, the decision was to avoid the bother and expense of a new site, and Belfast got the business. The figure of 700 internees, which had provided the templates in 1922 and 1939, had now been abandoned. From surviving documents, it is not clear why the projection had been so drastically reduced, but presumably RUC intelligence was reporting a much-diminished IRA.

With the release of all those detained or sentenced in connection with the IRA's activities during the war years, the demand for prison accommodation in Northern Ireland dropped to very low levels. Ordinary crimes (as reported by the police) rose gradually between 1940 and 1951 and then began to decline again.[10] When the closure of Londonderry and Armagh prisons was under discussion in 1951, a minute circulated in the Ministry of Home Affairs threw a further light on Northern Ireland's prisoners. The criminal character of the males was such that in the event of a national emergency (such as war), most could be released without serious threat to the community. 'Every single woman' in Armagh could be freed forthwith. Of some 200 convicted males, about half were serving sentences in excess of nine months. The remainder could be turned loose, in much the same way as the women.[11] Further confirmation of the quiet and entirely unremarkable nature of ordinary criminal justice in Northern Ireland in periods of IRA inactivity may be gleaned from the reports of the Board of Visitors of Belfast Prison. In 1953, before the arms raids preparatory to the Border Campaign got under way, Northern Ireland's main adult prison had an average population of 309 men.[12] This included all remands awaiting trial as well as short- and long-sentence prisoners. During the year, a Criminal Justice Act was enacted, bringing Northern Ireland into line with the various provisions of the English Criminal Justice Act, 1948. These included the abandonment of penal servitude and, with it, the term 'convict' for persons serving sentences of three and more years. The Act also introduced new preventive sentences for habitual or potentially habitual offenders. Other than recording the advent of this new legislation, the Board of Visitors dwelt on their appreciation of the work of the staff, the entertainment provided for the prisoners and the Christmas menu in the prison.

Within a few years, this placid scene was no more. The arrival of internees in the last weeks of 1956 had introduced a wholly new element into the chemistry of the prison.[13] Their presence was having a paralysing effect on normal administration, the Board reported. Expressing its customary support for the Minister for Home Affairs in the discharge of his onerous duties, the Board noted in particular his decision to order the release of two long-term political prisoners on their giving an undertaking to abstain from illegal activities.[14] This 'tallies with his nature and shows his great desire to restore order'. The Board hoped that the conditional releases would encourage other prisoners to follow suit and reported that its members had been approached by political prisoners seeking release. These had stated that whilst they still adhered to their former views (on Irish reunification) 'they now greatly disagree with the acts of terrorism which have been adopted'.[15] There was much relief when the last of the internees were released in April 1961. The Board reported that conditions had become 'more normal', allowing a better classification and separation in the arrangement of the remaining prisoners. There was also a greater amount of space available, and some refurbishment could consequently be undertaken.[16]

Some of the 1950s internees took a charitable view of the ordinary criminal prisoners. There was no question of internees being subjected to a penal regime or being forced to mix with other prisoners, so there was room for a more disinterested attitude. Leo Martin felt uneasy about describing the other prisoners as criminals: 'a wrong word, a terrible word to say'. He saw them as being more subjugated to prison staff because they were individuals, on their own, in contrast to the internees who always acted as members of and received the protection of the group. Improvements in internees' conditions sometimes meant changes that benefited all prisoners. There was also a willingness by internees to pass some cigarettes and food to the non-politicals, 'foods that they wouldn't have been allowed to get in'.[17] The brotherhood of captivity eroded a number of divisions.

Belfast Prison had proved to be remarkably adaptable in accommodating a considerable increase in numbers, swollen by prisoners, sentenced IRA men and a gradual growth in committals of ordinary criminal prisoners. Since it was a multi-purpose prison, however, with a number of different classes of inmates who each had to be separately housed, there was a limit to the intensification of use of the prison. This point was reached in the autumn of 1958. The particular problem was a growth in long-sentence prisoners during the preceding year. As we have seen, the Governor argued and the Ministry agreed that it was not desirable to accommodate the long-termers two to a cell. The only solution was to decant some of the short-sentence men (two years or less) to Armagh, which hitherto had been an exclusively female establishment. The necessity to maintain absolute separation of male and female prisoners and the configuration of Armagh prison meant that the intake had to be limited to fifty-eight men.

Regime and conditions

Neither having been convicted nor charged, internees could not be subject to the normal prison regime. There was no question of their wearing prison uniforms, nor could they be compelled to labour. They were expected to take a hand in the domestic routines of the prison, cleaning their cells and the common areas, but this was a matter of custom and usage, and mutual convenience, rather than law and regulation. Whatever the intention of the Ministry of Home Affairs, however, internment was a penal experience. There was no question of handing the wing over to the men to run as they saw fit: the state's interest was their safe and orderly custody, and, in a conventional prison, that entailed close control as well as security. Instead of a lax regime within a secure perimeter (the usual camp experience), men were locked in their cells for sixteen and a half hours out of twenty-four: close confinement as well as orderly custody, and unquestionably punitive. It is remarkable that they did not challenge this depressing and onerous arrangement at the outset, but by now it had evolved into republican tradition and expectation.

Internees' responses to the regime were nevertheless more vigorous than those of their convicted comrades in A Wing. The reception process was institutionally necessary, yet inevitably offensive to men who had not been charged with a criminal offence, never mind convicted, and who were now being treated as though they had been. Handing over personal property, being stripped, weighed and medically inspected is hugely invasive and intrinsically undignified. There was a testing process on both sides. The prison authorities would have had an easier life if the men had submitted to the usual regime. One example of this was the matter of names. Each man was given a prison number. This was put in the card-holder on the cell door, and staff initially referred to the internees by their number rather than by their name. The men destroyed the door cards and, not unreasonably, refused to respond to their assigned numbers.[18]

Not all internees were IRA members, but, as a body, they followed republican tradition and IRA procedures. They accordingly elected their OC and supporting leadership. This consisted of an adjutant and quartermaster appointed by the OC, as well as other functionaries. These handled correspondence, records and supplies. The OC also designated an internee to take charge of each of the landings of the wing and to report to him. Using this structure, the internees decided collectively on certain aspects of the daily regime.[19] It is routine at lock-up time for prisoners to be ordered to bang shut their doors, the order being 'Bang up.' The internees refused to comply: 'They were the jailors, and if they never closed them, that suited us. We just ignored the doors.' Internees also followed the long-established practice of awaiting orders from their own elected staff rather than obeying those of the prison officers. At evening lock-up, staff would order internees to cells, but the men would not comply until the command had been given by one of their own people.[20]

Like remanded or convicted prisoners, internees were not allowed to have cash in their possession. Any money that was taken from them on arrest, as well as sums sent in by relatives or friends, were held by the prison and made available in book transactions for the purchase of approved goods. These included cigarettes, confectionary or certain supplements to their food, such as jam or sugar. An ordinary prisoner with a balance in his favour in the prison shop (known as the canteen) would make a request via a prison officer and the item would be delivered to him. The internees adopted their own procedure, handing a note of the required items to their quartermaster who took it to the canteen and collected the goods.[21]

Internees tidied and cleaned their own cells but not initially the common areas in the wing. This work was assigned to ordinary sentenced prisoners, some of whom the internees suspected of acting as observers and informers. After about eighteen months, during which time the internees constantly demanded their own cooking facilities, a kitchen was provided. Thereafter, the food was supplied in bulk and cooked by internees.[22] Getting their own kitchen, Billy McKee remembered, made a big difference to the quality of the food: 'We had no complaints once we got [it].'[23]

As on many previous occasions, the prison authorities were in a difficult position regarding the internees' structure of command. Any explicit recognition would have been leaked by staff and thence into the newspapers. The Ministry of Home Affairs would then have come under fire from the more militant unionist and loyalist elements. At the same time, there were practical management problems. The few convicted IRA men were easy enough to handle, and, if they ever attempted to challenge the rules under which they served their sentences, they could be punished. (They did not have the numbers to pose a threat.) Internee numbers were large (just under 200 by October 1958), and their cooperation was essential for the running of the prison.[24] Lack of cooperation, never mind obstruction or sabotage, would have been a major problem. Staff numbers were comparatively small, and simply to get through the business of the day the internee command structure had to be used. As time passed, and as it became clear that the internees were not going to launch a concerted attack on the conditions of confinement and discipline, the Governor and staff became more confident in this approach of mutual accommodation.[25]

The management style of Major Thompson, rather surprisingly given his martinet reputation, was flexible enough to allow a degree of give and take. His background made this seem unlikely. He had been an A-Special, a full-time member of the Ulster Special Constabulary, a body whose foundation and entire purpose was to defend Northern Ireland from the IRA.[26] He had subsequently joined the Prison Service as an ordinary prison officer, and Billy McKee, in Belfast Prison in the 1940s, remembered him as 'the Devil out of Hell'.[27] When, after his years of service, he was eventually promoted to Governor, however, according to McKee, Thompson totally changed. A prison officer who had served in the 1940s confirmed the change. Speaking to Billy McKee, he had recalled that Thompson "'was on our backs for to punish you all then, watch you and not give you any concessions of any sort… He's the complete opposite… If I reported you now, and brought you down and you denied it, he would take your word for it.'"[28] Another officer, however, recalled that Thompson would back staff against prisoners (this may have been in the matter of complaints or accusations). Thompson's response was to tell the prisoner that he was entitled to make an accusation, 'but you must prove that they are right. If you are wrong you will be charged with making a false accusation against an officer. I want you to go away and think about it.'[29]

The house was not entirely harmonious, however. The internees decided from time to time to show their independence (or to resolve internal differences and tensions) by subtle forms of go-slow and non-cooperation. This seems never to have been taken to the point where they could be accused of staging a protest but was nevertheless effective as a tug on the reins to remind the rank-and-file staff that the workplace could be made difficult for them, and personally inconvenient. Billy McKee gave the example of evening lock-up, at 9 p.m., when staff were hoping to get off duty and go home. This was an opportunity to apply pressure: 'We were messing about, they weren't getting out until maybe half nine.' He described this as 'a gradual process, working on their nerves the way they tried to work on ours'.[30] Another tactic was the en-masse submission of applications to see the Governor. This was called 'flooding the system' and was intended to soak up official energies and to inconvenience, a skirmish in an extended, low-intensity campaign of attrition. Because of their lack of solidarity, it was impossible for a group of ordinary criminal prisoners to engage in such joint actions, but, had any ventured, there would have been a swift and unhappy comeback. With internees, it would have been unwise for the Governor and staff to initiate a tussle in response. There would have been reports to the Ministry, possible leaks to the press, and the whole thing too easily portrayed as the pettiness and bullying of gaolers. And the alternative was so much more attractive: staff off the premises on time and the Governor obliged to deal with only a few internees, principally the internees' OC.[31]

From the other side of the counter, Sydney Wolfe, a basic-grade prison officer at the time, recalled his experiences with the internees: 'They were awkward to work with. They could be very, very awkward, and you had to be careful.' His account matches that of Billy McKee, and he recalled that '[l]ocking up at night was the worst. When it was time to lock up[, the internees] would run all over the place. They would put matchboxes in the hole for the lock to go into. You slammed the door [and] it didn't lock. Another trick… was to get a steel knife, they put it in the hinge and broke the door. There were doors lying all over the place.' He also agreed that the internees were not amenable to the usual disciplinary process: '[w]e couldn't give them orders. You just had to ask them. And you knew they had their leaders.' He added, nonetheless, that the internee leader worked with staff as much as possible and that Father McAlister was an effective conciliator: '[a] go-between. If there was any trouble he would sort it out.'[32]

But whatever ameliorations they wrung from the regime, and whatever privileges they enjoyed over ordinary prisoners, internment was imprisonment. Being in prison rather than in a camp drove that home. Ó Rahallaí remembered the sense of confinement and control: '[p]rison life is like that [pointing to a dog] – that dog is depending on me to open that door, and letting him in and letting

him out, and feeding him – and that's the position they put a human being in…
It's do-what-you're-told, and if you can't put up with the heat get out of the
kitchen, which means "sign up and get out".[33]

In the wake of an attempted escape in March 1958, a collective punishment was
imposed on the internees.[34] Following a briefing by republicans, the Nationalist MP
Eddie McAteer lodged a complaint about the conditions and regime in Belfast
Prison, thereby providing a prisoners' view of its main defects.[35] Apart from the
extended lock-up period, McAteer referred to unsatisfactory sanitary conditions.
In common with all other prisons in Britain and Ireland at the time, during the
extended hours of lock-up there was no access to lavatories, and men (and
women) had to use chamber pots in their cells. At Belfast Prison, disinfectant for
these was issued only once a week. Even when out of their cells for recreation
and association, sanitary provision was inadequate since only four toilets were
available in the yard for use by 240 men. The century-old cookhouse contained an
open lavatory cubicle for the use of kitchen staff and workers, and there were no
washing facilities on the landings of the wings. This meant that the officers and
convicted prisoners who served internees' food to them in their cells had no
means of washing their hands. Internees were lucky to get a bath once every
three weeks, in contrast to the weekly bath provided for convicted men. The
cells were dark and unhealthy, and slop-out sinks (into which the chamber pots
were emptied every day) were located in recesses alongside. Cell lighting was
provided only between the hours of 8 and 10 p.m. and between 8 to 9 a.m.
While the internees were at exercise, convicted prisoners, who at that time
served as cellhouse orderlies, appeared to have accessed cells, and personal items
had gone missing. The exercise yard was provided with only one draughty shed
for the men to shelter in if the weather were inclement. There were complaints
about the food, some of these perennial and seemingly ubiquitously attached
to prison food everywhere. Until the internees were allowed to have their own
kitchen, food was prepared centrally, and meals took up to twenty minutes to
reach the cells. The food was steam-cooked and was deemed by McAteer (it is
not clear if he had tasted it) to be unpalatable. There was only one qualified
cook in the kitchen, and his prisoner assistants were accused by McAteer of
being of 'dubious personal cleanliness'. Foreign bodies such as cockroaches were
'often' found in the food.[36]

The Ministry of Home Affairs, unsurprisingly, disputed this recital. It agreed,
however, that internees were confined to their cells for sixteen hours a day and
were generally denied access to lavatories from 8 p.m. lock-up to unlocking at
8 a.m.; but the Ministry denied that educational facilities had been withdrawn. It
was true that basic educational classes, such as were provided to ordinary prisoners,
were not provided for internees, but they were permitted to organise their own
classes, and approved lecturers were allowed to come into the prison. There were a
number of privileges over and above those extended to ordinary prisoners.
Internees had two letters in and out each week in contrast to the allowance of
one letter per fortnight to ordinary prisoners. They could receive a visit by not

more than three persons every two weeks, the duration of which was at the Governor's direction. Visitors could come any day except Sunday, and the layout was open (as distinct from the closed visiting box). The Ministry listed other privileges – positive benefits unless one applied the standards of civil detention as opposed to criminal imprisonment. Internees could wear their own clothes and could receive books, newspapers, cigarettes and toiletries; they were issued with one free razor blade a fortnight. They had a well-stocked library of their own and a monthly film showing. Concerts could be organised, musical instruments were allowed, and a gramophone was provided for dancing and other music. There were facilities for approved correspondence courses, and a reasonable quantity of paper was provided for educational purposes. Outdoors, there were facilities for football and other games. In describing of this cornucopia it was further noted that men were entitled to free medical care. No comment was passed on the several complaints about poor hygiene, but it was confirmed that D Wing had eight baths and four showers and that these were available three days a week.[37]

In lodging his criticisms, McAteer confessed that he was 'not at all cocksure' on all his points and did not expect to be 'as crisply authoritative' as he had been in a similar crusade on such issues some years previously. William Topping, Minister for Home Affairs, had agreed to meet him to discuss the complaints, and, in submitting them, McAteer emphasised that his case would draw on John Warnock's 'quite inspired phrase' that 'there was no such thing as triviality in the life of a man in prison'.[38] He was concerned only with prison conditions and would turn away from 'all the tempting bye-paths and stock debating material' such as how the internees had got where they were, why they were being kept there, police methods and the like: 'I want to try and awaken even in the forbidding bosoms opposite me a sense that it is not cricket to try to degrade an enemy prisoner.'[39]

Classes and recreation

Irish-language classes, as always, came top of the list for the internees and catered for a range of abilities and attainments, from beginners to those who were fairly fluent. French was also available, as was music; there were classes in aspects of the building trade. All of these drew on the men's own skills, as no provision for course-teaching (as distinct from occasional lectures) was made by the Ministry of Home Affairs. Music was popular and useful, since the men had to make their own entertainment.[40] Instruction was given in the tin whistle, and, eventually, a concert was put on, with some thirty musicians.[41]

As a gesture of defiance and reaffirmation of solidarity, the internees conducted parades in the exercise yard. How often this was done is not clear, but there could be no doubt as to their character. Sunday (with its lower level of staffing) was the day usually chosen for these displays. The men were ordered into military formation, four deep, and were addressed by the OC. On Easter Sunday, the high holiday of the republican year, the parade took on the character of a commemoration, with all the prisoners wearing Easter lilies, a symbol of republicanism.[42] Without massive reinforcement, the prison authorities could not have prevented or broken up these demonstrations, which do not appear to have been reported by the Governor to the Ministry of Home Affairs. As with other pragmatic accommodations and instances of Nelson's eye, had information about these parades leaked out, opponents of the government might well have found useful ammunition for attacks in Stormont or in the press. From a management perspective, however, a parade, peacefully dispersed, was easier to accept than disturbances of another character.

Visits

From an early stage, it was agreed that the internees be allowed to receive fortnightly visits of one or two (later three) approved persons. They were originally conducted under much the same conditions as those for prisoners, but over time these were changed, and internees negotiated more open arrangements, with no wire screen or mesh.[43] The internee had to lodge an application, submitting the names of his proposed visitors; these were then forwarded to the RUC for vetting.[44] Provided there were no police objections, the prison issued a visiting permit. For the greater part, the system worked smoothly, but there were some differences between the Ministry and the RUC as to the standards to be applied when judging visitors' suitability. This became a formal disagreement in April 1957, when the RUC submitted a negative report on two brothers of John Hegarty of Draperstown, Co. Londonderry. The brothers appealed the matter to the Ministry (exactly how is not clear), which decided in their favour. There had been a similar case (McKnight) a few weeks earlier, and it was apparent that the criteria of the Ministry and those of the RUC were out of kilter. Where there was some, but not compelling, concern, the Ministry was content to grant the application but to exercise extra vigilance, instructing supervising staff to stop the visit should there be an attempt to speak 'in Irish or any other foreign language' or if any unlawful statement were made.[45] The RUC took a much more stringent view and wanted to exclude any person who had doubtful associations or who had otherwise unfavourably come to their attention.

The differences were the subject of a rather testy exchange. The matter was first submitted to the Secretary at the Ministry of Home Affairs, R. F. R. Dunbar, by J. B. O'Neill of the Prison Division. There had been three cases where relatives had been deemed to be unsuitable visitors. Upon O'Neill looking more closely into these, he concluded that the grounds for objection had not appeared to be 'of such substance as would justify depriving a close relative from visiting an internee'. He proposed that the Ministry should write officially to the RUC, pointing out that the Ministry would have trouble in justifying the exclusion of close relatives from visits. RUC attention was to be drawn to the stringent security exercised during visits. They were to be requested to review their criteria for objecting to visitors and told that only 'in very exceptional circumstances and where a strong case exists' should close relatives be refused permission to visit.[46] Dunbar concurred, and, on 18 April 1957, a letter was drafted and sent to County Inspector J. G. T. Nelson at RUC headquarters. The Ministry made the point that objections to visits from close relatives could not be sustained on grounds of political affiliation and past political activity, if they were considered republican in outlook, or indeed associated with Sinn Féin. To prohibit a visit from a close relative, there had to be 'good evidence of an active interest in the IRA'. RUC headquarters accordingly ought to review the grounds on which local police submitted their objections.[47]

The RUC conceded that 'on some occasions we may have appeared rather severe in our recommendations against visits by relatives'. There was an explanation for this. An arrested person might, at the time of his detention, be the only person to know the location of an arms dump and might then wish to pass the information to some trusted messenger who would know what to do. This was given only as an example, but no cases were cited. In deference to the Ministry's wishes, special consideration would be given to cases where local police objected to a visit by an internee's close relative, 'and if thought desirable you will be consulted before the Prison Governor is given a reply'.[48]

In truth, there had been a deal of sloppy or at least unreflective police thinking, which Nelson's rationale was intended to remedy. An internee who held and wished to pass on details of an arms cache, or anything else, simply had to use another internee and his visitors. The only way to prevent this was to put the man in solitary confinement, and that was all but impossible with an internee. It was, moreover, highly probable that many internees' families would, to varying extents, share their incarcerated relative's political views, and to exclude them on such grounds alone would have been inhumane and unacceptable. A growing point of difference between the Ministry and the police was beginning to emerge in this exchange. Times had changed, and the standards being promulgated as the world pondered its appalling experience of totalitarianism no longer fitted comfortably with notions of steamrolling opponents of the state, even those who used, supported or sympathised with violence. Dunbar and other senior officials knew this as they contemplated the declarations of the United Nations and as the agenda of the Council of Europe took shape. The European Convention on Human Rights had been drafted in 1950 (coming into force in September 1953), and the UK was one of the strong proponents and early signatories. Dunbar had also been perceptive when he noted that internment had changed since it was last imposed, in the wartime years. Now Northern Ireland was alone in the UK in exercising this most extreme form of civil restraint and had to be careful to keep it above reproach: UK standards had to be applied in all its component parts.

Extending a degree of latitude to internees' close relatives did not preclude the close scrutiny of others who sought to visit. The wives of two Derry internees applied to visit a third man, Eamon Timoney. The RUC showed no hesitation in opposing the request. The women were in no way related to Timoney, and during the period before his arrest, while Timoney had been on the run, one of the women had acted as his courier: 'One may now correctly assume that she is endeavouring to renew the intelligence link with Timoney.' The report was emphatic: 'Under no consideration would the local police agree to either of these persons being allowed to visit Eamon Joseph Timoney.'[49]

Some applications were so obviously doomed that only wild optimism or a desire to vex the authorities could explain them. Kevin Stewart, a former internee, applied to visit Joseph Madill. Both had been members of Saor Uladh, although Stewart claimed that he had terminated his membership a few months before arrest. He had signed himself out of internment after only five days, admitting past membership and giving and undertaking as to his future good behaviour. His desire to visit Madill raised an obvious question about his relationship with him and, indeed, Saor Uladh. The RUC already knew that, unlike the IRA, Saor Uladh had no problem with its members giving undertakings to secure release. Considering all these factors, it strongly opposed a visit being granted.[50]

But while non-relatives could be excluded because of police objections to their political background and associations, the exchanges between the Ministry and the RUC firmly established the rule that close relatives could visit unless there were specific (and probably immediate) intelligence to support a case to the contrary. This policy was altered only once, in March 1958, when a tunnel and plans for a mass escape were uncovered.[51] At that point, all visits were suspended.[52]

Internment entailed the particularly onerous feature of indeterminacy, and, as we have repeatedly noted, this was difficult for all the men.[53] Some became obviously depressed, withdrew from activities and stayed in their cells. Members of the internee command would visit and counsel. The simple duration of confinement was reason enough to be depressed, but suggestions from prison staff that a man could put an end to the waste of his life by signing out added to the pressure. To be torn between loyalty to comrades and a desire for freedom was undoubtedly a strain, varied by personality, commitment to the movement and by the needs and support of one's family. The last was an issue that arose especially at visits. O Rahallaí recalled some families putting great pressure on internees, saying "'Sign out, what are you doing in here? Nobody cares.'" He knew of men who had to put a stop to their visits to avoid such encounters, 'because they were tortured'.[54]

By the end of 1957, IRA inmates (internees and convicted men) were receiving about twenty-five visits on weekdays and forty on Saturdays. This last had gone as high as sixty early in November and caused problems for the prison. Thompson considered that his staff could comfortably handle about twenty-five visits a day and granted permits accordingly. Numbers were considerably increased, however, when permits were issued directly by the Ministry – especially since such visitors usually chose to come on Saturdays. He asked that the issuing of permits be left in his hands so that he could match numbers to times and resources.[55]

The tunnel and its aftermath

One of the major events in the 1956–61 period of internment was an attempted mass escape from Belfast Prison. This was a decision by the internees' leadership, sanctioned by IRA GHQ. A security defect in many prisons of Victorian design following the Pentonville model was that ventilation shafts ran behind the wall of each end cell in a wing.[56] This weakness had been found in Mountjoy.[57] Apparently independently (but possibly through shared information), the Belfast prisoners also discovered this design weakness, and the prison command decided to exploit it. In the last weeks of 1957, an opening, some 18 inches square, was made into the air shaft from an end cell on the ground floor of D Wing. The cell was fitted with a wall-mounted mirror, conveniently positioned. When this was removed and the opening made to the maximum area that it covered, it was evident that not even a small person could squeeze through. A larger hole was made, but, since this was greater than the area of the mirror, a number of postcards were used to conceal the gap. Even so, because of its limited dimensions, not all the internees would have been able to enter the shaft.[58] From this entrance, undiscovered despite regular cell searches, there was a drop of some 19 feet to the tunnel proper. By mid-March 1958, this had been driven 95 feet horizontally below the D Wing basement, in the direction of St Malachy's College at the rear of the prison.[59] This was a significant work of excavation, and the 30-inch-diameter tunnel produced almost 600 cubic feet of soil. Since removal from the prison was impossible, this had to be dispersed, allowing the authorities, had they been sufficiently vigilant, and sufficiently energetic and imaginative in their searches, yet another chance to discover what was going on.[60] This work had apparently been undertaken with minimal equipment – one chisel and a shovel – and, at the point of discovery, had been under way for between four and six months.

Impatience and a failure in control (after a long period in which internee discipline seems to have been meticulous) brought disaster. Staff finally noticed that D Wing's ground-floor cell 1, occupied by Denis Toner, was never empty and was the hub of constant comings and goings. Suspicion may also have been stoked by a demonstration by D-Wing prisoners earlier in the day on 11 March 1958. The commencement of the Antrim Assizes in the courthouse directly across the Crumlin Road from the prison, was, as usual, marked by some ceremony and traditional display. Shouts of 'Up the Rebels' were heard and were intended to be taken as a counter-demonstration. At least in retrospect, staff suspected that the hubbub may have provided cover for a difficult and noisy part of the tunnelling.[61] While Toner was out of his cell that evening, a search was made, and the opening into the air shaft was discovered.[62] Principal Officer Robert (Bob) Truesdale ordered Toner's cell to be locked. This was done, but, as the internees were returning from association about this time, Toner requested that his cell be opened. When this was refused, he called out to the others. That the project was lost was immediately clear to them. A group of about sixty was mustered outside the cell and, through concerted effort, were able to smash the door off its hinges. This allowed the organisers to spirit away two of their comrades who had been working on the tunnel when it was discovered, thus avoiding their being taken and punished.[63] It also seems that tools and other escape items were retrieved and secreted during the tumult.

The internee recollection is somewhat at odds with the official report. One version differs from Thompson's on a significant detail. According to this, the men were out in the exercise yard, playing hurling or football at the time of the tunnel's discovery. Word came out, and all the men re-entered the wing. At that point, the internees blockaded the cell, and the officers who were conducting the search were trapped inside. The internees refused to release the prison officers. This, if an accurate account, was a very serious matter and was omitted from Governor Thompson's report. The stand-off, according to O Rahallaí's recollection, continued until evening lock-up.[64] It is likely that neither the staff nor the internee account is entirely accurate, given the melee and confusion, as well as the passage of time. It is possible that, at some point, officers were being held in the cell while internee diggers waited in the tunnel. Whether a stand-off was agreed is not clear, but it is possible that some understanding was reached. What is common to the different versions is that no internee was captured in the tunnel or the cell and that no one was subsequently punished for the incident, not even Toner, whose cell was being used.[65]

The immediate worry of the Governor was not who to punish but rather the knowledge that tools, escape items and possibly weapons were loose in the prison. Given that the internees were in an angry mood, deeply disappointed, frustrated and apparently ready to resist, reinforcements had to be summoned before a cell-to-cell search could commence. It is also indicative of poor levels of security and control, and faltering staff confidence, that a regular programme of systematic surprise searching had not previously been implemented. The fact that a substantial body of specially trained police had to be brought in suggests that staff had, to some extent, been physically intimidated and psychologically conditioned by the internees.[66]

On the following evening, after lock-up, a cell-to-cell search was mounted in D Wing by parties of prison officers, supported by twenty-five police. The latter consisted of five sergeants, sixteen constables and four special constables. Twenty-one of the men were from the RUC Reserve Force, a special mobile body. The remainder were from the Glenravel Street barracks, Belfast.[67] The cells were each searched by three prison staff, with police in attendance. In addition, each man was required to strip down to his underwear while outer clothing was examined. There was no discovery of importance, apart from two small hacksaw blades. According to Thompson, however, about a third of the men were found to have equipped themselves with weapons of some sort. These ranged from wooden coat-pegs and their mounts, torn from the cell walls, to the legs of tables and chairs.[68] Accounts diverge completely as to what happened at this point. The Governor reported that some fifteen men refused to submit to a personal search. The police had then intervened: 'Only necessary force was used and no injuries of a serious nature were sustained by any of them, and none have made any complaint to me.'[69] The brief issued to the press was misleading (or deliberately ambiguous), suggesting that police had been called in subsequent to disorder breaking out.[70]

The men, or at least some of them, offered a very different account. P. J. McGrory, a Belfast solicitor, asked for an independent medical examination for his client, James Martin, and for a solicitor's visit and interview. The family claimed that Martin had been beaten so badly that bones had been broken. A similar application had previously been lodged on behalf of David Morgan, to which the Ministry had not replied. On receipt of the second letter, a visiting permit was issued for Martin, but an independent medical examination was deemed to be unnecessary.[71]

A threatening cloud of suspicion formed when, as a collective punishment, the Governor stopped all letters, visits and food parcels for one month.[72] This was a development that, for a short time, could have created a deal of unease in the Catholic community and perhaps allowed the internees to gather sympathy and help the IRA break out of its political isolation. Collective punishments are rare in prison management, though sometimes there can be a punitive element in security restrictions that affect all inmates. In this instance, Thompson may have had a moral case. The internees had demanded to be treated collectively, not individually, and therefore all could be deemed to be complicit in the escape attempt, even if not directly participating. But whether or not collective punishment could be justified morally, it was poor politics and public relations, and probably of questionable legality. The unannounced cancellation of visits had immediate practical consequences for visitors, some of whom had come long distances with parcels (and children), only to be turned away. Alarm and suspicion were increased when staff informed the visitors that the men's laundry would not be handed out and exchanged for fresh apparel. According to newspaper reports, some women shouted, 'You cannot give it out because it's all bloodstained. You beat up our men.'[73] Realising the seriousness of the allegation and the likelihood that the rumour would have legs and gain credence within the nationalist community, the Governor relented and directed that laundry be exchanged with those women who sent their names into the prison. The *Irish News* reported on futile visits by a number of women, including four Derry women who wished to see their husbands. All would-be visitors were questioned by detectives about their relationship to the internees.[74]

More broadly concerned with community relations and political hazards, the Ministry took a different tack, distancing itself from the Governor's collective-punishment decision. Topping insisted that the stoppage of privileges was a matter of prison discipline and therefore reserved solely for the Governor.[75] Rumours flew over the walls, and Topping and his advisers were undoubtedly conscious that there was a growing possibility of nationalist feeling becoming inflamed by the notion of men being ill-treated and beaten behind prison walls – and untried men at that. This was entirely counter to the government's stance that the men were a tiny and dangerous minority, isolated and representing no one but themselves. Were they thought to be victims of cowardly ill-treatment, the community might reach out to embrace them. Such allegations would inevitably gain weight the longer a ban on communication was maintained. A week after the incident, therefore, and apparently against his wishes, Thompson was instructed to issue writing paper and an envelope to each internee.[76] When the internees' letters were collected for censorship and processing, they were, according to Thompson, 'found to be of such a scurrilous nature that they were not allowed to go out'. Fresh sheets were then offered. Only ten men accepted the new paper, and all these subsequently changed their minds, doubtless on orders from Paddy Maguire, their OC.[77] The authorities were no longer fully in control of events, and, had the IRA any but the most vestigial existence and even a modicum of political skill and leverage, a degree of volatility could have been created and exploited – and then what?

This potentiality was to be discerned when, on St Patrick's Day, wives and families demonstrated outside the prison, assembling at 2 p.m. at the courthouse. They hoisted the Irish tricolour on the court gates and sang the Irish National Anthem. As Alec Taylor, the Deputy Governor, and a police van tried to drive into the prison, the women surged past the opened outer gate of the sally port and thus into the space between the outer and inner gates.[78] A spokeswoman for the demonstrators said that they wanted an interview with the Governor: 'there had been a riot the previous week and they had not heard from their menfolk and wanted to know how they were'.[79] Matters took yet another turn when a group of Protestant women from nearby housing tried to stage a counter-demonstration, singing 'The Sash' and other Orange tunes. Police immediately hustled them away. All in all, the gatehouse confrontation was a nasty incident and could have been nastier still. Joe Connellan, the Stormont Nationalist MP for South Down, telegraphed the Ministry, protesting that the stoppages were a severe punishment of all for the actions of the few. The order would further embitter feelings in the community and would cause much anxiety to families of the internees.[80]

Nationalist and Labour politicians across the board shared the worries of their constituents. Francis Hanna, a solicitor and Independent Labour MP for Belfast Central, wrote to Thompson (with a copy to the Minister for Home Affairs) emphasising considerable public concern about what was happening in Belfast Prison and noting that rumours were spreading about beatings by police and prison officers.[81] He also drew attention to the fact that a number of the internees' friends who had turned up with parcels had not been allowed to hand them in. These were internees, not convicted men, Hanna reminded Thompson, asking that all privileges be reinstated.[82] This was one of a slew of letters addressed to the prison and Ministry by solicitors and politicians in the days following the searches.

Father McAlister and his assistant chaplain also took a hand. In a private interview with Thompson they expressed concern about the number of head wounds inflicted and the blood they had seen on cell walls. Even in private Thompson stuck to his line: only when the search was resisted had there been any manhandling. He also insisted that up to a third of the internees had armed themselves. Only the minimum of force had been used.[83] Replying to Francis Hanna a few days later, Topping endorsed Thompson's account of the incident – as indeed he had to: there was no independent evidence for any other course. By implication, he retracted his initial statement that the lockdown and withdrawal of contacts lay entirely within the province of the Governor by asserting that the various suspended privileges 'would be restored as soon as I am satisfied that they will not again be abused and that normal conditions again prevail in the prison'.[84]

There are indications that both sides gilded the lily. Thompson's rationale for calling in the police – in retrospect an inflammatory step – was that his staff would have to continue working with the internees and it would be better, therefore, that someone else handled any violent resistance that might arise. The intention had been that prison staff would conduct cell and personal searches, but, where a man resisted, the police would take over. This ran counter to the usual course that prolonged persuasion was preferable to the use of force. Quite apart from the fact that the police were unfamiliar with and untrained to work in prison conditions, Thompson's account omitted an important fact. The RUC reserve were not part-time or ordinary constables but a specially trained quasi-military unit normally used to patrol country areas where the IRA was active.[85] That being so, their introduction into the prison, given the animus that would inevitably arise between them and the IRA and pro-IRA internees, was an error of judgement. The apportionment of blame between Thompson and the RUC was probably unclear at the time and is even more difficult now.

Thompson offered an additional, albeit post-hoc, justification for his decision. As soon as searches began and the men in the first cells shouted a warning to their comrades, it became generally known to the internees that the police were present. It was only because of this, he contended, that all the internees did not resist the search and that only a few who possessed weapons attempted to use them. Only thirty out of 163 refused to be searched, and half of these capitulated when confronted by the police. Seven were forcibly stripped and were not harmed in any way, but eight who offered violent resistance 'had to be overpowered'.[86] Nine internees had reported to the medical officer, of whom one was found to have no visible sign of injury and another refused to be examined. Four men requested to see their family doctor, and six asked for their solicitor. This last rose to fourteen when the press report of John Mellon's case became available in the prison.[87] As we shall see, subsequent legal action against the prison authorities and police failed.[88]

That there had been a more general confrontation, moreover, was partly indicated by Thompson's praise for his staff who had carried out their duties in such a manner that, in his version of events, no internee received more than minor injuries. It was repeatedly asserted that the men had been armed with table and chair legs, coat-pegs torn from walls and pieces of wood shaped to spear points.[89] Some of the last, it was claimed, had pieces of iron affixed to them or nails driven through and protruding from them. Staff and police had conducted the search with 'wonderful restraint' despite 'the sneers, jeers, slogans and threats hurled at them'.[90]

If this account (a thoroughly chagrined and highly charged staff and a police unit to whom the IRA and its works were a particular abomination behaving with exemplary restraint) seems improbable, so too do the various accounts offered by internees in the 'scurrilous' letters which were suppressed and collected in Ministry files. Common phrases, adjectives and numbers suggest that when given sheets of paper, the men had agreed to send out individually an exaggerated account of the search and the confrontations with police and prison staff. Letters had not been dictated, but common points were highlighted in what has the discernable character of a letter-writing campaign: on their part nothing but polite reasonableness; on the other police and prison staff enraged and out of control.[91] Neither the Governor's account of staff and police behaving with 'wonderful restraint' nor the letter-writers' portrayal of meek and submissive internees wantonly attacked is credible.

It was clear, and to be expected, that where there were clashes between some of the internees and the search parties the internees came off worse. Cells were searched one at a time, and occupants who were deemed to be resisting were completely outmatched by physically fit and well-trained police, acting in concert and equipped with batons. Looking back some forty years to the event, Joe Cahill (even at the time of the confrontations a senior IRA figure) went no further than this in recalling the incident for his biographer. The search, he asserted, was undertaken with the deliberate intention of being destructive. Personal items, family photographs and religious pictures were all smashed to the floor and trampled on. Prisoners objected and fought back. As a result, '[q]uite a few' got badly beaten, he claimed, and '[i]n fact, they knocked the shit out of us'.[92]

As often is the case where tempers are discharged and loyalties rule, and independent witnesses are not available, there must be a fog – or at least a mist – of uncertainty and lies. The truth about the incident lay somewhere between the two versions. The background was the evolving state of discipline and control in the prison. An implicit stand-off had been agreed between staff (including the Governor) and the internees. In return for conducting themselves in an orderly and trouble-free fashion, the men would be given a degree of latitude to organise their days as they wished. Thompson, whose basic responsibility was safe custody, saw the tunnel as a breach of this agreement and a betrayal of trust: he had been naive and should have remembered the tale of the scorpion and the frog. He had perhaps conflated his duty to reassert control with a desire to settle accounts, to show who was master, to punish the men for taking advantage of what now seemed like a foolish willingness to loosen control.

Following the confrontations, Father McAlister, who had the confidence of the staff and the Governor, attempted to mediate. After discussion with Thompson, McAlister visited D Wing, where he spoke to the internees' OC, Paddy Maguire, and to Joe Cahill. He told them that the Governor was 'pretty sore' about the tunnel.[93] Thompson had good reason to feel disgruntled. He had been taken for a fool – and possibly looked like one to his superiors. There was little consolation in the tunnel's eventual discovery, which, after many weeks, possibly months, of hammering, chiselling and digging, the removal and concealment of a vast quantity of soil and a veritable works' assembly in cell 1, had tapped staff on the shoulder and begged to be noticed. The internees had bungled the escape rather than its having been baulked by a proper schedule of searches and organised intelligence-gathering. Thompson's supervision and control of the police-backed search had also fallen short: safe custody also meant care. He should have anticipated the volatility of the confrontations and that injuries were likely. It was chance that no life had been lost or life-threatening injuries inflicted. His collective punishment of all the internees had been reflexive, ill-considered and heavy-handed, more retribution than prevention. By cutting off communications between the men and their families he had played the IRA's game and had created a toxic miasma of suspicion.[94] That was why he had relatively gently but surely been reined in by the Minister for Home Affairs. At the end of the affair, scores were much closer to being equal than they should have been. The IRA had lost a tunnel but had (to a modest degree) energised its supporters, sympathisers and internees' families and had made an appeal to its broader community. As a case study in prison administration, the episode could scarcely have been bettered, but the aftermath showed scant sign that Thompson, or even the Ministry, wanted to reflect.

It was beyond question that a number of internees had been hurt, but there was no record of injuries to staff or to the RUC squad, or indeed reports thereof. Dr S. W. McComb, the Medical Officer, reported examinations of eight internees on 14 March 1958. These showed a series of injuries consistent with internees' raising hands and arms to defend themselves and also being struck on the back and shoulders. One man, who refused to be examined, was observed by the doctor to be suffering from an arm injury.[95] At Governor's Applications on 14 March 1958, ten men variously applied to see their solicitors and doctors; one applied to see Father McAlister.[96] It was generally the case at that time in relation to convicted prisoners that an application to consult an outside medical practitioner was refused, unless supported by the prison medical officer. These men, however, were not convicted and should have been allowed all the privileges extended to civil detainees, including access to their professional advisers.

There was a further twist when John Mellon, aged twenty, a detainee rather than an internee, was produced on 13 March 1958 before Resident Magistrate John M. Campbell, at Belfast custody court. This was the committal stage in proceedings against Mellon under the Explosives Substances Act and the Special Powers Act. Mellon was represented by R. H. Conaghan, QC, and his Junior, F. G. Harty, instructed by R. H. O'Connor, an Omagh solicitor. During the lunch break, Conaghan visited Mellon in the courtroom cell. Immediately after, Conaghan approached the prosecuting police officer, District Inspector O'Brien, complaining that his client had been assaulted; he asked O'Brien to come with him to the cells. On examining Mellon, O'Brien found clear signs that he had indeed been beaten. There were marks on his left forearm, on his shoulders, back and legs and on his right knee. He complained of pains in his back and head; he was also limping slightly. Mellon told O'Brien that at about 8.30 the previous evening he had been in his pyjamas and in bed in his cell on C Wing. On hearing a commotion, he had gone to his cell door and called to a neighbouring cell, asking what was going on. When he got no reply, he kicked his cell door to attract attention. A prison officer had come, asked for keys to be brought and opened the cell door; Mellon had, by this time, returned to his bed. Six policemen came in, dragged him out of it and beat him with batons; they had also beaten and kicked his seventeen-year-old brother Marshall, with whom he shared the cell.

Conaghan at this point said that because of the complaint and Mellon's condition he could not agree to continue the committal proceedings and that he wanted Mellon to be examined by a doctor. He told O'Brien that he did not want any publicity and hoped that the matter could be dealt with quietly. Both men then went to the Resident Magistrate Campbell's chambers. On hearing the complaint, Campbell offered to have Mellon examined by the prison doctor. When Conaghan refused this, O'Brien offered an examination by the RUC medical officer. This was also refused, and Conaghan asked for an independent doctor. After some consultation with his clerk, Campbell reopened the committal proceedings. Conaghan then applied for and was granted an independent medical examination for his client; presumably in keeping with his counsel's advice, he asked the magistrate to make an order that the proceedings should not be reported. Taking the view that the matter should receive as much publicity as possible, Campbell refused the application, noting also that there existed the basis for a civil action.[97] Conaghan asked for bail, and, although District Inspector O'Brien expressed his opposition, Campbell granted it. A doctor was called on Mellon's behalf and the police doctor on behalf of the RUC. An examination was then conducted.[98]

The Ministry immediately called for a report from the prison. Principal Officer John Foster, who had been in charge of C Wing on the evening of the disturbance, gave his account of events, as did Constable H. S. Beckett. Foster's version was that both Mellon brothers had been hammering on their cell door, shouting 'Up the Rebels'. The door was opened, and the brothers were told they would be searched; both, Foster insisted, were armed with chair legs and had refused to comply. They attempted to attack Foster, who then called in the police. While the men were being disarmed, John Mellon tripped and fell over a bed and thus injured himself; no undue force was used. Constable Beckett's account was virtually identical, including the contention that Mellon had injured himself by tripping over a bed. Beckett did concede that he had struck Mellon once with his baton.[99] Both statements failed to account for Mellon's extensive injuries and, taken together, were not only implausible but smacked of collusion.

Although John Mellon had been granted bail, his brother Marshall remained in prison, at first a detainee and then an internee. His solicitor, H. O'Connor, attempted to visit him with his barrister but found that legal visits, as others, had been prohibited by Thompson as part of the collective punishment.[100] At this point, the most plausible reading of the refusal – and it was probably unprecedented for a legal visit to be stopped – was that access was being denied to stop the men speaking about their ill-treatment and to give time for their injuries to heal. On 29 March 1958, the Maghera, Co. Londonderry, firm of Agnew & Sons wrote on behalf of the relatives of ten internees. The firm had asked the prison for an independent medical examination but had been told that ministry authorisation was required. Could it be carried out as soon as possible, the firm enquired, since it would have no purpose after 'any considerable lapse of time'.[101] The reply was uncompromising: the Prison Medical Officer was responsible for the treatment of internees, and no other examination would be permitted. Denying that any inmate had been subjected to ill-treatment and abuse on 12 March 1958, the Ministry also noted that none of the ten listed in Agnew's letter had complained to the Governor or had asked to see either the Prison Medical Officer or his own doctor.[102]

A number of other solicitors were now in contact along similar lines. Concerned that events were taking a turn that could further generate corrosive publicity and growing scepticism and anger in circles of the Roman Catholic community well beyond republicanism, Dunbar wrote to the Crown Solicitor. He outlined the events of 12 March (sticking to Thompson's version) and asked for the Attorney General's opinion as to whether the legal and medical visits sought by the various solicitors should be granted. This was perhaps more of an exercise in risk-spreading than a genuine request for legal advice, and, fittingly, the reply was more political than legal. Although the purpose of the examinations seemed clear (to embarrass the Ministry), it might be better to grant them in view of the publicity that might follow a refusal. Another consideration was that a refusal 'might well be misrepresented in Great Britain and America, whereas if we accede to the demand, it will be a demonstration that we have nothing to hide'.[103]

Taking the view that an independent expert was sometimes hard to find in Northern Ireland, this was not what Dunbar had wanted to hear, but, since it was political rather than legal advice, he was able to disregard it. Writing to P. J. McGrory the following day, he agreed to a legal but not medical visit. The line was the same: the Prison Medical Officer alone was responsible for the internees' medical treatment. The adverse publicity to which the Attorney General referred had already occurred in the USA, and the Northern Ireland Prime Minister had begun to receive telegrams and letters from Irish societies there. A determination to weather such protests (which were regarded as being republican-inspired), awaiting the healing of bruises, cuts and injuries, and the hope that the whole thing would go off the boil with the passing of time led to the conclusion that the best course was to hold firm.[104]

The internees, their families and sympathisers could do little more than protest. On 15 April 1958, McGrory condemned the Ministry's stonewalling: 'You must know quite well that I asked for an independent examination because it is alleged by my clients that the Prison authorities permitted them to be abused.' If other than a prison were involved, a complainant would be entitled to an independent medical examination, and a refusal would result in certain conclusions being drawn. Because of the delay, the Ministry had 'effectively debarred any opportunity for independent medical testimony'. This refusal, which might have upheld the Ministry's version of events, 'can only remain as a matter of comment to the Court'.[105]

Over the succeeding weeks, McGrory added more clients to his list of intended litigants. There was more petty obstruction by the prison. When, for convenience, he asked to see more than one client at a time, permission was refused, and when one of the other members of his firm came to conduct an interview, he was refused entry because McGrory was named on the visiting permit. McGrory's protests that members of his firm had been admitted on his visiting permit many times over the previous ten years were met with a recital of the regulations.[106] The Ministry could not stop a legal action, but it was certainly not going to smooth the way. In all, eight internees sued the RUC Inspector-General and Governor Thompson. Three additionally took action against William Topping, the Minister for Home Affairs.[107]

A test case came to court with comparative speed. Evidence was taken on Monday, 30 June 1958, and judgment was reserved. A decision against the named plaintiff, Francis Card, a thirty-five-year-old docker, interned since January 1957, was given in the Belfast Recorder's Court on 10 July 1958.[108] Recorder Fox recited the facts as given by Card and by the defendants.[109] He found that the authorities had a legal right to search Card and accepted that prison staff had warned Card that if necessary he would be searched by force. Crucially, as to intent, he found that when police had entered the cell they had not drawn batons. He also accepted Principal Officer Joseph Myers's account as to what subsequently happened and rejected Card's claim that he had been struck with batons several times around his shoulders and arms.[110] Some doubt had been raised about the authority of the police to search within the prison, but the Recorder was satisfied that they had been asked to assist the prison staff, and, in so doing, they were acting under their common-law powers (and indeed obligation) to prevent a breach of the peace. Finally, Fox concluded that no unnecessary force had been used by the constables to strip Card. The action, accordingly, fell.

Four more cases were in the pipeline, and the Recorder now turned to these on a crucial point of law. The defendants (the Governor of Belfast Prison and the Inspector-General of the RUC) argued that their relationship to police officers was not that of master and servant and that therefore they could not be responsible for their actions. The Recorder, agreeing, cited the Constabulary (Northern Ireland) Act, 1922, and the Constabulary (Ireland) Act, 1846: 9 & 10 Vict., c.97. These established that a policeman in Northern Ireland held a public office, that his duties arose from common law or statute and that he was required to take an oath to carry them out. Case law confirmed that a police officer was not in a master-and-servant relationship to the government or constabulary authority. It followed that neither the Governor of Belfast Prison nor the Inspector-General of the RUC had such a relationship to the police constables and, therefore, in law, were not responsible for their searching of the defendant 'or for the manner in which they carried out the search'.[111] In the absence of a successful appeal, this judgment, in substance and in detail, effectively blocked the way to further litigation on the events of 12 March. The internees decided not to appeal. Eleven months later, the Ministry decided that it would be futile to pursue the internees for legal costs.[112]

In the prison, there was a gradual easing of the atmosphere. As with most escapes and escape attempts, there had been a deal of stable-door slamming. Had the escape succeeded – even partly, either in a number of internees getting away or even getting outside the prison – the repercussions for staff would have been considerable. This was a far greater lapse than a failure to prevent an opportunistic escape, the sudden exploitation of a weakness. It was worse than the success of a carefully planned escape by one or two individuals. A large number of internees had taken part in the operation, and the signs of what had been under way had not been hard for an alert staff to discern. An inquiry by the Ministry would have followed a deal of political embarrassment. On previous form, subordinate members of staff would have taken a disproportionate share of the plentiful blame, but it is also possible that Thompson may not have been invulnerable and, at the very least, would have been reprimanded. These reflections, and the fear that the internees might have another attempt in hand, made for a tense atmosphere. But, looking back on the episode, Billy McKee was fairly sanguine: 'It was hard for about three or four months, they gave us a really rough time and then it eased off again... As we were internees... they couldn't get away with it, you know.'[113]

Support groups

As during earlier periods, support groups were organised by Sinn Féin and other republican bodies. Máire Drumm of Sinn Féin raised funds both in Northern Ireland and in the USA but had little success outside those organisations and circles already sympathetic to or in support of the IRA. Some finance was available, however. Virtually all the men were smokers (as was true for a large section of the adults of that generation), and some of the funds provided were expended on these and other comforts. Families were aided directly by grants to provide necessities and also by being relieved of the need to send money and goods to their relatives.[114] Much of the fund-raising had to be done by women and also discreetly, since all republican activists feared internment. Equally, all fund-raisers had to be trusted by the IRA because of the information they inevitably gathered and the personal connections they made.

Support was severely limited by public attitudes towards internment. There was little media interest, North or South, and sometimes the internees felt that they had simply faded away, of concern to nobody but their families and the immediate organisation. Even in relatively close communities neighbours sometimes assumed that a young man who had disappeared had gone to Britain to work. As the months went by and the Border Campaign spluttered pointlessly on, the indifference of the Catholic community became demoralising: '[i]t was like a fool's paradise to the public – what were we doing up there lying in jail… People didn't realise the principle of it all, and the protest of it all.'[115]

The internees themselves acted as something of a support group for the convicted men in A Wing, principally it seems, as a pipeline for tobacco. As noted, the chapel was used by both categories of prisoner, but at different times, and so served as a depository and exchange point for concealed parcels and messages.[116] Cigarettes were given by the internees to their quartermaster, who reserved some for the small number of A-Wing men and distributed the rest equally. The cigarettes were also used as barter by both internees and sentenced men, to buy services or goods from other prisoners.

There was ambivalence and disagreement among the internees about the nationalist politicians and the support they offered. Some saw MPs such as Eddie McAteer and Harry Diamond as helpful checks when they raised internment and prison issues at Stormont; others thought that any assistance had to be paid for in the coin of electioneering by these men. O Rahallaí spoke for the more sceptical group when he portrayed Harry Diamond's involvement with internee releases as a cynical exercise in electoral politics. He would not allow Diamond (who he saw almost as a member of the Stormont government) to use his name or to become involved in his case: 'I wouldn't tolerate it. Not that I was a hard man, I just wouldn't do it.'[117]

The chaplaincy

The Bishop of Down and Connor issued particularly strict instructions to his chaplain as to the convicted men in Belfast Prison.[118] The internees were in a different position, having been confined on suspicion rather than because guilt had been proved in court. Internees attending confession were, nevertheless, asked by Father McAlister if they were members of the republican movement; in this he was presumably acting on the instructions of his superiors. Confirmation that they were, equivocation or anything short of a robust denial meant that absolution would be refused.[119] As time passed, there was a considerable reduction in men attending confession, and this may have prompted some reconsideration on Mageean's part. A priest was brought in from the Ardoyne parish who made it clear that there would be no political discussions in the confession box. This 'don't ask, don't tell' approach served the pastoral and political needs of the bishop and, at the same time, avoided what would have been an embarrassing reversal on his part or that of his chaplain.

The chaplain's pastoral duties were general as well as individual. It was customary for the ministers of the various denominations to arrange concerts and entertainment. For those whose days were lived out according to institutional routine and whose social and personal relations combined familiarity, predictability and a degree of emotional intensity, these visits of outsiders could mean a lot. Besides the entertainment, there was a change in routine and the chance to be an audience rather than simply an association of captives. A prison officer recalled that 'Father Pat' (McAlister) undertook the duties of prison impresario alongside his fellow chaplains but that his concerts were the best.[120]

Parish clergy were entitled to visits, but only to their parishioners. (Father Tomás Ó Fiaich – later Cardinal – was a visitor at this time.) Prison staff, having the internees' addresses, would know if a man fell within the priest's parish. When at liberty, O Rahallaí was a member of a confraternity (a lay society attached to a church), and the priest who conducted the group attempted to visit but was refused.[121]

Internee discontent had grown appreciably by the end of 1957. A significant portion of the group had been held for twelve months or more and release was nowhere in sight. Some frustration and anger was vented on Father McAlister. He had been mildly critical of overcrowding in his confidential report to the authorities and had urged that the Advisory Committee deal more rapidly with applications. At the same time, he recognised the increased pressures on staff of greater prisoner numbers.[122] Whatever his *sub rosa* observations to the internees, McAlister was a member of the prison hierarchy, more disposed to the authorities than to themselves, and theirs was a Manichean world.

Ill-feeling boiled up at a point when the internees were more than usually disheartened, in January 1958. Several men had recently joined their ranks, betokening a prolongation of incarceration and a confirmation that internment was still going strong. This, combined with the open-ended nature of internment, was hard to bear. The Governor reported internee disagreements, observing that the hard weather (which restricted outdoor exercise) had contributed to making them feel 'really miserable'.[123] The assistant Roman Catholic chaplain had obtained permission from the Ministry to conduct a mission – a sequence of twice-daily sermons and services throughout the week – and this entailed some departures from the daily routine (which may have been part of his thinking). In addition, another priest, from the Republic of Ireland, stayed locally in order to participate and help. Following a morning service, the men were ordered to their cells for breakfast. They refused to comply unless cell doors were left open, since they had reached the point in the daily routine normally set aside for exercise. Thompson would not countenance disobedience and staged a show of force, entering D Wing with extra staff. All but a few then returned to their cells, and those who did not were manhandled into them.[124] The men subsequently tried to enlist the assistant chaplain in a protest, but he refused to support them. Alarmed that his mission was being made an occasion of protest, the assistant chaplain then decided to call it off, telling the Governor that the protesters were no good and were 'prepared to use religion to suit their purpose and could only be described as Anarchists'. Such was the hostility directed at McAlister and his assistant, and the men's generally unsettled temper, that the Governor cancelled a scheduled withdrawal of the police reserve guard from the prison.[125]

Release

Signing out

Some men were released shortly after arrest, others at the preliminary detainee stage, with little more ado, when it became clear that they had been picked up in error. One of the ways in which intelligence was collected also lent itself to an over-wide casting of the net. Many republican activists – not necessarily members of the IRA – were known to the police. Through normal police patrolling and observation, persons were seen in company with known activists. Efforts would then be made to identify these, and some were added to the list of republican suspects. Back-up intelligence that would point either way was probably unavailable in many if not most cases. The difficulty with this method – especially simple observation – is to keep off the list those who are merely casual contacts. As much as anyone else, republican activists have a range of friends, acquaintances and associates – all lived in geographically and socially compact communities – and should mere contact indicate a degree of guilt the lists would snowball unmanageably. Even when other checks were possible, however, it was inevitable that some men with little or no interest in republican politics would become suspects. And with those whose sympathies were nationalist, shading into republican, a well-run intelligence system should have stipulated the thresholds to be crossed before such persons were deemed to merit police attention.

A number of those arrested were assessed and released during the detainee period; another group needed further review. One internee remembered these persons over whom suspicion lingered as part of a small group 'picked up because they had been knocking about with the likes of me, they had no real affiliation – they might have had sympathies towards the attitudes we had'.[126] These were subjected to a test which, at face value, might be taken as decisive: were they willing to renounce all connection with republicanism and promise to be of good behaviour? After several weeks in custody, most who were not members of Sinn Féin or the IRA would have signed, but some completely unaffiliated men, as we shall see, refused on principle to sign the required declaration.[127] The police attitude was one familiar to their profession: why would an innocent man refuse to sign? Unfortunately, the recalcitrant detainee's view mirrored that: why should an innocent man be required to sign?

There was, as we have noted previously, a visceral reaction to signing out that extended beyond active republicans and those who accepted IRA discipline. Paddy Joe McClean was not a member of the IRA or Sinn Féin, though he had been active in Liam Kelly's political organisation, Fianna Uladh, in 1953 and had worked then for Kelly's election in the Mid-Tyrone constituency. McClean was working as a primary-school teacher at the time of his arrest and was not affiliated to the IRA. Shortly after being served with an internment order, he was inclined to apply to the Advisory Committee. He decided not to do so because the internees, as a body, had decided against any recognition of the Committee. He recalled that 'it went further than that because, if you did go to the Board, then you were ostracised from your own, and then you had to be changed into isolation, into another part of the prison'.[128] A man who went to the Advisory Committee and who was released, McClean contended, 'politically castrated himself... because in the nationalist culture of internment, and the aftermath, you didn't give [a signature] and if you did you were ineffective as a political... forever'.[129]

Billy McKee, much imprisoned, would doubtless have agreed with McClean that signing out branded a man or woman within the nationalist and certainly the republican community. At the same time, he recognised the pressures that could come from families, especially where something had gone wrong: sickness, death, privation. A man might respond by signing out: 'You regret it a couple of hours afterwards, but you've done it and that's it... It's hard on lads that are interned, I pitied some of them.'[130]

The Advisory Committee

For those who entered into internment proper, and who would not sign an undertaking, the path to release was far from easy. As we have seen from the earlier uses of internment, the Special Powers Act provided for an Advisory Committee to consider individual cases. This quasi-judicial mechanism was necessary to defend against the charge of detention by mere executive fiat. Critics said that the Advisory Committee merely threw a cloak of equity over a process that removed liberty on the basis of information secretly collected and laid, and secretly reviewed, and which therefore was unchallengeable by the normal methods of the law. It is certain that internment would not have been acceptable to many far beyond active nationalist and republican circles without the safeguard of a scrutinising committee. This body was accordingly reconstituted and met on 11 February 1957, some two months after the first round-ups of the Border Campaign. It was chaired by F. A. L. Harrison, QC. The two other members, D. Andrews and R. W. F. T. Berkeley, were Justices of the Peace.[131]

By the time the Committee held its first session, there were sixteen appeals on the table.[132] A total of twenty men had appealed by mid-March 1957, of whom four were successful.[133] The IRA's prohibition on any dealings with the Committee was absolute, so the ratio of twenty applications from almost 120 detainees could be read as some kind of confirmation that RUC intelligence, which had guided the arrests, had been broadly accurate.[134] Equally, the fact that a man had submitted an application could conveniently be taken as *prima facie* evidence that he did not have or had severed connections with violent republicanism, though that deduction was, in itself, not enough to ensure release.

As during previous periods of internment, police influence was critical. Special Branch drew up arrest lists, decided on which detainees should be recommended for internment, reported to the Advisory Committee, responded to its queries and had an effective veto on release.[135] As far as can be discerned from surviving papers, their attitude towards the internees seems to have remained professional throughout, though fraught with all the difficulties and possible injustices inherent in the use of informants, supposed facts and observations which the accused could not challenge.[136] It was a one-sided process, and nothing would remedy that. As the campaign wore on and its failure became evident to all, police attitudes eased, and it was sometimes they who had to prompt the Advisory Committee in a release decision. Indeed, the *Manchester Guardian*, obviously on the basis of a briefing, reported that direct appeals to the police were more useful than a normal Advisory Committee application.[137] This created the possibility of police favouritism or prejudice determining freedom or incarceration, or indeed an understanding that there would be some kind of quid pro quo. But since police information was the basis of the system, these were, to some extent, unavoidable possibilities. Both the Committee and the Ministry seem to have been willing to take some notice of the reputation of the police officer who made the internment recommendation (which appears to have been at district inspector level).[138]

This was not the position at the outset, however, when Special Branch cautioned that the IRA had possibly changed its policy on signing out. This assessment was probably on the basis that this had been decided by the Saor Uladh group, and police understanding of the relationship between it and the IRA was hazy (quite remarkable and instructive in itself). Up to that point, a refusal to apply to the Advisory Committee had been taken as confirmation that a man had been correctly interned: the IRA general order and republican culture thus provided the authorities with a quality guarantee. If this new intelligence were correct (it was not, as soon became evident) then everyone connected with the internment process was faced with a much more complicated task of evaluation.[139] This concern, together with a belief that detainees would lie about past and future membership of, or association with, the IRA, would, unless there had been an act of public renunciation, have embargoed any release of any man who had at any time become known to the police as a member, supporter or possibly even a sympathiser of the IRA. Dunbar worried about this sweeping approach. It was possible, he observed, that in the period of IRA quiescence, from 1946 until 1954, some younger men might have joined the organisation as a matter of course rather than intending to take part in warfare. And where Sinn Féin rather than the IRA was the reason for internment (as it was in a few cases), he pointed out that until December 1956 this had not been an illegal body. The element of risk involved in releasing applicants needed to be weighed against 'the risk of turning them into embittered Republicans'.[140]

To some extent, Topping accepted Dunbar's reasoning. On 20 March 1957, he recommended the release of seven men, having sought advice from the police and also from Major Thompson. The latter reported that applicants, being known as such, were in 'an embarrassing position'. There was no open hostility from other internees, and a few even joined in football games. They nevertheless stayed together during association periods, probably because they feared ostracisation.[141] Of the seven applications presented to the Minister, only one had carried a recommendation for refusal. Topping generally took the view that if a man admitted past membership of the IRA, gave undertakings as to his future behaviour and was prepared to enter into a recognisance, he had substantially purged himself and, by the very fact of submitting to procedures, had cut past ties and thus might be released. In some instances even this act of submission was not required. One man, reported by a district inspector to have made a credible statement that he was not a member of the IRA, refused on principle to give his recognisance but was nevertheless released. Another had come to police attention as an active IRA man, but only during the recent upsurge. Dunbar did not like the implication in the police report that his internment would teach his family a lesson. Major Thompson also observed that the man was not in sympathy with the current campaign and that 'his impending marriage will keep him out of trouble'. He too was recommended for release on recognisance, and the Minister concurred. The police proposed that another man's release be delayed for two months, to see if the IRA campaign subsided. If the applicant were fit to be released in two months, Dunbar contended, there was no point in continuing to hold him. In another case, a former member of the Lurgan unit of the IRA was recommended for release. Dunbar argued that this was a risk to be preferred to his becoming hardened in his views. The IRA unit of two men under consideration had broken up and its members were on the run: this was a disincentive to their resuming IRA activities. In this case Topping agreed with the line of reasoning, but he did not automatically follow advice. Two men recommended by Dunbar were turned down, despite favourable comments from Thompson. Exactly why Topping took a contrary view is not clear, since no comment was given, but even the fact that they were at the end of the list may have counted against them.[142]

Like many predominantly or substantially rural societies, Northern Ireland is a collection of small communities and local knowledge, and reputation and connections were crucial during the release-assessment process. Close to the ground, county inspectors were listened to carefully. They recommended for release on the basis of detailed information about the man in question, his family and associates and underwrote this by sometimes requiring that those who wished them to intervene should sign a declaration that they were not members of the IRA. The signature itself served as a material guarantee of future good behaviour – presumably because the document could be made known should a released person revert to IRA activities.[143] Nationalist MPs, reviled by many republicans, were also able to make representations on a man's behalf, and a number of releases were secured in this way.[144]

One of the strangest recommendations came from an RUC district inspector in October 1960. By this point it was clear to all – except the much depleted and several-times-replaced IRA GHQ – that the campaign was beyond its terminal stages. The cases of two Maghera men (McKenna and McCuskar) were brought to the Advisory Committee. They were thought to have fired a Thompson sub-machine gun at an RUC sergeant but had never been charged. The Committee, understandably, saw this as a clear-cut case: there could be no question of releasing such violent men. The District Inspector attended the next committee meeting to argue the men's case. He had received information that while they had indeed fired at the sergeant they had deliberately aimed high so as not to hit him and that locally the deed was recognised as having arisen from a desire by the pair to have done their bit 'for the cause'. To retain them any longer, perhaps releasing them only at the last, the District Inspector contended, would turn them into martyrs; public safety would not be endangered by their release. Taken aback by the recommendation, the committee chairman insisted that anyone who fired a Thompson sub-machine gun 'could only be regarded as dangerous and should be held until the very last'. The two lay members of the Committee had, however, been persuaded by the RUC man, the bizarre nature of the recommendation and the incongruity of such an advocate perhaps exerting its own weight, and a favourable recommendation was therefore made.[145]

RUC influence notwithstanding, the Ministry, from the outset, sought to bolster the authority of the Advisory Committee. We have seen how, during previous periods of internment, police or political considerations could cut across a committee decision.[146] But times, and the international legal environment, were changing, and notions of civil and human rights were beginning to influence official thinking and procedures. Writing to Topping on the basis of his review of the first batch of appeals, Dunbar proposed that the Ministry should depart from the Committee's recommendation only in the 'exceptional circumstance' when the RUC was willing to reveal to the Minister information it would not share with the Committee. Matters were now very different from the operation of internment during the wartime years. Regulation 18b of the DORA had then been in operation in England and had provided an element of cover and support for internment in Northern Ireland: this was no longer the case. Then, 'on top of all this we have this confounded United Nations with their document of Human Rights and all the rest of it'.[147] The Advisory Committee was, therefore, crucial. As long as it was active and made up of well-known members of the community, 'it cannot possibly be said that it is simply a piece of play-acting which means nothing'. With this important proviso, government could justify the stance of being willing to intern anybody 'against whom we have any grounds for suspicion'.[148]

There were other cautionary concerns. As we have seen, a man might be thought by the police to be mixed up with the IRA or Sinn Féin simply because of his friends, even though he might not have the slightest sympathy with their political theories or affiliations. Then again, the process could be vulnerable to malice and grudge, Dunbar noted. An informer might have proved himself extremely reliable, giving the police all the information he could, but that would not stop him 'working off bits of personal spite on the side'. Much would also turn on the applicants' demeanour before the Committee, which 'it is completely impossible to get down on paper'.

There had been a change in the conduct of appeal proceedings. During the wartime years, the Committee had sat with its clerk and shorthand writer present but giving the applicant a binding promise of confidentiality. F. A. L. Harrison (now Chairman) proposed a preliminary interview without clerk or shorthand writer. When that was completed, officials were brought into the room, and from that point all proceedings were on the record.[149] Dunbar welcomed the new format, believing it more likely to get internees talking freely and to produce a more reliable and valuable recommendation. The absence of a verbatim record would necessarily make it more difficult for the Ministry to evaluate the Committee's recommendation. Dunbar did not consider this a great defect and urged Topping to scrutinise the appeals as rapidly as possible.[150]

Dunbar stuck by this straightforward approach, even when it was queried by Topping. The Committee based its decisions on the confidential interview, and, unless the Ministry had information not available to the Committee, its finding must be accepted: '[o]therwise the appointment of the Committee is completely insincere and means nothing'. Most of the release recommendations involved two-year recognisances with various sums, ranging from £10 (the usual amount) to £50, forfeit in default. Where more complicated conditions were proposed, Dunbar urged caution on Topping. In two cases, the Committee proposed to defer release for a month. Dunbar argued for immediate release: internment was not meant to be a punishment, and a man either had to be kept in or let out. Another case carried as the condition for release that the man should leave the country and take his family with him. The Ministry could not impose such an order, Dunbar insisted, though the Governor of Belfast Prison might be asked to talk to the man and strongly suggest that he go to England on release, since this was a factor that had favourably influenced the Ministry in his case.[151]

The hearing of appeals proceeded at a reasonable pace, though, to a man awaiting a decision on his freedom, any delay was agonisingly slow. By the end of July 1957, thirteen committee meetings had been held, reviewing thirty-five appeals. Of these, in twenty-eight cases there were recommendations for release, all but one requiring recognisances. On the Minister's orders, three men who had received favourable recommendations were retained for further consideration, one for additional police enquiries.[152] From time to time in the files there is mention of the current state of the IRA campaign, suggesting that in quiet periods it was easier for Topping to accept release recommendations. A statistical round-up showed that forty-one meetings of the Committee were held up to the first week in June 1958, by which time 466 persons had been detained. Of these, ninety-three were released by the police and eighty-eight were charged. A total of 100 men had been released from internment, and, on 23 June 1958, 183 were held under internment orders, with a further two in detainee status. There had been 117 appeals and ninety-six releases. Two men had been refused release and did not re-appeal; nineteen cases remained under consideration, and five had been released without going to appeal.[153] Besides the usual police recommendations, the files show that some of these cases had been decided on compassionate or medical grounds. The highest proportion of internees were from the southern and western parts of Northern Ireland where the IRA was most active: counties Armagh, Fermanagh, Tyrone and Derry. Belfast (in proportion to its population) was under-represented. This reflected the virtual exclusion of the IRA's Belfast Battalion from Operation Harvest. With very few exceptions (one being a man from Clones, Co. Monaghan; another coming from Co. Donegal and another from Dublin), the internees were from Northern Ireland. Certain towns and villages contributed significant numbers (Coagh, Cookstown, Coalisland and Trillick, Co. Tyrone; Swatragh, Co. Londonderry; Newry, Co. Down; Enniskillen, Co. Fermanagh), suggesting that entire IRA units and networks had been rounded up.

How to end it?

As we have seen, by the end of 1958, the Border Campaign had dwindled into sporadic acts of sabotage, although there would be periodic upsurges in the three years before it was formally called off. Yet, as long as it continued, at whatever level, internment would not be ended. This realisation inevitably had a depressing effect on the remaining internees, one of whom, Canice Kane, of Limavady, Co. Londonderry, had been the very first man interned (on 18 December 1956). He and others, described as 'dyed in the wool' types, were, according to Major Thompson, on the verge of submitting applications to the Advisory Committee. Were they to do so, other hold-outs would follow. Among the internees and convicted men generally, he observed, there was no longer any great enthusiasm for the campaign: 'funds are drying up, and relatives and people outside are fed up with the whole affair'. The internees lacked both cohesion and determination. They were very disappointed that in the recent debate on their conditions none of the Nationalist MPs had taken a general stand against internment.[154]

But just as the campaign ground pointlessly on so did internment, and, a year later, feeling had grown in the Ministry that something should be done about those who, for whatever reason, had not submitted an application to the Advisory Committee.[155] There was no benefit in detaining men who could no longer be a risk to the state, and internment had both political and financial costs. The hold-outs had in their detention ceased to be security assets and were becoming political liabilities, throwing a critical spotlight on internment. Topping and Dunbar, and other Home Affairs officials, met to consider what might be done. As Chairman of the Advisory Committee, Harrison counselled against unconditional releases, which, he insisted, would make the Committee's future work abortive. Topping gave assurances that no general release was contemplated, and unconditional releases would be confined to the few cases which the police were satisfied would pose no further public danger. To deal with men who would not initiate an appeal, it was proposed that in appropriate cases they be summoned and told that they might be released subject to their entering into a recognisance. Those who were unwilling to do so themselves might have sureties sign on their behalf. Alternatively, a man could simply give an undertaking as to his future conduct.[156] The consensus was to reduce numbers to an absolute minimum, so much so that if a man were unwilling to seek release in one of the three ways listed, Harrison suggested, and provided the police were satisfied, he might nevertheless be freed on humanitarian grounds such as adverse domestic circumstances.

Two interesting points concluded this discussion. To get around the IRA prohibition of applications to the Advisory Committee, and the implementation of that policy by the prisoners' command structure in Belfast Prison, it was proposed to summon men before the Committee in batches of ten or twelve. The men would be told that they were being considered for release, and at least some would be freed. If those to be released were judiciously chosen, Harrison thought that the exercise would undermine the IRA – the 'yard committee' – in the prison. A distinction was also proposed between members of the IRA and of Saor Uladh. The latter were 'usually of a more intelligent and better class than the average member of the Irish Republican Army'. The Advisory Committee considered Saor Uladh men to be much more dangerous and – of considerable importance when considering them for release – they were known to be willing to sign any undertaking.[157]

A tussle developed between senior members of the RUC and the Committee, which, following the lead of its chairman, remained adamantly opposed to unconditional release. At a meeting in early January 1960, the Deputy Inspector-General of the RUC and Nelson observed that from their knowledge of the remaining internees, the great majority would refuse to give any undertaking whatsoever, even a verbal one. To insist on this before release would therefore mean that 'with the exception of perhaps a few weaklings', all the internees would remain in custody, awaiting unconditional release, 'which was inevitable'. The police recommendation for release, moreover, had been made most carefully, and the men concerned were 'definitely finished in every way possible with the movement and any future activities', but would nevertheless not give any type of undertaking.[158]

The police view was that internment was drawing to a close, and its ending would make the issue of undertakings moot. The IRA was a spent force with no capacity to renew itself or to recharge its campaign. In 1959 there had been only nineteen major and six minor incidents in Northern Ireland, as compared to 126 incidents in 1958, 341 in 1957 and twenty-five in the first two weeks of the campaign in 1956. Such events had taken place ever since the establishment of Northern Ireland, but three years had passed since the introduction of internment, and there was no danger to the security of the state. It was therefore difficult – especially to those outside Northern Ireland – to justify the continued detention of a mere residue of internees. The RUC was confident that there was no risk in releasing the men they had recommended. To free them now, moreover, would discredit them with their sympathisers, withhold martyr status and pre-empt any publicity and effusive welcome home.[159]

The case was cogent, and the RUC's authority was considerable, but the Minister had political concerns.[160] Were internees released unconditionally it would be very difficult for him to answer questions in Stormont and elsewhere. He also worried about the possibility that unconditional releases might cause retaliation by the 'extreme element' (amongst loyalists), something that had hitherto been avoided. The RUC Deputy Inspector-General countered by pointing out how long internment had lasted and suggesting that it was better to get a gradual release under way rather than wait until the issue was forced and there had to be a general release. An immediate start, moreover, would strengthen the Minister's hand when pressure was brought to bear, as he felt it would soon be. Topping's response showed that he felt that the RUC was being too forceful in presenting its case. He referred to an approach he had had from the *Belfast Telegraph*, hinting that he had suspicions that the journalist in question may have had a police briefing.[161] Like many politicians he had a dislike of being 'bounced', especially by officials.

Discussion was resumed at a meeting of the Advisory Committee, the RUC and the Ministry (but with Topping absent) the following week. Arguments were simply repeated, with the Committee opposing unconditional release and the RUC and Ministry urging a programme of gradual general releases. Eventually it was agreed that the Committee would review dossiers presented by the police, thus avoiding the necessity to bring a man before them. Harrison also proposed that each man to be freed should be interviewed by the police and warned 'most firmly' as to future conduct, such warning 'of course' stopping short of a threat of re-internment. The police agreed to do this and indicated that the internee's local district inspector would be the best person to conduct the interviews. Harrison then raised the question of whether releases should take place in batches or as a trickle. He favoured the former, waiting for a month or so to see how those who had been freed behaved. Dunbar preferred the trickle approach as a means of limiting publicity; he also diplomatically evaded Harrison's suggestion that the men be released with movement, residence and other controls under Section 12 of the Emergency Powers Act.[162] His strategy was adopted. Releases proceeded as a trickle and without conditions, the last men walking on to Belfast's Crumlin Road on 25 April 1961.

Pleas and consequences

Before leaving this aspect of internment, it should be noted that there were informal approaches to the authorities and by some families. An undertaking from a senior member of the family that the man in question would break IRA contacts, that he would move away, or was to marry, may have worked in some cases; in other instances the police appear to have steered proceedings towards release.[163] These confidential approaches and undertakings had the great advantage that they did not involve a formal application to the Advisory Committee and therefore a loss of face for the person under detention or in internment.

The Minister was approached by Stormont MPs, both Nationalist and Unionist.[164] The former was to be expected while the latter may seem surprising. Although the community was divided on religious and political grounds, there existed, especially in rural areas, ties of neighbourliness and civility that transcended or eased these divisions. Thus, in late December 1957, Topping received a letter of intercession from James McSparran, MP for Mourne. Paul McCarry was in detention, and his father had asked for help. He would enter into any bond, however substantial, and, McSparran added, 'I am quite satisfied that if this young man… were released he would have no more to do with the people who gave him the posters. I am so convinced of this after seeing his father, that I would go to bail for him myself.' He also added that were Paul released it would 'do a lot of good in the district, apart from anything else, and I imagine that the Police would not be against his release'.[165]

On occasion, the approach was woman to woman. In September 1959, Dame Dehra Parker, MP, wrote to Topping. Mrs McKenna, a Swatragh woman, had come to her home (Moyola Park, Castledawson, Co. Londonderry) by taxi from 'Crumlin Gaol'. She had three small children, and her husband, a small farmer, had been interned the previous month. Parker emphasised that she had no information other than that given to her by the woman, who had been in a distressed state. She asked for the case to be reviewed and if it were true that no income support was provided in such instances.[166] The reply was unpromising: McKenna had been arrested when 'articles of an explosive nature' had been found at his house, and his case was being examined by the Attorney General. As far as the family was concerned, Topping believed that National Assistance was available.[167]

Finally, it was sometimes evident that a mistake had been made. The Nationalist MP Edward (Eddie) G. Richardson wrote to Topping about a young man from Castleblaney (just across the border in Co. Monaghan) who had been detained in mid-September 1959. He had had in his possession a military book which Richardson believed to be the property of his brother, who had been in the Irish Army: 'This man I can assure you has nothing to do what-so-ever with any organisation. I am sure by now you have found out, that he has not his full sense.' The plea in this case was direct (and somewhat abrupt): 'Will you please see that this man gets justice, and is released at once.'[168] There was no notation as to decision.

And, for some, that there was cause for bitterness against the authorities could scarcely be disputed. The consequences of detention that did not proceed to internment, even if followed by speedy release and a confirmation of innocence, were devastating and could be long-lasting. This had been shown in the case of Brendan Fee of Enniskillen, who, in January 1957, had been detained for twelve days under the Special Powers Act. Cahir Healy, the veteran Nationalist MP, and P. J. O'Hare, a Nationalist Senator, intervened. The RUC eventually concluded that Fee had no IRA connections and released him. Immediately upon release Fee was told by his employers, Taylor-Woods, a nylon hosiery manufacturer, that his job was secure but that he should delay his return to work because of feeling among fellow employees. Fee, who was a skilled worker, several times promoted within the firm, nevertheless reported for work a few days later, on Monday, 4 February. The workforce (three-quarters Protestant) stopped work in protest.[169] Subsequent appeals by the Northern Ireland Prime Minister, the local Unionist Association, the Nationalist Union of Hosiery Workers and nationalist politicians failed to secure Fee's reinstatement.[170] Taylor-Woods were faced with a total stoppage, and the Union of Hosiery Workers was unable to persuade its members to desist from a course that all agreed was unjust. Fee's mistaken detention has cost him his livelihood in an economy and area of the country where well-paid employment was desperately hard to come by.

The end of the end

As internment entered its final stages, in parallel to the dwindling disarray of the Border Campaign, the remaining internees (those considered by the police and the Ministry to be the most militant men) were caught in a tangle of frustrations. Loyally, they would have insisted otherwise, but each futile explosion at an electricity transformer or petrol-rag arson at a wooden customs hut was a deadly hammer blow: their confinement was being uselessly prolonged. Billy McKee shifted the blame to the Ministry of Home Affairs. The staggered releases, with their stops and starts, were 'psychological warfare'. Two or three were being released each week, '[t]hen, if there was an explosion at the weekend, there were no releases the next week at all, you know'. He insisted that the stops and starts were deliberate and intended to punish: 'it was not only the men inside, they were using that against the families outside… women with families and all, waiting, waiting, waiting'.[171] Whatever individual police officers and ministry officials may have thought about the phasing out of internment, there is no indication whatsoever in the files that those who directed policy – Topping and Dunbar – sought to punish by any type of cat-and-mouse exercise. The emphasis, in all the documents and case files, once the final phase of releases began, was on the individuals under consideration and whether they posed a risk. There was no mention of the IRA's evaporating campaign of explosions and arson.[172] It might be presumed, of course, that the Minister would be unlikely to commit to paper his day-to-day political calculations and estimate of the effect of the latest IRA actions. Against this, by the end, these events had become so trivial, and the public so indifferent, that the political repercussions of releasing a handful of detainees were negligible.

Even though the internees were wrong to suppose that the releases were being used in a repressive and punitive way, an elaborate exercise in breaking the internees' spirit and that of their families, it was understandable that they should harbour such suspicions. Intrinsically and unavoidably, internment was opaque. Internees were not allowed to test the evidence against them, and even the appeal process, on which their freedom turned, was only partially open. Conjecture and rumour multiplied each other and further removed many internees from any possibility of seeing Northern Ireland as a state based on the impartial rule of law. This left visible only the incapacitatory, deterrent and retributive elements in internment. These were undoubtedly of service to the state in the short term, but at the price of further reinforcing a core of republicans in their beliefs and the circle surrounding them in their sympathies. And for those who were hostile to the state, opacity in proceedings and results confirmed their belief that the exercise of power was arbitrary and unaccountable.

More than a decade after the last release from internment arising from the Border Campaign, the measure would again be employed. The Prime Minister of the day was Brian Faulkner, and it was said that he drew heavily on his experience of the Border Campaign. His advocacy of the policy was critical to his ascent to the leadership of the Ulster Unionist Party, and he staked his political future upon its success as a keystone of security and conciliation measures. But his direct experience of internment had been extremely limited. It was not until December 1959 that he was asked by Lord Brookeborough, the Prime Minister, to become Minister for Home Affairs.[173] By this point, the Border Campaign was effectively over, and all that remained of internment was a phased and acceptable release of the diehards and hold-outs. Paddy Joe McClean (a hold-out rather than a diehard) remembers Faulkner coming into Belfast Prison's A Wing. He came without the usual retinue of staff and police and spoke directly to the internees. McClean had intended to approach him about various improvements in conditions, and had a list. An exchange of words ensued: "'Put that [list] down. I'm here to get you fellows out.'" When McClean said he found that hard to believe, Faulkner responded, "'Proof. Within two weeks, there'll be people released and, from that on, there'll be people released. I'm against internment.'"[174]

Notes

1 *Irish News*, 17 December 1956, 1b–c. Detention and internment had never been off the scene for long in Northern Ireland, no more than had paramilitary organisation and incidents. On New Year's Eve 1950, a Mills grenade had been placed in the back yard of the RUC barracks on Hastings Street, Belfast, and four men had been detained for a short time (*Northern Whig*, 1 January 1951, 1d; *Irish Times*, 1 January 1951, 1c). For six days on and around a royal visit in 1 June 1951, thirteen prominent IRA men were detained in Belfast, as a precautionary measure (*Irish Times*, 1 June 1951, 7b–c; PRONI HA/32/1/991, Memorandum, 1951). Sydney Wolfe, a prison officer who joined in 1947 and served at Belfast prison after 1971 and who had subsequently served at the Maze until 1973, observed, 'Well, we were always used to political prisoners. There was always some there at some time because if there was a royal visit or anything they used to throw a lot of these republicans in and they were just treated as internees… We were used to them' (interview).

2 PRONI HA/32/1/991, Memorandum, Ministry of Home Affairs, 31 January 1957. A total of 116 men had been detained since 15 December and seventeen released. Internment orders had been made against sixty-two of the ninety-nine; thirty-seven remained under detention. Charges were pending against thirteen of the detainees.

Only one woman was interned during these years, Brigid O'Neill. She was released from Armagh Prison in February 1960.

3 See Special Powers Act 1922 and 1933, Regulations 23B, *et seq*. Breandán O Rahallaí recalled that, following his arrest, he was held for five weeks before being served with internment papers. At that point he was offered for signature a document renouncing all connections with republicanism, with the understanding that speedy release would follow: 'Here's your chance of showing us we're wrong… sign up and go home boy.' It must have been a tempting offer after five weeks in prison, 'but on principle I wouldn't sign it'. (Interview.) A young Co. Londonderry man, whose name was not given but who most probably was Canice Kane, was reported in the press to be the first to be served with an internment order, on 18 December 1956 (*Irish News*, 19 December 1956, 1b; *Northern Whig*, 19 December 1956, 1f).

4 Not all arrests progressed to detention and internment. Thus, two men arrested in Maguiresbridge, Co. Fermanagh, were arrested on the night of 17 December 1956 but were released after questioning (*Irish News*, 18 December 1956, 1a–b).

5 It is apparent from the lists of internees that the fortnight of detention status was often used to the full, before the internment order was served. Especially in the wake of the first round-up, the police struggled to complete the interrogations and case-papers. Even so, presumably on the basis of a completed intelligence dossier, some individuals were served with full internment orders shortly after their arrest. Well-known IRA men such as Joe Cahill, Jimmy Steele and Patrick Devlin fell into this category, but so also did some lesser-known figures (see PRONI HA/32/1/177, Advisory Committee Meetings, Report of Cases, 3 December 1957). As noted, detention was occasionally used to take activists out of circulation for a time. In 1961, two Fermanagh men said to be 'very much involved in IRA activities' were detained on 2 March, and it was decided to hold them until after Easter (a time of republican commemorations and other activities) (PRONI HA/32/1/1268, Home Affairs memorandum, 21 March 1961).

6 Paddy Joe McClean was arrested as he returned home for the Christmas holidays in 1956. (He worked elsewhere as a teacher.) I asked him about his arrest. There had been no ill-treatment, he responded, 'just bad language, bad songs. The Sergeant was drunk: "We'll put you where the crows'll not shite on you" – all that sort of stuff' (interview).

7 O Rahallaí interview.

8 Details of the search for accommodation are taken from a Ministry of Home Affairs minute of 24 January 1957 (PRONI HA/32/1/748).

9 PRONI HA/32/1/748, RUC memorandum, 25 January 1957.

10 During the first part of the 1950s, the daily population averaged around 340 (*NIPD*, vol. 33, col. 129, 8 March 1949; vol. 38, col. 2131, 18 May 1954). This figure included those on remand as well as Borstal trainees.

11 The paper was a rather fanciful attempt to fend off the closure proposals by arguing that, in the event of an attack on Northern Ireland with atomic weapons, only Armagh would be safe and therefore should be kept open (PRONI HA/9/2/935).

12 PRONI HA/9/940, Report of Board of Visitors, Belfast Prison to Governor General of Northern Ireland. Boards of Visitors were lay people empowered to enter the prison at any time and to report to higher authority (in England to the Home Secretary; in Northern Ireland, at this time, to the Governor General). It was rare at this time for Boards to take any view critical of authority, and their independence and impartiality were questionable. For a discussion of the origins of Boards of Visitors and Visiting Committees, see Seán McConville, *English Local Prisons, 1860–1900: Next Only to Death* (London and New York: Routledge, 1995), Chapters 10 and 11; see also Seán McConville, 'Legislators, Judges and Jurors: Bureaucratic Processes

and Law in Victorian England', *Law in Context*, 7 (1) (1989). Londonderry Prison would be closed as from 1 April 1953. Armagh Prison held not many more than twenty women (PRONI HA/9/2/935).

13 The internees did not see the Board as an independent body. Billy McKee had a vague and not overly impressed notion of its function. He thought that it was constituted of businesspeople and others (including the Labour MP Jack Beattie). Unlike the usual run of criminal prisoners, internees were willing to complain that they were not being treated humanely. McKee did concede that, partly through the Board's intervention, 'things were changing gradually, you know' (McKee, contribution to Leo Martin interview).

14 See Chapter 15, p. 864.

15 PRONI HA/9/940, Report of Board of Visitors, Belfast Prison to Governor General of Northern Ireland, 1958. Despite the difficulties caused by the internees, the Board noted that during the year there had been no offence serious enough to be brought before them for adjudication. The two who had been released were Phil Clarke and Patrick Kearney (see above, p. 864).

16 Prison administrators normally distinguish between maximum and operational capacity, when calculating available space. The former is largely notional since a margin of spare capacity is needed to allow for repairs and refurbishment. It might be possible for a short period to use all available space, but somewhere around 10 per cent vacancy is needed to allow for repairs, refurbishment and emergencies. All residential institutions need this flexibility, but places of detention are prone to outbreaks of destructive violence by inmates, as well as vandalism or hard wear and therefore cannot operate for long without some element of flexibility in space usage. Sydney Wolfe believed that the internees set out to destroy as much as possible and instanced the smashing of cell doors. On another occasion, a group came together and, by shaking the landing railings ('big, strong iron railings') destroyed them. 'They did as much damage as they could to cause expense to the Government. That was all they could do; it was part of their war' (interview).

17 Martin interview.

18 O Rahallaí interview.

19 Billy McKee, the veteran IRA activist, who had been imprisoned both as an internee and under sentence, was emphatic that the authorities recognised the internees' OC during the 1956–61 period: 'Oh, they recognised him in internment, you see, it was a different kettle of fish there' (interview). The implicit bargain had, by definition, considerable benefits for both sides. For the prison administration there was the important assurance that housekeeping duties would be carried out and that, organised protests and confrontations apart, order would prevail and discipline be enforced. In turn, the internees gained a considerable measure of control over the regime and the way in which they could associate and organise. We have seen this compact, with a number of embellishments and balances in the power ratio, in the various episodes of internment and imprisonment examined throughout this book.

20 O Rahallaí interview.

21 O Rahallaí interview. It is significant that, although the authorities insisted that they had not and would not recognise the internee structure of command representation, they agreed to accept this and similar arrangements.

22 O Rahallaí interview. Leo Martin recalled that the internees eventually took over all the cleaning on the wing (interview). It is unclear when and why this was done, but it may have been attractive to exclude the ordinary prisoners because of suspicions about their gathering information.

23 McKee intervention in Martin interview.

24 See *NIDP*, vol. 43, cols. 83 and 94, 21 October 1958.

25 Billy McKee, an experienced prisoner, recalled how the internees wore down the initial assumptions and attitudes of the staff and how the prison management came to use the internee command structure. McKee, contributing to Martin interview.

26 There is a sizeable literature on the Ulster Special Constabulary, much of it fairly partisan. See, for example, two quite different perspectives: Michael Farrell, *Arming the Protestants: The Formation of the Ulster Special Constabulary and the Royal Ulster Constabulary* (London: Pluto Press, 1983); Sir Arthur Hezlet, *The 'B' Specials: A History of the Ulster Special Constabulary* (London: Tom Stacey, 1972).

27 Referring to his imprisonment as a teenager, McKee claimed that Thompson 'could put a fear in you' and was one of the staff that supported physical attacks on the prisoners, 'a real brutish man' (McKee speaking in Martin interview).

28 McKee in Martin interview. Sydney Wolfe recalled Thompson as 'Very hard, very, very strict. You daren't put your hands in your pockets or anything' (interview).

29 Wolfe interview.

30 McKee in Martin interview. After 9 p.m. lock-up, the lights were left on for another hour. This could also cause difficulties. On one occasion, rather than go around and turn the lights off cell by cell, allowing, where necessary, a few extra minutes for a man to finish whatever he might be doing, the Principal Officer on duty ordered that the control switch be thrown, turning off all the lights simultaneously and without consultation. This caused an immediate commotion on all the landings of D Wing. 'There was banging on the doors and the bolts were rattled… The doors were liable to come in. They were old doors, old hinges.' The police were called in, but the disturbance died down and they were not deployed (Wolfe interview). The incident demonstrates how easy it was for a minor demonstration to acquire quite a different character and outcome and perhaps to spiral out of control.

31 Internees had to have permission from their OC to make an application to see the Governor. Such occasions were restricted to personal family matters (Wolfe interview).

32 Wolfe interview. But it was not always smooth going: 'They were awkward with the priest.'

33 O Rahallaí interview. 'Sign up and get out' is a reference to the procedure for signing an undertaking in order to obtain release.

34 See below, p. 904.

35 Eddie McAteer (1914–86) had a long career of involvement in nationalist politics at a local level and at Stormont. He was, in 1947, a founder member of the Anti-Partition League. McAteer's younger brother Hugh (1917–72) had been IRA Chief of Staff from 1941 to 1942 and had escaped from Belfast Prison with three other IRA men on 15 January 1943. Eddie McAteer, in the later stages of his career, lost out to the emerging SDLP.

36 PRONI HA/32/1/1339, Eddie McAteer, MP, to R. F. R. Dunbar, Secretary, Ministry of Home Affairs, 30 June 1958. McAteer also complained about several elements in the collective punishment that had been inflicted on the internees in the wake of the escape attempt. Heating had been turned off on 13 March, and education classes had been stopped and only partly restored. McAteer returned to these matters in an early day motion debate at Stormont on 21 October 1958 (*NIPD*, vol. 43, col. 59 *et seq.*)

37 PRONI HA/32/1/1339. Ministry memorandum responding to Eddie McAteer's complaints. Internees were allowed permitted items in their cells, but joiner tools had been withdrawn because of damage to prison property. With the passage of time, there were further ameliorations. Kitchen facilities were provided in D Wing to permit the men to cook their own food, the prison providing the supplies. A former mailbag workshop was converted into a dining and recreation room, and a billiard table was installed in a nearby corridor.

38 John Edmund Warnock, KC (1887–1972) had been called to the English Bar in 1911 and to the Northern Ireland Bar in 1921. Elected to Stormont in 1938, representing Belfast, St Anne's, he held his seat until his retirement thirty-one years later. Minister for Home Affairs, 1944–6, was briefly Deputy Attorney General and was again Minister for Home Affairs (September 1946–November 1949). Attorney General, 1949–56. Privy Council (Northern Ireland) 1944. Relaxed, even liberal views on ordinary (non-political) aspects of penal administration. The remarks recalled by McAteer came in a surprisingly bi-partisan debate on prison conditions on 17 December 1946: 'I fully agree… that in the life of a man who is suffering a long term of imprisonment there is no such thing as a triviality' (*NIPD*, vol. 30, col. 3667, 17 December 1946).

39 PRONI HA/32/1/1339, Eddie McAteer to R. F. R. Dunbar, Secretary, Ministry of Home Affairs, 30 June 1958. See also *NIPD*, vol. 30, cols. 3664–72, 17 December 1946, for Warnock's general penal observations.

40 Wolfe recalled that, among the internees, there was an outstanding musician, 'Sean Maguire, "Fiddler Maguire", one of the greatest fiddler musicians in Ireland… and he played the fiddle at night. And you could hear the boys singing and all.' He also remembered an evening visit by a local dignitary (who had received authorisation, necessarily) and who passed over a small bottle of whiskey for Maguire (interview).

41 O Rahallaí interview.

42 O Rahallaí interview.

43 Martin interview. The supervising prison officer was instructed to report anything of particular significance that occurred, or was said, during the interview. Wolfe supervised many visits over the years, but, when asked about his experience, responded, 'No, I never heard anything, because they were usually careful. They knew they were being listened to' (interview).

44 Nationalist MPs McAteer and Joe Connellan visited without difficulty from the outset. It is probable that they were visiting constituents and that other MPs were admitted with similar ease. The purpose of the RUC vetting was to ensure the exclusion of republican activists and to avoid the danger of transmitting IRA orders and information.

45 PRONI HA/32/1/1296, Ministry of Home Affairs to Governor, Belfast Prison, 31 January 1957; Governor, Belfast Prison to Ministry of Home Affairs, 3 April 1957.

46 PRONI HA/32/1/1296, Memorandum, 29 March 1957.

47 PRONI HA/32/1/1296, R. F. R. Dunbar, Secretary of Home Affairs, to County Inspector J. G. T. Nelson, RUC Headquarters, 18 April 1957.

48 PRONI HA/32/1/1296, J. G. T. Nelson to R. F. R. Dunbar, 24 April 1957.

49 PRONI HA/32/1/1296, E. Frazer, RUC Headquarters to J. F. McIlwrath, Ministry of Home Affairs, 17 April 1957.

50 PRONI HA/32/1/1296, RUC, Crime Special Office, to Ministry of Home Affairs, 28 November 1957.

51 PRONI HA/32/1/1329. See below, p. 904.

52 PRONI HA/32/1/1296, letters to Mrs Dorothy Maguire and Mrs Daly, 25 March 1958.

53 Billy McKee, imprisoned under sentence and as an internee at different periods, spoke of indeterminacy as a test, to be met a day at a time: 'The only way you can beat internment is, say to yourself, "Well I'm in, and I'm in until I get out"' (contributing to Martin interview).

54 O Rahallaí interview. Billy McKee (unmarried himself) remembered a man who, showing a photograph of his children, responded to McKee's compliments, asserting, 'I don't deserve any credit. It was herself. She did all the rearing of them.' Reflecting on this, McKee said that most men who had spent substantial time inside would say the same. He added that, for many of the men, 'their wives were good, stood by

them and they didn't put any pressure on them. There were other women who did, you know' (McKee interview).

55 PRONI HA/32/1/1338, Governor, Belfast Prison, to Secretary, Ministry of Home Affairs, 18 November 1957.

56 For the background to the mid-nineteenth-century penal debates and the eventual dominance of the Pentonville model in architecture, see Seán McConville, *A History of English Prison Administration, Vol. I: 1750–1877* (London: Routledge & Kegan Paul, 1981), Chapter 8.

57 This was a ubiquitous feature of Pentonville-type prisons.

58 O Rahallaí interview. The required postcards were contributed by a number of internees. Knowledge of the project seems to have been fairly widespread.

59 The extent of the tunnel was fully acknowledged in Thompson's report to the Ministry, but, either through speculation or a misleading briefing, the *Irish Independent* reported that the tunnel extended only a few feet when it was discovered 'under a rhubarb patch in the garden' (13 March 1958, 9e–f).

60 These details, and many that follow, are taken from the report by Governor Thompson to the Ministry of Home Affairs, 13 March 1958 (PRONI HA/32/1/1329) and also interviews with men who were interned in the prison at the time.

61 *Irish Independent*, 13 March 1958, 9e–f.

62 See *Belfast Newsletter*, 13 March 1958, 5b–c; *Irish Times*, 13 March 1958, 1a–c; *Irish Independent*, 13 March 1958, 9e–f. That staff had to wait until the cell was unoccupied suggests that they operated in the wing under constraint and were unwilling to take actions that could provoke the internees en masse. According to O Rahallaí, the rope (made from prison blankets), used to lower and raise the diggers in the access shaft, was found in the cell, and from that the opening was discovered.

63 Brendan Anderson, *Joe Cahill: A Life in the IRA* (Dublin: The O'Brien Press, 2002), p. 148. They would undoubtedly have faced charges of prison breaking and, following conviction (a plausible defence seems unlikely), heavy sentences.

64 O Rahallaí interview. 'So to an extent we had hostages – they weren't named that way at the time.'

65 The failure to punish Toner, the occupant of the cell, seems curious, but not to O Rahallaí: 'if they had done that, they were asking for trouble' (interview). Elsewhere, he noted, 'if they wanted physical trouble there were nearly 300 of us altogether and they didn't have that many screws' (interview). It may have been that Toner's punishment was simply deferred. He was kept in internment until the very end and was among the last fifteen to be released, on 25 April 1961. See Eamonn Boyce, *The Insider: The Belfast Prison Diaries of Eamonn Boyce, 1956–1962*, ed. Anna Bryson (Dublin: Lilliput Press, 2007), p. 344. It is possible as well (or alternatively) that Toner was considered by the authorities to be a significant IRA activist whose extended detention was necessary.

66 The Governor reported that in the preceding months of 'inclement weather' a number of the internees had refused to go to the exercise yard, insisting that the shelter provided for them there was inadequate. Too late the Governor discerned what had been happening: 'They developed the habit of congregating in groups in the area in the proximity of this particular cell some awaiting being called for visits others awaiting the arrival of mail and no ulterior motive was then ascribed to their so doing, but I am now satisfied that their purpose was to form a cover up for those engaged in the tunnelling.' This was, of course, a classic conditioning and deception technique and points to an operation of some sophistication (PRONI HA/32/1/1329, Governor's report to Ministry, 13 March 1958).

67 For a full list, see the papers in the case of *Francis Card* v. *Inspector General and Thompson* (PRONI HA/32/1/1331).

68 An account of the riot and photographs of the weapons used by internees appeared in the *Northern Whig* (15 March 1958, 1d–e, photograph 1b–d). See also *Irish Independent*, 15 March 1958, 6d–e (photograph) and 11c–d.

69 Someone at Home Affairs had underlined these last words, possibly displaying scepticism. The whole sentence, however, is heavily qualified. See also *Northern Whig*, 15 March 1951, 1d–e.

70 'A number of internees and detainees armed themselves with chair legs, table legs and other pieces of wood to which nails and pieces of iron were attached and resisted the search. Police were called in to deal with the disturbance and order was restored' (*Irish Independent*, 15 March 1958, 11c–d). Sydney Wolfe's recollection was that the internees' injuries were not too bad, that they were 'a bit bruised'. He also observed that, when the men refused to be searched, 'they knew they were going to get a hiding' (interview).

71 PRONI HA/32/1/1296, P. J. McGrory to Ministry of Justice, 10 April 1958, and annotations.

72 PRONI HA/32/1/1329, L. F. Thompson to Ministry of Home Affairs, 13 March 1958.

73 *Irish Independent*, 18 March 1958, 9e–g.

74 *Irish News*, 14 March 1958, 1g–h.

75 *Irish News*, 14 March 1958, 1g–h. The prison at first increased the atmosphere of uncertainty by refusing to confirm or deny the ban on visits, letters and parcels. This was truly inept public relations.

76 PRONI HA/32/1/1329, L. F. Thompson to Ministry of Home Affairs (wrongly dated 15 March).

77 PRONI HA/32/1/1329, Thompson to Ministry of Home Affairs.

78 Entrances to prisons are almost universally arranged as sally ports to ensure that there can be no inward or outward rush. Only one gate is opened at a time – in this instance the outer gate. The demonstrators were able to get into the area between the two gates but could go no further since the inner gate was closed. Staff closed the outer gates to prevent the entry of more demonstrators. The women and children who had been trapped in the sally-port area were then pushed out of the prison via the wicket gate (a door-sized gate set into the large outer gate). For a photograph of the incident, see the *Irish Independent*, 18 March 1958, 9g–h; *Irish News*, 18 March 1958, 1f; photograph 1d–f.

79 *Irish News*, 18 March 1958, 1f–g; *Northern Whig*, 18 March 1958, 1d; PRONI HA/32/1/1331, Governor, Belfast Prison to Ministry of Home Affairs, 17 March 1958.

80 PRONI HA/32/1/1329, Joe Connellan to Ministry, 14 March 1958 (telegram). Joe Connellan (1889–1967) was a journalist, editor and proprietor of the *Frontier Sentinel*. Represented South Armagh, 1929–33, and South Down from 1949 until his death in 1967.

81 Francis Hanna (1914–87) established the firm of Francis Hanna & Co. in Belfast and specialised in employment and personal-injury cases. Originally a nationalist, he moved, in 1942, to the Northern Ireland Labour Party and, under its colours, was first elected in 1946 (Belfast Central) but later sat as an Independent Labour member, retiring in 1969.

82 PRONI HA/32/1/1331, Francis Hanna to Lance F. Thompson, Governor, Belfast Prison, 18 March 1958.

83 PRONI HA/32/1/1331, L. F. Thompson to Ministry of Home Affairs, 16 or 17 March 1958.

84 PRONI HA/32/1/1331, William Topping to Hanna, 20 March 1958.

85 Anderson, *Joe Cahill, op. cit.*, p. 149.

86 PRONI HA/32/1/1329, L. F. Thompson to Ministry, 15 March 1958. The nature of the 'violent resistance' was not specified.

87 *Ibid*. Two brothers, John C. and Marshall Mellon (aged twenty and seventeen respectively), who shared a cell, had a particularly violent encounter with police and staff (see below, pp. 908–9). John Mellon had to be produced at Belfast petty sessions on 13 March 1958, and a press report of his appearance confirmed that he had been roughly handled. The *Irish News* (14 March 1958, 2d–e) reported that John Mellon, a man of slight build, limped into court.

88 See reports of the case of Frances Card (*Irish News*, 1 July 1958, 1a e; 1 July 1958, 7a–b; 11 July 1958, 2d–f). The authority of the police to conduct a search inside the prison was challenged.

89 A photograph purporting to show the items used as weapons was released to the press (see *Irish Independent*, 15 March 1958, 6d–e).

90 PRONI HA/32/1/1329, L. F. Thompson to Ministry, 15 March 1958.

91 A selection of the letters may be found in PRONI HA/32/1/1329. Jim McWilliams and B. McLaughlin both agree that thirty men were beaten up. J. J. McMillen claimed that the only wood involved was in the form of pieces which the men used for carving into harps. He described police and prison staff as 'crazy criminals'. These and other letters advised the recipients to ignore press reports and promised that what they were about to relate was the truth of what happened. There are a number of indications of a common hand at work, both in agenda and tone.

92 Anderson, *Joe Cahill, op. cit.*, p. 149. Cahill recalled that one man suffered a broken leg and ribs. O Rahallaí was convinced that staff had identified particular cells for tough treatment. He and a man from a neighbouring cell in D Wing had agreed just before the tunnel was discovered to swap cells with two others in C Wing and so missed a beating. He was told by the two with whom they had swapped that the beating was stopped when a sergeant said, 'it's not them, it's two older ones' (interview).

93 Anderson, *Joe Cahill, op. cit.*, p. 150.

94 O Rahallaí was injured playing football some time after the discovery and search. He had to be taken to hospital and was seen by demonstrators at the prison gate. They, not unreasonably, believed that he had been injured during a search or protest and so told the story to nationalist Belfast (interview). There is no mention of this incident in official papers, but had it come to the notice of the Ministry it would have lent weight to the arguments of those who said that the sequestration of the prison was bound to multiply rumours and accelerate their circulation. Openness was not only the right but also the best policy.

95 PRONI HA/32/1/1331, Medical Officer's Report, 18 March 1958.

96 PRONI HA/32/1/1331, L. F. Thompson to Ministry of Home Affairs, 14 March 1958.

97 See *Irish News*, 14 March 1958, 2d–e.

98 These details are taken from a report of 15 March 1958 to the Ministry of Home Affairs by District Inspector O'Brien, PRONI HA/32/1/1330. Dr W. G. Gibson, who examined John Mellon on behalf of the police, concluded that while he had been struck, 'in the circumstances' no more force had been used than was absolutely necessary. How he could make this assessment was far from clear, and his opinion on non-medical issues was irrelevant. See *Northern Whig*, 14 March 1958, 5g–h.

99 PRONI HA/32/1/1330, Reports of Principal Officer Foster and Constable Beckett, 14 and 15 March 1958, respectively.

100 PRONI HA/32/1/1331, H. O'Connor to William Topping, Minister for Home Affairs, 4 April 1958. The request to visit had been made as soon as O'Connor had heard of the men's condition.

101 PRONI HA/32/1/1331, P. J. Agnew & Sons to Secretary, Ministry of Home Affairs, 29 March 1958.

102 PRONI HA/32/1/1331, Ministry of Home Affairs to P. J. Agnew & Sons, 2 April 1958. This last point was disingenuous since the internees saw the Governor as

complicit in their ill-treatment and the Medical Officer as anything but independent. The Ministry had evidently decided that adverse comment about the stoppage of communications was preferable to the testimony of independent medical witnesses.

103 PRONI HA/32/1/1331, R. F. R. Dunbar to Crown Solicitor, 10 April 1958; annotated reply same date.

104 See ministry statement at PRONI HA/32/1/1331.

105 PRONI HA/32/1/1331, P. J. McGrory to Secretary, Ministry of Home Affairs, 15 April 1958.

106 PRONI HA/32/1/1331, McGrory to Ministry of Home Affairs, 15 April 1958, 25 April 1958, 8 May 1958 and 14 May 1958; ministry reply, 13 May 1958.

107 The other plaintiffs were James G. Devlin, aged twenty-one, a farmer's son, of Moneymore, Co. Londonderry; James P. McCorry, twenty-five, joiner, of Stewarts-town, Co. Tyrone; John McCormack, twenty-one, cobbler, of Belfast; James McReynolds, thirty-four, labourer, of Dungiven, Co. Londonderry; J. J. Martin, twenty-four, stove machinist, of Belfast; Daniel Morgan, twenty, clerk, of Belfast; and William O'Neill, thirty-two, lorry driver, of Belfast.

108 Judge Fox had declined to hear the cases in aggregate. This was not unreasonable since the procedural and evidential complexities of an eight-handed trial are con-siderable. Having decided that the legal issues could be tested by taking a specimen case first, Fox possibly hoped to avoid protracted cases and excessive costs.

109 The defendants were Lance F. Thompson, Governor of Belfast Prison, and Sir Richard Pim, the Inspector-General of the RUC. Their evidence was given by prison staff and police officers. See *Belfast Newsletter*, 1 July 1958, 6a–b; 11 July 1958, 8a–b; *Irish News*, 1 July 1958, 7a–b; 11 July 1958, 2d–f. The *Irish News* made the story its lead under the strapline '"Batons Not Necessary": Warder Agrees' and the headline '"RUC Attacked Me," Internee Claims'.

110 Myers had, however, agreed in cross-examination that Card had not assaulted the police in such a way as to justify their having drawn batons and, indeed, that it had been unnecessary to draw batons (*Irish Independent*, 1 July 1958, 8b).

111 PRONI HA/32/1/1331, Transcript of judgment in *Francis Card* v. *Inspector General and Thompson* (see also PRONI HA/32/1/1334 for further papers in the case).

112 PRONI HA/32/1/1334, Ministry of Home Affairs memorandum, 8 June 1959.

113 McKee interview.

114 O Rahallaí interview.

115 O Rahallaí interview. Although after the first two years O Rahallaí (and others) recognised that the campaign had been broken, he withheld comment on those who were continuing the action: 'You didn't criticise them. I felt I had no right to criticise them. I felt that they were doing what they believed but that it was wasted because there was no chain of command to direct things' (interview).

116 See above, p. 843.

117 O Rahallaí interview. O Rahallaí was particularly offended by Diamond's condemnation of the IRA in the Northern Ireland Parliament.

118 See above, pp. 847–8. Daniel Mageean (1882–1962) had been educated at St Malachy's College, Belfast, and St Patrick's College, Maynooth. He became Bishop of Down and Connor in 1929 and was, in the 1930s, active in promoting Roman Catholic rights in Northern Ireland. Failing to attract the interest of Westminster, he apparently took the view that engagement with the Stormont government would produce little ben-efit for his community. He was incensed by Craigavon's often (and sometimes inac-curately) quoted speech of 24 April 1934 (*NIPD*, vol. 16, col. 1095). From this came the injudicious observation, '[t]hey still boast of Southern Ireland being a Catholic State. All I boast of is that we are a Protestant Parliament and a Protestant State.' This was garbled to become the much more offensive and provocative 'A Protestant

Parliament for a Protestant People'. In this form, the remark was used by Mageean as justification for disengagement from the civil powers. Mageean, nevertheless, anathematised the IRA. This, in turn, was a factor (but certainly only one) in the emergence of a dangerous state of political sterility for Northern nationalism.

119 O Rahallaí interview.

120 Wolfe interview. McAlister brought a well-known Italian singer into the prison, as well as leading sportsmen.

121 O Rahallaí interview.

122 PRONI HA/32/1/177, Revd Patrick McAlister to Ministry of Home Affairs, 21 January 1958.

123 PRONI HA/32/1/626, L. T. Thompson to Secretary, Ministry of Home Affairs, 27 January 1958.

124 Sydney Wolfe has a slightly different recollection, according to which the men returned to chapel and told the assistant chaplain (Father Timothy) that they would not continue to participate in the mission (interview).

125 PRONI HA/32/1/626, L. T. Thompson to Secretary, Ministry of Home Affairs, 27 January 1958. The assistant chaplain had spoken to the Governor, contrasting the friendly and supportive attitude of the staff to the sneers and ingratitude of the internees.

126 O Rahallaí interview.

127 See below, p. 922.

128 McClean interview. Although at the time of his arrest Fianna Uladh had been a legal organisation, it was proscribed just weeks later, in January 1957. McClean's internment was thus retroactive, justified because he was a leading member of Fianna Uladh. This was the initial reason given in his personal file, released under the thirty-year rule. (For the background to Fianna Uladh and Saor Uladh, see above, pp. 836–9.) Another allegation was made: that he had participated in a post-office raid on 9 October 1956. This was untrue, McClean insisted, as could have been checked, had the attendance roll at his school been examined. He was teaching in a Christian Brothers' School in Enniskillen. The ninth of October 1956 was a Tuesday, certainly a school day.

129 McClean interview. Personality factors came into the calculation as well. McClean admitted that he was and remained a stubborn man.

130 McKee interview.

131 The Committee held its meetings in Belfast Prison, attended by its secretary, J. F. McIlwrath.

132 PRONI HA/32/1/177.

133 *Manchester Guardian*, 18 March 1957, 3a–b; PRONI HA/32/1/177, Advisory Committee Memo, 15 February 1957.

134 O Rahallaí, who had been a member of the IRA when arrested, recalled that some prison staff worked on the younger internees, attempting to persuade them to sign out. Knowing that a friend had signed out, they might use that as a lever to persuade the one still in internment to follow: 'Oh, I saw your mate in the town yesterday, and he had a girl with him, and he was saying to me you know, what a great change it was. Why don't you follow him out? Sure, he's working now.' Older IRA men warned the prison officers off. They did not themselves attempt to stop an application for release but tried to persuade waverers to stick it for another, then another week (interview). The advent of handicraft work filled the time and distracted internees from incessantly pondering their situation, thus heading off inclinations to seek release by signing out, O Rahallaí noted.

135 This was evident from the outset. The Committee at its initial meetings had sought the assistance of County Inspectors Kennedy and Peacock. Seven cases were reviewed on 11 and 13 February and the views of the two officers sought. One man

was then released unconditionally, three conditionally and two more were put back for consideration in three months. Only one application was rejected outright (PRONI HA/32/1/177, Memo on meetings of 11 and 13 February 1957).

136 Cahir Healy, by this time a Nationalist MP but in 1922–3 an internee on board the *Argenta*, recalled that one of his comrades at that time had been interned on the say-so of a man who was a rival in the courtship of a young woman (*Manchester Guardian*, 18 March 1957, 3a–b).

137 *Manchester Guardian*, 18 March 1957, 3a–b.

138 Thus, on 20 February 1957, Dunbar, in comments for the Minister, noted that one district inspector was 'a very sound and reliable officer who would not recommend internments unless as absolutely necessary'. The officer in question was opposed to release, and Dunbar was disposed to accept his judgement. In another case, however, the local district inspector opposed release but could offer no evidence beyond that already seen. Dunbar did not think the case against the man was very strong, and, despite police opposition, proposed the man might be released on compassionate grounds (PRONI HA/32/1/177, Memo to Minister, 20 February 1957).

139 PRONI HA/32/1/177, County Inspector A. H. Kennedy, RUC, to R. F. R. Dunbar, Secretary, Ministry of Home Affairs, 20 March 1957.

140 PRONI HA/32/1/177, R. F. R. Dunbar to Minister for Home Affairs, 4 April 1957.

141 PRONI HA/32/1/177. Patterns of prison association would have provided a strong (though not infallible) test of applicants' good faith, but although staff observed and reported on such matters no systematic routine of observation, reporting, collation, analysis and distribution was established, an indication not only of the managerial style of Major Thompson but also of the limitations of intelligence organisation in Northern Ireland.

142 PRONI HA/32/1/177, with ministerial annotation.

143 There often was no standard form, the wording being provided by the police according to their knowledge of the detainee (see PRONI HA/32/1/176, RUC to Secretary, Ministry of Home Affairs, 15 April 1957).

144 *Manchester Guardian*, 18 March 1957, 3a–b. This eventually caused some resentment among loyalists, it was reported. Press accounts had made it appear that the MPs had directly obtained the internees' releases whereas what they had done was to put the case before the Advisory Committee with favourable comment and evidence (PRONI HA/32/1/177, RUC to Ministry of Home Affairs, 10 July 1958). Representations could include the death of a close relative, as was the case on 20 August 1957, when Topping, having been told by Joseph Stewart, MP (Nationalist, East Tyrone) that a man's grandfather had died, decided on release without again referring the case to the Committee. The intervention of politicians was also, as we have seen, resented by some internees, who took it as cheap politicking.

145 PRONI HA/32/1/176, Secretary of Advisory Committee to Ministry of Home Affairs, 19 October 1960.

146 See above, p. 537.

147 PRONI HA/32/1/177, R. F. R. Dunbar to William Topping, 14 February 1957. The Universal Declaration of Human Rights had been adopted by the United Nations in 1948. Despite his tone of mock exasperation, Dunbar wisely recognised the still-unfolding implications of the Declaration and other instruments which were developing international law and formulating and reinforcing the rights of citizens.

148 PRONI HA/32/1/177.

149 Police officers were also summoned to discuss certain cases with the Committee.

150 PRONI HA/32/1/177, R. F. R. Dunbar to William Topping, 14 February 1957. In the cases that Dunbar forwarded to the Minister with the memo, there were two that demonstrated that having a verbatim account would certainly not assist in second-guessing

the Committee. In one of these cases, they recommended immediate release for a man who, on principle, refused to enter into recognisances, arguing that a totally innocent man should not need to do so. By contrast, the Committee recommended total and final rejection of an appeal by a man who categorically stated that he had never been a member of the IRA, that he never knew anything about it, did not know that it existed in his area and would enter into any recognisance the Committee might require. Notwithstanding Dunbar's general policy of accepting the Committee's decision, in some cases the Minister refused to order release.

151 PRONI HA/32/1/177, R. F. R. Dunbar to Minister, 21 February 1957. He also pointed out that the Home Office was likely to have taken a dim view of the man being forced to move to England and that a condition of expatriation could be used politically against the Ministry.

152 PRONI HA/32/1/177, Memo of 5 August 1957. One of the men whose appeal was turned down (D. P. McIlone) went on hunger strike on 3 July 1957. The files are not clear, but it appears to have been of short duration (PRONI HA/9/2/933, Governor, Belfast Prison to Ministry of Home Affairs, 5 July 1957).

153 PRONI HA/32/1/177, Summary of 23 June 1958, 10 February 1957.

154 *NIPD*, vol. 45, cols. 358–84, 27 October 1959; PRONI HA/32/1/177, Memorandum to Secretary, Ministry of Home Affairs, 3 November 1958. These men did then appeal and were considered at the Committee's December 1958 meeting.

155 Two Northern Ireland Labour Party MPs (T. W. Boyd, Belfast Pottinger) and W. R. Boyd (Belfast Woodvale) raised the matter of the undertaking, pointing out that this would be a difficult step for someone who, throughout, had insisted on his innocence. To this, Minister Topping confidently replied that 'there is no one in Crumlin Road [Belfast Prison] who is innocent' (*NIPD*, vol. 45, col. 369, 27 October 1959). At this point, 160 men and one woman remained in internment.

156 PRONI HA/32/1/177, Minutes of meeting, 26 December 1959.

157 PRONI HA/32/1/177.

158 PRONI HA/32/1/177, Minutes of meeting to consider the release of internees, 4 January 1960. The unwillingness to give an undertaking was in some cases stubbornness, but in others it was an overriding fear of the lifelong stigma of 'signing out'.

159 PRONI HA/32/1/177. Nelson instanced the case of Christopher Loy, whose sons were interned with him. When eventually released with the ending of internment, Loy would be met at Newry station with bands and treated as a martyr for Ireland. Were he 'thrown out of internment now' he would be much discredited.

160 William Topping attended this meeting. Brian Faulkner had recently been appointed Minister for Home Affairs but may not at this point have completed the handover.

161 The Committee agreed, however, that the information that a general release was imminent could not have come from the police. The *Belfast Telegraph* journalist (Tommy Roberts) had probably just exercised 'intelligent anticipation' in the matter. It is unlikely that this dispelled Topping's suspicions. (Roberts later turned gamekeeper and was appointed by Northern Ireland Prime Minister, Terence O'Neill, to be his Press Secretary.)

162 PRONI HA/32/1/176, Minutes of meeting on proposed release of internees, 8 January 1960.

163 The record of a statement by James McAllister, a Larne solicitor, is instructive. He had been detained on the basis of a range of contacts, going back to his support for the Sinn Féin candidate for North Antrim in the 1951 general election and involvement again in 1955. The police knew that he had met a number of prominent IRA figures, including Joe Cahill, but he explained this was in the context of his election activities. Joe Cahill he claimed to know because his family had holidayed locally for many years. McAllister affirmed that he had never been a member of the IRA and would

never in future be involved with prohibited organisations. The overriding impression is that this was a sympathetic interrogation, conducted by the astute and highly experienced District Inspector Fannin, who took him through all the points that would reassure the Ministry, including his education and respectable family background (PRONI HA/32/1/991, Statement of James McAllister, recorded by District Inspector Fannin). It is likely, of course, that McAllister and Fannin had a prior, and would have a continuing, professional relationship.

164 An unidentified Stormont MP submitted a long letter concerning two Omagh boys aged seventeen who had been interned as a consequence of putting up IRA posters in the town. The MP had discussed their cases with their families and was convinced that it was a matter of being easily led astray. The boys' release would be universally approved locally (PRONI HA/32/1/991, Letter to William Topping, Minister for Home Affairs, 13 February 1957).

165 PRONI HA/32/1/991, James McSparran to William Topping, 23 December 1957. McSparran, a barrister, sat for Mourne (Nationalist) from 1945 until his retirement in 1958. Chairman of the Nationalist Party (1945–58) and of the Anti-Partition League (1945–53) and thereafter President of the League until his death.

166 PRONI HA/32/1/991, Dehra Parker to Minister for Home Affairs, September 1957. Dame Dehra Parker (née Chichester) (1882–1963). MP (Unionist) for Londonderry (1921–9) and South Londonderry (1933–60). Minister for Health and Local Government (1949–57). Privy Council (NI), 1949. One of a handful of women to become members of Stormont and the only one to achieve such a senior appointment. Her Stormont seat was, in 1960, in an uncontested by-election passed to her grandson, James Chichester-Clarke, who would, in May 1969, win the Ulster Unionist Party's leadership election (beating his opponent, Brian Faulkner, by one vote). He thus became the penultimate Prime Minister of Northern Ireland. Dehra Parker was a person at the very heart of the Ulster unionist establishment.

167 PRONI HA/32/1/991, William Topping to Dame Dehra Parker, 17 September 1957.

168 PRONI HA/32/1265, Edward G. Richardson to Minister for Home Affairs, 18 September 1959. The man lived quite alone. Father and mother were dead and his brother now worked in England.

169 *Irish Times*, 5 February 1957, 1d.

170 PRONI HA/32/1/1278.

171 McKee in Martin interview. Martin agreed that the slow and interrupted releases were hard on the families. Rumours of impending releases were also constantly circulating in D Wing, inevitably a source of strain in itself.

172 Some thousands of pages of ministry files have been examined. These have been selected entirely on research criteria.

173 Brian Faulkner, *Memoirs of a Statesman*, ed. John Houston (London: Weidenfeld & Nicolson, 1978), p. 23. He took office on 15 December 1959 (*Irish Independent*, 16 December 1959, 11h).

174 McClean interview.

17

BE CAREFUL WHAT YOU WISH

The Republic of Ireland in the 1950s

As we have seen, social, economic and cultural currents in the Republic of Ireland had come together in the mid-1950s in a particularly oppressive fashion. Unemployment, underemployment and limited employment opportunities seemed designed to thwart even the most modest expectations and ambitions of youth. The education system, dominated by the Roman Catholic Church, was stunted and misshapen. A disproportionate portion of primary-school time was devoted to the learning of Irish, and to religious instruction.[1] Further and higher education were limited and largely unrelated to vocational needs and economic growth. The university with the highest status, longest history and greatest international recognition, Trinity College Dublin, had been proscribed for their flock by the Catholic hierarchy.[2] Duty was an omnipresent theme in religious, political and public discourse; challenge, discussion, innovation and social nonconformity – or even laxness – were objects of suspicion and targets of disapproval.[3]

In an economy which was stagnating when not contracting, employment was a treasured prize: security and the prospect of a pension gave immense reassurance. With central and local government so prominent in the economy, patronage – the life blood of Irish political parties since Emancipation – was inescapable.[4] By its nature, patronage is a bargain: fealty in return for grace and favour. Any quick scan of proceedings in the Dáil conveys this element in national life: questions about a sub-postmastership here or there, various minor civil-service or state-sector positions throughout the country and, of course, related pensions and allowances. In a no-growth economy, zero-sum, beggar-my-neighbour, dog-in-the-manger politics, driven by envy and fear, clientism cannot but flourish.[5] Patronage and submission were an indispensable and unavoidable portion of adult life for many citizens. For those outside the fold, these could be years of insecurity and thin living.

The Catholic Church played a full part in patronage.[6] For an unskilled or semi-skilled man, a note from a priest to a prospective employer was a testimony to character – respectability and steadiness as measured in church attendance and compliance. Even for those with more skills and qualifications, church approval could be important. A clerical query was to be feared, and a veto was insurmountable.[7] As in many countries, Catholic and Orthodox, where the population was almost entirely homogeneous in religion, the Church was a parallel system of authority and, indeed, lead partner in several key areas of public administration and provision. Nor did this authority baulk at entering the private lives of citizens: the word 'pastoral' became almost literal in meaning. In the Ireland of the mid-1950s, Philip Larkin's *Annus Mirabilis* was inconceivable, though chronologically only eight years off.[8]

Employment is perhaps the most important civic measurement. In times of plenty, when demands for labour are high, the working man or woman has a higher degree of independence, often manifested in rising wages and labour mobility. When the economy falters or contracts, the process reverses. This is not to say that the Irish worker in the 1950s was hopelessly downtrodden. It was a heavily unionised economy, and there was a pressure on those who offered employment to be decent and fair. Catholic social doctrine also called for balance in employer–employee relations, and this helped to set a context. But unemployment was high, masked by extensive underemployment and the statistical and social opacity of small-scale agriculture.[9] None of the political parties appeared to have an answer, but the centrality of the issue was not in doubt. Fianna Fáil contested the 1957 general election under the slogan, 'Wives, put your husbands to work.'

Since at least the early nineteenth century, Ireland had been a country of emigration, and conditions in the post-war period were apt for a surge. The establishment of sturdy Irish communities overseas, in the USA, in Australia and, most of all, in the ferry-hop-away neighbour, Britain, eased the path for those who found no solutions to their problems at home and who had none but faint and uncertain prospects. Migration is always a push–pull process, and this worked perfectly: the absence of employment pushed, while family and friends already settled overseas, together with near-full employment in the host countries, pulled.

Emigration was an extremely sensitive topic. Rural areas were undergoing large-scale depopulation, visible in the abandoned cottages and homestead plots, whilst in cities and towns, its effects, less visible, were still known. Quite apart from its social consequences, which included divided families and the growth of an isolated, elderly and vulnerable section of the population, there were other implications. The Catholic Church was apprehensive for the religious well-being and spiritual welfare of those who left the folding-pen in Ireland and who came under the influence of secularism, materialism, individualism, scepticism and a shedding of deference in other countries.

There was a political dimension that became increasingly heated as the outflow of the young continued.[10] As the only country in the developed world in which the population was declining, Ireland's political establishment and business leadership had a unique if unwanted distinction.[11] For many, conventional politics offered no hope, and its practitioners were seen as self-seeking, cynical and profoundly corrupt. This certainly was the long-term assertion of physical-force republicanism, and its truth seemed inescapable to young men who were drawn to the IRA in the mid-1950s.

To those gripped by love of country, emigration had a special horror. It was evident that the nation was haemorrhaging: were the flow not staunched, further enfeeblement and even extinction could be avoided only by outside assistance and oversight. Within a decade, solutions would begin to emerge, and courage and confidence would be found, but with the predominant doctrines of stasis, protectionism and corporatism facing no challenge from within the political and state establishment, it was hard, in 1957, to imagine where these benign forces would come from – and imagination was the key.

There was a spring of hope, which also happened to be accepted wisdom: the unification of Ireland would somehow (and exactly how was rarely or ever specified) transform economic prospects. Nationalism, like many other single-issue political doctrines, necessarily hangs from a spine of millenarianism. When the cause has triumphed, the believer knows, all dependent problems (and almost all problems are thus defined) will be resolved. This faith and received wisdom, spanning the range of political parties, would have been impossible to resist by those already fervent. Eamonn Boyce (who would subsequently be sentenced to twelve years' imprisonment for leading the Omagh raid) was himself in employment (and securely so) but was convinced beyond a doubt that drastic action was necessary:

> There was no work here… it was one of the motivations that would make you join the IRA – anything to stop this – the mail boat sailing every night at a quarter to nine and it practically down to the gills with people going off. They were terrible times.[12]

Globalisation has substantially altered perspectives on emigration and immigration. Despite acute problems in international trade, commerce and finance during the past several years, migration between states has acquired a more positive character: opportunity-seeking and life enhancement on the part of the emigrant and enrichment and stimulation for the receiving country. The paradigm has its flaws and certainly its critics, but it needs to be emphasised that emigration from Ireland (and indeed from other poor and peripheral countries) did not fit into the still-developing paradigm of the free movement of populations. Those who emigrated in the 1950s went, in general, to low-level and low-skill occupations, or to assist with post-war building and reconstruction, or to train and fill vacancies in such organisations as the National Health Service in Britain.[13] Many individuals flourished, but probably the majority went to (and were happy with) humdrum and sometimes quite grinding work, which they would, of course, have been even more happy to have at home.

Nationalism and republicanism and their traditions throughout the nineteenth century incorporated the plight of the emigrant into a definitive account of Ireland's suffering. That emigration could be a brutal and heart-wrenching process can scarcely be contested: separation, sometimes a lifetime of feeling torn and incomplete, loss and longing. In the 1950s the reach and thoroughness of the phenomenon at times passed from the depressing and disheartening to the frightening.

Early in 1959, for example, questions were raised about the unsupported emigration of boys and girls under the age of sixteen. No verifiable information was available on this movement of children, but it was known that, on occasion, they used the birth certificates of other family members.[14] A nation whose children leave in such circumstances is in desperate straits.

This was the dismal scene surveyed by those entering and finding themselves in early adulthood in the 1950s. As with most generations, they were, for the most part, apolitical, and interested in public affairs only to the extent that they affected their own lives, those in their circle, or kin and neighbours. But also, as in most generations, there was a minority which had an inescapable sensitivity to and affinity with the problems of the day. Some accepted what seemed to be the settled order of things: others were moved to indignation and action. Many and varied were the ways in which they sought solutions, and, within that minority, an even smaller group, recruited through all of life's chances and happenstance, embraced violence.

Youth in general favours simplicity and directness and is apt to be intolerant of ambiguity, yet ambiguity, fudge and compromise make politics possible. Revolutionary doctrine, by contrast, is meticulously uncompromising and scornful of backsliding of any kind, of those who fret and procrastinate. The message of the IRA was in this regard, as in others, appealing and immediately rewarding: revelation, justification and freshness after despair-inducing staleness. This was a state born of violence and poetic gesture; secular and sacred, the notion of sacrifice had an unassailable place in the national identity: the prevailing Whig history ennobled it as an aspiration. Recruitment, indoctrination, training, the prospect of action, action itself, danger, survival, comradeship – sheer intensity – all worked their chemistry, and, for however short or long a time, the inertia, thin hopes and mill-race politics of the everyday were pushed or swept aside. On whatever scale, war possesses a transformative quality that sweeps up the warrior spirit in many, and boldly dissolves doubt, as the voice of another generation in another place proclaimed:

> Now, God be thanked Who has matched us with His hour,
> And caught our youth, and wakened us from sleeping
> With hand made sure, clear eye, and sharpened power,
> To turn, as swimmers into cleanness leaping,
> Glad from a world grown old and cold and weary,
> Leave the sick hearts that honour could not move,
> And half-men, and their dirty songs and dreary,
> And all the little emptiness of love![15]

To all of this, had they been asked, politicians would have spoken about national dangers and the spectre of civil war (of which many had personal experience). They might, to varying degrees, have denied accusations of self-interest in their political careers, and they would certainly have deflected or rationalised the world of favour-taking and favour-giving: the closed economy of patronage, public service as the bestowal of favours on constituents. But had they been angry and honest, the rebuttal could have been blunter. Politics, they might have said, are that part of the continuum of competition and conflict of interest that stops short of war; and war, indeed, is the fearful extension of politics. Whether their experience was direct or indirect, all but a few Irish politicians would have condemned conflict as an evil: destruction of order, property, life and limb and prospects of prosperity for the country. They might, some of them, have liked to wrap themselves in the flag and to sing of past wars lost and won, but very few wanted such events to replace the ordinary, peaceful and often disappointing times of peace.

To those who accused them of hypocrisy, the politicians had an answer that yet none dared give: 'You pay us to cant and compromise, to enter into deals that are personally as well as politically questionable; we are the indispensable recipients of obloquy. You know what we do; you know it has to be done – from the extravagant promise in an election leaflet, the expediency of late-night fudge, the continual grubbing and granting of favours. Knowing this, you still direct your frustrations, your own self-absorption and sectional interest, at us as a group and as individuals; you do not hold back. Who, truly, can escape the charge of hypocrisy?' But these exchanges never took place, and young men made the swimmer's leap, trained and planned and hoped, and took themselves to the border and beyond, their battle-chariots – turf and cattle trucks – trailing broken clouds of glory.

Dithering and mithering

As the Border Campaign unfolded, there were increasingly firm representations from the British government. Dublin, however, went little beyond warnings to the IRA to desist or face certain (largely unspecified) consequences. Blatant acts within the jurisdiction were not condoned. Generally, men taken in arms or in suspicious circumstances in border areas were, as far as we know, arrested and dealt with under the OASA. Sentences of up to six months were imposed, usually for the catch-all offences of refusing to answer questions, or the possession of documents.[16] Notwithstanding an unrelenting and bitter antipathy between Dublin's Special Branch and the republican movement, a less stern line was sometimes taken by other divisions – the local gardaí. This may have amounted to little more than a considered lack of zeal or an unspoken understanding that, provided they exercised some discretion and did not embarrass locals, IRA men would be left alone.[17] The attitude of Irish army units along the border was generally less tolerant, very likely a mixture of clearer orders, military discipline, insulation from politics, impatience with irregulars who set themselves up as rivals, action as relief from ennui and an absence of some of the ambiguities of civil policing. Yet, with an apparently unchallenged consensus across the mainstream political parties on the evils of a divided Ireland, many in public service at more junior levels could hardly be expected to make fine distinctions in their day-to-day duties.

An incident following the attacks on Derrylin and Lisnaskea RUC barracks on 13 December 1956 demonstrated the degree of toleration that gardaí then extended to the IRA. A party of twelve or thirteen men, led by Charlie Murphy, was surrounded and captured on the night of 16 December 1956, at a safe house at Knockatallon on the Republic's side of the Monaghan–Fermanagh border. There were various incriminating documents at the house, together with a mine, which Murphy helpfully disabled for the arresting gardaí and soldiers. The twelve were then taken to Co. Monaghan Garda Headquarters, fully expecting it to be the first leg in a swift transition to prison. The police officer in charge telephoned his superiors (exactly who is not clear) and, having confirmed that the men had held no ammunition, was directed that they should be released.[18]

The second element in this irresolution and tergiversation was the curious structure of the Irish government, cobbled together on an 'absolutely anyone but de Valera' basis. The difficulties with this lowest-common-denominator approach were acutely felt in the management of Anglo-Irish relations and responses to IRA and other republican activities. On 2 June 1954, John Costello had taken office for the second time as head of a coalition.[19] His position was much weaker in the Dáil than it had been in the 1948–51 period. Then he had led an equally improbable government with Fine Gael as the major coalition part-ner, certainly right of centre on many issues, and Labour, hard to characterise but generally somewhat left of centre. The most controversial part of the government had been Seán MacBride's Clann na Poblachta, comprising republicans and ex-IRA members and supporters, teetering on direct action and left-leaning but accepting the 1937 Constitution. Not above shouting encouragement to would-be combatants from the sidelines, the party was willing to work within the Southern settlement. It occupied a position between Sinn Féin, which would not enter the abode of apostates it called Leinster House, and Fianna Fáil, which was seen by militant republicans to be soaked in the compromises of electoral politics and office, the corruption of patronage and the blood guilt of the wartime executions. As Labour took issue with its partner, Fine Gael, on some economic and social matters, so Clann na Poblachta challenged it on national issues. A small farmer's party, Clann na Talmhan, was given one portfolio to complete this oddly shaped and flimsily tied parcel. The arrangement had to work within a narrow Dáil majority.[20]

This preceding administration, the first coalition government in the state's his-tory, had established the terms of trade which would apply as the Border Campaign developed. With the loss of a Dáil confidence motion needing no more than a few abstentions or switched votes, there was bound to be a process of continuous bartering and of TDs trading support for various constituency and other favours and concessions. Inevitably, for the 1954 government, one of the commodities of exchange was the treatment of the IRA – episode by episode and individual by individual. This political fluidity in turn required an amount of operational caution from the Republic's security forces, since, especially during the preparatory stages of the Border Campaign, they could not be certain of ministerial and political support in the face of controversy and sniping in the Dáil. Quite apart from parliamentary wheeling and dealing, the unremitting anti-Partition campaign had established an orthodoxy from which few appeared to dissent, and Costello, whatever reason may have told him about the need for firmness, simply could not afford to be cast in the role of Dame Britannia's gendarme.

For its part, London took time to work out its approach to the Irish government. It was thought unwise to lodge an official protest: this could simply have put Dublin on the defensive. Lord Brookeborough had visited the Home Office on 15 July 1954. Besides reporting on IRA activities, he had warned that loyalist feeling was running high – this was, of course, the marching season – and that, especially were there an incident in which life was lost, there was a danger that hotheads might dictate the pace of events.[21] This was a view that Whitehall took seriously, at least in internal exchanges, throughout the autumn of 1954.[22] Both the Home and Commonwealth offices agreed that for the sake of British domestic politics a contact with Dublin, even if it did not lead to increased practical cooperation, was now imperative. The CRO judged, quite correctly, that Costello's coalition would not be as effective as de Valera in the matter. The attention of the Irish government would be drawn to IRA activities: the Ambassador would do so orally rather than in a note.[23]

The British Ambassador Walter Hankinson agreed with this approach. Indeed, a protest to Dublin at an earlier point might not have been disadvantageous. The IRA was a thorn in the flesh there also. More than that, 'We have the most direct evidence possible that they are detested by the Army of the Republic, and I am pretty confident that the Garda Siochana do keep their activities constantly under close observation, even if they do not or cannot often do much about them.' It was also important to avoid giving the impression that London was weak and politicians uncertain of themselves. The Fine Gael-led government was less well placed to deal with the IRA, but, against that, Fine Gael had the sympathies of the great bulk of the regular armed forces and of the Gardaí. Hankinson proposed one change in the proposed course of action: rather than have the British Embassy make the contact, the Irish Ambassador Frederick Boland should be asked to call on the Commonwealth Office to receive the communication.[24]

This was fairly promptly done, and, on 31 August 1954, Boland heard what Sir Percivale Liesching, Permanent Under-Secretary at the CRO had to say: the matter was still being kept at official rather than political level, with its attendant publicity. Boland responded that he was glad that Liesching had raised the issue, which, he agreed, held dangers. The IRA had been an embarrassment to all Dublin governments. There were, nevertheless, difficulties in attempting its suppression because this would evoke both material and oral support from sections of the community, who, 'while they disliked the IRA, would dislike government efforts at its complete suppression even more'. The movement would be driven underground and would attract support.[25] No less than de Valera, the coalition government was keeping it under constant surveillance and control within those political limits. London was looking for rather more than a watching brief, Liesching observed, and wanted Dublin to take positive control of the situation.

The conversation took a turn that showed the contradictions in Dublin's position. Until the autumn of 1953, Boland suggested, de Valera's policy in pursuing the abolition of Partition by peaceful means had been bearing fruit. 'The aim had been gradually to re-establish more normal relations between the two parts of the country and this policy had been, on the whole, successful and encouraging.' There had been an exchange of visits between the lord mayors of Dublin and Belfast. The policy of conciliation had, however, received a sad setback when 'the more extreme section' in the North had opposed it and had brought pressure to bear on Brookeborough and Brian Maginess, his Minister for Home Affairs. Since then, Boland had noticed a deterioration in relations which he hoped might be reversed. Pressed, however, as to whether the desire for good neighbourly relations did not require contacts between the security forces, north and south of the border, Boland parried. When he had been Secretary of the Department of External Affairs, such contacts had been made secretly 'though he took no official cognisance of them'. Liesching wanted to pursue this point but, as he had not been briefed, felt unable to do so.[26] The exchange, however, demonstrated the coalition government's reluctance to act against the IRA, even when faced with dangerous, armed and potentially incendiary raids from the territory of the Republic on another jurisdiction. This despite the fact that Boland had confirmed that the IRA remained an unlawful organisation in the South.[27] On 28 October 1954, the Dáil gave a much stronger signal to the IRA and also, of course, to London and Belfast. This took the form of strong speeches from John Costello and Éamon de Valera – a united front – and was followed up by Frederick Boland in a confidential briefing to Liesching.[28] This was the first of several detailed discussions on developments that continued throughout the autumn.

The Roman Catholic hierarchy, better informed about Northern Ireland's divisions and potentials, was also deeply concerned and acted more decisively than the Dublin government. In his Christmas Day address, 1954, Cardinal John D'Alton, Archbishop of Armagh and Primate of the Roman Catholic Church in Ireland, strongly appealed to young Irishmen not to join any 'unauthorised' forces.[29] This was followed up in the Lenten pastorals of several of the bishops.[30] The IRA issued a counter-statement: it was a voluntary body, not a secret organisation, and a strict watch was kept to identify 'subversive' (that is, Communist) individuals.[31] In reality, most young men drawn to the IRA were unlikely to be deterred by episcopal proscription. As on past occasions, sympathetic clergy could always be found to confer the sacramental comforts of the Roman Catholic Church when required.[32]

The Irish government embodied, in its make-up and membership, the various ambivalences and fault lines that existed across the Irish electorate. There was condemnation of violence but, at the same time, a degree of unspoken toleration of the IRA. Costello's notion of conciliating or even incorporating physical-force republicanism, which had been one of the motives (or rationalisations) behind the 1948 coalition with Clann na Poblachta, had not worked, but neither had the hope quite been extinguished. De Valera and Gerald Boland, his former Minister for Justice, stood ready on any and all occasions to recite their barren experience of trying to draw the IRA away from its military traditions. Costello and Norton (Fine Gael and Labour, respectively) perhaps thought that de Valera's dominant personality and domineering style had been the impediments to a reconciliation between the strands of republicanism. Fearful for their own fragile unity and inhibited by what they saw as public opinion, policy-makers in Dublin seemed paralysed as the autumn of 1954 passed into the spring of 1955.

Besides the conversations between Frederick Boland and Liesching (and then with Sir Gilbert Laithwaite, the latter's successor) there was a curious and worrying exchange at Strasbourg on 10 December 1954, which might have been interpreted as an opportunistic attempt by Dublin to derive advantage from IRA activities. Two of the Irish delegates to the Council of Europe, acting on Costello's express instructions, sought out the leaders of the British delegation. The only thing that would stop the militant republicans, they contended, was 'some indication that partition would not go on forever'. They wished to initiate tripartite talks between Northern Ireland, the Republic of Ireland and Great Britain to seek an agreement, perhaps in the first instance, on defence, and then, it was vaguely expressed, a united Ireland 'within the Commonwealth principle'.[33]

This was another example of the bellows-and-flute approaches that had been made by de Valera to the British Representative to Dublin throughout the 1940s, with, on this occasion, the addition of an extremely vague reference to the Commonwealth. It showed no appreciation whatever of the political and social realities within Northern Ireland and, essentially, assumed that London could (and would wish to) force a deal on Belfast. It also showed a worrying willingness to ride on the coat-tails of violent republicanism and therefore diminished the Dublin government's credibility and assumed good faith. Seeking to deflect what it correctly anticipated would be the British government's repetition of its earlier requests for action against the IRA in the South, the Strasbourg delegates solemnly informed their British counterparts that the incidents in Northern Ireland were not the work of the IRA but of 'a new organisation known as the Physical Force Movement'.[34]

The Commonwealth Office was bemused by the contact but, rather than give it a sinister import, was disposed to take it as some kind of smokescreen to cover what was becoming evident beyond concealment: Dublin's earlier promise of concerted action against the IRA had not been honoured, for whatever reason. Frederick Boland was left to peddle improbabilities in meetings with his British counterparts – possibly to his own embarrassment. By the end of January, no one on the British side took his valiant efforts at all seriously. Following his meeting with Boland in January 1955, the Secretary of State for Commonwealth Relations, Viscount Swinton, was blunt in his assessment: 'I have little doubt myself that the [Irish] Government did get cold feet, that they had trouble inside their Cabinet, and that they felt they were not strong enough to carry out their original intention.'[35]

The consequent difficult but necessary balancing act ran the risk, scarcely unusual in politics, of masking an inability to do much with an array of declarations of suitably urgent, definitively definite and militant intentions. The first occasion when this was deemed necessary by the Costello-led government was in response to the Saor Uladh attack on Rosslea RUC barracks on Saturday, 26 November 1955.[36] Further scandal was created when, with what appears to have been political interference and garda acquiescence (if not complicity), a secret inquest was conducted on Connie Green, one of the raiders.[37]

Up to this point, incidents on the border – slogan-painting, destruction of signs and even the burning of unoccupied customs posts – seem to have been accepted by the Costello government as a kind of background noise. A determined raid on a police barracks, with what can only have been murderous intent, using both firearms and explosives, took these events beyond political vandalism. The death of a young man served to underline what might have been a far greater and more inflammatory tragedy, and warned of what might lie ahead. The raiders had shown nerve and audacity; an attack such as Rosslea was leagues away from creeping about the deserted countryside with oily rags and cans of paraffin or petrol, setting unmanned customs posts alight.

In a speech a few days after the Rosslea raid that, quite unintentionally, lit up the Republic's contradictory doctrines of state, Costello condemned what he described as 'an unlawful use of force' – a circumlocution that would have been noted in Belfast, if not London. The lengthy preamble to this condemnation indicated why he had chosen to characterise an armed attack on a police station in the adjacent jurisdiction in a manner that was oddly detached. Partition was also condemned, as was Britain, '[a] country that held itself out as the champion of freedom'. The Partition of Ireland had been maintained by Britain's military and financial power, even while British leaders 'find it possible to condemn the evils of territorial partition in other lands'. This was a cynical stance, a 'disregard for principle and consistency'.[38] Costello condemned discrimination against Northern Ireland's nationalists (using the term 'six counties'), including acts of 'petty intolerance that outrage every principle of justice and good government'.[39] The division of the country was a 'grievous wrong', and that it was an injustice was recognised by fair-minded people in many countries, including Britain itself. There was no true peace in 'the separated part' of Ireland, and there could be no true remedy 'except the removal of the parent cause'.

It was not surprising, Costello ventured, that 'some of our people' should despair of non-violent tactics and turn to force. The responsibility for this 'particular evil' rested with government and Parliament in Britain and with 'the subordinate rulers of the Six Counties'. Were these last to join with the Irish government in working out 'a constitutional solution of Partition' that would be acceptable to the majority (that is, the majority of nationalists on the island of Ireland) and with safeguards for those 'at present opposing reunion', then political offenders who infringed those rights would, with 'universal assent', be subject to the treatment 'deserved by people who had manifestly dishonoured the nation and its Constitution'.

So far, this was a predictable statement, expected and doubtless deemed unremarkable by those listening: a word-perfect recitation of the catechism of anti-Partitionism. Costello, however, and those around him, were edging closer to a version of the necessity defence. Those who engaged in violent actions had been driven to it by the unrelenting suppression of nationalists in the North. Britain and the Belfast government were, therefore, the cause of the violence, with those who had taken to bomb and gun-bearing only a consequent and contingent part of the blame. Realising perhaps how such an approach could drift and be deemed inflammatory, the drafters of the speech sought to have it both ways and had Costello declare that '[i]n stating where the responsibility for the evil lies, I do not condone the evil itself.' Here listeners were invited to move from the evils of Partition to the evils of armed raids: it was an unconvincing sleight of hand. But the inconsistency of blaming Britain and the unionists rather than those who had taken to the gun had somehow to be squared with what Costello had further to say: that such actions were intolerable and a possible threat to the Southern state.

Referring to a statement that he had made the previous year, shortly after his coalition had taken office, Costello reminded his colleagues that physical force could not be employed, except by the government, acting with the assent of the Dáil, and that only the forces of the state could act in this way.[40] When leading the 1948 government, Costello pointed out, he had declared more than once that he wished to take the gun out of Irish politics: 'No object has been more earnestly desired and sought after by me in the course of my political life.' He believed, and would not otherwise have accepted the office of Taoiseach, that with the cooperation of his colleagues in government (here he was referring to MacBride's reluctantly constitutional Clann na Poblachta) that this object could be achieved. Before leaving office at the head of that earlier administration, it seemed to him that his goal had been achieved.[41]

When the current series of incidents began to occur, Costello noted, the reaction of his government had been 'patience and forbearance'. It had hoped that within a short time the men responsible for the actions would realise, by reflection and conscience and by sensing public opinion, that their challenge to democratic institutions 'could not indefinitely be tolerated'. Notwithstanding the government's 'detestation of repressive measures', there would be consequences should his appeal to desist from violence not be heeded. In that event, the government had a clear duty: 'We are bound to ensure that unlawful activities of a military character shall cease, and we are resolved to use, if necessary, all the powers and forces at our disposal to bring such activities effectively to an end.'[42]

On behalf of Fianna Fáil, the largest party in the Dáil and the principal opposition party, de Valera was brief. His views and those of his party were well known and unambiguous. It was necessary only to endorse the Taoiseach's appeal and warning and to hope that those to whom it was addressed would heed it and that those who could influence public opinion 'will realise fully the direction in which we have been drifting'.[43]

In a somewhat rickety fashion, Seán MacBride bridged the gap between a type of constitutional politics and direct-force republicanism, and he had a more complicated minuet to perform. Although not a member of the government, he had agreed to support it in the Dáil (and, indeed, a good portion of Costello's speech had been directed at MacBride and his two Dáil colleagues). His own political position was uncomfortable and, inevitably, a good deal of what he had to say also concerned the iniquity of Partition. He traced the same causal chain from that prime iniquity to the actions of young men prepared to use any means at their disposal to rectify it. He could understand 'and sympathise even' with this attitude but had no such feelings with those who, at a distance, encouraged them 'to endanger their lives and their liberty'. At the same time, he insisted that the government should not act 'as the instruments of British policy in Ireland'. For more than twenty years, successive governments had been placed in the position 'of virtually fighting a civil war against a section of its own people in an effort to maintain a limitation of the sovereignty of the Irish people in Ireland'.

So where did those observations take MacBride? He slid past Costello's stipulations while claiming to support the appeal that Costello had made. His own message to republican militants was a good deal more conditional. Those who were 'in an attitude of open revolt' should 'refrain from creating a situation in which they will come into conflict with our own people here'.[44] These were carefully chosen lawyer's words, vague and intentionally ambiguous, allowing those who wished to read them an unavoidable flimflam to continue what they were doing but to keep violence north of the border. There was a further implicit appeal to both the government and Fianna Fáil (always the government in waiting) to enter into some kind of compact with physical-force republicanism on that basis. MacBride was careful not to dwell on detail, but he had been explicit in stating that the Irish government was entitled to use every means at its disposal 'including, if needs be, and in certain circumstances, the use of the armed forces of the state'.[45]

MacBride was in some ways more consistent than either Costello or de Valera. Both had referred to the state's monopoly of force as an expression and condition of democracy. But, in their delineation of causes of the unlawful use of force, neither had looked to their own doctrines, political careers and moral responsibilities. Were they and their parties blameless, when, for a generation, they had made Partition a defining issue in Irish politics, almost a test of citizenship, and certainly of public office, accompanying this by denunciations of the state of Northern Ireland (a geopolitical and legal term so completely repugnant to them that they effectively forbade it in political discourse and official use)? Unionists were variously represented as dupes or oppressors, and the Old Adversary, in robes of guile and gule, was regularly and ritually trotted across the stage. To a large extent, this political view was reflected in the school curriculum, and certainly a critical approach to national issues was not remotely encouraged.[46] How then could Costello and de Valera, and all of their senior colleagues, overlook themselves when looking for the causes of young men losing patience and their middle-aged commanders seizing chances to complete their life's work? If the discrimination and injustices perpetrated against the Roman Catholic minority in Northern Ireland were ingredients in the broth that nourished the IRA and Saor Uladh, what of those who had elevated anti-Partitionism to totemic status in Irish politics – in Irishness itself – and who periodically loosed salvos of patriotic rhetoric, never wondering about impact and damage? Their own political histories – biographies indeed – showed the killing power of words.

This Dáil debate, in the statements of the major figures, held a significance that went far beyond the issues at hand. It backlit a political landscape, bleak and unpromising, and devoid of sources of nourishment, in which both main parties stood in the ruins of their anti-Partitionist rhetoric and policies. There was the barrenness of de Valera's wartime policies and the isolation of the post-war years. An arrogant disregard for the new forces in Europe and beyond, and, indeed, a volume and quality of evil unparalleled in any age, had led him to find acceptable and urgent the signing of a book of condolence for the universally loathed Hitler.[47] The internal politics of the first coalition government had led to the declaration of a republic in 1948.[48] Beyond that, social, political and constitutional steps undertaken by both Cosgrave and de Valera had emphasised the Catholic nature of the Irish state and had pushed the island's two communities further apart.

These political decisions and policies – some little more than sleepwalking – were followed through with a compulsiveness that had created a culture. The civil service and other public agencies, thoroughly permeated with anti-Partitionist orthodoxy, were held to a lexicon of acceptable terms with a strictness that would become familiar as West and East confronted each other in the bitter Cold War years. Compare the alternative terms for Northern Ireland – 'the Six Counties' or 'the North' – with 'Soviet Zone', 'East Germany' and 'German Democratic Republic' and all the other sternly enforced but intrinsically absurd variations in nomenclature (lower and higher case included) for the opposing parts of Korea, Vietnam and China. The Irish political establishment had, for some decades, embraced a type of cold war with Northern Ireland. So little did de Valera think of the unionist and Protestant population of 'the Six Counties' that in a Europe teeming with displaced persons he was minded to urge a forced movement of population on the British government as a solution to the problem of Partition.[49]

This lack of respect was shown in the unvarying terminology of Dáil debates. The governments of Northern Ireland were referred to as 'the subordinate rulers of the Six Counties', 'the Six County rulers' and 'the Six County authorities'. It is true that the term 'Twenty-Six Counties' was used, but this was not intended to display any degree of equality between the two entities but rather the opposite: that the Irish State was incomplete and comprised thirty-two counties. Thirteen months before the debate prompted by the Rosslea attack, a motion had been considered by the Dáil that proposed a right of audience in the Dáil or Seanad for representatives from Northern Ireland ('the six north-eastern counties'). Costello had initially thought that the measure 'might give comfort to our own people in the North'.[50] He had rejected force to unite Ireland, whether it be state or irregular, because even if the nationalist cause prevailed it would be at the price of civil war and of bringing into the unified state '800,000 people sullen and recalcitrant and feeling that they are suffering injustice'.[51] This was a sober and undoubtedly correct estimation of the consequences of unification by force, but Costello could not bring himself to speak of unionism, much less of Ulster unionists, referring instead to 'the 800,000 Partitionists or whatever you may like to call them'.[52] That this group had an historical and cultural identity and a coherent political doctrine apparently could not be acknowledged, much less addressed as a substantive issue. Yet it was that fiercely held identity and its resolute defence rather than the deeds of the British, or the likely tally of a vote taken throughout the island, that was the basis of Partition.

Three years later, there was a revealing allusion to this doctrine and an intimation that it was the transcending orthodoxy of party politics in the Republic, as the Border Campaign began to provoke reactions and rancour. The comment came from the strongly republican Jack McQuillan, but, taken in its context, one can see that he was pointing to what he considered to be a surprising and even shocking stance of a minority within the Dáil: 'It would appear from some of the speeches made by some of the Deputies that they have the idea in their minds that until the majority in the Six Counties decide they want to come in here, they have an absolute right to say they will stay out.'[53]

Challenge is youth's gift to age and authority. That it often has a wrapping fully intended to provoke, irritate and dethrone should not obscure the fact that a society that smothers youth smothers the future. It is, of course, a broad generalisation, but that was the Ireland of the 1950s: shedding energy, ambition and talent through extraordinary levels of emigration and wrapping in toils of conformity those who stayed. There existed no doubt, in pockets of subculture, counterculture and approved and harmless recreation, a range of alternatives for some of the frustrated and baulked. The high walls of convention, restraint and social control had one important gateway and that, paradoxically and ironically, held open by the orthodoxy of State: the removal of British rule in Ireland and the absorption into the Republic of the Northern Ireland state.

One may disagree with the substance of Jack McQuillan's arguments in his 135-minute attack on the government for its introduction and use of emergency measures, but his charge of historical inconsistency had more persuasiveness than he knew or could ever acknowledge. It was, he proclaimed,

> [a] terrible tragedy that men in this House, who themselves were interned and under sentence of death by the British Government for trying to secure the freedom of the 32 Counties, should reach the state of interning young Irishmen for trying to secure the very same thing. It is bad enough that it should have been done to them without their doing it to young men who have read the history of this country through Fianna Fáil glasses.[54]

Dublin Acts

The weeks passed, and, as the extent and intensity of the attacks across the border fully registered and the IRA's ambition became clearer, Costello had to harden his stance. The Northern Ireland government was understandably angry and apprehensive and made urgent representations in London, to which matters of external defence were reserved. The British Ambassador in Dublin, Sir Richard Clutterbuck, called on Liam Cosgrave, Minister for External Affairs, and delivered a formal note.[55] The following day, 19 December 1956, the British Prime Minister, Sir Anthony Eden, assured the Commons that the British government accepted all its responsibilities and would safeguard Northern Ireland's position within the UK.[56] Eden's statement was measured and, though far from bellicose, was not without an element of threat. No sane government could allow an illegal organisation to push it into conflict with a neighbour, especially one with such an incontestable military capability: Costello had to act or stand down. Irish troops had been deployed along the border, together with extra garda and Special Branch patrols. By 5 January 1957, there had nevertheless been three additional fatalities. Twenty-three-year-old Constable John Scully (a Catholic) had been shot dead at Derrylin barracks on the night of 30 December and Seán South and Feargal O'Hanlon (aged twenty-seven and nineteen respectively) were mortally wounded in the disastrous raid on Brookeborough barracks on 1 January 1957.[57] Despite (or because of) an enormous turnout for the cortège of Seán South, in a radio address to the nation on 6 January 1957, Costello declared that the authority of his government had been challenged and that it would respond.[58] Political ambivalence resolved, at least for the time being, and, to an extent, arrests followed swiftly.

It may not have been comprehensive, and it was sometimes behindhand, but Special Branch intelligence more than outmatched IRA security measures. The number and quality of arrests following Costello's statement suggested that detectives had previously been hampered by some form of political control – direct, implicit or presumptive. The IRA obviously still hoped for some kind of understanding, deal or stand-off, and, at a large republican rally in central Dublin, Tomás MacCurtáin, IRA Adjutant General and a nationally known republican, insisted that the IRA was not challenging the Dublin government and that, even if they came under fire, IRA men would not shoot at Irish soldiers.[59] Were this intended as a prophylactic, it showed extraordinary political naivety: the rally itself was effrontery that was bound to trigger a reaction. By mid-January, almost the entire Army Council and GHQ staff had been netted. Processed under the OASA, sentences were limited, ranging between two weeks and six months.[60] This was somewhat beyond an inconvenience but was far short of a fatal blow. For some time, Dublin's dilatoriness, and what were seen as derisory sentences for leading figures in a destructive and murderous campaign, had further inflamed opinion in Northern Ireland.[61] Belfast wanted drastic as well as decisive measures from its neighbour, and light sentences – not much more than one could expect for a drunken brawl – simply underlined the Southern government's weakness, pusillanimity and unwillingness to match words with actions. Despite its institutional ignorance of Northern Ireland, Dublin could not disregard the possibility of sectarian retaliation, no more than a British reaction.

The Southern state had faced such challenges from the moment of its foundation and had in its locker a number of legal and preventive security measures of proven effectiveness. Were the Special Criminal Court reactivated, for example, its impact – deterrent and preventive – would have been immediate. But the fragility of the coalition impeded such a step. The strains and urgent pressures of national security could not be addressed by this weak government. On 28 January 1957, six weeks into the IRA's campaign, Seán MacBride indicated that he would move a Dáil vote of no confidence. This referred to two conspicuous failures of the Costello government (and indeed of all post-war Irish governments): progress in the economy and on national reunification.[62] The Dáil was accordingly dissolved on 12 February and a general election on 5 March 1957 restored Fianna Fáil to power two weeks later, with an additional fifteen seats, allowing it to form an administration without the assistance of any other party.[63]

By far the dominant political and public figure of his times, and now in his seventy-sixth year, and almost blind, de Valera headed a government for the eighth time. He assembled around himself a familiar Fianna Fáil family of ministers, once more in confident command of all the instruments of state. The IRA had fashioned its own scourge, and MacBride had handed it to someone who would use it.

There was anger enough in store as the Republic's authorities reacted to the Joe Christle–Saor Uladh raid on an explosives store in Moorestown, Co. Dublin, on 13 January 1957.[64] This action, south of the border, was a significant departure, which the IRA had been scrupulously careful to avoid. Worse was to follow. When the suspects were brought to trial, it became evident that witnesses, who at earlier proceedings had given identification evidence to the police, had been intimidated. The men were consequently acquitted. Three days before the general election, two IRA men had carried off an audacious and novel attack by crashing a train into buffers at Londonderry Great Northern Railway Station.[65] Thereafter, there was a decline in activity, to the point that Dublin's new government felt able to begin releases of the political prisoners.[66] The coming of longer days and the very thorough and effective round-up of republicans in the North persuaded de Valera and his colleagues to wait and see if the campaign would simply dwindle away. Sensitive to the ambivalences of some of their constituents, they knew well that in past episodes a political price had been paid for locking up IRA men. That the campaign still had deadly force and intent was demonstrated in the early hours of 4 July 1957. An RUC mobile patrol was ambushed at Carrive Grove, near Forkhill, Co. Armagh. Constable Cecil Gregg was killed and Constable Robert J. Halligan wounded.[67] The IRA's commitment and ruthlessness could not have been clearer. The consequence was inevitable and swift. The following day, the government took internment powers under Part II of the OAS(A)A. Throughout the weekend of 6 and 7 July 1957, a general round-up got under way in Dublin, Cork, Dundalk and elsewhere.[68] Incredibly (and not for the first time in such circumstances, the last being only six months previously), the IRA leadership continued to misread or disregard the government's intentions and took no precautionary steps. Seven members of the Army Council conveniently assembled themselves at the Sinn Féin national headquarters, ostensibly conducting the business of the Sinn Féin Ard Coimhairle (central committee). All, together with five colleagues, were arrested.[69] Those present at a raid of the *United Irishman* offices were also put in the bag.[70] Within a week, most of the remaining GHQ staff had joined them. Altogether, sixty-three were arrested in that first wave, and as many again by early November 1957.[71]

Between November 1956 and July 1957 there were some 300 incidents in which arms or explosives were used.[72] On 25 July 1957, de Valera issued a press statement, emphasising that there was no question of his reining back. Echoing the bishops' pastoral letter of 19 January, he stressed that action had been taken only after other means had failed and in the face of a possible war with another state and 'a hateful civil war as well'. Over the previous two or three years, the coalition government had issued warnings, which he, as leader of the opposition, had supported. Internment was necessary to foil those who, by intimidation and secret conspiracy, defeated the normal legal processes which were 'not designed to deal with private armies'. Partition was an evil, but to permit private armies to act against it could lead only to anarchy and chaos. He implicitly – and possibly for the first time in a public statement – accepted the need for the consent of the people of Northern Ireland to end Partition. Even were military action successful, 'the use of force would leave behind a nation more deeply divided than it is now'.[73] The IRA's action, in other words, was wrong morally, legally, politically and in terms of likely outcome. This statement left the IRA no ground whatsoever to imagine that an accommodation could be reached south of the border, even at the level of nods, winks and Nelsonian eyes.

Rather than reduce its profile and challenge to Dublin, the IRA leadership (now nearly all new men, second or, indeed, third echelon), like a mastodon on its ancestral trail, pressed on. Signed by the IRA Army Council, a manifesto was issued in August that condemned 'the 26-County authorities [for] embarking on a policy of coercion and expression'. More ominously, it threatened the RUC and the Special Constabulary, despite earlier IRA assurances that they would not be attacked, provided they did not allow themselves to be used to support British forces: 'The Resistance can hardly be expected to differentiate between men, trained, organised and equipped along military lines (although clad in police uniforms) and British troops.'[74] Further killings were thus promised, and fellow Irishmen would be among the targets.[75] All Dublin governments claimed *de jure* responsibility for the whole of the island of Ireland, and the loss of life in Northern Ireland could only reinforce Dublin's determination to suppress the IRA.

There was a further telling incident on 21 January 1957, in connection with arrests on the border, which would underline the difference between the approach of Fianna Fáil and that of the coalition government. A group of men were brought before District Judge Michael Lennon. He made some disparaging remarks about the activation of the OASA as well as the Explosive Substances Act, 1883.[76] Having dealt with the case, Lennon directed that property belonging to two of the men, Tomás MacCurtáin and Tony Magan (leading and well-known IRA figures) be returned to them. Detective Inspector Philip MacMahon, who had appeared in court to give evidence of the arrests, pointed out that the property was ammunition and refused to obey the judge's order.[77] Judge Lennon had form, to which this behaviour added. Many in Costello's government were annoyed, and Chief Justice Conor Maguire was requested to reprimand Lennon informally. When Fianna Fáil came into office on 20 March 1957, the issue of Lennon's remarks was reopened; reprimand was deemed to be too lenient a sanction. Lennon was told that were he not to resign, the government would initiate the necessary process in the Dáil and Senate to effect his removal.[78] De Valera and his colleagues, having taken a stand and incurred the opprobrium of executions in the 1940s, were not prepared to allow any ambiguity as to the criminality of IRA activities, least of all in judicial ranks.

The new government's attitude towards the IRA had been tested by means of a Dáil question put down by deputies Jack McQuillan and Patrick Finucane (intermittent Independents, with periods respectively in Clann na Poblachta and Clann na Talmhan – in many ways the voices of the abstaining and absent Sinn Féin).[79] This referred to political prisoners at first, but when the government objected to the term it was omitted. The final version referred to 'members of Dáil Éireann who are imprisoned and of other persons imprisoned under the Offences Against the State Acts'.[80] The new Minister for Justice, Oscar Traynor, speaking in the Dáil, repeated de Valera's basic line: 'There can be only one Army in the State and that shall be the Army established by this Parliament.'[81]

In October, when the Dáil resumed after summer recess, Finucane and McQuillan returned to the issue of prisoners, dealing with the OASA, but also internees. This time they chose to put down a motion rather than to ask a question. McQuillan spoke for two and a quarter hours. He was organised, penetrating and struck home on several issues, raising a number of specific points and cases, addressing conditions of confinement and the traditions of republicanism and emphasising the political character of the IRA prisoners and internees. He used the violent origins of the state and the state ideology of anti-Partitionism to indict the government. The authorities in 'the occupied part of Ireland' described the raiders 'as thugs, murderers, criminals and all the rest', and the weight of the British Empire was being used to crush them. In the Republic, the IRA activists were being described as misguided young men, 'but we are taking the same action as the British Government are taking through their puppet in Stormont'. He also drew upon the European Convention on Human Rights to make a number of telling points, some of which, as we shall see, anticipated important issues in human rights and the procedures of the European Commission and Court.[82]

Traynor used his right of reply to review the continuing campaign of violence being waged across the border, the death, wounding and destruction that had resulted as well as the intimidation in legal proceedings. Documents produced to the courts in evidence showed 'the very widespread nature of the conspiracy'. Short sentences of imprisonment had not deterred, and most of those released resumed plotting and training with a view to renewing their offensive in the autumn. Internment had been introduced since the normal processes of the law had proved insufficient. Did Deputy McQuillan, or any other member of the Dáil think that these men should be released 'to carry on a so-called war which might well end in the loss of the liberty that exists in this part of the country today?' Was the government to release these men 'and stand idly by while they plan and carry out armed raids resulting in loss of life and destruction of property and in activities likely to embroil our people not only in war with another country but in a possible civil war as well?' The electorate had voted, and the government had its mandate and its duty: 'I wish to assure the House that the policy which operates at the moment will continue until these people allow reason and understanding to replace hatred and violence.'[83]

Jack McQuillan had introduced a consideration relatively new to such debates. He did not attempt to challenge the Minister's description of IRA activities or his chronology of shootings, bombing and witness intimidation. His line of attack was directed at internment rather than at imprisonment under the OASA. It was to the credit of the previous (coalition) government that when they had decided to act, they had done so through the courts and men had had a fair trial. Internment, by contrast, ran contrary to the European Convention for the Protection of Human Rights. The government had taken the action because of 'the direct and indirect pressure, the threats and intimidation brought to bear by the British government'.[84] McQuillan had sidestepped the Minister's contention that the IRA's activities were on a scale that threatened the security of the state and justified Ireland's temporary derogation from Article 5 of the Convention.[85] He also failed to address the problems of using the normal processes of law when faced with the resources of a paramilitary organisation. He had, however, indicated that the criteria of the Convention might be used to restrict the government's freedom on action. It was significant that before the new Dáil session this line of criticism was trailed by John Desmond in the generally republican *Kerryman*.[86] Although brushed aside at this point, the legality of internment and the importance of the procedures for derogation would eventually be tested and found in some regards to fall short of European standards.[87]

Push and pull

The IRA's activities, and those of the smaller armed groups, were watched with concern by both Belfast and London. The interests of these two governments were almost exactly, but not totally, the same. Since external affairs was one of the functions not devolved to the Northern Ireland government, and in the absence of bilateral relations between Dublin and Belfast, all representations from the latter had to pass through London. Even there, the process was convoluted, since Northern Ireland matters were handled by the Home Office. That branch of government, however, had no authority to communicate with a foreign country and so had to work with Dublin through the CRO.[88] The line of communication was perceptibly frustrating to Belfast at times. This was not simply a matter of complication and delay but of the different objectives and cultures of the two departments of state. The CRO worked on a broader canvas to address complex international interests of the UK; the Home Office, an astonishingly multitasked body, had as its core objective the preservation of domestic law and order, balancing security with democracy and accountability. One worked within the conventions, restraints, nuances and sensitivities of diplomacy; the other had the authority and flexibility that came from working to one chain of state command and political cover. Inevitably, therefore, perceptions and approaches to policy would differ between the branches of the British government, and this would add to the complicated exchanges and balances of the Dublin–Belfast–London troika. In dealing with the Border Campaign, officials and politicians in Belfast must sometimes have felt that their anger and concern were robbed of some of their urgency and passed through a distancing and denaturing filter.

The British Ambassador in Dublin, Sir Alexander Clutterbuck, was London's prime assessor of Irish matters. To perform this task, he and his staff had to form and cultivate relationships within political, official, cultural and journalistic circles. This was conventional diplomatic work, always apt to be sensitive, requiring much thought and control. Words, expressions and silences would all be gauged, and a diplomat's constant concern was to not misrepresent his government's policy. He had, moreover, to confine himself to revealing and discussing only that part of policy for which he had been given authority or direction. At the same time, he had to conduct informal as well as formal conversations and had to engage in the courtesies and exchanges necessary to build and develop relationships. To do this, Clutterbuck had to take a measure of trustworthiness and, sometimes, to take a chance. It was tricky work. There was always the possibility of inadvertent or malicious disclosure by some of those with whom he and his colleagues worked. Another danger, inevitable in all such positions, not just public but also commercial, was over-identifying with local parties and concerns and failing to give primacy to the priorities of the organisation he represented. Throughout the Border Campaign, we see these tensions, sometimes explicit and perceptible, sometimes less so, but always there.

The British Embassy in Dublin had significant contacts in and around the Irish government. Its intelligence, in consequence, was reasonable, though certainly incomplete and probably not as effective as Clutterbuck assumed.[89] Even though they had some foreknowledge of impending action, both the British and the Irish were taken very much by surprise by the initial raids of the Border Campaign on the night of 11/12 December. There were numerous constraints and delicacies in communications. Some of the British contacts (there was one in the Dublin Special Branch) were *sub rosa*; others were apparently of that kind but may have been fully authorised communications, known perhaps to a small group of ministers and given a confidential hue to lend emphasis. All had to be handled and acted upon with the utmost discretion and care. The Costello government, frail in itself, was constantly lambasted by republican critics, constitutional and physical force alike, for being too ready to dance to the British tune. Any acknowledgement that London was receiving confidential information and assurances from Dublin would have delighted and reinforced those who, for a range of reasons, wished to limit or smother British influence.

Operation Harvest's launch date, and indeed its extent and structure, had eluded both Irish and British intelligence, but there had been some exchanges on the preceding Saor Uladh–Christle raids of the night of 11 November (which had damaged six customs huts along the border).[90] Sean Murphy, Secretary General of the Department of External Affairs had, in a confidential conversation with Clutterbuck, shared Dublin's meagre information and speculations about the incident. It is interesting that, at this stage, there was no direct intelligence but only deductions that could have been made by anyone reading public reports of the incidents.[91]

Army intelligence was apparently somewhat better at this stage, and, on 5 November 1956, General Patrick Mulcahy, Chief of Staff of the Irish Army, passed a confidential warning to his opposite number, General Sir Brian Kimmins, GOC Northern Ireland, that there were plans to sabotage one of the large Service oil tanks near the coast.[92] The warning was passed, Mulcahy said, 'as from one soldier to another'. The perpetrators of the intended attack would come mainly from the North, though one or two from the South might join them. This was evidently another Saor Uladh–Christle operation. The exact timing was not known, but it was likely to be during the week of 5–11 November 1956. Precautions were immediately taken, and, whether because of these or some other reason, the attack did not materialise.[93] It seemed, following a meeting with Sean Murphy, that the Department had not been aware of the information passed on by Mulcahy or of his action in providing it to the British. Clutterbuck emphasised that, in order to protect Mulcahy's position, knowledge of the nature of the contact and information 'should be confined to the narrowest possible circle'.[94]

At this point, Clutterbuck was satisfied that the Irish government had taken effective steps against the IRA: located as it was in the North, Saor Uladh was primarily Belfast's responsibility. Mulcahy's intelligence had confirmed a view held for some time by the Dublin Embassy that any British representations implying a lack of effectiveness or cooperation by the Irish government would undermine existing good relations and 'would be ill-timed and only do harm'. Clutterbuck also urged his superiors in London that everything possible be done to dampen down recriminations by the Northern Ireland authorities, 'in order not to prejudice the goodwill and cooperation being built up behind the scenes'.[95] For several reasons, this would be a difficult matter to manage, particularly because the extent of Dublin's cooperation could not be revealed beyond a narrow circle.

The delicacy of the position was emphasised a few weeks later, when Clutterbuck saw Gerard Sweetman, the Fine Gael Minister for Finance. In the course of a financial discussion, on 20 November 1956, Sweetman suddenly switched to the acts of sabotage in Northern Ireland. He indicated that he knew of General Mulcahy's warning to General Kimmins and said to Clutterbuck, 'You will see I have kept my word to you, and I will always keep it.' He reminded Clutterbuck that he had passed on a similar warning earlier in the year and promised that '[w]henever we have any grounds for thinking that anything troublesome is being planned, you will be told, through one channel or another'. Apart from the Taoiseach, none of his cabinet colleagues knew that information was being passed on. Secrecy was essential, otherwise sources would dry up, 'and we should be landed into a first-class political row into the bargain'.[96] It was clear that, in the interests of preserving Anglo-Irish relations, a very small group within the Irish government had, despite the considerable political risks involved, decided to establish an intelligence conduit. Given that it was an inter-party administration, inevitably prone to leaks and continuing differences of a political nature, this was the only way to handle these contacts.

This link was not the Embassy's only source of intelligence. In a further secret letter to Ian Maclennan, Assistant Under-Secretary at Commonwealth Relations, Clutterbuck revealed that a detailed account of the 11 November attacks on customs posts had been obtained from 'one of our most reliable Police contacts' in Special Branch. This confirmed that the operation had combined the resources of Saor Uladh and the Southern (Christle) splinter group and gave a detailed account of events (including the hiring of four cars from Ryan's self-drive agency in Dublin).[97]

The CRO now found itself in a delicate and difficult position. It was receiving indications of firm support and resolute action from an authoritative group at the heart of the Irish government. These were backed by offerings of intelligence, with promises of more to come. In both Irish political and official circles, and within Whitehall, all of this information had to be tightly restricted, lest there would blow up a political row in Dublin that could drive the government from office. It was thus almost impossible, without disclosing more than was healthy, to placate the Northern Ireland government and Unionist and Conservative concerns in Parliament. Neither the Northern Ireland Prime Minister, Lord Brookeborough, nor the Home Affairs Minister, Captain Terence O'Neill, had been told about the Dublin link. For that matter, neither had the War Office nor the Home Office (the principal part of the UK government responsible for Northern Ireland affairs) been kept wholly in the picture. Within Northern Ireland, an official noted, few people trusted anyone else, and, 'as a result the military, the RUC and Northern Ireland government do not keep in sufficiently close touch'. All of this led to a certain amount of paralysis. Were the knowledge obtained secretly from the Irish government and police used to persuade Northern ministers to refrain from criticising Dublin, 'they would feel entitled to use the information to justify themselves and then the cat would be out of the bag'. But if this risk could be overcome, there was something to be said for taking Brookeborough and O'Neill into the confidence of the CRO. That, in November 1956, remained a dilemma.[98] The CRO concluded, however, that Dublin was, within its limits, honestly trying to keep its bargain, 'and we are anxious to avoid queering their pitch'.[99]

The CRO may have over-persuaded itself of the value and scope of its Dublin intelligence and of the confidential undertakings given by Irish ministers. Only a week before the launch of Operation Harvest, Maclennan wrote to his counterpart at the Home Office (Sir Austin Strutt) pointing out that the recent raids in Northern Ireland had been undertaken by a group from within that jurisdiction, 'the culprits having received some assistance from adherents in the South'. Those involved had, no doubt, crossed into the Republic before returning home. Were this true, then the hut-burning operation of 11 November 'hardly gives grounds for complaint to the republican authorities'. Costello's speech of 30 November 1955, and the subsequent pronouncements of the Catholic hierarchy on 18 January 1956, had, in retrospect, been 'a turning point in so far as terrorist activity in the Republic is concerned'. The IRA had been driven underground and had lain low. Splinter groups had broken away, intent on more activity, but these were 'of very minor importance and have accomplished nothing'.[100]

In conversation with British officials, O'Neill had claimed that IRA drilling had intensified in the Republic over previous months. This, wrote Maclennan, was contrary to CRO information. There had been a 'small outbreak of drilling in parts of Donegal in September', but this had been the work of members of 'an insignificant splinter-group' and had been broken up by the police.[101] The Irish government was in earnest in its determination to prevent force being used against Northern Ireland but could not be expected to accept any publicity for its actions in that regard. For this reason, the CRO believed that, were it to press Dublin further for cooperation, it would run the risk of making things worse rather than better. O'Neill had also asked for financial and economic pressures to be brought against Dublin, but the CRO, having examined the possibilities, found little scope for such sanctions. This was a complacent, slightly patronising position to take, and events would, within days, show that it was based on a mere smidgen of knowledge of the IRA's capacity, state of preparedness and intent.

With the launch of the Border Campaign on 12 December 1956, some of the CRO's credibility came into question, and the focus, in any event, had to shift to Northern Ireland, relations with which were conducted by the Home Office rather than with Commonwealth Relations. The immediate and strong statement by Costello on the evening of 14 December (following a long cabinet meeting) pre-empted what would have been a formal British protest.[102] In its place came the aide-memoire that welcomed Dublin's statement of condemnation and determination to take action.[103] There was also, as we have seen, the statement delivered in the House on 19 December 1956 by Prime Minister Eden.[104] This was welcomed by Hugh Gaitskell on behalf of the Labour Party.[105]

This strong affirmation of London's position produced an irritated and indeed somewhat angry response from the Irish government, undoubtedly drafted to secure the agreement of the component political parties and to continue to secure the support of the republican Clann na Poblachta. Replying to the aide-memoire the following week, Dublin confirmed its intention to suppress unlawful activities. All necessary means would be employed, but what form these might take were solely for it to determine. The memorandum went on to assert that responsibility for 'the root cause of unlawful military activities in Ireland' rested with 'the British parliament and Government and on the Government of the Six Counties'. It was a matter of 'deepest concern' that there had been no change of attitude towards Partition. On the contrary, the position that had already had 'such deplorable consequences' had been reaffirmed in recent public statements. Eden's statement in the Commons on 19 December 1956 had had a regrettable effect on public opinion in Ireland. In particular, his statement that the Six Counties were 'an integral part of the UK' was completely rejected and 'could never in any cir-cumstances be accepted by an Irish government'. These counties, the note declared, were part of the national territory of Ireland, 'and it remains the profound conviction of the Irish government that the evils attendant on Partition can be eradicated only by the removal of their basic cause'. Territorial unity should be restored in accordance with the wishes of the majority of the people of the island. It would be in the interests of all those whose peace and freedom were threatened were the British Government to take the initiative to end Partition for the existence of which that Government is primarily responsible'.[106]

This was a classic expression of nationalism, and only the timing and tone of the memorandum need comment. It was also most unlikely that Dublin was genuinely surprised by Eden's Commons statement, which contained nothing new. The coalition could not afford to be outflanked by Fianna Fáil, or any other party, in the fervour of its nationalism. Shaky, fissured and buffeted, it was apparent to all observers that it could not survive for much longer without acquiring a fresh mandate. When that happened, its green credentials would be challenged, and the text of a note firmly rebutting British claims to Irish territory could become a talisman. In the meantime, a bit of tub-thumping might help to bolster the wavering loyalty of Clann na Poblachta and some of the Independents. The British had heard all this before and bilateral relations should not suffer, were the text of the memorandum to be glossed and amplified by means of confidential briefings: London knew and understood that anti-Partitionism was an essential term of political trade in Dublin.

There was no likelihood of a public riposte. London's primary interest was, in practical measures, to counter the armed campaign, and Dublin had already shown willingness to act. But, at the same time, timing and tone were not right. The insecurities of Northern unionists had again been stoked. Resentment was rising about the renewed use of Southern territory as launching pad and safe haven. An outrage, or even a continuation of a campaign of attrition, could ignite intercommunal violence. Seen from this perspective, therefore, this was precisely the wrong time to beat the anti-Partitionist drum. Once again, more-over, Dublin had shown how little it knew about Northern Protestant sentiment and how very much less it cared. In the longer term, that blindness and neglect would have consequences a deal more important than the calculation of elec-toral advantage.

It was time for something of a post-mortem in Dublin: how could the assessments of November 1956 have been so far off the mark? The Rugby International between Ireland and France on Saturday, 26 January 1957, provided an occasion to bring Generals Mulcahy and Kimmins together. A considerable crowd of spec-tators had travelled down from Northern Ireland, and in this number, incognito ('and rather to the consternation of the RUC'), came Kimmins. Clutterbuck arranged for a quiet dinner at his residence, and the two men had a long conversa-tion. Some of what Mulcahy contributed to the conversation that evening was fact (such as the reactions of the Irish Cabinet); some was judgement (likely future developments). Six full and detailed foolscap pages minuting the con-versation were transmitted to London as top-secret material.[107] Much of what Mulcahy had to say related to the actions and perceptions of the Irish government and Army and is discussed elsewhere.[108] What we must note here is the extra-ordinary willingness of the Chief of Staff of the Irish Army to speak not only to a foreign representative but to his opposite number in the adjacent jurisdiction with whom, over the decades, there had been so much ill-feeling and bad blood.

The launch of the attacks on Northern Ireland (the opening salvo of the Border Campaign) had, Mulcahy conceded, taken the Irish authorities completely by surprise. Available intelligence had suggested that nothing was likely to happen for some time. Since that assessment, it had been learned that splinter-group activ-ities had forced the IRA to bring forward actions that had been in preparation for some time. There had been an undoubted failure in intelligence, and the government had not picked up even a hint of what was in the wind. The arrangement hitherto was that the police should be the prime intelligence agency and that they should keep the Army informed. Because of the Border Campaign failure, consideration was being given to having the Army mount its own intelligence-gathering.

Mulcahy, conceding past failures, gave some comfort to the British, both by his frank admission of Irish shortcomings and by outlining further steps and intentions. The Irish Army had so far taken a back seat, held in reserve to assist the civil power as and when required, but, if need be, it could be given a more active role. In dealing with IRA cases, for example, district judges had been 'a bit wobbly' (possibly because some or all had been threatened). If this nervousness spread and if the police did not succeed in preventing further trouble, the Army would take a more active role and Special Courts would be instituted.[109]

Clutterbuck also took it as a positive indication that Mulcahy had spoken highly of the RUC stance in the face of the IRA attacks and 'the exemplary restraint which they had shown'. This had helped to explain to potential sympathisers (pre-sumably in political circles) the futility of the campaign 'as well as the iniquity of exploiting young ill-trained boys'. Mulcahy thought that the campaign had already run out of steam; that it was unlikely to be turned against targets in the South or in Britain; that there was a fair hope that it would be called off or, if not, that it would be confined to fairly minor acts of sabotage. He acknowledged that there was 'an excessive measure of sympathy' for the raiders, particularly in areas where, for one reason or another, there was discontent with the government. He did not, however, think that sympathisers would be willing to go a step further and to volunteer themselves. People were beginning to realise that the encouragement of violence could pass beyond the 'cowboys and Indians' phase and into civil war – and they did not want that. Mulcahy also took comfort from his assessment that women, who had supported rebellion in 1916 and in 1920, were now opposed to violence.

Clutterbuck described the after-dinner conversation with Mulcahy to the CRO, pointing out its considerable value to both sides. He emphasised the high value he put on the Mulcahy link: 'a thoroughly genuine fellow... out to be as helpful as he can'. There was clearly a deal of rapport between the two men, Clutterbuck putting on record his personal respect for Mulcahy: 'He pulls no punches, but equally does not try to hide anything.' In general terms, what had passed was reassuring but, of course, had to be treated with the strictest confidence.[110]

Clutterbuck was given further assurances in another meeting with Gerard Sweetman towards the end of January 1957. Once more the conversation, which had principally concerned financial issues, switched to the IRA. Sweetman was confident that in recent operations (including in a round-up of the IRA Army Council when the Sinn Féin and *United Irishman* offices were raided on 6 July) most of the leading figures were in custody, either serving sentences or awaiting trial. Only three men of importance, Sweetman calculated, remained at large. Except in a few places ('hot spots'), public opinion was strongly against violence. The situation was much better than in previous years, and it was an indication of how far sentiment had moved against the IRA that it had now become possible, for the first time, to try and convict in ordinary courts persons engaged in 'patriotic' acts of violence. Hitherto, judges could not have been relied on to face the odium (Sweetman did not mention intimidation) of these cases, and it was only in Special Courts that convictions could be obtained. The successful use of ordinary courts was therefore a great advance as well as an indication of what Sweetman termed 'the essential soundness of public opinion'.[111]

The Embassy was able to report continued firmness in the administration of ordinary criminal law. By the middle of March 1957, it concluded that the situation was 'not unsatisfactory considering the peculiar circumstances of this country' and drew attention to the fact that two-thirds of those suspected of IRA activities had been convicted. When the Border Campaign had first got under way, some of the district judges had shown hesitancy in taking a firm line, which had caused the police in their districts to become impatient. While the British side might have preferred longer sentences, it should not lose sight of the importance of IRA offences being dealt with by the ordinary courts. That that had been done with little public criticism was cause for long-term satisfaction. Every Irish government wished to avoid creating martyrs, and if the men brought before the courts had been given long sentences, there would have been a considerable risk of arousing popular sympathy: 'the hysterical scenes over the funerals of Sean South and Fergal O'Hanlon show what can so easily happen in this mercurial country'.[112]

With the experience of rather less than two months of the Border Campaign, the CRO had come to accept that the Irish government had acted in good faith and had done what it could to counter the IRA 'as far as their peculiar circumstances admit'. Writing from the CRO to the Foreign Office, a senior official made the case. The Irish government had increased patrols on the border, had kept in touch with the Northern Ireland authorities, had passed on useful information and had rounded up leading IRA figures in the Republic. There was a desire to maintain good relations with the UK and a willingness to soft-pedal on the issue of Partition until North–South confidence had been built up at the administrative level.[113]

We have repeatedly seen how, in condemning IRA violence, Irish politicians of all shades of green had felt obliged simultaneously to condemn Partition and to identify it as a prime cause for Ireland's economic ills, the frustrating and seemingly intractable factor that had animated and propelled the IRA's young recruits into violence.[114] The British recognised that no party in government in Dublin could afford to be hesitant or lukewarm on this issue: this would have left it exposed and vulnerable on a core belief in post-independence party politics, a founding myth of the state.

But it was not all electioneering, flimflam and window dressing. In private conversations with the British Ambassador – and with exquisite ill-timing – both Fine Gael and Fianna Fáil continued to try to lever advantage from the activities they condemned and to present a case that the IRA could be outflanked by some movement towards the removal of Partition. This was, in Dublin's view, a matter exclusively for bilateral discussions: the government of Northern Ireland, and all it stood for, was avoided as one would an unpleasantness in the corner of the room.

There is not space here, nor is it necessary, to provide any kind of complete account of the number and nature of private exchanges on Partition. It is worth noting, however, an attempt by Clutterbuck to persuade his superiors back in London, and the politicians under whose authority they worked, to reward Irish cooperation with slight movement, a change in the usual stonewalling words and a somewhat more encouraging response to Dublin's pleas. London seems to have concluded that Clutterbuck was perhaps being oversensitive to the concerns and problems of the Irish government. It certainly thought that he was giving insufficient weight to Belfast's likely reaction, should it get word of any softening of the position on Partition, however nuanced and minimal that shift might be. Westminster wished to avoid any further complication of its relationship with unionist politicians and especially to avoid triggering any concerns about an

Anglo-Irish deal. Realities also intruded, and they were sharp and many-angled. Only when viewed from the redoubt of nationalist orthodoxy could it have seemed appropriate to raise a basic issue of Anglo-Irish relations and the constitutional structure and territorial integrity of the UK in the midst of an open-ended campaign of violence.

The timing of Dublin's initiative was all the more ill judged, coming as it did rather less than a week into the Border Campaign. When Clutterbuck delivered the British government's aide-memoire to Liam Cosgrave on 18 December 1956, the Irish Minister for Foreign Affairs recited the mantra that terrorism would never be eliminated until the territorial unity of Ireland had been restored.[115] Reporting this, Clutterbuck confirmed that he had emphasised that the British government stood firmly by the terms of the Ireland Act, 1949. This had long been London's position, and the 1949 Act was Belfast's guarantee that no change would be made in the status of Northern Ireland without the consent of its people. Clutterbuck nevertheless wanted to be able to offer some comfort and encouragement. A bolstering of democratic politicians, after all, could enable them to act with more vigour and confidence in suppressing the IRA. His proposal, therefore, was that, in addition to affirming commitment of the 1949 Act and the constitutional status quo, he should be authorised to say that if, at any time, the Irish government had specific ideas they wished to outline to the UK government 'as a preliminary to a possible approach to the North', he would be at their disposal.[116]

This proposal was as ill judged and ill timed as Costello's had been and, in the circumstances, inflammatory in its potential. In the usual neutral and courteous language of the civil service, it was explained to Clutterbuck why such a statement, however minimal it might seem, whatever comfort it might bring to Irish politicians and whatever effect it might have in bolstering them against the IRA, could lead to very unwelcome complications. Given the continuing acts of violence, Henry Lintott, Deputy Under-Secretary at Commonwealth Relations (and shortly to be appointed as High Commissioner to Canada) wrote, were it to become known in Northern Ireland that the British government had gone so far as to consider orally Dublin's ideas for the possible future development of a united Ireland, 'the Government in the North would certainly react very unfavourably'.[117] Cabinet had considered the matter, and Clutterbuck was directed that the oral response to Irish representations should be confined to a reiteration of London's adherence to the Ireland Act, 1949, and advice that building cooperation with Northern Ireland on practical administrative matters was the best way forward. Should Dublin have such proposals, they would receive 'ready and careful consideration'.[118]

As the spring of 1957 wore on, the Embassy continued to receive assurances that the coming of longer days and the waning of support for the IRA would mean a reduction in the incidence and severity of violent incidents.[119] This assessment was made in the face of the return, in the March general election, of four Sinn Féin candidates to the Dáil.[120] How politicians, journalists or, indeed, any member of the clergy could assess the level of IRA support, tacit or more active, is unclear. There were no opinion polls, and, given that the Roman Catholic hierarchy had anathematised the organisation, it is unlikely that parishioners would raise the topic with the clergy or that any but a hardy few would admit to their priests anything but compliance. Much the same was probably the case of conversations between many constituents and their political representatives. And, to some extent, these were irrelevant considerations. Again and again through its history, moreover, the IRA had shown a stern indifference to popular opinion. Its defining doctrine was that it would put the interests of the true republic above all considerations, save those of principle. It was, moreover, a relatively low-cost and certainly lean organisation, able to make do on a small budget.[121] Public opinion was not altogether an irrelevance, but it was a relatively peripheral concern in the IRA's continued operation.

We know, in retrospect, that, within a month or two, Operation Harvest had stalled and had no hope of regaining – never mind increasing – its momentum: apogee and perigee were never far apart. But this was hardly clear to observers in the first half of 1957, when, despite a host of emollient predictions, and the operational difficulties arising from the coming of long days, the IRA continued to conduct operations. On 13 May, there was a spectacular raid, not by the IRA but by the Saor Uladh–Christle group. Lock gates on the Newry Canal were destroyed with explosives. Repairs cost £50,000 and the loss of trade connected to the Port of Newry was estimated at £100,000. The IRA issued a statement denying its involvement in the raid and absurdly suggested that it had been carried out with the connivance of the authorities in Northern Ireland.[122]

The various forecasts of an ebbing in the tide of violence and destruction, which Clutterbuck had, with some conviction, passed on to London, now acquired an embarrassing patina of gullibility. Following the Newry raid, Clutterbuck saw Sean Murphy, Secretary of External Affairs, and expressed concern about the incidents 'which contrary to our hopes show no sign of stopping'. The greatest restraint had been shown by the North in the face of continuous provocation. But there were limits, and what no one could dismiss was that, 'one of these days', people in the North might lose patience and embark on reprisals. Murphy at first parried this by contending that the incidents were diminishing but, when pressed by Clutterbuck, agreed that it was deplorable that they were continuing at all. This led to the question of the efficacy of the measures being taken in the Republic. They had some effect, Clutterbuck agreed, but not enough: sentences of three months were of little consequence. Murphy, in Clutterbuck's opinion, rehearsed all the old do-not-create-martyrs arguments against severity but, significantly, could not be drawn on the intentions of the new government.[123]

How the Fianna Fáil government would act to end the Border Campaign was not at this time clear, but, from both de Valera and Frank Aiken (Minister for External Affairs) came strong indications that it wished to have high-level negotiations on Partition. The village hall had opened its doors, and it seemed as though the first round of a much-played card game had started again. But there were expectations that de Valera would act with vigour when choices had to be made. Certainly, he was less constrained by parliamentary or party factors than his predecessors. It was not unreasonable to conclude that, once again, de Valera was seeking to ride on the IRA's coat-tails, and this certainly was London's inclination. London was unmoved. Any initiative on Partition had to come from Dublin, and 'HMG [Her Majesty's Government]... could not do anything publicly which appears to coerce the North to the advantage of the South.'[124]

As we have seen, the Fianna Fáil government's policy continued on much the same lines as those of its predecessor for some three and a half months. Attacks continued, and both London and Belfast continued to fret and fume: it seemed as though, with slow rotations, the IRA's campaign would grind on. The Forkhill ambush, on Thursday, 4 July 1957, in which Constable Cecil Gregg was killed and Constable Robert Halligan wounded, broke Dublin's inertia.[125] Politicians in Northern Ireland were outraged, and there were immediate reactions in Stormont.[126] Particular ire was directed at the Irish government for failing to take adequate preventive action. The Secretary of Home Affairs wrote to his counterpart in the Home Office warning that feelings had become greatly embittered across Northern Ireland and that, in the view of the Northern Prime Minister, Lord Brookeborough, 'the position has been reached where it would take very little more to spark off a serious outburst, the effects of which it would be impossible to foretell'.[127] To anyone with even the slightest familiarity with Northern Ireland, it was alarmingly obvious that the shooting of Constable Gregg, just a week before the Twelfth of July celebrations, held particular potential for intercommunal strife. Brookeborough was not only within his rights but was fulfilling a basic duty of his office in asking the Home Office to ensure that the seriousness of the situation be impressed on the Dublin government. No British government could afford to neglect such a strong and specific warning.

To a large extent, the wishes of London and Belfast were met when, on Monday, 8 July 1957, the Irish government brought into effect Part II of the OAS(A)A. In Dublin, Clutterbuck recalled with evident relief that the Act had been used by de Valera during the Second World War 'with crushing effect'. Arrests had begun on Saturday, 6 July, even before the Act came into effect, and this swift response to Forkhill was described by Clutterbuck as 'a most heartening development'.[128] It was, nevertheless, clear that the Irish government, at last having taken a drastic course to limit and, as far as possible, to close off the Republic as a place of refuge, and to hold out to IRA members and active supporters the prospect of years in custody, now expected a quid pro quo. Clutterbuck recognised that, having suppressed political violence in the cause of anti-Partitionism, the Irish government would want to demonstrate that there were other and effective ways of making progress in the cause. In the course of a meeting between Aiken and Clutterbuck to discuss the Armagh ambush, the former had once again held forth on the injustice of Partition. He offered no new ideas, and Clutterbuck, having heard the message many times before, found the exercise tedious. Aiken desired that a British minister should, in the course of a public speech, declare that, once past the present troubles, and looking ahead, it was clearly a British as well as an Irish interest that Ireland should eventually be reunited. Clutterbuck thought that it might have become evident to Aiken that such a statement was an unlikely possibility but equally feared that he would keep returning to it until he had received a definite 'no' in a personal meeting with a minister in London.[129]

De Valera's willingness to use internment and the strong lead thus given to the Army and the Gardaí was another stone added to the pile that was crushing the much enfeebled IRA in what seemed like a protracted *peine forte et dure*. But, like the obstinate defendant, who, in the eighteenth century, refused to enter a plea, the IRA showed surprising reserves of determination and refused to give in. London may have been broadly satisfied that the Irish government was doing all that could reasonably be expected, but Belfast was not convinced. In February 1958, Phelim O'Neill (Unionist MP for North Antrim in the Westminster Parliament) articulated the irritation of many in his party, and in Northern Ireland. It must have seemed that London and the British public more generally were largely unmoved by the continuing low level of IRA activity. This point was driven home by what seemed like a disproportionate amount of political and media noise when (very rarely) the IRA conducted an operation in Britain. Thus, when IRA men carried out an unsuccessful raid on Blandford Camp in Dorset in the small hours of Sunday, 16 February 1958, the Irish press carried the incident at the top of their news reports.[130] At around the same time, the IRA attacked two police stations on the border (Belleek, Co. Fermanagh, and Middleton, Co. Armagh).[131] These raids received almost no coverage in the British press, but, in the Commons, Christopher Soames, the Secretary of State for War, announced that there would be an Army Board of Inquiry.[132]

Writing to Cuthbert Alport, Parliamentary Under-Secretary at the CRO, Phelim O'Neill pointed out the telling disparity in concern or even attention. Was the British government maintaining pressure on the 'Southern Irish Authorities' to become more active in their campaign against the terrorists? O'Neill had heard that levels of police energy on the border varied a great deal, according to the convictions of the local commander. Initiative and countermeasures were left without much central direction, and he did not think this was good enough. With negotiations on the European Free Trade Area in the offing, 'H.M.G. have all four aces and the Joker in their hand, or are they becoming the victims of Southern Irish blarney?'[133] Alport replied in kind, 'I think the English tend to be susceptible to the charm of the Irish whether they come from the North or the South of the border.' He went on to insist that representations were being made to the Irish government about the need for more cooperation from the Irish security forces and pointing out the restraint shown by the government and people of Northern Ireland. Alport was less certain about the leverage afforded by the free-trade negotiations but assured O'Neill about Westminster's continuing anxiety to suppress violence and terrorism.[134]

But the attacks continued and, in mid-July, clustered in a way that further stoked Northern alarm. On 12/13 July, there were two unsuccessful bomb attacks in

Newry and another at a drill hall in Skelga, near Fintona, Co. Tyrone.[135] The significance of these operations lay not in their individual seriousness but in the fact that they continued to be made, were well coordinated and took place in several places. There were two further considerations: the attacks had been attempted when nights were short, thus raising fears of what might happen in the seasons of more prolonged darkness; they also fed worried reassessments about the supposedly waning strength of the IRA. At a human level, much more tragic was the killing of Constable Henry Ross, near Carrickbroad, Co. Armagh around midday on 16 July. On this occasion, unlike the haphazard death and injury of a firefight, the killing had been deliberate.[136] Customs huts at Killeen, Middleton, Co. Armagh, and Clontibrit, Co. Monaghan, were destroyed or badly damaged earlier that day.[137] In addition to these attacks, there was an IRA fatality, which occurred when, on 15 July, twenty-eight-year-old Patrick MacManus, IRA OC for South Fermanagh (and a member of the Army Council) died when handling a gelignite bomb. Two of his comrades had been injured in the blast.[138] Taken together, it seemed impossible to think otherwise than that a new wave of attacks was forming. In spite of all the countermeasures and optimistic predictions, had the Border Campaign drawn second wind?

A fortnight after these events, two Ulster Unionist Westminster MPs met Cuthbert Alport to express their concerns. Sir David Campbell, leader of the Westminster Ulster Unionists, and Colonel Robert Grosvenor, MP for Fermanagh and South Tyrone, raised concerns about the upsurge in IRA activity as well as the political situation in the Republic. The feeling was growing that de Valera was growing too old to be fully effective and that no obvious successor was yet in sight. This, they conjectured, had had a knock-on effect. Gardaí in the border counties were cooperating less with their RUC counterparts: despite the fact that they were well equipped, with good transportation and communications equipment, they did not seem to be effective. Senior RUC officers had the impression that their Southern colleagues were unsure of themselves and were not getting results because of uncertainties about political succession: after de Valera, would they get the same strong HQ backing as before? These concerns, Campbell and Grosvenor contended, had to be set within another one: would there continue to be popular restraint in the North, or might there be retaliation?[139]

To this, Alport pointed to the strong steps Dublin was taking in the wake of the recent incidents. There had been arrests, and a number of individuals were being sought. In addition, the IRA could take little comfort from recent events. An RUC constable had been killed, but on the IRA side a man had blown himself up; two had been seriously wounded, and three had been captured in Armagh Cathedral. The Southern authorities thought that those taking part in the raids had little or no training in handling explosives. The two MPs demurred from this view of developments, insisting that extensive drilling was taking place in the South. Alport observed that if further representations were to be made to Dublin, they would be far more effective were they to be backed up with concrete instances, whether they concerned police cooperation on the border or law and order elsewhere. Unsubstantiated assertions were likely to be met with unsubstantiated replies about cooperation.[140]

The events of 16/17 July continued to reverberate. Sir Richard Pim, Inspector-General of the RUC, protested about Southern inaction about Liam Kelly, who, although not involved in this instance, was thought to be active in other operations. Why had he not been interned and why had Saor Uladh not been proscribed? From the Dublin embassy, Clutterbuck pointed out that matters were not as straightforward as they might seem from Belfast. The Gardaí were convinced that Kelly was no longer active. He had signed an undertaking to respect the Republic's law and constitution and had, in addition, given an oral undertaking not to plan operations against the North. Simple assertions that Kelly was a dangerous man were unlikely to influence the Southern authorities without concrete evidence that he was violating his undertakings. For Dublin to intern without such evidence someone who had given his undertaking would undermine the useful instrument of 'signing out'. As to Saor Uladh being declared illegal in the South, the reality was that whether an organisation had formally been proscribed did not affect internment decisions. Several Saor Uladh members were currently in the Curragh, and that was one of the reasons why Aiken was confident that Saor Uladh were ceasing to be of any importance. Clutterbuck, nevertheless, thought there was much to be said for another approach, before the winter, on security matters. He cautioned that this would have to be handled informally and without publicity.[141]

Following this, there was a general reassessment by the Dublin embassy of the IRA's durability, and of Dublin's policy responses. Matters had certainly improved since the activation of Part II of the OAS(A)A in July 1957. Yet, despite internment, and with all but one of its known leaders in the Curragh, the organisation had continued its operations. While most of these were acts of sabotage, there were other more daring actions from time to time. Recruits were still coming in, and finance was available to support operations. This led to the conclusion that a further turn of the screw was needed to get on top of the organisation. De Valera, in a speech on 17 July, had indicated that, if necessary, additional powers would be sought.[142]

Thinking how to approach the Irish government, Clutterbuck returned to the matter of occasion. There had been a lull in activities after the mid-July upsurge, and he could not, without evidence and specific examples, urge further measures. Further actions by the IRA would supply a peg; otherwise, he needed dates and places of drilling and of preparation for attacks. It was most important to keep any approach informal and unpublicised, lest the Irish government face difficulties should it have to go to the Dáil for additional powers. Clutterbuck also thought it 'only too likely' that any approach to de Valera would bring on another 'impassioned restatement of the anti-Partition case'. This would not matter much, but it was also possible that de Valera might use the occasion to press again for a personal meeting with the British Prime Minister (Harold Macmillan). (He did not need to spell out the difficulties this might entail with Stormont.) On the basis of a deal of experience (his own and representatives long before him), Clutterbuck reminded the CRO that 'we cannot expect any interview with [de Valera] to be plain sailing'. He was not opposed to a further approach, but it could entail a cost of some kind, even if only embarrassment.[143]

The Dublin embassy (and Clutterbuck had indicated that there had been a general discussion among the senior staff there) also doubted whether it would be useful to seek assistance from the Catholic Church. Its position had been made clear by Cardinal D'Alton and by Archbishop McQuaid. Should further incidents occur, the Church might speak; otherwise it was best to leave things alone since such statements, if repeated too often, could cause resentment. It was, of course, open to the Northern authorities to approach Cardinal D'Alton directly.[144] Whether this was tongue in cheek is hard to say, but Clutterbuck knew well that relations between the Roman Catholic hierarchy and Northern unionist politicians were, if they could be said to exist at all, of the most insubstantial kind. Neither will nor means existed to improve them, and they only too accurately reflected the dangerous political and social paralysis of which the IRA was but one outcome.

Notes

1 For the background, see Department of Education, *Report of the Council of Education as Presented to the Minister for Education (1) The Function of the Primary School; (2) The Curriculum to Be Pursued in the Primary School from the Infant Age Up to 12 Years of Age* (Dublin: Stationery Office, 1954), especially pp. 94, 130–2, 140 and 142–4.

2 See J. V. Luce, *Trinity College Dublin: The First Four Hundred Years* (Dublin: Trinity College Press, 1992). The ban dated to 1875 and was regularly reinforced, with Archbishop John Charles McQuaid of the Dublin archdiocese reminding the faithful in a Lenten Pastoral in 1967 that there had been no relaxation in the proscription. A synodal statute of 1956 proclaimed, 'we forbid under pain of mortal sin… Catholic youths to frequent the College… Catholic parents, or guardians, to send to that College Catholic youths committed to their care.' Only the Archbishop of Dublin could decide 'in what circumstances and with what guarantees against perversion attendance at that College may be tolerated' (Luce, *Trinity College Dublin*, *op. cit.*, pp. 181 and 196). It should be noted, however, that a number of Catholics, with or without episcopal permission, did attend Trinity College, the proportion of the student body rising from 23 per cent in 1950 to 29 per cent in 1960.

3 There was, across a surprisingly wide social spectrum, a degree of intolerance of religious dissent that occasionally verged on hysteria and worse. This was epitomised in the case of three street preachers who were badly assaulted in Killaloe, Co. Clare, on 26 June 1958. The assailants (three local farmers in town for a fair) were prosecuted for causing actual bodily harm and, in due course, appeared before District Justice Gordon Hurley who remarked, *inter alia*, that the preachers were abusing their constitutional rights, and 'such action is bound to draw down the rod of the people whose hospitality they have received'. The judge's remarks, the lightness of the sentence (probation) and the refusal of costs provoked a deal of concern, justifiable among non-Catholics (and, it must be said, prominent Catholics). When the matter was raised in the Dáil by Lionel Booth (Fianna Fáil TD for Dun Laoghaire and Rathdown – a constituency which had a sizeable Protestant population), the government expressed concern but drew the line at a direct criticism of the judge. The principle of freedom of expression, guaranteed by the Constitution, would be upheld,

the Minister said. This led to an intervention from Fintan Coogan (Fine Gael, Galway West) demanding to know if freedom of expression permitted 'provocation or abuse'. Dr Owen Sheehy-Skeffington tried and failed in the Senate to secure a motion asking for a judicial inquiry. *Dáil Debates*, vol. 171, cols. 37–8, 29 October 1958; *Senate Debates*, Vol. 50, cols. 150–65, 10 December, 1958; see *Irish Times*, 16 September 1958, 1d; *Manchester Guardian*, 1 October 1958, 6f–g.

4 See Elaine Byrne's examination of the distortion of the Irish state through cronyism and corrupt patronage. Elaine Byrne, *Political Corruption in Ireland, 1922–2010* (Manchester: Manchester University Press, 2012). See also Tom Garvin, *Preventing the Future: Why Was Ireland So Poor for So Long?* (Dublin, Gill & Macmillan, 2004).

5 Sometimes taking a bizarre turn as, for example, when repeated questions were asked about the presence of a French lawyer on the Irish government's legal team at Strasbourg in the Lawless case. The issue, apparently, was not political, but a matter of employment.

6 And could of course receive it, collectively and individually. Elaine Byrne described how Archbishop McQuaid made a fortune by using insider information to trade in railway stocks.

7 A theme powerfully and poignantly explored in John McGahern's *The Leavetaking* (London: Faber & Faber, 1974).

8 'Sexual intercourse began / In nineteen sixty-three / (Which was rather late for me)—/ Between the end of the *Chatterley* ban / And the Beatles' first LP.' Philip Larkin, 'Annus Mirabilis', *Collected Poems* (London: The Marvell Press and Faber and Faber, 2002), p. 146.

9 See OEEC, *Economic Conditions in Ireland and Portugal* (Paris: OEEC, 1955), p. 5; OEEC, *Economic Conditions in Member and Associated Countries of the OEEC: Ireland* (Paris: OEEC, 1961), pp. 28–9. See also OECD, *Economic Surveys by the OECD: Ireland* (Paris: OECD, 1962), p. 28.

10 Because no exit figures were kept, it was all but impossible to calculate emigration figures on an annual basis, nor could they be known in the inter-censual period. A 1960 estimate by Dr James Ryan, Minister for Finance, put emigration at 100,000 between 1957 and 1960. There seemed to be general agreement that 1956–7 was a peak in the rate of outflow. A modern academic estimate is that one-eighth of the population emigrated in the 1950s: 'This rate of emigration in both absolute and relative terms, was the highest recorded since the 1880s, and at the end of the period, the population of the state had shrunk to an all-time low of just over 2.8 million.' Gerry O'Hanlon, 'Population Change in the 1950s: A Statistical Review', in Dermot Keogh, Finbarr O'Shea and Carmel Quinlan (eds.), *Ireland in the 1950s: The Lost Decade* (Cork: Mercier Press, 2004), p. 72. See also *Dáil Debates*, vol. 184, cols. 677–8, 9 November 1960.

11 See OECD, *Economic Surveys*, *op. cit.*, p. 16. See also OEEC, *Economic Conditions in Ireland and Portugal* (Paris: OEEC, 1954), p. 11.

12 Eamonn Boyce, *The Insider: The Belfast Prison Diaries of Eamonn Boyce, 1956–1962*, ed. Anna Bryson (Dublin: Lilliput Press, 2007), p. 10. See also OEEC, *Economic Conditions*, p. 5.

13 See Enda Delaney, 'The Vanishing Irish? The Exodus from Ireland in the 1950s', in Dermot Keogh, Finbarr O'Shea and Carmel Quinlan (eds.), *Ireland in the 1950s: The Lost Decade*, Cork: Mercier Press, 2004, pp. 80–6.

14 *Dáil Debates*, vol. 172, cols. 1131–2, 28 January 1959. Besides the practical problems of intervening to prevent this worrying (and indeed deplorable) outflow, action was thought inadvisable by the government because 'It would... be open to criticism as infringing the rights of parents and guardians, on whom the responsibility for the welfare of these young persons primarily rests.'

15 Rupert Brooke, '1914: Peace', in *The Collected Poems of Rupert Brooke: With a Memoir* (London: Sedgwick & Jackson, 1918), p. 71.

16 See above, pp. 283–6, for this legislation. Refusing to answer questions amounted to police imprisonment at only one remove since even were an initial question answered satisfactorily follow-up questions would be put on such matters as the names of persons the interviewee had met and what had been said. On the first refusal, the suspect in effect convicted himself. Possession of almost any document with an IRA connection would also ensure conviction; weapons and ammunition hardly required discussion.

17 See above, pp. 819, n. 63.

18 Tim Pat Coogan, *The IRA* (London: Fontana, 1980), pp. 394–5. According to the account that Coogan received, the IRA men then refused to leave Monaghan garda barracks unless transport were provided. After some haggling, gardaí provided and paid for taxis to Dublin. Bell gives a slightly different account (date and number of men involved) and implies that the release decision was made at a political rather than an official level. J. Bowyer Bell, *The Secret Army: The IRA, 1916–1979* (Cambridge, Mass.: MIT Press, 1983), p. 293.

19 As sometimes happens in parliamentary politics, de Valera had called the 1954 election to renew his mandate in the face of by-election losses. He had miscalculated, and the results went against him, reducing Fianna Fáil to its lowest number of seats (at sixty-five) in the Dáil since 1932. Fine Gael increased its representation from forty to fifty seats; Labour regained three seats to achieve a total of nineteen. The smaller groupings were much diminished: Independents fell to five seats, Clann na Talmhan to five; Clann na Poblachta won only three. Seán MacBride refused to join government, though he agreed in effect to support it passively.

20 The results of the general election of February 1948 had been Fine Gael, thirty-one seats; Labour, nineteen; Clann na Poblachta, ten; Clann na Talmhan, seven; Independents, twelve. Against this, Fianna Fáil had sixty-eight seats.

21 This scenario would have been particularly worrying for Brookeborough, whose role in establishing the Ulster Special Constabulary in October 1920 had laid the foundations of his political career.

22 This concern was also taken up by Frederick Boland, the Republic's Ambassador to London. In a conversation on 22 February 1955, he told the new Permanent Under-Secretary at the CRO (on whom he had called to express his good wishes) that he was 'disturbed' at the prospect of reprisals (by the majority community) in Northern Ireland. These would greatly complicate the Dublin government's task of dealing with public opinion in the South, 'which while condemning, was not wholly sympathetic' to the IRA campaign (PRO DO/35/4985, Record of conversation between F. H. Boland and Sir Gilbert Laithwaite, 22 February 1955). Frederick H. Boland (1904–85) was one of the Republic's most able and talented diplomats, with a broad educational background that, in the late 1920s, had taken him, by way of a Rockefeller Fellowship, from Trinity College Dublin to Harvard, the University of Chicago and the University of North Carolina. Joining the Department of External Affairs in 1929, he became Assistant Secretary within ten years and Secretary in 1946. He was the Republic's first Ambassador to the Court of St James (1950–6). Ireland gained UN membership in 1955, and Boland became his country's first permanent representative in 1956. He served as President during the UN's momentous and turbulent Fifteenth General Assembly (1960–1).

23 PRO DO/35/4984, Draft letter, A. F. Morley, Permanent Under-Secretary CRO, to Sir Walter Hankinson, British Ambassador, Dublin, 10 August 1954. When Brookeborough had visited the Home Office, the tensions inseparable from Northern Ireland's marching season and pressures to which he was being subjected by loyalists sharpened his assessment of the political and public-order dangers.

24 PRO DO/35/4984, Sir Walter Hankinson to A. F. Morley, 16 August 1954. By the conventions of diplomacy, this raised by one notch the strength of concern being expressed.

25 There had been confirmation of these points in Irish press reports. Dundalk Urban Council had adopted a resolution (albeit by a narrow majority) congratulating the Gough Barracks raiders. It also urged the Irish government not to cooperate with the Northern authorities. The proposer of the motion wanted the government to form a liberation army to march on Northern Ireland and conduct guerrilla war against those 'who occupied the stolen six counties until they were driven back to the land from which they had come'. The motion's opposers pointed out that 1,600 Dundalk men were employees of the Great Northern Railway and half their wages came 'from their friends in Stormont and the much-despised Northern Ireland' (*Irish Times*, 26 August 1954, 7h). See also *Connacht Sentinel*, 15 June 1954, 1d; *Nenagh Guardian*, 19 June 1954, 7c; *Anglo-Celt*, 19 June 1954, 1h; 26 June 1954, 1b.

26 PRO DO/35/4984, Activities of the Irish Republican Army: Record of a conversation between Mr. F. H. Boland, Ambassador for the Irish Republic in London and Sir Percivale Liesching on 31 August 1954. When informed by the Home Office of the reference in the conversation to the question of closer relations between the RUC and the Gardaí, the Northern Ireland government confirmed that it would greatly welcome such contacts, recognising 'that they would necessarily have to be arranged with great care and secrecy' (PRO DO/35/4984, J. H. Walker, Home Office, to F. A. K. Harrison, CRO, 11 October 1954). Six months later, there had been so little progress in contact between the two police forces that Belfast had to ask, by means of the Home Office writing to the CRO, to pass on intelligence about an IRA training house in the 'Monaghan bulge', a Southern salient on the Northern Ireland border (PRO DO/35/4954, Brian Maginess, Minister for Home Affairs to Gwilym Lloyd-George, Home Secretary, 14 February 1955). RUC intelligence (although later corrected) seems to have been only partly accurate on this occasion. The house was a training base operated by Saor Uladh, rather than the IRA (PRONI HA/32/1/955, Special Branch briefing on Liam Kelly, July 1958).

27 London had checked separately and found that the Unlawful Organisation (Suppression) Order, 1939, had not been repealed by Dublin.

28 *Dáil Debates*, vol. 147, cols. 171–202, 28 October 1954. See PRO DO/35/4985, November 1954. Boland, *inter alia*, argued that it was better that London made no public representations to Dublin since this would impede the mobilisation of public opinion against the IRA, as would 'anything which conveyed the suggestion that the Dublin Government were acting under pressure from or at the instigation of the Government of this [i.e. Britain] country'. Boland also pointed out that the IRA leadership 'in a mood of excessive confidence' were holding public recruiting meetings 'and generally showing their hands'. The Irish police found this helpful in making identifications in preparation for later round-ups. For the Dáil speeches, see *Dáil Debates*, vol. 147, col. 160 *et seq.*, 28 October 1954.

29 See *Weekly Irish Times*, 25 December 1954, 1e–f; see also *Irish Times*, 25–8 December 1954, 5b. The form of denunciation had been used for more than 100 years against physical-force nationalism. John Francis D'Alton (1882–1963), extensively educated in Ireland, Rome and England, was a lifelong friend of Éamon de Valera, his schoolmate at Blackrock College. In the 1930s, he was interested in easing Free State–UK relations.

30 *Meath Chronicle*, 26 February 1955, 2a. Dr Quinn, the Bishop of Kilmore, managed to spear both nationalism and Communism and to associate the IRA with the latter: 'History had left examples from every age of the use the enemies of the Church had made of nationalism to do her injury... fidelity to the faith was held to be the profession of a foreign allegiance... It seems to have had a measure of success nearer home. It always remains something of a mystery how many who have a genuine love of country, as our people have, can ever be deceived by the pretence of the Communist

to share that love.' With varying degrees of emphasis, much the same line was followed by Quinn's colleagues. See *Southern Star*, 26 February 1955, 2f–g (Dr C. Lucey, Bishop of Cork); *Connacht Sentinel*, 22 February 1955, 2c–d (Dr Browne, Bishop of Galway).

31 *Kerryman*, 16 April 1955, 3c–d; *Nenagh Guardian*, 16 April 1955, 5a–b. The latter reported that the IRA statement was read out in Banba Square in Nenagh, Co. Tipperary, following a commemorative mass for the Easter Rising and the recital of the rosary in Irish.

32 Mick Ryan (who became Director of Operations in 1960–2) recalled that his girlfriend of the time, who held strong religious beliefs, urged him to make his confession before returning to the North on active service, facing the chance that he would be killed. He attended confession at the Jesuit church in Gardiner Street, Dublin: 'I'd go down, knock on the door and they'd bring you into a room, you would kneel on the kneeler and the priest would sit there. You wouldn't be in the confession box even. And you'd sometimes feel embarrassed with revealing some of your sins but the need for a clear and clean conscience was paramount so you'd overcome the embarrassment for absolution! [The priest would say] "Absolved." And out the door.' (Interview.)

33 PRO DO/35/4985, Memorandum on Strasbourg talks of 10 December 1954.

34 PRO DO/35/4985, Memorandum, 10 December 1954. This evasiveness might – had words been stretched to the very limits of meaning – have been an attempt to blame republican splinter groups for the developing campaign in Northern Ireland and to minimise the IRA's well-advanced preparations for a more substantial one.

35 PRO DO/35/4985, Memorandum of meeting between the Secretary of State for Commonwealth Relations and Mr F. Boland, Ambassador for the Republic of Ireland, 24 January 1955.

36 See p. 787.

37 See Coogan, *The IRA*, *op. cit.*, pp. 363–5 and 375. These raids had been undertaken by what, in effect, were splinters from the IRA: Saor Uladh, led by Liam Kelly, and a breakaway group led by Joe Christle. The latter group had initially come from the Dublin IRA but had then gathered in frustrated young activists from across the country and an ally, rather than follower, of Christle, Gerry Lawless. (The background to the breakaway groups is sketched by Bell in his *Secret Army*, *op. cit.*, Chapter 14.) The *Irish News* (28 November 1955, 1a–f) headlined its report 'Double Mystery in Raid on Roslea Barracks'. Who had carried out the raid (the IRA had immediately denied responsibility) and had one of the raiders been killed in the firefight? The newspaper also pointed out that the wife and two children of a sergeant lived in the barracks (28 November 1955, 6h). The following day, the newspaper reported the inquest 'on an unknown man' and the RUC theory that an organisation called Saor Uladh was involved in the attack (29 November 1955, 1a–f). The story ran in the *Irish News* for several days following. See also *Northern Whig*, 28 November 1955, 1a–f; 29 November 1955, 1a–h; 30 November 1955, 1a–e. The *Whig* also covered aspects of the story for several days: Ulster grit and determination and Southern inactivity were the principal themes.

38 *Dáil Debates*, vol. 153, col. 1336, 30 November 1955.

39 *Dáil Debates*, vol. 153, col. 1337. All following quotations are taken from the *Dáil Debates*, as shown.

40 *Dáil Debates*, vol. 147, col. 171, *et seq.*, 28 October 1954. The line taken in the earlier speech was identical with that of the later one. Partition was an 'evil', and the Belfast government discriminated against the minority, engaged in gerrymandering and was in breach of elementary justice. At the same time, the use of force would not solve the national problem and there was no basis for any usurpation of the authority of the state.

41 *Dáil Debates*, vol. 153, col. 1349, 30 November 1955.

42 *Dáil Debates*, vol. 153, cols. 1349–50.

43 *Dáil Debates*, vol. 153, col. 1350.

44 *Dáil Debates*, vol. 153, col. 1352.

45 *Dáil Debates*, vol. 153, col. 1352. Earlier, he had said that he did not believe that Partition could be brought to an end by violence 'unsupported by the resources of the State'. The link was clear: Partition was such an evil that even state force could be contemplated to end it. The extent to which MacBride and his colleagues were in contact with Kelly, Christle and others is not clear. Tim Pat Coogan, whose sources were manifold, refers to Dáil deputies parking outside Leinster House with their car boots full of arms and ammunition which they were transporting for the IRA. He adds that, '[o]n at least one occasion a ministerial car was used to transport ammunition for Thompson guns from Kerry to Dublin' (Coogan, *The IRA*, *op. cit.*, p. 375).

46 For the background to schooling in post-independence Ireland, see *Report on the Council of Education*, *op. cit.*, p. 98. Discussing training in citizenship, the authors asserted that, '[n]ext to the religious motive, the most powerful influence in creating and fostering those virtues is the study of history'.

47 On this grotesque incident, see Robert Fisk's succinct summation, *In Time of War: Ireland, Ulster and the Price of Neutrality, 1939–45* (London: André Deutsch, 1983), pp. 461–3. See also Clair Wills, *That Neutral Island* (London: Faber & Faber, 2007), pp. 389–90.

48 The Republic of Ireland Act, 1948, came into operation on Easter Monday 1949.

49 See above p. 770.

50 *Dáil Debates*, vol. 147, col. 173, 28 October 1954. Costello concluded, however, that granting a right of audience would damage the cause of anti-Partitionism.

51 *Dáil Debates*, vol. 147, col. 185.

52 *Dáil Debates*, vol. 147, col. 173.

53 *Dáil Debates*, vol. 164, col. 623, 6 November 1957.

54 *Dáil Debates*, vol. 164, col. 622, 6 November 1957.

55 PRO DO/35/4987, Telegram, HM Ambassador, Dublin, to Commonwealth Relations, 15 December 1956, with draft aide-memoire (subsequently approved). The aide-memoire was a level below a formal protest.

56 5 *Hansard*, vol. 562, cols. 1265–7, 19 December 1956. The declaration was delivered in the midst of great international turmoil. Suez and the Hungarian uprising had brought an increase in tensions with both the Soviet Union and the USA, as well as UN condemnation of Anglo-Franco-Israeli collusion. Suez itself confirmed the drastic diminution in imperial power. That Ireland should, in whatever form, shoulder its way onto the agenda again was both an increase in ministerial concerns and a considerable irritation. Eden (ailing, and in his last weeks as prime minister) reiterated his government's commitment to the maintenance of Northern Ireland's position within the UK; he also praised the 'courage and resource' of the Special Constabulary and the RUC as well as the 'exemplary restraint' of the people of Northern Ireland.

57 See *Northern Whig*, 1 January 1957, 1c and 2a; *Irish News*, 1 January 1957, 1a–h. On Brookeborough, see *Northern Whig*, 2 January 1957, 1a–h; *Irish News*, 2 January 1957, 1a–h; 3 January 1957, 1a–e. Bell gives a detailed account of the Brookeborough attack. He makes the point that while it was an operational shambles it aided the IRA by creating martyrs and thus momentum (*The Secret Army*, *op. cit.*, pp. 297–9). See also Coogan, who interviewed participants on the IRA side (*The IRA*, *op. cit.*, pp. 395–9) and p. 792 above.

58 The consequences of the attacks were now clear to the whole nation, Costello declared. In so far as they originated from within the Republic, the government was obliged to prevent their continuance: 'That duty we are resolved to perform. No Irish

government could permit the rich achievements of past generations to be squandered in the hands of ruthless or reckless men' (NAI JUS/8/1063, Lawless case papers). For Northern comment, see *Northern Whig*, 7 January 1957, 1a–d and 3d–e.

59 *Sunday Press*, 13 January 1957, 5h; *Sunday Independent*, 13 January 1957, 9b.

60 NAI JUS/8/1040, Table of political prisoners and offences. The most common offences were refusing to account for movements, membership of an unlawful organisation and possession of incriminating documents. Possession of firearms and of ammunition were less common. Some men were convicted of more than one type of offence. See also *Dáil Debates*, vol. 164, cols. 608–60, 6 November 1957.

61 *NIPD*, vol. 40, cols. 3188–93, 18 December 1956. The Nationalist opposition absented itself from the House in anticipation of the inevitable statement of condemnation. This may, in fact, have been a beneficial step, since Unionist tempers were understandably high. Nat Minford (who would later be described by Ian Paisley as 'an extreme right-wing unionist'), in particular, was beside himself, referring to 'those damned scoundrels, who are a disgrace to any country', calling for Sinn Féin to be banned from any Northern Ireland election and proclaiming that 'we Protestants run this country and we are going to continue to run it'. The Minister for Home Affairs, William Topping, was more circumspect in his language but left no doubt that government would respond to the raids with all firmness, including detention and internment under the Special Powers Act. The blocking of certain border roads was in hand, and curfews and other measures were under consideration. Topping condemned the inaction of the Dublin government even though recruitment for the IRA had been going on openly 'and bands of armed men have been seen training at camps along the border for all to see'. He also complained that at a meeting in the centre of Dublin the previous night a man had boasted before a large crowd of the part he had played 'in the recent dastardly attack on our police station at Lisnaskea'. Police watched but took no action, and the Irish government had attempted to prevent the publication of any report of the meeting. As Topping saw it, the attempt to muzzle the press on this occasion was further confirmation of Dublin's unresponsiveness to the IRA threat and its desire to conceal this.

62 In a ten-year retrospect, John Costello considered that neither of MacBride's reasons for the withdrawal of Clann na Poblachta's support from the government (the economy and national reunification) was as important as the Coalition's attitude towards the IRA (*Irish Times*, 7 September 1967, 10a–d). For the MacBride motion, see *Northern Whig*, 29 January 1957, 1f–h; *Irish News*, 29 January 1957, 1a–h; 30 January 1957, 1a–h and 2b–c; 31 January 1957, 1d.

63 The distribution of seats was as follows: Fianna Fáil, seventy-eight; Fine Gael, forty; Labour, twelve; Sinn Féin, four; Clann na Talmhan, three. Clann na Poblachta's support collapsed from 51,069 first-preference votes in 1954 to 21,615, securing the party one seat only. (This was not held by Seán MacBride. The party descended into oblivion, winning only one seat in the 1961 and 1965 elections and thereafter nothing.) There was a small increase in the number of Independents in the Dáil, from five to nine seats (*Irish Times*, 8 March 1957, 1a–h).

64 *Irish Times*, 14 January 1957, 1c. This was not an IRA action, but it added appreciably to a sense of armed disorder in the state. During the preliminary hearing for the men accused of the explosives raid there was a demonstration outside the court. This was of such a ferocious nature that witnesses, rather than leave the premises for lunch, asked gardaí to bring food into them. Later, the witnesses were visited in their homes by men who gave them 'friendly' advice about their testimony (NAI JUS/8/1063; see also *Dáil Debates*, vol. 164, cols. 648–9, 6 November 1957).

65 *Irish News*, 4 March 1957, 1d–f and 5c–f; *Northern Whig*, 4 March 1957, 1e–h. Another part of the operation, intended to disable Northern Ireland's railway system, failed to come off.

66 See NAI TAOIS/CAB/2/19, item 5.

67 *Northern Whig*, 5 July 1957, 1a–g and 2b; Irish News, 5 July 1957, 1a–f and (editorial) 2b. Cecil Gregg was aged twenty-seven and Robert Halligan twenty-nine. Gregg was killed by a bullet to the heart.

68 *Irish Times*, 8 July 1957, 1a–d; *Iris Oifigiúil*, Special Issue, 8 July 1957.

69 In its subsequent campaign of protests, Sinn Féin made much of the fact that those arrested were meeting, as it said, as part of the legitimate business of Sinn Féin, a legal organisation (see *United Irishman*, September 1957, 1c–d). De Valera brushed aside as specious the notion that the round-up had been directed at a constitutional organisation and the implication therefore that it had been politically motivated. Those arrested at Sinn Féin HQ were, indeed, leaders of the IRA. They included 'the so-called "Chief of Staff" and so-called "Adjutant General" as well as other members of what they call the "Army Council"'. Was it contended that by joining a movement 'Constitutional, or professing to be so', persons engaged in illegal armed activity could secure immunity? He answered his question: 'If this were so, every group of law-breakers has at hand an easy alibi and a ready sanctuary' (*Irish Press*, 26 July 1957, 4b; *Dáil Debates*, vol. 164, col. 649, 6 November 1957).

70 See *Irish Times*, 8 July 1957, 1a–d; *Irish Independent*, 9 July 1957, 7a–e. At a late point, Charlie Murphy received warning of the impending arrests from a friendly military policeman. He immediately left his house by the back door and, with the assistance of a local garage owner, was able to leave the district. As the car drove past Murphy's house, Special Branch was going in. Murphy phoned a warning to Seán Cronin and sent his brother-in-law to alert the Sinn Féin Árd Chomhairle, which was then ostensibly in session at its Wicklow Street office. It was too late. Arrests had already started, and the messenger was himself detained for a short time (Murphy interview).

71 *Dáil Debates*, vol. 164, col. 608, 6 November 1957. Between December 1956 and 1 July 1957, 103 men were sentenced to between fourteen days and six months under the OASA (*Dáil Debates*, vol. 164, col. 648).

72 NAI JUS/8/1063, Lawless case, government observations on statement of claim, 27 January 1958.

73 *Anglo-Celt*, 3 August 1957, 1c. The full text is given at NAI JUS/8/1040, 'Detention of Members of Unlawful Organisations: Statement by the Taoiseach, Eamon de Valera.' This was poorly received by the republican-inclined section of the press. The *Kerryman* (3 August 1957, 8a–b) condemned de Valera's statement as hypocritical. He should ask himself what he was doing when he was the average age of an internee. The seeds of his party, Fianna Fáil, were sown in the Civil War internment camps. That experience could boomerang: 'what of the youth, eager, idealistic, questioning, who believe that men should do what they say and say what they think. Pity the patriotic youth who are in a minority and who are striving to find their way through the maze without guidance or help.'

74 'IRA Manifesto', August 1957. A copy of this handbill may be found at NAI JUS/8/ 1070, Lawless case, papers.

75 This was a fanciful distinction, in any event. The IRA Chief of Staff, Tony Magan, had been insistent that there should be no sectarian element in the Border Campaign. He directed that engagements with the B-Specials (an exclusively Protestant force) were to be avoided and that the campaign should focus on the British military occupation. But since the British Army was not deployed and the RUC was in paramilitary mode throughout, Mangan's intentions were swept aside. They had been extraordinarily naive and unappreciative of the political and social circumstances prevailing in Northern Ireland (see Boyce, *The Insider, op. cit.*, p. 13, *bis*).

76 *Irish Independent*, 23 January 1957, 8a–b; *Evening Herald*, 22 January 1957, 1c–d. In an exchange with Walter Carroll of the Chief State Solicitor's Office, Lennon asked

whether the *Iris Oifigiúil* proclamation bringing into effect Part V of the OASA ended with the words 'God Save the King'. Carroll asked, 'Am I supposed to comment on that?' Tomás MacCurtáin then shouted from the dock to Lennon, 'Hang that one on us, Sir, and it will do us.' Coogan gives a slightly different account of the incident (*The IRA, op. cit.*, pp. 381–2). Describing Lennon as 'an eccentric but humane judge', he noted that in 1932 Lennon had attacked James Joyce in the American *Catholic World*. The Explosives Act had been brought in to deal with the dynamiting campaign in Britain by a breakaway group of Irish-American Fenians. See Seán McConville, *Irish Political Prisoners 1848–1922: Theatres of War* (London and New York: Routledge, 2003), Chapter 7. There were certain problems in applying the Act in Ireland under the 1937 Constitution, and, on 19 February 1940, an Adaptation Order was submitted to the Dáil to amend the terminology of the Act, removing uncertainties as to its application in Éire (NAI 90/8/166, Department of Justice to Attorney General's Department, 8 February 1940).

77 Coogan, *The IRA, op. cit.*, p. 381. Lennon's judgment did not pass unnoticed in London, which had received from the Dublin Embassy news reports of the case. An official at the CRO noted that the men's discharge had been ordered on the basis 'of what appears to be somewhat specious technicalities'. Whatever protestations of good intent the Dublin government was prepared to give in private, 'it is events such as these which cannot fail to convince Northern Ireland opinion (if it needed convincing) of the existence of collusion between the Republic and the IRA' (PRO DO/35/4992, E. G. Le Tocq to Walsh-Atkins, 30 November 1956).

78 Paddy Terry interview. In the Dáil on 12 June 1957, Oscar Traynor, the Minister for Justice, in response to a question from the tireless Jack McQuillan, explained why the government had called for Lennon's resignation and, in the event that it was not forthcoming, deemed his case subject to Article 5 of the Constitution for removal by means of a process of Dáil and Senate. Judge Lennon's conduct was 'calculated to bring the law into contempt and was inconsistent with the obligation to uphold the Constitution of the State and its laws' which Lennon had assumed when taking office. There could be no doubt about the misconduct since it had occurred in open court, and 'the public would have just cause for complaint of misconduct of this kind were it to be passed over or condoned' (*Dáil Debates*, vol. 162, col. 567, 12 June 1957). See also *Evening Mail*, 25 May 1957, 5g–h. Lennon's background was substantially republican. He had joined the Irish Volunteers in 1914, fought in the 1916 Rising and was interned in Frongoch Camp. In the run-up to the Anglo-Irish War he had again been active and was interned in Mountjoy and Lincoln prisons between May 1918 and March 1919. Upon release he had taken up a position as a justice in the republican courts (see *Irish Independent*, 25 May 1957, 11a–d). The *Irish Independent* subsequently criticised the government's action in Lennon's case as interfering with judicial independence (27 May 1957, 12b–c).

79 Sinn Féin had secured four seats but since it stood by its policy of refusing to enter the Dáil, issues which it might have tackled were taken up by members such as McQuillan and Finucane. Jack McQuillan (1920–98), who had a distinguished Gaelic football background, began a career in the Irish Army as an officer but left it for work in local government. In the general election of 1948 he was returned to the Dáil for Roscommon, under the colours of Clann na Poblachta. When, in 1951, his close colleague Noël Browne resigned as Minister for Health (in the face of Church-driven opposition to his Mother and Child Scheme, opposition which was supported by sections of the medical profession), McQuillan resigned in sympathy from Clann na Poblachta. Thereafter, until 1958, McQuillan sat as an Independent. In May 1958, he and Browne founded the National Progressive Democrats and played a vigorous opposition role in the Dáil. In 1963, both men joined the Labour Party.

McQuillan lost his Roscommon Dáil seat in 1965 but was elected to the Senate; he did not contest the 1969 election. Patrick Finucane (1890–1984) was a member of the Dáil for Kerry North from 1943 until 1969. He stood on behalf of Clann na Talmhan in 1943 and in two successive general elections. He was elected as an Independent in 1951 and, after a spell again with Clann na Talmhan, was returned in three successive general elections as an Independent. In political hue, McQuillan was green and red, Finucane was purely green. Both men were vigorous and resilient debaters.

80 NAI JUS/8/1040, Note to Minister.

81 *Dáil Debates*, vol. 161, col. 99, 26 March 1957.

82 *Dáil Debates*, vol. 164, cols. 638 and 608–56, *passim*, 6 November 1957.

83 *Dáil Debates*, vol. 164, cols. 645–57, *passim*. See also *Irish Independent*, 7 November 1957, 7a–c and 8a–b.

84 *Dáil Debates*, vol. 164, cols. 614–15.

85 See above, p. 803, for a discussion of the derogation procedure which was permitted under a procedure set out in Article 15.

86 *Kerryman*, 10 October 1957, 7a–b.

87 See above, pp. 801–3.

88 The Republic of Ireland was not a member of the Commonwealth, but it had been, and its business remained with the CRO. At a deeper level of perception, the British (and probably the Irish) did not regard each other as fully foreign entities: the relationship was sui generis. When, in British public administration, rationality and convention clashed, there was always a good chance that the latter would be victorious.

89 There are hints that it may have included a covert contact, if not in the IRA then in the republican movement close to it.

90 *Northern Whig*, 12 November 1956, 1d–h. The raids spanned three counties (Armagh, Fermanagh and Tyrone), and that, and the coordination in timing, showed a deal of organisational and command capability. Five of the huts were destroyed by explosives, the sixth by fire (see also *Irish News*, 12 November 1956, 1f–h).

91 PRO DO/35/4992, Sir Alexander Clutterbuck to CRO, 14 November 1956. This is suggestive as to the intelligence available to the Department of External Affairs at this stage and the degree to which it was excluded from information available to other departments of government. It would be surprising indeed if Dublin's Special Branch had not been aware that the attacks had been carried out by the Saor Uladh–Christle group – not least because the IRA would have made sure that they did. But neither at official nor police level were there contacts between the two jurisdictions. The RUC did not inform their garda colleagues about the incidents, nor did they seek assistance.

92 Patrick Anthony Mulcahy was Chief of Staff from 1955 until 1959. He had served in the British Army (Royal Engineers) but joined the Volunteers in 1916. He subsequently fought in the War of Independence and took the pro-Treaty side in the Civil War. He was brother to Richard Mulcahy, one-time (Old) IRA Chief of Staff and, at the time of the initial meeting with Clutterbuck, leader of Fine Gael and Minister for Education. Patrick Mulcahy, therefore, spoke with both military and (at least during the period of coalition government) political authority. Lieutenant General Sir Brian Kimmins had been GOC, Northern Ireland, since 1955. This was his last posting before retirement in 1958.

93 PRO DO/35/4992, Sir Alexander Clutterbuck, HM Ambassador, Dublin, to Ian Maclennan, Assistant Under-Secretary of State, CRO, 15 November 1956.

94 PRO DO/35/4992, Clutterbuck to Maclennan. He also observed that the British were in Mulcahy's debt, and that the fact that he gave the information, despite the IRA not being involved, was 'further proof that the Irish security authorities are genuinely out to play the game with us and to live up to the unwritten assurances which I have previously reported'.

95 PRO DO/35/4992, Clutterbuck to Maclennan.

96 PRO DO/35/4992, Sir Alexander Clutterbuck, HM Ambassador, Dublin, to Ian Maclennan, Assistant Under-Secretary of State, CRO, 22 November 1956. Sweetman had continued, 'I cannot stress too highly the extreme delicacy of the whole business. I know I can rely on you to see on your side that the utmost secrecy is preserved.'

97 PRO DO/35/4992, Clutterbuck to Maclennan, 22 November 1956. The name of the Special Branch man is still redacted in the files available for public consultation. Clutterbuck noted a certain difference of emphasis between police and army intelligence, observing that the latter was inclined to be less concerned about the activities of the splinter group, commenting that this was hardly surprising, since the Army's main concern was 'to watch and contain the IRA itself'.

98 PRO DO/35/4992, E. G. Le Tocq to Walsh-Atkins (CRO), 30 November 1956. In the meantime, Le Tocq proposed to send to the Dublin Embassy a copy of the minutes of the recent meeting between Lord Brookeborough and the Home Secretary (Gwilym Lloyd-George).

99 PRO DO/35/4992, Ian Maclennan to Sir Alexander Clutterbuck, 5 December 1956.

100 PRO DO/35/4987, Ian Maclennan to Sir Austin Strutt, Assistant Under-Secretary of State at the Home Office, 5 December 1956.

101 PRO DO/35/4987, Maclennan to Strutt. Participants had been disarmed, and four men had been charged with the illegal possession of arms. It was regrettable that they had been discharged by the judge 'on what appears to be a very specious technicality'.

102 See PRO CAB/84, Memorandum for Cabinet, 17 December 1956.

103 This expressed 'very great concern' about 'the recrudescence of violence', much of it claimed 'by an organisation which apparently has its headquarters in Dublin but which for some time has been illegal'. Welcoming the 'forthright statement' of 14 December, the British government conveyed its 'anxious hope' that the Irish government's objective would be 'effectively and successfully secured' (PRO DO/35/4987, 15 December 1956). This fell short of a formal protest. See also PRO CAB/129/84, British Cabinet Minutes, 17 December 1956.

104 Clutterbuck (whose credit was inevitably diminished because of his previous sanguinity) was able to secure some toning down of the statement, having argued that the original version would have undermined his position in Dublin.

105 5 *Hansard*, vol. 562, cols. 1265–7, 19 December 1956. Clutterbuck had argued, *inter alia*, that 'it would be fatal for them [the Irish government] to be seen to be acting under pressure from us' (PRO DO/35/4987, Telegram from Sir Alexander Clutterbuck, 19 December 1956).

106 PRO DO/35/4987, aide-memoire of Irish government, 24 December 1956 (transmitted by telegram from the Dublin Embassy).

107 The notes are so comprehensive that it seems probable that the conversation was taped. No fourth person was present, and Clutterbuck could not have taken such detailed minutes of a conversation so ostensibly informal.

108 See pp. 963–5.

109 The note of the Mulcahy, Kimmins and Clutterbuck conversation is to be found at PRO DO/35/4987, Sir Alexander Clutterbuck to Henry Lintott (Deputy Under-Secretary of State at the CRO), 28 January 1957. All details and quotations in this section are taken from this source.

110 PRO DO/35/4987, Clutterbuck to Lintott.

111 PRO DO/35/7811, Clutterbuck to Henry Lintott, 30 January 1957. Seán MacBride's action in withdrawing support from the coalition government was, Sweetman said, 'a stab in the back'. He conjectured, nevertheless, that the general-election campaign

that must inevitably follow might distract attention from the campaign of violence and allow people to let off steam by means of ordinary political agitation.

112 PRO DO/35/7811, Garth Kimber (Counsellor, Dublin Embassy) to G. W. St J. Chadwick, CRO, 21 March 1957.

113 PRO DO/35/7811, G. W. St J. Chadwick, CRO, to B. T. Holmes, Foreign Office, 4 February 1957.

114 See above, pp. 948–51.

115 PRO CAB/128/31, Cabinet Meeting, 1 February 1957.

116 PRO DO/35/4987, Henry Lintott to Sir Alexander Clutterbuck (reviewing communications), 13 February 1957.

117 Lintott's letter clearly followed the terms of a paper jointly prepared for Cabinet by the CRO and Home Office and was approved on 28 January 1957 (PRO DO/35/4987).

118 PRO DO/35/4987, Lintott to Clutterbuck, 13 February 1957. Lintott added that once the make-up of the next Irish government were known, Clutterbuck's instructions would be looked at again. In the meantime, he was to make 'no communications whatsoever' with Irish ministers. It was a mild but telling rebuke, possibly reinforced by the information that a long-delayed appointment of a military attaché to the Dublin Embassy would remove from Clutterbuck some of the work relating to the collection of information about IRA activities.

119 Besides political assurances along these lines, Clutterbuck met Archbishop McQuaid, on 3 May 1957. Although the upsurge in violence (which McQuaid correctly traced back to 1954) had not yet subsided, McQuaid was confident that it had passed its peak. The latest reports he had received (presumably from clergy) showed 'that the IRA had ceased to enjoy any significant support' (PRO DO/35/7811, Sir Alexander Clutterbuck to Sir Gilbert Laithwaite, 7 May 1957).

120 Its four successful candidates were Ruairí Ó Brádaigh (Longford–Westmeath); John Joe McGirl (Sligo–Leitrim); Eighnarchán Ó hAnnluain (Monaghan) and John Joe Rice (Kerry South). McGirl and Brady would each hold the position of IRA Chief of Staff. Rice was an IRA notable in Kerry and Ó hAnnluain was Feargal O'Hanlon's brother.

121 Bell, whose sources for this period seem particularly knowledgeable, estimated that the Border Campaign was costing about £100 per week. This sum supported men, on active service and on the run, and the dependants of both active men and prisoners (The Secret Army, op. cit., p. 320).

122 Irish Times, 14 May 1957, 1d–f.

123 PRO DO/35/7811, Telegram, Sir Alexander Clutterbuck to CRO, 18 May 1957.

124 PRO DO/35/7811, Note from Cuthbert Alport, Parliamentary Under-Secretary of State for Commonwealth Relations, n.d. but c.29 May 1957.

125 See above, p. 793.

126 NIPD, vol. 41, cols. 1951–73, 4 July 1957. There were calls for corporal punishment and for the death penalty for carrying arms; there were also pleas for community restraint. There was no doubt that feelings were running high. The Dublin government was repeatedly condemned for its inadequate response to the raids.

127 PRO DO/35/7812, Secretary for Home Affairs to Sir Austin Strutt, Home Office, 5 July 1957.

128 PRO DO/35/7812, Sir Alexander Clutterbuck to Sir Gilbert Laithwaite, 9 July 1957. He added that the Saturday haul of arrests was just a preliminary and that others would follow. De Valera, he observed, 'whatever his other defects, is not lacking in the courage of his convictions. He has suppressed these people before and has not shrunk from doing so again, even if this can only be achieved by extra-judicial methods which are politically unpalatable.' The killing of Constable Gregg had been a turning point.

129 Frank Aiken had no immediate plans for a visit to London, and could not make one without political cover. Transit to New York for a UN meeting might offer a suitable opportunity.

130 Led by Seán Cronin (the architect of Operation Harvest, whose deployment was a sign of how very depleted the pool of activists had become), the team had intended to break into the armoury. Shots were fired and the raiders had to bolt. They eluded police searchers and made it back to Ireland. Despite having been aborted, the audacity of the raid apparently had a positive effect on IRA morale, and on that of their supporters. *Irish News*, 17 February 1958, 1a–h; 18 February 1958, 1a–c; *Northern Whig*, 17 February 1958, 1b–d.

131 *Irish News*, 17 February 1958, 1a–h; *Northern Whig*, 17 February 1958, 1a.

132 5 *Hansard*, vol. 582, cols. 860–2, 17 February 1958.

133 PRO DO/35/7813, Phelim O'Neill to Cuthbert Alport, 20 February 1958.

134 PRO DO/35/7813, Cuthbert Alport to Phelim O'Neill, 25 February 1958.

135 *Northern Whig*, 15 July 1957, 1b–d; *Irish News*, 15 July 1957, 1a. Much more could have been made of the fact that one of the bombs had been placed at the base of a war memorial (at Trevor Hill, Newry). Had it exploded and destroyed the memorial, this would undoubtedly have added to the combustibility of community relations in the midst of the marching season.

136 A mine was detonated by control wire as Constable Ross came past on a motorcycle. Badly injured, he was able to get to a nearby house, where he waited for an ambulance. He died of his injuries in hospital the following day, leaving a wife and child. See Coogan, *The IRA*, *op. cit.*, p. 416; *Northern Whig*, 17 July 1958, 1f–h. The Coroner for South Armagh described the attack as 'callow and cowardly murder' (*Northern Whig*, 18 July 1958, 1f–h).

137 *Irish News*, 17 July 1958, 1f–g; *Northern Whig*, 17 July 1958, 1f–h.

138 *Irish News*, 17 July 1958, 1f–g; *Northern Whig*, 17 July 1958, 1f–h.

139 PRO DO/35/7814, Minute attached to note of meeting of 29 July 1958 from A. W. Snelling, CRO to Sir Austin Strutt, Home Office, 31 July 1958. Intercommunal violence was prominent in news reports in the form of Turks versus Greeks in Cyprus. Turks being the minority group on that island, the parallels were worryingly close.

140 PRO DO/35/7814. Alport mentioned that when Aiken had recently seen Lord Home, Secretary of State at the CRO, Aiken 'had been shaken' when presented with a dossier showing the encouragement of IRA activities by certain Southern newspapers, including articles on the art of ambush and similar topics. He also said that the CRO would ask the Home Office whether they could gather 'any convincing detailed instances' to be included in representations to Dublin.

141 PRO DO/35/7814, Sir Alexander Clutterbuck to G. W. St J. Chadwick, 4 August 1958. De Valera's recent strong statement to the Dáil about the IRA might, Clutterbuck suggested, form part of an approach to the Irish government (see *Dáil Debates*, vol. 170, cols. 1072–5, 17 July 1958).

142 See pp. 804–5 for the context.

143 PRO DO/35/7814, Sir Alexander Clutterbuck to G. W. St J. Chadwick, 22 August 1958.

144 PRO DO/35/7814, Clutterbuck to Chadwick, 22 August 1958. 'After all', he concluded, 'the Cardinal lives in the North and rarely comes down here, and they no doubt have close relations with him'.

18

INTERNMENT IN THE REPUBLIC OF IRELAND

July 1957–March 1959

The Offences Against the State Act

The killing of Constable Cecil Gregg at Carrive Grove on the night of 3/4 July 1957 was yet another indication that the IRA intended to press on with its campaign and that it had dealt with whatever scruples it may initially have had about shedding Irish blood.[1] The British Army was largely unavailable to be engaged, impregnable in its now heavily guarded bases. The campaign was based on the destruction partly of state and public installations and partly of communication networks. These targets were, however, ancillary to the principal objective: the destruction of crown forces. With the British Army begarrisoned, this could only mean attacks upon the RUC and the Special Constabulary. Any violent attacks in Northern Ireland were liable to increase intercommunal tension, of course, but the targeting of the police and the Special Constabulary was especially apt to do so: these were men with community ties, and, if not quite as vulnerable as the unarmed police of the Republic and Britain, they were regarded as relatively easy targets because they were dispersed and because they served the community in all the routine ways of crime prevention and law enforcement.

For all its ambivalences about Northern Ireland, de Valera's government was firm in its belief in the rule of law. Attacks on and in Northern Ireland threatened domestic and international order, and the killing of police officers was murder, whatever uniform they wore. These and other considerations were debated at a long meeting of the Irish government on Friday, 5 July 1957.[2] It was agreed that the ordinary processes of the law were insufficient to deal with the IRA campaign and that Part II of the OAS(A)A should be brought into operation. Notice of this was given in a special issue of *Iris Oifigiúil* on the following Monday (8 July 1957), and sixty-three arrests were made forthwith.

By this point, internment had been in operation in Northern Ireland for seven months. It was, of course, largely a preventive measure, and, apart from the sometimes unreliable and incomplete intelligence on which it was based, Northern internment was to some extent nullified by the existence of a nearby and effortlessly accessible haven in the Republic. Looking back at his experience of internment from a vantage point of almost two decades, Brian Faulkner claimed that internment had generally been very successful, 'helping to demoralise the terrorists, break up their organisation, exhaust their finances, and improve police intelligence'. He added a coda: 'The fact that it was operated on an all-Ireland basis was of course an important element in its success.'[3]

There is no indication in the surviving papers that the Irish government had this last consideration in view when it turned once more to internment. Political contacts between the two jurisdictions – certainly in the direct sense – were as close to zero as it was possible to get between two geopolitically entwined neighbours. But explicit understandings were not necessary, and both sides had their constituency reasons for avoiding and being able to deny them. What was more important was unspoken intent, and Dublin knew that if the IRA were to be suppressed, as it devoutly wished, the organisation had to be denied Southern redoubt.

In de Valera's Ireland, very little stirred in public administration without the relevant minister knowing. This was particularly the case in sensitive matters such as policing and national security. We may safely infer, therefore, that cross-border cooperation between the police and special branches of the two jurisdictions was conducted with the tacit permission (and possibly encouragement) of higher authority and, ultimately, of politicians. There may have been few paper trails and many nudges, winks, expectant silences and Nelsonian gazes, but there was a strong common interest in order and a shared fear that all kinds of things could unravel.

The Irish government had resisted the introduction of internment as long as it could safely do so. The measure carried an unavoidable weight of opprobrium with a section of Fianna Fáil voters, and the previous coalition government, an always-improbable alliance of right-of-centre and green left, could not have contemplated it. It was, indeed, a De Gaulle measure, and in de Valera Ireland had such a figure. Only those who claimed custodianship of the tabernacle of national interest had the authority to declare it so imperilled that internment was imperative.

Regarded from a different angle, however, internment was a logical extension of hidden North–South cooperation already under way. In the November 1957 debate on internment, Jack McQuillan, the Clann na Poblachta TD, challenged Minister for Justice Oscar Traynor with the claim that high-level Special-Branch conferences had taken place frequently 'on the Border and elsewhere'.[4] It was notable that Traynor did not refute the claim.[5] Nor did he deny or offer evidence to contradict McQuillan's other assertion that 'We have extradition going on behind the scenes quietly, persistently and in a similar manner.' There could not, McQuillan further insisted, be cooperation between 'the occupation forces in the Six Counties and the Special Branch here without the Government knowing it'.[6]

There was indeed a connection between this covert cooperation and internment. McQuillan gave an example of three men taken into custody in a farmhouse in Dunleer, Co. Louth (about halfway between Dundalk and Drogheda, and some twenty miles south of the border) on 8 September 1957. Earlier, Special Branch or Gardaí had discovered a substantial arms dump in a haystack on the farm.

The men, who had addresses in Co. Armagh, in Northern Ireland, were taken to Drogheda Garda Station from which, by some process, they were released the following day and taken to the border. Whether they were pushed across it or simply handed from one policeman to the other, they found themselves in RUC custody, and liable to internment.[7]

The incident, whatever the nature of the communication between the two police forces, and whoever knew of it (or chose not to know) further up the chain of authority and command, demonstrates the greatly increased impact of simultaneously enforced internment, North and South. Police officers operating on the border, or even at some distance from it, who liaised with their counterparts, could determine which force could deal the more effectively with a detained suspect – which, in other words, was in a position more certainly and with the greater ease to remove an activist from circulation for the longer period. In this matter, ironically, the benefits of North–South unity of purpose were demonstrated beyond all doubt.

The Southern door had been closed – never hermetically, of course – and the pressure on the IRA was increased by several notches. Besides internment and North–South cooperation, there was the steady undercut of accumulating Special-Branch intelligence. No one who was active, or even substantially connected, with the IRA could have been unaware of this shift in the balance of forces. Faulkner's claim about demoralisation, disruption, straining finances and enhanced police intelligence would have been hard to dismiss. After the introduction of internment in the Republic, no one who honestly, and with reasonable intelligence, looked to the IRA's campaign objectives could possibly have expected success – or could have imagined that future failure would be less than complete.

Back to the Curragh

Layout and physical conditions

The Curragh received its first internees on Monday, 8 July 1957, following the execution of the sixty-three internment orders mentioned above. At the end of that week, orders were issued against a further fifteen men who had completed sentences under the OASA. Rearrested at the gates of Mountjoy, they (and two men who had been separately arrested and held in the bridewell) were immediately taken to the Curragh.[8] Located in the Detention Barracks (the Glasshouse) for less than a week, by the middle of August, 114 men were behind the wire in the internment camp proper.[9] A total of just over 200 men would pass through internment in the twenty months during which it was enforced.[10] The huts that had been used for the previous (wartime) IRA internment were now derelict, and, in any event, that compound was too large for the anticipated intake. A smaller compound, which had been used for Allied and Axis military internees, on 2 or 3 acres and containing six large residential huts, had been under frantic renovation.[11] Much remained to be done, but, were internment to proceed, this was the only suitable accommodation. The compound contained some fifteen huts, including sheds and other structures in various states of repair and readiness. The men were to be housed in three of the huts, each 163 feet long and 20 feet wide.[12] A fourth billeting hut was built after the camp was occupied.[13] These huts were stripped-down affairs. They had no ceilings, and, at its apex, each roof rose to 13 feet. Within three months of being brought into use, each hut could accommodate just over forty men.[14] The partitions that had divided the huts into cubicles during the war years were removed. The ostensible reason was security, but it is more likely that the alteration had more to do with maximising bed space, avoiding the expense of renovating cubicles and having to erect or renovate other huts. Dispensing with partitions reduced privacy and increased the onerousness of confinement. There was a spare residential hut, and, from time to time, on a rotating basis, one of the occupied huts would be decanted into it, to permit a thorough search of the vacated one.[15] From the outset, staff were particularly on the lookout for signs of tunnelling and for suspicious contraband. Other huts were used for ablutions, latrines and laundry, dining and recreation, and there was a separate chapel.[16] Army engineers and the Department of Works, respectively, had installed a formidable array of security fences and had put the camp into some kind of order.

In contrast to Mountjoy and the Glasshouse, there was considerable freedom of movement within the camp, and security therefore depended on the perimeter. Six barbed-wire fences enclosed the compound, with a seventh, some fifty yards beyond these, acting as a screen to prevent outside inspection, intrusion or the throwing in of contraband. Between the second and third fences, a tank-trap trench, about 10 feet in depth, guarded against tunnelling and was an additional barrier to a surface escape. On the other side of this trench and inside the fourth fence, there was a footpath, constantly patrolled. Initially, the camp had four watchtowers (raised posts, in army parlance), but another three were added to cover the playing field; these were equipped with searchlights. Entry and exit were controlled by an extended sally-port arrangement of four linked barbed-wire gates, each with its own sentry, armed with a sub-machine gun.[17] Another soldier, carrying only a baton, was posted inside the gate. To foil any mass rush on the inner gate, a further barbed-wire barrier inside the compound kept internees at a distance. Additional protection and deterrence were provided by a tower overlooking the inner gate compound and the huts. Guards in the perimeter towers were armed with rifles, allowing accurate fire to be directed to any part of the camp.

After some months, it was decided that a space should be provided for sport and physical recreation. Access to this area, on the camp's south side, was tightly controlled. A footbridge crossed the protective trench. This was festooned with barbed wire, in effect turning it into a covered passageway – a bridge of sighs – through which internees were admitted twice a day. When in use, the field was guarded in the same way as the inner compound and was overlooked by three watchtowers.[18] The assembly of the entire population of the camp, able to move around freely and in groups of various sizes, always compliant to the commands of their officers, presented obvious problems of control and security.

Despite the hurried preparatory work, the camp was not wholly ready when the first men arrived. Army huts are built for an immediate solution rather than for durability, their usual purpose being to augment the permanent, brick-built barracks, to cope with a rapid expansion in army numbers, a new deployment or an influx of prisoners. The renovated huts had been vacant, unheated and without repair and maintenance for some twelve years. When they were brought into use on 13 July 1957, they were still in a fairly dire condition, and for some weeks their residents had to cope with leaky roofs in what some remember as a particularly wet summer and autumn. Beds were shifted away from leaks, and, where leaks could not be entirely avoided, plastic raincoats were used to cover bedding.[19] The huts were originally unlined, and draughts cut through the walls and partitions. The combination of dampness and chill, it was claimed, caused men to suffer from colds.[20]

It was a hardship (and certainly impeded hygiene) that there were no proper laundering or drying facilities. The men had only fourteen washbasins in which to hand-wash their clothes. By the spring of 1958, this amounted to rather less than one basin to each ten men. These basins, it was admitted by the camp authorities, were too shallow in which to wash clothes, and their small number meant that they were in constant demand and could not be used for soaking. There were nine deeper basins at Arbour Hill, and it was proposed to move these to the Curragh, but authority had to be sought at a higher level for the estimated expenditure of £30. Much the same penny-pinching governed the provision of showers. Only ten men could use them at a time, and the boiler heated enough water for only thirty showers a day. Complaints led to the purchase of a second 2-kilowatt immersion heater (a small domestic capacity) but not, it was decided, a second hot-water cylinder. The total amount of hot-water capacity for showering 150 men was therefore not much more than would be available in two family dwellings.[21] Hot water for ablutions other than showering was also said to be a problem by the internees. This supply was met by a 50-gallon cistern, which, again, the camp authorities said was adequate – though this was also on a domestic rather than an institutional scale. The Adjutant General directed that the men be issued with additional galvanised washbasins. This, he said, would encourage economy in the use of hot water.[22]

The drying of laundry was also a problem. For the first several weeks, this important matter of housekeeping and personal hygiene went unaddressed. Only in the accommodation huts, which were overcrowded, could clothes be dried. It takes little imagination to understand the depressing effect of underwear, socks and outerwear draped around accommodation in which, by reason of their custody and the prolonged spell of inclement weather, men were obliged to spend so much time. The complaints put forward by the internees on this (as with other matters of practical importance) were palpably genuine, and, within two or three months of the opening of the camp, hot pipes were installed in the laundry hut, and there were no further complaints about drying facilities.[23]

There were other defects in sanitary provision. The men were locked in at night, and, therefore, access to lavatories was extremely important. The two huts in which they were initially held had flush lavatories. On 1 August 1957, however, one of the huts was evacuated because of fears of tunnelling. The men were held for one night in a hut without plumbed sanitation and had to make do with a bucket – a particularly unsanitary practice that Sinn Féin insisted caused an outbreak of diarrhoea. There was little privacy in the use of this revolting facility, which was cut off from the rest of the hut by little more than some low boarding. Some unfortunate soul drew the evil card of having his bed immediately adjacent to the bucket. Later, each hut had three latrines available, used mainly at night, when the men were locked in. An inspector found these to be 'extremely clean' when he visited. Old-style military palliasses were provided. These consisted of three planks resting on 3-inch-high trestles, the whole no more than about 8 inches above the floor. Blankets were bound to overspill, drag and become soiled by mud tramped in from outside the huts and, inevitably, by traces of urine walked from the lavatory area.[24]

Such a packed and confined space entailed a further hardship (and for some it was considerable): a complete lack of privacy. Daytime freedom of movement had a price in that the open dormitory arrangement denied the respite from others that could be had in a cellular prison.[25] This was the test that many found most challenging. Especially during the first year, when a hut was packed with beds – and the months of low trestles – a man could have touched his neighbour's bed. Tomás Mac Giolla was emphatic that 'there was absolutely no privacy. Privacy was totally out of the question and that was very traumatic for some… There were some people there that lay all day long in their beds or trestles, and never went outside the hut at all.'[26] So disagreeable were conditions that the internees themselves did what they could to provide some relief. With the authorities providing tools and gravel, the men laid walkways between and around the huts, helping to reduce the amount of mud being trampled into the living areas. The Board of Works continued its piecemeal efforts, re-roofing huts and eventually finishing the fitting of flush lavatories and washbasins.

The administrators of prisons and camps (as well as residential homes, hospitals and all similar institutions) have a duty to protect the health and safety of their charges. The issues involved are numerous, touching on all aspects of the environment from water and sewage to kitchen hygiene. The legal and moral responsibility in these matters is particularly heavy in custodial or high-dependency situations since captives are unable to take precautions or make arrangements for themselves in most aspects of their lives. As we have seen, the timber-and-felt construction of the Curragh huts and the exposed, heath-like location, made them particularly vulnerable to fire.[27] At an early point in the reoccupation of the huts, it was apparently agreed between the IRA OC and the Camp Commandant that the threat of fire was such that the hut windows should not be barred. The internees protested when, in November 1958, the authorities began to install strong mesh coverings on the windows. They pointed out that this left only one door through which the occupants would have to escape in the event of a fire.[28] From the surviving papers, it is not clear whether the camp authorities took advice from the fire service, civil or military, or submitted their fire precautions and evacuation plans to expert scrutiny. The handling of such matters has to be considered in context, of course, and health and safety legislation and regulation were not as well developed at the time as they are now. But these were residential units, warmed by solid fuel stoves and occupied by men the majority of whom were smokers. A tragedy was in the offing, as it was in many similar institutional settings.

The Red Cross inspection

The incomplete works and somewhat makeshift conditions gave Sinn Féin an opening, which, with a spurt of deftness generally lacking during the Border Campaign, it was quick to exploit. On 13 August 1957, it issued a statement describing and condemning conditions at the Curragh. The document contended that the huts in which the internees were held were crowded, unclean, leaking and draughty. There was a lack of privacy, and sanitary, ablution and laundry facilities were inadequate. All of this was little more than a statement of facts. The organisation also complained that the last meal of the day was at 5 p.m., which, it insisted, was unreasonable. Inadequate arrangements had been made for recreation and education, for medical, dental and optical treatment and for visits. Clothing and footwear allowances did not meet the genuine needs of internees.[29] De Valera recognised that this was a damaging account of facilities for persons who had not been tried or convicted. He directed that a rebuttal statement be prepared and issued immediately.[30]

The government had to concede the validity of some of the complaints. There had indeed been leaks in the huts and gaps in their timbering, and sanitary facilities had initially been defective. When vacated by workmen, the huts had needed cleaning. It was also true that when there was a crush on visits times were curtailed to fifteen minutes. There was no waiting room for visitors, who had to stand in the open, even in inclement weather. In response to all other complaints, the working party of civil servants and army officers insisted that facilities were adequate or reasonable and that, in the matter of crowding, privacy and clothing, the conditions and allowances were the same as for serving soldiers. All the admitted material defects were rapidly being put right.[31]

Improvement works had been largely completed when the internees managed to contact the Red Cross. An approach to the Irish Red Cross, at the time active in providing support for the Hungarian refugees fleeing from the failed rising of October and November 1956, had initially failed to produce a response. Contacts were then made by the Irish Red Cross, and by others, with the ICRC in Geneva, and, in February 1958, a delegate arrived in Ireland with permission to inspect the Curragh.[32]

The ICRC delegate, Melchior Borsinger, came to the camp on 20 February 1958, accompanied by Mrs Leslie Barry, President of the Irish Red Cross and wife of Tom Barry, the famous republican figure of the Anglo-Irish and Civil wars.[33] She conducted an inspection alongside the ICRC delegate but did not contribute to the report and had no responsibility for its contents.

The ICRC had great moral authority, and the internment of civilians was a particularly sensitive issue just twelve years after the defeat of Nazi Germany. The report of the delegate would remain confidential, but adverse comments of any consequence might leak, to the great embarrassment of de Valera and his government. As it turned out, none of the queries or critical comments seriously condemned conditions at the Curragh, and fears of leakage were unfounded.

In all such circumstances and settings there is room for improvement, and Borsinger's comments, in his report of twenty-six paragraphs, addressed various of the domestic and organisation arrangements at the camp. Some substantiated the complaints lodged by Tomás MacCurtáin, Internee OC, on behalf of the internees, then and later.[34] One of the most interesting points to emerge was that the government had plans to increase the camp's capacity from 155 to 285 if that were necessary.[35] Most of the other observations dealt with the details of institutional life. Camp medical staff consisted of one medical officer and four orderlies (two non-commissioned and two other ranks). Borsinger found this level of medical care to be adequate. Following his observations, nevertheless, two more orderlies were added to the staff. The visit took place during an exceptionally cold spell, and Borsinger had addressed this. The Adjutant General (Colonel Pádraig Ó hAilche) emphasised that even before the visit every man had been issued with six blankets. He also noted that each hut had four stoves, not three, as the ICRC document claimed: heating in the huts was adequate. There were comments on the supply of hot water. The Army's view was that this was satisfactory and allowed every internee to have a bath once a week, the standard allowance for serving soldiers. Internees continued to insist that the hot-water supply failed to meet their needs.[36]

Food, which internees agreed was adequate in quantity and quality, was nevertheless criticised as being monotonous.[37] Colonel Ó hAilche did not demur, simply stating that he was satisfied every effort was being made to address this problem. Complaints about the supply of clothing were simply rejected. The internees' position had always been that they should all be issued with clothing, irrespective of their needs, but the camp command insisted that clothing would be issued only when, in the opinion of the medical officer, a man needed it. Ó hAilche noted that '95% of the internees are able to turn out respectably dressed on occasions (e.g. for Mass and visits). At other times many of them wear ragged and worn clothing... and generally do not try to present a well clothed appearance.'[38]

Borsinger had erred in some relatively minor details. These, quite properly, were pointed out by Ó hAilche. One such arose from Borsinger's misreading of the Statutory Instrument that embodied the camp rules.[39] He had thought that the restriction on letters out of the camp (one per week) also applied to incoming mail. This was not so, Ó hAilche pointed out: there was no restriction on the number of letters and parcels that an internee might receive. Visiting privileges remained at one family visit per month, but since the ICRC inspection, facilities had been improved, and the average duration of visits, even at weekends, was around one hour.

Another set of comments had proved somewhat irritating to the authorities. Borsinger had criticised the equipment available for classes. The rebuttal very much reflected the mind of a soldier of 1950s Ireland: 'A blackboard and sufficient chalk have been issued to internees for classes. The statement that the equipment for classes is inadequate is not understood.' There was much the same briskness in response to complaints about sports facilities. Since the inspection, a larger field had been made available, and Gaelic football and hurling could be played there at agreed times, now four hours a day. Borsinger had also suggested that there should be better gymnastics equipment. A gym had been set up in the recreation hut, but its equipment was 'rudimentary and inadequate', consisting of thin coconut matting, basketballs and medicine balls. Ó hAilche did not see any need for improvement. The internees had never complained about the inadequacy of equipment, 'and seldom use what they have'.

Arrangements for releases and parole had also raised concerns. Ó hAilche noted that from the commencement of internment up to 20 February 1958 (the day of the inspection), twenty-one men had been released. Four of these had been by order of the Minister for Justice, on submission of medical reports.[40] Of the remainder, fourteen had signed the required undertaking; one had given a verbal undertaking; and two had been freed whilst on parole.[41] Parole itself had been a subject of comment, and Ó hAilche noted that up to June 1958 there had been seventy-two applications, of which twenty-two had been refused. Borsinger had had a private meeting with Tomás MacCurtáin, who had raised other matters with him. One of these concerned legal visits, and Ó hAilche noted that of twenty-four such applications two had not been granted.

Borsinger had evidently misunderstood the way in which the daily routine was organised. He suggested that 'Free time and internees' time table could be improved upon.' This led Ó hAilche to point out that since the camp's inception the internees had been left to organise their own free time. Requests for special facilities for instruction, hobbies or recreation were dealt with on their merits. This was so fundamental to the running of the camp and to staff–internee relations that it is surprising it was not grasped by Borsinger. He was probably right to point out that internees' days could have been organised in a more purposeful way, and one can imagine how unimpressed he must have been by the tempo of camp life and by so many ruggedly dressed men apparently lolling around. (Photographs of POW camps during the Second World War were not so different in many cases.) But within a secure perimeter and with the many hours of free association, the organisation of the regime was, on their insistence, substantially in the hands of the internees.

In his private conversation with Borsinger, MacCurtáin had touched on some other matters, but, overall, he seemed to provide backing for the camp administration. Borsinger noted that MacCurtáin had expressed 'no complaints with regard to treatment, discipline or food'.[42] But he had reservations, and one of these surprised Ó hAilche. This was vaguely set out as 'the attitude of officiating clergymen' and presumably referred to some kind of hostility or brusqueness on the part of the clergy. The matter had never been raised with the Camp Commandant or with his predecessor or with any of the camp's officers.[43] It may have been that MacCurtáin was reacting to some sermons or to other comments to which the internees had taken particular exception. Another possibility is that he found the army chaplaincy to be insufficiently zealous. In a report to Ó hAilche nine months after the ICRC visit, the Camp Commandant noted that MacCurtáin had applied for daily mass at the camp. The chaplaincy responded that it had insufficient clergy to provide this service, and MacCurtáin had then appealed to the Bishop of Kildare to provide an extra chaplain.[44]

Aftermath

Although there may have been some minor irritations, and there certainly were points of fact in dispute, the Irish government was no doubt relieved with the tenor of the ICRC report. Had it been strongly critical, and had that leaked, there could well have been inter- and intra-party political reactions, as well as popular concern. As it was, none of the comments rose above the mildly critical, and many of the suggestions could have been made following a visit of inspection to any custodial or similar residential institution, especially one established in a hurry and with a limited lifespan. It is hard when looking at the document and at the character of the observations to believe that Borsinger told MacCurtáin that the camp was worse than British and French equivalents he had visited. It was run as economically as possible with a minimum of expenditure and amenities: this was Ireland in the straitened 1950s. Perhaps it had a drab and depressing atmosphere about it, especially in a bleak late-February Curragh.[45] If the internees looked down at heel or even ragged, that was some reflection of how a section of the Irish population had to live at the time.

But certainly the Irish government was concerned about public opinion and international publicity. This was in part shown by the seriousness with which they treated the ICRC visit. Having concluded his Curragh inspection, Borsinger was invited to meet Taoiseach de Valera, Frank Aiken (Minister for External Affairs) and Kevin Boland (Minister for Defence) as well as camp and command officers and to report verbally on his findings to them. The respect and cooperation was well advised and well rewarded. Borsinger commented on the support and understanding he had received from the authorities and commended the authorities' 'humane attitude towards this problem'.[46]

This was a good report, but the government fretted that it might somehow leak. Assurances had been given by the ICRC, and its approach to reports of this kind was well known. Further enquiries were made, however. The Irish Legation in Berne was instructed to approach the ICRC to discover what was proposed by way of circulation of Borsinger's report. A reassuring reply was received: 'Possibility of leakage most unlikely.' A verbal report had been made to the ICRC's Presidential Committee, and the document itself had been circulated as confidential to the heads of section at the ICRC headquarters. A copy had also been sent to the Irish government and to the Irish Red Cross.[47] As far as can now be ascertained, there were indeed no leakages.

There was, however, an enquiry from an unlikely interested party. The British Embassy in Dublin telephoned the Department of External Affairs. They wanted to know about the background to the ICRC visit. Had it taken place? How had it been arranged? And had the report been given to the Irish government? The British interest arose from a possible ICRC visit to the internees at Belfast Prison. The Secretary at the Ministry of External Affairs agreed that the British should be given the background information they requested.[48] The interest was not academic since the Northern Ireland government had agreed that a like visit should be made to Belfast Prison a few weeks after the Embassy's enquiry.[49]

A year after Borsinger's visit, the ICRC mooted the possibility of another visit to the Curragh. Writing to Mrs Barry, as Chairman of the Irish Red Cross, the President of the ICRC also suggested that on this occasion the visit could be extended to 'persons undergoing sentences at Mountjoy Camp'.[50] The first part of the ICRC request was easily and swiftly resolved. By the time the Department of Defence received the ICRC note, via Mrs Barry, and considered it, the last of the Curragh internees had been released: there was no point in a further visit. And although Borsinger had been allowed to visit both prisoners and internees at Belfast Prison the previous June, the Irish authorities decided not to grant a visit to Dublin's Mountjoy.[51]

The inspection spurred improvements, but a number had already been made.[52] The walls of the huts (only one plank thick) were lined with hardboard to increase insulation. The plank and trestle beds were replaced by more substantial bedsteads identical to those used by the Irish Army.[53] Three blankets were provided for each bed (with more in winter), together with sheets and a pillow. Every man also had a wooden locker for personal property. The adjoining camp (No. 1), used for the 1940s internment, was derelict, and a portion was fenced off for use as a football field. Ruairí Ó Brádaigh noted that the ICRC inspection was a significant difference between internment in the 1940s and in the 1950s, showing the restraining influence of the European Convention on Human Rights and of the Red Cross.[54]

Revolutionaries, even part-timers, frequently do not live the settled lives or have the priorities that allow for basic health maintenance; health and life chances are also significantly affected by social class. Ireland had a very limited amount of publicly funded health provision in the 1950s, and by coming into army custody the internees may have been better off than the average citizen and civil prisoners. Many had apparently neglected their health while at large, through ignorance, indifference or need.[55] Through internment they had, albeit limited, access to army medical, dental and optical services, and where necessary, hospital treatment – all free of charge. Consideration was given, in the first months of internment, to the supply of spectacles, dentures and surgical appliances, which, in the meantime, had to be paid for by the internee or his family.[56] As in a civilian prison, the Camp Commandant was obliged, as far as reasonably possible, to implement any recommendation of the medical officer for health-related changes in the regime.[57] No extra medical staff were recruited, however, and some services were subject to a long delay.[58] Between 8 July 1957 and 25 November 1958, fifteen internees were released on medical grounds.[59]

Whatever urgency Sinn Féin's August 1957 press release may have stimulated in the departments of Defence and Justice, once the moment passed, a certain lethargy and indifference returned to the way in which internee complaints were handled. This was only partly true of the camp authorities, who had to face the irascible, articulate, dogged and formidable Tomás MacCurtáin but who also, quite independently of MacCurtáin's complaints and representations, seem to have had a clear view of their own duty of care. The lines of communication to the Department of Defence, within the department and onward to the Department of Finance, however, made decision-making protracted, at times incomprehensible and nearly always frustrating for all who waited on the outcome. Irish public finances were in a parlous state; austerity was the watchword for officials and ministers alike; and it was hens'-teeth difficult to get authority to spend. Both the departments of Defence and Finance would have been apt to point to the temporary nature of internment: by the autumn of 1958, numbers were already in decline. It was not wholly unreasonable to resist expenditure on a temporary facility soon to be disused.[60]

But camp life had to be lived in the meantime, and some conditions were deteriorating. In November 1958, Camp Commandant B. G. Maguirc wrote a brisk note to the Adjutant General Pádraig Ó hAilche. Tomás MacCurtáin had paid another admonitory visit, and it seemed that there was a deal of substance in the complaints. Thirty-three men required jackets and sixty-six needed trousers. In view of the weather and the bleak and exposed situation of the camp, these were needed at once, but the usual delays meant that they would not be issued until January. There had been an outbreak of influenza the previous year, and Commandant Maguirc suggested that an adequate supply of clothing might avoid a recurrence. In September, he had made proposals for the improvement of food, but decisions were still awaited. A decision was similarly awaited in improvements to hut lighting. MacCurtáin had proposed weekly instead of monthly visits, but this was impossible: 'Staff and accommodation here is NOT sufficient to permit weekly visits from persons regardless of relationship.'[61]

Behind this fairly blunt approach to higher authority by the Commandant lay a fear that MacCurtáin might be forced to adopt more militant tactics because of restiveness among the internees. In his meeting with the Deputy Commandant, MacCurtáin had protested at the poor response to the men's requests and representations. Their complaints centred on making the camp more comfortable as another winter settled in, replacements for clothing that some had worn since their arrest, better food and more visits. Were there no movement on these matters, MacCurtáin had said, 'it was likely that the internees would, in the near future, start a row'. In the course of this, he warned, 'many may be injured and the Camp burned'. He did not wish this to happen, but there were the feelings of many internees who believed that nothing could be achieved without a row (by which he presumably meant a riot). MacCurtáin was no lightweight, and the Deputy Commandant took his warning seriously: 'It may be the beginning of a new policy to gain more favour by the Internee Captain, who is for a long time hard pressed by certain elements to adopt a bolder attitude with the Authorities.'[62]

Staff–internee relations

Staff–inmate relations were relatively good – 'very benign' as one leading internee put it.[63] Borsinger had noted in February 1958 that discipline did not appear to be too harsh and that there was 'no question' of inhuman treatment, cruelty or bullying: 'The attitude of officers, non-commissioned officers and other ranks towards the internees is strictly humane.' Borsinger also noted that both sides 'appear to be doing their utmost to avoid friction'.[64] Eighteen months into internment, Tomás MacCurtáin observed that staff generally wanted to cooperate with internees in the smooth administration of the camp and 'to construe the regulations in a manner giving the prisoners the benefit of any doubt that may exist'.[65] A number of factors contributed to this. Once past its opening weeks, the Border Campaign began very obviously to lose momentum and, thus, credibility. Whatever initial sense of crisis there had been in the Republic dwindled with it. And, as we have seen, the IRA's endlessly repeated refrain was that the Border Campaign was directed exclusively at the British and their Stormont satraps. The personal bitterness, some of it arising from the executions of comrades, that had shaped staff–internee relations during the war years, had gone. In principle, the IRA was committed to the overthrow of the Southern state, but at that point, in the late 1950s, there was a strict no-conflict policy embodied in the IRA's General Army Order No. 8.[66] And Curragh internees did not have the same animus as those in Belfast: 'We felt we were being imprisoned on behalf of the British, but not by them.'[67] Neither was there the same disposition on the side of the authorities to make the experience of imprisonment and internment punitive and deterrent, as in the 1930s and 1940s.[68] There was neither need nor desire to confront the internees by refusing to recognise their command structure or by imposing any conditions, such as menial housekeeping services for the guard, that would have been personally humiliating, implied criminal status and provoked conflict. As in Mountjoy, the internees' OC was an accepted channel for doing business. Indeed, the position was stipulated by the Detention Regulations. Long experience (on both sides of the counter) left ministers in no doubt that one way or the other, and sometimes after a deal of trouble, the internees' command structure would have to be recognised.[69] The authorities called the OC the Internee Captain; internees called him OC – both parties lived with that.[70] This reasonableness extended to prisoners' requests, a well-trampled battleground in earlier years. In a confrontational atmosphere, the point of requests – demands – was not the item, facility or issue in question but the provision of an anchor point from which to kedge forward to another stage of what would always be an open-ended struggle. A request denied could provide the basis for accusations of victimisation and action inside and outside the camp or prison. Were the demand met, another point of purchase would be chosen. By contrast, in the Curragh's more cooperative atmosphere, this strategy and associated battle plans were decidedly irrelevant.

Some of the guards regarded their charges with a degree of respect. Emphasising that the Army had no political views, that soldiers did not consider the politics of the situation and that their duty was to ensure that internees remained in custody, Dick Reade, a military policeman, commented, 'I suppose 90 per cent of them were fine, decent people, just they got mixed up in the wrong trade, as far as we were concerned.' They were, he noted, 'very disciplined people'. A colleague remembered them as 'honourable people'.[71] The internees, Reade contended, did not look on their guards as the enemy: 'They knew you were there with a job to do; we knew what they were there for.' The internees' military command structure made the guards' job easier because they handled complaints through their OC rather than individually and because they understood the military way.[72]

During his visit, the Red Cross delegate had questioned MacCurtáin about the relations between the internees and staff, noting an absence of hostility. MacCurtáin explained that there was no armed conflict in the South.[73] While a relaxed ethos made the camp management go smoothly, such conditions could create other problems, especially if internees and members of staff became too close. The IRA's insistence that all communications with internees should be channelled through its command structure should have avoided that difficulty, and this was reinforced by the authorities' prohibition of any but the exchange of a few necessary words between soldiers and internees. Men living in such conditions, on opposite sides, but neither certain when it would all end, were nevertheless bound to get around the no-speaking rule: the tedium of the days, the monotony of guard duty and common humanity ensured that. Ruairí Ó Brádaigh recalled that soldiers wishing to talk to internees would step into an alcove or recess (where they could not be seen by comrades or superiors). Not looking at the hidden soldier, the internee, were he willing, would listen and reply. Ó Brádaigh used to speak to one man who asked advice about his children and their education.[74] MacCurtáin had ordered that guards were not to be subjected to abusive language or provocation. In the event of a dispute, no altercation was allowed. The internee had to report the matter to his OC, who would, were it deemed sufficiently important, take it up with the camp authorities.[75]

Speaking in the Dáil for more than two hours about the wickedness of internment, in conception as well as execution, Jack McQuillan found very little upon which to comment favourably, and certainly nothing to praise. The one exception was the camp staff, whom he was 'not for a moment criticising'. They were merely carrying out the duties imposed upon them and (he added a significant phrase) 'to my knowledge' were doing so 'as favourably as they possibly can from the internees' point of view'. (Since McQuillan had never been in the camp, his knowledge was entirely derived from a brief whose ultimate origin was the IRA.) The staff, he noted, were trying to make things as easy as possible, but if they did not have the necessary facilities, they could do nothing about it.[76]

Looking back on internment, Tomás Mac Giolla concluded that though they did their duty, soldiers were ambivalent about it. His escort on the way down from Mountjoy gave him the impression that they did not consider internment to be their business and did not want to be involved in it. He wondered nevertheless whether they had been picked because they did not share a general army distaste for the work: perhaps by involving the Army at that juncture, the government had got it wrong, and, in consequence, internment had to be ended even though the Border Campaign was continuing. There may have been a crumb of comfort for an IRA man in this line of reasoning, but it hardly holds, since the Irish Army did not have the luxury of selection: it cobbled together the Curragh staff as best it could. But, given the flimsy and speculative nature of their enterprise, it is understandable that in the 1950s a leading IRA figure, and apparently a number of his colleagues, hoped that some distinction could be drawn between army and government.[77]

Life in internment

Ireland was at peace, and its standard of living, low by the standards of more developed nations, had nevertheless advanced through the post-war years. Nationally and internationally the country was more secure than it had ever been. A number of aspects of life in the Curragh were in consequence superior to those of the 1940s. The camp did not skimp on food, though it followed the usual institutional practice and offered little variety.[78] Internees received a slightly enhanced version of the dietary scale of private soldiers in the Irish Army. In addition to camp rations, food could be sent in, and the huts were equipped with very basic cooking facilities.

The contrast between the custodianship of the civil authorities and the Army was wholly favourable to the latter. Noel Kavanagh remembered:

> In the 'Joy' it was terrible initially, it was a culture shock… you got a can of lamb stew with about an inch of grease on top of it… it was terrible. But by goodness I can tell you after a month in there, you'd eat the can and all! But down at the Army Base in the Curragh the first decent breakfast we got was when we arrived… they sat us down and gave us an Army breakfast, and we got an Army lunch and an Army dinner and we got Army food right through the internment. We had no problems with the food.[79]

Any experienced prison administrator knows that the grouses and disaffections of captivity whirl around and periodically light upon a predictable set of issues, food especially. Army rations helped to establish a sound and politically justifiable basis for the peaceful management of the Curragh.[80] By October 1957, the camp administration was able to report that there had been no complaints about the food or about how it was cooked.[81] A year later, opinion was rather more divided. There were objections to its monotony and to the lack of fresh ingredients such as vegetables, tomatoes and cheese. One man wrote to his mother that after his experience with boarding-house food, dishes needed to be particularly bad before he refused them, but some Curragh offerings were beyond even his capacity: 'The Free State soldiers got somewhat the same as we do, but as one man pointed out, they are paid to eat it.'[82] A month later, however, another man was reassuring his mother about camp conditions: 'Most of the food here is very good for a prison and even though none of it is as nice as we would get at home, it is eatable in any case.'[83]

Apart from temperament, the other significant factor affecting one's reaction to imprisonment and internment was prior experience, both immediate and general. Charlie Murphy had grown up in the testing times of the 1940s, and, even with an ingenious, intelligent and resourceful mother, his family had experienced 'really hard circumstances'. This background made life at the Curragh 'relatively tolerable'. Like others, he initially found the camp something of a haven, having been on the run for the previous eighteen months: 'it was something of a surprise to have regular meals and a roof over your head – to be able to sleep in bed every night and be dry, and not be a burden on the sometimes poor people who put them up'.[84]

Mick Ryan, Director of Operations in the campaign's closing and utterly hopeless phases, recalled that the condemnation of the Curragh as a concentration camp (*campa na geibheann*) was 'because it was wired in, that kind of stuff'.[85] When Ryan came into custody he had been operating on the run along the Cavan–Monaghan border and in Leitrim. Host families were as generous as possible, but they did not have much:

> It was basic bread and tea most of the time, and you would be glad to get it – and then you would be staying in barns and stuff like that and you would go out of a house at night to maybe lie in ambush somewhere and you wouldn't have a sandwich with you, or a flask of tea, and you could be there all night and then maybe break up and head back wet and soaking into a barn. And you would be waiting then for someone to bring you a cup of tea, if the house was friendly. But in the camp, as far as I know, we had rations that were similar enough to the army personnel. I ate everything that was put in front of me.[86]

A full stomach and a good and safe night's sleep went some way, at least initially, to ease the pains of captivity and certainly made it hard to raise a head of steam against the inoffensive guards.

Concurrent with its proclamation of reactivation of Part II of the OASA, the government also issued and brought into force the Detention Regulations,

1957.[87] This document comprised some sixty-four paragraphs and set out the nature of the camp, its regime, the behaviour required of internees and the authorised privileges and punishments. It governed the administration of the Curragh Camp and provided the legal basis for the authority and actions of its commandant. Given that those who were to be detained were uncharged, untried and in custody through executive rather than judicial action, it was important that as many aspects as possible of the regime should be explicitly stated. This provided a measure of protection for the internees as well as for their custodians. The latter wanted to know the exact delineation of their powers and immunities, both for operational reasons and because of the possibility of a civil suit and liability.

The most sensitive part of the Regulations set out a variety of offences against camp discipline and provided for sanctions and punishments. Behaviours that were prohibited included infringements of security but beyond that simply set out the basics that would be required of any body of men or women living in a collectivity, albeit one which was custodial. Paragraph 30 listed offences in fourteen sub-sections. There was a catch-all provision, used in most prison systems and known as GOAD, that is, any action which offends against *good order and discipline*. This confers discretion on the administrator of a custodial institution to deal with any action not specifically prohibited in the regulations but which, nevertheless, undermines discipline. Given the scope for subversive or challenging actions, and the capabilities of human inventiveness, the managerial leeway is essential: the scope for barrack-room lawyers would otherwise be limitless.

As much as the Irish government, through its officials, drew upon precedent and experience in devising its regulations, so also did the IRA. Its experience of internment was as long as that of the Irish and its predecessor British governments. Apart from the matter of custody itself (at least in theory the IRA would have committed its members to escape from and certainly to subvert custody), there was a deal of congruence between the objectives and even interests of captors and captives. The IRA, above all, had to maintain its imprisoned and interned members as a disciplined body. For this there had to be order, submission to the collective will, basic standards of personal hygiene and decency, the avoidance of disorder and tumult and civilised relations between all members of the organisation. These requirements, although from a different source of authority, were almost identical with those of the institution.

Given MacCurtáin's determination to avoid unnecessary trouble with the camp authorities, their reciprocation, and the IRA's own strong code of discipline, few internees broke the camp's rules and regulations. Formal disciplinary procedures and punishments were available, but no action of this kind could be taken against an internee by anyone other than the Camp Commandant or, were he absent, his deputy.[88] All disciplinary matters entailed formal hearings, with evidence being offered and subject to challenge. A full record had to be kept of findings and any punishments awarded by the Commandant.[89] Since the men were untried detainees, not subject to penal discipline, sanctions were limited. The most severe was close (solitary) confinement, which would be served in the detention barracks and which could not exceed three days.[90] A period of forfeiture of various facilities, such as parcels, letters, visits and recreation could also be ordered. More severe, at least in theory, was deprivation of the mattress. These punishments were also limited to three days.[91] By early October 1957, the Commandant had dealt with sixteen breaches of camp discipline, a rate not much more than one a week for the entire camp. It is not clear from the records, but it is probable that some of these cases went no further than reprimand or warning.[92]

It would have been agreed by all that the acts and omissions that were prohibited and punishable were such that no residential community could have tolerated them. They included disobedience and disrespect of any member of staff or visitor; irreverent behaviour at divine service or prayers; abusive, insolent, threatening or improper language; indecent language, acts or gestures; assault; leaving cell, hut, room or place of work without permission; making unnecessary noise ('or gives any unnecessary trouble'); damaging or defacing any part of the camp; committing any nuisance; and possessing any prohibited article. Escape or conniving at another's escape were, not surprisingly, prohibited, as was attempting to do any of the prohibited actions. In addition to the actions of individuals, there was a regulation covering 'collective insubordination' to deal with which the Commandant had available to him all the punishments set out for individuals. Those living forty-three to a hut, cheek by jowl, would have agreed their own Regulation No. 17, had it not been provided. This required internees to keep themselves clean and decent in their person and to obey orders as to washing, bathing and hair-cutting. Every man was also obliged to keep his cell, utensils, clothing and bedding 'clean and neatly arranged'.[93] Given what M. Borsinger saw at the Curragh – a ragged peat-bog army – the sartorial regulations appear to have been liberally interpreted and laxly enforced.

As in any prison, the threat of sanctions depended in part on what a man had to lose. Contact with home was perhaps the most important of privileges. As noted, internees were entitled to send out one letter a week, and the Commandant could allow more; there was no restriction on incoming post. A man could receive one visit a month from relatives and more at the discretion of the Adjutant General; he could also receive visits (no limit was mentioned) from lawyers.[94] At the discretion of the Minister for Defence, visits were allowed from persons other than relatives and lawyers. The administration insisted that no genuine application had been refused, although 'a particular solicitor' had for security reasons been refused visits.[95]

Internment was intended, above all, to disrupt IRA activities and to curtail the activities of messengers and couriers, and so visiting privileges and arrangements were tightly controlled. The allowance itself was miserly. These were untried men, who by analogy should have received the same allowance of visits as those available to remand prisoners. If that were impracticably high because of its staffing requirements and army resources, an entitlement that was at least approximate to that scale would have been appropriate. It is noteworthy that the

IRA, although it would later oppose a tightening-up of visiting arrangements, did not make the allowance itself an issue. Given that relatives sometimes used visits to urge their men to sign out or to tell them about home conditions, it might well have suited MacCurtáin and the IRA camp command, intent on keeping the internees together, to have a low rate of visiting. And perhaps there was a more humane consideration. The camp, whilst not remote, was an inconvenient and relatively expensive destination: families had burdens and problems enough.

The monthly visit was restricted to relatives (a maximum of three on each occasion), but since the degree of kinship was not specified and no procedure was laid down for verifying family connections, there was scope for abuse or evasion.[96] Requests for additional visits had to go to the Adjutant General's office for decision and reasons had to be given. A man's behaviour in the camp was noted on the application. The Minister's authority was necessary for a visit from persons other than relatives. These applications were first routed through military intelligence and the Special Branch. There was concern that some legal practitioners would be willing to act as IRA couriers, and there were past instances of this, as members of the government were well aware. A solicitor had to submit his application in writing, specifying the precise legal business he wished to discuss with his client. This went to the Adjutant General and, if granted, was subject to the condition that the legal practitioner signed an undertaking on his professional honour 'that the interview… will be concerned solely with the legal business in respect of which the internee made application'.[97]

In the last months of internment, the Commandant attempted to tighten up visiting procedures. The arrangements had been that relatives' visits were not prearranged, and, unlike the procedure in a civilian prison, no visiting order was required. Visitors simply turned up, stated that they were relatives and filled out a form. If the man were entitled to a visit, and wished to see them, they were admitted. For reasons not detailed in the files, and without consultation with his superiors or the internees, the Commandant decided to change the rules. This decision was made just before Christmas 1958, to come into operation on 12 January 1959. The IRA issued a protest about restrictive measures imposed on visits, including the impending new requirements. By 12 January no applications had been received, and it looked as though there would be a non-cooperation protest. A few applications came in at the last moment, and Tomás MacCurtáin advised the men at a camp general meeting to comply with the new requirements. The Commandant received information, however, that some were not disposed to follow this advice.

At this point, army intelligence began to be alarmed, taking the view that a confrontation was unnecessary and unprofitable, given that the Curragh was now the IRA's only effective publicity tool. After a deal of discussion, the issue was referred to the Adjutant General. The Commandant adhered to his decision, but Ó hAilche, offering him the face-saver that he did not need to tell the internees that the order had been withdrawn, concluded that the proposals were too rigid and that in exceptional circumstances visits that had not been prearranged should be allowed. The Commandant still resisted, and a direct order was then issued.[98] Tomás MacCurtáin's reaction was somewhat curious, but he may have concluded that were the men to lose a battle with the authorities the rate of defection from the ranks could increase, with men either signing out or moving over to the splinter group. There may also have been a realisation on the part of the IRA that by January 1959 its resources were so depleted and the public so indifferent that a dispute over visiting regulations at the Curragh was unlikely to rally supporters and sympathisers.

Despite the no-confrontation policy, there was a certain amount of testing of the camp authorities, but this never assumed sufficient mass and weight to drive a campaign such as those waged in earlier (and indeed later) years. Various minor requests had been made and granted at Mountjoy, and it was evident that for broader political reasons, as well as reciprocation of MacCurtáin's cooperation, the authorities had decided to go as far as possible to be accommodating, within the limits of their budget and, of course, security and control. There was a deal of irony in one request. In Mountjoy there was an absolute insistence that IRA men would never accept prison uniforms, even though they had been convicted. At the Curragh, they insisted that suitable clothing be provided, on the basis that they should be spared the expense of replacing their own civilian clothing as it wore out. The relevant regulation made no mention of providing clothing at public expense, referring only to 'supplies of necessary clothing by friends'.[99] The request was nevertheless granted, and outfits of brown-coloured clothing, called 'Martin Henrys' were provided.[100] Some in authority may have drawn a deal of sly satisfaction from the fact that parts of these outfits were also issued to mental patients in public institutions.[101] Some internees had been arrested on active service on the border in makeshift quasi-military clothing, unsuitable for camp life. Others were simply poor and consequently ill-clothed. Yet others may have wished to conserve their own clothes and to take what the state provided. Boots were the main item requested. By mid-October 1957, the camp command reported that it had issued 106 pairs, fifty-four of which were part-worn. Only three jackets and fifteen pairs of trousers had been provided during that time.[102] But the largesse was not restricted to clothing. Seán Cronin, architect of Operation Harvest, and sometime Chief of Staff, had developed a taste for coffee during his years in the USA. At that time, coffee was not a widespread taste in tea-drinking Ireland. This did not stop it being raised as an official request from the internees – and it was granted.[103]

The austerity of the times, however, meant that some requests were turned down. As part of his long-running attritional campaign against internment, the Clann na Poblachta TD Jack McQuillan asked whether winter clothing, razor blades, stamps and stationery and toothpaste could be provided at public expense. The reply from Kevin Boland (Minister for Defence) was negative on each point. Internees should provide their own clothing and could additionally be supplied by friends; cases of necessity were dealt with by the camp medical officers, as they arose.

Postage for letters had to come from internees' private funds. Where there was no credit in their account, letters were allowed to go out unstamped.[104] (This meant that the addressee would have to pay postage, plus a small surcharge.) Razor blades, stationery and toothpaste also had to be paid for by the internees, and Boland had no intention of changing that arrangement.[105]

In the outcome of requests and demands, much depended on the chain of responsibility for decision-making. Where other army or civil departments were involved, it was difficult to effect improvements in the camp. As we have already noted, even modest expenditure additional to the camp's budget required protracted exchanges and, it sometimes seemed, interminable delay in decision-making; certainly the difficulty in getting a decision, even a negative one, was usually not proportionate to the sum of money involved. The internees complained, more or less from the outset, that there was insufficient hot water for cooking, laundry and showering. As the population of the camp increased in the spring of 1958, the continuing inadequacy of these facilities became more apparent. Improvements were made, but always at a minimum level.[106]

As we have noted, the possibility of day-to-day friction and conflict was reduced by the limited interactions between internees and staff. Food was collected by internee orderlies and served by them in the dining hut. Internees also did the cleaning-up and dishwashing. The only regular contact most individuals had with their guards was their escort to and from visits. The visiting rooms were outside the perimeter fence. Remarkably, neither the internees nor their visitors were searched.[107] A certain amount of contraband was bound to be passed, but since the men were not under penal discipline and could legitimately receive a wide range of goods, and since there was no question of an armed attack on staff, the no-search policy was a reasonable way of reducing the occasions for conflict, with apparently little risk.[108]

Education, recreation and amenities

The internee command was conscious of the need to keep the men occupied, as constructively as possible. Internment, the more experienced knew, was going to be a protracted grind, and the sense of uselessness had to be kept at bay. There may have been some attempts to consolidate the basic instruction and orientation that all received on joining the IRA, but there is no indication of covert military training in the documents that survive, or in the recollections of former internees we have interviewed. Among the camp leaders there were some who were teachers or instructors, and a substantial programme of classes could be mounted, morning, afternoon and evening. These were set out for the approval of the Camp Command in a *clár na ranganna* (schedule of classes).[109]

Recreation and exercise times varied with the season, being set officially as 9 a.m. until sundown. During the short winter evenings, the men were allowed to move around in a restricted area close to their huts, from dusk until 9 p.m. Morning classes began at 9.45 a.m. and ran every day of the week, including

Sunday. Servicing such an extensive programme (preparing and conducting classes and assisting class members) required a great deal of commitment and energy from the tutors. Six Irish-language classes were offered, Monday to Friday, including three for beginners.[110] Junior English was also offered on those days, with one session for more advanced students on Tuesday mornings and Friday evenings. There were four sessions of Irish dancing each week, and classes were available on public speaking, economics, electrical engineering, journalism and Irish history. On Sunday mornings there were social-study groups, and one day each week a visiting Jesuit priest gave a class on social ethics. On one evening, the Fáinne group (for those more advanced in the Irish language) met, and on Tuesday evenings the Sinn Féin cumann held its meetings.[111] Alongside all these activities, the various housekeeping duties of the camp had to be performed, with tasks allocated by rota by the internee command.

There were discussions and debates, mainly on historical matters. Noel Kavanagh remembered that political debates were on a 'very, very low-level'. Reviewing his notes of the discussions after release he reflected 'My God, they weren't up to much!' Despite the high unemployment level in the country, destructive emigration levels and areas of grinding urban poverty, the political debates remained 'very airy-fairy'.[112]

In addition to classes and discussions, there were the perennially popular craft and leatherwork classes and groups. Handicrafts were a major feature of camp life, apparently concentrated on woven woollen belts (*croises*), Celtic crosses or ornamented wallets. These were sent outside, either as keepsakes for family or friends or to raise funds for prisoners' relief.[113] Rug-making was available, and, after some time, woodworking classes were added to the curriculum. Some of Tim Pat Coogan's interviewees reported that, the wire fences apart, the place was more like a factory than a camp.[114]

As the internees entered their first winter, MacCurtáin approached the camp authorities with proposals for entertainments. The principal one was a weekly film show. The proposal was backed by the Commandant and went to the Secretary of the Department of Defence with the further approval of the Adjutant General. The Army had projectors and trained operators, and the main cost was the hiring of the films and whatever extra electricity was involved – no great expense. The request was accordingly agreed.[115] A more cautious approach was taken a week or so later when MacCurtáin asked permission to allow a theatrical group, Coisde Leasa, to organise a Christmas concert. More details were required by the Adjutant General ('Internee MacCurtáin to inform you what exactly the proposal entails'). There was concern that the entertainment should not become a political event.[116] This would be a constant issue in all the requests for entertainment, education and hobbies. The camp authorities were perhaps being over-cautious and under-imaginative. The experience of those in charge of POW camps during the Second World War showed that camp concerts and live entertainments raised morale, gave an outlet for energies otherwise frustrated and generally stabilised staff–inmate relations.[117]

In putting forward proposals, MacCurtáin constantly probed the limits of his own authority and the Camp Commandant's willingness to deal with him. He wanted to be allowed to meet an outside prisoners' welfare committee (an IRA sponsored and controlled body), but this was blocked by the Commandant: all dealings with outside bodies had to be done through him. Likewise, emphasising his pastoral role as OC, MacCurtáin asked to be allowed to visit internees who had been removed to the military hospital. This was turned down because, Colonel R. J. Callanan, Director of Intelligence noted, MacCurtáin had abused the privilege on a previous visit to the hospital 'by deterring another internee from accepting parole which had been granted to him'.[118]

The Army was at first disposed to reject the internees' request for a library.[119] In early September 1957, however, Traynor approved of classes in Irish, journalism and leatherworking, adding, 'I am anxious that everything possible should be done to provide suitable reading material and if a library service can be provided from any source this should be done.'[120] This settled the matter, and the following month an informal approach was made to Kildare County Council (the relevant local authority) for the supply of library books.[121] Despite strong ministerial support, the request dawdled through the various bureaucracies. It was not until January 1958 that the operating conditions for the library were agreed, and a formal request was submitted to Kildare County Council for the location of a sub-branch at the camp. The library began to operate in the early spring of 1958. The initial consignment of books somewhat predictably turned out to be the county library service's discards. These were sent back, and a detailed request list was drawn up by Seán Cronin, Noel Kavanagh, Bob Russell and Tomás MacCurtáin. Literary works, from the Irish revival, to English classics, to Turgenev and the other Russians were requested, and delivered. The choices were high-minded, reflecting not just the tastes but also the hopes of the selectors and their desire to educate their comrades. Pulp fiction seems to have had no place in the collection. One-third of the refectory hut was converted into a library (equipped with a fireplace). Internees could read there or they could sign a book out. At the end, with the camp closing, the librarian Noel Kavanagh found that only two volumes had gone missing.[122] In the early autumn of 1958, however, there was a hitch in the arrangements with Kildare County Council. Books returned in September had still not been replaced by November, leaving the stock in the camp quite depleted. Repeated letters from the internees to the Council had no effect, and the camp authorities, for some reason now not clear, refused to intervene.[123]

Sports were a particularly useful outlet for pent-up energies and frustrated emotions, and there were inter-hut competitions in football and hurling. The GAA had, for some, been a gateway into the IRA, and some men had played for their counties and had set high standards. There was also a deal of music. Songs were taught and much enjoyed (including a strong representation of republican ballads, no doubt). There were several good singers as well as a number of accomplished instrumentalists. A further outlet was given in gardening – vegetables rather than flowers. Dick Reade remembered how attentive his charges were to this patch; the marrows in particular were very big.[124] MacCurtáin was keen to keep the men in a good state of health – perhaps the most basic obligation of a soldier. Paradoxically, this turned out to be as difficult at the Curragh as it was in Mountjoy. There was certainly more freedom of movement and many more opportunities for exercise, but camp life also allowed men to do very little, 'not to move at all, to flop about and be stupid'.[125]

The ostensibly wholesome recreation of gardening opened the way to one of the common temptations of imprisonment. Forgoing tarts, internee brewmasters decided that rhubarb could better be used as a basis for home-brewed alcohol. Mac Giolla remembered it as 'desperate stuff' (adding 'I believe'). Such brews became something of a disciplinary and morale problem. Other internees had their alcohol smuggled in to them. One man was always drinking lemonade out of small bottles, which, somehow, he had contrived to have generously mixed with alcohol. The internees' command could not report him to the camp authorities but had to find some other way to manage to control his consumption of 'lemonade'.[126]

As in a civil prison, no cash circulated. Since the early nineteenth century, gaolers had seen this as a guard against a number of possible breaches of security and discipline: subornation of staff, escapes, extortion, gambling and the like. Ordinary prisoners on remand at Mountjoy and elsewhere could ask for approved purchases to be made from their private cash. The Curragh had a slightly different scheme. Money could only be sent in to the authorities, who banked it, issuing the recipient with equivalent tokens, known as camp coinage. With this specie, food, cigarettes and other goods could be bought from a van that visited the camp daily. Ordinary prisons invariably insist that purchases have to be made as a book transaction only, to avoid circulating an alternative currency with its attendant evils, including extortion. These problems apparently did not arise in the camp, given the character of the internees and the scrutiny and discipline of the IRA.

A cash control and accounting system that would protect against abuse and any suggestion of impropriety was essential, and the camp authorities set up a fairly complex procedure for receiving, holding and disbursing funds. Money received in letters addressed to internees was handed to the accounts' officer, who provided a receipt. The censor then authorised a credit to the internee's account. Money handed in on visits, or which the internee had when he arrived at the camp, was handled in the same way. Total receipts by the censor's office were checked by balancing the internees' account and general account books. Internees could use their credits in two ways. A purchase could be made on the authority of the censor, or the internee could use his camp coinage to make canteen purchases.[127] Internees could check their accounts weekly, and all received a twice-monthly statement. It was essential to protect against mistakes and any accusation or actual instances of misappropriation. Soldiers stealing from internees would not have made a pleasant story, and even an apparatus as feeble as Sinn Féin's could have made much of it, with much justification. To ensure that camp coinage was kept under control, no more than £100 was put into circulation.[128]

Apart from private cash, there was a camp fund, to provide additional shared amenities. This derived from profits on internees' purchases in the camp canteen, which, it was agreed from the outset, should be at a rate of 4 per cent of turnover. By May 1958, £70 had accrued in this account. Several camp purchases were then made by MacCurtáin, but a balance of about £50 was retained in the account. In the spring of 1958, Hut 5 was opened to provide additional accommodation for an expected additional influx of internees. The other huts had, by this time, each been equipped with electrical water heaters to allow the internees to make tea and other hot beverages. The cost of this equipment had been met by prisoner-support organisations. MacCurtáin applied to use some of the internees' camp fund to provide a water heater for Hut 5. Considering himself bound by a military standing instruction of 1958 which did not authorise the purchase of this equipment, the Commandant refused to allow the purchase. This angered MacCurtáin, who argued, not unreasonably, that the fund had been accumulated by the prisoners' purchases and was their property. It took a protest by the internees to shift the Commandant. His solution was deft, if late: MacCurtáin was allowed to seek permission to purchase items for handicraft and would buy a water-heater for the preparation of papier mâché. This boiler could then serve a dual function. The request (probably in an amount not exceeding £30) went first to the Adjutant General and then to the Minister for Defence: both approved the purchase of the boiler, for papier mâché, of course.[129]

Religion

As with chaplains in civil prisons, and as we have previously noted, the Curragh chaplain was subject to two systems of authority: he was licensed and assigned by the bishop and employed and remunerated by the secular authority, civil or military. There are a number of reasons why membership of the IRA would stand as no impediment to receipt of the sacraments at the Curragh but would continue to be a bar at Mountjoy prison. A different episcopal approach, possibly implicit rather than explicit, was one explanation; the conscience and determination of the chaplain was another. But it is also possible that the army authorities made it clear that they wanted a quiet life at the Curragh and would not be pleased by over-punctiliousness by the chaplain in this aspect of his duties. The stance of the state, after all, was that everyone at the Curragh was an active member of the IRA, whose custody by non-judicial authority was essential for national safety and international security. But to have this statement of necessity deprive all at the camp of the spiritual consolations and disciplines of their faith was politically inexpedient, managerially counter-productive and perhaps morally unacceptable to a government composed almost entirely of practising Roman Catholics, who, as private individuals, accepted the centrality of the sacraments to their lives. 'Don't ask; don't tell' is a compromise that enables many organisations to avoid conflict and turmoil – and so it was here.

There was a regulatory background to the chaplain's ministrations, and this may also have been significant. The Detention Regulations emphasised that these duties had to be carried out in a manner that supported the camp administration. The chaplain was obliged to conform with the camp rules and regulations, 'and shall not interfere with the working of them as regards the safe custody, discipline and labour of the internees but shall support the Commandant in the maintenance thereof'.[130] This meant that even had he been so inclined the chaplain could not have relied on his judgement of spiritual or moral necessity in a way that disrupted the running of the camp. Withholding the sacraments could well have provided a cause for disruption; it would also have allowed the internees, uncharged and unconvicted, to emphasise to the broader community how thoroughly and vindictively they were being subjugated and oppressed.

The prescribed duties and subordinate position of the chaplain did not pass unchallenged in the outside world, even though Tomás MacCurtáin may have been happy enough with the resultant fudge in the camp. Jack McQuillan, as part of his lengthy Dáil speech on internment on 6 November 1957, insisted that the regulation dealing with the chaplain was questionable. Having spelt out the chaplain's obligation to support the camp administration and regime, he asked, with a flourish of incredulous sarcasm, 'Is that not a nice function for a chaplain?'[131]

That nuance was irrelevant to MacCurtáin, whose priority was to hold his men together and to maintain their morale. Indeed, religion was as prominent in camp as in national life, North and South, and he used his authority to ensure a maximum turnout for Sunday church parades. Noel Kavanagh recalled, however, that as time went by there was a falling-off in attendance. A religious retreat was organised, bringing a preacher into the camp to deliver a series of sermons and to conduct special devotions and services. The purpose of this was to remind and instruct internees regarding certain important principles of their religion and to remotivate them. Attendance failed to reach expected levels.[132] That the Roman Catholic authorities were prepared to countenance such a venture, however, apparently indicated a more forgiving and liberal attitude (at least at the pastoral level) than they had shown during the earlier periods of political imprisonment and internment. At the same time, however, the hierarchy did not waver in its public condemnation of the IRA and the Border Campaign.[133] Ruairí Ó Brádaigh, who had served a sentence of six months at Mountjoy, had been refused the absolution of the confessional by the prison chaplain. On arrival at the Curragh he asked about chaplains and was told that they were 'no bother at all'. He took an early opportunity to test this, prefacing his confession (as was required) by the revelation that he had been refused absolution at Mountjoy. The response, as he recalled, was direct. 'Look', said the chaplain, 'will you get on with your confession and tell me your sins.' No difficulty was made about giving the internees full access to the sacraments.[134]

Security and control problems

The most effective means of preventing escape or disorder, given the basics of physical security, are control, supervision and the collection of intelligence by observation, eavesdropping, mail censorship, tip-offs and the cultivation of informants. Camp staff could and did enter any part of the camp at any time: no-go areas were not tolerated. Regular roll-calls and searches were supplemented by occasional surprise inspections and tallies. The latter were usually conducted in the evening and morning but sometimes a duty officer would direct that they be conducted in the middle of the night. This served a security function but it also reminded the internees who was in control and reinforced staff morale. 'You see, the camp was run by the Commanding Officer of our crowd, not theirs, and we didn't give two hoots about them. We were there to do a job. If we felt [that] if the Commanding Officer felt like having an inspection at two in the morning, it was done.'[135]

In an ordinary civilian prison in Ireland or Britain (and most other European jurisdictions), staff move among the prisoners, inspecting, supervising, opening and closing doors, issuing orders and receiving requests, but also conversing on a number of topics from sports to sentences to family matters. This mixing maintains the stable relations so critical to the running of such establishments and also allows in the collection of information. The latter is sometimes given by a prisoner in anticipation of a return favour, but it also arises out of staff observations, drawing of inferences and making of connections.[136] This approach has many advantages, but to work well it requires an alert, motivated, well-supervised and regularly de-briefed staff. It also has its dangers, principally that staff will give away as much or more information than they collect and that they will be lulled and gulled. Occasionally, staff will be 'turned' altogether and will behave corruptly or maliciously against the institution. As noted, Curragh guards were under a standing order to confine their conversations to routine pleasantries: sustained conversation was forbidden. Dick Reade remembered the order being strictly enforced. If an internee asked for something, the guard was to reply that he would find out and pass the request to his superiors.[137]

Advantages of close staff–inmate interaction were thus largely forgone to avoid the pitfalls. That relegated the collection of intelligence to observation and occasional eavesdropping supplemented by information gleaned from visits or through the censorship of correspondence.[138] These are labour-intensive activities, and, throughout much of the Curragh camp's existence, there were repeated complaints from its commanders that it was understaffed. To work to advantage, moreover, staff must be kept to their task, and there must be a strong system of collation and dissemination.

No army is at ease when dealing with civilians, and the military approach can appear alien and abrupt to those outside the ranks. That they professed to be members of an army and to a considerable extent behaved as POWs did not alter the fact that the Curragh internees were civilians in law and likely to be seen as civilians by politicians and by the public. There was a deal more to their custody and the comfort of the government than ensuring that they did not escape. There had to be some type of bridge between them and the Army and between the camp and the government, the civil service, police and public. A large portion of this complex duty fell to the camp liaison officer, who was appointed shortly after the first internees were received.

The liaison officer handled applications from relatives for visits beyond the basic monthly allowance, as well as applications from non-relatives and lawyers. He was also responsible for dealing with enquiries from the civil service, with parliamentary questions, visits by outside bodies such as the Red Cross and telephone enquiries from civilians. Other duties included oversight of the paperwork concerning reception and releases, the handling of internee complaints forwarded to him by the Camp Commandant, findings of courts of inquiry into escapes and any allegations made by outside bodies. With such a wide knowledge of the camp and its contacts it was inevitable that he would be the contact point for the Army's Rannóg Faisnéise (Intelligence Section). He kept a personal file for each internee, together with a nominal register. His oversight required a host of other files, almost thirty in number. Working with the camp censors, he prepared for the Intelligence Section, the civil service and the Minister extracts from internees' correspondence and notes of conversations during visits. His was a critical post in enabling senior civil servants and ministers to gauge the mood of the camp.[139]

Security and control were apparently hampered by low staffing levels. The staff establishment on 20 February 1958 was eighty officers, non-commissioned officers and other ranks and was thought by a commandant of the camp, Commandant Mac Eilgeóid, to be insufficient. In December 1958, in the wake of a large-scale escape, he wrote to his superior in Curragh Command insisting that he and the staff were doing their utmost to prevent escapes but were hampered by the poor resources.[140] Dick Reade recalled the effect of low staffing levels: 'they were hard times, that's the best way of putting it. Staff were working unbelievable hours. You could be on twenty-four hours a day, without a break.' After one such spell on duty, Reade remembered being called in the following day, supposed to be a rest period, because of staff shortages.[141] The camp required substantial deployments throughout the twenty-four-hour cycle to meet the requirements of the various functions: perimeter patrols, watchtowers, compound duty, fire pickets and other duties. Sickness or leave drained what was already a very shallow reserve. This may have been the principal weakness that enabled the mass breakout on 2 December 1958 to take place. It was certainly a matter of the stand-to (rapid-response) squad being less than rapid, but the necessary reserve was not mobilised and deployed in time because it was not available.[142] In addition to their inadequate strength in numbers, staff were poorly equipped. There were insufficient arms for them and, although they were required to patrol in all weathers, not enough protective clothing.[143]

Intelligence

In the early months at the Curragh, security and control were almost exclusively physical, apparently without much of an observational or intelligence component. No systematic handover intelligence was provided to the Curragh reception staff, but some of the Special Branch escorts did provide background information on individuals.[144] A further difficulty was that the military police had been drafted into the Curragh from the Army's various commands, so they were both inexperienced and also unused to working with each other.[145] These defects apart, there was, in contrast to the 1940s, a more developed system of gathering information about internees, their activities in the camp, their relatives and friends outside and shifts in opinion and sentiment. At one level it is not too difficult to assemble such information since, although they were aware of being under surveillance and took some precautions, prisoners and their contacts were relatively easy targets. Much more difficult is the management of information: the process of selection, analysis and dissemination and the always fraught business of sharing with other agencies. The Curragh operation reported to the Army's Director of Intelligence, but what his purpose was in assembling intelligence is unclear. Was it to support security at the Curragh; to assist the Irish Army in its operations on the border; to give the Minister for Defence an appreciation of the IRA; to support Special Branch with another stream of information about IRA membership, supporters and sympathisers, and related activities; or was it all of these? And to what extent was information exchanged with Special Branch?[146] No precise answers can be given from the records that are available, but it is clear that, from a relatively early point, there was a structured attempt to develop intelligence at the Curragh.[147]

One obvious and important source was the internees' correspondence into and out of the camp. The extent and significance of this stream is not simple to determine. We do not know, for example, the extent to which the IRA camp command, being aware of this scrutiny, operated its own mechanism for censorship and control, and how effective that was. We have seen how in the 1940s the IRA camp command required internees to submit outgoing post for its own censorship before anything was handed over to the camp authorities. Incoming post, already opened by the camp censors, went through a similar examination.[148] From the camp censor's abstracts and reports in 1957 and 1958 it does not seem that internees' mail was subject to this level of double censorship, or at least that this was done systematically and effectively.

That the IRA camp command did not have control over internees' outgoing correspondence to anything like the same extent as in the 1940s is apparent from a general meeting in May 1958. Ten months into internment, and rather late in the day to be taking precautions, Tomás MacCurtáin warned the men not to say anything at all about the republican movement in their letters since the camp authorities were passing extracts on to Dublin, and thereafter to the British. The internees' newspaper *Barbed Wire* repeated the message.[149]

Some internees corresponded in fairly stereotypical terms about the IRA's morale and prospects, and others wrote guardedly, aware that their letters were to be doubly scrutinised.[150] It is possible that secret messages were passed in code, that some of the persons mentioned in correspondence referred to others and that the matters discussed were simply a cover for other activities altogether. There were some instances of misinformation being planted in the letters either as an individual initiative or on the direction of the IRA camp leaders. It is certain that some names and addresses functioned simply as mail forwarders, to prevent Special Branch adding yet another associate to their list. All said, however, there was a surprising amount of fairly frank discussion in the correspondence. The tone was often stronger and more direct in inward correspondence, but outgoing letters could be very open about conditions, even when this contradicted the IRA's approved line that the Curragh was a concentration camp and its inmates were united and confident.

Abstracts prepared for the Director of Intelligence showed the topics of interest for which camp censors had been briefed to watch out. Names, addresses and movements of relatives of associates were recorded, as were contacts with the prisoners' support organisation and constituency politicians. Developments in the camp, especially internees' opinions and attitudes, were highlighted. A particular interest was internees' statements on favourable treatment. (These were not so rare because some aspects of the regime, such as food, were good, and also because, as we have seen, internees had an understandable wish to reassure relatives.) With a view to refuting, if need be, accusations that camp conditions were poor, the censor group noted all comments praising conditions or good relations with staff. It was evident that some of the outgoing letters were attempts to mislead by giving supposedly frank assessments of outside units or activities. There were also attempts to rile, such as the frequent references to the Dublin Special Branch as 'Specials' (a conflating reference to the detested Northern Ireland Special Constabulary). Inward correspondents frequently referred to developments in Sinn Féin (usually increases in membership) and in the strength, activities and collections of prisoner-support groups, and these were noted by the censors, with details of names and addresses.

It was also fruitful to observe and listen to internees, and to observe their visits. The difficulty for the Army was to train and motivate its men to observe and listen to give them sufficient confidence to report what they had learned and to believe that this was a valuable activity. Something as basic as the soldiers' ability to write English may have affected the quantity and quality of information coming in. Civilian prison staff have as part of their stock in trade the continual observation of their charges, although any prison administrator will admit that performance is uneven. This is a skill of subtlety as well as attentiveness that is acquired over a number of years, and not all staff have the motivation or ability for this. There was also a major limitation at the Curragh in that, unlike a civilian prison, conditions substantially separated internees and their guards. Despite these limitations, guards did report conversations, and the authorities were able to send to Dublin fairly full reports of the general meetings of internees – either because the proceedings were eavesdropped or because of information received. MacCurtáin and others in the internee command took whatever precautions they could. Shortly after arrival in the camp, a general meeting was held at which MacCurtáin ordered that in the presence of soldiers there should be no mention of IRA men still at liberty. Disciplinary action was threatened should anyone breach the order.[151]

Visits yielded much information. Relatives and friends were generally much less alert and constrained than internees, and even general statements on republican activities and attitudes were of interest.[152] By January 1958, MacCurtáin and other senior IRA men realised that the collection of intelligence within the camp was much more systematic and comprehensive than hitherto imagined. He complained to the Camp Commandant about notes of conversations between internees and visitors being passed on to gardaí, together with the index numbers of visitors' cars. This information, MacCurtáin protested, was being used to 'persecute' relatives and friends. Around this time there were other references in visits and in correspondence to the camp authorities 'collaborating' with gardaí.[153]

Particularly experienced staff were assigned to supervise MacCurtáin's own visits, and detailed reports were submitted to the Director of Intelligence. Tom Landers's instructions were to 'Listen for every move and every word.' Since Irish was (at least in aspiration) the primary language of the Republic, there could be no question of forbidding its use (as in Britain and Northern Ireland) during visits. The difficulty was that few camp staff had Irish to any level of fluency. The problem was addressed, in part and occasionally, at least, by using the skills of a Galway military policeman – presumably a native speaker. He was able to understand what was going on and to submit his report in Irish.[154] Had the IRA been in better condition, or spoiling for a fight, control of the visits could have been a useful focus for conflict.

Peter Brennan remembered supervising visits, a duty he 'avoided like the plague, as far as I could'. His unease did not come from an expectation of confrontations with visitors, who, in many cases, were 'quite nice'.[155] Rather, it was impossible to prevent items – particularly notes – being passed. Tables were not partitioned or divided, and the supervising soldier sat in the corner of the visiting room. Supposedly he would intervene if anything untoward took place, but, in practice, a lack of training, experience and confidence meant that many items were passed without sanction.[156] Support or other weaknesses would not have saved the unfortunate in charge of a visit from disciplinary consequences had sinister contraband been passed and later used, and were its source traced.

Speaking in the Dáil debate on internment on 6 November 1957, Traynor rejected the claim that visiting facilities were inadequate. That they were originally rather skeletal he simply chose not to acknowledge. In the first months of the camp, visitors awaiting their turn simply congregated in the open, without cover or a place to sit. This was a remarkable oversight and could not be defended, or indeed excused. Funds were found, and a hut was erected outside the camp perimeter where up to twenty visitors could wait to see internees. The hut was provided with seating and had been newly decorated. There were two rooms set aside for the visits themselves, also freshly decorated and furnished. Should there be a rush of visitors, the Commandant's office and an adjacent room were used. Traynor claimed that visits varied from between thirty minutes and an hour, depending on the number of people waiting to see their relatives.[157] That this was misrepresentation, or at least an overly sanguine view of the visiting facilities, was suggested by comments made during a visit conducted almost a year later, when the population of the camp had fallen, and with it, one might reasonably suppose, pressures on visiting space. Brian O'Hagan complained to his parents and sister that there were only five visiting rooms, and, at busy times, visits lasted only five minutes. People who were waiting still had to stand outside for hours, sometimes in the rain. He urged his relatives to seek publicity in the GAA, the newspapers and elsewhere. In forwarding a note of this conversation to the Adjutant General's department, the Camp Commandant noted that all internees were raising the issue in outgoing correspondence (indicating IRA coordination). He did not address O'Hagan's claim that visitors had had to wait outside, merely noting the availability of the waiting room, nor did he directly refute the claim that visits could be as short as five minutes, simply noting that they averaged one hour.[158]

All prisoners, political or ordinary, are intensely suspicious of any individual staff–inmate interaction. The abiding fear is that information will be given (and prisoners are always engaged in forbidden activities) either in exchange for favours or simply through inattention or stupidity. The informer is among the most reviled of prisoners (called 'snitch', 'grass', 'rat') and a constant threat to his comrades. This may have underpinned MacCurtáin's insistence that for meals and religious services the internees should assemble and march together. On the surface it was an affirmation that they remained disciplined soldiers, that they were under the command of their own officers, that they were captive but not cowed – all versions of the MacCurtáin doctrine of imprisonment. But there was another level of reasoning: anyone who remained behind, alone in the huts, was a danger: was he perhaps making contact with the staff?[159]

It is only within the past two decades, following the escape of six IRA men from the Whitemoor maximum security prison in Cambridgeshire on 9 September 1994, that staff have been trained to recognise conditioning and subtle intimidation and to report and resist it.[160] Conditioning was described by a psychologist who was able to observe the social dynamics in parts of Whitemoor (especially the Special Security Unit, a prison within the prison) as akin to brainwashing: 'Prisoners deliberately set out to condition staff to behave the way they want them to.' Another source of the failure of control was the inability of staff to acknowledge and discuss with colleagues attempts by prisoners to undermine them, 'to make subtle inroads into their authority'.[161] These and other patterns of staff–inmate relations were analysed in the wake of the Whitemoor and Parkhurst prison escapes, and counter-conditioning training was incorporated into the curriculum of uniformed staff and governor grades.

No such training was conceived of in the 1950s, and there was certainly not the remotest hint of it at the Curragh. But neither had the IRA advanced much beyond its traditional repertoire of confrontation and protest. Had it done so, a considerable range of possibilities for subverting authority may well have opened for it.

Bridge-building between inmates and staff was one such opportunity. Here the IRA proscription of informal contacts with staff enhanced the security of the camp. How could staff be suborned and weaned away from their loyalties when the IRA itself maintained a very effective ban on informal contacts? Men more reflective and flexible than MacCurtáin and his senior associates might have explored these possibilities. But to the internee commanders, the prime task was guardianship of the rubrics and rituals of orthodoxy and the prescriptions for conducting oneself in captivity: purity in the cause rather than inventiveness and effectiveness. We shall return to this point.

An obvious danger to security, imbued with subversive possibilities, perhaps not exclusive to the place and time but certainly very much a part of it, was prior personal acquaintance between a member of staff and an internee. Charlie Murphy, one of the upcoming generation of IRA leaders, had been at school with one of the military policeman. Neither openly recognised the other, for which the policeman was very grateful.[162] Tom Landers recalled another aspect of the issue. Staff were indeed asked if they knew any of the internees, but Landers contended that none would admit to it. 'It was a bad system… a terrible bad system.'[163] Staff could ask to be removed from compound duties if pressures were being brought to bear. That worked for a while, but some of the Dublin staff, who did not like Curragh duty, complained of pressures or of knowing a prisoner in order, Landers thought, to be returned to their units.[164]

Getting out

Parole

It had been accepted in the various periods during which internment was in use that temporary parole would be granted on compassionate grounds, almost always for urgent family matters (though there was sufficient ambiguity to allow that to extend to farming difficulties).[165] Only an application and a promise to return were required, so no political engagement or submission was involved; republican integrity was thus uncompromised.[166] The wording for the parole undertaking was fixed by the Cabinet at its meeting on 6 August 1957, as follows:

> I,…, of…, now in…, in consideration of my release on parole for… for the purpose of… do hereby undertake on my honour (1) that I will not convey any message, written or verbal, into or out of…; (2) that, while on parole, I will not allow myself to be interviewed by members of the Press and will not take part in the activities of any organisation, which is an unlawful organisation under the Offences Against the State Act,

1939; and (3) that I will surrender myself to the... not later than... on the... day of...

As with all other camp communications or business, applications were submitted through the internees' own command. The authorities were unconcerned about the risk of absconding since in order to preserve the privilege the IRA would, if necessary, ensure that a person who was tardy in returning, or who otherwise misbehaved, was brought to heel: Ireland was a small country and there was nowhere to go. There was also some uncertainty as to parole criteria. Since the reason for applying was normally a family emergency, the questions in most cases would have been specific to the degree of urgency and of kinship. By early October 1957, fifteen applications had been submitted, of which two were refused and two had been passed to the Minister for Justice for a decision.[167] These last concerned senior IRA men, whose possible linking up with the outside organisation whilst on parole raised broader issues of national security.

As we have seen, the form of words for parole applicants was fairly prescriptive. Reasons for the request had to be specified and it was required that the applicant agree that, were it granted, he undertook 'on my honour' not to convey any message, written or verbal, into or out of the camp or prison. In addition, he had to promise not to conduct an interview with the press. He also undertook not to take part in the activities of any organisation deemed to be unlawful under the provisions of the OASA. Finally, he would surrender himself to his place of custody within the allotted time.[168] But the non-communication clauses were vague. Unlike the blunt fact of failing to return to custody on time, they could not be policed or even precisely defined. Exactly what constituted a 'message' could in most instances be debated, and even MacCurtáin's punctiliousness had limits.[169]

Whether the non-communication portion of the undertaking was as scrupulously observed is another matter. Certainly, there was no on-the-record talking to the press, and the smuggling out or in of documents may have been too risky. Paradoxically, parole was more fraught with difficulty for MacCurtáin and his colleagues than for the authorities. His persistent concern was that demoralisation would lead to more men signing out. Were that to happen, a momentum could gather that would cause a mass desertion, with dire and long-term consequences for the republican movement, and immediately and directly for the Border Campaign: all could melt away, leaving only a forlorn rump. Less than a year into internment, the camp authorities were picking up information that confirmed that the internee command had good reason to worry. Men were saying that it was a worse experience to return to the camp than to be refused parole. For obvious reasons – the tug of two sets of loyalties – this was particularly the case with married men. The camp intelligence officer commented that whereas the refusal of parole appeared to steel internees in their convictions, '[a] period at home reveals to them the true state of affairs with their wives and families, not the "good face" which is put on in incoming letters and in visits'.[170]

MacCurtáin was experienced in the dynamics of captivity and, though not an obviously imaginative man, had over his many years as an activist given the various dimensions much thought. A man in the camp had to be constantly reinforced in the faith. The daily routine was tailored as far as possible to emphasise and re-emphasise the substantive existence and continuity of the IRA, the sacred nature of its demands for loyalty on behalf of the Irish nation, the feasibility of its goals and lack of alternatives to its programme and, withal, the urgent need to support men in peril in the North. In an effort of will commingled with virtue and self-denial, shared belief turned into reality, and this could be maintained as long as no other vision intruded. A man's family struggling and in need was undoubtedly a potent rival for heart and mind. Monastic orders cut themselves off from the world in varying degrees to intensify a sense of spirituality, the undoing of which is distraction and then temptation. MacCurtáin's band must at times – perhaps at all times – have seemed to him to be equally vulnerable. Barbed-wire fences were monastery walls.

With any kind of reasonable case, a man, apart from one of the leaders, could be hopeful that the camp authorities would be amenable to a parole applica-tion.[171] By this point, readers will scarcely be surprised to learn that the men's real hurdle was the IRA camp command, which had developed its own strict rules, camels to pass through the needle's eye. An internee, convalescing in the camp hospital after an operation for appendicitis, applied to the IRA Camp Council for a short parole at home to assist his recovery. MacCurtáin wrote back: 'in our movement there are a few definite rules governing parole. Your case is bound by them and does not allow me to give the o.k. to an application by you for parole.'[172] Another man, on parole because of problems on his farm, wrote to MacCurtáin asking for a few weeks' extension because of his wife's poor state of health. The Camp Council considered the application, but agreed to only one week.[173] The father of another internee sought his son's parole on grounds of ill-health, but the son wrote out to a friend asking him to tell the father that 'a lad in a more serious condition… was refused'.[174] Scruples extended even to legal proceedings. A man who was a witness to an accident would neither apply for nor accept parole to attend court. He was willing to attend as a prisoner under escort, but could not give his parole: 'I have no masters in Ireland or out of it, and never will have.'[175]

The cardinal notion that internment in itself was service in the national struggle was severely tested in the first year of internment when the government shifted its ground regarding a general grant of parole. On 26 November 1958, the Minister for Justice indicated that he would seek the support of his cabinet colleagues for amending legislation to allow selected prisoners to return home for Christmas week.[176] With internees, there was no legislative barrier, and parole was simply a matter of executive decision. All internees were again offered leave to be with their families over Christmas, provided that they sign the usual undertaking to return and, in addition, to refrain from illegal activity during the period of parole.[177] Many surprised and delighted families must have exerted strong pressure on their men to come home for Christmas. The government had two objectives: first, to disarm its critics on the republican and civil liberties flank with a show of leniency; and second, to begin to unravel the internees' discipline.[178] Some of those who sat by a Christmas hearthside would very likely have decided to call it a day and, giving a full undertaking as to their future behaviour, to not return to the Curragh.

The renewed parole offer was unwelcome to the IRA leadership who well understood the dangerous possibilities of domestic reunions during the festive period. It was this, as well as an ineluctable scruple about giving an undertaking to refrain from paramilitary activity whilst at liberty (at this stage more of a theoretical than a practical possibility) that made it all but inevitable that MacCurtáin and the camp leadership would reject the government's liberal terms and would instead opt to sit out another Christmas in the Curragh.[179] That there had been some wavering and hard discussion on the issue was apparent in MacCurtáin's speech to a camp general meeting on 1 March 1958. He emphasised the need for unity. The government's one weapon was to get the internees fighting amongst themselves since 'with dissension they might sign out'. This, he pointed out, 'had happened before in history. The Government were hoping it would happen again, but the Government will not succeed this time – when we did not fall out over the parole at Christmas. We will stay here and break the Government instead of they breaking us.'[180] This was a sentiment cherished and frequently repeated and reasserted since the earliest days of the IRA – Terence MacSwiney's assertion that he who endured most would triumph and Eoin MacNeill's triumphant paradox: 'Imprisoned, we are their jailers.'[181]

Whatever his capacity for endurance as revolutionary duty and perhaps mode of personal fulfilment, MacCurtáin had a constituency to whom he had to answer in some fashion, and by the spring of 1958 it was evident that it was restive. The vigour with which he lodged his complaints and representations noticeably increased, and he began to hint that he might be displaced as internee leader or that more direct and violent methods might be used to pursue the internees' objectives.[182] He needed some successes and, on 7 May 1958, lodged a raft of complaints. A sense of irony was certainly absent when these extended to a protest that there had been an increase in the number of parole refusals. 'The urgency and necessity of all parole applications', he wrote, 'can be, and is vouched for, by the prisoners' Camp Council'. Notwithstanding this, and even in cases where medical certificates had been produced, 'parole is unjustly refused'. This was redirected to the Minister for Justice, since it was at his discretion that parole was granted.[183] It is not clear what reply, if any, was given, but since internment was an exceptional measure, intended to disrupt the organisation, activities and operations of the IRA, there could be no question of granting it more or less automatically on the say-so of a camp council made up of IRA leaders and activists. MacCurtáin and his colleagues seem to have seen themselves almost as partners of the authorities in handling applications and were surprised to discover that their winnowing and sorting was disregarded.

Release

As in the past, there was provision for case review for those who thought they had been detained without good reason or who wished to break their connections with the republican movement. Unlike Northern Ireland, where a declaration of intent was not in itself sufficient to obtain release, and where all such applications still had to be scrutinised by the Advisory Committee and the Special Branch, Dublin released anyone who gave an undertaking and signed the relevant form.[184] A Detention Commission was nevertheless provided, in accordance with Section 8 of the OASA.[185] The Detention Commission held its first session at the Curragh on 17 September 1957.[186] It started what was to be a very limited programme of work. Gerry Lawless, who would prove to be a major legal and public-relations headache for the Irish government, was represented by Seán MacBride.[187] Challenges were immediately lodged regarding the status of the Commission, particularly asking whether or not it was a court. If it were a court, it had to adhere to the rules of due process, including the discovery of all relevant evidence. But the Commission was un-court-like in that it could not take sworn evidence; neither could it hold a rebuttal hearing on evidence submitted by the authorities, and its proceedings were not public. MacBride argued that whatever latitude the government may have had in 1940 when provision was made for internment in the OASA, it was now constrained by having submitted itself to the jurisprudence arising from the European Convention of Human Rights. The Irish High Court was accordingly persuaded to issue a conditional order for Lawless's release.[188] The following month, the case was determined against Lawless, but this was merely the start of a protracted legal battle at Strasbourg.[189]

Sinn Féin helpfully but unwittingly aided the government when it declared that an internee who applied for release automatically broke his links with the republican movement: members would not 'purchase their personal liberty nor their livelihood at the cost of betrayal of those who died to make us free'.[190] At a stroke, the statement confirmed that all those in internment, if not active, were certainly obedient members of a violent movement unreconciled to the Irish state. It also characterised as traitors those who did seek release. Justification for continued detention shifted from the government to the detainees themselves.

The wording of the release application had been given to the internees by the Camp Commandant on 18 August 1957, together with the government's promise that anyone who signed it would be released. To ease the burden, persons who had been in public employment would not be required to sign the declaration again as a condition of reinstatement. The form itself was straightforward: 'I... undertake to respect the Constitution of Ireland and the laws, and I declare that I will not be a member of or assist any organisation which is an unlawful organisation under the Offences Against the State Act, 1939.'[191] The form, as we have seen, was much disliked, and the act of 'signing out' was excoriated. De Valera's government, several ministers of which had themselves been prisoners or internees (or both) well understood this and, on 6 August 1957, decided in Cabinet that the Minister for Justice could direct release from internment without requiring any undertaking where 'the circumstances warrant that course'. He could alternatively direct that an oral undertaking be accepted, provided that it was formally given before a witness and that a record of the oral record was retained and signed by the witness.[192]

Despite a degree of toleration for those who decided that they no longer wished to serve in the IRA, or perhaps because of it, and the emphasis constantly placed on its being a volunteer body, those who signed out were anathematised. In some cases of acute family need the IRA leadership gave permission to a man to sign the declaration, but since the dependants of all those interned were being made to pay a price, these approvals were very rare.[193] Looking back on it, Mick Ryan thought that the ostracisation of those who signed out was a bad thing.[194] The IRA, he observed, produced two strong and opposing sentiments: 'very close friendship and loyalty and comradeship; but then that can turn to the exact opposite – hatred and bitterness'.[195]

No gaoler, civil or military, wishes a prisoner to die in his hands. Such deaths, no matter how natural or explicable, always feed suspicions: hard-heartedness and a lack of compassion at the least, malign wrong-doing as a possibility. A number of regulations were intended to guard against concealment, actual, apparent or supposed.[196] There were a few persons in poor health among the internees, but for the most part the men were young and healthy. Problems of mental well-being did arise, however, especially as the months of internment wore on. An instance of this occurred in the summer of 1958. A man had seemed increasingly unwell to his comrades, on the verge of a complete breakdown. A hut-mate described the symptoms: 'Every night he used to do all sorts of queer things, get on the floor, make speeches and sometimes get hysterical, either laughing or crying. I earnestly hope he will get well again and don't forget to say a prayer for him.' The sick man was released on 19 September 1958.[197]

Another man wrote to a correspondent in Canada at some length about his chest problems and declining appetite which meant that he had little to eat but bread and butter. The camp censor commented that the man definitely appeared to have something wrong with him and indeed ate very little food.[198] On 22 September 1958, referring to such notes, the camp authorities observed that there were several older men in the camp. The greater number did not complain, but 'the danger of a heart attack cannot be ruled out'. There were eight men aged over fifty in the camp, the oldest being fifty-nine.[199] Prior to the end of September 1958, fourteen men had been released. Of these, an internee claimed, nine had been released on health grounds. Another forty-five were released in October and November, seven of whom had been freed on health grounds. This made sixteen such cases in six months, 'and they weren't released until their health was very bad'. Things were not as good at the Curragh as the Minister for Justice had claimed, but, on the other hand, the internee wrote, 'I don't mean to infer that we are all at death's door.'[200] When the pattern of releases for the entire duration of internment is considered, it shows that twenty-eight men were released on medical grounds, the first on 14 November 1957 and the last in January 1959. This is a rate of just under 15 per cent of all releases.[201] Some of these may have been a compassionate or convenient application of the medical label to get men home, but considering that this was predominantly a group of younger men, the rate of medical discharges seems rather high.

A small number of internees had, by this time, been released unconditionally, either because they had been arrested in error or because it had been decided that they were no longer a significant threat to public security.[202] Four were freed on 19 August 1957; two came from Northern Ireland and one was the law student, Michael Davern.[203] Two weeks previously, four men who had completed their Mountjoy sentences were freed, instead of being taken from the gates to the Curragh. In these cases, the men's youth had been a factor as was the government's stated reluctance to unnecessarily 'interrupt their training or education for particular careers'.[204]

But on other matters a harder line was taken. In the autumn of 1957 there was an enterprising attempt to secure temporary release and at the same time to twist a tail or two. A by-election had been announced for the North-Central constituency in Dublin, for 14 November 1957, and five IRA men, the list headed by Seán Garland, applied to the Curragh Commandant to be allowed to vote. Since there was no postal voting at this time, this was a bid to be taken or (even more unlikely) to be allowed to travel to the relevant voting station in the constituency. It was a bit of cheek, since all rejected the legitimacy of the Irish legislature. Peter Berry, the formidable and long-serving Secretary of the Department of Justice, put it before his minister, and the men were informed that their request could not be granted.[205]

As Christmas 1958 approached, rumours and expectations of release abounded in the camp.[206] From the time that the British released the Easter Rising rank and file from Frongoch Camp to be home in time for Christmas 1916, this was a season of the year when freedom was most expected. A gesture of conciliation and humanity would have political advantages for the government and would be in line with this tradition. Seán MacBride visited the camp on 6 December 1958 to deliver a lecture on proportional representation. One of the internees spoke to him afterwards and later reported that MacBride had told him that in order to avoid a complete capitulation when the Court of Human Rights ruled against the government (and he was certain that would happen), all internees would be released before Christmas or shortly thereafter.[207]

Speculation along these lines had been going on throughout the autumn. Writing to Emily Scullion, the secretary of the prisoners' aid association, An Cumann Cabhrach, internee T. Doyle reported that releases had encouraged speculation that a more general move was in prospect: 'The most popular theory is that the Devil-era gang realises that the case about Human Rights is going against them and that the final verdict is likely to be for MacBride.' Rather than be faced with a general release, it had, he speculated, been decided to reduce numbers gradually. The final decision might not come for six months, and 'even if it is against

Devil-era there is no guarantee that he will even then close the place as he may decide that his obligation to the British would still be too great to allow him to do so'.[208]

The government had to consider several matters as it settled on a release policy. There had been little trouble in the Republic, it was true, and none was anticipated. The Border Campaign had failed and could not now be revived. Southern public opinion could easily veer, however, and by the late autumn of 1957, some men had been inside for almost eighteen months. Against that, the IRA had not declared a cessation, had used the Republic as a haven, and continued its sporadic attacks in Northern Ireland. The British and Northern Ireland governments would not react well to a general release. As for the IRA itself, a general release would be portrayed as a capitulation by the government, a backing-down in the face of supposed public indignation. At a practical level, many of the organisation's most experienced and committed operatives would be freed to return to their work on its behalf – assuming of course that the organisation had the means to deploy them.

But while a general release had little merit, there were several advantages in one that was phased. That section of public opinion which might actually or potentially harbour sympathy for the internees would be neutralised. There were clear signs that the IRA organisation within the camp was under strain and there had been some splintering. A selective policy of releases might assist that disintegration whilst providing good reason for the continued detention of the leaders and the more militant rank and file. Men freed in small batches, moreover, were unlikely objects of mass demonstrations, not least because they would be conscious that any misbehaviour would slam and bolt the gates on those left behind.

From July 1957 until the beginning of December 1958, 205 men had been interned and seventy-five released.[209] Fifteen were released on 23 December 1958. Most of these had been imprisoned and then interned in the summer of 1957. Only one was freed on medical grounds (after five months' internment); the others were released because they were no longer judged to be a significant risk. All but three were from Dublin or the immediate area.[210] It may have been a testing of public opinion or a bid for a good press reaction, especially with Dublin families on hand to express their gratification, but at this stage there was little journalistic interest.[211] After the Christmas release, fairly small batches followed in January and February 1959. By the beginning of March 1959, there were only forty-two left at the Curragh. Seven were released on 3 March, thirteen on 6 March, ten on 9 March and the last twelve on 11 March.[212] Leaders and known militants were kept until last. Seán Cronin, Tony Magan and J. B. O'Hagan were in the last batch; Tomás MacCurtáin, the OC, had been released the previous week.[213]

Solidarity and signing

Internment could not claim to be always accurately targeted. By its covert nature, intelligence was sometimes impossible to check, and minnows and wholly unconnected or disengaged men were picked up along with militants and members of the leadership.[214] From the commencement of internment up to the end of December 1957, fourteen men had been released on their signing undertakings. Some of these signed out of dire necessity or because they were unconnected with the IRA, but ten were noted as being members of the splinter group – the official term for the Saor Uladh group and for those who followed Joe Christle.[215] These men did not share the IRA's objection to recognising Southern courts and to signing out. Deducting these ten from the total, perhaps four men gave the undertaking during the first months of internment – a rate so low that it is possible that some men who had only loose connections with the IRA preferred to remain in the Curragh rather than become known as signers.[216] Indeed, of the 200 or so men who passed through the Curragh, only sixteen in total (counting the ten dissidents) signed the undertaking; this was a rate of around 8 per cent and demonstrates a high level of solidarity and commitment. Gerry Lawless, the most notable of the splinter-group internees, could not bring himself to sign the undertaking but was willing to give a verbal undertaking, which the authorities accepted.[217]

The rate of signing out was particularly low considering the urgings of some wives and other dependants and relatives. The unrelenting tug of loyalties where a wife and children were experiencing hardship must have been considerable. Parents, whether or not they were dependants, were wont to voice their frustrations. A mother, writing about a month after the commencement of internment, was definitely vexed and puzzled: 'Why don't you tell them you had nothing to do with the activity in the North, they can't expect men to sign papers they would not sign themselves if they were in.'[218] Sometimes the pressure was indirect but intense nevertheless. A father urged his son not to send any more IRA men up to the family home. These visits upset his mother, whose health was not good:

> You all seem to have got the same brain wash as you all have the same litany to repeat. You will learn in your own time what a mug you have been. Of course you want to free Ireland but just wait and see who reaps the benefit of your suffering.[219]

When Seán MacBride brought the Lawless case there was further speculation and pressure, one mother endorsing the view that if it failed the only thing left to do would be 'to come out[,] as you would be fools… to do anything else but come out'.[220]

Another man was directly coerced by his wife, who wrote threatening that if he did not sign out she would have their children placed in a children's home. The husband wrote back: 'I served my time in jail for what I had done and if I had been let go, I am sure I would have given up all to save the kids from going into a home… However I will not sign out.'[221] In this and in other cases it was not only loyalty to the IRA that stood in the way of a man signing out but the sense of personal betrayal in giving the undertaking while others remained staunch and resolute. There was also, as we have seen, a strong and vivid fear of lifelong stigmatisation. Rural or urban, communities in Ireland were honey-combs of family and neighbourhood networks, and reputation, good or bad, had consequences – and could be passed on to the next generation. Moving on was hardly an option: Ireland was a small country, and new neighbours, friends or workmates were apt to be curious about antecedents.

Such repugnance arose from signing out that rumours immediately spread when a release was made without the undertaking. A man who had been released on completing his prison sentence wrote to an internee friend. He and four others released from Mountjoy without passing into internment had not signed out. The decision to let him go was, he contended, a ploy on the part of Special Branch to create false impressions – presumably to sow discord.[222] The same reasoning was applied by an internee writing to a comrade recently freed:

> Needless to say we were all very surprised at your release. Of course we guessed the real reason behind this. But they will have to try a lot harder if they expect to spread confusion in the Movement or if they expect to be led back to unknown members of the organisation in Wicklow.[223]

For all the urgings of family and friends, camp loyalty was generally stronger. This was all the more remarkable given the collapse of the campaign outside. The signer acquired a taint that was deeply damaging, even beyond immediate republican circles.[224] This was so feared that when a man was unconditionally released he and his friends would ensure that the fact that he had not signed became known.[225] But there was another process at work. The longer one spent in internment the more difficult it might become to sign the undertaking. No matter how it was dressed up, signing was an act of submission and renunciation; it also made a nonsense out of time already served and all the sacrifices and hardship suffered by one's family. The undertaking that brought release wrote in capital letters the foolishness of weeks and months of discomfort and deprivation, of life suspended, earnings and opportunities needlessly forgone. As internment began to be phased out, the rate of signing out increased – not great numbers, but more than there had been. The camp was acceptable as a place of internment, Dick Reade reflected, but not for many who came from good families, 'so they would have been getting browned off… and they would have been anxious to get out'.[226]

The grinding nature of the experience was captured in a letter to his wife by the veteran IRA leader Michael Traynor, sometime Secretary of Sinn Féin, as he neared the end of his first Curragh year. His health was not good, and he had lost weight. Tests were being carried out to learn more about his various symptoms, but Traynor had no doubt that his ills were a product of internment:

> The lack of suitable food for my age, the psychological effects created by the loss of necessary solitude; the uncertainty of the future; you see

there is no guarantee that I won't end my days here. A man for instance sentenced to 10 years or 15 even can, after a couple of months' adjustment settle down to live at normal tensions; but here release might be next month, next year, or as I said never; therefore life is lived at high nervous tension which must have serious effects on general health.[227]

Internment was exhausting and deeply demanding, even for a man as committed and experienced as Traynor. Apart from the special pressures of being middle-aged in a population of much younger men, the sheer boredom of internment was unavoidable and debilitating. The uncertain duration of it all made it hard for men to commit to the various classes and camp activities and thus to achieve adjustment: all were awaiting the arrival of a train, one that was certainly on the way but whose timing was unknown. An internee complained to a friend that there had been no film show for four months: 'An Fear Fada [de Valera, the Long Fellow] says we are deprived of nothing… I would dearly love to see some of those people… living in these huts with 43 to each hut. I guarantee half of them would need mental treatment after it.'[228] Despondency and a penetrating weariness had overtaken the enterprise, and whether they signed themselves out or awaited release, many men walked away from the movement as well as from the camp when they were released.

Some twenty months of internment ended on 11 March 1959 when the last man left the Curragh.[229] The OASA remained available to deal with anyone who showed too much enthusiasm for IRA activities.[230] By this time, IRA, Sinn Féin and ancillary organisations' resources were utterly exhausted, both in terms of finances and manpower; only a type of automatism kept up the appearance of things going. The command structure was so depleted that it was unable to re-engage released men, some of whom, Mick Ryan remembered, took to meeting up together, visiting the National Museum and other Dublin venues that offered free admission. Without unemployment dole and help from the IRA, they had to rely on their families.[231] Ignored by the republican movement, Mick Ryan remembered that the men were 'in a kind of limbo, not knowing what was going to happen to the IRA'.[232]

Civil servants and others in public employment (teachers, postal workers, transport and utility workers and the like) were in some ways in a better position than those who had either been in private employment or who were unemployed at the time of arrest. The assumption with civil servants and public employees was that they would be re-employed. Since they had not been charged or convicted of any offence, that right of return to employment was a matter of justice. But, of course, it was not quite so simple or automatic. Where possible, the authorities sought to extract a written undertaking. With those employed directly by the government in the civil service, the undertaking may have been pursued fairly vigorously, but for those in other branches of public service – the semi-state companies or local government – ministerial authority was much more limited.

The numbers involved were, as far as can be discerned from the records, not very great. It may have made the giving of an undertaking more palatable in some cases, since it was taken only when applying for release, and permission was given to authorise reinstatement on this basis alone.[233]

Mountjoy Prison

Between December 1956 and 1 July 1957, 103 IRA men were sentenced to terms of imprisonment ranging from fourteen days to six months. Most were convicted under the OASA, but some had been found guilty of firearms' offences. When Fianna Fáil entered office on 29 March 1957, there were fifty-three men serving sentences under the OASA. Before internment began, forty-one completed sentences and were released without further action.[234] Sixty-one remained in prison when internment was brought in on 5 July 1957, and, with few exceptions, as their sentences expired they were served with internment orders and transferred to the Curragh. Anticipating and heading off a campaign on the issue, the government did not oppose demands for political status for these prisoners and accepted the inevitable consequences for discipline and regime. Thus, whilst serving sentences, the men wore their own clothes, were exempt from labour and communicated with the prison authorities through an OC. They were confined to their own part of Mountjoy and rarely brought into contact with ordinary prisoners. No grounds were provided for protests and agitation, nor did the prisoners want to pick a fight. The doctrine behind the Border Campaign emphasised at every turn that this was a war with Britain only. Prison protests – and grounds could always be found, if wanted – would simply obscure this message. In consequence, the terms of imprisonment served at this time were the most trouble-free in the history of the republican movement.

Our knowledge of Mountjoy at this time would probably be increased had the Irish government allowed the ICRC to visit. The proposal was put in February 1959 and was debated within the government over the following two months. The Department of Defence was neutral on the matter, the Department of Justice against; External Affairs was somewhere in between. A memorandum from the last briefly examined the advantages and drawbacks of a visit. In the final lines of his report on the Curragh, Borsinger had indicated that there might be a visit to Mountjoy, 'and there does not seem to be anything to lose by permitting a visit'. Yet it might be undesirable to create a precedent for such prison visits 'at the prompting of groups in Ireland anxious to make political propaganda'. If such visits were, however, carried out in other European countries, the case against a Mountjoy visit would be weaker.[235]

But Kevin Boland, Minister for Defence, and Oscar Traynor, his counterpart in Justice, were having none of it; Mountjoy was a prison to which persons were admitted by order of the court, either to await trial or under sentence. The prison was administered in accordance with a variety of statutory rules and was provided with a Visiting Committee to which prisoners might submit their complaints. Various documents were supplied that gave chapter and verse of the prison's governance.[236] The conclusion left not a chink of doubt: there would be no ICRC visit to Mountjoy.

But it was certainly not a matter of easy conditions, despite the claims for good governance. Mountjoy was (and is) a Victorian institution and, in the 1950s, offered near Victorian amenities and an amount of residual and not unintentional discomfort. Opened in March 1850 and designed for the separate system by which prisoners spent all their time, but a daily hour or two, in their cells, Mountjoy then needed little in the way of workshops or spaces where the prisoners could assemble for association and recreation.[237] Over the years, the regime was modified and the building was adapted to some extent. Such was the closeness of design and the footprint of the establishment to the original purposes and discipline, however, that modifications were more difficult to effect. Since they refused to conform to the rules for convicted prisoners, politicals forwent remission of sentence for good behaviour. This was of little importance to them or to the authorities since almost all were destined for the Curragh. There would be more freedom of movement at the Curragh, and the constant company of comrades, but, as we have seen, some found a total lack of privacy more wearing by far than the prolonged solitude of the cell.

Tomás Mac Giolla recalled his time in Mountjoy with a degree of equanimity: 'the conditions in Mountjoy were just the conditions in Mountjoy, slopping out and all that type of thing, except that everyone had their own cell'.[238] Lock-up was prolonged. In 1957, Mac Giolla remembers being locked in his cell for twenty-two hours a day, although by 1961–2 an evening association period of two hours had been introduced. By this time also, there was a reasonable amount of exercise available, with 'a couple of fine handball alleys'.[239] These easements notwithstanding, there were prolonged periods of solitude. Personality and background determined how well one coped. Those who could not or who did not wish to read fared worse than those who could pass time with a book or with some form of study. Unlike the Curragh, no handicrafts were permitted, and there were none of the other diversions of camp life.

Although the IRA prisoners were not obliged to perform prison work, they were expected to clean their own cells and the immediate living area, and they did not contest this arrangement. The work was hard and menial since at first it entailed their kneeling with a scrubbing brush and cloth, but eventually long-handled deck-scrubbers were provided. They also cleaned the wing lavatories and the landing outside their cells. Ordinary prisoners were brought in to clean the larger space on the ground floor.[240]

From long experience, the Department of Justice had a well-developed policy for IRA prisoners. As we have seen, after the May 1946 death by hunger strike of Seán McCaughey, it was decided to avoid confrontations on what were essentially peripheral issues.[241] The IRA was not to be given ground for manoeuvre and allowed to pick a fight on matters such as prison uniforms, labour and mixing with ordinary prisoners.[242] Such struggles could rarely be prevented from acquiring a David and Goliath quality, with consequences seemingly disproportionate to the issues immediately in contention. The Fine Gael-led coalition government of 1954–7 contained parties hostile to Sinn Féin and the IRA. It was, however, dependent on the support of Clann na Poblachta and was, in consequence, anxious to avoid hunger strikes or anything of the kind. James Everett, Minister for Justice, saw the party-political dangers of giving a purchase point for an IRA campaign.

This did not mean that IRA demands were explicitly accommodated. There was a deal of double-speak and semantic evasion. They were not to be referred to in official transactions and documents as political prisoners and, supposedly, were not entitled to any special privileges or treatment. All prisoners, ordinary as well as republican, could wear their own clothes – a policy that was at odds with the more general insistence on prison uniform that went back to the eighteenth century. The change was nevertheless effected without fanfare.[243] In the same oblique way, separate accommodation was provided for IRA prisoners, certainly when more than a handful were in custody. The rationale, which the Minister could defend if pressed, was that the governor had responsibility for ensuring good order and discipline and these would be threatened were IRA men to be mixed with ordinary prisoners.[244]

A thornier issue, especially at the political level, was that of collective representation and communicating with the prisoners through their OC. Here the Minister was to some extent buffered by the official fiction of the Department of Justice which held that prisoners made representations entirely on their own behalf. The day-to-day reality was ignored because the Department's policy simply would not have worked: IRA members insisted in dealing only through their OC and command structure, and to refuse to accept that would have entailed protest and confrontation. A senior official in the Department of Justice, Paddy Terry, recalled, 'never wanted to enquire… we knew what was going on'.[245] Politicians were equally willing to look the other way.

The men were held in Mountjoy's D Wing, cut off from other prisoners except when being brought out through the Circle – the focal point of the prison's radiating wings. Once a week they were taken to the bathhouse, and at that point there would be passing contacts with other inmates, though this did not extend beyond casual greetings.[246] All male prisoners were mustered in the chapel for mass, with the various categories – political, remands, star class and recidivists – sitting in their respective sections. The same applied to Saturday-night film shows, which the female prisoners also attended. At that point, Ireland's crime rates were low, accommodation was plentiful, and the cells on the upper tiers were unoccupied.[247] Most IRA men wore the clothing in which they had been arrested. This varied from the military-style boiler suit and kindred outfits of those arrested on the border to the ordinary civilian clothing of those taken from their homes, 'So it was quite picturesque around Mountjoy', Ruairí Ó Brádaigh recalled, 'a variety of bits and pieces on us'.[248]

Only a few republican women were held in Mountjoy at this time, and it would have been impractical (and oppressive) to separate them from the rest of the female population. May Mac Giolla was remanded in custody for her part in a protest at the British Passport Office in Dublin. As with many other female republicans, she did not seek or emphasise a divide between herself and the ordinary prisoners: 'They were poor – they were just prostitutes and people in for stealing things, but they were poor little girls.' A friendly woman prison officer attempted to provide May and her cellmate, Janice Williams, with freshly made tea. This was some kind of well-meant acknowledgement of their social status. Extraordinarily for a prison, this came with a teapot; the officer also provided white china cups. May and Janice rejected the offer because the other women prisoners were having to take their tea from the tea-urn and to use tin mugs: 'We kicked up a row, we wouldn't take it, and the poor woman, I often think since, she was doing us a good turn.'[249]

Discipline and organisation

All IRA prisoners lost rank with imprisonment, whatever their outside seniority. When the leadership arrived – Tomás MacCurtáin, Tony Magan, Larry Grogan and others – they reinforced this doctrine. Ó Brádaigh was impressed: 'They were just the same as the rest of us and indeed they gave very good example because of their experience as to what you did and all that kind of thing... All you had to do was watch them and follow on.'[250]

The rules for the IRA's prison organisation were equally clear. Where numbers warranted, a council was elected. This was not of a fixed size but varied depending on the number of prisoners. It was, however, supposed to be of an uneven number, in order to avoid a tied vote. The OC, elected separately, met the Council and decided on the various issues that concerned them. Other officers – an adjutant, a quartermaster and an intelligence officer – were appointed by the OC. The quartermaster, in addition to whatever military duties he might perform (and the scope of this was extremely small in Mountjoy), allocated the various housekeeping duties. As in any male team-type activity, a considerable premium was placed on comradeship, fitting in and uncomplaining submission to the routines and discipline that the men had imposed on themselves.[251] The military spirit was addressed by organised physical exercises in D Wing's outside yard in the mornings (weather permitting) and by regular parades at which the men fell in under verbal command.

The Mountjoy routine made it difficult to organise classes. They were not prohibited, but with such long lock-up times only forty-five minutes of association was available in which they could be held. In that time it was not possible to deliver a lecture or to conduct a debate. There was another reason why classroom activities did not develop. Men locked in their cells for twenty-two hours a day were unlikely to be attracted to the notion of sitting down in a classroom for the time they were allowed out. 'When you had time', Mac Giolla observed, 'you wanted to get out and run around and play handball. Exercise was what you wanted.'[252]

Even had more frequent discussions been possible at Mountjoy they would have been confined to uncontroversial topics. Charlie Murphy noted that there was no question of analysing and debating how the Border Campaign was going. Since by far the most interesting topics would have been current affairs and the campaign in particular, what was left as acceptable topics were bound to be abstract and dry – especially to young men in their twenties with little political knowledge or background. Murphy remembered a discussion on agriculture: 'God, I hadn't a clue.' The men were so bored at times that he managed to negotiate a concession with the authorities to allow his mother to send in projectors and films: 'That will tell you the level of boredom… So, we were able to get films in, war films, of course.'[253]

How one conducted oneself in prison was important as a determinant of the esteem of fellow inmates and, longer term, one's reputation in the movement. Prison puts a man (or woman) under the microscope of social intensity, testing and continuous observation. Both strengths and weaknesses of character were apt to be revealed. Ó Brádaigh considered that imprisonment helped to build the IRA because 'it created a sense of – as long as you weren't too long there – a sense of comradeship and all that type of thing'. Under favourable conditions it could help leaders to emerge and develop their skills. A limited amount of military training (theoretical necessarily) did go on, but it was the experience of living at close quarters with comrades and earning their respect by self-control, stoicism and commitment that constituted the selection and confirmation process.[254]

Imprisonment and internment also winnowed out those who, for whatever reason, did not wish to continue with the struggle, and this process could in itself be seen as a strengthening mechanism. Continued adherence in conditions of adversity signified determination and commitment. In the circumstances of the Border Campaign, however, with manpower a persistent problem, there was another side, and men dropping out was a further weakening, both in itself and through its effect on morale. But, unless a man signed out, thus pledging, whatever might have been his mental reservations, to break his association with the IRA, his intention to leave the ranks would not have been apparent. That would come after release, when many declined to attend parades, drills and training or to return to active service, and drifted away. This was a world away from signing out. The understanding seems to have been that such men (and women) had paid their dues and could make this choice without stigma. Mick Ryan noted that imprisonment could be an implicit selection device but also insisted that several men who chose not to return to an active role did so 'mostly for very good, sound reasons… there was no shame in them quitting the struggle'.[255]

In the first year or so of the Border Campaign, chronically short of trained men and losing momentum by the day, the IRA leadership nevertheless expected its members imprisoned in the Republic to do their time with minimum trouble and to return to active ranks as quickly as possible. Internment was intended to block this process, but even before it was introduced, the refusal to accept penal discipline meant that all republicans forfeited the one-third remission they would otherwise have earned. In the first swathe of prison sentences in early 1957, there were no confrontations with the authorities, and there were no escape attempts. They were, Charlie Murphy recalled, 'never contemplated, because we felt it would rock the political boat… bring us into conflict with the authorities in some shape or form. [The attitude was] do your time, three months, get out and renew the struggle.'[256]

There was some minor agitation, but this was kept to the minimum, a rattling of the bars to remind prisoners and the authorities what was possible. One such stirring concerned electric shavers. The men generally did not use these, but in what Murphy calls 'an act of perversity' they decided to have them sent in and then successfully pressed the authorities to install the sockets. It was simply an act of attrition, Murphy admits, 'Now whether I ever used it after that I can't remember anyway.'[257]

Food and privileges

Food in Mountjoy was much what was expected of a 1950s urban prison. Prisoners queued at a serving point, collected their meal and returned to their cells to eat. Quite apart from the solitude and cramped surroundings, some men complained that the standard backless stool made it uncomfortable to sit or eat at the cell's table. The food itself was 'pretty rough' and came on chipped enamel plates, of sometimes questionable cleanliness. The stew, Ruairí Ó Brádaigh remembered, was called 'lucky dip' because of uncertainty as to its contents. There were periodic complaints, but Ó Brádaigh's attitude was probably that of the majority. 'I just used to close my eyes and eat it.'[258] Prison and its hardships were part of what it meant to be in the IRA: far better therefore to lower one's expectations and thereby make it easier to serve the sentence.

Not all prisoners were able to achieve Ó Brádaigh's state of detachment. Looking back on the food after almost fifty years Tomás Mac Giolla remained indignant, recalling it as 'dreadful'. Ireland at the time was not renowned for the general standard of cooking, and its prisons and other residential institutions funded from the public purse were at the lower end of an already basic scale. There were two types of main meals: stew and bacon and cabbage. Men would wake up in the morning to the smell of the cabbage boiling. By the time it got to the cells, the accompanying bacon was 'like strips of leather'. As for the stew, 'you would get a bowl of potatoes and you would search for the meat, and sometimes you would find a bit and sometimes you would didn't'.[259]

The authorities would, quite naturally, have given a different account of the Mountjoy dietary but would probably have conceded its institutional nature. A Dáil statement of mid-1959 is instructive as to quantity, variety and cost but leaves quality to be inferred. More than half a century has passed since then, and the quality of school and other institutional food has become a frequent topic in public debates and policies whilst the consumption of food (and its cooking) has become part of popular culture. The Mountjoy dietary reminds us that the prison was an austere institution in austere times. Prisons had moved on from an era of penal policy when food was intended to be an instrument of deprivation and a key part of the deterrent character of the prison.[260] There nevertheless remained an implicit understanding that prison food should not be excessive in quantity and should be plain, without any hint of indulgence. The cheaper cuts of meat, plenty of starches, pulses, cooked root vegetables and cabbage were the main ingredients of the main meal of the day – called dinner, and always served around noon. Breakfast was stirabout (watery porridge) and half a pound of bread, with margarine or jam. Two other small meals were served: tea (in the afternoon) and supper (early evening). The former was another half pound of bread with jam or margarine; the latter a quarter pound of bread with less than an ounce of jam. A mug of tea was issued with all meals.[261]

There survived more than a vestige of the eighteenth- and nineteenth-century doctrine of less eligibility when it came to food. This, first clearly articulated by nineteenth-century penal reformers, held that the condition of the prisoner (or inmate of the workhouse) should not be more favourable than that of the poorest free man.[262] In Ireland in the 1950s, this comparison and computation was not put into plain words but it was nevertheless fairly explicit. TDs of various political persuasions would have recognised it. From the republican and left-inclined, there was a concern that prisoners, and especially political prisoners, were not being subjected to undue hardship; their opponents sought reassurances that prisoners were not enjoying food, at the public expense, that in quantity, quality and variety the working man would strain to afford. Both sides were reasonably assured by the publication of the Mountjoy dietary. On 22 June 1959, the daily allowance of food was costed at just over 3 shillings.[263] This was probably not far off the amount that could be afforded by a man in unskilled or semi-skilled employment, on a modest wage.

In the dietary there was a shortage of two items which all who live in consumer societies know are a particular source of gratification and enjoyment: sugar and fat. Fairly minute quantities of jam and margarine were issued. A very small (2-ounce) portion of cheese could be issued to prisoners deemed by the medical officer to be unwell. Rather less than 2 ounces of sugar was issued daily to each prisoner, mostly in the mugs of tea. The lack of variety and the lack of the most gratifying and enjoyable forms of food would have been felt as a deprivation. Not so with an omission most noticeable to modern eyes: fresh fruit and uncooked vegetables. Of these there were none whatsoever in the Mountjoy dietary.

Going back to the days of British administration, there had been a tradition, albeit not uninterrupted and always subject to the political temper of the times, of allowing those serving sentences for political offences to receive parcels of food items and other small luxuries from families and friends. Following the attempted escape from Mountjoy on 25 July 1957, this privilege was withdrawn, along with certain others.[264] These ameliorations were greatly valued, and in protest at their withdrawal, both because of the deprivation and on the principle that they were customary and due to political prisoners, there were various protests. Towards the end of 1957, a hunger strike was staged by some of the IRA men. Of the twenty-two then serving sentences, nine refused all food for periods of between three and eight days. Seven others staged a partial hunger strike, accepting milk or tea and porridge with some milk.[265] Six men took no part in the action. The object of the protest was the restoration of lost privileges, in particular the food parcels and extra visits and cigarettes; the prisoners also demanded better recreational facilities. Possibly because few of those currently serving sentences had been in the prison at the time of the July 1957 escape attempt, the concessions were restored. Traynor may have reflected that it would be hard, on equitable grounds, to maintain the collective punishment; he was also well acquainted with the history of hunger-striking in Irish prisons. Finally, by any criteria, it was a weak and ragged protest, and, paradoxically, this probably made it easier to make a concession and to show leniency. Facing the daily round of monotonous food and close confinement, the restored privileges were no doubt very welcome indeed. Both sides would have marked well another lesson of the action: privileges can be given and taken away.

One of the reasons that the IRA man could be given privileges was that they were almost totally separated from the other prisoners, who did not receive food parcels or the other privileges. It would have been impossible, had ordinary and political prisoners been mixed, to avoid jealousies, quarrels and even fighting: administratively, therefore, mixing was one of the last things to be attempted. Somewhat larger than usual parcels were allowed at Christmas, such festive foods that friends and relatives could afford and that the authorities would tolerate. One of the prisoners of the time recalled the reaction of an ordinary prisoner to these gifts. Whilst in the Circle, Tomás MacCurtáin, was approached by a prisoner from another wing. Speaking through the bars, the prisoner, an Englishman, wanted to know how he could join the IRA. MacCurtáin outlined the procedure and then asked why he wanted to know. The answer was immediate and emphatic: 'To get parcels.'[266]

Like its Belfast counterpart, Mountjoy was a multi-purpose prison, holding remand and convicted, long and short term, male and female. The various classes were each kept in their own wings and floors, but there were some opportunities for the men to see the female prisoners. They had separate religious services, but women attended the Saturday-night film show, being brought in to sit at the front once the men had taken their places.[267] Prisoners also waved from their cell windows to the nurses coming off duty in the nearby Mater Hospital. The nurses' accommodation overlooked part of the prison, and the prisoners (as young men inevitably would) devised a way of communicating: 'getting a white handkerchief and doing a reverse blackboard thing to them'. (Letters would be formed by the fingers against the background of the white hankerchief.) Some of the nurses were sufficiently interested or sympathetic to visit.[268]

Staff–prisoner relations

Relations with staff were reasonably good, the general nationalistic and anti-Partitionist temper of the times having its effect behind as well as outside the walls. Some staff came on duty at Easter 1957 wearing the republican lily. This was a general expression of sentiment about the republican origins and character of the state and distant from any kind of declaration of support for the IRA. The former would have been hard to suppress, even if the government had had a mind to do so; the latter would have been taken as an act of subversion and threat to security, meriting disciplinary action up to dismissal. Staff also told the prisoners that when in local public houses, where they were recognised as prison officers, other customers would remark that they hoped staff were not giving the IRA men a hard time. And, indeed, the majority appear to have dealt professionally with their charges, political and non-political alike. Those who may have been warmer and more accommodating to the republicans were balanced by others who were cynical and withdrawn. One or two of these were sarcastic to Ruairí Ó Brádaigh when he was elected to the Dáil, noting that they had previously seen men coming in as IRA and Sinn Féin members and then moving on into constitutional politics.[269]

Tomás Mac Giolla put prison staff in much the same category as ordinary gardaí – a very different one from Special Branch. They did their job, and nobody got pushed around: 'They gave us the normal respect due to us, and did whatever had to be done... they weren't down on us at all.' However, should a prison officer single out and bully a man, the other prisoners would turn on him and have him removed.[270]

The Governor of Mountjoy at this time was Seán Kavanagh, who, as an active republican in the Anglo-Irish War, had been imprisoned by the British authorities in Kilmainham and then in Mountjoy itself. He took the Free State side in the Civil War and, as an army officer, served as Deputy Governor of Newbridge and Governor of Hare Park internment camps. In 1924, he transferred into the civil service as Deputy Governor of Mountjoy. A short spell as Governor of Limerick Prison was followed, in 1928, by his return to Mountjoy as Governor. Thereafter, with one short interruption in 1933, he remained at Mountjoy until his retirement in 1962. This thirty-eight years was unique (he was the longest-serving governor in the 112-year history of Mountjoy) and was rendered all the more extraordinary by his having started this long connection as a prisoner.[271] Thousands of men and women had passed through his charge at Mountjoy by the time the Border Campaign men arrived there in the 1950s. Their talk, attitudes, hopes and outcomes fell into repetitive patterns, which, with Kavanagh's style and banter, given edge by a close knowledge of republicanism, inevitably made for a degree of sardonic detachment mixed with mordant humour. Ó Brádaigh found Kavanagh 'a bit cynical', adding, 'I wouldn't find fault with him at all.'[272]

The chaplaincy

The prison chaplaincy was certainly more engaged. The bishops' statement of 19 January 1956 drew on theological concepts of the just war and the authority of the state to denounce the Border Campaign.[273] The basis for condemnation was the concept of just war, set out by St Augustine and developed by St Thomas Aquinas. War gave rise to very great evils, 'physical, moral and social' and was not lawful unless declared and waged by the supreme authority of the state. No private citizen or organisation could usurp this power. Were individuals to take such measures, the outcome would inevitably be tyranny and oppression. War also had to be waged in a just cause, with all peaceful methods tried first: 'No private individual has authority to judge these issues or to involve the people, from whom he has received no mandate.' Civil war, which caused most damage to a nation, was the one most to be avoided. On this basis, the hierarchy proclaimed it to be a mortal sin to become or to remain a member of an organisation that arrogated to itself the right to bear arms against another state.[274] Moreover, 'it is also sinful for a Catholic to cooperate with, express approval of, or otherwise assist, any such organisation'. Were such assistance significant, the sin was mortal.[275]

At the heart of IRA doctrine, this teaching was not contradicted but was circumscribed by the political and moral claim that the IRA, and it alone, was the legitimate government of Ireland. It claimed title to the authority proclaimed in 1916, reconfirmed by the Second Dáil and passed to it in 1938 by survivors of that body. It followed that it had every right to take armed action and that, in doing so, it did not transgress the teaching on just war. Indeed, given that the true government was being denied its right in what the IRA called the 'twenty-six counties' and that a foreign power occupied the remaining 'six counties', the organisation was obliged to wage war. Short of embracing the IRA's claims to exclusive legitimacy, however, the clergy had been left little room for manoeuvre by the bishops' pastoral, which had been drafted to avoid ambiguities and to close all doors.

The Mountjoy chaplain, Father MacCurtáin, vigorously promulgated the bishops' teaching and directions. Not surprisingly, the result was a stand-off. More difficult was the issue of access to the sacraments. Roman Catholics are obliged to make confession and receive communion at least once a year, at Easter, the holiest festival in the Christian year. Ruairí Ó Brádaigh made his confession in preparation for Easter communion in 1957. At the point in the sacramental dialogue when the priest would customarily pronounce the words of absolution, Father MacCurtáin asked Ó Brádaigh if he were a member of the IRA. It was a formal question only. Ó Brádaigh, sitting in the confessional in the military-style clothing in which he had been arrested, confirmed that he was indeed a member and would remain one. Absolution was accordingly refused.[276]

Tomás Mac Giolla had a slightly different memory of encounters with the clergy. Whereas at the Curragh, under internment, the prisoner had not been convicted and could therefore apparently deflect a priest's enquiry, Mountjoy prisoners had been convicted under the OASA. Even then, however, if the confessor did not put the question, the prisoner had no reason to raise the issue and so most men could successfully complete their confession and receive absolution. On at least one occasion there was a confrontation between the chaplain and a group of prisoners. Mac Giolla remembered men queuing up to enter the confessional and to argue their case: 'They would say, "If I raped a woman it would be all right. Is that the way it is with you?"'[277]

The clergy took a vow of obedience to their superiors, as unconditional as the obligation undertaken by those who entered the IRA.[278] Charlie Murphy, almost fifty years later, remembered Father MacCurtáin with an undiminished strength of feeling: 'I hated him.' He, with all the IRA men, understood that prison staff at all levels were simply doing their duty, 'but this guy was obnoxious'. The men attended mass but were always happier when Father MacCurtáin was not officiating. This coloured Murphy's subsequent view of the Roman Catholic Church, as did the bishops' pastoral letter of January 1956.[279]

Although Ó Brádaigh was soured about the clergy as a result of his Mountjoy experience, he adhered to his Roman Catholic faith.[280] He and other IRA men who were strong in their attachment to the Church were doubtless much consoled by clergy other than the chaplain who attended the prison. With a number of others, he remembered the sympathetic Capuchin, Father Livinius, 'who was fine'. Other visiting priests, who, the chaplaincy might argue, did not have specific pastoral responsibility for the men or a direct duty to the bishop in that regard, were able to take a more liberal approach. Some of these clerical visitors themselves probably held republican views or were sympathetic towards them.[281] Looking back, it is hard to see how the Roman Catholic hierarchy and clergy reasoned. They wanted to win the men away from political violence, but these were individuals who, by definition, were opposed to and not overawed by established authority. Edicts were certainly the style of the Roman Catholic Church in Ireland at the time. It was the most respected institution in the Republic, and the laity were indeed disposed to respond to its pronouncements. That the same manner might not work with rebellious young men and hardened veterans, that it might indeed be counterproductive, does not seem to have been considered in instructions to the prison chaplaincy.

Escape

Internment greatly changed the prospect and perspective for IRA men serving sentences. As soon as it came into effect, and they realised that freedom could be deferred for years, escape moved up the agenda and an attempt was made. On the evening of 25 July 1957, four men dragged an insufficiently secured ladder to the perimeter wall. Using this and sheet-ropes, two of them clambered onto the wall. They had been spotted, however, and escape was blocked by armed Special Branch men and by prison staff.[282] Army General Order No. 8 and the whole orientation of the campaign forbade any act of violence towards the security personnel of the Republic, and, in consequence, the escape was thwarted.[283] Traynor was deeply concerned and pressed for the dismissal of Governor Seán Kavanagh, on grounds of negligence. An inquiry by Paddy Terry, then Principal at the Department of Justice in charge of prisons, mollified the Minister, but various steps were taken to prevent any repetition. Traynor, an Old IRA man, had himself been interned and imprisoned in Mountjoy in the early 1930s and took a close interest both in the details of the escape and in the proposed improvements in security.[284]

Closing down the campaign

Even when it became clear that the notion of building guerrilla momentum was fanciful and stood not the slightest chance of being realised, the Border Campaign meandered on because no one in the IRA had the authority to bring it to an end. Those who had conceived it and those who had launched and shaped it had left the leadership or, indeed, the organisation itself. Second, third and fourth echelons of leaders had come and gone. As measured by arrests and sentences in the Republic of Ireland, the twin effects of the OASA and internment can be seen to have had a devastating effect. In 1957, 122 persons were charged under the OASA, of whom 116 were convicted. The following year, the respective figures were fifteen charged and fifteen convicted.[285] The trend continued, and, by May 1960, only twelve men were imprisoned following OASA convictions.[286]

Not all IRA activities were dealt with under the provisions of the OASA. Other offences fell under the Firearms Act, 1925, and the Explosive Substances Act, 1883. A list of offences committed by the thirty-three IRA men serving sentences (all in Mountjoy) in February 1962 showed that they ranged from the baseline 'refusal to account for movements' (the normal sentence for which was three to six months) to the possession of firearms and ammunition with intent. For this latter offence, sentences were as high as eight years (Michael McEldowney) to as low as three years (Denis O'Riordan). Other offences included refusal to give information (three to six months), membership of an unlawful organisation (between six months and two years), possession of incriminating documents (three to six months) and possession of arms and ammunition – but where intent could not be proved. This last attracted a sentence of between six months (where the case was heard and sentenced in a District Court) and eighteen months (Special Criminal Court).[287]

Sentences varied with the circumstances of each case, though the baseline of refusal to account for movement and possession of incriminating documents received, on conviction, standard sentences with few exceptions. The details of the offence and the character of the offender became more important with serious offences. Thus, Michael McEldowney's hefty eight-year sentence for the possession of firearms and ammunition with intent, reflected the court's view of both the offender and the circumstances of the offence.[288] Richard Nagle and Alphonsus Larkin received heavy sentences for the same offence (seven years each) but were deemed not to have been in the same category.[289] There is insufficient data to support a thorough analysis, but it seems improbable that the political and security context of each offence would not have had an influence. The logic is hard to recreate, however. How would a sentencer treat a serious offence in a period of calm, for example? Would it be more or less serious because it was a relatively isolated event?

Five years into the Campaign, the Irish government (now headed by de Valera's Fianna Fáil successor, Seán Lemass) acting on garda intelligence that the IRA had undertaken a measure of regrouping and was planning new activities, opted for far stronger measures. Three considerations lay behind this decision. First, although the Campaign had diminished to the level where policing alone was necessary to contain it, that in itself was a costly item. Only a small group was involved, Lemass told the Dáil, but some 600 gardaí were engaged solely in anti-IRA activities, with 250 on special duties in the border counties. These deployments, the government estimated, were costing around £400,000 per annum.[290] Closely related to the question of cost, and outweighing it in several respects, was the fear of injury and death along the border. Any government, never mind one that claimed *de jure* authority over the territory and citizens under attack, had a moral obligation to protect life and property. The international consequences, practical and reputational, of the injury or death of RUC or Special Constabulary members were always likely to be unpleasant and could have grave and unexpected consequences at an intergovernmental level. Finally, at this point Lemass was beginning to shape his post-de Valera policy towards Northern Ireland (the first meeting with the Northern Ireland Prime Minister, Terence O'Neill, was little more than three years away).[291] It was a long-standing Northern grievance that the Republic was insufficiently vigorous in its response to the IRA (and many in Northern Ireland accused the South of bad faith as well as torpor). A demonstration to the contrary had to be made.

On 23 November 1961, Dublin announced that it would exercise its powers and reconstitute the Special Criminal Court. This step, Lemass announced, was justified only because of the 'grave circumstances'.[292] Offenders brought before the District Court were not being subjected to sentences of a weight which their offences merited. In a carefully worded reference to judicial leniency in such cases, Lemass noted that use of the District Courts 'may have occasioned some misunderstanding amongst those concerned with them as to the seriousness with which the Government view the position and their determination to deal with it'. The difficulty of bringing matters before a higher, non-summary court (the Central Criminal Court) was that this would entail the use of a jury, and, given the IRA's record, this meant the intimidation of jurors and witnesses. Lemass assured the Dáil that the only cases which would be brought before the Special Criminal Court (which was, of course, manned exclusively by military officers and therefore immune from intimidation) would be those arising from 'this armed conspiracy of violence'. This was not all. Should this drastic step be insufficient to suppress the IRA's activities, his government 'will not hesitate to take still further steps'.[293] In response to questions, Lemass pointed out that the Special Criminal Court would follow the same rules of procedure and of evidence as civil courts. Though he did not spell it out, the principal distinction between the Special and the Central Criminal Courts was that, in the former, the panel of army officers were both finders of facts and sentencers and, as sentencers, had available to them the full range of disposals of the higher civil court.

The Dáil received the Taoiseach's statement relatively calmly. James Dillon, on behalf of Fine Gael, accepted the government's decision, taken in the light of confidential information available only to them, adding the caveat that normal operation of the criminal law should be restored as soon as possible. Joseph Barron (Clann na Poblachta) and Jack McQuillan (at this point National Progressive Democrats) asked critical questions with a republican tilt, but Brendan Corish, speaking for the Labour Party, simply sought reassurance about the rules, procedures and fairness of the Special Criminal Court.[294] Sniping continued in the Dáil over the succeeding months, but it was confined to those very few with even a residual sympathy for the IRA.[295] In the meantime, as we have seen, cases were brought before the Special Criminal Court, and sentences which had been denominated in months by District Courts were now handed down in years. (McEldowney's sentence exemplified the shift.) This was as the government had intended and, compounded with the many other difficulties of the IRA, helped to smother the embers of the Border Campaign.

The IRA's formal statement of the cessation of the Campaign came on 26 February 1962. It largely blamed the Irish people for the failure and, avoiding all self-criticism, left the door open for a re-run, should conditions be propitious.[296] On 8 March 1962, probably the earliest possible date to get on the order paper, four deputies raised questions about the release of prisoners with Charles Haughey, now Minister for Justice.[297] For the Labour Party, Seán Treacy asked whether any of those convicted of offences under the relevant Acts had 'indicated a willingness to respect the Constitution and if so, whether it was intended to free them?' This was a long way short of an amnesty, especially since it was established practice in most cases for an act of renunciation of violence to be rewarded with early release. Treacy, Noël Browne and McQuillan wanted to know whether the end of the IRA's campaign, confirmed in its statement of 26 February, was sufficient to persuade the government to discontinue the operation of the Special Criminal Court and to release the prisoners: they clearly thought that one followed the other.[298]

Just as the IRA had kept its options open, so Charles Haughey, on behalf of the government, refused to offer leniency for what he saw as the IRA's pig-in-a-poke statement. He pointed out that it was not true to claim (as had Browne and McQuillan) that the IRA had eschewed the use of force to end Partition: 'The statement specifically stated that the organisation is to remain in being and it went on to speak of a period of consolidation, expansion and preparation.' The existence of unlawful organisations claiming the right to use force if and when it suited them would not be tolerated. The IRA's confession of failure (in line with Fianna Fáil's unvarying policy Haughey avoided referring to the IRA, preferring 'the illegal organisation concerned') and its further admission that its campaign of violence had been rejected by the Irish people 'should bring home to the individual members the futility of the continued existence of the organisation itself'.[299] On the matter of releases, either as a consequence of individuals signing undertakings or by way of general release, Haughey refused to be drawn.

It was not the practice to disclose when a prisoner had given an undertaking. As for other forms of release, were the government at any time satisfied that there was no remaining threat to the Constitution or to law 'they would be prepared to review the situation'.[300]

This chapter has, in the main, looked at the part of the Curragh and its life that was most visible. Although I have drawn on internees' letters and on interviews, the source materials have predominantly been drawn from official archives and from the public record. Like all custodial institutions, the Curragh and Mountjoy had another and less visible life. It is to that we turn in the final chapter. The hidden life has been uncovered and discussed throughout the book, and it is time to draw together a number of our insights and questions.

Notes

1 See above, p. 793. It is telling that, in a Dáil debate four months later, Jack McQuillan, the pro-IRA Clann na Poblachta deputy, in a Private Member's motion debate, managed, without mentioning the death of Constable Cecil Gregg, to refer to the attack on Forkhill (*Dáil Debates*, vol. 164, cols. 608, *et seq.*, 6 November 1957). In the same speech, he referred, apparently without irony, to internment as de Valera's 'policy of repression against young Irishmen' (col. 621).

2 NAI TAOIS/G3/23.

3 Brian Faulkner, *Memoirs of a Statesman*, ed. John Houston (London: Weidenfeld & Nicolson, 1978), p. 117. The memoir was written in the mid-1970s, when the final and most contentious use of internment (which Faulkner had introduced when he assumed the Stormont Premiership) had been widely criticised and deemed a failure. One must therefore read his qualification that to be successful internment had to be introduced on both sides of the border, in that context.

4 Oscar Traynor (1886–1963) had taken part in the Easter Rising and was, as a consequence, interned in Frongoch Camp, North Wales. During the Anglo-Irish War he led the attack on the Custom House. He was a leader of the anti-Treaty forces in the Civil War (OC in Dublin on the outbreak of hostilities), was captured and imprisoned. He sided with de Valera when Sinn Féin split in March 1927, having been elected to the Dáil in March 1925 (though at this point an abstentionist). He was elected as a Fianna Fáil TD in 1932 and in 1936 entered the Cabinet. At a later point in his career he served as Minister for Defence in a number of de Valera's administrations, eventually becoming Minister for Justice.

5 *Dáil Debates*, vol. 164, col. 639, 6 November 1957.

6 *Dáil Debates*, vol. 164, col. 640.

7 *Dáil Debates*, vol. 164, col. 640. McQuillan made the point that it was difficult to understand why men, against whom there was such strong circumstantial evidence of arms possession, should be released. It may well have been that legal advice was taken that suggested the case could fail were it taken to court: the men were not taken in actual possession of the arms.

8 *Evening Herald*, 13 July 1957, 1a–g. To avoid a demonstration by supporters, the men were formally released from Mountjoy an hour early, at 6 a.m. Two army trucks and a strong complement of Special Branch men effected the transfer. Ruairí Ó Brádaigh was one of the rearrested.

9 The Irish Army soldiers who had been in the Glasshouse, under punishment, were removed to another barracks.

10 MA PM/I/ADM/30-29, Curragh Releases, July 1957–March 1959. This document also gives the date of reception into the camp, and other useful information. See also NAI JUS/8/1100, c.3 December 1958.

11 Aerial photographs were taken of the camp on 4 November 1957 and are held in the MA PM/30/23; there is also an explanatory sketch at PM/30/20.

12 The ICRC delegate gave different dimensions, averaging 40 yards (120 feet) by 15 yards (45 feet). This gives a total of 5,400 square feet as against the Army's 3,260 square feet. Since the Army had reason to maximise the footage, its lesser figure might be preferred to that of the ICRC. See Report at NAI DFA/417/39/19/4/2/1.

13 MA PM/I/ADM/19, Statements on Internment Camp, memo 'Curragh Detention Camp', 25 November 1958. See also NAI JUS/8/1099, Memorandum on Curragh Detention Camp, 26 September 1958. This calculated the space allowance per internee as between 834 and 860 cubic feet. The Army pointed out that the optimum space recommended for soldiers was 800 cubic feet. Some of this space, however, rose into the apex of the roof and was of little direct use to the internees (although it did increase breathing space).

14 Hut No. 1 was not in use. No. 2 was divided, with thirty-eight men of the IRA in the larger portion and five men of Saor Uladh (referred to in the files as the 'splinter IRA group') in the smaller. Huts 3 and 4 each held forty-one men.

15 The internees objected to these transfers as irritating and inconvenient, a tactic 'which could be construed' to provoke trouble between the prisoners 'and those whose unpleasant task it is to keep them in confinement'. MA PM/I/ADM/21, MacCurtáin (IRA OC) to Camp Commandant, 1 January 1958.

16 NAI JUS/8/1040, Memorandum on Curragh Internment Camp, 8 October 1957. The men undertook their own laundry, soap and hot water being provided. More adventurously, they also did their own haircutting for which three sets of equipment were available. Sixteen months into internment, the security of the huts was increased by installing wire mesh over the windows. This led the internees to fret and agitate that in the event of a night-time fire they would be trapped. Given that the huts themselves were of a relatively flimsy construction, easy to break out of, the danger was possibly exaggerated (though smoke as well as fire is a remarkably swift killer). Against that, a high proportion of the internees were smokers, with the attendant risk of accidental fire (MA PM/I/ADM/12, Report, 18 November 1958). A formal letter of complaint was lodged by Tomás MacCurtáin on 19 November and reported to army headquarters.

17 The raised posts (watchtowers) were manned by infantry. Only the military police came into contact with the internees (Peter Brennan interview).

18 These details are taken from Noel Kavanagh's short and unpublished account of the escapes of Dáithí Ó Conaill and Ruairí Ó Brádaigh.

19 Ruairí Ó Brádaigh interview. While these defects were being corrected, soldiers spoke to internees' visitors about them. One visitor subsequently wrote to an internee. 'The soldiers had said that the huts leak terribly in winter or any wet weather for that matter.' He urged the internee to give his mother the details in his next letter out and they could then be given to the *United Irishman* (MA PM/I/ADM/12, Letter of 14 September 1957). In a report of 25 November 1958, the Camp Commandant listed all the complaints about leaks in the sixteen months that the camp had been in operation. On 17 October 1957, there had been nine leaks after a night of heavy rain. All had immediately been repaired. Thereafter, several leaks were reported in January and February 1958 and were dealt with promptly. Instances of leaking then became few or less frequent (MA PM/I/ADM/19, Statements on Internment Camp, memo 'Curragh Detention Camp', 25 November 1958).

20 *Dáil Debates*, vol. 164, col. 627, 6 November 1957. By mid-autumn, the inside hardboard lining of the huts had been completed, and interior porches had been

constructed in order to reduce draughts; each hut had also been re-roofed (*Dáil Debates*, vol. 164, col. 653).

21 MA PM/I/ADM/21, Complaints of Internee MacCurtáin of 7 May 1958, annotated by Camp Commandant, Adjutant or Quartermaster General and Minister.

22 *Ibid.*

23 Oscar Traynor also told the Dáil about these improvements, and reported that the soap allowance for laundering clothes had recently (mid-autumn 1957) been increased (*Dáil Debates*, vol. 164, col. 654, 6 November 1957).

24 Ó Brádaigh interview. The layout of the huts meant there were at least five unfavourable bed-spaces: those nearest the lavatory (even with flush basins) because of the smell and traffic; opposite the door, because of the draught; and nearest the fire, because of the lack of privacy. As the camp population declined and more space became available, the Commandant agreed to MacCurtáin's request that these bed positions be kept empty (MA PM/30–11, Captain P. Ó Riada, Deputy Commandant to Adjutant General, 19 April 1958). Jack McQuillan supported IRA claims that, as a result of these conditions, there was, within weeks of the camp being occupied, an outbreak of dysentery. If true (and the claim was not challenged), this would have contributed to further strains on the facilities and to a degradation in conditions (see *Dáil Debates*, vol. 164, col. 627, 6 November 1957).

25 'You weren't in cells... I've forgotten how many were in the hut, and... in many ways you begin to long for a cell, the privacy of a cell. I know that sounds strange' (Charlie Murphy interview). Mick Ryan contended that the lack of privacy was a hardship and deprivation: 'In a cell it was okay. Mountjoy was good from that point of view' (interview). John L. McCormack, who had been interned in the 1940s, served a short sentence in Mountjoy in 1956. Prison was preferable to the camp, he insisted: 'Ah, we had privacy and you had your cell and the warders were very, very helpful, yes; but the PAs [Military Police] and the military weren't in the same class at all' (interview).

26 Tomás Mac Giolla interview. During his time at the Curragh, eight or ten people were released on health grounds, and Mac Giolla noted, 'I know of one or two who never really recovered.'

27 See above, pp. 705–7.

28 NAI JUS/8/1101, Statement of Sinn Féin Publicity Committee, 25 November 1958.

29 *Sunday Independent*, 18 August 1957, 1b–c. Many of these claims were repeated by Deputy Jack McQuillan (probably drawing on a briefing document) in the Dáil debate of 6 November 1957 (see *Dáil Debates*, vol. 164, cols. 626–8).

30 NAI JUS/8/1056, Conditions at Curragh Detention Camp, 18 August 1957. The degree of urgency in the matter was shown by the fact that the meeting to prepare the rebuttal was convened on Sunday, 18 August 1957 at the Curragh – the same day that Sinn Féin's accusations were reported in the *Sunday Independent*. A statement was produced that day, in time for the following day's newspapers. See *Irish Independent*, 19 August 1957, 1b–c, 2e. The following year, when the Irish Association for Civil Liberty applied for permission to send a small group to visit the camp (Dr W. B. Stanford, Dr Owen Sheehy-Skeffington [a member of the Senate] and Dr Roger McHugh [a former member of the Senate]), their request was refused (NAI JUS/8/1099, Memorandum on Curragh Camp, Appendix B).

31 NAI JUS/8/1056, Conditions in Curragh Detention Camp, 18 August 1957. A draft statement was immediately prepared for ministerial approval.

32 There survives a note of the way in which the visit came about. At a meeting of the ICRC in Delhi in 1957, attended by Mrs Barry in her capacity as Chairman of the Irish Red Cross, the President of the International Committee raised with her complaints that had been received regarding the Curragh internment camp. He asked

whether a visit to the camp by an ICRC delegate might be arranged. On her return to Ireland, Mrs Barry put the request to the Department of Defence. The Minister put the matter to Cabinet, and a visit was agreed. NAI DFA/417/39/19/4/2/1, Secretary, Department of Justice to Secretary, Department of Defence, 30 May 1958.

33 NAI PRES/1/P/1331; NAI DFA/417/39/19/4/2/1. Leslie Barry (née Price; 1893–1984) married Tom Barry in 1921. She had been Director of Organisation for Cumann na mBan. In 1950, she was appointed President of the Irish Red Cross. She had a solidly republican background, going back to 1916, when she received orders from Thomas Clarke. She was a trained teacher, but in 1917 became full-time Director of Cumann na mBan. Both she and her husband took the anti-Treaty side. She ceased to be politically active in the 1930s and in 1939 was a founder member of the Irish Red Cross, becoming Chairman in 1950. In later life she would receive many international awards for her humanitarian work. She was a distinguished and able woman, by any measure. Melchior Borsinger was then the Personal Assistant to the President of the ICRC.

34 At the conclusion of the inspection, Tomás MacCurtáin obtained a private interview. In the course of conversation he asked Borsinger to rank the Curragh. According to MacCurtáin's account, the delegate told him that he had inspected British camps in Cyprus and French camps in Algeria. There may have been camps which those two governments had not allowed him to see, he acknowledged, but he judged the British and French camps to be much better than the Curragh (Ó Brádaigh interview). The delegate, no doubt drawing on experience, had told MacCurtáin that if the report favoured the government it would be published, otherwise not. The ICRC report was not published. (Ó Brádaigh interview.)

35 See NAI DFA/417/39/19/4/2/1 for the full report. In the nature of such reports, attention is going to focus on weaknesses in the arrangements, and there will be few comments on satisfactory provision. The Adjutant General responded to criticism and suggestions, which further shifted the focus from satisfactory to less satisfactory aspects of camp life (MA PM/I/ADM/19, Report from the ICRC, Geneva, on a visit to the Curragh Camp on 20 February 1958). The Adjutant General's response was dated June 1958. The four-month gap between the visit and the response is not unreasonable and was largely due to the length of time it took the ICRC to complete and authorise the report, which was sent from Geneva on 11 April, and the time after receipt for the Camp Commandant and his colleagues to prepare their response.

36 See below, p. 1050.

37 'Food is abundant and of good quality… the only complaint in this respect was monotony. There were no complaints with regard to quality and quantity' (ICRC Report, *op. cit.*, p. 3). Army dietary scales, of which the internee allowance was an enhanced form, may be found in a Dáil written answer (*Dáil Debates*, vol. 171, col. 840, 25 November 1958).

38 NAI JUS/8/1056, Response to report from the ICRC, *op. cit.*

39 *Dáil Papers*, SI No. 146/1957, OAS(A)A, (Detention) Regulations, 1957 (hereafter Detention Regulations), Regulation No. 27(1).

40 By November 1958, there had been fifteen releases on medical grounds, as follows: nerves (eight); asthma (two); lumbar complaint (two); stomach trouble (one); general debility (one); bad sight (one) (MA PM/I/ADM/19, Statements on Internment Camp, memo 'Curragh Detention Camp', 25 November 1958, Appendix A).

41 The verbal undertaking had been given by Gerry Lawless, see p. 803 above.

42 ICRC Report *op. cit.*, p. 6, para. 25.

43 Former internees we have interviewed have not made unfavourable comments on the Curragh clergy, all army chaplains. Their recollections, rather, have referred to the Curragh chaplains being willing to give them access to the sacraments without requiring an undertaking to forsake the IRA (see pp. 1009–10).

44 MA PM/I/ADM/19, Statement, on Internment Camp, memo 'Curragh Detention Camp', 25 November 1958.

45 The weather on the day of the visit was anticipated to be 'mainly cloudy, some outbreaks of light rain… north-westerly winds, occasionally fresh' (*Irish Independent*, 20 February 1958, 6d). Borsinger noted that the Curragh climate was 'raw, windy and damp, with frequent ground mist and a damp soil' (ICRC Report, *op. cit.*, p. 1).

46 ICRC Report, *op. cit.*, p. 7.

47 NAI DFA/417/39/19/4/2/1, Secretary, Ministry of External Affairs to Secretary, Ministry of Defence, 11 June 1958.

48 NAI DFA/417/39/19/4/2/1, memoranda, 30 May 1958 and 2 June 1958. The British Embassy had not asked to see the ICRC Report.

49 This visit took place on 25 June 1958. A further inspection had been scheduled for May 1959.

50 NAI DFA/417/39/19/4/2/1, J. S. Pictet, President ICRC, to Leslie Barry, Irish Red Cross, 18 February 1959.

51 NAI DFA/417/39/19/4/2/1, Kevin Boland to Leslie Barry, 17 April 1959. On Mountjoy, see below, p. 1028.

52 Hut lighting had been upgraded and electrical sockets installed to allow the heating of water and some cooking (*Dáil Debates*, vol. 164, cols. 653–4, 6 November 1957, statement by the Minister for Justice, Oscar Traynor).

53 The Camp Commandant had presented a strong case for the replacement of the bed boards and trestles, arguing that they posed problems of hygiene and security. In addition, the Medical Officer had deemed them to be unsuitable for sitting on for prolonged periods. There were some former Irish Army soldiers among the internees, and they were aware that the usual provision for soldiers was the spring bed. No extra expenditure would be required (a crucial point) since there were sufficient beds in the army stores (MA PM/I/ADM/21, Commandant B. G. Maguirc to Adjutant General, 25 January 1958).

54 Ó Brádaigh interview. The Adjutant General, supporting a strong case submitted by the Camp Commandant for the replacement of the unsatisfactory trestle and bed boards with spring beds, had pointed out that a Red Cross inspection was imminent. The beds should be issued immediately since were that done after the Red Cross visit it 'would give the impression to the internees that the Red Cross were responsible for this improvement' (MA PM/I/ADM/21, Adjutant General to Quartermaster General, 8 February 1958). The Adjutant General wanted the Quartermaster's comments before making a submission to the Minister.

55 By early December 1958, a sufficient number of men had passed through the camp and its medical services to support a fairly comprehensive overview of internees' health. The number of internees admitted to the Curragh General Military Hospital between 8 July and 3 December 1957 was sixty-nine; the number of admissions (some men were admitted more than once) was ninety-two. Length of stay ranged from two to eighty days (the latter a man with sciatica, eventually released on medical grounds). Twenty-seven operations were performed on internees, from the minor (ingrown toenail) to the fairly serious (appendectomy). The sixty-nine men admitted to hospital included twenty-five within a short period, due to an outbreak of influenza. No internee was admitted to an outside hospital, but a number were examined by outside specialists (NAI JUS/8/1099, Statistical Memorandum, 25 November 1958).

56 Four months into internment, the government was still considering the matter, with an indication that dentures, spectacles and surgical appliances would be provided on the Medical Officer's certification of necessity (*Dáil Debates*, vol. 164, col. 656, 6 November 1957).

57 Detention Regulations Nos. 43, 50 and 60; NAI JUS/8/1040, Memorandum on the Curragh, 8 October 1957. By the time this memorandum was issued, seven internees had received hospital treatment.

58 Writing to his father, an internee complained that he would have to get private dental treatment since he had been unable to see the dentist for eight months or more, always being told that he was busy (MA PM/I/ADM/12, Letter, 14 July 1958). The complaint was noted by the camp censors and passed on to a senior officer in the Army's medical department. See also Tomás MacCurtáin's list of complaints about inadequacy and delay in providing services (MA PM/I/ADM/21, MacCurtáin to Camp Commandant, 1 January 1958).

59 See above, p. 1054, n. 40.

60 John Tully (Clann na Poblachta) continued to raise questions about Curragh conditions, particularly overcrowding and leaks in the roofs and the effect these had on the health of internees. These were stonewalled by Minister for Defence Kevin Boland (see *Dáil Debates*, vol. 171, cols. 292–3, 30 October 1958 and col. 818, 25 November 1958).

61 MA PM/I/ADM/21, Commandant B. G. Maguire to Adjutant General, 7 November 1958.

62 MA PM/I/ADM/21, Captain P. Ó Riada, Deputy Commandant, to Commandant Internment Camp, 6 November 1958.

63 Murphy interview. Gus Cronin, a military policeman, drew a distinction between internees from the North and the South, with the former being more vicious towards the guard (interview).

64 ICRC Report, *op. cit.*, p. 6.

65 MA PM/I/ADM/21, MacCurtáin to Camp Commandant, 1 January 1958.

66 Brendan O'Brien, *The Long War: The IRA and Sinn Féin* (Dublin: The O'Brien Press, 1995), Appendix 2: IRA General Army Orders, p. 407.

67 Murphy interview. He continued, 'I know it's semantics.' But such formulas, as the worlds of politics and commerce constantly demonstrate, can be crucial in allowing an accommodation.

68 See pp. 302–11; 617–52.

69 Detention Regulation No. 51(1) dealt with complaints from internees. The Commandant was directed to provide facilities for individuals to make complaints or to submit a request. It also allowed for complaints and requests other than by individuals. For this purpose, 'the internees shall elect or appoint a "Captain" to represent them'.

70 This acceptance of collective representations was also a recognition that a dual structure of authority would exist within the camp, a circumstance that had far-reaching consequences. It also meant that no individual or group could opt out of the representations that were being made on their behalf. No ordinary prison countenances collective representations, except perhaps in minor matters of housekeeping, and then through an approved committee. This principle that an individual speaks only for himself is intended to avoid or curtail the chances of concerted action. Here at the Curragh, however, concerted action worked in favour of the administration.

71 Brennan interview.

72 Dick Reade interview. This was to some extent reciprocated: 'But you also knew that they had their own discipline and they had their own code of conduct, you kind of respected them for that.'

73 NAI JUS/8/1056, Report from the International Committee of the Red Cross, Geneva.

74 Interview. Ó Brádaigh was a teacher, and in 1950s Ireland the profession was highly respected. As ill-luck would have it, a man who had sought his advice sometimes had the duty of counting the prisoners in and out of the camp to the playing field. He was on gate-guard duty the night that Ó Brádaigh escaped. At the time, Ó Brádaigh

reflected, 'You poor devil you, pulling this off, you're going to be in trouble now.' The guard was not seen again in the camp after the escape.

75 Ryan interview.

76 *Dáil Debates*, vol. 164, col. 628, 6 November 1957.

77 Mac Giolla interview. En route to the Curragh, soldiers in his escort had said 'Don't blame us.' Many internees (correctly) thought that in the event of an escape soldiers would not open fire with lethal intent, and, indeed, during the mass escape of 2 December 1959, nobody was fired upon with intent to kill, minor leg-wounds being the only injuries. (And these, it appeared, had been caused by casings from tear-gas granades.) Mac Giolla suggested that, pleading a fault on the telephone line, sentries in the immediate vicinity of the escape deliberately did not summon the Speedy Reaction Squad. The fact that the Irish Army in the border areas had never opened fire was, Mac Giolla contended, another indication of their ambivalence. That may have been true, though it is unlikely. The legal consequences of inflicting injury or death were more important constraints, as were political considerations.

78 Charlie Murphy recalled that the food was good. Irish Army rations were issued, 'and if you've never seen a military sausage you would have to see it, because it's determined by weight or calorific value or something' (interview).

79 The reception breakfast was important in setting the tone, and, intentionally or otherwise, it was good psychology. It was not too obvious a device either, since it was the practice to take the prisoners from Mountjoy to the Curragh in the early morning of the day that their sentences expired. Kavanagh emphasised the importance of the rations: 'We got exactly the same food as the army soldiers. We didn't get the fare that they were getting up in the officers' mess, but we got very good food. I had no complaints about that period, food-wise' (interview). He was not to know it, but internees actually got a more comprehensive allowance than ordinary soldiers. In addition to the meals a soldier would have received, internees were allowed a supper ration of bread, butter, tea, sugar and milk. NAI JUS/8/1040, Memorandum on Curragh, 8 October 1957; *Dáil Debates*, vol. 164, col. 654, 6 November 1957.

80 Detention Regulation No. 11. That in turn had been submitted to the legislature in the form of a Statutory Instrument.

81 NAI JUS/8/1040, Memorandum on Curragh, 8 October 1957.

82 MA PM/I/ADM/12, S. Ryan to mother, 15 September 1958. The camp censor noted that there had been a number of complaints about food the previous month.

83 MA PM/I/ADM/12, internee to mother, 13 October 1958. He added that there were plans in hand to increase menu choices. By the early part of 1958, however, internees were less responsive to the camp authorities' line that in food, living space, footwear and other matters, internees were on a par with Irish Army soldiers. Such comparisons, Tomás MacCurtáin bitterly observed, did not help: 'No prisoner entered this Camp of his own free will and none remains within it of his own volition' (MA PM/I/ADM/21, MacCurtáin to Camp Commandant, 1 January 1958).

84 Murphy interview, additional written response.

85 See, for example, 'Inside the Curragh Concentration Camp', *United Irishman*, September 1957, 12a–e.

86 Ryan interview. Tomás Mac Giolla described the food as 'very acceptable – for so many people it was better than they had been getting at home' (interview).

87 Much of the document could be traced back to old DORA internment regulations. The additional provisions, Jack McQuillan sardonically observed, were 'the product of the native, brilliant, penal intellect. They were actually an improvement, if such is the correct word to use, on the work of the experts the British used' (*Dáil Debates*, vol. 164, col. 624, 6 November 1957).

88 The regulations for the administration of the camp were set out in the Detention Regulations. Regulation No. 29L 'Persons authorised to award punishments' restricted the imposition of 'punishment or privation of any kind' to the Commandant or, in his absence, the officer appointed to act for him.

89 Detention Regulations, Nos. 33 and 34.

90 Other punishments included a restricted dietary along military lines and, as provided for in the Rules for Military Prisons and Detention Barracks, 1954 (SI No. 291/ 1954), deprivation of mattress for up to three days and loss of privileges such as parcels, association, visits, correspondence and classes and instruction. Quite apart from these punishments, the use of 'irons or mechanical restraints' was authorised. It was clear that this could not be for punishment but only 'in case of necessity'. Any use of irons or other restraints had to be entered in the Commandant's journal. As far as can now be determined, this power (intended for a person who became violent or uncontrollable) was never used. From the surviving documents, it also appears that the detention barracks was rarely used for punishment (MA PM/30–19, PM Strength of Internment Camp). That it was sometimes used, however, was indicated by memoranda that resulted in an order to the Commandant to ensure that where a man had been sentenced to close confinement his next of kin were notified. This arose from a case where a mother visited but was unable to see her son because he was under punishment. This was to avoid relatives making a fruitless trip to the Curragh, only to learn – perhaps after a lengthy and expensive journey – that the visit could not take place. (Such a case had been raised by the Deputy Adjutant, Colonel P. S. O'Faolain, on 17 February.) Besides a humane wish to avoid such loss and inconvenience, the authorities no doubt had in the mind the protests that relatives might well lodge with their TD. The Order stipulated, however, that in writing to the family the words 'close confinement' should not be used (MA PM/I/ADM/1, General Correspondence, Memo 17 February 1957, order 21 February 1957). Parcels, correspondence visits and other privileges were suspended whilst a man was in close confinement.

91 See Regulation No. 32. As in civilian prisons, the Medical Officer had to be informed of the names of any prisoners under punishment (Regulation No. 44; see also No. 59[2]). The concern was that a person who was unfit for punishment should not be subjected to it.

92 NAI JUS/8/1040, Memorandum on the Curragh, 8 October 1957. The rate of offending seems particularly low, considering the age distribution of the internees. On 20 February 1958, when Melchior Borsinger visited, there were 125 men in the camp. Of those ninety-one (73 per cent) were aged up to thirty years. Only fifteen (12 per cent) were between thirty and forty, and nineteen (15 per cent) were aged above forty (NAI DFA/417/39/19/4/2/1, ICRC report).

93 Detention Regulations Nos. 30(1–14) and 17(1–3). Internees also had to take a bath on reception and submit to a medical examination. If a man were suffering from a skin disease or if he were verminous, he was to be given appropriate treatment. Power was given to the Commandant, on the advice of the Medical Officer, to deal in an appropriate manner with internees who were in weak health or suffering from physical or mental infirmity (Regulation No. 20). (More to the point, perhaps, might have been to question why such men were interned.)

94 Detention Regulations Nos. 27(1), 25 and 27(3).

95 *Ibid.* The solicitor was Myles P. Shevlin of Carlow. No reason was given in the file for the ban, but presumably it was because of his IRA connection or suspicions of his willingness to act as a courier. J. Bowyer Bell notes that on 11 November 1957, Shevlin had been brought onto the IRA GHQ staff. J. Bowyer Bell, *The Secret Army: The IRA from 1916* (Cambridge, Mass.: MIT Press, 1983), p. 313. This appointment

would certainly have been known to Dublin's Special Branch. See also MA PM/I/ ADM/12, Note of 7 September 1957.

96 Detention Regulation No. 25. The Camp Intelligence Officer noted in a report to HQ that a particular man 'has visited a number of internees as an Uncle' (MA PM/I/ADM/ 12). If the evasion were not too blatant the authorities seemed willing to condone it.

97 MA PM/I/ADM/4, Extract from Standing Instruction No. 16, 1957. Legal practitioners (solicitors, solicitors' clerks and barristers) had to be given security clearance by military intelligence and Special Branch.

98 Detention Regulation No. 26(3); MA PM/I/ADM/3, Memorandum, Commandant P. MagCanna to Adjutant General, 19 January 1959. The Commandant also considered at this time refusing to send out any internee letter headed 'Curragh Concentration Camp'. This proposal, another sure way of stirring up the internees and their supporters, was also dropped. MA PM/I/ADM/12, memorandum 8 January 1959.

99 Detention Regulation No. 14.

100 I have been unable to identify the origins of the name. The internees were expecting a stay of some five years, so the provision of replacement clothing was a reasonable request.

101 Murphy interview. The sentenced prisoners in Mountjoy were amused: 'here we are saying we won't wear state clothing, and our other brethren are demanding them' (Murphy interview). Tomás Mac Giolla confirmed that the clothes were issued on request to internees whose own clothing was wearing out and who could not replace it (interview).

102 In addition to items which were issued on request, all internees on induction received two pairs of socks, two pairs of underpants, two shirts and two towels (NAI JUS/8/ 1040, Memorandum on Curragh, 8 October 1957). Complaints about inadequate clothing nevertheless continued throughout much of the period of internment.

103 It is not clear if the camp supplied the coffee or simply allowed it to be brought in (Murphy interview).

104 Regulation No. 27.

105 When pressed by McQuillan, Boland denied that any hardship had arisen on these issues (*Dáil Debates*, vol. 171, cols. 1762–3, 10 December 1958). Given that funds were raised by the IRA to provide internees with these amenities (they can hardly be said to be luxuries), the Minister was correct in claiming that no hardship had arisen. It was unthinkable, moreover, that, in the community of the camp, a comrade would be denied a razor blade, toothpaste or stationery. The issue here may have been on whom the burden should fall: the IRA and its supporters or the public purse. Had it shifted to the state, the expense, whilst not large, would have been significant, and there would have been the need for rationing and account-keeping at the camp. The further result would have been to free funds available to the IRA – very welcome in those hard times.

106 MA PM/I/ADM/21, Adjutant General to Department of Defence, 20 May 1958.

107 Noel Kavanagh interview. The Detention Regulations (No. 26[1]) provided that the Commandant, should he have grounds for suspicion, could direct that a visitor be searched and, should the visitor refuse, refuse admission into the camp. The power seems to have been little used. This is hardly surprising since a high proportion of those visiting were women and children and the Commandant had no female staff to conduct any such search.

108 Noel Kavanagh was emphatic on this. No arms or other materials were smuggled in because Army Order No. 8 prohibited armed action in the South. He considered the order to have been '[v]ery, very, sensible, and it would have been a very, very fractious situation if the IRA had been – it would have brought them back to the twenties, thirties, forties' (interview). Tom Landers, whose duty included the supervision of visits, remembered the difficulty of preventing items being passed. The visits were

open, with no barrier (such as mesh or glass) across the table. Should children visit with their mother, fathers were allowed to hold them. This made the task of intercepting contraband 'ridiculous', Landers insisted (interview). Internees returning from parole were searched. One such turned up an ordnance-survey map of Co. Kildare, including the camp. The report to the Adjutant General noted that the man in question 'was anxious that MacCurtáin should not know of this' (MA PM/I/ADM/12, Report, 12 November 1958).

109 Detention Regulation No. 28 governed hobbies, handicrafts and instruction, authorised the Commandant to fix the times for these activities and stipulated that they should not exceed four hours daily.

110 Since a number of the IRA leaders were fluent Irish speakers, there was no shortage of tutors. Tomás MacCurtáin, Ruairí Ó Brádaigh and Seamus Hughes all conducted classes. MacCurtáin provided a course of lectures on the Irish-language classic *Cúirt an Mheán Oíche*. He had studied this text at a German university and had translated it from Irish into English. Mick Ryan recalled that, in general, language classes were taught by men who had enjoyed a better education than most internees, and those with an incomplete education were not able to benefit from them (interview). A former member of staff commented, 'They were no eejits, none of them' (Tom Landers interview).

111 MA PM/I/ADM/13, Classes for Internees, *Clár na Ranganna* (undated).

112 Kavanagh thought that the lack of political knowledge was due to the strict segregation of IRA volunteers and Sinn Féin. But even Sinn Féin made it a matter of pride and principle to attribute all social and economic ills to the division of the country and to the iniquities of 'Leinster House' – the illegitimate (as they would have it) Dáil, Senate and government.

113 Some prisoners desperately needed money for their families. Tomás Mac Giolla recalled one internee with a large family (a wife and eight children), 'and he used to work from morning until night. He set up his own workshop. He used to do everything – leatherwork, needlework and all sorts. The lights would go off in the huts at 10 o'clock, but there were lights outside and I often saw him at 10 o'clock up at the little window trying to get the light from the outside, working away' (Mac Giolla interview). This man's handicrafts were entirely for sale, providing some family income. There was a pathos here, which irresistibly evokes Dickens's Monsieur Manette, unceasingly making shoes in his isolated garret in the Bastille's North Tower (*A Tale of Two Cities*, Chapter 6). The affinity is in the image, of course, rather than the substance.

114 Tim Pat Coogan, *The IRA* (London: Fontana, 1980), p. 405.

115 MA PM/I/ADM/20, Canteen and Welfare Facilities, 18 November 1957.

116 MA PM/I/ADM/20, Canteen and Welfare Facilities, 29 November 1957.

117 There is a very considerable literature on this. A recent book deals with camp entertainment in a particularly interesting manner: Midge Gillies, *The Barbed Wire University* (London: Aurum, 2012), Chapters 14, 34 and *passim*.

118 MA PM/I/ADM/20, Director of Intelligence to Adjutant General, 14 October 1957.

119 This is a basic amenity in any custodial institution, and it was a major omission from the Detention Regulations, and perhaps another indication that they were cobbled together in something of a rush, without time for consultation (with, for example, the Mountjoy and Portlaoise governors) or review.

120 MA PM/I/ADM/13, Minute of Minister regarding the question of Organisation of Educational and Vocational Classes, 2 September 1957.

121 MA PM/I/ADM/21, Captain P. Ó Riada, Deputy Commandant to Commandant, 6 November 1958.

122 'I don't know whether Kildare Library has as good a record!' Kavanagh was nostalgic about the library, which he pictured almost like a clubroom or college sitting

room; 'I used to ensconce myself there, especially in the winter, at the big turf fire and all the books I wanted to read, all English literature. I was reading the Irish authors and the likes of *Hamlet*, and Turgenev and Dostoevsky, to my heart's desire. And that was very educational to me, as a young fellow' (interview). It was a precondition for the establishment of the library that the internees should provide a librarian, that he should keep a record of the receipt and issue of books, that the cost of lost or damaged books would be met by the individual responsible or, in default, by the Camp Fund. All books were to be examined and censored by camp staff 'with particular reference to ideological content' (MA PM/I/ADM/13, Commandant P. MagCanna [for Adjutant General] to Commandant, Internment Camp, 13 October 1957).

123 MA PM/I/ADM/20, Canteen and Welfare Facilities, Memorandum, 29 November 1957.

124 Years later, long after internment, soldiers digging their own garden on the spot uncovered a large sealed jar inside which was a pair of pliers, wire-cutters and other tools. It was uncertain whether the cache dated from the 1950s or from the 1940s (Reade interview).

125 Mac Giolla interview.

126 Mac Giolla interview.

127 There was no specific provision in the Detention Regulations for camp coinage, but the Commandant was the accounting officer for the internees' money (Regulation No. 37).

128 MA PM/I/ADM/20, Canteen and Welfare Facilities, undated memorandum.

129 MA PM/I/ADM/21, Complaints of Internee MacCurtáin of 7 May 1958, with annotations.

130 Detention Regulation No. 24.

131 *Dáil Debates*, vol. 164, col. 625, 6 November 1957. It was, he said, 'a new and novel function, at any rate, for a spiritual advisor'.

132 Kavanagh interview.

133 Individual priests remained sympathetic, especially if, as Noel Kavanagh pointed out, they came from a republican or a nationalist background.

134 'And from when we went to the Curragh until it was closed, there was never any difficulty in the wide earthly world with any of them, which was a breath of fresh air' (Ó Brádaigh interview). Father Livinus, a Capuchin friar from Church Street in Dublin, was mentioned by Ó Brádaigh and many others (including IRA prisoners in Belfast) as being especially sympathetic in his ministry. Priests who had served abroad generally took a more flexible view of their duties than those who had simply gone from Maynooth Seminary to a parish in Ireland.

135 Reade interview. He continued, 'you went in and did it, and that's it. They knew bloody well it was going to be done.'

136 On this, broadly, see Michael Parker (ed.), *Dynamic Security: The Democratic Therapeutic Community in Prison* (London: Jessica Kingsley, 2006).

137 Reade interview. But some staff disobeyed the order (see above, p. 998).

138 The unit that dealt with censorship also kept an account of internees' funds – money sent or handed in and purchases (see above, p. 1008). Censorship of correspondence was governed by Regulation No. 27(3).

139 MA PM/I/ADM/1, General Correspondence, Commandant P. MagCanna to Adjutant General, 11 April 1959. See below, p. 1013.

140 MA PM/I/ADM/1, Commandant Mac Eilgeóid to Curragh Command, 11 December 1958. In many modern civilian prisons, the total operational staff number (that is, excluding clerical and specialist posts) is normally divided by 2.3 to arrive at the number of deployable staff. This calculation is intended to take account of shift working, leave, sickness and training. Accordingly, the commandant of the internment camp

would have had approximately thirty-five full-time equivalent positions at his disposal. This seems a sparse allowance.

141 Interview. 'The staff problems were terrible... We didn't have enough staff.' Another member of staff (Peter Brennan) was on duty on Christmas Eve, 1958. The normal arrangement was for a guard to be on duty for two hours, followed by four hours rest (or one hour on and two off). On that Christmas Eve he had been on duty for twenty-six hours without relief. At that point he was instructed to supervise a visit and had no option but to report sick to the hospital. 'I was incapable of staying awake any longer' (interview).

142 To deal with the escape, Dick Reade calculated, another twenty men would have been necessary (interview).

143 Reade interview.

144 Landers interview. Landers had joined the Irish Army in 1950 and transferred to the military police three years later.

145 Landers interview.

146 The registration numbers of visitors' cars were passed to the Kildare gardaí. MA PM/I/ADM/12 (1957), Memorandum of 20 October 1957.

147 In the 1940s, the Irish Army was on an emergency footing, with several grave possibilities in its planning. Manpower and resources were directed to national survival. By 1957, there were no such dangers evident and sufficient men were available to provide the basics of an intelligence-collection system at the Curragh.

148 See above, p. 714.

149 MA PM/I/ADM/12 (1957), Report to Director of Intelligence, 6 May 1958. MacCurtáin instanced his own experience where a letter he had posted in the camp containing a copy of his correspondence with the Red Cross had reached his wife a week later, postmarked Dublin. (Those were the days of three postal deliveries a day and of next-day delivery for almost all letters and postcards.)

150 MA PM/I/ADM/12 (1957), Correspondence: Extracts Internees.

151 MA PM/I/ADM/12 (1957), Report of general meeting held on 8 September 1957.

152 Relatives could visit once a month for between thirty minutes and one hour. (Regulation No. 25). See also *Dáil Debates*, vol. 164, col. 657, 6 November 1957, statement of Oscar Traynor, Minister for Justice.

153 MA PM/I/ADM/12 (1957), Report to Director of Intelligence, 8 January 1958. The Camp Intelligence Officer noted that in its use, gardaí had 'inadvertently or otherwise' revealed its source. In a long letter of 1 January 1958 (obviously some weeks in the drafting), MacCurtáin listed internee grievances, down to the provision of sufficient fire irons for each stove. He drew particular attention to visits and correspondence being used 'as a medium for collecting information for Government and Police agents' (MA PM/I/ADM/21, Complaint Internee MacCurtáin: MacCurtáin to 'Governor', 1 January 1958).

154 Landers interview. Whether many officers at HQ were able to understand these reports was not mentioned.

155 In the early weeks of internment, a man urged his wife to avoid topics that were not permitted during her visits. No comment had been made on his previous visit, but 'it causes embarrassment both to the PA [Military Policeman] on duty and to the duty officer. Relations with the powers that be are first class at present and we wish them to remain that way' (MA PM/I/ADM/12, letter from internee to wife, 29 August 1957). It would appear that she had made anti-government statements or had been critical of the camp authorities.

156 Interview.

157 *Dáil Debates*, vol. 164, col. 657, 6 November 1957.

158 MA PM/I/ADM/12, Note on O'Hagan visit, 14 September 1958.

159 Landers interview: 'They would say themselves that, if somebody didn't go to Mass, they'd be looking out, to see was he colluding with staff.'

160 *Report of the Enquiry into the Escape of Six Prisoners from the Special Security Unit at Whitemoor Prison Cambridgeshire, on Friday 9th September 1994* (London: HMSO, 1994), Cm 2741 (Woodcock Report), p. 71 *et seq*. See also *Special Security Units* (Home Office Research Study No. 109) (London: HMSO, 1989). This study explicitly warned about the dangers of staff conditioning by inmates. These issues were further explored following the escape of three prisoners from Parkhurst Prison (another maximum-security institution) on 3 January 1995. See *Review of Prison Service Security in England and Wales and the Escape from Parkhurst Prison on Tuesday 3rd January 1995* (London: HMSO, 1995), Cmd. 3020 (Learmont Report), especially pp. 53–60, paras. 2.180–82.217. Learmont observed that '[a] phoney stability was achieved at Parkhurst but only by surrender to the prisoners of control over their daily existence' (Learmont Report, para. 2.182).

161 Woodcock Report, *op. cit.*

162 Murphy interview.

163 Landers interview.

164 Landers interview.

165 Decisions were made by the Department of Justice. Up to 31 October 1958, 115 applications had been submitted, of which thirty-one had been refused (NAI JUS/8/1099, Memorandum on Curragh Camp, f. 9).

166 MA PM/I/ADM/12, General Correspondence, Memorandum, Department of the Taoiseach, 6 August 1957. Because parole applications might involve a degree of urgency (a relative who had been injured, or who was seriously ill or dying), a procedure had long been established for after-hours' applications. This involved the senior officials of the Department of Justice, the camp authorities and the Garda Síochána or Special Branch (NAI JUS/8/1096, S921/40, Parole, Procedure Outside Office Hours, July 1940).

167 NAI JUS/8/1040, Memorandum on Curragh Camp, 8 October 1957. Granting or withholding parole was a matter for the Department of Justice and its minister. There is, accordingly, no mention of parole in the Detention Regulations.

168 MA PM/I/ADM/1, Department of Taoiseach Circular S16274, 6 August 1957.

169 But in notes for a speech to be delivered by the Minister for Justice, there is reference to detainees obtaining parole for family bereavements or for serious illness. Some had been paroled more than once, and there were 'some, whose conduct outside elide their parole undertakings' (NAI JUS/8/1100, Notes for speech on Senator Owen Sheehy-Skeffington's motion regarding detainees, n.d., but c.3 December 1958).

170 MA PM/I/ADM/12, Note on parole, 12 May 1958.

171 Family emergencies could sometimes cover livelihoods, and parole was granted to deal with farming problems. A man was allowed to go home from 16 August to 2 September 1957 because of disease in his livestock. That the leadership were unlikely to receive parole was confirmed when Patrick McLogan, formerly of the IRA General Staff, was turned down in March 1958. Unneeded and unwanted, the government had in December 1957 offered Christmas parole because of public pressure. But now that he needed it for personal reasons, he wrote to this wife, he had 'been subjected to the humiliation of having to ask' and the 'further humiliation of having to accept a refusal' (MA PM/I/ADM/12, letter of 29 March 1958).

172 MA PM/I/ADM/12, Tomás MacCurtáin to applicant, 7 September 1957.

173 MA PM/I/ADM/12, Letter of 26 September 1957 and reply.

174 MA PM/I/ADM/12, Letter of 9 November 1957.

175 MA PM/I/ADM/12, Letter of 13 December 1957. The internee advised his correspondent (an insurance company) to contact 'the Minister or the people here to produce me in Court and I will be delighted to give evidence if brought… for me to give an

undertaking, putting myself in a position of turnkey and prisoner at the same time is much below my height'. Another man, a witness in a manslaughter case, discussed the matter with MacCurtáin and took the same line. He would not accept parole, and, whilst he was willing to give a statement under oath to a member of the firm of solicitors, 'under no circumstances will I make any statement to any member of the Police Force' (MA PM/I/ADM/12, Letter to John P. Ward, Solicitors, Co. Donegal, 10 February 1958).

176 *Dáil Debates*, vol. 171, col. 971, 26 November 1958. The offer had also been made the previous year, three days before Christmas. See *Irish Independent*, 23 December 1957, 4f; 28 December 1957, 8c; *Irish Press*, 23 December 1957, 5h; *Irish Times*, 24 December 1957, 1e.

177 See the statement concerning 'the usual conditions' in the offer that was made on 22 December the previous year (*Irish Independent*, 23 December 1957, 4f). See also *Dáil Debates*, vol. 171, col. 2232, 16 December 1958.

178 The offer was mentioned in the Dáil on various occasions. When Patrick Finucane (Independent, but formerly of Clann na Talmhan) asked, during the Dáil's last sitting before the Christmas break, whether the Curragh visiting regulations could be relaxed over Christmas, Kevin Boland asserted that this was not necessary. He added that the internees had been advised that, should any of them apply for parole for the Christmas period, their applications would be considered (*Dáil Debates*, vol. 171, col. 2232, 16 December 1958).

179 When first offered (December 1957), Sinn Féin had commented that the gesture 'was obviously a hurried face-saving attempt on the part of the Fianna Fáil administration to make some gesture in the hope of allaying the steadily increasing criticism of their resorting to concentration camp methods in dealing with political opponents' (*Irish Independent*, 28 December 1957, 8c).

180 MA PM/I/ADM/12, Note of General Meeting of Internees, 1 March 1958. When one of those attending the meeting complained about camp food, MacCurtáin ruled him out of order, noting that 'the food they were getting was better than what some of them got at home'. Patrick McLogan supported MacCurtáin's stand. Even the hardship of the camp, real or supposed, had to be minimised in order to maintain unity of purpose.

181 In his speech on being elected as Lord Mayor of Cork, Terence MacSwiney declared that 'it is not they who can inflict most but they who can suffer most can conquer… Those whose faith is strong will endure to the end and triumph.' In 1920 (or thereabouts), Eoin MacNeill, former Commander-in-Chief of the Irish Volunteers, summarised his organisation's experience of punishment and politics in an epigram: 'Imprisoned, we are their jailers / On trial, their judges / Persecuted, their punishers / Dead, their conquerors.' For the provenance and context of these remarks, see Seán McConville, *Irish Political Prisoners, 1848–1922: Theatres of War* (London and New York: Routledge, 2003), pp. 4 and 738.

182 See above, p. 996.

183 MA PM/I/ADM/21, Complaints of Internee MacCurtáin of 7 May 1958, and annotations.

184 At a meeting of the Irish government (Cabinet) on 6 August 1957, it was decided, *inter alia*, that *every person* detained under the OAS(A)A should be informed 'that he will be released if he gives the required undertaking and that this information should be conveyed to the detained persons individually in writing' (my italics). De Valera and his colleagues were well acquainted with the opprobrium that attached in IRA circles to anyone who signed such a document. By refusing to sign, they confirmed implicitly the justness of their detention and became their own gaolers. Such logic did not hold for the dissident but pragmatic Saor Uladh–Christle groups (see below, p. 1025).

MA PM/I/ADM/12, General Correspondence, Memorandum, Department of the Taoiseach, 6 August 1957.

185 The Detention Commission consisted of a commissioned officer of the Defence Forces with not less than seven years' service. Each of the other two members had to be barristers or solicitors of not less than seven years' standing, or be or have been a judge (from District to Supreme Court rank). The Commission had decision-making powers, independent of the government, and was obliged to consider each application submitted to it. Should it decide that no reasonable grounds existed for continued detention of an applicant, the government was obliged to release him. The Commission was a largely pointless body since it was clear from the outset that, in practice, release powers had been reserved for the Department of Justice. In a memorandum prepared for Cabinet and dated 3 December 1958, it was noted that since the commencement of internment (July 1957) 205 men had been held. Seventy-nine of these had been released, 'none as a consequence of a report of the Detention Commission established under Section 8 of the Act' (NAI JUS/8/110, Memorandum for the Government, 3 December 1958). The point being made, presumably, was that the Department of Justice had acted with such a degree of clemency and liberality that the intervention of the Detention Commission was unnecessary. The figures could just as plausibly have suggested the toothlessness of the Commission. On the other side, it might have been argued that it did act as a backdrop – at least in theory.

186 Circuit Court judge Barra Ó Briain presided. The two other members were District Justice Eamon O Riain and Colonel J. V. Joyce (*Evening Herald*, 17 September 1957, 1e).

187 Lawless was not a member of the IRA and had been ostracised by the IRA camp command.

188 *Irish Independent*, 19 September 1957, 3c–d.

189 *Irish Times*, 19 October 1957, 9c. Lawless was released on 12 December 1957, on giving an undertaking. This rendered moot the issue of his continued detention, but he then sought damages for unlawful detention (see above, p. 802). No damages were awarded.

190 *Irish Press*, 24 August 1957, 9e.

191 *Irish Press*, 24 August 1957, 9e.

192 MA PM/I/ADM/12, Department of Taoiseach Circular, S16274, 6 August 1957.

193 Mick Ryan emphasised that IRA discipline was 'absolutely strict' but that a man could opt out at any time. Even men about to go on an operation could leave if they couldn't face going through with it. He had sent a couple of men home because he thought they were not up to the demands of the operation and would have been a danger to others. Men had the right not to accept an order, and if they did so, membership was terminated. If such a man could help in another way, he might be asked to do so: 'There was no cruelty involved, or boycotting, except for people who "signed out" – they were just ignored' (interview).

194 Some men, Ryan remembered, signed out 'because their families were in terrible straits, married men, and the poor fellows, they were silently boycotted... And I just didn't feel anything about it one way or the other [at the time]' (interview).

195 Ryan interview. The splits produced those intense feelings 'when people won't talk to you and regard you as a traitor and all kinds of stuff like that. So it's a very cruel kind of thing.'

196 The Commandant was directed to notify the Medical Officer of any instance of mental or physical ill-health. In addition, he had to inform higher authority of any case of insanity or apparent insanity or of any case in which the Medical Officer had formed an opinion that an internee's life would be endangered by continued custody, or that the mental state of an internee was 'becoming impaired or enfeebled' by internment (Detention Regulations Nos. 43[1] and 46). The Chaplain and Medical Officer had to be informed of any man whose life was in danger, 'or whose state of

health in mind or body appears to require their attention' (Regulation No. 47). In cases of dangerous illness (in the opinion of the Medical Officer), the Commandant, where practicable, also had to notify relatives (Regulation No. 51). Finally, the Commandant had the usual reporting obligations in case of death: the Coroner, Garda Síochána and, 'where practicable', next of kin (Regulation No. 48).

197 MA PM/I/ADM/12, Internee to wife, 19 September 1958.

198 MA PM/I/ADM/12, Internee to correspondent, 20 September 1958 and censor's note.

199 MA PM/I/ADM/12, Comment on internee correspondence, 22 September 1958.

200 MA PM/I/ADM/12, Internee to correspondent (in Irish), 21 November 1958. A week later, however, another man assured his mother that 'whatever else they say the Medical care we get here is as good if not better than what you would get in a civvy hospital' (MA PM/I/ADM/12, 28 November 1958).

201 MA PM/30-29, Curragh Releases, 15 July 1957–11 March 1959. See p. 996 above. On 20 February 1958, 73 per cent of the 125 in the Curragh were aged up to thirty years. Only 15 per cent were forty or older.

202 One man, John A. Kelly, appears to have been arrested because of mistaken identity. On arrival at the Curragh, he claimed he had asked for, but had not been given, the form of undertaking which would have ensured his release (MA PM/30–18, Memoranda, 21 February 1959).

203 Michael Davern, from Cashel, Co. Tipperary, was a twenty-two-year-old law student, who had been arrested on 18 July 1957. Studying at UCD, he was President of the National Students' Council. In the November debate on internment, Jack McQuillan pointed out that Davern was not a member of an illegal organisation. He seems to have come to the attention of Special Branch because of his language in condemning the activation of Part II of the OASA and for his part in organising protests against the Act (*Dáil Debates*, vol. 164, col. 633, 6 November 1957).

204 *Irish Times*, 22 August 1957, 1b. This report was based on a Department of Justice briefing.

205 NAI JUS/8/1089, Peter Berry to Commandant, Curragh Camp (probably 13 November 1957). Quite apart from the merits of the application, which was almost certainly submitted to provoke, Berry and his minister would have been aware of the danger of creating a precedent which could (in the event of a general election) have carried security and logistical implications of unmanageable proportions. It is of interest that, in Northern Ireland, the courts had found that internees could not be deprived of their votes (see *Derry Journal*, 14 January 1958, 1c–d). Had Garland and his comrades pursued their request in the Republic's courts, they may well have secured a similar result.

206 Questions about a Christmas amnesty were put in the Dáil on 30 October (John Tully, Clann na Poblachta TD for Cavan) and 25 November 1958 (Fintan Coogan, Fine Gael, Galway West). The reply in each case was the same: if internees wanted to be released, it was at any time available to them 'by giving an undertaking to respect the Constitution and the laws' (*Dáil Debates*, vol. 171, col. 280, 30 October 1958 and cols. 786–7, 25 November 1958).

207 MA PM/I/ADM/12, Internee to ex-internee, 9 December 1958.

208 MA PM/I/ADM/12, T. Doyle to Emily Scullion, 8 October 1958. In another letter, two days later, he anticipated that in the event of success in the Lawless case, compensation would have to be paid to all internees for wrongful imprisonment. 'Some people' (in government) were going to have sore heads, worrying about their blunder, 'especially as in some instances the Minister himself can be held personally liable for payment of compensation' (MA PM/I/ADM/12, T. Doyle to Breda Kearns, Women's Union of Ireland, 10 October 1958).

209 NAI JUS/8/1100, Notes for Senator Sheehy-Skeffington's motion regarding detainees, *op. cit.*

210 MA PM/30-29, Curragh Releases, 15 July 1957–11 March 1959.

211 *Irish Independent*, 24 December 1958, 3g; *Irish Press*, 24 December 1958, 7f. Both newspapers reported the releases, placing the items inconspicuously and without comment. The *Irish Times*, 24 December 1958, 1d, gave rather more space to the releases, but still below the fold, observing that the Government was reviewing the position 'fairly often', and that young men interested mainly in the political side of the movement were likely to be favoured for release. This report was probably based on an official briefing.

212 Three were released on 8 January 1959, two on medical grounds. Between 16 January and the end of the month, four were freed, all for medical reasons. The closest to a general release was in February 1959, when forty-three men had their internment orders lifted. None was a medical case, and one who was already at large on parole was notified that he did not need to return to the Curragh (MA PM/30-29, Curragh Releases, *op. cit.*).

213 *Ibid.*

214 One man arrived at the Curragh on 3 February 1958 and was released on the same day on signing the undertaking. The register of releases noted 'Not in any movement'. This was an obvious case of mistaken identity or baseless intelligence (*ibid.*).

215 *Ibid.*

216 A few men were released whilst on parole and some others who were not applicants, on the Minister's direction. It is possible that these were recognised by the authorities to be unnecessary or mistaken internments where the men could not bring themselves to sign the undertaking.

217 See above, p. 1056, n. 189.

218 MA PM/I/ADM/12, Mother to son, 29 August 1957.

219 MA PM/I/ADM/12, Letter of 20 August 1957.

220 MA PM/I/ADM/12, Letter of 26 August 1957.

221 MA PM/I/ADM/12, Letter of 28 March 1958.

222 MA PM/I/ADM/12, Letter of 2 September 1957.

223 MA PM/I/ADM/12, Letter of 7 September 1957.

224 One man sought an interview with the Camp Commandant and told him that he was not a member of the IRA but that he was unwilling to sign the undertaking that would secure his release 'because of fear of his father and of people in his own locality'. The Commandant suggested that the man should seek advice. This was emphatically rejected, the man insisting that he did not wish to see Inspector McMahon of Special Branch 'under any circumstances' (MA PM/I/ADM/12, Report to Director of Intelligence, 14 September 1957).

225 Thus, in August 1957, a Mayo man was released. Two outgoing letters emphasised that he did not sign out and that he was 'a grand lad' (MA PM/I/ADM/12, Letter of 28 August 1957). The man's release, it was reported, 'had caused a certain amount of dissatisfaction among the internees', presumably because they also wished to be released without signing.

226 Interview.

227 MA PM/I/ADM/12, Michael Traynor to wife, 20 June 1958. The intelligence officer commented that Traynor's comments 'puts the feeling of the internees, very well, regarding the indefiniteness of internment and the question of *releases*. Traynor is 51½ years of age.'

228 MA PM/I/ADM/12, Letter of 7 July 1958. He found it 'maddening' to see seventeen- and eighteen-year-olds growing to manhood in such unnatural surroundings. 'They have no outlet for youthful energies, the confinement helps to make them very bitter and is bound to affect them all their lives.' The camp's old men should be enjoying 'peace and happiness at the end of their days', and the younger married

men were unable to provide for the rearing and educating of their families. 'No matter', he concluded, 'it is all for a good cause'. It is hard to say whether the last comment was declaratory, ironic or despairing.

229 The last twelve out were Joe Conway (Newry), Seán Cronin (Dublin), Frank Driver (Kildare), Hugh Heaney and Joe O'Hagan (both of Lurgan), Tony Magan, Dan Merrius, Andy Nathan, Bob Russell, Brendan Seeley (all of Dublin), Frank Skuse (Cork) and William Stewart (Dundalk).

230 Following the final collapse of the Border Campaign and the doubt cast by the Lawless case on the legal assumptions behind internment, the power to intern under Part II of the OASA was relinquished when, on 6 March 1962, the measure was repealed.

231 Having served a prison sentence or term of internment inevitably had consequences for employment prospects, though the degree and extent of this is unclear. Some of the reluctance to employ or re-employ may have been purely practical, based on a calculation that an IRA activist would put cause before employment and (given that the Border Campaign continued) was liable to rearrest or a possible call to service by the organisation. This line of reasoning would make any such man a potentially unreliable employee. In other instances, there may have been an element of political distaste or antagonism in the employer's judgement. Jack McQuillan gave some examples of the employment problems of former prisoners and internees, including the Sinn Féin Deputy Ruairí Ó Brádaigh. See *Dáil Debates*, vol. 164, cols. 631–6, 6 November 1957.

232 Interview. Ryan confirmed that there was no organised support for the ex-prisoners and that 'you just had to live off [supporters]'.

233 MA PM/I/ADM/1, Department of Taoiseach Circular, S. 16274, 6 August 1957.

234 *Dáil Debates*, vol. 164, cols. 647–8, 6 November 1957. In mid-March 1957, a return compiled for Oscar Traynor, the incoming Minister for Justice, showed that there were fifty-two IRA men under sentence in Mountjoy, with terms ranging from two to six months. There had been thirty-one convictions for failing to account for movements; twenty-six for membership of an unlawful organisation; twenty-four for possession of incriminating documents; ten for possession of firearms and ammunition and two for possession of ammunition. Most of the fifty-two prisoners had been convicted of multiple offences. NAI JUS/8/1040, Secretary, Department of Justice to Minister, 23 March 1957.

235 NAI DFA/417/39/19/4/2/1, Department for External Affairs, memorandum, 8 April 1959. The denial of a visit might also mean passing up a chance to poke others in the eye, it was suggested: 'Our decision in regard to Mountjoy might perhaps influence the Six-County or British authorities in their attitude to this proposal [for an ICRC visit to Belfast Prison].'

236 NAI DFA/417/39/19/4/2/1, Kevin Boland to Leslie Barry, 17 April 1959.

237 The prison was constructed according to the design principles developed at Pentonville, London, and, like that prison, Mountjoy was at first intended to be 'a portal to the colonies'. Convicts (persons sentenced to transportation) were selected for several months' separate confinement – a purgative and deterrent experience – prior to their removal to Australia. See Tim Carey's informative account of the prison, *Mountjoy: The Story of a Prison* (Cork: Collins Press, 2000), Chapters 2 and 3. On Pentonville's origins and the convict regime, see Seán McConville, *A History of English Prison Administration, Vol. I: 1750–1877* (London: Routledge & Kegan Paul, 1981), Chapters 7 and 12.

238 'Slopping out' was a particularly revolting part of the routine. Although separate-system prisons had originally been equipped with in-cell WCs in order to avoid prisoners leaving their cells, these were of a defective design (lacking a water valve) and emitted the effluvium of the sewer. They were removed on health grounds from

most prisons in the 1880s (ironically just a few years before that much improved modern-type water-valved lavatory basins came on the market). In their place, 'slopping-out' was introduced. When cells were unlocked early in the morning, the prisoners came out and queued along the prison landings, chamber pot or slop-bucket in hand. These vessels were emptied into sinks on each landing. Anyone who experienced the ritual – staff, prisoner or visitor – would confirm that the smell was appalling, the practice most unhygienic and the overall effect degrading. Slopping out continued in some prisons until very recent years. See Seán McConville, *English Local Prisons, 1860–1900: Next Only to Death* (London and New York: Routledge, 1995, pp. 283–4).

239 Interview.

240 Ó Brádaigh interview.

241 See above, p. 652.

242 Paddy Terry interview.

243 Because it did not have a fanfare I cannot be certain of dates, but it may have been in the mid-1940s. It was certainly in effect when the Border Campaign men came into custody.

244 Terry interview.

245 Terry interview. He also recalled that at a later point (1972), the fact that the Mountjoy Governor had been dealing with the IRA OC received publicity. Terry was instructed to summon the Governor ('an absolutely principled Governor... really a first class official'). Although he and other senior justice officials knew that what had been done 'was absolutely in accordance with practice', he had been directed to issue a severe reprimand: 'It was most embarrassing.'

246 'Ah, you weren't snooty or anything like that', Ó Brádaigh emphasised (interview). Tomás Mac Giolla was even warmer: 'They were called lags, only the lags were great when you got to know them. It was always the same people every time I went in. They would say, "Oh, are you back again?"' (interview). Mick Ryan remembered relations with the ordinary prisoners as being quite friendly. There seemed to be fewer horrific crimes (such as attacks on the elderly) then. His attitude towards them was also conditioned by childhood memories of his father throwing a few cigarettes to Mountjoy prisoners as they swept the road outside the prison (interview).

247 Ó Brádaigh interview.

248 Ó Brádaigh interview. He also remembered that on going to see the prison governor a tie was requested: 'There would be a warder outside with a lot of ties draped over his arm which he gave out to you. You put on the tie when you went in and you took it off when you came out again, handed it to him.' Not unlike the dress-code requirement of the smarter hotels and restaurants of the time.

249 May Mac Giolla interview. 'We turned against her because she was giving it to us and she wasn't giving it to the poor people... we were all in the prison. Why should we have got china cups?' That women were treated rather more informally and even sympathetically by the authorities was confirmed by another recollection. A companion arrested at the Passport Office protest had a baby. The republican women asked the Governor to release her because of this since she had nobody to care for her baby. Whatever process was followed (or not), the young mother was freed.

250 Ó Brádaigh interview.

251 During his period of imprisonment Ó Brádaigh was elected to the Dáil in the Sinn Féin interest. Since the party was resolutely abstentionist, there was no question of his taking his seat, but he was careful nevertheless not to hint at superiority in front of the other prisoners. He wished 'to just be myself, be totally normal, and not to be getting any ideas about myself, that when anything arose I just made sure I was treated the same as any other prisoner' (interview).

252 Mac Giolla interview.

253 Murphy interview.

254 Ó Brádaigh remembered talking to veteran leaders such as Tomás MacCurtáin who had been through so much in the 1940s. MacCurtáin had been on hunger strike, under sentence of death and within a few hours of being hanged. His father was a major figure in the republican pantheon, recognised and respected across the political spectrum of Irish nationalism. The interest was intense, a type of reverence, 'because you weren't going to get a chance to get to close quarters with people like that again'. He commented that the prisoners had a saying that experience of this type of imprisonment made a man a better or a worse republican: 'You don't come out as you went in' (Ó Brádaigh interview).

255 Ryan interview.

256 Murphy interview.

257 Murphy interview.

258 Interview. It is fair to record that not all agreed that the Mountjoy food was dire. Manus Canning served a long sentence in Wormwood Scrubs (London) for his part in the Felsted raid. He was later in Mountjoy, where he found the food to be much better. The favourable comparison was, however, due more to particularly low standards in Wormwood Scrubs (interview). Another view was given by John L. McCormack, interned at the Curragh in 1940–2 and sentenced in 1956 to six months for the illegal possession of a document. For him, the Mountjoy food seemed to be almost a different category of substance, called prison food, but 'it was grand. It was good enough. You could survive on it' (interview).

259 Interview. He agreed with others that the Curragh food was very much better: 'fantastic – army food'. The army chef who prepared the food made it very acceptable, 'for so many people it was better than they had been getting at home'.

260 I have explored this topic in my *English Local Prisons, op. cit.*, pp. 303–19. Both Oscar Wilde (imprisoned in Reading Prison) and the Fenian Michael Davitt (who served time in convict prisons at Dartmoor and Portland) wrote about the debilitating effects of the penal dietary in, respectively, the 1890s and the 1870s. Davitt was characteristically excoriating, holding that 'men are driven, by a system of half-starvation, into an animal-like voracity and anything that a dog would eat is nowise repugnant to their taste'. See Michael Davitt, *The Prison Life of Michael Davitt, Related by Himself; Together with His Evidence to the House of Lords Commission on Convict Life*, 2nd edn (Dublin: J. J. Lawlor, 1882), p. 18. See also, Francis Sheehy-Skeffington, *Michael Davitt: Revolutionary, Agitator and Labour Leader* (London: MacGibbon & Kee, 1967), p. 47.

261 See *Dáil Debates*, vol. 176, cols. 161–4, 30 June 1959.

262 See McConville, *English Local Prisons, op. cit.*, pp. 310–11, 316–17 and *passim*. For an alternative approach to less eligibility by the great Utilitarian, Jeremy Bentham, see Alexander Taylor Milne (ed.), *The Correspondence of Jeremy Bentham*, 9 vols. (London: Athlone Press, 1981), vol. IV, pp. 226 and *passim*. The doctrine became one of the most hotly debated in public policy as a consequence of the Poor Law Amendment Act, 1834.

263 Calculated from 'Dublin Prison Food Statistics' (written answer), *Dáil Debates*, vol. 176, col. 161, 30 June 1959.

264 The food parcels were, at the Governor's discretion, allowed to well-behaved prisoners. These items could be used to supplement the prison dietary, subject to what was probably a notional oversight and approval by the Medical Officer. Other privileges withdrawn at this time were additional visits, cigarettes on request and extended periods of outdoor recreation. On the escape, see pp. 1038–9 below.

265 *Dáil Debates*, vol. 165, col. 37, 12 February 1958.

266 Murphy interview. MacCurtáin had passed on the story.

267 Ó Brádaigh interview. He remembered one Protestant girl who would traverse the male wing on her way to religious service 'very demure with the hat on and her prayer book'.

268 Ó Brádaigh interview.

269 Ó Brádaigh interview.

270 Mac Giolla interview. He continued, 'I hadn't any problems with the guards; very few of us had any problems with the guards.'

271 Carey, *Mountjoy*, *op. cit.*, p. 232. I know of no similar career in any jurisdiction.

272 Ó Brádaigh interview.

273 See the *Irish Press*, 19 January 1956, 1a–h. The statement was issued by the Standing Committee of the Hierarchy, to be read by the clergy after mass on Sunday, 20 January 1956.

274 In Roman Catholic teaching, a mortal sin is a degree of iniquity so grave that were one to die unshriven (without sacramental absolution) there would be eternal damnation.

275 *Irish Press*, 19 January 1956, 1a–h. 'With paternal insistence', the statement went on to warn young men to be in their guard against such organisations.

276 There ensued an exchange only possible between the devout. Ó Brádaigh protested that he had complied with all the conditions of confession yet absolution was being withheld. He insisted that were anything to happen to him that night (were he to die and be brought before the Judgement Seat), 'I'll call you as a witness that you denied me absolution.' The priest replied that Ó Brádaigh was threatening him, to which the response was, 'No, that is the situation' (interview). The bad blood between the two men persisted, and when Ó Brádaigh returned to Mountjoy a second time, there was an exchange following which he asked the priest to leave the cell. As Ó Brádaigh remembered it, Father MacCurtáin drew his attention to a small wedding photograph and asked if he had been married since his last time in Mountjoy. When Ó Brádaigh said that he had (and it was only weeks before), the chaplain asked whether his wife was not lonely for him. At this point, Ó Brádaigh asked him to leave. 'You know, he was going to leave me there on my own in the cell, thinking about this kind of thing… and so on.'

277 Mac Giolla interview.

278 The 'Green Book', the IRA training manual for recruits, set out the obligation for obedience: 'All recruits entering the army declare that they shall obey all orders issued to them by their superior officers and by the Army Authority' (cited in O'Brien, *The Long War*, *op. cit.*, p. 402). In slightly different wording, this is set out as General Order No. 7 (O'Brien, *The Long War*, *op. cit.*, p. 407).

279 Murphy interview. He found the inaccuracies in the pastoral letter, that the IRA was a secret and oath-bound society, telling. If the bishops could get that wrong, he asked himself, in what else had they erred?

280 He drew comfort from an observation of his mother on the excommunication of IRA men during the Civil War. She commented that 'the Irish people are wonderful, the way they have clung to their religion in spite of the bishops'. Taking this view, Ó Brádaigh decided to cut out the clergy, as middlemen, and to deal directly with God. People had told him that this was a very Protestant idea, but 'so be it'. He had much less resentment of other prison officials. The Prison Medical Officer he regarded as 'a joke' because of the cursory examinations the men were given on reception. Returning to Mountjoy in November 1959, the Medical Officer asked, 'You got married since you were here last?' Ó Brádaigh confirmed that he had, and the Medical Officer, looking at his private parts, commented, 'I don't see that it did you any harm.' Rather than take offence at such a personal comment, Ó Brádaigh was indulgent: 'It was his joke, you know. I just passed it off. There was no malice in it' (interview).

281 Charlie Murphy, also angered by Father MacCurtáin's hard line, agreed that there were individual sympathisers among the clergy. He recalled a Fermanagh curate who would hear the confessions of IRA men in his car before they headed off on an operation: 'I don't want it be said that he was approving, but, as far as he was concerned, this was an active service unit, and the idea was they would want confession, you know' (interview).

282 *Evening Herald*, 26 July 1957, 1b. No details have survived of the escape, but it has every appearance of being an inside-only job, without IRA support. It is significant that no other escape attempt was made at Mountjoy. The IRA wanted a quiet life in the South.

283 General Order No. 8 was emphatic: 'Volunteers are strictly prohibited to take any military action against 26 County forces under any circumstances whatsoever' (O'Brien, *The Long War, op. cit.*, p. 407).

284 Terry interview.

285 *Dáil Debates*, vol. 174, cols. 266–8, 9 April 1959. In 1957 there were two peaks in Offences Against the State charges: January (fifty-two charged and forty-eight convicted) and June (thirty-eight charged and convicted). There was another, smaller upsurge in December (eighteen charged and convicted). Other than that, monthly totals ranged from nil to five. The picture in 1958 was completely different, with five being the greatest monthly total of arrests and convictions (April). Six months had no arrests at all and the rest a handful or far less.

286 *Dáil Debates*, vol. 181, col. 1258, 12 May 1960.

287 These figures are taken from an answer and tabulation provided to a Dáil question by Charles Haughey, Minister for Justice, on 15 February 1962 (*Dáil Debates*, vol. 193, cols. 376–82).

288 See *Irish Times*, 15 December 1961, 11g–h. The newspaper reported that five men had appeared before the Special Criminal Court the previous day on arms offences charges. Three wore green and khaki battledress with tricolour shoulder flashes. A *nolle prosequi* was entered against one of the defendants, Gerard Crossan, at the direction of the Minister for Justice. Crossan had signed a declaration that he would obey the Constitution and laws. It is not clear what happened to the other man against whom it was decided not to proceed (Charles Carolan), but the allegation against him was simple possession of a rifle and ammunition. Michael McEldowney had already served two sentences under the OASA and Firearms Acts, and had only recently been released from a six-month sentence. In the charges, 'with intent' referred to the possession of firearms and ammunition with intent to endanger life or cause serious injury to property, or with intent to enable any other person by means of arms and ammunition to endanger life or to cause serious injury to property (Firearms Act, 1925, s.15). McEldowney denied allegations that he had pointed a gun at a garda.

289 The men were arrested on the Monaghan–Fermanagh border in possession of sub-machine guns, a rifle and ammunition. The court heard that one of the men had asked a local farmer 'Are we in the North or the twenty-six counties' before police closed in (see *Evening Mail*, 14 December 1961, 9f–g; 14 December 1957, 9c–d. For sentencing, see *Evening Herald*, 22 December 1961, 3d–e).

290 *Dáil Debates*, vol. 192, col. 839, 23 November 1961.

291 The meeting was in January 1965.

292 *Dáil Debates*, vol. 192, col. 839, 23 November 1961. Other quotations from Lemass are taken from this source.

293 Since, for various reasons, a revived use of the death penalty was unlikely to have been contemplated, Lemass was probably intimating that sentences would be very substantially increased for IRA-related offences. On the Irish state's use of the death penalty (the last execution was on 20 April 1954) and the shift in attitudes thereto,

see David M. Doyle and Ian O'Donnell, 'The Death Penalty in Post-Independence Ireland', *Journal of Legal History*, 33 (1) (2012): 65–91.

294 *Dáil Debates*, vol. 192, cols. 839–42, *passim.*, 23 November 1961. These exchanges degenerated into undignified name-calling between Jack McQuillan and Brian Lenihan of Fianna Fáil: 'You are a professional agitator' (Lenihan to McQuillan) and 'You are a professional chancer' (service returned).

295 See, for example, *Dáil Debates*, vol. 192, cols. 1213–14, 6 December 1961 (Noël Browne and Jack McQuillan); vol. 193, cols. 73–4, 14 February 1962 (Browne, McQuillan and Michael Mullen of the Labour Party).

296 See *Irish Independent*, 27 February 1962, 1a–h; *Irish Press*, 27 February 1962, 1a–b and 5a. The *Kerryman*, traditionally sympathetic to the republican movement, carried the statement in full.

297 The four were Browne and McQuillan, Michael Donnellan (Clann na Talmhan) and Seán Treacy (Labour Party).

298 See *Dáil Debates*, vol. 193, cols. 1306–7, 8 March 1962.

299 *Dáil Debates*, vol. 193, col. 1307. See also NAI TAOIS/GIS/1/172, C. J. Haughey, 1961–2.

300 *Dáil Debates*, vol. 193, col. 1307.

19

THE DESOLATED SHRINE

We have come almost to the end of this tale, long and tortuous, revealing, and drawn together by a number of persistent and layered themes. I reluctantly prolong the narrative, aware that a volume of this size tests the reader's patience and endurance. But there is one more sequence to be laid out and examined before we can claim to have a conspectus of the reciprocal relationship between prisons and politics during the four decades of romantic physical-force republicanism.

We know that revolutions have a strong tendency to devour their own children: this observation, most often made when analysing the course of events that constituted the French Revolution, is not universally validated, but it may be that it applies most frequently when the revolution is doctrinally driven and its claims are general, perhaps universalist. We see this in the 1917 October Revolution and today in some of the Islamic revolutions and insurgencies. The mechanism is relatively simple: the revolutionary comes out of the desert – literal or figurative – preaching a message of purity and redemption. The call may, by force of arms or other means, triumph, but in doing so it cannot shed its destructive force and possibilities. Purity of doctrine is always open to challenge and interpretation and, by its very nature, generates accusations of backsliding and apostasy. And, indeed, since life rarely lives up to doctrine, or matches it, and since individual gain and comfort are such widespread motivations, the pure soul – the seagreen incorruptible Robespierre – will find backsliding and apostasy in abundance.

When we focus on the revolutionist himself or herself, the dynamics are much the same. When all the compromisers, trimmers, deserters and traitors (as he or she would have it) are winnowed away, the doctrine remains, more precious and cherished than ever, a truly intimate and sustaining possession. The scenarios vary, of course, but in many the intensity with which the doctrine – the idea – is promulgated and defended drives yet others away. Far from sobering or checking the purist, this falling-off confirms and strengthens his or her beliefs and tightens the sense of intimate possession. Here is evidence not of the fallibility of doctrine and programme but an utterly convincing explanation for its lack of success. Greater devotion, more complete submission are required and have been withheld: this explains all failure. Enmity, which is directed against the greater, supposedly universal enemy, is turned and focuses on the enemy within. Comradeship magnifies rather then moderates enmity and revulsion. Could it be, indeed, that the now-uncovered foe was intent from the outset on destroying the revolution and its movement? Even when successful in seizing power, revolutions find (and may perhaps need) that to maintain momentum apostates and traitors must be conjured up.

Whilst not inevitable, this morbid sequence has possessed, and consumed, revolutionary movements, both secular and religious, those of physical as well as intellectual (and spiritual) force. Combine this mechanism with the gravitational forces, the innumerable pressures of imprisonment, the special strains of internment, and we begin to see the cogs and gears, pulleys and levers, the engine and the fuel of self-destruction.

It would be futile to dispute with historical, social and economic determinists the question of voluntary action. There are some whose circumstances make them apt for revolution, but many others similarly placed who choose a different path: chance, temperament and opportunity all intervene. We may, however, agree that becoming active in revolutionary activities is not like catching a bus: waiting for the one displaying the right destination and then hopping aboard. To break the law, to contemplate overthrowing it, involves, even for the most shallow of personalities, a significant shift in self-perception. The dangers cannot be avoided (and in its induction training, the IRA, for example, underlines them), and one crosses a threshold that would cause all but a few of one's fellow-citizens to shy. The vast majority of revolutionists are therefore conscious and determined volunteers, albeit swept along to varying extents by circumstances and chance – as with events and fortune in all our lives.

We see in this concluding scene of the last episode of romantic Irish nation-alism: the combination of the internal forces of revolution, the needs and drives of the revolutionary personality, the testing to destruction of the volunteer spirit and the corrosion of prolonged and seemingly indeterminate captivity. All of this is set within a self-sustaining, middle heavens' type of politics, a set of axioms that exponents either see no need to test against reality or refuse to do so. This with-holding is not one of neglect or indolence or indeed ignorance but is an act of will and, in itself, a statement of principle. Those living out their days of deprivation and servitude at the Curragh had at some point undergone a type of conversion experience, and to let it go would entail cost and pain, existential tragedy and a stripping of the soul. Their commitment and self-abnegation came from the same impulse as that of the religious who had answered the Gospel invitation: 'Come unto me, ye that are heavy laden and I will give you rest… for my yoke is easy and my burden is light.'[1] They had placed trust, hope and faith in the organisation. Surrender and submission had freed them of responsibility and regret, absorbed them into a vision of justice and freedom and of marvellous promise.

The freedom within

The state of the IRA in the free world largely determined what happened behind walls and wire fences. A body united, intact, active and able to command at least some degree of public support, could motivate its prisoners, give them (and their dependants) assistance in various forms and enlist them as a reserve battalion in the contest for hearts and minds. This was the function of prisoners and internees during the Anglo-Irish War. Bitter divisions within the organisation and the ebbing away of support had, as we have seen, dire effects on republican prisoners during the Civil War, the 1930s, and the years of the Second World War. Northern and Southern prisoners and internees had different experiences. Prisoners and internees in Northern Ireland could count on humanitarian support from within the Catholic community, despite the majority probably not favouring the IRA's use of violence. There was also at least a halo of support from this source, always thin and fading away at times. This sentiment had various elements, including alienation from the Northern state and a lack of faith in electoral politics within it. On the other side of the community divide, and unlike Dublin, the Belfast government faced no dissension on internment from within the ranks of its electoral supporters. This polarity in the broader society aided cohesiveness among the internees and prisoners. Dissension, weariness and departures from the ranks were bound to increase as the campaign ebbed and dwindled away, but rancour was more contained in Belfast Prison than in Mountjoy and the Curragh.

By insisting on strict segregation between Curragh staff and internees, the IRA failed to identify and exploit some useful opportunities. The camp staff were unprepared to be gaolers and, to the extent that they could, learnt that complicated job by trial and error. For the most part, even established military policemen had little relevant preparation other than crowd control and limited use of force; their basic training lasted about six weeks.[2] Such was the division between the ministries that no one in Defence or Justice apparently thought it worthwhile to second to the Curragh a cadre of senior and experienced prison officers to assist with the establishment of the regime and to train staff.[3]

As we have repeatedly noted, IRA rules and customs – its carceral template – provided a military command structure for any establishment in which its men were held. The exact form this took varied with the size and layout of the prison or camp, the number of prisoners and the type of confinement (a sentence of imprisonment, or internment). A substantial body of men, a degree of freedom of movement and the flexibility of an internee regime meant that the IRA's Curragh arrangements were quite elaborate. Describing the system as 'self-government', an internee outlined it to an IRA prisoner. There was a general assembly of internees every three months at which an OC was elected. During his term, the OC was the internees' supreme authority: 'We are responsible to him and he is responsible to the leaders of the Movement.' The OC selected his own staff, including adjutant and quartermaster. Other staff included an intelligence officer and an officer and assistant in charge of orderlies.[4] In addition to staff appointments, the OC also nominated a representative committee which had an advisory function. Each hut had an OC who reported to the camp OC. A weekly meeting of internees was held at which the OC issued orders and heard proposals and complaints. Committees were each responsible for a different facet of camp life – education and entertainment, sport and the like. All internal camp services were manned by the internees, who had their own barbers, a librarian, meal servers, cleaners and others assigned by rota to a range of duties.

The IRA's self-imposed regime and system of discipline did not include much that a regular army would have considered essential – kit and bed inspections, marching and foot-drill, and coordinated physical exercises. This had never been part of the IRA's tradition, nor its style. The only armies that could have served as models for such spit and polish were those of adversaries – the British or Free State/Republic of Ireland forces. This was a rebel body, and, although rebels may choose to subordinate themselves to a hierarchy and conventional military scheme of discipline, one gains the impression that any IRA leader who adopted such a style in the 1950s would have been laughed out of office. The IRA man embodied self-discipline, internalised soldierly qualities and adhered to a system arrived at by agreement. Marching columns, shouted orders and the cat-and-mouse structured humiliation of kit inspection had no place in that type of order.[5]

Acceptance of its command structure by the authorities satisfied the IRA demand that the men be treated as political or military prisoners rather than criminals or civilians. An important consequence of this approach – the full implications of which were seemingly not grasped by IRA members – was that the men became their own gaolers, and some took up the role with zest. The assignment by rota of internees to housekeeping duties such as food service, cleaning and the issue of linen meant that captors, whether North or South, conserved manpower and husbanded finances. The organisation considered that autonomy inside the wire or wall was always more advantageous than the attritional possibilities of forcing the authorities to provide manpower for the many operational tasks of custody. Go-slow, sabotage and minimal cooperation would all have exacted a significant administrative cost. It was as though MacCurtáin and the other veterans entered the camp gates as persons returning to a home of sorts, a battalion to its depot, a column at the end of a route-march, billets waiting, knowing how to behave, drawing reassurance from custody's intense familiarity, the veterans able to induct and guide.

These leaders were the purposeful pilgrims, leading the way, sharing knowledge, offering advice and encouraging the novice. Purpose, destination, rubric and conduct were held to be self-evident. Tradition provided all answers and the sacrifices of those who had trodden the path before imposed obligation and confirmed legitimacy. On both sides of the border there was at this time no questioning of the proposition that the internees were political, not criminal, in status, so that battle did not have to be won. The deal had attraction for the established leadership of the internees and for officials alike. A policy of non-cooperation could have obliged the authorities to double or treble manning levels and costs. There would have been some, but not many, disadvantages for the internees, and the opportunities for propaganda stunts would have more than compensated for these. As we shall see, the Curragh was thinly staffed, and a multiplication of demands would not only have been costly but was possibly beyond the Irish

Army's resources. Cooperation could have been bartered for concessions or even the curtailment of internment. At the very least it would have been an embarrassment to the Irish government, and an administrative drain.[6] But drawing on familiar archetypes, both the IRA and the Irish Army reflexively stepped into roles for which their personal education in a nationalistic state, and their common republican heritage, had prepared them: it was the traditional village marriage, all known, nothing unexpected. The IRA enjoyed the trappings of its military structure with its moral validation, unchallenged. The Irish Army acquired a group of prisoners who cooperated easily and generally seemed to find *de facto* POW status an acceptable consolation prize for not being able to be soldiers. Some individuals enjoyed this; nearly all uncomplainingly acquiesced in it. Yet beyond the immediate ease and lack of conflict a personal as well as an organisational price had to be paid: the internee was enmeshed in two demanding disciplinary systems, as firmly grasped within the IRA's demands and minutely arranged injunctions as if in a prison of wires, walls and searchlights. The resultant tensions stressed the organisation and tested loyalties up to and into destruction. 'Self-government' added another and indeed more intrusive bureaucracy to the official one. Since it was supposed to be voluntary, there could be no withholding of self, no domain of privacy. Tensions and confrontations were bound to increase and, finding no outlet, to coalesce around the establishment of a series of priorities and needs that inevitably would involve the control of escape attempts and, indeed, any confrontation with the camp authorities. As the months passed it became evident that a blanket of assumptions had been thrown over the internees. A suffocating and intolerable situation had been created and could only intensify: many of the bold and the able had little choice but to flee it; the rest, disheartened, folded into themselves.

Tomás MacCurtáin, who would be much criticised for his authoritarian style of leadership, had a detailed knowledge of the IRA's resources. His credentials were impeccable and the lustre of his father descended easily upon him. He had been within hours of the hangman's early morning greeting and had faced the prospect with stoicism. With Tony Magan and Patrick McLogan he had rebuilt the organisation in the post-war years and over a decade had painstakingly put together the plans and *matériel* for the Border Campaign. He insisted that, with the very limited manpower and resources available, any distraction from the principal objective – attacking British forces in Northern Ireland – must be avoided. The point of prison protests was largely to rally outside opinion, reinforcing supporters and encouraging sympathisers, aiding the armed struggle by encouraging recruitment and funding and throwing obstacles in the government's way. These actions, prison and camp protests, moreover, had always to be approached as sideshows, subordinate in every respect to the Border Campaign. Within the IRA's strategic and tactical concerns, no other approach made sense, in the opinion of MacCurtáin and the senior men. The other reason for prison protests (to mount what were skirmishes of attrition against the authorities), was not on the agenda, since the Dublin government was not the current target. Irish independence was well established, in its third generation of citizens. Rants about 'Staters' were vapor-ous political moonshine. How would the Irish public react were there con-frontations that led to the injury of Curragh staff? Time, moreover, was against the movement, and it would take months or even years to build up a worthwhile head of pressure on prison issues, could it be done at all. Malignity and cruelty on the part of captors would be hard to conjure up. The armed campaign did not have months or years: losing momentum it must die.

From this line of reasoning it followed that there was little purpose in picking fights with the authorities, and much to gain by avoiding them. How then should IRA members in internment conduct themselves most effectively to support the continuing armed struggle? The camp leadership's answer was subtle, neither meat nor drink for young men of action: it would test followers grievously and ultimately split the ranks. Its consequences would bring the IRA close to extinction and change its character for ever. MacCurtáin drew (as so many did) on MacSwiney's dictum from the Anglo-Irish War. MacCurtáin's father (also Tomás), as Lord Mayor of Cork, had been murdered in his home, almost certainly by members of the RIC. His close comrade, and successor as Lord Mayor, had been Terence MacSwiney, whose death on hunger strike in Brixton Prison dealt a heavy blow to British authority in Ireland.[7] MacSwiney, as we have noted, was the author of one of the most influential aphorisms of Irish republicanism: 'It is not they who can inflict most but they who can suffer most can conquer... Those whose faith is strong will endure to the end and triumph.'[8] Proceeding from this, MacCurtáin's strategy seemingly reconciled the need not to distract attention from his organisation's armed actions against Northern Ireland, with the need to preserve the internees from passivity and demoralisation. They would exert moral and political pressure on the Irish government simply by being – by the very shameful fact of internment – and the longer they were held the greater the pressure. They were guilty of no offence other than seeking the freedom of their countrymen in Northern Ireland – state policy since the foundation of the Southern state. Disciplined and committed, not seeking trouble, they would shove de Valera's government into the moral spotlight. But for this, structure, discipline and unity were essential. And thus, supposedly, 'Sweet are the uses of adversity / Which, like the toad, ugly and venomous, / Wears yet a precious jewel in his head.'[9]

As internee OC, MacCurtáin presented his men's grievances to the camp authorities. A whole range of deficiencies arise when the state – and a comparatively poor state, at that – runs a residential institution. Details are overlooked, needs swept aside and human foibles are dismissed. Luxury was certainly not the issue since basics were poorly provided or neglected. These deficiencies ranged from a failure or tardiness in the supply of items such as spectacles and dentures to the number of washbasins in the ablutions room and everything between and beyond. When MacCurtáin put these to the administration he was conscious that the lack of some amenities and supplies directly affected the lives of his men: nothing in a prisoner's life is petty. He was aware that dissatisfaction intensified when such requests and complaints were acknowledged, when action was promised and when nothing was delivered. But he was indignant at another level: the authorities were acting in bad faith. His men, he insisted, had 'contributed in fair measure to establishing and maintaining conditions within the Camp, on a plane which has made administration of Camp Affairs as tolerable as the circumstances would permit for all concerned'. This had called for 'a high sense of duty and discipline on the part of all the prisoners'.[10] The very minimum quid pro quo was attention to the men's minimal requests. Were delays to continue to frustrate and irritate, relations between staff and internees would deteriorate. What he did not say – and may not have acknowledged even to himself – was that this souring would have reflected on his own leadership and his strategy of serving by enduring, fighting by being, as much as on the camp authorities. He might have joined de Valera in the moral spotlight.

And as it turned out, MacCurtáin's strategy was at the same time too limited and too ambitious. Of such a pedigree and experience, and age, he could with equanimity contemplate the claim that 'the race is not to the swift, nor the battle to the strong'. Schooled in the virtues of an unquestioning and wholehearted obedience, willing and grateful submission, MacCurtáin and his senior colleagues pressed stoical endurance, obedience and a belief in the waiting game to a body of men a generation or two younger than they, for many of whom the most attractive order of the day would be summarised as 'have a scrap now, in whatever way possible and damn the consequences'. The resultant clash between control and restraint as example and weapon and the yearning for action was inevitable. The internees re-ran the divisions and personality conflicts that had erupted and persisted during the years of the Second World War and that cut as channels of acid through the movement. In accordance with his strategy, MacCurtáin demanded obedience to his non-confrontation policy in all the details of camp life: this was his right as leader; this was their duty as inheritors of sacrifice.[11]

The Curragh experience of the 1940s had blighted and gutted the IRA for his generation, and now, by holding his men together, MacCurtáin sought to bring them to the day of liberation, intact and safe, emblem and example, ready for other battles. There was much but inevitable irony in the fact that factionalism would indeed be repeated and that MacCurtáin's policy would be its engine and he its principal and most energetic stoker. Backed by senior comrades, he seemed to revel in a perverse 'never apologise, never explain' style of leadership: loyalty, like love, never questions. This was authoritarianism approaching cult-like levels. Even had he not rubbed against the human grain and the mettle and impulses of youth, the fact that confrontation, splits, schisms and bitterness are their most dangerous and pressing enemies is hard to explain to men devoured by the wasting of their days, increasingly tortured by fears of futility and beset by doubt. Frustration found its outlet in criticism of the leadership and in calls for action; the alternative, it appeared, was to settle down with the equivalent of a knee-rug and comfortable slippers, sitting out indefinite detention, sustained by rarefied notions of the effects of noble endurance. Among the internees there were no doubt philosophers and stoics, but there were many more of an audacious and impetuous disposition for whom action was eloquence and the only form of dignity.

Internee politics

Internees accepted their organisation's discipline for several reasons. It was a quality that defined the IRA tradition from its emergence at the time of the Easter Rising and maintained over the years by men all internees admired as legends and models. It was a privilege to belong, at whatever remove, to such a company. Republican authority was based on the Petrine rock of Easter 1916, and its passing on was as familiar to the republican devout as the genealogy of the Old Testament was to religious fundamentalists. Structure and routines made life easier; solidarity and a sense of belonging gave meaning to incarceration and – underpinning all – most continued to be committed to the IRA and its purposes. Despite the camp leadership's martinet style, the discipline of internment in the 1950s had aspects of toleration – certainly in comparison to the war years. There was, according to Tomás Mac Giolla, a degree of freedom of speech: 'Anyone could come up with ideas about escapes or anything they wanted to do… ideas which would then be discussed.'[12] Some topics were off-limits: criticism of the leadership and espousal of ideas that might be seen as having an explicit Communistic tinge (even though the hysterical anti-Communism of the war years seemed to have faded). The Cold War was in an intense phase and its outcome far from certain. Internment in the Republic of Ireland commenced in the year of Sputnik.[13] In the camp were Sputnik-watching contests at night; the pot-bellied stoves that heated the huts were known as sputniks; and there seems to have been some speculative discussion of the Soviet Union and its achievements – as there was in the broader society. The peace and anti-imperialism elements in Soviet rhetoric, and the fact that it was opposed in foreign policy to all that Britain stood for, could not be dismissed. Mac Giolla did not remember camp discussions as having an ideological outcome or that there was a growth in socialist ideas at this time, 'but you felt that there were differences of opinion, and there were a whole lot of new ideas being spun about Irish history… There was the working-class idea coming out into discussions of historical events.' But the exchanges were not pressed to the point where significant differences of doctrinal opinion emerged, or a new school of thought surfaced, or such ideological dissent began to shape camp life. There was constant discussion and pondering on the Border Campaign, but because it was still under way none felt able to call for a stop. There was, according to Mac Giolla, a growing sense that it was not the best way forward and that there were better means of promoting republicanism, but 'We were in here because we were supporting the IRA and they were still out there fighting, and therefore you dare not say that they were wrong.'[14]

Among the camp's organisations was the Legion of Mary, a Roman Catholic lay body founded in Dublin in 1921 by Frank Duff.[15] Whilst pursuing its spiritual purposes, the Legion also served inmates' more immediate needs. Because it was part of their obligations and spiritual discipline, its members were allowed, as an exceptional privilege, to congregate for meetings in the various huts after lock-up. Since movement between huts was then otherwise prohibited, Legion membership was a useful means of getting around restrictions and convening meetings or conducting business of a distinctly non-spiritual kind.[16] But, like Legion membership, religious convictions were scarcely a factor in camp life and did not shape the prevailing republican ideology.

Outside perceptions

Apart from occasional and isolated press stories, the internees failed to keep their plight before the public. North and South, the general political climate was unreceptive. The IRA and related organisations did what they could, and the *United Irishman* ran prisoner and internee pieces in every issue, but all this reached a small and declining readership. In theory, imprisonment and internment personalised and illustrated a number of evocative issues and accessed powerful nationalist currents. In the past these had varying degrees of success, going beyond immediate and routine techniques of petitions, demonstrations and appeals, to acquire broad sympathy and significant political leverage.[17] Republicanism had attracted a number of journalists of talent who had projected the message, full of colour, sharp with invective and satire, and wrapped in indignation, well beyond the ranks. That zenith had passed, and the dreary orthodoxy of the organisation – its self-indulgent isolation and comfortable inertia – was repetitively and unimaginatively and, one feels, routinely, indifferently and hopelessly presented. Flair could so easily have offended 'the movement'. Yet the more general state of politics and the preoccupations of public opinion were critical and largely unaddressed.

During the war years, as we have seen, any expression of sympathy or support for prisoners, North or South, meant almost certain attention from the respective Special Branches and, if persisted in, the distinct possibility of consequences extending to a closer acquaintance with internment and the objects of one's sympathies.[18] The blanket of press censorship and sense of acute national peril lay over all. This was remote from the conditions of the 1950s, and yet internment failed to produce anything approaching sympathy, much less indignation, outside republican circles. Press indifference, on whatever that was based, was one reason for this. Just as importantly, however, was the lack of issues around which to develop a general grievance. Apart from the unready state of the camp when they first arrived (but tell that sad tale to anyone in the hands of builders), internees had little to grouse about beyond the fact of their rather Spartan captivity. They were treated well, food was good, conditions reasonably liberal, and there was no attempt to humiliate, oppress or punish them. They could at any time secure freedom by giving an undertaking to do what all other citizens did (respect the Constitution and laws), and thus liberty was in their own hands. This version of internment wrapped in mildness blocked hopes of drawing into republican ranks those who lay just beyond their outer fringes and certainly of creating any kind of political momentum.[19] When the Border Campaign was finally terminated, the IRA acknowledged this and castigated the public.[20]

As in other periods of internment, two different accounts were given: one for public and the other for relatives' consumption. Letters out and in often referred to the 'Curragh Concentration Camp' in headings or text, and the *United Irishman* always did so. It suited the organisation to conjure up, however improbably, the suffering and injustice of a concentration camp. Not much more than a dozen years had elapsed since the world was horrified by the revelations of what had been going on in extermination camps across eastern Europe and Germany. To put the Curragh in this category was grotesque, as one hopes internees and the wider public knew. There was a counter-pressure: some internees were uncomfortable with their relatives and friends believing the Sinn Féin propaganda and worrying unnecessarily. A number of letters addressed this. To a woman friend, a man referred to such reports: 'I wish to emphatically state that at no time have we been treated harshly or unjustly. The punishments we have incurred to date, well let us be fair, have we not "earned" them?' This was not a statement of submission but of fact and was intended 'to counteract the insidious remarks which I'm sure must be worrying the parents of the internees'.[21] When in November 1957 it was alleged in the Dáil that internees were being escorted to visits with a bayonet in their backs, internees and their visitors were heard by camp guards to say that this was not true and that they would tell their friends the truth.[22] There was more such. The following month, an internee commented that '[t]he food here – army rations – is exceedingly well cooked and that makes up for a lot'. He also remarked on the good relations with staff that made for the smoother working of the camp.[23]

Dependants' funds

The IRA had shaken the last pennies from the purse to fund the Border Campaign, and there was little for internees' and prisoners' relief. Some sympathisers, willing to donate for the prisoners and their families, would not give for the running of the military campaign. An Cumann Cabhrach dealt with prisoners' relief in the Republic, and the more respectable and ostensibly apolitical Green Cross served the same function in Northern Ireland.[24] Mick Ryan's family received no financial assistance whilst he was active in the campaign, or even during his imprisonment. He remembered a certain localism in donations. Places such as Armagh and Lurgan and other Northern areas had a solid base of supporters, some perhaps dating to the 1940s, and these would always contribute to 'look after their Lurgan men, their Armagh men, their Derry men or whatever'.[25]

A fixed scale of dependants' support payments was established by An Cumann Cabhrach. According to Irish army intelligence, this was fixed at half a man's former wage in the case of a married man. The dependants of single men were more difficult to assess for payment, but some did receive support. Funds were tight, and information was demanded from applicants in order to prioritise giving. Only a generation or so away from the Poor Law and its workhouses, such means-testing was always a sensitive matter and could cause considerable offence. A father reported to his Curragh son that on applying for assistance he got back a reply 'asking for all particulars as regards dependants and what other income is coming into the house. I have no intention of giving such information nor will I look for charity from them so you can realise what you are wasting your time for. *Get a load of that.*'[26]

Another dissatisfied relative wrote in, this time a mother. She had applied personally to An Cumann Cabhrach, but the official had become angry with her. He told her that it was public money and that since her son had been unemployed at the time of his arrest she was not entitled to any support payments. She replied that had it not been for the IRA her son would still be in employment. She also reproached her son, 'So... you see I have been right all the time. I told you they were a bad lot but please yourself.'[27]

Apart from payments to dependants, An Cumann Cabhrach provided comforts to the internees and help to their visitors. Committees were established in various towns to collect funds for parcels. Those included tobacco and cigarettes, food, clothing and footwear and cooking equipment.[28] Arrangements were made to save postage by setting up collection points for parcels, which were then taken to the Curragh by car. Transport was also provided for visitors, and car-owners who were prepared to take other visitors with them to the camp were given money for petrol. As the first Christmas in internment approached, a supply of cards for the internees was sent in by a sympathiser who wisely declined an offer by the *United Irishman* to acknowledge his generosity in its columns.[29]

Fund-raising was tolerated by the government (and was doubtless useful for Special Branch), although there were attempts to discourage newspapers from accepting advertisements from the Republican Dependants' Committee. Not all that long out of the censorship of the war years, there was some timidity, and a number of editors sought advice on this, but the line taken by the Department of Justice was that they could not issue legal advice. At the same time, it pointed to Sections 2, 10, 11 and 18 of the OASA which might have a bearing on the matter. Short of legal advice, it did not hesitate to describe as 'mischievous or contrary to the public interest' certain items for publication.[30] In practice, there seems to have been little interference with editors' discretion in the matter of dependants' committee advertisements. On their part, editors had to be careful not to reject the advertisements, thus risking republican criticism and condemnation, only to see the material carried in a rival and equally respectable title. The same applied to reporting on the activities and solicitations of the dependants' committee.[31]

The dependants' funds were not conducted on a philanthropic basis. Recipients had to toe the IRA line, the internee within the camp and his dependant outside. One man insisted that, in maintaining its control within the camp, the IRA's disbursement of funds was 'the main weapon'.[32] Collectors and organisers of An Cumann Cabhrach may not have been IRA members, but they were approved auxiliaries – former members, associates or kin, republicans in good standing. No clandestine organisation could have risked giving access to dependants' families to persons other than known friends and supporters: the opportunities for making mischief and collecting intelligence were far too many. Activists would have known that when in 1916 Michael Collins joined with others after his release from Frongoch internment camp to reconstruct the IRA, he first took up the position of secretary of the Sinn Féin relief committee.[33] That such a position could work for malign as well as benign ends was obvious.

In Ireland's depressed and unpromising economy, even small sums were immensely important to some families. It was also important to the IRA, and to its active members, that the fund workers should support families and dependants politically and psychologically as well as materially. Visiting, explaining and defending IRA activities, giving the message of 'just hang on – support the lads in the North and those behind the wire', brought comfort and perhaps reassurance to some. For those who were worried about conditions in the Curragh, perhaps taking too literally the concentration-camp tales of the *United Irishman*, regular visits were also important. And at the heart of this was the need for the IRA to do all it could to prevent or ease family pressures on internees. Even were they not to sign out, men who were not supported by their families made poor camp-mates.[34] Disaffection could spread in many ways.

Escapes

As might be expected, members of the Saor Uladh–Christle group were the first to attempt a breakout, and this ratcheted up restiveness among the more action-minded IRA internees. At the time, nine members of the minority group were housed in a section of Hut 5, half of which also accommodated the infirmary and chapel. Limited facilities may have dictated the decision to locate them there, but it was an unwise one, since Hut 5 was only a matter of feet away from the first of the camp's array of barriers. Given that part of its justification for existence was greater effectiveness than the allegedly sclerotic IRA, the dissident group was bound to make a demonstration.

Work must have started almost as soon as the men were assigned to Hut 5. By the time the tunnel was discovered, on 14 August 1957 (not much more than a month after the camp's opening), it had made considerable progress. The spade had been enthusiastically wielded while the basics of deception were ignored. Staff had reported that the occupants of Hut 5 were acting suspiciously, apparently on edge. One man stayed inside all day, and another sat reading on the doorstep, despite it being unseasonably cold. On the morning of the 14th, Captain P. Reidy, Acting Commandant, became even more suspicious when he found one of the men still in bed at 10 a.m. He covertly noted that the boots of the other occupants showed light traces of brown soil. Searching at lunchtime (when all were in the dining hall), a hole about eighteen inches by twelve was found under the fireplace (a supposedly clever but actually very obvious location). Later in the day, Reidy and other senior officers deliberated whether to let the tunnel (which at that point posed no risk) proceed, while keeping the men under observation. It was decided to take the safer course, and the men were paraded outside and confronted that afternoon. All were warned about damage to property and removed immediately to Hut 1. On closer examination it was discovered that two openings had been made: one (possibly a decoy) was under the fireplace, but the entrance to the tunnel itself started inside a cupboard: there had been a double-bluff. Various tools were recovered, together with a candle that staff pointedly noted had been taken from the chapel altar. The tunnel had been dug back under the hut to avoid making too obvious a path to the wire. The vertical shaft had been sunk to a depth of only three feet at that point.

The nine occupants of Hut 5 were brought before the Commandant, charged with two offences. The first and more serious was attempting to escape and the second was damage to property, a trivial misdemeanour. The Commandant found the men not guilty of the first offence, presumably on the grounds that on the day in question the tunnel could not have provided a means of escape. Whatever the quibble on which he acquitted them, he had evidently decided not to make too much of the incident, perhaps judging that to do so would have boosted the men's view of themselves as well as elevating their status in the camp. He did find them guilty of damage to property and deprived them of visits, letters, parcels and other privileges for a fortnight. This was only a couple of steps above a verbal warning.[35]

Someone on the staff seems to have been willing, as American cop movies of the day would have had it, to 'drop a dime' (make a telephone call). A garbled account of the incident accordingly appeared in the press, together with the claim that the men had gone on hunger strike against their punishment.[36] Since the other details in the report were incorrect it is hard to know what to make of the hunger-strike claim – certainly if there was one it came to nothing.

The Hut 5 incident was relatively unimportant in itself, but it was the opening passage in a complicated and (for the IRA) sombre symphony. The question of escapes became critical, exposed deep flaws in doctrine and organisational structure and would have effects far outlasting internment. The first successful break by IRA internees was an opportunistic and go-it-alone affair. During the evening of Tuesday, 27 May 1958, Vincent Conlon (who had driven the lorry in the Brookeborough raid) and Terence O'Toole took advantage of their stay in the camp infirmary to break out through a lightly barred shower window. Joined by James Anthony Kelly, they managed to flee from the camp area. Without a getaway plan, contacts or a safe house, they were reduced to knocking on doors and asking for shelter. On the first night, sheer luck took them to the house of a Sinn Féin supporter, but Conlon and O'Toole were picked up by the Army two days later.[37] The escape had not been authorised, and they had therefore committed an offence against the IRA as well as against the law of the land. Nevertheless, on their return to camp their indiscipline was dealt with leniently by the IRA camp command. The mildness may have been due to the novelty of the escape – and possibly their low rank. But their exploit stimulated the appetites of other adventurers. The camp leadership insisted on its right to control all such activity. Freelance ventures, at least in theory, could jeopardise other plans, prospective or in train, and might also, should they include an element of force or violence, sour relations with camp staff. Equally, or perhaps more importantly, the camp leadership required total submission and saw unauthorised initiatives as subversive of their authority. It would become apparent that obedience had become a goal in itself, a leadership-created fetish. Four months would elapse before another break succeeded. This was on 27 September 1958, when Ruairí Ó Brádaigh and Dave O'Connell slipped through the wires and evaded detection. They were well gone when missed at roll-call the following morning.[38] Outside, all but three members of the Army Council had been taken at an IRA safe house on Dublin's Serpentine Avenue in September, so Ó Brádaigh and O'Connell remained prudently out of touch with contacts for almost a month.[39]

These unauthorised escapes and attempts, and the fact that several non-escapers had been involved, created turmoil and bad feeling. Into this increasingly noxious mix of resentment and suspicion came Charlie Murphy, former IRA Adjutant General, interned at the end of his three-month sentence of imprisonment.[40] Whatever his intentions, Murphy was destined to become a catalyst. Those dissatisfied with the camp leadership cast him in the role of a Brutus around whom they could rally.[41] The camp leaders were cold and hostile towards him as a member of a GHQ who they thought had made a number of errors and who had ignored and snubbed their good advice. For his part, Murphy considered that camp policy on escapes had been too restrictive. Accepting *de facto* leadership of the disenchanted, Murphy and his followers occupied their own hut, which came to be called 'Little Rock'.[42] Entirely bypassing the camp leadership, a very basic and bold escape plan was concocted. This entailed a group rush on the fence. Under cover of the milling crowd the wire would then be cut. On 2 December 1958, the attempt was made.

This, the largest escape from the camp, was a demonstration of what the internee leadership could have done had it chosen to make a break.[43] From its inception, the recreation field had been an obvious security weakness. The risk was recognised but outweighed by the counterbalance of giving frustrated and bored men a chance to discharge their energies and to disperse the ennui of confinement. As we have seen several times, the congregation of large numbers of prisoners tests staff abilities to control and multiplies the possibilities for disorder, on a small or large scale. This is the case within a conventional walled compound, but even more so when the perimeter is secured by wires and watchtowers. Add to this the customary and inevitable melee of internees rushing about in team sports, other forms of exercise, or as spectators, and the chances of things getting out of control increase still further. But the most critical element was the fact that these men had agreed a plan and were prepared to act in a coordinated fashion. On the afternoon of Tuesday, 2 December, all these factors blended. The guard had collected no intelligence and were unprepared and vulnerable.

At a prearranged signal, some sixty internees who had been engaged in Gaelic football and in hurling broke into groups and, running in different directions, attacked the wire security fences with cutters. The field, as we have noted, was overlooked by watchtowers and manned by armed guards. Lethal force simply to prevent an escape was out of the question. Warning shots and gas grenades were fired but the key group managed to get through the fences. The authorities took only small consolation from the almost immediate recapture of two men.[44] The government information service declared that only warning shots had been fired and that five men had received minor injuries from gas grenades.[45]

The escape lifted the spirits of IRA men at large and in captivity and predictably embarrassed and infuriated both the government and the Curragh IRA leadership. Jack McQuillan, the semi-official republican out-player and goad, put questions in the Dáil, further intended to wring advantage from the event. What was the nature of the men's injuries and had their next of kin been notified? He was also solicitous and concerned about the hours on duty of the soldiers in the pursuit operation. Kevin Boland's responses were tight-lipped.[46] Carelessness meant that there had been a discrepancy between the government's initial statement of the number injured and the number given a few days later. None of the injuries was serious, and the confusion of the escape's aftermath was easily enough understood. There was no political mileage in the event. The government and the Army may have reflected that the loss of fourteen internees was no great loss to bear if the alternative (had lethal force been used, even accidentally) were serious injuries or deaths. That most certainly would have entailed a heavy moral and political cost.[47]

The escape, quite understandably, attracted a deal of public attention. John Joe McGirl, a Sinn Féin (abstaining) TD, held a press conference at which he announced that legal action was being considered on behalf of the injured men.[48] This was routine tinsel and tambourine-shaking and, as expected, came to nothing. Ten days later, the IRA was demonstrably irritated when the *Irish Times* ran a report claiming that it had taken disciplinary action against the escapers.[49] The newspaper, whatever its sources, had got the story more or less correct: 'the older leaders had decided on a policy that precluded escapes, at least for the time being, but that the younger men ignored this decision'. In response to this, MacCurtáin issued a statement through the Republican Publicity Bureau. The statement certainly did not refute the *Irish Times* story and thus served to confirm it: 'All Republican prisoners here stand shoulder to shoulder in a united front against our jailors, and, knowing their scheme, will ignore all provocative and aggressive behaviour on the part of the military. In this camp the victory will not be achieved by those who can inflict most.'[50] The audience for such a statement cannot have been the general public but only the ever-evaporating rock pool of IRA purists, supporters and sympathisers.

The nub of this escape was a gamble, informed or otherwise, on the guards' terms of engagement. They could open fire only if their lives or those of comrades were threatened. Should they do so outside those specific conditions, disciplinary proceedings would inevitably have followed, and, had there been injuries or death, criminal charges would have been all but inevitable.[51] A military police-man, on duty on the day of the breakout, recalled that neither his life nor the lives of his colleagues were threatened, and, in consequence, he decided not to open fire. As well as his revolver, he was carrying tear-gas grenades, and he threw some of these. Several internees were affected by the gas, he recalled, but 'I think I was affected even worse.' Shots were fired in the air, and some of the internees were manhandled back into the camp. But for this, more would have escaped.[52] The escape showed the Army's weakness in their role as guards. They were, by law, extremely restricted in their use of lethal force and had not been given sufficiently clear and specific guidance. In addition, they were not deployed in adequate numbers and were without the necessary equipment and training to use methods short of lethal force to prevent mass escapes.[53]

It was much more acceptable to the endurance-sweat-and-toil cast of mind and the revolutionary trade-guild approach of MacCurtáin and his senior comrades to organise that most traditional of camp escape methods: the tunnel. Intensive teamwork and discipline were required, and the structure of command was an essential part of the enterprise. Tunnels may have seemed more respectable than taking one's chances: escape, if it came, would have been earned. A revolutionary bank-manager would doubtless have approved. An authorised tunnel had been started, but evidence of soil disposal was found during one of the regular searches. The only way of getting rid of the very considerable amount of material was to spread it around the compound. Special bags were made, some knitted and some sewn together. Internees filled these, put them down their trouser-legs and walked around the compound using drawstrings to release small amounts as they went. (This method had been shown in the 1950 film, *The Wooden Horse*, which may have provided the inspiration.)[54] The camp guard had been briefed and was alert for digging and on the lookout for soil of a different texture and colour. Proof that something was under way came more directly and conclusively, however, when a still-full soil-disposal bag (made from a piece of blanket) was found under a bed, its owner awaiting a chance (or having forgotten) to empty it. Although the tunnel remained hidden (and it may be there to this day), the discovery of the soil-bag had much the same effect as if the tunnel had been found. The approved escape had been a time-wasting dud, but, Noel Kavanagh remembered, 'We paid for it, as we were shifted [from one hut to another] sometimes twice a week and even one Christmas Eve.'[55]

Reactions to the mass escape

The Army

Commandant B. G. Maguirc, Commanding Officer at the time of the mass escape of 2 December 1958, was immediately removed and a black mark was no doubt entered in his file. There followed bitter and rather undignified exchanges between Curragh Command and Commandant S. Mac Eilgeóid, who now took charge and who much resented being passed the poisoned chalice. The escape had been a national sensation suggesting massive incompetence, and there was abundant blame to go around.[56] Stricken by the fate of his predecessor, Mac Eilgeóid was determined not to follow him into career extinction. His survival strategy was to lay down a barrage of paperwork and to skirmish with his superiors on several fronts. Should there be a repeat of the 2 December fiasco, he wanted company when blame and recrimination were doled out. Writing nine days after the escape, he lodged a protest at Curragh Command's decision to remove the stand-to rapid-reaction party that (stable-door-wise) had been deployed after the escape. The Adjutant General had agreed to this reinforcement, and it was anticipated that the party would have a billet inside the internment camp. Since it was prohibited to fire on internees to prevent an escape, and because of 'the proven speed with which wire fences can be breached', Mac Eilgeóid pointed out that he could not hope to hold back another mass assault on the fences unless immediate reinforcement was at hand. It had been established that it took fifteen minutes from the receipt of the alarm code word for the stand-to party, stationed elsewhere in the Curragh complex, to reach the internment camp. The fences, however, had been breached in only two minutes.[57] Mac Eilgeóid did not say, possibly because it was obvious to all, that the December escape had given any future escapers, should they be sufficiently focused, at least a notion of the Army's powers and restraints.

The response to Mac Eilgeóid's protest failed to mollify or reassure him, and he despatched another warning the following day, making a number of general criticisms in even more heated language: he feared that there could be another incident at any time. There had been only 'a niggardly half-hearted response' to the report on the escape and to his subsequent recommendations. Apparently Curragh Command was 'indifferent to the security of An Campa Imtheorannachta'. Certain officers had said '"You are getting paid for doing this job, why should we worry, you can hold the baby."' This was a dangerous attitude, to be eliminated at once: 'The Army has suffered sufficient adverse publicity by the National Press.' Staff morale was low and deficiencies in numbers had not been remedied. A fifth of the soldiers were not content with their posting and were looking for opportunities for getting away: they should be replaced. Mac Eilgeóid repeated his objections to the withdrawal of the stand-to party: 'If a two or three point breach [in the fences] using mattresses is attempted more than half the internees will be a minimum 12 minutes ahead of any recovery attempt.' Recommended upgrading of the fences had not yet been undertaken. In summary, he wrote, 'I cannot accept the situation which exists, which is in effect that if an escape attempt or attempts on the previous lines are made, I shall merely be a scapegoat and the subject of jocose and sarcastic references in the National Press.'[58] As indeed he would have been.

This was unseemly squabbling and certainly ran contrary to the military tradition that an officer did his best with the resources that were made available to him by his superiors. The language showed a degree of desperation, presumably based on the calculation that anger towards superior officers was less career-threatening than another escape. And Mac Eilgeóid had a point, both professionally and personally. Had the internees been fully aware and sure of the sentries' very restricted terms of engagement, and had they had the will, a two- or three-point rush on the fences could have procured escape on an even greater scale – perhaps even emptying the camp. A break could have turned into something like a great walk-away. Even minimal outside organisation and assistance could have spirited a considerable number of men away from the Curragh area. Although Mac Eilgeóid was trying to immunise himself, he was surely right to point to what could have been a national scandal, perhaps even a crisis of government.

The IRA

In parallel, there was as much confusion and disarray within the IRA command, inside and outside the camp. Unbeknownst to Mac Eilgeóid and his senior colleagues – and it would certainly have come as a very great surprise – their best safeguard against further escapes was Tomás MacCurtáin and his leadership group, whose disapproval of the 2 December escape was probably as great as that of Mac Eilgeóid himself.[59] Bizarrely, this was deemed a time for the internee command to reinforce discipline and condemn the escapers rather than to make their own and even more powerful and organised rush on the fences. If rancour and buck-passing were setting the tone for official correspondence, as much and more was apparently under way in the councils of the internees and in their messages out of the camp to GHQ.

Despite their condemnation of the escape as unauthorised, and their belief that it undermined IRA operations in some fashion (how is unclear), MacCurtáin and his associates had to be careful. Even within the inner circle there had to be doubts. It would be all too easy to respond reflexively, to appear to begrudge the escape and by doing so to declare, however vaguely and circuitously, an implicit agreement with the authorities. Less than happy with his opportunistic and rebellious comrades, MacCurtáin nevertheless lodged a protest that escapers had been shot; he also objected to the camp's collective punishment: the suspension of visits and newspapers and the withdrawal of wireless sets from the huts. (Mac Eilgeóid wisely did not stop correspondence: to have done so would have fed rumours of ill-treatment – as on past occasions in prisons and camps.) MacCurtáin also objected, on the ground that it had put escapers at risk, to the burning of furze in the area surrounding the camp.[60]

MacCurtáin had immediately informed IRA GHQ that the escape of the sixteen was unauthorised and that those who had taken part were, to varying degrees, dissidents who had taken themselves outside his command. The response of the organisation was therefore conspicuously lacking in triumphalism; indeed, not the smallest drop of praise was bestowed. It was as though a visiting editorial team from *Pravda* had been put on the spot by some embarrassing incident that was not in their script. Yet there had to be some IRA reaction, if only because of press coverage. This had been critical, and the Army's action in firing on and imperilling the wholly innocent driver of an Electricity Supply Board lorry at Newbridge, Co. Kildare, added to the impression of incompetence and ham-fistedness.[61] This was surely a moment when determination and derring-do on the IRA side could have been trumpeted: some hero-making was possible, and certainly a few celebratory ballads could have been run up. But the lack of per-mission to escape and an unwillingness to compromise or improvise blocked this approach entirely: all was looking away and a shuffling of feet.

In consequence, IRA publicity was strangulated and verged on the ludicrous. Again, *Pravda*-like, the escapers were damned with a touch of the airbrush. How then to deal with this imbroglio? A leaflet was issued, concentrating on the supposed overreaction of the guards and camp command. Two men had been wounded, gas grenades had been used, 'round after round' had been directed at the escapers, and, in an attempt to flush out any who may have been hiding, the furze around the camp had been fired.[62] The break itself was not portrayed as a successful attempt to rejoin the IRA's campaign but as a reaction (with the hint that it was a foolish one) to the camp regime. It had, indeed, been engineered by the authorities to serve their own ends: 'when prisoners' rights are denied it is a well-known tactic on the part of their jailers to get them to do something which is apparently unjustifiable and thus – in retrospect as it were – attempt to "justify" the original misdeeds of their jailers!' But, once the prisoners understood this their 'high standard of unity and discipline would be maintained'.[63] In a statement issued through the Republican Publicity Bureau, MacCurtáin fell back on the sentiments of his father's comrade and predecessor in office: 'In this camp the victory will not be achieved by those who can inflict most.'[64]

Revolutionary organisations are apt to tie themselves into ideological knots, but this was something altogether different: fealty to the organisation was to be demonstrated by staying inside the camp and not escaping. It is likely that MacCurtáin himself wrote the leaflet or, at the very least, had a major hand in the final text. Certainly he is generously quoted. In the aftermath of the escape, he had told Mac Eilgeóid that it was the internees' 'firm intention', as in the past, to avoid conflict with the authorities. If there were trouble, therefore, the responsibility would be the Commandant's.[65] What the IRA rank and file at large made of this bizarre document is hard to say, but it would be safe to conjecture that it failed to inspire them. For some in whom the revolutionary sap was high was there a whiff of the Molotov–Ribbentrop Pact?

The split

The escape was a catalyst, an historic juncture in the IRA's complicated history. Reinforcing division, it transformed recrimination and mistrust into split. MacCurtáin and the camp leadership took the escape as a calculated affront to their steward-ship: it was almost as though the challenge was the break's principal objective. The dissidents saw it in much the same way, but as confirmation that the leadership had been timid to a perverse degree, hidebound and stubborn, so that sound and committed men had no option but to go against them.[66] There were further consequences. Whilst the escapers had disobeyed the orders of their OC, they had shown themselves to be audacious, determined – and successful. Now at liberty, were they to be excluded from the IRA as delinquents or accepted as men of proven ability, much-needed reinforcements? GHQ chose the latter course, thereby enraging the camp leadership. The *reductio ad absurdum* would have had the men submitting and making their way back to the camp, petitioning at the front gate for readmission. A row turned into a feud, an endless spiral of recriminations like those that had come out of the Curragh in the war years. Bitterness intensified and ate into the organisation for years thereafter.

Escapes are perhaps the most effective demonstrations by prisoners that captivity has failed to rob them of spirit and initiative, that brio and guts remain intact.[67] We have seen how previous breaks were used by the IRA to mock the government and to rally the membership and supporters.[68] This was scarcely possible at this juncture. Convinced that the Border Campaign had run out of steam, and wishing to show that the IRA was no longer a serious threat to its authority, Dublin began to release the internees, unconditionally and (to minimise any chance of homecoming celebrations and triumphalist publicity) in small batches.[69] Even had the IRA leadership seized the opportunity and taken the Curragh escape to its heart, praising the men and mocking the government, glee may have been short-lived. Such glory may have appeared to be more spangles and glue than substance if by waiting for three months the men could have joined their colleagues and walked out through the front gate, government-provided train or bus ticket in hand. The last internee left the Curragh on 11 March 1959, and the camp closed a few days later.[70] The great breakout may have shifted into a different perspective – a bit more like youthful high-jinks than the derring-do of fearsome revolutionaries.

Dogma and dissent

Immured in his certainties, Tomás MacCurtáin continued to insist that IRA escapes be matched to the needs of the outside organisation and that timings be synchronised. To spring from prison or internment a man who had skills or contacts that could be put to immediate use in the campaign was justifiable, but had a price. Breakout would inevitably trigger an official inquiry and review and lead to additional precautions. Each escape, therefore, could be expected to ratchet up security and to limit the options for another. In addition, escapes could entail disciplinary proceedings against camp staff. The resultant resentment would, at least for a time, make camp life more difficult by increasing vigilance and reducing willingness to countenance minor evasions of the rules. Outside, intensified police activity might disrupt IRA activities and searches turn up documents and even arms. There was in this line of reasoning much that was practical and obvious. But it was not the doctrinal issue centring on rank and discipline that lent such heat to the arguments about escapes, even though a cool view might have conceded that, while MacCurtáin's orthodoxy was not without merit, revolutionary activities have much more of the pell-mell than procession about them. To the camp leadership (in a backhanded compliment to Special Branch), the internees were not randomly assembled individuals but soldiers under discipline. Any failure to keep that in mind would prove disastrous, the first phase of a great unravelling. The experience of republicanism, going back to the Fenians, was that the entire organisation, captive and free, survived and prospered by maintaining its structure and discipline in prison. Actions that undermined this, such as unauthorised escapes, were not simply rash but an injury to all. They were, therefore, to be condemned as a type of sabotage, whatever the immediate practical benefit and temporary rise in morale an unsanctioned action might bring.

Such was the orthodoxy. But, as we have seen (and it is far from unique to revolutionaries), structure and discipline all too easily become and displace ends. Permission granted or withheld may be the badge and frisson of authority, just as submission becomes the cardinal or even sole test of loyalty. And there was another danger to be avoided, the opposite of the buccaneering spirit. Confinement, especially when it is of indefinite duration, produces torpor as adaptation, a type of hibernation. Expectations are lowered to match surroundings and prospects. Even the boldest and most committed of internees could thus come to prefer routine, inertia and stoical resignation. One easily assumes the role of the pro- phet in winter. Organisational erosion thus comes by seemingly opposite means: escape from the camp and withdrawal into one's self.

The issue of escapes migrated into the broader body as a source of persistent rancour and division. An underground organisation, as we have noted, has none of the tangible supports of conventional bodies: legal underpinnings, public acceptance and prestige, cash in the bank, uniforms, barracks, career structure, achievement badges and visible ranks – and therefore structure and procedures become central and definitive. From the IRA's very earliest days, these had been matters of critical importance – inevitably so since it was drawn from and oper- ated in a religiously observant society. Without founding authority, discipline, rules, standing orders and a chain of command, the organisation would be little more than an informal association or gang; it would lack a moral basis on which to command the loyalty of its members, to legitimise its actions and to present itself to fellow-citizens. Its bombings would be criminal damage, its confiscations robbery and its assassinations foul murder.

An additional source of strain was that a significant portion of the Army Council, figures who had for years nurtured the organisation at uncounted and unstinted personal cost and who had undertaken the endless detailed preparations for the Border Campaign, now found themselves in the Curragh. Tony Magan, former Chief of Staff, a key figure in the IRA's post-war reconstruction, was one such. He had been a single-minded, iron-disciplined leader, impatient of any opposition and Leninist in exerting control at all levels. Some veteran activists had found it impossible to work with him and had left the movement. His close associates on the Army Council, Tomás MacCurtáin and Patrick McLogan (they were known together as 'the three Ms'), had fully supported this centralising style of leadership, believing that only through effective and ineluctable discipline could the IRA succeed.[71] This dogmatic model of revolution was imported into the camp, without modification and untested by discussion. It was also inevitable that these men should have a proprietorial and defensive attitude towards the organisation they had rebuilt and the campaign they had set in motion. They caused a great deal of offence when they attempted to steer the current (and younger) leadership outside from behind the wires – and were rebuffed.[72] Even were a highly controlling style of leadership effective in a revolutionary body preparing for action, it was certain to provoke ill-feeling. It went to the limits of internees' thin and sorely tested toleration. They were already tormented by living at such close quarters, missing and sometimes reproached and pressured by their families and psychologically depleted by their indefinite term of confinement. The cistern of personal irritations and grudges notwithstanding, here was another source of conflict. And there was an additional unpleasant (and largely unspoken) conundrum: the more active the IRA was in its ambushes, raids and bombings, the more prolonged internment would be; on the other hand, IRA inactivity and lack of success might hasten the day of freedom. But that called into question the purpose and worth of the internees' captivity. The very worst circumstance was a campaign ticking over enough to secure public acceptance of internment but which had no chance of success. It was this dismal and futile level of activity that had been reached by the autumn of 1957. Escape, therefore, at almost any price, was the only way of dissipating the billows of gloom and passing beyond the barriers of despair. To be chided and chastised for this was beyond endurance.

The lack of public interest, much less understanding or support, was especially dispiriting. Charlie Murphy recalled one telling incident. A man from a rural area who had been granted compassionate parole was quizzed on his return to camp as to what local people were saying. His comrades would no doubt have hoped for a modicum of admiration and perhaps some anger against the government, but the returnee replied that neighbours had asked him what it was like to work in England. His parents, who were not republicans, not wanting it to be known that he was in the Curragh, had put it about that he was in England. There was no pride in 'our boys behind the wires'. Murphy commented how affected men became as such stories came back.[73]

With the campaign and the movement itself in the doldrums, prisoners' black moods and dissatisfaction almost inevitably focused on the OC and his staff. In these circumstances, twenty-five-year-old Ruairí Ó Brádaigh was approached in August 1957 to stand for election as Camp OC. He realised that were he elected he would be in for troubled times. MacCurtáin sourly described the job to him: "'You're a sink where all the dirt accumulates and you're identified in the end with the prison regime, because you are the person that goes and deals with them".'[74] Ó Brádaigh turned down the nomination.

Bile, vituperation and personal abuse erupted as the split widened. Less than two months after the revival of internment in the Republic, Gerry Lawless, one of five ostracised on MacCurtáin's orders, wrote to a friend. Exclusion had been hard on them at first, he wrote, but now they were happy with it since, with the exception of about twenty of the majority (114 strong at that point), 'they are a bad lot'. If Ireland were to look to them, it would have poor prospects: 'I would as soon see the present [de Valera] regime in power than them, as I'm sure they would make the country into a police state, the likes of which has never been seen before.' He supported this claim by noting that in the Curragh, where they claimed all their key activists were being held, 'they have a setup, in which 20% are doing little all day but spying on the other 80%. And in which a small clique of about 7 men with Tony [Magan] at the top keep an iron hold on the rest, with the Republican Aid Money [for families] as the main weapon.'[75]

Anathema was pronounced with bell, book and candle and enforced with assiduous devotion. Writing to a friend who had told him that Tony, another internee, was asking after him, Liam Walsh, a dissident, disclosed that he had not recently been able to speak to Tony in the camp: 'he's being watched by IRA intelligence, ever hear the likes of it in all your life'. He went on to discuss Paul, another internee. MacCurtáin had discovered that Paul was talking to members of the splinter group and warned him that the next time he would be thrown out of the camp.[76] Members of the majority group saw benefits in expelling those who did not accept MacCurtáin's discipline. Writing to his wife, however, Michael Traynor noted that there was much better feeling in the camp than in the 1940s. He appeared to compare the minority with the 'undesirables' that had been in the Curragh in the 1940s: 'Commies and touts [informers] & what not – they were like a lot of wolves among a flock of sheep.'[77]

But whatever the instructions about writing out of the camp (and they were bound agitprop-wise to emphasise the internees' resoluteness and solidarity), neither group was shy about spilling their grievances about the other to the authorities. With threats of punishment, MacCurtáin had instructed his men not to discuss IRA matters within the hearing of camp staff yet he was himself expansive in discussions with the Assistant Commandant. The dissidents, MacCurtáin told him, had been expelled for their lack of discipline. They were linked to Liam Kelly, and they (it was not clear if he meant the dissidents or Kelly) had 'carried out a raid on a police barracks, in which there was a woman and a child, against the wishes of the IRA proper'. He was emphatic that under 'no circumstances' would they be readmitted and believed that in any case they had as few as forty followers outside. MacCurtáin seemed determined to deliver this type of information to army intelligence: 'Liam Kelly's crowd were responsible for the recent affair where shots were fired across the Border. He [MacCurtáin] was inclined to scorn their efforts. He also thought that McChrystle [*sic*] had gone to France.' His message was that the IRA could be trusted to act with discipline and only against the British: 'under no circumstance will they fire on a fellow Irishman, even if they are fired on – they do not want a civil war'.[78]

Liam Walsh (of the splinter group) did not pass information about the IRA but was more openly abusive, telling the Assistant Commandant that 'the spleen we have is not with you but the 120 bastards inside, the same bastards who were willing to shake the hands of myself, Atkins and Doyle a few months ago when we had done the work and who now scorn the very ground we walk on'. Because he made fewer problems for them, the camp authorities were understandably more comfortable with MacCurtáin than with Walsh and his colleagues. The splinter group, the Assistant Commandant reported, had for some time past been the only source of trouble in the camp; 'however their attempts at tunnelling, hunger strike, escape, etc., may be only for the purpose of seeking notoriety, as it appears that they know just how far to go, and are docile enough when caught out'.[79]

And here solid information runs out, and we leave Curragh. As noted, the last internees were freed on 11 March 1959, and they and many freed before them took into the outside organisation the bile and bitterness distilled so zealously in the Curragh. This, arguably, was the last of the IRA that had grown out of the 1916 Rising, that had split over the Treaty and that, in search of a role, had stumbled through the three decades and more that followed. The duty exacted by the dead and by doctrine had been pursued to the very end by diminishing numbers and by an ever more self-contained ideology.

The story of physical-force nationalism and republicanism had not come to an end. Others would find in its tropes and traditions, colours and sounds, expression for their passions. This had, however, been the last hurrah of romantic Irish nationalism. It had sought the test, prepared for it and had drawn the conclusion of many such movements in other times and other places: the people were not worthy. And since the people had failed, a new people would have to be found.

Dispersal

Stepping back to look at the broader canvas, the culmination at the Curragh acquires more shape and colour and becomes familiar. We realise that we have seen its elements elsewhere across the picture that we have variously glimpsed. As the years and decades passed, in all their complexity of ideas, events and people, a simplicity was also discernible, just as by shifting our vantage point a little what was jumble becomes a pattern. The simile only holds in part, for history is multilayered, and we need to apply our imagination accordingly. But when the image repeatedly forces itself we must pay attention. In colour, shape and sound, as we scan the decades of internment and imprisonment, we begin to find and assemble the elements of pilgrimage, and we see our prisoners assuming, for the most part unconsciously, but sometimes with surprising awareness and clarity, the pilgrim role.

The metaphor of life's passage as a pilgrimage is familiar and is used both in sacred and secular thought and commentary. As some use it, the notion relates to ontology, the consideration of being. Some find cause for hope and reinforcement of humane values in the belief that individuals are in a constant process of coming into being, never wholly fixed and determined. This enables us to envisage the pilgrimage as an internal process as well as an activity in the external world. To regard ourselves as a creative work in progress, through choice and circumstance, means that we must view others similarly.

Pilgrimage takes various forms. It may be a journey shared as well as one taken alone. It is a time out of ordinary life, connections and preoccupations, a progress of submission, self-discovery and change, swapping the ordinary and immediate for an exultation and celebration of a greater thing. It contains a promise of merit gained, defects and vices shed, of connection with the transcendent. But this is more than individual wish and striving. It is a thing of custom and order. It has a known destination, of a precious and sacred nature, a place or state of being commonly revered. The pilgrim progresses through stages, follows a sequence and is bound and thus assisted by custom. He or she will have companions, guides, staging posts and refuges along the way. Those that have passed that way before encourage by example and achievement. One of the most famous allegorical and metaphorical depictions of pilgrimage, John Bunyan's *The Pilgrim's Progress*, sets out the temptations, adversities and obstacles that face the pilgrim but shows that, in the end, through fidelity and will, and though many fall away or are diverted, some will persevere. As one of the pilgrims, Mr Steadfast, stands on the threshold of his goal, he rejoices and declares that it was with great difficulty he got hither but that he did not regret the effort or his troubles:

> My sword I give to him that shall succeed me in my pilgrimage, and my courage and skill to him that can get it. My marks and scars I carry with me, to be a witness for me that I have fought His battles who now will be my rewarder.[80]

Surely among the most affecting lines of prose in the English language, emanating from profound religious convictions, written in Bedford Prison almost three centuries previously, but not an inapt expression of the belief of Tomás MacCurtáin and men who journeyed with him and before him; so close that Terence MacSwiney's dictum about endurance could be a paraphrase.

Suffering on behalf of another is at the core of Christian thinking (and that of other religions) and has long been an element in Irish culture. The sufferings of illness or adversity are 'offered' to a greater good or, this being a closed moral economy, for the relief of another. The fallen nature of man, original and all subsequent sin, demand penitence: human suffering and death itself are 'the wages of sin'. The inevitability of suffering, as well as taking on suffering, have easily migrated and adapted to become powerful values within physical-force Irish republicanism.

The leadership that found itself in the Curragh during the Border Campaign was the group that had painstakingly pieced the venture together. They had, between them, decades of imprisonment, commitment and sacrifice. For what they saw as an overriding goal and body of principles they had lived in uncomplaining renunciation of the smaller things. Their reputations within the republican family went before them: stoicism, loyalty, fixity of purpose, abhorrence of compromise, immersion in the movement, hardness and bravery. With these and other qualities, and possessed of strong personalities and unfailingly serious dispositions, they were in a powerful position to command and inspire. At the Curragh they exercised authority that was at once traditional, legal and charismatic. One may utterly reject their beliefs, but it would be dishonest and futile to deny that they were figures of character and consistency, seeking a moral path within the range of their convictions, and willing to stand fast, as Bunyan would have seen it, faithful unto death. This, of course, does not mean that they were persons of virtue: one may persevere in a wicked course as in a good and benign one. Fidelity is a powerful and usually admirable quality, but it is morally neutral. The nature of the cause and object of devotion must still be judged.

For these men, the notion of pilgrimage, never, as far as I know, acknowledged, was an underlying source of strength. They trod a path on which others, whom they could enumerate and describe, had passed before. It sustained and encouraged them that their journey would be taken by people still to come, generation by generation until the end. The cause and destination they knew beyond all questioning and doubt to be sacred, all-consuming and all-excluding. As a novice embarking humbly and gratefully, instructed by the example of those who had gone before, the difficulty of the journey was gradually disclosed and the mysteries and ways of the order were unveiled. Language, ways of behaving, routines, new ways of thinking – a reformation of personality – demanded a different way of being but offered a new life. A number could be expected to fall by the wayside, challenging but ultimately strengthening those who persevered. Among these, the sense of honour and privilege and of being in the best of company intensified. Still some dropped away, the company becoming more select, and conscious of it. The distance travelled became as important as that which was still to come: to give up was to give away so much.

By stages, imperceptibly and largely unexamined, gradually and organically, the revolutionary life withdraws into itself. External points of reference diminish or are disregarded, the imagined and longed-for goal acquires a spiritual intensity, an intimate proximity, unspeakingly known to be shared with others of the company: words do not comprehend it. Tests, checks and questions cease to refer outward and instead to turn in, to assay purity. Reality at this point is brittle, and still some apostatise with fearful personal consequences, open to vistas of lives consumed and laid desolate, utter hopelessness for some. Yet even defections and betrayals can reinforce those who press on. Never can they find a place to stop, and all contemplation has to be of things to come: to falter is to fail. These are romantics, selected by chance, advanced by opportunity, several times self-selected and refined. We may wonder, behind the granite walls they offered to the world, how many doubted, lost faith but could not lose face and pressed on with Yeats's warning, terribly understood: 'Never give all the heart.'

The Border Campaign roughly coincided with the centenary of Fenianism. The IRA leaders, from what we can tell, rarely referred to these forerunners, yet the affinities were inescapable and numerous.[81] It may be that Fenianism offered a lesson that IRA leaders did not wish to ponder. It had been a bright and spectacular comet in its time, involving tens of thousands, extending its operations to three continents, causing dismay in London, becoming in the popular mind a fiendish threat. There came the end of its journey across the sky, no more remarkable, intangible. Like the post-Treaty IRA, Fenianism was largely an exercise in political imagination and will, rhetoric and fervency far outstripping deed and effect. Part of its ancestry was to be found in the secret revolutionary groups of Paris with which the Fenian leader James Stephens and others were familiar during their early exile. Those revolutionaries – and who knows the detail of their ancient pedigree – would have recognised the qualities and personas of MacCurtáin, Magan and McLogan as those of confrères. They would have been familiar spirits also to the dynamitards of the 1880s, to some at least of the Nihilists and could easily have found a place within the album so persuasively opened by Joseph Conrad in *The Secret Agent* (1907). This may seem an improbable claim, but when the carapace of conspiratorial Irish nationalism is stripped away, the creature that dwells within can be seen to have family features not unknown in pre- and post-Revolutionary Paris, St Petersburg and London's old East End.

Romantic republicanism got its best and final opportunity under the leadership of this dedicated, austere group of conservative revolutionaries who saw through the last months and weeks of internment in the Curragh. There had been years of planning for their great venture, years of accumulation, of training and of testing. No premature displays or adventures were permitted to damage the project, and, to the extent that was possible in a milieu of rumour, surveillance, informers and agents, a degree of secrecy (or at least uncertainty) was preserved. And not all the omens and circumstances were unfavourable. The political class in the Republic agreed one and all that Partition was more than a disputed policy and possessed iniquity that took it to the level of national evil, a maiming inflicted solely through the malignity of foreign oppressors. For many young men (and some young women), passage between the national legend and the republican programme was easy, and censure lacked coherence and consistency and was delivered, it may have seemed, without conviction.

Not all recruits were poorly educated, but many were; not all had had parochial vision, but many had: both conditions were common in mid-twentieth-century Ireland. For lives which were ordinary and humdrum, which had the few prospects and limited choices of the 1950s, a promise of full-blooded action and sweeping change could attract and intoxicate. Entering a hidden world of clandestine organisation and rules, introduced to a world view that combined a venerable tradition with the imperatives of action, recruits could be drawn effortlessly along. But this was never a mass movement, could not be one, and on its fringes people came and went. When all the winnowing was done – the distractions of courtship, ambition, domesticity and work, the deterrents of the black mark, closed doors and police attention – there remained a serious-minded group from which could emerge those willing to translate thoughts into action, not dismayed to travel from declaration to commitment to consequence. This was the human material of the Border Campaign, an answer to the existential questions with which physical-force republicanism had wrestled since the dump-arms order of 24 May 1923.

In all of this, as we have seen, reality was held at bay and bent to the wheel of conjectured history. The virtual Republic was alive, trampled, dishonoured and wronged, but a power that would come again – pity, protectiveness, anger and vengefulness combining in a powerful wave. The religious and political loyalties of Northern Ireland's Protestant majority were but ghostly figments, whisked away in a magician's cloak, lost in a deft display of the three-card trick or condemned as wholly oppressive, foreign and heretical. For the philosophical and political romantic realities do not precede thought and action. However contradictory, challenging or repugnant, they can do no more than confirm that the idea alone makes reality. Only the idea is pure enough for the test of creation; all else is corruption.

We return now to the familiar setting of prison, to the camp's bleakness and to the heartache of both. All who have experience of captivity, as captor or prisoner, would agree that this is a testing condition, sometimes supremely so. For Irish political prisoners, the well-known and much-documented pains of all imprisonment – loss of freedom, of privacy, of choice, of goods, of domestic and sexual intimacy, and more – were to some extent moderated by preparation (suffering described, shared and anticipated), by outlook, by fellowship, and in the communion of ideas. We have explored these processes, their dynamics and their outcomes in a variety of settings. In some circumstances and under favourable conditions, these forces can be so strong as to transform the nature of imprisonment; captors can become hostage to their prisoners; and the prison or camp is turned inside out, becoming a battering ram to be used against the state. This optimal outcome for organised, disciplined and committed prisoners was achieved during the Anglo-Irish War but not thereafter. The qualities of the prisoners are a necessary condition for this transformation, but they are not sufficient: if not a majority, then a significant section of the population at large must withdraw legitimacy from the government to make possible this custodial alchemy. It is a rare event, but its potentialities gripped the imagination and exerted a pervasive influence over republican prisoners and internees during the years that we have traversed. They thought of the Anglo-Irish War and of the almost triumphant Republic. A freak spring tide had swept the beaches and the shore beyond and never in a lifetime would come again – but none knew it.

And when a prison or camp cannot be transformed; when a campaign flickers and hope gutters, existing but ever failing; and when public opinion blows cold or is indifferent, what then for those who must eat captivity's bitter herbs? Zion is not gained, and its graces and comforts imperceptibly fail to answer the summons of the mind. The companionship of trust and honour cannot be sustained. It had never seemed that one was submitting to a second captivity beyond that of the enemy. Treading in the footsteps of an earlier generation of strivers and captives had been a privilege and (following the prophet) the IRA's custodial discipline was a yoke willingly assumed and light to bear. To have another allocate duties was no hardship but a thing of brotherhood, were the system open and equitable, and by and large it was. But go further, to the topics, words and sentiment of letters to wives, sweethearts, parents and other family, the manner of conversations during visits, to requests for parole and parole's justification and duration, and one is indeed behind a second wall, a second fence: something alien becomes discernible. This world within a world was, as we have seen, bound round with injunctions and sanctions, what in the everyday world would pass as humiliations and invasions of the self. Here we have the stuff of religious orders and a life to be lived by those who have received and are sustained by the force of an extraordinary will. But below our group of dedicated and self-abnegating leaders, as we have seen, was an array of less extraordinary characters. The common quality was the voluntary nature of their custody: all held the key to the gate. North and South of the border the lock of liberty could be turned and the bolts withdrawn by a signature (sometimes merely a word) promising no more than citizenship. Past the ranks of political detainees and internees, some guilty men, convicted and long-sentenced, were also offered leniency for a promise. But, as we have repeatedly seen, to take this clemency was to sin in deepest scarlet, to go widdershins against all that was known and valued. The possession of the key must have been a torment to many, an undetachable incubus, too often roused by the urgings of family, friends and voices in the broader community.

At various points we have heard the internee's complaint that in one cardinal respect his or her lot was worse than that of the sentenced prisoner, the absence of a horizon of freedom to which once could make passage through the dreary days, however protracted. Indeterminacy is a hard notion properly to convey in the abstract. In the course of our ordinary private lives we join the company of strangers who are waiting, with little or no information and with no sense of control. Most commonly, and trivially, we encounter this frustration with delayed transportation (planes, trains and traffic jams) but also sometimes find it in a place of service: a busy emergency ward or an ill-organised public-service office. Time drags and grinds, information is tantalisingly sparse, frustration mounts and strains, yet eventually there is resolution: emotions calm and we gratefully resume the routines of life, momentarily more valued. These are common experiences, rarely rising above the level of unremarkable irritation.

But imagine these frustrations projected onto internment's larger screen. Life is lived in a waiting room, all other possibilities closed off. One lives with similarly afflicted others, and perhaps this provides some balm, but maybe not. A bargain of brotherhood was made and now is cast in hardest moral metal: the fate of all is the fate of one. As in the transport queue or in the crowded but unattended waiting room, rumour and speculation thrive. From time to time a companion is freed. The comparison of antecedents can become frantic as a pattern is sought and chances are calculated. Imagine further that somewhere beyond this waiting place others are committed to actions that will prolong your suspended condition. These actions are futile, counterproductive and have descended to the merely ritualistic, but you cannot gainsay them: that is the pact among you.

This was the multi-gravity pressure on the Border Campaign prisoners and internees: all hope of success gone and a harvest of continued severity daily gathered in. It was indeed a torment of rare qualities to be able to open the door and step through it but to hold back in deference to a vow or fear of lifelong rejection and disdain from those, in the whole world, whose esteem is most valued. No ordinary criminal prisoner, outcast and despised, self-accusing or wrapped in foolish braggadocio, is thus loaded with anguish. And in all of this the pilgrim is recalled to duty and submission, mind and spirit as well as body.

In the manner of a specimen stripped and stained for the microscope, captivity lays bare the individual's fine tissues and anatomy's faintest shadows. It brings to bear its powers of magnification in several ways. In Goffman's fruitful characterisation, it is a total institution: all the otherwise separate segments of a life are cast together in one place.[82] This creates visibility and possibilities for intense control. Devices and tactics that allow us to create social shelters and retreats – choosing our company, being alone, doing this instead of that – are no longer available. Add to these characteristics of prisoners and camps a further agency of social magnification – the organisation of an army – and demands and stresses intensify. The magnification screw is twisted again by the pervasive suspicions of a clandestine and terminal conspiratorial organisation. Is there still commitment? Is discipline being upheld? Is there backsliding or indeed betrayal? Is a coup being prepared against the leadership? Are splinter groups being formed? Who had said what? Where did this rumour start? Was there derision, caricature and scatological disrespect? What did that laugh mean? Paranoia blossoms and casts out further seeds. Appeals for loyalty and conformity were hobbled not only by personality conflicts and petty quarrels but most of all by the failure of the Border Campaign, lost beyond dispute and long past the reach of wildest hopes. With that incontestable fact daily to be confronted, the question of primary purpose could not be evaded or silenced. There rose within the age-old chant of the soldier: 'we're here because we're here because we're here'.

There was justification of a kind, but it was subtle, serpentine and tenuous: the prisoners and internees could, by enduring, reverse the hostage relationship. Simply by being they would capture, embarrass and expose their captors. This venerable republican stratagem had at other times and in other circumstances been effective. It now seemed unconvincing, the more so that government's unlikely discomfiture had to be paid for in the currency of lost days, weeks and months, in love strained and lost, and in the dowsing of pity. This had not been in the original prospectus. What of honour, of personal dignity, of that old down-country favourite, payback through stubbornness? Well, much the same: it was a thin market, increasingly a fool's one.

And so it ended, as it had a decade and a half before. Feuds laid down and revetted, gall and enmity in plentiful supply, the pages of the grudge book turned down for further perusal. The Border Campaign was no longer the issue, though bizarrely it stumbled on and around like some badly wounded beast. The battles now to be fought, and the prizes to be gained, concentrated on orders, ranks, procedure and the sour detritus of camp life, backward-looking, inward-facing, irrelevant to the people, disconnected from the times, confirming that the long quest of romantic republicanism had ended. Words hardly mattered.

Thus the pilgrimage dispersed. In progress, the fellowship never doubted that history and spirit had converged with grace upon them, pointing to a destination supremely worthy. The path was well worn and reverenced. Custom and usage made tangible the sense of passing from the ordinary into greater history. But between a journey and a pilgrimage there lies only the effort of mind and spirit, a mere tilting of the glass. And, despite every trick of mind and reflex, should that shift occur, the vision shatters. The pilgrim finds himself in the world of ordinary little cares, the longing of the spirit unsatisfied but quenched.

Notes

1 Matthew 11:28–30 (King James Version).
2 This was too short, according to Peter Brennan, who joined the Irish Army in 1952 and became a military policeman two years later (interview). A small number of military police would have had experience of running a detention barracks and of basic custodial techniques.
3 This was the comment of Tom Landers, a military policeman of several years standing when he was assigned to the Curragh in 1957. Reflecting (after half a century) he suggested that should internment ever again be necessary, 'they should get Prison Warders in Mountjoy… civilians, to come down and train them, if it's only a week, or four or five days even, and give them an idea of what they have to do, and what they can't do' (interview). Peter Brennan agreed. Camp staff were not briefed properly when they arrived: 'You landed straight in and that was it.' His enduring memory of the period remains the unsuitability of staff because of their lack of training (interview).
4 MA PM/I/ADM/12, S. Ryan to T. R. Atkins, 15 September 1958. Tomás MacCurtáin remained OC throughout the period of internment. For the first year, Tomás Ó Dubhghaill was his Adjutant, Seamus Slattery was Quartermaster and Brendán Sealy was OC of camp orderlies.
5 Two observations on the Spanish Civil War (one from an unlikely source) come to mind (though the IRA of the 1950s would have been horrified by the comparison): 'And, having as their ideal a self-discipline requiring no external authority to perfect it, genuine Anarchists were necessarily difficult to control.' Duchess of Atholl, *Searchlight on Spain* (Harmondsworth: Penguin, 1938), p. 111. The maverick duchess (née Katharine Ramsay) had been a Scottish Unionist MP for thirteen years and was the first woman to serve in a Conservative government in the UK, but she was drawn to the independent-minded and free of spirit. For more on the military training of the fiercely libertarian, see George Orwell, *Homage to Catalonia* (London: Folio, 1970), Chapter 1.
6 There was a curious concurrence of government and IRA opinion on the matter of housekeeping and maintenance, and, of course, a number of senior politicians who had entered the mainstream and had attained high office had direct or indirect

experience of camp or prison life and of the conventions that had grown up. Thus, Oscar Traynor, the Fianna Fáil Minister for Justice, gave it, in axiom form, that '[i]t is the custom that detention camps should be kept clean by the detained persons themselves' (*Dáil Debates*, vol. 164, col. 654, 6 November 1957). As noted, Traynor had been a Volunteer during the Easter Rising and was interned in Frongoch in North Wales. He took the anti-Treaty side in the Civil War and, after streetfighting in Dublin, escaped to Co. Wicklow, where he was captured in September 1922 and imprisoned until the releases following the republican ceasefire. He thus had a substantial experience of imprisonment and of the republican usages and mores attaching to it.

7 See Seán McConville, *Irish Political Prisoners, 1848–1922: Theatres of War* (London and New York: Routledge, 2003), pp. 735–54 for an account of MacSwiney's hunger strike and its aftermath.

8 PRO HO/144/10308.

9 William Shakespeare, *As You Like It*, Act II, Scene 1, lines 12–14.

10 MA PM/I/ADM/21, Tomás MacCurtáin to Camp Commandant (addressed as 'Governor'), 1 January 1958. MacCurtáin's approach had elements of Colonel Nicholson's in David Lean's film *Bridge on the River Kwai*, which appeared in cinemas in 1957. (The Curragh Camp commandants, one must hastily add, were improbable simulacra of Nicholson's brutal opponent, Camp Commandant Colonel Saito.)

11 Gus Cronin, a military policeman then posted to the Curragh, remembered MacCurtáin intervening when one of the internees became fractious: "'Get away from them. They're only doing their duty… That won't help us in here… to have a thing like that happen'" (interview).

12 Interview.

13 The Russian satellite was launched into orbit on 4 October 1957. The achievement was a surprise, galvanised the Western powers, especially the USA and fascinated ordinary men and women across the globe.

14 Mac Giolla interview.

15 The purpose of the Legion of Mary is primarily spiritual. It aims to enable its members to live within the Roman Catholic Church in an organised manner, with a structure of spiritual discipline and support. Members take a pledge of allegiance to the Holy Spirit and to Mary, attend weekly meetings and recite daily the prescribed prayers. The organisation of the Legion is loosely modelled on that of the Roman Army.

16 Mac Giolla interview. The Legion at the Curragh was run by Eamon Thomas (MA PM/I/ADM/12, Internee S. Ryan to T. R. Atkins, 15 September 1958).

17 See McConville, *Irish Political Prisoners, op. cit.*, pp. 480–92 and 722–6, for example.

18 See above, pp. 533–4.

19 Apart from Jack McQuillan and one or two other hard-line republicans, a few politicians did take up prisoners' issues from time to time but usually for constituency reasons. Relatives or friends made an approach, and some TDs were willing to ventilate their grievances within a general nationalist and moderate republican format.

20 See above, p. 1041.

21 MA PM/I/ADM/12, Letter, 9 September 1957.

22 MA PM/I/ADM/12, Intelligence report on visits, November 1957. See also *Dáil Debates*, vol. 164, cols. 654–5, 6 November 1957.

23 MA PM/I/ADM/12, Extracts from internee letter, 12 December 1957.

24 On the Green Cross, see above, pp. 534, 728–30.

25 Mick Ryan interview.

26 MA PM/I/ADM/12, Letter of 20 October 1957 (italics in original).

27 MA PM/I/ADM/12, Letter of 9 September 1957.

28 The last included cooking rings and a small cooker to use in the preparation of the internees' suppers. MA PM/I/ADM/12, Letter of 23 September 1957. Water heaters (for beverages) were also provided.

29 MA PM/I/ADM/12, Memorandum, 19 October 1957.

30 James Everett, Minister for Justice, to Thomas F. O'Higgins, Minister for Health, January 1956. O'Higgins had asked about policy in the matter, having been approached by Austin O'Reilly, editor of the *Leinster Express*, an important provincial newspaper.

31 See, for example, complaints by the *United Irishman* that the Department of Justice had suppressed news items and advertisements (January 1957, 7a–c). The Department denied the accusation.

32 See below, p. 1087.

33 This was the Irish National Aid Association (see McConville, *Irish Political Prisoners*, *op. cit.*, p. 484); see also Caoimhe Nic Dháibhéid, 'The Irish National Aid Association and the Radicalisation of Public Opinion in Ireland, 1916–18', *Historical Journal*, 55 (September 2012): 705–29.

34 See below, p. 1075.

35 These details are taken from an account of the escape prepared at the time. MA PM/I/ADM/22, Camp Disciplinary Actions, 14–16 August 1957.

36 The government and the press made little of the incident. The *Irish Independent* carried the Government Information Bureau denial that there had been an 'attempted mass escape' from the Curragh and that the internees had gone on hunger strike because of a consequent loss of privileges (19 August 1957, 10c). The *Irish News* led on a Sinn Féin Publishing Committee statement that the Curragh huts were in ill-repair and were leaking, but it also carried Dublin's denial of a mass escape attempt (19 August 1957, 1a). The *Irish Times* followed suit (19 August 1957, 1c–e). Two days before, the *Longford Leader* (17 August 1957, 3c–d) had carried a long and convoluted statement from Sinn Féin which had every appearance of a MacCurtáin pronouncement. The flavour may be taken from the following sample: 'The Republican movement and the members of that movement at present in the Curragh Concentration Camp, ever conscious of the determination of the movement to avoid any incidents which might give an appearance of truth (in the public mind) to the Civil War catchcries of the politicians, wish it to be clearly understood that they will not permit themselves to be inveigled into any occurrence which might involve a clash between them and their fellow-Irishmen who have been given the unpalatable task of acting as their jailors.'

37 *Limerick Leader*, 28 May 1958, 1e; *Anglo-Celt*, 31 May 1958, 1d–e; *Leinster Leader*, 31 May 1958, 1a–b. Kelly was recaptured a week later (*Irish Press*, 7 June 1958, 12b).

38 Permission had been given during the summer months for a sports day to be held. Grass, cut to clear a running track, was left to lie in piles. As time passed, these turned into drifts of hay. Dave O'Connell suggested that some of this should be thrown over the inner fence, apparently just clearing it out of the way. The hay accumulated between the inner fence and the next one. O'Connell's idea was that somehow the escapers would get through the inner fence and conceal themselves under the hay until dark. The escape was classic in its simplicity. Groundsheets were joined with press buttons and straw, grass and other camouflage materials glued onto them. The two men practised compressing and rolling themselves by crawling under the curtains of the camp concert hall. A football match was arranged, to provide cover near the fences. The wire was cut in preparation and rejoined with an additional length, to conceal the break. A coloured hat was dropped near the spot, to distract the sentry. Ruairí Ó Brádaigh and O'Connell squeezed under the wire, wrapped themselves in their camouflage cover and waited for two hours until darkness. Another man (Noel Kavanagh) made sure they were properly covered. He then

backed into the compound and rejoined the fence. Dummies were placed in the men's beds to make up the count. Under cover of darkness the two men made their way through the remaining barriers and kept their rendezvous with a waiting car (Noel Kavanagh interview and unpublished article). As can be seen, a number of internees took part in supporting the escape.

39 Ó Brádaigh remembered the escape: 'Oh, it was very sweet to leave the likes of that place behind you.' The day after they had got away, O'Connell suggested to an innocent civilian in their company that they listen to the 1 p.m. news '"till we find out is there any sign of those two fellows being caught"' (Ó Brádaigh interview).

40 Charlie Murphy was arrested in Clontarf, Dublin, on 31 May 1958, in company with Frank McDonnell, as he kept a rendezvous with Lieutenant Patrick Joseph Dolan, a renegade Irish Army officer (*Sunday Independent*, 1 June 1958, 1c; *Irish Independent*, 5 June 1958, 3e). Neither report named Lieutenant Dolan, probably for legal reasons – but perhaps also on government advice.

41 Murphy recalled that he was exhausted physically and mentally by the time he reached the Curragh. A dissident group had already formed, around J. B. O'Hagan. O'Hagan was an Armagh man who had earned much respect for his leadership of the group that had extensively damaged the Dungannon Territorial Army barracks on 18 January 1957. Although he was not particularly inclined to do so, Murphy was propelled into the dissident (perhaps more accurately *activist*) group. These men considered the camp leadership as 'too inactive and prepared to sit it out', and they wanted to escape and take their place in the struggle. (Murphy interview.)

42 This was a reference to the conflict that had erupted when Arkansas Governor, Orval Faubus, attempted to resist the integration of public education in Little Rock.

43 Tim Pat Coogan, drawing on his extensive interview material, provides a detailed account of the escape: *The IRA* (London: Fontana, 1980), pp. 408–10. Charlie Murphy recalled that he 'wasn't fussed' about getting away. Two men had been wounded and caught on the wire, and he was trying to release them (interview). Tom Landers, one of the camp guard, emphasised that the military police, having been drafted in from various commands, were unknown to each other: 'We knew they were Military Police but what their capabilities were, we didn't know. We knew our own crowd alright, but not the outsiders.' He also referred to the watchtowers: 'We didn't know who was up on the elevated posts.' (Landers interview.) This lack of staff cohesiveness was a weakness in camp security and doubtless contributed to indecisiveness on the day of the mass escape.

44 There was extensive press coverage, all giving it front-page headlines. Dublin's *Evening Herald* was the first off the mark (2 December 1958, 1g–h) under the banner 'Curragh Mass Escape'. It managed to spice things up by juxtaposing the Curragh report with one about an unknown submarine sighted off the Wexford Coast, heading northwards. The sensational tone persisted the following day: 'Biggest Manhunt of Recent Years' (*Evening Herald*, 3 December 1958, 1a–f; see also the *Anglo-Celt*, 6 December 1958, 1d–e).

45 *Leinster Leader*, 6 December 1958, 1f–h. The first announcement, on 3 December, stated that only two men had been injured. On 5 December, however, that number was increased to five (*Evening Herald*, 6 December 1958, 1g–h). The five injured men were Brian Boylan, James Columb, Liam Fagan, Patrick McGirl and Patrick O'Sullivan (*Dáil Debates*, vol. 171, col. 1763, 10 December 1958). The *Longford Leader* (27 December 1958, 3d–e) carried a statement by the Irish Republican Publicity Bureau. This denied that there had been any assaults on camp staff and claimed that detonator grenades as well as tear-gas grenades were used: 'It is certain that at least one man had a chunk of metal deeply embedded in his body.'

46 *Dáil Debates*, vol. 171, cols. 1764–5, 10 December 1958.

47 McQuillan also probed the matter of an Electricity Supply Board truck which, in the aftermath of the escape, had accelerated through an army cordon and had been fired upon. His attempt to portray the army action as disproportionate and as a threat to public safety was fanciful in itself and was easily swatted away by Minister for Defence Kevin Boland (*Dáil Debates*, vol. 171, cols. 1907–12, 10 December 1958). See *Irish Press*, 11 December 1958, 3a–c; *Irish Independent*, 11 December 1958, 12a–b.

48 *Evening Herald*, 22 December 1958, 5a–b.

49 *Irish Times*, 3 January 1959, 1c. 'Yesterday, from one unofficial source it was learned that some of the men [who escaped] actually have been expelled and others suitably reprimanded because, it is said, they acted against "orders" in attempting to escape… The story goes that the older leaders had decided on a policy that precluded escapes, at least for the time being, but that the younger men ignored the decision.'

50 *Irish Times*, 5 January 1959, 1f. The statement went on to denounce the *Irish Times* report of 3 January as 'a whole tissue of falsehood and misrepresentation'. But the *Irish Times* had been, as Hollywood might have had it, right on the button.

51 This was based on common-law doctrine that, whilst lethal levels of force could be used to prevent the escape of a felon, it was unlawful to act thus against other prisoners (misdemeanants, remands, civil prisoners and, by extension, internees; see above, p. 853). Staff could have been authorised to use lethal force and indemnified against any consequences, but such legislation had not been put on the books and would probably and quite properly have had a controversial passage in the Dáil.

52 Peter Brennan interview. A Court of Enquiry was conducted on the escape, and a number of critical comments were made. Although the escapers had gambled that the guards would not open fire, they almost certainly did not know the terms of engagement; neither, indeed, did some of the guard. Whilst the sentry in the raised post nearest the point of escape did not fire, other guards opened fire with revolvers. Tim Pat Coogan's interviewees confirmed that a confused melee developed. At one point, it was claimed, an officer disarmed one of the guard who had already inflicted leg wounds and was preparing to fire again (*The IRA, op. cit.*, footnote, pp. 409–10).

53 The Detention Regulations were unsatisfactorily vague, casting back on the Commandant the decision as to the type and degree of force to be used. He was, by Regulation 44(2), directed to take 'every precaution' to prevent escape and was authorised to 'use such force as may be necessary'. It is doubtful if this regulation would in itself have provided a defence against a criminal charge of using unlawful force or against a civil suit. Those matters would almost certainly have gone to trial to consider necessity and proportionality. See SI, No. 206/1936, Article 1a of the Constitution, Consolidated Regulations.

54 For the earlier Curragh tunnels, see above, pp. 706–7. *The Wooden Horse*, a British POW epic featuring an ingenious tunnelling scheme, was released in January 1950. The script was based on Eric Williams's book of the same title (London: Collins, 1949) and showed the importance of cooperation, teamwork and discipline.

55 Kavanagh article. In consequence of the discovery, Hut 3 was closed up. The sewing machine that had been provided for use in the internees' leather work was removed since it had been misapplied to make the soil-disposal bag.

56 The Irish Republican Press Bureau issued a four-page booklet, *The Curragh Escape*. See also *Dáil Debates*, vol. 171, cols. 1763–4, 10 December 1958. The *Leinster Leader* (6 December 1958, 1f–h) pointed out that this had been the third escape of internees that year, but the *Ulster Herald* (13 December 1958, 5e–f) thought that the escapes had been 'inevitable': 'it has happened since the days when the British first began to put men behind barbed wire on this same site'.

57 MA PM/I/ADM/1, Commandant, Internment Camp to Curragh Command, 11 December 1958. Since the removal of the stand-to party, the fences were protected

only by the sentries in each tower. Given that they could only fire warning, not disabling or lethal shots, they could not prevent another rush on the fence. Mac Eilgeóid copied this and other angry correspondence to the Adjutant General. It is instructive that the quest for preventive intelligence was not re-energised at this point.

58 MA PM/I/ADM/1, Commandant Internment Camp to Curragh Command, 12 December 1958.

59 It is hard to understand why Army Intelligence did not offer an appreciation and some suggestions at this point, other than that no one in the Army wanted to touch the tar-baby. The lack of information, however caused, shows that security at the camp was concentrated on physical barriers and whatever deterrence the guard could offer. It seems unlikely that informers had been recruited or were forthcoming and even less likely that an agent had been infiltrated.

60 MA PM/I/ADM/21, Complaint of MacCurtáin of 8 December 1958. The file itself has been removed, and only a summary remains, but large quotations from MacCurtáin's letter to the Commandant appeared in the IRA leaflet, *The Curragh Escape*. A copy of this is at MA PM/I/ADM/19, Statements on Internment Camp.

61 See *Irish Times*, 4 December 1958, 1a–c.

62 The Camp Command did not agree with MacCurtáin's version of what had happened. The wounded men (Brian Boylan and James Columb, both from Cavan) had not been wounded by revolver shots but by fragments of the gas grenades striking their legs. A total of five men had been injured, but none seriously: the longest stay in hospital had been nine days. This was a critical point for the Army, given its clear restrictions under the terms of engagement. At this distance, it is impossible to be sure which version of events is correct: both sides had a direct interest in representing events in their favour.

63 'The Curragh Escape', *op. cit.*, p. 3.

64 *Irish Times*, 5 January 1959, 1f.

65 'The Curragh Escape', *op. cit.*, p. 3.

66 The escape was condemned as 'unofficial'. Murphy remembers that the camp leadership argued that by escaping the men had dismissed themselves from the IRA: 'That was the leadership's view, that the men and people like me who had planned this, by so doing we had automatically dismissed ourselves. It was of no consequence, but it gave you an idea of the mindset.' (Murphy interview.) Relations between the factions deteriorated further with the leadership enforcing its harsh view of the dissidents. It all took on the characteristics of the shunning practices of a rigid chiliastic religious sect or the protracted silences of an utterly dysfunctional family. Conciliation was the more difficult because of the age gap between the two groups. MacCurtáin and others in the leadership were in their fifties and the bulk of the dissidents were in their twenties. Besides their rigid insistence on procedure, the camp leaders may also have been hurt and angered because insufficient respect was being paid to their age, years of service and sacrifice and seniority. The dissidents reacted equally strongly, incensed that the leadership was improperly pulling rank. Despite Murphy's anxiety not to remember it as such, it did become very personal: 'in the dining hall they wouldn't speak to you. It was very hurtful. I don't want to over-personalise it' (interview).

67 As I write this, some of the last obituaries are appearing of the RAF officers, who, when POWs, took part in the Great Escape, the break of seventy-six men from Stalag Luft III at Sagan, Germany, on 24/5 March 1944. The mass breakout, after which fifty escapees were murdered on Hitler's orders, became and has remained emblematic of ingenuity, indomitability and bravery.

68 See above, pp. 586–97.

69 See above, p. 1024.

70 See the *Kerryman* (14 March 1959, 19d). Providing a short history of internment, the newspaper suggested that the expected decision in the Lawless case at Strasbourg

may have been a factor in the closure of the camp, as well perhaps as the pending presidential election. Much of the regional and local press comment chose to focus on Harold Macmillan's criticism of the Irish government's decision (see *Anglo-Celt*, 14 March 1959, 1d–e; *Donegal News*, 14 March 1959, 3a–d; *Leitrim Observer*, 21 March 1959, 3d). Commandant Mac Eilgeóid no doubt put the poisoned chalice back in the cupboard and may have raised a celebratory vessel instead.

71 See J. Bowyer Bell, *The Secret Army: The IRA, 1916–1979* (Cambridge, Mass.: MIT Press, 1983), pp. 245–52.

72 Bell, *The Secret Army, op. cit.*, p. 323. Charlie Murphy (one of the few IRA leaders to have evaded arrest in January 1957) describes the communications sent out of the Curragh as 'directions… beautifully typed up instructions'. After six months in custody, Murphy contended, 'you become divorced from reality'. The flow of directives 'created a level of tension' (interview).

73 Murphy interview.

74 Ó Brádaigh interview. He decided to turn down the nomination but was accepted for a place in the successful escape of 27 September 1958 (see above, p. 1078). As it happened, one of the leaders of the dissident groups, J. B. O'Hagan, stood against MacCurtáin in the election for OC, and MacCurtáin barely won. In the election of 29 March 1958, MacCurtáin had been returned without opposition, and the implied rebuff of a contested and closely run election now increased ill-feeling between the two factions (Murphy interview). Within IRA tradition, there appears to have been two procedures for choosing the OC: appointment and election. Under the first, the Army Council would make the choice, and the appointed OC would then select his own staff within the prison. (Ryan interview.) The second procedure, followed in the Curragh at this time, was for the internees to elect their OC. It is not now clear when, why and where which of the two procedures was adopted. Election was the method most mentioned by interviewees.

75 MA PM/I/ADM/12, Gerry Lawless to friend, 2 September 1957. The reference to prisoners' aid funds is significant. Totally controlled by the IRA they were available only to members in good standing and their dependants. See above, p. 1087.

76 MA PM/I/ADM/12, Liam Walsh to friend, 9 September 1957. 'Thrown out of the camp' meant the camp as defined by the IRA. Walsh's correspondent responded to this news with some anger. Paul, she wrote, 'is only a kid. Its [*sic*] terrible the way MacCurtáin treats him however he won't always get away with it' (MA PM/I/ADM/12, 12 September 1957). It all increased general anger, and Walsh was overheard by staff to remark 'if I had my hands on that fellow from Limerick [de Valera] I would teach him a thing or two' (MA PM/I/ADM/12, annotation).

77 MA PM/I/ADM/12, 16 September 1957. Traynor, adhering to the instruction not to discuss the details of camp life, was not explicit about the split.

78 MA PM/I/ADM/12, Summary of conversation between MacCurtáin and Assistant Commandant, 16 September 1957. The note concluded, 'McCurtain [*sic*] is inclined to be talkative.'

79 MA PM/I/ADM/12, Summary of conversation between Liam Walsh and Assistant Commandant, 15 September 1957.

80 John Bunyan, *The Pilgrim's Progress* (London: 1678–83).

81 Uinseann MacEoin's *The IRA in the Twilight Years, 1923–1948* (Dublin: Argenta, 1997) is probably the best and most comprehensive collection of first-person reflections and narratives of twentieth-century romantic Irish republicanism. Despite its loving detail, mentions of Fenianism are remarkably few. On Fenianism, see McConville, *Irish Political Prisoners, op. cit.*, Chapters 3 and 4.

82 See Erving Goffman, *Asylums* (Harmondsworth: Penguin, 1968).

BIBLIOGRAPHY

Order of bibliography

Archives
Unpublished, privately held material
Cases, statutes, parliamentary papers and official publications
    United Kingdom
        Cases
        Statutes
        Statutory Instruments and Orders
    Ireland
        Statutes
        Statutory Instruments and Orders
Parliamentary Papers, Official Papers and Reports
    United Kingdom
    Ireland
Other reports
Books, essays and journal articles
Journals, newspapers and works of reference
Libraries
Interviews

Archives

In addition to material listed in the general catalogues of the repositories below, special collections were consulted, as follows:

Frank Aiken Papers: University College Dublin Archives
Sir John Anderson Papers: Public Record Office (National Archives)
Todd Andrews Papers: University College Dublin Archives
Robert C. Barton Collection: Irish Defence Forces Military Archives
Ernest Blythe Papers: University College Dublin Archives
Bureau of Military History, 1913–21: Irish Defence Forces Military Archives

Margaret Burke Papers: University College Dublin Archives

Cabinet Conclusions: Public Record Office of Northern Ireland

Cabinet Papers (CAB): Public Record Office (National Archives)

Cabinet Secretariat: Public Record Office of Northern Ireland

Joseph Campbell Papers: Trinity College Dublin Archives

Robert Erskine Childers Papers: Trinity College Dublin Archives

Papers of Sir Winston Churchill: Churchill Archives Centre, Churchill College Cambridge

Civil War Captured Documents: Irish Defence Forces Military Archives

Máire Comerford Papers: University College Dublin Archives

Contemporaneous Documents Collection: Irish Defence Forces Military Archives

Eithne Coyle Papers: University College Dublin Archives

Craigavon Papers: Public Record Office of Northern Ireland

Madame Czira Collection: Irish Defence Forces Military Archives

Joe Dennigan Papers: University College Dublin Archives

Records of the Ministry of Defence Cabinet Committees (DEFE): Public Record Office (National Archives)

Department of Defence '2/' files, 1925–47: Irish Defence Forces Military Archives

Department of Defence 'A/' files from 1922: Irish Defence Forces Military Archives

Department of Defence 'MS' Files: Irish Defence Forces Military Archives

Sinead de Valera Papers: Trinity College Dublin Archives

Éamon de Valera Papers: University College Dublin Archives

Records created or inherited by the Dominions Office (DO): Public Record Office (National Archives)

Simon Donnelly Collection: Irish Defence Forces Military Archives

Christina Doyle Papers: National Library of Ireland

Gavin Duffy Papers: University College Dublin Archives

Executive Council Minutes: National Archives of Ireland

Department of External Affairs: National Archives of Ireland

Department of Finance: National Archives of Ireland

Desmond FitzGerald Papers: University College Dublin Archives

Department of Foreign Affairs: National Archives of Ireland

Records of the Foreign and Commonwealth Office and Predecessors (FCO): Public Record Office (National Archives)

Frank Gallagher Papers: National Library of Ireland

Frank Gallagher Papers: Trinity College Dublin Archives

General Prisons Boards Reports: National Archives of Ireland

C. D. Greaves Collection: Working Class Movement Library, Manchester

George Harrison Papers: Archives of Irish America, New York University

Cahir Healy Papers: Public Record Office of Northern Ireland

Ministry of Home Affairs: Public Record Office of Northern Ireland

Home Office (HO): Public Record Office (National Archives)

Sighle Humphreys Papers: University College Dublin Archives

Irish Collection Pamphlets: Working Class Movement Library, Manchester

Department of Justice: National Archives of Ireland

Hugh Kennedy Papers: University College Dublin Archives

Local Authority Files: Public Record Office of Northern Ireland

Dorothy Macardle Collection: Irish Defence Forces Military Archives

Dorothy Macardle Papers: Trinity College Dublin Archives

Seán MacEoin Papers: University College Dublin Archives

Joseph McGarrity Papers: National Library of Ireland

Mary MacSwiney Papers: University College Dublin Archives

Kathleen Barry Moloney Papers: University College Dublin Archives

Maurice Moore Papers: National Library of Ireland

Richard Mulcahy Papers: University College Dublin Archives

Jane Conlon Muller Oral History Collection: Archives of Irish America, New York University

Annie Mary Constance Murphy Papers: University College Dublin Archives

Fintan Murphy Collection: Irish Defence Forces Military Archives

Records created or inherited by the NIO (CJ): Public Record Office (National Archives)

North Dublin Poor Law Union and Rural District Council Papers: National Archives of Ireland

Lily O'Brennan Papers: University College Dublin Archives

Art O'Brien Papers: National Library of Ireland

James L. O'Donovan Papers: National Library of Ireland

Sean O'Mahony Papers: National Library of Ireland

Ernie O'Malley Papers: Trinity College Dublin Archives

Elgin O'Rahilly Papers: University College Dublin Archives

Bernard O'Rourke Papers: University College Dublin Archives

Sean Prenderville Collection: Archives of Irish America, New York University

Dorothy Price Papers: National Library of Ireland

Prime Ministers' Office Collection (PREM): Public Record Office (National Archives)

Records created or inherited by the Prison Commission and Home Office Prison Department (P.Com.): Public Record Office (National Archives)

Prison Locations Book: Civil War: Irish Defence Forces Military Archives

Provost Marshall files: Irish Defence Forces Military Archives

Provisional Government Minutes: National Archives of Ireland

Desmond Ryan Papers: University College Dublin Archives

James Ryan Papers: University College Dublin Archives

Sheehy-Skeffington Papers: National Library of Ireland

Austin Stack Papers: National Library of Ireland

Alice Stopford Green Papers: National Library of Ireland

Department of the Taoiseach: National Archives of Ireland

Moss Twomey Papers: University College Dublin Archives

War Office (WO): Public Record Office (National Archives)

Unpublished, privately held material

Eamonn Boyce memoir

Charlie Casey prison letters

Joe Collins (alias Conor McNessa), prison memoir

Noel Kavanagh's material on the Curragh Internment Camp

Art McMillan (letters and memoir)

Seamus Murphy (Collins memoir)

Cases, statutes, parliamentary papers and official publications

United Kingdom

Cases

Bernardo v. *Ford*, HL 1892 AC 326

Francis Card v. *Inspector General and Thompson*

Leigh v. *Gladstone and Others* (1909), 26 *Times Law Reports*, 139

R. v. *Secretary of State, Ex Parte O'Brien* (1923), 39 *Times Law Reports*, 487

Morris v. *Winter* (1930), 1 KB 243

R. v. *Vickers* (1957), 2 QB 664 (CCA)

Statutes

Treason Act, 1351: 25 Edw. III, c.2

Habeas Corpus Act, 1679: 31 Cha. II, c.2

Act of Settlement, 1701: 12 & 13 Will. III, c.2

Habeas Corpus Act, 1816: 56 Geo. III, c.100

Suppression of Insurrections (Ireland) Act, 1822: 3 & 4 Geo. IV, c.1

Habeas Corpus Suspension (Ireland) Act, 1822: 3 & 4 Geo. IV, c.2

Prisons (Ireland) Act, 1826: 7 Geo. IV, c.74

Poor Law Amendment Act, 1834: 4 & 5 Will. IV, c.76

Constabulary (Ireland) Act, 1836: 6 & 7 Will. IV, c.13

Central Criminal Lunatic Asylum (Ireland) Act, 1845: 8 & 9 Vict., c.107

Treason Felony Act, 1848: 11 & 12 Vict., c.12

Penal Servitude Act, 1853: 16 & 17 Vict., c.99

Convict Prisons (Ireland) Act, 1854: 17 & 18 Vict., c.76

Prisons (Ireland) Act, 1856: 19 & 20 Vict., c.68

Penal Servitude Act, 1857: 20 & 21 Vict., c.3

Malicious Damage Act, 1861: 24 & 25 Vict., c.97

Habeas Corpus Act, 1862: 25 & 26 Vict., c.20

Security from Violence Act, 1863: 26 & 27 Vict., c.44 (Garotters Act)

Prison Act, 1865: 28 & 29 Vict., c.126

Capital Punishment Amendment Act, 1868, 31 & 32 Vict., c.24

Forfeiture of Property Act, 1870: 33 & 34 Vict., c.23

General Prisons (Ireland) Act, 1877: 40 & 41 Vict., c.49

Prison Act, 1877: 40 & 41 Vict., c.21

Prison (Officers Superannuation) Act, 1878: 41 & 42 Vict., c.63

Explosive Substances Act, 1883: 46 & 47 Vict., c.3

Prisons Act, 1898: 61 & 62 Vict., c.41

Inebriates Act, 1898: 61 & 62 Vict., c.60

Post Office Act, 1908: 8 Edw. VII, c.48

Prevention of Crime Act, 1908: 8 Edw. VII, c.59

Children Act, 1908: 8 Edw. VII, c.67

Prisoners (Temporary Discharge for Ill-Health) Act, 1913: 3 & 4 Geo. V, c.4 (Cat and Mouse Act)

Defence of the Realm Act, 1914: 4 & 5 Geo. V, c.29
Criminal Justice Administration Act, 1914: 4 & 5 Geo. V, c.58
Army Act, 1916: 6 & 7 Geo. V, c.5
Larceny Act, 1916: 6 & 7 Geo. V, c.50
Constabulary and Police (Ireland) Act, 1916: 6 & 7 Geo. V, c.59
Representation of the People Act, 1918: 7 & 8 Geo. V, c.64
Restoration of Order in Ireland Act, 1920: 10 & 11 Geo. V, c.31
Firearms Act, 1920: 10 & 11 Geo. V, c.43
Government of Ireland Act, 1920: 10 & 11 Geo. V, c.67
Irish Free State Constitution Act, 1922: 13 Geo. V, c.1
Irish Free State (Consequential Provisions) Act, 1922: 13 Geo. V, c.2
Irish Free State (Agreement) Act, 1922: 12 & 13 Geo. V, c.4
Civil Authorities (Special Powers) Act (Northern Ireland), 1922: 12 & 13 Geo. V, c.5
Constabulary (Ireland) Act, 1922: 12 & 13 Geo. V, c.56
Restoration of Order in Ireland (Indemnity) Act, 1923: 13 & 14 Geo. V, c.12
Local Government (Northern Ireland) Act, 1923: 13 & 14 Geo. V, c. 31
Irish Free State (Confirmation of Agreement) Act, 1924: 15 & 16 Geo. V, c.77
Statute of Westminster, 1931: 22 & 23 Geo. V, c. 4 (Act to Give Effect to Certain Resolutions Passed by Imperial Conferences Held in the Years 1926 and 1930).
Civil Authorities (Special Powers) Act (Northern Ireland), 1933: 23 & 24 Geo. V, c.12
Summary Jurisdiction & Criminal Justice (Northern Ireland) Act, 1935: 25 & 26 Geo. V, c.13
Public Order Act, 1936: 1 Edw. VIII & 1 Geo. VI, c.6
Prevention of Violence (Temporary Provisions) Act, 1939: 2 & 3 Geo. VI, c.50
Education Act, 1944: 7 & 8 Geo. VI, c.31 (Butler Act)
Constabulary (Ireland) Act, 1946: 9 & 10 Vict., c.97
Criminal Justice Act, 1948: 11 & 12 Geo. VI, c.58
Ireland Act, 1949: 12 & 13 Geo. VI, c.41
Prison Act (Northern Ireland), 1953: 1 Eliz. II, c.18
Homicide Act, 1957: 5 & 6 Eliz. II, c.11
Murder (Abolition of Death Penalty) Act, 1965: 13 & 14 Eliz. II, c. 71

Statutory Instruments and Orders

Prison (Amendment) Rules (Northern Ireland) 1955 (Statutory Rules and Orders of Northern Ireland, 1954)
Prison Rules (Northern Ireland) 1955 (Statutory Rules and Orders of Northern Ireland, 1957)

Ireland

Statutes

Dáil Éireann Courts (Winding-up) Act, 1923
Indemnity (British Military) Act, 1923
Local Government (Temporary Provisions) Act, 1923
Courts of Justice Act, 1924
Public Safety (Powers of Arrest and Detention) Temporary Act, 1924

Firearms Act, 1925
Prisons (Visiting Committees) Act, 1925
Treasonable Offences Act, 1925
Public Safety (Emergency Powers) Act, 1926
Electoral (Amendment No. 2) Act, 1927
Public Safety Act, 1927
Constitution (Amendment No. 10) Act, 1928
Juries (Protection) Act, 1929
Constitution (Amendment No. 17) Act, 1931
Army Pensions Act, 1932
Constitution (Removal of Oath) Act, 1933
Garda Síochána Pensions Act, 1933
Electoral (Revision of Constituencies) Act, 1935
Connaught Rangers (Pensions) Act, 1936
Constitution (Amendment No. 24) Act, 1936
Superannuation Act, 1936
Emergency Powers Act, 1939
First Amendment of the Constitution Act, 1939
Offences Against the State Act, 1939
Emergency Powers (Amendment No. 2) Act, 1940
Offences Against the State (Amendment) Act, 1940
Offences Against the State (Forfeiture) Act, 1940
Republic of Ireland Act, 1948
Criminal Justice Act, 1964
Criminal Justice Act, 1990

Statutory Instruments and Orders

SI 2 October, 1922: Military Courts: General Regulations as to Trials of Civilians
SI 72/1931 Constitution (Operation of Article 2A) Order, 1931
SI 172/1936 Constitution (Declaration of Unlawful Association) Order, 1936
SI 206/1936 Article 2A of the Constitution, Consolidated Regulations, 1936
SI 249/1939 Detention Regulations, 1939
SI 288/1939 Detention Military Custody Regulations, 1939
Emergency Powers (No. 20) Order, 1940
SI 146/1957 Detention Regulations, 1957

Parliamentary papers, official papers and reports

United Kingdom

Report on the Organisation of the Permanent Civil Service, PP, 1854 (1713), XXXVII, 1.
First Report of the General Prisons Board, Ireland, PP, 1878–9 [C.2447], XXXIV, 353.
Report of the General Prisons Board, Ireland, PP, 1899, c. 9439, XLIII, 585.
Thirty-Seventh Report of the General Prisons Board, Ireland (Dublin: HMSO, 1917).
Arrangements Governing the Cessation of Active Operations in Ireland (London: HMSO, 1921) Cmd.
    1534.

Articles of Agreement for a Treaty between Great Britain and Ireland (London: HMSO, 1921), Cmd. 1560.

Annual Report of the Prisons Board for Ireland, 1919–20.

Forty-Second Report of the General Prisons Board, Ireland, 1919–1920, PP, 1921, XVI [Cmd. 1375], 469.

Report of the Commissioners of Prisons and the Directors of Convict Prisons, PP, 1922 (Sess. 2), II, Cmd. 1761, 1017, 53.

Report of the Commissioners of Prisons and the Directors of Convict Prisons, PP, 1923, Cmd. 2000, XII, Pt. 2, 379.

Imperial Conference, 1926: Summary of Proceedings, PP, 1926, XI [Cmd. 2768], 545, 14.

Report of the Inter-Departmental Committee on Social Insurance and Allied Services (London: Stationery Office, 1942), Cmd. 6404.

Report of the Inquiry into Prison Escapes and Security (Mountbatten Report) (London: HMSO, 1966), Cmd. 3175.

The Regime for Long-Term Prisoners in Conditions of Maximum Security (Radzinowicz Report) (London: HMSO, 1968).

Disturbances in Northern Ireland: Report of the Commission Appointed by the Governor of Northern Ireland (Cameron Report) (Belfast: HMSO, 1969), Cmd. 532.

Special Security Units (Home Office Research Study No. 109) (London: HMSO, 1989).

Report of the Enquiry into the Escape of Six Prisoners from the Special Security Unit at Whitemoor Prison Cambridgeshire, on Friday 9th September 1994 (Woodcock Report) (London: HMSO, 1994), Cmd. 2741.

Review of Prison Service Security in England and Wales and the Escape from Parkhurst Prison on Tuesday 3rd January 1995 (Learmont Report) (London: HMSO, 1995), Cmd. 3020.

Report of the Bloody Sunday Inquiry (Saville Report) (London: HMSO, 2010).

Ireland

Forty-Third Report of the General Prisons Board, Ireland (Dublin: Stationery Office, 1922).

Forty-Fifth Report of the General Prisons Board, Ireland (Dublin: Stationery Office, 1924).

Annual Report of the General Prisons Board, 1923–1924 (Dublin: Stationery Office, 1925).

Report of the Council of Education as Presented to the Minister for Education (1) The Function of the Primary School; (2) The Curriculum to Be Pursued in the Primary School from the Infant Age up to 12 Years of Age (Dublin: Stationery Office, 1954).

Other reports

Report of a Commission of Inquiry Appointed to Examine the Purpose and Effect of the Civil Authorities (Special Powers) Act (Northern Ireland) 1922 & 1933 (London: National Council for Civil Liberties, 1936).

Books, essays and journal articles

Ackroyd, Peter, *Tudors* (London: Macmillan, 2012).

Adair, Lynne and Murphy, Colin (eds.), *Untold Stories: Protestants in the Republic of Ireland* (Dublin: Liffey Press, 2002).

Ahamed, Liaquat, *Lords of Finance: 1929, The Great Depression, and the Bankers who Broke the World* (London: Windmill Books, 2010).

Alighieri, Dante, *The Divine Comedy*, trans. Henry Wadsworth Longfellow (London: George Routledge & Sons, 1886).

Alleg, Henri, *The Question* (London: John Calder, 1958).

Anderson, Brendan, *Joe Cahill: A Life in the IRA* (Dublin: The O'Brien Press, 2002).

Andrew, Christopher, *The Defence of the Realm: The Authorized History of MI5* (London: Allen Lane, 2009).

Anon., *The Future Is Orange and Bright* (Glasgow: Grand Lodge of Scotland, c.2003).

Atholl, Duchess of, *Searchlight on Spain* (Harmondsworth: Penguin, 1938).

Babbington, Anthony, *The Devil to Pay: The Mutiny of the Connaught Rangers, India, July 1920* (London: Cooper, 1991).

Bailey, Victor, *Delinquency and Citizenship: Reclaiming the Young Offender, 1914–1948* (Oxford: Clarendon, 1987).

Banks, J. A., *Victorian Values: Secularism and the Size of Families* (London: Routledge & Kegan Paul, 1981).

Barnett, Hilaire, *Constitutional and Administrative Law*, 8th edn (London and New York: Routledge, 2011).

Barry, Denis, *The Unknown Commandant: The Life and Times of Denis Barry, 1883–1923* (Cork: Collins Press, 2010).

Barry, Tom, *Guerilla Days in Ireland* (Dublin: Anvil Books, 1999).

Bartlett, Thomas, *Ireland: A History* (Cambridge: Cambridge University Press, 2010).

Barton, Brian, *Brookeborough: The Making of a Prime Minister* (Belfast: Institute of Irish Studies, 1988).

Béaslaí, Piaras, *Michael Collins and the Making of a New Ireland* (London: Harrap, 1926).

Beccaria, Cesare, *An Essay on Crimes and Punishment*, 5th revised English translation (London: E. Newbery, 1801).

Beevor, Anthony, *Berlin: The Downfall* (London: Viking, 1945).

Behan, Brendan, *Borstal Boy* (London: Arrow Books, 1990).

Bell, J. Bowyer, *The Secret Army: The IRA, 1916–1979* (Cambridge, Mass.: MIT Press, 1983).

Bell, P. M. H., *The Origins of the Second World War in Europe* (London: Longman, 1997).

Bew, Paul, Peter Gibbon and Henry Patterson, *Northern Ireland, 1921–2001: Political Forces and Social Classes* (London: Serif, 2002).

Black, John Bennett, *The Reign of Elizabeth, 1558–1603* (Oxford: Clarendon Press, 1959).

Block, Brian P., *An Introduction to Judicial Decision-Making* (Chichester: Barry Rose, 1998).

Bourke, Seán, *The Springing of George Blake* (London: Cassells, 1970).

Bowen, Elizabeth, *Notes on Éire* (Aubane: Aubane Historical Society, 2009).

Bowman, Timothy, *Carson's Army: The Ulster Volunteer Force, 1910–22* (Manchester: Manchester University Press, 2007).

Boyce, Eamonn, *The Insider: The Belfast Prison Diaries of Eamonn Boyce, 1956–1962*, ed. Anna Bryson (Dublin: Lilliput Press, 2007).

Boyd, Andrew, *Holy War in Belfast* (Tralee: Anvil Books, 1969).

Bradley, A. W. and K. D. Ewing, *Constitutional and Administrative Law*, 15th edn (London: Longman, 2011).

Breen, Dan, *My Fight for Irish Freedom* (Dublin: Anvil Books, 1989).

Bretherton, C. H., *The Real Ireland* (London: Black, 1925).

Broderick, Marian, *Wild Irish Women* (Dublin: The O'Brien Press, 2002).

Brooke, Rupert, '1914: Peace', in *The Collected Poems of Rupert Brooke: With a Memoir* (London: Sedgwick & Jackson, 1918).

Buckland, Patrick, *The Factory of Grievances: Devolved Government in Northern Ireland, 1921–39* (Dublin: Gill & Macmillan, 1979).

——*James Craig, Lord Craigavon* (Dublin: Gill & Macmillan, 1980).

Byrne, Elaine, *Political Corruption in Ireland, 1922–2010* (Manchester: Manchester University Press, 2012).

Byrne, Sandie, *The Unbearable Saki: The Work of H. H. Munro* (Oxford: Oxford University Press, 2007).

Callanan, Mark and Justin F. Keogan (eds.), *Local Government in Ireland: Inside and Out* (Dublin: Institute of Public Administration, 2003).

Campbell, Colm, *Emergency Law in Ireland* (Oxford: Clarendon, 1994).

Campbell, Fergus, 'The Last Land War? Kevin O'Shiel's Memoir of the Irish Revolution (1916–21)', *Archivium Hibernicum*, 57 (2003): 155–200.

Campbell, Flann, *The Dissenting Voice: Protestant Democracy in Ulster from Plantation to Partition* (Belfast: Blackstaff Press, 1991).

Card, Richard, *Criminal Law* (London: Butterworths, 1995).

Carey, Tim, *Hanged for Ireland: A Documentary History* (Dublin: Blackwater Press, 2001).

——*Mountjoy: The Story of a Prison* (Cork: Collins Press, 2000).

Carroll, James, *One of Ourselves: John Fitzgerald Kennedy in Ireland* (Lancaster: Gazelle, 2003).

Carroll, Joseph T., *Ireland in the War Years, 1939–1945* (Newton Abbot: David & Charles, 1975).

Churchill, Winston S., *The Second World War: The Hinge of Fate* (Harmondsworth: Penguin Books, 1985).

Clark, Wallace, *Guns in Ulster* (Upperlands: Wallace Clark, 2002).

Collins, Michael, *The Path to Freedom* (Dublin: The Talbot Press, 1922).

Coogan, Tim Pat, *The IRA* (London: Fontana, 1980).

——*Michael Collins* (London: Arrow Books, 1991).

——*De Valera: Long Fellow, Long Shadow* (London: Hutchinson, 1993).

Coogan, Tim Pat and George Morrison, *The Irish Civil War* (London: Orion, 1999).

Cotter, Cornelius P., 'Emergency Detention in Wartime: The British Experience', *Stanford Law Review*, 6 (2) (1954): 238–86.

Cronin, Mike, *The Blueshirts and Irish Politics* (Dublin: Four Courts Press, 1997).

Cross, Rupert, *Punishment, Prison and the Public: An Assessment of Penal Reform in Twentieth Century England by an Armchair Penologist* (London: Stevens, 1971).

Cruise O'Brien, Conor, 'The Embers of Easter', in O. Dudley Edwards and Fergus Pyle (eds.), *1916: The Easter Rising* (London: MacGibbon & Kee, 1968).

Cullen-Owens, Rosemary, *Louie Bennett* (Cork: Cork University Press, 2001).

Curran, Joseph M., *The Birth of the Irish Free State* (Tuscaloosa, Ala.: University of Alabama Press, 1980).

Cuthbert, Norman, *An Economic Survey of Northern Ireland* (Belfast: HMSO, 1957).

Daly, Mary E., 'Local Appointments', in Mary E. Daly (ed.), *County and Town: One Hundred Years of Local Government in Ireland* (Dublin: Institute of Public Administration, 2001).

——*The Slow Failure: Population Decline and Independent Ireland, 1920–1973* (Madison, Wisc.: University of Wisconsin Press, 2006).

Darby, John, *Conflict in Northern Ireland: The Development of a Polarised Community* (Dublin: Gill & Macmillan, 1976).

Davies, Joseph E., *Mission to Moscow* (London: Victor Gollancz, 1942).

Davitt, Michael, *The Prison Life of Michael Davitt, Related by Himself; Together with His Evidence to the House of Lords Commission on Convict Life*, 2nd edn (Dublin: J. J. Lawlor, 1882).

——*Leaves for a Prison Diary; or, Lectures to a 'Solitary Audience'*, 2 vols. (London: Chapman & Hall, 1885).

Dawson, Robert MacGregor (ed.), *Constitutional Issues in Canada* (London: Oxford University Press, 1933).

de Vere White, Terence, *Kevin O'Higgins* (Dublin: Anvil Books, 1986).

Doherty, Richard, *The Thin Green Line: The History of the Royal Ulster Constabulary* (Barnsley: Pen & Sword, 2004).

Donnelly, Dónal, *Prisoner 1082: Escape from Crumlin Road, Europe's Alcatraz* (Cork: Collins Press, 2010).

Doyle, David M. and Ian O'Donnell, 'The Death Penalty in Post-Independence Ireland', *Journal of Legal History*, 33 (1) (2012): 65–91.

Duce, Alan, 'A Christian Approach to Punishment', in Seán McConville (ed.), *The Use of Punishment* (Cullompton: Willan, 2003).

Edmunds, Sean, *The Gun, the Law and the Irish People: From 1912 to the Aftermath of the Arms Trial 1970* (Tralee: Anvil Books, 1970).

Elliott, Marianne, *The Catholics of Ulster* (London: Allen Lane, 2000).

Ellison, Graham and Jim Smyth, *The Crowned Harp: Policing Northern Ireland* (London: Pluto Press, 2000).

English, Richard and Walker, Graham (eds.), *Unionism in Modern Ireland: New Perspectives on Politics and Culture* (Basingstoke: Macmillan, 1996).

Ervine, St John Greer, *Craigavon: Ulsterman* (London: Allen & Unwin, 1949).

Evans, Richard J., *Rituals of Retribution: Capital Punishment in Germany, 1600–1987* (London: Penguin, 1997).

Fairfield, Letitia (ed.), *Trial of Peter Barnes and Others* (London: William Hodges & Co., 1953).

Fallon, Charlotte H., *Soul of Fire* (Cork: Mercier, 1986).

Fanning, Ronan, *The Irish Department of Finance, 1922–58* (Dublin: Institute of Public Administration, 1978).

——*Independent Ireland* (Dublin: Helicon, 1983).

Fanning, Ronan, Michael Kennedy, Dermot Keogh and Eunan O'Halpin (eds.), *Documents on Irish Foreign Policy*, vol. I: *1919–1922* (Dublin: Royal Irish Academy, 1998).

Farrell, Michael, *Northern Ireland and the Orange State* (London: Pluto, 1976).

——*The Poor Law and the Workhouse in Belfast, 1838–1948* (Belfast: Public Record Office of Northern Ireland, 1978).

——*Arming the Protestants: The Formation of the Ulster Special Constabulary and the Royal Ulster Constabulary, 1920–7* (London: Pluto, 1983).

Faulkner, Brian, *Memoirs of a Statesman*, ed. John Houston (London: Weidenfeld & Nicolson, 1978).

Finnare, Mark, 'A Decline in Violence in Ireland? Crime, Policing and Social Relations, 1860–1914', *Crime, History and Societies*, 1 (1) (1997): 51–70.

Fisk, Robert, *In Time of War: Ireland, Ulster and the Price of Neutrality, 1939–45* (London: André Deutsch, 1983).

Fitzpatrick, David, 'The Logic of Collective Sacrifice: Ireland and the British Army, 1914–18', *Historical Journal*, 38 (4) (1995): 1017–30.

——'Militarism in Ireland, 1900–22', in Thomas Bartlett and Keith Jeffrey (eds.), *A Military History of Ireland* (Cambridge: Cambridge University Press, 1996).

——*Politics and Irish Life: Provincial Experience of War and Revolution* (Cork: Cork University Press, 1998).

——*The Two Irelands, 1912–1939* (Oxford: Oxford University Press, 1998).

Flynn, Barry, *Soldiers of Folly: the IRA Border Campaign 1956–1962* (Cork, Collins Press, 2009).

Follis, Bryan A., *A State under Siege: The Establishment of Northern Ireland, 1920–25* (Oxford: Clarendon, 1995).

Fox, Richard Michael, *Rebel Irishwomen* (Cork: Talbot Press, 1935).

Fuller, Louise, *Irish Catholicism since 1950: The Undoing of a Culture* (Dublin: Gill & Macmillan, 2002).

Gallagher, Frank, *Days of Fear* (London: John Murray, 1928).

Garvin, Tom, *1922: The Birth of Irish Democracy* (Dublin: Gill & Macmillan, 1996).

——'Democratic Politics in Independent Ireland', in John Coakley and Michael Gallagher (eds.), *Politics in the Republic of Ireland* (London and New York: Routledge, 1999).

——*Preventing the Future: Why Was Ireland So Poor for So Long?* (Dublin, Gill & Macmillan, 2004).

Gibson, Ian, *The English Vice: Beating, Sex and Shame in Victorian England and After* (London: Duckworth, 1992).

Gillies, Midge, *The Barbed Wire University* (London: Aurum, 2012).

Girvin, Brian, *The Emergency: Neutral Ireland, 1939–45* (London: Macmillan, 2006).

Glynn, Sean and John Oxborrow, *Interwar Britain: A Social and Economic History* (London: George Allen & Unwin, 1976).

Goffman, Erving, *Asylums* (Harmondsworth: Penguin, 1968).

Goodwin, Doris Kearns, *Team of Rivals: The Political Genius of Abraham Lincoln* (London: Penguin, 2009).

Graves, Robert and Hodge, Alan, *The Long Weekend: A Social History of Great Britain, 1918–1939* (London: Faber and Faber, 1940).

Greenberg, Karen J., 'The Rule of Law Finds Its Golem', in Karen J. Greenberg (ed.), *The Torture Debate in America* (Cambridge: Cambridge University Press, 2006).

Greg, Patrick, *The Crum: Inside the Crumlin Road Prison* (Dublin: Gill & Macmillan, 2007).

Grivas, Georgios, *Memoirs*, ed. Charles Foley (London: Longmans, 1964).

Groves, Patricia, *Petticoat Rebellion: The Anna Parnell Story* (Dublin: Mercier Press, 2009).

Hanley, Brian, *The IRA, 1926–36* (Dublin: Four Courts Press, 2002).

Hanley, Brian and Scott Millar, *Lost Revolution: The Story of the Official IRA and the Workers' Party* (Dublin: Penguin Ireland, 2009).

Harbinson, John F., *The Ulster Unionist Party, 1882–1973: Its Development and Organisation* (Belfast: Blackstaff Press, 1974).

Hardy, Thomas, 'The Withered Arm', *Wessex Tales* (London: Macmillan, 1888).

Harford, Judith and Claire Rush (eds.), *Have Women Made a Difference? Women in Irish Universities, 1850–2010* (Berne: Peter Lang, 2010).

Harkness, D. W., *The Restless Dominion: The Irish Free State and the British Commonwealth of Nations, 1921–31* (London: Macmillan, 1969).

Harrington, Niall C., *Kerry Landing: August 1922* (Dublin: Anvil Books, 1992).

Harris, Mary, *The Catholic Church and the Foundation of the Northern Ireland State* (Cork: Cork University Press, 1993).

——'Church, State and Minority Rights', in Dermot Keogh and Michael H. Halzel (eds.), *Northern Ireland and the Politics of Reconciliation* (Cambridge: Cambridge University Press, 1993), pp. 62–83.

Harrison, Henry, *Ulster and the British Empire 1939: Help or Hindrance?* (London: Robert Hale, 1939).

Hart, Peter, *The IRA and Its Enemies: Violence and Community in Cork, 1916–1923* (Oxford: Clarendon Press, 1998).

——*The IRA at War, 1916–1923* (Oxford: Oxford University Press, 2003).

——*The Somme* (London: Weidenfeld & Nicolson, 2005).

Hassan, John (pseud. G. B. Kenna), *Facts and Figures: Belfast Pogrom, 1920–1922* (Belfast: Donaldson Archives, 1997).

Hayes, Maurice, *Minority Verdict: Experiences of a Catholic Public Servant* (Belfast: Blackstaff Press, 1995).

Hennessey, Thomas, *A History of Northern Ireland, 1920–1996* (Basingstoke: Macmillan, 1997).

Hezlet, Arthur, *The 'B' Specials: A History of the Ulster Special Constabulary* (London: Tom Stacey, 1972).

Hirst, Catherine, *Religion, Politics and Violence in Nineteenth Century Belfast: The Pound and Sandy Row* (Dublin: Four Courts Press, 2002).

Hogan, Gerald, *The Origins of the Irish Constitution, 1928–1941* (Dublin: Royal Irish Academy, 2012).

Hood, Roger, *Borstal Reassessed* (London: Heinemann, 1965).

Hopkinson, Michael, *Green against Green: The Irish Civil War* (Dublin: Gill & Macmillan, 1988).

——*The Irish War of Independence* (Dublin: Gill & Macmillan, 2002).

Horne, John (ed.), *Our War: Ireland and the Great War* (Dublin: Royal Irish Academy and RTÉ, 2008).

Hostettler, John, *Torture Trial in Belfast* (London: Connolly Association, 1958).

Hyde, H. Montgomery, *Carson: The Life of Sir Edward Carson* (London: Constable, 1974).

Inglish, Tom, *Moral Monopoly: The Rise and Fall of the Catholic Church in Modern Ireland* (Dublin: UCD Press, 1998).

Isles, K. S., in Thomas Wilson (ed.), *Ulster under Home Rule* (Oxford: Oxford University Press, 1955), pp. 116–17.

Jenkins, Roy, *Churchill* (London: Pan, 2002).

Jones, Jack, *My Lively Life* (London: John Long, 1928).

Jordan, Anthony J., *Sean MacBride: A Biography* (Dublin: Blackwater Press, 1993).

Kee, Robert, *The Laurel and the Ivy: The Story of Charles Stuart Parnell and Irish Nationalism* (London: Penguin, 1994).

Kelly, James, *Bonfires on the Hillside* (Belfast: Fountain Publishing, 1995).

Kennedy, Kieran A., Thomas Giblin and Deirdre McHugh, *The Economic Development of Ireland in the Twentieth Century* (London and New York: Routledge, 1988).

Keogh, Dermot, Finbarr O'Shea and Carmel Quinlan (eds.), *Ireland in the 1950s: The Lost Decade* (Cork: Mercier Press, 2004).

Kilcommins, Shane, Ian O'Donnell, Eoin O'Sullivan and Barry Vaughan (eds.), *Crime, Punishment and the Search for Order in Ireland* (Dublin: IPA, 2004).

Kinnear, Michael, *The Fall of Lloyd George: The Political Crisis of 1922* (London: Macmillan, 1973).

Kissane, Bill, *The Politics of the Irish Civil War* (Oxford: Oxford University Press, 2005).

Kleinrichert, Denise, *Republican Internment and the Prison Ship Argenta 1922* (Dublin: Irish Academic Press, 2001).

Lawrence, R. J., *The Government of Northern Ireland: Public Finance and Public Services, 1921–1964* (Oxford: Oxford University Press, 1965).

Livades, Vias, *Cypriot and Irish Political Prisoners Held in British Prisons, 1956–1959* (Nicosia: Power Publishing, 2008).

Lloyd, C. (ed.), *Captain Cook's Voyages of Discovery* (London: Dent, 1920).

London, Jack, *People of the Abyss* (New York: Macmillan & Co., 1903).

Long, S. E., *The Orange Institution* (Belfast: House of Orange, 1978).

Longmate, Norman, *The Workhouse: A Social History* (London: Pimlico, 2003).

Loomis, Stanley, *Paris in the Terror* (Philadelphia, Pa.: J. B. Lippincott, 1964).

Lucas, Norman, *The CID* (London: Barker, 1967).

Luce, J. V., *Trinity College Dublin: The First Four Hundred Years* (Dublin: Trinity College Press, 1992).

Lyons, F. S. L., *Ireland since the Famine* (London: Fontana, 1973).

——*Charles Stuart Parnell* (London: Fontana, 1978).

Macardle, Dorothy, *The Irish Republic* (London: Victor Gollancz, 1937).

McBride, Lawrence W., *The Greening of Dublin Castle: The Transformation of Bureaucratic and Judicial Personnel in Ireland 1892–1922* (Washington, DC: Catholic University of America Press, 1991).

McCluskey, C., *Up Off Their Knees: A Commentary on the Civil Rights Movement in Northern Ireland* (Galway: Conn McCluskey and Associates, 1989).

McConville, Seán, *A History of English Prison Administration, Vol. I: 1750–1877* (London: Routledge & Kegan Paul, 1981).

——*English Local Prisons, 1860–1900: Next Only to Death* (London and New York: Routledge, 1995).

——'Hearing, Not Listening: Penal Policy and the Political Prisoners of 1906–21', in Lucia Zedner and Andrew Ashworth (eds.), *The Criminological Foundations of Penal Policy: Essays in Honour of Roger Hood* (Oxford: Oxford University Press, 2003).

——*Irish Political Prisoners 1848–1922: Theatres of War* (London and New York: Routledge, 2003).

McCoole, Sinéad, *No Ordinary Women: Irish Female Activists in the Revolutionary Years, 1900–1923* (Dublin: The O'Brien Press, 2003).

McCullough, David, *A Makeshift Majority: The First Inter-Party Government, 1948–51* (Dublin, Institute of Public Administration, 1998).

McDermott, Jim, *Northern Divisions: The Old IRA and the Belfast Pogroms, 1920–22* (Belfast: Beyond the Pale, 2001).

MacEoin, Uinseann, *Survivors: The Story of Ireland's Struggle as Told through Some of Her Outstanding Living People Recalling Events from the Days of Davitt, through James Connolly, Brugha, Collins, Liam Mellows, and Rory O'Connor, to the Present Time* (Dublin: Argenta, 1980).

——*Harry: The Story of Harry White as related to Uinseann MacEoin* (Dublin: Argenta, 1985).

——*The IRA in the Twilight Years, 1923–1948* (Dublin: Argenta, 1997).

McEvoy, F. J., 'Canada, Ireland and the Commonwealth: The Declaration of the Irish Republic, 1948–49', *Irish Historical Studies*, 24 (1985): 506–27.

McGahern, John *The Leavetaking* (London: Faber & Faber, 1974).

McGuffin, John, *Internment* (Tralee: Anvil Books, 1973).

McIntosh, Gillian, *The Force of Culture: Unionist Identities in Twentieth Century Ireland* (Cork: Cork University Press, 1999).

Maclean, Fitzroy, *Eastern Approaches* (London: Cape, 1949).

McMahon, Paul, *British Spies and Irish Rebels: British Intelligence and Ireland, 1916–1945* (Woodbridge: Boydell Press, 2008).

Macmillan, Harold, *Winds of Change, 1914–39* (London: Macmillan, 1966).

Magill, Charles W. (ed.), *From Dublin Castle to Stormont: The Memoirs of Andrew Philip Magill, 1913–1925* (Cork: Cork University Press, 2003).

Maguire, Martin, *The Civil Service and the Revolution in Ireland, 1912–38: 'Shaking the Blood-Stained Hand of Mr Collins'* (Manchester: Manchester University Press, 2008).

Mao Zedong *Quotations from Chairman Mao Tse Tung* (Peking: Foreign Languages Press, 1972).

Marsh, Edward, *A Number of People: A Book of Reminiscences* (London: Heinemann, 1939).

Martin, Peter, *Censorship in the Two Irelands, 1922–39* (Dublin: Irish Academic Press, 2006).

Matthews, Ann, *Renegades: Irish Republican Women, 1900–1922* (Cork: Mercier Press, 2010).

Memendez, Albert J., *The Religious Factor in the 1960 Presidential Election: An Analysis of the Kennedy Victory over Anti-Catholic Prejudice* (Jefferson, NC: McFarland & Co., 2011).

Millar, Michelle and David McKevitt, 'The Irish Civil Service System', in A. J. G. M. Bekke and Frits M. Van Der Meer (eds.), *Civil Service Systems in Western Europe* (Cheltenham: Edward Elgar, 2011).

Milne, Alexander Taylor (ed.), *The Correspondence of Jeremy Bentham* (London: Athlone Press, 1981).

Milroy, Sean, *Memories of Mountjoy* (Dublin and London: Maunsel & Co., 1917).

Mitchell, Arthur and Pádraig Ó Snodaigh (eds.), *Irish Political Documents, 1916–1949* (Dublin: Irish Academic Press, 1985).

Mooney Einhacker, Joanne, *Irish Republican Women in America: Lecture Tours, 1916–1925* (Dublin: Irish Academic Press, 2003).

Moroney, Michael, 'George Plant and the Rule of Law: The Devereux Affair, 1941–42', *Tipperary Historical Journal*, 1 (1988): 1–12.

Mulholland, Marc, 'Why Did Unionists Discriminate?', in Sabine Wichert (ed.), *From the United Irishmen to Twentieth-Century Unionism: A Festschrift for A. T. Q. Stewart* (Dublin: Four Courts Press, 2004).

Murphy-O'Connor, Cormac, *At the Heart of the World* (London: Darton, Longman & Todd, 2004).

Murray, Patrick, *Oracles of God: The Roman Catholic Church and Irish Politics, 1922–37* (Dublin: University College Dublin Press, 2000).

Myers, Kevin, *Watching the Door: Cheating Death in 1970s Belfast* (London: Atlantic Books, 2006).

Ní Aoláin, Fionnuala, *Law in Times of Crisis: Emergency Powers in Theory and Practice* (Cambridge: Cambridge University Press, 2006).

Nic Dháibhéid, Caoimhe, 'The Irish National Aid Association and the Radicalisation of Public Opinion in Ireland, 1916–18', *Historical Journal*, 55 (September 2012): 705–29.

Ó Cadhain, Máirtín, *Cré na Cille* (Dublin: Sáirséal & Dill, 1949).

——*As an nGéibheann: Litreacha Chuig Tomás Bairéad* (Dublin: Sáirséal & Dill, 1973).

Ó Longaigh, Seosamh, 'Emergency Law in Action, 1939–45', in Dermot Keogh and Mervyn O'Driscoll (eds.), *Ireland in World War II: Diplomacy and Survival* (Cork: Mercier, 2004).

——*Emergency Law in Independent Ireland* (Dublin: Four Courts Press, 2006).

O'Brien, Brendan, *The Long War: The IRA and Sinn Féin* (Dublin: The O'Brien Press, 1995).

O'Brien, John A., *The Vanishing Irish: The Enigma of the Modern World* (London: W. H. Allen, 1955).

O'Connor, Emmet, 'Communists, Russia and the IRA, 1920–23', *Historical Journal*, 46 (1) (2003): 115–31.

O'Donnell, Peadar, *The Gates Flew Open* (London: Jonathan Cape, 1932).

——*There Will Be Another Day* (Dublin: Dolmen Press, 1963).

O'Donoghue, David, *The Devil's Deal: The IRA, Nazi Germany and the Double Life of Jim O'Donoghue* (Dublin: New Island, 2010).

O'Halpin, Eunan, *Defending Ireland: The Irish State and Its Enemies since 1922* (Oxford: Oxford University Press, 1999).

——*Spying on Ireland* (Oxford: Oxford University Press, 2008).

O'Hanlon, Gerry, 'Population Change in the 1950s: A Statistical Review', in Dermot Keogh, Finbarr O'Shea and Carmel Quinlan (eds.), *Ireland in the 1950s: The Lost Decade* (Cork: Mercier Press, 2004).

O'Malley, Ernie, *On Another Man's Wound* (Dublin: Anvil Books, 1962).

——*The Singing Flame* (Dublin: Anvil Books, 1992).

O'Neill, Joseph, *Blood-Dark Track* (London: Granta, 2001).

O'Sullivan, Donal, *The Irish Free State and Its Senate* (London: Faber & Faber, 1940).

Oakeshott, Michael, *Experience and Its Modes* (Cambridge: Cambridge University Press, 1995).

OECD, *Economic Surveys by the OECD: Ireland* (Paris: OECD, 1962).

OEEC, *Economic Conditions in Ireland and Portugal* (Paris: OEEC, 1954).

——*Economic Conditions in Ireland and Portugal* (Paris: OEEC, 1955).

——*Economic Conditions in Member and Associated Countries of the OEEC: Ireland* (Paris: OEEC, 1961).

Orwell, George, *Down and Out in Paris and London* (London: Victor Gollancz, 1933).

——*Homage to Catalonia* (London: Folio, 1970).

Osborough, Nial, *Borstal in Ireland: Custodial Provision for the Young Adult Offender, 1906–1974* (Dublin: Institute for Public Administration, 1975).

Pagel, Mark, *Wired for Culture* (London: Allen Lane, 2013).

Parker, Michael (ed.), *Dynamic Security: The Democratic Therapeutic Community in Prison* (London: Jessica Kingsley, 2006).

Parkinson, Alan and Eamon Phoenix (eds.), *Conflicts in the North of Ireland, 1900–2000* (Dublin: Four Courts Press, 2010).

Pearse, Padraig, *Collected Works of Patrick Pearse: Political Writings and Speeches* (Dublin, Talbot Press, 1922).

Pearson, John, *The Profession of Violence* (London: Panther, 1973).

Pellow, Jill, *The Home Office, 1848–1914: From Clerks to Bureaucrats* (London: Heinemann, 1982).

Phoenix, Eamon, 'Cahir Healy (1877–1970): Northern Nationalist Leader', *Clogher Record*, 18 (1): 32–52.

——*Northern Nationalism: Nationalist Politics, Partition and the Catholic Minority in Northern Ireland, 1890–1940* (Belfast: Ulster Historical Foundation, 1994).

Pollock, Sam, *Mutiny for the Cause* (London: Sphere, 1971).

Prunty, Jacinta, *Dublin Slums, 1800–1925: A Study in Urban Geography* (Dublin: Irish Academic Press, 1998).

Questier, M. C. and E. H. Shagan, *Elizabeth and the Catholics* (Manchester: Manchester University Press, 2005).

Radzinowicz, Leon, *A History of the English Criminal Law and Its Administration from 1750*, 5 vols. (London: Stevens & Sons, 1948–1986).

Radzinowicz, Leon and Roger Hood, *A History of the English Criminal Law and Its Administration from 1750*, vol. V: *The Emergence of Penal Policy* (London: Stevens & Sons, 1986).

Rafferty, Oliver P., *Catholicism in Ulster, 1603–1983: An Interpretative History* (London: Hurst, 1994).

Rakove, Milton L., *We Don't Want Nobody Nobody Sent: An Oral History of the Daley Years* (Bloomington, Ind.: University of Indiana Press, 1979).

Randle, Michael and Pat Pottle, *The Blake Escape* (London: Harrap, 1989).

Regan, John M., *The Irish Counter-Revolution 1921–1936: Treatyite Politics and Settlement in Independent Ireland* (Dublin: Gill & Macmillan, 1999).

Reidy, Conor, *Ireland's 'Moral Hospital': The Irish Borstal System, 1906–1956* (Dublin: Irish Academic Press, 2009).

Rousseau, Jean-Jacques, *Du contrat social* (Paris, 1762).

Ryder, Chris, *The RUC, 1922–2000: A Force under Fire* (London: Arrow Books, 2000).

——*The Fateful Split* (London: Methuen, 2004).

Sagarra, Eda, *Kevin O'Shiel: Tyrone Nationalist and Irish State-Builder* (Dublin: Irish Academic Press, 2013).

Salt, Henry Stephens, *The Flogging Craze* (London: Allen & Unwin, 1916).

Sexton, Brendan, *Ireland and the Crown, 1922–1936: The Governor-Generalship of the Irish Free State* (Dublin: Irish Academic Press, 1989).

Shakespeare, Geoffrey, *Let Candles Be Brought In* (London: MacDonald, 1949).

Sheehy-Skeffington, Francis, *Michael Davitt: Revolutionary, Agitator and Labour Leader* (London: MacGibbon & Kee, 1967).

Sinott, Richard, *Irish Voters Decide: Voting Behaviour in Elections and Referendums since 1918* (Manchester: Manchester University Press, 1995).

Solomon, Peter H., 'Soviet Criminal Justice under Stalin', *American Historical Review*, 103 (5) (1998): 1657.

Spindler, Karl, *Gun Running for Casement in the Easter Rebellion, 1916* (London: Collins, 1921).

Steele, James, *Resurgent Ulster* (Belfast: Republican Publicity Bureau, 1952).

Stephan, Enno, *Spies in Ireland* (London: Four Square, 1965).

Stopes, Marie, *Married Love: A New Contribution to the Solution of Sex Difficulties* (London: A. C. Fifield, 1918).

Strickland, Agnes, *The Life of Queen Elizabeth* (London: Dent, 1924).

Stuckey, M., 'The Evolution of the "Star Chamber"', *Australian Law Journal*, 68 (9) (1994): 670.

Szymborska, Wisława, *Views with a Grain of Sand: Selected Poems*, trans. Stanisław Barańczak and Clare Cavanagh (London: Faber and Faber, 1995).

Taswell-Langmead, T. P., *English Constitutional History*, ed. T. F. T. Plucknett, 11th edn (London: Sweet & Maxwell, 1960).

Taylor, A. J. P., *English History, 1914–1945* (Oxford: Oxford University Press, 1965).

Taylor, Rex, *Michael Collins* (London: Hutchinson, 1958).

Thomas, D. A., *Principles of Sentencing*, 2nd edn (London: Heinemann Educational, 1979).

Thompson, E. P., *The Making of the English Working Class* (Harmondsworth: Penguin, 1968).

Tubridy, Ryan, *Four Days That Changed a President* (London: Collins, 2011).

Tuchman, Barbara W., *The Guns of August* (London: Constable, 1962).

'An Ulster Presbyterian', *Ulster on Its Own; or An Easy Way with Ireland, Being a Proposal of Self-Government for the Five Counties Round Lough Neagh* (Belfast: Carswell, 1912).

Vidler, John, *If Freedom Fail* (London: Macmillan & Co., 1964).

Walker, Graham, *A History of the Ulster Unionist Party: Protest, Pragmatism and Pessimism* (Manchester: Manchester University Press, 2004).

Ward, David A. and Gene G. Kassebaum, *Women's Prison: Sex and Social Structure* (London: Weidenfeld & Nicolson, 1966).

Ward, Margaret, *Unmanageable Revolutionaries: Women and Irish Nationalism* (London: Pluto Press, 1983).

Whyte, John, 'How Much Discrimination Was There under the Unionist Regime, 1921–68', in Tom Gallagher and James O'Connell (eds.), *Contemporary Irish Studies* (Manchester: Manchester University Press, 1983).

——*Interpreting Northern Ireland* (Oxford: Clarendon Press, 1990).

Wiener, Martin J., *Reconstructing the Criminal: Culture, Law and Policy in England, 1830–1914* (Cambridge: Cambridge University Press, 1990).

Williams, Eric, *The Wooden Horse* (London: Collins, 1949).

Wills, Clair, *That Neutral Island* (Cambridge, Mass.: Harvard University Press, 2007).

Wood, Peter, *Poverty and the Workhouse in Victorian Britain* (Stroud: Allan Sutton, 1991).

Yeats, W. B., *The Poems*, ed. Richard J. Finneran (New York: Macmillan, 1983).

Journals, newspapers and works of reference

Anglo-Celt
Armagh Guardian
Banbridge Chronicle and Downshire Standard
Belfast Gazette
Belfast Newsletter
Belfast Telegraph
Connacht Sentinel
Connacht Tribune
Cork Examiner
Dáil Debates
Daily Chronicle
Daily Express
Daily Herald
Daily Mail
Daily Telegraph
Derry Journal
Derry Standard
Dictionary of Irish Biography
Dictionary of Irish History, 1800–1980, ed. D. J. Hickey and J. E. Doherty
Dictionary of National Biography
Donegal News
Down Recorder
Eire
Encyclopaedia Britannica (11th edn)
Evening Herald
Evening Mail
Evening News
Fermanagh Herald
Fermanagh Times
Freeman's Journal
Glasgow Herald
Hansard
History Ireland
History Today
Iris Oifigiúil
Irish Democrat
Irish Historical Studies
Irish Independent
Irish News

Irish Police News
Irish Studies Review
Irish Times
Kerryman
Leinster Leader
Leitrim Observer
Limerick Leader
Liverpool Daily Post
Liverpool Echo
Longford Leader
Manchester Evening News
Manchester Guardian
Meath Chronicle
Midland Daily Telegraph
Morning Post
Nenagh Guardian
New Grove Dictionary of Music and Musicians
New York Times
Newry Reporter
News Chronicle
Northern Ireland Parliamentary Debates
Northern Standard
Northern Star
Northern Whig
Notable British Trials
Oxford Companion to Irish History, ed. J. S. Connolly
Oxford Companion to Philosophy, ed. Ted Honderich
Oxford Dictionary of Quotations
Poblacht na hÉireann
An Phoblacht
Reynold's News
Scotsman
Southern Star
Standard, The
Star
Sunday Dispatch
Sunday Independent
Sunday Press
Sunday Review
Times, The
Times Pictorial
Ulster Herald
United Irishman
Weekly Irish News
Western Morning News
Westminster Gazette
Who Was Who
Who's Who

Interviews

Eamonn Boyce
Peter Brennan
Manus Canning
Joe Clarke
Gus Cronin
Hugh Cunningham
Dónal Donnelly
Dan (Bally) Keating
Eddie Keenan
Noel Kavanagh
Tom Landers
Jack Lavin
Paddy Joe McClean
Madge McConville
John L. McCormack
Willie-John McCorry
Uinseann MacEoin
May Mac Giolla
Tomás Mac Giolla
Pat McGirl
Tony McInerney
Billy McKee
Leo Martin
Charlie Murphy
Donal Murphy
James Andrew Mary Murphy
Ruairí Ó Brádaigh
Dessie O'Hagan
Breandán O Rahallaí
Christy Quearney
Dick Reade
Mick Ryan
Paddy Terry
Sydney Wolfe

Libraries

Bodleian Library, University of Oxford
British Library (Euston and Colindale)
Cambridge University Library
Institute of Advanced Legal Studies, University of London
Institute of Historical Research, University of London
Library of Congress
Linenhall Library, Belfast
London Library
Manchester Central Library

National Library of Ireland
Queen Mary, University of London, Library
Reform Club Library
Senate House Library, University of London
Squire Law Library, University of Cambridge
Trinity College Dublin Library
University College Dublin Library
Working Class Movement Library, Salford, Manchester

INDEX

706; failed Glasshouse protest 704–5; on hunger strike 696; removed 708

Grogan, Thomas: on hunger strike 695

Grosvenor, Colonel Robert (MP): on Southern uncertainties 970

Guckian, Father Daniel (chaplain): appointed to *Argenta* 330

Guiney, Commandant James: Curragh welcome speech 713; on final releases 733; on splits 720–21

gun-running: 13

Haccius, M. (ICRC): and prison conditions 261–63

Haldane, Colonel M. M.: on female internment 327; on internee interviews 332

Hales, Seán (TD): assassinated 26

Hallet, Mr Justice: sentences Behan 448

Halligan, Constable Robert J.: killed 954

Hallinan, Bishop Denis: on prison conditions (1922–23) 196

Hamill, Seán: criticises comrades 719; and final releases (1945) 734–35

Hamilton, Special Constable Samuel: killed 550 n. 36

Hankinson, Sir Walter (ambassador): and Border Campaign 945; converses with de Valera 773

Hanna, Francis; biographical note 932 n. 81; on collective punishment 905–6

Hanna, Joseph: assassinated 508

Harbourne, John: wounded in Mountjoy 187

Hare Park camp: accommodation at 192; poor conditions in 197–98

Harrington, Dr John: possible escape involvement 588

Harris, Father (chaplain): note on 670 n. 82

Harris, Major (governor): and Morgan Report 394

Harrison, F.A.L.: and Advisory Committee 916

Harrison, County Inspector Richard: on prison corruption 582

Harte, Thomas: executed 656–57

Hartnett, Noel: and McCaughey 638

Harty, F.G.: and Mallon case 908–9

Harvey, J.T. (governor): appointed to *Argenta* 526

Haughey, Charles (minister): refuses leniency 1041–42

Hayes, Major-General A.: on MacSwiney hunger strike 251

Hayes, Maurice: on civil service recruitment 98–99 n. 16

Hayes, Stephen: 'arrest' and torture 607–8 n. 122; effect of allegations against 90, 703, 718

Healy, Cahir (MP): biographical note 364 n. 92; conditions removed 360; detention case 924; endorses Green Cross 534; House of Commons ruling 40 n. 11; internment (1922) **352–60**; moved to Larne Workhouse 355; and postal censorship 96; privilege case **353–55**; visits Parkhurst prison; mentioned 331, 335

Healy, Con: at Portlaoise 296

Healy, Timothy Michael: activates Boundary Commission 7; biographical note 40–41 n. 12; and prisoner releases 133

Henderson, Commandant General Leo: 'arrested' 24

Henry, Colonel F.J.: on Curragh disintegration 720

Henry, Sir Denis: dismisses 'Cushendall Massacre' claim 82

Hewitt, Joseph: and Coventry bombing 480

Hewitt, Mary: and Coventry bombing 480

Hill, J.G.: 854

Hoare, Sir Samuel (Home Secretary): circulates 'S Plan' 433

Hogan, Annie: alleges ill-treatment 252–53

Hogan, John: at Portlaoise 296

Holderness, Sir Ernest: on Northern internment (1939) 516

Holland, Kevin: 305

Hostettler, J.: on Mallon and Talbot trial 799

House of Commons: excludes Northern Ireland matters 40 n. 11; and Irish affairs 7, 40 n. 10

Huddleston, General Herbert: on Londonderry internees 524

Hueston, Thomas: pleas for release 133; pleads guilty 161 n. 142; and Wattlebridge ambush 136, 160 n. 128; mentioned 414

Hughes, Seamus: gives classes 1051 n. 110